BLACK HERITAGE SITES

An African American Odyssey and Finder's Guide

Nancy C. Curtis, Ph.D.

American Library Association
Chicago and London
1996

Project editor: Joan A. Grygel

Proofreader: Joyce Petersen

Indexer: Pam Hori

Cover design: Richmond Jones

Interior design: Dianne M. Rooney

Composition by Publishing Services, Inc.
using Xyvision/Linotype 330

Typefaces: Palatino and Antique Olive

The paper used in this publication meets the minimum requirements of American National Standard for Information Sciences—Permanence of Paper for Printed Library Materials, ANSI Z39.48–1992. ♾

Printed on 50-pound Arbor, a pH-neutral stock, and bound in Roxite B-grade cloth by Edwards Brothers, Inc.

Library of Congress Cataloging-in-Publication Data

Curtis, Nancy C.
Black heritage sites : an African American odyssey and finder's guide / by Nancy C. Curtis.
p. cm.
Includes index.
ISBN 0-8389-0643-5 (alk. paper)
1. Historic sites—United States—Directories.
2. Afro-Americans—History. I. Title.
E159.C65 1996
973'.0496073—dc20 95-5788

Printed in the United States of America.

00 99 98 97 96 5 4 3 2 1

Contents

Preface

My father's mother, Martha Chevis, was born before the Civil War in rural, nineteenth-century Kentucky. Martha, who probably was born in slavery, lived in Bourbon County, Kentucky. My father, who died when I was twelve years old, never talked about his childhood, his mother, or his other ancestors. His reluctance to talk about his family history was typical of all of the adults whom I knew when I was growing up—my adult relatives and my parents' friends never talked in my presence about their family heritage, their childhood experiences, or their genealogy.

In home and at church we learned about outstanding Black Americans—Carter G. Woodson, Marian Anderson, George Washington Carver, Mary McLeod Bethune, Paul Robeson, A. Philip Randolph—and we took pride in their achievements. In contrast, personal family histories were shrouded in secrecy. The adults I knew believed that stories about the past dredged up harsh memories of slavery and the decades that followed—the hard times, the racial hatreds, the lynchings and other outrages against individuals, the shame, and the bitter experiences that they believed were best forgotten. They wanted to shield the young from these hard memories because they felt the burden of those memories should not be carried forth as impedimenta into the future. They wanted to provide us with a fresh slate because they were optimistic that the future would be better.

When Alex Haley published *Roots* and thousands of families saw the video drama that followed, our family watched, too. Haley's story stirred old memories and impelled the asking anew of old questions. Families that previously had been silent about their heritage began to talk about the subject. As my mother told the stories that started with my great-grandmothers, the panorama of my family history began to unfold. Years later I traveled to Kentucky, where I first gleaned bits of information about my father's family. I spoke with a Black woman, Mrs. Mary Reeves, who had seen "Aunt Martha," as she called my grandmother, through the eyes of a small child. My grandmother was tall and slender, she said; her brown skin was touched with a reddish hue, and she had a friendly smile as she spoke to children who passed by each morning on their way to school. They always saw her standing on her porch, early, hanging up items she had laundered and ironed for white families in her town.

From a visit to the Bourbon County Courthouse, I gathered a little more information. By the time she was twenty-three, or even before, Martha was married. At twenty-three she could not read or write. Although her parents were born in Kentucky, both of her maternal grandparents (my great-great-grandparents) were born in Virginia. Her paternal grandmother was born in Virginia, and her paternal grandfather (my great-great-grandfather) was born in Africa.

After traveling west across the rolling green hills of the Western Kentucky Parkway, I sat in the Todd County Courthouse and began to learn about my maternal great-grandmothers, Ann and Alice, who were born in slavery. I found Alice's name in a large will book in the courthouse. She was regarded as property to be transferred as her owner wished. When she was a young child, her master had willed her to be a servant to his young daughter. Fortunately for Alice, the Civil War ended four years after the will was written. Although she later experienced other sorrows, she and other African Americans no longer were forced to serve as slaves.

After learning about Alice, I began to hunger for some visible evidence of my ancestors' existence. I wanted to see some of the places they had lived or at least places that resembled those they had known. Ann and Alice had remained in southwestern Kentucky after emancipation. Their children, along with other African Americans, owned and tilled rich farmland in Todd County. Decades ago the farms were sold. When I visited the family's former land for the first time in 1988, only one of the family houses, built around 1916, remained. The schoolhouse where my grandfather and his brother-in-law taught part-time was no longer standing. Their original church was demolished long ago and replaced by a more modern building. My grandfather sold his farm and moved his family from their rural Todd County farm to Hopkinsville, Kentucky, when my mother was entering third grade—my grandparents believed their children could get a better education in the city. Although my grandfather died before I was born, I visited my grandparents' house in Hopkinsville at the ages of four and six and never forgot how the house looked. The gray, frame, two-story house was located midway up a sloping hill. The long, wide, gracious porch had a comfortable swing. On one visit my brother and I sat on the porch floor cradling a quartet of wiggling puppies in our laps. Grandma's house had cool rooms with muted light and a wide lawn in back punctuated with grapevines and a tall walnut tree. One day when we were standing under the tree, a walnut fell on my brother's head, sending us into endless gales of laughter. There were chickens, too, that we very often fed handfuls of grain.

In 1988 I returned to Hopkinsville with a camera, seeking to record the bit of history that I remembered so well, but my grandmother's house had been torn down. No family member had a photograph of the house. The feeling of loss led me to wonder again what kinds of houses my great-grandparents had lived in before emancipation and after freedom. How did other Black families live in slavery? Did examples of their houses still stand? What did their schools, their churches, and the stores where they bought goods look like? The search for my family tree had opened up a flood of wishing and wanting for some visual record, something to show me some of the things that I had learned in words. The work of this book had begun.

The search for structures associated with Black history began with the mailing of more than five hundred letters to national, state, and local historical associations and museums in the United States, to every historically Black college in the country that I could identify, to Black history departments in colleges nationwide, and to other historic sites across the country. The search, designed to be as comprehensive as possible, included a review of manuscripts, books, and articles about Black history and about historic sites in America. The questionnaires began to return, many with references to additional sites or to other knowledgeable individuals. The highlight of the search, however, came with my own personal visits to towns throughout Michigan, Indiana, Kentucky, Ohio, California, Oklahoma, Tennessee, Louisiana, Mississippi, Alabama, Georgia, South Carolina, North Carolina, Virginia, and Canada—to see and photograph many of the sites for myself. Seeing the history was a moving experience, as those who take the journey will learn for themselves; it gave a connection with the past that could have been obtained in no other way.

As the manuscript took shape, it included homes, schools and colleges, churches, commercial buildings, cemeteries, and monuments. By publication time almost half of the sites had to be deleted—some because too little information was available, others because of space limitations. Those that remained provided a comprehensive view of a wide range of Black American structures built primarily from the last half of the nineteenth century through the first half of the twentieth century. They included some surprises—I learned for the first time about the iron furnaces where Black slaves labored in Pennsylvania and about the religious campgrounds in North Carolina where Black families had gone after harvest time each year for more than one hundred years. With the exception of some museums, most of the structures included are at least fifty years old. Some buildings were associated with famous African Americans; others belonged to people whose names may be forgotten but who struggled, fought, sacrificed, protested, and marched to attain freedom and advance or who simply lived their lives in dignity, providing as best they could for their children and the well-being of their communities. This book honors the humble as well as the famous.

Tragically, many buildings from the Black heritage already have been lost. As the project was ending, I spent months making personal telephone calls to many of the sites. The calls garnered unexpected information about the status of Black historic sites across the country. While some of the sites have been restored and are well-maintained and cared for, in too many instances sites have been lost to neglect, abandonment, vandalism, or demolition by urban renewal projects, many of which had no direct benefit to Black communities. Urban renewal projects often demolished close-knit neighborhoods to make way for gleaming new office buildings or to make space for highways that cut through Black communities to rush white commuters home to the suburbs. After wholesale demolition, which was promulgated as eliminating slums, Black residents often were crowded into high-density housing that confined large numbers of minorities to one geographic area of town. Black historic sites were demolished to provide land for shopping centers, for expansion of predominantly white college campuses, or simply to provide parking space for downtown buildings. As I made calls across the country, I listened to people who grieved about the loss of their historic sites and who felt they had no choice in the taking of their buildings. To be fair, it should be stated that many other sites were lost because Black people themselves, enchanted by the new vistas opened up by desegregation, left the old parts of town as fast as they could and never looked back. Unfortunately, as they moved away to newer parts of town and to the suburbs, many interesting older buildings, even some designated as historic, fell vacant and were destroyed. In the mid-1990s some of the most precious of historic sites, the irreplaceable Black colleges and universities, were on the verge of closing for lack of financial support.

Counterbalancing the losses, however, were shining examples of communities working diligently to preserve and restore their historic buildings. The task, never easy and rarely inexpensive, was accomplished in several ways, and it can be accomplished in other communities if citizens work together. Many routes are available to historic preservation. For example, volunteer groups can write grants or sponsor fund-raising events for restoring one-by-one the historic buildings in their communities. Fraternities and sororities can adopt a local historic site, working with senior citizens and other groups to rejuvenate it. Architects and historians can ensure that restoration is done in harmony with the historic era in which the structures were built. School classes, or even an entire school, may wish to adopt a site, clearing overgrown brush and creating historically harmonious gardens. Community groups can purchase informative plaques for sites in towns where few signposts exist to guide visitors and tell the history of the structures. The homeless people who advertise that they will work for food may be willing to clean up the sites, help with painting and carpentry tasks, and perform interior decorating jobs for food and a modest wage. Some historic sites have been abandoned but are structurally sound. If they could be cleaned up and made habitable according to local codes and insurance regulations, a responsible couple in need of shelter might be happy to live in the house, to help to rehabilitate it, and to show the house to visitors two or three days a week in exchange for low rent. Donations from visitors could assist with upkeep of the houses. Articles in local papers can draw visitors to the houses and attract possible donors who wish to see these areas make a comeback.

In many cases old schoolhouses, closed after 1954 desegregation laws were passed, could be turned into community centers and filled with interesting activities for youth and the elderly. Where organizations already exist to provide programs for youth, they may be willing to lease the houses as extension sites. There are several examples in this book of former schools that have been transformed into community centers or into office space for multiracial community programs —read about the Booker T. Washington School in Rushville, Indiana; the Pleasant Plains Rosenwald School in Ahoskie, North Carolina; the McCray School in Burlington, North Carolina; the East End School in Harveysburg, Ohio; the Sumner School in Washington, D.C.; the Ferry Street School in Niles, Michigan; and the Limerick Historic District's Central Colored School in Louisville, Kentucky. Communities also have restored buildings and have sold or rented them to caring organizations. For example, read about the Jewell Building in Omaha, Nebraska; Fisk Chapel of the African Methodist Episcopal Bethel Church in Fair Haven, New Jersey, now a community center; the African Meeting House in Boston, now a museum; the early Frederick Douglass Home in Washington, D.C., now the home of the Caring Institute; the Whitelaw Hotel in Washington, D.C.; the Dunbar (Somerville) Hotel in Los Angeles, California; the Orchard Street United Methodist Church, restored as a museum and now home of the Baltimore, Maryland, Urban League; and the Avalon Hotel in Rochester, Minnesota, now the Hamilton Music Company. This book describes other examples of sites that have been restored. Each new historic site does not detract from the others but adds to the attractiveness of the entire area. Families that take the time to travel to see a historic site probably would enjoy the trip even more if they could see several sites in the same area.

This introduction closes with a caveat or caution—in the mid- to late 1990s, social conditions have changed in a way that has made many homeowners and renters more cautious about strangers who appear to be inspecting or photographing their property. In the early 1990s I spent months visiting sites, almost always in the oldest sections of cities and towns, and, with few exceptions, was met with friendliness. Today, a few years later, visitors need to be cautious and careful not to trespass on private property, to keep a respectful distance from private homes, and to explain their interest if people ask why their property is being inspected. I remember being amazed when two young ladies walked onto the porch of a private home across from Dr. Martin Luther King Jr.'s birthplace in Atlanta, Georgia, and peered at length into the living room window. Such behavior could create a very stressful conflict today. If the text notes that a site is private and the interior is not accessible to the public, drive or walk by *but do not go onto the property unless invited to do so.* If visitors are respectful, most tenants will appreciate the public's recognition of the value of their property.

If our Black historic sites (and they belong to all Americans) are not saved, a precious part of our history will be lost to future generations. This book will have served its purpose if it encourages armchair travelers as well as travelers who actually visit the sites to appreciate and treasure this part of our country's heritage and to renew their connections with this history that we share.

Introduction

In 1619 sixteen Africans who had been captured from a Spanish ship were brought to Virginia on a Dutch warship. The Africans, the first of their race recorded in the English colonies, may have been brought in as indentured servants rather than as slaves to be bound for a lifetime. Their arrival in Jamestown set in motion a series of events that would result in centuries of bondage for an estimated 11 million sons and daughters wrested from the African homeland.

Although some scholars date African American history from that fateful arrival in the colonies, those who arrived on Virginia's shores in 1619 were not the first Africans to come to the Americas. Ivan Van Sertima, professor at Rutgers University, has provided evidence that large African sculptures and pyramids in Mexico and Central America show the influence of African civilizations long before the seventeenth century. The huge African sculptures, called the Olmec Heads, show African influences in the Americas as early as c800 to c400 B.C.E.[1] Ancient statues with African features still stand at La Vanta, Mexico. In addition to the facial features, the sculptures show cultural items—tattoos, earrings, and helmets—associated with Africa. Van Sertima, in his book *They Came before Columbus,* gives additional evidence of contact between Africa and the New World long before Columbus "discovered" America.

Other Africans visited the Americas long before the arrival of the Jamestown sixteen. They came as skilled sailors, soldiers, and servants who accompanied Spanish explorers. One of the early explorers, Estevan de Dorantes (Estevanico), was the first African known to have entered the land that is now the United States of America. He was born near the Moroccan coast of Africa. The conquistador Andres Dorantes de Carranca purchased Estevanico to be his servant, and in 1527 the two men traveled together in a six-hundred-person expedition to the Americas. After facing hurricanes, disease, and attacks by Indians in Florida, Estevanico and four other men spent six years as captives of the Indians.

The arrival of the African men and women in Jamestown represented the beginning, in the colonies, of a way of life that would become associated with the wholesale buying and selling of human beings for use as slaves. The Africans who were brought to the colonies in 1619 and those who came later on slave ships did not arrive devoid of a cultural heritage. They came from a continent immense in size, many from civilizations that had excelled in literature, sciences, the arts, and agriculture. Africans had worked as skilled teachers, artisans, oral historians of their tribes, miners, ironworkers, and agronomists. The men and women brought to America in chains came primarily from West African communities that for centuries had evolved stable traditions and patterns of kinship. They had developed religious, political, and legal systems complex and sophisticated enough to maintain order and viability amid the vicissitudes of daily life. Their continent was one of the world's most bountiful in agricultural and mineral resources.

The advent of the slave trade disrupted the natural growth and evolution of African societies. The European interlopers with their superior weapons, trickery, and deceit seized power and then carved up the continent for themselves. With the collusion of some African leaders, themselves consumed by greed, the Europeans drained the country of both material and human resources.

The Atlantic slave trade that began on a small scale grew in scope following the events that brought the first Africans to Jamestown. The same slave trade also initiated a centuries-long quest for freedom that started with rebellions on the slave ships and moved in an unending line to the slave rebellions of Gabriel Prosser, Nat Turner, and Denmark Vesey; to the search for freedom through the deep woods, guided by the shining North Star; through the escape by plunging into the swamps of Florida where the Seminoles lived and fighting with them in the Seminole Wars; to the search for freedom through fighting in the War for Independence, the War of 1812, and the Civil War; to the marches and demonstrations of the twentieth-century civil rights movements—all part of a protracted, determined, and magnificent intent to escape from bondage and to be treated with dignity as human beings. The quest of the Africans eventually impelled the country to redefine the meaning and scope of natural and national laws, rights, and privileges, and it illuminated the meaning of humanity, human worth, and freedom throughout the world.

Wherever circumstances permitted, and in spite of powerful barriers, African Americans established themselves as leaders and active participants in this struggle. The tangible symbols of their fight for freedom are the sites and structures described in this book. Many African Americans who sought freedom and equality from the seventeenth through the early twentieth centuries stayed in or near the underground railroad structures described here. Others lived in the slave cabins, shotgun houses, cottages, and spacious dwellings shown in these pages. They bought and sold goods and developed professional practices in commercial buildings ranging from small, frame buildings to substantial, multistory structures.

After emancipation their children attended school in churches, in one-room schoolhouses, in the Rosenwald schools that replaced the crowded and dilapidated old schoolhouses, and in some larger schools that, though segregated, were architecturally distinguished. Using their own resources and assisted by the American Missionary Association and philanthropists, African Americans developed a system of quality colleges unmatched in number by any other ethnic minority group in America. Fisk University, Howard University, Hampton University, Morehouse College, Spelman College, and Tuskegee University are but a few of the distinguished institutions of higher education that enrolled many of the nation's future leaders.

From the Revolutionary War period on, the African Americans established their own churches. There the congregations met not only their spiritual needs but also the needs of the community by sheltering fugitive slaves, by helping newcomers to communities, and, later, through leading demonstrations and boycotts that led to enfranchisement and the right to participate in decision-making processes.

Scope and Organization

Black Heritage Sites: An African American Odyssey and Finder's Guide describes a wide variety of historic African American sites. Some are in fine condition; others show signs of neglect. Many sites are in the oldest parts of town or in rural areas, to be found most easily with maps or by telephone calls to local chambers of commerce or city halls. Some sites are designated as state or national historic sites and have regular visiting hours; others are private and may be viewed from the exterior only. While exterior viewing may not be as satisfying as interior tours, the exteriors, even when they are in less-than-ideal condition, still radiate a sense of history and place and resonate with the lives of their former inhabitants.

This book is divided into five regions: South, Northeast, Midwest, Southwest, and West and Noncontiguous States. A few sites in Canada are included as special features following the Detroit, Michigan, sites because they are a short trip from Detroit and because the hospitality of many Canadians created an inviting setting for establishing the northernmost terminus of the underground railroad. Many fugitives settled there in peace, and many of their descendants still live in Canada today.

Each section of this book is introduced with a brief description of the states in that region and highlights of the types of structures a visitor might see—churches, schools, dwellings, commercial buildings, battlefields, cemeteries, and monuments. By using the table of contents, visitors can explore by geographic region or, by using the index, by type of structure or by theme. For example, one family, heading south for a family reunion, may wish to explore all of the Black heritage sites in the reunion area. Another group may wish to explore sites in several states associated with the Civil Rights Movement of the 1950s and 1960s. Another family may wish to drive through several states, visiting the homes or birthplaces of famous Black leaders. Groups may organize to travel anew over old underground railroad routes that wind through several states. Teachers may take their students on a tour of historic African American schoolhouses. The index will prove helpful to families or schools that are arranging geographical or theme tours.

Certain conventions are used throughout this book. For example, headings for sites of national significance are followed by an asterisk (*). These sites are important because of their association with a nationally known leader or because of their association with a civil rights, educational, or social movement of national significance. Other sites are highlighted with an asterisk because the structure at the site is architecturally unique and shows an important aspect of African American life. Over time the names of some sites have changed. The site name given is the name with historical significance to the African American heritage. Sites that would be of interest to children are indicated by following the visiting-hours information.

In addition, shortened forms of print and computer sources are given after sites; more-complete bibliographic citations are in a list of works consulted at the end of each state. Site sources include books, journals, newspaper articles, site brochures and fliers, research manuscripts, dissertations, and information compiled from more than 500 questionnaires and 700 telephone calls and numerous personal visits.

Two sources frequently used were the National Register of Historic Places Inventory Nomination Form (NRHPINF) and the National Register of Historic Places Registration Form (NRHPRF). Although these forms were widely used, consistent attempts were made to update the information through telephone calls and through written information from other sources. The National Register forms, compiled by different individuals or groups, describe the location, architectural style and date of construction, historical significance, and bibliographic references for thousands of individual sites. The NRHPRF certifies that the property has been accepted in the National Register. In the 1970s information was compiled and published in summary form in a book titled *The National Register of Historic Places.* However, the information became too voluminous to be published as a whole in book form; therefore, the entire listing currently is accessible through computer listings through the National Register Information System or by accessing the individual nomination or registration forms. Site listings may be obtained for a copying fee from the individual states. Limitations of staff time in the state offices may determine the staff's ability to respond.

The National Register forms are used by various individuals or groups to obtain information about houses, schools, commercial buildings, battle sites, and other places of historical significance in the fifty United States as well as in American Samoa, the Federated States of Micronesia, Guam, the Republic of the Marshall Islands, the Commonwealth of the Northern Mariana Islands, the Republic of Palau, the Commonwealth of Puerto Rico, and the Virgin Islands. A list of the State Historic Preservation Officers may be obtained from the Department of the Interior, National Park Service, Preservation Assistance Division, Grants Administration Branch, P.O. Box 37127, Washington, DC 20013-7127.

Visiting hours and fees were verified by telephone calls; however, such information may change from the time of this printing. The information included in this book is the best and the latest that I could gather before publication, but I strongly recommend that visitors call each site in advance to obtain the latest visiting information.

Acknowledgments

This book could not have been written without the help of countless individuals who were generous in sharing valuable information. Members of state, county, and city historic associations, individual site administrators, librarians, church officers, business leaders, and community residents responded with information about sites and geographic locations. Many guided me to other individuals who had valuable information.

State historic preservation officers were generous in taking the time to send written information, and when I prepared to visit and photograph sites, they answered my questions about travel conditions in their states and helped me select the sites that would be most visually interesting to photograph.

Hundreds of individuals spoke with me by telephone, providing updated visiting information and, equally important, providing personal viewpoints and historical data about the sites that could have been obtained in no other way.

Several skilled editors—Bonnie Smothers, Robert Cunningham, and Joan Grygel—made the book a better one in several ways. They gave helpful suggestions about including or deleting individual sites according to their significance in Black history, uniqueness of architecture, or accessibility. The extensive pruning was difficult at times because many interesting sites had to be left out, but the deletions made the work more consistent in quality and focus. The editors clarified sentences and paragraphs, checked for consistency, and improved the flow of the words. I am grateful for their considerable help in these areas. Material gathered from many sources showed occasional inconsistencies in dates, in spelling of names, or in other factual information. The editors and I searched for such inconsistencies, but responsibility is my own if any inadvertently were overlooked.

The preparing of this work took longer than expected due to the need to gather additional data to round out the description of certain sites and the need to make personal contacts to verify and update information. I am grateful to my mother, Dorothy A. Curtis, and to my brother, George Russell Curtis, and his wife, Betty, for their unfailing assistance and encouragement through these years of compiling information, writing the text, and verifying information. They never wavered in their belief that this specific story about Black historic sites needed to be told; their assurances sustained me every step of the way.

Note

1. Ivan Van Sertima, *They Came Before Columbus, The African Presence in Ancient America* (New York: Random House, 1976).

PART 1

THE SOUTH

Alabama
Arkansas
District of Columbia
Florida
Georgia
Kentucky
Louisiana
Maryland
Mississippi
North Carolina
South Carolina
Tennessee
Virginia
West Virginia

The ship sailed into Jamestown Harbor in August 1619 manned by pirates and other unsavory characters and carrying a cargo of sixteen Africans. The crew of the pirate ship had seized the Africans from a Spanish vessel bound for the West Indies and had sailed through a violent storm before reaching Jamestown, exchanging the Africans for badly needed food. Although little is known about the Africans other than that they had Spanish names, they became an important part of American history as the first of their race recorded as permanent settlers in the original English colonies.

When the Africans arrived, dark skin color as a distinguishing characteristic had not yet been firmly equated with notions of inferiority. The Africans were regarded as indentured servants. Their status was essentially equal to that of white indentured servants, the poor of England who had been released from jails, orphanages, and poorhouses and who were bound to seven years of servitude to pay for a voyage to America. For many years after the arrival of the Jamestown sixteen, Black indentured servants worked side by side with their white counterparts in houses and fields, intermingling and sometimes intermarrying. Although some distinctions were made on the basis of race, racism and prejudice based on skin color were not yet firmly entrenched.

When the first African indentured servants were freed, they bought land and property and sometimes owned servants themselves. Once free, they lived a better life than those who were still bound, although their status was not as high as that of free white men and women.

The status of Africans changed, however, as the slave trade became highly profitable and as huge plantations created an insatiable need for cheap labor. White planters began to recognize that it was to their economic advantage to own their servants for life rather than for a fixed period of several years. They realized that white servants came from a politically powerful country and had allies in England in those men and women who spoke out against human bondage. As Christians, they were accorded a measure of dignity and respect. Because their skin was white, they were difficult to identify if they escaped.

Indians also proved unsuitable as slaves; they knew the countryside well and could easily flee, and they often were regarded as hard to subdue. Only the Africans stood out in their helplessness to fight against bondage. They were in a strange land where the language was not their own, their homeland lacked political power, and they had no national leaders with the military power to oversee their welfare. Although some Africans had been baptized into Christianity, this status was often ignored when the political realities of greed prevailed. The Africans were easily visible, and they lacked a knowledge of the geography of the new country. These factors mitigated against the possibility of escape.

Within just a few decades these differences led the landowners to increasingly and cunningly weave a web of justifications for keeping Africans in bondage for a lifetime. Landowners determined that slavery would be good for "heathen" Africans because white people would care for them and introduce Christianity to them. As new British colonies came into existence, white leaders threaded ideas of racial inferiority into their ideologies and laws, creating an image of the African as a different and lower being whose rightful place was in a subservient role and whose labors could be justifiably appropriated for the white community's gain. White landowners passed laws that consolidated their right to own slaves and that separated the races into different status levels. By the 1660s Virginia and Maryland had enacted laws that instituted lifetime slavery and that made intermarriage between Black and white people illegal. Georgia established the institution of lifetime bondage through slavery in 1754. Although the system of white indentured servitude continued, most Black people who had not already been freed were designated servants for life with no rights that white people had to respect.

In South Carolina in 1701, in North Carolina in 1715, and in Virginia in 1723, Africans were denied the right to vote. The five original colonies in the South—Georgia, Maryland, South Carolina, Virginia, and North Carolina—which later would fight for their own freedom from tyranny, increasingly denied freedom to human beings. The slave trade flourished, making it possible to farm large acreages that earned enormous wealth for landowners. The men, women, and children who had come from caring, developed societies in Africa now labored in the fields under brutally harsh conditions. In Virginia slaves advised their owners that the land was suitable for growing rice and showed how this cultivation was best done. Their reward for giving such knowledge was being forced to do the cultivation with no compensation for their labor.

In spite of the cruelty of slavery, most Africans managed to retain both humanity and dignity. Some already were skilled artisans when they arrived; they and others were the skilled carpenters and masons who built many of the beautiful mansions, churches, and commercial buildings still standing in the South. On the larger, self-sufficient plantations they worked as carpenters, wheelwrights, shoemakers, barbers, weavers, and tailors. They worked in the coal mines of Alabama and the iron mines of South Carolina.

For a century after the Jamestown men and women arrived, they never forgot Africa and the loved ones they had left behind; many dreamed of returning to the homeland, and some gave their children African names. They named the first church denomination established as their own the *African* Methodist Episcopal Church. Gradually, however, the new generations realized that they were to remain forever in the new land, which they accepted as the only home that they would ever know. They had become African Americans. Their original dreams lived on in stories, customs, traditions, religion, and song, while at the same time another dream grew in insistent intensity—the dream of freedom.

Free African Americans before the Civil War

Long before emancipation, significant numbers of free African Americans lived in the South. In 1790,

32,000 of the 59,000 free Black persons in the United States lived in the South. They had attained freedom in different ways. Some had been indentured servants who were released after completing their term of service. Others had been allowed in slavery to spend part of their free time working for wages: by saving their share over a period of many years, they bought their freedom. Some were emancipated because of the owner's self-interest—an old or infirm slave was often set free and left to find food and shelter as best he or she could. This happened frequently enough that some towns passed laws making owners responsible for the welfare of their emancipated slaves. In Alabama some Black families of mixed heritage, called Creoles, were free because of provisions of the Louisiana Purchase. Occasionally an African was freed because he or she was the master's own child, and there was some bond between them.

Although free Black persons lived under restrictive laws, they possessed more freedom than slaves did, including the freedom to own property. Some of their pre-Civil War dwellings are still standing in the South.

Slave Housing in the South

By 1790, the date of the first U.S. census, Black Americans made up approximately 19.3 percent of the population of the United States. By far, the majority of African Americans lived in the South either as slaves or as free Black individuals. In cities the servants lived in the same houses with their owners, often in a back room protected outside by the high walls of a courtyard. City factories provided dormitory-style housing or built communities of small houses for their workers. Large farms had both house servants and field slaves. Housing for field slaves often was of a lower quality, and much of it has not survived. It included one-room log cabins, small cottages finished with clapboard siding, and brick, "tabby," or stone houses. Some were single houses, while others were one- or two-story duplexes. Some of the one-story cabins had a sleeping loft accessed by a ladder. Closed shutters or small windows provided little light but conserved the heat of a central fireplace. Some plantations had a kitchen separate from the main house to keep the main house cool and to protect against fire; sometimes the kitchen had a room above that served as the cook's living quarters. A slave's house of log construction at Belle Meade in Nashville was built in an unusual two-room "dog-trot" design with an open-air passageway between the two rooms. This house style was so named when someone said that a dog could trot back and forth between the two sections.

House servants often slept in the main house, using a back room on the second or third floor or a room located directly over the kitchen. Many houses had a back stairway for use by servants. Occasionally slaves, like some at White Hall in Richmond and the Grange near Paris, Kentucky, slept in barred rooms in the basement of the main house. The slave trader-owner of the Grange kept slaves being held for sale chained in a barred room in the basement. The room, which had little light or air, came to be known as the dungeon.

Some slave houses were well constructed; others were rude, windowless structures with dirt floors and the most rudimentary of furnishings—beds with rope slats and straw mattresses, plank tables, and a few utensils for cooking and eating. House servants often had dwellings of a higher quality because they lived near the main house and often had the same pleasant view of the grounds that their owners had. Boone Hall near Charleston, South Carolina, had rows of brick slave houses arranged on each side of an elegant, tree-shaded drive leading to the main house.

Although the poorest of the slave cabins have been demolished, many of the quarters are still standing and are used today for storage, office space, rental rooms, or tenant-farmer housing.

Housing after Emancipation

Following emancipation, African Americans lived in a variety of dwellings that reflected their resources and opportunities. Unfortunately, many had to return to their former masters and plead for work to keep from starving. When the Civil War ended, many families in the South, both white and Black, were impoverished, and whole areas were in debt. Prior to the Civil War, wealthy Southern planters had a large portion of their wealth invested in their slaves; because the labor was free, they had no need for cash to pay wages. The former slaves had no cash either; they had set out with no more than a few worn belongings and high hopes for a better life. Too often those hopes were soon crushed by those who intended for them to remain subservient.

With memories of the war still fresh, there were hostilities at every turn. New state laws were passed in the South providing for the capture of wandering "vagrants"; once jailed, the men and women were forced to work off their sentences on farms, railroads, and other places that needed laborers. The Freedmen's Bureau, an association established by the federal government to help freed slaves, sought to establish a system of paid labor for former slaves but found there was little capital with which to pay wages. The planters then turned to the sharecropping, or tenant-farming, system. Black workers provided labor for the plantations, and the landowners provided housing, food, clothing, and farming implements for the laborers. Since the planters often were deeply in debt themselves, some borrowed money for the farm equipment and other supplies from merchants. Bankers, in turn, lent money to the merchants who advanced the supplies; interest rates at the banks sometimes approached 50 to 90 percent. Those on the lowest rung—the Black tenant farmers (and sometimes white tenant farmers, too)—often found themselves trapped in a system of peonage akin to slavery. Those who could be imprisoned before for vagrancy now could be imprisoned for debt; they could be forced to work off the debt in place of cash payment for their work. The cycle of debt was never-ending. Living conditions were poor, too; the tenant farmers often lived in the same cabins they had known in slavery.

Other former slaves were more fortunate and were able to improve their lives. Sometimes a former master helped by providing land and a little cash, and a former slave was able to build a small house that was better than the one known in slavery. Some were able to capitalize on skills they had acquired in slavery as carpenters, coopers, blacksmiths, bricklayers, barbers, nurses, midwives, and cooks. They started small businesses or hired themselves out for different jobs. They and their children often became the business leaders; some of their homes were the equal of those of white citizens. By the early 1900s many African Americans were living in attractive, elegant homes.

Another type of housing consisted of dwellings built by companies for their workers. In factory towns in the South, Black and white workers often lived in the same neighborhoods in company-built homes.

Black Americans and Religion in the South

When Africans came to the Americas, they brought with them a religious heritage and a set of beliefs that had evolved over many centuries in Africa. Diodorus Siculus, a Greek historian from the first century B.C., stated that the Ethiopians conceived themselves to be the inventors of every religious practice. The kingdom of Ethiopia, which traces its lineage back to the Queen of Sheba, took Christianity as its official religion in the fifth century when the kingdom was at its height. Black Africans had traveled widely and were acquainted with different forms of religion, including Christianity and Islam. Some of the people of Ghana, Mali, and Songhay converted to Islam in the eleventh century.

Even before converting to those religions, Africans had been deeply religious. They believed in a supreme God, in a variety of lesser gods, and in a life force believed to be present in all people and objects. They also had a religious attitude of reverence for ancestors. Religion, which permeated all aspects of life in Africa, continued to be a part of the African experience across the Atlantic. The preference for certain styles of worship included the call-and-response pattern present in Black spirituals and in the interaction between preacher and congregation that characterizes many Black congregations to the present.

Religious practice took many forms for slaves and free Black individuals. Some slaves came to America from England, Spain, Portugal, or the West Indies, where they had been baptized into Christianity. Those who came directly from Africa adapted their own religious beliefs to the instruction they received in their new land. The form of religion presented to them was determined by the presence or absence of state and local laws regarding religious assembly by Africans, by guidelines of white denominations and individual white churches, and by the wishes and whims of individual slave masters. Some planters banned the teaching of religion to slaves. Others allowed only house slaves to attend church services with them; their slaves, however, sat in separate seats in the gallery. Many of the original slave galleries still exist in the South.

Former slave Adele Frost, who attended her master's church before emancipation, said, "Colored people had no preacher, but they had leaders. Every slave go to church on Sunday, 'cause they didn't have any work to do for Marster. My grandma used to teach the catechism and how to sing."[1]

Where field hands were barred from attending church services, they sometimes received religious instruction from an itinerant preacher or from a Black slave who was permitted to preach under the guidance of the white master. Former slave Rebecca Jane Grant of South Carolina recalled that for most of the three or four hundred slaves her master owned, there were no "colored churches." Only the house servants, drivers, overseers, and craftsmen attended the master's church; Black preachers led services for the field hands.[2]

Where itinerant preachers were allowed to give special services for slaves, some of the listeners were adept at remembering the Scriptures and presenting them to others. After emancipation they often became the first Black preachers, or they became leaders wherever they lived.

Some slaveowners built small chapels for their slaves. Several of these became the forerunners of the praise houses that still exist on the Sea Islands of South Carolina. In North Carolina and South Carolina some planters allowed slaves to attend a week of religious celebration following the August harvest. Although this was a time of rest and rejoicing, the Africans took the religious intent of the campground meetings very seriously. After emancipation some of the religious camp meetings continued; generations of Black families have attended August camp meetings at the same sites. These campgrounds, which date back to the late 1800s, include very old wooden "tents" where families live during camp meeting week and arbors where they worship.

Slaveowners often taught religious principles to their house slaves as a regular part of family activities. Adeline Johnson, a former slave who was raised in her owner's house, had daily morning duties of making a fire and helping the young white girls dress and comb their hair. With these tasks completed, she had to lay the Bible on the table by Master Williams's chair. After the meal was finished, they all listened to Williams read from the Bible and say a prayer.[3]

Bible passages were carefully selected to teach obedience and loyalty to the master and his family. The idea of loyalty to the master was taught in prayers, too, thus ensuring the repetitions of words of loyalty and gratitude to slave owners. Sylvia Cannon, a slave in South Carolina, was taught as a child to pray as follows:

> The angels in heaven love us,
> Bless Mamma and Bless Papa,
> Bless our Missus,
> Bless the man that feeding us
> For Christ Sake.[4]

Slaves were repeatedly admonished to remember the Bible injunctions from 1 Peter 2:18, "Servants, be subject to your masters with all fear" or from Colossians 3:22, "Servants, obey in all things your masters." Of course, certain words directed at masters were not presented to slaves, as the verse from Colossians 4:1, "Masters, give unto your servants that which is just and equal; knowing that ye also have a master in heaven." Once the idea of obedience to the master was accepted, some slaveowners allowed slaves to have prayer meetings in their own cabins. Even where religion was forbidden to them, however, many slaves held their own prayer meetings in secrecy in brush arbors in the woods. W. L. Bost, a former slave from North Carolina, remembered that families on his plantation were never allowed to go to Sunday school or church because the owners were afraid they would get education or religion. In spite of this, they would sneak off for prayer meetings, even continuing the practice after patrollers caught and beat some of them.[5]

Although the slave masters used religion to teach docility and obedience, the human mind could not be controlled. Slaves who learned how to read passed on the knowledge that the Bible offered a kind of hope not taught by their masters. Although the teaching of religion was used primarily as a means of teaching obedience and loyalty to the slaveowner, African Americans found their own message in the Bible—a message of hope that they would be free some day, not in the indefinable hereafter, but on earth and within their lifetimes or their children's lifetimes. White preachers taught the verse "Slaves, obey your masters," but Africans were beginning to hide other, more revolutionary ideas in their spirituals (religious slave songs): "Tell old Pharaoh to let my people go!" There was a defiant message to "old Massa" when they sang, "You say your Jesus set-a you free; Why don't you let-a your neighbor be?" When they sang about meeting family on the other side of the River Jordan, the slave master may have thought they were singing about a heavenly reunion, but they also were singing about a wish to meet their brothers and sisters on the other side of rivers here on earth, for rivers were symbols of freedom—the Ohio River was the boundary of Kentucky and freedom, and the Detroit River led to safety in Canada.

As early as the 1700s some slaves and free Black families started their own churches. At first these churches remained under the sponsorship and direction of white denominations that closely monitored and supervised their assemblies. They were governed by white church laws and discipline in ways that did not treat them as equals. Not surprisingly, they began to prefer their own churches. Between 1776 and 1780 Black churches were established in Petersburg, Richmond, and Williamsburg, Virginia. In Savannah, Georgia, George Leile, a Black preacher licensed by the Baptist church, established a Baptist church and trained an assistant, Andrew Bryan. Leile later left Georgia when the British forces withdrew, and Reverend Bryan continued the work Leile had started. Their church, First Bryan Baptist Church in Savannah, Georgia, is still in existence.

Prior to the nineteenth century, many congregations in the South were integrated, although seating in the churches was segregated. As the Civil War approached, however, fears, hostilities, and divisions developed as white and Black members of congregations began to support different sides in the war. Northern and southern branches of the same denominations separated over this issue. Once the northern influence decreased, some slaveowners erected chapels for slaves and paid the salaries of mission preachers, hoping to maintain order among the slaves. After congregations split along racial lines, African American churches began to flourish. At first the new churches had little freedom to operate as their members wished. In Mobile, Alabama, for example, when Black members of the First Baptist Church withdrew in 1830 to form their own church, the white church continued to supervise them. There was, however, an unstoppable trend toward independence.

At the end of the Civil War, Black churches developed at a rapid pace. Of all the African American institutions, these were the most enduring because the churches were the heart of the communities. In addition to providing spiritual activities, the congregations sponsored a variety of social activities. Churchgoing was a way to relax and socialize with neighbors who otherwise were seen infrequently. Churches provided networks of help that ensured that families in trouble could receive assistance from caring friends. Furthermore, churches sometimes provided assistance to fleeing slaves, and they provided meeting places for discussing community business. Especially important, they provided a training ground for leaders who now had opportunities to preach, to raise funds for themselves, to procure supplies, to pay bills on a regular basis, and to lead auxiliary groups within the church. One of the most important functions of the early churches was to provide for schooling of Black children where no other schools existed. It is not by chance that a large percentage of the early African American schoolhouses were located beside a church and associated with it.

Growth of African American Commercial Enterprise in the South

During slavery African Americans were involved not only in agriculture but also in many types of work that later would serve them well in developing commercial enterprises. Especially on the larger, self-sufficient plantations they worked not only in the fields but also as carpenters, cooks, nurses, bricklayers, blacksmiths, barbers, weavers, porters, stevedores, and bondsmen. In large cities slaves and free Black men and women worked in a variety of occupations. In New Orleans they were butchers, vendors, and fishmongers. In Baltimore's harbor they loaded ships and repaired vessels. They worked in the cotton docks of Mobile and Savannah. They built railroads through the countryside.

By 1820 slavery was thriving in southern cities as well as on rural farms and plantations. River cities such as Richmond, Charleston, Savannah, New Orleans, Mobile, Baltimore, Louisville, and St. Louis were important distribution centers for transporting goods to and from agricultural areas. Docks at the mouth of the Mississippi in New Orleans bustled with commerce. Cotton transformed Mobile into a busy port and brought commerce to Savannah. Charleston, with its spacious harbor, became a favorite resort town for cotton and rice planters and required many laborers to support their lavish style of life. Richmond, Virginia's state capital on the James River, had brick warehouses and factories crowding the river banks where Black men and women processed tobacco. Slaves also worked in Virginia processing iron and mining the coal that fueled the iron furnaces. Railroads in the large cities owned slaves. Slave women usually worked in domestic tasks—cleaning house, nursing, caring for children, cooking, sewing, laundering, and going to market. They were expected to be available at all times to care for every large or small need of the owner. In cities throughout the South, slaves drove wagons, repaired roads, tended stores, went shopping, dug sewers, and completed construction projects. By keeping labor costs low and the quality of work high, slaveowners competed successfully with northern industries.

As the Civil War approached, slavery began to lose its grip in the cities. Under such crowded conditions, slaves were hard to supervise and control. As they went about their business, they were free much of the time from the direct supervision of their slaveowners. They met free Black people who showed by their existence that slavery was not universal or inevitable. Some were allowed to find extra jobs during free hours and to keep a portion of the money they earned. This relative freedom allowed slaves in cities to hold responsible positions in various commercial enterprises. With emancipation their marketable skills gave them a distinct advantage.

After the Civil War, African American leaders began to encourage the development of business enterprises. In the forefront was Booker Taliaferro Washington, the head of Tuskegee Institute in Alabama. Born a slave in 1850, Washington attended Hampton Institute in Virginia, taught there, and directed a night school before he was invited to become principal of Tuskegee Institute in 1881. He stressed the importance of training young people for jobs that were open to them in agriculture, industry, and homemaking. Although the quality of the industrial curriculum he espoused was challenged, he continued to emphasize a practical education. He also inspired many families across the country to start businesses; across the South commercial areas sprang up with rows of shops operated by African Americans. The years of the Great Depression and those following desegregation took a toll on Black businesses. Consumers lacked money to spend, and customers began moving to outlying areas. Many businesses, however, were highly successful. For example, several insurance companies developed into major enterprises. This book contains examples of the businesses founded in the decades from emancipation through the twentieth century, as well as examples of structures associated with community enterprises—stores, libraries, and buildings of fraternal organizations.

Schools and Education for African Americans in the South

Southern Schools before Emancipation

In the earliest years of slavery in America, the choice of providing or withholding instruction to slaves was left to individual slaveowners. During this early colonial period southern regions provided no systematic, universal instruction for children of any race. Wealthy families who chose to do so hired tutors or set up small schools on their own for educating their children. In the new country, clearing the land, protecting settlers from ruthlessly displaced Indians, building houses, raising crops, and caring for livestock took up so much time that education was not a top priority.

For most Black children an education in reading and writing was out of the question. Once slavery became institutionalized in law, the teaching of slaves was severely discouraged. Ideas of racial inferiority were dredged up, including notions that literacy skills were inappropriate for a race with limited mental capacity. Ironically, in contrast to that idea, slaveowners seemed to have a greater fear and understanding that Black slaves might learn only too well. If this happened, they said among themselves, slaves would become dissatisfied with their lot and would be more difficult to control. The slaves would be able to read abolitionists' arguments against slavery in pamphlets and newspapers. They would read the laws for themselves and discover that statutes regarding slavery came from humans rather than from God. If bondsmen and women could write, they could forge their own passes, making it easier to escape. Worse, an educated slave would not be as docile as one who remained illiterate.

One of Frederick Douglass's masters, Hugh Auld, clearly understood the subversive nature of teaching a slave to read. As a young boy Frederick had been sent to Baltimore to live with Hugh and Sophie Auld to care for their young son, Tommy. As Sophie read to Tommy and Frederick listened, the young slave boy became curious about the letters and asked Sophie to teach him to read. She did so, and one day, she proudly showed the boy's accomplishments to her husband. Enraged, Hugh demanded that she stop the instruction. Douglass recalled that Hugh Auld exploded with anger and said:

> If you give a n----- [author's deletion] an inch, he will take an ell; he should know nothing but the will of his master, and learn to obey it. Learning would spoil the best n----- in the world; if you teach that n----- . . . how to read the Bible there will be no keeping him; it would forever unfit him for the duties of a slave; and . . . learning would make him no good, but probably a great deal of harm—making him disconsolate and unhappy. If you learn him how to read, he'll want to know how to write; and this accomplished, he'll be running away with himself.[6]

Frederick, who was about eight years old at the time, clearly understood what his master was saying and became even more determined to learn to read. He bribed some hungry white street playmates with bread, and the boys continued the lessons that Sophie Auld was told to stop.

Five years after Frederick's incident with reading, a dramatic slave uprising in Virginia changed the lives of slaves across the South. Nat Turner, a Black preacher who had learned to read as a child and whose owner had given him further reading instruction when he was a young man, initiated and led a fierce slave uprising. As a child he had read and interpreted the Bible and he believed that he, like Moses, was a prophet who would lead his people from bondage. He gathered a group of slaves together, and in August 1831 they moved from house to house in a rebellion that ended in the death of more than sixty white men, women, and children. Ultimately, Turner, with three free Black men and thirteen slaves, was tried and hanged. Even though the rebellion was quelled, white people throughout the South felt a sense of terror and panic. Word spread that Turner had been influenced by abolitionist publications he had read. As a result, states began to pass even more restrictive slave laws as a deep-seated fear grew of both educated *and* illiterate Black people. Alabama had come into the Union in 1819 and had immediately adopted a slave code based on Georgia's laws. Alabama did not, however, forbid educating slaves until after Nat Turner's rebellion. As a result, Alabama passed new laws making it a crime to teach any Black person, slave or free, to read and write and making it a crime for Black people to assemble for any purpose.

Under such restrictive laws few Black children learned to read or write in the South before the Civil War. Those who tried to learn received severe punishment. Milton Marshall, a former slave in Newberry County, South Carolina, remembers that:

> Us chaps did not learn to read and write; that is why I can't read and write today. Marster wouldn't allow us to learn.
>
> I was small in slavery time and played with the white chaps. Once he saw me and some other chaps, white chaps, under a tree playing with letter blocks. They had the ABCs on them. Marster got awful mad and got off his horse and whipped me good.[7]

In 1826 Alabama legislation first provided for establishing a public school system, but it was not until 1854 that the state attempted to set up a state-wide public school system; with the possible exception of one or two schools for the Creole children, who were exempted under a Louisiana Purchase treaty with the French, the system was for white children only. Where schools did exist for Black children before emancipation, they existed only as classes that met in a home or church. Although several Black college campuses have one or two buildings built before the Civil War, they usually were built for white students and already were standing when the Black college received the property. For example, Swayne Hall in Talladega, Alabama, was built by slaves in 1857 for a white school and was used only after emancipation for Talladega College. In South Carolina on St. Helena Island the Brick Church, built by slaves in 1855 for white planters, later was used as an early building of the Penn School, which was established for slaves during the Civil War.

Southern Schools after Emancipation

After the Civil War, local communities were in no mood to provide funding for Black schools. Nevertheless, schools sprang up all over the South, reflecting the strong desire of African Americans to gain the literacy skills that previously had been denied them. Black churches founded many of the early schools, even providing classroom space for them. Parents provided supplies and labor for building one-room schoolhouses. The Freedmen's Bureau and the American Missionary Society provided funds, buildings, and teachers. This was a prime period for a remarkable accomplishment: the establishment of African American colleges in each southern state.

Students not only helped with fund-raising, they also helped to construct many of the buildings. They were responsible for much of the maintenance and housekeeping at their schools. All of the teachers had to begin at the level of the entering students, but they had strong beliefs that the former students, whether slave or free, were teachable.

Some schools and colleges presented a practical, industrial curriculum; others featured a classical curriculum in which students studied science, mathematics, Latin, Greek, history, and literature. Both types of curricula existed in the South depending on the school leadership, the training and orientation of the teachers, and sometimes, political necessity, which meant the will of donors to the school. Booker T. Washington understood the need for students to receive a practical training to prepare for jobs that were available to them, and he also understood that he would be better able to attain both funding and goodwill of white citizens if he prepared students for the farming and industrial work that met local needs. Whether students received an industrial or a classical education, they were taught to accept, in a sense, a curriculum that did not openly challenge the racial status quo. In addition, according to Black historian Carter G. Woodson, in both curricula, students failed to gain a strong enough sense of Black history. In spite of this, the colleges did a magnificent job of moving students from slavery to literacy; with limited means they educated a disproportionate share of the future leaders of the race. The work of student activism would be left to students in the twentieth century—those in the nineteenth century did a masterful job of laying the groundwork for the future.

Twentieth-Century Southern Schools

During the first half of the twentieth century, many of the old attitudes still prevailed in which white lawmakers in the South almost universally refused to adequately fund Black schools. There were great disparities in salaries, buildings, supplies, and almost every aspect of funding. White citizens still held tight to the old slavemaster views that schooling was inappropriate for Black children. In a pamphlet distributed in 1933, an author expressed his resentment:

> The taxing of poor white people to furnish "HIGHER EDUCATION" for negro wenches and sassy bucks, is an OUTRAGE upon the WHITE and an injury to the negroes. The schools and colleges are turning loose on the country thousands of negro men and women who have been taught the smattering of the higher branches and who, in consequence consider it beneath their dignity to work with their hands. There is absolutely no place in this land for the arrogant, aggressive, school-spoilt Afro-American, who wants to live without manual labor.[8]

That education was able to proceed at all for Black students in many counties was due in large part to the determination of Black parents and to gifts from individuals and philanthropic organizations. These included the Peabody Fund, the John F. Slater Fund, the Anna T. Jeanes Fund, and especially the Julius Rosenwald Fund. The Carnegie Fund was important in building libraries in southern towns.

The Rosenwald Fund helped local communities build schoolhouses for Black children throughout the South. Local school boards and Black communities contributed funds and the Rosenwald Fund gave matching monies. By the time Rosenwald funding stopped in 1932, North Carolina had constructed 813 Rosenwald buildings, more than any other state. Unfortunately, many local governments took advantage of this resource, providing less funding for Black schools where Rosenwald funds became available. In spite of this, many communities for the first time had attractive, structurally sound, professionally designed schools for African American children.

Many Rosenwald schools closed after school integration of the 1950s created consolidations, and the last of these schools shut down in 1966. They had been built in small, rural Black settlements. Even though some schools were substandard for the 1960s, they had raised the quality of school buildings for their day and had improved education for Black students within a segregated framework.

The twentieth century was a major period of awakening of Black college students to the burgeoning Civil Rights Movement of the 1940s, 1950s, and 1960s. Although protest was not new, the scope of the mass participation of students in demonstrations and marches was new. The era began with smaller-scale civil rights battles, often fought in the courts. For example, in 1943 Dunbar Junior High School, a segregated Arkansas school, was involved in a successful legal battle for equal pay for Black teachers and white teachers who performed the same work.

More widely publicized, however, was the turbulent period of the 1950s and 1960s. For the first time, television instantly involved the nation in the drama of desegregating schools. In the fall of 1957, when nine Black students tried to enroll in Little Rock's Central High School, they were turned aside by a hostile, jeering crowd. A Black journalist, James Hicks, traveled with two other African American reporters to cover the first day of school for the nine Black students. Suddenly he saw that

> This was a mob all around us; we were outnumbered I guess about five hundred to one. And so they started getting smart and whatnot. And pretty soon this one man, he was a one-armed man, he put his arm around my neck, and the others started attacking me. But I was able to look up and see that whereas I was being held and my clothes torn off, Alex Wilson was being attacked by somebody who had a brick in his hand. Instead of throwing the brick, 'cause he was too close and he didn't want to, I guess, throw it, he hit Wilson up the side of the head with this brick. I mean a full brick. He picked it up and slapped Wilson like that. Wilson was more than six feet tall, and an ex-Marine. He went down like a tree. Newsome, he was mauled. I was mauled.[9]

Even when later protected inside the school by federal troops, the nine students experienced a year of hatred and harassment. They had to be watchful for acts of random violence directed at them and had to forgo the typical fun-filled activities that are usually a part of the high school years. The African American student who was a senior, Ernest Green, graduated in May 1959; then Governor Orval E. Faubus challenged again the right of Black students to integrate schools by closing all of Little Rock's public schools for a school year. In August 1959 the U.S. Supreme Court ruled the closing evasive and unconstitutional, but white citizens continued to evade desegregation laws through the 1970s. By that time many Black citizens had left the state seeking better opportunities in other regions.

African American Participation in Battle

African Americans fought for the United States in battles throughout our country's history. Their participation started in the colonial era when colonial militias called for all able-bodied males between the ages of seventeen and sixty to serve in defense of the colonies. In the early 1800s, however, some colonies barred Black men from serving, fearing that they could become involved in armed insurrections of their own. Virginia later amended the laws, permitting free Black men to serve as laborers, as drummers, and as similar unarmed workers. In 1703, during Indian attacks in South Carolina, slaves were armed and sent to serve in the defense. During the early 1700s, South Carolina promised freedom to slaves who killed Indians, but the promises often were not kept.

When the War of Independence started in 1775, the old fears about arming slaves arose again. White citizens argued that Black soldiers would prove cowardly in war; ironically, they feared arming the same Black men they had called cowardly. In November 1775 General George Washington banned the recruitment of Black men for service as soldiers even though some already were fighting in the Revolutionary War. His policy later was reversed as the Americans became aware that the British, through a proclamation from Lord Dunmore, Virginia's Royal Governor, promised freedom to slaves who would fight against the colonists. Eventually, 5,000 Black troops served in the Revolutionary War, although those in the South served primarily as laborers and servants.

Black Americans who thought they would be rewarded for their service in the War for Independence were bitterly disappointed to learn that the country regarded the struggle as a white man's war. In 1792 Congress restricted military service to white citizens only. The Navy, however, did recruit Black men during this period, and a group had a chance to train in Louisiana, a state that already had trained a militia of free Black citizens when the state was under French and Spanish rule. The men offered their services during the War of 1812 against Great Britain and fought courageously with General Andrew Jackson in the Battle of New Orleans. The men in the militia never received the land and other compensation they had been promised, and they did not become a part of the regular United States Army.

This section on the South lists many sites at which Black soldiers fought in important military battles, primarily those associated with the Civil War. When the Civil War began in 1861, most states in the North had abolished slavery, but more than 75 percent of the Black population in the United States lived in the southern states of North Carolina, South Carolina, Virginia, Georgia, and Alabama. Most white Northerners at first did not associate the Civil War with efforts to free slaves but considered it a war to preserve the Union. Southern leaders, however, believed that Abraham Lincoln's policies would weaken the power of the South, and their states began to secede from the Union. In February 1861 a group of southern states formed the Confederacy.

The South went to war to defend its institutions, including slavery. For African Americans, too, the issue was clear—their freedom was at stake. At the time of the 1860 elections, there was no political party that promised relief for their oppression. The four major parties had failed to promote the cause of freedom for the slaves. The Republican party sought only to prevent the extension of slavery into the new territories, and Abraham Lincoln not only failed to oppose slavery as a whole but also stated that the South was entitled to a Fugitive Slave Law that made it easier to capture escaping slaves and return them to their owners.

Although the outcome of the Civil War affected them deeply, at first African Americans were not permitted to join the Union Army as soldiers. In spite of being barred from service, slaves ran to Union lines anyway and sought refuge there. By May 1861 Union General Benjamin Butler began to call the fugitives "contraband of war," and began to use them as laborers. By August of that same year, Congress passed an act providing for seizure of property used in aiding the rebellion; this property included slaves. Although the slaves seized under this act were not emancipated, they were a step above slavery. Even though their treatment was sometimes abusive, the escaped slaves still preferred it to life on the plantations. They began to serve as laborers and, even more important because of their knowledge of the land, as spies and scouts. They found food and hiding places for Union soldiers and often led them through unfamiliar terrain.

The Confederate states believed at first that slavery would help them win the war. They reasoned that their economy would be less disrupted than the North's economy because slaves could continue the work of the plantations while white men went off to fight. They believed that the economy in the North would be disrupted because no one would be available to fill the industrial positions when white men in the North went off to fight.

Although neither side wanted to arm Black men, it was inevitable that they should do so. The President saw that the war effort was becoming unpopular and that winning would be far more difficult and costly than Northerners had first imagined. White men were tiring of the war, and by summer 1862 the Union had begun to suffer a series of defeats. On July 17, 1862, Congress repealed the 1792 act that barred Black men from serving as soldiers, and Congress empowered the President to enlist African Americans. When President Lincoln issued the Emancipation Proclamation, which became law on January 1, 1863, the abolition of slavery became tied to the aims of the Union cause. Black men, who for years had volunteered to serve, now officially began to enroll in the U.S. Army. Frederick Douglass was one of the primary recruiters, and two of his own sons, Charles and Lewis, enrolled.

When the Civil War ended, there was such rejoicing, celebration, and anticipation as most people only experience as a group once in a lifetime. Although Black men and women learned about the end of the Civil War in many different ways, they universally hoped that the war that had ended slavery would bring a peace that had eluded them—they wanted a better life economically and access to the rights and privileges the Constitution had secured for others but had denied to African Americans.

Too often, however, in the South they encountered a bitter determination of former slaveowners and those who sympathized with them to control people whom they saw as a resource wrested from them. The hard times were balanced to a degree by some acts of kindness from former masters and by assistance from the Freedmen's Bureau and northern philanthropists. During the Reconstruction period, African Americans moved ahead making gains in the political arena, in education, in business, and in general living standards. At the same time, however, the U.S. government released control over affairs of the South, former abolitionists declared success for their cause and turned away, and former proslavery forces in the South regained control. The Ku Klux Klan and other groups increased their terrorist tactics, and white lawmakers in the South regained control of the political process and passed "Jim Crow laws" that instituted another century of repression. Black Americans found themselves involved in the struggle anew.

Notes

1. Belinda Hurmence, ed., *Before Freedom When I Just Can Remember* (Winston-Salem, N.C.: John F. Blair, 1989), 39–40.
2. Hurmence, *Before Freedom,* 60.
3. Hurmence, *Before Freedom,* 56.
4. Hurmence, *Before Freedom,* 126.
5. Belinda Hurmence, ed., *My Folks Don't Want Me to Talk about Slavery: Twenty-One Oral Histories of Former North Carolina Slaves* (Winston-Salem, N.C.: John F. Blair, 1984), 95–96.
6. William S. McFeely, *Frederick Douglass* (New York: Touchstone, Simon & Schuster, 1991), 30.
7. Hurmence, *Before Freedom,* 43.
8. G. Woodford Mabry, *A Reply to Southern Slanderers: In Re the Nigger Question* (Grove Hill, Ala.: the Author, 1933), quoted in Horace Mann Bond, *Negro Education in Alabama: A Study in Cotton and Steel* (New York: Atheneum, 1969), 245.
9. Henry Hampton and Steve Fayer with Sarah Flynn, "The Little Rock Crisis 1957–1958," in *Voices of Freedom: An Oral History of the Civil Rights Movement from the 1950s through the 1980s* (New York: Bantam, 1990), 44–45.

Works Consulted

African Americans, Voices of Triumph: Perseverance. Alexandria, Va.: Time-Life, 1993.

Against All Opposition: Black Explorers in America. Jim Haskins. New York: Walker, 1992.

Historical and Cultural Atlas of African Americans. Molefi K. Asante and Mark T. Mattson. New York: Macmillan, 1992.

Slavery in the Cities: The South 1820–1860. Richard C. Wade. New York: Oxford University Press, 1964.

Alabama

Auburn

Ebenezer Missionary Baptist Church

Ebenezer Missionary Baptist Church, a frame church with clapboard siding, is one of Alabama's finest surviving examples of a church built by African Americans in the post–Civil War years. Fine craftsmanship is shown in the details of the double entrance doors and in the square bell tower, which is capped with a pyramidal roof and embellished with wooden circular designs.

During the period of slavery, many African Americans in Alabama had worshiped in their "owners'" churches but not as equals. Before 1866, however, this unequal arrangement began to change in the Auburn area. Reverend Thomas Glenn came from Columbus, Georgia, to preach to local freedmen and freedwomen. He led community members in establishing the Ebenezer congregation and, in 1870, members constructed the church with their own hands. Their great achievement took place only five years after slavery ended. Community members financed its construction with their own money and built the church on land that they themselves owned.

More than a century later, church membership had declined significantly. To save the building, the Auburn Heritage Association acquired Ebenezer Church and restored it. The historic structure is in use today by the Unitarian Universalist Fellowship.

DATE ESTABLISHED:	Congregation, before 1868; church, 1870
ADDRESS:	Thach Street and Auburn Drive S, Auburn
TELEPHONE:	Dr. Ann Pearson, (205) 821-3660
VISITING HOURS:	Sun. services, 10
SOURCES:	Telephone conversation Mar. 13, 1994, Dr. Ann Pearson. NRHPINF. *Alabama's Black Heritage. Keepers of the Faith.*

Birmingham

Fourth Avenue Historic District
Alabama Penny Savings Bank

On Birmingham's Fourth Avenue, African American businesses once flourished in spite of the segregation that gripped the city. Commercial buildings housed businesses catering to the cultural, entertainment, and business needs of the Black community. Although many of the buildings have been razed by urban renewal, several landmarks remain as a testament to the vibrant business district that once existed here. Major landmarks—the Alabama Savings Bank (now the Pythian Temple), Colored Masonic Temple, Famous Theatre, and Carver Cinema (one of Birmingham's best examples of the art-moderne architectural style)—provided offices for business leaders and community organizations as well as entertainment facilities for the community.

The Fourth Avenue district developed between 1908 and 1941, when, in response to segregation, African Americans developed their own professional offices, businesses, cultural institutions, and social activities. Large and small businesses sprang up side by side in this downtown area, which was the heart of the African American business community. The 1600 and 1700 blocks of Fourth Avenue North contained restaurants, hotels, dry cleaners, and beauty and barber shops.

The major landmark in the district, the Alabama Penny Savings Bank, was founded in 1890 as Alabama's first Black-owned bank. Bank officers chose an established company, the Black-owned Windham Construction Company, as contractor. By 1913 a distinctive six-story, buff-colored brick building rose in this hub, a building whose projecting cornice lent an air of distinction to the busy commercial district.

Business leaders and professionals had office space in the Alabama Penny Savings Bank Building, and a newspaper was published there. The bank grew by 1907 into America's second-largest Black bank, one that provided construction loans for thousands of homes and churches in the African American community. By 1915, however, the community was struck by financial hardship, the bank failed, and ownership of the landmark building passed to another community organization, a fraternal society called the Grand Knights of Pythias.

It was desegregation that hastened the decline of the district as a whole. As boundaries fell in other parts of the city, many business owners and their clients moved to more distant neighborhoods. Some of the Fourth Avenue buildings became vacant; others burned; still others were demolished. The buildings remaining in this historic business district stand as visual reminders of a once-thriving commercial, social, and cultural center of Birmingham's African American community.

DATE BUILT: Alabama Penny Savings Bank Building, c1913; Colored Masonic Temple, 1922; Famous Theatre, 1928; Carver Cinema, 1941; other buildings, 1908–1941

ADDRESS: Alabama Penny Savings Bank, 310 Eighteenth Street N; Masonic Temple, 1630 Fourth Avenue N; other buildings, 1600 to 1800 blocks of Fourth Avenue N and part of the 300 blocks of Seventeenth and Eighteenth Streets N, Birmingham

TELEPHONE: Masonic Temple, (205) 328-9078

VISITING HOURS: Private, visitors may walk or drive by

SOURCES: NRHPINF. Personal visit, summer 1990. *Alabama's Black Heritage.*

Sixteenth Street Baptist Church*

Sixteenth Street Baptist Church has a permanent place in Black history, both for the proud history of its congregation and church structure and for its role in the civil rights era of the 1960s. The congregation was first organized in 1873. Within a decade it had constructed the first sanctuary on this site, designed by a well-known African American architect from Birmingham, Wallace A. Rayfield, and built by the Windham Brothers Construction Company. Rayfield's design featured large, round-arched windows, arched openings, twin bell towers, and a central cupola.

Sixteenth Street Baptist Church was thrust by tragedy into the international limelight on September 15, 1963. On that Sunday morning, fifteen sticks of explosive were hurled into the church, killing four children: Addie May Collins, Denise McNair, Cynthia Wesley, and Carol Robertson, whose ages ranged from eleven to fourteen. In the riots that followed the explosion, two more Black youths were killed.

For months the church and Kelly Ingram Park, located just northwest of the church, had been gathering points for demonstrators determined to end segregation through nonviolent confrontations and boycotts. The nonviolence was one-sided, however. There had been as many as fifty bombings in the city between the end of World War II and the 1960s. A white Lutheran minister, the Reverend Joseph Ellwanger, later noted that in the ten years preceding 1963, there had been approximately forty bombings in Birmingham. On May 11, 1963, Klansmen had rocked the A. G. Gaston Motel and the Reverend A. D. King home with bombs. By September of 1963, police with clubs and police dogs and firefighters with high-pressure hoses were responding swiftly and brutally to demonstrators. Across the nation, shocked Americans watched on their television sets as dogs and fire hoses were turned on peacefully demonstrating men, women, and children. The attacks enraged the Black community, and many of its members began to return violence for violence.

That Sunday morning in September 1963 was a turning point. The four young girls at the Sixteenth Street Baptist Church had just changed into their choir robes in preparation for services. Moments later they died in the loud explosion that rocked the church, shattering the portion of the basement where they stood and injuring twenty-four others in a cloud of smoke, fire, and debris.

After the bombing, a change of heart took place among many in the white community, and they began to accept a conciliatory plan for desegregating Birmingham. The 1964 federal Civil Rights Act eventually outlawed segregation in public accommodations. There were, however, no easy or quick resolutions to the incident at Sixteenth Street Baptist Church. Eight years after the bombing, the police had made no arrests in the case. That same year the people of far-off Wales, moved by compassion, gave a stained-glass window to the church to commemorate the tragedy. Finally, the case was reopened. In 1977 a former Ku Klux Klan member was convicted of first-degree murder of Denise McNair and sentenced to life in prison.

DATE ESTABLISHED:	Congregation, 1873; present church, 1911
ADDRESS:	1530 Sixth Avenue N at Sixteenth Street N, Birmingham
TELEPHONE:	(205) 251-9402
VISITING HOURS:	By appointment; inquire at the parsonage located just west of the church
SOURCES:	NRHPINF. *Alabama's Black Heritage. Keepers of the Faith. Before the Mayflower.* "Birmingham, 1963."

Smithfield Historic District

Birmingham's earliest and largest concentration of middle-class African American homes and buildings is found in the suburb called the Smithfield Historic District. The community began in the nineteenth century when developers carved lots out of the flat land of the Joseph Riley Smith plantation. By 1898 the area had the largest concentration of Black families of any of Birmingham's suburban communities. Prominent African American families moved to Smithfield, where, because of segregation, the affluent families built beside low rent industrial housing. This gave a wide variety of housing types in the same community, a neighborhood that today has 194 buildings in the historic district. Visitors to the area will be able to trace the development of a professional "white-collar" group early in this century.

The Dr. Arthur McKinnon Brown House, the Edward A. Brown House, and the Windham Construction Company are community landmarks. Other historic buildings include the Pilgrim Lutheran Church, a tiny Gothic-style church built about 1930 of clinker brick laid in fancy patterns; the Dobbins Service Station (later named Pure Oil), an early gas station type from about 1935; and the Trinity Baptist Church. This latter building, which currently houses the New Mount Pilgrim Baptist Church, dates from about 1920 and was the earliest and most substantial church building in the Smithfield district. It is distinguished by its proportions and twin bell towers. There are notable residences on the 400 to 600 blocks of First Street, the 300 and 500 blocks of Fourth Terrace, and the 400 and 500 blocks of Sixth Avenue. Together, all of these structures give a view of how a wide variety of African American families lived in early twentieth-century Birmingham.

DATE ESTABLISHED: Community, 1893–1930

ADDRESS: Roughly bounded by Eighth Avenue N, Sixth Street N, Fourth Terrace N, and First Street N, Birmingham

TELEPHONE: New Mount Pilgrim Baptist Church, (205) 252-9603

VISITING HOURS: Private, visitors may drive by

SOURCES: NRHPINF. *Keepers of the Faith. National Register of Historic Places,* 10. Alabama Department of Archives and History. *Alabama's Black Heritage.*

Dr. Arthur McKinnon Brown House

The Dr. Arthur McKinnon Brown House (now the A. M. Brown Community Center for Arts and Crafts) was constructed about 1909. The nine-room bungalow located at 319 North Fourth Terrace is the most impressive residence in the district. Dr. A. M. Brown was born in North Carolina in 1867, studied at Lincoln University, and then continued his graduate studies in surgery and ophthalmology, graduating with honors from Michigan Medical School. He founded Children's Home Hospital in Birmingham, which for many years was the only hospital in the area for Black doctors and their patients.

The Brown House was designed by W. A. Rayfield, an African American architect born in 1870. After attending Howard University, Rayfield graduated from the Pratt Institute at Columbia University with a degree in architecture. He taught at Tuskegee Institute before coming to Birmingham. In designing Brown's home, Rayfield created a tasteful and comfortable residence. Its porch extends across the front of the house and halfway around both sides. Stained-glass windows and glass areas above and to the sides of the front door add decorative embellishments. When Brown died in 1939, his son, Dr. Walter Brown, granted a free lease to the Birmingham Art Club, allowing the organization to use the home as an arts and crafts community center.

DATE ESTABLISHED: c1909

ADDRESS: 319 Fourth Terrace N

Edward A. Brown House

The Edward A. Brown House, a cottage at 526 Fifth Street North, is another Rayfield design. This two-story, pressed-concrete structure was constructed between 1906 and 1909 for a prominent Birmingham attorney.

ADDRESS: 526 Fifth Street N
TELEPHONE: (205) 252-8587

Windham Construction Company

The Windham Construction Company is a two-story brick office building on Eighth Avenue. It is the earliest known commercial building in the Smithfield Historic District. Thomas C. Windham, born in 1880, founded the company in 1895, and his brother Benjamin, an honors graduate of Leland University in New Orleans, joined the business in 1897. The brothers constructed the office building in 1912, and corporate offices were moved into it in 1917 or 1918. Thomas Windham and his wife lived in one of two apartments on the second floor until the mid-1920s. This building, now vacant, served as the home office of the firm until 1966, when Lewis, Thomas Windham's only son, died. Other small businesses also were located in the Windham Building.

The Windham Construction Company, in cooperation with architect Wallace Rayfield, built many significant buildings and structures in Birmingham, including the Sixteenth Street Baptist Church; the Sixth Avenue Baptist Church; the Birmingham Railway, Light and Power Company; the Alabama Penny Savings Bank; and the Trinity Baptist Church.

DATE ESTABLISHED: c1912
ADDRESS: 528 Eighth Avenue N

Florence

W. C. Handy "Father of the Blues" Birthplace, Museum, and Library*

Composer W. C. Handy was born on November 16, 1873, in a log cabin high in the Alabama hills near the Tennessee River. His birthplace was in Florence, a town that provided many places for a child to walk, explore, and especially listen to music. As a boy, when Handy visited his grandfather's farm, he would walk down to the locks along the river and listen to the songs of the laborers. He loved the sounds of their voices. Although his father and grandfather were ministers and urged him to follow in their footsteps, Handy went down a different path because of his love of music.

Handy studied music with Y. A. Wallace, who came to Florence from Fisk University to teach in the Black public school where he drilled his students in singing and music techniques. After studying with Wallace for eleven years, Handy was ready to combine his formal training with memories of the music he had heard along the river. In the end he created his own unique blues form—a composite of spirituals, African melodies and rhythms, and the songs he remembered from his childhood.

Running away from home at the age of eighteen, Handy struggled through financially lean years but continued to produce songs. In Memphis, he wrote the song "Mr. Crump" during a political campaign in which E. H. Crump ran for the office of mayor of Memphis. He later rewrote the song and gave it new words, and it became the widely known "Memphis Blues," the first popular song to include an improvised jazz break. In St. Louis, during a period when he was out of work, Handy lay down on a cobblestone levee on the riverfront and overheard a man express words of misery. He later used some of the words in his 1914 "St. Louis Blues." Songs he composed during this period were among the more than 150 compositions he wrote during his lifetime.

To advance his musical career, Handy moved north and founded a publishing firm in New York

City in 1918. He died there on March 28, 1958. Today the Handy Museum in Florence has the world's most complete set of his personal papers as well as his library, piano, photographs, trumpet, handwritten sheet music, and other memorabilia. The restored cabin contains furnishings as they might have appeared when Handy lived in Florence.

DATE BUILT: Cabin, c1845

ADDRESS: 620 W. College Street, Florence

TELEPHONE: (205) 760-6434

VISITING HOURS: Tues.–Sat. 9–noon, 1–4; closed Sun., Mon., and major holidays

FEES: Tour, $1.50

SOURCES: Alabama Department of Archives and History. Telephone call to site, Nov. 25, 1994. *Alabama: A State of Surprises. Alabama's Black Heritage.*

Greenville

Frank Ward's Corner Store

The Frank Ward's Corner Store, although closed now, is a reminder of an era that emphasized the growth and development of Black businesses. When Reverend Frank Ward opened his little corner store around 1885, he was carrying out the self-help ideas of Booker T. Washington and other Black leaders who had emphasized Black independence through business ownership. Ward's Corner Store is the earliest remaining example of the neighborhood businesses established in Greenville.

Reverend Frank W. Ward (1857–1925), a prominent and respected African Methodist Episcopal Zion Church minister, opened his neighborhood grocery store to serve the people of his community. In addition to being a place for buying groceries, the store also served as a place for chatting, socializing, and catching up on community news. The Wards lived in a nineteenth century, one-story frame house behind the store. After Ward died, his wife operated the store until her death in 1930. Mrs. Nobie Price then purchased the business and continued to operate it as a corner store through the 1960s, occasionally leasing the building out for social events.

Frank Ward's Corner Store was built on a corner lot rise in a folk-style version of the Greek-revival country store. The one-story frame building has a narrow "shotgun" shape, projecting display windows, and steps that lead up to the center entrance. The corner store is the best nineteenth-century building of this type remaining in Greenville.

DATE BUILT: c1884

ADDRESS: 219 W. Parmer, Greenville

VISITING HOURS: Interior, closed; visitors may walk or drive by

SOURCES: Personal visit, summer 1990. *National Register of Historic Places. Multiple Resources of Greenville, Butler County, Alabama.*

Marion

First Congregational Church of Marion

When slavery ended, one of the greatest desires of the freedmen and freedwomen of this area was for a school for their children. In July 1867, with financial support from the American Missionary Association, they erected a small building, the Lincoln Normal School of Marion. In 1870 the newly organized First Congregational Church also began using the schoolhouse as a chapel. A year later, after the American Missionary Association donated a building site and $800, church members built the present chapel.

The First Congregational Church of Marion, a strong influence in the community over the years, is the last remaining symbol of the cooperation that existed between Marion's Black community and the American Missionary Association during the Reconstruction period. Completely restored, the First Congregational Church is listed in the *National Register of Historic Places.*

DATE BUILT: 1871
ADDRESS: 601 Clay Street, Marion
TELEPHONE: Mrs. Idella Childs, (334) 683-6981
VISITING HOURS: Contact the church
SOURCES: NRHPINF. The Honorable Mrs. Idella Childs, city council member. *Alabama's Black Heritage. Keepers of the Faith.*

Lincoln Normal School
Phillips Memorial Auditorium

A determined group of former slaves, in cooperation with the American Missionary Association, established the Lincoln Normal School in 1867. The idea for a school was born when a crippled Union soldier, who had been left behind during the Civil War, began teaching local Black children. His instruction unleashed among community members a desire for education that could not be quenched. In 1867 a group of freedmen asked the state government for permission to incorporate the Lincoln Normal School of Marion.

Trustees moved quickly to acquire a lot and a small building. They also petitioned the American Missionary Association for help and received a commitment from the association to pay the teachers, to keep the building in repair, and to operate the school at least seven months each year. In return, members of the Black community agreed to assist in maintaining the school.

Lincoln Normal School opened in a predominantly rural, Black, and impoverished county of Alabama. The American Missionary Association bought an old plantation house—formerly the headquarters of the local Ku Klux Klan—and transformed it into a teachers' residence. In 1874 the state of Alabama took over the teacher-training department, while the association continued to operate the primary department. In 1887 the teacher-training department moved to Montgomery, where it eventually became Alabama State University. The primary school continued to function in the old farmhouse and in an adjacent old barn. With the help of members of the community, boxes and benches were installed to turn the meager buildings into classrooms.

The school struggled financially through every year of its existence. Finally, the American Missionary Association, which was called on to finance schools through the entire South, reviewed the poor facilities at Lincoln Normal School and decided that it would be best to cut the school from its budget. Noting the crowding of 150 students into the small house, the association directors saw little hope for the school.

Members of the local community, however, felt otherwise. To keep their school open, adults pledged $1,300 to pay its debts; even the children made a pledge to raise at least $100. Staying out of school at the beginning of the term, some students picked cotton to pay for their tuition and books. Teachers who returned to work without salaries received their pay instead in eggs, milk, vegetables, and meat. Writing to friends in the North, the teachers pleaded for help, and they prayed together that funds would arrive. Finally, the American Missionary Association relented and agreed to continue its support of the Lincoln Normal School.

During the Great Depression the school encouraged continued attendance by reducing annual tuition from $25 to $4. Parents raised money by selling old clothing that the Congregational Church in the North sent south in barrels. From miles around people came to purchase clothes and goods from the school's storeroom. Those who had no money paid with farm produce.

Miss Elizabeth Phillips-Thompson, a Northerner and the school's sixth principal, guided Lincoln Normal School through its most difficult period. When she died in 1927, her will provided money for the school. Alumni began a fund to initiate the building of an auditorium that Miss Phillips had wanted to be her next project. Black and white contributions led to construction of a stately Classical Revival building that was named Phillips Memorial Auditorium in memory of Miss Phillips's service and generosity. For years this building served as the primary meeting place and social center for Marion's African American community.

In 1943 the Perry County Board of Education began providing financial support. As a result, the board also changed Lincoln from a private school to a segregated county public school. White faculty members who had worked side by side with Black faculty members were forced to leave. The American Missionary Association sold the buildings to the state of Alabama in 1960.

Lincoln Normal School, in its one hundred years of existence, produced many graduates who went on to attain high levels of education and accomplishment. In an era when vocational and industrial education was recommended for Black students, Lincoln Normal School challenged the norm by providing a quality private, liberal arts education in Perry County.

Lincoln Normal School celebrated its one hundredth anniversary on May 7, 1967. After antisegregation laws were enforced in Perry County in 1970, the county closed the institution and sent the children to a formerly white school. In the 1970s all of the Lincoln Normal School buildings were demolished except the Phillips Memorial Auditorium. The auditorium is still in use for community meetings.

DATE BUILT: 1935–1938

ADDRESS: Lincoln Avenue and Lee Street, Marion

TELEPHONE: Mrs. Idella Childs, (334) 683-6981

VISITING HOURS: Private; to see interior, contact Mrs. Childs

SOURCES: Personal visit, summer 1990. NRHPRF. Telephone conversation Aug. 5, 1995, Mrs. Idella Childs, city councilwoman and president, Lincoln School National Alumni Association. "Lincoln Normal School."

Mobile

Dave Patton House

Dave Patton was born in 1879. As an adult he was influenced by Booker T. Washington's ideas that Black people should develop their own economy in which they would trade with each other. Patton diverged somewhat from Washington's philosophy because he had many white clients. He founded one of Mobile's most successful hauling companies, having some eighty men to transport goods on mule-drawn vehicles around the city. As his hauling business grew, he added wrecking and contracting services. He also began to acquire real estate. After Patton died in 1927, his son continued to operate the business.

The Dave Patton House, built in 1910, is an unusually large and well-constructed residence. In contrast to other houses in the neighborhood, which are modest, one-story structures, the Patton House appears to have been designed by an architect. The frame residence has a two-story front porch with elaborately turned balusters at the second-story level. There is a porte-cochere on the east side of the building. The interior has paneled alcoves with bench seats, a built-in bookcase in the living room, detailed moldings, and the original ceiling light fixtures.

The Patton family owned the house until 1979, when the Stewart Memorial Christian Methodist Episcopal Church purchased it for use as a parsonage.

DATE BUILT: c1915
ADDRESS: 1252 Martin Luther King Jr. Avenue, Mobile
TELEPHONE: Stewart Memorial C.M.E. Church, (334) 432-3791
VISITING HOURS: Private, visitors may drive or walk by
SOURCE: NRHPINF.

St. Louis Street Missionary Baptist Church

The St. Louis Street Missionary Baptist Church, the mother church of many Alabama churches, has been the setting that inspired many to become members of the Black clergy. It was one of four Black congregations established in Alabama before the end of the Civil War.

Members of Mobile's Black community organized their own congregation as early as 1836. After worshiping in a variety of locations, they constructed the Stone Street Baptist Church in 1839. Ten members left that church and organized the St. Louis Street Baptist Church in 1854. They worshiped in a small church for years and completed the present two-story, stuccoed brick church in 1872.

In 1874 the Colored Baptist Convention met in this church and passed a resolution to sponsor a school that would educate young people to become teachers and ministers. The school eventually became Selma University.

DATE BUILT: Present building, 1872; renovations, 1897 and 1910
ADDRESS: 108 N. Dearborn Street, Mobile
TELEPHONE: (334) 438-3823
VISITING HOURS: Restricted access, telephone ahead
SOURCES: NRHPINF. Telephone conversation Mar. 13, 1994, Mr. Booker T. Green, member, Board of Trustees. *Keepers of the Faith.*

State Street African Methodist Episcopal Zion Church

State Street A.M.E. Zion Church is one of America's oldest remaining church structures built and maintained by a Black congregation. It was built in 1854, one of two Black Methodist churches established in Mobile prior to the Civil War, and it is the oldest Methodist church building in Mobile.

A nineteenth-century photograph of the church shows a ten-foot spire that was added during an 1890s renovation. The spire was removed in the twentieth century, leaving emphasis on the original Romanesque details of round-arched windows and door woodwork. The structure shows the idealism and determination of the congregation members who constructed the edifice before emancipation.

DATE BUILT: 1854

ADDRESS: 502 State Street, Mobile

TELEPHONE: Office, (334) 432-3965

VISITING HOURS: Office hours, Tues.–Fri. 10:30–4:30; Sun. school 9:30, Sun. service 11

SOURCES: Telephone conversation July 29, 1995, Michael Lemmon, minister of music, State Street A.M.E. Zion Church. NRHPINF. *Alabama's Black Heritage. Keepers of the Faith.* Historic Mobile Preservation Society. Alabama Department of Archives and History.

Stone Street Baptist Church

Stone Street Baptist Church, built by its members, is one of Alabama's oldest African American congregations, which traces its history to the early nineteenth century. It was organized under the influence of the white Baptist church, and church members held their first meetings in a brush arbor. The church building was redesigned in 1931.

DATE BUILT: 1820; redesigned 1931

ADDRESS: 311 Cleveland, Mobile

TELEPHONE: (334) 433-3947

VISITING HOURS: By appointment, Mon.–Fri. 11–5; Sun. service, 11

SOURCES: Alabama Department of Archives and History. Telephone call to site, Nov. 25, 1994. *Alabama's Black Heritage. Keepers of the Faith.*

Union Baptist Church
Cudjoe Lewis Memorial Statue

The Africa Town settlement in Prichard is the oldest African American community in Alabama. It was established in 1859 when the vessel *Clotilde* sailed into harbor carrying an illegal cargo of Africans bound for slavery. Although the U.S. Congress had enacted legislation forbidding the importing of slaves into the United States after January 1808, some illegal slave ships continued to smuggle slaves into ports throughout the South. The *Clotilde* was the last to smuggle Africans into America to be sold into slavery.

Timothy Meaher, a white man, had commissioned the schooner to sail to Africa in 1859, and William Foster was the schooner's builder and captain. The *Clotilde* returned with 130 Black men, women, and children who had been captured from a West African village. The captors took the Africans to the slave market at the corner of St. Louis and Royal Streets in Mobile and prepared to display them for sale. Then Meaher and Foster found out that authorities had been alerted to the illegal sale. Knowing that they could not sell the slaves with authorities in the area, they decided to abandon them.

The freed Africans remained together, settling in the east-of-Mobile area of Plateau. They called their community "Africa Town," and many attended the Union Baptist Church. Cudjoe Lewis, the last African survivor brought to America on the *Clotilde,* lived next door to the Union Baptist Church until his death in 1935. A bronze bust located in front of the church honors him. It was sculpted in 1959 by a teen, Albert Williams, under the direction of Henry C. Williams of Plateau. Lewis and many of his descendants are buried in Plateau Cemetery on Cut Off Road.

Each year in February/March, Union Baptist Church members join others in celebrating an annual Africatown Folk Festival.

ADDRESS: Church, 506 Bay Bridge Road, Prichard; Cudjoe Lewis Memorial, in front of the Union Baptist Church

TELEPHONE: Church, (334) 456-6080; Africatown Folk Festival, Mrs. Arealia P. Craig, (334) 456-4331

VISITING HOURS: Sun. school, 9–10; Sun. services, 10:30–12:30

SOURCES: Personal visit, summer 1990. Telephone conversation Sept. 14, 1993, Reverend Arthur J. Crawford. Telephone conservation July 18, 1990, Mrs. Mary West Lumbers, descendant of Cudjoe Lewis. Telephone conversation July 26, 1995, Henry C. Williams, president, Progressive League, Inc., Plateau. Telephone conversation Aug. 7, 1995, Mrs. Arealia P. Craig, coordinator, Africatown Landmark Association. *Alabama's Black Heritage.*

Montgomery

Alabama State University

Alabama State University was founded in Marion, Alabama, as the Lincoln Normal School, a private school for Black youth. The state began supporting the secondary portion of the school in 1874, and this department moved to Montgomery three years later. In 1927 the school, now called the Alabama State College, began offering extension courses for Black elementary and secondary teachers who lacked college degrees. Students enrolled for two years in Mobile, and then transferred to Alabama State College in Montgomery to complete work for the bachelor's degree.

Most campus buildings at Alabama State University have been constructed in the past thirty years. The older buildings feature Georgian architecture and have beautiful slate roofs with dormer windows.

The university features the E. D. Nixon Civil Rights Collection, named for an outstanding Montgomery civil rights leader and activist. In the 1920s Nixon founded the Montgomery branch of the Brotherhood of Sleeping Car Porters. In 1943 Nixon was president of the National Association for the Advancement of Colored People. Later, he posted bond for Mrs. Rosa Parks after she was arrested. He also urged Dr. Martin Luther King Jr. to accept the leadership of the Montgomery bus boycott. During the boycott Nixon's home was bombed. Nixon was a leader in breaking down barriers that prevented Blacks from voting in Montgomery.

DATE ESTABLISHED: 1874

ADDRESS: 809 S. Jackson Street, Montgomery

TELEPHONE: Library, (334) 293-4100; to arrange visit, (334) 293-4290

VISITING HOURS: Nixon Library, Mon.–Sat. 8–6, Sun. 1–6; closed major national holidays

SOURCES: Robert G. Forbus Jr., coordinator of news services, Alabama State. The Honorable Mrs. Idella Childs, city council member, Marion, Alabama. *Alabama's Black Heritage. Keepers of the Faith. Rosa Parks: My Story.*

Civil Rights Memorial*

This stark and graceful black granite monument honors forty martyrs who died in the 1955–1968 struggle for racial equality. The Southern Poverty Law Center commissioned the memorial, choosing as architect Maya Lin, the designer of the Vietnam War Memorial in Washington, D.C. On a black granite wall, a waterfall cascades over the etched words used by Dr. King, which came from Amos 5:24, "Until justice rolls down like waters and righteousness like a mighty stream."

A circular stone has inscribed the names of forty individuals murdered during the civil rights era. Some were nationally known, while others are remembered only by their families and local communities.

DATE DEDICATED: 1989
ADDRESS: 400 Washington Avenue, corner of Hull Street, Montgomery
TELEPHONE: (334) 264-0286
VISITING HOURS: Daily, 24 hours
SOURCES: Alabama Department of Archives and History. Personal visit, summer 1990.

The Dexter Avenue King Memorial Baptist Church and Pastorium*

Dr. Martin Luther King Jr. had accepted the call to become pastor of the Dexter Avenue Baptist Church in 1954, leading a congregation of 600. This was his first pastorate. The church is one of the birthplaces of the Civil Rights Movement of the 1950s and 1960s. In Montgomery the movement began in a sweeping way in December 1955, when Mrs. Rosa Parks, a seamstress, boarded a city bus. By custom Black patrons sat in the back of the bus and white patrons in front. If there were not enough seats for white passengers, the bus driver demanded, often in a rude manner, that African Americans move to the back or give up their seats to whites. On this particular day Parks refused to move when told to do so and was arrested. According to Parks, the story was not true that she refused to move because she was physically tired. The weariness that she felt was of a different kind, one that welled up inside her from experiencing years of injustice:

> People always say that I didn't give up my seat because I was tired, but that isn't true. I was not tired physically, or no more tired than I usually was at the end of a working day. I was not old, although some people have an image of me as being old then. I was forty-two. No, the only tired I was, was tired of giving in.[1]

Labor leader and community activist E. D. Nixon joined other Black leaders in calling for a boycott of the city's bus system, and Nixon urged Dr. Martin Luther King Jr. to accept leadership of the boycott. Reverend Ralph David Abernathy, who helped organize the Montgomery Improvement Association, nominated King as president of the association.

On the boycott's first evening, hundreds crowded into the Dexter Avenue Baptist Church to talk about the crisis and a possible boycott. Although some were fearful that a boycott might not succeed, King's speech so electrified and inspired the audience that the idea gained solid support, and the boycott began.

There were threats and retaliations, but Black people avoided the buses in spite of great sacrifices they had to endure. They walked to and from work or formed motor pools. The city buses continued to roll, nearly empty. In retaliation, white citizens formed the White Citizens Council. City authorities, finding an old city ordinance that prohibited destroying income of a business through a boycott, arrested King for violating the ordinance. Some employers fired their workers.

On the evening of January 31, 1956, at approximately 9:15 a bomb ripped a hole in the front porch of the Dexter Church Pastorium, shattering front windows in the explosion and hurling glass shards inside. The incident received national attention, and a horrified public, shocked at the act of violence against a nonviolent family and horrified to think what might have happened, began to show support for the bus boycott and for King's leadership in the nonviolent movement.

African Americans continued the boycott for over a year, steadily gaining national support and sympathy for their cause. In 1956 the Supreme Court declared bus segregation illegal; following the federal court injunction, Montgomery integrated its city buses in December of that year. Many of the boycott meetings had been held in the Dexter Avenue Baptist Church. A mural in the church office shows the highlights of the Civil Rights Movement during those years.

When the pastorium was being restored in 1990, the front porch still bore a scar from the 1956 bombing. In mid-1995 the King family furnishings were put in storage to protect them for a day when the cottage may be open to the public. Church members had not, however, made a decision to open the pastorium to the public.

DATE BUILT: Church, 1878; pastorium, c1912, remodeled 1990

ADDRESS: Church, 454 Dexter Avenue; pastorium, 309 S. Jackson Street, Montgomery

TELEPHONE: (334) 263-3970

VISITING HOURS: Church, Mon.–Fri. 8–4; guided tours Mon.–Thurs. 10 and 2, Fri. 10, Sat. 10:30 and 2; pastorium interior not open at present but call for information update

FEES: None

SOURCES: Personal visit, summer 1990. Telephone conversation May 29, 1994, Richard Smiley, deacon. Telephone call to church, July 28, 1995. NRHPINF. Convention and Visitor Division, Montgomery Chamber of Commerce. Alabama Department of Archives and History. *Rosa Parks: My Story. Alabama's Black Heritage. Keepers of the Faith.*

North Hull Street Historic District

The North Hull Street Historic District (also called "Old Alabama Town Historic District") is an area of carefully restored structures. Two of the buildings relate to African American history: the First Colored Presbyterian Church and the Ordeman-Shaw Townhouse.

The **First Colored Presbyterian Church** dates from 1890, a year when Black and white members of the Presbyterian Church formed separate congregations. The church has been restored to its original state.

Another structure, the **Ordeman-Shaw Townhouse,** contains slave quarters dating from before the Civil War. These rooms, which are located above the kitchen, contain sturdy furniture made by the slaves. A third structure, a "shotgun" house, also is part of the Black history displayed in this site. A shotgun house is one room wide with each room behind the next.

DATE BUILT: 1820s–1890s

ADDRESS: 310 N. Hull Street, Montgomery

TELEPHONE: (334) 240-4500

VISITING HOURS: Tours, Mon.–Sat. 9:30–3:30, Sun. 1–3:30

FEES: Adults, $5; students 6–18, $2; children under 6, free; group discount of $4 per person to groups of 10 or more with reservations

SOURCES: Telephone conversation Mar. 12, 1994, Mary Ann Neeley, executive director, Old Alabama Town Historic District. *Alabama's Black Heritage.*

North Lawrence—Monroe Street Historic District

Six business buildings located between two busy downtown streets remain from an era when Black-owned businesses thrived. The impetus and inspiration came partly from the National Negro Business League, which was organized in 1900 under Booker T. Washington's direction at Tuskegee. This movement encouraged African Americans to look within their own community for ways to become more independent. By 1911 two buildings on Monroe Street were associated with Black businesses, which inspired other Black entrepreneurs to settle in the area. In a segregated city this district became the center of Black commercial, professional, and social life.

In 1955, when the onset of the Montgomery bus boycott provided the first serious and sustained challenge to segregation, several businesses in the North Lawrence—Monroe Street area played a major supporting role by offering dispatch and pick-up services to the boycotters. However, when racial barriers began to fall and business leaders began to move to the suburbs, the viability of downtown establishments was threatened, and commercial activity declined in the historic district.

DATE BUILT: 1860–1916; significant in the Black community, 1900–mid-1940s

ADDRESS: 132–148 (even numbers), 216, 220 Monroe Street and 14, 22, 28–40 (even numbers), and 56 N. Lawrence Street, Montgomery

VISITING HOURS: Restricted access; information not available

SOURCE: NRHPINF.

Selma

Brown Chapel African Methodist Episcopal Church King Monument*

Brown Chapel A.M.E. Church, founded in 1866, was Alabama's first African Methodist Episcopal Church. Its members constructed the present church between 1906 and 1908. Brown Chapel, an imposing red-brick building, is the only remaining example of the fine church architecture of A. J. Farley, a Black builder from Beloit, Alabama. The chapel has twin square towers and large intersecting barrel vaults. The tower interior has wooden wainscoting and wooden stairways with spool baluster railings.

Brown Chapel played a major role in the Civil Rights Movement of the 1960s. In 1964 Selma's Black citizens were pressing for the right to register and vote. Although the Civil Rights Act of 1964 protected the voting rights of Blacks, local officials in Selma used all kinds of violence to keep Black citizens from registering. Community leaders invited Dr. Martin Luther King Jr. and the Southern Christian Leadership Conference to help plan their strategy, and King spoke to a large crowd at Brown Chapel, initiating the campaign.

Demonstrations were met with violence by Sheriff James Clark and his deputies, who used cattle prods and bullwhips against the demonstrators. At one point Clark and his men surrounded approximately 150 children who were demonstrating downtown and herded them out of town and along country roads with cattle prods. Two thousand protestors who had marched to the courthouse were jailed in 1965. Leaders then called for a more dramatic demonstration—a fifty-mile march from Selma to the state capital in Montgomery along U.S. 80. There was strong commitment from the community, and Brown

Chapel served as the staging area where hundreds of demonstrators gathered to prepare for the march.

Today Brown Chapel honors Dr. King and the marchers with a bust of King on the grounds in front of the church. Within the chapel the Martin Luther King Room contains mementos from the civil rights era.

DATE ESTABLISHED: Congregation, 1866; present building, 1906–1908
ADDRESS: 410 Martin Luther King Jr. Street, Selma
TELEPHONE: (334) 874-7897
VISITING HOURS: By appointment Mon.–Fri. 10–noon, 2–4
FEES: None
SOURCES: Department of Archives and History. NRHPINF. Alabama Historical Commission. *Rosa Parks: My Story. Alabama's Black Heritage. Keepers of the Faith.*

Edmund Pettus Bridge*

The Edmund Pettus Bridge is where the historic Selma-to-Montgomery civil rights march began. Despite the Civil Rights Act of 1964, local officials used threats and violence to prevent Black people from registering to vote. African-Americans in Dallas and Petty counties finally planned a dramatic demonstration in which they would march across the Pettus Bridge and follow the highway from Selma to the state capital in Montgomery. On Sunday, March 7, 1965, as three hundred demonstrators began the fifty-mile trek, Governor George Wallace gave orders forbidding the march. When he saw that the demonstrators would not stop, he ordered state police to mass along the Alabama River. As soon as the unarmed demonstrators reached the river, troopers assaulted them with tear gas and clubs.

Two weeks later the marchers set out again, this time under federal protection ordered by President Lyndon B. Johnson. Thousands of supporters from across the country joined local marchers, and together they walked to the Montgomery State Capitol building in five days. The resulting publicity awakened sympathetic reaction across the nation and hastened the passage of a new voting-rights bill.

The Pettus Bridge on Highway 80 was the site of dramatic and pivotal moments in modern civil rights history. An explanatory marker is located at the foot of the bridge near Broad Street.

DATE BUILT: 1940
ADDRESS: Broad Street, US 80, Selma
SOURCES: Personal visit, summer 1990. Convention and Visitors Division, Selma Chamber of Commerce. *Alabama's Black Heritage. Keepers of the Faith. Tourist Guide to Downtown Selma.*

First Baptist Church

When Dave Benjamin West, a local contractor and architect, constructed the present Victorian-style First Colored Baptist Church in 1894, it was regarded as the finest church in Alabama built for a Black congregation. A century later the church was known for its role as a site associated with the 1960s Civil Rights Movement. Black leaders, including members of the Dallas County Voters League and the Student Nonviolent Coordinating Committee, held meetings in the First Baptist Church. Although Dr. Martin Luther King Jr. and the Reverend Ralph Abernathy had their headquarters in the nearby Brown Chapel, they spoke each night to young people at the First Baptist Church. These meetings culminated in the Selma-to-Montgomery march described in the Edmund Pettus Bridge coverage.

DATE BUILT: 1840; present structure, 1894; restored 1979
ADDRESS: 709 Martin Luther King Jr. Street, Selma
TELEPHONE: (334) 874-7331
VISITING HOURS: Contact the church
SOURCES: NRHPINF. Personal visit, summer 1990. *Alabama's Black Heritage. Keepers of the Faith.*

Talladega

Talladega College

The Talladega campus originally was created in 1857 for a white Baptist academy. Although the Baptists individually pledged to raise money for the project, some fulfilled their pledges by ordering their slaves to labor on the construction. Ambrose Headen was one of the slaves assigned to build the three-story academy. Forced to work out his master's pledge of $900, he did so with sadness, knowing that his own four children could not attend the school he helped to build.

Eight years later, however, the Civil War had ended and Headen and other slaves were free. A group of freed persons, including William Savery and Thomas Tarrant, made a commitment that their own children would receive the education that the parents regarded as vital to the preservation of their children's liberties. With the help of General Wagner Swayne of the Freedmen's Bureau and the American Missionary Association, the freed men and women established Talladega College. Joyfully they began to fulfill their commitment to their children's education. Using salvaged lumber, they constructed a one-room schoolhouse, a place of learning that soon overflowed with students.

Aware of the crowded schoolhouse, community leaders began to look at the three-story Baptist Academy that had been constructed with slave labor. They sought General Swayne's help again, and he persuaded the American Missionary Association to purchase the Baptist Academy along with twenty acres of land. Ambrose Headen, the freedman who had helped to build Swayne Hall, was overjoyed. While building the structure years earlier he had prayed that his own children one day would be free; now he realized that the building that he had been forced to erect for white students only would serve his own children.

Grateful parents renamed the building Swayne Hall in honor of the generous assistance of General Swayne; today the building is a national historic landmark. Savery Library, completed in 1939, was named in honor of William Savery, the carpenter who made a commitment to build a school for Black students and who helped to build Swayne Hall.

DATE BUILT: Swayne Hall, 1857; campus transferred to Talladega College, 1867
ADDRESS: 627 W. Battle Street, Talladega
TELEPHONE: (205) 362-0206
VISITING HOURS: Contact the college; closed Martin Luther King Jr.'s Birthday, Good Friday, Easter Sunday, July 4, Thanksgiving break, Christmas break
SOURCES: Public Relations Department, Talladega College. NRHPINF. *Alabama's Black Heritage.*

Tuskegee

Tuskegee Institute National Historic Site*

According to educator/historian Dr. Horace Mann Bond, Tuskegee Institute came into being as the result of a political pact between two men, both of whom were politicians. Lewis Adams, a Black politician and a prominent leader in Tuskegee, Alabama, was approached by a white politician who also was an ex-Confederate colonel. The white politician, a Democrat, was a candidate in 1880 for a seat on the state legislature. Needing the support of Black voters to win the election, he was willing to offer something in return for the support. He approached Adams, a Republican, and asked what Adams would want in return for securing the support of Black voters.

There was no doubt that attempts were made to manipulate the Black vote during that period, especially among those who previously had owned slaves. The Reconstruction period had brought attempts to provide former slaves the same type of education that white people received, but as the sharecropping system of tenant farming grew, there also grew a vested interest in keeping a pool of uneducated Black laborers who might be more satisfied with laboring in the fields. The proper place for the laborers, the planters believed, was behind the plow.

To the credit of Adams, he responded to the question by stating that what Black people most wanted was a school. He promised to help get the Black vote in exchange for a bill appropriating money for a normal and industrial school in Tuskegee. Both individuals kept their parts of the bargain. The following year the Alabama legislature appropriated $2,000 for the Tuskegee Institute.

Booker T. Washington, then twenty-six years old and a former teacher at Virginia's Hampton Institute, was selected as Tuskegee Institute's first principal. When Washington arrived, he learned, probably to his dismay, that the $2,000 had been appropriated from the "Negro public school fund" and that it could be used only for teacher salaries. With the resourcefulness that would aid him through the years, Washington moved ahead with the formidable task, holding classes at first in the shanty and church that were available to him. He skillfully guided Tuskegee in its early devel opment as a normal (teacher training) school and an agricultural and vocational school, basing the early curriculum on his philosophy that practical knowledge was the route to economic success.

Students constructed buildings after working in the Tuskegee brickyard to make building materials. They also worked on the school farm. Female students also studied practical housekeeping. All students learned practical skills designed to help them find employment. The curriculum was nonthreatening to white citizens who would have objected to any type of higher education for Black students.

Washington became a nationally influential and powerful leader. He was able to meet and speak with some of the wealthiest of Americans, yet he retained the ability to speak to poor Black plantation workers in a relevant manner. He invited them to conferences where they learned about saving money, building schoolhouses, using better methods of agriculture, and improving living conditions for their families.

Washington also was responsible for making faculty appointments for the institute. Dr. George Washington Carver came to Tuskegee at Washington's request and remained there as a faculty member from 1896 to 1943. He taught students and conducted experiments that benefited agriculture as well as human nutrition and health.

Today Tuskegee University has more than twenty-seven landmarks associated with Booker T. Washington and George Washington Carver. They include:

Booker T. Washington's home, the Oaks, constructed about 1899 by Tuskegee students, one of the few surviving Black-constructed and designed structures of this era, now operated as a museum by the National Park Service

The Booker T. Washington Monument portraying Washington lifting the veil of ignorance from his fellow man

The grave site of Booker T. Washington

The Old Administration Building, which housed Dr. Washington's original office

Tuskegee University Library and a collection that highlights Dr. Booker T. Washington's life

The Carver Museum exhibits include samples of products that Dr. Carver derived from peanuts and the sweet potato as well as examples of Dr. Carver's paintings and needlework

DATE ESTABLISHED: 1881

ADDRESS: 1 mile N.W. of Tuskegee on US 80 (Old Montgomery Highway), Tuskegee

TELEPHONE: (334) 727-3200

VISITING HOURS: Booker T. Washington home tours, daily and hourly 9–11 and 2–4, closed Thanksgiving, Christmas, New Year's Day; Carver Museum, daily 9–5, closed Thanksgiving, Christmas, New Year's Day

FEES: None

SOURCES: Alabama Department of Archives and History. *National Register of Historic Places,* 11. Historical Society of Macon County, Alabama, Convention and Visitors Division. *Alabama's Black Heritage. Tuskegee Institute National Historic Site. Negro Education in Alabama,* 139, 140, 196, 197, 215–19.

Note

1. Rosa Parks with Jim Haskins, *Rosa Parks: My Story* (New York: Dial, 1992), 116.

Works Consulted

Alabama: A State of Surprises. Alabama Bureau of Tourism and Travel, 1993.

Alabama's Black Heritage: A Tour of Historic Sites. Montgomery: Bureau of Tourism and Travel, n.d.

Before the Mayflower: A History of Black America. Lerone Bennett Jr. New York: Penguin, 1982.

"Birmingham, 1963." Henry Hampton and Steve Fayer. In *Voices of Freedom: An Oral History of the Civil Rights Movement from the 1950s through the 1980s.* New York: Bantam, 1990.

Keepers of the Faith: Alabama's Historic Black Churches, A 1989 Calendar. Shirley Qualls Range, comp. Montgomery: Black Heritage Council, Advisory Committee to the Alabama Historical Commission, 1989.

Lincoln Normal School. Idella Childs. Marion, Ala.: the Author, n.d.

Multiple Resources of Greenville, Butler County, Alabama.

National Register of Historic Places. Washington, D.C.: National Park Service, 1976.

Negro Education in Alabama. Horace Mann Bond. New York: Atheneum, 1969.

Rosa Parks: My Story. Rosa Parks with Jim Haskins. New York: Dial, 1992.

Tourist Guide to Downtown Selma. Selma: Downtown Selma Assoc., 1989.

Tuskegee Institute National Historic Site. National Park Service, Dept. of the Interior.

W. C. Handy Birthplace, Museum, Library: "Father of the Blues" Tour. Florence, Ala.: City of Florence and Florence Historical Board. [pamphlet]

Arkansas

Doddridge

Kiblah School

In 1866 soon after emancipation, former slaves began to homestead the East Kiblah community. Although this community was primarily an agricultural area, settlers in this African American town also operated timber and milling industries.

By 1870 Kiblah's children attended school for three months each year, studying in a church building. The state of Arkansas later approved schools for the north and south districts and consolidated the schools in 1905. Kiblah School was constructed in 1917 as a plain, single-story, wood-frame building. The central front porch provided access to the school. Inside, hinged doors eight feet high extended the width of the building, separating the classrooms and auditorium. Two decades later, the site included an elementary school, a junior high school, and a homemaking building.

Kiblah School provided a central educational facility. The physical plant was better than the space formerly provided by the church. State support enabled the school to expand the length of the three-month term. In addition, the schoolhouse provided a convenient place for community meetings.

After World War II the economy of the area declined. As residents left to seek work outside the community, school enrollment began to drop. Until 1970 students from neighboring Doddridge and Caney also attended school in the Kiblah buildings, but the state then consolidated a number of school districts. Kiblah was absorbed into the Bright Star School District and the original Kiblah school building was sold for use as a private home. Although the interior is not open to the public, the exterior retains its traditional appearance, and visitors may drive to see the old schoolhouse in this historic rural community.

DATE BUILT: 1917

ADDRESS: From Doddridge take US 71 south about 1.5 miles to the crossroads (the Church of Christ is on the right, but turn left), go about 2.5 miles, passing by some houses, and you will see the old Kiblah School, now a community center

VISITING HOURS: Private, visitors may drive by

SOURCES: NRHPRF. Telephone conversation Mar. 14, 1994, Mr. Leo Garrison, superintendent, Bright Star School District.

Little Rock

Arkansas Baptist College Main Building

In 1884 the Negro Baptist Convention of Arkansas established a school to educate students for the ministry and for teaching. Classes met in Mount Zion Baptist Church and other churches in Little Rock until the college purchased land at Sixteenth and High Streets for $5,000. After the first central building was destroyed by fire, it was replaced by Main Building, the first brick building constructed by the college. Although the architects intended Main Hall to be a four-story building, funds collected were insufficient for a building of that size. As a result it was completed as a two-story structure.

Main Hall and Arkansas Baptist College are associated with the Reverend Joseph A. Booker, who was born in Arkansas in 1859 to slave parents. He led the college through a period of growth and also provided leadership in the community. When Arkansas passed a "Jim Crow" law in 1891 establishing racial segregation in railroad coaches and railroad waiting rooms, Dr. Booker led the protest against the new law. Although unsuccessful in abolishing segregated facilities, he continued to be in the forefront of protests against segregation.

Arkansas Baptist College is the state's only college that was controlled by African American leaders in the nineteenth century. Main Building, also known as the Old Administration Building, is the oldest building on a Black college campus in Arkansas.

DATE BUILT: Begun in 1893
ADDRESS: 1600 High Street, Little Rock
TELEPHONE: (501) 374-7856
VISITING HOURS: By appointment during academic year, Mon.–Fri. 9–5:30
SOURCES: NRHPINF. Telephone conversation Mar. 14, 1994, Mr. William C. Teaton, president, Arkansas Baptist College.

Dunbar Junior and Senior High School and Junior College

Dunbar Junior and Senior High School, which opened in an era of strict racial segregation, served African American students in Arkansas from 1929 through 1955. Although the school's first name was "Negro School of Industrial Arts," the curriculum provided a strong academic foundation as well as training in manual skills.

The school was designed by the same architects who had helped design Central High School in Little Rock. The architectural plan was distinguished; interior corridors featured terrazzo floors of black, yellow, and white marble.

Dunbar has served as a junior high school, high school, and junior college. In 1931, when Dunbar School received accreditation from the North Central Accreditation Association, it was one of only two industrial arts schools in the South to achieve a junior college rating.

A landmark legal decision, *Morris* v. *Williams*, brought attention to Dunbar. In 1943 the school was involved in a challenge to the Little Rock School system in which Black teachers sought pay equal to that of white teachers. The case, brought before the United States Eighth Circuit Court of Appeals, established the precedent that teachers who have the same professional qualifications and who provide the same services should receive equal pay regardless of race. The last high school and junior college classes graduated from Dunbar in 1955. Today Dunbar Magnet School is a junior high school that serves gifted and talented students and students in international studies. Once a segregated school, Dunbar today has a student body that is approximately 60 percent African American.

DATE BUILT: 1929
ADDRESS: Wright Avenue and Ringo Street, Little Rock
TELEPHONE: (501) 324-2440; Mr. Richard Davis, (501) 324-2300
VISITING HOURS: Call Mr. Davis for appointment Mon.–Fri. 8:30–3:45
SOURCES: Telephone conversation Mar. 14, 1994, Mr. Richard Davis, counselor, Dunbar Magnet School. NRHPINF.

Little Rock Central High School

When nine African American students tried to enroll at Central High School in the fall of 1957, a threatening, shouting, jeering crowd of white citizens awaited them, intent on forcing the young Black students to turn away. Three years earlier, on May 17, 1954, the United States Supreme Court had handed down a decision in *Brown* v. *Topeka Board of Education* declaring that the principle of "separate but equal" education was no longer valid.

Shortly after the Supreme Court decision, the Little Rock School Board resolved to comply with the new law, although minimally, by phasing in integration at Central High School on a grade-by-grade basis starting in 1957. They intended to keep the Black school open while accepting a token number of African American students into Central High School. School board members sought support from Governor Orval Faubus, but he would not take the politically unpopular step of publicly stating support for school integration. Little Rock's white citizens considered Central High School to be the pride of the state and one of the most beautiful schools in the country. The five-story building, the state's second-largest building, was constructed in 1927 to accommodate 3,000 white students. Central High School also had something else according to Black student Melba Pattillo Beals: "I wanted to go to Central High School because they had more privileges. They had more equipment, they had five floors of opportunities."[1]

Daisy Bates and other Black citizens, however, were not satisfied with the idea of a gradual integration that would have forced Black students to wait years before becoming eligible to enroll at Central. As state president of the National Association for the Advancement of Colored People, Bates already had brought pressure on Little Rock's school board to admit the Black students. Now she and others began legal action against the plan for gradual integration.

At first, the white community showed little opposition to integration in Little Rock. However, in 1956, when several Black students attempted to enroll in white schools a year ahead of the proposed schedule, hostility surfaced. Segregationist groups voiced their outright opposition.

In the fall of 1957, nine Black students, selected for their high academic ability, came forward as the first African Americans to integrate Central High. Governor Faubus, however, called out the Arkansas National Guard to block their entry to the school. Later these African-American students tried again to enroll, but the atmosphere became violent. They could not enroll until President Dwight D. Eisenhower federalized the Arkansas National Guard and sent a detachment of the 101st Airborne Infantry Division to the city. Under heavily guarded conditions on September 25, the nine Black students walked into Central High School. Their next challenge was to tolerate the hostility that they met and that continued even after troops were assigned to protect them in the schools. Melba Pattillo Beals said of the troops:

> They couldn't be with us everywhere. They couldn't be with us, for example, in the ladies' bathroom, they couldn't be with us in gym. We'd be showering in gym and someone would turn your shower into scalding. You'd be walking out to the volleyball court and someone would break a bottle and trip you on the bottle. I have scars on my right knee from that. After a while, I started saying to myself, Am I less than human?[2]

Although the students attended school in a hostile and rejecting atmosphere, some of the white students began to accord them respect. Ernest Green was the first Black student to graduate from Central High School in 1958. Daisy Bates and her husband found their participation costly—their home was bombed, and they lost their newspaper. Yet, the students never forgot the courage of Mr. and Mrs. Bates. In 1958 when the NAACP honored the nine students who had courageously entered Central High School in 1957, the students accepted the honor on the condition that Mrs. Bates would be honored, too.

DATE BUILT:	1927
ADDRESS:	1500 Park Street (Fourteenth and Park Street), Little Rock
TELEPHONE:	(501) 324-2300; for appointment, (501) 324-2304
VISITING HOURS:	By appointment, Mon.–Fri. 8:45–3:30
SOURCES:	NRHPINF. *International Library of Negro Life and History,* 162–63.

Pine Bluff

University of Arkansas at Pine Bluff

A legislative act of 1873 created this university "for the convenience and well-being of the poor classes." In 1875 the institution, which opened with one professor and seven students, was known as the Branch Normal College. When the Morrill Act of 1890 charged the institution with providing instruction in agriculture, the mechanical arts, and military science, the school became one of the original Black land-grant colleges. Its curriculum also included scientific and classical studies.

By the 1920s the expanding school, renamed Arkansas Agricultural Mechanical and Normal College, was in the process of becoming a four-year college. In fact, certification as a standard four-year college was received in the 1930s. In 1982 Arkansas AM&N merged with the University of Arkansas and was named University of Arkansas at Pine Bluff. This merger joined the two oldest public higher educational institutions in the state.

The bell tower, Caldwell Hall, and the Administration Building are historic structures on campus. The bell tower was constructed in 1945 to house the school bell, which had formerly been located at Old Branch Normal. The Isaac Hathaway Fine Arts Center on campus houses the "Persistence of the Spirit" exhibit, a collection that chronicles the history of Black men and women in Arkansas from pioneer days through 1986. A marker describing the school's history is located at the original site in Pine Bluff, on Second Avenue between Elm and Oak Streets.

DATE ESTABLISHED: Branch Normal College, Apr. 25, 1873; opened, 1875

ADDRESS: 1200 N. University Drive, Pine Bluff

TELEPHONE: University, (501) 541-6500; planning and public information office, (501) 541-6678

VISITING HOURS: University, by appointment through planning and public information office; museum Mon.–Fri. 9–noon, 1–4; closed weekends and all national holidays

FEES: None

SOURCES: Dr. Victor D. Starlard, professor of history, University of Alabama at Pine Bluff. Eva M. McGee.

Notes

1. Henry Hampton and Steve Fayer, *Voices of Freedom: An Oral History of the Civil Rights Movement from the 1950s through the 1980s* (New York: Bantam Books, 1990), 39.

2. *Voices,* 48.

Work Consulted

International Library of Negro Life and History: Historical Negro Biographies, Wilhelmena S. Robinson, New York: Publishers Co., 1970.

District of Columbia

Washington, D.C.

Anacostia Museum, Smithsonian Institution*

The Smithsonian's Anacostia Neighborhood Museum features frequently changing exhibits and programs on African American history and culture. The museum's exhibits are of interest to individuals and families. Some past topics have included Black women achievers, Africa from kingdoms to colonization, Harlem Renaissance writers, and artists and musicians. The research department has reference materials of interest to scholars. The small gallery features art shows; the large gallery features displays of historical and cultural significance.

The building adjoins a wooded area and has picnic tables, benches, grills, and ample parking close by.

DATE BUILT: 1987

ADDRESS: 1901 Fort Place SE, Fort Stanton Park

TELEPHONE: For educational programs and activities, (202) 357-1300, (202) 357-2020, and (202) 357-2700

VISITING HOURS: Daily 10–5; guided tours Mon.–Fri. 10, 11, and 1; closed Christmas

FEES: None

SOURCES: Robert L. Hall, education specialist, Anacostia Museum. Harriet W. Lesser, curator of exhibits, Mr. James Walker, associate director, The Charles Sumner School Museum and Archives. Telephone call to site, Nov. 30, 1994. Black History Resources in Washington, D.C.

Mary McLeod Bethune Council House National Historic Site*

Mary McLeod Bethune—a well-known twentieth-century leader in education, civil rights, and the Black women's movement—was born in South Carolina in 1875, the fifteenth of seventeen children. Her parents and the older children in the family were born in slavery, but she was born free. Although she didn't start school until the age of nine, her promise as a student eventually led her to study in South Carolina, North Carolina, and Illinois.

In 1904 Bethune opened her own school in Daytona Beach, Florida, for only six students, including her own son. Like all gifted innovators, she had a dream. Money always was scarce for the fledgling institution, which later merged with Cookman College and was acknowledged as an accredited college.

Bethune became more widely known when she served as president of the State Federation of Colored Women's Clubs. In 1935 she founded the National Council of Negro Women. She served also as an adviser on minority affairs to President Franklin Delano Roosevelt, residing in Washington, D.C., at 316 T Street (probably at an earlier house on the site) and later at 1812 Ninth Street NW. The National Council of Negro Women originally had its headquarters in Bethune's home. Council House, the nineteenth-century townhouse on Vermont Avenue, served as the headquarters of the National Council of Negro Women from 1943 to 1966. The surrounding Logan Circle Historic District began as a white residential area, but by 1940 many prominent African Americans had moved into the area.

In 1979 the townhouse became home to the Bethune Museum and Archives, America's largest collection of manuscripts on the contributions of Black women in the Americas. The restored three-story brick townhouse has a small front yard and a staircase with iron balustrades.

DATE BUILT:	House, c1885; museum and archives, 1979
ADDRESS:	1318 Vermont Avenue NW
TELEPHONE:	(202) 332-1233
VISITING HOURS:	Mon.–Fri. 10–4 and for special programs one weekend day each month; guided tours and archive access by appointment
FEES:	Free for individuals; for scheduled tours of 15 or more, adults $1, children 12–18 $.50, children under 12 $.25
SOURCES:	Telephone call to site, Mar. 14, 1994. *Washington, D.C., Black History National Recreation Trail.* "The Office of Minority Affairs Presents a Black Heritage Tour of Washington, D.C., for the American University Community." Black History Resources in Washington, D.C.

Blanche K. Bruce House and Plaque

The home of Blanche Kelso Bruce, the first African American U.S. senator to serve a full term (1875–1881), is in the historic area where some houses and commercial buildings were constructed as early as 1833. Many were built in alleyways behind middle-class housing. Even before emancipation, some African Americans owned real estate in this neighborhood. One of the outstanding residents was Senator Bruce, who was born a slave in 1841 in Farmville, Prince Edward County, Virginia. As a child, he learned to read along with his master's son. After emancipation he taught in a school for Black children in Kansas and later helped to establish a similar school in Missouri. Although he attended Oberlin College, financial difficulties kept him from completing college studies.

Bruce later settled in Mississippi, where he purchased significant amounts of land, amassed wealth, and became involved in political affairs. In 1874 the Mississippi legislature elected him to a full six-year term as a U.S. senator. He followed Senator Hiram Revels, another African American senator, who had served one year before resigning to become president of Mississippi's Alcorn University. In March 1875 Bruce was sworn into office and served until March 1881.

In 1879 Bruce became the first Black person called to preside over the U.S. Senate. He advocated many changes to improve the lives of all citizens.

After losing his senatorial seat in the 1880 Mississippi election, Bruce remained in Washington. President James A. Garfield appointed him as register of the Treasury in 1881, a post he held through 1885. After his reentry into private life, Bruce continued to serve in political and civil activities, working as recorder of deeds for the District of Columbia from 1888 to 1893, as a trustee of the District of Columbia Public Schools, and as a trustee of Howard University. When Bruce died in 1898, 3,000 mourners attended his funeral at Metropolitan African Methodist Episcopal Church.

Senator Bruce once lived in the four-story home at 909 M Street NW, a residence with mansard roof and interior fireplaces. The house has been restored as have many in the neighborhood around it.

DATE ESTABLISHED: Community, c1833–1941; Bruce House, 1865 or 1873

ADDRESS: Historic district bounded by Ninth, Tenth, M, and O Streets NW; Bruce House, 909 M Street NW

VISITING HOURS: Private, visitors can drive by

SOURCES: Telephone conversation May 22, 1994, community resident. NIHPINF. District of Columbia Inventory of Historic Sites. *Before the Mayflower.*

Mary Ann Shadd Cary House

Mary Ann Shadd Cary was born free in 1823 in Delaware. She grew up in a household where her family often sheltered runaway slaves. Although her parents wanted her to receive an education, schooling was forbidden to Black people in Delaware at that time. The Shadd family, therefore, moved to Pennsylvania, where they enrolled their daughter in a Quaker boarding school. On her return to Wilmington in 1839, Miss Shadd conducted a private school for Black children.

In 1850, Shadd, her brother Isaac, and some associates moved to Canada to seek better opportunities and refuge from dangers posed by the Fugitive Slave Law of 1850. She became the first Black woman in North America to co-edit a newspaper. Shadd started out by publishing pamphlets that encouraged Black people to emigrate to Canada. Later she co-edited a newspaper, *The Provincial Freeman,* and also operated a school in Chatham, Ontario. Between 1850 and 1860 she was a leader in encouraging thousands of Americans to emigrate to Canada.

While living in Chatham, Shadd met John Brown, a white abolitionist who later led the famous raid on Harpers Ferry. (For further information on the raid, see Harpers Ferry, West Virginia.) Brown spoke with many groups about his plan to free the slaves, and in 1858 he held one of his meetings at Isaac Shadd's house. Although Brown was not successful in freeing the slaves, he inspired many abolitionists to continue to fight for their cause. Shadd already was lecturing against slavery and impressing audiences with her logic and her great sense of dignity.

When the Civil War began, Mary Shadd Cary, now a married woman, was appointed to the position of recruiting officer for the Union Army. Widowed during the Civil War, she moved with her daughter to Washington, D.C. She taught in the city school system and at Howard University and continued to lecture on women's rights and the improvement of life for freedpersons. Cary studied law at Howard University and graduated in 1883 as one of the first Black women to receive an LL.B. degree in America.

Mary Shadd Cary was an activist, lecturer, and lawyer who lived in this three-story brick house on W Street between 1881 and 1886.

DATE OF SIGNIFICANCE: Cary residence, 1881–1886

ADDRESS: 1421 W Street NW

VISITING HOURS: Private, visitors can walk or drive by

SOURCES: NRHPINF. *Historical and Cultural Atlas of African Americans. When and Where I Enter.*

Frederick Douglass National Historic Site*

The twenty-room Cedar Hill house was home to the prominent orator, author, and abolitionist Frederick Douglass. Born in slavery in Maryland in 1817, Douglass learned to read as a boy with help from his master's wife. After she was ordered by her husband to stop teaching him, Frederick resolved to continue to learn.

Douglass escaped from slavery at the age of twenty-one. Carrying an official-looking paper, he made his way north in a borrowed sailor's uniform and settled in Rochester, New York, where he began publishing a newspaper. An eloquent speaker, he soon was in demand at antislavery meetings. He was acquainted with many of the outstanding white abolitionists of his day and became in his own right a leader of the city's underground railroad.

When the United States finally accepted African Americans as soldiers in the Civil War, Douglass worked hard to recruit Black men for the Union cause. Two of his sons served in the Union Army.

Frederick Douglass made a final move to Washington, D.C., in 1872. After his Rochester, New York, house burned, he moved his family irrevocably to Washington, where they lived in the house at 316 A Street NE. (See following site information.) In 1877 he moved to Cedar Hill, setting a precedent by moving to a neighborhood restricted by covenant to white residents. In that same year Douglass was appointed U.S. Marshal of the District of Columbia. He later served as recorder of deeds and as U.S. minister to Haiti. He lived at Cedar Hill for the last seventeen years of his life until his death in 1895.

The brick house at the top of Cedar Hill overlooks the Anacostia River. It has several shuttered windows, a second-story bay window, and a full-length columned front porch. Many of the original furnishings and some of the personal belongings of Frederick Douglass are on display.

Tourmobiles to the Frederick Douglass Home depart from the Washington Monument twice daily, June through Labor Day, with the route passing the Mary McLeod Bethune Memorial in Lincoln Park.

DATE BUILT:	c1855–1859; additions in the 1890s; restored 1962–1964
ADDRESS:	1411 W Street SE
TELEPHONE:	(202) 426-5960; for group reservations, (202) 426-5961; tourmobile service from the Mall, (202) 554-5100 or (202) 426-5960
VISITING HOURS:	Daily, Oct.–Apr. 9–4, Apr.–Oct. 9–5; closed Thanksgiving, Christmas, and New Year's Days
FEES:	None
SOURCES:	Telephone call to site, Apr. 24, 1994. NRHPINF. *National Register of Historic Places,* 126. *Frederick Douglass National Historic Site. Washington, D.C., Black History National Recreation Trail. The Life and Times of Frederick Douglass.* District of Columbia Inventory of Historic Sites. Black History Resources in Washington, D.C. *Welcome to Washington.*

Frederick Douglass Museum

Frederick Douglass, a nationally known Black leader and abolitionist who escaped from slavery, once lived in this home on A Street. The neighborhood is very old—two other houses on the same street are considered to be two of the oldest dwellings on Capitol Hill. Douglass is believed to have purchased the house at 316 A Street in 1871; two years later he add the structure at 318 A Street. Douglass stayed in Washington, D.C., before he made the final move of his family to that city. Douglass received the telegram about the fire at his Rochester, New York, house on June 3, 1872, while he was in Washington. In spite of pleas from his family to remain in Rochester, he moved his family irrevocably to the house on A Street in Washington. In 1878 he moved to Cedar Hill, a major site today that is open to visitors. The house on A Street remained in the Douglass family until 1920; Joseph Douglass, Frederick's grandson, was the last family member to live there. The Museum of African American Art occupied the site from 1964 to 1985.

The restored historic property now is occupied by the Caring Institute, an organization that honors caring people. The institute leaders believe that few Americans were more caring than Frederick Douglass, a man who attained his own goal of freedom, who was an ardent enthusiast for Black men's enlistment as soldiers in the Civil War, and who spent his entire life speaking out for equal opportunity for Black Americans. Today the Caring Institute encourages the highest human qualities of philanthropy, sacrifice, and compassion by recognizing and honoring on a national basis each year the ten most caring adults and children in America.

Restoration of the Frederick Douglass House took place between 1990 and 1993. The two adjoining houses were combined to provide office space as well as areas that are rented out for community events. Visitors to the site learn about Frederick Douglass and other caring Americans and see museum collections that include some of Douglass's personal items as well as artwork depicting caring Americans. The rooms have been restored to the period when the Douglass family lived here. During the restoration, in tearing down walls workers found an original fireplace and an original stairwell. Although the flooring is not original to the house, it is from a house built in the same period. Visitors see Douglass's original desk, a photograph of him and his family standing in front of the house, and a drawing of Douglass by his grandson, Joseph Douglass, a concert violinist. In a great irony, there is a chandelier in the house that came from the home of Confederate General Robert E. Lee.

DATE OF SIGNIFICANCE:	Douglass residence, 1871/1872–1878
ADDRESS:	316–320 A Street NE
TELEPHONE:	(202) 547-4273
VISITING HOURS:	The Caring Institute, Mon.–Fri. 9:30–5:30, visitors may make appointments, although they are not required
FEES:	None
SOURCE:	Telephone conversation May 3, 1994, and Nov. 30, 1994, Angie Halamandaris, wife of president of the Institute.

Ebenezer United Methodist Church

Ebenezer Church is one of the earliest African American congregations on Capitol Hill. The Ebenezer congregation has occupied this site continuously since 1838 and built the present church in 1897.

The congregation originated in the "mother church," Ebenezer Church. The mother church, the Methodist Episcopal Church, first met in a dwelling on South Capitol and N Streets in 1805. There were sixty-one white and twenty-five Black members. The congregation moved several times, changing its name in 1819 to Ebenezer Church. Seating was segregated, and by 1827 the African American membership had outgrown its assigned gallery space. By 1838 the church purchased a lot on Fourth and D Streets SE, and the Black congregation built a small frame church for its own use. The mother church, assisted by three African American ministers, administered the new church, which was called Little Ebenezer from 1838 until 1858, when it became known as the Ebenezer Church.

By 1860 Black trustees began administering the church, and in 1864 the first Black pastor was appointed. Since public schools were segregated, church officials in 1864 opened a private school for Ebenezer's children. Miss Emma Brown was hired as teacher at a salary of $400. This was the first Black school in the District of Columbia. In spring 1864 the first government-sponsored school for Black children in Washington, D.C., was housed in the church.

The first church on this site was a small, frame structure. The present Ebenezer United Methodist Church was constructed in 1897. The present church, a one-story, red-brick building, has a tower, a double-arched entrance, stained-glass windows, and Indiana-limestone details. The interior has a pressed-tin ceiling, and many of the original interior fixtures remain.

The mother church, now named Capitol Hill United Methodist Church, is located at 421 Seward Square SE.

DATE BUILT: 1897

ADDRESS: 420 D Street, corner of Fourth Street SE

TELEPHONE: (202) 544-1415

VISITING HOURS: Sun. school, 9:30; Sun. service, 11; call for visiting information

SOURCES: Telephone call Mar. 13, 1994, Ebenezer Church. Telephone conversation Nov. 30, 1994, Mrs. Audrey Gilbert, secretary, Ebenezer United Methodist Church. Telephone conversation Dec. 1, 1994, Mrs. Shirley Chavis, Capitol Hill United Methodist Church. NRHPINF. District of Columbia Inventory of Historic Sites. "History of Ebenezer United Methodist Church."

Evans-Tibbs House

This residence was home to Lillian Evans-Tibbs, a performer known in the world of opera as Madame Evanti. She sang opera and classical music in an era in which the world expected Black singers to limit their repertoire to spirituals, blues, or minstrel melodies. In spite of her considerable talent, the United States offered few opportunities for Evanti to perform operatic music, so she traveled to Paris to study and perform, adopting her stage name in that city.

When Evanti performed in France, Italy, and Germany with the Paris Opera Company, she became the first African American opera singer to gain international recognition. In spite of her success and growing stature in Europe, when she returned to the United States, she was not invited to join any American opera company. Some national leaders, however, recognized her talent and provided opportunities for her to perform. Evanti performed in the White House for Eleanor Roosevelt and later performed for Presidents Harry S. Truman and Dwight D. Eisenhower. Evanti traveled throughout South America with Arturo Toscanini's orchestra as part of the Roosevelt Administration's Goodwill Ambassador Program. During World War II she gave morale-building vocal performances for Black troops.

Most of Evanti's appearances, however, were in local theaters. Recognizing that other Black singers needed opportunities to perform classical music, she helped to establish the National Negro Opera Company in 1942. She also participated in the Pan-African movement by promoting knowledge of African American culture in Latin America.

Evans-Tibbs died in 1967. Her house, which was decorated under her direction, later served as a gallery, a library, and a research center. Visitors to the house will see paintings and sculptures and have access to a major library with books about Black artists.

DATE BUILT: 1894

ADDRESS: 1910 Vermont Avenue NW

TELEPHONE: (202) 234-8164

VISITING HOURS: By appointment

FEES: None

SOURCES: Telephone conversation Mar. 14, 1994, Thurlow Tibbs, curator and grandson of Lillian Evans-Tibbs. NRHPINF. District of Columbia Inventory of Historic Sites.

Archibald and Francis Grimké House

Archibald Grimké (1849–1930) and his brother Francis (1850–1939) were born in slavery in Charleston, South Carolina. Their mother, Nancy Weston, was a Black slave, and their father/owner was Henry Grimké, a prosperous white planter. Before he died, Henry Grimké made known his wish that his sons Archibald and Francis would be freed. Their white half-brother, however, ignored his father's instructions and forced the boys and their mother back into slavery.

In spite of the hardships of slavery, Archibald Grimké later graduated from Lincoln University. His white aunts, Angelina and Sarah, heard about Archibald's successful studies. They were abolitionists, and they shocked Washington society by acknowledging their relationship with their Black nephews, Archibald and Francis. Angelina even provided financial assistance to enable Archibald to study law at Harvard University. After graduating in 1874, he established a law office in Boston. He edited *The Hub*, a weekly newspaper, and wrote articles for another newspaper, the *Boston Herald*. Appointed to a high-level position as United States consul to Santo Domingo, he served in that position from 1894 to 1898.

Because of advantages received from his family and his education, Archibald Grimké could have chosen a life apart from his people. Instead, he worked for the goals of the Black community. He served for ten years as president of the Washington, D.C., chapter of the National Association for the Advancement of Colored People, and he led the American Negro Academy from 1903 to 1916.

Francis Grimké also studied at Lincoln University at the close of the Civil War. After graduating with honors, he entered Princeton Theological Seminary. He graduated in 1878 and became the widely influential pastor of the Fifteenth Street Presbyterian Church. He spoke out for equality and justice and against Booker T. Washington when Grimké felt that Washington had avoided speaking out on civil rights issues. Reverend Grimké married Charlotte Forten, a schoolteacher who dedicated her life to opposing slavery and discrimination. Reverend Francis Grimké lived at two other sites in the city: briefly at 1419 Swann Street NW and at 1608 R Street NW (see Charlotte Forten Grimké House, following).

ADDRESS: 1930 Eleventh Street NW

VISITING HOURS: Private, visitors may drive by

SOURCES: *The Washington, D.C., Black History National Recreation Trail. International Library of Negro Life and History: Historical Negro Biographies,* 85–7.

Charlotte Forten Grimké House

"I find the children generally well-behaved, and eager to learn; yes, they are nearly all most eager to learn, and many of them make most rapid improvement. It is a great happiness to teach them."[1] Thus Charlotte Forten wrote in her journal a description of her work in teaching the newly freed slaves on St. Helena Island near Beaufort, South Carolina.

Charlotte Forten Grimké was born to wealthy, free Black parents. She was the granddaughter of James Forten, a successful sailmaker who also was an abolitionist and prominent leader in Philadelphia. Charlotte grew up in a household that emphasized both education and personal service to the community.

When the local white school refused to admit Charlotte, her father provided her with private tutors. At the age of sixteen, she journeyed to Salem, Massachusetts, to attend public schools in that town. After graduating with honors, she was offered a teaching position at the integrated Epes Grammar School in Salem. Forten became the first African American teacher at that school.

Charlotte Forten met many well-known abolitionists in New England, including William Lloyd Garrison and poet John Greenleaf Whittier.

She met accomplished, active African Americans, and their conversations influenced her to join them in working for the antislavery cause. Forten kept a diary, leaving an invaluable description of her life as a privileged, involved Black woman.

When the Civil War began, Forten learned that thousands of slaves were left destitute as their masters fled the sea island plantations in South Carolina. As the plantations fell to Union occupation, the federal government began an experiment in preparing the former slaves for freedom, including obtaining an education. Forten made arrangements to go south with Quaker friends. When Forten traveled to Port Royal, St. Helena Island, South Carolina, to teach, she and her Quaker friends were among the first Northern educators to teach former slaves in the isolated areas of South Carolina that had been ravaged by war. Ten thousand Port Royal slaves had been abandoned by their owners, who fled the island when it was captured during the Civil War. Forten taught on St. Helena Island from 1862 to 1864. She kept a journal that described her life and work on the island.

In 1878, at the age of fifty, Charlotte married the Reverend Francis J. Grimké, pastor of the District of Columbia's Fifteenth Street Presbyterian Church. They resided at 1608 R Street NW. When she died in 1914, the example of her work had encouraged hundreds of Black men and women to become involved in civil rights work and teaching.

The Charlotte Forten Grimké House, a two-story, brick rowhouse, has wrought-iron steps leading to the entry door. Although there have been renovations to the interior, the house still retains much of its nineteenth-century character.

DATE BUILT: c1880

ADDRESS: 1608 R Street NW

VISITING HOURS: Private, visitors may drive by

SOURCES: NRHPINF. *A Documentary History of the Negro People in the United States.* District of Columbia Inventory of Historic Sites.

Howard University*

The Missionary Society of the First Congregational Church saw a need for educating former slaves after the Civil War and proposed the establishment of a school. Congress chartered Howard University in 1867 as a "university for the education of youth in the liberal arts and sciences." The charter called for educating all youth regardless of race, and the first four Howard students were white women who were daughters of the founders. Three Chinese students enrolled in 1870, starting the tradition of a cosmopolitan institution open to all. By the 1900s, however, the school was predominantly Black.

University operations began in a frame structure on a one-acre lot, but the school soon purchased a 149-acre farm. General O. O. Howard, a commissioner of the Freedmen's Bureau, a university founder, and first university president (1869 to 1873), bought a lot. His brick residence, **Howard Hall** (General Oliver Otis House) was privately built for him from 1867 to 1869. Today, Howard Hall is the only survivor of the four original buildings on campus. The residence has retained many of its decorative elements: mansard roof, dormer windows, cast-iron balustrade capping the roof, and a three and one-half–story tower. The house has been used by the music department, the African Language Center, and the University Press.

Other historical buildings include **Andrew Rankin Memorial Chapel** (1895); **Freedmen's Hospital** (1909), where Dr. Charles Drew did pioneering research on blood plasma, now the C. B. Powell Building; and **Founder's Library** (1939). In addition, the university has other ties to Black history. Alpha Kappa Alpha Sorority was organized at Howard University during the 1907–1908 academic year. Howard's students at that time included eight women in the class of 1908 and two in the class of 1909. Today, the sorority's records are located in the archives of the Moorland-Spingarn Research Center. The stained glass Alpha Kappa Alpha sorority founders commemorative window in the Andrew Rankin Memorial Chapel lists names of the organization's founders.

Visitors to the campus may want to see the **James V. Herring Gallery of Art,** which features a collection of African art and works by contemporary Black artists. Exhibits and programs are for visitors grade one through adult.

The Howard University **Moorland-Spingarn Research Center** attracts visitors to the campus from elementary age through adult. Many items are of interest to visitors who are doing research in Black history. The collection includes books, photographs, old newspapers, and some exhibits. These items, as well as materials from a fine arts picture gallery, are in the museum's permanent collections. The center also has a collection of historic catalogs from Black colleges.

Howard University has produced many outstanding graduates, including Supreme Court Justice Thurgood Marshall; Andrew Young, former mayor of Atlanta; Jessye Norman, world-acclaimed opera soprano; and performing artists Debbie Allen and her sister Phylicia Rashad. Other outstanding Howard University graduates include Toni Morrison, Pulitzer-Prize-winning journalist; Vernon Jordan, Washington lawyer and former head of the National Urban League; L. Douglas Wilder, former governor of Virginia; David Dinkins, former mayor of New York City; and the late Patricia Roberts Harris, secretary of the United States Department of Health and Human Services. Dr. Ralph Bunche and Dr. Charles Drew are among the distinguished individuals who have served on the faculty.

DATE ESTABLISHED: University, 1867; Howard House, c1867–1869

ADDRESS: University, 2400 Sixth Street NW; Howard Hall, 607 Howard Place; Herring Gallery, 2455 Sixth Street NW; Moorland-Spingarn Research Center, 500 Howard Place NW

TELEPHONE: University, (202) 806-6100 or 686-5400; Herring Gallery, 806-7070; Moorland-Spingarn Research Center, 806-7239

VISITING HOURS: University, call for appointment; Herring Gallery, Mon.–Fri. 9:30–4:30, Sun. 1–4 for programs, closed holidays; Moorland-Spingarn Research Center, Mon.–Fri. 9–4:30, closed holidays

FEES: None

SOURCES: Telephone calls to site, Mar. 14, May 1. Telephone conversation Dec. 7, 1994, Joyce Rose, secretary, African American studies department, Howard University. Telephone conversation Dec. 8, 1994, Eileen Johnston, registrar, Howard University. Telephone conversation Dec. 8, 1994, Janet Sims-Wood, assistant chief librarian for references, E. Ethelbert Miller, director, Afro-American Resource Center, Howard University. Howard University. Scott W. Baker, museum docent, Moorland-Spingarn Research Center. Howard University department of university relations. NRHPINF. *National Register of Historic Places,* 127. *Washington, D.C., Black History National Recreation Trail.* Black History Resources in Washington, D.C. *Towards the Preservation of a Heritage.*

Lincoln Memorial*

On several occasions the Greek-styled temple honoring President Abraham Lincoln has been the site of dramatic gatherings in Black history. In 1939 the Daughters of the American Revolution (DAR) refused permission for famed contralto Marian Anderson to sing in Constitution Hall in Washington, D.C. First Lady Eleanor Roosevelt resigned her membership in the DAR because of the outrageous act of discrimination, and her example influenced many other Americans to denounce the decision. Anderson then accepted an offer to perform on Easter Sunday at the Lincoln Memorial. An audience of 75,000, including some of America's leading officials, came to hear the moving performance. In 1953 Anderson performed in Constitution Hall, giving the first of six concerts at the site that once had barred her.

In 1963 the Lincoln Memorial was the backdrop for another unforgettable moment in Black History when some 250,000 people gathered in a multiracial assemblage for the August 28, 1963, March on Washington—the largest civil rights demonstration in U.S. history. At the Lincoln Memorial, before an immense and enthusiastic audience, Dr. Martin Luther King Jr. delivered his moving speech, "I Have a Dream." Here he reaffirmed the ideal that brotherhood would win in the battle against racism.

DATE DEDICATED: 1922

ADDRESS: Foot of Twenty-third Street NW in West Potomac Park on the Mall

TELEPHONE: (202) 426-6895

VISITING HOURS: Interpretive services daily 8 A.M.–midnight; building, daily 24 hours

SOURCES: Telephone call to site, May 1, 1994. *Encyclopedia of African-American Civil Rights,* 22. *The Black 100.* District of Columbia Inventory of Historic Sites. "The Office of Minority Affairs Presents a Black Heritage Tour of Washington, D.C., for the American University Community." *Welcome to Washington.*

Lincoln Park
Freedom's Memorial
Mary McLeod Bethune Memorial

In 1862 slavery was abolished in the District of Columbia. Several years later, just after the end of the Civil War, President Abraham Lincoln was assassinated. The Black community was stunned and sorrowed at the loss, and a former slave, Charlotte Scott, vowed to give her first earnings for a monument to Lincoln's memory. In 1876, the statue of Lincoln was unveiled in this park, paid for exclusively with funds donated by freed slaves. The statue was called *Freedom's Memorial.* It portrayed President Abraham Lincoln life-sized, holding the Emancipation Proclamation in his right hand and extending his left hand to a kneeling Black man who is breaking free of his shackles.

A century later, in 1974, the National Council of Negro Women erected a statue of educator and civil rights leader Mary McLeod Bethune. The Bethune Memorial in Lincoln Park was the first erected in a public park in Washington, D.C., honoring a woman.

Lincoln Park, located one mile east of the Capitol, is in one of the oldest residential neighborhoods in Washington. Many of the fine old homes nearby have been renovated.

ADDRESS: East Capitol Street between East Eleventh and East Thirteenth Streets

VISITING HOURS: Daily, 24 hours

SOURCES: Black History Resources in Washington, D.C. *Washington, D.C., Black History National Recreation Trail.* "The Office of Minority Affairs Presents a Black Heritage Tour of Washington, D.C., for the American University Community."

National Museum of African Art*

The National Museum of African Art of the Smithsonian Institution has exhibits, research facilities, and public programs relating to the arts and cultures of sub-Saharan Africa. The museum has more than 6,000 works in wood, metal, fiber, ivory, and fired clay. Exhibits are of interest to all ages from preschool children through adults.

ADDRESS: 950 Independence Avenue SW
TELEPHONE: Recorded message, (202) 357-1300; Visitors Center, (202) 357-2700
VISITING HOURS: Daily 10–5:30; closed Christmas
FEES: None
SOURCES: Jacqueline E. Wilson, executive director, Archdiocese of Washington, Office of Black Catholics. Telephone call to site May 1, 1994. Black History Resources in Washington, D.C.

St. Luke's Episcopal Church

St. Luke's Episcopal Church was founded in 1876 by Reverend Alexander Crummell and members of his congregation. Together they previously had worshipped at St. Mary's Episcopal Church, but learning that the land on which St. Mary's stood had not been willed to them as they had expected, they purchased land with clear title and built St. Luke's Church. A few members remained at St. Mary's, which reverted to its former status as a small mission outreach of the white St. John's Episcopal Church.

Alexander Crummell was born free in New York in 1819. He grew up in a deeply religious family that was committed to the antislavery cause. After attending the African Free School in New York City and the Black-operated Canal Street School in New York, Crummell studied at Noyes Academy in New Hampshire until local racial prejudice and violence forced him and other Black students to leave. He then attended the Oneida Institute in New York, a school that emphasized both classical studies and manual subjects.

Since the Episcopal Church Seminary in New York had rejected Crummell because of his race, he studied privately and was admitted to the priesthood. Then he met more bigotry in his efforts to gain admission as a priest of the diocese of Philadelphia. Next he studied in England and then traveled to Africa. His experiences in Africa led him to believe that educated Black Americans could help to create a new civilization in Africa, and he became a citizen of Liberia. Although his plan never gained adequate support, he continued to hold a dream for the development of Africa.

Leaving Africa in 1872, Crummell returned to the United States and became a permanent resident of Washington, D.C. In 1876 he established St. Luke's Church with some members who wanted to leave St. Mary's Church (see next site) to form their own parish. Reverend Crummell believed the church was an important influence in the Black community because it was the only institution that Black people controlled. He understood the importance of education, too. In 1897 he founded the American Negro Academy, an organization that established a tradition of scholarship and developed the talents existing among Black people.

Black architect Calvin T. S. Brent drew the plans for St. Luke's Church, which is listed in the *National Register of Historic Places.*

DATE ESTABLISHED: Founded, 1876; constructed, 1879
ADDRESS: Fifteenth Street and Church Street NW
TELEPHONE: (202) 667-4394
VISITING HOURS: Sunday Mass, 7 and 10; by appointment Mon.–Fri. 10–3
SOURCES: Telephone call to site May 1, 1994. NRHPINF. *Washington, D.C., Black History National Recreation Trail.* "District of Columbia Inventory of Historic Sites."

St. Mary's Episcopal Church

St. Mary's Church, organized as a Black mission of another church, St. John's in Lafayette Square, dates back to 1867. The church is significant as Washington's first church for Black Episcopalians and is significant as a church designed by James Renwick, a leading nineteenth-century architect who also designed the Smithsonian Institution building.

St. Mary's Church grew out of a struggle for rights and dignity for African Americans. Before the Civil War, many free Black people lived in Washington. They came seeking opportunities in this seat of the national government and the equality they believed should exist in the city. Even before the Civil War, 75 percent of African Americans in Washington were free.

Washington, however, was not the paradise they had expected to find. Strict policies of segregation extended even to worship services in churches. Black seating was on the periphery, and Holy Communion for African Americans came after white worshipers had completed the rite. White churches refused to perform weddings and funeral services for Black members.

During this period the African American congregation members learned that a chapel attached to a hospital was about to be demolished and sold for lumber, and they requested the chapel. They carefully took it apart, transported it on wagons to a new site in the Foggy Bottom area, and rebuilt it on land donated by Mrs. Catharine Pearson, a St. John's parishioner. When the new church, called St. Barnabas Mission, had its opening service in June 1867, it was the first Black Episcopal congregation in Washington. The name later changed to St. Mary's Mission and to St. Mary's Episcopal Church.

In 1873 the church welcomed its first Black rector, Dr. Alexander Crummell (see St. Luke's, Washington, D.C., site). Crummell attracted so many African Americans to St. Mary's from other Episcopal churches in the city that within a year the church was capable of operating in an autonomous manner and was admitted into the Diocesan Convention. Unfortunately, for an unknown reason, the land on which St. Mary's Church stood never was legally conveyed to St. Mary's. Desiring to have church property with a clear title, Crummell and most of the St. Mary's congregation left to establish another church; they named it St. Luke's. When St. Luke's Church held its opening service in 1879, St. Mary's was left with only a few communicants who found themselves once again under the supervision of St. John's Church.

St. Mary's began building its congregation again by sponsoring outreach programs for impoverished residents of the neighborhood. The St. Mary's Industrial School opened in the church and by 1882, 128 girls were studying cooking and sewing there. In the same year 150 children were attending Sunday School there. With the programs outgrowing the small church and the one-story brick schoolhouse that had been added behind the chapel, a lot adjacent to the Pearson lot was purchased and a new St. Mary's Church was constructed. The opening service was held in January 1887.

St. Mary's Church is a brick structure with a two-story tower and lancet windows. One window has a deeply colored Tiffany glass design executed by the Lorin firm of Chartres, France. The interior has carved oak furniture, patterned-tile and red-marble floors, and stenciling on the walls. The church has had minor alterations but remains much as it was when constructed over a century ago.

DATE ESTABLISHED:	Founded, 1867; opened, 1887
ADDRESS:	728 Twenty-third Street NW
TELEPHONE:	(202) 333-3985
VISITING HOURS:	Mon.–Fri. 9:30–3
FEES:	None
SOURCES:	Reverend John F. Evans, interim rector, St. Mary's Episcopal Church. *St. Mary's Episcopal Church. National Register of Historic Places*, 132. *Washington, D.C., Black History National Recreation Trail.* District of Columbia Inventory of Historic Sites.

Strivers' Section Historic District

In the late-nineteenth and early-twentieth century, a Black middle class developed in the area called the Strivers' Row. Many Black leaders lived in the row of houses in the 1700 block of U Street, a neighborhood that symbolized pride and accomplishment. They were leaders in government, architecture, education, business, religion, and art. Frederick Douglass, one of the most prominent men of the nineteenth century, built three of the five houses at 2000–2008 Seventeenth Street and owned two of the houses until his death.

The rowhouses and apartment buildings, constructed from about 1875 to 1925, have a variety of architectural styles and a variety of ornamental moldings and cornices. The Strivers' Section Historic District contains approximately 450 buildings. The 1700 blocks of T and U Streets are the focal points of the historic community. Brick rowhouses in the 1900 block of New Hampshire Avenue NW date from around 1875. The elegant Albemarle apartment building at 1830 Seventeenth Street NW and the brick apartment buildings at 1918 and 1930 Eighteenth Street NW are two of the area's outstanding apartment buildings.

DATE BUILT: c1875–1925

ADDRESS: 1700 blocks of T and U Streets NW, roughly bounded by Swann Street on the south, Florida Avenue on the north and west, and the Sixteenth Street Historic District on the east

VISITING HOURS: Private, visitors can drive or walk by

SOURCES: NRHPINF. District of Columbia Inventory of Historic Sites.

Charles Sumner School

The first school constructed for Black children on the site of the Charles Sumner School was vastly different from the imposing building that stands today. Using lumber salvaged from wartime barracks, the Black community, under the sponsorship of the Freedmen's Bureau, constructed the earliest school in 1866. The M Street School was demolished in 1871, and an outstanding and internationally recognized architect, Adolph Cluss, was chosen to build a substantial and distinguished new school for Black children. Erected in 1872, the new school was one of the first built in Washington, D.C., for Black students. Today it is one of America's oldest Black public school buildings still standing and substantially unaltered. (For information about other early Black schoolhouses, read the sections on the East End School in Harveysburg, Ohio, built in 1831; the Ferry Street School in Niles, Michigan, built in 1868; and Central Colored School in Louisville, Kentucky, built in 1873.)

Sumner School was impressive when it opened—it had three full stories with a tower sixteen feet square and a basement that provided playrooms, washrooms, and rooms for the janitor. The first story contained four schoolrooms, the second story housed schoolrooms and offices for the trustees and the superintendent, and the third floor contained a 3,000-square-foot public hall large enough to accommodate all of the pupils. The water closets (bathrooms) were in a separate building in the yard. In 1871–1872 the superintendent of Colored Schools of Washington and Georgetown included in his annual report the description of the building as prepared in 1872 by the architect Adolph Cluss. One section of the report boasted that

> The gas fixtures are of the latest and most improved style, being made to order specially by Shepherd & Bros. The large hall, as well as the teacher's platform, is covered with rich and tasty carpets, which together with the delicate and chaste tints of the frescoed walls give the rooms a very cheerful appearance. The superintendent's office, as well as the trustees', are marvels of neatness, there being a complete blending of taste and uniformity.[2]

Sumner School, built at a cost of about $70,000, stood near Metropolitan African Methodist Episcopal Church in what is now one of Washington's most historic districts. The school, which produced its first graduates in 1877, was named for Senator Charles Sumner (1811–1874) of Boston, Massachusetts, an outspoken white opponent of slavery and a fighter for equal-rights causes—the right of Black people to use the District of Columbia's streetcars, equal pay for Black soldiers, and creation of a Freedmen's Bureau that would provide assistance to often-destitute newly freed former slaves. Sumner's attacks in Congress on slavery one day drew the wrath of Representative Preston Brooks of South Carolina, who physically attacked him, causing injuries from which Sumner never recovered.

In 1979 the collapse of a portion of the school's roof led to efforts by the District of Columbia board of education and the district government to save and restore the historic building. By 1986 the resulting cooperative efforts had restored Sumner School to its old glory, garnering major national and local awards along the way for the excellence of the restoration. Today the school houses a museum that honors the life and works of Charles Sumner as well as the achievements of the Washington, D.C., community and its Black residents. The museum sponsors lectures, tours, exhibits, performances, and film showings. On a scheduled basis community groups can use the galleries and the great hall. Visitors can see antique furnishings, a District of Columbia Women's Hall of Fame, an exhibit on Black abolitionist and leader Frederick Douglass, and a room with school memorabilia from the 1920s and 1930s—trophies and high school sorority and fraternity items.

DATE BUILT: 1871–1872; renovated 1984–1985

ADDRESS: 1201 Seventeenth Street NW

TELEPHONE: (202) 727-3419

VISITING HOURS: Mon.–Fri. 10–5; concerts, meetings, receptions, and other special events during evening hours and on Saturdays; closed summer from the time classes end until Labor Day and on holidays

FEES: None

SOURCES: Telephone call to site Mar. 14, 1994. NRHPINF. *The Charles Sumner School. Webster's New Biographical Dictionary,* 961. District of Columbia Inventory of Historic Sites. "The Office of Minority Affairs Presents a Black Heritage Tour of Washington, D.C., for the American University Community."

Mary Church Terrell House

One of the best-known and most-respected African American advocates of civil rights and the rights of women, Mary Church Terrell (1863–1954) lived for a number of years in this house at 326 T Street NW. (Another Mary Church Terrell Home is located at 1632 S Street NW; it is also private.) Terrell was born in 1863 in Memphis, Tennessee. Her father, Robert Church, was born in slavery but after emancipation became rich as a result of purchasing extensive property in Memphis. In fact, he was one of the first Black millionaires in the South. During the Memphis riot of 1866, a saloon owned by Church was vandalized; he himself was shot and left for dead. Despite all expectations, however, he recovered and then showed great courage by testifying in court against the men who had attacked him. All his life he was a persistent campaigner for the fair treatment of African Americans.

Even though Robert Church was a strong activist on behalf of African American causes, he wanted his daughter Mary to enjoy a life of ease. He vigorously opposed her desire to go to work and even threatened to disinherit her when she accepted a teaching position at Wilberforce University in Ohio. Undeterred, Mary pursued her career by moving to Washington, D.C., where she taught Latin at the M Street High School. There she fell in love with one of her fellow teachers, Robert Terrell (1857–1925), who was also a lawyer.

After their marriage Mary and Robert Terrell became prominent leaders of Black society in Washington. Robert served for a while as principal of the M Street High School and was later appointed the first African American district judge in Washington. He served the court from 1901 to 1925. Mary was appointed a member of the board of education of the District of Columbia—possibly the first Black woman to be asked to serve on a school board.

When Mary was twenty-nine years old, two tragic events impelled her to a life of social activism. A man who had been a guest at Mary's wedding, Thomas Moss, became the victim of racial violence in Memphis. Moss, who was a childhood friend of Mary's, with two friends had started a food store known as the People's Grocery. Fiercely resentful over losing his Black customers, a white store owner instigated a series of provocative incidents against Moss's store. One Saturday night a gang of white ruffians started to attack the People's Grocery. Armed Black men in the store fought back, shooting three white people in the process. Although the three white men recovered from their wounds, the three Black store owners were arrested and put in jail. Afterward a mob broke into the jail, seized Moss and his companions, and lynched them. The People's Grocery was ransacked and destroyed; remnants of its inventory were auctioned off by white authorities. Moss's death deeply upset Mary Terrell, who was expecting her first child at the time. Shortly afterward, Mary Terrell's newborn infant died in a segregated, poorly equipped hospital. She felt that with proper care the child would have survived.

Upset by the two tragedies, Mary Terrell started her career as an activist by approaching Frederick Douglass, the well-known Black abolitionist leader. Together they spoke with President Benjamin Harrison at the White House, requesting him to take a firm public stand against the lynchings in the South. For political reasons Harrison refused to do so.

Despite this setback, Terrell continued to be a staunch worker for civil rights and women's rights. Selected in 1896 as the first president of the National Association of Colored Women, she urged the association to place emphasis on day-care programs that would strengthen the family. In 1903 Mrs. Terrell gave an acclaimed presentation in Germany at the International Congress of Women, and many speaking engagements followed in cities across the United States. Terrell published articles in newspapers and magazines and wrote her autobiography, *A Colored Woman in a White World.*

Mrs. Terrell sought to provide recreational facilities for Black veterans of World War I. When she was eighty-six, she and her friends, two Black and one white, entered a restaurant in downtown Washington and were refused service. Terrell then campaigned to integrate public facilities in Washington, even initiating a suit to end such segregation. The lawsuit, called the Thompson Test, went to the Supreme Court in 1954. The court's decision resulted in an end to segregated public accommodations in Washington.

As of mid-1994, the Terrell House and parts of the surrounding neighborhood had deteriorated, but visitors may drive by to see the exterior. Someone may even wish to initiate restoration efforts.

DATE BUILT:	1907
ADDRESS:	326 T Street NW
VISITING HOURS:	Private, visitors may drive by
SOURCES:	Telephone conversation, May 22, 1994, with local resident. NRHPINF. *When and Where I Enter.* District of Columbia Inventory of Historic Sites. Black History Resources in Washington, D.C.

Whitelaw Hotel

The Whitelaw Hotel once stood as a proud example of Black enterprise in the District of Columbia. Built in 1920, it may have been the first Black-owned-and-developed hotel in the United States. John Whitelaw Lewis financed the construction by selling shares to the Black community, and he exclusively used Black tradesmen in the construction.

At the time of the hotel's construction, U Street was known as the "Black Broadway." The area remained vibrant and attractive through the 1940s but gradually began to decline in the 1950s and 1960s. After the race riots of 1968 ravaged Fourteenth Street one block away, the area plunged in attractiveness. Code violations were found at the Whitelaw, which was abandoned in 1973. To add to the misfortune, squatters at the hotel caused a fire there in 1981. The Whitelaw had to be boarded up.

In 1981 the Manna Whitelaw Limited Partnership, a local developer of low-income housing, acquired the hotel. Assisted by low-income-housing tax credits and additional funding, the group began restoration. The building was converted into apartments, and the first tenants took occupancy in December 1992.

The five-floor Whitelaw Apartments, with an exterior finished in yellow clay brick, boasts a first-floor ballroom that has been beautifully restored. The ballroom is used now as a common room for the apartments and as an elegant setting for community events. In July 1993 the Whitelaw Hotel was listed in the *National Register of Historic Places.*

DATE BUILT: 1920

ADDRESS: 1839 Thirteenth Street NW at T Street

TELEPHONE: (202) 234-5857

VISITING HOURS: By appointment

SOURCE: Telephone conversation, May 5, 1994, Mr. Adrian Bishop, property coordinator, Manna, Inc.

Carter G. Woodson House

Dr. Carter Goodwin Woodson (1875–1950), often called the father of Black history, was widely known for his trenchant criticism of what he called the "mis-education of the Negro." In his collected writings under that same title, Woodson noted that neither the industrial education nor the classical education that Black students received prepared them for the world in which they would live. Their industrial curriculum used outmoded equipment and methods, he believed, and failed to give them the preparation white apprentices received for work in modern factories. Moreover, those few Black students who were well prepared were barred by trade unions from using their skills. On the other hand, Black students who were taught the classical curriculum found themselves the objects of contempt in history classes; in language classes they were taught to scoff at, rather than to understand, their own dialect and linguistic history. They were excluded altogether from learning about the rich heritage of African proverbs and folklore as well as travel literature about Africa. In medical school they were reminded of their role as germ-carriers. In history classes African history was omitted except when presented as the subject of white exploitation. In a series of essays compiled in 1933, Woodson strongly objected to the results of this form of education:

> The "educated Negroes" have the attitude of contempt toward their own people because in their own as well as in their mixed schools Negroes are taught to admire the Hebrew, the Greek, the Latin, and the Teuton and to despise the African. Of the hundreds of Negro high schools recently examined by an expert in the United States Bureau of Education, only eighteen offer a course taking up the history of the Negro, and in most of the Negro colleges and universities where the Negro is thought of, the race is studied only as a problem or dismissed as of little consequence.[3]

Carter G. Woodson was born in New Canton, Virginia, the first of nine children of former slaves. At an early age he went to work in the coal mines, which delayed his entrance into high school until the age of twenty. Later, Woodson attended Berea College in Kentucky, one of the first colleges in the United States to educate both Black and white students. At Berea he worked his way through school like many other students. He attended the college during the turbulent years when legislation was being written and passed in Kentucky to end the integrated education at Berea College.

In 1912 Carter G. Woodson became one of the first Black students to receive a doctorate from Harvard University. After his graduation, he continued his research and publications in the field of history, showing the need to teach both Black and white Americans about the contributions of Africans and African Americans to civilization. He established the Association for the Study of Negro Life and History and founded the association's *Journal of Negro History.* In 1922 he established Associated Publishers, an organization designed to present an accurate history of African American life and culture.

Dr. Woodson served as dean of Howard University from 1919 to 1920 and as dean of West Virginia State College from 1920 to 1922. For his outstanding contributions, he was awarded the Spingarn Medal in 1926 from the National Association for the Advancement of Colored People. Because of Woodson's influence, Black parents across the United States began teaching their children their own history that had been denied them in their schools.

Woodson resided in this house on Ninth Street from 1915 until his death in 1950. He lived on the top floor, used the lower floors for his office, and turned the basement into a warehouse for books from the Association for the Study of Negro Life and History. Woodson spent his career educating people about the history and contributions of African Americans. In 1971 the Association for the Study of Negro Life and History moved from this Ninth Street location to 1407

Fourteenth Street NW at Rhode Island Avenue. The following year the organization changed its name to the Association for the Study of Afro-American Life and History. The association still owns the historic Woodson House and intends to restore it and open it to the public.

DATE BUILT:	c1890
ADDRESS:	1538 Ninth Street NW
TELEPHONE:	Association for the Study of Afro-American Life and History, (202) 667-2822
VISITING HOURS:	Contact the society for this information
SOURCES:	Telephone conversations, Mar. 14, 1994, Gerald R. Warren, director, Association for the Study of Afro-American Life and History; call to site May 2, 1994, and Dec. 1, 1994. *The Mis-Education of the Negro. Webster's New Biographical Dictionary,* 1070. *Washington, D.C., Black History National Recreation Trail.* District of Columbia Inventory of Historic Sites.

Notes

1. Herbert Aptheker, ed., *A Documentary History of the Negro People in the United States,* vol. 1 (New York: Citadel, 1990), 492.

2. *The Charles Sumner School Rededication* (Washington, D.C.: District of Columbia Public Schools, 1986), 5.

3. Carter G. Woodson, *The Mis-Education of the Negro* (Philadelphia: Hakim's, 1933), 1.

Works Consulted

Before the Mayflower: A History of Black America. Lerone Bennett Jr. New York: Penguin, 1982.

Black History Resources in Washington, D.C. Education Dept. Staff and the Research Dept. of the Anacostia Museum, Smithsonian Institution. Washington, D.C.: The Institution, 1987. [list]

The Black 100: A Ranking of the Most Influential African-Americans, Past and Present. Columbus Salley. New York: Citadel, 1993.

The Charles Sumner School. District of Columbia Public Schools. Washington, D.C.: The District, 1986.

District of Columbia Inventory of Historic Sites. Historic Preservation Division, District of Columbia Dept. of Consumer and Regulatory Affairs. Washington, D.C.: The Department, 1990, 1991.

A Documentary History of the Negro People in the United States. Vol. 1. Herbert Aptheker. New York: Citadel, 1990.

Encyclopedia of African-American Civil Rights: From Emancipation to the Present. Charles D. Lowery and John F. Marszalek. New York: Greenwood, 1992.

Frederick Douglass National Historic Site. Parks and History Assoc., Washington, D.C., with the National Park Service, U.S. Dept. of the Interior. Washington, D.C.: National Parks Service. [pamphlet]

Historical and Cultural Atlas of African Americans. Molefi K. Asante and Mark T. Mattson. New York: Macmillan, 1992.

"History of Ebenezer United Methodist Church." Helen V. Dyson. Washington, D.C.: Capitol Hill United Methodist Church, 19 Mar. 1989. [manuscript]

International Library of Negro Life and History: Historical Negro Biographies. Wilhelmena S. Robinson. New York: Publishers Co., 1970.

The Life and Times of Frederick Douglass Written by Himself: His Early Life as a Slave, His Escape from Bondage, and His Complete History. Frederick Douglass. New York: Collier, 1962.

The Mis-Education of the Negro. Dr. Carter G. Woodson. Philadelphia: Hakim's, 1933.

National Register of Historic Places. Washington, D.C.: National Park Service, 1976.

"The Office of Minority Affairs Presents a Black Heritage Tour of Washington, D.C., for the American University Community." Office of Minority Affairs. Washington, D.C.: The American University. [manuscript]

St. Mary's Episcopal Church. Washington, D.C.: the Church, n.d. [brochure]

Towards the Preservation of a Heritage: Inaugural Exhibition of the Howard University Museum. Thomas C. Battle, Glenn I. O. Phillips, Michael R. Winston. Washington, D.C.: Moorland-Spingarn Research Center, Howard University, 1979. [booklet]

Washington, D.C., Black History National Recreation Trail. Parks and History Assoc. with the National Park Service. Washington, D.C.: National Park Service, 1988. [booklet]

Webster's New Biographical Dictionary. Springfield, Mass.: Merriam-Webster, 1988.

Welcome to Washington. Washington, D.C.: National Park Service, U.S. Dept. of the Interior. [brochure]

When and Where I Enter: The Impact of Black Women on Race and Sex in America. Paula Giddings. New York: William Morrow, 1984; New York: Bantam, 1988.

Florida

Bushnell

Dade Battlefield State Historic Site

In December 1835, slaves who had escaped from Georgia and the Carolinas joined Seminoles in a war ambush at this site. Earlier the African Americans had escaped to Florida, where they lived among the Seminoles. It is estimated that there were several thousand Seminoles in Florida at the time. Some of the Black people living in the state were free; others were slaves of the Seminoles; still others were allies of the Seminoles. Many remembered the first Seminole War of 1817–1818 caused in part by the Seminoles' harboring of runaway slaves.

Andrew Jackson, who had become well known as an Indian fighter, was President of the United States from 1829 to 1837. Known as "Old Hickory," Jackson had in Tennessee a very large number of slaves and was open about his anti-Indian and pro-slavery sentiments. In 1817 he had been called to fight the Seminoles, and the following spring he had pursued Indians into Spanish Florida. He strongly backed the Indian Removal Bill of 1830. U.S. authorities as well as Florida slaveowners joined in the long and costly Seminole War designed to move the Indians across the Mississippi and reclaim the Black fugitives as slaves. Launched in December 1835, the Second Seminole War raged for seven years. The Black fighters proved to be formidable foes. Many of them had been free for more than a generation, and they used their superior knowledge of the swamps in the Everglades to defend their freedom fiercely. At one point they ambushed U.S. Major Francis Dade and a troop of white soldiers. In the massacre that followed, Louis Pacheco, a Black slave who had served as interpreter for Major Dade, was one of only four survivors.

In the end, however, the superior power of the national government and militias from several states prevailed. When the Seminole War ended in 1842, many of the defeated Indians and African Americans were forced to go on a cruel march from Florida to a new territory in Oklahoma.

DATE OF SIGNIFICANCE:	1835
ADDRESS:	Off FL 476, west on US 301
TELEPHONE:	(904) 793-4781
VISITING HOURS:	Daily, 8–sunset; Visitors Center, daily 9–5
FEES:	Vehicle with up to 8 persons, $2; pedestrian or bicyclist, $1
SOURCES:	Telephone call to site, Mar. 15, 1994. *Florida Black Heritage Trail. There Is a River,* 108–10. Academic American Encyclopedia.

Daytona Beach

Bethune-Cookman College
Mary McLeod Bethune Home

Mary McLeod Bethune—educator, administrator, presidential adviser, and civil rights leader—was one of the best-known Black American leaders from the 1920s through World War II. She was born in 1875 in a small wooden cabin near Mayesville, South Carolina, the fifteenth child of parents who were former slaves.

As a child, Mary yearned for an education but was not able to start school until she was nine years old. She excelled in her studies at a missionary school established by the Presbyterians in Mayesville; she then continued her education at the Barber-Scotia Seminary in North Carolina and the Moody Bible Institute in Chicago.

Mary McLeod taught at Haines Institute in Augusta, Georgia, before moving to Sumter, South Carolina, where she married a fellow schoolteacher, Albertus Bethune. They had one child, Albert. Later the Bethunes moved to Savannah, Georgia, where Mrs. Bethune continued her missionary and education work among the poor. After Albertus died in 1904, Mary Bethune moved to Daytona Beach. Realizing that her true mission in life was in the field of education, she opened the Daytona Normal and Industrial Institute for Negro Girls in a community of Black railroad construction laborers. The first six pupils were taught in a dilapidated cabin. To obtain much-needed support, Bethune launched a series of fund-raising appeals to northern philanthropists and industrialists and to merchants in Daytona Beach.

In 1923 the school merged with the Cookman Institute for Boys of Jacksonville and eight years later changed its name to the Bethune-Cookman College. At first it was a junior college, but in 1941 it was accredited as a four-year teacher training and liberal arts college.

As the school grew, Bethune received national recognition for her work in addressing the intellectual, social, and religious needs of Black youth. She was known as a major leader in the realm of civil rights and education. In 1936 President Franklin Delano Roosevelt appointed her Director of Negro Affairs in the National Youth Administration. In 1947 Bethune stepped down from her position as president of Bethune-Cookman College. She died in 1955 at the age of eighty.

Bethune-Cookman College has continued to expand. In 1989–1990 the college, which is located on a fifty-two-acre campus, enrolled 2,145 students, 97 percent of whom were African Americans. The Bethune residence on the college campus was Mrs. Bethune's home from the time of its construction until her death. The two-story frame house and all its furnishings remain as they were when she lived there. The residence is maintained as a museum, while an attached, small brick building serves as an archive for the Bethune papers.

DATE ESTABLISHED:	College, 1904; house, 1920s
ADDRESS:	Bethune-Cookman College, 640 Second Avenue, Daytona Beach
TELEPHONE:	(904) 255-1401, Ext. 372
VISITING HOURS:	College, Mon.–Fri. 8–5; library, Mon.–Thurs. 8 A.M.–10 P.M., Fri. 8–5, Sat. 9–1, Sun. 3–11 P.M., closed holidays; Bethune home, by appointment
FEES:	None
SOURCES:	Dr. Bobby Henderson, director, Library/Learning Resources Center, Bethune-Cookman College. NRHPINF. *National Register of Historic Places,* 152.

Howard Thurman Cultural Park

A two-story frame house among dense foliage and oak trees provided the serene setting for Dr. Howard Thurman's childhood home. His autobiography, *With Head and Heart,* describes the Daytona home and the strength he received from looking out upon the large oak tree in his backyard.

Daytona Beach had three Black neighborhoods. Thurman was born in 1900 in the Waycross community, an area of unpaved, tree-lined streets. There he grew up in his grandmother's house. African Americans, who made up more than 33 percent of the population of Daytona Beach, worked on the estates of wealthy industrialists and rich northern families who came south for the winter. After dark the servants and laborers had to leave their places of employment to return to the Black neighborhoods of Newton, Midway, and Waycross.

Following the Civil War, Black children in Florida had few opportunities to obtain a good education. Wealthy white children attended privately funded schools while poor white and Black children attended public elementary schools. By 1915, for every $11.50 spent per year to educate a white child, Florida spent only $2.64 to educate a Black child. As late as 1917, white teachers were legally barred from instructing Black students, and 95 percent of Black children who received instruction did not proceed past the elementary school level.

The Black school in Daytona Beach was funded by white winter residents and was one of the few "public" schools for Black children in Florida. Because Daytona's Black students were not instructed past the seventh grade, they were unable to pass the eighth-grade examination required for high school entrance. Howard Thurman was an exception. Although his grandmother was a former slave who could not read or write, the young boy showed an ability to learn from an early age. His principal recognized his talent and on his own time instructed Thurman in eighth-grade courses. With this help, Thurman became the first Black student in Florida to pass the high school entrance examination.

The young graduate had to attend high school in Jacksonville, thirty miles away from home. James Gamble of the Procter & Gamble Company, a man who had winter estates in the Daytona area, paid for Thurman's high school costs and part of his college education. When Thurman left for high school in Jacksonville, a stranger paid the freight on his luggage.

After graduating from high school, young Howard Thurman worked his way through Florida Baptist Academy and Morehouse College in Atlanta, where he majored in economics. He entered the Colgate-Rochester School of Divinity, which at that time admitted only two Black students each year.

After serving as a pastor in Ohio, Thurman decided to continue his studies with Rufus Jones, a Quaker philosopher, at Haverford College in Haverford, Pennsylvania. He moved into the academic realm, accepting a joint appointment at Morehouse College and Spelman College in Atlanta. During this period he met Sue Bailey, whom he married in 1932; later he was appointed as the first dean of Rankin Chapel at Howard University in Washington, D.C.

In 1935 Dr. Thurman led an African-American delegation to India, Burma, and Ceylon. During this trip he met the poet Rabindranath Tagore and India's political and spiritual leader, Mahatma Gandhi. On returning to the United States, Thurman preached one Sunday in Philadelphia, describing the teachings of Gandhi and his philosophy of nonviolent resistance. The sermon, and Thurman's book, *Jesus and the Disinherited,* deeply influenced Dr. Martin Luther King Jr. and helped to shape King's philosophy of leadership in the Civil Rights Movement.

In 1953 Thurman accepted an invitation to become the dean of Marsh Chapel at Boston University—the first time a Black man held such a post at a predominantly white university. He remained at Boston University for twelve years. *Life* magazine named him one of the best preachers of the year.

Thurman retired to San Francisco in 1964. Over his distinguished career, he became a nationally known theologian and author of twenty-two books. He supported many intercultural activities and founded an educational trust to provide college scholarships. Thurman died of a respiratory illness on April 10, 1981. Because he had spent most of his working life in housing provided by universities, the Daytona Beach house is the only residence directly associated with him—the place he lived from birth to his departure for high school in 1917. Bethune-Cookman College and the

New Birth Corporation plan to open the house to the public on a regular basis. Restored to reflect its appearance when Thurman lived there with his grandmother, the interior contains Thurman's bed, his favorite sofa, a chair from his days at Boston University, an organ, and pictures that portray his life beginning with high school graduation. The Howard Thurman Cultural Park will have research, rather than museum displays, as its primary emphasis.

DATE ESTABLISHED: c1888

ADDRESS: 614 Whitehall Street, Daytona Beach

TELEPHONE: To leave a message on tape, (904) 258-7514; Daytona Beach Visitors Bureau, (904) 255-0415

VISITING HOURS: Information not available; visitors may drive by

SOURCES: NRHPINF. Telephone conversation Mar. 16, 1994, Reverend Jefferson Rogers, New Birth Corp.

Fernandina Beach

Fort Clinch State Park

Prior to the Civil War, slave owners in the area contracted out their slaves for seasonal work at Fort Clinch. As part of the contract, the owners received wages for each slave working there. The slaves received food, medical care, and some personal equipment.

During the Civil War, Union troops occupied the fort. Some commanders wrote reports depicting the role of Black slaves and freedmen at the site. Escaped slaves who made their way to Fort Clinch soon found employment there. Fort Commander A. F. Sears commented that at twenty-five cents per day the fugitives would work a day or two; then they would loaf or pretend to be sick for a while. He began paying seventy-five cents per day while applying penalties for absenteeism or tardiness. As a result, he had fewer, but more reliable, workers. His report did not say how the wages and work assignments of the Black workers compared with those of the white workers.

The following is a list of some activities of African American troops stationed at Fort Clinch during the Civil War:

The First South Carolina Volunteers (Colored) brought back to the fort from a raid in Georgia a shipload of cut lumber and brown bricks. These soldiers were mustered into the Union Army on Amelia Island, Florida, in July 1863 and stationed at Fort Clinch until January 1864.

The Thirty-fourth United States Colored Troops stationed two companies at the fort from February 1864 until February 1866. According to an October 24, 1864, report, the regimental recruiter had kidnapped four Black men from the Fort Clinch workforce and enlisted them into a company he was forming on Amelia Island.

From November 1864 until May 1865 the Third United States Colored Troops stationed Company G at the fort.

Although the soldiers of Fort Clinch never saw action, the bastions, barracks, and other restored buildings remain, showing a site where Black slaves and freedmen were stationed and worked.

The fort is interesting because of its historic walls and bastions. The site also includes a parade ground, soldiers' barracks, and quartermaster building. Occasionally volunteer units dress as Civil War soldiers. A museum display shows the system of fortifications.

DATE ESTABLISHED: 1847; as seen today, 1867

ADDRESS: 2601 Atlantic Avenue, Fernandina Beach (enter off FL A1A on Atlantic Avenue)

TELEPHONE: (904) 277-7274

VISITING HOURS: Fort, daily 9–5; park, daily 8–sundown

FEES: Park, $3.25 per vehicle with up to 8 people and $1 per person for each additional person; fort, $1 per person in addition to the park entry fee

SOURCES: Roy Kemp, park manager, and George Berninger, ranger. Telephone conversation Mar. 16, 1994, Park Ranger Boyette.

Fort Pierce

Zora Neale Hurston House

Harlem Renaissance writer Zora Neale Hurston was born in Eatonville, Florida, in 1903. As a college student, she studied anthropology with Franz Boas at Barnard College, where she was one of the few Black students. When she studied the lives of African Americans in small communities, her sharp observations moved her to begin writing novels. Some of her works, including the novel *Their Eyes Are Watching God,* have gained wider recognition in recent years.

Zora Neale Hurston moved to Fort Pierce in 1957. She wrote for the *Fort Pierce Chronicle* and worked on her manuscript *Herod the Great.* Her worst period, financially, came after her manuscript on King Herod was rejected. She died in 1960 in a welfare home, nearly penniless.

Hurston was the first tenant to live in this one-story, concrete-block house, and it is the only known still-existing residence associated with her life.

ADDRESS: 1734 School Court Street, Fort Pierce

VISITING HOURS: Private, visitors may walk or drive by

SOURCES: William N. Thurston, historic preservationist supervisor, Florida Department of State Division of Historical Resources, Tallahassee, Florida. Dr. Deidre H. Crumbley, coordinator, African and African American Studies, Rollins College. Tulie Wheeler Taylor, assistant supervisor, Florida Master Site File, Florida Department of State, Division of Historical Resources. *Florida Black Heritage Trail,* 2, 8, 9. "The History of Eatonville, Florida." *Webster's New Biographical Dictionary,* 501. *International Library of Negro Life and History,* 208–9. *Their Eyes Are Watching God.*

Jacksonville

Masonic Temple

September 18, 1912, was a proud day for the Free and Accepted Masons of Florida, Colored. Groundbreaking ceremonies took place for the new Masonic Temple building, and crowds had gathered to hear the oration by Jacksonville's Mayor W. S. Jordan.

emonies continued
te the placing of the
Masonic Lodge, the
s League, Ladies of
ch Mason, Heroines
Templar had helped
of them were there
uition.

decided as early as
downtown Jackson-
in 1901, many new
ucted. The Jackson-
nal Negro Business
ancing in return for
ssmen, and affiliated
raising construction
ole.

has a classical design,
ornamentation and a
ior features a decora-
wainscot in the lobby.

The building housed professional offices, the *Jacksonville Journal* newspaper, and the state Young Men's Christian Association. The Masonic Temple became a gathering point for the Black community's commercial and fraternal activities.

Several years after construction, however, the lodge was $109,000 in debt, and members' spirits were low. Davis Powell was inducted as Grandmaster in 1916, and within five years, he transformed the lodge, reinvigorated the membership, and retired the entire mortgage and other debts amounting to $200,000.

By 1921 the Masonic Temple building, described by a contemporary as palatial and magnificent, was valued at a half-million dollars. The NAACP's *Crisis Magazine* of January 1942 described it as among the leading buildings of the South, regardless of the owners' race. Today the Masonic Temple is one of the few remaining twentieth-century buildings in Jacksonville associated with the development of the Black community.

Street, Jacksonville
368
by appointment
. Telephone conversation Mar. 15, 1994, Mrs. Sampson, Masonic Temple.

Edward Waters College
Centennial Hall

Florida's Black students
er learning. In 1872 the
opal (A.M.E.) Church in
Florida tried to establish a college, Brown's Theological Institute, that would prepare young men to become preachers. Construction proceeded in Live Oak, Florida, in 1873, but mismanagement caused the project to come to an end. Church trustees lost their land and materials to a high bidder.

The church established another school in Jacksonville in 1883. This time the college grew rapidly. In 1892 officials renamed the institution Edward Waters College, in honor of the third bishop of the A.M.E. Church. In 1901 a disastrous fire destroyed nearly all of Jacksonville, including the three-story building on East Beaver Street that housed Edward Waters College. Administrators rented buildings for three years before purchasing the Kings Road property where the college stands today.

Centennial Hall survives as the oldest building on the campus. The historic structure, built in 1916, was named to commemorate the 100th anniversary of the A.M.E. Church. Reverend Richard L. Brown, one of the few Black architects of the era, built the three-story brick building, capping it with a small octagonal cupola and locating it in a large, green, open setting. The exterior of Centennial Hall remains unaltered, and changes to the interior have been kept to a minimum. The building, which symbolizes A.M.E. Church efforts to ensure quality higher education for Black students, now houses the college library.

DATE ESTABLISHED: 1916

ADDRESS: 1658 Kings Road, Jacksonville

TELEPHONE: (904) 355-3030

VISITING HOURS: Mon.–Fri. 9–4:30; contact college for tours

SOURCES: NRHPINF. Telephone call to site, Dec. 22, 1994. *Florida Black Heritage Trail,* 10.

Miami

Black Archives History and Research Foundation of South Florida
D. A. Dorsey House
Dr. William A. Chapman House

The Black Archives History and Research Foundation conducts research on the multicultural roots of Miami's Black population, presents exhibits and tours of Miami's African American heritage sites, and leads in the preservation of local historic sites. The foundation is associated with two local historic buildings described in this listing, the D. A. Dorsey House and the Dr. William A. Chapman House.

The Foundation is located in a building named for Black artist Joseph Caleb, whose works are on display here. Collections include photographs of historic sites in Black communities of Dade County and a collection of 119 old lobby posters from hotels. The posters, which advertised early local presentations of such well-known performers as Count Basie and Aretha Franklin, give a panoramic view of local business from the 1930s through the early 1960s. The foundation also has extensive manuscripts about Dade County's Black history.

The foundation led in efforts to reconstruct the **D. A. Dorsey House,** which belonged to a pioneer African American Miami businessman. The house is located in the Overtown district, one of Miami's oldest neighborhoods, a community that began developing in 1896. Dana A. Dorsey, who was born in Quitman, Georgia, in 1872, came to Miami about 1896 as a truck farmer. He purchased lots for $25 each and then began to develop large real estate parcels into the early "Colored Town." His land holdings were considered to be the largest ever acquired by a Black man in Dade County.

Dorsey also helped to organize the Mutual Industrial Benefit and Savings Association, Florida's first Black bank, and he chaired the Colored Advisory Committee to the Dade County School Board.

The house at 250 N.W. Ninth Street is on the site most closely associated with Dorsey's productive life in Miami. Mr. and Mrs. Dorsey lived here until his death in 1940. The Black Archives History and Research Foundation, the current owners of the house, spearheaded efforts to reconstruct the original Dorsey House, which no longer was habitable. Architects completed measured drawings and precisely reconstructed the house with the kinds of building materials used in the original dwelling. Dorsey House will be a children's museum with a focus on pioneers who were associated with labor.

The Black History Archives also is associated with the **Dr. William A. Chapman House,** a restored seventeen-room house built in 1923 for Dr. Chapman. Chapman was a graduate of Meharry Medical School in Nashville. The Dade County Public School District owns the house, which was restored at a cost of $1.5 million, and the Black Archives Foundation operates it as an ethnic heritage children's center that emphasizes oral history. Visitors will see an elegant house containing masks from various countries in Africa as well as flags and materials from the 120 countries represented in the Dade County School District's student population. Schoolchildren are collecting oral histories neighborhood-by-neighborhood, and these are to be deposited in Chapman House.

Visitors may see these three sites by appointment with the Black Archives Foundation.

DATE BUILT: Dorsey House, c1914; Chapman House, 1923

ADDRESS: The Black Archives History and Research Foundation of South Florida, in the Joseph Caleb Community Center, 5400 N.W. Twenty-second Avenue, Building B, Suite 101; Dorsey House, 250 N.W. Ninth Street; Chapman House, next to the Booker T. Washington High School on N.W. Sixth Avenue, Miami

TELEPHONE: For appointment to visit the three sites, (305) 636-2390

VISITING HOURS: Archives office, Mon.–Fri. 9–4; closed Sat., Sun., and days when public schools are closed

FEES: None

SOURCES: Telephone conversation Mar. 16, 1994, Ms. Dorothy Jenkins Fields, social studies specialist, Dade County Public School District, and founder and certified archivist, Black Archives, History and Research Foundation of South Florida. NRHPINF. *Florida Black Heritage Trail,* 15–16.

Ocala

Mount Zion African Methodist Episcopal Church

Mount Zion A.M.E. Church, which has served the Black population of Ocala since 1891, stands as Ocala's only surviving brick, nineteenth-century church. A Black contractor, Levi Alexander Sr. (1854–1939), designed and built the church in 1891. Alexander, who was born in Palmer Springs, Virginia, learned carpentry in Raleigh, North Carolina. He moved to Ocala between 1880 and 1885 and constructed several houses, a hardware building, a store, an academy, and the Mount Zion A.M.E. Church. When his son, Levi Jr., joined him in the business, they operated under the name "L. Alexander and Son—Contractor and Builder." Father and son worked together until the father retired in the early 1930s.

The care that Alexander took in his design was shown in the spaciousness and fine acoustics of the Mount Zion church. The interior has a high ceiling of dark mahogany-stained decking, white plaster walls with wainscoting stained to match the ceiling finish, and carved wooden pews. The acoustics and seating capacity of approximately 600 persons made the church an ideal location for commencement and baccalaureate ceremonies of Howard Academy and Howard High School. Concerts and state meetings of fraternal organizations were also held at the church.

Mount Zion A.M.E. Church was built on one of the major thoroughfares in the city. At the time of construction, it was near the town limits. Although commercial and residential buildings have grown around it, the church, renovated in 1992, retains its historic appearance and remains a community landmark.

DATE BUILT: 1891

ADDRESS: 623 S. Magnolia Avenue, Ocala

TELEPHONE: (904) 351-2008; pastor's residence, (904) 371-6178

VISITING HOURS: Sun. school, 9:30; Sun. service, 11; Bible study, Wed. 8 P.M.

SOURCE: NRHPINF. Telephone conversation Aug. 14, 1995, Reverend Oliver Simmons, Mount Zion A.M.E. Church.

Olustee

Olustee Battlefield State Historic Site

The Union Army campaign that climaxed in the Battle of Olustee began in February 1864 when more than 5,500 troops embarked at Hilton Head, South Carolina. Their objective was to occupy Jacksonville, disrupt transportation and supply lines, and restore Florida to the Union. They intended to deprive the Confederacy of food supplies, capture other supplies, and gain Black recruits for "Colored" units of the Union Army.

On the afternoon of February 20, Union troops commanded by General Truman A. Seymour made contact with Confederates two and one-half miles east of the hamlet of Olustee. They met approximately 5,200 men under Confederate General Finegan and fought for five hours in an open virgin pine forest before the Union forces retreated.

The Eighth Colored Troops had never been under fire, yet the soldiers maintained discipline and advanced toward the enemy lines as directed. Confederate cavalrymen pursued the men until dark and returned with 150 prisoners. The victory went to the Confederates when, having lost nearly a third of their strength, Union forces had to withdraw toward Sanderson.

Black soldiers from the Massachusetts Fifty-fourth Volunteers then went into the battle, and the First North Carolina Colored Regiment followed. The men fought steadily and inflicted great losses on the enemy. Men from the Fifty-fourth Massachusetts Regiment held the area until dark and were the last to leave the site.

Battle casualties included 1,861 Union and 946 Confederate soldiers. Corporal James Henry Gooding from the Fifty-fourth Massachusetts Volunteers was one of the Black men wounded and taken prisoner at the Battle of Olustee. In 1863 Gooding had written to President Lincoln to protest the injustice shown in providing Black soldiers lower pay than that given to white soldiers. The proud Black men of the Fifty-fourth Massachusetts chose to take no pay at all rather than to accept less than white soldiers received. Corporal Gooding did not live to see this equality corrected. He died in June 1864 at the Andersonville Prison in Americus, Georgia, where prisoners of war were kept under terrible conditions of exposure and privation. A month after Gooding died, Congress enacted legislation providing equal pay to Black soldiers. Union forces remained in Jacksonville and other Florida sites until the end of the war. They carried out frequent operations against Confederate forces defending East Florida but did not come out in significant force again.

The site was acquired by the state of Florida in 1901. Although there is little to see in terms of physical land features, visitors see the general area where the battle occurred. The battlefield is marked along the battle lines, and an interpretive museum offers exhibits and artifacts that interpret the Confederate victory. The battle is reenacted each February. A museum, a monument, and a walking tour of the battlefield commemorate the largest Civil War battle in Florida. There was a mass grave, but the exact site has been forgotten. One-third of the 5,500 Union troops who fought at Olustee Battlefield were Black; they came from the First North Carolina Colored, the Fifty-fourth Massachusetts Volunteers, and the Eighth U.S. Colored Troops of Pennsylvania.

DATE OF SIGNIFICANCE:	1864
ADDRESS:	42 miles west of Jacksonville and 2 miles east of Olustee on US 90, Olustee
TELEPHONE:	Olustee Battlefield, (904) 758-0400; Stephen Foster State Folk Cultural Center (managers of the battlefield), (904) 397-1919
VISITING HOURS:	Battlefield, Thur.–Mon. 8–5 including July 4, closed Tues.–Wed. and Nov.–Apr.; Cultural Center, Mon.–Fri. 8:30–4:30, closed holidays
FEES:	None
SOURCES:	Telephone call to site, May 29, 1994. Telephone conversation Dec. 22, 1994, Darlene Sawyer, secretary specialist, Stephen Foster State Folk Cultural Center. Information sent by ranger on site. NRHPINF. *International Library of Negro Life and History. The Negro's Civil War.*

Opa-locka

Opa-locka Historic District

The predominantly Black community of Opa-locka is noted for its buildings in the Moorish-revival architectural style. Sixty-five of the original 100 buildings remain, and three of these are listed in the *National Register of Historic Places.* The Harry Hurt Building, constructed in 1926, is a shopping and service center highlighted by a central dome with minarets on each side. In 1939 the town acquired an existing structure for use as a city hall. The building may have been used as a fanciful advertising attraction during the city's heyday. A third attraction, the railroad station, has a design based on the stories of *Aladdin* and *Ali Baba and the Forty Thieves.* Many visitors come to Opa-locka to see the railroad station.

Visitors with a love of words will be interested to know that the town's name is derived from the Indian word *opatishawokaloca,* which means "big island covered with many trees in the swamp." In 1990 the population was 96.8 percent Black and Hispanic American.

DATE ESTABLISHED: 1926

ADDRESS: Harry Hurt Building, 490 Ali-Baba Avenue; Opa-locka City Hall, 777 Sharazad Boulevard; Opa-locka railroad station, 500 block of Ali-Baba Avenue, Opa-locka

TELEPHONE: City Hall, (305) 688-4611

VISITING HOURS: Buildings are private, visitors may drive by

SOURCES: Telephone conversation Mar. 15, 1994, city manager's office. Telephone conversation Dec. 22, 1994, Edna Griffin, library director, Opa-locka Public Library. *Florida Black Heritage Trail,* 17.

Orlando

Orlando Museum of Art—African Gallery

The African Gallery at the Orlando Museum of Art depicts the Black heritage through art. The Paul and Ruth Tishman Collection includes masks, figures, beaded divination bags, and other West African artifacts.

Another part of this museum, the Art Encounter Gallery, is set up specifically for children and includes a section of African art. There, young visitors can press one button and hear African music and a talk about the music or press another button that starts a recording of an African story. The gallery also has African musical instruments for hands-on use by children.

DATE ESTABLISHED: 1985

ADDRESS: 2416 N. Mills Avenue, Orlando

TELEPHONE: (407) 896-4231

VISITING HOURS: Tues.–Sat. 9–5, Sun. 12–5, closed holidays

FEES: Adults, $4; children 4–11, $2; children under 4, free; members, free

SOURCES: Jan Clanton, assistant educator, Orlando Museum of Art. Telephone conversation Mar. 15, 1994, Hansen Mulford, curator of exhibitions.

Pensacola

Julee Cottage Museum

Julee Cottage, one of the oldest houses in Pensacola, was owned by Julee Panton, who was described as a "free woman of color." Tradition maintains that Julee Panton helped to purchase the freedom of enslaved Blacks and assisted them in their new lives as free men and women. Her name has persisted as a symbol of altruism. Although the cottage was Panton's first purchase, she also owned several other properties in Pensacola. This cottage was later sold to another freed woman named Angelica and then to several different Black families.

Some time ago Julee Cottage was removed from its original location at 214 West Zaragoza Street to keep it from being demolished. In addition to its role in African American history, the residence is significant in Pensacola's architectural heritage as the only surviving house reminiscent of the Creole cottages of the French Quarter in New Orleans. Many of the original features of this 200-year-old structure were lost in the move, but enough of the original structure remains to merit a visit. Rehabilitation has prepared the cottage for use as a center for Black history; it contains an exhibit on Black history in West Florida.

DATE BUILT: 1805

ADDRESS: 210 E. Zaragoza Street, Historic Pensacola Village, Pensacola

TELEPHONE: Office, (904) 444-8905; recorded information, (904) 444-8587

VISITING HOURS: Visitors Center (across the street from Julee Cottage), Mon.–Sat. 10–4

FEES: Admission tickets to the entire village purchased at 205 E. Zaragoza Street (tickets to Julee Cottage not sold separately), adults, $5.50; seniors and active military, $4.50; youth 4–16, $2.25; children under 4, free

SOURCES: Telephone call to site, Mar. 15, 1994. Telephone conversation July 31, 1995, Dora Johnson, administrative assistant. *Historic Pensacola Village; Julee Cottage, Historic Pensacola Village: Blacks in West Florida.*

St. Augustine

Castillo de San Marcos National Monument
Fort Mosé

The Castillo de San Marcos was first established in St. Augustine in 1672 to protect the Spanish colony from British attacks by sea. Construction on the fort continued until 1756. In Spanish Florida the governor granted freedom and protection to slaves, and those who escaped from North Carolina, South Carolina, and Georgia in the 1700s often found refuge with the Spaniards at San Marcos.

Fort Mosé, a small fortified community located two miles north of Castillo de San Marcos, was inhabited almost entirely by Black men, women, and children. The small community was established in 1738 and became part of the outer defense of St. Augustine. The Black men and women who lived in St. Augustine, because of their family heritage as former slaves, had a strong reason to want to protect St. Augustine and Fort Mosé. Slavemasters to the north still wanted to recapture their runaway slaves, and British victories could return the former slaves to bondage. Having converted to Catholicism, Black men were considered part of the local militia, and they fought both inside and outside the forts to protect St. Augustine and their own freedom.

Two of the notable early battles in which they fought were the War of Spanish Succession in 1702 and the Battle of Jenkins' Ear in 1740. The War of the Spanish Succession started in Europe in 1701. The English colonies in America became involved in 1702 when an expedition from the Carolinas moved against the Spanish settlement of St. Augustine. Although the English siege was not successful and the attackers returned to the Carolinas, Florida was weakened by the battle and by later attacks. Black men from St. Augustine fought again with the Spanish in the War of Jenkins' Ear (the Spanish were said to have mutilated an English sea captain, giving the war its name). The war began in 1739, the result of commercial rivalry between Britain and Spain. In 1740 James Edward Oglethorpe, founder and first governor of the new colony of Georgia, led men from Georgia and the Carolinas against St. Augustine, but his siege of several weeks was a failure.

Fort Mosé is considered to be the first free African American settlement in North America. The community was destroyed about 1740 but reestablished in 1758. In 1759 a priest left records indicating that Fort Mosé contained approximately twenty houses and nearly one hundred men, women, and children. The fort was destroyed when the Spanish left Florida, and most of the inhabitants are believed to have left for Cuba with the Spanish. Today nothing remains of Fort Mosé except underground archaeological artifacts.

In 1819 Spain ceded Florida to the United States, and the transfer of territory was ratified by the U.S. government in 1821. Still the fight for control of the Black and Indian peoples of Florida raged on in the Seminole Wars from 1835 to 1842 (see Bushnell, Dade Battlefield).

Today, Castillo de San Marcos is the oldest masonry fort in the United States. It stood in the northeast corner of the old city of St. Augustine. When the whole city was invaded in the eighteenth-century conflicts, the stone building withstood a number of attacks but was never captured. It appears much as it did three hundred years ago. One of the exhibits at the fort describes Fort Mosé and the role that free Black people played in Spanish Florida.

DATE ESTABLISHED: 1672

ADDRESS: Castillo Drive and Avenue Menendez, St. Augustine

TELEPHONE: (904) 829-6506

VISITING HOURS: Daily 8:45–4:45, closed Christmas

FEES: Adults, $2; seniors who have paid a one-time fee of $10 for a Golden Age pass to all national parks, no charge; children 16 and under, free

SOURCES: Telephone conversation Mar. 15, 1994, Mr. Gordie Wilson, superintendent, Castillo de San Marcos. Telephone conversation Dec. 4, 1994, Mr. Joseph Brehm, interpretative park ranger, Castillo de San Marcos. *The Smithsonian Guide to Historic America,* 389. The Academic American Encyclopedia.

Lincolnville Historic District

This neighborhood in St. Augustine had its origins as a Black community in 1866, when former slaves began settling in a three-block area that they called *Africa.* Later named Lincolnville, the district began to develop as a residential and business neighborhood. St. Augustine's greatest collection of architecture from the late nineteenth century is located in the Lincolnville historic district.

One building, at the corner of South Street and Blanco, may have once been a slave cabin or outbuilding from a plantation. Today it is used as a garage.

The historic community was a turbulent center of the 1964 Civil Rights Movement. When Dr. Martin Luther King Jr., his assistant, Reverend Ralph Abernathy, and other civil rights leaders arrived in St. Augustine for the 1964 summer demonstrations, Dr. King was moved from house to house each night for safety. For decades before, the Ku Klux Klan had openly conducted meetings in St.

Augustine. The major confrontation, however, came in 1964, when city officials sought federal funds for celebrating the 400th anniversary of the founding of St. Augustine. A local Black leader, NAACP member, and dentist, Robert B. Hayling, protested to federal authorities, including President Lyndon Johnson, that such a rigidly segregated city should not receive federal assistance for the celebration. White citizens regarded the protest as audacious and were enraged. Violence followed; bricks were thrown and gunshots fired at Dr. Hayling's home, and he and others were beaten. Armed white ruffians drove through the Black section of town, shots were exchanged, and an armed white man was killed. Four Black men were arrested and charged with murder. At this point Southern Christian Leadership Conference officials came to St. Augustine to give workshops in nonviolent protest. They sent out nationwide calls for volunteers to join their protest. After SCLC demonstrations interrupted the lucrative tourist business, the white people became infuriated again and erupted in brutal, unprovoked attacks. The scenes were televised to a shocked nation. SCLC leader Ralph Abernathy later read an FBI report revealing that St. Johns County Sheriff L. O. Davis indicated that he would rely on the help of Ku Klux Klan members to help control Black demonstrators.

SCLC leaders, aware that the escalating violence could lead to deaths, agreed to leave St. Augustine if white leaders would establish a biracial committee to deal with the problems. They left after governor Farris Bryant called a press conference and announced that he had appointed such a committee. They later learned that no committee had been appointed—a bitter lesson showing that segregationists would go to any lengths to prevent desegregation from becoming a reality.

DATE ESTABLISHED: 1866

ADDRESS: Bounded by Cedar, Riberia, Cerro, and Washington Streets and DeSoto Place, St. Augustine

SOURCES: Telephone conversation Dec. 20, 1994, Charles Tingley, assistant librarian, St. Augustine Historical Society. *Florida Black Heritage Trail*, 21. *And the Walls Came Tumbling Down*, 282–96. *Encyclopedia of African-American Civil Rights*, 489.

Sumatra

Fort Gadsden State Historic Site
Negro Fort

During the War of 1812, the British built Fort Gadsden at Prospect Bluff on the Apalachicola River. They intended to recruit runaway slaves and Seminole Indians to fight against the Americans, and the fort provided a useful assembly point for these forces. After the end of the war, the British abandoned the fort. Since they had promised freedom to those who joined them, they took with them some Black men as they withdrew. Most of the Black men, their families, and some Indians, as well as recently escaped slaves, continued to use the fort as a hideaway. A Black fugitive named Garson and a Choctaw chief led a group of more than 300 individuals at the site, which they called Fort Negro. Other groups began to settle along the river because they felt safe under the protection of the fort.

White slaveowners in the area were irate about the community of defiant Black people, for they knew that such a beacon of freedom would encourage other slaves to escape. Soon the slaveowners pressured the U.S. government to help them regain the slaves, whom they regarded as their property. Agreeing to the demand, General

Andrew Jackson sent federal troops and gunboats to attack the fort. After the fort's defenders refused to surrender, the American gunboats opened fire on July 27, 1816. When cannon balls struck an open magazine, the gunpowder ignited, and a tremendous explosion followed, killing 274 of the 334 men, women, and children at the fort. The terrible carnage that ended the four-day siege was a factor in precipitating the First Seminole War.

Today this state park still contains a network of trenches as well as the earthen outlines of the old fort. The site gives witness to the slaughter that was meant to keep Black people in bondage forever. Known variously as Fort Gadsden Historic Memorial, British Fort, or Negro Fort, the park commemorates a brutal siege and its tragic end. A local resident, Mrs. Helene Square, who visits the site occasionally, describes it as "quiet—a beautiful place on the banks of the Appalachicola river, a place where I walk among the wildflowers, a place that is eerie when I look at the indentations of all those graves and think of all of the people who died there."

DATE ESTABLISHED: 1814–1818

ADDRESS: 6 miles southwest of Sumatra on FL 65; 24 miles northeast of Appalachicola on US 98 east, then FL 65 north and follow the signs to the park

VISITING HOURS: Daily, 24 hours

FEES: None

SOURCES: Telephone conversation Mar. 15, 1994, Ms. Helene Square, secretary at St. George Island State Park. *Florida Black Heritage Trail. National Register of Historic Places,* 144, 145. *The Smithsonian Guide to Historic America,* 373. *There Is a River,* 63–65.

Tallahassee

Florida Agricultural and Mechanical University Carnegie Library Black Archives, Research Center, and Museum

The Carnegie Library, a small but prominently located building, is one of the oldest buildings on the campus of Florida Agricultural and Mechanical University. The college started out as the Florida State Normal and Industrial School for Negro Youth and received its charter in 1887. It was organized as part of Governor Bloxham's program to improve public education in Florida. The normal school soon became a land-grant institution funded by the 1890 Morrill Act, and it was moved in that year to the highest hill in Tallahassee on land that was once a plantation belonging to the governor of Florida.

A committee of the General Alumni Association approached philanthropist Andrew Carnegie in 1904 with a request for funds to build a library. In 1905 a fire consumed the main building containing the existing library and administrative offices, and the loss made the request all the more urgent. Carnegie agreed to provide $10,000 for construction of a library building, stipulating that the college would have to stock the library with books.

When the completed facility was dedicated in 1908, it was the only Carnegie library located on a Black land-grant campus. By 1913 the library's collection of books had grown to 8,000 volumes. The college became known as Florida Agricultural and Mechanical College in 1908 and was recognized as a university in 1953.

Although a new library was constructed in 1947, the original Carnegie Building, a two-story, square, white-brick structure with a hipped roof and pedimented portico, remains and now houses the Black Archives, Research Center, and Museum. Inside, there is an extensive collection of African art, slave irons, and other African American cultural artifacts. The center has been visited by outstanding Americans, including Booker T. Washington, Marian Anderson, W. E. B. Du Bois, and George Washington Carver. The Carnegie Library is listed in the *National Register of Historic Places.*

DATE ESTABLISHED: College, 1887; library, 1908; Black Archives, 1975

ADDRESS: Near the intersection of Gamble and Boulevard Streets, Tallahassee

TELEPHONE: (904) 599-3020

VISITING HOURS: Mon.–Fri. 9–4; closed weekends and all holidays except by appointment

FEES: None

SOURCES: NRHPINF. James N. Eaton, Black Archives, Research Center and Museum, Florida A & M University.

Union Bank Building

The Union Bank Building, located just east of the state capitol, is the oldest surviving commercial building in Florida. It was chartered in 1833 but operated in private residences at first until this building was completed in 1840. The business opened to the public as a planters' bank whose success depended on slave labor in a cotton-producing region. The bank went bankrupt in 1843–1844, however, and the structure later developed an entirely new function that favored Black people.

Starting in 1869, four years after the end of the Civil War, the structure began to house the Freedmen's Savings and Trust Company. This business, however, was as ill-starred as Union Bank, and by 1874 also was bankrupt. In succession the building was used as a boarding house, a bakery, and a feed store. Then in the late 1920s the site again became part of Black history when Willis Giles, a cobbler educated at Tuskegee Institute in Alabama, opened a shoe factory here. His association with the building was so strong that in 1985 the Willis Giles-Susie Baker Giles family held its family reunion in the historic place.

Even today, Black history remains an emphasis in programs here. The Museum of Florida History houses its African American history teacher in-service programs in this building, one of the museum's four main sites. Thus, the structure that served from 1867 to 1874 as one of Florida's two Freedmen's Bureau banks and that once housed the shoe factory of a Black cobbler has retained its association with Black history.

Visitors today see the building restored as a bank of 1841. Sensitive renovations include the original colors on the walls and period reproductions of a cashier's desk and other furnishings.

DATE BUILT: 1840

ADDRESS: 219 Apalachee Parkway, corner of Calhoun Street, Tallahassee

TELEPHONE: (904) 487-3803

VISITING HOURS: Tues.–Fri. 10–1, Sat. and Sun. 1–4; closed Mon.

FEES: None

SOURCES: Telephone conversation Mar. 15, 1994, Peter Cowdrey, museum program superintendent, Museum of Florida History. *The Smithsonian Guide to Historic America,* 513.

Tampa

Museum of African American Art

The museum highlights African art and African American art from many areas of the United States. Collections range from African sculpture to modern-day impressionistic paintings and include some of the oldest examples of African American art in the United States (one item dates from 1851). The Barnett/Aden Collection is a premiere collection of art portraying African American history and culture.

ADDRESS: 1308 Marion Street, Tampa
TELEPHONE: (813) 272-2466
VISITING HOURS: Tues.–Sat. 10–4:30, Sun. 1–4:30; closed Mon., Christmas, New Year's Day
FEES: $2 donation
SOURCES: Telephone conversation Mar. 15, 1994, Uwezo Sudan, museum docent. *Florida Black Heritage Trail*, 22.

West Palm Beach

Mickens House

The Mickens House is one of the oldest continuously Black-owned residences in West Palm Beach. Haley Mickens built the house in 1917, the year he married Alice Frederick. Mickens, who was employed by the Beach Club, a casino in Palm Beach, was responsible for one of the concessions—a novelty in which guests were transported in wicker carriages propelled by bicycles. In his own community he was active as a founder of Payne Chapel A.M.E. Church in West Palm Beach.

Alice Mickens was born in Bartow, Florida. After graduating from Spelman College in Atlanta, she attended the College of the City of New York and Agricultural and Technical College of Greensboro, North Carolina. Dr. Alice Mickens was devoted to civic improvements, education, and to finding ways to decrease juvenile delinquency. In her work she was acquainted with many leaders, including Mary McLeod Bethune, Dr. Howard Thurman, A. Phillip Randolph, Philippa Schuyler, and Dr. Ralph Bunche. The Mickens House served on many occasions as the focal point of meetings of community and nationally known leaders.

Mickens House is a two-story, frame dwelling with wide front porch, awnings, and narrow weatherboard siding. The ceilings in the living and dining rooms have raised geometric plasterwork moldings created by a craftsman named Thomas Wilkens. This home, one of the oldest surviving residences in West Palm Beach, has been maintained in excellent condition. Many furnishings are those purchased by Haley and Alice Mickens shortly after they moved into the house.

DATE BUILT: 1917

ADDRESS: 801 Fourth Street, West Palm Beach

VISITING HOURS: Private, visitors may walk or drive by

SOURCES: Telephone conversation Mar. 15, 1994, Ms. Alice Frederick, West Palm Beach resident. NRHPINF.

Works Consulted

The Academic American Encyclopedia. New York: Grolier, 1993. [electronic version]

And the Walls Came Tumbling Down: An Autobiography. Ralph David Abernathy. New York: Harper, 1989.

Encyclopedia of African-American Civil Rights: From Emancipation to the Present. Charles D. Lowery and John F. Marszalek, eds. New York: Greenwood, 1992.

Florida Black Heritage Trail. Gary Goodwin and Suzanne Walker. Tallahassee: Florida Bureau of Historic Preservation, 1992.

Historic Pensacola Village. Pensacola: Historic Pensacola Preservation Board, 1988. [brochure]

"The History of Eatonville, Florida." Suzanne Douglas and Charles A. Hooper. Tallahassee, Florida: Florida Dept. of State, Div. of Historical Resources, n.d. [manuscript]

International Library of Negro Life and History: Historical Negro Biographies. Wilhelmena S. Robinson. New York: Publishers Company, 1970.

Julee Cottage, Historic Pensacola Village: Blacks in West Florida. Pensacola: Historic Pensacola Preservation Board, 1988. [program bulletin]

National Register of Historic Places. Washington, D.C.: National Park Service, 1976.

The Negro's Civil War. James M. McPherson. New York: Ballentine Books, 1991.

The Smithsonian Guide to Historic America: The Deep South. William Bryant Logan and Vance Muse. New York: Stewart, Tabori, & Chang, 1989.

Their Eyes Were Watching God. Zora Neale Hurston. Philadelphia: J. B. Lippincott, Inc., 1937. Reprint, New York: Perennial Library, Harper & Row, 1990.

There Is a River: The Black Struggle for Freedom in America. Vincent Harding. New York: Vintage Books, 1983.

Webster's New Biographical Dictionary. Springfield, Mass.: Merriam-Webster, 1988.

Georgia

Athens

Chestnut Grove School

Chestnut Grove School, a frame structure, was built in 1896 as a one-room schoolhouse. Although built for Black children, it was typical of rural schools erected in Georgia for both races. One teacher instructed children in all grades, and attendance usually was higher in the winter months when there were fewer farm duties to keep children at home.

The one-story structure had a wood stove for heat. There was no inside plumbing or lighting; the outhouse is still standing in a wooded area behind the school. The Black community provided land, labor, and many of the materials to build this school, and the charming, historic structures remain a source of pride to the community. In recent years a committee has formed to restore the schoolhouse as a community center to be opened on special occasions for children and for church members of the Chestnut Grove Baptist Church. Committee members have painted the structure and given it, as Deacon Kenney of the Chestnut Grove Baptist Church says, "a good new roof and steps." (Kenney once attended the little school.) Mrs. Roberta Barnett, committee chair, notes that three generations of her husband's family attended Chestnut Grove School.

DATE BUILT: 1896

ADDRESS: 610 Epps Bridge Road, Athens

TELEPHONE: Contact Mrs. Roberta Barnett, restoration committee chair, (706) 543-8761, or Chestnut Grove Baptist Church, (706) 548-1741

VISITING HOURS: Visitors can drive by or make an appointment to see the interior

FEES: Donations appreciated

SOURCES: Personal visit, summer 1990. Telephone conversation Mar. 19, 1994, Mack Kenney Sr., deacon, Chestnut Grove Baptist Church and former student at Chestnut Grove School. Telephone conversation Mar. 23, 1994, Mrs. Roberta Barnett, chair, restoration committee. NRHPINF.

Morton Building

The Morton Building, Union Hall, and Samaritan Building (no longer standing) once formed the core of the downtown Black business district in Athens. The four-story Morton Building remains as a landmark in Athens and is a symbol of a prominent Black businessman, Monroe Bowers Morton (1853–1919). Morton purchased this lot in 1909 and erected the building within a year. His other business included ownership of twenty to thirty-five other buildings in Athens. He was selected as the contractor for the Wilkes County Courthouse in Washington, Georgia. Morton's interests also included publishing and politics. He edited and published the *Progressive Era* and served as a delegate to the Republican National Convention in 1896.

The building that bears Morton's name housed many Black-owned businesses, including insurance companies, restaurants, a jewelry store, cleaners, and professional services. Dr. William H. Harris, one of the founders of the Georgia State Medical Association of Colored Physicians, Dentists, and Druggists, housed his practice in the Morton Building. Dr. Ida Mae Johnson Hiram, the first Black woman to be licensed as a dentist in Georgia, also had an office here.

The Athens community enjoyed many entertaining programs in the Morton Theater, which opened here in 1910. In an ironic reversal of the traditional practice in the South, a separate section in the theater's balcony was reserved for white patrons. Vaudeville acts were brought to the stage in 1914 and by 1927, the audience was enjoying performances by artists from New York's Cotton Club. In the 1930s the same space was transformed into a movie theater. The theater came to an unfortunate end after a fire in 1954; inspectors, finding that the theater had only one exit, padlocked the auditorium. Although the theater formally closed in 1955, businesses continued to operate in other sections of the Morton Building.

In 1973 the Morton family sold the historic building to Bond Properties, Inc. The structure had been neglected for a period of years and needed extensive restoration to be put into use again. The Morton Theater Corporation (a nonprofit, multiracial organization) purchased the building in 1980. In 1987, through a bond issue, voters approved a referendum to provide 1.5 to 1.8 million dollars for restoration, specifying joint ownership by the Athens-Clark County Government and the Morton Theater Corporation.

Workers began converting the entire building to a performing arts center. While cleaning out old debris, they found old ticket stubs showing that nationally known performers had entertained at the Morton Theater in its heyday—Duke Ellington, Cab Calloway, Ma Rainey, Bessie Smith, and Louis "Satchmo" Armstrong. By 1993 restoration was completed and the theater, located on the second floor with balcony on the third floor, was once again in use by performing artists.

DATE BUILT: 1910

ADDRESS: 199 W. Washington Street, Athens

TELEPHONE: Ticket and event information, (706) 613-3771

VISITING HOURS: Visitors may drive or walk by, or contact ticket office for schedule of events

SOURCES: Personal visit summer 1990. NRHPINF. Telephone conversation Dec. 20, 1994, Billy Evans, former owner of Evans Brothers Furniture and Antiques, located near the Morton Building. Telephone conversation Dec. 21, 1994, Susan West, volunteer, Athens Welcome Center. Telephone conversation Dec. 21, 1994, Rodney Thomas, administrative secretary, Morton Theater Corp.

Atlanta

Atlanta University Center District*

The Atlanta University Center District, listed in the *National Register of Historic Places*, includes a distinguished group of African American colleges and universities: Clark Atlanta University, the Interdenominational Theological Center, Morehouse College, Morris Brown College, and Spelman College. These colleges and universities, collectively known as the Atlanta University Center, provide an excellent education for Black students. Their distinguished faculties included, among others, Horace Mann Bond, sociologist and first African American president of Lincoln University; W. E. B. Du Bois (1868–1963), recipient in 1896 of a doctorate from Harvard University, historian, author, and one of the founders of the National Association for the Advancement of Colored People; E. Franklin Frazier (1894–1962), noted sociologist, author, and president in 1948 of the American Sociological Society; and Whitney M. Young Jr. (1921–1971), dean of the Atlanta University School of Social Work from 1954 to 1960 and appointed in 1960 as executive director of the National Urban League.

The colleges also produced outstanding alumni, including James Weldon Johnson (1871–1938), poet, novelist, lawyer admitted to the Florida bar in 1898, and executive director of the NAACP; Walter White (1893–1955), 1916 graduate of Atlanta University, executive secretary of the NAACP, fighter for antilynching legislation, and author; Dr. Martin Luther King Jr. (1929–1968), national civil rights leader and Nobel Peace Prize winner; Maynard Jackson Jr. (1938–), Morehouse College graduate, elected first Black Mayor of Atlanta, Georgia, in 1973; Selina Butler, first national President of the National Congress of Colored Parents and Teachers; and Mattiwilda Dobbs, renowned opera singer.

The universities of the center provided outstanding educational services and today represent the most extensive concentration of nineteenth-century buildings of this type still existing in Atlanta. Morehouse and Spelman have buildings from the 1880s and 1890s that retain their original appearances.

The surrounding streets have residences that date from the period when the college buildings were erected. These residences include homes on Beckwith Street, where faculty members once lived, and the impressive Herndon Mansion, built by the late Alonzo Herndon, founder of the Atlanta Life Insurance Company. The historic district also includes structures not directly associated with the colleges—the E. A. Ware School, University Homes, Friendship Church, and West Hunter Street Baptist Church.

DATE ESTABLISHED: See individual sites

ADDRESS: Roughly bounded by transit right-of-way and Northside, Walnut, Fair, Roach, and West End Drives and Euralee and Chestnut Streets, Atlanta

TELEPHONE: See individual sites

VISITING HOURS: Contact the colleges; visitors can walk through campus areas at any time

FEES: None

SOURCES: Personal visit, summer, 1990. NRHPINF. Telephone conversation Dec. 21, 1994, Dr. Nattalyn Tolbert, principal, Oglethorpe School. Telephone conversation Dec. 21, 1994, Rose Howell, special affairs coordinator, Housing Management, City of Atlanta. *National Register of Historic Places*, 165. *Encyclopedia of African-American Civil Rights. And the Walls Came Tumbling Down.*

Atlanta University

Atlanta University, chartered in 1867, was established by the American Missionary Association with financial assistance from the Freedmen's Bureau. Classes for freed slaves were first held in a boxcar on the railroad tracks. Between 1869 and 1893 the trustees of Atlanta University purchased seventy acres of land, including Diamond Hill, one of the highest elevations in the Atlanta area. They laid the cornerstone for North Hall (Gaines Hall) in 1869 and built several other buildings in the next decades.

The university provided elementary through secondary education at first and gradually introduced college-level courses. The association with the American Missionary Association ended in 1892. In 1929 Atlanta University, with its strong academic tradition, joined Morehouse College and Spelman College in establishing the Atlanta University Center. Atlanta University dropped its undergraduate programs and concentrated on graduate education. After Atlanta University moved into new quarters closer to Morehouse and Spelman Colleges, the original structures associated with Atlanta University became a part of Morris Brown College. In 1988 Atlanta University merged with Clark College to become Clark Atlanta University.

DATE ESTABLISHED: 1865–1867
ADDRESS: 223 James P. Brawley Drive SW, Atlanta
TELEPHONE: (404) 880-8000
SOURCE: NRHPINF.

Clark College

The Methodist Episcopal Church sponsored Clark College, which opened in 1869 in Clark Chapel Methodist Episcopal Church in south Atlanta. The college moved to its present site in 1941 and became affiliated with the Atlanta University Center in that year. In an era when many Black schools concentrated on industrial and agricultural training, Clark College sought to produce an academic elite. Early university leaders such as Edmund Asa Ware, John Hope, and W. E. B. Du Bois, rejected the notion of racial inferiority and insisted on a curriculum comparable to those in other fine American colleges and universities. In 1988 Clark College merged with Atlanta University to become Clark Atlanta University.

Visitors to the college complex may wish to stop by the **Trevor Arnett Library** on the Clark Atlanta University campus. The library contains a variety of papers and artifacts in its collection—rare items from the days of slavery, manuscripts from leading Black Harlem Renaissance writers, and papers from the Civil Rights Movement.

The **Clark Atlanta University Art Gallery** on the lower level of the Trevor Arnett Library contains one of America's most significant collections representing contemporary Black artists. The main part of the permanent collection is based on art originally displayed here in annual exhibitions between 1942 and 1970. The art is historically significant because it represents the condition of Black society for three decades as seen through the eyes of African American artists. This gallery provided the artists an opportunity to display their work when other galleries were closed to them because of race. Additional artwork acquired creates a collection of paintings, prints, and sculptures that span the years 1916 through 1980. Many school groups have viewed the collections. The Clark Atlanta University Art Gallery, formerly called the Waddell Art Gallery, closed in 1995 for renovations, to reopen in 1996 in conjunction with the Olympic games in Atlanta.

DATE ESTABLISHED: Clark College, 1869
ADDRESS: 223 James P. Brawley Drive SW, Atlanta
TELEPHONE: University, (404) 880-8000; art gallery, (404) 880-8671
SOURCES: Telephone conversation Dec. 21, 1994, Tina Dunkley, director, University Art Collections. NRHPINF.

Friendship Baptist Church

Friendship Baptist Church, one of Atlanta's oldest Black churches, started out in 1862 by offering services in a boxcar. The boxcar was shared with a school for former slaves that later became Atlanta University. The congregation began erecting the present building in 1871 and remodeled it in

1944 and 1975. The church also became associated with educational programs by providing the first home for Spelman and Morehouse Colleges. Morehouse College held classes in the basement of this church after moving from Augusta, Georgia. Spelman College was founded in this church building.

Friendship Baptist Church is finished in white stucco and has three stories, including the basement. The sanctuary, which seats four hundred, has lovely stained-glass windows on the sides and in the balcony and features a pipe organ behind the pulpit.

DATE ESTABLISHED: 1862; current structure, 1871
ADDRESS: 437 Mitchell Street SW, Atlanta
TELEPHONE: (404) 688-0206
SOURCES: Telephone conversation Dec. 21, 1994, church secretary, Friendship Baptist Church. NRHPINF.

Interdenominational Theological Center

In 1946 four schools of theology joined together to form the Interdenominational Theological Center. The center moved to its present site in 1957, and three additional seminaries later joined the original schools. The school originally represented several denominations—African Methodist Episcopal, Baptist, Christian Methodist Episcopal, Church of God in Christ, Presbyterian, and United Methodist. Approximately four hundred students study at this center, preparing for service in the ministry.

DATE ESTABLISHED: This location, 1957
ADDRESS: 671 Beckwith Street SW, Atlanta
TELEPHONE: (404) 527-7794
VISITING HOURS: By appointment, Mon.–Fri. 9–4
SOURCES: Telephone conversation Dec. 21, 1994, Barbara Holton, administrative secretary to the vice president, Interdenominational Theological Center. NRHPINF.

Morehouse College

Morehouse College was established as the Augusta Institute in 1867 and moved to Atlanta in 1879. The college held classes on a temporary basis in the basement of Friendship Baptist Church. In 1888 the Augusta Institute bought its third and present site, a location that had been an important Civil War battle site during the siege of Atlanta. Officials changed the name to Morehouse College in 1913 to honor the secretary of the American Baptist Home Mission Society. Morehouse has always had a strong academic reputation. Dr. Martin Luther King Jr. was one of Morehouse College's outstanding graduates.

DATE ESTABLISHED: Augusta Institute, 1867; in Atlanta, 1879
ADDRESS: 830 Westview Drive SW, Atlanta
TELEPHONE: (404) 681-2800
SOURCE: NRHPINF.

Morris Brown College

Morris Brown College, founded in 1881, was named for the second consecrated bishop of the African Methodist Episcopal Church. The school constructed its first building in 1885. In 1932 the college moved to the old Atlanta University campus.

Fountain Hall (formerly Stone Hall), a noted Atlanta landmark located on the Morris Brown University campus, was constructed in 1882 when the land belonged to Atlanta University. Its three and one-half–story brick building is the oldest structure in the complex and is the building most closely associated with the history of Atlanta University. The ground level has an entrance recessed under round-arched openings, and a distinctive four-story clock tower with a spire rises in the front center of the building. Stone Hall was Atlanta University's administration building until the merger took place in 1929 with Morehouse College and Spelman College. Now the structure is used by Morris Brown College as an administration building.

DATE ESTABLISHED: 1881
ADDRESS: University, 643 Martin Luther King Drive NW; Fountain Hall, 643 Martin Luther King Drive NW, Atlanta
TELEPHONE: (404) 220-0270.
SOURCE: NRHPINF.

Spelman College

Spelman College originated in 1881 in the basement of Friendship Baptist Church; it was sponsored by the Women's American Baptist Home Missionary Society. In 1883 the college purchased nine acres of the present campus. The grounds were on Civil War land, the site of a camp hospital and four barracks for federal troops. Several generations of the Rockefeller family contributed to the college, and in 1884 the institution's name was changed to Spelman College in honor of Laura E. Spelman Rockefeller.

DATE ESTABLISHED: 1881
ADDRESS: 350 Spelman Lane SW, Atlanta
TELEPHONE: (404) 681-3643
SOURCES: Telephone conversation Dec. 20, 1994, Nicole Christopher, admissions clerk, Spelman College. NRHPINF.

University Homes Housing Project

John Hope, Atlanta University's first Black president, provided much of the initiative for developing the University Homes Housing Project. One of the first federally funded, low-cost housing projects in America, University Homes is part of the historic district. The complex has both two-level and three-level buildings that contain 24 efficiencies, 92 one-bedroom units, 302 two-bedroom units, 76 three-bedroom units, and 6 four-bedroom units. Originally there were 675 units, but some have been demolished. The brick buildings, which border Clark Atlanta University, were modernized in 1991. Formerly flat on top, they now have rooflines that vary. Although the beautiful aluminum-finished balconies were modified and windows in corner units were bricked in, the buildings still have the original doors and beautiful brass in the stairwells.

DATE ESTABLISHED: 1937
ADDRESS: University Homes Office, 685 Fair Street SW, Apt. 1, Atlanta
TELEPHONE: (404) 332-1529
SOURCES: Telephone conversation Dec. 21, 1994, Charlotte Wheeler, manager, University Homes. NRHPINF.

E. A. Ware School

The Edmund Asa Ware School, at the corner of Martin Luther King Drive and Walnut Streets, originated around 1922 when Atlanta University sold land for this elementary school building to the city of Atlanta. The school's name honors the first president of Atlanta University (1869–1885). Ware originated the idea of establishing a university to educate teachers and to train talented young people. His strong belief in the right of Black people to receive a liberal education was a guiding philosophy in the development of Atlanta University. The E. A. Ware School is now used as a classroom building by Morris Brown College.

DATE ESTABLISHED: c1922
ADDRESS: corner of Martin Luther King Drive (formerly Hunter Street) and Walnut Streets, Atlanta
TELEPHONE: Morris Brown College, (404) 220-0270
SOURCE: NRHPINF.

West Hunter Street Baptist Church

Although the congregation of the Grace Covenant Baptist Church now owns this building, it was the home of the West Hunter Street Baptist Church from 1881 to 1973. The building is associated with its former pastor, the late Reverend Ralph David Abernathy, a nationally known civil rights leader who was associated with sweeping social changes from the 1950s through the 1980s.

Ralph David Abernathy Sr. (1926–1990) was born in Linden, Alabama, the grandson of a slave and the tenth child of a respected farming couple. He graduated from Alabama State College in 1950, then earned a master's degree in sociology in 1951 from Atlanta University. A close associate of Dr. Martin Luther King Jr., Abernathy helped to organize the Montgomery bus boycott in 1955. He was a founder of the Southern Christian Leadership Conference in 1957 and headed SCLC after the assassination of Dr. King in 1968. In that same year he continued the civil rights cause by directing the Poor People's March on Washington.

Abernathy served as pastor of the West Hunter Street Baptist Church in this building and in the congregation's later location at 1040 Gordon Street SW in Atlanta. He led the congregation until he suffered the first of a series of strokes in 1983. In 1989 he published his autobiographical description of the Civil Rights Movement, *And the Walls Came Tumbling Down*. Reverend Abernathy died in 1990.

DATE ESTABLISHED: West Hunter Street congregation, 1881

ADDRESS: 775 Martin Luther King Jr. Drive North (formerly Hunter Street); congregation's present address, 1040 Ralph D. Abernathy Boulevard SW, Atlanta

TELEPHONE: Grace Covenant Church, (404) 525-8571; historic West Hunter Street Baptist Church congregation, (404) 758-5563

SOURCES: Telephone conversation Dec. 20, 1994, Ivyleander Smith, church secretary, West Hunter Baptist Church. NRHPINF. *And the Walls Came Tumbling Down.*

Herndon Home

Alonzo F. Herndon was born a slave in 1858 in Social Circle, Georgia. Because he spent his youth in field labor, he received less than two years of schooling as a child. After moving to Atlanta and learning the trade of barbering, he bought and operated three barbershops. With his savings he began to acquire extensive real estate holdings and by the turn of the century had become one of the wealthiest Black men in America.

Herndon began to acquire some of the benevolent and protective associations that provided a form of insurance to the sick and needy in the Black community, and in 1905, he reorganized them as the Atlanta Life Insurance Company.

Adrienne McNeil Herndon, Alonzo Herndon's wife, was born in Augusta and grew up in Savannah. She graduated from Atlanta University and taught elocution at the university. Her training in the dramatic arts led her to establish the tradition of producing Shakespearean plays at Atlanta University.

Alonzo and Adrienne Herndon designed this fifteen-room house and hired African American contractors to do most of the construction. Tragically, in 1910, Adrienne Herndon died of Addison's disease the week the house was completed. Alonzo Herndon married again in 1912. His second wife, Jessie Gillespie Herndon, served as vice president of Atlanta Life until her death in 1947.

The Herndon family members were philanthropists and community leaders as well as business leaders. The son, Norris Bumstead Herndon, graduated from Atlanta University and earned a master's degree in business administration from Harvard University. After his father's death in 1927, Norris Herndon assumed leadership of the Atlanta Life Insurance Company. He began to envision the Herndon House as a museum to honor his parents. He traveled extensively in different countries to find furnishings for the residence and in 1950 established a charitable trust that would operate the house as a museum. He died in 1977.

Today the Herndon Home is an example of a turn-of-the-century, upper-income dwelling. The showplace home, which is listed in the *National Register of Historic Places*, contains antique furniture, Roman and Venetian glass, silver, and decorative artwork.

DATE BUILT: 1910

ADDRESS: Herndon Home, 587 University Place NW; headquarters of the Atlanta Life Insurance Company, 100 Auburn Avenue NE, Atlanta

TELEPHONE: (404) 581-9813

VISITING HOURS: Tues.–Sat. 10–4; home tours on the hour; closed Sun.–Mon.

FEES: None

SOURCES: Personal visit, 1990. Atlanta Convention and Visitors Bureau. Telephone conversation Dec. 20, 1994, Stephen Glass, museum associate, Herndon Home. Brochure from the Herndon Home. Survey by Carole Merritt of the Herndon Home.

Martin Luther King Jr. National Historic District*

Dr. Martin Luther King Jr. was born in 1929 at 501 Auburn, in the Atlanta neighborhood known as "Sweet Auburn." He rose to international prominence in the 1950s and 1960s Civil Rights Movement in which he played a leading role through his philosophy of nonviolent social confrontation.

Following the Civil War, Auburn Avenue, one of Atlanta's oldest neighborhoods, had no racial barriers. As early as the 1880s, Black and white residents lived as neighbors. From the 1890s and through the early 1920s, white people began to move to other areas of town. Their departure may have been hastened by Atlanta's race riot of 1906. Auburn Avenue gradually became the center of the Black business and professional community. Although the Atlanta fire of 1917 leveled much of the district, some buildings and businesses remained. Alonzo Herndon, founder of the Atlanta Life Insurance Company (see Clark Atlanta University Center District), put much of his money back into Sweet Auburn, including his own insurance company's building. Atlanta Life Insurance Company became one of the largest Black insurance companies in America (100 Auburn Avenue).

Sweet Auburn was one of America's most prosperous Black communities in the early twentieth century, providing homes for a mix of doctors, ministers, lawyers, educators, bankers, politicians, and unskilled laborers. Local Black builder Alexander Hamilton II lived in Sweet Auburn. He owned a construction company and built more buildings in Sweet Auburn than any other contractor. In the 1880s he built and owned the house at 102 Howell Street.

Some houses on the block were quite modest, like the "shotgun" style Victorian duplexes across from the King birthplace. A textile company built the duplexes in 1905. The shotgun house is a narrow, one-story structure often with three rooms, one behind the other, and no hall. A person enters the living room, then goes through the bedroom into the kitchen. Other Victorian houses near the King birthplace were erected in the 1880s as single-family homes.

Business was at its height in the 1930s, and as young Martin Luther King Jr. grew up he saw many Black-owned commercial businesses, including beauty and barber shops, laundries, insurance agencies, dry cleaners, shoe repair shops, restaurants, funeral homes, and real estate agencies. The community also included one of Georgia's earliest Black Catholic parishes, Our Lady of Lourdes Catholic Church Mission, which was built in 1912 as a three-story church, school, and Catholic hall. The mission's backyard is next to the King birthplace.

After the 1930s Atlanta's west side became a newer growth area for Black families, and the Sweet Auburn community began to decline. Recent restoration has returned many of the historic structures to their former fine appearance.

DATE ESTABLISHED: Nineteenth and twentieth centuries

ADDRESS: Upper Auburn Avenue bounded roughly by Irwin, Randolph, Edgewood, Jackson, and Auburn Avenues, Atlanta

VISITING HOURS: Residences are privately owned, visitors may walk or drive by but should be careful not to go on private property

FEES: None

SOURCES: Personal visit, summer 1990. NRHPINF. Cleveland Dennard, former acting director, Martin Luther King Jr. Center for Nonviolent Social Change. *National Register of Historic Places,* 166. "Experience Atlanta." *Let the Trumpet Sound.*

Ebenezer Baptist Church

Ebenezer Baptist Church, a Gothic-revival building completed in its present form in 1922, is part of the historic district. Reverend John Parker founded the church in 1886 and served as pastor until his death in 1894. From 1894 to 1975 a member of the King family preached at Ebenezer Baptist. In 1894 Reverend Adam D. Williams, Martin Luther King Jr.'s grandfather, was pastor of the church. When he died in 1931, Reverend King Sr. became pastor. Dr. King Jr. served with his father as co-pastor from 1960 to 1968, and the senior Reverend King was pastor until 1975.

Dr. King Jr.'s gravesite occupies much of the area east of Ebenezer Baptist Church toward Boulevard Street. The memorial park consists of a plaza with an arch-covered walkway and a chapel partially surrounding a reflecting pool. The King crypt rests in the center of the pool on a raised pedestal. An engraved inscription contains an adaptation of Dr. King's words, "Free at last, free at last, thank God Almighty, I'm free at last."

DATE ESTABLISHED:	Congregation, 1886; present church, 1914–1922
ADDRESS:	407 Auburn Avenue NE, corner of Jackson Street, Atlanta
TELEPHONE:	(404) 688-7263
VISITING HOURS:	Mon.–Fri. 10–4; worship services Sun.
FEES:	Donations accepted
SOURCES:	Telephone conversation Dec. 20, 1994, Beverly Miles, church secretary. NRHPINF.

Martin Luther King Jr. Birthplace

This two-story Queen Anne-style house was built in 1895, and Reverend Adam D. Williams, Dr. Martin Luther King Jr.'s grandfather, purchased the fourteen-room house from a white family in 1909. He may have been the first Black person to purchase a home in this section of Auburn Avenue.

M. L. King Sr. left his father's sharecropper farm and came to Atlanta, a city containing a community of proud, industrious, and successful Black residents. He worked as a mechanics' helper in a repair shop and as a railroad fireman until he was called to the ministry. Then he met and fell in love with Alberta Williams, daughter of the Reverend Adam D. Williams, pastor of Atlanta's Ebenezer Baptist Church. They married and lived in this house with the Reverend and Mrs. Williams, an arrangement that continued throughout the lifetime of Mrs. King's parents. When Dr. Williams died in 1931, Reverend M. L. King became pastor of Ebenezer Baptist church in the area. He also earned the doctor of divinity degree from Morris Brown College in Atlanta.

Dr. King Jr. was born in an upstairs middle room in 1929 and lived in this house during the first eleven years of his life. He was a brilliant child who could, at the age of five, recite whole Biblical passages from memory. He received his bachelor's degree at nearby Morehouse College (which he entered at the age of fifteen), graduating at the age of nineteen. After graduating with honors from Crozer Theological Seminary in Pennsylvania with a B.A. in divinity, he enrolled at Boston University, where he earned a Ph.D. degree in 1955. While in Boston, he met Coretta Scott, who had grown up near Marion, Alabama, and was studying music at the New England conservatory. The young couple dated, fell in love, and married in 1953. They returned South, where Dr. King accepted a call to be the pastor at Dexter Avenue Baptist Church in Montgomery, Alabama.

Dr. King Jr. was a leader in the 1955 fight against segregation on public buses in Montgomery. His leadership of the Montgomery bus boycott rallied the community and helped to lead to the passage of the Civil Rights Act of 1963 and the Voting Rights Act of 1964. He continued to be a leader in different campaigns of the Civil Rights Movement of the 1950s and 1960s.

Dr. King Jr. was a founder and the first president of the Southern Christian Leadership Conference. In 1964 he became the youngest and the first Black person to receive the Nobel Peace Prize. In April 1968 King traveled to Memphis, Tennessee, to support sanitation workers in their bargaining with city government. On April 4 he was assassinated by a sniper's bullet.

The Martin Luther King Jr. Center for Nonviolent Social Change acquired this residence in 1974 and restored it to its appearance at the time of Dr. King Jr.'s birth.

ADDRESS: 501 Auburn Avenue, Atlanta
TELEPHONE: (404) 331-3920
VISITING HOURS: June–Labor Day, daily 10–4:30; Labor Day–May, daily 10–3:30
FEES: None

Martin Luther King Jr. Center for Nonviolent Social Change

The Martin Luther King Jr. Center for Nonviolent Social Change, established in 1968, is adjacent to Ebenezer Baptist Church. It houses exhibits concerning the mid-twentieth-century freedom movement in the United States. A film shows Dr. King Jr.'s life and philosophy, and there is an interesting display of some of his personal effects. The center also houses the Freedom Hall Complex—the Rosa Parks Room, Gandhi Room, gift shop, and restaurant.

ADDRESS: 449 Auburn Avenue NE, Atlanta
TELEPHONE: (404) 524-1956
VISITING HOURS: Mon.–Fri. 9–5:30, Sat.–Sun. 10–5:30
FEES: Donations appreciated; film presentation, $1

Booker T. Washington High School

In nineteenth-century Atlanta the Black community struggled to gain adequate education programs for its students. Although public education started in Atlanta in 1872, and although a bond issue had created sixteen schools by the 1920s, the city had no public high schools available for Black students. Private high school departments in colleges at the Atlanta University Center provided the only high school instruction for African American students, and only those who could pay a fee were able to attend.

The Booker T. Washington High School was built on a trail of broken promises. Black people lobbied several times for bond funds to build a school for their children. They had been encouraged by school board members who promised the Black community a high school in return for its support of the general bond referendum. The Black community helped to pass the referendum in 1903 and 1910, but the school board broke its promise both times.

In 1919 the school board again sought the African American community's help. This time the National Association for the Advancement of Colored People completed a successful voter registration drive, and Black voters worked successfully to defeat the school bond referendum.

In the 1921 bond campaign the school board pledged $1,290,000 for Black schools. Stung by past defeat and recognizing the power of the African American community, the board finally kept its promise. Booker T. Washington School opened in 1924. It was the first Black junior/senior high school in Atlanta and, until 1947, was Atlanta's only high school for Black students.

Booker T. Washington was completed at a cost of $325,300. The school's name honored Booker T. Washington (1856–1915), who had been a slave in Virginia. Booker T. Washington founded Tuskegee Institute in Talladega, Alabama, in 1881, and became one of the most influential leaders and educators in the United States. A statue of Washington was added at the front entrance in 1927. The sculpture, which was created by nationally known artist Charles Keck, is an exact duplicate of the original statue at Tuskegee Institute. It shows Booker T. Washington lifting the veil of ignorance from the head of a former slave.

The massive four-story school has five arches in two tiers at the main entrance, terra-cotta trim, and Venetian-style columns. The building's main block contains forty classrooms, an administrative suite, a library, cafeteria, and science laboratories.

The high school, on opening, offered both academic and vocational subjects. Charles L. Harper (1875–1955), the first principal, and his faculty members required excellence of the students, and many out-of-town students enrolled because of the school's fine reputation. Some noted graduates include Dr. Asa Yancy, surgeon; Judge Romae T. Powell; and Dr. Martin Luther King Jr.

DATE BUILT: 1924; additions, 1938, 1948

ADDRESS: 45 Whitehouse Drive SW (bounded by Martin Luther King Jr. Drive on the north, Whitehouse Drive on the east, and Beckwith Street on the south), Atlanta

TELEPHONE: (404) 688-7263

VISITING HOURS: By appointment

SOURCES: Personal visit, summer of 1990. Telephone conversation Mar. 17, 1994, Dr. Lowe, principal. NRHPINF.

Augusta

Paine College

The Methodist Episcopal Church, South, and Reverend H. Lucius Holsey of the Colored Methodist Episcopal Church (now the Christian Methodist Episcopal Church) cooperated in establishing Paine College in 1882. Officials selected Augusta as the site because of that city's proximity to a majority of the members of the C.M.E. Church, and they named the college Paine Institute in honor of Bishop Robert Paine.

In 1884 the faculty began meeting with classes in rented quarters. A year later Paine Institute purchased the present fifty-four-acre site. Through 1920 most instruction was on the elementary and secondary levels. By 1926 grades one through six had been eliminated, leaving grades seven through high school and the college department. Paine offered secondary education until 1944, when the first public school for Black students opened in Augusta.

The historic Bell Square located on the campus is a monument to the old Haygood Hall, which was destroyed by fire. The square houses the original bell from the Haygood clock tower. Paine College Special Collections include the Frank Yerby Collection, Martin Luther King Collection, and Howard Thurman Cassette Collection. Frank Yerby, an African American author, graduated from Paine College. He wrote 32 books that have sold more than 55 million copies and have been translated into 22 languages. Howard Thurman was a noted twentieth-century African American theologian. The Collins-Callaway Library and Learning Resource Center at Paine College contains 23 books written by Yerby and 124 cassette tapes of Reverend Thurman's sermons.

Paine College is associated with outstanding graduates such as Dr. Charles G. Gomillion who, for decades chairman of the Social Science Department at Tuskegee University, was a civil rights activist. His efforts led to the landmark Supreme Court decision in *Gomillion* v. *Lightfoot*, which outlawed gerrymandering in the United States. The case began in 1957 when the Legislature of Alabama redrew the boundaries for the city of Tuskegee in a way that drastically limited the ability of the town's Black residents to vote. The city originally had a square shape, but the legislature, through Local Act No. 140, drew a boundary that gave an irregular twenty-eight-sided shape. The new plan removed all but four or five of the Black voters from the city but did not remove any white voters or residents. A lawsuit ensued. The lower court ruled that no improper legislative intent had been shown and upheld the boundary change. The Supreme Court, however, reversed the decision. Supreme Court Justice Felix Frankfurter, writing for the Court, focused on the effect of the plan rather than its intent. He noted that depriving a racial minority of the right to vote in municipal elections in a discriminatory manner violated provisions of the Fifteenth Amendment.

Paine college graduate Louis Lomax excelled in literature and history. He wrote *The Negro*

Revolt, which is used as a textbook in many colleges and universities. His book *The Reluctant African* won the *Saturday Review* Avisfield-Wolf Award. He also wrote *To Kill a Black Man* about the assassinations of Malcolm X and Dr. Martin Luther King Jr.

DATE ESTABLISHED: 1882
ADDRESS: 1235 Fifteenth Street, Augusta
TELEPHONE: (706) 821-8200
VISITING HOURS: All weekdays, 9–5; weekends or holidays by appointment; campus tours arranged through the Admissions Office or Public Relations Office
SOURCES: Personal visit, summer of 1990. Telephone conversation Aug. 1, 1995, Willie Mae Jordan, catalog librarian, Paine College. Telephone conversation Dec. 20, 1994, Cassandra Norman, director, Collins-Callaway Library and Learning Resource Center, Paine College. Public Relations Office, Paine College. *Paine College. Race, Racism and American Law.*

Macon

Harriet Tubman Historical and Cultural Museum*

The Harriet Tubman Historical and Cultural Museum has four galleries in a two-story building. Tubman was a courageous, nationally known leader who, after escaping from slavery, returned again and again to the South to lead others to freedom. The museum contains portraits of Tubman as well as exhibits that focus on Black art and other achievements of African Americans.

The mural gallery contains a sixty-three-foot mural that shows African American history from its background in Africa to present-day America. The mural contains three hundred faces of individuals who have contributed to African American progress in areas ranging from slavery, the Civil War, and inventions to sports, the blues, and the Civil Rights Movement. An African artifacts gallery contains musical instruments, money, statues, clothing, and jewelry. Another gallery shows portraits and wood carvings by African Americans, including the wood carvings of O. L. Samuels. More portraits are on exhibit in the halls that lead from gallery to gallery. Exhibits in the upper level change each month, and one or two outstanding pieces from the rotating exhibits are purchased each month for the museum's permanent collection.

DATE ESTABLISHED: 1985
ADDRESS: 340 Walnut Street, Macon
TELEPHONE: (912) 743-8544
VISITING HOURS: Mon.–Sat. 9–5; Sun. 2–5; closed major holidays
FEES: $1
SOURCES: Telephone conversation Mar. 17, 1994, Anita Ponder, director of education. Telephone conversation Dec. 20, 1994, Angie Brooks, operations manager.

Nicholsonville

Nicholsonboro Baptist Church

Rural Southern Georgia has lost most of the early Black churches built after the Civil War. The frame structures were demolished over time and replaced in the twentieth century by concrete-and-brick structures. The Nicholsonboro Baptist Church, along with an older church building on the same property, are rare surviving examples of the earlier churches.

Members of the original congregation were slaves on St. Catherines Island off the Liberty County coast. Jacob Waldburg owned 19,000 acres of land, making him one of the region's wealthiest planters. In 1860 he had 225 slaves working on his land producing crops and animal products. Some of them later became the founders of this church.

In 1865 Waldburg lost the land for a time and his slaves gained their freedom. General William T. Sherman, the victorious Union commander, issued Special Field Order No. 15 that provided that the sea islands from Charleston, South Carolina, to Florida were to be used for freedmen's settlements. This promise, however, did not hold. The ex-slaves never received the land, and Waldburg eventually regained control of his land on St. Catherines Island.

The former slaves remained on the island for a few years, but eventually nearly two hundred of them left to start a new settlement. In 1877 eighteen of the African Americans signed a mortgage to buy 200 acres of land for $5,000. They paid off the mortgage in five years. The settlers raised and sold vegetables in the summer, and in winter they caught and sold fish and oysters.

In 1883 the settlers deeded one acre of land for a church site, and the older church on this land may have been built at that time. However, the older building may have been constructed in the late 1870s before these settlers arrived or at a much earlier date as a slave church. By 1890 the community laid the cornerstone for the present Nicholsonboro Baptist Church. The older church, seventy feet away, continued in use as a feasting house. Eventually the older church deteriorated, and the congregation stopped using it on a regular basis. Each year, however, in a celebration, the older church is opened for Friends and Members Day and another church, St. John, joins the Nicholsonboro congregation for this open house.

Both the older and the newer churches on the grounds are frame structures, painted white. The earlier church is a small, one-room structure with two side windows and one window above the area where the choir stands to sing. There is no permanent seating area for the choir. When its members sing, they rise and ascend a few steps to a platform. The 1890 church is a two-story structure. An educational building stands between the two churches. Both churches are significant in Black history because their congregation dates back to the days of slavery and is associated with the events initiated by Sherman's field order. The Nicholsonboro Baptist Church is listed in the *National Register of Historic Places.*

DATE BUILT: Older structure, perhaps in late 1870s; newer church, 1890

ADDRESS: White Bluff Road, Nicholsonville (approximately 10 miles from Savannah; from Savannah take Bull Street to the White Bluff area of Nicholsonville)

TELEPHONE: (912) 921-0566

VISITING HOURS: Call for an appointment to see the interior

SOURCES: NRHPINF. Telephone conversation Mar. 19, 1994, Mr. James Balcom, deacon.

Savannah

First African Baptist Church

First African Baptist Church—one of the oldest Black churches in North America—was established in 1777 in the British North American colonies by George Leile, the slave of a British officer stationed in Savannah. During the American Revolution when the British occupied Savannah, the British officer, recognizing Leile's talent, permitted him to preach on different nearby plantations. Leile was ordained as a minister in 1775; in 1777 he organized a church at the Brampton Plantation site and called it the Ethiopian Baptist Church. The church later moved to a Yamacraw site where it became known as the First Colored Baptist Church. When American forces regained control of Savannah, Leile had to flee to Jamaica with his master and with other British people who had occupied Savannah. He continued his work in Jamaica, establishing one of the first African churches there.

Fortunately, during the Reverend Leile's stay at Brampton he had baptized a slave, Andrew Bryan. Bryan was ordained as a minister in 1788 and served as Leile's assistant. After Reverend Leile left the country, Reverend Bryan became the spiritual leader of the church, serving as pastor until his death in 1812.

The early congregation of First Colored Baptist Church met in barns and arbors. In 1793 they purchased a lot on West Bryan Street and began to worship in a praise house that they may have moved to that location. Around 1822 the congregation changed its name to the First African Baptist Church.

By 1832 there was a rift in the congregation. Church historians from the two ensuing congregations still disagree on the sequence of events. Harry B. James, historian of First Baptist Church, maintains that in 1832 the entire congregation, led by third pastor Andrew Cox Marshall, purchased the lot in Franklin Square where First Baptist now stands and moved to that site. A division soon occurred over a doctrinal matter. The church gave 155 letters of dismissal to the dissenters but permitted them to return to the West Bryan Street site, giving them a quitclaim deed to their old church there. The congregation that returned to West Bryan Street was called the Third Baptist Church until the end of the Civil War, when the name was changed to First Bryan Missionary Baptist Church (see the following listing).

The present sanctuary of First Baptist Church is of neoclassical design. It was erected in 1859 by members of the congregation who did the construction work themselves. This was the first Black-owned building in Georgia that was constructed of bricks. Restored in 1975, the church houses archives and memorabilia dating back to the eighteenth century.

DATE ESTABLISHED: Congregation, 1773; present building, 1859

ADDRESS: Franklin Square, 23 Montgomery Street, Savannah

TELEPHONE: (912) 233-6597

VISITING HOURS: Fri. 10–2; Mon.–Thurs. by appointment

FEES: None

SOURCES: Personal visit, summer 1990. April Scott-Walsh, Georgia Historical Society. Carolyn M. Viafora, Historic Savannah Foundation Tours. Telephone conversation Mar. 17, 1994, Pearl F. Holmes, church secretary. Telephone conversation Dec. 23, 1994, Harry B. James, deacon and chairperson of the historic group and public relations, First African Baptist Church. *The Shaping of Black America.*

First Bryan Missionary Baptist Church

In 1988 the congregation of First Bryan Missionary Baptist Church celebrated its two hundred years of history in the Savannah community. Deeds dated September 4, 1793, show that the parcel of land on which the church stands is the oldest parcel of real estate in the United States continuously owned by African Americans.

As indicated in the previous entry, the church began in the eighteenth century with George Leile, a slave who showed unusual talent and leadership ability. He became converted around 1774 and was received into the membership of the white Baptist Church in Burke County. His master permitted him to visit neighboring plantations along the Savannah River to preach to the slaves.

On a visit to Brampton Plantation, Liele converted and baptized four slaves, one of whom was Andrew Bryan, another talented and intelligent man. Opposition grew at the end of the Revolutionary War as many white Southerners proved hostile toward the Black churches. They feared that Black people might seek to end slavery. Because of this opposition and because his master was British, Reverend Leile had to flee the country. Reverend Bryan was imprisoned for a time after the American colonists' victory in the War of Independence, but he continued his missionary work upon his release.

Reverend Bryan was ordained to the ministry of the Baptist Church and his owner permitted him to visit plantations along the river as far as Yamacraw, preaching to Black groups and to white groups who gathered to hear him. Edward Davis, a white landowner, permitted the worshipers to build a rough building on his land in Yamacraw. In 1799 Bryan became the pastor of a congregation, organized in 1788, called the Ethiopian Baptist Church and later First Colored Baptist Church, that would become First Bryan Baptist Church.

After purchasing his freedom for a small sum, Bryan devoted himself to the ministry. At first the congregation worshiped on Mill Street, then it bought for thirty pounds sterling (or approximately $150) the lot upon which the church now stands. A praise house—a small, modest structure used for religious services—was rolled onto church grounds in 1793.

Bryan served as pastor of the church until his death in 1812. According to records of First Bryan Missionary Baptist Church, church members later became divided on doctrinal matters. In 1832 the second pastor, Andrew C. Marshall, and a large group of members left the mother church and organized the First African Baptist Church in Franklin Square. The remaining members stayed on to worship at the original site. Their church still was partially controlled by the white Baptist church denomination that named the congregation Third Baptist Church. After the Civil War, however, when the congregation became independent, it took the name First Bryan Missionary Baptist Church.

Since the praise house of 1793 had became dilapidated, the congregation erected a new building in 1865, but the new building soon needed repairs. In 1871 police entered the church and fired their pistols. The congregation, believing the church had been desecrated, razed the building in 1873 and made plans to erect a new church. A photographer took pictures at the last service in the old building, and church members sold copies for one dollar to help with the building fund.

A white civil engineer from Savannah, John B. Hogg, designed the new church in the Corinthian style, similar to the Wesley Chapel in London, England, and the Trinity Methodist Church in Savannah. The design called for an interior with a lower audience room and a spacious gallery on three sides.

The Grand Lodge of Colored Masons in the state of Georgia laid the cornerstone in 1873, and Black mechanics, under the architect's supervision, completed all of the construction work by 1888.

On January 20, 1988, church members held a ceremony to open the old cornerstone. Although documents had dissolved from seepage of water and the passage of time, the cornerstone contained the black leather covering of a Bible, more than 400 old coins found on pulling down the old church building, earrings and necklaces, and colored stones. At the ceremony, Mrs. Lillian W. Ellis, wife of Reverend Ellis, gave a prayer for "the privilege of being a part of the Mother Church of all Black Baptist people in the United States."

First Bryan Missionary Baptist Church has a monument to Reverend George Liele, the first American Black Baptist missionary, the man who converted and baptized Reverend Bryan.

DATE ESTABLISHED: c1788
ADDRESS: 575 W. Bryan Street, Savannah
TELEPHONE: (912) 232-5526
VISITING HOURS: Contact church for information
SOURCES: Personal visit, summer 1990. Telephone conversation Dec. 24, 1994, Reverend Edward Ellis Jr. April Scott-Walsh, Georgia Historical Society. *Bicentennial Celebration, Historic First Bryan Baptist Church. Before the Mayflower. The Historical and Cultural Atlas of African Americans.*

King-Tisdell Cottage
Beach Institute

The charming King-Tisdell Cottage is significant in Black history as a nineteenth-century home owned by Black people. The cottage, built in 1896, is interesting in architectural details that include an unusually intricate gingerbread ornamentation on the porch and dormers. The wheel-and-spindle pattern may be unique. W. W. Aimar, a white millowner, built the cottage in 1896. The house later changed to African American ownership. Eugene Dempsey King and his wife, Sarah, purchased it in 1910. Mr. King died in 1941, and his widow married Robert Tisdell, a longshoreman. After Sarah Tisdell's death in 1943, Tisdell married again and he and his wife moved away a few years later.

In 1980 the King-Tisdell Cottage was in an area of the city marked for urban redevelopment. Seeing that the heritage and architecture of Wheaton Street would be lost, a man named W. W. Law began a campaign to save the cottage. Law, who grew up in Savannah, developed an interest in Black historical sites at an early age. His grandmother, who worked as a laundress, told him stories about Black history and Black culture. He pulled the wagon for her as they made deliveries of laundry to white-owned homes, and she pointed out Savannah's Black historical sites as they walked along.

Law began to read at an early age, and avidly read books on Black history. He earned a bachelor of science degree in biology, but because of his extensive activities with the NAACP, he was unable to find work as a teacher. He became a mailman and continued his activities to gain recognition for Black historical sites. In 1981 he succeeded. The city of Savannah responded to his efforts by donating the King-Tisdell Cottage to the Association for the Study of Afro-American Life and History. The city contributed $104,700 for renovations and resettled the cottage in the Beach Institute neighborhood.

Today the King-Tisdell Cottage is a starting point for Savannah's seventeen-site Negro Heritage Tour. The Savannah-Yamacraw Chapter of the Association for the Study of Afro-American Life and History operates the cottage as a museum and hosts a variety of cultural events there. The museum contains two floors of exhibits associated with the black heritage of Savannah and the sea islands. The association also shows visitors the Beach Institute, a historic Black school in Savannah established in 1865. The school, transformed into a cultural museum, has exhibits, lectures, films, and a variety of programs. Children enjoy the sculptures of the late Ulysses Davis, a wood carver who lived for forty years in Savannah. They are charmed by the collection of two hundred carvings representing people, animals, fanciful creatures, and Biblical themes.

DATE ESTABLISHED: Cottage, 1896; Beach Institute, 1865
ADDRESS: Cottage, 514 E. Huntingdon Street; Beach Institute, 502 E. Harris Street, Savannah
TELEPHONE: (912) 234-8000

VISITING HOURS: Cottage, Mon.–Sat. 1–4; Beach Institute, Tues.–Sat. noon–5, closed Sun.–Mon.

FEES: Cottage, $2; Beach Institute, $3; Negro Heritage Tours, $10 when the cottage vehicle is operating; on other days, "step-on" tour (the guide from the cottage accompanies the group in your vehicle) for groups of five or more persons, $5 per person; tours must be scheduled two or three days in advance

SOURCES: Telephone conversation Dec. 20, 1994, Alloceia Hall, site guide, Beach Institute. Personal visit, summer 1990. April Scott-Walsh, Georgia Historical Society. Carolyn M. Viafora, Marketing Manager, Historic Savannah Foundation Tours. *The Negro's Civil War,* 303–4. "Making History Live."

Savannah State College

Savannah State College opened as a department of the State University and was called the "Georgia State Industrial College for Colored Youths." Requirements of the Morrill Land-Grant Acts of 1862 and 1890 were adhered to in starting the college in 1891. The Morrill Act, introduced by congressman Justin Morrill, offered tracts of land to states as incentives to establish colleges with agricultural, industrial, military, or scientific studies. In the second Morrill Act of 1890, states that practiced racial segregation were required to establish Black colleges as a condition for receiving funds. The Black colleges usually stressed agriculture, but they also developed higher-education curricula in addition to the agricultural programs.

In 1892 the school moved to its present site, located in part in Savannah and in part in Thunderbolt, Georgia. In its first years of operation, teachers offered instruction in agriculture, natural sciences, mathematics, English, and the mechanical arts.

Savannah State College is situated on a beautiful 165-acre campus with 38 buildings, including both the original 1890s buildings. Hill Hall, built in 1901 by Savannah State students, has served as a men's dormitory, college student union, post office, and college library. Extensively renovated in recent years, Hill Hall is listed in the *National Register of Historic Places.*

DATE ESTABLISHED: 1890

ADDRESS: College Drive, Savannah

TELEPHONE: (912) 356-2286; Admission and Records Office, (912) 356-2212

VISITING HOURS: Call the Admissions and Records Office, 9–5; closed two weeks Christmas/New Year break

SOURCES: Office of Development and College Relations, Savannah State College. April Scott-Walsh, Georgia Historical Society. The Academic American Encyclopedia.

Second African Baptist Church

The Second African Baptist Church was witness to freedom in several ways. Before the Civil War church members hid slaves in the church basement, whose walls were four feet thick. They sheltered fugitives until they could leave safely. According to tradition, General William T. Sherman read the Emancipation Proclamation in front of this church or in the sanctuary.

The church has an archives section that contains its first organ, some early furniture, and communion trays. The lower level is used as an assembly hall and once was part of the underground railroad. The assembly hall still contains holes in the floor that led to a still-lower level. The hiding place is not open to the public.

ADDRESS: 123 Houston Street, Greene Square, Savannah
TELEPHONE: (912) 233-6163
VISITING HOURS: Mon.–Fri. and for Sun. service; call for information
FEES: None
SOURCES: Telephone conversation Mar. 18, 1994, Reverend James Cantrell. Telephone conversation Dec. 23, 1994, Elaine McIntosh, church secretary.

Thomasville

Church of the Good Shepherd

The Church of the Good Shepherd houses one of Georgia's few Black Episcopal congregations. The small, late-Victorian church in southwest Georgia is significant architecturally as a late-nineteenth-century church structure built for a small congregation.

The church was organized in 1893 under the leadership of the rector of Saint Thomas Church. The frame church was built in 1894 in a style featuring stained-glass windows with pointed arches and finely detailed carved shingle work in the gable end. Interior details include wainscoting and a ceiling with exposed beams. The church has the original furnishings.

The church once housed a parochial school, which was started by John W. "Jack" Carter, a Black community leader, in an era when no public education was available for Thomasville's Black students. The Church of the Good Shepherd operated the school from 1894 to 1964. The two-story vicarage is a frame building, built in 1908 next to the church complex. Today the church has a small congregation, numbering twenty-five to thirty people. Their vicar, Father Bernard Rosser of Albany, Georgia, who is African American, leads the service once a month; Reverend Frederick A. Buechner, of All Saints Episcopal Church, and another local priest lead the services three Sundays a month.

DATE BUILT: Church, 1894; parish addition, c1896
ADDRESS: 511–519 Oak Street, Thomasville
TELEPHONE: (912) 228-6415
VISITING HOURS: Sun. 9–10
SOURCE: NRHPINF.

Woodbury Vicinity

Red Oak Creek Covered Bridge

The Red Oak Creek covered bridge, possibly Georgia's oldest covered bridge, is attributed to Horace King, a freed slave who was a prominent area contractor and builder. The covered bridge has a frame construction with vertical siding, a town lattice with a truss of 412-foot single span and stone abutments. This is one of Georgia's twenty-one remaining covered bridges.

DATE BUILT: c1840

ADDRESS: North of Woodbury on Huel Brown Road (between Gay and Woodbury, almost in Imlac); take GA 85 to Imlac, go over railroad tracks to end of road, turn left and go to bridge

SOURCES: Telephone conversation Dec. 20, 1994, Joann Gay, local resident. *National Register of Historic Places*, 169.

Works Consulted

The Academic American Encyclopedia. New York: Grolier, 1993. [electronic version]

And the Walls Came Tumbling Down: An Autobiography. Ralph David Abernathy. New York: Harper, 1989.

Before the Mayflower: A History of Black America. 5th ed. Lerone Bennett Jr. New York: Penguin Books, 1988.

Bicentennial Celebration, Historic First Bryan Baptist Church. Savannah, Ga.: First Bryan Church, 1988.

Encyclopedia of African-American Civil Rights: From Emancipation to the Present. Charles D. Lowery and John F. Marszalek, eds. New York: Greenwood, 1992.

Experience Atlanta. Atlanta: Atlanta Convention & Visitors Bureau. [brochure]

"General Management Plan, Development Concept Plan and Environmental Assessment." Atlanta: U.S. Dept. of the Interior/National Park Service, Martin Luther King Jr. National Historic Site & Preservation District, 1985.

The Historical and Cultural Atlas of African Americans. Molefi K. Asante and Mark T. Mattson. New York: Macmillan, 1991.

Let the Trumpet Sound: A Life of Martin Luther King, Jr. Stephen B. Oates. New York: Harper, 1982, 1994.

"Making History Live: Memories of Black Savannah." Lauren Adams De Leon. In *Emerge* (Sept. 1991).

National Register of Historic Places. Washington, D.C.: National Park Service, 1976.

The Negro's Civil War. James M. McPherson. New York: Ballentine, 1991.

Paine College: The Right Choice. Augusta, Ga.: Paine College Board of Trustees and Office of the President, 1987.

Race, Racism, and American Law. Derrick A. Bell. Boston: Little Brown, 1973.

The Shaping of Black America. Lerone Bennett Jr. New York: Penguin, 1975.

Kentucky

Berea

Berea College
Lincoln Hall

Berea College has a lovely green setting in the foothills of the Cumberland Mountains. The serene setting hardly hints of the furor caused when Berea opened as the first college in America founded for the specific purpose of educating Black and white students together. Other colleges had admitted Black students in the nineteenth century. Cheyney State College and Lincoln University in Pennsylvania and Wilberforce University in Ohio, for example, were established as Black colleges or as colleges that would admit Black students. Berea, however, was founded for the purpose of integrating the races for classroom instruction and work experiences, and it opened in a state that had accepted slavery.

The school had its origins in 1855 when Reverend John Fee, a white abolitionist, opened a small elementary school in a church. He named the location "Berea" after a biblical town in which people were tolerant and open-minded. Reverend Fee had written a pamphlet entitled the *Antislavery Manual.*

Cassius Clay, a white abolitionist (see the listing for White Hall State Historic Site, Richmond, Kentucky), read the manual and was so impressed that he urged Fee to spread his abolitionist views among the people of western Kentucky. As these views became widely known, proslavery forces began to see the church and school as hated symbols. In spite of threats, Fee and his associate, J. A. R. Rogers, struggled to keep the school alive.

Shortly after the constitution for Berea was written, abolitionist John Brown and his followers raided the arsenal at Harpers Ferry, West Virginia, in October 1859. Their intent was to free the slaves and establish a stronghold in the mountains. The raid increased the slaveholders' fear and anger, and reprisals swept the South. In December 1859 sixty-five armed men rode into Berea and ordered Fee and Rogers to leave Kentucky within ten days. Since the state governor refused to provide protection, the men had no choice but to flee. In spite of this hostility, by 1867 the school reopened; ninety-six Black and ninety-one white students were attending elementary classes at Berea.

The school remained an irritant until the turn of the century when the southern and border states enacted Jim Crow laws. Kentucky's segregationists turned to the state legislature in 1904, pressuring legislators to pass the Day Law. This new legislation, which specified that Black and white students could not be taught on the same campus, was specifically aimed at Berea. The college fought the law for four years, but in 1908 the Supreme Court, in *Berea College* v. *Commonwealth of Kentucky,* ruled that the state could require a private institution to segregate students of different races.

Bitterly disappointed, African American students had to leave the campus, and Berea remained segregated until 1940, when the state of Kentucky removed the ban. During the period of segregation, Berea used its funds to establish an all-Black school in Simpsonville, Kentucky (see Lincoln Institute site).

Today Berea College is a racially integrated college with a student body that is approximately 11 percent African American (the highest Black enrollment of any private college in Kentucky). The college has produced many outstanding Black individuals, including 1903 graduate Dr. Carter G. Woodson, who was the father of Black History Week and the founder of the Association for the Study of Afro-American Life and History, as well as Julia Britton Hooks, an 1873 graduate who became a member of the college's teaching faculty and taught composer W. C. Handy. Mrs. Hooks's grandson, Benjamin Hooks, served as executive director of the National Association for the Advancement of Colored People. James Bond, grandfather of Georgia legislator Julian Bond, paid his tuition at Berea with a young steer that he led to the school. A Berea graduate, he served as a member of the Berea College Board of Trustees from 1896 to 1914. Berea graduate John Henry Jackson was the first president of the State Normal School for Colored Persons, which later became Kentucky State University.

Of the forty-four buildings on campus, **Lincoln Hall** is the last surviving structure from the old college. The three-story brick building, constructed in 1878, was named after President Abraham Lincoln. The structure originally contained classrooms, a library, a museum, meeting rooms, and laboratories, but it is used today for administrative offices and activities. Although the interior has been altered, the exterior remains as it originally appeared. Lincoln Hall is listed in the *National Register of Historic Places.*

DATE ESTABLISHED: 1855

ADDRESS: College, Chestnut Street; Welcome Center, 201 N. Broadway, Berea

TELEPHONE: (606) 986-9341; Welcome Center, (606) 986-2540

VISITING HOURS: Welcome Center, Apr.–Oct., Mon.–Sat. 8–5, Nov.–Mar., Mon.–Sat. 9–5; student guided tours June–Aug., Mon.–Fri. at 9 and 2; tours Sept.–May, Sat. at 9 from the Boone Tavern hotel lobby

FEES: None

SOURCES: Personal visit, summer 1990. NRHPINF. Brochure and survey returned by Andrew Baskin, director, Black Cultural Center and Interracial Education Program, Berea College. *National Register of Historic Places,* 266. *The Uncommon Wealth of Kentucky. Historical Sketches of the Kentucky Bluegrass Area.*

Elizabethtown

Severn's Valley Baptist Church

First Baptist Church is one of the few remaining structures of Elizabethtown's early Black community. Built to house a white congregation, it was originally named Severn's Valley Baptist Church. This congregation opposed slaveholding from an early date. The second pastor spoke out against slavery, and the third, Josiah Dodge, refused fellowship to slave holders.

The present church structure was completed in 1834 at a cost of $1,200, and both Black church members and white church members worshiped here. Although the white congregation had opposed slavery, their church seating was segregated. Black worshipers sat in the balcony of the new building, while white worshipers sat in the first-floor pews.

In the 1850s the African American members built a log house and began holding their services there. Although they had a Black pastor, at first the Severn's Valley church supervised the Black congregation's worship services. When the Severn's Valley white congregation built a larger church in 1897, the Black Baptists purchased the old building for $500. They used this structure until 1974, when they moved to a new building.

First Baptist Church is a one-and-a-half-story brick Greek-revival structure, with a front octagonal cupola capped with a low spire. The historic structure, located in an area that has become Elizabethtown's central business district, is used today by a white civic organization, the Riasok Shrine Club. It is listed in the *National Register of Historic Places.*

DATE BUILT: 1833–1834

ADDRESS: 112 W. Poplar Street, Elizabethtown

TELEPHONE: Riasok Shrine Club, (502) 765-7777

VISITING HOURS: Private, visitors may drive or walk by

SOURCES: NRHPINF. *National Register of Historic Places,* 263. Personal visit, summer 1990. Letter, Mar. 1994, James D. Deneen, the Riasok Shrine Club.

Frankfort

Kentucky State University

Kentucky State University is a historically Black university that was chartered in May 1886 as the State Normal School for Colored Persons. The school's mission was to train African Americans for teaching positions in Black schools. When the college was being organized, several cities competed to be its location. The residents of Frankfort showed a high level of interest, and their city offered to donate a site and $1,500. As a result, Frankfort won the contest, and the new school opened with three teachers and fifty-five students in 1887 on a scenic bluff overlooking Frankfort.

In 1890 the institution became a land-grant college and added home economics, agriculture, and mechanics departments. The five members of the class of 1890 were the school's first graduates. In 1938 the school was named the Kentucky State College for Negroes. Kentucky State College became a university in 1972. Today, the university is a coeducational, liberal arts institution with an African American enrollment of approximately 47 percent.

Kentucky State University maintains its African American heritage by collecting books, records, and artifacts relating to the Black history of the college and the state. The 1982 book, *The Fascinating Story of Black Kentuckians: Their Heritage and Tradition* by Alice Dunigan, is typical of the type of material in the university collections. It is found in Blazer Library, located adjacent to Jackson Hall.

Jackson Hall, erected in 1886–1887 as Recitation Hall, was the university's first building. It was named for John Henry Jackson, a graduate of Berea College and first president of the State Normal School for Colored Persons. Jackson Hall is a two-story building with a stone base, a flat roof with parapet, and a three-story tower with turrets. It is listed in the *National Register of Historic Places.*

Hume Hall, the visual center of the campus, was the most important building on campus for fifty years. Constructed in 1908–1909, it housed administration offices, a library, and a chapel. The 500-seat auditorium provided a place for community activities. The structure was named for Edgar Enoch Hume, a physician and legislator who influenced passage of legislation that founded the university. Architect Sidney Pittman, a son-in-law of educator Booker T. Washington, designed Hume Hall. The two-story stone building is constructed of Kentucky limestone. The exterior, with arched entrance and windows, remains as it appeared when constructed. Most other early buildings on this campus have been altered, leaving Hume Hall as the most important link with the university's early history.

DATE ESTABLISHED: University chartered 1886 as a normal school; Jackson Hall, 1887; Hume Hall, 1908–1909

ADDRESS: E. Main Street, Frankfort

TELEPHONE: (502) 227-6000

VISITING HOURS: Visitors may walk through or join a tour conducted by the Office of Records, Registration, and Admissions, by appointment Mon.–Fri. 8:30–4

FEES: None

SOURCES: Personal visit, summer 1990. D. W. Lyons, associate director/associate professor, Library Services, Kentucky State University. NRHPINF. *Kentucky State University Catalogue, 1988–1990. Onward and Upward. Kentucky's Black Heritage,* 40. National Register Information System.

Gamaliel

Mount Vernon African Methodist Episcopal Church

The log church, one of the oldest African American religious structures in Kentucky, is empty now except for an annual reunion. Most of the members have died or have moved away, with only one or two remaining in Gamaliel.

Mount Vernon Church is associated with William Howard, a wealthy farmer and slaveowner who settled in Monroe County in 1802. Although Howard owned slaves, he did not fully approve of slavery and freed his slaves when they reached the age of twenty-one. Later he gave the freed people 400 acres of land on which to build their own homes. They established the community of Free-Town several miles west of Howard's residence, living in freedom at a time when others still lived in slavery. As late as 1860, there were 922 slaves and 17 free Black people in the county.

Some of the freedmen established Mount Vernon Church. In 1848 George Pipkin, Albert Howard, and Peter West built the log structure on a slight rise, one-fourth mile southwest of Free-Town and five miles north of the Kentucky-Tennessee border. The structure also served as a school.

Except for the tin roof and double pane sash windows that were installed at a later date, Mount Vernon Church still has most of the original building material. The one-room, one-story structure has hand-hewn logs joined by wooden pegs and chinked with clay. Clapboarding covers the north and south ends. The interior has the original floor on log sleepers and rustic benches that appear to be the original ones.

A white resident recalls:

> They had a Maypole—it was around the time I married, in 1930—and it was such a pretty sight. They had a big dinner there in front of the church with white and Black there. They still have funerals there sometimes but most of them are done and dead and gone.

Some residents of surrounding communities still have memories of activities at the log church. Ms. Edith Howard, an African American resident of Gamaliel, made the following statement: "I used to go to the church way back yonder. They had big dinners on the ground. Enjoyed it. They fixed the church up later and got it looking good." After adding that "most of them down here are dead and gone," she noted that there is a reunion each year.

Ruth Craig Proffitt of the Gamaliel Senior Center also has a vivid memory of the church.

> I remember the Maypole. Everyone went from miles around to see it. The girls wore frilly white dresses. They held on to streamers that were red, white, and blue, I think, and they plaited them. They danced in and out, their dresses blowing in the wind, and when they finished, the pole was braided with the pretty streamers.
>
> It was the best settlement of colored people in the world. They were all straight and honest people. They had to go to Hickory Ridge for high school. Sometimes, too, they had to walk to Fountain Run—they would walk or go by in buggies. My mother would have a bucket of water for them because they would be thirsty. Nobody looked down on them, but I didn't know until I was in high school that Black people had to sit in the back of the bus and couldn't eat in the restaurant. When I asked why I was told it was just that way.[1]

Mrs. Joyce Thomas, a school teacher in Louisville, Kentucky, and a descendant of founders of Mount Vernon Church, is writing a book about her family in Monroe County and about Mount Vernon Church. Her great-grandfather, Peter West, one of the builders of the church and its preacher, was a freed Methodist minister from Tennessee. Thomas said the Free-Town people were:

> very proud and honest, people who believed that you do what you say you will do and look out for each other. The Pipkins and Wests originally came from Tennessee, and most were teachers. My uncle, Roscoe Pipkins, and my Aunt Elmer taught school in the log church. When the school first started they chopped down trees and made desks, some of which are still there. For school supplies, they used whatever the white students had rejected.[2]

Mrs. Thomas leads an annual reunion to celebrate this heritage. Beginning in 1982–1983, former members of the Mount Vernon Church and their families began to return to the log church for an annual reunion on the second Saturday in June. Thomas and her sister hope to open the church as a museum.

DATE BUILT: 1846–1848

ADDRESS: From Gamaliel take KY 100 west approximately 1½ miles

VISITING HOURS: Not presently occupied; visitors can drive by; to see the interior, visit during reunion week, the second Saturday in June

SOURCES: NRHPINF. Kentucky state historical marker. Telephone conversation Mar. 29, 1994, Reverend Charles Kevin Pruitt, pastor, Gamaliel United Methodist Church. Telephone conversation May 23, 1994, Ruth Craig Proffitt of the Gamaliel Senior Center. Telephone conversation May 23, 1994, Mrs. Joyce Thomas, former member of Mount Vernon Church and author of upcoming book about the church.

Hodgenville

Abraham Lincoln Birthplace National Historic Site

President Abraham Lincoln was born on a farm at this site on February 12, 1809. Because of a defective land title to the property, his family lived on the property less than three years. The grounds include a restored one-story log cabin that has been dismantled and moved numerous times before being preserved in this setting.

The site is operated by the National Park Service. (For additional information about President Lincoln, see the Lincoln home and Lincoln tomb in the Springfield, Illinois, section.)

DATE BUILT: Early-nineteenth century
ADDRESS: Hodgenville vicinity, 3 miles south of Hodgenville on US 31E and KY 61
TELEPHONE: (502) 358-3137
VISITING HOURS: Apr.–May, Sept.–Oct., daily 8–5:45; June–Aug., daily 8–6:45; other months, daily 8–4:45
FEES: None
SOURCES: Telephone conversation Dec. 21, 1994, Thelma Weedman, park ranger. *National Register of Historic Places,* 266.

Hopkinsville

Freeman Chapel Christian Methodist Episcopal Church

Ministers B. Newton, David Ratcliffe, and George McClain organized the congregation of Freeman Chapel C.M.E. Church in 1866, just after the end of the Civil War. The second oldest Black congregation in Christian County, it was named after Peter Freeman, a steward in the church.

From 1866 to 1926 the congregation occupied a building downtown on the corner of Eleventh and Liberty Streets. Construction of the present church began in 1923, but only the stone foundation was completed in the next two years. Work resumed in 1925, and the congregation held its first service in the new building in 1926. The structure served as a church and a community center, providing meeting space for lodges, fraternal organizations, and other community groups.

Freeman Chapel is a large, two-story building in the classical-revival style. Fine craftsmanship shows in the stone ornamentation and stained-glass windows. Inside, the original wood flooring has been carpeted, but the pews, altar, and window moldings remain unchanged. Freeman Chapel C.M.E. Church is listed in the *National Register of Historic Places.*

DATE ESTABLISHED: Congregation, 1866; present building, 1923–1925
ADDRESS: 137 S. Virginia Street, Hopkinsville
TELEPHONE: (502) 886-2186
VISITING HOURS: Contact the church
SOURCES: Personal visit, summer 1990. NRHPINF. Kentucky Historic Resources Inventory.

Jeffersontown

Jeffersontown Colored School

Jefferson County maintained thirteen elementary schools for Black children in the late 1920s. Most were small, frame buildings dating from the early 1900s—segregated facilities that were unequal in structure and in funding. The first "colored" school on this site was housed in a frame residence already present when the Board of Education purchased the site in 1912. The present

Jeffersontown Colored School, first known as School # 2A, was built in 1929–1930 for Black elementary school children from Jeffersontown and surrounding areas. When School # 2A opened in 1930, the modern, art-deco brick school replaced the existing substandard frame building.

The Jeffersontown School accommodated three teachers and an average of 120 students per year. The school operated until the 1954 *Brown* v. *Board of Education* Supreme Court decision made segregated schools illegal. Jefferson County gradually began integrating schools, and the Jeffersontown Colored School closed in 1961. By 1963 all of the county schools for Black children had closed. The Jeffersontown School and Central Colored School in Louisville may be the county's only remaining schools that were built for Black children.

After the schoolhouse was closed, it provided office space for the Standard Electric Company. The building has been well maintained and still resembles a school. Slate blackboards are on the walls; on the top floor, bifold doors that once opened to create an auditorium are still there. The lower-level kitchen and restroom area has been converted to office space. The Jeffersontown Colored School is listed in the *National Register of Historic Places.*

DATE BUILT: 1929–1930

ADDRESS: 10400 Shelby Street, Jeffersontown

VISITING HOURS: Private; exterior easily seen from the road

SOURCES: Personal visit, summer 1990. Telephone conversation Mar. 16, 1994, Mrs. Lois McCoy, owner. Kentucky Historic Resources Inventory.

Lexington

Chandler Normal School Building
Webster Hall

Chandler Normal School Building and Webster Hall are two of the most important structures associated with Black education in central Kentucky. The complex is located on Georgetown Street, the main street in a predominantly Black residential area of northwest Lexington. The neighborhood also includes the former Colored Orphan's Home complex, the former Booker T. Washington Public School, Douglass Park, and a variety of modest, older homes.

Chandler Normal School grew out of an educational program for Lexington's Black children. Reverend James Turner, pastor of St. Paul's A.M.E. Church, established the school just after the Civil War, and the white Ladies' Missionary Society provided teachers. Many prominent members of Lexington's Black community attended Chandler, and the school educated many of Lexington's teachers before it closed in 1923.

Chandler is the only remaining school building in Fayette County built in the Richardson Romanesque architectural style. The three-story brick structure has a square tower in front. Its main auditorium wing was added around 1960.

Webster Hall, a two-story frame structure built around 1914, originally served as a teachers' and principal's home for the school. It was the first building in Lexington designed by African American architect Vertner W. Tandy Sr. Vertner Tandy was born in 1885, the son of Henry Tandy, who owned a brick masonry and building firm in Lexington. The son was educated at the Chandler School, Tuskegee Institute, and Cornell University School of Architecture. Vertner Tandy was the first Black person registered as an architect in the state of New York and one of the first to be admitted to the American Institute of Architects. Tandy practiced architecture in New York for more than forty years and designed many fine homes and institutions in Harlem.

For many years after 1960 Webster Hall served as the parsonage of the National Temple of the House of God. Much of the original school property has been developed as Lincoln Terrace, a public housing project.

DATE ESTABLISHED: c1914
ADDRESS: 548 Georgetown Street, Lexington
VISITING HOURS: Private, visitors may drive by to see the exterior but *should not go on the grounds*
SOURCES: Personal visit, summer 1990. U.S. Department of the Interior, National Park Service.

Kentucky Horse Park, Isaac Murphy Memorial

Isaac Murphy, one of the greatest jockeys in the United States, was the first man to win three Kentucky Derby races. His 628 wins out of 1,412 starts gave him a lifetime winning percentage of 44 percent. He was born Isaac Burns in 1859 (varying sources give birth dates of 1856 and 1861) in Fayette County, Kentucky, but his mother changed his name to Murphy to honor her father. Eli Jordan, a Black trainer, began to teach Murphy racing skills at the age of twelve, and Murphy began riding professionally by the age of fourteen. He was known for his integrity in racing, which was as important to him as winning.

When Isaac Murphy died in 1896, 500 mourners of all races attended his funeral—the largest attendance at a funeral in Lexington's history. Through the years his grave became neglected and almost forgotten. In 1967 after an awakening of interest in his story, Murphy's grave was found and moved to its present location outside the front gate of the Kentucky Horse Park.

Visitors to the park can see two movies about horses, a museum with displays about horses, a horse farm, a farrier shop, and a parade of horses. There are several retired champion horses at the farm. Children delight in the horse-drawn tour that is available in the summer.

ADDRESS: North of Lexington at 4089 Iron Works Pike (take I-75 exit 120)
TELEPHONE: (606) 233-4303
VISITING HOURS: Apr.–Oct., daily 9–5; Nov.–Mar., Wed.–Sun. 9–5; closed Dec. 24, 25, 31, and Jan. 1
FEES: Summer, adults, $8.95, children 7–12, $4.95; winter, adults $5, children, $3
SOURCES: Telephone conversation Mar. 17, 1994, staff at the Kentucky Horse Park. Information from JoD Neace Place. Brochure from Office of Tourism and Development. *Webster's New Biographical Dictionary*, 719.

Pleasant Green Baptist Church

Pleasant Green Baptist Church is the fourth oldest Black Baptist church in the United States and is the oldest west of the Allegheny Mountains. The church is remarkable in that its congregation has worshiped continuously at the same site since 1822. It was founded by Peter Duerett, a slave called Brother Captain. Brother Captain learned in Virginia that his wife was to be taken to

Kentucky, and he petitioned his master to be allowed to go with her. A trade was arranged that allowed him to go to Kentucky as a slave of Lexington pioneer John Maxwell. Brother Captain preached in Kentucky and organized a congregation. In 1822 he and the congregation purchased the land on which the present church stands. Three trustees, all slaves, received the land deed from a white Lexington surgeon, Dr. Frederick Ridgely. A year later their pastor, Brother Captain, died.

Reverend George W. (Pappy) Dupee, a slave, was the fourth minister of Pleasant Green Baptist Church. In 1826 the congregation heard that Reverend Dupee's owner was planning to sell him. Greatly troubled, they asked a white minister, Reverend William Pratt, to buy their pastor for them, and Pratt purchased Dupee off the auction block. Every Monday morning the church members made a payment on the debt to Pratt with their Sunday offerings until Dupee was free. Dupee became a widely known and respected preacher. In 1858 he left Lexington to become pastor of Washington Street Missionary Baptist Church in Paducah, Kentucky, where he served for thirty-nine years.

DATE ESTABLISHED:	Land conveyed, 1822
ADDRESS:	540 W. Maxwell Street, Lexington
TELEPHONE:	(606) 254-7387
VISITING HOURS:	Mon.–Fri. 9–4; Sun. school, 9:30, Sun. service, 11
SOURCES:	Personal visit, summer 1990. Telephone conversation Mar. 16, 1994, Reverend Thomas Peoples, pastor, Pleasant Green Baptist Church. *Kentucky's Black Heritage,* 13, 14.

Waveland State Historic Site

Although many people think of slaves in the South only as laborers working in the fields, many were skilled artisans employed in constructing some of the beautiful southern mansions. Their individual names seldom were recorded, but their fine workmanship on numerous mansions remains as a testament to their skill.

Waveland, now the Kentucky Life Museum, is one of Kentucky's finest examples of Greek-revival architecture. The builder and foreman was Washington Allen, but the actual construction was performed by slaves working as stone and brick masons, carpenters, and cabinet makers.

Waveland was an 1847 hemp/tobacco plantation that consisted of many buildings—a Greek-revival mansion, slave quarters, a smoke house, an ice house, a carpenter's shop, a blacksmith's shop, and other outbuildings. The slave quarters are still standing and may be seen by visitors.

DATE BUILT:	Main house, 1847
ADDRESS:	225 Higbee Mill Road, Lexington, off US 27 South
TELEPHONE:	(606) 272-3611
VISITING HOURS:	Mar.–Dec. 22, Mon.–Sat. 10–4, last tour starts 3; Sun. 2–5, last tour starts 4; closed Thanksgiving, Dec. 22–Mar. 1
FEES:	Adults, $3; senior citizens, $2; students kindergarten through college, $1; children under 5, free
SOURCES:	Personal visit, summer 1990. Telephone conversation June 1, 1994, Jack Bailey, staff assistant. Sara L. Farley, Park Manager, Waveland Historic Site. *The Uncommon Wealth of Kentucky. Historical Sketches of the Kentucky Bluegrass Area.*

Louisville

Kentucky Derby Museum

The Kentucky Derby Museum has a collection of materials relating to Black jockeys of the late nineteenth and early twentieth centuries. Black jockeys were a significant part of thoroughbred racing at that time. Isaac Murphy, a Black man, was the first jockey to ride three Kentucky Derby winners (see Lexington, Isaac Murphy Memorial), and fifteen of the first twenty-eight winning Derby horses had Black jockeys.

ADDRESS: Churchill Downs, 704 Central Avenue, Louisville
TELEPHONE: (502) 637-1111
VISITING HOURS: Daily; serious researchers should call for appointment 9–5; closed Thanksgiving, Christmas, Oaks Day, and Derby Day (first Fri. and Sat. in May)
FEES: Adults (age 12 up), $3.50; senior citizens, $2.50; children 5–12, $1.50; children under 5, free; check for group tour rates
SOURCES: *The Uncommon Wealth of Kentucky. Kentucky's Black Heritage*, 66.

Knights of Pythias Temple

The order of Knights of Pythias was founded as a white men's organization in 1864. By 1893, however, two Black lodges were listed in the Louisville City Directory. The African American lodge built this building in 1914–1915 as their state headquarters, locating in an area that had been a Black residential neighborhood since the late nineteenth century. The six-story brick structure with limestone trim was said to have cost $130,000.

By 1916 there were thirteen African American chapters of the Knights of Pythias in Louisville, most of which met at the new Pythias building. The temple also housed professional offices, social facilities including a USO, and hotel rooms for men. Civil rights leader James Bond had an office there. The first floor housed a drugstore, a movie theater, and a restaurant. Lodge groups met on the second floor, and the sixth floor contained a ballroom and roof garden for private parties and dances.

Although approximately 25,000 African Americans attended the National Pythian Convention in Louisville in 1925, the Depression years saw a decline in activities. Eventually the facility was converted into apartments, offices, and the Davis Trade School for Negroes. The prominent leaders who had organized the Lodge also established the Chestnut Street Young Men's Christian Association. In 1953 the Knights of Pythias Lodge sold the Temple to the Chestnut Street Y.M.C.A.

Today, reflecting a change in need, forty-one rooms at the "Y" are used to shelter the homeless. The Knights of Pythias Temple/Chestnut Street Y.M.C.A. building is listed in the *National Register of Historic Places.*

DATE ESTABLISHED: Organized, 1893; building, 1915
ADDRESS: 928–932 W. Chestnut Street, Louisville
TELEPHONE: (502) 587-7405
VISITING HOURS: Mon.–Sat. 8 A.M.–11 P.M.; call in advance to see the interior
SOURCES: NRHPINF. Personal visit, summer 1990. Telephone conversation Mar. 16, 1994, Ronnie Smith of the Y.M.C.A.

Limerick Historic District

The Limerick historic district is a central Louisville neighborhood with residences and other buildings that date from about 1860. The district includes a variety of residential styles ranging from lavishly constructed late Victorian houses to modest frame and brick shotgun dwellings. Central Colored School and the former Municipal College Campus are important Black historic sites in this community.

The Irish first settled Limerick community when they came to the area looking for jobs in the Kentucky Locomotive Works. Prior to the Civil War, a large plantation existed between the present Broadway and Kentucky Streets. A small Black community lived in the area, with many of their dwellings along the alleys of the Irish households. The African Americans worked as slaves or servants in local households or worked for the Louisville and Nashville Railroad.

The existence of the Black families was an important factor in locating Central Colored School and the Kentucky Normal and Theological Institute in this community. After a series of name changes, the campus of the Kentucky Normal and Theological Institute became known as Municipal College for Negroes. Today, the campus is called Municipal Park. Although some Irish-American residents still live in the Limerick District, most homes west of Seventh Street are occupied by Black residents.

DATE ESTABLISHED: c1860

ADDRESS: Between Breckinridge and Oak, Fifth and Eighth Streets, Louisville

VISITING HOURS: Private, visitors can drive by

SOURCES: NRHPINF. Personal visit, summer 1990. Telephone conversation Mar. 18, 1994, Bonnie McCaferty of Creative Resources at the Central Colored School Building. *Kentucky's Black Heritage*, 37, 42, 86.

Central Colored School

Central Colored School was erected in 1873 at the edge of the sparsely developed Limerick residential neighborhood. The school attracted Black residents to the neighborhood and later led to construction of the Kentucky Normal and Theological Institute in 1879 and Louisville's first public housing complex.

The landmark Central Colored School is a symbol of progress that was made in educating Black children during Reconstruction. Before the 1840s, African American children received an education only if an exceptional slave master allowed them to learn; then they learned only by instruction from a private tutor. A few schools opened for Louisville's Black children in the early 1840s, but most were operated by churches or by teachers who operated independently. Many free Black children in Louisville attended the independently operated schools, and a few slaveholders sent slave children to the schools.

After the Civil War, the freed people began to pay taxes but were denied their fair share of revenues for educating their children. An integrated committee of citizens formed to seek more equitable school funding. As a result, officials constructed a two-story building, but the facility was inadequate. By 1870 the appeal for better school facilities for Black children began anew, with some prominent white citizens joining the campaign. The school board again gave an inadequate response, using tax money from the Black community to establish three primary schools in rented church space. The facilities were poor, and the schools provided instruction only in the lower grades.

After years of effort, city commissioners released the Louisville school board from paying an obligation of $64,000 owed for a bond repayment. In return, the school board was directed to provide better education for Black children. When the Central Colored School was dedicated in 1873, the Louisville *Courier-Journal* described it "as neat and handsome a school structure as there is in the city."[3]

The facility operated as an African American school until 1894, when students moved to a larger building at Ninth and Magazine. Central School, which from the beginning was located in a largely white neighborhood, then became a school for white students only. Later, after several years of disuse, the school reopened as the Hill Adult Learning Laboratory.

Central Colored School is a substantial brick, three-story building. Cross halls allow twelve corner classrooms with abundant window lighting. Privately owned now, the interior remains much as it was when the school was constructed. The school is listed in the *National Register of Historic Places*.

DATE BUILT:	1873
ADDRESS:	542 West Kentucky Street, Louisville
TELEPHONE:	For appointment to see interior, Mr. Dan Stewart of Stewart Lopez Bonilla & Associates, (502) 583-5502
VISITING HOURS:	Privately owned

Municipal College (Simmons University) Campus

Another landmark facility in the Limerick historic district is the Municipal College (Simmons University) campus. There have been several name changes of the educational institutions located on this site. Names changed from Kentucky Normal and Theological Institute in 1873 to State University in 1884, Simmons University about 1918, Municipal College for Negroes in the 1920s, Municipal Park today. These schools educated Black students from Reconstruction until the 1950's repeal of school segregation.

Four years after the end of the Civil War, Black Baptists from Kentucky held a series of conventions at which they proposed the establishment of a literary and theological school that would train African American students for the ministry. They purchased the present site in 1879, commenting on the high, dry land, the fruit and shade trees, winding tanbark walkways, and the good water supply. In addition to the school, they wanted a park because such facilities did not exist for the Black community. They bought the land and an existing brick house for $1,857.

The Kentucky Normal and Theological Institute was chartered in 1873 and opened in 1879. The college later was named for William Simmons (1849–1890), a man who had served with the Forty-first Colored Troops in the Civil War. Simmons graduated from Madison University in New York and Howard University in Washington, D.C. He served as president of the Kentucky Normal and Theological Institute until shortly before his death.

During Simmons's tenure, the institution received university status. In the 1880s, it became known as State University. By 1919, State University had ten departments, including a medical school.

Two of the major surviving buildings are the Girls' Dormitory and Domestic Science Building (now the Mary B. Talbert School) and Steward Hall, built as the boys' dormitory. The girls' dormitory, built in 1909, is believed to have been built and designed by Samuel Plato, a graduate of Simmons College and one of Kentucky's best-known Black builder/architects. Plato learned the construction business through a correspondence course. He spent his early years in Marion, Indiana, before coming to Kentucky in the 1920s. His Plato construction company built several buildings in Louisville.

The boys' dormitory, constructed in 1924, was named for William H. Steward, a man hired in 1876 as the first Black letter carrier in Louisville. Steward was elected in 1882 by his primarily white coworkers as their representative to the National Letter Carriers Association.

Simmons University began to have financial problems and sold this campus to the University of Louisville in 1930. Simmons University moved a year later to Eighteenth and Dumesnil Streets. The facilities at this site then became the Municipal College for Negroes. Municipal College provided important access to higher education in an era of segregation when the only higher education opportunities for Black students in Kentucky were provided by Berea College (*see* Berea), Kentucky State University, and the Lincoln Institute (*see* Simpsonville). Municipal College operated at this site until 1951, when the University of Louisville opened all its divisions to Black students.

The Municipal College Campus is known today as Municipal Park and is owned by the Louisville School District. Municipal Park buildings are used for educational purposes by the local school district and are not generally open for tours.

DATE ESTABLISHED: 1873
ADDRESS: Municipal Park, 1018 S. Seventh Street (between Kentucky and Zane, Seventh and Eighth Streets), Louisville
VISITING HOURS: Visitors can inspect the building exteriors

Louisville Western Branch Library

The Carnegie-endowed Western Colored Branch of the Louisville Free Public Library was one of the first in the nation to extend privileges to the Black community. The Louisville Free Public Library, Western Colored Branch, was established in 1905. Although construction of the main library building of the Louisville Public Library began in 1905, Black citizens were denied access. The African American community established a free library, open to all, in three rooms of a home, but it was inadequate in size.

Philanthropist Andrew Carnegie then provided a gift of a construction allowance for the Western Colored Branch, a gift that had to be matched by guarantees that other financial obligations would be met. After the state of Kentucky committed public funds for the project, construction began. The library opened in the present structure in October 1908 and Thomas Blue joined the branch as librarian. The library science training program that he designed for Black librarians later was adopted on a national scale.

The Western Branch Library is a substantial brick structure with extensive stone ornamentation. The community viewed the library with pride because it represented a tangible result of their efforts to extend the benefits of a free public library to all citizens.

DATE BUILT: 1907–1908
ADDRESS: 604 S. Tenth Street, Louisville
TELEPHONE: (502) 574-1779
VISITING HOURS: Mon.–Tue., Thur. noon–8; Wed., Fri.–Sat. 10–5
SOURCES: Personal visit, summer 1990. NRHPINF. Information from Ms. Carmen Samuels, manager, Carnegie Library Branch.

Russell Historic District

The Russell historic district is located to the west of Louisville's central business district. The area began to develop at the end of the Civil War, when trolley cars enabled people to move out of the crowded downtown area. The large, beautiful homes were fashionable from the 1870s through the 1890s.

Before Russell became a predominantly Black district, many shotgun and small frame houses lined the alleys. Oral history maintains that these were dwellings of Black people who worked for white property owners. A few surviving structures are on Plymouth, Eddy, Esquire, and Green Alleys.

In the first quarter of the twentieth century, the district became a residential, social, and commercial area for middle-class Black families. The area was named for Harvey Clarence Russell, dean of Kentucky State College and president of West Kentucky Industrial College and West Kentucky Vocational School. Russell was elected president of the Kentucky Educational Association and served as a specialist in Negro Education in the United States Office of Education.

A high proportion of the Black families owned their homes. Black professionals purchased large, expensive residences on Jefferson, Walnut, and Chestnut Streets. Around 1929 Samuel Plato, one of Louisville's few Black architects, built for his own use a yellow brick house at 2509 West Chestnut Street. From 1910 to 1930 families with more modest incomes began to move onto Cedar, Madison, Magazine, and Elliott Streets, where homes generally had been constructed between 1870 and 1880.

The Russell district contains 1,700 structures, primarily residences, in a variety of architectural styles including Italianate (2510 West Muhammad Ali Boulevard), Victorian (2110 West Chestnut Street), Queen Anne (2100 West Chestnut Street), Richardsonian Romanesque (1633 West Jefferson Street), and shotgun style. The shotgun style—the most common style in the district—offers here a greater variety than in any other section of the city. The basic shotgun is one room wide and three rooms deep. Many shotgun houses built between 1890 and 1900 are located on Magazine Street. Numbers 2323 to 2329 on West Chestnut Street are the only examples of row-shotgun houses in the city. These four houses are all connected by the two-story rear sections of each house.

The old Twelfth Ward School at Twenty-second and Magazine Streets is a three-story Victorian structure built in 1889 to serve the Russell community. The building currently is used for commercial purposes. The Russell historic district is listed in the *National Register of Historic Places*. The neighborhood, an African American center of residential, social, and cultural activity for more than fifty years, still retains many of the original features—brick alleys and sidewalks, cast-iron fences, and cast-iron porches—that are rare in other areas of the city.

DATE ESTABLISHED: Late nineteenth century

ADDRESS: Roughly bounded by S. Fifteenth, S. Twenty-sixth, Congress, and W. Broadway Streets, Louisville

VISITING HOURS: Private, visitors may drive or walk through

SOURCES: Personal visit, summer 1990. NRHPINF.

Mammoth Cave

Mammoth Cave National Park

Mammoth Cave, with its three hundred miles of explored passageways, is perhaps the longest cave system in the world. African Americans were among its early explorers and mappers.

Early Woodland Indians, the earliest cave explorers, visited Mammoth Cave more than 2000 years ago and left charred remains of their torches throughout the passageways. Europeans and African Americans came to the site in the late 1700s, as a succession of European owners began to mine the caves for saltpeter. Their Black slaves worked in the darkness, digging and leaching out the saltpeter for gunpowder.

When the need for saltpeter declined, curious visitors came to explore. Dr. John Croghan, the owner of the cave from 1839 until 1849, had a slave named Stephen Bishop who, in fact, came with the property when Croghan purchased it. Bishop possessed an expert knowledge of the cave and helped to map and make known the vast extent of the underground trails. He is credited with crossing the area called the "Bottomless Pit" for the first time in 1838. Before he took a ladder down and crossed the pit, the cave was thought to end at that point.

Bishop discovered another wonder in 1848 when he saw for the first time the "eyeless" fish in the underground Echo River. In the 1800s, when he was still a slave (although well-known), Bishop led tours of the cave. In the 1840s he published one of the earliest and most complete maps of Mammoth Cave.

Stephen Bishop died in 1859 and was buried within the park. Two African American brothers, Matt and Nicholas Bransford, also had explored the cave before the Civil War. Matt Bransford became chief guide after Bishop's death. William Garvin, another Black man, served as an early guide for exploring groups. An 1871 newspaper sketch shows him holding a lantern up for a group of visitors. The National Park Service has some artifacts associated with Stephen Bishop.

DATE DISCOVERED: c1798

ADDRESS: Mammoth Cave (halfway between Louisville and Nashville off I-65 at Exit 48 or 53) Note: Several caves in the area have similar names; be sure that you are visiting the one in Mammoth Cave National Park

TELEPHONE: (502) 758-2251

VISITING HOURS: Daily, year round; Visitors Center 8–6:30 summer months (first tour 8:15, last tour 5); winter, spring, fall 8–5:30 (first tour 9, last tour 4); closed Christmas; some of the walks are long and strenuous; summer tours can last from one and a quarter to four hours; bring a warm sweater

FEES: Depending on length of tour, adults, $3.50 or $5.50; children, $1.75 or $2.75

SOURCES: Personal visit, 1990. Telephone conversation Aug. 2, 1995, Vicki Carson, public affairs officer, Mammoth Cave. Larry Z. Scott, director, The Kentucky Museum. *The Uncommon Wealth of Kentucky. Mammoth Cave Inside Out.* "The Stephen Bishop Story."

Paris Vicinity

The Grange

The lovely elegance of the nineteenth-century house called "the Grange" belies the misery experienced by Black slaves who suffered there. The house was built for slave trader Edward Stone, who chained slaves below his own living quarters while he awaited their sale.

Edward Stone, his wife, and their eleven children settled on Stone's father's Revolutionary War land grant. He began to build the one and one-half–story main house in 1800 and completed it in 1816. The elegant brick main house known as "Oakland" has a deep-set doorway with a fanlight and side lights and Palladian windows in delicately curved walls. The carved, reeded woodwork throughout the interior is said to have been created with an eight-foot gouge chisel operated by a talented carpenter and pulled on chains by slaves. Stone kept slaves due for sale in a 24-foot-by-12-foot masonry-walled cellar.

When Stone built this house, his neighbors owned slaves, too, but they did not regard slave trading as an honorable profession. He was the only person in the community to openly advertise his trade. On July 24, 1816, for example, he placed an advertisement in the *Western Citizen:*

> "Cash for Negroes"—I wish to purchase twenty negroes, boys and girls from 10 to 25 years of age. A liberal price will be given for those answering the description on early application to the subscriber, Edward Stone.
>
> Living on the Limestone Road, 4 miles from Paris leading to Millersburg.[4]

In 1882 a Reverend James H. Dickey met one of Stone's coffles (that is, a group of slaves chained together) on the Paris-Lexington Road. Forty men and thirty women were in the coffle, and Reverend Dickey described them as marching with sad countenances. Owners often sold Stone their unruly slaves or those who had committed crimes. To break their spirits, Stone chained them to rings set in the walls of the dungeon and left them in complete darkness. They were fed nothing but bread and water, and their only breath of fresh air came from one iron-barred window under the back porch. This window was approached by a 4-foot-by-4-foot doorway raised two feet off the ground and guarded with a solid iron door.

By 1826 Stone had developed a lucrative business, but the community still rejected him because of his slave-trading practice. Stone finally announced that he would give up slave trading and become a planter. He planned a final trip to New Orleans with a cargo of seventy-seven surplus slaves and loaded his human cargo on a flat-bottomed boat. Ignoring a servant's warning that a rebellion might take place, he began a fateful trip down the Ohio River. Approximately ninety miles below Louisville, the slaves overwhelmed Stone and other white men on board, killing them and throwing their bodies into the river. The servant who had given the warning fought to save Stone, but when he could not, he escaped and eventually returned home. The slaves who had rebelled were determined to be free, but were eventually captured. Their mutiny was unsuccessful in freeing them, but it left no doubt in the minds of Kentucky citizens of the strength of the impulse toward freedom. The fate of Stone's rebellious slaves is not known; as a rule, such slaves were either executed or very harshly punished.

The Grange today is a private home, and its interior is not accessible to visitors. There is a one-story brick cabin on the site that once was used as slave quarters, and the slave-holding cellar is still there. Despite the fact that the house is not open to visitors, it is worthwhile to drive by because of its tragic history.

DATE BUILT: 1800–1816

ADDRESS: 4 miles north of Paris on the Lexington-Maysville Pike, US 68, Paris vicinity

VISITING HOURS: Privately owned, not accessible to the public

SOURCES: Personal visit, summer 1990. Colonel G. C. Brown. NRHPINF. Telephone conversation June 1990, Mrs. Joe Allen, preparer of the NRHPINF. *National Register of Historic Places,* 259.

Richmond

White Hall State Historic Site

This forty-four room, three-story mansion was the home of Cassius Marcellus Clay, an outspoken and idiosyncratic white abolitionist. The site also contains slave quarters of stone located near the main house.

Cassius Clay was the son of General Green Clay, one of the richest men in Kentucky. At the time of his death in 1828, General Clay owned more land, slaves, and personal property than anyone else in the state. When his sixth child, Cassius

Marcellus Clay, was born in 1810, slavery was a well-accepted institution in Kentucky, and Cassius grew up in a world of wealth and privilege.

Two incidents, however, caused Cassius to turn against slavery. The first occurred when he was approximately eight years old. A slave named Mary, who had been Clay's companion and playmate, was punished by Green Clay for a minor misdeed. She was transferred from her position in the Clay household and sent to work for the family of the overseer on another of Green Clay's estates.

The overseer was known for his cruelty, and when he ordered Mary to an upstairs room, she hid a butcher knife under her skirt. As the overseer raised a whip to strike her, she plunged the knife into his heart, then she ran out of the house and ran to the Clay house screaming. The other slaves were horrified at the sight of the bloodied woman. Mary was tried for murder. Although a jury of white men acquitted her on the basis of self-defense, unwritten rules required that any Black person who attacked a white person had to be sold away. Mary was sold down the river to Mississippi, far from everyone she had known.

The eight-year-old Cassius understood the unwritten rule, but he believed the harsh punishment was unjust. Years later these feelings were reinforced when he heard his first antislavery speech while a student at Yale. White abolitionist William Lloyd Garrison gave a lecture that impelled Clay to speak out against slavery. Clay asked that his name be removed from the church roll because he disagreed with the members' views on slavery. When he graduated from Yale, Clay was selected to deliver the Washington Centennial Address, and he made his first antislavery speech at that time.

After graduation, Cassius freed approximately fifty of his own slaves at great financial cost. In 1845 he began publishing an antislavery paper, *The True American,* in Lexington. Within a month he received death threats and had to arm himself and barricade the doors of his newspaper office for protection. On an occasion when he was ill, a mob of about sixty men broke into his office, dismantled the press and equipment, and shipped them to Cincinnati. Clay continued to publish the paper from Ohio, circulating it throughout Kentucky.

Cassius Clay also helped to found Berea College, one of the first colleges in the United States established for the purpose of educating an integrated student body. This activity drew more hatred and enmity from Kentucky's proslavery forces.

Clay's last years were saddened. Divorced from his wife and deeply in debt, he sold much of his property. Ironically, in spite of his antislavery views, he still owned some slaves, whom he now sold to pay his creditors. He lived almost alone in his large house, armed for his own protection. On July 22, 1903, at the age of ninety-three, he died nearly alone.

For sixty-five years White Hall stood empty and in ruin. The fine furnishings were sold at auction for a little more than $3,000. Walls and floors buckled, and vandals destroyed parts of the house. Tenant farmers who lived in sections of the house stored grain and hay in the elegant ballroom. In 1968 the Commonwealth of Kentucky bought White Hall and thirteen acres of land from the Clay heirs for $18,375 and began to restore the main house.

The old stone slave quarters behind White Hall were built in the early 1800s. Slaves also lived in the basement of the main house, where bars remain across a window in one room. In another room a tunnel still exists where slaves owned by General Green Clay tried to dig their way to freedom by tunneling under ground. Apparently the escape plot was discovered.

DATE BUILT:	1798; added to in 1864–1868
ADDRESS:	500 White Hall Shrine Road, Richmond (7 miles north of Richmond on Clay Lane off US 25; I-75, exit 95 on US 25/421)
TELEPHONE:	(606) 623-9178
VISITING HOURS:	Apr.–Labor Day, daily 9–5; Labor Day–Oct., Wed.–Sun. 9–5
FEES:	Adults, $3; children, $2
SOURCES:	Personal visit, 1990. Carolyn Jones, park manager, White Hall Historic Site. *The Uncommon Wealth of Kentucky. National Register of Historic Places,* 266. *Historical Sketches of the Kentucky Bluegrass Area. White Hall, Kentucky, State Shrine.*

Simpsonville

Lincoln Institute Complex

Lincoln Institute opened as a result of a landmark Supreme Court decision supporting segregated education in Kentucky. Berea College had been integrated until 1904 when the Kentucky Legislature passed the Day Law, making integrated education illegal. Berea College spent four years fighting the case in the courts, but the Supreme Court ruled that Berea, as a private college, had to obey the laws of Kentucky.

Berea then used part of its own funds to open the Lincoln Institute for Black students who had to leave the college. The Carnegie Foundation paid half of the $400,000 needed to create Lincoln Institute. The newly established school opened classes in 1911 on a campus twenty-five miles east of Louisville. For more than fifty years Lincoln Institute played a major role in educating Kentucky's Black students. The curriculum followed the recommendations of leading Black educator Booker T. Washington by focusing on agricultural and industrial education.

After Whitney M. Young Sr. became director in 1935, he obtained state funding and began to improve the facilities, persuading counties with small Black populations to pay for educating their students at Lincoln Institute. Although the institute grew after World War II, school desegregation in the late fifties and early sixties made the school obsolete, and it closed in 1965. In the early nineties the campus was used as a job training center for young people.

The Lincoln Institute Complex Historic Site consists of Berea Hall, Belknap Hall, and Norton Hall. Berea Hall, a two and one-half–story brick building on the crest of Lincoln Ridge, was built for academic and administrative activities. The hall has a five-story tower and the original wrought-iron chandeliers. Norton and Belknap Halls are dormitory buildings standing on each side of Berea Hall.

The three buildings are approached by a drive with maple trees planted for one thousand feet on each side. The campus landscaping was designed by the nationally known Olmsted firm of Brookline, Massachusetts. Some of the buildings were designed by the New York firm of Black architects, G. W. Foster and V. W. Tandy.

Another building on campus significant in Black history is the early twentieth-century house that was the birthplace of the late Whitney M. Young Jr. He was born on the Lincoln Institute campus in 1921, the son of distinguished educator and Lincoln Institute Director Dr. Whitney M. Young Sr.

Whitney Young Jr. graduated from Kentucky State College in 1941. He was nineteen and ranked first in his graduating class. After serving in the U.S. Army in World War II, he earned his master's degree from the University of Minnesota. He directed the Urban League in Minnesota and Nebraska between 1947 and 1954, and then served six years as dean of the School of Social Work at Atlanta University.

Young became director of the National Urban League in 1961. A primary accomplishment was his work in finding employment for thousands of individuals. In 1968 he declined a cabinet post with the federal government because he believed he could accomplish more with the Urban League, which he directed until his death in 1971.

Today a historical marker honoring Young is located at the entrance to the Lincoln Complex, which now serves as the Job Corps Residential Manpower Center. The Young birthplace is a lovely frame clapboard home in a serene setting of a large lawn on the Complex grounds. A one-story side wing of the birth home contains a display of Young's papers, correspondence, and awards. This house, Young's birthplace and his home for twenty years, was a comfortable residence and a symbol of a well-educated middle-class Black family that provided leadership on both a local and a national basis.

DATE ESTABLISHED: 1911

ADDRESS: South side of US 60 West at Simpsonville (southwest of Simpsonville, off US 60 West); historic marker, on the open road near the entrance to the complex

TELEPHONE: (502) 722-8862

VISITING HOURS: Open by appointment with the supervisor at the Whitney M. Young Jr. Job Corps Training Center

SOURCES: Personal visit, summer 1990. NRHPINF. Larry Z. Scott, director, the Kentucky Museum. Yvonne V. Jones, Ph.D., Associate Professor, University of Louisville. *Kentucky's Black Heritage. National Register of Historic Places*, 270.

Notes

1. Telephone conversation May 23, 1994, Ruth Craig Proffitt, Gamaliel Senior Center.

2. Telephone conversation May 23, 1994, Joyce Thomas, former Mt. Vernon Church member.

3. Louisville *Courier Journal*, 1873, as quoted in NRHPINF.

4. *Western Citizen*, July 24, 1816, as quoted in NRHPINF.

5. NRHPINF.

Works Consulted

Historical Sketches of the Kentucky Bluegrass Area. Robert A. Powell. Lexington, Ky.: Kentucky Images, 1990.

Isaac Burns Murphy. Famous Kentuckians Series. JoD Neace Place. Frankfort, Ky.: Office of Tourism Development.

Kentucky State University Catalogue, 1988–1989. Frankfort, Ky.: The University, 1988.

Kentucky's Black Heritage. Frankfort, Ky.: Kentucky Commission on Human Rights, 1971.

National Register of Historic Places. Washington, D.C.: National Park Service, 1976.

National Register Information Systems. Washington, D.C.: National Park Service. [computer database]

Mammoth Cave Inside Out 11, no. 2. Mammoth Cave, Ky.: National Park Service, summer 1990.

Onward and Upward: A Centennial History of Kentucky State University, 1886–1986. John A. Hardin. Frankfort, Ky.: The University, 1987.

"The Stephen Bishop Story: The Man and the Legend." Harold Meloy. Mammoth Cave, Ky.: files of Mammoth Cave, 1974. [manuscript]

The Uncommon Wealth of Kentucky: The Traveler's Guide to Kentucky. Frankfort, Ky.: The Kentucky Dept. of Travel Development, 1989.

Webster's New Biographical Dictionary. Springfield, Mass.: Merriam-Webster, 1988.

White Hall, Kentucky, State Shrine. David C. Greene. Richmond, Ky.: Print Shop, 1972. [booklet]

Louisiana

●●●●●●●●●●●

Alexandria

Arna Bontemps African American Museum

Noted American author Arna Bontemps was born in the house at 1327 Third Street in Alexandria in 1902, but within six years virulent racism in Alexandria caused his family to move to California. In 1923 Bontemps graduated from Pacific Union College in California; he later earned a master's degree in library science from the University of Chicago. Entering the creative life of the writer, Bontemps won the NAACP's *Crisis Magazine* Poetry Prize, the Alexander Pushkin Prize, and Rosenwald and Guggenheim Fellowships. In some of his works he collaborated with writer Langston Hughes and composer W. C. Handy.

Bontemps never forgot Alexandria, Louisiana, always considering it to be, in a sense, his home. He returned again and again to learn about his family heritage. Today, a museum, established in 1988 and housed in the Bontemps home in 1990, appropriately honors the author by honing the creative writing skills of local Black youth and by teaching them their history.

Arna Bontemps wrote *Why I Returned* to trace the steps of his journey home. A museum room that is named for him showcases his collected writings and his family heritage. His wife is donating to the museum furnishings that he used, including an early typewriter.

The former dining room of the house has become a community room where a Junior Writing Guild meets on Saturdays, taught by a teacher from the local school district. In 1994 nine of the young writers published their first book and sold more than seventy copies at their book-signing celebration. Another group of students meets on Saturdays for an African American history class; they are preparing for the museum-sponsored "African American Quizbowl," a test about Black history facts and concepts.

DATE BUILT:	House, 1879; museum, 1990
ADDRESS:	1327 Third Street, Alexandria
TELEPHONE:	(318) 473-4692
VISITING HOURS:	Tues.–Fri. 10–4, Sat. 10–2; closed Thanksgiving weekend, one-half day on Christmas Eve, Christmas Day, one-half day on New Year's Eve, New Year's Day, July 4, and Labor Day
FEES:	None
SOURCE:	Telephone conversation June 7, 1994, Barbara Epps, museum director.

Baton Rouge

Louisiana State University Rural Life Museum

The LSU Rural Life Museum, an outdoor folk museum, includes Black history in its representation of groups who settled in Louisiana. The museum shows the preindustrial lifestyles of Native American, French, Black, German, Spanish, Anglo-American, and Acadian groups. Displays include tools, furniture, utensils, and farming implements as well as some original buildings moved to this site.

The museum re-creates the back yard of a large plantation with everything except the big house. The site includes an overseer's house, slave cabins, a sick house, a blacksmith shop, a church, a schoolhouse, and other buildings. Most structures in the complex known as the "working plantation" are authentic and are authentically furnished. The museum shows major activities on a typical nineteenth-century plantation.

That white people of the day rewarded their servants for hard work and loyalty to the white community is indicated by a bronze figure of "Uncle Jack" at the museum entrance. The people of Natchitoches erected the statue in 1927 in recognition of the hard and faithful service of Black Louisiana workers. At the time the award was made, African Americans, of course, were advancing in a much wider arena. The statue can be regarded as a comment on the times.

The museum's sick house and other cabins are of special interest. The sick house, built between 1830 and 1840, originally was a two-room slave cabin. The other slave cabins were built about 1835 and housed slaves before the Civil War. Tenant farmers and sharecroppers used the cabins after the war. Each cabin has a fireplace, a few simple hide chairs, and a bed.

The Rural Life Museum has a variety of artifacts. A voodoo exhibit includes items related to some African religious rituals. Another collection shows plantation bells that awakened field hands in the morning and announced special events.

The museum also displays some paintings of Clementine Hunter, an African American woman who worked at Melrose in the Natchitoches area. Hunter's paintings of Black plantation life are displayed now at the Rural Life Museum, the Louisiana Arts and Science Center, and the new State Capitol.

DATE ESTABLISHED:	1970
ADDRESS:	6200 Burden Lane (entrance is at Essen Lane at I-10, Burden Research Plantation), Baton Rouge
TELEPHONE:	(504) 765-2437
VISITING HOURS:	Mon.–Fri. 8:30–4; guided tours for groups of 8 or more on a "first-come" basis by appointment at least two weeks in advance; closed weekends and university holidays
FEES:	$2 per person, 12 years and up; children 11 and younger, $1
SOURCES:	John E. Dutton, director, The LSU Rural Life Museum. Kay Harrison, tour coordinator, and Fleurette Aucoin, tour guide, Lagniappe Tours, Foundation for Historical Louisiana, Inc. *The LSU Rural Life Museum.*

Southern University and A & M College

Southern University, the parent campus of America's largest predominantly Black university system, was chartered in 1880 by the state of Louisiana. A year earlier, Pinckney Pinchback, T. T. Allain, T. B. Stamps, and Henry Demas had sponsored a movement in the state constitutional convention to establish an institution for educating "persons of color." Their efforts were rewarded when the Louisiana General Assembly chartered Southern University, creating one of the first African American colleges to receive federal land funds for agricultural and mechanical courses.

Trustees purchased the former Hebrew Girls School in New Orleans, and in 1881 Southern University opened there with twelve students. In 1914 Southern University in New Orleans was closed and sold, and the university was reestablished on a plantation in the Scotlandville area of Baton Rouge. The new 512-acre campus was on Scott's Bluff overlooking the Mississippi River. Lake Kernan flows through the center of the campus.

When Southern University opened in Baton Rouge, the present Archives Building was the only usable building on the site. Constructed about 1840, the raised cottage originally may have been a support building for a large plantation house. The cottage originally had three rooms arranged one room deep and had a gallery in front. In the early 1900s rear rooms and a corridor were added and windows and floorboards were modified.

The president of the university and his family lived in the cottage in the early years, and the building later housed a conference center, a girls' dormitory, a dining hall, and a social center.

Southern University, which opened in 1881 with twelve students, in recent years has enrolled more than 9,000 undergraduate and graduate students with a student body that is primarily African American. As visitors tour the campus and see the Archives Building, they also may wish to visit the university library to peruse some of the books of poetry by Pinkie Gordon Lane, professor emeritus of English at Southern University and Poet Laureate of Louisiana from 1989 to 1991. A graduate of Spelman College and Atlanta University, Gordon was, in 1967, the first Black woman to receive a Doctor of Philosophy degree at Louisiana State University. Her volumes of poetry include *Wind Thoughts* (1971), *The Mystic Female* (1978), *I Never Screamed* (1985), and *Girl at the Window* (1991).

DATE ESTABLISHED: 1880; first part of the Archive Building, c1840

ADDRESS: Scenic Highway at Harding Boulevard, Baton Rouge

TELEPHONE: (504) 771-2430

VISITING HOURS: Guided tours by appointment; visitors can drive the loop during daylight hours

FEES: None

SOURCES: Kay Harrison, tour coordinator, and Fleurette Aucoin, tour guide, Lagniappe Tours. Foundation for Historical Louisiana, Inc. Personal visit summer 1990. NRHPINF. Mary E. Norris, Baton Rouge Area Convention & Visitors Bureau. Telephone conversation Dec. 27, 1994, Dr. Pinkie Gordon Lane, professor emeritus, Southern University. *Southern University and A & M College Catalog; Southern University, Baton Rouge, Louisiana; The Flavor of Louisiana—Baton Rouge: A Visitor's Guide,* 24. "Pinkie Gordon Lane Named Poet Laureate."

Bunkie

Edwin Epps House

This frame house, once the property of a planter named Edwin Epps, now commemorates the life of Solomon Northup, his slave. Northup was born free in New York in 1808. His father, Mintus Northup, had been born a slave of the Northup family of Rhode Island but was freed by the

Northup family and took their name. Mintus Northup, a hard-working farmer, was able to give his two boys an education better than that of most Black children; for this reason, Solomon was able to read, write, and play the violin with skill. Solomon married Anne Hampton at the age of twenty-one, and they moved to Saratoga, New York. (For information on another Northup site, see the listing for Solomon Northup House in Fort Edward, New York.) They were the parents of three children who were their pride.

Once when Anne was away for the week working as a cook, Northup wandered around Saratoga looking for work for himself. He was introduced to two men who offered to hire him for short-term work playing his violin in a circus in Washington, D.C. They seemed kind and generous, and Solomon went with them, not bothering to notify his wife because he believed he would return before she completed her week's work at the tavern.

Instead of taking him to a circus in Washington, the two men betrayed Northup by selling him into slavery. He was kidnapped, beaten, whipped, and sold to the first of his masters in Louisiana, where he spent the next twelve years of his life in heavy labor. Having been severely whipped with a hardwood paddle and with a large rope called a cat-o'-nine-tails, and having been threatened with death if he ever mentioned that he had been free, Northup did not dare speak out about freedom. He thought of freedom every day, but knew he might never see his family again.

Northup had an incredible memory for names and details, which he later used to give poignant descriptions of his life in slavery; his delineations left no doubt that slavery was cruel and dehumanizing.

Northup's violin provided solace at times. His carpentry skills, his inventive talent, and his air of assurance caused other slaves and some white people to respect him, even though they did not know his history. His strong spirit resembled that of a slave in Maryland, who later took the name Frederick Douglass. Just as Douglass once had done as a slave, Northup, too, whipped a white man. The man, named Tibeats, had raised a three-foot-long rawhide whip, loaded with lead at the base, to whip Northup, but the slave snatched the whip from Tibeats, pushed him to the ground, and whipped him until he screamed for mercy.

Northup eventually was sold to Edwin Epps whom he described thus:

> Edwin Epps is a large, heavy man with a sharp expression. His language is vulgar, and I've often seen him drunk, sometimes for two weeks at a time. But lately he has gotten better, and when I left him, he didn't drink at all. But when he was drunk, he would love to dance with his slaves or whip them just to hear them shriek and cry.[1]

After a day of picking cotton, the slaves always dreaded having their cotton weighed:

> No matter how tired a slave may be at the end of the day, he never goes to the millhouse without fear. Here the cotton is weighed. If he did not pick enough that day, he knows he will be whipped. If he picked more than expected, he will have to pick that much more every day from then on. . . . After the weighings come the beatings.[2]

Every day Northup thought of escaping, but everyone he knew who had tried to escape had failed. After twelve years, Northup was assigned to work on a construction job where he met Bass, a white carpenter born in Canada. Eventually Northup felt he could trust the man and risked everything by telling his story. Bass promised to help and he wrote and mailed a letter for Northup. After several turns of events, Northup was freed months later and reunited with his family. At the request of others he soon dictated his story, published in 1853 as *Twelve Years a Slave.* Northup died about 1863.

The simple white house of Northup's owner, Edwin Epps, is nearly empty of furnishings now; but it is filled with history because it is the same house that Northup helped to build six months before his escape from Epps and from Louisiana. Members of the Belmont Foundation and its managers are waiting for the day when they can obtain funds to turn it into a museum that will tell the story of the two men whose lives intersected more than a century ago.

DATE BUILT: 1852

ADDRESS: US 71 (Jefferson Highway), Bunkie, coming from Alexandria into Bunkie, the Epps House is just past Chevy Lane

TELEPHONE: Bunkie Chamber of Commerce, (318) 346-2575

VISITING HOURS: Private, but visitors can drive by, park, and view the exterior

SOURCES: Telephone conversation Mar. 20, 1994, Judy Descart, Bunkie Chamber of Commerce. Betty Williams, branch manager, Avoyelles Parish Library. *The Smithsonian Guide to Historic America: The Deep South,* 98. *African Americans: Voices of Triumph,* vol. 1, 36. *The Shaping of Black America,* 151–2. *In Chains to Louisiana. Twelve Years a Slave. Avoyelles Homes.*

Derry

Magnolia Plantation

Tax records from 1850 indicate that there once were 250 slaves working at Magnolia Plantation and at the owner's other plantation across the river. The plantation is still a working farm where cotton and soybeans are grown. The historic site contains a twenty-seven-room plantation house and several outbuildings, including eight slave cabins with tin roofs, an overseer's house, a gun house, a blacksmith's shop, and a store.

Although as of December 1994, the slave cabins were not open to the public, they were in the process of being restored. The two-room cabins each have a large central fireplace. Most have a front and back porch and a kitchen. There are windows on both sides and in back of the structures, and some have two doors. Visitors can view the slave cabins from the road, and they can visit the interior of the main house. The barnyard animals are appealing to children.

DATE BUILT: 1784

ADDRESS: LA 119 (approximately 32 miles north of Alexandria; from I-49 take exit 119 and follow the Cane River Plantation sign to the right for approximately one mile), Derry

TELEPHONE: (318) 379-2221

VISITING HOURS: Daily 1–4 or by appointment; closed major holidays

FEES: Adults, $5; students, $3; children, $2

SOURCES: Telephone conversation Dec. 24, 1993, Betty Hertzog, manager/owner. Telephone conversation Dec. 27, 1994, Barbara Bayonne, tour guide. *The Smithsonian Guide to Historic America: The Deep South,* 103.

Lafayette

Holy Rosary Institute

Holy Rosary Institute opened in 1913 at a time when many Black people in the South lived in poverty and under conditions of strict segregation. African Americans were denied the right to vote, and they could only attend school in poorly equipped buildings.

In 1895 Booker T. Washington gave a speech in Atlanta in which he proclaimed the importance of economic advancement in Black communities and spoke of the progress that could come about through industrial and technical education. Washington maintained that this kind of education program should precede efforts to gain social or political equality.

Within this context Father Philip Keller founded the Holy Rosary Institute, a Catholic high school for Black women. The school provided vocational, technical, and teacher training for work in rural Black schools. Sisters of the Holy Family staffed the Holy Rosary Institute. This religious order of Black women was founded in the 1850s in New Orleans.

The oldest campus building is a structure three stories in height with a main block, end wings, and a chapel. Although the hall is surrounded at present by new school buildings, its central position creates an important focal point on the campus. The Holy Rosary Institute enrolled about 400 students at its peak. Enrollment declined, and the institute closed. Today the campus houses other educational programs such as Project Independence, a GED diploma program.

DATE ESTABLISHED: 1913
ADDRESS: 421 Carmel Avenue, Lafayette
VISITING HOURS: Interiors, private; visitors may view the exteriors from the driveway
SOURCE: NRHPINF.

Melrose

Yucca Plantation

Yucca Plantation was established by Marie Thérèse Coincoin, who was born about 1742. Coincoin grew up working as a household slave. When she was thirty-four, her owner's household dissolved, and she and her four children were sold to a French plantation owner, Thomas Pierre Metoyer. A bond grew between them, and Coincoin had ten more children by Metoyer. She and her children were freed in the last quarter of the eighteenth century.

A new priest in the area was instrumental in breaking up the arrangement by which Coincoin and Metoyer lived together unmarried. Although Metoyer later took a white widow as his lawful wife, he continued to assist Coincoin, especially helping with her applications for land grants.

In 1794, when Coincoin was in her fifties, she began to establish a large plantation complex called Yucca Plantation (known as Melrose Plantation after 1875). Her achievements as a plantation owner and businesswoman were remarkable for a woman of this period, regardless of race. By the 1830s her plantation encompassed 12,000 acres. She and her family are said to have owned at least forty-five slaves as well as some sawmills that produced lumber for sale.

The plantation complex is located on a back road along the Cane River. It consists of nine buildings, including Yucca House, the African House, the big house (constructed in the 1830s), the Ghana House, and the barn. Yucca House and the African House—the buildings of the original plantation—show an African influence in their design. Yucca House has cypress beams and walls of river mud mixed with Spanish moss and deer hair. African House may be the only house still standing in the United States built in an African style by Black people and for Black people.

Generations of the Metoyers, who were free Black people, developed Yucca Plantation. After Marie Thérèse died in 1817, her descendants prospered for years. Eventually, though, a financial depression swept across the United States, and after 1847 ownership passed from the Metoyer family.

When Melrose Plantation was sold in 1970, some of the furnishings were sold at auction. Fortunately, many Metoyer possessions are still on view in the house. Also on display are some paintings by Clementine Hunter, an African American worker at Melrose who painted scenes of Melrose plantation activities. Her paintings provide a valuable record of Black life in rural Louisiana a century ago.

DATE ESTABLISHED:	1794
ADDRESS:	LA 119 and 494 (0.1 mile east of junction with LA 493, 15 miles southeast of Nachitoches), Melrose
TELEPHONE:	(318) 379-0055, or (318) 379-0171
VISITING HOURS:	Daily 12–4, with 90-minute tours available; closed major holidays and on Fridays preceding special events
FEES:	Adults, $5; children 13–18, $2.50; children 6–12, $2; those under 6, free
SOURCES:	NRHPINF. Telephone conversation Aug. 2, 1995, Leslie Cooper, curator, Melrose Plantation. *American Negro Art. National Register of Historic Places,* 279. *The Smithsonian Guide to Historic America: The Deep South,* 100.

New Orleans

Amistad Research Center, Tulane University

The Amistad Research Center is a major archive of African American history. Its library contains 8 million documents about African American culture in the United States and specifically about Black people in New Orleans, including the free people of color. The center also houses African art objects and African American works of art.

A nearby site also of interest is the William Ransom Hogan Jazz Archives, also located at Tulane University.

ADDRESS:	Tilton Hall, Tulane University, 6823 St. Charles Street, New Orleans
TELEPHONE:	Research Center, (504) 865-5535; Jazz Archives, (504) 865-5688
VISITING HOURS:	Daily 8:30–5
FEES:	None
SOURCES:	Lester Sullivan, senior archivist, The Amistad Research Center. Greater New Orleans Black Tourism Center Points of Interest.

Chalmette National Historical Park

Black soldiers were among the participants on both sides in the Battle of New Orleans, the final battle of the War of 1812 and the last fought between Britain and the United States. While Major General Andrew Jackson's victory restored American pride and unity and made Jackson a hero, the victory also highlighted the courage of men in the Louisiana Battalion of Free Men of Color who fought with Jackson.

British forces sought to capture New Orleans by taking the city by surprise, thus gaining a foothold along the Mississippi River, but Jackson was prepared. His men widened the canal between the Chalmette and Macarty plantations, built a protective mud rampart, and waited there for the British attack. With the Americans were two Black battalions, men who were until then the largest group of African Americans ever assembled to fight for the United States.

On January 8, 1815, British commander Major General Sir Edward Pakenham made a frontal assault, but his forces soon had to retreat under fire from the Americans. Pakenham fell, mortally wounded by a musket ball. Under heavy fire the British had no chance of winning. In a battle that lasted less than two hours, British casualties exceeded 2,000 while the Americans reported only 13. Jackson later stated that he believed Pakenham had died from the bullet of a free man of color.

Today's visitors can read brochures and see exhibits in the Visitors Center, including replicas of American and British uniforms. There also is a twenty-eight-minute film. Outside on the lawn are cannons and the Chalmette monument—122 steps that lead up to a site where visitors can look out over the battlefield. At stop number four, visitors stand where the battery supported by the Battalion of Louisiana Free Men of Color strongly repulsed the attacking British. The free men of color were described in one account as having "fought like desperadoes." For this bravery, however, they received little reward after the battle. Only a few were awarded lump sums of money or pensions. Some of the "free colored" veterans and their descendants were later asked—as proslavery feelings arose—to leave the state.

DATE ESTABLISHED: January 1815

ADDRESS: on LA 46 (6 miles east of central New Orleans by way of St. Claude Avenue and St. Bernard Highway), part of the Jean Lafitte National Historical Park, New Orleans

TELEPHONE: (504) 589-4428

VISITING HOURS: Daily 8–5; buildings, 8:30–5; closed Christmas

FEES: None

SOURCES: *Negro Soldiers in the Battle of New Orleans.*

French Quarter

Slaves constructed many of the buildings in the French Quarter, the original walled city of New Orleans. They created much of the brick masonry, ornamental iron works, and elaborate woodwork. Many buildings in Jackson Square in the French Quarter are decorated with beautiful wrought- and cast-ironwork created by Black artisans.

ADDRESS: Roughly bordered by Esplanade Avenue, N. Rampart Street, N. Peters Street, and Canal Street, New Orleans

VISITING HOURS: Both public and private; tourists may walk through the area

SOURCE: *Greater New Orleans Black Tourism Center Points of Interest.*

Hermann-Grima Historic House

The Hermann-Grima House is a restored mansion with slave quarters. The lavishly decorated house in the French Quarter was built by Samuel Hermann, a Jewish immigrant who built a vast merchandising and shipping operation in Louisiana. He had to sell the house after losing large amounts of money in the panic of 1837.

The slave quarters at the site are built in the style of the French Quarter, one room deep with no hallway. The three-story slave quarters has four rooms to each floor and a balcony on each of the upper two levels. The first floor has a kitchen area, a washroom, an ironing room, and a wine room, all with furnishings from the 1830s to 1860s. The upper two stories contain the living quarters. Both the main house and the slave quarters overlook a courtyard. There is no information on how many people lived at the same time in this building. The upper stories are used today as offices and are not open to visitors. The regular tour includes the main house and the first floor of the slave quarters.

DATE BUILT:	1831
ADDRESS:	820 Saint Louis Street, New Orleans
TELEPHONE:	(504) 525-5661
VISITING HOURS:	Mon.–Sat. 10–3:30
FEES:	Adults, $4; senior citizens and children 8–18, $2; children under 8, free
SOURCES:	Telephone conversation Dec. 29, 1993, Harriet Bos, director. *The Smithsonian Guide to Historic America: The Deep South*, 35.

Historic New Orleans Collection

The Historic New Orleans Collection, including manuscripts, a gallery with changing exhibitions, and a library, is housed in a complex of historic buildings in the French Quarter. It also contains records of Black troops in Louisiana during the Civil War as well as original documents and a study guide describing the Cane River Colony. The colony consisted of families of Black-French heritage who had extensive holdings along the Cane River. The library also has books about the free Black community in New Orleans and Louisiana.

DATE ESTABLISHED:	Townhouse, c1880; collection, 1966
ADDRESS:	533 Royal Street, New Orleans
TELEPHONE:	(504) 523-4662
VISITING HOURS:	Tue.–Sat.; Williams Gallery, 10–4:45; research reading rooms, 10–4:30; tours, 10–3:15
FEES:	Williams Gallery and reading rooms, free; tours, $2
SOURCE:	Mrs. Pamela D. Arceneaux, reference librarian, Historic New Orleans Collection.

New Orleans Jazz Museum

One of the world's largest jazz museums is located in the old U.S. Mint Building. Collections include musical instruments, sheet music, photographs, and artifacts that belonged to famous jazz musicians. There also are presentations on well-known musicians such as Louis Armstrong and Bessie Smith.

ADDRESS:	400 Esplanade Avenue, 2nd Floor, New Orleans
TELEPHONE:	(504) 568-6968
VISITING HOURS:	Wed.–Sun. 10–5; closed holidays
FEES:	Adults, $4; senior citizens and teens, $3; children under 12, free
SOURCES:	Telephone conversation Dec. 5, 1994, Deandria McGee, receptionist, Louisiana State Museum. *Greater New Orleans Black Tourism Center Points of Interest.*

Pontalba Buildings, Cabildo Museum

The Louisiana State Museum operates the 1850 House (or Lower Pontalba Building), which is part of the Pontalba buildings and Cabildo Museum, a Black history site. Slaves constructed the Upper and Lower Pontalba buildings, structures that were considered, when built, to be the first apartment buildings in the United States. The apartments are situated on each side of Jackson Square, a landscaped park in New Orleans. They were financed by Micaela Almonester de Pontalba, a wealthy woman who wanted to replace dilapidated commercial buildings with the apartments. Each room in the 1850 House, including those in the top-floor slave quarters, is furnished as it would have appeared in the 1850s.

Cabildo Museum is near the 1850 House. It is located on Chartres Street facing Jackson Square. Inside visitors see many artifacts including a slave collar, a slave block, and African drums.

DATE BUILT: Lower Pontalba, 1851; Cabildo, 1794

ADDRESS: 1850 House, 523 Saint Ann Street, Jackson Square; Cabildo, 701 Chartres Street, New Orleans

TELEPHONE: Both sites, (504) 568-6968

VISITING HOURS: Tues.–Sun. 10–5; closed holidays

FEES: To see two buildings, adults, $3; senior citizens and students, $1.50; children 12 and under, free

SOURCES: Telephone conversation June 7, 1994, Glenda Washington, secretary, Marketing and Public Relations, Louisiana State Museum. *Greater New Orleans Black Tourism Center Points of Interest. The Smithsonian Guide to Historic America: The Deep South,* 32, 98.

St. Francisville

Cottage Plantation

Two of the slave quarters still survive on Cottage Plantation, one of Louisiana's oldest and largest sugar plantations and one of the South's few remaining complete antebellum plantations. Although the two cabins are now used for storage and are not part of the tour and interpretation of the site, visitors may ask to walk over to see the exteriors of the cabins. They are small structures probably built of cypress wood and painted white.

A portion of the plantation house is used today as a bed-and-breakfast inn. The thirty-minute tour, arranged by calling in advance, includes four downstairs rooms of the main house and four outbuildings: a law office, smokehouse, milk house, and carriage house.

DATE BUILT: 1795–1850

ADDRESS: 10528 Cottage Lane at US 61, 5 miles north of LA 10, St. Francisville

TELEPHONE: (504) 635-3674

VISITING HOURS: Daily 9:15–4:30; call to arrange a tour

FEES: Age 13–adult, $5; children under 12, free

SOURCE: Telephone conversation Dec. 29, 1993, Frieda Young, tour guide leader, Cottage Plantation.

Oakley Plantation

In the early 1820s the artist John James Audubon was employed as a tutor at Oakley Plantation in St. Francisville. The site, therefore, also is called the Audubon State Commemorative Area. He completed a number of his bird studies while living there. Slavery was a part of plantation life before the Civil War years, and four donated one-room slave cabins have been moved to an area behind the plantation's "big house" where slave quarters may previously have existed on the plantation.

The cabins have been restored so that each interior shows a different aspect of slave life: one has displays showing the events of slave life, a second shows furnishings of a slave family, a third illustrates how the buildings were constructed, and a fourth shows the life a sharecropper might have lived shortly after the Civil War.

Extensive volumes of plantation records remained at Oakley Plantation telling about the slaves who lived here. The volumes even include sermons preached to the slaves. A planned trail will lead to a slave graveyard and a pond where slaves were baptized.

DATE BUILT:	Nineteenth century
ADDRESS:	LA 965, off US 61, in the Audubon State Commemorative Area, St. Francisville
TELEPHONE:	(504) 635-3739
VISITING HOURS:	Daily, 9–5; closed Thanksgiving, Christmas, New Year's Day
FEES:	Adults 13–61 years, $2; 62 years and over and 12 years and younger, free
SOURCES:	Telephone conversation Dec. 27, 1994, Sheila Varnado, librarian, *Morning Advocate.* Telephone conversation July 29, 1995, Mike Varnado, manager, Audubon State Commemorative Area. "Slave Cabins Added to Oakley Exhibit." *The Flavor of Louisiana—Baton Rouge: A Visitor's Guide,* 14.

Thibodaux Vicinity

Laurel Valley Village Museum

Sixty-five structures at the Laurel Valley complex contribute to this site today—the largest surviving nineteenth- and twentieth-century sugar plantation in the United States. Although rice, cotton, and potatoes were raised here, sugar cultivation was the major plantation activity for 160 years.

The interesting village complex contains twenty-six shotgun houses dating from the 1840s (the shotgun-style house is one room wide and two or three rooms deep with no interior hall). Slaves lived in the cypress houses before the Civil War, and laborers lived in them after the war. Although the interiors of the slave cabins are not open to visitors, the exteriors are easily visible. The village also contains a school, built in 1906 for children of the village (closed in 1952), and the remains of a sugar mill, built about 1845 with bricks made by people on the plantation. The mill closed in the 1920s.

The village started about 1790 when an Acadian, Etienne Boudreaux, obtained a Spanish land grant containing fifteen-by-forty arpents of land. Little is known about the Boudreaux family. The next owner, Joseph Tucker, came to the valley in 1832 and expanded the holdings by purchasing additional land from the United States land office. Between 1835 and 1845 he built the mill, introduced sugar cultivation, and brought in slave labor with twenty-two slaves. After Tucker died in 1832, his family tried unsuccessfully to continue the plantation. Different owners cultivated the land until 1926, when mosaic disease destroyed the sugar crop here and throughout southern Louisiana. The financial disaster lasted eighteen years for this plantation.

Between 1893 and 1951, 450 people lived in Laurel Valley Village. In 1903, there were 305 employees working in the field. Today Laurel Valley exists as a rural life museum operated by a nonprofit association, the Friends of Laurel Village. Since 1978 the Friends of Laurel Village have led restoration efforts, resulting in the rehabilitation of more than a dozen structures. The Louisiana State Department of Labor has provided funds for summer employment at the site, and local residents from the Bayou Lafourche area have crafted and donated items for sale in Laurel Village's country store.

Although a public road goes through the village, there is a fence around it. Visitors start their tours at the country store on LA Route 308.

DATE BUILT:	1840s
ADDRESS:	595 LA 308, 2 miles south of Thibodaux
TELEPHONE:	Laurel Valley Village Store, (504) 446-7456; Mrs. Ruby Landry, head volunteer, (504) 447-2902
VISITING HOURS:	Tues.–Fri. 10–4, Sat.–Sun. noon–4; closed Mon., holidays
FEES:	$2 per person, any age, for tours in the English language; special arrangements may be made for free tours in French or Cajun French
SOURCES:	Telephone conversation Dec. 2, 1994, Mrs. Ruby Landry, volunteer tour guide of French language tours, Laurel Valley. Telephone call to site, July 29, 1995. *The Smithsonian Guide to Historic America,* 55. "Laurel Valley Village."

Zachary

Port Hudson Battlefield

Port Hudson, considered the second most important Confederate position on the Mississippi River, was the battleground of the longest single Civil War conflict between the North and the South. Three regiments of free Black men and former slaves fought under Black leadership at this site. Although their attack was not successful, they fought Confederate troops in a brave and worthy manner.

The First and Third Regiments of the Louisiana Native Guards of Free Colored participated in the Union assault on Port Hudson. The First Regiment included free Black men who were skilled, intelligent, wealthy, and influential in their community. The Third Regiment soldiers were former slaves who had enrolled in 1862 in New Orleans. The third Black organization at Port Hudson was the First Regiment of Engineers of the Corps d'Afrique.

Before the two regiments of the Louisiana Native Guards of Free Colored fought in the Union assault on Port Hudson, military leaders had questioned their courage and willingness to fight. The men were aware that the battle was a test of their courage and were prepared.

On May 14, 1863, Federal General Nathaniel Banks headed for Port Hudson. On May 27, the First and Third Regiments of Black troops prepared for battle, but because of poor timing and communications, they could not proceed as planned. As they advanced, they took the brunt of the enemy's fire and suffered severe losses. When they came to a seemingly impassible stream, some swam across under heavy enemy fire. Some men in the regiment fell back, regrouped, and charged again into the sheets of fire.

There were heavy losses. Captain André Cailloux, an intelligent, Paris-educated Black man, exemplified the courage and caliber of the troops. He died in battle after courageously moving ahead of his troops, even though his arm had been shattered. Cailloux had a public funeral; after he was buried with military honors in the Bienville Cemetery, the American Flag in New Orleans flew at half-mast for thirty days in his honor.

On May 27, 293 Union troops died and 1,545 were wounded; 235 Confederate troops died on that day. Of the Black men, 37 were killed, 155 were wounded, and 116 were reported missing.

Although the Union troops did not take Port Hudson that day, there was no longer any doubt that Black soldiers would perform courageously in battle. The fighting continued. On June 14, approximately 6,000 federal troops attacked, but the Confederates withstood the assault. On June 28, Port Hudson was still under siege, but it was not until July that the Confederates, after hearing of the fall of Vicksburg to Union troops, surrendered Port Hudson. All of the Mississippi River was henceforth under federal control.

At the Port Hudson State Commemorative Area and Museum today six miles of trails show the battlefield and fortifications. The commemorative area consists of 643 acres of paths on rugged terrain. The area includes a hike up a steep slope and approximately one mile of earthworks, where the battle occurred. At the top of the slope, visitors may view the terrain where Black soldiers, for the first time in America, fought in large numbers as members of the U.S. Army. Many Black soldiers who died in the Battle of Port Hudson are buried in a common unmarked grave at Port Hudson, but the exact site of the grave is unknown. A complete tour of the public areas at Port Hudson takes one to three hours, including museum audiovisual presentation and exhibits.

DATE ESTABLISHED:	1863
ADDRESS:	756 W. Plains, Port Hudson Road, Zachary (along US 61, E. Feliciana Parish, about 17–20 miles north of Baton Rouge)
TELEPHONE:	(504) 654-3775
VISITING HOURS:	Museum, Wed.–Sun. 9–5; grounds, Apr. 1–Sept. 30, Wed.–Sun. 9–7; grounds, Oct. 1–Mar. 31, Wed.–Sun. 9–5; closed Mon., Tues., Thanksgiving, Christmas, New Year's Day
FEES:	Adults, $2; children 12 and under, free; senior citizens over 65, free
SOURCES:	Kay Harrison, tour coordinator, and Fleurette Aucoin, tour guide, Lagniappe Tours, Foundation for Historical Louisiana, Inc. NRHPINF. Telephone conversation Dec. 5, 1994, Kathy Tarver, interpretive park ranger, Port Hudson Battlefield. *The Civil War Almanac,* 147–9, 153, 157, 161. *The Flavor of Louisiana—Baton Rouge: A Visitor's Guide,* 22. *National Register of Historic Places,* 278. *The Smithsonian Guide to Historic America: The Deep South,* 89.

Notes

1. *In Chains to Louisiana: Solomon Northup's Story,* adapted by Michael Knight, New York: Dutton, 1971, 69.

2. *In Chains to Louisiana,* 70.

Works Consulted

African Americans: Voices of Triumph. Vol. 1, *Perseverance.* Alexandria, Va.: Time-Life, 1993.

American Negro Art. Cedric Dover. New York: New York Graphic Soc., 1960.

Avoyelles Homes: A History of Avoyelles Parish as Seen through Its Architecture. Randy P. De Cuir, ed. Marksville, La.: Gremillion, 1975.

The Civil War Almanac. John S. Bowman, ed. New York: World Almanac/Bison, 1983.

The Flavor of Louisiana—Baton Rouge: A Visitor's Guide, 1988–1989. Baton Rouge: Baton Rouge Area Convention and Visitor's Bureau.

Greater New Orleans Black Tourism Center Points of Interest. New Orleans: Greater New Orleans Black Tourism Network, 1991.

In Chains to Louisiana: Solomon Northup's Story. Adapted by Michael Knight. New York: Baron/Dutton, 1971.

"Laurel Valley Village: A Rural Life Sugar Plantation Museum." Thibodaux, La.: Friends of Laurel Valley Village. [manuscript]

The LSU Rural Life Museum. Baton Rouge: LSU Public Relations, 1989.

National Register of Historic Places. Washington, D.C.: National Park Service, 1976.

Negro Soldiers in the Battle of New Orleans. New Orleans: Battle of New Orleans 150th Anniversary Committee of Louisiana and the Eastern National Park Association, 1965.

"Pinkie Gordon Lane Named Poet Laureate." Sarah Sue Goldsmith. The Baton Rouge *Morning Advocate,* 30 July 1989.

The Shaping of Black America. Lerone Bennett Jr. New York: Penguin, 1993.

"Slave Cabins Added to Oakley Exhibit." James Minton. The Baton Rouge *Morning Advocate,* 30 May 1989.

The Smithsonian Guide to Historic America: The Deep South. William Bryant Logan and Vance Muse. New York: Stewart, Tabori, & Chang, 1989.

Southern University and A & M College Catalog. Baton Rouge: The University, Oct. 1987.

Southern University, Baton Rouge Louisiana. Julie R. Wessinger and others, eds. Baton Rouge: Southern University Business and Industry Cluster, n.d.

Twelve Years a Slave. Solomon Northup. 1853. Sue Eakin and Joseph Logsdon, eds. Baton Rouge: Louisiana State University, 1968.

Maryland

●●●●●●●●●●●

Annapolis

Banneker-Douglass Museum

The Mt. Moriah congregation was organized in 1803 by a group of free Black people. Their church was built in 1874. The brick two and one-half–story structure has High Victorian architectural elements that include small turrets and an entrance beneath a pointed arch. This historic building is listed on the *National Register of Historic Places.*

The Banneker-Douglass Museum, housed in the old Mt. Moriah Church, took its name from two African Americans of notable achievement—Benjamin Banneker (1731–1806) and Frederick Douglass (1818–1895)—both of whom were born in Maryland. Banneker was born free near Ellicott's Lower Mills, Maryland. Although he worked as a tobacco farmer, he also managed to find time to read and study, and he acquired extensive knowledge of mathematics and science. Between 1791 and 1802 Banneker published six almanacs that were widely distributed. In 1791 he served as an assistant to Major Andrew Ellicott in surveying boundaries for the new site that would become the District of Columbia. Banneker attended the Mount Gilboa Church in Oella, Maryland (see the listing for Mount Gilboa Church).

Twelve years after Banneker died, Frederick Bailey (later Douglass) was born in slavery on a Maryland Plantation, where he grew up on the banks of the Tuckahoe Creek. Although he experienced hardship and witnessed brutality to slaves, the young Frederick also had opportunities to explore his physical surroundings and to reflect on his condition as a slave. When Frederick was eight years old he was sent to Baltimore to care for Tommy, the two-year-old son of Hugh and Sophia Auld. Douglass learned to read and write in Baltimore. He also learned about abolitionists and freedom, and he began to plan his escape, which was accomplished in 1838. For years he lived in Rochester, New York, where he founded a newspaper, the *North Star* (later renamed *Frederick Douglass's Paper*). A man of many achievements, Douglass was best known as one of the nineteenth century's most effective abolitionists; he was a powerful speaker who moved audiences deeply with his descriptions of slavery. After emancipation Douglass achieved still more fame as he worked for civil rights and women's suffrage. (For more information about Douglass, read the listings Frederick Douglass National Historic Site and Frederick Douglass Museum and Hall of Fame for Caring in the Washington, D.C., section and Frederick Douglass Gravesite and Susan B. Anthony House in Rochester, New York).

The Banneker-Douglass Museum is a state-operated museum. The museum displays document the Black experience in the history of Maryland as well as the Black experience on a national and international basis.

DATE BUILT: 1874

ADDRESS: 84 Franklin Street, Annapolis

TELEPHONE: (410) 974-2893

VISITING HOURS: Tues.–Fri. 10–3; Sat. 12–4; closed Sun.–Mon., Thanksgiving, Christmas, Easter, July 4, Labor Day

SOURCES: Barbara Jackson, former acting director, Banneker-Douglass Museum. Madelon N. McDonald, Historic Annapolis, Inc. Telephone conversation Dec. 1, 1994, Karen Eldridge, office manager, Banneker-Douglass Museum. *Frederick Douglass*. The Academic American Encyclopedia.

Baltimore

Baltimore City Life Museums 1840 House

The 1840 House (so-named because its programs focus on the social history of Baltimore of the 1840s) is a part of the Baltimore City Life Museums, the city's museums devoted exclusively to showing how people lived in the past. The three-story house once was home to a white wheelwright, John Hutchinson, his wife, Mary Ann, their three daughters, a grocer, two boarders, and a free Black servant and her child.

In portraying the emerging middle class, the hands-on museum displays examples of African American life in urban Baltimore. Many free Black people lived in Baltimore in the 1840s, and they frequently had conflicts with Irish immigrants over jobs. Black stevedores on the docks often had to protect themselves from gangs of immigrants who wanted their jobs. Professional playwrights have turned the stories of their lives into living-history dramas portrayed in 1840 House. A primary program, *Steps in Time: Scenes from 1840 Baltimore,* highlights race relations before the Civil War. As visitors move through the house, they see small dramas in the rooms that tell about the way of life of the occupants of the house. For example, in the dark basement kitchen we see Sarah West (Sarah was a free African American who actually was a domestic worker for the Hutchinsons) mediate an argument between her fiancé, who has lost his job to an Irish immigrant, and her brother, who is a business success. Based on extensive research on nineteenth-century Baltimore, the scenes include such issues as abolition, colonization, and other concerns of Black people in that period.

The 1840 House is one of four structures on the main campus of the Baltimore City Life Museums. Another center, the Courtyard Gallery, also has live theater—*Heroes Like You*—that portrays the struggles of African Americans as they sought to overcome barriers in the workplaces of Baltimore. The chronologically organized exhibits, geared to school-aged children from the inner city, move from the late nineteenth century to the twentieth century showing a variety of jobs from the domestic to the industrial and clerical.

DATE ESTABLISHED: House, 1796; museum, 1985

ADDRESS: 800 E. Lombard Street, Baltimore

TELEPHONE: (410) 396-3279

VISITING HOURS: Tues.–Sat. 10–5, Sun. noon–5; reservations encouraged for performances; closed Mon., Christmas, New Year's, Easter

FEES: One admission fee to 4 museum sites: adults, $5; children 4–18, $3.50; children under 4, free

SOURCES: Dale Jones, director of education, Baltimore City Life Museums. Telephone conversation Dec. 2, 1994, Andrew Reiner, public relations manager, Baltimore City Life Museums. "Baltimore's Magical History Tour." "Steps in Time: Drama at 1840 House Alters Its Route through Past."

Great Blacks in Wax Museum

The Great Blacks in Wax Museum is the first in the United States to display more than one hundred wax figures of Black people in history in a permanent museum collection. Located in a renovated fire station, the museum dramatically depicts figures and scenes showing the achievements and contributions of African Americans.

Professionally designed displays show the Black struggle from early history through the Civil Rights Movement. The figure of Hannibal astride an elephant greets visitors in the lobby. Other displays show outstanding Black women including Ida Wells-Barnett, the courageous writer who led a crusade against lynching, and Mary Church Terrell, an organizer of the Women's Club movement. In medicine the figure of Dr. Charles Drew represents the doctor's achievement in developing a method of separating blood from plasma, making blood transfusions possible.

Familiar leaders shown include Booker T. Washington, Dr. Martin Luther King Jr., and Malcolm X. Included also are Dr. Carter G. Woodson, the outstanding pioneer Black historian, Bessie Coleman, the first Black licensed pilot in the United States, and the legendary railroad worker John Henry.

A segregation scene depicts a Black woman at a water fountain labeled "Colored." One showcase displays items invented by, or improved upon, by Black Americans. The museum's displays are designed to instill a sense of pride and to provide role models for young people.

DATE ESTABLISHED: 1983

ADDRESS: 1601 E. North Avenue, Baltimore

TELEPHONE: (410) 563-3404

VISITING HOURS: June–Aug., Mon.–Sat. 9–6; Sept.–May, same hours but closed Mon.

FEES: Adults, $5.50; senior citizens and college students with ID, $5; youth 12–17, $3.50; children 2–11, $3; children under 2, free

SOURCES: D. Tulani Salahu-Din, Great Blacks in Wax Museum. Telephone conversation July 30, 1995, Jennifer West, receptionist, Great Blacks in Wax Museum. *The Great Blacks in Wax Museum Newsletter.*

Frances Ellen Harper School

The Frances Ellen Harper School is a brick structure in a traditionally Black neighborhood surrounded by nineteenth-century townhouses. It was built for Black students and staffed by Black teachers.

In 1867 the city of Baltimore began to provide for the education of African American students, but they had to attend school in rented buildings or in old buildings no longer needed for white children. When Colored School #9 opened in 1889 in this brick building, it was a pleasant contrast to the former makeshift surroundings.

Although the school has had several names over the years, eventually it was named for Frances Ellen Watkins Harper. Frances Ellen Watkins Harper (1825–1911) was a writer and a widely respected activist who worked in the antislavery movement, the Reconstruction period struggle for civil rights, and the universal suffrage movement. Born Frances Ellen Watkins in Baltimore, Maryland, she was an only child whose mother died before Frances was three years old. She was raised by her aunt. Until the age of thirteen, Frances attended a school for free Black children in Baltimore that was operated by her uncle, the Reverend William Watkins. At the age of thirteen she was sent to work for a living in a household where she learned sewing and child care. When she had some leisure time, she read books and began to write poetry, some of which was published in newspapers.

In 1851 Frances Watkins moved to Ohio and taught school there; after a short period, however, she moved to Philadelphia. There, her difficulties in teaching fifty-three unruly children led her to realize that teaching was not her true calling. Philadelphia was a center of underground railroad activity, and Frances Watkins began to learn firsthand there about the terrible effects of slavery. She was aware of passage of the 1850 Fugitive Slave Law that made it easier for slaveowners to capture runaway slaves. She read and was deeply moved by Solomon Northup's story of his twelve years in slavery (see the Bunkie, Louisiana, listing for the Edwin Epps House). One incident, however, impelled Watkins to devote her life to the antislavery cause. In 1853 the state of Maryland enacted a law providing that any free Black person from the North who entered Maryland would be imprisoned and sold into slavery. A Black man, unaware of the law, entered Maryland and was captured and sold into slavery; he died soon after from harsh treatment. On hearing about this tragedy, Watkins pledged to spend her life working to end slavery. Soon she was recognized as one of the most effective speakers on the antislavery meeting circuit.

When white abolitionist John Brown was jailed for leading a raid on the arsenal at Harpers Ferry, Frances Harper wrote a letter to Brown's wife to express sympathy, and she stayed for two weeks with Mrs. Brown who was awaiting the execution of her husband. (For additional information about John Brown read listings for the Jefferson County Courthouse in Charleston, West Virginia; Harpers Ferry National Historic Park in Harpers Ferry, West Virginia; John Brown Farm New York State Historic Site in Lake Placid, New York; John Brown Statue in Kansas City, Kansas; and John Brown Memorial State Park in Osawatomie, Kansas.)

Frances Ellen Watkins married Fenton Harper in 1860, but he died four years later. Unable to forget the work she had started years earlier, she began traveling extensively again, visiting Black communities in all of the southern states except Texas and Arkansas. She visited plantations, constantly observing the plight of the former slaves, and she spoke in churches and schools and lecture halls. When the Civil War ended, Harper continued to speak about the need for African Americans to develop stable families and to grow in wealth and influence. She described the heavy double load of Black women who toiled in the fields, then labored again in the home. Recognizing that racism could not be stopped by a disenfranchised people, Harper worked for ratification of the Fifteenth Amendment (the last of the Reconstruction amendments proposed after the Civil War) that prohibited governments from infringing, on the basis of race, color, or previous condition of servitude, on the right of a citizen to vote. Harper believed that with passage of this amendment, Black citizens would use the ballot to work against racial injustice.

Harper was respected for her work and her lectures were well-received. One listener at the State Street A.M.E. Zion Church in Mobile, Alabama (see the listing for this church in Mobile), gave this description:

> The lecturer was then introduced as Mrs. F. E. W. Harper from Maryland. Without a moment's hesitation she started off in the flow of her discourse, which rolled smoothly and uninterruptedly on for nearly two hours. It was very apparent that it was not a cut and dried speech, for she was as fluent and as felicitous in her allusions to circumstances immediately around her as she was when she rose to a more exalted pitch of laudation of the Union, or of execration of the old slavery system. Her voice was remarkable—as sweet as any woman's voice we ever heard, and so clear and distinct as to pass every syllable to the most distant ear in the house.[1]

Although the interior of the school has been converted into apartments for the elderly, the exterior retains its original appearance as a red-brick, two-story school with a sloped roof. The schoolhouse, which is listed in the *National Register of Historic Places*, is worth driving by because it is one of the few surviving schools in Maryland built for Black students and staffed by Black teachers and because it is a reminder of Frances Ellen Watkins Harper.

DATE BUILT: 1889
ADDRESS: Southwest corner of North Carrollton Avenue and Riggs Road, Baltimore
VISITING HOURS: Interior not accessible to public, visitors may drive by
SOURCES: Telephone conversation Mar. 4, 1994, Joseph Henley Sr., architect, facilities dept., Dept. of Education, Baltimore City. NRHPINF. *The Underground Railroad. When and Where I Enter.*

Henry Lee Moon Library/NAACP National Civil Rights Archives

The National Association for the Advancement of Colored People has a civil rights library and archives at its headquarters building. The library contains papers on microfilm from the civil rights struggle, original papers of local leaders and units involved in front lines of the struggle, and book collections that describe the Civil Rights Movement. The library serves as an educational resource and a focal point to keep alive the message of the Civil Rights Movement.

DATE ESTABLISHED: 1988–1990
ADDRESS: 4805 Mt. Hope Drive, Baltimore
TELEPHONE: (410) 486-9126
VISITING HOURS: By appointment, call in advance
FEES: None
SOURCES: Letter from the NAACP National Civil Rights Archives. Martha Ruff, Librarian. Telephone conversation Mar. 4, 1994, James Murray, archivist.

Morgan State University
James E. Lewis Museum of Art

The James E. Lewis Museum of Art at Morgan State University is housed in a modern building. The collection of European, African, African American, and American art is accessible for viewing by university students and visitors.

DATE ESTABLISHED: 1951; gallery 1960; below-ground section 1970
ADDRESS: Murphy Fine Arts Building, Cold Spring Road and Hillen Road, Baltimore
TELEPHONE: (410) 319-3030
VISITING HOURS: Mon.–Fri. 9–5, Sat.–Sun. by appointment only
FEES: None
SOURCE: Professor James E. Lewis, director, James E. Lewis Museum of Art.

Orchard Street United Methodist Church

A Baltimore resident recently described the restored Orchard Street United Methodist Church building as "Beautiful! A sight to behold." The original church, once called Metropolitan Methodist Episcopal Church, and Sunday School structures were built by African Americans in an area once known as "Scrabbletown."

The church organized in 1825 when a West Indian man, Truman LePratt, began holding prayer meetings in his home. As the group of worshipers grew, LePratt was first to donate money to build a church. LePratt's wife worked for the Moore family, wealthy property owners who gave land to the Black congregation for a church. The congregation built the main church from 1837 to 1839 and a classroom and auditorium building attached to the rear between 1840 and 1853. Unfortunately, there was no legal deed executed in the transaction, and church members had to go to court years later to secure clear title to the property. Misfortune came again as a result of several fires. The smaller Sunday School/auditorium structure was rebuilt in 1879 and 1903, the second church structure was built between 1853 and 1859, and the present spacious church was constructed in 1882.

After the congregation moved away from Orchard Street Church in the 1970s, the building was vacant for two decades. The fine old structure suffered from neglect, deterioration, and vandalism. Community concern, however, impelled rescue efforts; eventually the city of Baltimore, the state of Maryland, the Maryland Historical Trust, and private donors came to the support of the Urban League in its efforts to restore the structure for use as its headquarters and as a museum. November 6, 1992, marked the gala reopening of the historic church. After three years of planning and renovations, the Baltimore Urban League took occupancy of the 22,000-square-foot complex. The organization plans to maintain the structure as a memorial to the heritage of Baltimore's African American community.

DATE BUILT: 1882
ADDRESS: 510 Orchard Street, Baltimore
TELEPHONE: (410) 523-8150
VISITING HOURS: Call to arrange to see the interior
FEES: None
SOURCES: Telephone conversation Mar. 4, 1994, Anne Chase, Urban League. NRHPINF. *Commemorative Booklet for the Restoration and Opening of Orchard Street Church.*

Bowie

Bowie State University

The Baltimore Colored Normal School was established in 1865 to educate teachers for Black schools. In 1908 the school offered its assets to the state of Maryland on the condition that the state would maintain a permanent school for training Black teachers. In response, the state purchased a 187-acre tract near Bowie and began to construct buildings for the school, known in 1908 as the Maryland Normal and Industrial Institute. The college opened in 1911 with fifty-eight students.

Students at the college did their practice teaching in Black elementary schools in Bowie. In 1938 the school began to offer a four-year degree program. Its name was changed to Bowie State College and later to Bowie State University. Maryland's first Black postsecondary school grew from a one-building school to a multimillion dollar racially integrated college that confers liberal arts degrees.

Today the original buildings no longer are standing. Principal buildings include Harriet Tubman Hall, Martin Luther King Arts Center, the Administration Building, and Pullin Library.

DATE ESTABLISHED: 1865
ADDRESS: 13900 Jericho Park Road, Bowie
TELEPHONE: (301) 464-6560
VISITING HOURS: Contact college to arrange a visit Mon.–Fri. 8–6
SOURCES: Susan M. Fitch, historian, The Maryland-National Capital Park and Planning Commission, Riverdale, Maryland, 1989. Telephone conversation Dec. 28, 1994, Herbert Mills, assistant to the registrar, Bowie State University.

Harriet Tubman Birthplace Marker

Harriet Tubman was born in a small cabin on the Brodas Plantation south of Cambridge, Maryland. Only a marker remains to honor the courageous woman who led so many out of slavery to freedom.

Tubman was born around 1820 and named Araminta. She escaped from slavery in 1849 and became a leader among abolitionists, practicing her belief in freedom by returning to the South to help more than 300 slaves escape on the underground railroad. She served as a nurse, laundress, and spy in the Civil War. After the war ended, she settled in Auburn, New York, where she died in 1913.

Although the plantation and its structures no longer exist, a historical marker honors Harriet Tubman at the site of her birthplace. (For additional information on Harriet Tubman, see Auburn, New York.)

ADDRESS: 8 miles south of US 50 on MD 397
SOURCES: *Webster's New Biographical Dictionary,* 1002. *Hippocrene U.S.A. Guide to Black America,* 155.

Columbia

Maryland Museum of African Art

The Maryland Museum of African Art, founded in 1980, is dedicated to promoting a better understanding of traditional African art. Doris H. Ligon, the museum founder, notes that this is the second museum in the United States devoted exclusively to traditional African art and the first of its type started by an African American female. The museum is housed in downtown Columbia, a planned town that grew up around a manor.

Museum offerings include exhibits, lectures, tours, and workshops. Examples of programs presented at the museum include "African Art of Adornment" and "Talking Drums—Art and Culture of West Africa." The museum curator is Dr. Kwaku Ofori-Ansa, who has also served as professor of African Art and Culture in the College of Fine Arts at Howard University, Washington, D.C. Dr. Ofori-Ansa was born in Ghana, West Africa.

DATE ESTABLISHED: 1980
ADDRESS: Oakland Manor, 5430 Vantage Point Road, Columbia
TELEPHONE: (410) 730-7105
VISITING HOURS: Tues.–Fri. 10–4; Sun. 12–4; closed Mon., Sat., and selected holidays, including Christmas and Thanksgiving
FEES: None
SOURCE: Doris H. Ligon, executive director.

Cumberland

African Methodist Episcopal Church

The African Methodist Episcopal Church on Decatur and Frederick Streets stands as a symbol of an early community of free Black people. For many years its members had to sit in the balcony of the Centre Street Methodist Episcopal Church to worship. In 1847 they finally decided to separate from the white congregation and build their own church. Their elected board of trustees, described as "free men of color," bought a lot in Magruder's Addition to Cumberland.

The congregation completed the first church, a plain, brick building, by the end of 1848. They rebuilt and enlarged it twice and then decided to build the present church in 1892 to meet the needs of their growing membership.

The substantial, two-story brick building has a gable roof. Its sanctuary is on the second floor, and there is a meeting room below. The church has several stained glass windows, some with pointed and others with lancet arches. The African Methodist Episcopal Church, now called the Metropolitan A.M.E. Church, is an important part of the history of the free Black people of Cumberland, Maryland.

DATE BUILT: 1892
ADDRESS: 413 Decatur Street, corner of Decatur and Frederick Streets, Cumberland
TELEPHONE: (301) 759-6398
VISITING HOURS: Sun. school, 10; Sun. service, 11
SOURCES: NRHPINF. Telephone conversation July 30, 1995, Garland Kearney, administrative assistant, African Methodist Episcopal Church.

Hollywood

Sotterley Plantation

A surviving slave cabin on Sotterley Plantation, is one of a row that once extended along the road to Sotterley Creek. The slave house, built with early English-construction methods, has a steep-pitched roof with an elegant freestanding brick chimney for the central fireplace. Early English methods of construction were used for the log cabin. A narrow stairway leads upstairs, where there is a shutter window on one side and very small shelves for clothing on the other side. Some of the furniture is authentic. Visitors can look into the cabin but cannot go inside.

The plantation overlooks the Patuxent River. In 1650, Lord Baltimore granted the original tract of land to Thomas Cornwallis. After a 1710 subdivision James Bowles bought part of the land. He began constructing Sotterley Mansion several years later. Established in 1717, this has been the nation's longest continuously operating plantation. Many years ago hogsheads of tobacco were rolled down the road to waiting ships, and imported goods were brought up to the former customs house.

Visitors today may see the slave cabin, mansion, tenant houses, smokehouse, tobacco shed, and barn. The plantation has a list of Black people who lived and worked there. During James Bowles's lifetime, there were forty-one Black people at Sotterley. On the plantation there were free Black people, slaves, indentured servants, and free white people. The African Americans included seventeen field hands and six house servants at the home plantation and eighteen field hands at two other sections of the plantation, one of which was named Hog Neck Quarter. The widowed Mrs. Bowles later married George Plater. A total of four generations of Platers lived at Sotterley (one was the governor of Maryland in 1791). During these years there were sixty-three field hands and house servants at Sotterley.

A Black man, Hilary Kane, worked at Sotterley. A complete history of his family, compiled by Mrs. Agnes Kane Callum, one of Kane's descendants, is included in the document closet at the plantation.

Visitors may view the plantation and learn about its history and those who lived there. School groups enjoy hearing about the mansion's ghost, the secret passage, and pirate attacks that actually happened here.

DATE ESTABLISHED: c1730

ADDRESS: From the center of Hollywood (MD 235 and 245), go south on MD 245 (Sotterley Road) 4–5 miles; follow the signs to the plantation

TELEPHONE: (301) 373-2280

VISITING HOURS: By appointment, Apr.–May, June–Oct., Mon.–Sat. 11–4; closed mid-Dec.–Mar. 31

FEES: Adults, $5; senior citizens, $4; children, $2

SOURCES: Telephone conversation Dec. 6, 1994, Mrs. Elizabeth Harmon, curator, Sotterley Plantation. Donna L. Ely, administrator, Sotterley. Telephone call to site, July 30, 1995. *Sotterley since 1717.*

Oella

Mount Gilboa African Methodist Episcopal Church

According to a plaque on its front gable, Mount Gilboa Church, a small, stone building, dates from 1859. The sanctuary is on the first floor, and space in a high basement is used for Sunday School and social activities.

Mount Gilboa A.M.E. Church has served the same community of Black families since the eighteenth century. The church is significant also for its association with Benjamin Banneker, a Black astronomer/mathematician who was born in 1741 on a farm in Oella, not far from this church. He worshiped at the earlier Mount Gilboa Church on this site and attended school in the same structure.

Banneker published an almanac between 1792 and 1806. He made weather predictions and astronomical calculations for his almanac, having taught himself mathematics and astronomy in the limited free time he had left from his farming duties. The Ellicott brothers, members of a local family prominent in the milling industry, befriended Banneker and shared their science and mathematics books with him. Banneker was hired as a surveyor and worked with the Ellicotts on developing plans for the District of Columbia.

The Ellicott family deeded property to the Black community for the purpose of erecting an African meeting house and schoolhouse. The resulting Mount Gilboa Church is the sole remaining site strongly associated with Benjamin Banneker's life. His one-hundred acre farm at the corner of Oella and Westchester Avenues has been divided into many tracts and has been completely altered, and his house site is not known. Thus, Mount Gilboa Church, where he was a member of the earlier congregation and church, remains as a memorial to a free Black man who was recognized for his work in mathematics and astronomy.

DATE BUILT: 1859
ADDRESS: 2312 Westchester Avenue, Oella
TELEPHONE: (410) 461-7126
VISITING HOURS: Sun. school, 9:30; Sun. service, 11
SOURCES: NRHPINF. Telephone conversation Dec. 28, 1994, Julie De Matteis, librarian, Catonsville Public Library.

Oxon Hill

St. Paul's Methodist Episcopal Church

The congregation of St. Paul's church dates to the 1790s, which would make it the first documented Black congregation in Prince George's County and one of the first in the United States. In 1791, a group of Black people in Oxon Hill built a small preaching house where Ezekiel Cooper preached to the group. The present congregation has its first records in the period immediately following the Civil War, when the Freedmen's Bureau built a school used for both school instruction and church services.

In 1887 minister Daniel Wheeler and trustees purchased a lot a mile from the school and built a small, frame church that was used until 1915. They built the present church in 1915 near the older church. The church is a one and one-half–story frame building with three pointed-arch windows and a small Palladian window in the gable end. The two-story steepled tower rises at the northeast corner of the church. With the exception of upgraded siding, the structure has retained its basic appearance.

St. Paul's Methodist Episcopal Church began its recorded history shortly after the Civil War with a small rural congregation. The church has made a transition to an urban middle-class congregation. Church members may be descendants of the congregation that began worshiping in Oxon Hill in 1791.

DATE ESTABLISHED: Congregation, 1791; church, 1915
ADDRESS: 6634 St. Barnabas Road, Oxon Hill
TELEPHONE: (301) 567-4433
VISITING HOURS: Mon.–Fri. 9–1; Sun. school 10, Sun. service 8, 11:15; call in advance to arrange to see interior
SOURCES: Susan M. Fitch, historian, The Maryland-National Capital Park and Planning Commission, Riverdale, Maryland. Telephone conversation Mar. 13, 1994, Edward Dorsey, St. Paul's Methodist Episcopal Church.

Rockville

Beall Dawson House

The Beall Dawson House, built around 1815 by Upton Beall, still has the original slave quarters above the kitchen. The house was built in two sections, and a staircase (now blocked off) led from the kitchen to the slave quarters. The house and slave quarters are open to the public. Both have period furnishings that show how the residents once lived. The property is operated by the Montgomery County Historical Society.

DATE BUILT:	1815
ADDRESS:	103 W. Montgomery Avenue, Rockville
TELEPHONE:	(301) 762-1492
VISITING HOURS:	Tues.–Sat. 12–4; first Sun. each month 2–5; closed Mon., major holidays, most Sun.
FEES:	Adults, $2; seniors or scholars, $1; members of the Montgomery County Historical Society, free
SOURCES:	Barbara Holzapfel, Beall Dawson House. Telephone conversation June 4, 1994, Bettina Curtis, volunteer docent.

Ruxton

St. John's Church

St. John's Church in Ruxton and the accompanying buildings—the parsonage and the social hall—are examples of buildings associated with Black religious history in Baltimore County. The church building is a modest interpretation of the Gothic revival style with some Queen Anne decorative details. The small frame structure, approximately 36 feet by 21 feet in size, has a sharply pitched gable roof, board-and-batten siding, and lancet-shaped windows. The interior has narrow-board flooring and oak pews.

The site includes two other early structures and a cemetery. The parsonage, believed to date from around 1835 when the first church was built, is a one and one-half–story, stuccoed-stone house. The walls remain intact but the interior was heavily damaged by fire in the 1880s. A third building is a rectangular frame social hall, possibly dating from the 1890s. A cemetery dating from the 1830s lies between the church and the parsonage.

The St. John's congregation, which was formed in the 1830s, acquired the site in 1833. The congregation always was small, and most members of the congregation worked for wealthy white people who had estates and large houses nearby.

The church has a long association with a Black family, the Scott family. In 1858, Minister James Aquilla Scott died at the age of seventy-six while in prayer at the church. His son, James Aquilla Scott II, became the next minister. James Scott II worked also as a blacksmith as his father had done. He bought a slave wife from a landowner to rescue her from a life of abuse. Three generations of Scotts served as trustees of the church.

St. John's congregation built the present church in 1886, locating the 20-foot-by-35-foot frame building on a hill overlooking Lake Roland. The size of the congregation began to decline in the 1950s after transportation patterns changed in the community; other churches were established, and fewer individuals worked as live-in-help in the large houses in Ruxton that bordered the church complex. Eventually the congregation could no longer support a minister. Although the church was closed for a period, it is in use again today.

St. John's Church is an important example of nineteenth-century rural church architecture in Maryland and represents a congregation that formed in the 1830s.

DATE BUILT: Church, 1886; parsonage, c1835
ADDRESS: 7538 Bellona Avenue, Ruxton
VISITING HOURS: Contact the church for time of Sun. service
SOURCE: NRHPINF.

St. Mary's City

Slave Quarters
Mathias de Sousa Monument

St. Mary's City, the first capital of Maryland, was the fourth permanent settlement in British North America. Today the former frontier town is a living-history museum on 800 acres with reconstructed seventeenth-century buildings, a tobacco plantation, and a square-rigged ship. Actual remains of the early seventeenth-century settlers' homes form a layer under the ground of the present historic St. Mary's City.

Two areas are associated with Black history: the slave quarters structure in the Governor's Field Exhibit area (part of an exhibit of a nineteenth-century plantation) and the monument to Mathias de Sousa (located on the bank of St. Mary's River). The monument consists of a large stone placed under a mulberry tree, containing a plaque with the following inscription:

> Mathias de Sousa was the first Black Marylander. Of African and Portuguese descent, he was one of nine indentured servants brought to Maryland by Jesuit missionaries and was on the ARK when Lord Baltimore's expedition arrived in the St. Mary's River in 1634.[2]

De Sousa finished his indenture in four years and became a mariner and fur trader. He went to sea as a merchant in 1641. The following year he became the master of a ketch. De Sousa next moved to St. Johns, where he was the colony's first Black voter. He also served in the 1642 legislative assembly of freemen as the colony's first Black legislator.

DATE ESTABLISHED: 1634
ADDRESS: Off MD 5 in southern Maryland, St. Mary's City
TELEPHONE: (301) 862-0960; (301) 862-0990; public relations, (301) 862-0962
VISITING HOURS: Visitors' Center, weekends Mar. 25–Memorial Day and Labor Day–Nov. 26 10–5; daily 10–5 Memorial Day–Labor Day; closed Thanksgiving, Christmas, and New Year's Day
FEES: Adults, $5; children 6–12, $2; children under 6, free; special rates for groups and schools
SOURCES: Karin B. Stanford, director of public affairs, Historic St. Mary's City. *Historic St. Mary's City Visitor Guide. Mathias de Sousa Memorial.*

Notes

1. William Still, *The Underground Railroad* (reprint, Chicago: Johnson, 1970), 807.

2. Monument inscription reproduced in *Mathias de Sousa Memorial,* St. Mary's City, 1987. [flier]

Works Consulted

The Academic American Encyclopedia. Danbury, Conn.: Grolier, 1993. [electronic version]

"Baltimore's Magical History Tour," *Southern Living* (Feb. 1989).

Commemorative Booklet for the Restoration and Opening of Orchard Street Church. Baltimore: Baltimore Urban League (Nov. 1992).

Frederick Douglass. William S. McFeely. New York: Touchstone/Simon & Schuster, 1991.

The Great Blacks in Wax Museum Newsletter 1 (Aug. 1989), 1.

Hippocrene U.S.A. Guide to Black America: A Directory of Historic and Cultural Sites Relating to Black America. Marcella Thum. New York: Hippocrene, 1992.

Mathias de Sousa Memorial. Maryland Department of Economic and Community Development. [flier]

St. Mary's City Visitor Guide. Maryland Department of Economic and Community Development, Mar. 1987. [pamphlet]

"Steps in Time: Drama at 1840 House Alters Its Route through Past." Michael Anft. Baltimore *Evening Sun,* 11 Feb. 1989, 1D.

Sotterley since 1717. Hollywood, Md.: Sotterley Mansion Foundation, Inc. [brochure]

The Underground Railroad. William Still. 1872. Reprint, Chicago: Johnson, 1970.

Webster's New Biographical Dictionary. Springfield, Mass.: Merriam-Webster, 1988.

When and Where I Enter: The Impact of Black Women on Race and Sex in America. Paula Giddings. New York: Morrow, 1984; New York: Bantam, 1988.

Mississippi

Calhoun County

Memorial Garden Cemetery and Historical Marker

A historical marker at this site states: "This is the resting place of freed Black people and their descendants. The members of the Hawkins, Pearson, Reese, Steen and Shipp families established the Mt. Pleasant Church, Bryant School, a cotton gin, grist mill and a blacksmith shop in Calhoun County."

A Black community in Paris, Mississippi, once existed nearby and not far from Water Valley, Mississippi. The families of the community were slaves who labored in the cotton fields, some dreaming of freedom as they worked. Although each owner in the region had a whipping post, one man, in spite of the threat of flogging, managed to escape on his second attempt.

One of the slaves was permitted to work for pay. After emancipation he bought land with money he had saved. This was the start of the new community. Families built a church, a school, a gin, and a blacksmith shop; they began to raise sheep, primarily for wool and hides. The women carded and spun the wool into thread and knit wool socks for the men and cotton stockings for themselves and the children.

The church and Bryant School were about 1,000 feet from each other, and the cemetery was about one-half mile from the church and school. The men used to make the coffins and carry the deceased from the church to the cemetery. Family members of every deceased person had a marker made as soon as possible after death. Years later the children, proud of their heritage, often would take noon recess time to run to the cemetery to read the different markers.

Some Bryant School graduates attended Mississippi Industrial College in Holly Springs, Mississippi (see that listing), but usually only for just a portion of the term because they couldn't afford to spend more time away from the land. Then, as the land became impoverished, the parents began an exodus, seeking better opportunities for themselves and their children. Soon there were too few children left in the school to justify paying a teacher, and there were too few remaining in the congregation to support the church. Finally, the town was deserted.

Ownership of the land passed into new hands, and the land including the cemetery was converted to cattle pasture. Years later, when descendants of the original families returned to visit the cemetery, they had to crawl through a barbed wire fence only to find that many of the markers had been overturned and broken. Many older members of the families whose relatives were buried there agonized for the rest of their lives over this situation.

At last, family members from Detroit began to organize efforts to reclaim the cemetery. They raised funds, sought legal assistance, and finally saw the cemetery designated as a Mississippi historic site. They commented, "We believe that is as it should be in honor and memory of the people who lived there as slaves until the bells of freedom rang. They built a community with a church and a school. Their great-great-grandchildren are now participating in every phase of honorable life."[1]

The marker is a tribute to a Black family that has sought to preserve its cemetery and its history. Descendents of the original family still visit the site, where a marker reads, "Former Mt. Pleasant C.M.E. Church 1863–1926, Memorial Garden, In Memory of our loved ones whose remains lie here. H. P. R. S. S. Family Org. 1981."

DATE ESTABLISHED: Shortly after the Civil War

ADDRESS: Near town of Paris, vicinity of Water Valley (from Water Valley take MS 315 east to Hawkins Crossing and Liberty Street; turn right; approximately 3 miles to the historic marker; go up the hill to the cemetery site)

VISITING HOURS: Daily

SOURCES: Mrs. Essie Kennedy of Detroit, Michigan, descendant of the original Shipp family of Paris, Mississippi. Denise Miller, museum secretary, State Historical Museum, Mississippi Department of Archives and History.

Clarksdale

Delta Blues Museum

The Delta Blues Museum is located in the main library building, the Carnegie Public Library, in downtown Clarksdale. Visitors have access to videotapes, slide-and-sound programs, photographs, recordings, books, performances, memorabilia, archives, and other sources of information about the blues. The Carnegie Public Library Board of Trustees established the Blues Museum in 1979 for the purpose of making this type of historical material accessible to the public. The museum attempts to increase understanding and appreciation of the blues and to show its influence on jazz, country, rock and roll, and popular music in general.

The blues, one of America's unique music forms, had its birth in the Mississippi Delta. Clarksdale and Coahoma County were home to many famed blues musicians, including W. C. Handy, Muddy Waters, Howlin' Wolf, John Lee Hooker, and others. Muddy Waters (born McKinley Morganfield in 1915) grew up on the Stovall Plantation near Clarksdale and later moved to Chicago. He died in 1983. W. C. Handy (1873–1958) lived on Issaquena Street in Clarksdale (*see also* Florence, Alabama, W. C. Handy Birthplace, and Memphis, Tennessee, Beale Street Historic District).

DATE BUILT: Library, 1914; museum, 1979

ADDRESS: Carnegie Public Library, 114 Delta Avenue, Clarksdale

TELEPHONE: (601) 624-4461

VISITING HOURS: Mon.–Fri. 9–5

FEES: None

SOURCES: Sid F. Graves Jr., director. *Delta Blues Museum.* Denise Miller, Mississippi Department of Archives and History.

Corinth

Corinth National Cemetery

African American men from the 14th, 40th, 106th, 108th, and 111th Colored Infantry regiments are among the 6,000 Civil War soldiers buried at Corinth National Cemetery.

On April 11, 1862, Union troops began to marshal forces to push toward the Confederates at Corinth, Mississippi, a town located at the junction of two important railroads along which Confederate soldiers and their supplies moved. By May 22, skirmishes flared between the federal forces led by General Henry Halleck and the Confederate troops commanded by General Pierre Beauregard.

On May 30, Union troops entered Corinth and took more than 2,000 prisoners. During the battle, the Confederates destroyed much of the valuable property in the city. By October fierce fighting was taking place again in Corinth. On October 4, in the Battle of Corinth, Van Dorn's Confederate troops mounted an intense offensive against General Rosecrans's federal troops. But in the end, the Southern troops were forced to retreat before nightfall.

The entire town of Corinth was a battlefield. Today, there is no Visitors Center or ranger on duty at this site, but the Corinth Chamber of Commerce will provide a map with battle areas marked. Visitors provide their own self-driving tours following markers along the way that tell the history of individual locations. There is an original earthen fort with a rifle pit at Robinette, which was part of the battlefield.

DATE ESTABLISHED: Civil War era

ADDRESS: 1551 Horton Street, Corinth (battlefield, crossroads of US 72 and US 45)

TELEPHONE: (601) 286-5782

VISITING HOURS: Corinth National Cemetery, Mon.–Fri. 8–5; gates open 24 hours

SOURCES: Telephone conversation Mar. 31, 1994, Tom Shillings, caretaker, Corinth National Cemetery. *The Civil War Almanac,* 95, 100, 101, 115. *Hippocrene U.S.A. Guide to Black America,* 188.

Greenwood

Cottonlandia Museum

Black reunion groups are beginning to hear about Cottonlandia, and some of them tour this museum, showing the younger generations a way of life that their parents and grandparents once knew in Mississippi. Between 1910 and 1920 the region's farms were equally divided between Black and white ownership, and the implements seen at Cottonlandia could have been used by farmers of either group. Visitors see mule-drawn farm implements such as plows, harrows, disks, seeders, and planters. Between 1880 and 1920 two photographers roamed the Delta, taking photographs of cottonfields and all aspects of growing and processing cotton and the steamboats that transported it. Many of the twenty Couvert and Moore photographs displayed in Cottonlandia show the Black workers who were a part of this process. There is a souvenir and gift shop, and the bookstore has a good selection of Black history books.

ADDRESS: Greenwood (2¾ miles west on US 82W bypass)
TELEPHONE: (601) 453-0925
VISITING HOURS: Mon.–Fri. 9–5, Sat.–Sun. 2–5
FEES: Adults, $2.50; children, $.50
SOURCE: Telephone conversation Mar. 26, 1994, Peggy McCormick, executive director, Cottonlandia.

Florewood River Plantation State Park

The Florewood River Plantation is a re-creation of 1850s plantation life in the Mississippi Delta, which was populated in that era by small farmers, entrepreneurs, and a few large planters. Slaves worked the soil and provided the domestic labor. In 1972 the 1,000-acre Florewood River Plantation was deeded to the state of Mississippi to become a park administered by the Department of Natural Resources.

On the re-created plantation, the cookhouse shows the working environment of the slave who served as cook for the "big house." Food generally was kept under lock and key, but the cook was held in relatively high esteem and trusted with the keys to the food bins. The cookhouse at Florewood, as on many other plantations, was located in a building adjacent to the big house. This separation minimized heat in the big house and reduced the risk of fires to it. At Florewood Plantation the cookhouse has a collection of period cooking utensils. The cook was skilled not only in preparing standard meals but also in preparing intricate pastries and desserts, wild game, and foods that required canning, salt curing, smoking, and drying.

The plantation contains a laundry house, where slaves boiled clothing in large black wash pots or used scrub boards along with soap made from animal fat and lye. Visitors to Florewood can view some of the domestic servants' living quarters. The bed in the servant's house has rope as a support for the straw-and-cornshuck mattresses.

The communal kitchen/nursery shows how meals for slave workers were prepared in the area of the slave quarters. Young children often were cared for in a setting near the work sites or the communal kitchen.

A double house divided by a wall provided living quarters for two slave families. The slave house has pine floors and contains beds, pallets, primitive tables, utensils, and wood-burning fireplaces.

Children especially will enjoy exploring Florewood's thirty-one interesting areas. The domestic servants' quarters, double slave house, cookhouse, laundry house, communal kitchen/nursery, and slave driver's house are most relevant to African American history because Black people lived in or worked at sites such as these. Other areas of interest include the planter's mansion, the tutor's residence, the poultry house (where children can feed the pigeons, chickens, and peacocks), the church/school, the blacksmith shop, the livestock shed (where children may pet the goats), and the cotton field, where visitors can pick cotton in season.

DATE ESTABLISHED: Museum, 1976
ADDRESS: Fort Loring Road (2 miles west of Greenwood off US 82), Greenwood
TELEPHONE: (601) 455-3821
VISITING HOURS: Mar.–early Nov., Tues.–Sat. 9–12 and 1–5, Sun. 1–5; tours every 30 minutes; Dec.–Feb., same visiting hours but tours every hour through the "Big House" only; closed Mon., New Year's Day, Thanksgiving, Christmas
FEES: Adults, $3.50; children 5–18, $2.50; children under 5, free; senior citizens, $3
SOURCES: Nettie Williams, clerk, Florewood River Plantation State Park. Telephone conversation Dec. 29, 1993, Bonita Staten, interpreter.

Holly Springs

Asbury United Methodist Church

In 1866 before Rust College was formally established in its own buildings in Holly Springs, classes met here at the site of the original Asbury Church. Reverend A. C. McDonald of the Freedmen's Aid Society and Reverend Moses Adams, a local minister, taught the first classes in the first church on this site. By 1870 the school was chartered as Shaw University and had moved to its own site in Holly Springs.

The present church, constructed about 1891, has a sanctuary with a divided chancel and eighteen pews.

DATE ESTABLISHED: 1866; building, c1891
ADDRESS: 225 W. College Drive, Holly Springs
TELEPHONE: (601) 252-1766
VISITING HOURS: Mon.–Sat.; contact church office about visiting hours
FEES: None
SOURCES: Pastor F. H. Brown, Asbury United Methodist Church. Information from state historical marker. Denise Miller, museum secretary, State Historical Museum, Mississippi Department of Archives and History.

Mississippi Industrial College Historic District

Mississippi Industrial College was established in 1905 by the Colored Methodist Episcopal Church (now named the Christian Methodist Episcopal Church) as an educational institution for Black students. Its original mission was the education of students from preschool age through college. Bishop Elias Cottrell (1855–1937), a prominent theologian of the C.M.E. Church, helped to found the college.

Upper-level courses first included theology, vocational subjects, and music. Later, the college added arts and sciences, business management, and teacher training. During the World War II teacher shortage, education students were able to earn college credits by living and teaching for a month in a rural community.

In 1903 the citizens of Holly Springs donated 120 acres to the school. An existing antebellum structure apparently was incorporated in 1905 into the Greek revival building called Catherine Hall. The Mississippi Industrial College Historic District consists of five buildings, four of which reflect the period from 1905 to 1923. The five historic buildings are Catherine Hall, 1905; Washington Hall, 1910; Carnegie Auditorium, 1923; Hammond Hall, 1907; and Davis Hall, 1950. Carnegie Auditorium, which seats 2,000, remains the largest auditorium space in Mississippi constructed by and for Black people.

Mississippi Industrial College closed in 1982, but the buildings are easily visible from the street.

DATE BUILT: 1905
ADDRESS: Memphis Street, Holly Springs
VISITING HOURS: Closed, but visitors can walk or drive by
SOURCES: NRHPINF. Telephone call Dec. 29, 1994, Rust College.

Rust College
Oakview Mansion

When Rust College was founded in 1866, it was the first college established by the Methodist Episcopal Church and Mississippi's first Black "normal institute." During Reconstruction, the Freedmen's Aid Bureau, a part of the Methodist Episcopal Church North, took on the responsibility of preparing former slaves for freedom. This college was the bureau's earliest effort to educate Black children and prepare Black teachers.

The founders, missionaries from the North, opened a school in Asbury Methodist Episcopal Church. They accepted both adults and children, instructing them in elementary subjects. The first building on the present campus was erected a year later.

The school was chartered as Shaw University in 1870; however, in 1892 its name was changed to Rust University to avoid confusion with another Shaw University. The name honored Richard Sutton Rust, a Methodist clergyman, educator, abolitionist, and secretary of the Freedmen's Aid Bureau. Rust College started with an elementary school curriculum reflecting the needs of newly freed slaves; later it added high school and college courses. The school regarded it as a milestone when two students graduated from the college department in 1878, twelve years after the opening of the school.

During the first decades after the Civil War, Black colleges traditionally were led by white presidents. It was not until 1920 that Rust University appointed its first African American president, Dr. M. S. Davage. The next two presidents were Rust graduates. By 1901, 132 male students and 127 female students were enrolled. In the early years many Rust students completed only their elementary or secondary studies. By 1930, however, public schools for African American students had become more widespread. The need for private schools decreased, and Rust's grade school was discontinued in that year.

More than 5,000 students have graduated from the college department. One of Rust's graduates was Kate Price, mother of renowned opera singer Leontyne Price. To honor her mother and to repay a debt of gratitude for the inspiration her mother gave her, Leontyne Price gave a concert at Rust, raising $50,000 for the college. The artist's portrait hangs in the library named in her honor.

Rust College is located in Holly Springs, on a 120-acre campus in the northwestern part of Mississippi. Oakview Mansion, a one and one-half–story brick cottage, stands on a site where slaves once were auctioned. One of Mississippi's earliest buildings associated with the education of Black students, Oakview is believed to have been built as a kitchen house for a plantation. The outbreak of the Civil War halted construction of the plantation's main house and other buildings.

Oakview Mansion formerly housed the infirmary and administrative offices. The house was renovated in 1985 to house female students. The mansion, listed in the *National Register of Historic Places,* is the only nineteenth-century building on campus.

DATE ESTABLISHED:	College, 1866; Oakview Mansion, c1860
ADDRESS:	150 E. Rust Avenue (US 78 and MS 7), Holly Springs
TELEPHONE:	(601) 252-4661
VISITING HOURS:	Mon.–Fri. 9–5
SOURCES:	Rust College General Catalog. State historical marker. *Encyclopedia of Mississippi History.* Mississippi Department of Archives and History.

Jackson

Farish Street Neighborhood Historic District

The Farish Street historic district consists of more than 800 buildings in a 125-acre area, the largest economically independent Black community in Mississippi. Many outstanding African American professionals, business leaders, and artisans lived in the community and owned shops here. Black artisans constructed many of the buildings in the district. Robert Rhodes built the stucco cottages on Cohea and Blair Streets, and contractor George Thomas built many buildings throughout the city. Reverend Scott constructed the Scott Building at 705 North Farish Street to house his printing company. Later, his family moved to Atlanta, where they started the Black daily newspaper *The Atlanta Daily World.*

Most of the houses are one-story frame structures, while most of the commercial buildings are brick, one- or two-story structures. Much of the historic area belonged to large estates before the Civil War, and the houses at 154 Monument Street and 208 East Cohea Street may have been built before the Civil War. They appear to be too substantial to have been slave houses and may have belonged to free Black families or families associated with the estates.

By the 1890s the area was segregated. African Americans had begun to purchase homes and establish businesses. Dr. Sidney Redmond of 229 East Church Street, a prosperous African American resident, was president of one of Jackson's two Black banks, a stockholder in several white-controlled businesses, and chairman for twenty-four years of the state Republican Executive Committee. He was president of the Mississippi Medical and Surgical Association and a delegate to the 1919 Pan-African Congress.

The commercial brick buildings that line Farish Street, later known as Beale Street, housed many successful businesses. The narrow streets and the mixture of commercial buildings create an early twentieth-century atmosphere that no longer exists in Jackson's other commercial areas.

DATE BUILT: c1860–1940
ADDRESS: Roughly bounded by Amite, Lamar, Mill, and Fortification Streets, Jackson
VISITING HOURS: Both public and private buildings; visitors may drive by
SOURCES: NRHPINF. Mississippi Department of Archives and History.

Jackson State University
Ayer Hall

Jackson State College was established in Natchez after the Civil War. In 1877 the American Baptist Home Missionary Society of New York authorized the establishment of a school in the Mississippi Valley. The school, named Natchez Seminary, was to train Black teachers and ministers and to develop leadership within the Black community.

By 1882, larger accommodations were needed. The society purchased fifty-two acres in Jackson, a more centrally located area within the state. In 1892, as African Americans began to move to new areas of the city, the college responded to the new population trends by buying the present site. Ayer Hall, constructed in 1903, was the first academic building on the Jackson College campus and is the only structure still standing from the early period of what is now Jackson State University. It replaced temporary facilities used until that time.

The American Baptist Home Missionary Society was beset by financial problems and discontinued operating Jackson College. Community leaders, however, acted to save the university, and the state legislature voted to make the college a training school for Black teachers. Today, Jackson State University is one of Mississippi's eight state-operated institutions of higher education.

Ayer Hall originally served as a men's dormitory but has housed classrooms, a chapel, the president's and dean's quarters, and other university departments over the years. The centrally located brick building, now painted white, overlooks a shaded plaza. The building originally contained three stories, but the third story was removed following severe fire damage in 1938.

In 1970 Jackson State University became the focus of national attention when city and state police fired round after round of bullets into Alexander Hall, the women's dormitory. Twelve students were wounded, and a college student and a high school student were killed. Ongoing antiwar protests had been taking place at the university, and police were called after a report of sniper fire. They surrounded the women's dormitory and opened fire after angry students confronted them. Although relatives of the victims sought damages, the Supreme Court in 1975 dismissed the case on grounds of sovereign immunity, a principle by which governmental bodies and their agents are exempt from legal punishment (including civil lawsuits) and free from most local laws unless they consent to be sued or subject to such laws.

DATE BUILT: 1877; present site, 1902–1903

ADDRESS: Institute for Black Studies, 1400 Lynch Street, Jackson

TELEPHONE: Main office, (601) 968-2100; Ms. Jacqueline Magee, (601) 968-2911; Mr. Larry Belton, (601) 968-2912; Ms. Linda Rush, (601) 968-2914

VISITING HOURS: Contact one of the people listed above to arrange a visit

SOURCES: NRHPINF. Telephone conversation Dec. 28, 1994, Ganon Coates, work study program student, Jackson State University. Denise Miller, Mississippi Department of Archives and History. *Historic Landmarks of Black America,* 176.

Old Capitol Restoration

The Old Capitol, considered one of America's most outstanding examples of the Greek revival style of architecture, has a variety of associations with Black history. The passage of the Ordinance of Secession took place in this building. Years later, eighteen African Americans were among the ninety-seven delegates to the Constitutional Convention of 1868, which conservative newspapers called the "Black and Tan Convention." At this convention, in a hotly contested vote, the Constitution of 1868 that attempted to disenfranchise ex-Confederates, was at first defeated. A second vote in 1869 eliminated the clause regarding the ex-Confederates, and the Constitution was ratified.

Under the provisions of the new Constitution, all men, including Black men, were to be equal in the right to life, liberty, and the pursuit of happiness. However, in 1868, a writer in the *Vicksburg Daily Times* protested, maintaining that white men should stand by their own race in the contest to determine whether Mississippi would be ruled by "Negroes and Radicals" or by white men. "If there is a white man who refuses to affiliate with his own race, in maintaining the rightful supremacy of white men in the South, we have no use for that man."[2]

The Old Capitol is significant in Black history because this struggle, reflected in the Constitutional Convention of 1868 held in this building, was the beginning of decades-long efforts of white Mississippians to regain economic and social control over African Americans. The racist practices established at that time lasted an entire century.

The South's first comprehensive and permanent exhibit on the Civil Rights Movement is installed at this site. The exhibit describes slavery, Reconstruction, and the Jim Crow era. The focus is on the periods of resistance to integration (1954–1961), confrontation (1961–1964), and compliance (1964–1970). As visitors reach a certain point in the exhibit, a television monitor turns on and shows twelve minutes of footage on the Civil Rights Movement. The remainder of the story is told through memorabilia—banners, remnants from bombed buildings, a voting booth, and a charred cross. The site is listed in the *National Register of Historic Places.*

DATE ESTABLISHED:	1839
ADDRESS:	100 S. State Street, Jackson
TELEPHONE:	(601) 359-6920
VISITING HOURS:	Mon.–Fri. 8–5, Sat. 9:30–4:30, Sun. 12:30–4:30; closed major holidays
FEES:	None
SOURCES:	Denise Miller, Mississippi Department of Archives and History. Brochure from the Mississippi State Historical Museum with exhibit notes.

Smith Robertson Elementary School

The Smith Robertson Elementary School is located on the site of Jackson's first public school building for African American students. It is considered the "mother school" for Jackson's Black community. A distinguished graduate of the school is the well-known author Richard Wright.

The first school was a wood-frame building erected in 1894. Before it was built, Jackson's Black children, if they attended school at all, attended church schools or learned through informal arrangements made by their families. The school originated with Smith Robertson, born a slave in Fayette, Alabama, in 1840, who moved to Jackson in 1874. He became a community leader, serving as a city alderman from 1893 to 1899. Robertson devoted himself to improving the education of Black youth. Mississippi had given little support for Black education; thanks to Robertson's influence, the city fathers decided to establish this school. After the building burned in 1909, it was rebuilt the same year, receiving a front addition with an art deco frontispiece. This two-story 1929 structure remained in service until June 1970 when it closed after a court order directed the integration of Jackson's public schools. A museum now occupies the site. In 1984, through community efforts in cooperation with the city of Jackson and the Mississippi Department of Archives and History, the school was renovated for use as a museum named for Smith Robertson.

Smith Robertson houses 22,000 square feet of space, including exhibit galleries, an atrium, and a performance area accommodating 250 to 300 persons. Artifacts in the museum portray the Black Mississippian's experience from Africa to the present day.

DATE BUILT:	1894; present building, 1909 and 1929
ADDRESS:	528 Bloom Street, Jackson
TELEPHONE:	(601) 960-1457
VISITING HOURS:	Mon.–Fri. 9–5, Sat. 9–noon, Sun. 2–5; closed New Year's, Memorial Day, July 4th, Labor Day, Thanksgiving, Christmas, Dec. 26
FEES:	Adults, $1; Children $.50
SOURCES:	NRHPINF. Dr. Jessie Mosley, executive director. Telephone call Dec. 2, 1994, to site. Brochure from the museum.

Lexington

Booker-Thomas Museum

A telephone call to the Booker-Thomas Museum reached Mrs. Fannye Thomas Booker, then eighty-seven years old, the founder and director who lovingly created the museum out of a dream. Many years ago she built a fourteen-room home for the elderly, and many of the residents, who had moved out of their own homes in this rural Mississippi area, left her assorted items from their cherished possessions. Family, neighbors, and friends began to contribute more items. The collection grew over the years until the assorted memorabilia, stored here and there, seemed to form the nucleus for a museum that would show a disappearing way of life. Booker wanted to show the way of life she had known as a child, including the country store her family operated. In 1980 she built her museum, setting it up as an old-fashioned country store. She also moved two log cabins to the site, with plans to renovate them.

Today the Booker-Thomas Museum contains a delightful assortment—a plow, old cast-iron pots, iron beds, old record players, and a walking stick once used by a man who walked through the streets selling whiskey.

The one large room, 150 feet by 150 feet, includes implements used in curing meat and grinding sausage, ox yokes from the days when mules were used, and beautiful cut glass. Thomas began collecting the glass after she saw local white people buying it. She took a closer look, liked it, and began purchasing it. She also acquired a preacher's library for the museum—a suitcase with books and papers that a Methodist minister carried from place to place. The museum also has a one-hundred-year-old pulpit and four pews from the former Poplar Springs Baptist Church.

DATE ESTABLISHED:	1980
ADDRESS:	From Lexington, take MS 17 to MS 12, west to Tchula Road; after the State Barn go downhill to the house with large wheels around it
TELEPHONE:	(601) 834-2672
VISITING HOURS:	By appointment
FEES:	Donations appreciated
SOURCE:	Telephone conversation Dec. 30, 1993, and Dec. 28, 1994, Mrs. Fannye Thomas Booker, founder and director.

Lorman Vicinity

Alcorn State University Historic District

Alcorn Agricultural and Mechanical College is the oldest land-grant college for Black students in the United States. Eight buildings contribute to the historic district at Alcorn State University, an African American institution of higher learning established in 1871. The buildings are located in the center of a beautiful campus, facing a large, tree-shaded historic green.

Alcorn was founded on the site of Oakland College, an 1828 Presbyterian school for white students from Mississippi, Louisiana, and Arkansas that closed during the Civil War. The state, in

1871, purchased the Oakland campus and converted it to a college for educating African American youth. This decision came about because of the unusual circumstances of the Reconstruction era. In 1871 Black legislators and those who sympathized with them held the balance in the Mississippi legislature. Prompted by the Morrill Act of 1862 that provided for the sale of public lands to fund agricultural colleges, the legislators allocated $50,000 for a Black land-grant school, known as the Alcorn Agricultural and Mechanical College, on the former Oakland campus.

Historic buildings on the campus include the 1928 colonial-revival style Administration Building, the Dormitory (c1885), Oakland Chapel (c1838), and President's House (c1830). The President's House, a two and one-half–story, federal-style building, has beautiful interior woodwork. Additional buildings in the historic district include Harmon Hall (1929), a second dormitory (c1855), Lanier Hall (c1939), and the Belles-Lettres Building (c1855).

Oakland Chapel, the oldest building on campus, is a beautiful Greek-revival structure. Ironically, it was constructed by skilled Black artisans. Of the three buildings remaining from Oakland College, only the Oakland Chapel has not had extensive alterations and retains the character of the original campus. The rectangular, brick, three-story chapel has a temple front with center entrance, sidelights, transom, and twelve-sided chimneys. Some of the striking features are the full-width, two-story portico and a square clock tower with pilasters. This building with its decorative woodwork was altered and restored in 1958.

The **President's House** is associated with Alcorn's first president, Hiram R. Revels, who served intermittently from 1871 until 1882. Revels was born free in Fayetteville, North Carolina, in 1825, and became an ordained minister in the African Methodist Episcopal Church. He organized Black units during the Civil War, and later founded a school for freedmen in St. Louis. He was the pastor of churches in Vicksburg and Jackson. Revels, the first Black person to serve in the United States Senate (1870–1871), was elected to the vacated seat of Senator Jefferson Davis, the president of the Confederacy during the Civil War. Revels died in 1901 at Aberdeen, Mississippi, and was buried in Holly Springs, Mississippi.

In the twentieth century, following the Depression years, the college curriculum became more diverse, and classical studies were offered in addition to the traditional agricultural offerings. Alcorn A & M has graduated many of Mississippi's Black leaders, including most of the state's Black physicians and dentists.

DATE BUILT: Oakland Chapel, c1838; Alcorn University, 1871

ADDRESS: MS 552, 7 miles northwest of Lorman and south of Port Gibson (from US 61 and the Natchez Trace Parkway, take westbound MS 552 to the university)

TELEPHONE: (601) 877-6100

VISITING HOURS: University, call for information; Oakland Chapel, Mon.–Fri. 8–4 or by appointment

SOURCES: Personal visit, summer 1990. NRHPINF. State marker. *National Register of Historic Places,* 390.

Meridian

Wechsler School

The Wechsler School was constructed in 1894 to house primary through eighth grades. It was the first brick building in Mississippi constructed for Black children with public funds from a bond issue. A high school was established at Wechsler in 1888, and by 1920 high school diplomas were offered. In the early years of operation, Wechsler was the only school in east central Mississippi where Black students were able to earn high school diplomas.

The building has been renovated with a 1914 annex and a 1951 addition. After desegregation the structure was used as a junior high school, then as a kindergarten building. It closed in 1981 but was reopened for use by a theater group from 1980 to 1986. After Wechsler closed in 1986, the building, vacant for four years, suffered from vandalism. The school had been loved, however, and was not forgotten. Community leaders worked to acquire the means of restoring the historic building, and in 1990 they formed the Wechsler Community Arts Center. A board of directors led renovation projects. The roof of the large, two-story, off-white building was repaired, heating and air-conditioning systems were installed, and local citizens cleaned and painted the rooms. In May 1994, the Reed Memorial Museum, named in honor of W. A. Reed, a beloved teacher, principal, and superintendent of Meridian's Black school district, opened in five rooms on the school's first floor. Collections include memorabilia from the local city and county.

Wechsler School stands in an area of town that contains other Black historic sites. They are either closed or open on an irregular basis and are best seen by driving by the buildings. The Carnegie Branch Library, now closed, was constructed for Black citizens in 1913 with aid of an $8,000 grant from the Carnegie Foundation. St. Paul United Methodist Church donated the land. The two-story Masonic Temple was erected in 1903 by three Black fraternal lodges and is still in use. The Meridian Baptist Seminary was founded in 1896 and was one of the early educational institutions for Black students in Eastern Mississippi. The existing brick structure was erected in 1921. The school flourished through the 1940s. Although the Baptist Seminary no longer operates, the building is used occasionally by community groups.

DATE BUILT: School, 1894; library, 1913; Masonic Temple, 1903; Seminary, 1896, 1921

ADDRESS: School, 1415 Thirtieth Avenue; library, 2721 Thirteenth Street; Masonic Temple, 1220 Twenty-sixth Avenue; Meridian Baptist Seminary, Sixteenth Street and Thirty-first Avenue, Meridian

TELEPHONE: Wechsler School, call Mrs. Melba Clark, (601) 483-4919; Masonic Temple, (601) 482-5067

VISITING HOURS: School, weekends only; call for information

SOURCES: Telephone conversation Dec. 28, 1994, Carol James, adult services librarian, Meridian Library. Telephone conversation Mar. 30, 1994, Dr. Larry Drawdy, Superintendent of Meridian School District. Telephone conversation Mar. 31, 1994, Mrs. Melba Clark, Wechsler Community Arts Center and Reed Memorial Museum. NRHPINF. Historic Sites Survey, State of Mississippi Department of Archives and History.

Mound Bayou

I. T. Montgomery House

The town of Mound Bayou, Mississippi, was established in 1887 by a group of African Americans in search of economic and political independence. The founders were former slaves Isaiah Thornton Montgomery and his cousin Benjamin Green.

At the end of the Civil War, Montgomery and Green had established a settlement south of Vicksburg at Brierfield, the former Jefferson Plantation. Although the settlement lasted eighteen years, its members were eventually forced to move to Vicksburg. Montgomery and Green never abandoned their dream of establishing another settlement, believing that in the hostile post-Reconstruction environment of Mississippi, they could thrive only by establishing their own self-governing Black community.

When a railroad received a land grant for the purpose of developing agriculture and commerce in Mississippi, its managers sought Black workers, believing they were resistant to malaria and best adapted to working in the hot climate. When the railroad managers sought Montgomery's assistance in recruiting workers, he was enthusiastic about the possibility of finding another site for the former colonists. He selected a swampy wilderness site, and many settlers from the former colony, as well as others from Louisiana, Alabama, and Georgia, joined in establishing the new settlement of Mound Bayou in 1887.

In 1892 Montgomery and Green donated land for a school, and Mary Montgomery, Isaiah's sister, became the first teacher. For years the American Missionary Association sent money, supplies, and teachers. The school, eventually called the Mound Bayou Normal and Industrial Institute, was the only one in the county serving Black children. In 1920 it expanded into a three-story brick building and became known as the Mound Bayou Consolidated Public School.

By the turn of the century, townspeople were erecting shops, institutional buildings, and homes. They established a bank in 1904 and an oil mill and manufacturing company in 1907. The town's proximity to the railroad facilitated trade, and the fertile delta land produced an abundance of cotton. At one time the town was one of the most prosperous in the state.

Montgomery became one of the wealthiest men in the county. He had interests in accounting, real estate, engineering, and politics. He was also a member of the 1890 Mississippi Constitutional Convention. Montgomery constructed his own home in 1910, a two-story, red-brick residence on Main Street that stood as a symbol of progress. When he died in 1924, he left a legacy of achievement and inspiration.

DATE BUILT:	1910
ADDRESS:	W. Main Street, Mound Bayou (on US 61, south of Clarksdale)
TELEPHONE:	City Hall, (601) 741-2193
VISITING HOURS:	Private; check with city hall concerning visits to the Montgomery House and request permission to take photographs
SOURCES:	Personal visit, summer 1990. NRHPINF. Denise Miller, Mississippi Department of Archives and History. State historical marker.

Natchez

Dunleith Mansion

John R. Lynch, who once worked as a house servant in the Dunleith Mansion, rose from slavery to become a noted businessman and politician. He was born in 1847 in a cabin on Tacony Plantation in Louisiana, where his mother was a servant and his father a plantation manager.

A few years before the Civil War, young Lynch and his mother were moved to Dunleith, his master's lavish estate and home at Natchez. John worked as a servant, running errands and assisting at the table during dinner. One of his duties was to fan guests in the dining room.

Lynch's master, Alfred Davis, appeared to recognize the boy's mental ability, but Mrs. Davis may have resented this favoritism. As a result, when Alfred Davis left Natchez to join the Confederate cause, Mrs. Davis returned the fifteen-year-old youth to Tacony to work as a field hand. A year later, in 1863, Union troops occupied the Natchez area, and the slaves were freed.

Lynch returned to Natchez, and he and his mother lived on Market Street. Working as a waiter, cook, messenger boy, and printer in a photography studio, he gradually took over more responsibilities in the studio, acting as its operator, printer, and bookkeeper. He also attended night school in a program sponsored by the Freedmen's Bureau.

The second-floor photography studio where Lynch worked had a window that opened across an alley to the Natchez Institute, a school for white children. Lynch often sat near the window and followed the children's lessons. He learned to solve arithmetic problems from viewing their chalkboards.

Lynch became an eloquent speaker, and at age twenty-one was appointed justice of the peace for Natchez. Within two years he was serving as Speaker of the House in the Mississippi House of Representatives. In 1873, at the age of twenty-five, Lynch was the first Black man from Mississippi to serve in the U.S. House of Representatives and the youngest man ever elected to that body. Congressman Lynch spoke out eloquently in favor of civil rights legislation and freedom and independence for all people.

Lynch had many other accomplishments. He incorporated a printing company and was president of the first Black bank in the United States, the Capital Savings Bank of Washington, D.C. He was admitted to the Mississippi bar in 1894, and President Harrison appointed him Auditor of the Treasury for the Navy Department in 1889. In 1898 he was commissioned a major in the United States Army and served for ten years in Puerto Rico, San Francisco, and the Philippine Islands.

The Honorable John Lynch published a book in 1913, *The Facts of Reconstruction*. In his eighties he began work on his autobiography, *Reminiscences of an Active Life*. He died in Chicago in 1939 at the age of ninety-two. The mansion on Homochitto Street, where John Lynch once worked as a slave, symbolizes the rise of an African American leader from bondage to freedom.

ADDRESS: 84 Homochitto Street, Natchez

TELEPHONE: (601) 446-8500

VISITING HOURS: Mon.–Sat. 9–5, Sun. 12:30–5; last 20-minute tour at 4:40; closed holidays

FEES: Adults, $4.50; children, $2.50

SOURCES: Personal visit, summer 1990. Telephone conversation Mar. 26, 1994, Mrs. Heims of Dunleith. "Natchez Rich in Black History," 2–3. "John R. Lynch Remembered during Black History Month," 4.

William Johnson House

Former slave William Johnson of Natchez left a rare document, a 2,000-page diary describing his thoughts and activities as a free Black man in the South. The diary documents his rise from bondage to freedom and depicts his day-to-day life, including his successes and failures in business. His account is believed to be the first complete journal kept by a free Black man in the South before the Civil War.

Mr. Johnson was born a slave in Natchez in 1809. In 1820 his owner, also named William Johnson, freed his mother and sister. When William was eleven years old, his owner successfully petitioned the state to give the boy his freedom.

A free adult, William Johnson began working as an apprentice in his brother-in-law's barber shop. He prospered, purchased land and a few slaves, and became a respected member of the Natchez business community. He owned three barber shops and operated a bathhouse. Other business interests included farming, real estate rentals, land speculation, and moneylending.

As a free Black man, Johnson was a member of the highest social group among African Americans of his day. Free African Americans in Natchez could enter into business deals with white citizens, have their marriages recorded, and own slaves. There were restrictions, however. They were not allowed to vote or to testify in court against white persons.

Johnson's businesses were operated by free Black people and by slaves. Some of his employees worked as apprentices until they became journeymen at the age of eighteen. From 1832 until his death in 1851, Johnson owned thirty-one slaves. Because Johnson was highly respected in Natchez, he had more latitude in his relationships with the white community than other free Black people had. He was able to employ white workers and also to bring civil suits to court, something other African Americans were not allowed to do. His relatively high status could not protect him, however, in a long-standing boundary dispute with Baylor Winn, a neighboring landowner, who murdered Johnson in 1851. Because Johnson's murder inflamed the people of Natchez, who held him in high esteem, the trial had to be moved to neighboring Jefferson County. After two years of litigation, Winn was released under the finding that a case could not be brought against a white man who murdered a Black person.

In 1951, one hundred years after Johnson's death, Louisiana State University published his diary. His attic, less than a block from the Adams County courthouse, also contained personal letters, family papers, rare newspapers from before the Civil War, and a large collection of nineteenth-century sheet music.

William Johnson built this two and one-half–story brick townhouse in 1840 and lived here from 1841 to 1851. The house is typical of the area's middle-class, nineteenth-century dwellings. The house has had some remodeling over the years, but the dormers with the windows of six panes over six and the tin roof are believed to be original. The William Johnson House is listed in the *National Register of Historic Places.* In 1994 the house was under full restoration by the National Park Service, a process expected to take two years. The first floor will house an African American history exhibit; the second floor will show Johnson's residence restored to look as it did when he lived there. Johnson rented out the first floor, but the type of shop housed there is not known. The attic loft once contained rooms for the children. The McCallum family, a white family, once lived in the house next door, which has an adjoining wall. The McCallum House will serve as the Visitors Center for the Johnson House.

DATE BUILT:	1840
ADDRESS:	210 State Street (between Canal and Wall Streets), Natchez
TELEPHONE:	National Park Service, (601) 442-7047
VISITING HOURS:	Visitors may drive by; restored house should be open in 1996
SOURCES:	Personal visit, summer 1990. Telephone conversation Mar. 29, 1994, Gerry Gaumer, chief of interpretation, National Park Service. NRHPINF. Jim Barnett, director, Division of Historic Properties, Mississippi Department of Archives and History. *The Historic Natchez Foundation's Natchez.* "Natchez Rich in Black History," 2–3.

Natchez National Cemetery

Natchez National Cemetery officials are uncertain about the number of African American Civil War veterans interred here; one estimate is more than 2,000. Senator Hiram Revels is buried in this cemetery. Revels, born in Fayetteville, North Carolina, in 1822, was a chaplain to a Black regiment in the Civil War and was the first Black person elected to the U.S. Senate (see the earlier entry for Alcorn State University at Lorman, Mississippi, for further information on Revels).

Another gravesite is of Wilson Brown, an African American and the only veteran in the cemetery awarded the Medal of Honor for heroism. Born in Natchez, Mississippi, about 1843, Brown enlisted on the Mississippi River in May 1863. In August 1864, during the naval engagement at Mobile Bay, he was serving as a shell boy on board the *USS Hartford* during successful Union attacks against rebel gunboats near Fort Morgan. Suddenly the *Hartford* was bombarded with shells. A shipmate climbing a ladder above Brown was struck by the enemy shellburst and fell back mortally wounded, knocking Brown into the hold of the ship where he lay unconscious. On regaining consciousness, Brown quickly returned to the shellwhip (a block and tackle device probably used here to hoist shells) on the berth deck and proceeded to perform his duties with an intensity of purpose, even though enemy fire had killed four of the six men at his station.

At the Natchez National Cemetery John Bacon, director, found records that told Brown's story. Brown was discharged May 19, 1865, from the *USS Washington,* due to a disability. He had a wife, named Lizzie. He died January 24, 1900.

After learning Brown's story, Bacon walked out to find Brown's grave in section G, grave number 3151. The stone was somewhat worn, Bacon thought, so he began making plans to redo the surface by having it sanded down and by ordering a gold inlay for the letters, thus making it more befitting for a hero.

The twelve-acre Natchez National Cemetery is bordered by private property. The cemetery has a design once compared to a wedding cake with a top level, a tier that slopes down, and another tier that slopes down again. Of the more than 6,000 graves in the cemetery, more than 3,000 are of Civil War veterans and 2,000 are graves of unknown soldiers. The 3,000 men who fought a terrible war over the issue of slavery were not segregated by race in their burials.

DATE ESTABLISHED: 1866

ADDRESS: 41 Cemetery Road (from Louisiana cross the Mississippi-Louisiana Bridge; take the first left to Canal Street; follow Canal Street until it ends; take a left, then the first right on Cemetery Road; go approximately 1 mile after the City Cemetery to the Natchez National Cemetery), Natchez

TELEPHONE: (601) 445-4981

VISITING HOURS: Gates open 24 hours; office, Mon.–Fri. 7:30–4

FEES: None

SOURCES: Telephone conversation Jan. 5, 1994, William A. Trower, director, Natchez National Cemetery. Telephone conversation Jan. 9, 1995, and July 31, 1995, John Bacon, director, Natchez National Cemetery. *Webster's New Biographical Dictionary,* 845. *Hippocrene U.S.A. Guide to Black America,* 192.

Smith-Buntura-Evans House

The Smith-Buntura-Evans House was a residence/business establishment built by a successful free Black businessman. Robert D. Smith built the home in stages between 1851 and 1858 for his home and livery business, and the rear wing of the building still has the arched openings that served as carriage entrances. Through his success in his carriage business, Smith achieved both social success with the Black community and professional success within the larger Natchez community.

The Smith-Buntura-Evans House is a two and one-half–story brick townhouse. A two-story cast-iron porch was added to the front of the home in the 1890s. The house is a rare survivor of a residential-commercial complex in this region.

DATE BUILT: 1851–1858

ADDRESS: 106 Broadway (directly across from the gazebo), Natchez

VISITING HOURS: Private, visitors may drive by

SOURCES: Personal visit, summer 1990. Mississippi Department of Archives and History. *The Historic Natchez Foundation's Natchez.*

Zion Chapel African Methodist Episcopal Church

The Zion Church is significant in Black history as an early post-Civil War African Methodist Episcopal church, one of the city's first Black congregations. The church also is significant for its association with Reverend Hiram R. Revels, the first African American to serve in the U.S. Senate.

The congregation of Second Presbyterian Church constructed the church in 1858, and in 1866, the A.M.E. Church purchased the building. The minister, Reverend Revels, was born free in North Carolina. He worked as a barber in his early years, and later became a minister. Reverend Revels came to Natchez as pastor of the Zion Chapel A.M.E. Church, and the congregation purchased this building during his pastorate.

DATE BUILT: 1858
ADDRESS: 220 Martin Luther King Street, Natchez
TELEPHONE: (601) 442-1396
VISITING HOURS: Sun. school, 9:30, Sun. service, 10:50
SOURCES: Personal visit, summer 1990. Mississippi Department of Archives and History. *The Historic Natchez Foundation's Natchez.* "Natchez Rich in Black History," 2–3.

Oxford

University of Mississippi Blues Archive

The Blues Archive is a library-research collection devoted to photographs and videos of blues musicians as well as archival collections concerning the music industry, radio, and blues throughout the world. The archive is primarily a research facility, but it also contains some exhibits. It is appropriate for adult researchers only.

The University of Mississippi Blues Archive opened full-time in 1984. Three major collections formed its nucleus: a folklore collection with a strong emphasis on Southern folklore and music; the B. B. King Collection with materials about B. B. King as well as his personal collection of phonograph records; and a Living Blues Collection containing thousands of classic phonograph records.

Numerous record companies and collectors in the United States and abroad have contributed gospel and blues recordings to this center. The archive also maintains videotapes, television documentaries, film footage, and taped interviews.

The site is relevant in Black history because the blues as an art/music form originated with African Americans. The Blues Archive collects and preserves information and documentation about this music and the community that created it.

DATE ESTABLISHED: 1984
ADDRESS: Room 340 Farley Hall, Grove Loop, University of Mississippi, Oxford
TELEPHONE: (601) 232-7753
VISITING HOURS: Mon.–Fri. 8:30–5; closed Sat.–Sun., 2 weeks at Christmas vacation, Easter weekend, national holidays

FEES: None

SOURCES: Suzanne Steel, University of Mississippi Blues Archive. Telephone conversation Dec. 6, 1994, Edward Komara, librarian/archivist, University of Mississippi Blues Archive.

Philadelphia Vicinity

Mt. Zion United Methodist Church*
Freedom Summer Murders Historical Marker

The burning of Mt. Zion Church at this site led to the tragic murder of three civil rights activists: James Chaney, Andrew Goodman, and Michael Schwerner. The three young men had come here to investigate the burning of the church. They were murdered on June 21, 1964, by Ku Klux Klan with police complicity.

The murder ripped into the heart of a summertime campaign to register Black voters in Mississippi. Civil rights leaders from Mississippi and volunteers from many parts of the country converged for the historic summer mission: to open up the voter registration process to local Black citizens who had been discouraged from voting through threats and cunning artifices. Although local civil rights groups had debated the wisdom of bringing white Northerners to Mississippi, Chaney, Goodman, and Schwerner were a racially integrated trio. Andrew Goodman (1943–1964), white, a junior at Queens College in New York, came to Mississippi to volunteer for the Council of Federated Organizations (COFO) Freedom Summer program. Michael Schwerner (1939–1964), white, grew up in New York City. After graduating from Cornell University he studied social work at Columbia University. Schwerner and his wife, Rita, joined the Congress of Racial Equality (CORE), and then prepared in Meridian, Mississippi, to join other Freedom Summer workers. James Chaney (1943–1964), a Black man from Meridian, Mississippi, was a student, a plasterer, and a civil rights worker with CORE and COFO.

On June 21 the three men went to visit a church that had been burned by the Ku Klux Klan—a target because plans had been made to house a freedom school there. (Freedom schools were alternative schools set up by civil rights workers in the South during the 1960s. In churches or other informal settings, they taught voting rights and citizenship as well as reading, writing, and arithmetic. They provided a setting where African Americans could discuss local problems and their solutions.) As the men returned to Meridian, a sheriff's deputy arrested them on a speeding charge. That evening, after their release from the Neshoba jail, Ku Klux Klan members stopped them in the dark on a country road, savagely beat them, shot them, and buried them in a dam.

On August 4, after a massive FBI investigation, the bodies were found. Citizens across the nation were outraged, and the ensuing investigation led to the first federal prosecution in Mississippi of a civil rights case. Although there was no murder conviction, seven men were found guilty in 1967 of conspiring to deprive the murdered volunteers of their civil rights. The seven members of the Ku Klux Klan were later paroled and set free.

The former Mt. Zion Methodist Church structure, one of the centers where Black people came to register, was blown up in 1964. The destruction of this church was one of sixty-seven incidents of bombings and arson that summer in Mississippi. A memorial marker at the church honors the memory of the three slain civil rights activists who lost their lives in the Freedom Summer campaign. During the Freedom Summer campaign, thousands of African Americans registered to vote and received health and education services.

DATE OF SIGNIFICANCE: June 21, 1964

ADDRESS: On County Road 747 about 1 mile off MS 482, approximately 5 miles northeast of Philadelphia

SOURCES: State of Mississippi historical marker. *Encyclopedia of African-American Civil Rights.*

Piney Woods

Piney Woods Country Life School

Dr. Lawrence Clifton Jones (1882–1975), founder of Piney Woods Country Life School, was born in St. Joseph, Missouri. He came to Mississippi in 1907 and taught at the Utica Institute; two years later he established a school in Simpson County, Mississippi. The school's curriculum combined the industrial form of education that prevailed in many African American schools in the South with rigorous academic studies. By the early 1920s Piney Woods School was preparing future teachers in its junior college program.

Providing leadership in the community as well as on the campus, Jones served as a board member of the Mississippi State Department's Expanded Food Distribution Program.

Although buildings on the Piney Woods campus include an old slave cabin, they generally date from the 1920s through 1930. Students arrive today from as far away as Alaska, attracted by a school that emphasizes personal responsibility, ethical standards, and quality instruction. Piney Woods School has had remarkable success in motivating indifferent students to achieve at high academic levels. Staff members strongly believe that students can achieve in academics and work experiences. The school is a memorial to Dr. Jones, who directed its development until his death in 1975.

DATE ESTABLISHED: 1909

ADDRESS: 5096 MS 49 (20 miles south of Jackson), Piney Woods

TELEPHONE: (601) 845-2214

VISITING HOURS: Call to arrange a tour

SOURCES: Denise Miller, Mississippi Department of Archives and History. Telephone conversation Mar. 1994, Marvin Jones, special assistant to the president, Piney Woods Country Life School.

Tougaloo

Tougaloo College

Tougaloo College, Mississippi's first accredited Black college, was established by the American Missionary Association in 1869 as a coeducational liberal arts institution to educate freed slaves for their new role in society. The association purchased a 500-acre farm, including its preexisting mansion and outbuildings. The mansion had been the residence of J. W. Boddie, a successful planter who died at the end of the Civil War. It became the nucleus of Tougaloo College in 1869 and today is one of the most historic sites on campus.

The Freedmen's Bureau provided funds to erect Washington Hall, which later burned down, and a women's dormitory in 1870. The state and the missionary society jointly operated the college. Its first president was Senator Hiram R. Revels (see full information on Revels in the previous entry on Alcorn State University). At that time many Black colleges were directed by white presidents in their first decades, so the choice of Revels was notable.

In the early years Tougaloo offered primary, grammar, and intermediate grades; a three-year preparatory course; a four-year normal course; and industrial and agricultural courses. In the late 1950s and early 1960s, many of Tougaloo's students led demonstrations and sit-ins, giving the college a prominent place in the twentieth-century Civil Rights Movement.

DATE ESTABLISHED: College, 1869; Mansion House, c1850
ADDRESS: 500 E. County Line Road, Tougaloo
TELEPHONE: (601) 956-4941
VISITING HOURS: Open during regular days of the college's operation
SOURCES: Denise Miller, Mississippi Department of Archives and History. State historical marker.

Tupelo

Natchez Trace Parkway Battle Sites*

The Natchez Trace Parkway, once known as the Old Natchez Trace, was an ancient trail once used by prehistoric Native Americans. It stretches 450 miles from Nashville, Tennessee, to Natchez, Mississippi. Hernando DeSoto, the ruthless Spanish explorer who arrived in Mississippi in 1540, was the first European to record this area. By 1785 settlers and merchants were using the trail for commercial transport. African American history became a part of the trail in the Civil War when Black soldiers fought at nearby Brices Cross Roads and Tupelo. Those battle sites today are part of the Natchez Trace Parkway operated by the Department of the Interior. Visitors to battle sites may also wish to see the Corinth National Battlefield, which is not part of the Parkway but is located to the northwest of Brices Cross Roads.

ADDRESS: Visitor Center for both Brices Cross Roads and Tupelo National Battlefield, Tupelo Headquarters, Natchez Trace Parkway, mile marker 266
TELEPHONE: Tupelo Headquarters, (601) 842-1572
VISITING HOURS: Daily 8–5; closed Christmas
FEES: None

Brices Cross Roads National Battle Site

In 1846 at Brices Cross Roads near Baldwyn, Mississippi, Confederate General Nathan Bedford Forrest defeated the Union forces commanded by General Samuel D. Sturgis. The Union plan had been to bisect the South east of the Mississippi, to occupy Atlanta, and to move on to Savannah and Charleston. The Confederates, however, believed that from Mississippi they could attack General William T. Sherman's vulnerable point—a railroad line carrying crucial supplies from Nashville to Chattanooga. Sherman, aware of this vulnerability, charged General Sturgis to move from Memphis to northern Mississippi and hold General Forrest there. Forrest hurried to Tupelo and began concentrating his forces of approximately 3,500 men along the railroad. On June 10, 1864, soldiers from both sides began to march at dawn. Sturgis's cavalry passed Brices Cross Roads before the Confederates arrived, and by noon the armies met and began fighting. The Confederates had good reinforcements, but the Union forces were at a disadvantage—due to torrential rains the night before, making the roads nearly impassable, the march along the muddy way had exhausted them. The Union soldiers began to withdraw but were beset by misfortune again when, as they recrossed the stream at Tishomingo Creek, a wagon overturned on the bridge, blocking their retreat. The Federals abandoned much of their artillery and their wagon train in their rush to move back; nevertheless, more than 1,500 of their men were captured in the retreat. The victory that day went to Confederate General Forrest, but it was only a partial one. Sherman managed to forestall more attacks on the railroad by sending small commands into northern Mississippi. He won the Atlanta campaign and later campaigns, too, and ultimately won victory for the Union.

At Brices Cross Roads, although the battle was not successful for the Black soldiers in the Fifty-fifth and Fifty-ninth Colored Infantry Regiments and Battery F of the Second Colored Light Artillery, these men fought valiantly with cool courage. Remembering the massacre of the Black soldiers at Fort Pillow (see the listing for Fort Pillow in Henning, Tennessee), these African Americans had vowed to avenge that outrage. Their mission was to check the Confederate advance until the Union artillery had passed. Later, when the Union forces had to retreat, some men from the Fifty-ninth Regiment were assigned to cover the rear. Moved by the memory of the Tennessee massacre, the Black soldiers fired until they had no more ammunition; then they fought with bayonets and muskets as if they had no intention of surrendering. Although this was the first battle experience for many of the soldiers, they fought valiantly. Men whose uniforms were soaked with their own blood marched with the rest of their regiments without showing signs of pain. An Illinois officer later claimed that General Forrest would have been more successful if it had not been for the actions of the Black troopers.

Today Brices Cross Roads National Battle Site is part of the Natchez Trace Parkway. Although there are no signs of the battle on the terrain of this one-acre site, the event is commemorated with a flag and two cannons, a granite memorial that commemorates both armies, and an interpretive marker. From this site much of the scene of action of the battle is within view. Next to the battlefield in the Bethany Church Cemetery are graves of 105 Confederate soldiers who died at Brices Cross Roads.

DATE OF SIGNIFICANCE: Battle, 1864; national battlefield site, 1929

ADDRESS: 6 miles west of Baldwyn on MS 370 (from Tupelo to Baldwyn take MS 45 north to Baldwyn; at the traffic light take a left to MS 370 and continue approximately 6 miles)

VISITING HOURS: Daily, 24 hours; closed Christmas

SOURCES: Telephone conversation Mar. 27, 1994, Cal Callinan, park ranger. Telephone conversation Dec. 31, 1994, Rick Putt, staff member, dispatch office, Tupelo Headquarters. "Military and Civilian Service during the Civil War: Brices Cross Roads, Mississippi," 177–8. *National Register of Historic Places,* 394. *Brices Cross Roads/Tupelo.*

Tupelo National Battlefield

In this Civil War engagement, also known as the battle of Harrisburg (near Tupelo), Confederate forces under General Stephen D. Lee and General Nathan Bedford Forrest tried to cut General Sherman's supply lines during his Atlanta campaign. The Battle of Tupelo took place five weeks after the Battle of Brices Cross Roads, and the hot sun and parched land had replaced the torrential rains and muddy roads of the earlier campaign. The Union soldiers had to protect the railroad that brought them food and ammunition from Louisville. The Confederates were not successful in this campaign but were repulsed by Union troops led by General Andrew J. Smith.

Union forces included Battery One of the Second Colored Light Artillery as well as the Fifty-ninth, Sixty-first, and Sixty-eighth Colored Infantry Regiments. The African American soldiers were eager to fight. Men of the Fifty-ninth Infantry had suffered a defeat at the battle of Brices Cross Roads and remembered the cruelties inflicted upon their African American brothers at Fort Pillow (see Henning, Tennessee).

Confederate soldiers in the battle that took place near Harrisburg were angered at the sight of the Black soldiers, and they concentrated their efforts on defeating the Black brigade. The Black soldiers, however, fought well; when the battles ended, their regiments were praised. Because of the courage of the Black soldiers and their importance in completing the mission, the commanding general later requested that they be included in the forces used to capture Mobile, Alabama.

The Tupelo National Battlefield site, a small park and a monument within the Tupelo city limits, commemorates this engagement where Black soldiers fought among others with courage. It is listed in the *National Register of Historic Places.* A park service brochure notes that there are hazards at the site that require alertness and vigilance. Children should not be allowed to stray.

DATE OF SIGNIFICANCE: 1864

ADDRESS: W. Main Street, Tupelo (on MS 6 about 1 mile west of its junction with US 45 and about 1.2 miles east of the Natchez Trace Parkway)

VISITING HOURS: Daily, 24 hours

FEES: None

SOURCES: Telephone conversation Mar. 27, 1994, Cal Callinan, park ranger. Ray L. Claycomb, assistant chief, Interpretation and Visitor Services, Natchez Trace Parkway. Official map and guide, National Park Service/U.S. Department of the Interior, 1989. "Military and Civilian Service during the Civil War: Brices Cross Roads, Mississippi," 186–7. *National Register of Historic Places,* 394. "Brices Cross Roads/Tupelo."

Vicksburg

Old Court House Museum

This majestic columned structure was built of hand-made brick. Highly skilled slaves belonging to the Weldon Brothers Construction Company put up the Court House. Weldon Brothers was Mississippi's largest contracting firm before the Civil War; it owned more than 100 slave mechanics. Researchers have learned recently that one Black man worked at a higher level than all the other laborers in planning this building. He was John Jackson, a slave for the Weldon Brothers, who had been educated in the "mechanical pursuits." H. S. Fulkerson, in his 1885 publication *Early Days in Mississippi,* described Jackson as a genius in the field of draftsmanship. Jackson worked closely with the Weldons to develop designs for the Old Court House in Vicksburg.

The columned building contains a collection of Southern memorabilia with an emphasis on the Confederate way of life. The Court House was important for both the Confederate and Union armies during the Civil War. With its massive Ionic-columned porticos and finely detailed clock tower, the Court House is one of the most historic and majestic buildings in Mississippi. Although it was viewed by some as a symbol of Confederate resistance, the active participation in its design and construction by African Americans makes it a monument to the skill of Black artisans.

DATE BUILT: 1858

ADDRESS: Court Square, 1008 Cherry Street, Vicksburg

TELEPHONE: (601) 636-0741

VISITING HOURS: Mon.–Sat. 8:30–4:30, Sun. 1:30–4:30; closed Christmas Eve, Christmas Day, New Year's Day, Thanksgiving

FEES: Adults, $1.75; children, $1; senior citizens, $1.25; preschoolers, free

SOURCES: Gordon A. Cotton, director, Old Court House Museum. "Negro Builders and Architects in Antebellum Mississippi."

Vicksburg National Military Park

Two sites within the Vicksburg National Military Park are significant in Black history: the *USS Cairo,* a restored Union ironclad gunboat, and the Vicksburg National Cemetery. Several Black men served on the ironclad gunboat *Cairo,* one of seven Civil War ironclads built for the United States, which in December 1862 steamed up the Yazoo River north of Vicksburg. During the Vicksburg campaign the gunboat's objective was to destroy Confederate batteries and clear enemy obstructions from the channel. Suddenly the *Cairo* struck two Confederate mines. Two explosions tore holes in the keel of the boat and within minutes it lay on the bottom of the river, with only the tops of the smokestacks and flagstaffs showing.

The gunboat remained hidden until 1956. Over the next three years, the badly damaged vessel was raised in sections and stored at the Ingalls Shipyard in Pascagoula. The historic gunboat later was restored and now rests at this site in Vicksburg.

After General Ulysses S. Grant failed to capture the city, he began a siege that lasted forty-seven days until the Confederate surrender on July 4, 1863. African Americans worked in the Vicksburg campaign as soldiers, laborers, and intelligence informants. In 1862 General Thomas Williams had assigned them the task of constructing a canal across the peninsula opposite Vicksburg to divert the course of the Mississippi River away from the Confederates. After two attempts failed, the Black workers were returned to slavery. This was the first widespread use of slave labor by the Union army in the South. The Confederates also used slaves in the defense of Vicksburg.

Black informers provided information to the Union Army concerning positions of the Confederates. Black soldiers were involved in two major battles of the Vicksburg campaigns—one at Port Hudson, the last remaining Confederate fortification on the lower Mississippi. Slaves had built the Port Hudson fortification on an eighty-foot bluff that contained siege guns and artillery pieces.

For many of the Black soldiers, this was their first real battle, and their performance was closely watched. Although Black Union regiments fought well, there were 37 killed, 155 wounded, and 116 missing.

Black soldiers also were involved at Millikin's Bend, located about twenty miles north of Vicksburg. Former slaves, organized into the Ninth and Eleventh Louisiana Regiments, went into battle in May 1863. They fought first with muskets and then in hand-to-hand combat with bayonets and musket butts. Although inexperienced in reloading their muskets, the men fought gallantly. The Ninth Louisiana Regiment with 285 men had 66 killed and 66 mortally wounded.

Today the site of the siege of Vicksburg has the remains of nine Confederate forts; twelve Union approaches; miles of breastworks, gun emplacements, rifle pits; and a national cemetery. Visitors may begin their sixteen-mile tour of the battlefield at the Visitors Center, where exhibits and an audiovisual program show the campaign and the siege of Vicksburg. Vicksburg National Cemetery holds the remains of several thousand African Americans who served their country from the Civil War through the Korean conflict.

As for the *USS Cairo,* it was not until the 1960s that artifacts were recovered from the gunboat. The artifacts are now on display at the *USS Cairo* Museum adjacent to the Vicksburg National Cemetery.

DATE ESTABLISHED: 1873

ADDRESS: 3201 Clay Street (US 80), within one mile of I-20, northeast Vicksburg

TELEPHONE: (601) 636-0583

VISITING HOURS: Park, daily 8–5; Visitors Center and *USS Cairo,* daily; closed Christmas

FEES: $4 per vehicle; licensed guided tour in your vehicle by prearrangement (two hours), $20; cassette rental $4.50, cassette purchase, $5.99

SOURCES: Personal visit to Vicksburg National Cemetery, summer 1990. Telephone conversation Mar. 1994, Patrick Shell, supervisory park ranger. Terrence J. Winschel, historian, Vicksburg National Military Park. *National Register of Historic Places,* 395. Brochure from Vicksburg National Military Park; "Military and Civilian Service during the Civil War: Brices Cross Roads, Mississippi," 187–91.

Notes

1. Essie Kennedy, letter to author, 17 October 1990.

2. *Vicksburg Daily Times,* 1868, quoted in brochure for the State Historical Museum, Old Capitol Restoration, Jackson, Mississippi, n.d.

Works Consulted

Brices Cross Roads/Tupelo. Washington, D.C.: National Park Service, 1994. [pamphlet]

The Civil War Almanac. John S. Bowman, ed. New York: World Almanac/Bison, 1983.

Delta Blues Museum. Clarksdale, Miss.: Carnegie Public Library. [flier]

Encyclopedia of African-American Civil Rights: From Emancipation to the Present. Charles D. Lowery and John F. Marszalek, eds. New York: Greenwood, 1992.

Encyclopedia of Mississippi History. Dunbar Rowland. Madison, Wisc.: S. A. Drant, 1906.

Hippocrene U.S.A. Guide to Black America: A Directory of Historic and Cultural Sites Relating to Black America. Marcella Thum. New York: Hippocrene, 1992.

Historic Landmarks of Black America. George Cantor. Detroit: Gale Research, 1991.

The Historic Natchez Foundation's Natchez: Walking Guide to the Old Town. Mary W. Miller and Ronald W. Miller. Natchez, Miss.: The Foundation, 1985.

"John R. Lynch Remembered during Black History Month," *Progressive Preservation* 7, no. 1 (Jan.–Feb. 1985), 4.

"Military and Civilian Service during the Civil War: Brices Cross Roads, Mississippi." Department of History, Howard University. In *Afro-American History Interpretation at Selected National Parks.* Washington, D.C.: National Park Service, 1978.

"Natchez Rich in Black History—HNF Recognizes Black History Month," *Progressive Preservation* 10, no. 1 (Feb. 1988), 2–3.

National Register of Historic Places. Washington, D.C.: National Park Service, 1976.

"Negro Builders and Architects in Antebellum Mississippi." Jackson, Miss.: files of the Mississippi Department of Archives and History. [paper]

Rust College General Catalog, 1988–1992. Holly Springs, Miss.: Rust College, 1988.

Webster's New Biographical Dictionary. Springfield, Mass.: Merriam-Webster, 1988.

North Carolina

Ahoskie

Pleasant Plains Rosenwald School

The Pleasant Plains Rosenwald School, built about 1921, is one of the best-preserved examples of a rural Rosenwald school. Moreover, it was a true family school in which teachers and parents cooperated in various aspects of the school experience. According to former student Calvin Weaver, a family living across the road from the school provided wood for the pot-bellied stove in each classroom and made the fire early in the morning before teachers and students arrived. In summertime the mothers gathered together to can string beans, corn, lima beans, and tomatoes for their children's lunches. On cold winter mornings they took turns sending jars of food to school. After organizing the day's lessons, the teacher opened the jars, poured the contents into a large pot, and set the pot on top of the stove to warm. Because the room was cold, the contents took a long time to heat. By lunchtime, however, the pot was warm and everyone enjoyed the delicious soup made from vegetables their own mothers had canned. Individual lunches also included sandwiches, a slice of cake, and milk.

The white, clapboard-sheathed, single-story Pleasant Plains School is located on quiet, shaded grounds set back from the highway. The serene setting gives no hint of the challenges faced by North Carolina's Black families in gaining an adequate education for their children. Before Rosenwald schools were constructed, Black children attended school, if they were able to go at all, in churches, shanties, old log cabins, or schools abandoned by white children.

When the Civil War ended, the Freedmen's Bureau began to establish schools for North Carolina's African American children. After 1868 local communities began providing schools for both races. Typically the rural schools had only one room, and those designated for Black children received very limited state support. Although the 1896 *Plessy* v. *Ferguson* decision of the U.S. Supreme Court legitimized the doctrine of separate but equal, vast differences in funding created schools that were separate and unequal.

In the 1910s nationally known Black educator Booker T. Washington, with his Tuskegee Institute staff, conceived of a public-private partnership that would improve education for Black children in the South. Washington approached Julius Rosenwald, a prominent philanthropist and president of Sears Roebuck & Company. Rosenwald had read Washington's book *Up from Slavery* and was familiar with his ideas. After meeting with Washington, Rosenwald agreed to give matching funds for Black schools. In doing so, he hoped to improve cooperation between Black and white people in the rural South who jointly would contribute funds or labor for erecting the Rosenwald schools. By the early 1930s more than five thousand Rosenwald schools had been built in fifteen southern states, with more of them in North Carolina than in any other state.

Enrollment eventually declined, the three-room Pleasant Plains School closed, and Hertford County consolidated its schools. The county eventually deeded the schoolhouse to the Pleasant Plains Baptist Church, which today is located across the street from the school. In 1990 the structure was in danger of being condemned, but community members, cherishing the schoolhouse, began a restoration program. The historic building is used today for community gatherings, reunions, clothing giveaways for low-income families, and summer programs for children.

DATE BUILT: c1921

ADDRESS: Junction of NC 1132 and US 13, on US 13, Ahoskie

TELEPHONE: Calvin Weaver, trustee, (919) 332-3861

VISITING HOURS: By appointment

SOURCES: Personal visit, summer 1990. Telephone conversation Apr. 21, 1994, Jean Parker of Hertford County High School and Pleasant Plains Baptist Church. Telephone conversation Apr. 21, 1994, Samuel James, trustee, Pleasant Plains Baptist Church. Telephone conversation May 19, 1994, Calvin Weaver, trustee, Pleasant Plains Baptist Church. State of North Carolina Division of Archives and History Historic Sites Survey. "The Rosenwald Schools and Black Education in North Carolina," 387–444.

Asheville

St. Matthias Episcopal Church

St. Matthias Episcopal Church is one of the finest churches built for a Black congregation in North Carolina. The church stands as a landmark in a historic Black neighborhood of Asheville, high on the western slope of Beaucatcher Mountain. The Gothic-style brick church is significant architecturally for its outstanding, elaborately detailed interior woodwork. Outside the church, kudzu vines have crept over the mountainside, partially hiding the church from viewers on the street below.

St. Matthias serves the oldest Black Episcopal congregation in western North Carolina. The congregation was established after the Civil War when a church was needed to serve the freed people. Jarvis Buxton, an Episcopal rector, already had organized an Episcopal congregation for free Black people in Fayetteville in 1832; in 1865 he founded Freedman's Chapel, also called Trinity Chapel, as part of Trinity Church in Asheville.

The cornerstone of the present building was laid in 1894, and the building was completed in 1896. The first service in the new church was held on Easter Sunday in 1896. At this time the name was changed from Trinity Chapel to St. Matthias Episcopal Church.

St. Matthias Church is listed in the *National Register of Historic Places.*

DATE ESTABLISHED: Cornerstone, 1894; church, 1896

ADDRESS: One Dundee Street, Asheville

TELEPHONE: (704) 255-6021, or (704) 298-8549

VISITING HOURS: Sun. service, 11

SOURCES: Personal visit, summer 1990. Telephone conversation Mar. 28, 1994, Reverend Thomas D. Hughes. NRHPINF. *The Smithsonian Guide to Historic America,* 76.

Young Men's Institute Building

The Young Men's Institute Building has served throughout much of the twentieth century as a focal point of African American activities in Asheville. Richard S. Smith, the supervising architect for George Vanderbilt's fabulous Biltmore estate, designed this two-story pebble-dash and brick building for Asheville's African American citizens.

In 1891 Vanderbilt was employing several hundred Black workers during the construction of the Biltmore estate. At that time Edward L. Stephens, the principal of Asheville's first Black public school and a native of the West Indies, urged the wealthy philanthropist to establish an institution to serve "colored men and boys" in Asheville. As a result, Vanderbilt purchased land in the Pearson addition to the city of Asheville. Construction of the building began in 1892 and was completed the following year. The center served not only the Black workers who were constructing the Biltmore estate but Asheville's Black community as well. The elegant structure contained 18,000 square feet of space; it housed meeting rooms, residence rooms, and shops. Through the years the center served as a focal point for community activities.

For many years the Young Men's Institute served as a counterpart to the white Young Men's Christian Association. In the 1960s, however, the Black commercial district around the building declined. The YMI building was sold twice and closed for a period.

In 1980 community members began a project to regain ownership and to restore the building. Their efforts were rewarded. After a $1.3 million renovation that sensitively retained much of the original woodwork, the historic building reopened in 1988. Several small businesses have now returned to the area.

Today the YMI Cultural Center contains the African Heritage Center with 7,500 square feet of museum/exhibit space and a theater seating 350. It provides programs associated with economic and community development projects, cultural events, and Black history exhibits.

DATE BUILT: 1893

ADDRESS: 39 S. Market Street, Asheville

TELEPHONE: (704) 252-4614

VISITING HOURS: Mon.–Fri. 9–5

FEES: Charges for some activities and programs

SOURCES: Personal visit, summer 1990. NRHPINF. Robin Sloan, cultural arts coordinator, YMI Cultural Center. *Cornerstone. Broadening the Spectrum.*

Burlington Vicinity

McCray School

When asked directions to the McCray School, a customer in a small store answered, "Oh, that's that little itty bitty old school," then showed the way.

The McCray School, small, but possessing a full measure of charm, is located on open terrain close to a highway; it is one of two remaining schools built for Black students in rural Alamance County. In 1915, Albert Graham (1830–1916), a prosperous Alamance County landowner, donated property to the Black community. Andrew Nash, a local carpenter, with help from community volunteers, built the school between 1915 and 1916. The design was typical of the one-room schools that served children in rural North Carolina from 1869 through the mid-twentieth century.

The rectangular building had a gable-front roof, weatherboard sheathing, and no ornamental trim. Inside, students sat at high-backed desks for two and wrote with penny pencils on ten-cent tablets with rough paper.

The Alamance County board of education purchased McCray School in 1919 and operated it until four county schoolhouses consolidated in 1951. Local residents then used the building as a community center until 1981, when an oak tree fell on the structure and destroyed the rear addition that had served as a second classroom.

McCray School closed, but it was not forgotten. McCray residents and high school vocational students began restoring the structure around 1990, completing the work in 1992. A former student sketched pictures of the students' desks and teacher's desk; they were reconstructed. The teacher's desk is large—about four feet high—and has an opening for holding books. Students' desks, each meant to seat two students, have a back section that slopes up to a ledge; this opens out to provide a writing support for the students who sit behind. The one-room schoolhouse at first held 30 students, but parents petitioned for additional space. A second classroom was added, and the school then accommodated 60 students. The second classroom was destroyed in 1983 by a hurricane and has not been replaced.

Not satisfied with restoring the physical environment of the original room, community leaders sought one of the original lunch menus. A former student obliged; the menu included a ham biscuit, a baked sweet potato, an apple, a sugar cookie, and water or milk.

Today, each fourth grade student in Alamance County School has an opportunity to spend a morning studying at McCray School. The students have their lessons in the 1916 ambiance of the old schoolhouse. They sit in the desks with the high backs, and at lunch time they enjoy their old-time lunch.

The McCray School, listed in the *National Register of Historic Places,* still radiates the intimacy and warmth of the original schoolhouse. It is one of the best-preserved examples of an early twentieth-century one-room school. Oh, yes—one additional restoration was done that become one of the biggest hits with the children—it is the fully restored outhouse, the only "facility" available on the site.

DATE BUILT: 1916

ADDRESS: Northwest side of NC 62, 400 ft. south of junction with NC 1757, vicinity of Burlington

TELEPHONE: (910) 570-6647

VISITING HOURS: Contact Mr. Ted Henson, director of Elementary Education, Alamance County Schools, 8–5, to arrange visit

SOURCES: Personal visit, summer 1990. Telephone conversation Apr. 19, 1994, Ted Henson, Alamance County School District. NRHPINF.

Charlotte

Afro-American Cultural Center

The Afro-American Cultural Center is located in a historic building, a former Black church in Charlotte called Little Rock African Methodist Episcopal Zion Church. The museum/cultural center presents visual arts displays, musical and theatrical productions, and other community events. Galleries on the first and second floor feature exhibits that change every two months. A featured exhibit of 1994 was *River Road on the Mississippi* by African American photographer Roy Lewis.

DATE BUILT: 1911

ADDRESS: 401 N. Myers Street at E. Seventh Street, Charlotte

TELEPHONE: (704) 374-1565

VISITING HOURS: Tues.–Sat. 10–6, Sun. 1–5; closed Mon. and holidays

FEES: None; tickets needed for some events

SOURCES: Personal visit, summer 1990. Vanessa Green, director, and Gwen Jackson, administrative assistant, Afro-American Cultural Center. Madine Hester Fails, president/CEO, Charlotte-Mecklenburg Urban League, Inc. Telephone conversation Apr. 19, 1994, Jane Lewis, receptionist.

Johnson C. Smith University
Biddle Memorial Hall

Johnson C. Smith University has a quiet and beautiful 100-acre, tree-shaded campus. Founded in 1867 as a mission school for Black students, it started out with only two teachers and fewer than twelve students. It was first named Biddle Memorial in honor of Mary Duke Biddle, a tobacco heiress who had given a large cash donation to the school. After a Charlotte entrepreneur donated eight acres in 1868, the school moved to the present location.

The campus is dominated by Biddle Memorial Hall, an imposing structure in Romanesque style with a high clock tower and ornamental brickwork. Its front entrance has a double door, a ten-pane transom, and a handsome fanlight. The interior displays a profusion of Victorian ornamentation, including a vine design on the radiators, transoms above most of the doors, and wainscoting in the entrance area and along the stairway. Biddle Auditorium, a theater seating 508 persons, occupies a part of the structure. It is adorned with paneled beams supported by a series of arches. The $40,000 construction costs for the hall came from a number of sources including the Freedmen's Bureau, Mary Duke Biddle, and the Board of Missions for Freedmen of the Presbyterian Church. Students played an active part in constructing the hall, even firing the bricks used in the building.

Today Biddle Hall houses the offices of the president, admissions, development, the registrar, and student activities as well as the auditorium. The hall, a national historic site, symbolizes the drive of African Americans from the Civil War to the present to obtain an education.

Johnson C. Smith University has two other buildings of historic interest: Carter Hall, the oldest dormitory, built in 1895 and designed in Gothic style, has distinctive corner towers and a decorative cupola. The Carnegie Library Building, constructed in 1911 with matching funds donated by the philanthropist Andrew Carnegie, served as the university library from 1911 to 1978 and is the only Carnegie library left in Charlotte and Mecklenburg County. A special Archives Room inside the facility contains photographs, publications, memorabilia, newspaper clippings, and other historical items.

DATE ESTABLISHED: University, 1867; Biddle Hall, 1883

ADDRESS: 100 Beatties Ford Road, Charlotte

TELEPHONE: Public relations, (704) 378-1025; admissions office, (704) 378-1010

VISITING HOURS: Tours by appointment 8:15–5:15; closed Martin Luther King Day, Christmas week, Thanksgiving, Easter

FEES: None

SOURCES: NRHPINF. Scott Scheer, director, Public Relations, Johnson C. Smith University. Personal visit, summer 1990.

Creswell Vicinity

Somerset Place State Historic Site

Somerset Place was one of the most important rice plantations in North Carolina. In 1784 three residents of Edenton, North Carolina, purchased 100,000 acres of swamp and woodlands. Needing to drain the swamps to make rice cultivation possible, they brought in eighty slaves from Africa to dig a six-mile canal. The owners realized that the African slaves knew how to grow rice and for this reason planned to use them in developing the plantation after the land had been drained.

Extensive records have survived to document the slaves' experiences. A map of 1821 shows the size and location of quarters that once housed more than 200 slaves; archaeological excavations have uncovered remnants of articles used by slave families.

Dorothy Spruill Redford, an African American, has written in *Somerset Homecoming* about her decade-long search for her own roots at Somerset. Her search led to records describing the ordeal of the slaves as they dug through swamp to a freshwater lake. A group of Edenton business leaders formed a company to drain the swamp land. One was a doctor named Samuel Dickinson; another was Josiah Collins, who ended up controlling the company. According to Redford,

> The digging took two years. Two years of malaria-ridden mosquitoes and blood-gorged black flies feasting on the slaves' flesh. Two years of hacking through a primordial jungle, through trees and roots thick beyond comprehension. One ten-foot-thick, eight-hundred-year-old tree would be pulled aside only to reveal its roots wrapped around an even thicker tree more than a thousand years old. Collins almost never came near the site. Dickinson came once a month to care for sick or injured slaves. The day-to-day excavation was left to an overseer named Thomas Trotter, a Scottish engineer who had made his name landscaping gardens in Edenton. But this was no garden. And Trotter took no chances with his labor. He built cages around slaves as they dug, forcing them to pass the dirt and mud out through the bars.
>
> It took two years, and many of them died, some of sickness, some of sheer exhaustion. Slaves who were not able to leave the work at the end of a day "would be left by the bank of the canal, and the next morning the returning gang would find them dead." Those were Trotter's words.[1]

Redford's book is one of the best accounts by an African American of the process of discovering her own history. She gives an excellent description of how the slaves lived at Somerset. In 1830 the plantation housed 183 slaves in three two-story, lakefront quarters that measured forty by twenty feet. Several families lived barracks-style in each of the four rooms of the dwellings. By the next decade twenty-one additional cabins were built along the lakefront, most of them eighteen-foot-square, one-room structures.

Owner Josiah Collins had a system of controlling his slaves through a caste system that accorded better treatment to some than to others. House slaves were the best fed and clothed; they were the only ones allowed to talk directly with the white family. Artisans and skilled craftsmen were ranked in the middle; they took care of the grounds and construction work and at times were paid for special projects. Field hands at the bottom of the scale had to do the hardest and dirtiest work. Out of fear that the field hands might be involved in a plot or an uprising, the white owners did not allow them to come near. All three groups of slaves were considered socially inferior to their owners.

The artisans may have been held in high esteem because many were very skilled at their work. At Somerset, as was true throughout North Carolina before the Civil War, most construction tasks were not mechanized. Clay, stone, and timbers were shaped by hand. Before steam-powered mills came into use and even later, Black carpenters had to saw large pieces of timber into planks, weatherboards, and framing materials. The sawyers often worked in pairs, using muscle power to push and pull the saw through the timber. In some cases Black men led the crews. For example,

Joe Welcome, a highly skilled slave owned by Josiah Collins, led the other slaves in construction work.

More than one hundred slaves lived their entire lives at Somerset Place. Today, an interpretive tour of the site includes the main house, salting house, smokehouse, and kitchen. Dorothy Spruill Redford, descendent of Somerset slaves, heads a program to restore the plantation and to continue to record and tell the history of the slaves who lived on the plantation. The work will include archaeological searches and a possible reproduction of the slave quarters. The site is operated by the state of North Carolina.

DATE ESTABLISHED:	c1830s
ADDRESS:	Off NC 64, 7 miles south of Creswell, in Pettigrew State Park
TELEPHONE:	(919) 797-4560
VISITING HOURS:	Apr.–Oct., Mon.–Sat. 9–5, Sun. 1–5; Nov.–Mar., Tues.–Sat. 10–4, Sun. 1–4
FEES:	None
SOURCES:	Telephone conversation Apr. 20, 1994, Dorothy Spruill Redford. *Somerset Homecoming.* "Black Builders in Antebellum North Carolina." *The Smithsonian Guide to Historic America.*

Durham

North Carolina Central University

North Carolina Central University traces its origins to the small, private National Religious Training School and Chautauqua for the Colored Race established by Dr. James E. Shepard in 1909. The National Religious Training School provided a high school and college education to hundreds of students for several years, even though the institution faced continuing financial crises.

In 1923 the state of North Carolina took over the college, which first was named Durham State Normal School and two years later become the North Carolina College for Negroes.

Dr. Shepard guided the college through 1945, years of growth that saw more than a dozen fine brick buildings constructed in Georgian style. The college's growth reflected the determination of a people to have higher educational opportunities; it also mirrored the growth of a prospering Black community in Durham.

Today North Carolina Central University is one of the sixteen senior institutions of the University of North Carolina. The art museum at the university, dedicated November 4, 1977, contains displays that include African American works of art. The university is listed in the *National Register of Historic Places.*

DATE ESTABLISHED:	1925
ADDRESS:	Bounded by Lawson Street, Alston Avenue, Nelson Street, and Fayetteville Street, Durham
TELEPHONE:	University, (919) 560-6100; museum, (919) 560-6211
VISITING HOURS:	University, Mon.–Fri. 8:30–4:30; museum, Tues.–Fri. 9–5, Sun. 2–5; closed Labor Day, Thanksgiving, Christmas, Martin Luther King's Birthday, fall vacation, spring vacation
SOURCES:	Personal visit, summer 1990. Norman E. Pendergraft, director, NCCU Art Museum. State of North Carolina Division of Archives and History Individual Property Form.

Mechanics and Farmers Bank

This six-story brick building was Durham's second-tallest building when constructed in 1921. The white-brick structure was considered to be a symbol of Durham's progressive Black middle class.

The building was the home office of the North Carolina Mutual Life Insurance Company founded in 1898 in Durham. The company grew out of the tradition of Black mutual benefit societies and fraternal organizations that were influential from the eighteenth through the twentieth centuries. The seven Black organizers reflected Booker T. Washington's ideas of self-help in an era of segregation. Responding to Jim Crow practices, African Americans began to form separate businesses and institutions.

Because the first year was difficult for the company, only two of the seven founders stayed with the business beyond the initial year. John Merrick, an ex-slave and a prosperous Durham barber, provided the major capital and commitment. Black physician Dr. Aaron M. Moore also stayed with the project, which he viewed as a cooperative movement to uplift African Americans.

Under the energetic guidance of Moore's nephew, Charles Clinton Spaulding, the company became a flourishing firm. Soon North Carolina Mutual Life was the largest Black business in America. Its territory expanded from Maryland to Florida and Oklahoma.

Guided by Asa T. Spaulding, America's first Black actuary, the company operated through the Great Depression and gained financial strength in the 1940s. Its financial position was strengthened again in the late 1960s when the Black community felt a new interest in racial solidarity and worked to encourage Black capitalism. Another dramatic gain came when large corporations such as General Motors and IBM contracted part of their employees' group insurance with North Carolina Mutual. Between 1969 and 1972 the number of insurance policies written more than doubled, making the Mutual the first Black billion-dollar company.

From the beginning North Carolina Mutual stood for solidarity and self-help. Its leaders believed a firm economic base could help to cure social and economic ills. In time the company formed additional enterprises: Durham's first Black newspaper, a cotton mill providing employment for Black workers excluded from white mills, and such financial institutions as the Mechanics and Farmers Bank (1907) and the Mutual Savings and Loan Association (1921). Mutual's leader also founded the Durham Committee on Negro Affairs, one of the South's most effective organizations on behalf of economic welfare, civil rights, and political activism.

The North Carolina Mutual Life Insurance Company, as an internationally known billion-dollar company operated by African Americans, has had an enormous impact on the Durham community and upon Black people in other states who were inspired by the significant achievements of this enterprise.

North Carolina Mutual is listed in the *National Register of Historic Places.*

DATE ESTABLISHED:	Insurance company, 1898; building, 1921
ADDRESS:	114–116 W. Parrish Street, Durham
TELEPHONE:	(919) 682-9201
VISITING HOURS:	Not set up for visitors, lobby open during business hours
SOURCES:	NRHPINF. Personal visit, summer 1990.

Scarborough House

The elegant Scarborough House, constructed in 1916, reflects the accomplishments of businessman and community leader J. C. Scarborough and the rise of Durham's urban middle class. Durham was a center of African American progress in the early years of the twentieth century. Hearing of Durham's reputation, Scarborough moved to the city in 1906 and opened Hargett Funeral Home, the city's first funeral service for Black people. He remained active in the business until he died in 1972 at the age of ninety-four.

Scarborough was an eminent leader in Durham. He was a director of the Mechanics and Farmers Bank, secretary of Lincoln Hospital, and trustee of St. Joseph's African Methodist Episcopal Church. He established the Daisy E. Scarborough Home (now a nursery school) in memory of his first wife. Scarborough's second wife, Clydie Scarborough, developed the nursery school; she also worked to improve early childhood education on a statewide basis.

The distinctive Scarborough home was constructed largely from materials salvaged from one of Durham's finest Queen Anne houses. The interior displays the city's most extensive collection of "high style" Victorian-period architectural elements. The family has carefully preserved this fine neoclassical-revival house, which is listed in the *National Register of Historic Places.*

DATE BUILT: 1916
ADDRESS: 1406 Fayetteville Street, Durham
VISITING HOURS: Private, visitors may drive by
SOURCES: Personal visit, summer 1990. State of North Carolina Division of Archives and History Individual Property Form. National Register Information System.

Stagville Center
Horton Grove Slave Cabins

Stagville Center is located on what was once a plantation of several thousand acres. Before the Civil War the plantation complex included 30,000 acres owned by the Bennehan-Cameron family. Fairntosh and Stagville were the two residential seats of a vast family-owned plantation empire that included thousands of acres that were expanded over a period of several generations. Archaeological surveys indicate a wealth of potential information about the people who lived on this rich land between the Flat and Little Rivers. Over time, approximately 900 slaves—many of them masters of many trades—worked at different parts of the estate.

The complex today consists of two areas that are one mile apart—Stagville and Horton Grove. Historic plantation buildings at these two sites date from 1776 through the 1930s. The plantation "big house" and the great barn are at Stagville. When the west wing of the main house was added in 1799, a walking cane was wedged between the two sections in an east-west direction. There has been speculation that slaves placed the cane there as a curse or a blessing on the inhabitants of the house. Slaves from the Cameron Plantation built the barn in 1860. The massive timber structure, 135 feet long by 33 feet wide, was once one of the largest agricultural buildings in North Carolina.

The Horton Grove property is significant in Black history because it contains a row of two-story slave houses—rare survivors of a slave-house complex. The site is significant, too, for the preservation of oral and written family history associated with the slave houses. The quarters, one of several slave communities on the estate, housed eighty to one hundred people from the 1850s to the end of the Civil War. In 1851 slaves built the four slave cabins at Horton Grove that had four rooms per house, each measuring 17 feet by 17 feet. Apparently one slave family lived in each room. The slave houses are unusual because they were built in a substantial manner for this type of dwelling. Construction techniques for the slave houses are like those used in the Middle Ages—a heavy timber-frame construction joined with wooden pegs. The walls were filled with brick nogging, and the exteriors were covered with board-and-batten siding.

A fork-shaped stick or divining rod—possibly a remnant of African tradition—was discovered in the wall of one of the slave houses. Mortar was attached to the rod, suggesting that it was placed there at the time of the house's construction. The rod may have reflected the West African practice of insuring a dwelling place within the new home for the guardian spirit that was supposed to protect the home. Cowrie shells, used in some West African societies, were also discovered in the remains of one of the slave cabins.

After the Civil War, many freed Black people remained on the plantation, working the land as sharecroppers. Others moved to the nearby growing town of Durham.

Today Stagville Center and Horton Grove are operated by the North Carolina Division of Archives and History. Visitors start at Stagville, where they see a ten-minute slide show about the center and the Horton Grove slave cabins. They see the Benneham House (main house), then receive directions to Horton Grove. All visitors must start their tour at Stagville.

DATE ESTABLISHED: Stagville, 1787–1851; slave houses, 1850s

ADDRESS: Stagville and Horton Grove Complex, east and west sides of NC 1626, 0.1 mile north of NC 1004, Fairntosh, Durham County (after receiving authorization at Stagville, to reach Horton Grove, take the Old Oxford Highway past the Bahama-Stagville Road to Jack Road; follow the Jack Road 2 miles to Horton Grove)

TELEPHONE: (919) 620-0120

VISITING HOURS: Access to Horton Grove only with permission; visitors start the tour at Stagville and receive directions to Horton Grove, Mon.–Fri. 9–4; closed Sat.–Sun. (except for special programs), state holidays

FEES: None

SOURCES: Kenneth M. McFarland, Stagville Center. Telephone conversation Mar. 24, 1991, Kathleen Needham, Historic Interpreter II. NRHPINF. "Slave Life at Stagville."

Elizabeth City

Elizabeth City State University

Elizabeth City State University is located in the historic Albemarle region of northeastern North Carolina near the mouth of the Pasquotank River. The campus is located approximately forty-five minutes from Norfolk, Virginia. In 1991 Elizabeth City State University celebrated a century of providing education to the people of North Carolina.

The university began as a normal school charged with teaching and training teachers of the "colored race to teach in the common schools" of North Carolina. Hugh Cale, a Black representative from Pasquotank County, sponsored the bill that established the college, and Elizabeth City Colored Normal School opened on January 4, 1892. The school operated in rented quarters with a faculty of two, a student enrollment of twenty-three, and a budget of $900. The college moved to its present permanent location on September 9, 1912. In 1937 it changed from a two-year normal school to a four-year teachers' college. The college awarded the first bachelor of science degrees in elementary education in May 1939.

Today, Elizabeth City State University is a constituent institution of the University of North Carolina with a student body of approximately 1,771 students, 76 percent of whom are African American. The 190-acre campus is supplemented by 639 acres in neighboring Currituck County where scientific research is conducted in the Dismal Swamp area. The late Alex Haley, author of *Roots,* was an outstanding alumnus of ECSU.

DATE ESTABLISHED: 1891

ADDRESS: Elizabeth City (accessible via US 17 and 158)

TELEPHONE: Public relations, (919) 335-3246; admissions office, (919) 335-3305

VISITING HOURS: Students or prospective students, contact the admissions office, 8–5; others, contact the office of public relations; closed national holidays

SOURCE: Shelia A. Johnson, director of public relations, Elizabeth City State University.

Fayetteville

Evans Metropolitan African Methodist Episcopal Zion Church
St. Joseph's Episcopal Church

Evans Metropolitan African Methodist Episcopal Zion Church is unique in early nineteenth-century North Carolina church history. Henry Evans, a free African American shoemaker-preacher, founded the church on Cool Spring Street and preached to both white and Black members. By the 1870s the congregation had joined the African Methodist Episcopal Zion denomination. The present Gothic-style church, constructed between 1893 and 1894 by skilled Black artisans, is the fourth church to stand on the same site. The two-story structure has double front towers, colored-glass windows, and beaded interior woodwork. It occupies the site of the original Methodist Church founded in 1795.

St. Joseph's Episcopal Church, chartered in 1873, is the second oldest Episcopal congregation in Fayetteville. It is architecturally distinguished as a rare surviving example from a period of American architecture when buildings were arranged in a close grouping and were landscaped to give the character of a small country village. The complex, built in 1896, includes a chapel, a parish hall, and a parsonage all linked by wooden arcades. In 1916 a fire destroyed all buildings except the church, but the complex was rebuilt in a bold, green-shingled Queen Anne architectural style.

DATE BUILT: Evans Metropolitan, 1893–1894; St. Joseph's, 1896, 1916

ADDRESS: Evans Metropolitan A.M.E. Zion Church, 301 N. Cool Spring Street; St. Joseph's Episcopal Church, Ramsey and Moore Streets, Fayetteville

TELEPHONE: Evans Metropolitan, (910) 483-2862; St. Joseph's, (910) 323-0161

VISITING HOURS: Contact Evans Metropolitan Church for appointment; St. Joseph's Church Holy Eucharist Sun. 11, Group Prayer Meeting Wed. at 6, followed by Holy Eucharist at 6:40, Bible Studies Thurs. 6, for other days, call for appointment

SOURCES: NRHPINF. City of Fayetteville, Division of Archives and History, State of North Carolina Division of Archives and History Individual Property Form. *The Smithsonian Guide to Historic America,* 65.

Greensboro

Agricultural and Technical College of North Carolina Historic District

This college was established at Raleigh in 1891 as the Agricultural and Mechanical College for the Colored Race. It moved to Greensboro in 1893 after the city of Greensboro donated $11,000 and fourteen acres of land for a campus.

Although none of the nineteenth-century buildings survive, five of the oldest buildings are listed in the historic district. These are the Dudley Memorial, Noble Hall, Morrison Hall, Murphy Hall, and the Richard B. Harrison Auditorium. Dating from 1922 to 1939, they represent the second and third major building efforts. When the North Carolina legislature funded the 1920s buildings, the money represented the largest appropriation ever made for Black education in the South. The Public Works Administration built Harrison Auditorium in 1939.

The historic brick buildings are excellent examples of the classical-revival style and have retained most of their original appearance. Today they form the historic center of an expanding campus. When they were constructed, the school was moving from a college preparatory program to one focusing on college-level work and the preparation for graduate schools and careers.

Another center of interest on campus is the **Mattye Reed African Heritage Center,** a museum/gallery located in a house on the main campus. Displays include traditional African and African-American art, crafts, and jewelry. The artifacts show the heritage and culture of people of African descent, tracing their history from Africa to America.

The college gained national attention in 1960 when four of its students walked into the Woolworth Store on South Elm Street and sat down for a meal at the lunch counter. Although there had been a series of sit-ins in North Carolina between 1957 and 1960, the act still seemed astonishing because segregation still ruled. Although not served, the students remained seated until the store closed. Their demonstration spread to other stores in Greensboro and led to demonstrations in the South. Northern demonstrators then placed pressure on their local Woolworth stores, and the demonstrations became part of the great Civil Rights Movement of the 1960s. By July 1960 business leaders in Greensboro had desegregated their lunch counters. Eventually legislation and voluntary desegregation opened establishments across the country to Black patrons.

In 1972 the college was renamed the North Carolina Agricultural and Technical State University. Among the well-known alumni of this university are Dr. Jesse Jackson, civil rights leader; Congressman Edolphus Towns of New York; and astronaut Dr. Ronald McNair, mission specialist on the ill-fated flight of the *Challenger* in January 1986. This historic site represents the evolution of the state's first Black land-grant campus from a college preparatory school to an outstanding institution of higher education. The university is listed in the *National Register of Historic Places.*

DATE ESTABLISHED:	1891
ADDRESS:	E. side of Dudley Street between Bluford Street and Headen Drive, Greensboro
TELEPHONE:	Campus tours, (800) 443-8964; campus information, (910) 334-7411; admissions, (910) 334-7946
VISITING HOURS:	When college is open; museum, Tues.–Fri. 9–12, 2–3, closed Sat.–Mon. except by appointment
SOURCES:	NRHPINF. Personal visit, summer 1990. C. Ndege Frigillans, director, African Heritage Museum. *Encylopedia of African-American Civil Rights. NAFEO's 117 Historically and Predominantly Black Colleges and Universities.*

Bennett College

The state of North Carolina chartered Bennett College in 1889. Affiliated with the United Methodist Church, it had been already established in 1873 as a coeducational normal school with the mission of providing educational opportunities for African American men and women. In 1926 the institution became a liberal arts college for women.

The Bennett College campus consists of seven residence halls, four main classroom buildings, a gymnasium, a chapel, an administration building, a student union, a health-counseling center, and a library. The Carnegie Building is one of the historic buildings on campus.

Today Bennett enrolls approximately 572 female students, 97 percent of them African American. In keeping with this enrollment, the college maintains a special collection of papers written "by/for women of the African Diaspora."

DATE ESTABLISHED:	1873
ADDRESS:	900 E. Washington Street, Greensboro
TELEPHONE:	Main number, (910) 273-4431; Office of Admissions, (910) 370-8624; Office of Public Relations, (910) 370-8646
VISITING HOURS:	Mon.–Fri. by appointment; closed all major holidays and weekends (unless prearranged)
FEES:	None
SOURCE:	Survey form returned by Bennett College. Personal visit, summer 1990.

Machpelah (Iron Station)

Tucker's Grove Camp Meeting Ground

An arbor more than one hundred years old in an old oak grove, surrounded by a rectangle of wooden "tents," and a camp-meeting tradition stretching back more than one hundred and twenty years—these represent the spirit of the Tucker's Grove Camp Meeting Ground, a place that draws families home each year from as far away as New York and California. Possibly the oldest continuously operating Black campground in North Carolina, Tucker's Grove grew out of the western North Carolina camp-meeting movement of the late eighteenth and nineteenth centuries. It served the needs of former slaves who had worked on the vast four-hundred acre iron "plantations" in the area—plantations that gave the town of Iron Station its name. Sixty to one hundred slaves worked at each of the region's iron furnaces, complexes that operated twenty-four hours per day and bore names such as Vesuvius, Stonewall, and Mt. Welcome. The furnaces operated from the 1790s through the 1880s with labor provided by Black slaves. The names of the Black families that worked at the furnaces—Smith, Graham, Brevard—are associated with those who attend Tucker's Grove Camp Meeting Ground today.

During slavery, the workers were restricted in their comings and goings. Even though all the iron furnaces were located within ten miles of Iron Station, slaves were restricted to their own areas, and large meetings were banned. After emancipation the camp meetings, always a celebration of the harvest for Black people and white people alike, were for the former slaves an especially cherished time because they were able, at last, to gather in large numbers and to make friends with their neighbors from other plantations.

The camp meetings started before emancipation. Bishop Francis Asbury, a Methodist missionary in North Carolina, preached to frontier Methodist congregations in the state. As he moved from place to place between 1780 and 1816, he became concerned about the religious and educational welfare of the slaves whom he met because some owners would not permit their slaves to attend Methodist services. The practices varied, however. An earlier white meeting place called Rock Springs Campground was incorporated by the North Carolina legislature in the 1840s and operated by the Methodist Episcopal Church South; it was attended by both Black and white worshipers until 1867. About 1868 the Reverend W. G. Matton of the Methodist Episcopal Church North came south, and he and a Black minister encouraged some of the people to establish the integrated Seven Springs Campground. Reconstruction, with polarizing activities by the Ku Klux Klan and similar groups, led to a split, and by 1873 most white members had pulled out of the Seven Springs Campground.

About 1871 negotiations began to buy land from William Clay Tucker, a white landowner; the deed was completed by his widow in 1875. For the first time the Black worshipers, whose trustees came primarily from Brevard Chapel, a local church, owned their own campsite in a serene oak grove. Since 1876 Tucker's Grove has operated as a Methodist Episcopal camp-meeting site operated by several local churches.

The complex is designed on a communal plan. Individual shelters are situated around a central arbor, which is the most sacred area. The original arbors were true brush arbors—frames with branches of trees on top to shelter from the sun; they had to be renewed each year. Today the open rectangular shelter has a deep pyramidal roof held up on braced tree trunks; in the original building plan no nails were used, showing the masterful skills of the builders. Inside is a pulpit platform with a long wooden mourners' bench at its front. The choir has three short rows of seating, and worshipers are seated in three sections of pews constructed from wide planks.

Families come to the campground for one week each year (enthusiasm and anticipation of seeing old friends have stretched the visit to two weeks or three weeks for some families), and they live in individual frame structures, called "tents," which surround the arbor. In the early years of the campground, tents were made of cloth or pine bark; now they are frame structures, each owned by an individual family. The oldest of still-standing tents date back to about 1875. Inside, the tents have unfinished walls, dirt floors, and ventilation gaps in the lower walls and beneath the eaves. The front room has a low wooden platform, and sometimes an upper platform, where sleeping pallets are placed.

Rudolph Young, avid collector and scribe for more than twenty years of the region's Black history, remembers coming to the campground as a child. The Black community, he said, was called Tucker's Grove and the white community was called Machpelah, but both were located in Iron Station. Rules were more strict then. According to Young, "There were no booths on the fairway for the selling of food and trinkets, there was little social mixing of the younger people, and there was no strolling up and down through the evenings to meet and talk with others. Families arrived on wagons bringing their own food and wood; once they arrived, the emphasis was strongly on the religious experience."

Traditions are strong at Tucker's Grove, which is listed in the *National Register of Historic Places.* A strong sense of tradition draws families back to spend their vacations in the simple, rustic surroundings where they worship as their families have done for well over a century. Dorrie Abernathy, a man who died in 1966, attended the Tucker's Grove camp meetings for 95 of his 105 years.

Albert Sanders, now more than seventy years old, recalls, "When I was a boy, there were services morning, noon, and night. Now because so many are working, there is one service at 7 P.M. Back then everyone was farming, and they came after they would lay by the crops. It was a farmer's vacation. Now just those who are retired are there all day long. On weekends, though, everyone's there. They sleep there at night and get up in the morning and go to work. Young people and those of all ages still want to go to Tucker's Grove. We don't ever want to stop."

DATE ESTABLISHED: 1874

ADDRESS: Meeting ground, rural area east of Boger City, Lincolnton, and Iron Station and north of Charlotte (from Lincolnton, east on NC 27 to NC 73, east on NC 73 to NC 1360 [Beth Haven Church Road], turn left to Tucker's Grove Camp Meeting Ground; from Charlotte travel north on NC 16 to NC 73, turn west on NC 73 and go 4 or 5 miles to NC 1360 [Beth Haven Church Road], turn right to Tucker's Grove Camp Meeting Ground); Tucker's Grove United Methodist Church, affiliated with the campground, NC 73 across from Beth Haven Church Road

TELEPHONE: Tucker's Grove United Methodist Church, (704) 735-3713

VISITING HOURS: Private, always open; religious reunion first 3 weeks of Aug. each year, with the primary religious service held the last week in August; several local churches also hold a communion service at the campground the first week in Oct.

FEES: None

SOURCES: NRHPINF. Personal visit, summer 1990. Telephone conversations May 25, 1994, city clerk's office, Lincolnton; May 25, 1994, Ms. Jean Johnson of Christian Ministries, Lincolnton; May 25, 1994, Ms. Ola Mae Foster, social worker, Lincoln County Schools; May 28, 1994, Mr. Rudolph Young of Stanley, N.C.; May 28, 1994, Mr. Albert Sanders, Stanley, N.C.; Jan. 1, 1995, Reverend Albert O. Perkins, pastor, Tucker's Grove United Methodist Church.

Milton

Thomas Day House

Thomas Day, who was born free in Virginia in 1801, showed a remarkable artistic talent from an early age. When he was only ten years old, he was sent to deliver some produce to a fine house in the community. The owner invited him in to hear her parlor melodeon, but Thomas was more impressed by the fine furniture he saw than by the music. Intently, he studied the fine carved antiques and then he examined a footstool nearby. When he returned home, he took a knife and patiently carved in walnut a small replica of the footstool he had seen. Amazed, his mother showed the fine work to the family. They, too, recognized his extraordinary talent and began to provide three years training in cabinetmaking for him in Boston and Washington. When he returned to his shop on his mother's farm, he began producing fine mahogany furniture for sale in Milton. In 1823 he moved to Milton, where he converted an old yellow-brick tavern into a factory.

Day was so skilled at his work that wealthy white people sent their slaves to be trained under his direction. Once the slaves had learned their work well, however, their owners called them back. Day also trained some white apprentices, but in order to have steady help, Day, a Black man himself, became a slaveholder.

By 1834 Day's business was thriving; by mid-century he had the largest production and the greatest number of apprentices in the state. He was invited to stay in homes of wealthy citizens for several days at a time to plan designs and furnishings. The governor of North Carolina was one of his clients.

Day produced elegant and distinctive furniture and woodwork. The furniture had Empire styling with ornamentation that appeared to be African-inspired. His original carvings for architectural ornamentation were in demand in North Carolina, Virginia, and Georgia.

Day was a proud man and a leader who did not easily accept personal injustices. On marrying Aquilla Wilson, a free Black woman from Virginia, he learned that North Carolina law prevented free Black people from coming into the state. Day threatened to leave North Carolina if his wife could not come into the state to live. Since he was both an economic and a cultural asset to the town, Milton citizens successfully petitioned the assembly to exempt his wife from the law; she was able to join him in Milton.

Day, who was on the board of directors of the state bank and the board of Milton's Presbyterian Church, showed his pride on another occasion. Although he was on the church's board of directors, he was expected to sit upstairs in the segregated section. When asked to carve pews for the church, he agreed to do so only if he and his family could sit in a pew downstairs. This request was granted.

Union Tavern, once one of the finest taverns in North Carolina, is known today also as the Thomas Day House. The brick building had interior brick walls. Day's studio/showroom was downstairs, and he and his family lived upstairs. A shop in back included a kiln to dry lumber and a waterwheel. Severely damaged in a 1989 fire, the historic building is undergoing extensive restoration; the roof has already been reconstructed and the walls have been stabilized. The restoration is expected to be complete in 1996, Milton's bicentennial year. Although construction work prevents visitors from seeing the interior, tours come to the site often to view the building through the chain-link fence. Visiting groups also see a slide presentation at the Milton Presbyterian Church or the Women's Club that provides information about Thomas Day, his furniture, and the history of the town of Milton. The Restoration Committee owns a bureau, bed, and sofa crafted by Thomas Day; eventually they will be displayed in the house. The site is listed in the *National Register of Historic Places.*

DATE BUILT:	c1810
ADDRESS:	Main Street, south side between Lee Street and Farmer's Alley, Milton
TELEPHONE:	(910) 234-7215
VISITING HOURS:	Closed during construction, but visitors can drive by
SOURCES:	Telephone call Apr. 20, 1994, North Carolina Historic Preservation Foundation. Telephone conversation May 15, 1994, Marian Thomas, president of the Thomas Day House/Union Tavern Restoration. NRHPINF. *International Library of Negro Life and History,* 71.

Oxford

Central Orphanage

Central Orphanage is a pioneer North Carolina Black orphanage, one of Granville County's major early institutions. The cluster of buildings was built for Black orphan children in the early part of the century and continues in use as an orphanage today.

In 1882 members of the Shiloh and Wake Associations, two Black Baptist organizations, established the Colored Orphanage Association in Henderson, North Carolina. A year later the association purchased 23 acres of land and incorporated as the nondenominational Colored Orphanage Asylum of North Carolina.

The first superintendent, Reverend Robert Shepard, was born a slave in Raleigh. As a small child, Shepard, an orphan, was given to his owner's daughter as a wedding present. Reverend Shepard served initially as orphanage superintendent without pay. When he arrived at his post, the orphanage consisted of a dilapidated barn and a small house sheltering eight children and a matron. During his tenure the orphanage secured donations from churches, fraternal orders, associations, and the state legislature. As the association grew in size and stature, it purchased an additional 148 acres of land in 1895 for $1,440. The children raised cotton and corn as cash crops and grew other crops for food.

Shepard was succeeded in 1907 by former U.S. Congressman Henry Plummer Cheatham (1857–

1935). Cheatham, who was born a slave, graduated from Shaw University in Raleigh in 1882. He became the orphanage superintendent in 1907 and kept this position until his death in 1935. Cheatham supervised the construction of the major brick buildings and guided Central Orphanage's rise as an institution of statewide importance.

The centerpiece of buildings at this site—the 1915 Henry Plummer Cheatham Building—was named in honor of this very prominent Black resident. The building is the finest example of Italianate architectural style in Granville County.

DATE ESTABLISHED: Colored Orphanage Association, 1882; Cheatham Building, 1915
ADDRESS: Antioch Drive and Raleigh Road, Oxford
TELEPHONE: (919) 693-7617
VISITING HOURS: By appointment
SOURCES: Personal visit, summer 1990. Telephone call to site, Aug. 2, 1995. NRHPINF.

Raleigh

North Carolina Museum of History

The North Carolina Museum of History has a collection of furniture designed by Thomas Day, a free Black man and cabinetmaker from Milton, North Carolina. (See the entry on the Thomas Day House in Milton.) At the present time one item created by Day is on display in the museum's Chronological History Gallery—a dresser/bureau with mirror. Additional Day items are in storage, but the museum plans to display an entire room of his finely crafted furniture.

ADDRESS: One E. Edenton Street, Raleigh
TELEPHONE: (919) 715-0200
VISITING HOURS: Tues.–Sat. 9–5, Sun. 1–6; closed Mon.; open most holidays
FEES: None
SOURCE: Telephone conversation Apr. 18, 1994, Patricia Phillips, chief curator, Preservation Section, North Carolina Museum of History.

Shaw University
Estey Hall

Estey Hall, an impressive Victorian building built in 1873, is Shaw University's oldest surviving building and one of the first college structures intended for Black women in America. The college was established in 1865 when Henry Martin Tupper, a white Baptist preacher from Massachusetts, began teaching a group of former slaves and their children in a hotel room in Raleigh. As the class outgrew this setting, it moved to a building provided by the Freedmen's Bureau. Elijah Shaw, an abolitionist leader from Massachusetts, donated the funds, and students are said to have dug clay, molded bricks, and cut timber for the first building.

A catalog from 1875 described Estey Hall as the "finest building in the state" and "the pride of the colored people of North Carolina." The four-story brick structure is well located in a setting of large trees on the Shaw University campus. Off-white stucco provides a dramatic contrast to the red brick walls, and a frame cupola caps the cross-gable roof. Stuccoed brick surrounds the arched openings, and stuccoed brick quoins define each corner of the building.

Shaw University is the mother university of African American colleges in North Carolina and has produced many leaders in their fields. Shaw's graduates founded Elizabeth City State University, Fayetteville State University, and North Carolina Central University in Durham. Henry P. Cheatham, class of 1882, served as superintendent of the Colored Orphanage in Oxford. Two Shaw graduates served as heads of universities: Dr. James E. Cheek, Howard University, and Dr. Collie Coleman, Allen University. University archives contain memorabilia and artifacts associated with the university's history.

DATE BUILT: 1873
ADDRESS: 118 E. South Street, Raleigh
TELEPHONE: (919) 546-8200
VISITING HOURS: Private; telephone to arrange visit
SOURCES: Personal visit, summer 1990. NRHPINF. "Strides to Excellence." "Inaugural Address," 4. *National Register of Historic Places*, 554. *The Smithsonian Guide to Historic America*, 78.

St. Augustine's College Campus

St. Augustine's College in Raleigh has a beautiful campus with many lovely stone buildings. It opened during Reconstruction with support from the missions of the Protestant Episcopal Church and the Freedmen's Bureau. The first students had only the basics of literacy, but the school developed their scope of knowledge; eventually it attained the full status of a college. St. Augustine's curriculum gradually shifted from its initial emphasis on teacher training to a technical and trade orientation. Later its emphasis was on the liberal arts.

Some of the historic buildings on campus include St. Augustine's Chapel (1895), a Gothic stone building; Benson Library (1896), now part of Taylor Hall; and St. Agnes Hospital (1909), another stone structure.

DATE ESTABLISHED: 1867
ADDRESS: 1315 Oakwood Avenue, Raleigh
TELEPHONE: (919) 516-4016
VISITING HOURS: Mon.–Fri. by appointment
SOURCES: Personal visit, summer 1990. NRHPINF. Charlotte McKensie Hunter, secretary, St. Augustine's College.

Reidsville

North Washington Avenue Workers' Houses

The North Washington Avenue Workers' Houses are five almost-identical examples of early twentieth-century housing built for Black workers. In the late nineteenth and early twentieth centuries, the number of agricultural jobs in North Carolina declined. At the same time Black workers were drawn increasingly to employment opportunities in the state's cotton mills and tobacco factories. As the towns grew, the industries needed housing for their workers. The American Tobacco Company, which had constructed a large facility in Reidsville in 1912, soon began to put up small, inexpensive housing for its Black workers.

The cluster of five frame cottages in the 300 block of North Washington Avenue is representative of the kind of housing made available to workers across the state; their architectural design is typical of what was common in traditional rural houses in North Carolina. This group is the only surviving example of houses built for this purpose by the American Tobacco Company. The five houses are listed in the *National Register of Historic Places.*

DATE BUILT: c1917

ADDRESS: East side of the 300 block of N. Washington Avenue, Reidsville

VISITING HOURS: Private, visitors may drive by

SOURCES: Personal visit, summer 1990. National Register Information System. State of North Carolina Division of Archives and History Individual Property Form.

Salem

Historic Old Salem

Old Salem, Inc., is a living-history museum in the restored eighteenth-century village of Salem. The village was established in 1766 by the Moravians, a Protestant evangelical German immigrant group from Bethlehem, Pennsylvania. The Moravians owned slaves and also hired many free Black workers; both groups became an important and highly visible part of the community as early as 1771. In an unusual arrangement, the church, rather than the individual Moravian families, owned most of the slaves. The church then rented out the slaves only to those families that could justify needing them. Because this was a trading community rather than a farming community, few families could justify the need for slaves to the satisfaction of the church.

Old Salem incorporates the Black history of the site in many areas of its historical interpretation, showing how the Black experience here differed in many ways from that in other places. African Americans spoke English and German, for example, and Old Salem and the surrounding Moravian villages may have had the largest concentration of German-speaking Black people in America. The African Americans often joined the Moravian Church and were incorporated into the highly structured theocratic community. Some were buried side by side with white Moravians in the church graveyard.

Staff members have been translating German records relating to the Black experience at this site. These include highly detailed Moravian church reports and diaries that have made possible the reconstruction of detailed profiles of the eighteenth-century lives of slaves known as Abraham, Peter Oliver, Johann, Samuel, Anna, and Christian.

Although Black history is interpreted at several of the structures, two—the 1784 tavern and the 1861 St. Philips Church—are strongly associated with the Black experience. A room in the Salem Tavern has exhibit space showing where Black people once worked. A Black Moravian congregation worshiped in St. Philips Church until they moved to a new building in 1949. Plans are under way to restore the church, and to interpret the roots of Afro-American involvement in the Moravian Church. Because of heavy Moravian evangelizing in the West Indies, South America, and Africa since the eighteenth century, the church today is three-quarters Black worldwide.

Archaeological explorations are ongoing at Old Salem. High school students interested in Black history assist in the search for old artifacts and information. Old Salem has twenty restored buildings that are open to the public as exhibit buildings. Fifty-four other structures are residences. Costumed interpreters demonstrate trades and crafts of the 1766 to 1850 period, including cooking over an old fireplace, washing clothing by hand, and demonstrating the joiner and pewter crafts, among others.

DATE ESTABLISHED: 1766

ADDRESS: 600 S. Main Street, Winston-Salem

TELEPHONE: (800) 441-5305; main number, (910) 721-7300

VISITING HOURS: Mon.–Sat. 9:30–4:30, Sun. 1:30–4:30; closed Thanksgiving Day, Dec. 24–25

FEES: Adults, $12; children 6–16, $6; children under 6 with adult, free

SOURCES: Robert Stern, director of information, Old Salem. Jon Sensbach, Afro-American program adviser, Old Salem. Telephone conversation May 18, 1994, Joyce Knabb, assistant, Tour Office. Telephone call to site, Aug. 3, 1995. *National Register of Historic Places,* 544.

Salisbury

Livingstone College Historic District

The Livingstone College historic district remains nearly unchanged as an example of a late nineteenth- and early twentieth-century Black college campus and its surrounding community. Livingstone College is the result of the initiative and commitment of the Black church to build an institution of higher learning.

When the Civil War ended, education for Black students in the South often began with efforts led by white missionary groups or philanthropic organizations. In contrast, Livingstone College developed through the efforts of the African Methodist Episcopal Zion Church. Because of its strong interest in education, the church established Zion Wesley Institute, a church school in Concord, North Carolina. When the school moved from Concord to Salisbury, its name changed to Livingstone College. The early curriculum emphasized the training of teachers and ministers, self-help, and the trades. By the twentieth century, however, the curriculum had a more-academic emphasis.

The college has produced many leaders of the A.M.E. Zion Church. Missionary and educator James E. K. Aggrey of the Gold Coast (now Ghana) of Africa was associated with Livingstone College, as was leader Joseph Charles Price, the college's founder. Price is buried in the Poets and Dreamers Garden on the campus.

The historic district, which consists of the college campus and the surrounding residential area, is a nearly intact example of an early Black college community.

DATE ESTABLISHED: 1882

ADDRESS: 701 W. Monroe Street, Salisbury

TELEPHONE: Campus tours, (704) 638-5502; switchboard, (704) 638-5534 or (704) 638-5500

VISITING HOURS: Private residences, visitors may drive by; college hours, Mon.–Fri. 9–4:30; tours on Thurs., contact the college office to schedule tour

SOURCES: NRHPINF. Personal visit, summer 1990. Telephone call to site, Aug. 3, 1995.

Sedalia Vicinity

Palmer Memorial Institute Historic District

Palmer Memorial Institute was a well-known private school that reflected the vision and excellence of its leader, Dr. Charlotte Hawkins Brown. The school was established in South Carolina, a state that, prior to the Civil War, did not provide education for Black children whether they were slave or free. During the Civil War, missionaries from New England came south and taught small numbers of Black children. This type of education continued during the Reconstruction period in a few schools for African American children. Far greater numbers of white students, on the other hand, attended locally funded public schools. In the early years of the twentieth century, Governor Charles Aycock promised universal education, but there were great inequities in state funding, differences only partially reduced by contributions from civic, religious, and philanthropic organizations.

Dr. Charlotte Hawkins Brown, an African American, came to Sedalia in 1901 to teach at the Bethany Normal and Industrial Institute. She had lived in New England as a child and had attended normal school there before coming to Sedalia. After a short period, Bethany Institute closed and Brown returned to Massachusetts to raise money for a new school. In 1902 she returned and founded the Palmer Memorial Institute.

The Sedalia-based school emphasized agriculture, industry, and home economics in its early curriculum. However, Brown had a vision for a curriculum that included more college preparatory courses, and she gradually influenced a change in this direction. As word spread about the school, students from prominent Black families across the United States and from foreign countries enrolled; by the mid-1950s Palmer Memorial Institute had earned a national reputation as a college preparatory school for Black students.

Brown believed teachers and staff should live on the campus or near it in order to interact with students. She also believed in learning by doing. Two campus buildings reflected these philosophies. The Carrie M. Stone Cottage, built in 1948 as a residence for single female faculty members, enabled staff to live on campus. The Massachusetts Congregational Women's Cottage, built in 1948 as a home economics center, encouraged students to learn by doing.

The school had reached its height under Brown's leadership when she retired as president in 1952. When she died in 1961, the outstanding and well-respected leader was laid to rest in a serene place on the campus she had loved. Three more presidents followed, but financial problems, along with a devastating fire, led to a gradual decline in the school's fortunes. As a result, Palmer Memorial Institute closed in 1971.

The campus today is named in honor of Dr. Charlotte Hawkins Brown, the educator who played a prominent role in building a reputation for academic and cultural excellence. The state of North Carolina operates the attractive, tree-shaded campus, providing exhibits and audio-visual presentations on the contributions of Black citizens to education in North Carolina. Visitors who tour the campus can see the restored Canary Cottage, where efforts are ongoing to secure for the cottage furnishings that once belonged to Brown. Visitors can also pass by the colonial-revival and bungalow-style buildings where Palmer's students were taught.

DATE ESTABLISHED:	1902
ADDRESS:	6135 Burlington Road, vicinity of Sedalia (north and south sides of US 70, approximately 0.7–1.0 mile northwest of Junction with NC 3056 [Rock Creek Dairy Road])
TELEPHONE:	(910) 449-4846
VISITING HOURS:	Apr. 1–Oct. 31, Mon.–Sat. 9–5, Sun. 1–5; Nov. 1–Mar. 31, Tues.–Sat. 10–4, Sun. 1–4, closed Mon.; tours of campus available
FEES:	None
SOURCES:	NRHPINF. Personal visit, summer 1990. Telephone conversation May 21, 1994, Barbara Wiley, historic interpreter. *When and Where I Enter.*

Wilmington

Latimer House and Garden
Slave House

Zebulon Latimer, a prosperous Wilmington businessman, and his wife, Elizabeth, built this Victorian-Italianate-style house in 1852. The servants' quarters (now reconstructed) behind the main house was home to fifteen slaves over a period of years. It is not known how many lived in the house at one time. The two-story, five-room servants' house has a first- and a second-story porch and a courtyard with an attractive garden. A little information has been passed down about the slaves who lived here. On the one hand, Mrs. Latimer was remembered for choosing to keep the slave families intact; she refused to sell a slave child as some slaveowners in the area did. On the other hand, there is a letter still in existence, explaining to Mr. Lattimer (possibly Zebulon Latimer, but this is not certain) that one of his slaves is on the way to Canada. The letter, sent by Boyd's City Express with two cents postage, requested that a response be sent to an antislavery office, strongly suggesting that the slave had run away. The letter gave this information and request:

> Mr. Lattimer:
>
> Sir this is to inform you that the slave that was at the American Hotel which I was informed was yours is now on her way to Canada.
>
> I sent for her and told the man to tell her that I had a bundle for you and when she came myself and some friends just taken her up and put her in the cab and drove off with her so you need not give yourself any uneasiness she is safe enough but why I write is to inform you that I want her clothes in order to send them to her which therefoire [sic] that you would inform me whether you will let me have them. Just send your letter to the Anti Slavery Office 61 John Street and oblige your humble servant
>
> Juble Cain
> Oct. 13, 1853 [exact year is not entirely legible][2]

The Zebulon Latimer House, listed in the *National Register of Historic Places,* was home to three generations of Latimers until 1963, when it became the headquarters of the Lower Cape Fear Historical Society. Today it serves as a historic-house museum.

DATE BUILT: Main house, 1852; slave house, 1832, reconstructed 1972

ADDRESS: 126 S. Third Street, Wilmington

TELEPHONE: Lower Cape Fear Historical Society, which operates the Latimer House, (910) 762-0492

VISITING HOURS: Main house, Tues.–Sun. 10–4; slave quarters (rented) open for Christmas candlelight tour and early April for Azalea Tour (contact historical society for exact dates); closed Mon., Thanksgiving, Christmas, New Year's Day

FEES: Adults, $3; youth through high school age, $1

SOURCES: Diane C. Cashman, archivist. Telephone conversation May 25, 1994, Jean Scott, executive director of the Lower Cape Fear Historical Society. *Latimer House and Garden.* "Letter regarding a slave."

St. Stephen African Methodist Episcopal Church

In May 1865, a period when federal forces were occupying Wilmington, 642 African Americans withdrew from membership in the Front Street Methodist Church and joined the African church led by Reverend W. H. Hunter, an African American pastor. Although they constructed their first church on Red Cross Street in 1866, in 1880 they began to build a new church. White citizens also contributed to the building fund, while African Americans designed and built the structure. Lewis Hollingsworth drew plans for the church and served as contractor; Daniel Lee provided bricks from his own brickyard; and twelve master carpenters and master masons worked on the construction. The church on Red Cross Street was demolished.

Funds were limited, and four years passed before the new church was ready for occupancy. While work proceeded on the interior, the congregation worshiped in the basement. When the church reached its present form in 1888, its interior was one of the most elegant in Wilmington; it even displayed a new pipe organ operated by a water-powered motor. St. Stephen's still has the original gas chandeliers with polished mirrored reflectors as well as the fine stained glass, the ornate dark woods, and the richly colored red carpeting.

President William Howard Taft visited Wilmington in November 1909. He first greeted white schoolchildren at Market and Third Streets; then he saluted the county's Black schoolchildren from a stand on the steps of St. Stephen's Church. Today a state historical marker at the intersection of Third and Red Cross Streets describes St. Stephen A.M.E. Church; the present structure is located two blocks east of the marker.

DATE BUILT: Church, 1880–1888; annex, 1913

ADDRESS: 501 Red Cross Street, Wilmington

TELEPHONE: (910) 762-9829

VISITING HOURS: Office hours, Mon.–Fri. 10–3; July 1–Sept. 16, Sun. school 8:30, Sun. service 10; Sept. 17–June, Sun. school 9:30, Sun. service 11

SOURCES: Diane C. Cashman, archivist, Lower Cape Fear Historical Society. Telephone conversation May 29, 1994, Reverend Calhoun. Telephone conversation, Jan. 5, 1995, Elsie Tilson, administrative assistant, Junior League of Wilmington. Telephone conversation Aug. 1, 1995, Valerie McIver, secretary, St. Stephen Church. *Wilmington, North Carolina.*

Wilson

East Wilson Historic District

The East Wilson historic district, with almost one thousand contributing buildings, is one of the largest historic districts in North Carolina. This was a major manufacturing and commercial center in eastern North Carolina as well as a major community of African American people in the South.

By 1919 the city of Wilson had become the nation's leading tobacco market, and the predominantly residential neighborhood of East Wilson developed near the tobacco warehouse district. The variety of houses built from about 1890 to the beginning of World War II reflect the lifestyles of workers and well-to-do middle-class residents. Workers' homes include the "shanty," the "saddlebag," the shotgun, and the "square-built." The district has the state's largest collection of shotgun houses in one neighborhood. Homes of middle-class Black people include the Queen Anne, colonial revival, and bungalow styles from this period.

Many Black residents made significant contributions to the community. Dr. Frank A. Hargrave established Wilson's first hospital for Black people in 1905. Samuel H. Vick, the major landowner in East Wilson, was a businessman, educator, postmaster, and religious leader. Between the 1920s and 1940s, Nestus Freeman, a Black builder and Wilson's most skilled stonemason, built numerous bungalows as well as a group of five unusual stone houses and sheds. Freeman's own home is a stone-faced bungalow; his yard is decorated with an assortment of concrete fantasy creatures. East Wilson is one of North Carolina's largest intact neighborhoods that reflect the lifestyles of Black people in the early twentieth century.

DATE ESTABLISHED: c1890

ADDRESS: East of the Seaboard RR tracks, roughly bounded by E. Gold and Academy Streets, Ward Boulevard, Woodard, Elvie, Railroad, and Pender Streets, Wilson

VISITING HOURS: Private, visitors may drive by

SOURCES: NRHPINF. Personal visit, summer 1990.

Winston-Salem

Winston-Salem State University

Winston-Salem State University was founded in 1892 as the Slater Industrial Academy. The school began in a one-room frame structure with twenty-five pupils and their teacher. The state of North Carolina recognized the school in 1895 and chartered it in 1897 as the Slater Industrial and State Normal School. From the beginning the emphasis was on training elementary teachers who would teach students to be good citizens.

In 1925 the General Assembly of North Carolina granted a new charter that extended the curriculum above the high school level. The name changed to Winston-Salem Teachers College, and the school was empowered to confer appropriate degrees. A historical sketch of the college notes that Winston-Salem Teachers College was the first Black institution in the nation to grant degrees for teaching in the elementary grades.

DATE ESTABLISHED: 1892

ADDRESS: 601 S. Martin Luther King Jr. Drive, Winston-Salem

TELEPHONE: (910) 750-2070, or (910) 750-2000

VISITING HOURS: By appointment

SOURCE: Lelia L. Vickers, Winston-Salem State University.

Notes

1. Dorothy Spruill Redford with Michael D'Orso, *Somerset Homecoming: Recovering a Lost Heritage* (New York, Anchor, 1989), 106.

2. "Letter Regarding a Slave," c1853, from the archives of the Lower Cape Fear Historical Society, Wilmington, North Carolina.

Works Consulted

"Black Builders in Antebellum North Carolina." Catherine W. Bishir. *The North Carolina Historical Review* 61, no. 4 (Oct. 1984), 423–61.

Broadening the Spectrum. Asheville, N.C.: YMI Cultural Center, n.d. [pamphlet]

Cornerstone 3, no. 3 (Aug.–Sept., 1989). [newsletter of the YMI Cultural Center]

Encyclopedia of African-American Civil Rights: From Emancipation to the Present. Charles Lowery and John F. Marszalek, eds. New York: Greenwood, 1992.

Hippocrene U.S.A. Guide to Black America: A Directory of Historic and Cultural Sites Relating to Black America. Marcella Thum. New York: Hippocrene, 1992.

"Inaugural Address." Talbert O. Shaw. *Shaw University Focus* 6, no. 1 (winter 1989).

International Library of Negro Life and History: Historical Negro Biographies. Wilhelmena S. Robinson. New York: Publishers, 1970.

"Latimer House and Garden." Wilmington, N.C.: Lower Cape Fear Historical Soc., n.d. [flier]

NAFEO's 117 Historically and Predominantly Black Colleges and Universities. Vol. 8. Washington, D.C.: National Association for Equal Opportunity in Higher Education, 1988.

"Letter Regarding a Slave," from the archives of the Lower Cape Fear Historical Society, Wilmington, North Carolina.

National Register Information System. Washington, D.C.: National Park Service. [computer database]

National Register of Historic Places. Washington, D.C.: National Park Service, 1976.

"The Rosenwald Schools and Black Education in North Carolina." Thomas W. Hanchett. *The North Carolina Historical Review* 65, no. 4 (Oct. 1988), 387–444.

"Slave Life at Stagville." Alice Eley Jones, Black History Coordinator, Stagville. Fairntosh, N.C.: files of Stagville, n. d.

The Smithsonian Guide to Historic America: The Carolinas and the Appalachian States. Patricia L. Hudson and Sandra L. Ballard. New York: Stewart, Tabori & Chang, 1989.

Somerset Homecoming: Recovering a Lost Heritage. Dorothy Spruill Redford with Michael D'Orso. New York: Anchor, 1989.

"Strides to Excellence: Why Not the Best?" Raleigh, N.C.: Office of the President, Shaw University, n.d. [manuscript]

When and Where I Enter: The Impact of Black Women on Race and Sex in America. Paula Giddings. New York: William Morrow, 1984; New York: Bantam Books, 1988.

Wilmington, North Carolina: An Architectural and Historical Portrait. Tony P. Wrenn. Charlottesville: University Press of Virginia, 1984.

South Carolina

Beaufort

Robert Smalls House

Robert Smalls, a Civil War hero and a state legislator, was born a slave in 1839. He was raised at first in a small cabin on this property at 511 Prince Street and later lived in the household of Henry McKee, a planter who constructed the larger house on the same Prince Street lot in 1843. When Smalls was approximately twelve years old, his owner hired him out in Charleston. Smalls learned a seaman's skills and remained in Charleston until the Civil War began. The war had a special meaning to him because he believed it would free the slaves.

Although Smalls was assigned to serve as a pilot on the Confederate steamer, the *Planter,* his sympathies were with the Union side, and he began to plan a daring escape. In May 1862 Union forces were blockading Charleston. After the Confederate officers and white crew members on his ship were ashore for the night, Smalls smuggled his wife and children and families of other slave crewmen on board. At dawn he raised the Confederate flag, put on the captain's straw hat as a disguise, and guided the *Planter* past three Confederate forts on heavily guarded Fort Sumter. Once past the Confederate ships, he raised a white flag and guided his ship toward Union vessels, surrendering the *Planter* to Union officials on a Union blockade ship. The Union navy was delighted to have the ship, which was valued at $60,000. They rewarded Smalls with a sum of money, appointed him as a U.S. Navy pilot on the *Planter,* and used his skills in guiding Union ships in the sea island areas.

The abduction of the *Planter* was not the last of Small's heroic deeds. In December 1863 after the *Planter* came under Confederate fire, the ship's captain fled from his post. Smalls took the helm and, in spite of the danger, returned fire and guided the *Planter* to safety. For this deed he was promoted to captain, a position he held until the ship was decommissioned in 1866.

After the Civil War, Smalls entered the political arena and was elected to the state Constitutional Convention of 1868. He advocated rights for former slaves and worked to establish free education for children of all races.

Elected to the state assembly in 1868 and to the state senate in 1870, Smalls fought corruption in government. He continued to fight to improve conditions for African Americans, using legislation to consolidate gains and to counteract growing threats and hostility from white South Carolinians. His strong support for civil rights caused the opposition to fight against his reelection. Nevertheless, Smalls was elected to the U.S. Congress in 1874.

The challenges became more severe in 1895 when the Constitutional Convention of South Carolina sought to repeal the right of Black people to vote. The white legislators also proposed laws that effectively would have reenslaved Black people. In spite of the flood of racist sentiment, Smalls continued to work for equal opportunity. As a state legislator and a member of the U.S. Congress during Reconstruction years, he was a voice for equality.

Following his years as a legislator Smalls worked from 1889 to 1913 as a customs collector in Beaufort. He lived again in the house at 511 Prince Street, having purchased it at a tax sale in 1863. The purchase had become possible after Congress, from 1862 to 1863, enacted legislation calling for direct taxes on property in occupied territory. Apparently the owner was unable to pay the taxes and Smalls was able to purchase the house he had lived in as a slave. His ownership of the house later was contested on the basis of the validity of the taxation legislation. The case went all the way to the U.S. Supreme Court, where a decision was made establishing the validity of the legislation and in favor of Smalls. Smalls and his descendants lived in the house on Prince Street for approximately ninety years. Smalls died in 1915.

The Robert Smalls house is a large frame two-story house with a raised basement. The central entrances each have a transom. Shuttered windows flank the door downstairs and the door leading to the porch upstairs, and the two-story front porch has balustrades. Although the house has had extensive alterations, it still has much of its original character. It is listed in the *National Register of Historic Places.*

Smalls was a member of the First African Baptist Church near his home at 600 New Street. A Robert Smalls monument is located at Baptist Tabernacle Church, 907 Craven Street.

DATE BUILT: 1843
ADDRESS: 511 Prince Street, Beaufort
VISITING HOURS: Private, visitors may drive or walk by
SOURCES: Personal visit, summer 1990. NRHPINF. *The Smithsonian Guide to Historic America: The Carolinas and the Appalachian States,* 184. *National Register of Historic Places,* 682. *International Library of Negro Life and History,* 124–5. *African Americans: Voices of Triumph,* vol. 1, 82.

Camden

Bonds Conway House

Bonds Conway was born in slavery about 1763. His owner was Edwin Conway, and Bonds may have been a body servant to Edwin's son, Peter. In 1792 Peter Conway entered a notice at the County Court making it known that Bonds "having conducted himself in a just and faithful manner" had the right to travel back and forth on his own, to hire himself out to work, and to trade. Bonds took the Conway name as his surname and began to work as a carpenter.

When he was approximately thirty years old, he bought his freedom. Conway's earnings were substantial enough to be able to buy property, and he purchased land and built his house some time between 1812 and 1843.

When Bonds Conway died in 1843, he left a house to each of his own surviving children. The last person bearing the Conway name sold the family property in 1890. The Kershaw County Historical Society received the property in 1977 and moved it to the present location.

Bonds Conway was a skilled carpenter, and a careful restoration, completed in 1980, brought out the architectural detail he had created. Today the furnishings in the house are of a type appropriate in a nineteenth-century cottage.

DATE BUILT: Between 1812 and 1843
ADDRESS: 811 Fair Street, Camden
TELEPHONE: (803) 425-1123
VISITING HOURS: Thurs. 1–5
SOURCE: Kershaw County Historical Society.

Charleston

Avery Normal Institute

The American Missionary Association founded the Avery Normal Institute in 1865 as a college preparatory and teacher training institution. The school moved into its present location on Bull Street in 1867, and through the leadership of Francis Cardozo, it was transformed into a prestigious private school. Cardozo (1836–1903), a free Black man, served as South Carolina's secretary of state from 1868 to 1872 and as state treasurer from 1872 to 1876. It was natural for him to be interested in education. He attended school until the age of twelve when he was apprenticed to a carpenter. Over a period of nine years he saved his money for the purpose of attending school again. Receiving a scholarship, he studied at the University of Glasgow in Scotland for four years, winning prizes for achievement in Latin and Greek, then continued his studies in seminaries in Scotland and England. After returning to the United States in 1864 he served briefly as a minister in New Haven, Connecticut. In 1865, the American Missionary Association appointed him to head the Avery Institute that the association had just created in Charleston. In 1915 Benjamin F. Cox became the first Black principal of this school for African American students.

Avery Institute once included instructional levels from kindergarten through normal school. Until 1944 it served as the only college preparatory school for Charleston's Black community and was known as one of the finest Black private college preparatory schools in America. The school ended its proud history in 1954 when financial difficulties led to its closure.

Today the Avery Research Center for African American History and Culture is located in the historic building that housed the Avery Normal Institute. The research center was founded in 1985 as a result of joint efforts by alumni of the Avery Normal Institute and the College of Charleston. The historic building was renovated to house exhibits and documents that highlight "low country" African American history and culture. One room delights children with its arrangement and furnishings as a turn-of-the-century classroom. For the researcher, the downstairs area contains a reading room, archive area, and a rare-book room. The latter contains 4,000 volumes and periodicals, manuscripts, photographs, articles, and a file of newspaper clippings. The entire floor upstairs—once the school auditorium—features a floor exhibit with a map that traces African American roots from Sierra Leone to Charleston Harbor, from the Creole language of Sierra Leone to the Gullah language of the new world's southeastern coastal region. Here the visitor can trace key drop-off points along the Middle Passage. Background music is supplied by a recording of praise singers from the sea islands off the South Carolina coast.

The center also has a sea island exhibit of shrimp and fish nets as well as the works of sea island artist Jonathan Green. Together the exhibits document the story and language retentions of African Americans from Savannah, Georgia, to the South Carolina coastal regions.

DATE ESTABLISHED: Avery Normal Institute, 1867; museum, Dec. 1985

ADDRESS: 125 Bull Street, Charleston

TELEPHONE: (803) 727-2009

VISITING HOURS: Center, Mon.–Fri. 9–5; Reading Room, Mon.–Fri. 1–4:30; closed Sat.–Sun., state and federal holidays

FEES: Donation

SOURCES: Myrtle G. Glascoe, director, Avery Research Center. Telephone conversation Apr. 15, 1994, Alisandra Ravenel, student archives worker, Avery Research Center. *To Walk the Whole Journey*, 24. *International Library of Negro Life and History*, 60–61. *Encyclopedia of African-American Civil Rights*, 88–89.

Central Baptist Church

Central Baptist Church is believed to be one of the first Black churches founded and built entirely by Black Charlestonians. The congregation founded the church in 1891 and completed the building about 1893.

Central Baptist Church is located in a residential neighborhood with many Victorian-era houses. Built in an architectural style called "carpenter Gothic," the church features a copper roof, belfry, dome, and tower window with tracery. The interior has an unusual feature: ceiling murals depicting the life of Christ. The artist, Amohamed Milai, originally from India, began painting the murals in 1912 as a way to earn money to travel to Spain. He completed the work by November 1915 and was on his way. The murals, which depict several miracles, are a dominant feature of the church interior.

The adult education building of the church is a Victorian house built about 1875. The church and education building together are listed in the *National Register of Historic Places.*

DATE BUILT: c1893

ADDRESS: 26 Radcliffe Street, Charleston

TELEPHONE: (803) 577-4543

VISITING HOURS: Wed. 7 P.M.–9 P.M., prayer service Thurs. 6 A.M.–8 A.M., Sun. service 9:45–1; visits at other times by appointment with the pastor

SOURCES: NRHPINF. Telephone conversation Apr. 17, 1994, Reverend Charles Davis, associate minister.

Eliza's House at Middleton Place

Freed slaves built this house at Middleton Place, once a Charleston-area rice plantation. Today Eliza's House is part of a large and vibrant complex that includes many areas where slaves probably worked. Visitors view the historic gardens that slaves developed and see daily activities such as blacksmithing, weaving, pottery-making, and coopering.

Middleton Place listed 50 slaves in the 1790 census and 110 in the 1850 census. Many of the slaves were skilled artisans who performed the activities demonstrated today at Middleton Place. After emancipation, some freed persons wanted to remain at the place they knew as their home, and they built the duplex that today is called Eliza's House. Each family living in the dwelling had two rooms, and their two separate fireplaces had one central chimney stack. The clapboard dwelling was occupied continuously until the 1980s by African American families who worked at Middleton Place. The last occupant was Eliza Leach, and the house has been named in her honor. It has been restored to its appearance in the 1870s and is open to visitors.

DATE BUILT: 1870s

ADDRESS: 12 miles northwest of Charleston on Ashley River Road (SC 61)

TELEPHONE: (800) 782-3608, or (803) 556-6020

VISITING HOURS: Daily 9–5

FEES: For all areas in Middleton Place as well as to Eliza's House, adults, $10; children ages 6–12, $5; children under 6, free

SOURCES: Telephone conversation Apr. 14, 1994, Janan Jones, interpretive coordinator for stableyards and African American history, Middleton Place. *To Walk the Whole Journey,* 12.

Emanuel African Methodist Episcopal Church

According to Reverend John H. Gillison, present pastor of the church, the congregation of Emanuel A.M.E. Church is the oldest of this denomination in the South. The congregation became a separate one as a result of a rift between Black and white members of the local Methodist church. In 1817 and 1818 white Methodist churches increasingly placed discriminatory restrictions on their Black members. They capped the insult when they built a hearse house on the Black burial ground. Four thousand Black worshipers then left the white Methodist Church and established affiliation with the African Methodist Episcopal Church.

One of the best-known of the church leaders in this congregation was Denmark Vesey, an intelligent and charismatic free Black man who led an 1822 slave insurrection in Charleston. (See also Vesey House site in Charleston.) When the uprising was suppressed, Vesey and several of his followers were hanged. The city of Charleston then destroyed Vesey's church building, and the Black congregation had to worship in secret until they rebuilt the church at the present site between 1865 and 1872. The congregation's trials were not over, however; an earthquake demolished the church in 1886, and it was not until 1891 that the present structure was completed.

DATE BUILT: 1891

ADDRESS: 110 Calhoun Street, Charleston

TELEPHONE: (803) 722-2561

VISITING HOURS: Church office, Mon.–Fri. 9–1 and 2–4; Sun. services 7:30 A.M., 11 A.M.; call in advance to see the interior Mon.–Fri.

SOURCES: Telephone conversation Apr. 16, 1994, Reverend John H. Gillison, Emanuel A.M.E. Church. Telephone conversation Aug. 3, 1995, Norma Roberts, secretary, Emanuel A.M.E. Church. *To Walk the Whole Journey.*

Old Bethel United Methodist Church

Old Bethel United Methodist Church, the oldest Methodist church still standing in Charleston, was built cooperatively by white and Black members of the congregation, both slaves and free individuals. The multiracial congregation raised funds jointly. They started church construction in 1797 and completed it in 1809.

The Methodist church encouraged African Americans to join and to attend services. It conducted extensive mission work among African Americans in the South Carolina low country, even though its work caused hostility among those opposed to the abolitionist movement.

The congregation remained interracial until the 1840s when Black church members began to protest against having to sit upstairs in the galleries while whites sat in the twelve rows of pews below. As the conflict grew, nine Black members were expelled from the church. Some 165 others withdrew to form their own congregation, causing a severe setback for Methodism in Charleston.

After the white congregation built a new brick Bethel Methodist on the original site for its use, the Old Bethel building was presented to the Black congregation. Its members rolled the older building across the street to its present site at 222 Calhoun, opposite the newer church.

African American church members have contributed to the religious, educational, and political development of the Charleston community. Reverend Henry Cardozo, an African American minister at Old Bethel, served as state senator from Kershaw County from 1870 to 1874.

Old Bethel United Methodist Church originally was constructed as a simple white clapboard meeting-house styled church. A later alteration added a portico supported by four fluted columns. The church still has the original slave galleries, and, on the lower level, twelve pews around a central aisle. Old Bethel United Methodist Church, which presently serves an African American congregation of approximately 200, is listed in the *National Register of Historic Places.*

DATE BUILT: c1797

ADDRESS: 222 Calhoun Street, Charleston

TELEPHONE: Church, (803) 722-3470; Charleston Chamber of Commerce, (803) 853-8000

VISITING HOURS: Church, Mon.–Fri. 10–5; Sun. service, 11; for tours, coordinate with the city's Visitors Center

SOURCE: NRHPINF.

Old Slave Mart

The Old Slave Mart in Charleston's historic district is a commercial building that was used for slave trading and auctions before the Civil War. Few such buildings from prewar South Carolina remain. Thomas Ryan, a former sheriff, and his partner, James Marsh, an alderman, built the building in 1853. Traders sold stocks, bonds, real estate, and slaves at the mart, placing advertisements for the sales and auctions in newspapers in Galveston, Memphis, and New Orleans.

The front of the building has a stucco finish, and it has octagonal pillars at each end with an arch between the pillars, The salesroom had a twenty-foot ceiling. Because the space beneath the arch was open, visitors could stand inside the building or out in the street to watch the proceedings. The auction table, ten feet long and three feet high, could be placed near the arch, giving a good view to those inside or out. The mart originally included a jail to house slaves prior to sale as well as a kitchen and a morgue. Those structures were demolished in the twentieth century.

After the Civil War, this building was used as a tenement house. In the 1920s it was converted into an automobile salesroom. In 1937 the Old Slave Mart Museum set up shop here. The Old Slave Mart Museum was developed to preserve and interpret Black history and slave crafts. In 1960, however, the building was scheduled to be demolished and the property was to be developed into a parking garage. Two white sisters, Judith Wragg Chase and Louise Wragg Graves, who had arrived in Charleston that year, were ahead of their time in valuing the preservation of Black history. They pooled their money—$300 each—and made a down payment on the property. Although it took them twenty years to pay for the property, they organized the museum as a nonprofit association with an interracial board of directors. Unfortunately, the mart, listed in the *National Register of Historic Places,* was damaged by Hurricane Hugo, and the owners sold it to the city of Charleston. A committee has made some plans to open the structure as a Black history museum.

Chase and Graves also owned a unique Black history library on Sullivan's Island. Their library contained hundreds of books on Black history and culture—many very old and rare—as well as pictures, catalogs, and letters. Chase, an art teacher for forty years, also wrote a Black history book in 1971, *Afro-American Art and Craft.* Unfortunately, the building housing the library also was damaged by Hurricane Hugo, and the library closed for an indefinite period.

DATE BUILT: 1853

ADDRESS: Old Slave Mart Museum Building, 6 Chalmers Street, Charleston

VISITING HOURS: Visitors can walk or drive by

SOURCES: Personal visit, summer 1990. Telephone conversation Apr. 16, 1994, Ms. Judith Wragg Chase, former co-owner, Old Slave Mart Building. NRHPINF.

Denmark Vesey House*

Denmark Vesey (1767–1822) was a man who stunned and electrified Charleston and a much wider area of the nation by his bid for freedom for African Americans. Earlier he had won a lottery and purchased his freedom with the money, and he was able to read and write. Thus, he could have been satisfied with his life. White people trusted him. As a free Black man he was allowed to come and go as he pleased, and he accumulated considerable wealth in his carpentry business. He was not satisfied, however, because he identified with his African heritage and felt deeply the pain of those still in bondage.

Different authors claim that Vesey was born in Africa, on the island of Hispaniola, or on the island of St. Thomas in the Caribbean. By the time he was fourteen years old, however, he lived on St. Thomas, then a part of the Danish Virgin Islands. He would have spoken the Danish language there. In 1781 a slave trader from Charleston, Captain Vesey, who traded between St. Thomas and Hispaniola, brought 390 slaves, including Denmark, from St. Thomas to Santo Domingo, where they were to be sold. Although Captain Vesey sold Denmark, the boy was found to be epileptic, and by law the captain had to repurchase him. The captain kept the intelligent boy as his own slave, renaming him Denmark because he had come from the Danish colony of St. Thomas. Captain Vesey's ship visited many ports over the next fourteen years, and Denmark learned to speak English, French, and Spanish. However, Denmark remained deeply troubled by the cruelty of the slave auctions that he saw on these voyages.

As more restrictions were placed on the slave trade, Captain Vesey left the business, settled in Charleston, and continued to engage Denmark as his servant. In 1800 Denmark won $1,500 in a lottery. He purchased his freedom for $600, established a carpentry business, and set up residence at 20 Bull Street, now numbered 56 Bull Street.

Black people, slave and free, outnumbered Charleston's white population, and a fearful white community began to place restrictions on Black individuals. As a craftsman, however, Vesey was trusted to travel around the city. The white community did not know that he had read about the injustices of slavery, that he knew about rebellions in Santo Domingo, and that he was aware that Black people had successfully fought for their freedom in the Caribbean.

When he felt the time was right, Vesey began to formulate a plan. He carefully selected his followers, including Ned and Rolla Bennett, Jack Purcell, Peter Poyas, Gullah Jack, and African-born Monday Gell. A date for the uprising was set—July 14, 1822, a Sunday, when many white people would have left Charleston to escape the heat. This also was the day when slaves were allowed to go visiting. Another factor in the careful plan was the fact that there would be no moonlight. The leaders then brought about 9,000 slaves from a wide area around Charleston into the plan.

A slave who had learned about the plan informed his master's wife. From this moment the uprising was doomed. Although Vesey rescheduled the insurrection date for June 16, Governor Bennett ordered the militia to be ready for trouble. As a fear approaching hysteria gripped the white people of Charleston, thirty-four Black men, including Peter Poyas, one of the trusted leaders, were arrested. Denmark Vesey himself was taken into custody on June 21. At first none of the Black men would talk; later, however, three of Vesey's men testified against him in return for immunity from punishment. Eventually, as many as 313 Black men were arrested; of these, 67 were convicted and 34 (one source says 35) were executed. Denmark Vesey was hanged on July 2, 1822.

Although the rebellion was not successful, Black people learned of it. Vesey's tragic ending did not crush their hope but only fueled their desire to be free.

Because the house numbering system has changed in Charleston over the years, the identity of Vesey's house on Bull Street had to be determined through research. The 1822 city directory listed Vesey's address as 20 Bull Street. Through a series of steps, which included the inspection of insurance maps, completion of a title search, a match of names and addresses of everyone who lived on Bull Street, and use of information that Vesey's house was located just east of the northeast corner of Smith and Bull Streets, a determination was made that Vesey's House, then numbered 20, would be the house now numbered 56. The Greek-revival design was fashionable in the early 1800s, and the building had been built not long before Vesey lived there. The house is set back just a few feet from the sidewalk with its side turned to the street, as is true of many homes in Charleston. It is listed in the *National Register of Historic Places*.

DATE BUILT: Early 1800s

ADDRESS: 56 Bull Street, Charleston

VISITING HOURS: Private, visitors may drive by

SOURCES: NRHPINF. Personal visit, summer 1990. The Academic American Encyclopedia. *Denmark Vesey. Before the Mayflower,* 127. *International Library of Negro Life and History,* 137.

Columbia

Allen University Historic District

Allen University is one of several universities established by the African Methodist Episcopal Church after the Civil War. The college opened in Columbia in 1881 and purchased a four-acre lot on the site of the present campus. The first major building on the site was erected in 1888.

Although Allen was founded primarily to educate clergymen for the A.M.E. Church, it was one of the few southern Black colleges with a law department, which operated until the early 1900s. Daniel Augustus Straker, an outstanding lawyer in the 1880s, taught there. The graduates he trained scored so high on the state Supreme Court examination that judges gave them a special commendation. After some years of political activity in South Carolina, Straker moved to Detroit.

E. J. Sawyer was another outstanding graduate of Allen University. In 1879 he founded one of the strongest African American newspapers in South Carolina, the *Pee Dee Educator.* After graduating from the law department in 1882, Sawyer had several careers: practicing law, becoming a successful merchant, and serving as principal of the Bennettsville Graded School.

Another graduate, William Davis Chappelle, later became president of the university. An African Methodist Episcopal minister, he established the A.M.E. Printing House in Nashville, Tennessee. Reverend Chappelle later became a bishop in the A.M.E. Church.

Allen University's first curriculum followed the philosophy of Booker T. Washington by emphasizing agricultural and industrial studies. Each student had to complete some manual labor for an hour each day. All female students had to learn sewing. Although students of all ages attended the school in its early years, the elementary school closed in the mid-1920s and the high school department did so in 1929.

The historic district contains four major buildings situated around a campus green. Arnett Hall (the Ladies Industrial Hall) is the oldest building still standing on campus. Its cornerstone was laid in 1891, and the fifty-room building was in use by 1896. Over the years it has served as a women's dormitory, classroom building, men's dormitory, and industrial building. It was vacated in 1965. Coppin Hall, a three-story red-brick building, was completed in 1907. Chappelle Administration Building was completed in 1925. John Anderson Lankford, a leading Black architect of the day, designed the brick Georgian building. Flipper Library, named for an A.M.E. bishop, was erected in 1941.

Allen University is close to the downtown section of the city. Another historically Black college, Benedict College, is located just across Taylor Street, one of the boundary streets for Allen. Allen University was founded just four years after the University of South Carolina was closed to African American students. Allen may have been South Carolina's first private school founded by and for Black students and operated by Black administrators.

DATE ESTABLISHED: 1881
ADDRESS: 1530 Harden Street, Columbia
TELEPHONE: (803) 254-4165
VISITING HOURS: Contact college for visiting hours
SOURCES: NRHPINF. Ms. Rachel H. Cockrell, Historic Columbia Foundation. Personal visit, summer 1990. *The Smithsonian Guide to Historic America: The Carolinas and the Appalachian States,* 159.

Benedict College Historic District

The American Baptist Home Mission Society was influential in establishing Benedict Institute, one of several Black institutions that emerged during the Reconstruction period. Founded in 1870, the institute was named for Stephen Benedict, a Rhode Island businessman, abolitionist, and Baptist deacon, who bequeathed money for the new school. When Benedict opened its doors to students, the curriculum offered primary-level to college-level courses and had as its mission the education of ministers and teachers. The curriculum also prepared for the world of work, emphasizing agriculture, horticulture, and the industrial arts. In 1894, when it was chartered as Benedict College, it enrolled about two hundred students.

Benedict's first seven presidents were white ministers who served as missionaries as well as administrators. In 1929 Dr. J. J. Starks became the first Black president. One of the early graduates, Richard Carroll, was born a slave in Barnwell County during the Civil War. He worked his way through Benedict Institute and, after further education, became a Baptist minister. Carroll, considered one of the most eloquent and prominent ministers in South Carolina, spoke candidly about relations between Black and white people in the South.

In the twentieth century, Benedict College continued to play a role in race relations in the South. During the years of racial segregation, it was a center of activities for the Black community, hosting meetings, lectures, concerts, and other social affairs. When the National NAACP campaigned in 1937 for Congress to pass an antilynching bill, a branch of the NAACP was founded at Benedict. Although the bill did not pass, this action increased both the NAACP's stature and student involvement in its programs. In 1937 Benedict students participated in a nationwide youth demonstration against lynching, one of the first civil rights campaigns in the state prior to World War II.

Benedict College is located in a Columbia residential area. Many of the older structures on campus were demolished in the 1960s to build more modern facilities. Five buildings constructed between 1897 and 1937 remain, however, in the historic district.

The oldest building on campus, **Morgan Hall,** served as the president's residence. The three-story building has a first-story wraparound porch with turned posts and balustrades with sawn brackets. Today Morgan Hall is used for storage and for housing security personnel.

Pratt Hall, a two and one-half–story brick building, was built in 1902 as a hospital and training school for nurses. Today it houses administrative offices.

Duckett Hall was built in 1925 as a science building; it now houses business administration classrooms.

Antisdel Chapel was built in 1932 in honor of Benedict College's last white president, Reverend C. B. Antisdel. The brick one-story chapel has an octagonal steeple and a central portico with Doric columns.

Starks Center was built in 1937 as a joint library for Benedict College and Allen University, which adjoins the Benedict Campus.

The college is listed in the *National Register of Historic Places.*

DATE BUILT: 1895–1937

ADDRESS: Roughly bounded by Laurel, Oak, Taylor, and Harden Streets on Benedict College campus, Columbia

TELEPHONE: (803) 256-4220

VISITING HOURS: By appointment

SOURCES: Ms. Rachel Cockrell, Historic Columbia Foundation. Personal visit, summer 1990. NRHPRF.

Mann–Simons Cottage

The Mann–Simons Cottage symbolizes the history of a community of free Black people in Columbia. Celia Mann, who was born in 1799, built the cottage about 1850. According to local tradition, she was born in Charleston and reared in slavery. In the early nineteenth century, she purchased her freedom and walked to Columbia, a city with a population of approximately 200 free Black people.

Mann established Columbia's First Calvary Baptist Church, one of the earliest post-Civil War Black churches in South Carolina. The congregation first met in the basement of this cottage. Mann did not have a formal education, but she served as a midwife and, saving her money, used the funds to accumulate property.

Descendants of Celia Mann—the Simonses—describe the night of February 17, 1865, when Columbia was burned. The Simons family allowed several white families to hide in basement rooms of this cottage and to conceal their silver in the well. Since Union troops did not search the property of African Americans, the Black families, ironically, provided refuge for some local white families.

When she died in 1867, Mann owned more than $2,000 in real estate, a considerable amount at the time. Her oldest daughter, Agnes, a baker and laundress, inherited the cottage. Agnes married Bill Simons, a music teacher. Their son, Charles, also was a musician, and father and son gave music lessons to white children in Columbia. After Agnes Simons died, Charles, who at times was employed as a musician, a tailor, or a grocer, inherited the cottage. Together with his wife, Amanda, and her niece, Bernice, Charles lived in the cottage. After his death, Amanda Green Simons continued to reside there until her death in 1960. The niece (later known as Mrs. Bernice Conners) attended Benedict College and taught in public schools in South Carolina for thirty-eight years. She sold the house in 1970 to the Columbia Housing Authority.

The Mann-Simons house is a one and one-half–story frame cottage with clapboarding. Its center entrance has a transom, and there is a full-width balustraded porch. It is the only pre-Civil War structure still standing in this area, which was originally a neighborhood of free Black people. In 1978 a community project restored the structure to its appearance in the 1880s. The cottage, which today houses the Museum of African-American Culture, contains items that once belonged to the Mann–Simons family and other Black people of Columbia. The museum sponsors public school tours, exhibits of work of local artists, and an Annual Jubilee Festival in September celebrating African American music, dance, arts, crafts, and food. The house is listed in the *National Register of Historic Places* and is owned and operated by the Richland County Historic Preservation Commission.

DATE BUILT: c1850
ADDRESS: 1403 Richland Street, Columbia
TELEPHONE: (803) 252-1450
VISITING HOURS: Tues.–Fri. 10–4; Sat. 11–4; Sun. 1–4; tours during these hours by prearrangement
FEES: Adults, $3 or with AAA card, $2.50; children 6–18, $1.50; children under 6, free
SOURCES: Personal visit, summer 1990. Telephone conversation Aug. 20, 1995, Rickie Good, docent, Mann–Simons Cottage. *National Register of Historic Places,* 696. *The Smithsonian Guide to Historic America: The Carolinas and the Appalachian States,* 162.

Randolph Cemetery

Randolph Cemetery is named in honor of B. F. Randolph, a Black state representative from the Reconstruction era. Senator Randolph's tombstone is inscribed: "In Memoriam, B. F. Randolph, late State Senator for Orangeburg County and Chairman, Republican State Central Committee, who died at Hodges Station, Abbeville County at the hands of assassins on Friday October 16 AD, 1868."

After Senator Randolph was lynched, his body was left hanging. Nineteen brave Black men risked their lives to go to Abbeville County to retrieve the body and to return it to Columbia by mule. Pooling their money, they paid Elmwood Cemetery $300 for three acres of land; thus, the Black section of the cemetery began. Since that date eight representatives and senators as well as bishops, doctors, attorneys, ministers, and Columbia's only Black postmaster have been buried there.

One burial site has a marker inscribed: "Sacred to the memory of George Elmore, who through unmatched courage, perseverance, and personal sacrifice brought the legal action by which Black people may participate in South Carolina democratic party primary elections: '*Elmore* v. *Rice,* 1947.'"

As the years passed, the cemetery became overgrown with weeds and brush and was used as a dump. Clearing the land for a building site, bulldozers began to knock down some of the stones. Fortunately, some residents remembered the legacy of those buried in the cemetery, and a community group began efforts to restore and preserve Randolph Cemetery. Today lanes originally designed for horse-drawn carriages wind through a place that honors the memory of brave people.

DATE ESTABLISHED: 1871
ADDRESS: Two blocks west of Elmwood Avenue at I-126 (off the I-126 Elmwood Extension, adjacent to the Elmwood Cemetery; from the access road, drive by St. Peter's Cemetery and proceed to where the access road ends at Randolph Cemetery), Columbia
VISITING HOURS: Daily, dawn–dusk
SOURCES: Personal visit, July 28, 1990. "The Burial of Black American History." Description for the *South Carolinian,* written by Elaine Nichols, Guest Curator of History, South Carolina State Museum. "Randolph Cemetery to Be Showcased at the South Carolina State Museum."

South Carolina State Museum

South Carolina State Museum, the state's largest gallery, maintains a fourth-floor permanent exhibit on slave life. Here visitors can see examples of slave housing, slave tags, carpentry, pottery, basketry, and mortars and pestles as well as information about the Gullah language. Originating in the Charleston area, the slave tags were placed on the neck for identification when a slave was hired out to work for a period away from the home plantation.

Occasionally a slave was recognized for creative talent. For example, a literate slave from Edgefield County worked for a printer. He placed imaginative couplets on jars; now called "Dave Pots," they are considered rare and valuable. He confidently stated on one jar, "I'm sure this jar will hold 14 gallons."

The museum has a side-view model of a slave house and a model of another slave house with furnishings. Visitors can see traveling exhibits such as the Romaire Beardon exhibit that features the work of a Black artist from Charlotte. African American history is featured also in the museum's space-science exhibit.

ADDRESS: 301 Gervais Street, Columbia

TELEPHONE: (803) 737-4921

VISITING HOURS: Mon.–Sat. 10–5; Sun. 1–5; New Year's Day 1–5; closed Easter, Thanksgiving, Christmas

FEES: Adults, $4; senior citizens, military, and college students, $3; youth 6–17, $1.50; children under 6, free; South Carolina school groups with advance reservations, free; free first Sun. each month

SOURCES: Telephone conversation Apr. 18, 1994, and Aug. 10, 1995, Elaine Nichols, curator of African American Culture and History, South Carolina State Museum. *To Walk the Whole Journey,* 23.

Denmark

Voorhees College Historic District

Voorhees College grew out of the dreams and determination of a single Black woman, Miss Elizabeth Evelyn Wright, who had worked her way through Tuskegee Institute in Alabama. Even before graduation, she dreamed of establishing a school modeled after Tuskegee Institute to serve poor Black children being trained in the industrial arts. Wright founded Denmark Industrial School in 1897. She tried several times to establish roots for the school in small towns near Denmark, but prejudice, hostility, jealousy, and even arson caused her to move the fledgling institution to several different small towns.

In 1901 Denmark Industrial School moved to its present home just outside the town limits of Denmark. Although some benefactors provided badly needed support, Wright constantly had to seek money to keep the school alive. She communicated frequently with Booker T. Washington, Tuskegee's president, who provided instructions and letters of recommendation. In spite of this help, she had to walk from church to church seeking donations, sometimes walking the distances without shoes.

In 1923 the school affiliated with the Protestant Episcopal Church and the American Church Institute for Negroes. Shortly afterward, students began building St. Philip's Chapel on the campus.

Voorhees College did essential work in educating Black students, providing at one time the only high school education for Black students in the area. Students built many of the campus buildings themselves, using carpentry and masonry techniques learned in class. When the original frame buildings burned down, Wright had them replaced with safer brick buildings. Many of the new structures had fine details, including leaded-glass windows, cupolas, moldings, gables, and decorative brickwork.

The state legislature incorporated the school in 1904, and Voorhees established a normal and industrial school in 1929. These were years of racial segregation, and as late as 1948 Voorhees was the only high school in Denmark for Black students. In 1965 the high school was discontinued, and Voorhees College became the name of the institution. In 1968 it was fully accredited as a liberal arts college.

The thirteen buildings in the historic portion of the campus were built between 1905 and the mid-1930s. Key properties in the historic district include:

Booker T. Washington Hall (1905) is a two-story brick building that was constructed totally by Black people. It served as the Booker T. Washington Hospital, one of the first hospitals in the area.

Blanton Hall, a two and one-half–story building with tracery windows and portico, was built in 1914 as the administration building.

The **Menafee Trades Building** was constructed in 1907.

St. Philip's Episcopal Chapel (1935) has a steep gable roof and brick buttresses.

The one-story **Bedford Hall** was built in 1912 as a dining hall.

Other historic buildings on campus include Wright Hall (1932), named for founder Elizabeth Wright; Massachusetts Hall (1930); St. James Building (1932); Pine Grove Cottage (1914–1915); the Old Agricultural Building (1930s); and the Old Pump House (1925).

Elizabeth Evelyn Wright died in 1906, and was buried in a gravesite on the campus. The Voorhees College Historic District is listed in the *National Register of Historic Places.*

DATE ESTABLISHED:	Historic portion, 1905–mid-1930s
ADDRESS:	Voorhees College Campus, Voorhees Road, Denmark
TELEPHONE:	(803) 793-3351
VISITING HOURS:	Contact the college to arrange visit
SOURCES:	Personal visit, summer 1990. Dr. Leonard Dawson, president. NRHPINF.

Edisto Island

Edisto Island Baptist Church

In 1807 Hephzibah Jenkins Townsend, a white woman, founded one of the South's first missionary societies. When she established a Baptist church on Edisto Island, her ex-slave, Bella, assisted her in raising some of the building funds for the church by cooking pastries that were sold in Charleston. Construction began in January 1818, and craftsmen completed the church four months later.

When the church opened for services, the community followed the custom of having slaves attend their masters' churches. The slaves, however, had segregated seating in an area known as the slave gallery. In the Edisto Island Baptist Church, the original recessed-panel slave gallery, an area that lined both sides of the nave of the church, is still intact.

The end of the Civil War brought many changes to the island. Federal troops occupied the area, and most white church members dispersed. Since the church trustees felt that the African American members of the congregation had been faithful, they decided to turn the church over to them. To the present day African Americans have used the building. Eventually, however, the congregation erected a new sanctuary north of the original building, and they are now using the old Edisto Island Baptist Church for storage space and as a ceramics shop.

The original church is a two-story, square structure sheathed in weatherboard. Inside, the flooring is made of wooden planks. A two-story portico with a small belfry was added to the façade about 1880. Edisto Island Baptist Church is listed in the *National Register of Historic Places.*

DATE BUILT: 1818

ADDRESS: Approximately 1.2 miles north of the town of Edisto Island on the east side of SC 174 at its intersection with SC Secondary, Edisto Island

TELEPHONE: First New Baptist Church, (803) 869-2432; Reverend Tony Daises, (803) 869-2183; Ms. Bernice Meggett, contact person, (803) 869-1934

VISITING HOURS: Private, visitors may walk behind the new church to see the historic church; services in the newer building, Sun. 10

SOURCES: NRHPINF. Telephone call to site, Jan. 12, 1995.

Florence

Gregg Plantation Slave Houses

Although Francis Marion University is a predominantly white school founded in 1970, it has on its campus two houses associated with Black history. These are one-story log cabins that once housed slaves and that have remained from what was once a street of slave dwellings on the Gregg Plantation. From 1820 to 1930 Black people were in the majority in South Carolina's population. During the years of slavery, many of them lived in a setting like the Gregg Plantation, where slave houses were located on each side of a street leading to the main house.

Slaves on the Gregg Plantation built these two log houses before 1831. They illustrate an early practice of mass production of houses of the same type. The same Black artisans and craftsmen who erected the fine plantation houses also put up slave houses. Although the slave quarters were modest, the craftsmen built them carefully, using the unusual feature in slave houses of dovetailed hewn logs. The craftsmen also added an open front porch that had roof overhangs with pillar post supports.

Each house contains a single room about 20 feet by 17 feet. Each has a pine board door and shuttered window in front, a shuttered window on each side of the house, and a rear door. The walls inside and out are constructed of hand-hewn logs. Open ceilings show the beams, rafters, and cross-bracings. The floors are of pine floor planks. The houses originally had 5-foot-by-4-foot fireplaces, but these are now missing. The plain exteriors of the houses have no decorative features.

After the Civil War, the houses were moved from their original location to a different site on the plantation; the former slaves remained in their houses but worked as tenant and wage farmers. They continued their plantation work in the fields and hunted, fished, and raised livestock. Some worked at a trade. The slave houses were occupied until 1950 by the workers in the Black tenant community. Now they are part of the state-owned Francis Marion University campus.

DATE BUILT: c1831

ADDRESS: 5130 E. Palmetto Street, Florence

TELEPHONE: University relations, (803) 661-1231

VISITING HOURS: Visitors can walk or drive by

SOURCES: NRHPINF. Dr. Wayne King, Francis Marion University. Telephone conversation Apr. 13, 1994, Theresa Wachowski, assistant director of university relations, Francis Marion College. *National Register of Historic Places,* 692.

Georgetown

Joseph H. Rainey House

Joseph Hayne Rainey, the first Black person to serve in the U.S. House of Representatives, once lived in this house. He was born in 1832 at Georgetown, South Carolina, to former slave parents who had bought their freedom. He received some private instruction.

The Rainey family moved to Charleston, South Carolina, in 1846 and established a business there. When the Civil War began, Rainey was drafted to work as a steward on a Confederate blockade-runner. Later he worked on Charleston fortifications for the Confederate Army. Eventually he escaped to the West Indies and then settled in Bermuda. Rainey opened a barber shop and continued to study by reading books lent to him by neighbors and friends.

After the Civil War, Rainey and his wife returned to Georgetown in 1866. He became involved in politics and moved up in the Republican Party to the state Senate. In 1870 he resigned from the state Senate to fill a vacancy in the U.S. House of Representatives. Another African American, Hiram R. Revels, also began serving in the United States Senate in February 1870. Together, the two men made political history by initiating Black representation in the federal law-making process.

During the Forty-second Congress, Rainey spoke out in March 1871 in favor of legislation to enforce the Fourteenth Amendment. Designed to keep state governments from abridging the rights of former slaves, the amendment, among its other provisions, also required due process of law and equal protection of the law to U.S. citizens. In the following session of Congress Rainey spoke out for appropriations to enforce the Ku Klux Klan Act of 1871. From 1866 on, Klan members had terrorized African Americans in the South to wipe out gains made since the Civil War. The violence had become so serious that in 1871, Republicans in Congress had given President Ulysses S. Grant authority to use national troops to restore order in areas affected by the violence, but the authority needed to be used. Once trained soldiers were empowered to arrest suspects, the Klan rapidly declined, almost disappearing as a nineteenth-century organization by 1872. Rainey also helped pass the Civil Rights Act of 1875, which outlawed discrimination in transportation, theaters, restaurants, and hotels. With others, he fought for legislation to benefit all Americans, including tariff protection for farmers and manufacturers, fair treatment for Native Americans, federal funds for local improvements, and the establishment of a national board of health.

Rainey served on the Indian Affairs Committee and defended Chinese immigrants in California. He also spoke for white citizens, even proposing a bill to remove political restrictions from former Confederates. African American legislators sought to eliminate racial discrimination in the Army and to secure equal pensions for all Civil War veterans, regardless of race.

Rainey and Revels helped bring about gains for African Americans during the Reconstruction period. Many of these advances, however, later were wiped out by Jim Crow laws. By 1883 the Supreme Court had stripped the Civil Rights Act of its effectiveness. Former slaveowners and their friends influenced state legislators in a strong backlash. The state legislatures apportioned legislative seats in a way that diluted the strength of Black voters. The poll tax, the white primary, complicated registration procedures, and intimidation kept Black voters—and some white voters, too—away from the polls. Too few African Americans were elected to office, and they did not serve long enough to gain seniority and power. Their colleagues often regarded them with indifference and hostility.

The Reconstruction period ended in 1877 as federal forces were withdrawn from the South. Representative Rainey sought a fifth full term in 1878 but was defeated by a white Democrat. He then worked for the U.S. Treasury Department and engaged in banking and brokerage businesses. In 1886 he returned to Georgetown, where he lived until his death in 1887.

According to local tradition, Rainey was born in the house at 909 Prince Street, and lived there until 1846. He again settled in this house when he returned to the United States after the Civil War, and it was his principal residence from 1866 to 1870. He lived off and on at this site until his death in 1887. The house then remained in the Rainey family until 1896.

The Rainey House is a two and one-half–story frame structure. The interior has two rooms on each of the main floors, with a wide center hall. The original wide, pine floorboards are intact. Rainey House is listed in the *National Register of Historic Places.* The house, one of forty-nine structures in Georgetown's historic district, is on one of the main roads and is easily visible to those who drive by. On Sunday, April 17, 1994, a historic marker was dedicated in front of the Rainey House.

DATE BUILT: c1760; Rainey home, 1832–1887

ADDRESS: 909 Prince Street, Georgetown

VISITING HOURS: Interior not accessible; visitors may drive or walk by

SOURCES: NRHPINF. Telephone conversation Apr. 16, 1994, Linda Mock, executive director, Georgetown County Chamber of Commerce. *International Library of Negro Life and History,* 112.

Greenville

Greenville Cultural Exchange Center

The Greenville Cultural Exchange Center preserves Black history with an emphasis on achievements of African Americans from the Greenville area. Inside the converted two-story house there is room for a variety of exhibits and events. A conference room provides a meeting place for organizations and a site for events such as weddings and receptions. A resource room has memorabilia donated by local citizens, including doctors' and dentists' paraphernalia. Another room contains photographs and information about local African Americans and their contributions. A highlight of the center is the Jesse Jackson Hall of Fame honoring Reverend Jesse Jackson, a former aide of Dr. Martin Luther King Jr. and a native of Greenville. In 1971 Jackson founded People United to Save Humanity (PUSH). An eloquent speaker and influential political leader, he was at one time a candidate for President of the United States. The Hall of Fame contains items donated by Jackson and his mother. Artifacts include the uniform that Jackson wore when he was a bellhop at the local Poinsett Club, presidential campaign buttons and posters, and front pages of magazines that featured stories about the leader. The museum also contains a life-sized bust of Jackson commissioned by the museum.

DATE ESTABLISHED: Aug. 22, 1987

ADDRESS: 700 Arlington Street at Summer Street, Greenville

TELEPHONE: (803) 232-9162

VISITING HOURS: Sat. 11–5, Sun. 2–5:30; weekdays by appointment

FEES: Donation

SOURCES: Telephone conversation Apr. 16, 1994, Ruth Ann Butler, founder, Greenville Cultural Exchange Center. *To Walk the Whole Journey*, 16. *Before the Mayflower*, 437, 438, 594.

Heath Springs Vicinity

Mount Carmel African Methodist Episcopal Zion Campground

Established after the Civil War, the Mount Carmel Church and campground site is one of the few remaining campgrounds of this type in South Carolina. When the Civil War ended, African Americans sought to establish their own churches. At the same time the African Methodist Episcopal Zion Church, organized in New York in 1796, was spreading to areas in the South. Reverend Isom Caleb Clinton (1830–1904), a former slave and church leader in South Carolina, founded Mount Carmel Church in 1866; a year later the South Carolina Conference of the A.M.E.Z. Church came to South Carolina. Reverend Clinton was ordained a deacon and, in 1892, was consecrated a bishop in the church.

Reverend Clinton's younger brother, Frederick Albert Clinton, also an active leader in South Carolina, was one of the organizers of Mount Carmel. He became active in local political affairs and served as a South Carolina state senator from 1870 to 1877. Senator Clinton is buried in the Mount Carmel graveyard.

The campground has a rectangular form with fifty-five "tents," or cabins, arranged around an arbor. The arbor, a shelter with open sides at the center of the rectangle, is the central point for revival meetings. The A.M.E.Z. Church still sponsors the annual camp meeting at Mount Carmel in September, drawing individuals and families from several states. The Lancaster County landmark is listed in the *National Register of Historic Places*.

DATE ESTABLISHED: c1866

ADDRESS: SC 19, 500 yards south of SC 620 (from downtown Heath Springs go past the Middle School, take a left, and travel about 5 miles), Heath Springs

TELEPHONE: Mt. Carmel A.M.E.Z. Church, (803) 285-4254

VISITING HOURS: Private, but always open; camp meeting the first week of Sept. Wed.–Sun. evenings

SOURCES: Telephone conversation May 29, 1994, Willie McDow, chairman of the trustee board, Mt. Carmel A.M.E.Z. Church. NRHPINF.

Johns Island

Moving Star Hall

On the South Carolina sea island plantations, small, but important, structures called praise houses served as centers of worship and community meetings. Before the Civil War, a praise house was a plantation institution on the South Carolina sea islands. After the Civil War, most praise houses were supplanted by churches. Rural Johns Island, however, was isolated from the mainland,

and African Americans depended on each other for their social and charitable needs and for their religious life. Even before the Civil War, free Black people had formed mutual-aid societies to care for community needs. In 1920 Black people on Johns Island chartered the Moving Star Association for similar purposes. They purchased land and lumber to build a praise house, Moving Star Hall. The small frame building served as the meeting place for the association, which provided social, fraternal, and charitable activities. Throughout the mid-1970s its members assisted the sick, offered burial services, sponsored a secret fraternal order, and provided a place for worship services.

All members were required to spend time, night and day, caring for any sick member, and the society paid bills during the sick person's illness if this was needed. Families contributed $.25 to $1 per month. When a member of the family died, the family received $100 plus the service of members as pallbearers, gravediggers, and mourners. Religious worship was an important activity in Moving Star Hall. The society was interdenominational, and although its members belonged to local Black churches, they also attended one to three meetings per week at the hall.

Each individual had an opportunity to preach, lead songs, or testify at the prayer meetings. They kept the spirituals and other traditional Black songs alive through the years. Spirituals and shouts were performed unaccompanied, beginning in a minor key with slow rhythms, then increasing in speed with counterpoints of hand clapping and foot stamping. In the 1960s a group of Moving Star Hall singers recorded albums of songs from the islands and presented their music at local and national folk festivals.

The Moving Star Association continued to be active in the community. In the late 1940s many association members joined the New Progressive Club established to register Black voters. The Progressive Club had its early meetings in the hall. The club eventually established a community store, a recreation center, and a legal defense fund. Eventually there was no longer a need for many of the early functions. As many young people moved to cities, membership declined and the hall closed. In 1977 the association's charter lapsed.

Moving Star Hall is one of the few remaining praise houses on the South Carolina sea islands. The one-story, one-room, frame building appears much as it did when built—a rectangular structure on concrete block pillars with a hip-roofed porch; a privy is located outside in back. Inside, backless benches face a table at the west end, a silent reminder of many community meetings filled with plans, prayers, and joyous shouts.

DATE BUILT: c1917–1920

ADDRESS: SC River Road, Johns Island (about 6 miles south of Charleston)

VISITING HOURS: Visitors may drive by

SOURCES: Conversation at Moving Star Hall, summer 1990, with Mrs. Alice Wine of Community Pentacostal Church, current occupant of Moving Star Hall. NRHPINF.

Mayesville

Mary McLeod Bethune Birthsite Historical Marker

Mary McLeod Bethune was a well-known humanitarian and educator who was born five miles north of Mayesville on July 10, 1875. She was one of the first pupils to attend the Mayesville Mission School, which was located fifty yards west of this historical marker. Bethune knew at an early age that she wanted to be a teacher, and she later served as a teacher at the mission school.

Bethune founded the Bethune-Cookman College in Daytona Beach, Florida, and directed its policies for thirty years. She founded the National Council of Negro Women in 1935. President Franklin D. Roosevelt asked her to serve on the advisory board of the National Youth Administration. He also asked her to establish the Office of Minority Affairs and later gave her the title of Director of the Division of Negro Affairs. Bethune was the only woman to have held such a high position in Roosevelt's unofficial "shadow cabinet."

Mrs. Bethune, who was honored by four Presidents, was a consultant in drafting the charter of the United Nations. She died on May 18, 1955, and was buried at Bethune-Cookman College. (See the listing for Bethune-Cookman College, Daytona Beach, Florida, for additional information on her life.)

DATE OF SIGNIFICANCE: 1875

ADDRESS: US 76, Mayesville

VISITING HOURS: Always accessible

SOURCES: *Historical and Cultural Atlas of African Americans*, 70. *Official South Carolina Historical Markers*. Sumter County Historical Commission.

Mount Pleasant

Boone Hall Plantation

Slavery was not pleasant or desirable under any conditions, but the house servants at Boone Hall Plantation at least lived in a setting that was as beautiful as that which their owners enjoyed. The road, or allée, leading from the plantation entrance to the main house was three-quarters of a mile long. The slave houses were in rows on a wide lawn beside the road leading to the main house. Regularly spaced, moss-draped live oak trees lined the road.

A row of nine brick slave houses remains on the Boone Hall Plantation. The one-story dwellings dating from about 1790 show how the house servants lived. The houses are approximately 12 feet by 30 feet in size. Each has a central door and four windows in front, a single window on one side, and a single attic window on both sides. Each house originally had two rooms with a central hall between the rooms and plank or dirt floors. Although ceiling rafters and joists are exposed today, there may have been garrets at one time. Each house has a fireplace with a brick hearth to the rear. Although the slave houses have experienced some deterioration and have had some structural repair work, they retain much of their original appearance.

Boone Hall Plantation in rural Charleston County dates from the 1700s, and its surviving slave houses may date from between 1790 and 1810. House servants and the plantation's skilled craftsmen lived in these houses. Field slaves lived in clusters of small cottages elsewhere on the plantation; these cottages are no longer standing. The main house at the plantation today is not the original structure but was built in 1936 to replace it. There may have been twenty-seven slave houses at Boone Hall in the early years. The seven remaining houses on the slave street are a rare example in South Carolina of this type of slave house.

Today the plantation is open to visitors, who may walk up to the slave houses and look through some of the windows. Although the houses are not furnished, they retain a great deal of atmosphere. The slaves here used to make sweetgrass baskets needed in daily plantation work. The art of basketry continues at Boone Hall, and visitors may, at times, observe this craft.

DATE BUILT: c1790

ADDRESS: 1235 Long Point Road, north of Mount Pleasant off US 17, Mount Pleasant

TELEPHONE: (803) 884-4371

VISITING HOURS: Apr. 1–Labor Day, Mon.–Sat. 8:30–6:30, Sun. 1–5; the remainder of the year, Mon.–Sat. 9–5, Sun. 1–4; closed Thanksgiving, Christmas

FEES: Adults, $7.50; children 6–12, $3; seniors, 60 and older, $6; children under 6 years, free

SOURCES: Personal visit, summer 1990. NRHPINF. Boone Hall Plantation brochure.

Orangeburg

Claflin College Historic District

Claflin College grew out of the ideas and support of three different groups—the former slaves and other Black people of Orangeburg, members of the South Carolina Mission Conference, and Northern philanthropists and missionaries. Following the Civil War, African Americans strongly desired a school. In 1866 the South Carolina Mission Conference organized at the Baker Biblical Institute in Charleston, South Carolina. Its members contributed critically needed money and leadership to help organize then-named Claflin University in 1869. The Baker Bible Institute moved to Orangeburg in 1871 and merged with Claflin University. Two Northern Methodist ministers, Reverend T. Willard Lewis and Reverend Alonzo Webster, came South to serve as missionaries to former slaves. One of them, Dr. Alonzo Webster, played a prominent role in securing the property of the former Orangeburg Female Academy for the new school; Webster was named first president of Claflin University. Lee Claflin, a wealthy Boston philanthropist, and his son, Massachusetts Governor William Claflin, provided initial funding for purchasing the site for the college.

The first students at Claflin University (the name was changed to Claflin College in 1914) had to begin at a grammar-school level before they could progress to higher-level courses; by the late 1800s Claflin's students were studying a high school and normal (teacher training) curriculum. In 1872 the South Carolina General Assembly approved an act establishing the South Carolina Agricultural and Mechanics Institute as a coordinate department of Claflin University. The colleges, which separated in 1896, shared a president for twenty-six years.

Continuing into the early 1900s, African American students in Orangeburg attended grammar school and secondary courses at Claflin. This reflected a reluctance of the state of South Carolina to provide for the education of former slaves. In the early twentieth century the state provided only a few public schools for Black students; however, most of the schools typically supported only one teacher. As late as 1920, Black children in Orangeburg's public schools attended an average of only eighty-four days and had little instruction at the high school level. In the entire state there was not one Black public high school that offered a diploma for four years of study. Claflin stepped into this gap, graduating many students who eventually became teachers, physicians, ministers, and professionals in other fields.

Northern philanthropists continued to donate funds to the college in the late nineteenth and early twentieth centuries, providing the means to build several substantial brick buildings. **Tingley Hall** was put up in 1908 with donated funds. Originally the English and Pedagogical Department, it has served as the main building on campus from about 1913 to the present. Black pioneer architect William Wilson Cooke, its designer, was born in 1871 in Greenville. Educated at Claflin, the Massachusetts Institute of Technology, and Columbia University, he designed most of Claflin's buildings. Cooke became the first Black senior architectural designer for the U.S. Supervising Architects office in Washington, D.C. He spent twenty-two years overseeing federal government construction projects in several states. He also conducted a private practice in Illinois and Indiana.

Tingley Hall has such fine details as a Palladian window, an acanthus leaf keystone, bead-and-reel molding, and brick corner quoins. The interior staircases have their original massive balustrades. A two-story brick building with fourteen classrooms and an assembly hall, Tingley Hall is listed in the *National Register of Historic Places.*

DATE ESTABLISHED:	College, 1869; Tingley Hall, 1908
ADDRESS:	College Avenue NE (on US 601 next to South Carolina State University), Orangeburg
TELEPHONE:	(803) 534-2710
VISITING HOURS:	Call to arrange a visit
SOURCES:	Personal visit, summer 1990. NRHPINF. Claflin College brochure. *Claflin College Catalog, 1988–1990,* 15.

South Carolina State University

When South Carolina State College opened in 1896, it was associated with Claflin College and was known as the Mechanics Institute for Colored Students in South Carolina. The earliest students attended classes in frame buildings. After the two colleges separated, a Black architect, Miller F. Whittaker, was selected to design permanent buildings for South Carolina State's new campus. Three of the buildings he designed—Lowman Hall, Hodge Hall, and Dukes Gymnasium—are listed in the *National Register of Historic Places.*

Miller F. Whittaker was South Carolina's first registered Black architect. When he chose his profession, formal architectural training was not available to African Americans in South Carolina. Undaunted, he traveled to Kansas, where he enrolled in the architectural department of Kansas Agricultural College. He returned to become a faculty member on this campus, and Lowman Hall (1917) was one of his first designs.

The oldest intact building on campus, **Lowman Hall,** a substantial, brick, three-story structure, has a dormer with three multipaned windows centered on the roof, brick corner quoins, a central entrance with fanlight and sidelights, and a portico with Ionic columns at each end.

Whittaker's work and his high standards inspired Black students who wanted to become architects. As part of Whittaker's requirements to earn a master of science degree in architecture from Kansas Agricultural College, he had to design a building and supervise its construction. He designed **Hodge Hall,** selecting a Palladian style for his design. Students at South Carolina State College gained practical experience in helping to build the structure. The substantial brick building housed the agricultural and home economics departments. The two-story structure has large, multipaned windows, a double-door entrance sheltered by a columned portico, and concrete steps with cast-iron lamps on each side.

Whittaker collaborated with John H. Blanche, a mechanical arts student at South Carolina State College, in building **Dukes Gymnasium** in 1931. Blanche designed the building as part of his graduation thesis, and Whittaker supervised the project. Thomas J. Entzminger, a Black carpenter from Columbia, served as chief building supervisor, and college instructors in the mechanical arts department installed steel framing, plumbing, and electrical systems. Much of the funding came from student recreation fees. The well-proportioned, two-story brick building has a red tile roof. Under the front arcade are multipaned windows on each side of the entrances.

Visitors to this campus also may be interested in seeing the **I. P. Stanback Museum and Planetarium.** The museum highlights Black history and culture with a collection of photographs dating from the 1800s; it includes exhibits of African American art as well as bronzes and other African artworks from Benin and Cameroon.

DATE ESTABLISHED: College, 1895; Lowman Hall, 1917; Hodge Hall, 1928; Dukes Gymnasium, 1931

ADDRESS: Campus, on US 601, exit 145 off I-26 south in Orangeburg; museum, 300 College Street NE, Orangeburg

TELEPHONE: College, (803) 536-7013, or (803) 536-7185; museum, (803) 536-7174

VISITING HOURS: Contact the college to arrange a campus visit; museum, Mon.–Fri. 9–4:30, closed summers

FEES: Donations accepted at museum

SOURCES: National Register Information System. South Carolina Inventory Form for Historic Districts and Individual Properties. Personal visit, summer 1990.

Ridgeway

Camp Welfare

Camp Welfare, a historic camp meeting site of the African Methodist Episcopal Zion Church, is located in an isolated part of Fairfield County. Black families have long gathered here for camp meetings. After church trustees bought the property in 1878, the meetings, already started at an earlier date, continued each year during the last week in August. Families gathered between the traditional time of the final cultivation of the cotton and corn crops and the harvest time. Assembling each day in the arbor for religious services, they enjoyed meeting family members, friends, and relatives who had returned from other states for the annual reunion.

The campgrounds contain a church, an arbor, and approximately one hundred one-story frame cabins called "tents"; members built these shelters around the turn of the century. The one-room tents have an entrance in center front and a shed roof porch to provide shade from the sun. More-recent modifications include metal or plywood siding or concrete block construction. Traditionally families slept in the tents, cooked outdoors, and used community bathhouses.

The arbor, focal point at the campsite, originally was a brush arbor but evolved into a gable-roofed wooden shelter with wooden benches. Zion Church, built at the site around 1930, is a frame building with a belfry and a porch supported by wooden pillars.

Several A.M.E. churches in Great Falls, South Carolina, use the Camp Welfare meeting site; they are Fairview Church, Mt. Nebo Church, Paradise Church, Pleasant Grove Church, and Rossville Church. The Camp Welfare A.M.E.Z. Church is located at the campground site. Camp Welfare, listed in the *National Register of Historic Places,* is one of the few historic sites associated with the large African American population of Fairfield County, and it is one of the few remaining religious campsites of this type.

DATE ESTABLISHED: c1876

ADDRESS: Ridgeway vicinity on east side of County Road 234; 4 miles southwest of County Road 55 (from Great Falls take US 21 in the direction of Columbia; go about 6 miles, then take a right on Campground Road; on reaching a fork in the road, bear left)

TELEPHONE: Rossville A.M.E.Z. Church, Great Falls, (803) 482-2291; Pleasant Grove A.M.E.Z. Church, (803) 482-3544

VISITING HOURS: Campground always open; church services at Camp Welfare first and third Sun. all year; camp meetings, third week in Aug.

SOURCES: Lelar Douglas, church member, Rossville A.M.E.Z. Church, Great Falls. National Register Information System. NRHPINF.

St. Helena Island

Eddings Point Community Praise House
Mary Jenkins Community Praise House

The Eddings Point Community Praise House and the Mary Jenkins Community Praise House are two of four praise houses on St. Helena Island. Praise houses represent an architectural form that has survived since the pre-Civil War years, originating during slavery on many South Carolina plantations where slaves used small frame houses as places of worship. When emancipated, they often built similar buildings on or near the old plantations to serve the same people as before and sometimes named the structures in honor of the plantation or plantation owner.

There were a few main church buildings on the island. Although islanders walked or rode to services at the main churches on Sunday mornings, they held other meetings and services in the praise houses. Meeting as often as three times per week, and for a Watch Night service on New Year's Eve, they sang, prayed, and gave testimony in the praise houses. Services ended with a "shout," an unaccompanied call-response song form that began slowly and increased in speed and vigor, accompanied by hand-clapping and stamping of the feet in complex rhythms.

In addition to the religious services, members also gathered to take care of community affairs in the praise houses. By 1932 there were seven churches on St. Helena Island and as many as twenty-five praise houses. Today four praise houses survive including the Eddings Point Community Praise House and the Mary Jenkins Community Praise House.

DATE BUILT: Eddings Point Community Praise House and Mary Jenkins Community Praise House, c1900

ADDRESS: Eddings Point Community Praise House, on SC Secondary Road 183, 0.1 mile north of junction with SC Secondary Road 74, Frogmore; Mary Jenkins Community Praise House, SC Secondary Road 74, 2.1 miles north of junction with US 21, Frogmore, St. Helena Island

VISITING HOURS: Interiors not accessible, visitors may drive by

SOURCES: Personal visit, Mary Jenkins Community Praise House, summer 1990. NRHPRF. Telephone conversation, Aug. 6, 1995, Ms. Dorothy Seabrook and Mr. Benjamin Smalls of St. Helena Island.

Penn Center Historic District
Penn School

Philadelphia Quakers Laura Towne and Ellen Murray came to St. Helena Island in 1862 to open a school for freed people. The area had been occupied by troops of the Union Army, and the white islanders had fled to the mainland. About a mile from the town of Frogmore, Towne and Murray found an area of flat, sandy land with salt marshes and creeks, palmettos and wisteria, and live oaks covered with Spanish moss. They learned that former slaves were attending classes in deserted plantation houses, cotton houses, and cabins scattered over the island. The Quaker schoolteachers established their school at the Oaks, a house that federal troops had confiscated and occupied. Penn School was the first school for free Black people in the South.

Towne and Murray met with their first nine pupils in a back room at the Oaks. As enrollment grew, the school moved to the two-story Brick Church, a structure built by slaves for Baptist planters in 1855. The church was used as a church, a meeting hall, and housing for Penn School. In 1864 a prefabricated schoolhouse was shipped by boat from Philadelphia and reassembled on the island to serve as the new schoolhouse; it no longer exists.

The Penn School curriculum, following the example of Hampton Institute in Hampton, Virginia, emphasized vocational and community service. The name later changed to the Penn Normal, Industrial, and Agricultural School, reflecting the school's work; it then began to focus on working within the community to improve public health as well as agricultural and financial conditions for Black people on the island.

Penn School provided an excellent education to students at a time when public education in the area was poor. Many graduates later taught at Penn School or at other schools nearby. Dr. York Bailey, a Penn School graduate, completed his medical studies. He then returned to St. Helena, where he was the island's only doctor for fifty years.

Laura Towne supervised the school from its founding in 1862 until her death in 1901, and the school continued operating until 1948. The landscape has changed little since Union troops occupied St. Helena Island in 1861. Today, the Penn Center historic district is a fifty-acre site consisting of frame and brick buildings. With the exception of Brick Church, all Penn campus buildings were constructed during the twentieth century. Brick Church is unaltered and is still in use.

In 1948 the school was converted to Penn Community Services, Inc., which provides programs that include basic literacy, public health, agricultural demonstrations, and preservation of the unique cultural heritage of the region. The York Bailey Museum has a large collection of oral history recordings in the Gullah language, islanders' English influenced by the African language. The museum also exhibits African American history on the sea islands from slavery to the present.

During the 1960s, Penn Center played a role in the Civil Rights Movement by supporting school desegregation, voter registration, and training for community organizers in the South. Dr. Martin Luther King Jr. and his staff held meetings at the Conference Center, which also has been used for Peace Corps volunteer training.

The historic district is listed in the *National Register of Historic Places.*

DATE ESTABLISHED:	1862
ADDRESS:	SC 37, Lands End Road (from Beaufort take US 21 across Lady's Island into the village of Frogmore; turn right onto Land's End Road), Frogmore vicinity, St. Helena Island
TELEPHONE:	(803) 838-2432, or (803) 838-2235
VISITING HOURS:	Office hours, Mon.–Fri. 9–5, excluding holidays; museum, Tues.–Fri. 11–4; groups of twenty or more, Sat. by appointment; visitors must ask permission to photograph the buildings and grounds
FEES:	Individuals by donation; groups, adults, $2 per event, children, $1 per event (events: [1] lecture, [2] grounds tour, [3] museum tour)
SOURCES:	Vanessa Thaxton, coordinator of history and cultural affairs. Personal visit, summer 1990. NRHPINF. *National Register of Historic Places,* 683. *The Smithsonian Guide to Historic America: The Carolinas and the Appalachian States,* 185.

Works Consulted

The Academic American Encyclopedia. New York: Grolier, 1993. [electronic version]

African Americans: Voices of Triumph. Vol. 1, *Perseverance.* Alexandria, Va.: Time-Life, 1993.

Before the Mayflower: A History of Black America. 5th ed. Lerone Bennett Jr. New York: Penguin, 1988.

"The Burial of Black American History." Washington, D.C.: Committee for the Restoration and Beautification of Randolph Cemetery. [Files of the South Carolina State Museum]

Claflin College Catalog, 1988–1990. Orangeburg, S.C.: Claflin College, 1988.

Denmark Vesey. Lillie J. Edwards. Black Americans of Achievement Series. New York: Chelsea House, 1990.

Encyclopedia of African-American Civil Rights: From Emancipation to the Present. Charles D. Lowery and John F. Marszalek, eds. New York: Greenwood, 1992.

Historical and Cultural Atlas of African Americans. Molefi K. Asante and Mark T. Mattson. New York: Macmillan, 1991.

International Library of Negro Life and History: Historical Negro Biographies. Wilhelmena S. Robinson. New York: Publishers, 1970.

Mann-Simons Cottage. Columbia, S.C.: South Carolina Department of Archives and History, n.d. [brochure]

National Register of Historic Places. Washington, D.C.: National Park Service, 1976.

National Register Information System. Washington, D.C.: National Park Service. [computer database]

Official South Carolina Historical Markers: A Directory. Columbia, S.C.: Confederation of South Carolina Local Historical Societies, 1978.

"Randolph Cemetery to Be Showcased at the South Carolina State Museum." Elaine Nichols. (Columbia) *South Carolinian,* July 29–31, 1989.

The Smithsonian Guide to Historic America: The Carolinas and the Appalachian States. Patricia L. Hudson and Sandra L. Ballard. New York: Stewart, Tabori, & Chang, 1989.

To Walk the Whole Journey: African-American Cultural Resources in South Carolina. South Carolina Department of Parks, Recreation, and Tourism and the South Carolina State Museum.

Tennessee

Chattanooga

Chattanooga Afro-American Heritage Museum and Research Center

The Chattanooga Afro-American Heritage Museum and Research Center shows Black culture and history through artifacts, historical documents, and photographs. Exhibits—some permanent and some changing every six months—include an extensive collection of African art, photographs of early Chattanooga, Kwanzaa celebrations, and Women's History Month in March. One exhibit highlights the life of Bessie Smith, the "Queen of the Blues." Born Elizabeth Smith in Chattanooga in 1894 or 1898, the blues singer recorded almost 200 songs in her own intense style, reflecting the life she knew from her first hit, "Down Hearted Blues," to her final record, "Nobody Knows You When You're Down and Out."

The museum moves in fall 1995 to a restored historic building at 200 East Martin Luther King Boulevard and will be one of two tenants in the 30,000-square-foot structure. The museum displays items related to Bessie Smith's life, including her old upright piano.

DATE ESTABLISHED:	1983
ADDRESS:	200 E. Martin Luther King Boulevard, Chattanooga
TELEPHONE:	(615) 266-8658
VISITING HOURS:	Mon.–Fri. 9:30–4:30, Sat. 10–4, Sun. 1–5; call to confirm hours
FEES:	None
SOURCES:	Telephone call to site Apr. 11, 1994. Telephone conversation Jan. 10, 1995, Vilma Fields, director, Chattanooga Afro-American Heritage Museum and Research Center. *Webster's New Biographical Dictionary*, 925.

Martin Luther King Boulevard Historic District

The Martin Luther King Boulevard (called East Ninth Street until 1981) Historic District has been a center of African American life in Chattanooga since the mid-1800s. It is the only remaining cohesive, well-defined area of Black social, cultural, and commercial activity in the city. Settlement began in this community in the early 1800s. During the Civil War and afterward, Black families began to build houses in a section considered less desirable because it was low-lying and contained a pond. The families found work as government employees in the Commissary Department or as cooks and workers for both the Union and Confederate Armies. Some worked in the iron-furnace and rolling mills in the vicinity of Ninth Street—they were considered fortunate because they received higher wages than domestics and unskilled laborers. There were also a few Black professionals like Dr. O. W. James, who owned the Eastside Pharmacy in the James Building.

African Americans experienced segregation and Jim Crow laws, but they fought against discrimination. In 1905, after the Tennessee legislature passed a "Jim Crow" law for streetcars, Black Chattanoogans organized their own transportation system. Its horse-drawn cars connected different settlements and employment areas. When World War I ended, some Black residents continued to follow the ideas of independence and self-pride taught by Marcus Garvey.

Most buildings in the historic district were constructed in a relatively short period around the turn of the century and show the architectural development of that era's Black community in southeast Tennessee. Although most of the approximately twenty-three historic buildings, primarily of brick, are commercial in nature, some of them have apartments above the first floor. Ownership of property in this historic district has changed over the past twenty years. The University of Tennessee, a predominantly white institution, has become the primary owner of these properties. Several structures that were a part of this *National Register of Historic Places* district have been demolished, including buildings in the 300 block of Martin Luther King Boulevard that were razed and replaced with the state of Tennessee's new Client Service Building. Although the state-owned building may attract new businesses to an area that had been deteriorating, the architectural style is not in harmony with the rest of the structures.

The **Bessie Smith Hall,** formerly a large warehouse in the 200 block of Martin Luther King Boulevard at Lindsay Street, has been restored in harmony with other buildings in this neighborhood. Renovated at a cost of more than three million dollars, the 30,000-square-foot structure, Bessie Smith Hall, will house the Chattanooga African American Museum (as of fall 1995) and Bessie Smith Hall, Inc. The latter organization will sponsor educational events as well as workshops and exhibits that showcase the work of aspiring artists.

Some of the early buildings include

231–239 Martin Luther King Boulevard, stores and apartments c1893

303 Martin Luther King Boulevard, store c1906

411–413 Martin Luther King Boulevard, stores and other businesses c1900

423 Martin Luther King Boulevard, shop and apartment c1890

905–907 Douglas Street, apartments constructed c1890

915 University Street, originally a two-story building used as a city jail in 1893 and as an early firehall; second story removed after a fire in the 1920s

DATE BUILT: Late 1890s to about 1917

ADDRESS: Martin Luther King Boulevard (roughly bounded by McCallie Avenue on the north, Lindsay Street on the west, Eleventh Street on the south, and Central Avenue on the east), Chattanooga

VISITING HOURS: Restricted access, visitors may drive or walk by

SOURCES: NRHPINF. Telephone conversation Jan. 10, 1995, Gary Kelley, director, Martin Luther King Community Development Corporation.

Shiloh Baptist Church

Former slaves worked for thirty years to raise funds to purchase land and materials. Before they were able to build a church, the congregation held services in the residences of different members. They put up their first church on Tenth and Lindsay Streets. When it burned, they built another on the same site. By 1885 church members began building the new, one-story church with their own hands and completed construction ten years later. The church interior had a vaulted ceiling, a sloping wood floor, and fine benches crafted by church members who worked in a Chattanooga chair factory. The church is one of the few remaining Gothic-revival style churches in Chattanooga.

In the early 1890s the congregation adopted the name First Baptist Church. Over the years, divisions in the church occurred twice, with groups withdrawing and forming other churches. First Baptist Church has remained a source of pride for those who spent their time and labor building it and for their descendants. It has been the religious, cultural, and social center in their lives.

DATE BUILT:	Present building, 1885–1895
ADDRESS:	506 E. Eighth Street, Chattanooga
TELEPHONE:	(615) 265-3229
VISITING HOURS:	By appointment
SOURCE:	NRHPINF.

Henning Vicinity

Fort Pillow

The massacre of Black Union soldiers at Fort Pillow marked a tragic point in African American history. The brutal slaughter, however, strengthened the soldiers' resolve to fight for the Union.

When the state of Tennessee established Fort Pillow, Confederate engineers constructed the fort on a high clay bluff at the junction of Cold Creek and the Mississippi River.

After Confederates left the fort in May 1862, federal forces held the area. They found that defense of the fort was difficult, however, because gullies and ravines enabled attacking troops to move within two hundred yards of its perimeter without being visible. Once the troops were this close, they could rush the fort.

Of the 570 Union troops stationed at the fort when the Confederates attacked in April 1864, 262 were Black—ex-slaves recruited from Alabama for the first battalion of the Sixth U.S. Colored Heavy Artillery and Battery D Second U.S. Colored Light Artillery. They were ready to fight in spite of the discriminatory treatment they had received. White Tennessee Union soldiers, for example, bunked in log cabins or shanties while Black soldiers had to sleep in tents with plank floors covered by dry straw.

Confederate troops hated the white Unionists from Tennessee. They had an even greater hatred for the Black soldiers, regarding them as rebellious slaves rather than as soldiers.

Union defenders were outnumbered when Confederate sharpshooters attacked the fort. Some Union troops fled to a Union gunboat in the river; others surrendered. Southern troops, led by Major General Nathan Bedford Forrest, killed both fleeing and surrendering Union soldiers but concentrated their assault on the Black soldiers, refusing to accept the surrender of Black soldiers. When the slaughter ended, 238 Black soldiers lay dead (12 percent of the Black soldiers survived as opposed to 55 percent of the garrison as a whole).

When news of the massacre reached Black soldiers in other units, they realized what their fate would be if they were taken by Confederate troops. Instead of weakening in resolve, they fought harder. Black troops in Memphis took an oath on their knees to remember the massacre. Their battle cry rang out: "Remember Fort Pillow."

Fort Pillow State Park is located in western Tennessee near the Arkansas border. The site today is covered with undergrowth, saplings, and trees; most land features remain essentially the same as in Civil War days, with trenches and fortification walls clearly visible. Although there are no guides, a Visitors Center offers a brochure, a trail map, and a twelve-minute video on the history of the battle at Fort Pillow. A display gives some information about the role of Black soldiers at Fort Pillow but leaves conclusions to be drawn by the viewer. Some visitors, including Boy Scout troops, enjoy hiking one-half mile to the restored fortification. The trek includes two hills and a lofty swinging bridge (which for safety and reassurance has high sides). The self-guided driving tour takes thirty minutes to an hour.

DATE OF SIGNIFICANCE:	Battle, Apr. 12, 1864
ADDRESS:	18 miles east of Henning on TN 87, then north on TN 207
TELEPHONE:	(901) 738-5581
VISITING HOURS:	Park, daily; Visitors Center, Mon.–Fri. 8–4:30; Interpretive Museum, daily 8–4; closed Christmas
FEES:	None
SOURCES:	NRHPINF. Telephone conversation Apr. 4, 1994, and Dec. 6, 1994, Camille Petree, clerk, Fort Pillow State Park.

Alex Haley Museum

The Alex Haley Museum, also known as the Alex Haley Boyhood Home, is located in the quiet suburbs of Henning, Tennessee. Will Palmer, a prominent Black businessowner and community leader, built the one and one-half–story bungalow in 1918 or 1919.

The late author of *Roots,* Alex Haley, was born in Ithaca, New York, in 1921. Six weeks after his birth, his parents took him to his grandparent's house in Henning. His father, Simon, returned to Ithaca to complete graduate studies at Cornell University. Young Alex and his mother lived at that time with Will and Cynthia Palmer. After Simon Haley completed his graduate studies, he came back to Henning, where he operated the Palmer's family business. Although the family relocated about 1929, Alex and his brothers spent every summer in Henning.

In the 1920s young Alex sat on the porch of this house on summer evenings listening to his grandmother, his aunts, and his cousin George tell the history of their ancestors. He learned about the Mandingo youth, Kunta Kinte, who had been captured near the village of Juffure in West Africa. Traders transported him to Annapolis, Maryland, and sold him into slavery.

Haley's relatives spoke of Kizzy, Kunta Kinte's daughter, and they described Kizzy's son, "Chicken George," a gamecock trainer who won his freedom. George, Alex Haley's great-great grandfather, led twenty-nine families from Alamance County, North Carolina, to Lauderdale County in Tennessee. Their wagons reached Henning in the late 1860s or early 1870s. After clearing their land, the settlers began to plant cotton and corn. George's son, Tom Murray, became a successful blacksmith who set up a shop in Henning in 1886. When Murray's daughter, Cynthia, married Will Palmer, the wedding reception was held in this house. The Lane College choir (see the Jackson, Tennessee, listing) gave a recital at the reception. Bertha Palmer, Will and Cynthia's daughter, married Simon Haley.

In 1964, Alex Haley began research to trace his family background. Twelve years later he published *Roots,* an influential book that won the Pulitzer Prize in 1977.

Will Palmer built this ten-room house in the 1920s. It was the place where Alex Haley received his inspiration to trace his ancestry back seven generations and over more than 200 years to the small West African hamlet of Juffure on the Kamby Balongo.

DATE ESTABLISHED: 1918 or 1919

ADDRESS: Museum, 200 S. Church Street and Haley Avenue, off US 51; Haley family plot, Bethlehem Cemetery on Durhamville Road, 1 mile east of Henning (accessed by the second cemetery entrance)

TELEPHONE: (901) 738-2240

VISITING HOURS: Tues.–Sat. 10–5, Sun. 1–5

FEES: Adults, $2.50; students, $1

SOURCES: NRHPINF. Personal visit, summer, 1990. Telephone conversation Jan. 12, 1995, Thelma Winbush, tour guide, Alex Haley Museum.

Jackson

Lane College Historic District

Lane College grew out of a strong desire of leaders of the Colored Methodist Episcopal Church to sponsor a school. When church representatives met in 1870 to discuss church affairs and the possibility of starting a school, a former slave, Bishop Isaac Lane, was a leader in the planning. Lane was born in 1834 on a plantation near Jackson. Although a formal education was denied to him, he managed to teach himself to read and write and became a lay preacher. After the Civil War and emancipation, the church recognized him as a minister. Elected an elder and later a bishop, Lane traveled throughout Tennessee to raise money for a school. With eleven children, he had to supplement his income by raising cotton and cutting firewood for local families. Finally he had $240 with which to purchase four acres on the outskirts of Jackson.

Lane College began its first session in 1882 as the Christian Methodist Episcopal High School with Miss Jennie Lane as the teacher. By 1896 the school, now Lane College, offered a four-year educational program with a full range of courses. Bishop Lane continued to take a personal interest in the welfare of the students who now studied Latin, Greek, physics, algebra, history, and Christian education. The college developed a positive relationship with the community. In 1904, when fire destroyed three buildings, many students moved in with friends in Jackson, and St. Paul Chapel nearby provided space to hold classes. New buildings soon were erected including Hamlett Hall, a brick building designed by Moses McKissack, Tennessee's first Black architect.

In the early 1960s Lane students contributed to the successful desegregation of Jackson facilities by joining sit-ins and pickets and by sitting in front of city buses to gain the right of free access to public facilities.

The Lane College Historic District is centered along Lane Avenue. Five buildings in the historic district are oriented toward a large landscaped yard on the campus. The buildings, constructed between 1905 and 1927, include Daniels Library (1923), Bray Hall Administration Building (1905), Saunders Hall (1908), Cleaves Hall (1921), and Steam Heating Plant (1927), a one-story brick building with attached brick chimney, that originally housed the steam boilers, coal, and other mechanical equipment.

DATE ESTABLISHED: 1882
ADDRESS: 545 Lane Avenue, Jackson
TELEPHONE: (901) 426-7500
VISITING HOURS: Mon.–Fri. 9–4
FEES: None
SOURCES: Elizabeth P. Coleman, director, alumni affairs/public relations, Lane College. NRHPINF. Personal visit, summer 1990. *International Library of Negro Life and History,* 93.

Jonesborough

Jonesborough Historic District

Three sites in Jonesborough, Tennessee's oldest town, have an association with Black history and slavery. The first site, Jonesborough Presbyterian Church, was built before the Civil War and still has an intact slave gallery. The onset of the Civil War caused conflict in a congregation already divided on the slavery issue. Half of the members were Union loyalists who believed in abolition. They left and built their own church at the other end of the street. The church later fell into disuse and disrepair. Eventually the two congregations rejoined and rebuilt the church. For some reason the slave gallery was left intact.

A historic marker is all that remains to identify a second site related to Black history—Jacob Howard's Print Shop. Howard built the large frame building on Main Street about 1800. America's first periodicals devoted solely to the abolition of slavery were printed in this shop. Elihu Embree was the publisher. The *Manumission Intelligence* was published sporadically in 1819, and *The Emancipator* was issued from April to October in 1820. Embree, a Quaker, died in 1820. A photograph of the print shop can be seen in the Jonesborough-Washington County History Museum.

The third site is a two-story brick structure atop Rocky Hills—the Old Holston Female Institute. Now serving as a restaurant, it was at one time a Quaker school for newly freed slaves.

Historic Jonesborough, founded in 1779, has 152 religious, public, commercial, and domestic structures. As a result of restorations, much of the town appears as it did a century ago. The Jonesborough Historic District is listed in the *National Register of Historic Places.*

DATE ESTABLISHED: 18th–19th C.
ADDRESS: Visitors Center, 117 Boone Street, Jonesborough
TELEPHONE: (615) 753-5961
VISITING HOURS: Museum, Mon.–Fri. 8–5, Sat.–Sun. 10–5
FEES: Adults, $1.50; seniors, $1; children, $.50
SOURCES: Molly Thompson, curator, Jonesborough-Washington County History Museum. Telephone call to site, July 31, 1995. *A Strolling Tour of Historic Jonesborough.*

Knoxville

Beck Cultural Exchange Center

The Beck Cultural Exchange Center contains a collection of tape recordings, phonograph records, and old books and newspapers that highlight the achievements of Knoxville's African American citizens. This interesting archive also covers the first one hundred years of the history of African Americans in eastern Tennessee, including historical documents, oral histories, photographs, and other artifacts dating back to the 1800s.

The Hastie Room houses personal memorabilia of the late William Henry Hastie, first Black federal judge and first Black governor of the Virgin Islands. Judge Hastie was born at Knoxville in 1904. His family donated his personal memorabilia to the center in 1976.

DATE ESTABLISHED: 1975

ADDRESS: 1927 Dandridge Avenue, Knoxville

TELEPHONE: (615) 524-8461

VISITING HOURS: Tues.–Sat. 10–6; closed Sun., Mon., national holidays including Martin Luther King Day and the following day

FEES: None

SOURCES: Telephone conversation Apr. 9, 1994, Robert J. Booker, executive director, Beck Cultural Exchange Center. Marianne W. Beaty, executive administrator, Afro-American Studies Program, Knoxville College.

Knoxville College Historic District

After emancipation, Black children studied in informal tutoring arrangements or in small groups in makeshift accommodations. The first formally organized school for Black students in Tennessee began in 1862, when Reverend J. G. McKee, under sponsorship of the Freedmen's Mission of the United Presbyterian Church, founded the McKee School in Nashville. In 1872, church leaders resolved to discontinue McKee School in favor of establishing a college that would prepare Black students for ministerial and teaching careers. African American residents of Knoxville were interested in education, and the city seemed to provide favorable conditions for a new school. Their city was selected, and Knoxville College opened in 1875 in an old elementary school. A year later, the college moved to its present location on a hill overlooking downtown Knoxville.

Through the years the college has added new functions: training military cadets, serving as the Industrial Department for Black students at the University of Tennessee, and providing a college of Arts and Sciences. Between 1920 and 1950 Knoxville College excelled in preparing students to teach in Black schools in East Tennessee.

Knoxville College is approached by streets winding up a hill northwest of downtown Knoxville. The historic district on campus includes eight buildings:

Elnathan Hall (1898), a large, four-story brick structure that has served as a women's residence, a dining room, and as a classroom and office building; altered in 1905 and 1971

Faculty Residence at 1005 College Street (1906), a one and one-half–story building with brick-and-wood shingle walls and a veranda

Faculty Residence at 1009 College Street (1906), a one and one-half–story brick bungalow with arched windows and a recessed porch with balustrades

Giffen Alumni Memorial Building (1929), a two-story brick building that has housed offices, classrooms, and a gymnasium

McKee Hall (1895, altered 1954), a two-story brick building with Romanesque arches, Palladian windows, and a four-story bell-tower

McMillin Chapel (1913), a rectangular one-story brick building with Greek Doric columns and stained-glass windows

The **President's House** (1886–1889), a two-story residence built of wood but bricked in 1905 with bricks made by the students on campus

Wallace Hall (1890, altered in the 1920s), a three-story building built as a home for orphan boys that also has housed the Domestic Science Center, the Literary Society, teachers' offices, and the Basic Skills Learning Center

DATE ESTABLISHED:	1875
ADDRESS:	901 College Street NW, Knoxville
TELEPHONE:	(615) 524-6500
VISITING HOURS:	Tours by appointment, visitors may walk or drive through
SOURCES:	Personal visit, summer 1990. NRHPINF.

Memphis

Beale Street Historic District

Beale Street has an indelible place in history as the street where composer W. C. Handy gave life to the blues. However, the street was thriving long before Handy came to town in 1905. By the turn of the century, East Beale Street was a residential section with many fine mansions built by wealthy cotton planters. The western end of the street, which was close to the Mississippi River, hummed with commercial activity. The central part of the street was the entertainment district.

After the Civil War the wealthy planters began to move out. In the 1890s the street became more commercial with many shops operated primarily by Jewish merchants. In the 1900s the street became predominantly Black.

Entertainment palaces, theaters, saloons, and gambling places thrived on Beale Street. Prohibition changed this; in the 1930s the Memphis police were driving Beale Street bootleggers and gamblers out of business. By 1938 the heyday of the nightlife establishments was over, and World War II brought more changes to the street. In the 1960s many of the once-thriving establishments were closed; many of the historic buildings were demolished. The city of Memphis began a major restoration project in the late 1970s.

Composer William Christopher Handy worked in Memphis from 1905 to 1917. During this productive period he wrote the "Memphis Blues." Originally titled "Mr. Crump," it originated from a campaign tune composed in 1909 by Handy for mayoral candidate E. H. Crump. Handy's band played the tune with such spirit that upon hearing it people danced in the streets. Crump won the election. Since Handy did not receive the financial profit and recognition he deserved for the composition, he decided to create another song. Renting a quiet room on Beale Street, he began working on "St. Louis Blues." African-American music flourished on Beale Street. The street was close to the Mississippi River with its thriving steamboat traffic. It had a lively entertainment and commercial atmosphere with pawnshops, cafes, dance halls, theaters, and saloons. Among its attractions was the Palace Theater, the largest Black show house in the South, and Peewee's Place, a gathering place for musicians. Handy located the headquarters of his band on Beale Street. He left about 1917 or 1918 for Chicago and then moved his publishing company to New York City.

The historic section of Beale Street has boundaries between Main and Fourth Streets and contains a great number of pre-1938 buildings from the old entertainment district. One site of interest, located outside the historic district, is the W. C. Handy House and Museum, a wood-frame, shotgun house at 352 Beale Street, which is said to have been one of Handy's residences while he lived in Memphis. It is open to the public.

DATE ESTABLISHED: Early 20th C.

ADDRESS: Historic district, Beale Street from Main to Fourth Streets; Visitors Center, 207 Beale Street; Handy Home, 352 Beale Street, Memphis

TELEPHONE: Visitors Center, (901) 543-5333; W. C. Handy House and Museum, (901) 522-8300

VISITING HOURS: Historic district, both public and private, visitors can drive or walk by; Handy House, May 1–Sept. 1, Tues.–Sat. 10–5, Sun. 1–5

FEES: Handy House, $2 each; group of 10 or more, $1 each

SOURCES: NRHPINF. Telephone conversation Dec. 7, 1994, Janis Beck Taylor, administrator, Blues Foundation. *International Library of Negro Life and History.*

First Baptist Church

First Baptist Church once was a center of cultural activities for the Black population of Memphis. Many years before emancipation, the church evolved from a series of praise meetings conducted by Reverend Scott Keys at his residence.

A New York Baptist Society donated the land where the present church stands, and in 1869 Black people built the three-story brick church for $100,000. First Baptist Church of Beale Street has a white-painted exterior with some portions covered with stucco. A large rose window above the arched entrance contains small round stained-glass windows, creating a beautiful effect for the interior. The interior has balconies on three sides of the sanctuary and graceful wood vaulting. The church has retained its historic appearance.

Many significant cultural and civic events have taken place at First Baptist Church. During Reconstruction, General Ulysses S. Grant spoke to Black citizens from this pulpit as he triumphantly toured the South after the Civil War. Ida B. Wells published her newspaper, *Free Speech,* at this site, making known the injustices that Black people suffered. The church honors her with a plaque. (For more information on Ida B. Wells, see the listing for Chicago.)

Church Park is located immediately next to First Baptist Church. A prominent Memphis Black businessman and millionaire, Mr. R. R. Church, bought land on Beale Street in 1900 and built Church Park and Auditorium. The auditorium has been razed, but the park remains.

DATE ESTABLISHED: Congregation, c1854; church, 1869

ADDRESS: 379 Beale Street, Memphis

TELEPHONE: (901) 527-4832

VISITING HOURS: Sun. school, 9:30; Sun. service, 11; call for appointment at other times

SOURCES: NRHPINF. Telephone conversation Apr. 7, 1994, Deboraht Robinson, church member.

LeMoyne-Owen College

In 1862 the American Missionary Association opened an elementary school for runaway slaves, who were newly designated by the Union army as contraband of war, and for free Black men and women. Both groups of African Americans had gathered at Camp Shiloh, a Union army camp in Pittsburg Landing, Tennessee. In 1863 the college moved to Memphis, and in 1866 it became known as Lincoln School. When financial problems arose in 1867, a prominent Pennsylvania physician and life member of the American Missionary Association, Dr. Francis LeMoyne, gave $20,000 to the fledgling school. In 1868 the school merged with Owen Junior College. Three years later, the college was named for its benefactor—the LeMoyne Normal and Commercial School.

LeMoyne College has produced some outstanding graduates including Benjamin Hooks, executive director of the National Association for the Advancement of Colored People; Willie Herenton, superintendent of Memphis City Schools; and A. Maceo Walker, president of Universal Life Insurance Company.

Today more than one thousand students attend college on the beautifully landscaped, fifteen-acre campus. Steele Hall, built in 1914, is the oldest building on campus and for many years was the main classroom building.

DATE ESTABLISHED:	1870
ADDRESS:	807 Walker Avenue, Memphis
TELEPHONE:	(901) 942-7393
VISITING HOURS:	Mon.–Fri. 9–4 by appointment with David Valentine, director of enrollment management
SOURCES:	Anthony Hicks, director of public relations, LeMoyne-Owen College. Telephone conversation Jan. 10, 1995, Stella Davis, administrative assistant, LeMoyne-Owen College.

South Main Street Historic District
Lorraine Motel*
National Civil Rights Museum

The railroad was a primary focus for the small retail and wholesale businesses that developed around South Main Street. Trains brought commerce to the eleven-block area located immediately south of the central business district of Memphis, and hotels, restaurants, barber shops, furniture stores, and storage companies emerged to serve travelers. Brick, cast-stone, and terracotta buildings were constructed between 1900 and 1930. The Eureka Hotel, built about 1885, is one of the few Victorian Gothic houses remaining in Memphis. The three small shotgun houses on the same street, built about 1900, are examples of the modest homes that once existed here.

One of the most significant sites historically is the **National Civil Rights Museum** housed in the former Lorraine Motel. The motel, built in 1925, was open only to white people until 1942; by the end of World War II it had become a Black establishment. The Lorraine hosted famous African American guests—Cab Calloway, Count Basie, Roy Campanella, Nat King Cole, Aretha Franklin, and, in 1968, Dr. Martin Luther King Jr.

The motel gained tragic fame in 1968 following a strike by Memphis garbage workers. Demanding more pay, better working conditions, and better treatment from white supervisors, the workers sought the support of Dr. Martin Luther King Jr. The nationally known leader checked into the Lorraine Motel and on April 3 led a march downtown. That night he gave a stirring speech to an audience of two thousand at Mason Temple in Memphis. King was tired and in low spirits when he began speaking; however, as he looked out at the listeners their warmth began to lift his spirits. He spoke to them about the different ages of humankind and about the problems that had troubled people throughout history. Then, in sentences that seemed prophetic, King spoke of the difficult days ahead. Although he would like to live a long life, he said, he had been to the mountaintop; although he might not get to the Promised Land with his listeners, he knew that the brotherhood of man would become a reality. The following day, April 4, 1968, as Dr. King stood on the balcony of the motel, a rifle shot rang out, killing him. James Earl Ray was convicted of being the assassin in this crime. Days of riots followed the tragic assassination of a man who had spoken for peace and nonviolence.

The Lorraine Motel, which has been transformed into the National Civil Rights Museum, honors Dr. King by making known the history of the Civil Rights Movement in America.

DATE ESTABLISHED: Historic district, 1900–1930

ADDRESS: Historic District, S. Main Street between Webster and Linden Streets, and Mulberry Street between Calhoun and Vance Avenues; National Civil Rights Museum, 450 Mulberry Street, Memphis

TELEPHONE: National Civil Rights Museum, (901) 521-9699

VISITING HOURS: Both public and private ownership, access varies; museum, Mon., Wed.–Sat. 10–5, Sun. 1–5, closed Tues.

FEES: Adults, $5; seniors 60 years and over, $4; students 13–18, $4; children 6–12, $3; children 5 and younger, free

SOURCES: NRHPINF. Telephone conversation Apr. 7, 1994, Sedalia Brown, executive secretary, National Civil Rights Museum. *Let the Trumpet Sound.*

Morristown

Morristown College Historic District

Morristown College, one of only two colleges established for Black students in eastern Tennessee, is significant not only for its architecture but also for its role in educating Black Appalachian youth. The college began when Mrs. Almira Stearns, a missionary who had been widowed by the Civil War, came to Morristown with her twelve-year-old daughter. Supported by the Freedmen's Aid Society of the Methodist Episcopal Church, Stearns sought to teach the former slaves, who had been prohibited by law from learning to read during slavery.

The first president was Dr. Judson S. Hill, who came to Morristown with his wife, Laura Yard Hill. In the first year of operation, Dr. Hill and Mrs. Stearns taught 190 students in a building described as a 60-foot-by-40-foot three-room shack. Classes met in several locations, moving in succession to a former meeting house, a former slave mart, and a former hospital for those wounded in the Civil War. Funds were provided in part by the Board of Education for Negroes of the Methodist Episcopal Church.

Townspeople were hostile to the school and the Black students. They called out names, jeered, and spat at Mrs. Stearns's daughter. The president, referred to as "N----- Hill" was threatened with tarring and feathering. Often he had to walk in the gutter to keep from being shoved off the sidewalk. In spite of the hostilities, the school survived. Some students were received in a kind manner by white townspeople. A few white people opened their homes to students and staff after two terrible fires at the school.

Black students enrolled by the hundreds. The school was established primarily as an elementary and secondary-level institution; at times, three generations sat together on the benches. Some students walked ten and twelve miles round trip to their classrooms; some had to swim the river to get there. By 1915 the school enrolled 183 elementary and 75 secondary pupils.

By 1927 Morristown began to offer freshman and sophomore college-level courses. In 1930 Morristown College donated land for an elementary school for Black children, and the city began to provide for their education. The Judson S. Hill Grammar School opened in 1931 with worn-out books and materials passed down from the rest of the school system. Many Morristown College students completed their practice teaching at Hill Grammar School and remained there to teach.

The Morristown College Historic District contains thirteen brick-and-frame buildings dating from 1892 to 1928. New Jersey Home, built in 1892, is the oldest structure on campus. This building was conceived as a "model home" for teaching domestic skills to women students. Following are listed some other important buildings on the campus. The Administration Building is the best eclectic style structure in the county, and the Kenwood Refectory, Wallace Hall, and Crary Hall are the finest Georgian-revival group in the region.

The **Carriger House,** a modest two-story wood-frame structure built in 1925, serves as the president's home.

The original **Crary Hall,** completed in 1898, was destroyed by fire. Crary Hall was rebuilt but again partially destroyed by fire in 1926 and rebuilt in the same year. Following another fire in the 1970s there was a shortage of the original handmade brick, so the upper floor of the building was repaired with wood siding.

The **Laura Yard Hill Administration Building,** the oldest brick structure on campus, was begun in 1901 and completed in 1911. Limestone for the foundation was quarried on campus, and students produced the bricks. Woodwork was milled in the college shops, and much of the construction was provided by students working their way through school.

Kenwood Refectory, the campus dining facility built in 1923, has a belfry containing the bell recast after the Crary Hall fire.

The 60-foot-by-60-foot coal-fired **steam plant** was built in 1923 of handmade brick.

The three-story **Wallace Hall** was built in 1923 after a fire at Crary hall created a need for immediate dormitory space.

The historic campus serves now as the Morristown branch of Knoxville College, enrolling approximately one hundred students.

DATE ESTABLISHED: 1881; buildings, 1892–1928

ADDRESS: 417 N. James Street, Morristown

TELEPHONE: (615) 586-5262

VISITING HOURS: Call for appointment Mon.–Fri. 9–5

SOURCES: NRHPINF. Robert J. Booker, executive director, Beck Cultural Exchange Center. Telephone conversation Dec. 7, 1994, LaShawnda Patrick, student receptionist and granddaughter of Morristown College students.

Nashville

Belle Meade Mansion

Belle Meade was considered one of the finest antebellum plantations of the Old South—a place renowned in the 1800s for the breeding of thoroughbred racing horses. The plantation has a place in Black history as the home of former slave Bob Green, who was known worldwide for his expert knowledge of racing horses. He and his family lived in a log cabin at this site.

The log cabin, constructed in "dogtrot" style with an open passage between the two sections, is one of the oldest houses in Tennessee; it was constructed in the 1790s. John Harding and his family used the house from 1807 to 1820. After the Civil War many former slaves stayed on as paid employees at the farm including Bob Green, who had been owned by John Harding's son, William. Green and his family moved into the one and one-half–story cabin and lived there until the farm was sold in 1903.

Green had the title of head stallion groom. Visitors to Belle Meade usually wanted to talk to him because his knowledge of horses was legendary.

No one knew Bob Green's age. He had lived as part of the Harding-Jackson family at Belle Meade from the time he was three months old until a year before he died in 1906. According to one newspaper account, he lived to be seventy-five years old. In accordance with his request, Bob Green was buried at Belle Meade.

Today's tours of Belle Meade include the 1853 mansion, the log cabin, and the Victorian Carriage Museum. The primary focus of the tour is not on Black history; however, photographs and artifacts at the Visitors Center provide some information about slaves who lived at Belle Meade, including descriptions of excavations at locations where slaves lived. Although 130 slaves once lived on the 3,500-acre Belle Meade Plantation, their cabins have been demolished and most of the plantation land has been sold. One cabin remains, a dwelling passed from a white family to a Black family and a reminder of a Black man whose knowledge and skill were widely respected.

DATE BUILT:	1790s and 1807
ADDRESS:	5025 Harding Road, Nashville
TELEPHONE:	(615) 356-0501
VISITING HOURS:	Mon.–Sat. 9–5, Sun. 1–5; closed New Year's Day, Thanksgiving, Christmas
FEES:	Adults, $4; children, $3.50
SOURCES:	Personal visit, summer 1990. *The Belle Meade Farm.*

Fisk University Historic District

Fisk University opened in Nashville on January 9, 1866. Agents of the American Missionary Association, in collaboration with the Freedmen's Aid Commission of Cincinnati, established the school. They originally had planned to open it as a racially integrated, coeducational school, but the plan was thwarted when state legislation limited the student body to Black students.

By 1870 there were 900 students at Fisk. Operating with limited funds, the school used former Union hospital barracks as classrooms, dormitories, and offices. Just five years after the university opened its doors, financial troubles made closure seem imminent. To save Fisk, Professor George White and nine students, later called the Jubilee Singers, left Nashville to give fund-raising concerts. The group met ridicule and hostility at first because their dignified manner and style of singing did not fit the expected stereotypes: that their performances would resemble those of Black minstrel performers. As they persevered, however, audience attitudes began to change from hostility to respect and enthusiasm. At the end of the first three-month American tour, President Ulysses S. Grant invited the group to sing at the White House. In 1873 the singers toured in Europe, where they presented concerts to enthusiastic audiences. The Jubilee Singers had established the spiritual as a unique American art form.

Five years after their original departure, they had raised enough money to buy the land where Fisk now stands and to erect the magnificent Jubilee Hall. The Jubilee Singers saved the university.

Fisk University established itself as a preeminent university associated with a number of Black scholars who studied at or taught at the university. Included are social philosopher W. E. B. Du Bois; sociologist E. Franklin Frazier; historian John Hope Franklin; Congressmen William L. Dawson and Charles C. Diggs; Solicitor General of the United States Wade H. McCree; jurist Constance Baker Motley; poets James Weldon Johnson, Arna Bontemps, Sterling Brown, and Nikki Giovanni; tenor Roland Hayes; and novelist John O. Killins.

The Fisk University campus today, with its mature trees, stone walls, and historic buildings, retains its turn-of-the-century charm. Although several modern buildings are interspersed with the older historical structures, the campus still retains much of its original character. Of the seventy structures in the Fisk District that date from the 1860s, forty-one are in the historic district. Historical buildings on the campus include the following.

Jubilee Hall, 1711 Meharry Boulevard, at the historical heart of the campus, is the country's oldest permanent building for the higher education of Black students. The magnificent six-story brick building with spired tower was constructed 1873–1876 with funds raised by the Jubilee Singers. This high Victorian Gothic building is delineated by a limestone wall built about 1873. The hall's front door is of black walnut with bronze trimmings. The front halls and stairways are wainscoted with wood brought from the Mendi Mission, West Africa.

The **Academic Building** (formerly Carnegie Library No. 5), at 1720 Meharry Boulevard, is a two-story brick building constructed in 1908. Andrew Carnegie donated $30,000 for construction of this building and Black architect Moses McKissack III designed it. It was his first major commission in Nashville, and the building is one of the first major structures in America designed by a Black architect.

The three-story brick chemistry building, **Tally Brady Hall** at 1016 Eighteenth Avenue North, was built in 1931 with similar materials and details to those in the Administration Building.

The Administration Building, **Erastus Milo Cravath Hall** at 1015 Seventeenth Avenue North, is a neo-Gothic brick and stone building that formerly served as the university library.

The **Little Theater, Speech and Drama Department,** at 1006 Eighteenth Avenue North, is the oldest building on campus. The one-story, wood-frame building, constructed in the early 1860s, was put up by the Union Army during the Civil War for use as a hospital.

The **Carl Van Vechten Art Gallery,** 1720 Jackson Street, is one of the country's outstanding African American galleries. The two-story, red-brick building formerly served as the university gymnasium. The foundation was excavated by students, and the cornerstone was laid in 1888. The Victorian picturesque building houses important original works by Cézanne, Picasso, Renoir, and O'Keeffe.

The **Fisk University Chapel,** 1016 Seventeenth Avenue North, was constructed in 1892. The stone and stucco building is one of the most picturesque on campus. It has twin stone and stucco towers and a tall bell tower. The interior has a stage with a pipe organ, curved seating, and a high ceiling with exposed framework. Many historic figures have given speeches or concerts in the chapel including Dr. Martin Luther King Jr. and opera singer Leontyne Price.

Magnolia Cottage, 1615 Meharry Boulevard, is a red-brick Victorian building constructed in 1875 as a private residence.

Richardson House, 1017 Sixteenth Avenue North, is named for Reuben B. Richardson, one of Nashville's first Black fire department captains, who built the house in 1905. Three of the Richardson children attended Fisk University.

Many Fisk University graduates and friends contributed to the restoration of Richardson House. The restored dwelling received the 1989 Architectural Award by the Historical Commission of Metropolitan Nashville-Davidson County for outstanding restoration in the education and institutional category. The house currently is used as headquarters for the Fisk General Alumni Association.

Some other historic buildings on campus are

The **Urban Affairs Institute Building,** 1611 Meharry Boulevard, built about 1915 and the former residence of Charles S. Johnson, president of Fisk University, and later the residence of noted author and Fisk librarian Arna Bontemps (see the listing for Bontemps under Alexandria, Louisiana, African American Museum)

The **Music Building,** 1607 Meharry Boulevard, a one-story clapboard building constructed about 1890 as a residence

The **Honors Center (Boyd House),** 1603 Meharry Boulevard, c1915–1920, a two-story brick house with large bay windows on the sides

An 1878 Victorian structure at **1030 Seventeenth Avenue North** originally constructed by Adam K. Spence, one of the founders of the University, and later a residence of poet and professor Sterling Brown, sociologist and professor E. Franklin Frazier, and Dr. John W. Work II, director of the Jubilee Singers from 1948 to 1957

Music Annex Building, 1014 Seventeenth Avenue North, built in 1876, a single-story brick building in the Italianate style

The **Bell Tower,** built in 1927, Jackson Street between Du Bois Hall and Livingston Hall, houses a one-ton bell presented to Fisk in 1880 by Mrs. Clinton B. Fisk and the Jubilee Singers

Faculty Residence, 926 Seventeenth Avenue North, c1890, a two-story residence that formerly was home to the Reverend George W. Moore, 1881 Fisk graduate, and his wife, Ella Shepard Moore, one of the original Jubilee Singers

Ballentine Hall, Art Department, 913 Eighteenth Avenue North, c1880, a two-story brick building

DATE ESTABLISHED:	1866
ADDRESS:	1000 Seventeenth Avenue N (roughly bounded by Sixteenth and Eighteenth Avenues, Hermosa, Herman, and Jefferson Streets), Nashville
TELEPHONE:	(615) 329-8665; Van Vechten Art Gallery, (615) 329-8720
VISITING HOURS:	Contact the university to arrange to see building interiors; Van Vechten Art Gallery, Tues.–Fri. 10–5, Sat.–Sun. 1–5
FEES:	Art gallery: adults, $2.50; students, free
SOURCES:	NRHPINF. Personal visit, summer 1990.

Tennessee State University
Goodwill Manor

When the 1909 Tennessee Legislature authorized teacher training institutions in each major division of the state, the legislators decided to allocate one of the schools for Tennessee's "colored people." Nashville's Black citizens lobbied to have the state normal school built in Nashville. The site selected was part of an old plantation where thirty-four slaves had once lived. The school was to be located two miles west of Fisk University.

Tennessee Agricultural and Industrial Normal School for Negroes had an emphasis that was more in line with the ideas of Booker T. Washington, while Fisk University emphasized the classical curriculum, in line with the ideas of W. E. B. Du Bois. The state university, however, started with more generous funding than Fisk had seen. The first physical plant was built at a cost of more than $80,000. Booker T. Washington toured the facilities and praised the college.

Goodwill Manor, a two-story, red-brick house in Colonial revival style, was constructed as a residence for college President William Jasper Hale. Dr. Walter S. Davis became university president in 1943 and occupied the house until 1968.

Presidents Hale and Davis served during a period of enforced segregation. Nashville offered few satisfactory facilities for African American visitors, so the college presidents hosted many distinguished visitors, including Marian Anderson, Jesse Owens, and Booker T. Washington.

Of the four buildings constructed between 1909 and 1912, only Goodwill Manor remained into the 1980s. Then the building was torn down and replaced by a replica. The many add-on sections that the older building had accrued were not replicated. In the rebuilt structure, which opened in April 1992, the exterior has the original appearance, while the interior has been altered to accommodate current needs.

DATE BUILT: c1912; rebuilt Apr. 1992

ADDRESS: Goodwill Manor, 3500 Centennial Boulevard, Tennessee State University, Nashville

TELEPHONE: (615) 320-3386

VISITING HOURS: Mon.–Fri. 8–4; call to arrange a tour

SOURCES: NRHPINF. Ophelia Paine, public information coordinator, Metropolitan Historical Commission. Telephone conversation Apr. 5, 1994, Margaret Whitfield, director of alumni relations.

Smyrna

Sam Davis Home and Slave Cottages

The former home of Sam Davis, who was called the "boy hero of the Confederacy," was also the home site of his personal servant, a slave named Coleman Davis Smith. Smith, born in 1844, was brought from Virginia when he was a small boy and was given to Sam "as a playfellow." As young men, they worked together in the fields, plowing and hoeing the crops until the outbreak of the Civil War. In 1861 Sam Davis, who had attended military school, became a scout for the Rutherford Rifles, Company I, of the First Tennessee Volunteer Infantry. Smith joined Davis as his body servant. As the war progressed, Captain Davis became widely known and admired in the South for his courage. He was also hunted by Union soldiers. In an irony of warfare, the white man and his slave remained close in friendship. They eluded capture and once worked together to burn a Union ammunitions wagon train. They were caught in 1863 in Giles County. Revealing documents were found in the saddle and boots of Captain Davis, and the two men were jailed. The captors tried to make Davis reveal the source of the documents but he would not, even though the person was standing within ten feet of him at the time.

Smith had been inseparable from Captain Davis, but on November 27, 1863, he watched inconsolably as Davis was taken to the scaffold to be hanged. Later he said that it broke his heart when the trap door opened. After Davis was hanged, Smith was allowed to return home to Rutherford County. In spite of the tragedy, everyone in the Davis household was overjoyed to see him.

Although Smith kept the important secret of the documents, he agonized all of his life that Sam Davis had died for not revealing who gave him the documents while others around him who knew had kept silent.

After the war Smith continued to farm. Eventually moving away from this site, he raised a family of twelve children. He talked little about his wartime experiences; he had been told that it would be dangerous to do so because he had accompanied a spy, and he was afraid of punishment. Six decades passed before he gathered up enough courage to apply for a pension. On March 7, 1926, he went to the office of F. C. Featherstun at the *Commercial Appeal* in Senatobia, Mississippi, and asked for help in gaining a pension for his wartime service. Featherstun, a relative of Governor W. S. Featherstun, assisted Smith and sent his story to the Tennessee Historical Society.

Finally, Smith was placed on the pension rolls at the age of eighty-four. While Sam Davis was referred to as the boy hero of the Confederacy, Smith, the Black man who accompanied him, was all but forgotten. (Note: There is some confusion in the records as to just what year Smith turned in his questionnaire as a Tennessee war veteran.) When his questionnaire and pension documents came to light years later, many were surprised to learn that a Black man had accompanied Sam Davis in his work as a spy and to learn about this story of trust and friendship in the midst of a savage war.

Today this site contains original slave cabins that are a part of African American history. Included also are the original kitchen, a smokehouse, and the two-story Davis home. Although Smith lived here, he did not reside in any of these cabins. Three of the slave cabins were moved to this site from "Rattle and Snap," a large Tennessee plantation; a fourth was moved from Lascassus in Rutherford County, Tennessee. All of the log cabins have wooden floors. Three are one-room structures, and one is in dogtrot style—two rooms with a central open area. According to lore, a dog could trot across the open area from one room to another in a house of this style. The cabins are furnished to show the different types of work done at that time. One slave cabin is set up as it would have been in the 1850–1860 period. The two in the middle contain weaving and spinning items and old farming machinery.

There were fifty-one slaves at this site, including Smith. Another servant, Uncle Charlie, lived until his death in 1925 in the converted kitchen quarters outside the main house.

DATE BUILT: early 1800s

ADDRESS: 1399 Sam Davis Road (from Nashville take US 24 East to Smyrna, take exit 66B, follow the signs on San Ridley Boulevard), Smyrna

TELEPHONE: (615) 459-2341

VISITING HOURS: May–Aug., daily 10–5; Sept.–Mar., Mon.–Sat. 10–4, Sun. 1–4; closed Thanksgiving, Christmas Eve, Christmas, New Year's Day

SOURCES: Telephone conversation Dec. 29, 1993, Pat Kerr, docent and site interpreter. Kay Holley-Humble, docent/site manager, Sam Davis Home. Copy of handwritten letter from the office of H. C. Featherstun, dated Mar. 7, 1927. Questionnaire administered to Coleman Davis Smith c1927 by the Tennessee Historical Committee, Department of Libraries, Archives, and History. Files from the Sam Davis Home. "Sam Davis on the Gallows (His Bodyservant's Point/Counterpoint)." "Coleman Davis Smith, Sam Davis Inseparable."

Works Consulted

The Belle Meade Farm: Its Landmarks and Out-Buildings. W. Ridley Wills II. Nashville: Nashville Chapter Association for the Preservation of Tennessee Antiquities, 1986.

"Coleman Davis Smith, Sam Davis Inseparable." Frank B. Hammond and Robert Hatton. n.p.: Camp Sons of Confederate Veterans, n.d. [files, Sam Davis Home]

International Library of Negro Life and History: Historical Negro Biographies. Wilhelmena S. Robinson. New York: Publishers, 1970.

Let the Trumpet Sound: A Life of Martin Luther King Jr. Stephen B. Oates. New York: Harper, 1982; New York: HarperCollins, 1994.

"Sam Davis on the Gallows (His Bodyservant's Point/Counterpoint)." Carolyn A. Kent. *The United Daughters of the Confederacy Magazine,* n.d.

A Strolling Tour of Historic Jonesborough. Jonesborough, Tenn.: Preservation and Restoration Committee of the Jonesborough Civic Trust. [flier]

Webster's New Biographical Dictionary. Springfield, Mass.: Merriam-Webster, 1988.

Pre-Civil War

All photos by
Nancy C. Curtis, Ph.D.,
except as noted.

Slave quarters, Carter's Grove, Williamsburg, Va.

Interior, slave quarters,
Carter's Grove,
Williamsburg, Va.

African House,
Yucca Plantation,
Melrose, La.

Courtesy of The Historic New Orleans Collection, acc. #1974.25.26.84.

Slave quarters at The Grange,
vicinity Paris, Ky.

Slave house,
Boone Hall Plantation,
Mount Pleasant, S.C.

Servant's house, Belle Meade,
Nashville, Tenn.

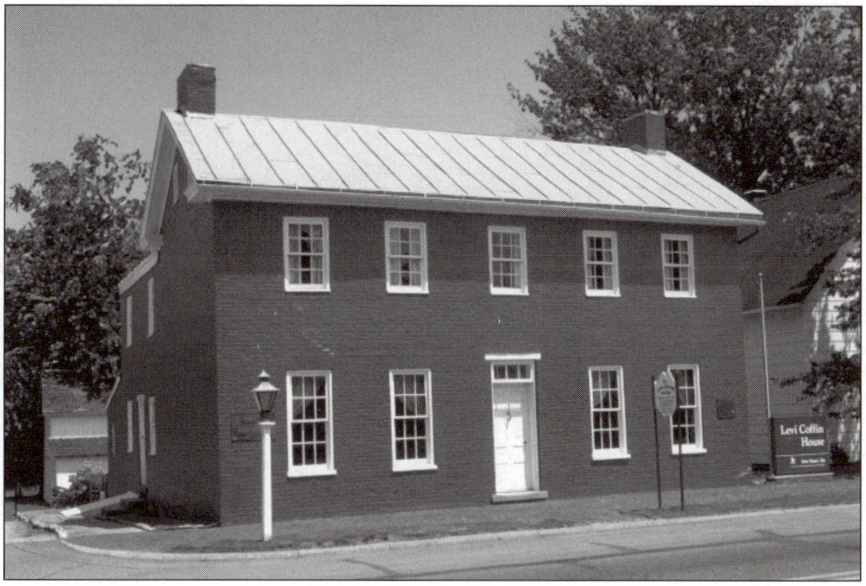

Levi Coffin House,
Fountain City, Ind.

Slave tunnel opening, lower level,
White Hall State Historic Site,
Richmond, Ky.

Slave quarters
(under restoration),
White Hall State Historic Site,
Richmond, Ky.

John B. Russwurm House,
Portland, Maine.
Courtesy of Maine Historic Preservation Commission.

Mount Vernon A.M.E. Church,
Gamaliel, Ky.
Countesy of Elizabeth Thomas Wilson, Gamaliel, Ky.

Cudjoe Lewis,
Mobile (Prichard), Ala.
Courtesy of the Erik Overbey Collection, University of South Alabama Archives and of Mary West Lumbers, great-great granddaughter of Cudjoe Lewis.

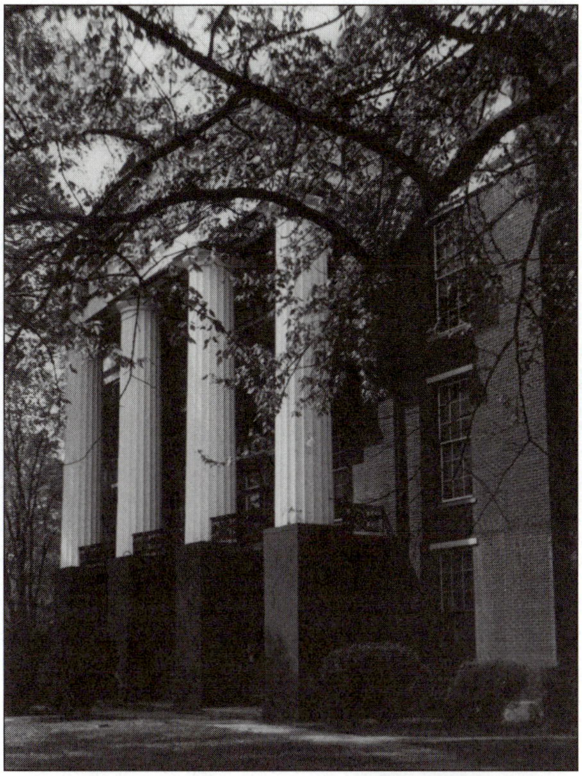

Swayne Hall, Talladega College,
Talladega, Ala.
Courtesy of Talladega College.

Waveland Mansion,
Lexington, Ky.

Interior, slave quarters, Waveland,
Lexington, Ky.

The Old Court House Museum,
Vicksburg, Miss.

Tower and clock,
the Old Court House Museum,
Vicksburg, Miss.

Entrance, Vicksburg
National Cemetery,
Vicksburg, Miss.

First African Baptist Church,
Savannah, Ga.

Oakland Chapel,
stair with
wrought iron railings,
Alcorn State University,
vicinity Lorman, Miss.

The Old Slave Mart Building,
Charleston, S.C.

Mann-Simons College, Columbia, S.C.

Virginia

Appomattox

Appomattox Court House National Historical Park*

When General Robert E. Lee surrendered to General Ulysses S. Grant at Appomattox Court House, a tiny village in south central Virginia, the Civil War was formally at a close. While the war's end was significant to the entire nation, it had special meaning to Black Americans. Not only had they fought for their freedom, but they also remembered well that Black men had been prevented from serving officially as soldiers at the beginning of the war. Later, when their services were considered essential for the Union to win, they were allowed to enlist in the U.S. Army. They played a large role in ensuring success for the Union cause. About 185,000 Black soldiers, called United States Colored Troops, served in the Union Army, participating in 410 military engagements.

The all-Black Second Division of the Twenty-Fifth Corps was one of the Union units that pursued Lee's army from Petersburg, Virginia. Lee's Confederates had endured a ten-month siege in the city of Petersburg and had seen their supply lines from the south gradually cut off. On April 1 Lee withdrew and headed west, moving over bad roads, through bogs and pine thickets, and across open fields. There would be nine days left until the surrender. When some of the Confederates finally reached the High Bridge spanning the Appomattox, their only route of retreat was threatened. The tired, famished Confederates had marched along the Lynchburg Road, hoping to catch up to needed supplies at Appomattox Station. The Federals, too, were racing ahead for the supplies at that station, and Sheridan's cavalry moved ahead and blocked the way. There was no open way left to the Confederates.

On April 7, 1865, General Grant sent a message to General Lee asking him to surrender. Lee, in turn, inquired about the terms of surrender. Grant responded that the one condition of surrender would be that "the men and officers surrendered shall be disqualified for taking up arms again against the Government of the United States until properly exchanged."[1] Lee balked against accepting the proposal at first, but by the following day he realized that his position was hopeless. His army was tired, tattered, and demoralized—along the way some even had stolen for themselves the hard corn intended for the horses. Lee knew that if the soldiers dispersed, each man for himself, they would become little more than bands of robbers and that the hostilities could be protracted over a period of years.

A towel, in lieu of a white flag, was carried through Union lines as a symbol of surrender. Lee requested a cease-fire until he could work out the terms of surrender with Grant.

Because the village courthouse was closed on Sunday, the day of the meeting, the McLean house, an impressively large, two-story brick residence close to the courthouse, was selected for the meeting. Here the two generals met on April 9, 1865, and General Lee surrendered the Army of Northern Virginia to General Grant. Grant graciously agreed to Lee's request to allow Confederate soldiers who owned a horse or a mule to take the animal with them to use when they returned to their farms. Lee accepted the surrender terms with dignity. The following day news of Lee's surrender swept through Washington, and a brass band led 3,000 people to the White House, where President Lincoln made a speech. Four days later Lincoln was assassinated.

The village of Appomattox Court House has been restored to its 1865 appearance. The 1,700-acre park includes thirteen of the buildings that existed in April 1865 and nine structures, including the McLean house, reconstructed on their original sites. A wallboard in the Visitors Center shows the position of Black troops in the battle and includes a listing of Black soldiers in the Confederate Army who surrendered here. In summer months African American residents join others in a re-creation of the 1865 village. They show how free Black people lived during the Civil War.

DATE OF SIGNIFICANCE:	April 1865
ADDRESS:	Between Richmond and Lynchburg on VA 24, just northeast of Appomattox
TELEPHONE:	(804) 352-8987
VISITING HOURS:	June–Aug., daily 9–5:30; Sept.–May 8:30–5; closed New Year's Day, Martin Luther King Jr. Day, President's Day, Thanksgiving, Christmas
FEES:	$2 per person, maximum $5 per vehicle; discount for seniors with a Golden Passport
SOURCES:	Tracy Chernault, supervisory park ranger. *Appomattox Court House. The Civil War Almanac*, 260–2. *Before the Mayflower*, 206.

Arlington

Charles Richard Drew House

Charles Drew, pioneer researcher in medicine, was born in 1904 to Richard and Nora Drew in Washington, D.C. He attended local schools including Dunbar High School, where he excelled in both scholarship and athletics. He won a scholarship to Amherst College in Massachusetts, where he decided on a career in medicine.

Drew studied medicine at McGill University in Montreal, Canada, and graduated second in his class, having earned the Doctor of Medicine and Master of Surgery degrees. He began to consider the need for having a system for preserving blood for use in emergencies. After teaching at Howard University, he received a scholarship to do research in characteristics of blood plasma at Columbia University. When Drew graduated from Columbia University in 1940, he was the first Black person in America to receive the degree of Doctor of Science in surgery. As director of a laboratory at Columbia, Drew and his coworkers showed that plasma could be preserved almost indefinitely, and they established uniform procedures for the collection of blood. During World War II his system for storing blood plasma was used in battlefields in Europe and the Pacific. He organized Blood for Britain, the world's first project of this type, and established the American Red Cross blood bank. Through Drew's efforts, plasma was available for battlefield victims, and it saved thousands of lives during World War II and in subsequent years. In spite of his achievement, Drew saw the Red Cross segregate blood drawn from Black donors; he resigned from the Red Cross because of this procedure.

Drew returned to the Department of Surgery at Howard University as a full professor and led the department to national prominence. He continued to fight the segregation that made it difficult for Black interns and residents to obtain medical internships in hospitals throughout the country.

While driving to a conference at Tuskegee and tired from an exhausting day, Drew fell asleep at the wheel of his car. The car overturned, and although efforts were made to save him, he died on April 1, 1950. A granite and bronze marker was placed on Interstate 85 between Greensboro and Durham, North Carolina, where the automobile accident cost him his life.

The Drew family bought the property on First Street in 1920. The two-story clapboard house originally had four rooms, but two rooms were added while Drew resided there. He maintained the house as his permanent residence until he married in 1939.

DATE OF SIGNIFICANCE: 1920–1939

ADDRESS: 2505 First Street S, Arlington

VISITING HOURS: Private, visitors may drive by

SOURCES: NRHPINF. Telephone conversation Mar. 6, 1994, Ms. Cathleen Drew. *Created Equal,* 138–43.

Charlottesville

Ash Lawn-Highland Slave Cabin

There is one remaining slave cabin on this site, which was once owned by President James Monroe (1758–1831). Monroe was one of the leaders who assisted in founding the Republic of Liberia. At that time the American Colonization Society was spearheading efforts to return former slaves to Africa, and in February 1820, the ship *Mayflower of Liberia* sailed from New York City with eighty-six Black passengers.

Most African Americans, however, rejected the idea of leaving the country they now regarded as home, a country they had helped to build. On July 5, 1832, Peter Osborne, a Black leader from Connecticut, spoke for thousands when he said:

> Let us all unite, and with one accord declare that we will not leave our own country to emigrate to Liberia, nor elsewhere, to be civilized nor Christianized. Let us make it known to America that we are not barbarians; that we are not inhuman beings; that this is our native country; that our forefathers have planted trees in America for us, and we intend to stay and eat the fruit.[2]

In spite of the protest, some African Americans did leave for Liberia. The capital of Liberia, Monrovia, a new home for former slaves, was named for President Monroe.

Ash Lawn-Highland consists of a mansion, a clapboard slave cabin, an overseer's house, and other outbuildings. The frame slave cabin has a stone foundation, two large rock chimneys, and three front doorways. It was reconstructed from a late 1860s photograph made of a slave building built on the site in the early 1800s and from archaeological evidence. Since the photograph did not show the interior, no attempt was made to duplicate the original inside area. Today, the three rooms of the slave cabin with its open-hearth fireplace are used for demonstrations of the cooking and spinning women slaves would have performed during President Monroe's era at Ash Lawn. There also are demonstrations of candlemaking, tinsmithing, and the herbal arts. One room has a small exhibit on slavery that includes some porcelain archaeological specimens and a few coins that probably belonged to slaves at Ash Lawn. There were forty slaves at the site, and perhaps two-thirds worked in the fields. An estimated three families lived in this dwelling; to their left was the overseer's cottage; to their right, the smokehouse.

ADDRESS: County Road 795, 2 miles past Monticello off VA 53

TELEPHONE: (804) 293-9539; Summer Festival Administration, (804) 293-4500

VISITING HOURS: Mar.–Oct., daily 9–6; Nov.–Feb., daily 10–5; closed Thanksgiving, Christmas, New Year's Day

FEES: Adults, $6; senior citizens, $5.50; children 6–11, $2

SOURCES: Telephone conversation Apr. 10, 1994, Earl Capel, curatorial assistant, Ash Lawn-Highland. *Before the Mayflower,* 453. *A Documentary History of the Negro People in the United States,* 138.

Monticello

Monticello, the home of Thomas Jefferson (1743–1826), America's third president, was built from 1769 to 1809; it is a place where slaves lived. Jefferson's ownership of slaves was ironic because he was the author of the Declaration of Independence. The slaves worked in the construction and maintenance of Monticello from its beginnings in the late eighteenth century and throughout Jefferson's life. As many as sixty adult slaves were engaged in farming and domestic work as well as in light-industrial shops.

Although the original slave houses no longer exist, the areas where they stood are marked. Tour guides describe the role Black servants played at the plantation, and the Thomas Jefferson Visitors Center has an exhibit on the life of slaves at Monticello.

DATE BUILT: 1769–1809

ADDRESS: Vicinity of Charlottesville (2 miles southeast of Charlottesville near the intersection of VA 20 and I-64; Visitors Center VA 20, just south of exit 24, off I-64)

TELEPHONE: (804) 984-9800

VISITING HOURS: Mar.–Oct., daily 8–5; Nov.–Feb., daily 9–4:30; closed Christmas

FEES: Adults, $8; senior citizens, $7; children 6–11, $4; group rates available

SOURCES: Sandra L. Richardson, education assistant, Monticello. Telephone call to site, Mar. 3, 1994.

Clarksville

Prestwould Plantation Slave House

The story of America as told from the perspective of a slave while in bondage would shed quite a new light on our history; therefore, the recent discovery of a large collection of slave writings at Prestwould (pronounced *prestwood*) Plantation has attracted attention. The process of transcribing the material is lengthy and at the time of this book's publication, the material had not yet been made available to the public.

Although the focus of interpretation at Prestwould Plantation is on the main house (which has furnishings used by four generations of the family that lived here) and gardens, the highlight for Black-history seekers is the recently restored two-family slave quarters. The frame, side-by-side duplex has separate entrances, and the double fireplace serves both sides with a single chimney made from stone quarried on the plantation. Prestwould once was a plantation of 10,000 acres, and this slave house is the only one on the site to survive.

DATE BUILT: Manor house, 1795

ADDRESS: 3 miles north of Clarksville on US 15; about 85 miles southwest of Petersburg via I-85 and US 58

TELEPHONE: (804) 374-8672

VISITING HOURS: May–Oct., Mon.–Sat. 12:30–4:30, Sun. 1:30–4:30; closed Nov.–Apr.

FEES: Adults, $4.50; senior citizens 65 and over, $3.50; children 6–12, $1.50; children under 6, free

SOURCE: Telephone call May 21, 1994.

Glen Allen

Virginia E. Randolph Cottage

This one and one-half-story rectangular brick building is named for Virginia Randolph (1874–1958), the founder of vocational education in the Virginia school system and the first Jeanes teacher. Virginia Randolph, born of former slave parents, taught in a one-room, rural school in Henrico County, Virginia. Along with the standard curriculum of reading, writing, and arithmetic, she devised unique methods of teaching practical, everyday skills. Using materials at hand, she taught students to fashion useful objects. They took cloth sugar and flour sacks, bleached out the letters, and made aprons and skirts from the fabric. Students made handkerchiefs from the small, leftover pieces. They created baskets from honeysuckle vines and doormats from cornshucks. Boys brought wooden boxes from stores and turned them into birdhouses. Sewing, cooking, and laundry work also were integral parts of the curriculum. Some of Randolph's techniques may have been passed on to her by her mother who had been a former slave and a housekeeper.

Jackson Davis, the white superintendent of Henrico County Schools, saw and admired Randolph's approach to teaching. At the same time, Anna T. Jeanes, a wealthy white philanthropist from Philadelphia, provided $1,000,000 to be spent on improving education for Black students in rural areas in the South. As Jeanes Fund trustees pondered how best to spend the money, Superintendent Davis recommended that it would be well spent by having Virginia Randolph show her methods to other teachers. The suggestion was adopted, and Randolph became the first industrial Jeanes supervisor in the Henrico Plan.

In 1939 the Henrico County School Board built this cottage as the home economics building of the Virginia Randolph Training School. Although Randolph did not teach students here, she was in and out of the site as a visiting teacher. The talented educator never married. Most of her possessions were sold after her death, and her house on Marshall Street in Richmond was later demolished.

After country schools were integrated in 1960, Black schools were closed, and their students were sent to white schools. In 1970 the cottage was turned into a museum named in Randolph's memory. The museum obtained four pieces of her furniture—a whatnot shelf, a large desk known as a secretary, a chair, and a small table fashioned from a piano leg and a piano top. The museum also has in its collections newspaper clippings, pictures, and articles about Virginia Randolph along with photographs of classes at the segregated training school that date back to 1926.

DATE BUILT: 1937

ADDRESS: Off US 1, 2200 Mountain Road, Glen Allen (from Richmond: take I-95 north to I-295; go west on I-295 to Woodman Road; take Woodman Road south to Mountain Road)

TELEPHONE: (804) 261-5029; Curator William Cosby (after 9 P.M.), (804) 360-2071

VISITING HOURS: Mon., Wed., Fri., Sat. 1–4; Sun. 3–5 or by appointment; closed Christmas, New Year's Day

FEES: None

SOURCES: Telephone conversations Apr. 23, 1994, and Jan. 11, 1995, William Cosby, museum curator. *National Register of Historic Places*, 796. *Virginia Museums and Historic Sites Guide Book*, 29.

Hampton

Fort Monroe

The Hampton area is rich in Black history. In 1619 two Black people, Anthony and Isabella, were among the first group of Africans to arrive in the English colonies. The group landed in Hampton at a location called Old Point Comfort (some historians still argue that the landing was at Jamestown). The son of Anthony and Isabella was baptized in the Second Church of Kecoughtan. Although the church no longer stands, a marker commemorates the site.

Ceaser Tarrant, a slave, was one of seven boat pilots appointed by the Virginia Navy Board during the American Revolution. He piloted an American gunboat in combat against larger British warships. An elementary school in Hampton is named in his honor.

Nearly a century after Tarrant's heroic deeds, the Civil War began. Many escaping slaves sought refuge at Fort Monroe in Hampton, Virginia, hoping for shelter under the Union flag. The Fugitive Slave Law of 1850, however, required that fugitive slaves be returned to their owners and made it illegal to give them assistance.

In May 1861 when three slaves escaped from a Confederate labor battalion and made their way to Fort Monroe, Union General Butler refused to send them back to slavery. He allowed them to stay at the fort and asked Secretary of War Simon Cameron to make a decision about the status of the former slaves as property. Butler argued that Virginia claimed not to be part of the Union. Therefore, Virginia was a foreign country, and its slave owners were at war with the United States. Butler reasoned that since the Confederates had put the slaves to work building fortifications, the slaves could be considered spoils or "contraband of war."

Two months after Butler made this controversial decision, 900 Black refugees, some from as far away as Richmond and North Carolina, had found their way to Fort Monroe and more were on the way. Although still not allowed to fight in the war, they were able to build roads and fortifications and to work on naval vessels. Eventually, Union leaders realized that Black soldiers were needed for victory and authorized their enlistment in the Union Army. Although nearly half of the inhabitants of the city now known as Hampton were slaves before the Civil War (there were a few free African Americans), by the time the war had ended, the influx of refugees had changed the ratio to two Black persons for every white person.

Fort Monroe's Casemate Museum is an interesting site, apart from its history, because it is entered by way of a live moat. The word *casemate* means "room within the wall of the fort." Inside the museum, the Freedom's Fortress exhibit tells the story through photographs of escaping slaves who found shelter at Fort Monroe. A gift shop has Black history publications, including the *Casemate Paper,* which describes General Butler and his definition of the escaping slaves as contraband. Tours here are popular with school groups of children in grades three and above.

DATE BUILT: 1819

ADDRESS: South of downtown Hampton, off I-64, exit eastbound VA 143

TELEPHONE: (804) 727-3973

VISITING HOURS: Daily 10:30–4:30; closed Thanksgiving, Christmas, New Year's Day; tours available for groups of schoolchildren in grades 3 and above

FEES: None

SOURCES: Telephone conversations Mar. 6, 1994, Carol Hanson, secretary, Fort Monroe, and Thornton Elliott Jr., museum staff, Syms-Eaton Museum, City of Hampton. *First Steps to Freedom. Before the Mayflower,* 193. *Highlights of Black History at Fort Monroe.*

Hampton Institute

As early as 1861 slaves fled to Hampton, Virginia, seeking protection within Union Army lines. As the Civil War progressed, the town of Hampton became a gathering place for hundreds of fugitive slaves. Although the Union encampment protected the grounds, the fugitives lived under conditions of great privation in tents or split-log cabins. A decade later, remnants of these settlements, called Slabtown and Sugar Hill, were still there. Their presence led to the need for a school.

Hampton Institute opened in 1868 under the guidance of Samuel Chapman Armstrong, chief of the local Freedmen's Bureau. General Armstrong, formerly colonel of the Eighth Regiment U.S. Colored Troops, was responding to requests from the former refugees for schools. When he urged the American Missionary Association to purchase land for a school, the farm at this location seemed ideal. The 200 acres were located near the mouth of the Hampton River on an area formerly known as Little Scotland Plantation. Moreover, Hampton had the largest settlement of fugitives, had federal protection, and had a hospital that the Union government had maintained during the war.

The school opened in 1868 in makeshift quarters. Its two teachers lived in one of the houses purchased with the farm. There were twenty students. Female students lived in deserted barracks or in a building formerly used as a grist mill. In winter of 1873–1874, male students lived through the icy season in tents. Mrs. Armstrong, one of Hampton's first teachers, described living conditions for male students.

> Last year we had the sorrow of turning away from our doors many an applicant whose only hope lay with us because our buildings were already more than full; and all through the chill Virginian winter, our boys, in squads of twenty-four to thirty at a time, are lodged in tents whose canvas walls are frail protection against the stormy winds which sometimes visit the open sea-coast. I have looked from my window, on many a frosty night, at those icicle-fringed tents, and through many a wild morning have watched the heavy Southern rain beating upon their gray roofs, wishing in my heart that those in North or South who tell us that "negro" is but a synonym for laziness and cowardice could see for themselves the testimony borne by that little settlement of tents standing unsheltered within a stone's throw of the sea. There is as much downright pluck under these black skins as under any white ones, and the admirable courage and ambition of the freed people deserve substantial recognition and encouragement; for, however heavy is the tax laid upon them, they have shown themselves ready to meet it, for the sake of the much-coveted prize of education.[3]

Soon a building program was under way that eventually established Hampton as one of the most beautiful of college campuses. By 1874 the massive Virginia Hall was completed. Nationally known architect Richard Hunt designed the building; white and Black mechanics and students, working under supervision, completed the construction work. Mary Lou Hultgren, a museum curator at Hampton, noted that Richard Morris Hunt, a white architect (1827–1895), designed the Vanderbilt Biltmore chateau near Asheville, North Carolina, as well as the pedestal for the Statue of Liberty. He also designed The Breakers in Newport, Rhode Island, and the Fifth Avenue facade and Great Hall of the Metropolitan Museum in New York. Before Virginia Hall was completed, there was a panic in the money markets and income for completing the building dried up. Fortunately, two

Boston benefactors donated the $10,999 needed for finishing the walls and roof.

Memorial Church, constructed in Romanesque-revival style and completed in 1886, still contains student-made pews. An early-nineteenth-century plantation building known as the Mansion House became the college president's residence.

Hampton Institute started out with a manual-labor curriculum. Students worked on the farm one and a half to two days each week, earning five to ten cents an hour. They also learned trades in the printing office, the carpenter and blacksmith shops, the shoe shop, and the paint shop. Female students learned to cut and fit garments in the Girls' Industrial Room and were taught household duties, including laundry work. Most students were expected to supply or earn their expenses.

Hampton's teachers worked evenings, if necessary, to give extra help in algebra, English, and other subjects. By 1874 nine-tenths of Hampton graduates were teachers in "colored" schools, helping to fill a great need for Black teachers. Mrs. Armstrong described what it was like to teach at Hampton.

> Such eagerness and earnestness of purpose make study what it should be, a delight to teacher and pupil, and fatigue and dullness are unknown conditions in the midst of scholars to whom the smallest fact is a treasure, and to whom every day shows change and growth.[4]

Booker T. Washington was one of the students who showed an eagerness to learn. He walked across Virginia to enroll at Hampton. Returning as a graduate in 1879, he assumed charge of the dormitory called the Wigwam.

The historic district includes five major buildings associated with the beginning of Hampton Institute: Virginia Hall, Mansion House, Memorial Chapel, Academic Hall, and the Wigwam. The Wigwam was constructed after the enrollment of American Indian students created a need for additional dormitory space. Assisted by federal funding, Hampton enrolled Indian students from 1878 to 1923. Indian students with good English-language skills entered the standard academic program; others entered a separate Indian department organized in 1879. The Indian department operated until 1901; after that date all students enrolled in the normal school program. The building called the Wigwam (constructed 1878–1879) housed male Indian students from the time of its construction until federal funding for the Indian program ended in 1912. Winona Hall (razed in the 1950s) was built in 1882 as the dormitory for female Indian students; later it also housed female African American students.

A magnificent live oak tree called the Emancipation Oak is part of the historic district. There were many free Black people in Hampton in the years leading up to the Civil War and through the Civil War. A free Black woman, Mary Peake, taught many slaves to read and write before emancipation at the site of the Emancipation Oak tree. She was a gifted teacher who taught from the 1850s until her death in 1862, and Hampton Institute evolved in part from these early lessons. In 1863 the Emancipation Proclamation was read to Hampton residents under this tree.

Also of interest are Hampton's Collis P. Huntington Memorial Library and the Hampton Museum. The library has a collection of original slave handbills, pamphlets about slavery, and personal papers of Black leaders. The Hampton University Museum has a collection of more than 9,000 objects and works of art, including important African, American Indian, Asian/Pacific, and African American art collections.

DATE ESTABLISHED:	1868
ADDRESS:	Northwest of the junction of US 60 and the Hampton Roads Bridge Tunnel, Hampton
TELEPHONE:	(800) 624-3328; (804) 727-5000; museum, (804) 727-5308
VISITING HOURS:	Mon.–Fri. 8–5, Sat.–Sun. noon–4; closed New Year's Day, Thanksgiving, Christmas
FEES:	None
SOURCES:	Personal visit, summer 1990. Jeanne Zeidler, museum director. NRHPINF. Thornton Ellicott Jr., Syms-Eaton Museum, Hampton. Telephone conversation Jan. 11, 1995, Mary Lou Hultgren, curator of collections, Hampton University Museum. The Academic American Encyclopedia. *Hampton and Its Students.*

Hardy

Booker T. Washington National Monument*

Booker T. Washington was born in slavery on the Burroughs farm in 1856. He spent the first nine years of his life on this 207-acre plantation. Plantation owner James Burroughs owned ten slaves, several of whom were Washington's relatives. Washington's mother, the plantation cook, prepared meals for both the white family and the slaves. At night, Booker, his mother, and his brother slept on the dirt floor of the kitchen cabin where they lived.

After emancipation in 1865, the family moved to West Virginia. At age sixteen Washington returned to Virginia to attend Hampton Institute. As a student and teacher at Hampton, he was influenced by philosophies of education that emphasized a strong industrial curriculum. Later, when he founded Tuskegee Institute as a normal school for training teachers in 1881, Washington put into practice his belief that industrial skills should be taught as well as the academic skills. In his opinion industrial education was more appropriate for a newly freed people who needed jobs. Tuskegee's students learned to manufacture bricks and built the school from the ground up. They also studied other crafts that Washington had seen taught at Hampton Institute.

Booker T. Washington became a national spokesman for Black people. At his famous speech in 1895 at the Atlanta Cotton States and International Exposition, he glorified common labor in agriculture, domestic service, mechanics, and business. His views assured the South a stable supply of Black labor; in return, white people were to support the education of Black people in those skills. There was a roar of approval when Washington raised his hand with the fingers wide apart and asserted, "In all things that are purely social, we can be as separate as the fingers, yet one as the hand in all things essential to mutual progress."[5]

Washington downplayed the wisdom of using agitation to secure gains and suggested that "severe and constant struggle" rather than artificial forcing would lead to enjoyment of privileges by Black people. Washington's speeches of appeasement angered many Black leaders, but they pleased white philanthropists who showered the educator with honors, recognition, and financial support. Instead of gaining privileges for their forebearance, however, less than a year later Black people saw passage of *Plessy* v. *Ferguson,* a Supreme Court decision that established "separate but equal" as the law of the land.

Washington continued to speak out, publicly advocating putting aside attempts to challenge white people on such issues as politics and civil rights. He advocated instead the accumulation of property and the acquisition of work values.

From the time of his Atlanta speech until his death, Washington was one of America's most influential Black citizens. He put the philosophy of self-help and racial solidarity into practice by founding the National Negro Business League in 1900. The league encouraged the development of Black schools, businesses, women's clubs, newspapers, and other self-help groups.

Because of his nonthreatening public posture, white philanthropists contributed extensively to Tuskegee and relied on Washington's recommendations of support for other Black institutions. Washington advised President Theodore Roosevelt on a southern political strategy. In turn, Roosevelt appointed several men recommended by Washington to high office. Washington at times used his extensive network and financial influence to promote his views and silence his critics.

Although he seemed to advocate the acceptance of social conditions, Washington secretly challenged some discriminatory practices, including the grandfather clause that limited Black voting. He also challenged railroad segregation and the exclusion of Black people from juries. He worked at a high level to abolish peonage contracts that former slaves had signed, binding themselves to work for plantation owners.

Two sites—the Booker T. Washington National Monument and Alabama's Tuskegee Institute—interpret Washington's life. The monument site uses replicas and interpretation to show the environment in which Washington lived from birth until the age of nine years. Tuskegee, with many of its original buildings still standing, shows how he worked and lived during his most productive years.

The Booker T. Washington National Monument offers a self-guided tour to the historical farm area. On summer weekends costumed interpreters show the activities of farm life. Woodlands and fields, a museum, replicas of buildings, and a remodeled school show how Booker T. Washington might have lived at this site. There is even a reconstruction of the one-room log kitchen cabin in which his family lived.

DATE BUILT: Mid-nineteenth century

ADDRESS: 15 miles east of Rocky Mount on VA 122; 20 miles southeast of Roanoke via VA 116, south to Burnt Chimney, then north on VA 122

TELEPHONE: (540) 721-2094

VISITING HOURS: Daily 8:30–5; closed Thanksgiving, Christmas, New Year's Day

FEES: None

SOURCES: NRHPINF. Connie B. Mays, Booker T. Washington National Monument. *Before the Mayflower*, 265. *National Register of Historic Places*, 793. *A Documentary History of the Negro People in the United States.*

Jamestown

Jamestown Settlement*

In 1619, approximately twenty Black people arrived in Jamestown on a Dutch ship. (This was a year before the Pilgrims landed at Plymouth Rock.) These Africans are widely regarded as some of the earliest Black individuals in America, although other men from Africa had earlier joined African, Spanish, and Portuguese voyages of exploration to the Western Hemisphere. The earliest arrivals from Africa in Virginia may have been treated as indentured servants. Eventually some of them were able to buy both their freedom and some land. Later, however, racism gradually changed the status of Black people in Virginia. In the late 1630s Black men and women were sold as slaves at Jamestown, and by 1669 most Africans brought to Jamestown were bound to slavery for life.

The indoor museum in the Jamestown Gallery has the story in words and drawings of Mary and Anthony Johnson, Africans who came to Jamestown as indentured servants and who worked their way to freedom. One exhibit emphasizes the change in Virginia from favoring servitude to favoring slavery. The exhibit features seventeenth-century documents as well as two life-sized figures of workers in a field—one an indentured servant, the other a slave—and describes similarities and differences in their status. The site is significant because Jamestown may have been the arrival place of the first permanent Black settlers in America.

DATE ESTABLISHED: Jamestown Festival Park, 1957; Jamestown Settlement, 1990

ADDRESS: Next to Jamestown Island on the Jamestown terminus of the Colonial Parkway

TELEPHONE: (804) 229-1607

VISITING HOURS: Daily 9–5; extended hours June 15–Aug. 15; closed Christmas, New Year's Day

FEES: Adults, $9; children 6–12, $4.25

SOURCES: Telephone call Mar. 6, 1994. *The Smithsonian Guide to Historic America: Virginia and the Capital Region*. "Introduction to Part IIA," 159–61.

Mount Vernon

Mount Vernon

Mount Vernon, the home of George Washington (1732–1799), is an accurately preserved eighteenth-century plantation that illustrates the living and working conditions of African Americans. President George Washington owned slaves, as did other early American presidents.

The plantation is restored to the year of Washington's death and includes, among other structures, the quarters, buildings, and grounds where slaves lived and worked. The site also includes a monument at the slave burial grounds.

At one time 317 slaves worked on the farm. Some had jobs requiring a high degree of skill. Women were house servants, spinners, or weavers. Some lived in the spinning house quarters, while others lived in the greenhouse quarters complex. Both buildings have been restored. Male slaves worked as coopers and distillers, blacksmiths, carpenters, shoemakers, and coachmen.

Washington's personal physician provided treatment for ailing slaves. His will provided that his slaves should be freed upon Mrs. Washington's death; it also stipulated that his estate should pay pensions to freed slaves for thirty years. Slaves lie buried fifty yards southwest of Washington's own tomb.

DATE BUILT: 1735

ADDRESS: 16 miles south of Washington, D.C., or 8 miles south of Alexandria, Virginia; on the George Washington Parkway

TELEPHONE: (703) 780-2000

VISITING HOURS: Mar.–Oct., daily 9–5; Nov.–Feb., daily 9–4

FEES: Adults, $5; senior citizens, $4; children 6–11, $2

SOURCES: Michael C. Quinn, director of information, Mount Vernon. Brochures from the site.

Petersburg

Petersburg National Battlefield*

Well-trained Black soldiers, ready to fight, participated in the long siege of Petersburg in 1864–1865. Like the white soldiers, the African Americans suffered terrible losses and served with tremendous courage under heavy fire.

In mid-June 1864, General Robert E. Lee's army was determined to hold Petersburg, Virginia. If the city fell, Richmond also would be lost. General Ulysses S. Grant, however, devised a strategy to cut off rail supplies to Richmond by digging a tunnel to the Confederate fort. Then the Union engineers would set off explosives below the fort prior to attacking its defenders. Grant's men tunneled under the Confederate defenses and detonated explosives that killed 278 Confederate soldiers in the initial blast.

Confusion reigned. Originally a Black division was trained to lead the attack, and its soldiers were ready and eager to do so. Major General Ambrose E. Burnside planned to use his Fourth Division to spearhead the attack right after the explosion, and all 4,300 Black men felt prepared for the mission. General George Meade, however, rejected this plan. He believed the Black troops did not have enough combat experience to carry out the mission, and he feared that the public would criticize the Union for placing Black troops in such a dangerous position. Therefore, he held the Black troops in reserve as the Ninth Corps attacked.

When the white soldiers were not able to break through, Burnside sent the Black troops into the crowded, dangerous crater left by the explosives. As they advanced, the Confederates trained artillery on them, sweeping the Black soldiers with steady fire. Although some soldiers retreated in the slaughter, others held their positions until almost all were killed.

Not only did the Confederates fire on the Black soldiers, some Union soldiers refused to follow them into battle; others attacked the Black men fighting on their own side, bayoneting them as they passed by. Incredibly, those white men later stated that they were saving the Black soldiers from Confederate vengeance.

Four thousand Federal troops were killed, captured, or wounded as opposed to 1,500 Southern casualties. General Burnside later gave the highest praise to the Black men who fought in the Battle of Petersburg.

After the battle Black soldiers performed other duties, including the construction of forts and breastworks and cutting timber. They continued to attack the enemy lines in skirmishes.

African Americans also served on the Confederate side. Some slave owners offered their slaves' service, other free Black men volunteered, and the General Assembly of Virginia and the Confederate Congress conscripted thousands of African Americans as laborers. The African American laborers at Petersburg constructed artillery batteries and earthworks. They also played a critical role in caring for those wounded in Petersburg's defense. In spite of the heroism of Black troops at Petersburg, only one Black man, Sergeant Decatur Dorsey, was honored by his country for heroism and was awarded the Congressional Medal of Honor.

The Petersburg National Battlefield today preserves miles of the original entrenchments, the crater, and the entrance to the tunnel. In the summer of 1993 a monument to the Black soldiers of this battle was erected at one stop of the tour. The granite monument features a description of the role the soldiers played. The tour includes eight stops within a four-mile radius of the Visitors Center. The site also has picnic facilities.

DATE OF SIGNIFICANCE:	1864–1865
ADDRESS:	2 miles east of Petersburg off I-95 on VA 36
TELEPHONE:	(804) 732-3531
VISITING HOURS:	June–Aug., daily 8:30–5:30; Sept.–May, daily 8–5; closed Christmas, New Year's Day
FEES:	$4 per car
SOURCES:	Telephone conversation Mar. 6, 1994, Jim Bell, park ranger, Petersburg National Battlefield. *The Smithsonian Guide to Historic America: Virginia and the Capital Region.* "Petersburg National Battlefield," 137–55.

Virginia State University

Virginia State University, established in 1882, had the mission of providing a college education for Black students. It offered a college-preparatory program, teacher training, and collegiate studies leading to a bachelor's degree.

Although an initial appropriation of $20,000 made this the first fully state-supported Black college in America, the collegiate program was later dropped for a period of twenty-three years, thus reducing the institution to the status of an industrial school.

In 1920 the state's land-grant program for Black students was located at Virginia State. By 1989–1990 the university enrolled approximately 4,073 students, 87 percent of whom were African Americans.

The university's 236-acre campus is located on a bluff across the Appomattox River overlooking Petersburg. More than fifty buildings reflect varying architectural styles including Colonial classical, Georgian revival, and Queen Anne. Storum Hall, constructed in 1907 as the president's house, was the second building erected on the campus. Vawter Hall was built in 1908. The two structures are listed in the *National Register of Historic Places.*

University archives contain Virginia's largest collection of documents by Black people about Black people. The collection is used extensively for research purposes.

DATE BUILT: 1882
ADDRESS: One Hayden Drive, Petersburg
TELEPHONE: (804) 524-5701
VISITING HOURS: Contact Office of Student Activities, Box 46, Virginia State University 23803 or call to arrange visits or tours
SOURCE: Cassandra D. Robinson, university relations director.

Portsmouth

Portsmouth Olde Towne African American Sites

This neighborhood in Portsmouth's Olde Towne Historic District includes five turn-of-the-century dwellings traditionally occupied by Black families, as well as the Emanuel African Methodist Episcopal Church. The Emanuel A.M.E. Church, the first Black church built by Black people for Black people in Portsmouth, houses the oldest Black congregation in southeastern Virginia. The church was erected in 1857 (one source lists 1791 as the date of construction). It is a stucco building with brick veneer on top. When the two-story church was remodeled in 1881, the new facade partially hid the original lines of construction. However, the original stained glass windows may be seen, and the original hand-carved wooden furniture remains in the sanctuary.

DATE BUILT: Church, 1791 or 1857; houses, late nineteenth to early twentieth century
ADDRESS: Church, 637 North Street; houses, 602, 610, 612–614, 616, 622 North Street, Portsmouth
TELEPHONE: Church, (804) 393-2259
VISITING HOURS: Houses are private; church, Mon.–Fri. 10–3 by appointment, Sun. service at 11
SOURCES: NRHPINF. Telephone conversation Jan. 11, 1995, Susie Wilson, church secretary, Emanuel A.M.E. Church. *The Olde Towne Walking Tour in Portsmouth, Virginia.*

Richmond

Fort Gilmer

The Seventh Regiment, a Black unit, was part of the Union forces in the September 29, 1864, engagement at Fort Gilmer. All the Northern soldiers were assigned to the Tenth Army Corps commanded by Major General David B. Birney. When the soldiers approached Fort Gilmer, they were met by fierce fire from the Confederates at the fort and nearby. The Confederates fired on the approaching soldiers at close range, killing, wounding, or capturing all but three of the 238 Union men who participated in the assault. None of the men who fought at Fort Gilmer was decorated for bravery, but several from battles at nearby Chaffin's Farm, Deep Bottom, and New Market Heights received the Congressional Medal of Honor.

Fort Gilmer includes intact earthworks and the remains of the Confederate Fort Gilmer. It has the original small, open-ended earthen fort with earthen mounds approximately 25 to 30 feet high from the bottom of the moat to the top. Viewers can see the earthen platforms where Confederate soldiers rolled their artillery up to fire at oncoming soldiers.

Although a Virginia state marker has been placed at New Market Heights, that section of the battlefield is on private land and is not accessible to the public. Visitors who seek additional information may obtain it at the Fort Harrison Visitor Center one mile from Fort Gilmer (east on Battlefield Park Road). Although there is no Visitors Center at the site, a recording in the parking lot gives the story of the battlefield. Brochures are at the same location.

DATE OF SIGNIFICANCE: Sept. 29, 1864
ADDRESS: Richmond vicinity, Battlefield Park Road off VA 5
TELEPHONE: Richmond National Battlefield Visitors Center, (804) 226-1981
VISITING HOURS: Daily dawn–dusk; Fort Harrison Visitors Center, May–Oct.
SOURCES: Telephone conversation Mar. 6, 1994, Robert Krick, park ranger. "Fort Gilmer, Virginia," 178–80. *The Smithsonian Guide to Historic America: Virginia and the Capital Region.*

Jackson Ward Historic District

One of the largest African American historic districts in America, Jackson Ward is a neighborhood of nineteenth-century townhouses and commercial buildings in the center of Richmond. Before the Civil War one in eight free Black individuals in America lived in Virginia, many in Jackson Ward. A number of them resided in a neighborhood called "Little Africa," located on West Leigh Street near Ebenezer Church and in the 200 to 400 blocks of Duval Street.

Before the Civil War, some Africans who lived in Richmond were slaves; others were free. Of those who were slaves, some were owned by their relatives; others had white owners who allowed them to hire out their own time, provided they paid the owner most of the earnings. Because the slaves kept all earnings above the amount due their owners, many acquired shrewd business and management skills that were useful to them when they were emancipated.

By the turn of the century, Richmond's Jackson Ward was considered the foremost Black business community in the nation. This hub of professional and business activity contained banks, insurance companies, fraternal organizations, barber shops, livery stables, catering shops, hotels, real estate companies, repair shops, and drugstores.

Most dwellings in the forty-two-block district were brick townhouses constructed between the early nineteenth and early twentieth century; there were also some free-standing homes. Built by middle-class families, many of the homes put up in the 1880s and 1890s have retained their interesting ornamentation, including elaborate Eastlake-style wooden carving on the porches. Clay Street contains one of the finest collections of ornamental cast-iron trim in America.

By the 1930s the last of the white residents had left Jackson Ward, and the area was home to 8,000 Black families. Many homes were subdivided as a larger proportion of lower-income families moved in. In spite of changes, the neighborhood has remained remarkably stable and today is one of the least-altered communities in Richmond. Between 1956 and 1976 the houses on the north side of the 600 block on St. James Street, all resident-owned, saw no changes in title.

Five sites in Jackson Ward—the Maggie Lena Walker Home, the St. Luke Building, the Black History Museum and Cultural Center of Virginia, the Luther Robinson statue, and the Sixth Mount Zion Baptist Church—are described in some detail. Other sites of interest in the Jackson Ward Historic District include the following.

Ebenezer Baptist Church, 216 West Leigh Street on the corner of Judah Street, is the first and largest Black church in Jackson Ward. The congregation formed in 1856 and held services in a small frame church building from 1858 into the 1870s. A public school for Black students operated from the basement in the late 1860s. The present church was completed in the 1870s.

Giles Jackson's Law Office, 511 North Second Street (traditionally the major commercial street in Jackson Ward), was owned by Giles B. Jackson, a leading entrepreneur and attorney. Jackson was the first African American admitted to the practice of law before the Supreme Court of Virginia. He drafted the charter for the True Reformers Bank, which survived the panic of 1893 to become, by 1907, America's largest Black-controlled financial institution. Jackson encouraged industrial growth in the African American community and promoted Black business interests in government circles. Booker T. Washington turned to Jackson for advice on challenging Virginia's segregation ordinances.

Mitchell Townhouse, 515–517 North Third Street, a two-unit townhouse row, was the home of John Mitchell, founder of the weekly newspaper *The Planet* in the late 1880s. Sometimes considered radical, Mitchell at one time was an officer and the sole African American member of the American Bankers' Association. He also served as grand chancellor of the Colored Knights of Pythias and opened his Mechanics Savings Bank under the auspices of the Pythians. Between 1899 and 1904, when Virginia began to pass Jim Crow laws about seating on common carriers, Mitchell protested in *The Planet.* The newspaper gained national circulation and merged in 1938 with the *Baltimore Afro-American.* It is still published in Jackson Ward.

Richmond Normal School, built in 1871 at 119 West Leigh Street, is currently used as the Richmond Public School's Adult Career Development Center. The two and one-half–story brick building once was the Old Armstrong High School, for many years the only high school for Richmond's African American students. To see the interior, call in advance.

Southern Aid Life Insurance Company Building, built in 1931 at 214–212 East Clay Street, is the largest commercial structure in Jackson Ward. Owned today by the Atlanta Life Insurance Company, the building is home to a variety of businesses and civic organizations including, among others, the Richmond Branch of the National Association for the Advancement of Colored People (#302), Williams Photography Studio (#312), Classic Theater Production (#310), and the Atlanta Life Insurance Company. The interior has been modernized, but visitors to Jackson Ward may want to drive by to see the exterior.

The former **Booker T. Washington School** at North First Street and East Leigh is an interesting structure; today it houses the Richmond Opportunities Industrialization Center, a job training program. It is worth driving by (21 East Leigh Street). The three-story, yellow-brick school has retained its basic appearance. To see the interior, call in advance.

The first Black-chartered bank was housed in the townhouse at **105 West Jackson Street.**

The Jackson Ward Historic District experienced many changes in the 1950s. Development of the Turnpike cut off the northern part of Jackson Ward while the Colosseum—an expansion of Virginia Commonwealth University—leveled the eastern portion. Although many displaced residents moved to the suburbs, Jackson Ward remained the place of residence, worship, and business for a substantial portion of Richmond's African American community, and many still participate in community efforts to preserve the character of this historic community.

DATE ESTABLISHED:	Nineteenth century
ADDRESS:	Roughly bounded by Fifth, Marshall, and Gilmer Streets and the Richmond-Petersburg Turnpike, Richmond
TELEPHONE:	Ebenezer Baptist Church, (804) 643-3366; Richmond Normal School (now Adult Career Development Center), (804) 780-4388; Southern Aid Life Insurance (now Atlanta Life), (804) 648-7234; Booker T. Washington School (now Richmond O.I.C.), (804) 643-5371
VISITING HOURS:	Many sites are private, visitors may walk or drive by

SOURCES: NRHPINF. Personal visit, summer 1990. Conversation Mar. 1994, Benjamin C. Ross, church historian, Sixth Mt. Zion Church. Telephone conversation May 31, 1994, Dorothy Perry-Hudgins, director, Richmond Community Action Program. Telephone conversation Mar. 31, 1994, Evelyn J. Davis, Grand Secretary of the Grand Chapter of OES of Virginia PHA. Lillie McMoore, secretary, Atlanta Life Insurance Company. Telephone conversations June 2, 1994, Wyona Staten, executive secretary, Richmond Opportunities Industrialization Center and Miss Bryan at the Adult Career Development Center.

Black History Museum and Cultural Center of Virginia

Built in 1832 by businessman Adolph Dill, the restored house has the original spiral staircase connecting the three floors. The house has pine flooring and a marble porch and steps. Since 1900 this historic structure has served different groups in Richmond's Black community. The Council of Colored Women bought the building in 1920; it later housed the Black branch of the Richmond Public Library. The site also has served as the Colored Navy Officers' Club and as an open high school. In early 1988 it became the home of the Black History Museum and Cultural Center of Virginia.

The Black History Museum and Cultural Center of Virginia has a collection of nearly 5,000 artifacts and documents. These include the papers of Dr. Carter G. Woodson, the "father of Black history," and the collection of Colonel Charles Young, the highest ranking Black officer in the U.S. Army prior to World War I. The museum also has initiated an oral history program that will provide a major documentation of the African American experience. It has sponsored children's workshops, exhibits of artwork, autographing parties, and one-person performances. Its gallery displays have included portraits of nationally recognized African American leaders, a special Michael Jordan display, a "Bojangles" Robinson exhibit, and a permanent display highlighting the history of the Jackson Ward district. The museum is located just three blocks from the Maggie Lena Walker house and the "Bojangles" Robinson statue.

DATE BUILT: House, 1832; museum, founded 1981, at present site, 1988

ADDRESS: 00 Clay Street (between First and Adams Streets), Richmond

TELEPHONE: (804) 780-9093

VISITING HOURS: Tues., Thurs., Fri., Sat. 11–4; tours for groups by arrangement; closed New Year's Day, Dr. Martin Luther King Jr. Day, July 4, Labor Day, Memorial Day, Christmas

FEES: Adults, $2; children, $1

SOURCE: Katrina M. Baxter, executive director, Black History Museum and Cultural Center of Virginia.

Luther (Bill "Bojangles") Robinson Statue

This impressive statue at Leigh and Adams Streets commemorates one of the world's greatest tap dancers. Luther Robinson (1878–1949) was born in the Jackson Ward neighborhood at 915 North Third Street. Although he never took dance lessons, he became a performer on the minstrel circuit and then starred on Broadway and in the movies.

Since Luther's parents died when he was a baby, his grandmother cared for him and his older sister and brother. The family was poor, and the children had to work much of the time to supplement their income. Luther worked first as a shoeshine boy; then he began dancing in shops and on sidewalks for the nickels and dimes thrown at him. Soon his talent was recognized, and he began dancing for a wider public—first in vaudeville acts, then on Broadway and in Hollywood movies. Many of his most popular films were made with child star Shirley Temple. Robinson, who started out in poverty, earned a fortune in his lifetime. Remembering his own childhood, he contributed generously to needy actors and to charities. On several occasions he watched schoolchildren cross an unsafe street to get to a school nearby, and he made sure that a traffic light was put up at that spot. Today he is remembered by a statue at the same intersection where the traffic light was placed.

ADDRESS: Leigh and Adams Streets, Richmond

SOURCE: *International Library of Negro Life and History,* 246.

St. Luke Building

Erected in 1902, the St. Luke Building was enlarged to four stories betwen 1915 and 1920. The brick office building, the oldest Black-affiliated office structure in Richmond, housed the national headquarters of the Independent Order of St. Luke.

An ex-slave, Mary Prout, founded the benevolent society. Like others of its time, it evolved from pre-Civil War burial societies that provided small sick benefits, burial funds, and a sum for survivors. The Independent Order of St. Luke carried on the tradition after the Civil War, giving financial aid to newly freed slaves. However, the association struggled financially until pioneering businesswoman Maggie Lena Walker improved the business structure and dramatically increased the membership.

Once located on the edge of Jackson Ward, the St. Luke Building today is separated from the district by an expressway. In the well-preserved interior the basement once housed the original press used to print the weekly magazine *St. Luke Herald.* The first floor housed shops, and the second and third floors contained meeting and storage rooms. Offices of the Independent Order of St. Luke were on the fourth floor. Maggie Lena Walker's office was preserved for a period as it was at the time of her death in 1934, with her desk, adding machine, and bookcases. Then a church moved in and used the building. Since 1986 the Richmond Community Action Program has been based in the St. Luke Building, and the Head Start Program uses the premises during the day. The fourth floor has been remodeled and the basement, once the printing shop, is now a kitchen and classroom. Yet hints of the old building still remain in the marble floors and bank cages.

DATE BUILT: 1902

ADDRESS: 900 St. James Street, Richmond

TELEPHONE: (804) 788-0050

VISITING HOURS: Business hours; call for appointment

FEES: None

Sixth Mount Zion Church

The Reverend John Jasper (1812–1901) and ten associates organized this church in 1867 on the shore of Richmond's James River. He was born in slavery, the twenty-fourth child of Phillip and Tina Jasper. Although Phillip Jasper died before John was born, he predicted that his unborn child would become a great preacher. Tina Jasper nurtured her child carefully, imbuing him with a sense of dignity and a love for humanity that remained with him all of his life.

In his early ministry Jasper preached to vast, racially varied rural congregations that included people in Richmond and Petersburg and even Confederate soldiers. Both before and after the Civil War he was widely known, especially for his old-time powerful oratorical skills. On the more than 250 occasions when Jasper preached his sermon, "The Sun Do Move and Earth Am Square," he drew standing-room-only crowds.

Sixth Mount Zion Baptist Church started in an unused Confederate horse stable. The congregation moved to the present site in 1869 and saw their church grow into one of the largest Black churches in Richmond. Jasper, who spent half of his life as a slave and half as a free man, served here as minister for more than thirty years. The church archives contain the pulpit from which he preached, his clothing, and other historical items.

DATE ESTABLISHED: 1867

ADDRESS: 14 W. Duval Street, Richmond

TELEPHONE: (804) 648-7511

VISITING HOURS: Sun. services or contact the church to arrange a visit

FEES: None

SOURCES: "Sixth Mount Zion Baptist Church." *Two Centuries of Christian Witness.*

Maggie Lena Walker House

Most houses in the 100 block of East Leigh Street are substantial, well-maintained nineteenth-century residences that have had few alterations. One of the most significant is the Maggie Lena Walker house at 110A East Leigh Street.

Born after emancipation, Walker (1867–1934) was the daughter of a former slave and a participant in two historical eras. Her mother, Elizabeth

Draper Mitchell, worked as a cook's helper and took in laundry to support the family. Maggie studied at the Lancaster School and the Armstrong Normal School. After graduating from Armstrong in 1883, she taught for three years. In 1886 she married building contractor Armistead Walker Jr. Mrs. Walker became active in business at first as an agent for Women's Union Insurance. Her leadership skills emerged when she joined a Black fraternal and cooperative insurance society, the Independent Order of St. Luke. When the Order of St. Luke met severe financial difficulties, Walker's guidance turned the situation around and led the association to new heights of prosperity. The organization operated an insurance company that owned a bank, a newspaper, and a department store. Walker became president of the St. Luke Penny Savings Bank, which later absorbed other African American banks in Richmond and changed its name to the Consolidated Bank and Trust Company. Walker served as its chairman until her death.

Maggie Lena Walker was active in education as well as business. She helped raise funds to establish the Virginia Industrial School for Colored Girls, which was later known as the Janie Porter Barrett School. For her accomplishments and service to the community, she received many honors including an honorary degree from Virginia Union University. A Richmond high school is named in her honor.

Maggie Lena Walker and her family lived in this elegant Victorian residence from 1904 to 1934. The twenty-two-room, two-story house has a facade of pressed brick painted red. The section fronting East Leigh Street has a series of narrowing ells behind it. The house contains a narrow library, a double parlor, and a dining room with a pressed-tin ceiling. A narrow ell containing the kitchen still has its original stove. The house, which contains the furnishings as Mrs. Walker left them, is an invaluable record of a distinguished American.

DATE BUILT: 1883; purchased by Walkers, 1904

ADDRESS: 110A E. Leigh Street, Richmond

TELEPHONE: (804) 780-1380

VISITING HOURS: Tours Wed.–Sun. 9–5; groups of 10 or more must make advance reservations; closed Christmas, New Year's Day

FEES: None

Valentine Museum

The museum about Richmond's history integrates the interpretation of Black history and culture into other exhibits. One of the early exhibits explored Richmond's antebellum Black community. A 1989 exhibit was entitled "Jim Crow: Racism and Reaction in the New South." For the latter exhibit, the museum obtained materials from the local African American community as well as from national and state repositories. Exhibit documents examine the evolution of racism from the close of the Civil War to 1940. The documents and materials have become a part of the museum's continuing program.

DATE BUILT: House, 1812; museum, 1892

ADDRESS: 1015 E. Clay Street, Richmond

TELEPHONE: (804) 649-0711

VISITING HOURS: Mon.–Sat. 10–5; Sun. noon–5; extended hours Memorial Day–Labor Day; closed Christmas, Thanksgiving

FEES: Adults, $3.50; seniors, $3; students, $2.75; children 7–12, $1.50

SOURCES: Karen Leutjen, director of public programs. *Perspectives.*

Virginia Union University

In Virginia before the Civil War, a state law forbade the teaching of slaves. When the war ended, most of the newly freed individuals, with the exception of Black ministers, were illiterate. The African American ministers, with support from some Northern philanthropists and missionaries, took on the responsibility of educating the former slaves. The Baptist Home Mission Society assisted in founding schools that later became the Richmond Theological Society and the Wayland Seminary. Their first campus was a complex of brick buildings in Shockoe Valley. Known as Lumpkin's Jail, these structures had served as a slave pen and as housing for slave traders.

By 1876 the Richmond Theological Seminary was formally incorporated. The school purchased an old hotel at Nineteenth and Main Streets. In 1896 Richmond Theological Society and the Wayland Seminary combined resources to become Virginia Union University. The university purchased land next to the already functioning Hartshorn Memorial College, a school founded in the 1880s for young Black women.

Wealthy Northern philanthropists provided funding for the extensive building campaign, and many of the buildings were named in their honor. Although funds for the seminaries came also from the Mission Society, the original schools were nonsectarian and Virginia Union has remained so.

Although Virginia Union developed architectural plans for new buildings, the Depression of the 1930s intervened, causing the plans to be canceled. Nevertheless, Virginia Union University grew into a beautiful sixty-five-acre campus along North Lombardy Street in Richmond. The seven oldest structures on campus were constructed between 1899 and 1901. They include Coburn, Huntley, Martin E. Gray, Kingsley, and Pickford Buildings; the old President's Residence; and the industrial building and power plant. The historic buildings, in an eleven-acre area, are constructed of rough-faced gray granite ashlar, hand-hewn by men newly freed from slavery. The campus, in Romanesque-revival style, has an outstanding grouping of college buildings.

L. Douglas Wilder, former governor of Virginia, is one of Virginia Union's outstanding graduates.

DATE ESTABLISHED: 1865

ADDRESS: 1500 N. Lombardy Street at Brook Road, Richmond

TELEPHONE: (804) 257-5600

VISITING HOURS: Call to arrange a visit

SOURCES: NRHPINF. Personal visit, summer 1990.

Roanoke

Harrison School

Harrison School, located within one of Roanoke's oldest African American neighborhoods, symbolizes the community's efforts to secure secondary education for its children. The school was built in 1916 in an era during which there were few Black public high schools in Virginia.

Prior to the Civil War, custom actively discouraged the teaching of slaves, and only two schools existed in the state for Black students. The Virginia Literary Fund offered limited public support for education of the poor but excluded African American children, slave or free, from this benefit.

As the Reconstruction period ended, Virginia instituted the first statewide system of public instruction. Two schools opened in the Roanoke area, one for white students, one for Black, with the latter housed in a one-room log house. The African American school was replaced three years later by a two-room building and, in 1882, by a school on Shenandoah Avenue.

In the early twentieth century, Black leaders from Hampton Institute (Hampton), Virginia Normal, Virginia Union University (Richmond), and St. Paul's College formed an organization for improving education for Virginia's Black students. Their lively discussions regarding the best curriculum led many to adopt the views of scholar W. E. B. Du Bois, who insisted that a college-educated Black elite was necessary to ensure full racial equality. This view was in opposition to views of white individuals who saw Black students as childlike learners who needed education for better discipline, good work habits, and manual skills that would make them economically successful. Their goal was to minimize integration of the races, and they did not encourage the establishment of high schools for Black students. In 1915 only 1,761 Black students were enrolled in Virginia high schools as opposed to 23,184 white pupils. Black pupils who wished to study beyond seventh grade had to travel the distance to Virginia State College.

Lucy Addison, an African American graduate of Philadelphia's public schools and Howard University, worked with other educators to open a high school for Black students. Addison had begun her teaching career in the 1880s in a two-room school for Black students. She and the community rejoiced when the Roanoke School Board authorized construction of the Harrison School. Addison was appointed principal when the school opened in the winter of 1917. Her philosophy was to provide an academic education, and she gradually extended the curriculum to the secondary level. In 1924 the first class completed four years of high school instruction.

After enrollment increased, the school board constructed a new high school for Black students. The Harrison School continued as an elementary school until the 1960s. Today, only two Black school buildings, Harrison and Addison, remain in Roanoke. Addison now serves as a school administration building. The ground floor of the historic Harrison School now houses the Harrison Museum of African American Culture.

DATE BUILT:	Building, 1916; wings, 1922; occupied as museum, Oct. 1985
ADDRESS:	First floor, 523 Harrison Avenue NW, Roanoke
TELEPHONE:	(703) 345-4818
VISITING HOURS:	Mon.–Fri. 10–5, Sat.–Sun. 1–5; closed major holidays except Christmas
FEES:	None
SOURCES:	NRHPINF. Melody S. Stovall, executive director, Harrison Museum of African American Culture. Telephone conversation Jan. 11, 1995, Filetha Bolden, curator, Harrison Museum of African American Culture.

Williamsburg

Carter's Grove Slave Quarter*

Carter's Grove consists of reconstructed eighteenth-century slave quarters: three slave houses, a corn crib, and a tobacco barn on the original site where the slave cabins once stood. The reconstruction employed building techniques from the eighteenth century, resulting in a slave quarter at Carter's Grove as it probably looked in the 1770s. Carter's Grove once was an estate of 300,000 acres that was worked by more than 1,000 slaves. Costumed African American interpreters guide visitors through the slave cabins and tell stories about the lives of slaves who lived on the plantation.

DATE BUILT: 1770s

ADDRESS: 8 miles southeast of Williamsburg via US 60 East

TELEPHONE: Ticket desk, (804) 229-1000, Ext. 2973; manager's office, (804) 220-7453

VISITING HOURS: Mid-Mar.–Oct. 31, Tues.–Sun. 9–5; Nov.–Dec., Tues.–Sun. 9–4; Grand Illumination (Christmas celebration of Colonial Williamsburg), first Mon. of Dec.; Christmas Day 11–4; closed Mon. except those that fall on holidays

FEES: Adults, $15; children 6–12, $9; children under 6, free; Patriot's Pass (for one year, includes Colonial Williamsburg and Carter's Grove), adults, $30; children, $18

SOURCES: Jerrold W. Roy, lead interpreter, Carter's Grove Slave Quarter. Personal visit, summer 1990. Wiley Smith III, acting chairperson, Department of Pan-African Studies, Kent State University. Telephone conversation Jan. 13, 1995, Louise Kelley, manager of operations, Carter's Grove.

Colonial Williamsburg

Colonial Williamsburg opened in 1934 as the first restoration in the country to employ costumed guides to interpret colonial life. The site contains one hundred restored buildings and another four hundred buildings reconstructed to show eighteenth-century architecture and arts.

In the 1770s, half of Williamsburg's residents were slaves and free Black individuals. Colonial Williamsburg has a Department of African-American Interpretation and Presentations (AAIP) that provides interpretations of eighteenth-century African American life and culture in a comprehensive way. They use first-person and third-person interpretative techniques to show how the African American community survived and contributed to the forming of American society.

A variety of experiences show African American history at this site. At the Wetherburn's Tavern and Benjamin Powell House, for example, visitors meet a slave from the eighteenth century and hear the personal feelings and perceptions of a slave.

AAIP also has a changing program schedule offering a variety of programs year-round to facilitate interpretations of African American culture. Past programs included

A one-hour Black music program of dance, music, and storytelling as experienced by African Americans in the eighteenth century

"Other-Half Tour," named for the half of the population of Williamsburg that were African Americans, a two-hour walking tour that offers a comprehensive look at the lives of slaves and free Black people in colonial Virginia

"The Runaway," in which the audience witnesses the plight of a young runaway slave

"Storyteller," an hour-long experience that combines African and African American storytelling in an enlightening and entertaining manner

"African American Children," a program that examines concerns of adolescent slaves and the ways they learned community, family, and survival lessons

"African Americans in Virginia," a program that uses music, storytelling, scenes, and vignettes to explore the beginning of the colonial Black culture

DATE BUILT: Eighteenth century; restoration began, 1934

ADDRESS: Colonial Parkway, Williamsburg

TELEPHONE: (804) 229-1000; information on current Black history programs, (804) 229-1000 or (804) 220-7212

VISITING HOURS: Mid-Mar.–Dec., daily 8:30–8; Jan.–mid-Mar., daily 9–5
FEES: Access to 12 historic buildings of choice, adults, $17; children 6–12, $9.75
SOURCE: Brochures from the Colonial Williamsburg Foundation.

Winchester

Old Stone Presbyterian Church

Old Stone Presbyterian Church, built in 1788, is the oldest public building and house of worship still standing in Winchester. The building became part of Black history in 1858 when it was deeded to the Old School Congregational Baptist Church of Color for $500. The congregation raised money to purchase the building by selling shares of stock at 50 cents a share and more to approximately 285 people. The African American community in that era included both slaves and free individuals, and this structure served as the first house of public worship for those who were free.

By 1871 Black community leaders were meeting with the Winchester School Board to plan the first public school for Black students. By 1875 the school board had acquired the old church building. The board made improvements and alterations and converted the building into three classrooms for the new Winchester Colored School. Students began attending classes in 1878. A wood stove heated their classrooms, and older boys took responsibility for keeping the fire going.

In 1916 the name was changed to Frederick Douglass School in honor of the abolitionist and civil rights leader. By the mid-1920s the school was overcrowded. The old stone structure lacked adequate ventilation, lighting, outdoor play facilities, and sanitation. The 183 children attending were on a half-day shift. If attendance laws had been enforced, 300 Black children would have been crowded into the three-room facility. African American community members announced that they would hold mass meetings until they received a new school building. Many white citizens supported their request.

The school in the old stone building served the African American community for fifty years until students moved into the new Douglass School building on North Kent Street. In 1927, when the cornerstone was laid for a new school building, a parade nearly a mile long and gala ceremonies accompanied the laying of the cornerstone.

DATE BUILT: 1788
ADDRESS: 116 S. Loudoun Street, Winchester
TELEPHONE: (703) 662-3824
VISITING HOURS: By appointment with the First Presbyterian Church
SOURCE: Rebecca A. Ebert, The Handley Library.

Notes

1. *Appomattox Court House* (Washington, D.C.: National Park Service, 1980).

2. Address of Peter Osborne, *The Liberator,* 1 Dec. 1832, quoted in Herbert Aptheker, ed., *A Documentary History of the Negro People in the United States,* vol. 1 (New York: Citadel, 1990), 138.

3. M. F. Armstrong and Helen W. Ludlow, *Hampton and Its Students* (New York: Putnam, 1874), 60–61.

4. Armstrong and Ludlow, 58.

5. Booker T. Washington, Sept. 18, 1895, speech delivered at the Atlanta Cotton Exposition, from Alice M. Bacon, *The Negro and the Atlanta Exposition* (Baltimore, 1896), 12–16, quoted in Herbert Aptheker, ed., *A Documentary History of the Negro People in the United States,* vol. 2 (New York: Citadel, 1990), 755.

Works Consulted

Appomattox Court House. Handbook 109. Washington, D.C.: National Park Service, 1980.

Before the Mayflower: A History of Black America. 5th ed. Lerone Bennett Jr. New York: Penguin, 1988.

The Civil War Almanac. John S. Bownman, ed. New York: World Almanac/Bison, 1983.

Created Equal: The Lives and Ideas of Black American Innovators. James Michael Brodie. New York: William Morrow, 1993.

A Documentary History of the Negro People in the United States. Vols. 1, 2. Herbert Aptheker, ed. New York: Citadel, 1990.

First Steps to Freedom. Sandra Gallop and Margo Gaither. Hampton, Va.: Hampton Institute, Hampton Assoc. for the Arts and Humanities, Syms-Eaton Museum, Hampton Bicentennial Committee, n.d. [pamphlet]

"Fort Gilmer, Virginia." Charles O. Johnson Jr. In *Afro-American History Interpretation at Selected National Parks.* Washington, D.C.: Research Team, Howard Univ., 1978.

Hampton and Its Students. M. F. Armstrong and Helen W. Ludlow. New York: Putnam, 1874.

Highlights of Black History at Fort Monroe. The Casemate Papers. Dr. Chester Bradley. Fort Monroe, Va.: Fort Monroe Museum, April 1972. [booklet]

International Library of Negro Life and History: Historical Negro Biographies. Wilhelmena S. Robinson. New York: Publishers, 1970.

"Introduction to Part IIA." Charles O. Johnson Jr. In *Afro-American History Interpretation at Selected National Parks.* Washington, D.C.: Research Team, Howard Univ., 1978.

National Register of Historic Places. Washington, D.C.: National Park Service, 1976.

The Olde Towne Walking Tour in Portsmouth, Virginia. Portsmouth, Va.: Portsmouth Convention and Visitors Bureau, July 1989. [brochure]

Perspectives: American Historical Association Newsletter 27, no. 4 (Apr. 1989).

"Petersburg National Battlefield. Charles O. Johnson Jr. In *Afro-American History Interpretation at Selected National Parks.* Washington, D.C.: Research Team, Howard Univ., 1978.

"Sixth Mount Zion Baptist Church Founded in 1867 by Reverend John Jasper." Keith C. Morgan. *Metropolitan Business Guide* 10, no. 5 (Feb.–Mar. 1994).

Smithsonian Guide to Historic America: Virginia and the Capital Region. Henry Wiencek. New York: Stewart, Tabori, & Chang, 1989.

Two Centuries of Christian Witness: The History of the Sixth Mount Zion Baptist Church of Richmond, Virginia. Geraldine J. Mills and others. 1986.

Virginia Museums and Historic Sites Guide Book. Virginia Assoc. of Museums, 1984.

West Virginia

Charleston

African American Sites of Charleston

Three sites in the same neighborhood have solid ties to West Virginia's Black history. They are the Garnet High School (now Garnet Adult Education Center), the Mattie V. Lee Home, and the Samuel Starks House. In different ways they represent the development of Charleston's African American community.

Garnet School

Garnet School (now Garnet Adult Education Center) is in the same neighborhood as the Starks House. The school was named for noted abolitionist, clergyman, and diplomat Henry Highland Garnet (1815–1882). Garnet, a descendant of the African Mandingo people, was born in slavery in Maryland. After he and his parents escaped from slavery, they settled in New York City. He graduated from Oneida Institute, a New York college that stirred controversy at an early date by enrolling Black students. Garnet became a leader in the abolitionist movement and a participant in the international peace movement. President Garfield appointed him Consul General to Liberia.

Garnet High School was one of three Black high schools in the Kanawha Valley. The first students attended the school in an era of segregation. Buses picked up Black students before daylight and delivered them to their school two or three hours before the start of school. The buses then picked up white students and delivered them at their destination just before the start of school. At the end of the school day, white students were returned home first while Black students were returned home after darkness fell.

In spite of inequities, Black faculty members worked hard and ensured that Garnet High School was respected for the quality of its curriculum and its graduates. Faculty members created a school spirit so strong and filled with love that every three or four years, 1,000 Garnet graduates returned to attend high school reunions. Tony Brown, host and president of Tony Brown Productions, an organization that produces video and educational materials, and Reverend Leon Sullivan, first Black member of the Board of Directors of General Motors Corporation, are among the outstanding graduates of Garnet.

After the U.S. Supreme Court declared the "separate but equal" principle unconstitutional, states began to close Black schools. May 25, 1956, was the date of Garnet's last commencement.

Garnet High School is the only remaining public school building in Charleston's commercial center. Visitors may drive by to see the original building and an addition designed by John C. Norman (1892–1967), a structural engineer and the second registered Black architect in West Virginia.

DATE BUILT: 1918–1929
ADDRESS: 422 Dickinson Street, Charleston
TELEPHONE: (304) 348-6195
VISITING HOURS: During school hours

Mattie V. Lee Home

The Mattie V. Lee Home is a historic place that provided shelter to young Black women in the early part of the century. Staff members at the home provided job training and assisted the young women in finding employment. The interior has been converted into apartments.

DATE BUILT: Early twentieth century
ADDRESS: 810 Donnally Street, Charleston
TELEPHONE: (304) 340-3693
VISITING HOURS: Daily 9–5
SOURCES: NRHPINF. Telephone conversation, Mar. 4, 1994, Mattie V. Lee Center staff. Telephone conversation, Mar. 4, 1994, Rodney Collins, historian, National Register Coordinator, West Virginia Division of Culture and History.

Samuel W. Starks House

The Samuel W. Starks House belonged to a community leader who reached national prominence through his work and leadership in the Knights of Pythias. Born in Charleston in 1866, Starks spent his boyhood as an apprentice to a cooper. As a young man he worked as a janitor for the railroad. In his railroad position he became fascinated with telegraphy and taught himself to use the equipment needed to send messages. He worked for a time as a telegraph operator but resigned when he felt that discrimination prevented his advancement.

Starks worked in several businesses. He was active in the Republican party, too. He became well known, however, for his leadership in the Knights of Pythias, a Black fraternal order that provided business, civic, and social activities for the Black community in the early years of the century. His achievements with the Knights of Pythias were so great that in 1907 George Atkinson, the governor of West Virginia, praised him for his work in building the organization. In 1897 the organization elected him supreme chancellor, its highest national office. Reelected unanimously term after term, he continued to hold the office until his death. As supreme chancellor, Starks organized the Pythian Mutual Investment Association that encouraged the acquisition of real estate in prime business areas in several cities in West Virginia. The association also encouraged the development of mercantile and insurance businesses.

After Starks died on an operating table in 1908 at the age of forty-two, hundreds came to Charleston for the service. The crowd filled the church to capacity and made the streets nearly impassable.

The Starks home is an architectural style called American four square. Inside there is a spacious foyer and a hardwood stairway leading to the second floor. The house has sixteen rooms and four baths and has hardwood trim throughout. The east end of Charleston, a neighborhood with historically strong Black associations, has become largely nonresidential, and this home is one of a few surviving free-standing houses in the area.

The house was rehabilitated and served as a shelter, but Sojourners, the organization that used it, moved to a larger facility and Starks House became vacant. Although visitors cannot see the interior, the house is well worth driving by. It is listed in the *National Register of Historic Places.*

In addition to the house, Starks is remembered by a thirty-two-foot obelisk that marks his grave at Spring Hill Cemetery in Charleston. Pythians and their friends donated $2,700 to purchase the granite monument that was dedicated in 1911. The monument, one of the few obelisks in the cemetery, is an example of Charleston funerary architecture.

DATE BUILT: c1906
ADDRESS: 413 Shrewsbury Street, Charleston
VISITING HOURS: Vacant, visitors can walk or drive by

Charles Town

Jefferson County Courthouse

The Jefferson County Courthouse (formerly known as the Charles Town Courthouse) is important in Black history as the site of John Brown's trial for treason in 1859. White abolitionist John Brown was well acquainted with many Black leaders and had a burning desire to see the slaves freed. Unsuccessfully he tried to enlist large numbers of Blacks in his attempt to raid the federal armory at Harpers Ferry. Although others agreed with his goal of freeing the slaves, most believed he could not be successful against the full power of the federal government. Brown ultimately was hanged for his role in the raid on the arsenal on Harpers Ferry, but he remained a revered hero to thousands of Black Americans.

The two-story, Greek-revival courthouse is brick, rectangular in design, with a square clock tower; it has been restored and enlarged.

DATE BUILT: 1836
ADDRESS: N. George and E. Washington Streets, Charles Town
TELEPHONE: (304) 725-9761
VISITING HOURS: Weekdays 9–5; closed Sat.–Sun., holidays
SOURCE: Debra Basham, archivist, Division of Culture and History, State of West Virginia.

Clifftop

Camp Washington-Carver

Camp Washington-Carver, a complex of major buildings and other facilities, was considered the first of its kind in the nation. Within the past fifty years the complex was the center of activities and events in West Virginia's Black history. It originally was built as the state's African American 4-H camp; later it was named Camp Washington-Carver to honor Black leaders Booker T. Washington and George Washington Carver.

A 1937 act of the West Virginia legislature authorized the creation of the "Negro 4-H Camp" to provide the state's Black youth with a recreation and camping area as well as recreational opportunities through extension services of West Virginia State College. Camp Washington-Carver was one of West Virginia's most ambitious Works Progress Administration (WPA) projects. The center of the facility, the Great Chestnut Lodge, is the largest log structure of its kind in the world. The facilities also included dormitories, a log cottage, and a pond. The interrelated structures were built of local hardwood and native stone to harmonize with the natural environment.

After construction of the camp from 1939 to 1942, management passed to West Virginia State College, a formerly all-Black institution. The college operated the camp until 1978. The center served Black youth in vocational agriculture, soil conservation, home economics, and 4-H standards.

Facilities are owned at present by the West Virginia Department of Culture and History, which uses the facilities to promote West Virginian arts and crafts, sponsors the Camp Washington-Carver African-American Arts Camp, and mounts exhibits showing African-American history related to the camp.

DATE BUILT: 1939–1942

ADDRESS: Just off US 60 adjacent to Babcock State Park, Clifftop

TELEPHONE: (304) 438-6429 or (304) 438-8625

VISITING HOURS: May–Oct., daily 10–5; closed Nov.–Apr.

FEES: None, except for special events

SOURCES: NRHPINF. George W. Jordon, director, Camp Washington-Carver. Debra Basham, Division of Culture and History, State of West Virginia.

Old Stone House

The Old Stone House in Clifftop, constructed in 1824, served as a tavern and a stagecoach station. The house also was the site of slave auctions—an unusual activity in this area. There was little slavery in western Virginia, and in 1863 West Virginia split from Virginia and joined the Union.

DATE BUILT: 1824

ADDRESS: 2 miles south of junction of US 60 and WV 41, Clifftop

VISITING HOURS: Jan.–Nov., daily 10–2; Dec., daily 10–4

FEES: None

SOURCES: "Black Cultural Sites in West Virginia." *Hippocrene U.S.A. Guide to Black America.*

Halltown

Halltown Union Colored Sunday School

The Halltown Union Colored Sunday School, now called the Halltown Memorial Chapel, is unique in the history of Black Americans in Jefferson County. Black artisans and workers erected the little stone chapel in 1901, working after their regular jobs and on their days off. They built the structure on the Old Smithfield–Charles Town–Harpers Ferry Turnpike, adjacent to the old Colored Free School. For sixty years after its construction, the congregation held church services, marriages, funerals, and social and community events at the chapel.

Halltown Chapel may be unique in West Virginia architecture. The one-story rubble-stone building is Gothic-revival style with a cathedral-like appearance. The four buttresses that reinforce the chapel walls and the pointed arch windows lend a Gothic influence. A shingle-covered belfry rises over the entrance stoop.

Although the Sunday School closed in 1967, the community restored the 40-foot-by-50-foot chapel to excellent condition in 1983. The setting is just as it was when the chapel was constructed, and the chapel appears much as it did originally. Halltown Union Chapel, listed in the *National Register of Historic Places,* is noted for its architecture as well as its important role in the religious and social life of Halltown's African American community.

DATE BUILT: 1901

ADDRESS: Off US 340, Halltown

VISITING HOURS: Open for special events; visitors can walk or drive by

SOURCES: NRHPINF. Telephone conversation Mar. 4, 1994, Rodney Collins, historian, National Register Coordinator, West Virginia Division of Culture and History. Telephone conversation Aug. 6, 1995, Stephen Luckett, local resident.

Harpers Ferry

Harpers Ferry National Historical Park*

Harpers Ferry, located at the confluence of the Shenandoah and Potomac Rivers in the Blue Ridge Mountains, was an important manufacturing and commercial town from 1803 to the Civil War. Its railroad and highway bridges across the Potomac made the town strategically important. George Washington visited Harpers Ferry in 1785. Ten years later, as President of the United States, he selected Harpers Ferry as the site for a proposed armory.

In 1859 Harpers Ferry was the site of a raid by white abolitionist John Brown and his followers. John Brown, a religious man and ardent abolitionist, conceived of a plan to free the slaves. First, he and his followers would seize the arsenal buildings at Harpers Ferry. They would then take the arms and with the help of newly freed slaves establish a base in the mountains of Virginia. From this base they would continue to free other slaves.

Of the original party with John Brown, five were Black: Shields Green, Dangerfield Newby, Sherrard Lewis Leary (sometimes listed as Lewis Sheridan Leary), Osborne P. Anderson, and John A. Copeland.

Leary was born in Fayetteville, North Carolina. He was an educated, literate man who designed saddles and played several musical instruments. Although a free man, he hated slavery. One day Leary saw a white man beating a slave and fought the white man. Forced to escape the wrath of the community, Leary fled to Oberlin, Ohio. He met John Brown in Cleveland and, without telling his family, joined Brown's group.

Brown reached Harpers Ferry on July 3, 1859. He and two of his sons established a base on the Kennedy farm in Maryland, just five miles from the town. He spent the summer recruiting men and collecting guns and supplies. By October 16, the band was ready. Leaving three men to guard the farm, Brown and eighteen men left in a wagon. At 10:30 P.M. they seized the watchmen at the bridge; then they seized the armory watchman and the arsenal. Brown and his men cut telegraph wires and barricaded themselves in the armory. They did not realize, however, that a train engineer had been warned about the trouble. The following day the engineer telegraphed an alarm from another location.

By noon on October 17 the militia arrived. In the fighting that broke out, several on both sides were killed or wounded. By nightfall only five of Brown's men remained unwounded. One of his sons died that night; his other son died later. Marines arrived and battered in the door. They bayoneted two men and captured all the others. Of the eighteen men who had started out with Brown for the arsenal, ten were killed, five were captured, and the other three escaped. Of the five Black men who took part in the raid, two were killed, two were captured, and only Osborne Anderson escaped. Anderson later told his story of the raid in *A Voice from Harper's Ferry.* He spoke of the bravery of the men, Black and white, who took part in the raid. He told how those inside the rifle factory were fired upon seven times and at last were forced to retreat to the river. They waded out to a rock, but pursuers hemmed them in, front and rear. They were fired at several hundred times, but kept fighting until all were killed, except John Copeland. At that point, Copeland surrendered.[1]

Although some had predicted that the slaves would be cowardly and afraid to join the raid, Anderson described the great joy of the slaves in learning that they could participate in the effort to free themselves. According to Anderson, the raid clearly demonstrated, "First, that the conduct of the slaves is a strong guarantee of the weakness of the institution, should a favorable opportunity occur; and secondly, that the colored people, as a body, were well represented by numbers, both in the fight, and in the number who suffered martyrdom afterward."[2]

John Copeland, who fought so gallantly, wrote to his family hours before his execution to reassure them that he had no regrets other than that "such an unjust institution should exist as the one which demands my life, and not my life only, but the lives of those to whom my life bears but the relative value of zero to the infinite. I beg of you, one and all, that you will not grieve about me; but that you will thank God that he spared me to make my peace with him."[3]

The raid on the arsenal captured the attention of the nation. Citizens and slaves watched as John Brown was brought to trial a week later. He denied everything except an intent to free the slaves. Yet he was convicted and sentenced to die. This abolitionist who acted on his beliefs that people should be free was hanged at Charles Town on December 2, 1859. The two Black members of the group, John Copeland and Shields Green, were hanged at Charles Town on December 16. Brown's associates who had been captured were also tried, convicted, and hanged for treason.

The nation, split on the subject of John Brown and his raid, fiercely debated about slavery and the raid. Brown had stirred the nation with his ideas about immediate emancipation. Although the raid was not successful, it focused attention and heightened feelings on both sides of the issue and helped lead to the Civil War. Soon armed men were marching to the tune of "John Brown's Body," and the town of Harpers Ferry was involved with other regions in the Civil War.

In the final campaign of that war, General Sheridan's Union army destroyed the Confederate army as a fighting force and conquered Virginia's Shenandoah Valley for the Union. Harpers Ferry was a ghost town. Because of the U.S. government decision not to rebuild the armory at Harpers Ferry and to dispose of the lands and ruined buildings, the town never fully recovered its industrial prominence.

Today Harpers Ferry National Park contains the original town center and surrounding area. Numerous structures have been restored and adapted to park use.

DATE OF SIGNIFICANCE:	1859
ADDRESS:	Harpers Ferry at the confluence of the Shenandoah and Potomac Rivers
TELEPHONE:	Park headquarters, (304) 535-6223
VISITING HOURS:	Park, daily 8–5; closed Christmas
FEES:	$5 per vehicle
SOURCES:	Telephone call to site, Jan. 13, 1995. *Before the Mayflower*, 463. *International Library of Negro Life and History*, 94–95. *The Autobiography of W. E. B. Du Bois*, 252. "Harpers Ferry National Historic Park, National Park Service," 14–62. *The Negro in the Making of America*.

Lockwood House
Storer College

Also part of Harpers Ferry National Historic Park is Storer College, located on Camp Hill overlooking the gap where the Potomac and Shenandoah Rivers meet. The college was founded at this mountain site immediately after the Civil War as West Virginia's first higher education institution for Black students. Most of the early students were refugee slaves or freed people.

Jefferson County once was a part of Virginia. By 1840 the free Black population in Harpers Ferry nearly equaled the slave population. By 1850 most of the free Black people had learned to read and write. With the onset of the Civil War the Harpers Ferry–Shenandoah Valley region, with its Union occupation of the area, became a haven for African Americans. They needed a school and in

1865, Reverend Nathan Brackett, supported by the Freewill Baptist Home Mission and the Freedmen's Bureau, established a grammar school for them at Harpers Ferry.

The land upon which the school was established initially belonged to the U.S. Armory, and the land encompassed a house built in 1848 for armory officials. The structure was named **Lockwood House,** for Brigadier General Lockwood who lived in the house for a few months during the Civil War. The U.S. government, through the Freedmen's Bureau, later donated the structure to Storer College. Although neglect and occasional shelling during the war had left Lockwood House in need of repair, the building was adequate for housing the small school. Teaching began in 1864.

Lockwood House provided both classroom space and living quarters. Teachers slept in the kitchen, and classroom benches doubled as student beds. Help came when philanthropist John Storer donated $10,000 to the fledgling institution. He stipulated that the church had to match the amount, and that all persons could enroll, regardless of race or sex. Although the church raised the matching funds, segregationist laws and customs hampered fulfillment of the goal of creating an integrated school. Storer College, named for its benefactor, received its state charter in 1868.

Many local white citizens expressed hostility toward the new college by verbally abusing teachers and students. When they began stoning them, the principal began allowing teachers and students to carry guns for protection. Eventually the townspeople became more accepting of the school.

As more buildings were added, the college became a center for educational, social, and cultural events. Frederick Douglass, former slave, noted abolitionist, and trustee of Storer College, gave a speech at Storer in 1881. In his speech he praised abolitionist John Brown and the Black men who fought and died with him at Harpers Ferry. Douglass also contributed to the endowment of a John Brown professorship at Storer College.

Black scholar W. E. B. Du Bois held the first public meeting of the Niagara Movement at Storer College. The association already had held its initial meeting in the summer of 1905 at Niagara Falls, Canada, attended by twenty-nine African Americans from thirteen states and the District of Columbia. At Niagara Falls, Du Bois, elected general secretary, had led members in creating a manifesto calling for the abolition of racial discrimination while supporting the principles of human brotherhood, freedom of speech, and freedom of the press. Members decided to hold annual meetings at sites significant in the march to freedom, including Faneuil Hall in Boston and Harpers Ferry. At the 1906 Harpers Ferry meeting Du Bois led a group on a barefoot pilgrimage to the engine house, the scene of John Brown's martyrdom. Du Bois later wrote that "we reconsecrate ourselves, our honor, our property, to the final emancipation of the race which John Brown died to make free."[4]

The Niagara Movement never had sufficient money. Although the initial group formed thirty branches, its membership remained small. Du Bois believed that the "talented tenth"—well-educated African American achievers—should help other African Americans to move up to a better life. Unfortunately the Niagara Movement received little support from the masses, and it failed to thrive. Although the association died in 1910, it did achieve some success in the fight against racial injustice, and it helped to lay the foundation for another group—the National Association for the Advancement of Colored People.

After a century of educating Black students, financial troubles beset the college. Enrollment declined following the 1954 *Brown* v. *Board of Education* legal decision that ended legal school segregation. The historic college closed its doors in 1955 and merged with Virginia Union University in Richmond in 1964. The restored buildings are used today for park services offices and for shops.

DATES OF SIGNIFICANCE: Lockwood House, 1848; college, 1867–1955

ADDRESS: Camp Hill, Hawks Nest, Harpers Ferry

SOURCES: Donald W. Campbell, superintendent, Harpers Ferry National Historic Park. Harpers Ferry: Storer College, the Lockwood House.

Institute

West Virginia State College

West Virginia State College was established in 1890 as the West Virginia Colored Institute, a land-grant institution for African American students. The college graduated many students who later became leaders in their fields. Two notable historic buildings here are East Hall and Canty House.

East Hall, the oldest building on campus, is a two-story frame house built about 1893. Originally used as a boy's dormitory, East Hall later housed several college departments. The college's 1898 catalog contained the following description of the house: "East Hall is a wooden structure painted white. It contains eight large rooms. Here are placed the printing department, the library, and chemical laboratory. It is nearly surrounded with porches. This building is heated with steam. It is furnished with water and its sanitation is good."[5]

East Hall later became the principal's residence, and it housed college presidents for more than seventy-five years. It was used for student and faculty receptions and housed numerous college guests in an era when suitable lodgings were not available elsewhere. The residence today retains its historic identity and associations with the development and growth of African American education in West Virginia.

Canty House is one of the most architecturally distinctive buildings in Institute. It was the home of "Colonel" James Monroe Canty, an early instructor and acting principal at the West Virginia Colored Institute. Canty was born in 1863 in Marietta, Georgia, the son of slave parents. He attended Tuskegee Institute, where he learned blacksmithing and pipe-and-machinery work. He used his skills at Tuskegee to install pipes for the first girls' bathroom at the Institute. After graduation he worked in Marietta in a carriage shop and also did machine work for two factories and a mill.

With a recommendation from Booker T. Washington, the head of Tuskegee Institute, Canty was appointed superintendent of mechanics at West Virginia Colored Institute. He taught blacksmithing, carpentry, and mechanical drawing; he also established the military training corps. As part of his work, he installed a sewerage system and a heating apparatus at the school.

Canty House, which James Canty called "The Magnolia," is valued as the surviving structure most closely associated with a remarkable instructor. The house is architecturally distinguished, differing from the other housing in the West Dunbar/ Institute area. Unlike the more typical tract housing in the area, Canty House is in the Classical style with fluted Corinthian columns, a fanlight over the double entrance doors, and a second-floor balcony above the entrance doors. The house is listed in the *National Register of Historic Places.*

DATE ESTABLISHED:	College, 1890; East Hall, c1893; Canty House, c1900, present form, 1923
ADDRESS:	WV 25, Institute
TELEPHONE:	(304) 766-3000
VISITING HOURS:	Call the college
SOURCES:	NRHPINF. Debra Basham, archivist, Division of Culture and History, State of West Virginia.

Lewisburg

Black Historic Sites of Lewisburg

Three sites in Lewisburg, West Virginia, have played a role in Black history. They are the John Wesley Methodist Church, six residences on Gospel Hill's Maple Street, and the Old Stone Church. Although all three sites are listed in the *National Register of Historic Places,* the churches are located in the Lewisburg National Historic District, which is a short driving distance away from the Maple Street Historic District.

Maple Street Historic District

The Maple Street Historic District consists of six single-family residences located atop "Gospel Hill" in Lewisburg. The terrain rises steeply behind the district, a slight ravine is in the center, and the yards feature trees, shrubbery, and assorted limestone outcroppings. The one- and two-story houses, which date from about 1900, are interesting as examples of workers' houses built by coal and timber companies in West Virginia company towns. The small, intact working-class neighborhood developed when railroads were coming into the Greenbrier Valley and the regional lumber boom was at its height.

When the Civil War ended, the Black community began to participate in kinds of community life that formerly had been closed to them. The Freedmen's Bureau moved into Lewisburg, and in spite of hostilities and discrimination, Black men began to vote and hold public office. The Black community supported the establishment of schools for their children.

Although much of the new freedom and opportunity ended after the election of 1872 when former Confederates came to power, African Americans continued to forge ahead economically. They took advantage of the lumber boom that began in the 1890s.

By the 1950s the Gospel Hill section had become more integrated with the rest of the city. Today Maple Street is the only remaining residential area that reflects nineteenth- and early twentieth-century housing of Black workers in this region. The remaining historic structures from the 1900s include the houses at 111, 113, 115, 117, 119, and 121 Maple Street. The houses provide a focal point of Lewisburg's Black history.

DATE BUILT: c1900

ADDRESS: 107–121 Maple Street, Lewisburg; to reach Maple Street from John Wesley Church, drive 2 blocks north to Randolph, turn left on Randolph to Oak Street, turn right 1 block to Gardner, turn left on Gardner and drive 1 block to Maple

TELEPHONE: Lewisburg Visitors Center, (304) 645-1000

VISITING HOURS: Private, visitors may drive or walk by

SOURCES: NRHPINF. John McIlhenny, director, Lewisburg Visitors Center.

Old Stone Church

The Old Stone Church is the largest and most distinguished church in the region that once was western Virginia. The church has the original slave balcony. Although the balcony featured beautiful hand-carved woodwork, it was an affront to dignity because it served to separate Black worshipers during church services.

DATE BUILT: 1796

ADDRESS: 200 Church Street, Lewisburg

TELEPHONE: (304) 645-2676

VISITING HOURS: Daily 9–4

FEES: None

SOURCES: John McIlhenny, director, Lewisburg Visitors Center. *Hippocrene U.S.A. Guide to Black America,* 369.

John Wesley Methodist Church

The John Wesley Methodist Church has the original slave gallery, which was built to provide segregated seating for Black worshipers. Following the Civil War, the church was taken over by five former slaves, and it remains a functioning Black church today. It is located in the Lewisburg Historic District.

DATE BUILT: 1820

ADDRESS: 209 E. Foster Street, Lewisburg

TELEPHONE: Lewisburg Visitors Center, (304) 645-1000

VISITING HOURS: Sun. school, 10; Sun. service, 11

SOURCES: Telephone conversation, Mar. 4, 1994, Rodney Collins, historian, National Register Coordinator, Division of Culture and History, West Virginia. Telephone conversation Jan. 11, 1995, John McIlhenny, director, Lewisburg Visitors Center. Telephone conversation Jan. 11, 1995, Reverend Henry James, pastor, John Wesley Methodist Church. *Black Cultural Sites in West Virginia.*

Malden

African Zion Baptist Church

African Zion Baptist Church, a charming, one-story frame church with clapboarding, is the mother church of West Virginia's Black Baptist churches. Noted members have included Booker T. Washington and "Father" Lewis Rice, church founder and leader of the early Black community in the Kanawha Valley.

The area known as the Kanawha Salines, located about one mile from the African Zion Baptist Church, flourished in the nineteenth century as a prime area for the production of salt. Slaves often were hired out by their masters to work for producers and shippers in the salt industry. After the Civil War many former slaves settled in the same area.

The African Zion Baptist Church was formally organized in 1863. For a short period members held services in the home of the Reverend Lewis Rice. In 1865 a structure was built for church meetings. By 1872 coal production had surpassed salt manufacturing as the leading industry, and the church moved to its present location in Malden. The present sanctuary was erected about 1872. Many of the Black settlers who worked in coal production formed branches of African Zion Baptist Church, and the individual units united in 1874 to form the Mt. Olivet Baptist Association.

After emancipation, Booker T. Washington migrated to the salines from Virginia with his mother, sister, and brother to join Washington's stepfather, who was working in a salt-packing house. Booker T. Washington and his relatives were part of the African Zion Church from the time he was nine years old until he left for Hampton Institute at the age of sixteen. He returned to Malden later, and his ties continued with the church.

African Zion Baptist Church is a rectangular frame structure with white weatherboard exterior, arched windows, and gable roof topped by a wooden bell tower. The lines of the church have remained intact since 1872. The sanctuary is not open on a regular basis because the African American population has dwindled in Malden to two or three individuals. This site, closely related to the history of the Black community in the Kanawha Valley, is listed in the *National Register of Historic Places.*

DATE BUILT: c1872

ADDRESS: 4104 Malden Drive, Malden

TELEPHONE: (304) 768-2635

VISITING HOURS: Call to visit interior

SOURCE: NRHPINF. Telephone conversation Jan. 12, 1994, Reverend Paul Gilmer, pastor, African Zion Baptist Church.

Notes

1. *A Voice from Harpers Ferry* (Boston, 1861), quoted in Herbert Aptheker, ed., *A Documentary History of the Negro People in the United States,* vol. 1 (New York: Citadel, 1990), 435–6.

2. *A Voice from Harpers Ferry,* 437.

3. *The Liberator* (New York: microfilm division of the Schomburg Collection, 13 Jan. 1869), quoted in Aptheker, *A Documentary History of the Negro People in the United States,* vol. 1, 445.

4. W. E. B. Du Bois, "Niagara Address of 1906," quoted in Herbert Aptheker, *A Documentary History of the Negro People in the United States,* vol. 2, 909.

5. *West Virginia State College Catalog,* 1898, quoted in *NRHPINF for East Hall, West Virginia State College* (Washington, D.C.: National Park Service, 1984).

Works Consulted

The Autobiography of W. E. B. Du Bois. W. E. B. Du Bois. New York: International, 1968.

Before the Mayflower: A History of Black America. 5th ed. Lerone Bennett Jr. New York: Penguin, 1988.

Black Cultural Sites in West Virginia. Michael Pauley and Peterr Jesus, comps. Charleston, W. Va.: Division of Culture and History, State of West Virginia, Feb. 1990.

Harpers Ferry: Storer College, the Lockwood House. Harpers Ferry, W. Va.: National Park Service.

"Harpers Ferry National Historic Park, National Park Service." Cassandra Smith-Parker. In *Afro-American History Interpretation at Selected National Parks.* Washington, D.C.: Howard University, n.d.

Hippocrene U.S.A. Guide to Black America: A Directory of Historic and Cultural Sites Relating to Black America. Marcella Thum. New York: Hippocrene, 1992.

International Library of Negro Life and History: Historical Negro Biographies. Wilhelmena S. Robinson. New York: Publishers, 1970.

The Liberator. Boston, 13 Jan. 1860. Quoted in *A Documentary History of the Negro People in the United States,* vol. 1, Herbert Aptheker, ed. (New York: Citadel, 1990).

The Negro in the Making of America. Benjamin Quarles. New York: Collier, 1964; New York: Macmillan, 1987.

"Niagara Address of 1906." W. E. B. Du Bois. Quoted in *A Documentary History of the Negro People in the United States,* vol. 2, Herbert Aptheker, ed. (New York: Citadel, 1990).

A Voice from Harpers Ferry. Boston, 1861. Quoted in *A Documentary History of the Negro People in the United States,* vol. 1, Herbert Aptheker, ed. (New York: Citadel, 1990).

PART

2

THE NORTHEAST

Connecticut

Delaware

Maine

Massachusetts

New Hampshire

New Jersey

New York

Pennsylvania

Rhode Island

Vermont

The experiences of African Americans in the South and their experiences in the Northeast had both parallels and differences. First, slavery and segregation were legal and were practiced in both regions. Although far more extensive and damaging in its effect in the South, slavery also enriched sea captains and slave traders in the Northeast and produced labor for the region's citizens.

A second parallel involved the existence of mitigating circumstances in both regions. In the South these were created primarily by differences in the character of individual slave owners and by the existence of some individuals who did not favor the cruel practices of slavery. In the North the institution of slavery was weakened by strong abolitionist and antislavery networks that included a secret underground railroad system.

A third parallel was that Black Americans made gains in both regions. Although conditions that were severe enough to break the will of some slaves existed in both the Northeast and the South, significant numbers of African Americans seized whatever opportunities they could find and rose to great achievements in education, religion, the arts, political affairs, and business. From the tests of adversity leaders arose to show ways out of the labyrinth of racism. Perhaps unexpectedly for those who created the racist laws and initiated the acts of hatred, destruction, and killing, such acts often had the effect of strengthening the will and determination of African Americans to overcome and to achieve in a way that brings to mind the Latin phrase *Virescit vulnere virtus* (wounds can increase courage). These ideas are explored in this introduction to the Northeast.

Slavery and Segregation in the Northeast

In the Northeastern states—Connecticut, Delaware, Maine, Massachusetts, New Hampshire, New Jersey, New York, Pennsylvania, Rhode Island, and Vermont—slavery and racial segregation were practiced beginning in the colonial period. This is surprising to many who regard slavery as a Southern phenomenon and who learned in school that the colonies were founded on principles of personal liberties. In the mindset of the colonial era, however, liberties were seen as encompassing white people, not Indians or Africans, and most colonists were untroubled by the contradiction of fighting for liberty for themselves while denying it to others. Thus, slavery did develop and spread in the Northeast. It was not as widespread as in the South because the land and growing conditions were not suitable for developing vast, labor-intensive rice, cotton, and tobacco plantations. Still, slaves were brought in, even in colonial days, to work the land and to labor as house servants.

On the Atlantic seacoast many sea captains earned their fortunes from profits gained in the slave trade. In Massachusetts eighteenth-century seaport towns prospered as ships carried timber and salt fish to the Caribbean and traded them for molasses and sugar. Returning with the molasses, they had it distilled into rum, took the product to West Africa, and traded it for slaves. In this triangle of trade, slaves then were taken to the Caribbean and South America to be sold, and more molasses and sugar were taken on board. Profits made from each point of trade were used to build many fine homes along the Massachusetts shores.

Sea captains in Maine and Rhode Island also joined the slave trade. Even though, according to provisions of the Missouri Compromise of 1820, Maine had joined the Union as a free state, slavery still benefited the state's economy. Maine's large forests provided lumber for building ships that were used for shipping cotton and other goods. The miles of inlets and coves provided convenient harbors for the cargo of human beings that the sea captains brought back to Maine on their return trips.

Such joint commercial ventures produced a sympathy for the South and for the institution of slavery, and many families in the Northeast purchased slaves for their own use. In New York both the Dutch and the English imported slaves from the West Indies and from Africa. The Dutch, who first brought slaves into New York in 1616 for agricultural labor, at first treated the Africans more like indentured servants than as chattels. Over the years, however, the form of slavery changed much as it had in the South, and the process of dehumanization began. Slave owners began to regard slaves as nothing more than property that could be bought and sold just as household goods or farm animals were bought, sold, and willed to others. In New York the importation of slaves increased until by 1698 there were more than 2,000 slaves in the New York Colony. By 1746 there were more than 9,000 adult slaves in the state.

In many ways slavery was as cruel in the Northeast as it was in the South. To increase control over the slaves, the New York Assembly passed a law in 1702 that forbade trading with slaves and that forbade slaves from assembling or carrying arms. In spite of the closer supervision, however, there was a slave uprising in New York City in 1712; it was not the last such conflict to occur in the state. In the Northeast slaves reacted as they had in the South—by trying to escape. In New York and Pennsylvania newspaper ads offered rewards for the return of runaway slaves. Between 1690 and 1730 Connecticut set up a series of laws to control and "protect" African Americans. Slaves who did not carry with them a pass from their masters were considered runaways. For stealing, a slave could receive up to thirty "strips" or lashes.

Although Maine never had a large Black population, slavery was as heartless there as it was in any other region. Families were separated in slave auctions with little thought to the anguish felt by family members. In an 1875 book, author Edward Bourne called slavery "the great sin of the South."[1] He described a house that once stood in York, Maine, and was used as a slave factory. Entire Black families were imprisoned for sale at the house, and buyers went there to purchase slaves. Bourne also noted that in the town of Wells, Maine, families were able to purchase slaves from the many small vessels that for almost a century traveled back and forth in the West India trade. He described the agony of a sale in which a mother and daughter were separated:

> Phillis had a little daughter of the age of five years, to whom she was bound by all the ties which take hold of a mother's heart. But a distinguished Revolutionary officer, with the same heartlessness which we have been wont to attribute to those engaged in the slave trade, took this little child from its mother, and, as he would any article of produce, carried her to Saco, and there sold her. The agony of the poor mother in this cruel separation, was said to be indescribable. Yet there were no relentings and no remorse on the part of the trader, which led to any attempt to rescind the unholy contract. It did not seem that our own townsmen had any more doubt, in the judgment of conscience, as to the legitimacy of this traffic; and that a negro was a mere chattel, subject to be bought and sold at the will of the master, than they had that the right of sale in the owner, was a condition or incident of any other property.[2]

The cruelty that could be displayed by slave owners, even in the Northeast, also was exemplified in the home of Colonel John Ashley and his wife, Hannah, in Ashley Falls, Massachusetts. When Hannah Ashley tried to burn a slave girl with a red-hot household implement, the slave girl's sister, Elizabeth, jumped between and took the searing burn instead. Elizabeth steadfastly refused to return to the house even though the Ashleys pleaded with her, and she eventually won her freedom through the Massachusetts state courts.

In New York, a Black man named Austin Steward also was treated cruelly by his master, a man who had brought him from Virginia to New York. Steward, who later wrote a book, *Twenty-Two Years a Slave and Forty Years a Free Man,* stated that it was as hard to have been beaten on the head with a piece of iron in New York as it was to have been beaten this way in Virginia.[3]

Even those slaves in the Northeast who lived in the master's home often lived in terrible conditions. As a child, Sojourner Truth, who later would become a famous spokesperson against social injustice, lived in a cold, damp basement in her master's house in Hurley, New York, sharing her living space with insects and rats.

Opposition to Slavery

Some opposition to slavery existed in the South, although it never was as open as it was in the Northeast. Protest in the Northeast consisted primarily of individual actions and of the strength of the abolitionist and antislavery movements in that region. Abolitionists worked to repeal laws that reinforced slavery, and they supported antislavery candidates. White and Black abolitionists established and maintained an underground railroad, a secret network of men and women who helped fugitive slaves to escape.

It was to the Northeast states that large numbers of slaves sought to escape. Although slavery existed in Maine, the underground railroad was there also. Surrounded on three sides by Canada and on the fourth side by the Atlantic Ocean, Maine provided a desirable route for runaway slaves who fled through Portland, Brunswick, Vassalboro, and China Lake before moving on to Canada. Sometimes boats transported them. A modest number remained in Maine, where they joined the relatively small population of slaves and free people already there.

In New York and Massachusetts several groups, including the Quakers and other religious sects, strongly opposed slavery. In their monthly meetings the Quakers spoke out against slavery, and they were prepared to disown individuals who would not set their slaves free. In New Bedford, Massachusetts, the Quakers worked to make the city hospitable to fugitive slaves and to free Black citizens. They were determined to see that no fugitive slave seeking refuge in New Bedford would be captured and returned to slavery. New Bedford created such a positive atmosphere that when Frederick Douglass arrived in that city, he was surprised to see that laboring Black people there lived better than many slave owners had in his native Maryland. He was surprised at the confident serenity of the Black men as they worked on the New Bedford docks. Douglass said:

> . . . almost every body seemed to be at work, but noiselessly so, compared with what I had

> been accustomed to in Baltimore. There were no loud songs heard from those engaged in loading and unloading ships. I heard no deep oaths or horrid curses on the laborer. I saw no whipping of men; but all seemed to go smoothly on. Every man appeared to understand his work, and went at it with a sober, yet cheerful earnestness, which betokened the deep interest which he felt in what he was doing, as well as a sense of his own dignity as a man.[4]

Both Black and white citizens worked against slavery in other areas of the Northeast. In Boston activists included African American leaders Lewis and Harriet Hayden and white abolitionist William Lloyd Garrison, one of the founders of the New England Anti-Slavery Society. The Farwell Mansion in Boston (now the property of the League of Women for Community Service) and the Dillaway-Thomas House in Roxbury, Massachusetts, were stops on the underground railroad. In New York, prominent abolitionists included Frederick Douglass, John Brown, Susan B. Anthony, and William Seward. Harriet Beecher Stowe, who lived in Hartford, Connecticut, wrote *Uncle Tom's Cabin*, one of the most effective books of the day in arousing sentiment against slavery. In Canterbury, Connecticut, Prudence Crandall showed uncommon courage in opening her school to Black students in the face of threats and actual violence directed her way.

Segregation and Achievement

Emancipation of slaves took place far earlier in the Northeast states than in the South. By 1799 New York had provided for the abolition of slavery by specifying gradual manumissions. By 1817 Governor John Jay of New York signed a law specifying that every slave born before July 4, 1799, was to be freed on July 4, 1827. Every child born after passage of the law was to be freed by age twenty-one. The importation of slaves also was prohibited. In 1827 all who still were slaves in New York were freed.

In Connecticut, which became the fifth state in 1788, most citizens opposed slavery. However, one impetus to abolishing slavery in Connecticut came not from philanthropic feelings but from self-interest. As more slaves began to acquire skills, white artisans began to lose their jobs to the unpaid Black workers. Fearful of losing more jobs, the white workers spoke out against slavery and against the importation of more slaves into Connecticut. A state law was passed providing that children of slaves who were born after March 1, 1784, were to be free by age twenty-five. In 1797 the age was changed to twenty-one years. By 1790 there were 2,759 slaves and 2,801 free blacks in the state. In 1848 all slavery was abolished in Connecticut.

With the abolition of slavery in the Northeast, Black citizens still lacked peace of mind. Fugitive slaves who escaped to the region feared being captured by slave traders to be returned to slavery in the South, and unscrupulous slave traders kidnapped free Black men and women to sell in the South. All of the United States was subject to the 1850 Fugitive Slave Law that allowed slave owners to enter Northern states to seize runaway slaves and that provided penalties for obstructing capture. Although American law had abolished the importing of slaves into the country in 1807, slave traders used stealth to get around this rule, and many continued to illegally import slaves.

As a further affront to free Black families, many white men and women wanted to send free Black people out of the country. The American Colonization Society was founded in Washington, D.C., in 1817 with this intent, and by 1829 the Society had a branch in New York. Most African Americans reacted negatively to the idea of emigration; having worked to build the country, they now considered it their home and its rewards their due. Some did, however, accept the idea of moving to Canada where slavery was abolished in 1833.

African Americans in the Northeast faced oppression and segregation in jobs, schools, and voting. In Maine, African Americans saw Irish immigrants take over their waterfront jobs; furthermore, with dwindling opportunities to work in Maine's shipping or lumber industries, many young Black people moved away from the state. In New York much anti-Black sentiment came from immigrants who felt an economic threat from Black workers and who resented being drafted to fight in the Civil War. The War was being fought, these immigrants claimed, to protect the rights of slaves and other Black people who might later compete with them for work. Enraged, they rioted, pouring violently through the streets of New York City, burning property, and lynching as they went. Some African Americans found a safe haven in the Weeksville section of Brooklyn, where they took up arms to protect themselves and their property.

In Boston, William Nell and other African American leaders protested state laws that forbade Black seamen to leave their ships when in Massachusetts ports. They also worked hard to end segregation in Boston's public schools. Schools were segregated, too, in Delaware, which in December 1787 became the first slave state in the union. Delaware's public school system, established as early as 1829, excluded African American children. Black children had to wait until 1907 to become part of a statewide compulsory education system, and they attended segregated schools until 1954.

Although most white citizens in Delaware supported the Union during the Civil War, they continued segregation after the war ended. Delaware instituted poll taxes in 1873, keeping impoverished Black citizens from voting. By 1897, when more African Americans could afford to pay the tax, a literacy test was substituted to bar them again from voting.

Both the South and the Northeast provided some opportunities for African Americans before and after emancipation. In the South such opportunities were more limited, but even segregation provided some niches where a few Black people could become wealthy by serving the Black community. Where slaves in the South had been allowed to preach, often they later provided a strong pattern of leadership in their communities that reached over generations. Some counties in the South encouraged the building of family strength by discouraging slave sales that separated families. In some instances, even though based on unequal status, a bond of affection existed between some slaves and their masters, and the white people helped the freedmen get a start after emancipation. Overwhelmingly, though, in the South, most slaves and freed people who rose to prominence did so through their own quiet diligence and determination.

In contrast, the Northeast states, even though prejudice existed, provided far more opportunities for advancement; this is why the escape route for slaves so often led to the Northeast. Here a person could keep the fruits of his or her labor. If conditions were not satisfactory, he or she could change jobs or move to a different state. Educational opportunities were superior. Savings could be kept to build for one's own future. For these reasons, many Black people in the Northeast rose to prominence, not only in the civil rights arenas but also in a variety of other fields. Lemuel Haynes, for example, preached to a white congregation. Paul Cuffe became wealthy through seafaring activities. In New Bedford, Massachusetts, and other seacoast areas, many African Americans sailed on whaling ships. In New York, Black artists, musicians, actors, and writers flourished during the Harlem Renaissance period, helped by the cultural opportunities that were available to them and that nourished and appreciated their talents. Some who had begun a pattern of achievement were born in the South but migrated to the Northeast and remained there.

Although the Northeast states were caught up in slavery and segregation just as the South was, slave labor was not needed as much, abolitionists spoke out more, and slavery ended earlier there. Furthermore, opportunities for achievement were greater for African Americans in the Northeast. At an earlier date some Black children attended school with white children. Black men, themselves both slave and free, fought for freedom beside white soldiers. One can only speculate what the contributions of these talented men and women would have been if their energies had not been constantly directed at eradicating social injustice. How much more might they have achieved?

Notes

1. Edward E. Bourne, *The History of Wells and Kennebunk from the Earliest Settlement to the Year 1820, at Which Time Kennebunk Was Set Off and Incorporated.* (Portland, Maine: B. Thurston, 1875), 406.

2. Bourne, 407.

3. Helene C. Phelan, *And Why Not Every Man? An Account of Slavery, the Underground Railroad, and the Road to Freedom in New York's Southern Tier* (Interlaken, N.Y.: Heart of the Lakes, 1987), 27.

4. Frederick Douglass, *Narrative of the Life of Frederick Douglass, an American Slave, Written by Himself* (New York: Penguin, 1968), 115–16.

Works Consulted

Academic American Encyclopedia. Danbury, Conn.: Grolier, 1993. [electronic version]

And Why Not Every Man? An Account of Slavery, the Underground Railroad, and the Road to Freedom in New York's Southern Tier. Helene C. Phelan. Interlaken, N.Y.: Heart of the Lakes, 1987.

"The Black Population of Maine, 1764–1900." Randolph Stakeman. *The New England Journal of Black Studies* 8 (1989): 17–35.

The History of Wells and Kennebunk from the Earliest Settlement to the Year 1820, at Which Time Kennebunk Was Set Off and Incorporated. Edward E. Bourne. Portland, Maine: B. Thurston, 1875.

National Register of Historic Places. Washington, D.C.: National Park Service, 1976.

The Underground Railroad in Connecticut. American Bicentennial Commission of Connecticut. Hartford, Conn.: Connecticut Historical Commission, 1976.

The Underground Railroad in New England. Richard R. Kuns and John Sabino, eds. Boston: American Revolution Bicentennial Administration, Region I, with Boston 200, the Bicentennial and Historical Commissions of the Six New England States, and the Underground Railroad Task Force, 1976.

Connecticut

Canterbury

Prudence Crandall House

When Prudence Crandall admitted Sarah Harris, a Black girl, to her school, the town of Canterbury erupted into violence. Angry townspeople directed their wrath at Crandall and at her girls school on Canterbury Green. There is an interesting background to this incident.

Prudence Crandall was well known in Canterbury, where she had lived from the time she was ten years old. As a young woman, Crandall moved to nearby Plainfield to teach at a girls school. Then, in 1831, a group of Canterbury citizens asked her to return there to establish a school. She agreed and opened the school in January 1832 with strong citizen support.

A few months later, Crandall, a Quaker, received a request from Sarah Harris to enter the school. Following is how Crandall described Harris's first visit to the school:

> A colored girl of respectability—a professor of religion—and daughter of honorable parents called on me sometime during the month of September last and said in a very earnest manner "Miss Crandall, I want to get a little more learning. If possible, enough to teach colored children and if you will admit me to your school, I shall forever be under greatest obligation to you. If you think it will be the means of injuring you, I will not insist on the favor.[1]

There were immediate reactions to Sarah's admission. Some parents threatened to withdraw their daughters if the Black girl did not leave; others withdrew their financial support. Crandall sought the advice of well-known abolitionist William Lloyd Garrison of Boston. After carefully considering the alternatives, she made a decision that would prove even more controversial. Instead of dismissing Sarah, Crandall dismissed the remaining white students and reopened the institution as a school for young Black girls. Even young women from other towns were allowed to enroll.

Local outrage and violence exploded. White citizens gathered outside to taunt the students as they left the school. They called out names and hurled eggs, mud, and rocks at the building and the students. The church across from the school refused to allow the girls to worship there. A shopkeeper refused to sell them food and supplies, and local physicians refused to give them medical treatment. When someone tried to set a fire at the school, white citizens accused a Black supporter of the school, George Olney, of starting the fire. He was tried and later acquitted.

Canterburians then encouraged state lawmakers to pass a law designed to destroy the school. The 1833 legislation known as the *Black Law* made it illegal to operate a school that brought Black or brown students into Connecticut. Crandall was arrested for breaking this law, and later released. When she returned to the school, violence erupted again. A mob attacked the building at midnight on September 9, 1834, using clubs and iron bars to break more than ninety windowpanes. Fearing that the girls were in great physical danger, Prudence Crandall and her husband finally decided to close the school. They fled from Connecticut. Prudence Crandall spent her later years in Kansas.

In 1886 the townspeople of Canterbury, recognizing the immense wrong the town had committed against Crandall and her students, granted an annuity of $400 per year to Crandall for the rest of her life. Sarah Harris later married and lived in Rhode Island. (See the listing for George and Sarah Fayerweather in Kingston, Rhode Island.)

The Prudence Crandall House opened as a state-operated museum in 1984. The sixteen-room, two and one-half–story house is a reminder of a period of segregation and racism in Connecticut. Today the museum has an exhibit that includes information about the Black experience in pre-Civil War Connecticut.

DATE ESTABLISHED: c1805; school, 1833–1834; museum, 1984

ADDRESS: Junction of CT 14 and CT 169, Canterbury

TELEPHONE: (203) 546-9916

VISITING HOURS: Jan. 15–Dec. 15, Wed.–Sun. 10–4:30; closed Mon., Tues., Thanksgiving

FEES: Adults, $2; senior citizens and children, $1; school groups, free; adult and youth groups, special rates

SOURCES: Ms. Kazimiera Kozlowski, museum curator I, Prudence Crandall Museum. *The Prudence Crandall House. National Register of Historic Places,* 102. *The Prudence Crandall Museum: A Teachers Resource Guide. The Underground Railroad in New England. The Underground Railroad in Connecticut. Classic Connecticut, Vacation Guide 1989–1990.* "Letter to the *Windham County Advertiser.*"

Farmington

Samuel Deming House

Fugitive slaves entering Connecticut at Stamford, New Haven, or Old Lyme usually next found their way to Farmington, called the "Grand Central Station" of Connecticut. Leaving Farmington, they traveled north to Westfield or Springfield in Massachusetts.

In Farmington Samuel Deming's house was a stop on the underground railroad. It also was associated with the Africans from the schooner *Amistad* (see First Church of Christ, Congregational and Austin Williams House, following). The Deming House later became the home of the headmaster of Miss Porter's School.

ADDRESS: 66 Main Street, Farmington

TELEPHONE: Miss Porter's School, (203) 677-1321

VISITING HOURS: Private faculty residence; visitors can drive by

SOURCES: Telephone call Apr. 5, 1994, Miss Porter's School. *The Underground Railroad in New England. The Underground Railroad in Connecticut.*

First Church of Christ, Congregational

A group of Africans who had been kidnapped from the West Coast of Africa for sale into slavery worshiped at this church while awaiting their trial to determine whether they would be slaves or free. Their ordeal began in 1839 when they were taken from Africa to Cuba. There they were purchased by two Spanish (Cuban) slave traders, Señores Ruiz and Montez, and were taken aboard the schooner *Amistad* to be delivered to Puerto Principe, Cuba. One of the slaves, Joseph Cinque, the son of a Mendi chief, was a man of high intelligence and leadership ability.

The Africans, numbering about fifty, were kept chained by the neck below deck, subsisting only on some bread, one plantain, and one cup of water per day. They had been terrified when the ship's captain killed a man with his knife, then used the knife to slash others among the Mendi. Moreover, the cook had threatened them with cannibalism. As a storm began to rage and the crew struggled to keep the schooner afloat, Cinque and his companions plotted their escape. Within four days some of the Africans broke loose from the hold, seized and killed the ship's captain and cook, and gave orders to Ruiz and Montez to return the ship to Africa.

During the day, the two Spaniards seemed to comply with their directions, but at night they sailed in a different direction, hoping to reach safety in a southern slave state. They had been at sea for weeks when crewmen from a Navy brig, the *U.S.S. Washington,* spotted the *Amistad* off Montauk Point in Long Island Sound. Seizing the schooner, the Navy crew captured the Africans and jailed them in New Haven, Connecticut. Later the Africans were transferred to Hartford, Connecticut, where they were to stand trial for mutiny, piracy, and murder.

An African slave from Mendi, who was working on a ship docked in New York, was brought in as an interpreter. Through the interpreter the prisoners told that they were not slaves but were freeborn Africans who had been kidnapped and sold to the Spaniards. After the Africans told their story, abolitionist sentiment rose for emancipating the group. The opening trial was scheduled for September 1839 in the State House at 800 Main Street in Hartford. The trial resumed in 1840 in the District Court of New Haven. When the Spanish government, regarding the slaves as property, demanded their return to the Cubans, the *Amistad* mutiny became an international affair. U.S. President Martin Van Buren sought to resolve the issue in favor of Spain, even offering to send a brig to take the Africans back to slavery in Cuba.

Meanwhile, the *Amistad* case was brought to the U.S. Supreme Court in 1841. While awaiting the decision, the Africans were taken to Farmington, where they became part of the community. They attended services at the First Church of Christ, Congregational during their nine months in Farmington. Former President John Quincy Adams served as counsel for the Africans before the Supreme Court. In March 1841 the Court declared the Africans to be free and upheld their right to return to their homeland. Sadly, on their return to Africa, they learned that members of their families had been sold into slavery.

DATE BUILT: 1771; *Amistad* Africans attended services, 1841

ADDRESS: 75 Main Street, Farmington

TELEPHONE: (203) 677-2601

VISITING HOURS: Mon.–Fri. 8–4; tours by request

SOURCES: David O. White, director of education, Connecticut State Library. NRHPINF. *International Library of Negro Life and History,* 63–64. *The Underground Railroad in Connecticut. The Underground Railroad in New England.* "Farmington Was the Grand Central on the Route North." *Race Racism and American Law,* 29–31.

Austin F. Williams House

When the Africans from the schooner *Amistad* came to Farmington, they lived in the carriage house of the Austin Williams House. Runaway slaves also stayed in the cellar under the carriage house. Twentieth-century owners of the house found five layers of flooring over the trap door leading to the cellar. The layers of flooring would have deadened any sounds made by the people hidden below.

DATE OF SIGNIFICANCE: 1839
ADDRESS: 127 Main Street, Farmington
VISITING HOURS: Private; visitors may walk or drive by
SOURCE: *The Underground Railroad in New England.*

Groton Heights

Fort Griswold State Park

Fort Griswold State Park is across the Thames River from New London, Connecticut, in the town of Groton. In September 1781 British troops under the leadership of the treacherous Benedict Arnold sailed up the Thames River, intent on burning the towns of Groton and New London. They attacked the small earthwork garrison called Fort Griswold. The British believed the attack was justified because ships from Connecticut towns along Long Island Sound had raided British shipping vessels throughout the war.

As the British soldiers sailed toward the fort, they were observed by a white farmer named Latham and his slave, Lambert Latham, who were tending cattle in a field. They rushed to assist fort commander Lieutenant Colonel William Ledyard and the other Americans at the fort. Latham and his slave were among those who refused to surrender even though they were surrounded by the enemy. Although Lambert Latham had a bullet wound in his hand, he was able to reload and fire again and again. During the attack Jordan Freeman, a Black slave and orderly, killed a British officer.

Although the Americans fought valiantly, they were outnumbered, and Colonel Ledyard finally offered his sword in surrender. The British officer, angered at the death of his colleague, took the sword and suddenly ran it through Ledyard to the hilt. Lambert Latham then stabbed the British officer with his bayonet, thus drawing upon himself the fury of the British, who pierced him thirty-three times with their bayonets. The British slaughtered eighty-four Americans, even though most of them had already surrendered. Both of the African American soldiers, Freeman and Latham, died in the massacre.

The 135-foot-high Groton Monument near Fort Griswold lists the names of the massacre victims. The placement of names on the monument reflects racism. The names of the white men who died were placed at the top while Lambert Latham and Freeman were listed below under the heading "Colored Men" and Latham, who had the nickname "Lambo," was listed as "Sambo."

DATE OF SIGNIFICANCE: 1781
ADDRESS: At the junction of Monument Street and Park Avenue, Groton Heights
VISITING HOURS: Park, daily 8–sunset; museum and monument, Memorial Day–Labor Day, daily 9–5, Labor Day–Columbus Day, weekends 9–5
FEES: None
SOURCES: David O. White, director of education, Connecticut State Library. William E. Hare II, curator, The New London County Historical Society. Jonathan Lincoln, park manager, Fort Griswold State Park. *Black Heroes of the American Revolution.*

Hartford

Harriet Beecher Stowe House and Library
Mark Twain Home

The residence at 73 Forest Street was home to Harriet Beecher Stowe (1811–1896), a white woman who influenced thousands through her stories about the horrors of slavery. After listening to African Americans describe their experiences, Stowe used some of the details they had supplied in her 1852 book, *Uncle Tom's Cabin*. Publishers translated the story into more than forty languages, and the narrative impelled many previously uncommitted readers to work actively against slavery.

Stowe lived in this home from 1878 until her death. Today the restored house is filled with original furnishings and family memorabilia, and visitors are offered guided tours. The Stowe-Day Library at 77 Forest Street, next to the Stowe House, is open to researchers studying the works of Harriet Beecher Stowe.

Visitors to the Stowe House have the opportunity to see the neighboring Mark Twain House where plans are proceeding to restore the third floor room of Black servant George Griffin. A former slave, Griffin came to the house in 1874 to wash windows and remained almost eighteen years as the household butler. A deacon in the Methodist Episcopal Church, he had a knack for making money and was remembered for lending funds to others in the African American community.

DATE BUILT: 1871

ADDRESS: Stowe House, 73 Forest Street; Carriage House, 71 Forest Street; Stowe Library in the Katherine Day House, 77 Forest Street; Twain Home, 351 Farmington Avenue, Hartford

TELEPHONE: (203) 525-9317; Twain Home, (203) 247-0998

VISITING HOURS: Stowe House, Tues.–Sat. 9:30–4, Sun. 12–4, June 1–Columbus Day and Dec., daily, last tour at 4, closed New Year's Day, Easter, Labor Day, Thanksgiving, Dec. 24–Christmas; Library, Mon.–Fri. 9–5, closed Sat.–Sun., holidays, Thanksgiving and the following Fri., Dec. 24–25

FEES: Admission for both the Stowe House and the Day House, adults, $6.50; children 6–16, $2.75

SOURCES: Telephone conversation June 9, 1994, Althea Sorensen, senior guide. The Stowe-Day Foundation. *National Register of Historic Places*, 97.

Wadsworth Atheneum

The Amistad Foundation of the Wadsworth Atheneum in 1987 acquired the Simpson Collection of African-American Art, a world-class record of the Black experience in America from the Middle Passage to the present. The Amistad Foundation Collection contains more than 6,000 paintings, sculptures, photographs, posters, books, historical documents, and artifacts. It began with Randolph Linsly Simpson who, as a boy, lived near the cemetery where Frederick Douglass was buried. Simpson's family had a strong antislavery tradition, and the boy became aware of the contributions of African Americans to American life. Deeply disturbed to realize that objects and pictures associated with Black history were rapidly disappearing, he became passionately dedicated to saving as much of this record as he could. The Simpson Collection found a permanent home in Connecticut's Wadsworth Atheneum.

The collection is extensive. More than 2,200 photographs, including some of Black abolitionists, show slave life in the early 1840s. The museum also includes slave narratives and objects made by slaves or used in the slave trade—from a pair of rare handmade chairs used in a slave cabin to shackles and chains. A bronze sculpture, *The Negro Looks Ahead, 1944*, was created by Richmond Barthe, who was born in Bay St. Louis, Mississippi, of African American, French, and American Indian parentage. Barthe was one of the first artists to use African motifs in his work.

The museum library includes historical documents such as letters, slave contracts, manuscripts, and more than 350 books.

DATE ACQUIRED: 1987
ADDRESS: 600 Main Street, Hartford
TELEPHONE: (203) 278-2670; information tape, (203) 247-9111; program/tour information, (203) 278-2670, ext. 323
VISITING HOURS: Tues.–Sun. 11–5; closed Mon., New Year's Day, July 4, Thanksgiving, Christmas
FEES: Adults, $3; students and senior citizens, $1.50; members and children under 13, free; Thurs. 11–1, free; Sat., free; annual student pass available
SOURCES: Barbara A. Hudson, African-American art curator, Amistad Foundation Collection. David O. White, director of education, Connecticut State Library. Telephone conversation Apr. 5, 1994, Eugene Gaddis and William G. Delana, archivist, Wadsworth Atheneum. *The Amistad Foundation.*

Milford

Black Soldiers from the Revolutionary War Marker

The town of Milford has erected a marker on the town green to honor three Black soldiers from the locality who fought in the American Revolution. During the Revolution African Americans made up about 3 percent of Connecticut's population and 2 percent of its armed forces. Some Black men were sent to serve in the army in the "master's" place, and of these, some were freed after completing their service in the army.

DATE OF SIGNIFICANCE: Revolutionary War
ADDRESS: Town Green, Milford
VISITING HOURS: Daily, 24 hours
SOURCES: David O. White, director of education, Connecticut State Library. "Town Records Tell Story of Black Residents."

New Haven

Connecticut Afro-American Historical Society

In 1971 a group of African American citizens formed the New Haven Afro-American Historical Society. Now called the Connecticut Afro-American Historical Society, the group operates a museum in a small turn-of-the-century house donated by a founding member. The original goal was to collect and preserve historical African American biographies, diaries, photographs, periodicals, and artifacts describing the early community of African Americans in New Haven, but the project expanded to include the state of Connecticut. The collections, displayed in five rooms on two levels of the house, include poster-sized photographs on the walls of each room, a Civil War rifle that belonged to an African American soldier from New Haven, uniforms from fraternal associations, and other items.

The historical association helped to plan the erection of a monument commemorating the *Amistad* incident (see the Farmington, Connecticut, listings for the Samuel Deming House; the First Church of Christ, Congregational; and the Austin F. Williams House). Dedicated in 1992 and rededicated in 1994, the triangular monument features three life-sized figures of Cinque, the leader of the African Mendi people who were kidnapped in Africa and who were later jailed in New Haven. Cinque is shown at three different points of his stay in America. Ed Hamilton, a nationally recognized African American artist and a resident of Louisville, Kentucky, won a national competition to create the sculpture. The *Amistad* monument is located in front of the New Haven City Hall on the New Haven Green, on the site where the jail once stood that housed the *Amistad* people.

As of January 1995 the Connecticut Afro-American Historical Society was seeking more space for its museum. Its most exciting project, however, is one recently initiated in conjunction with the Mystic Seaport Museum in Mystic, Connecticut, with $2.5 million in funding from the state of Connecticut. The museums plan to have built a full-sized replica of the schooner *Amistad* to serve as a floating museum. The home bases for the schooner, described as a Baltimore clipper, will be in New Haven and Mystic Seaport. If plans work out as desired, the ship will sail from port to port in Connecticut as well as throughout the United States, manned in part by inner-city youth trained to work on the schooner. The anticipated date of completion is summer 1998.

DATE ESTABLISHED:	1971
ADDRESS:	444 Orchard Street, New Haven
TELEPHONE:	(203) 776-4907
VISITING HOURS:	By appointment
FEES:	Donations appreciated
SOURCES:	Telephone call Mar. 16, 1990, Russell Hamilton, Connecticut Afro-American Historical Society. David O. White, director of education, Connecticut State Library. Edna B. Carnegie, volunteer, Connecticut Afro-American Historical Society. Telephone conversation Apr. 12, 1994, Lucinda Hamilton, board member, Connecticut Afro-American Historical Society. Telephone conversation Jan. 15, 1995, Khalid Lum, president, Connecticut Afro-American Historical Society.

Goffe Street Special School for Colored Children

Before 1869 Black children were barred from attending New Haven's public schools. Some African American children received instruction in private homes, but this arrangement was inadequate to meet the needs of the community. In 1864 a group of influential citizens met and resolved to establish a school for "the intellectual and moral well being of the colored people of the Town of New Haven and especially of their children."[2]

Henry Austin, one of Connecticut's most-influential architects of the mid-nineteenth century, designed the Goffe Street School, and starting in 1866, Black people used the facilities at night. By 1871 state and local leaders modified laws to permit the public education of Black children. Soon the African American community was using the building for sewing classes, a boys club, a masonry school, and an athletic club. The athletic club was chartered in 1895 as the Colored Young Men's Christian Association. After World War I, St. Luke's Episcopal Church used the building as a parish house and Black community center.

When the Dixwell Community Center was constructed nearby in 1924, use of the Goffe Street School decreased. The Grand Lodge of Negro Masons purchased the building in 1929 with the intent of preserving it for New Haven's Black community.

The Goffe Street School is a brick structure with two stories and attic. An interior staircase features heavy, turned balusters and an oak handrail. Although the exterior has been remodeled to serve as a parish house for St. Luke's Episcopal Church and later for use as a Masonic Lodge meeting hall, it still retains its basic original design.

Goffe Street School is significant in a state that has few remaining sites directly connected with Black history.

DATE BUILT: 1864
ADDRESS: 106 Goffe Street, New Haven
TELEPHONE: Prince Hall Masonic Lodge, (203) 865-9267
VISITING HOURS: Call for information
SOURCE: NRHPINF.

Yale University

The Beinecke Library at Yale University houses the James Weldon Johnson Memorial Collection of Negro Arts and Letters, historic items from African American literature and culture. Named for prominent Black author, composer, and civil rights leader James Weldon Johnson, the collection is a large and scholarly set of manuscripts, musical scores, prints, recordings, photographic slides, and letters written by well-known authors. It is open to researchers rather than to the general public.

ADDRESS: Beinecke Library, Yale University, 121 Wall Street, New Haven
TELEPHONE: (203) 432-2962
VISITING HOURS: Mon.–Fri. 8:30–5
FEES: None
SOURCE: Telephone conversation June 10, 1994, Suzanne Eggleston, reference librarian, Sterling Memorial Library.

Stratford

Judson House and Museum

The cellar of the Judson House once served as slave quarters. Today, the restored and furnished colonial home has a collection of farm and craft tools that fill the former slave quarters. An adjacent museum, operated by the Stratford Historical Society, has some Black history items, including manuscripts and a list of eighteen local Black men who fought in the American Revolution. One was Robert Freeman, whose descendants still live in Stratford. The museum also has an account of Jack Arabas, a local Black man who had been promised his freedom for joining the army. When his master, Thomas Ivers, refused to grant his freedom, Jack Arabas took his master to court. He won both his case and his freedom.

The museum library has such materials as a copy of the autobiography of Aunt Hagar Merriman, a local African American woman born in the 1790s; the secretary's book of the local abolition society, dating from the 1850s; and a rare collage silhouette and bill of sale, both of a slave named Flora who died in 1815.

DATE BUILT: c1750

ADDRESS: 967 Academy Hill, Stratford

TELEPHONE: (203) 378-0630

VISITING HOURS: Apr. 15–Oct. 31, Wed., Sat., Sun. 11–4; closed July 4

FEES: Adults, $2; children, $1; senior citizens, $1.50; $5 per family if more than $5 individually

SOURCES: Hiram Tindall, curator, Stratford Historical Society. *Classic Connecticut, Vacation Guide 1989–1990.*

Notes

1. Prudence Crandall, "Letter to the *Windham County Advertiser,*" May 1833. In Randy Ross-Ganguly, *The Prudence Crandall Museum: A Teachers Resource Guide* (Hartford, Conn.: Connecticut Historical Commission, 1988), 66.

2. Leroy Fitch, "History of the Goffe Street Special School," quoted in NRHPINF for Goffe Street Special School for Colored Children, 2.

Works Consulted

The Amistad Foundation: The Simpson Collection at the Wadsworth Atheneum, Hartford, Connecticut. Hartford, Conn.: The Foundation. [brochure]

Black Heroes of the American Revolution. Burke Davis. New York: Odyssey/Harcourt Brace Jovanovich, 1976.

Classic Connecticut, Vacation Guide 1989–1990. Rocky Hill, Conn.: Department of Economic Development, 1989.

"Farmington Was the Grand Central on the Route North." Lin Noble. *(Farmington) Herald,* Mar. 1989. Newcomers Section.

International Library of Negro Life and History: Historical Negro Biographies. Wilhelmena S. Robinson. New York: Publishers, 1970.

"Letter to the *Windham County Advertiser.*" May 1833. In *The Prudence Crandall Museum: A Teachers Resource Guide.* Randy Ross-Ganguly. Hartford, Conn.: Connecticut Historical Commission, 1988.

National Register of Historic Places. Washington, D.C.: National Park Service, 1976.

The Prudence Crandall House. Connecticut Historical Commission. Hartford, Conn.: The Commission, n.d. [brochure]

The Prudence Crandall Museum: A Teachers Resource Guide. Randy Ross-Ganguly. Hartford, Conn.: Connecticut Historical Commission, 1988.

Race Racism and American Law. Derrick A. Bell Jr. Boston: Little, Brown, 1973.

"Town Records Tell Story of Black Residents." Mary L. Nason. *(Simsbury) News,* 19 Feb. 1987, 22.

The Underground Railroad in Connecticut. American Bicentennial Commission of Connecticut. Hartford, Conn.: Connecticut Historical Commission, 1976.

The Underground Railroad in New England. Richard R. Kuns and John Sabino, eds. Boston: American Bicentennial Administration, Region I, with Boston 200, the Bicentennial and Historical Commissions of the Six New England States, and the Underground Railroad Task Force, 1976.

Delaware

Dover

Delaware State College

The historically Black Delaware State College opened in 1891 as a land-grant college that grew out of the Second Morrill Act of 1890. An earlier land-grant act of 1862, known as the Morrill Act because it was introduced by Congressman (and later Senator) Justin S. Morrill, had offered federal land tracts as an incentive for establishing college programs in science, agriculture, industry, and the military. The 1890 Morrill Act specified that states practicing racial segregation had to establish Black colleges in order to receive land-grant act funds; Delaware State College was established as a result of that second act.

The first African American colleges, whether they were publicly or privately funded, enrolled Black students who were former slaves or who had been free Black Americans with very limited opportunities to attend school; their students often had to begin their studies at an elementary school level. For this reason it was not until 1898 that Delaware State produced its first graduates, a fine achievement considering the starting point of its students.

The current student body is made up of approximately 58 percent African American students who study on a 400-acre campus that has 24 buildings. Loockerman Hall, constructed between 1772 and 1790, is one of the historic buildings on the campus. Restored in the 1970s, it retains some of the original interior woodwork.

DATE ESTABLISHED:	College, 1891; Loockerman Hall, c1772–1790
ADDRESS:	US 13, Dover
TELEPHONE:	(302) 739-4924
VISITING HOURS:	By appointment with the Public Relations Office, Mon.–Fri. 8:30–4:30; closed weekends and holidays
FEES:	None
SOURCES:	Drexel B. Ball, director, Office of Public Relations, Delaware State College. *National Register of Historic Places*, 109.

John Dickinson Plantation

Although the slave houses are no longer standing at the Dickinson Plantation, site interpreters give a comprehensive look at the lives of African Americans who lived here. The Delaware Bureau of Museums and Historic Sites has gleaned information from more than 400 documents pertaining to slavery and to John Dickinson's manumission practices. The researchers used tax-assessment records, orphans-court records, daybooks, account books, receipts, manumission records, probate inventories, period legislation, petitions, and newspapers to reconstruct the lifestyles of slaves and manumitted African Americans between 1750 and 1808.

The plantation belonged to John Dickinson (1732–1808), a lawyer of great wealth who was known as the "penman of the Revolution." He was a Delaware delegate to the United States Constitutional Convention. Although Dickinson wrote many essays on colonial rights and liberty, ironically slaves lived on his plantation.

DATE BUILT: Mansion, 1740, rebuilt 1804; opened as a museum, 1956

ADDRESS: 8 miles south of Dover on Kitts Hummock Road just off US 113 and southeast of the Dover Air Force Base

TELEPHONE: (302) 739-3277

VISITING HOURS: Tues.–Sat. 10–3:30, Sun. 1:30–4:30; group tours by arrangement; closed Mon., holidays

FEES: None

SOURCES: Letter Sept. 27, 1989, Madeline D. Thomas, curator of education, Bureau of Museums and Historic Sites. *The John Dickinson Plantation.*

Wilmington

Afro-American Historical Society of Delaware

The Afro-American Historical Society of Delaware has identified several sites in Wilmington associated with the Black history of the city. One of the historic sites is the Walnut Street Young Men's Christian Association. Referred to at one time as the "Colored Y," for years it was the only YMCA that allowed Black participation.

Today the YMCA of Delaware remains active, providing housing for young men in its rooms and sponsoring activities for young people including a day-care program, weightlifting, and swimming.

For more information about Delaware's Black historic sites, call the Afro-American Historical Society of Delaware.

DATE ESTABLISHED: 1939

ADDRESS: Historical society administrative office, 512 E. 4th Street; "Y," 1000A Walnut Street, Wilmington

TELEPHONE: Administrative office, Afro-American Historical Society of Delaware, (302) 571-9300; "Y," (302) 571-6935

VISITING HOURS: Mon.–Fri. 1–5

FEES: Contact the "Y" for information

SOURCES: Harmon Carey, executive assistant for African-American Affairs, Delaware Division of Historical and Cultural Affairs. Telephone conversation June 11, 1994, Mrs. Ruth Peebles of the YMCA. Potentially Significant Afro-American Historic Sites.

Works Consulted

The John Dickinson Plantation. Dover, Del.: Department of State, Delaware Division of Historical and Cultural Affairs. [brochure]

National Register of Historic Places. Washington, D.C.: National Park Service, 1976.

Potentially Significant Afro-American Historic Sites. Patricia B. Koeker. Dover, Del.: State of Delaware, Division of Historical and Cultural Affairs, Oct. 1989. [list]

Maine

Brunswick

Bowdoin College

Bowdoin College, located 25 miles northeast of Portland and a few miles away from Maine's rugged coastline, is the state's oldest institution of higher learning. Founded in 1794 as a college for men, the institution became coeducational in 1971. Among Bowdoin's illustrious nineteenth-century students were poet Henry Wadsworth Longfellow, novelist Nathaniel Hawthorne, and newspaper editor John Brown Russwurm, who in 1826 became Bowdoin's first Black graduate.

In 1827 Russwurm established *Freedom's Journal,* the nation's first newspaper edited by a Black person (see the entry on the Russwurm House in Portland, Maine). Today a center at Bowdoin is named in his honor.

The Little-Mitchell House, once a stop on the underground railroad, today houses the offices of the Africana Studies Program and the John Brown Russwurm Afro-American Center. The center's library contains archival materials on the Black experience including 2,000 volumes on the subject of the Black diaspora worldwide.

The Hawthorne-Longfellow Library contains the original manuscript of a Phillis Wheatley poem, records of the Freedmen's Bureau, and papers of General Oliver O. Howard, founder of Howard University. This library and the Russwurm Center library are used by researchers from across the United States.

DATE ESTABLISHED: 1794

ADDRESS: John Brown Russwurm Afro-American Center Library, 6–8 College Street; Hawthorne-Longfellow Library, Maine, Bath, and College Streets, Brunswick

TELEPHONE: (207) 725-3000

VISITING HOURS: Russwurm Center, summer Mon.–Fri. 8:30–5, winter Sun.–Fri. 7 A.M.–11 P.M.; library, during school sessions, Mon.–Sat. 8:30 A.M.–midnight, Sun. 10 A.M.–midnight, spring and summer breaks Mon.–Fri. 8:30–5

FEES: None

SOURCES: Telephone conversation Apr. 13, 1994, Harriet Richards, academic coordinator, Africana Studies Program, Bowdoin College. *Bowdoin, The Offer of the College. African-American Studies at Bowdoin.* The Academic American Encyclopedia.

Harriet Beecher Stowe House

Author Harriet Beecher Stowe awakened the conscience of thousands of Americans with her novel, *Uncle Tom's Cabin* (1852). During the eighteen years she lived in Cincinnati, Ohio, she met several fugitive slaves and listened to the stories of their lives. On a visit to Kentucky, she saw a slave auction site and learned more about the lives of slaves in the South.

In 1850 Stowe's husband became a professor at Bowdoin College, and the Stowes moved to the house at 63 Federal Street in Brunswick, Maine, where Stowe began writing her story using composite characters developed from true incidents that had been related to her. The resulting book, *Uncle Tom's Cabin,* was a moving story of slavery and flight from bondage. Sympathetic readers bought 10,000 copies in the first week, while slaveholders violently opposed the book, proclaiming that much of the content was false.

After two years in Brunswick, the Stowe family moved to Massachusetts. The house in Brunswick later was altered for use as a restaurant, motel, and gift shop. The first floor is used for the front desk and gift shop of the hotel, and private quarters are upstairs. The barn is used today as a restaurant. The exterior of Stowe house is largely unaltered, and much of the original woodwork remains inside.

DATE OF SIGNIFICANCE: Stowe residence, 1850–1852
ADDRESS: 63 Federal Street, Brunswick
TELEPHONE: (207) 725-5543
VISITING HOURS: Private; call to see interior
SOURCES: Telephone conversation Mar. 31, 1994, April Glass, front desk clerk, Stowe House Restaurant. NRHPINF. *National Register of Historic Places,* 289. *Uncle Tom's Cabin.*

Gardiner

Nathaniel Kimball House

Although Maine's sea captains were heavily involved in the slave trade, residents of some towns in Maine opposed the trade and gave assistance to fleeing slaves. Sometimes they used boats to transport individuals or families from one town to the next on the underground railroad.

The Lamb House, a large Colonial home, is located about 200 feet from the west bank of the Kennebec River. Captain Nathaniel Kimball, a sea captain, built the residence in 1846 as a wedding gift for his daughter. The house later became part of the underground railroad. After fugitives arrived by boat, the family hid them in a cellar archway or under the eaves in the large attic.

In 1912 Dr. Bert Lamb purchased the house. Since that time, the residence has been used as a convalescent home and an office building, and the cellar hiding place was converted to storage use. Today it houses the Gardiner Family Chiropractic.

DATE BUILT: 1846
ADDRESS: 220 Main Street, Gardiner
VISITING HOURS: Private office; visitors may view the exterior from nearby parking lots by permission
SOURCES: *The Underground Railroad in New England.* "An Architectural and Historical Survey of the Gardiner Area."

Portland

Green Memorial African Methodist Episcopal Zion Church

Green Memorial African Methodist Episcopal Zion Church is the oldest Black congregation in Maine. Its parent organization, the Abyssinian Society, was incorporated in 1828. When the church was organized, members first worshiped in a brick-and-stone meeting house on Newbury Street in Portland, a structure that no longer exists.

The present two and one-half–story structure was built in 1914, and when completed, it was considered one of the finest Black churches in New England. The church is constructed of rough-textured concrete block. Rectangular windows on the first floor admit daylight, while arched second floor windows create a diamond pattern in stained glass. A two-story, shingled rectory stands adjacent to the church.

The congregation named the church in 1943 for Moses Green, a man who was born a slave and who worked for fifty-two years at Portland's Union Station. Records indicate that Green Memorial A.M.E. Zion Church was the only all-Black congregation in Maine's history. This church and the John B. Russwurm House in Portland are the only sites where physical evidence remains of African American history in Maine.

By 1993 the congregation had dwindled to fifteen members, but there was a rewarding increase in membership and attendance starting in 1993 and 1994. Reverend Margaret R. E. Lawson, who became pastor in May 1993, noted that a recent video entitled *Anchor of the Soul* told of the struggle and survival of Black people in Maine. The videotape brought focus on Green Memorial Church, and some members of the Green family who were related to the original founders of the church were located. Many hundreds of viewers of the videotape have described it as a moving experience. Green Memorial Church is listed in the *National Register of Historic Places.*

DATE ESTABLISHED:	Congregation, 1828; church, 1914
ADDRESS:	46 Sheridan Street, Portland
TELEPHONE:	(207) 772-1409
VISITING HOURS:	Sun. school, 9:45; Sun. service, 11; other hours by appointment
FEES:	None
SOURCES:	Telephone conversation Apr. 10, 1994, Reverend Margaret R. E. Lawson, Green Memorial African Methodist Episcopal Zion Church. NRHPINF. *National Register of Historic Places,* 291. *Anchor of the Soul.*

John B. Russwurm House

John Brown Russwurm (1799–1851) was one of the first African Americans to graduate from a college in the United States. He was founder and editor of *Freedom's Journal,* the nation's first Black-owned newspaper, and through his press he sharpened the debate about the future of free Black people in America.

Russwurm's father was a white planter in Virginia; his mother, a slave on his father's plantation in Virginia. Father and son relocated to Portland in 1812. The boy already had received some schooling in Canada; in the 1920s he began attending Maine's Hebron Academy. When his father died in 1815, John continued to live in the Portland house as a family member except during the school year.

After graduating from Hebron Academy preparatory school in Maine in the early 1820s, Russwurm studied medicine at Bowdoin College in Brunswick. Perhaps because of discrimination, although this is not certain, Russwurm was the only student in his class to live off campus. He boarded with a blacksmith outside Brunswick. Graduating in 1826, Russwurm then moved to New York City, where he began his newspaper career by founding *Freedom's Journal.* The journal's coeditor and cofounder was Samuel Cornish, a man who had been born free in Delaware in 1790 and had attended school in Philadelphia.

The growth of *Freedom's Journal* coincided with the growth in the United States of an organization called the American Colonization Society, founded in 1816 to encourage former slaves to emigrate to Africa. The society established the colony of Liberia in 1822; in 1824 the colony was named for U.S. President James Monroe. More than 2,600 Black Americans migrated to Liberia in the next decade, settling in Monrovia or establishing separate colonies. The colonies amalgamated in 1847, making Liberia the first independent republic in Black Africa.

In the United States Black people and white people were debating the idea of Black emigration to Africa. As coeditor of *Freedom's Journal,* Russwurm was silent about his emigrationist views; after becoming editor, however, he gradually began using the paper as a forum to promote the idea of emigration. He admired and praised Paul Cuffee, a Black man from Massachusetts who also promoted colonization (see the Cuffe listing for Westport, Massachusetts). Some African Americans, however, harshly criticized Russwurm—they believed slaveowners wanted to eliminate free Black people from their communities by sending them to Africa because the slaveowners feared the influence of free Black people on their slaves. Those African Americans who were opposed to emigration knew they had helped to build America and had shed their blood in America's wars; therefore, they claimed their future was in America.

On the other hand, African American emigrationists believed Black people could never control their destinies in America. On a daily basis they faced hostility and indifference in both the North and the South, and they strongly felt the grip of the tentacles of slavery. These people believed their lives would be better in Africa where they could practice self-determination and live unmolested by daily rebuffs of discrimination.

In 1829 Russwurm acted on his beliefs and moved to the new colony of Liberia. He later became governor of the neighboring colony of Las Palmas. During his seventeen years as governor, Russwurm introduced currency and established education programs. He eventually merged his colony with others to create the Republic of Liberia. He died in Las Palmas in 1851. Although he did not live to see the emancipation of America's slaves, he contributed to the struggle for freedom and raised questions about self-determination that African Americans continue to debate today.

Russwurm resided in Portland between 1812 and 1827. The house, one of two sites in Maine directly related to African American history, is listed in the *National Register of Historic Places.*

DATE OF SIGNIFICANCE: Russwurm residence, 1812–1827

ADDRESS: 238 Ocean Avenue, Portland

VISITING HOURS: Private residence; visitors may drive by

SOURCES: Telephone call June 10, 1994, Maine Office for Historic Preservation. NRHPINF. *International Library of Negro Life and History,* 68. The Academic American Encyclopedia.

Works Consulted

The Academic American Encyclopedia. New York: Grolier, 1993. [electronic version]

African-American Studies at Bowdoin. Brunswick, Maine: Bowdoin College, Nov. 1990. [brochure]

Anchor of the Soul. Shoshanna Hoose and Karine Odlin, prods. Distr. by Northeast Historic Film. Buckport, Maine. 1994. [videotape]

An Architectural and Historical Survey of the Gardiner Area. Augusta, Maine: Maine Historic Preservation Commission, 1984. [booklet]

Bowdoin, The Offer of the College: The Bowdoin Viewbook 1993–1994. Brunswick, Maine: Office of Admissions and the Office of Communications, Bowdoin College, 1993. [booklet]

International Library of Negro Life and History: Historical Negro Biographies. Wilhelmena S. Robinson. New York: Publishers, 1970.

National Register of Historic Places. Washington, D.C.: National Park Service, 1976.

Uncle Tom's Cabin. Harriet Beecher Stowe. Bantam Books. 1981.

The Underground Railroad in New England. Richard R. Kuns and John Sabino, eds. Boston: American Revolution Bicentennial Administration, Region I, with Boston 200, the Bicentennial and Historical Commissions of the Six New England States and the Underground Railroad Task Force, 1976.

Massachusetts

Amherst

W. E. B. Du Bois Library, Special Collections and Archives

The University of Massachusetts at Amherst houses an outstanding collection of papers by and about W. E. B. Du Bois, an African American who was a Harvard University graduate, scholar and author, and a leader in establishing the NAACP and its journal, *The Crisis*. In an era when many leaders advocated an industrial model of education for Black students, Du Bois insisted on a quality classical curriculum, especially for the talented tenth of Black students who would lead others of the race in the struggle for equality.

The Special Collections Archives is located in the University of Massachusetts, Amherst, main library, recently renamed the W. E. B. Du Bois Library. The collection spans the years from 1803 to 1979 (1877 through 1963 for Du Bois's own writings) and includes manuscripts and printed versions of his speeches, newspaper columns and articles, pamphlets and leaflets, book reviews, petitions, essays, nonfiction books, and an eighty-nine-reel microfilm collection.

ADDRESS: University of Massachusetts, 154 Hicks Way, Amherst
TELEPHONE: (413) 545-2780, or (413) 545-0150
VISITING HOURS: Mon.–Fri. 10–3
SOURCES: Daniel Lombardo, curator of special collections, Jones Library, Inc. Telephone conversation June 11, 1994, Lori Mestere, education reference librarian, University of Massachusetts. Telephone conversation Jan. 20, 1995, Mike Milewski, archives assistant, Special Collections and Archives.

Ashley Falls

Colonel John Ashley House

The Ashley House, the oldest dwelling in Berkshire County, was home not only to a prominent white family, the Ashleys, but also to Elizabeth Freeman, a slave who changed the course of Black history in Massachusetts. Freeman was the first African American to win freedom under a court test of the Massachusetts Bill of Rights. The 1760s decision, known as *Brom & Bett* v. *Ashley,* was a landmark civil rights case.

The Ashley property, owned by John and Hannah Ashley in the eighteenth century, stood in an area of farmland, meadows, and the winding Housatonic River. John Ashley—a Yale graduate, attorney, surveyor, and justice of the peace—owned more than 3,000 acres of land. Although he had Black servants, John, Zack, and Harry, John Ashley appeared to have had some sentiment against the institution of slavery. He had been brought up in the tradition of the Congregational Church, which opposed slavery as an institution. His church urged slave owners to treat their slaves as indentured servants. John Ashley, in his will, referred to John, Zack, and Harry as servants rather than as slaves.

Mrs. Ashley, however, had a different, more harsh view of slavery. She had grown up with the beliefs of the Dutch Reformed Church, which taught that God approved the enslavement of Black people. Although Mr. and Mrs. Ashley had different beliefs, he may have accommodated himself somewhat to her beliefs, perhaps because of her strong personality. A neighbor, Catharine Sedgwick, once referred to Hannah Ashley as a "shrew untamable."[1] The harshness of Mrs. Ashley's character led to the conflict that caused Elizabeth to seek her freedom.

In September 1735 John Ashley married Hannah Hogeboom and purchased two children on the slave market, Elizabeth (later known as "Mum Bett") and her younger sister Lizzie, to serve as maids to his wife in her new home. The field and household servants lived in an east wing of the house, which had its own fireplaces for heat and cooking. Elizabeth became indispensable in the household and was respected as a nurse, midwife, friend, and counselor to the village children.

In the late 1760s, the Massachusetts Bay Colony was planning to adopt a new constitution. When Colonel Ashley and his friends discussed the details of the proposed constitution, Elizabeth served refreshments to visitors in the upstairs meeting room and listened. One day Mrs. Ashley became enraged at some transgression of Lizzie, Elizabeth's younger sister, and reached out with a red-hot kitchen implement to burn the girl. Elizabeth moved between the two and received the blow herself, suffering a severe burn on her arm. Although she had been a slave for thirty years, she left the house at once, walking three miles in freezing weather to the home of a neighboring family, the Sedgwicks.

Citing the provisions of the new Massachusetts Constitution of 1780 and its Declaration of Rights clause, Elizabeth asked Theodore Sedgwick to go to court on her behalf. She told him that she had overheard that the clause specified that all men were born free and equal. Sedgwick was surprised at Elizabeth's knowledge because he knew she was illiterate. When he asked how she knew about the provisions of the Constitution, she replied that she had learned by keeping still and minding things. Sedgwick took the case, even though he was John Ashley's friend. Ashley appeared to welcome the test case and did nothing about his wife's demand that Elizabeth should be brought back to their household. In fact, he resigned his lifetime appointment as a judge because he did not want a conflict of interest in a case in which he was part of the lawsuit.

Because women had no standing in court, a Black man called Brom was made codefendant with Bett. Sedgwick and another attorney, Reeve, argued that slavery had never received legal sanction in Massachusetts, and that regardless of the prior situation, slavery was now outlawed by the Declaration of Rights of the new Constitution. They won the case and won a later appeal, setting a precedent in the arena of human rights in Massachusetts. Brom and Bett were freed. Bett took the name Elizabeth Freeman at some point.

Theodore Sedgwick later became a judge, a member and speaker of the Continental Congress, a member of the United States House of Representatives, and a Justice of the Massachusetts Supreme Court. Even though Hannah Ashley never again allowed Sedgwick to enter her house, he and John Ashley remained friends.

The Ashleys pleaded with Elizabeth to return to their household, but she refused and went to work, instead, in the Sedgwick household. There she remained, a loved, respected, and valued member of the household, for twenty years. She later bought land in Stockbridge and raised a large family of children and grandchildren. Elizabeth Freeman died in 1792 at the age of eighty-five and was buried in the Sedgwick family plot in the old burying ground at Stockbridge next to Catherine Maria, the Sedgwick daughter.

The Ashley House is a museum today, open to visitors. The house, now the property of The Trustees of Reservations, has been moved one-quarter mile to its present location, and has been restored to its early character.

DATE BUILT: 1735

ADDRESS: Cooper Hill Road, Ashley Falls

TELEPHONE: (413) 229-8600

VISITING HOURS: Memorial Day–last Tues. in June, Sat.–Sun. and holidays 1–5; last Wed. in June–Labor Day, Wed.–Sun., and Mon. that fall on holidays 1–5; day after Labor Day–Columbus Day, weekends and holidays 1–5; days subject to change

FEES: Adults, $5; children 6–12, $2.50; members and children under 6, free; groups, reduced fees

SOURCES: Lisa McFadden, assistant director for public information, The Trustees of Reservations. Telephone conversation May 21, 1994, and Aug. 9, 1995, Don Reid, western regional ecologist, The Trustees of Reservations. Telephone conversation Jan. 20, 1995, Mark Miller, editor, *The Berkshire Eagle. Webster's New Biographical Dictionary,* 900. *W. E. B. Du Bois: Biography of a Race. The Ashleys: A Pioneer Berkshire Family.* "Mum Bett's Heroism." "A Monument to History and High Purposes."

Boston

Black Heritage Trail™*

The Black Heritage Trail is a walking tour of fourteen Black history structures known formally as the Boston African American National Historic Site. The fourteen structures on the trail were constructed before the Civil War and represent the largest grouping of pre-Civil War Black historic sites in the United States.

Among the structures are the African Meeting House, the oldest standing Black church in the United States, the Abiel Smith School, and the Phillips School, which was integrated in 1855.

Boston's first African Americans arrived as slaves in 1638, eight years after the city was founded. However, by the end of the Revolutionary War, more free Black individuals than slaves lived in Boston. By the nineteenth century, most of the city's African Americans had their homes in the West End between Pinckney and Cambridge Streets and between Joy and Charles Streets in an area known today as Beacon Hill's north slope. Many of their leaders lived in this community, including Prince Hall, founder of the African American Lodge of Masons.

Slavery was outlawed in Massachusetts by the end of the 1700s. By 1790 the federal census recorded no slaves in Massachusetts, the only state in the Union at that time to have no slaves recorded. Thus, African Americans belonged to a free Black community. They were concerned with improving their social and educational status and abolishing slavery in the rest of the country.

The sequence for visiting the sites as recommended in the *Black Heritage Trail* brochure is the African Meeting House, Smith Court Residences (and the house on Holmes Alley), Abiel Smith School, Middleton House, Robert Gould Shaw and Fifty-fourth Regiment Memorial, Phillips School, Smith House, Charles Street Meeting House, Lewis and Harriet Hayden House, Charles Street A.M.E. Church, and Coburn's Gaming House. Visitors also may take a guided tour led by rangers from the National Park Service. Of the fourteen sites in the historic area, five are listed in alphabetical order and described in greater detail. Four are associated with nineteenth-century African American leaders, and one is associated with soldiers who served in the Civil War. The following sites that have a briefer overview are listed in sequence by proximity. They are included for their historical value and for their architecture that shows how African Americans lived in this nineteenth-century Boston community. Of sites on the Black Heritage Trail, only the African Meeting House and the monument to Robert Gould Shaw and the Fifty-fourth Massachusetts Colored Infantry Regiment are public; the rest are private and may be viewed from the street.

In the nineteenth century there were alleys where back yards stand today; the alleys in the middle of the blocks contained houses. **Number 7A in Holmes Alley** is to the rear of Number 7 on Smith Court and is similar to several other houses that once stood in Holmes Alley. A mariner and a hairdresser once lived in 7A.

The **George Washington House** at 5 Smith Court was built between 1815 and 1828. Washington, a laborer and a deacon in the African Meeting House, purchased the house in 1849. The Washington family, which included nine children, lived in the upper part and rented out the first floor.

The **Joseph Scarlett House** at Number 10 Smith Court was originally owned by Black chimneysweep and entrepreneur Joseph Scarlett. Built in 1853, this house is next to the African Meeting House. Scarlett owned fifteen real estate parcels at the time of his death and left bequests to the African Methodist Episcopal Zion Church and to the Home for Aged Colored Women.

The **George Middleton House** at 5–7 Pinckney Street was built in 1797. Two Black men, George Middleton and Lewis Glapion, were the original owners. This is the oldest existing home on Beacon Hill built by an African American. Middleton was a veteran of the American Revolution and led an all-Black company from Boston, the Bucks of America, one of two all-Black units in the Continental Army.

The **Phillips School** at Anderson and Pinckney Streets was built in 1824. Until 1855 the school was open only to white children. When the state legislature abolished separate schools in 1855, this became one of Boston's first integrated schools.

The **John J. Smith House** at 86 Pinckney Street belonged to a man who was born free in Virginia in 1820 and moved to Boston at the age of twenty-eight. Smith's barber shop, at the corner of Howard and Bulfinch Streets, became a center for Black abolitionists and fugitive slaves. Smith worked in Washington, D.C., as recruiting officer for the all-Black Fifth Cavalry during the Civil War. He was elected between 1868 and 1872 to the Massachusetts House of Representatives and later was appointed to the Boston Common Council. Smith, who died in 1906, lived at this address from 1878 to 1893.

Charles Street Meeting House, at the corner of Mt. Vernon and Charles Streets, was built in 1807 for the white Third Baptist Church of Boston (later known as the Charles Street Baptist Church). In the mid-1830s an abolitionist member, Timothy Gilbert, challenged the segregated seating patterns in the church by bringing some Black friends into his pew. Expelled from the church, he with other white abolitionists founded Tremont Temple, one of America's first integrated churches.

The **Charles Street African Methodist Episcopal Church** used the old meeting house on Charles Street until 1939. The last African American institution to leave Beacon Hill, it moved in 1939 to Dorchester, a district of Boston, where it is located today.

John Coburn was born in Massachusetts in 1811 and worked as a clothing dealer. He hired Boston architect Asher Benjamin to design **Coburn's Gaming House** at Phillips and Irving Streets, which was built in 1843–1844, as a home for himself, his wife Emmeline, and his adopted son Wendell. He also established there a private gaming house. Emmeline Coburn died in 1872. When John Coburn died the following year, he left substantial holdings of real estate and cash, a testament to his financial acumen.

DATE BUILT: 19th century

ADDRESS: Sponsored by the Museum of Afro-American History located in Abiel Smith School, 46 Joy Street, Boston

TELEPHONE: (617) 742-1854

VISITING HOURS: Visitors can see the exteriors from street; rangers from the National Park Service lead guided tours Memorial Day–Labor Day at 10, noon, and 2 starting at the Robert Gould Shaw and Fifty-fourth Massachusetts Colored Infantry Regiment Monument at Beacon and Park Streets

FEES: None; donations are appreciated

SOURCES: Telephone conversation June 11, 1994, Kevin Wall, park ranger. The Black Heritage Trail concept was devised by Sue Bailey Thurman and refined by J. Marcus and Gaunzetta L. Mitchell. Marilyn Richardson, curator, Museum of Afro-American History. Maurice Nobles Jr., site manager, African Meeting House. Representative Byron Rushing, Commonwealth of Massachusetts, House of Representatives. NRHPINF. *Black Heritage Trail. A Documentary History of the Negro People in the United States,* 221, 244, 320–1, 336–41, 357–9, 376–7, 406, 481. *Before the Mayflower,* 171. *African Americans: Voices of Triumph,* Vol. 1, *Perseverance,* 65. *The Underground Railroad in New England.*

African Meeting House

The Museum of Afro-American History is the owner of the African Meeting House, the oldest extant Black church structure in the United States. Built in 1806 to accommodate the First African Baptist Church, it was the center of Boston's Black community for more than ninety years.

In the early nineteenth century members of the Black community needed a church of their own—in white churches they were required to sit in a segregated gallery and were denied voting privileges. Then Reverend Thomas Paul, a Black preacher from New Hampshire, began leading worship meetings for African Americans in Boston's Faneuil Hall. In 1805 Reverend Paul and the twenty members of his congregation purchased land in the West End; a year later they completed the African Meeting House, making it the first Black church in the United States.

The three-story brick building was designed by Asher Benjamin, an architectural designer of Federal-style buildings throughout Boston's Beacon Hill area. Located on Beacon Hill, which at one time was the heart of Boston's Black community, the church was constructed almost entirely by Black labor. Its two-story interior contained meeting space with a gallery on three sides. Ironically, when the congregation dedicated the new building in December 1806, Black members chose to sit in the gallery and reserved the seats below for white worshipers who had been friends to the Black community.

Beginning in 1808 the basement of the African Meeting House served as a school for Black children. It was the site of so many historic meetings that during the abolitionist era the building was called the Abolition Church and the Black Faneuil Hall. Here, in 1832, white abolitionist William Lloyd Garrison and his followers founded the New England Anti-Slavery Society, New England's first abolitionist organization. Frederick Douglass; U.S. Senator Charles Sumner, a white man who was a passionately outspoken member of the antislavery movement; and women's rights advocate Maria Stewart, an African American teacher and speaker who opposed slavery, racism, and sexism, were some of the noted Americans who spoke from the African Meeting House platform. When Black Americans finally received authorization to serve in the Civil War, members of the Massachusetts Fifty-fourth Regiment enlisted here. This regiment was portrayed in *Glory,* a much-acclaimed book and motion picture.

The congregation remodeled the Meeting House in the 1850s. By the end of the nineteenth century, the Black community had begun to migrate to the South End and Roxbury. They sold the building to a Jewish congregation, which used it as a synagogue until it was purchased by the Museum of Afro-American History.

This national historic site has been restored to its appearance in the mid-1850s and is open to the public. The red-brick, Federal-style structure, symbol of the early search for independence, now is called the Museum of Afro-American History. Although there are changing art exhibits inside, the primary emphasis is the historic structure itself.

DATE ESTABLISHED:	Congregation, 1805; Meeting House, 1806
ADDRESS:	8 Smith Court, Boston
TELEPHONE:	(617) 742-1854
VISITING HOURS:	Mon.–Fri. 10–4; closed New Year's Day, July 4 Thanksgiving, Christmas
FEES:	None; donations are appreciated

Lewis and Harriet Hayden House

This four-story building was home to Lewis and Harriet Hayden, outstanding Boston citizens of the nineteenth century. Lewis was born a slave in Kentucky in 1816 but escaped on the underground railroad. He and his wife, Harriet, lived in Detroit before moving to Boston. This home was built in 1833, and the Haydens moved into the dwelling about 1849.

Lewis Hayden became a leader in Boston's abolitionist movement. The Hayden home became a haven for fugitive slaves, even though passage of the 1850 Fugitive Slave Law imposed severe penalties for providing such assistance. Hayden operated underground railroad activities from his home and from his store on Cambridge Street. When William and Ellen Craft escaped from slavery by posing as master and slave, they lived for a period in the Hayden house. Craft and his wife first met as slaves in Macon, Georgia. Both had been separated from their families in childhood, and both yearned to live in a place where they would be able to raise and protect their own children. Ellen's skin was nearly white, and they based their escape on a plan in which Ellen would disguise herself as a white gentleman while William would pose as her slave. The dangerous plan worked, and they lived in Philadelphia and, for a period, in Boston. Other fugitive slaves as well were sheltered here. In one of the boldest actions in defiance of the Fugitive Slave Law, in 1851 Hayden and other Black men forcibly rescued a slave named Shadrach from United States custody.

When Harriet Beecher Stowe came to Boston to seek material for her *Key to Uncle Tom's Cabin,* she visited the Hayden home, and thirteen fugitive slaves were brought into a room for her to see.

Lewis Hayden was a leader in the Black community's efforts to become politically active and to gain equality of rights. When Boston's Jim Crow school, the Abiel Smith School, was closed in 1855, Hayden was one of those who sponsored a dinner honoring William Nell, who had led the struggle to close the school.

Hayden served as a recruiting agent for the Fifty-fourth Regiment during the Civil War. His only son died serving in the Union Navy. Hayden, who was one of two Black men elected to the state legislature in 1873, died in 1889. Harriet Hayden, who survived her husband, provided in her will a scholarship for African American students at Harvard Medical School.

DATE BUILT:	1833; Hayden residence, from c1849
ADDRESS:	66 Phillips Street, Boston
VISITING HOURS:	Private; visitors may walk or drive by

William Nell House

White bricklayers built this residence in 1799. Around 1825 or 1830 Black families rented the double house with its common entryway. William Nell, a prominent community activist and possibly the first published Black historian in America, boarded here from 1851 to 1856. Nell served on many committees that sought to gain equality for Black people, including one that sought rights for Black Americans in seafaring occupations. Beginning in 1822, after a slave rebellion led by Denmark Vesey, several states passed laws forbidding free Black seamen to leave their ships when at port. In 1842 Nell, with other African Americans in Boston, protested the laws and petitioned the Massachusetts legislature and the U.S. Congress to pronounce such laws unconstitutional.

Nell, who once had studied law, was one of the primary leaders in the pre-Civil War struggle to integrate Boston's public schools. For years Boston's Black community had petitioned the school committee to allow their children to attend school in the community where they resided, but the committee voted to continue separate schools. The African American parents held a series of mass meetings in 1844 and adopted a resolution recommending withdrawal of their children from Abiel Smith School, the only school Black students were allowed to attend. By 1849 Boston's abolitionists, led by William Nell, had collected funds to hire Charles Sumner as attorney to plead their case. Unfortunately the Boston court ignored Sumner's plea and delivered a "separate but equal" decision. Nell continued to lead the group in sit-ins and stand-ins until the state legislature finally passed a law banning segregation in schools.

Nell joined Boston citizens in protesting slavery and in protesting the ban on allowing Black Americans to serve in the U.S. Army. In 1865 an African American clothing dealer, James Scott, purchased the house.

DATE BUILT: 1799; Nell residence, 1851–1856
ADDRESS: William Nell House, 3 Smith Court, Boston
VISITING HOURS: Private; visitors may walk or drive by

Robert Gould Shaw Memorial Fifty-fourth Massachusetts Colored Infantry Regiment Monument

In 1863 President Lincoln's administration first allowed Black soldiers to officially join the Union forces in the Civil War. The North's first Black regiment was recruited in Massachusetts and was commanded by Robert Gould Shaw, a young white officer. Black men were eager to serve as soldiers. They understood that freedom for African Americans could depend on the outcome of the battle. Distinguished African Americans were involved in the recruiting, including the great Black abolitionist Frederick Douglass, who wrote a lengthy editorial in his newspaper on March 2, 1863. The editorial, entitled "Men of Color, to Arms!" said in part:

> There is no time to delay. The tide is at its flood that leads on to fortune. From East to West, from North to South, the sky is written all over, "Now or Never," "Liberty won by white men would lose half its luster." "Who would be free themselves must strike the blow." "Better even die free, than to live slaves." This is the sentiment of every brave colored man amongst us. . . .
>
> The day dawns; the morning star is bright upon the horizon! The iron gate of our prison stands half open, . . . while four millions of our brothers and sisters shall march out into liberty. The chance is now given you to end in a day the bondage of centuries, and to rise in one bound from social degradation to the plane of common equality with all other varieties of men.[2]

In July 1863 the all-Black regiment led an attack on Fort Wagner in South Carolina. The new troops were tired from marching and had received little food for two days. Nevertheless, they showed magnificent bravery in battle. Under the leadership of Colonel Shaw and under crossfire from Confederate guns, ninety men with Shaw made their way to the parapet of the fort. Shaw was killed and half of the 600 men in his regiment were killed, wounded, or taken prisoner.

Although the regiment was not successful in taking the fort, it had distinguished itself at Fort Wagner. Sergeant William Carney earned the Congressional Medal of Honor because he had saved the American flag from the Confederates by wrapping it around his body. He was one of nine Black men to be awarded the Congressional Medal of Honor during the Civil War. (See the listing for Carney House in New Bedford, Massachusetts.) That flag is now on display in the State House Hall of Flags in Boston.

Joshua B. Smith initiated the collecting of funds to build the memorial to the regiment. Smith, a fugitive from North Carolina, had worked in the Shaw household. He became a state representative in 1873–1874. Sergeant Carney, veterans of the Fifty-fourth and Fifty-fifth Regiments and the Fifth Cavalry, and speakers including Booker T. Washington were present for dedication ceremonies in 1897.

DATE OF SIGNIFICANCE: July 1863; monument dedicated 1897
ADDRESS: Memorial: entrance to the Boston Common, Beacon and Park Streets; State House Hall of Flags, Beacon Street across from the Memorial, Boston

VISITING HOURS: Memorial always accessible; Memorial Day–Labor Day, starting point for tour of Black Heritage Trail sites at 10, noon, 2; Hall of Flags, Mon.–Fri. 9–5

Abiel Smith School

Prince Hall, an African American leader in Boston, petitioned the Massachusetts legislature for access to the public school system for Black children. After this petition and others presented by Black parents were denied, the parents organized a grammar school. The school first met in a Beacon Hill home but moved in 1808 to the basement of the African Meeting House.

In the 1820s, the city of Boston established two primary schools for Black children. White businessman Abiel Smith left a bequest to the city for the education of Black children, and in 1834 the Abiel Smith School was constructed. The Smith School replaced the Meeting House School and served Black children from all over the city of Boston.

In 1848 Benjamin Roberts sued for the right of his daughter Sarah to attend any of the five white schools that stood between his home and the Smith School. Roberts sued on the basis of an 1845 statute that provided recovery of damages for any child unlawfully denied public school instruction. William C. Nell, a Black leader in the struggle to integrate the schools, sought the aid of abolitionists in obtaining funds to have the well-known abolitionist Charles Sumner represent Sarah Roberts. The case was a lengthy one, and Sumner and the Black community lost. Nell and his association then initiated a boycott, asking all of the Black parents to remove their children from the segregated schools. Within six months the state legislature passed a bill ending segregation in public schools in Massachusetts. In appreciation a dinner was given in honor of William C. Nell for his long efforts in leading the struggle to abolish segregated schools in Boston.

Black children were permitted to attend the school closest to their homes, and in 1855 the Smith School closed. For many years the building was used to store school furniture. In 1887 Black Civil War veterans began to use the building as their headquarters. Abiel Smith School currently is used for offices of the Afro-American History Museum and the National Park Service. Museum leaders hope to restore the interior and open the school to the public.

DATE BUILT: 1834

ADDRESS: 46 Joy Street, corner of Smith Court, Boston

TELEPHONE: (617) 742-5415

VISITING HOURS: Tours of interior not currently available; National Park Services offices on upstairs level, daily, 9–5 Memorial Day–Labor Day and Mon.–Fri. Labor Day–Memorial Day; closed Christmas, Thanksgiving, other holidays; closings vary, so check ahead

FEES: None; donations are appreciated

Bunker Hill Monument

During the American Revolution Black soldiers were among those who fought in an important battle that took place in Boston's Charlestown district. The site was actually Breed's Hill, but the battle is mistakenly known today as the Battle of Bunker Hill, after the name of a neighboring hill.

Among the Black soldiers who fought in this battle were Salem Poor, Peter Salem, Pomp Fisk, and George Middleton. Peter Salem's owner—a man who owned property at Framingham, Massachusetts—granted Peter his freedom so that he could fight in the Continental Army of the American colonists. By some accounts Peter Salem fired the shot that killed the British commander, Major Pitcairn.

Both Peter Salem and Salem Poor were cited as outstanding soldiers in this action. Fourteen officers later commended Poor for his bravery, commenting that he behaved like an experienced officer. His officers presented a petition to the

General Court of Massachusetts in 1775, saying, "We would only beg leave to say, in the person of this said negro, centers a brave and gallant soldier."[3] Poor later served in the battles at Valley Forge and White Plains.

Each year thousands of visitors come to see the Bunker Hill Monument, which is located in the Charlestown neighborhood of Boston. A lodge contains a diorama and other displays depicting the battle that took place on Breed's Hill. There are booklets, a free brochure, and an interpretive talk by a ranger. From the lodge visitors proceed to the monument itself, a 221-foot-high obelisk with 294 steps to the top. Those who are hardy enough to reach the top are rewarded with a view of the land on which the battle was fought. Although there is little to see and hear about Black history at this site, visitors have information from this entry about the role of some of the African Americans in the battle.

DATES OF SIGNIFICANCE: Battle, June 17, 1775; monument built 1827–1842, dedicated 1843

ADDRESS: Breed's Hill (from downtown Boston follow the Freedom Trail Line, painted on the street pavement, across bridge, past Charlestown Naval Yard), Monument Square, Charlestown District, Boston

TELEPHONE: (617) 242-5641

VISITING HOURS: Daily including holidays 9–5

FEES: None

SOURCES: Telephone conversation May 26, 1994, Joe Damico, park ranger. Telephone conversation June 11, 1994, Emily Prigot, interpretive ranger. *Before the Mayflower,* 62, 64. *International Library of Negro Life and History,* 28, 30.

Bunker Hill Pavilion

After seeing the Bunker Hill Monument and the land where the battle actually took place, visitors may wish to see a multimedia show that portrays some of the sights and sounds of the battle. The show, called *Whites of Their Eyes,* contains 1,000 slides, 14 screens, and 7 channels of sound.

DATE OF SIGNIFICANCE: 1775

ADDRESS: 55 Constitution Road, Charlestown (from Boston, follow the red line in the pavement, the Freedom Trail line, from the Boston Common to nearby Bunker Hill Monument)

TELEPHONE: (617) 241-7575

VISITING HOURS: Daily 9:30–4; shows every half hour starting at 9:30

FEES: Adults, $3; senior citizens, $2; children, $1.50; special school and group rates

SOURCE: Mary J. Morrissey, supervisor.

Charles Street African Methodist Episcopal Church

Charles Street African Methodist Episcopal Church is one of the historic Black churches in Boston. It is located in the Roxbury section of Boston in a residential neighborhood of Queen Anne and Victorian houses. A white congregation, Mount Pleasant Congregational Church (All Souls Church), erected the building in 1888–1889. In 1939 the Charles Street A.M.E. Church bought the building.

The African American congregation originated before Civil War days, meeting on Anderson Street in Boston. They held many antislavery meetings at the earlier site that included such outstanding speakers as Frederick Douglass, William Lloyd Garrison, and Wendell Phillips. The congregation owned the Charles Street Meeting House on Beacon Hill from 1876 through 1939. As population patterns changed and African Americans began to move from Beacon Hill to Roxbury, the Charles Street Church was the last Black congregation to leave Beacon Hill.

Architect J. Williams Beal designed the Roxbury church that the Black congregation purchased. He used a combination of Gothic-revival and Tudor-revival elements. The exterior features local materials such as Roxbury puddingstone and Quincy granite trim. The interior is finished in cypress. Although some of the stained-glass windows were removed when the church was sold in 1939, some remain, including windows by John LaFarge, an outstanding nineteenth-century stained-glass designer. The sanctuary, a broad, low space, has varnished wainscoting and roof timbers. The ceiling is supported by a complicated system of rafters and beams.

DATE BUILT: 1888–1889; purchased by African American congregation, 1939
ADDRESS: 551 Warren Street at Elm Hill Avenue, Boston
TELEPHONE: (617) 427-1298
VISITING HOURS: Office, Mon.–Fri. 10–4; Sun. services, 8, 11
FEES: None
SOURCES: Candace Jenkins, preservation planning director. Telephone conversation May 26, 1994, Lisa Radcliffe, secretary. NRHPINF.

Faneuil Hall*

Faneuil Hall originally was built as a market and meeting hall. It was given to the city by a merchant named Peter Faneuil in 1740. Destroyed by fire in 1761, it was rebuilt two years later and then enlarged and restored during the nineteenth century. The building was a focal point for Boston citizens protesting against English rule. Among the five men killed by British soldiers in Boston on March 5, 1770, the first to die was a Black man, Crispus Attucks. (See the listing for Old Granary Burying Ground in Boston.) Three days after the massacre a public funeral was held with a large procession starting from Faneuil Hall where the five men had lain in state.

Faneuil Hall became an important focal point for religious meetings of the African American community and for meetings of nineteenth-century abolitionists. Thomas Paul, a Black preacher from New Hampshire, led worship meetings here for the Black community. In 1805 his twenty-member group formed the First African Baptist Church. In that same year they purchased land and began building the African Meeting House (which still stands in Boston). Black abolitionist Frederick Douglass was a speaker at Faneuil Hall. Black Bostonians met here in 1850 and formed the Black Vigilance Committee to provide assistance to fugitive slaves. In August 1907 W. E. B. Du Bois addressed an audience of about 800 at Faneuil Hall at the third annual meeting of the Niagara Movement.

Faneuil Hall is a brick, three-story building with an octagonal cupola. It has a great hall on the second floor. This historic building currently is used as both a marketplace and a museum.

DATE BUILT: 1740–1742
ADDRESS: Faneuil Hall Square, Merchants Row, Boston
TELEPHONE: (617) 635-3105, or (617) 242-5675
VISITING HOURS: Mon.–Fri. 10–5

FEES: None

SOURCES: *National Register of Historic Places*, 345. *W. E. B. Du Bois: Biography of a Race*, 339. *The Negro in the Making of America*, 52.

Farwell Mansion/League of Women for Community Service

This fine old brownstone mansion twice has played a role in Black history—once as a site on the underground railroad and again, for the past seventy-five years, as the home of the League of Women for Community Service.

William Rice Carnes built the mansion about 1858. He had built another home nearby, but that one did not meet his high standards; he believed this represented his better effort. The mansion had gold and brass chandeliers and hand-carved furnishings.

The house is of interest in Black history because abolitionists hid fugitive slaves at this site. If they anticipated a dangerous situation, they would send the fugitives to the original Carnes mansion, which was kept in total darkness to make it appear uninhabited. The fugitives would be returned to this site at 558 Massachusetts Avenue when the danger was over.

Boston was a center of abolitionist activity, and the Farwell House, as it was known for the family that purchased it from the Carnes estate, was only one of many places in which slaves were hidden. Many Black abolitionists lived on Beacon Hill (then called West End) in the nineteenth century, and the African Meeting House was the center of many abolitionist meetings. White abolitionist William Lloyd Garrison lived in Roxbury.

The Farwell house was empty for about ten to fifteen years before it was purchased by an African American organization, the League of Women for Community Service, a benevolent society that used the house for many years as a temporary residence for young women.

DATE BUILT: c1858

ADDRESS: 558 Massachusetts Avenue, Boston

TELEPHONE: Answering service, (617) 536-3747

VISITING HOURS: By appointment; closed June and July

SOURCES: Telephone conversation May 22, 1994, Muriel Turk, League of Women for Community Service. Telephone conversation May 25, 1994, Jacqueline Arrington, League of Women for Community Service. *The Underground Railroad in New England.*

Museum of the National Center of Afro-American Artists

The Museum of the National Center of Afro-American Artists highlights contemporary and historical Afro-American art in displays that include thousands of items of African, African American, and Caribbean art. The structure housing the museum is worth seeing, too. Resembling an old stone castle, it was originally the Oak Bend mansion that was built in the early 1870s by Aaron Davis Williams. The 20,000-square-foot mansion is constructed of Roxbury puddingstone and Nova Scotia sandstone and is one of the best examples of neo-Gothic architecture in Boston. At a cost of more than $365,000, it was the most expensive house in Boston at the time of construction. The old "castle" served as a residence until the mid-1920s when it became a school for boys with discipline problems. Later it became an annex to the David Ellis School. The building closed and fell into ruin until the museum acquired it in the mid-1970s and began the still-ongoing process of restoration; the museum occupies half of the mansion. Visitors can also enjoy the surroundings that include a large lawn shaded by oak trees and surrounded by a low stone wall.

DATE ESTABLISHED: 1969
ADDRESS: 300 Walnut Avenue, Boston
TELEPHONE: (617) 442-8014
VISITING HOURS: Tues.–Sun. 1–5; closed New Year's Day, Thanksgiving, July 4, Christmas
FEES: Adults, $1.25; students and senior citizens, $.50; members, free
SOURCES: Edmund Barry Gaither, curator/director. Telephone conversation May 26, 1994, Mr. Gaither.

Old Granary Burying Ground

The Old Granary Burying Ground has a place in Black history because among the victims of the Boston Massacre buried here is Crispus Attucks, the first person to die in the struggle against Britain that led to the War of Independence.

In 1770 the antagonism between British troops and Black and white patriots reached a peak in Boston. The city was tense as a result of numerous fights and skirmishes. On March 5, as some soldiers emerged from their barracks near the center of town, a crowd gathered, trading insults with the soldiers and taunting them with snowballs and stones. Among the crowd was a Black man, Crispus Attucks (c1723–1770), who had escaped from slavery and had worked for twenty years as a merchant seaman.

According to one report, when the crowd began to draw back, Attucks rallied them to continue and a fight broke out. Soon the fire bell rang at the Old Brick Meeting House, and more frightened and angry citizens joined the crowd. The British troops panicked and opened fire. Attucks was the first to fall in the conflict that later became known as the Boston Massacre. A plaque in the middle of State Street commemorates the massacre.

The Old Granary Burying Ground, which contains the remains of Paul Revere and John Hancock, also contains the bodies of the five victims of the massacre. Crispus Attucks is further honored by the Crispus Attucks Monument, which citizens of Boston erected in 1888 on the Tremont Street side of the Boston Common.

DATE OF SIGNIFICANCE: Mar. 5, 1770
ADDRESS: Park Street District, Tremont, Park, and Beacon Streets, Boston
VISITING HOURS: Daily, dawn–dusk
SOURCES: *Before the Mayflower,* 61. *National Register of Historic Places,* 346. *International Library of Negro Life and History,* 8.

Dorchester

William Monroe Trotter Home

William Monroe Trotter was born in 1872 to a life of privilege in a Black family of Boston. He excelled in his studies and was elected president of his senior class at Hyde Park High School. After spending a year as a shipping clerk, Trotter attended Harvard College, graduating *magna cum laude* in 1895. He was the first African American elected to the Phi Beta Kappa chapter at Harvard.

The 1890s were a period of racial tensions and hatreds. Intimidation and a tangled web of restrictive laws were used to bar African Americans from voting. The 1896 U.S. Supreme Court decision in the *Plessy* v. *Ferguson* case established the infamous "separate but equal doctrine." Under it, Louisiana was entitled to segregate Black travelers in railroad cars. This decision led to a court-approved system of segregation for the next sixty years.

During the 1890s white Americans were raising Booker T. Washington to national prominence. They approved of his statements that the races could remain separate and that Black people should not concern themselves with political power, and they supported Washington's emphasis on industrial training in schools for Black students.

Trotter, however, vigorously opposed such ideas. He spoke out for political involvement against segregation, becoming more militant as he saw racist views spreading from the South into the North. In 1901 Trotter helped organize the Boston Literary and Historical Association, which served as a forum for expressing militant political opinion.

That same year Trotter and his friend George Forbes founded *The Guardian,* a weekly newspaper that opposed compromises on civil rights. Trotter spoke out against Booker T. Washington's ideas, which he believed relegated African Americans to a lower place in society, and he insisted on the right to vote as essential for achieving power.

On July 30, 1903, Booker T. Washington was the featured speaker at the Columbus Avenue African Zion Church in Boston. As Washington started to speak, Trotter stood on a chair and attempted to read nine questions he had prepared concerning Washington's program. Trotter and his sister were arrested, leaving Washington free to deliver his speech. The press, giving widespread coverage to the incident, called it the "Boston riot."

Trotter's sentence of thirty days in jail drew national attention to his views and encouraged another leader, W. E. B. Du Bois, to join forces with him. Trotter continued to work for justice, forming another group, the Boston Suffrage League, and assisting in founding the Niagara Movement in 1905. (See the listing for Harpers Ferry, West Virginia.) However, he would not join the 1909 initial meeting of the NAACP because he believed the association was dominated by white people.

Since Trotter devoted so much time to civil rights causes, he had less time for his business. As a result, he eventually lost the property inherited from his father and the house on Dorchester Avenue where he had lived from 1899 to 1909. He slipped into poverty, and many of his old friends abandoned him.

Although he lived in poverty, Trotter continued to fight energetically for better conditions for African Americans in *The Guardian.* Twenty thousand people from thirty-six states signed a petition on civil rights that he drafted and presented to President Woodrow Wilson. Although Trotter met twice with the President, Wilson made no commitment for a change.

When the Paris Peace Conference convened in 1919, Trotter was denied a passport that would have allowed him to attend and to place the plight of Black people before the world's leaders. Despite this setback, he found a job as a cook on a transatlantic steamer in order to reach France. There he attended the conference as a delegate of the National Equal Rights League and presented the cause of African Americans. Neither President Wilson nor the newly created League of Nations gave any response to Trotter's plea to end racial discrimination. In America conditions continued to deteriorate as white groups in 1919 took up arms against Black people in cities throughout America. Trotter continued his work, speaking out for racial justice before a Senate committee and supporting an antilynching bill.

Trotter's later years were overshadowed by financial problems and other disappointments, yet he never flinched from speaking out and never drew back from working for justice for African Americans. William Monroe Trotter died in April 1934. His home is listed as a national historic site.

DATE OF SIGNIFICANCE: Trotter residence, 1899–1909

ADDRESS: 97 Sawyer Avenue, Dorchester

VISITING HOURS: Private, visitors may drive by

SOURCES: NRHPINF. *Before the Mayflower,* 329–30, 333. *International Library of Negro Life and History, Historical Negro Biographies,* 154, 254–5.

Framingham

Old Burial Ground

Framingham was home to two Black men who gained fame in the Revolutionary War period. One was Crispus Attucks; he was born a slave but escaped from his owner in 1750. Attucks was the first person killed in the Boston Massacre, one of a series of events that led to the Revolutionary War. (See the entry on the Old Granary Burying Ground in Boston.)

The other Black man from Framingham was Peter Salem, whose master freed him so that Peter could serve in the Continental Army. Peter took part in the first conflicts of the Revolutionary War at Lexington and Concord in 1775. Later that same year Peter Salem and another Black man, Salem Poor, showed outstanding courage at Breed's Hill, in the conflict known today as the Battle of Bunker Hill. Peter is credited with shooting the British commander, Major Pitcairn, at Breed's Hill.

Peter Salem died in Framingham and was buried in that city.

DATE ESTABLISHED:	Prior to 1698
ADDRESS:	Main Street, Framingham
TELEPHONE:	Framingham Historical Association, (508) 872-3780; Framingham Public Library, (508) 879-3570
VISITING HOURS:	Daily dawn–dusk
FEES:	None
SOURCE:	Bonita M. Bryant, corresponding secretary pro tem, Framingham Historical & Natural History Society.

Great Barrington

W. E. B. Du Bois Boyhood Home

William Edward Burghardt Du Bois, one of the most brilliant scholars of his time, was born on Church Street in New Barrington on February 23, 1868, the son of Alfred Duboise and Mary (according to his birth certificate). Although there may have been fewer than thirty Black families in the village, Du Bois had a strong attachment to the region; he claimed that Burghardts had lived there for more than 200 years.

Du Bois spent the first seventeen years of his life in Great Barrington. Before he was two years old, however, his parents' marriage failed and his father left; his mother then had to leave the child with his grandparents on South Egremont Road. When Willie (as he was called then) was five years old, his grandfather died and his grandmother, Sarah, had to sell the family property to pay debts. She moved in with Willie's mother and his half-brother Adelbert above some stables on an estate south of Main Street. The family moved again, to a run-down house near the tracks on Railroad Street that they shared with a poor white family. By the time Du Bois was in high school, some townspeople who were interested in his family's welfare helped them to find a small house to rent on Church Street; it was located behind the property of a white family, the Casses.

Du Bois's mother encouraged him to do well in school. No one in his family had attended school beyond the elementary level, but he showed promise. The only Black student in his high school, he was recognized as the outstanding scholar in his graduating class. He attended Fisk University on a scholarship, graduating in 1888, then continued his studies at Harvard University, where he received his bachelor's degree with honors in philosophy in 1890.

Du Bois began studying for a doctorate degree at Harvard University. Before completing his dissertation at Harvard, he studied at the University of Berlin for two years. In 1895 he became the first African American to receive a Ph.D. degree from Harvard University. Harvard published his Ph.D. dissertation.

Du Bois began writing and publishing at an early age. He also taught at Wilberforce University in Ohio, the University of Pennsylvania, and Atlanta University. While teaching in Atlanta, he began to challenge the views of Booker T. Washington, who had recommended industrial training rather than a classical education. Du Bois believed that Washington's curriculum prepared for manual-labor careers rather than for leadership positions that would challenge the status quo. Moreover, Du Bois believed that Washington was too accommodating of racial segregation. In contrast, Du Bois sought to educate the "talented tenth" of Black people through a rigorous classical education. His ideas were widely influential at many Black colleges and universities.

In 1905 Du Bois called for a national meeting of leaders to initiate the Niagara Movement, which was superseded in 1909–1910 by the NAACP. In 1910 he became founder and editor of the NAACP magazine, *The Crisis.* Because of his independent stance, Du Bois at times came into conflict with NAACP fellow directors. In 1934 he resigned from the NAACP and returned to Atlanta University for a decade.

For most of his career Du Bois was interested in Africa. He gathered and shared valuable information about the European colonies in Black Africa and served as a consultant on matters about Africa.

In 1958 Du Bois made his fifteenth trip abroad, visiting the Soviet Union and the People's Republic of China. In 1961 he applied for membership in the American Communist Party and accepted an invitation from President Kwame Nkrumah of Ghana to reside in Ghana. He became a citizen of Ghana in 1963 and died there the same year. He was given a state funeral and buried in Accra.

The outspoken scholar, Du Bois, was the great-grandson by marriage of another intelligent, respected, and outspoken African American, Elizabeth Freeman. (See the listing for the Colonel John Ashley House in Ashley Falls, Massachusetts.)

Du Bois owned the Burghardt house from 1928 to 1954. He never acquired great wealth, and his friends, recognizing his love for the place in Great Barrington, purchased his boyhood home for him. The two-story clapboard house where he once lived is no longer standing. The property is a park today, five acres of land in an open field, clustered with pine, maple, and elm trees.

DATE OF SIGNIFICANCE:	1868–c1885
ADDRESS:	North side of MA 23, between Great Barrington and South Egremont Streets, Great Barrington
VISITING HOURS:	Privately owned, but accessible to the public as a park during daylight hours
FEES:	None
SOURCES:	Mr. Walter Wilson, W. E. B. Du Bois Memorial Foundation. NRHPINF. *W. E. B. Du Bois.*

Lynn

Jan Ernst Matzeliger Monument

A monument in Lynn honors the Black man who invented the mechanical shoe-lasting machine. As a young man, Jan Matzeliger worked for several years to perfect a machine that made possible the routine mass production of shoes. He worked on his model in between his regular working hours in a shoe factory. The device Matzeliger created was credited with improving wages and working conditions for thousands of people. While the manual method of shoemaking produced only fifty pairs of shoes a day, Matzeliger's method could turn out 150 to 600 pairs.

Matzeliger was born in 1852, the son of a Dutch colonial engineer father and a Black Guianese mother in Dutch Guiana (now Suriname). At the age of ten, he began an apprenticeship in his father's machine shop. At age nineteen, he left home to become a sailor and earned his passage to the United States. He worked in Philadelphia for five years, and then came to Lynn. He attended evening school and went to work in Lynn's major industry, the shoe industry. Matzeliger had worked in a shoe factory in Philadelphia, but in Lynn he began the painstaking process of creating a machine that could automatically fit leather over the sole of a shoe. Before his invention, this task had to be completed by hand.

Although he worked fourteen years to perfect the process, Matzeliger never gained the major financial benefit from his invention. He had to sell the majority ownership in the device to finance its production. The U.S. Shoe Company was the beneficiary and became the industry leader. Matzeliger died in 1889 of tuberculosis at the age of thirty-six.

ADDRESS: Pine Grove Cemetery, Boston Street, Lynn
TELEPHONE: (617) 593-0563
SOURCES: *I Have a Dream,* 25. *Webster's New Biographical Dictionary,* 666. *Hippocrene U.S.A. Guide to Black America,* 167. *International Library of Negro Life and History,* 99.

Nantucket

African Baptist Society Church

The historic African Baptist Church in Nantucket, built in 1830, may be the second-oldest surviving Black church in the United States. The church is a rectangular building with a double-door entrance. Its origins are associated with people from the west coast of Africa. In 1826 trustees of the African Baptist Society bought land at Pleasant and York Streets, and sea captain Absalom Boston and four of his crew built the church. Boston, who also put up a home for himself on Nantucket Island, had an all-Black crew on his ship, *Harmony.* The crew were representative of the many African Americans who worked aboard whaling vessels in the nineteenth century.

The African Baptist Church became important to runaway slaves who had escaped by becoming stowaways on vessels sailing north from Maryland and Virginia. Upon reaching Nantucket the runaway people became free. Many of them settled in a small area west of Orange Street and south of Silver Street known as New Guinea. There they developed their own community with shops, stores, and the African Baptist Church. The church provided a place of worship, a school, and a meeting center. From 1847 to 1888, the years when the church was active, Reverend James Crawford, also a barber, served as its minister.

The whaling industry prospered until 1850 or 1860 when the sailing ships became obsolete as steamships replaced them. Now unemployed, some of Nantucket's African Americans left for New Bedford or other ports. This may explain why the church ceased to operate by 1888.

In 1911 C. Chase bought the church for $250. He installed large garage-type doors, strengthened the floors, extended the building so that trucks could be parked inside, and transformed the house of worship into a warehouse and garage.

In 1933 Florence Higginbotham bought the church for $3,000 from the estate of Henry Chase. The building could have been torn down, but Mrs. Higginbotham's son, who was attending a

Black preparatory school in North Carolina at the time, learned the history of the building in a Black history course. Years later he donated the building to Boston's Museum of African-American History. Although the church is not yet open to visitors, the Boston museum intends to restore it and to research the history of the Africans who established it.

DATE ESTABLISHED: c1827

ADDRESS: North side of York Street at corner of Pleasant Street, Nantucket

TELEPHONE: Boston Afro-American Museum, (617) 742-1854

VISITING HOURS: Interior not open to public, but visitors can walk or drive by; contact the museum to find out when the restoration will be complete

SOURCES: Nantucket Historical Association. Historic American Buildings Survey HABS No. MASS-909, 1967 Historic American Buildings Survey summer project on Nantucket, Massachusetts. "Hub Museum to Restore Black Church."

Nantucket Historical Association

The collection of the Nantucket Historical Association includes portraits of sea captain Absalom Boston and Arthur Cooper, two of Nantucket's most prominent Black citizens. The library and research center has detailed information on Nantucket's Black history, including diaries, letters, and newspaper clippings.

Nantucket was the birthplace of Lucretia Coffin Mott, a white advocate of Black rights and women's rights. Mott lived in Nantucket throughout her childhood years and often returned to the island. (For additional information about Mott, see the La Mott, Pennsylvania, listing.)

ADDRESS: Peter Folge Museum Building, Broad Street, Nantucket

TELEPHONE: (508) 228-1655

VISITING HOURS: Portraits and facilities by appointment Mon.–Fri. 10–3; closed holidays

FEES: $5 per day research fee

SOURCES: Elizabeth A. Codding, assistant curator, Nantucket Historical Association. Telephone conversation May 12, 1994, Peter MacGlashan, audiovisual librarian.

New Bedford

New Bedford Heritage Trail

Five sites in New Bedford show the history of the city's Black and Cape Verdean citizens. Many runaway slaves found the city of New Bedford hospitable and decided to live here instead of continuing to Canada. A second and distinct Black population originated with the Cape Verdeans who also arrived in New Bedford in the nineteenth century. They came from the dry and infertile Cape Verde Islands off the most western point of Africa; the islands were Portuguese territory until independence in 1975. They had functioned for centuries as a way station and slave depot on slave routes to the New World and had served as an administrative center for the Portuguese colony of Guinea. Ethnically the Cape Verdeans were Black Africans or Black/Portuguese who spoke Portuguese or a Creole form of Portuguese called "crioulo."

Many Cape Verdeans came to New Bedford on whaling ships in the late eighteenth and early nineteenth centuries, and some chose to settle in that important whaling port. There they sometimes disagreed over their identity. Catholic in religion and with a language based on Portuguese, many considered themselves Portuguese; the white population, on the other hand, often saw the Cape Verdeans as Black. During the 1970s, an era of emphasis on racial pride, some Cape Verdeans formed alliances with Black Americans. They shared a common heritage related to working in seafaring occupations.

A group of New Bedford's Black historical sites follow in alphabetical order. Tina Furtado, archivist at the New Bedford Free Public Library, notes that all of the sites can be viewed in a pleasant two-hour walk.

ADDRESS: Visitors Center, 42 S. Second Street, New Bedford

TELEPHONE: (508) 991-6200

SOURCES: Tina Furtado, archivist, New Bedford Free Public Library. *We The People*. The Academic American Encyclopedia.

Sergeant William H. Carney House

Sergeant Carney of the Fifty-fourth Massachusetts Volunteers was the first African American to win the Congressional Medal of Honor. In the Union assault on Fort Wagner, South Carolina, in 1863, Carney rescued the colors from the mortally wounded standard bearer. Even though severely wounded twice, Carney held the colors as he led a charge to the parapet.

The Carney house was built in 1850 and until 1939 was occupied by members of the Carney family. Today the small frame, story-and-a-half home is owned by the Martha Briggs Educational Club, a Black women's organization founded in 1920 to provide scholarships to young people. Although the house generally is not open to the public, it is open once a year for a week when the local historical association gives tours of New Bedford's historic sites.

DATE BUILT: 1850

ADDRESS: 128 Mill Street, New Bedford

TELEPHONE: New Bedford Preservation Society, (508) 997-6425; New Bedford Chamber of Commerce, (508) 999-5231; New Bedford Free Public Library, (508) 991-6278; New Bedford Library, (508) 991-6275

VISITING HOURS: Not open to public except once yearly during tour of historic homes

SOURCES: Telephone conversation June 12, 1994, Annette Morton, president, Martha Briggs Educational Club. *Historical and Cultural Atlas of African Americans*, 88. *Before the Mayflower*, 94.

Nathan Johnson Home

When New Bedford was a refuge for slaves who ran away via a sea route, this house was a safe haven and a stop on the underground railroad. One of the most famous fugitives to stay at this house was Frederick Augustus Washington Bailey who, at the age of twenty-one, escaped from slavery and arrived in Newport by sea with his wife. They were transported to New Bedford where they were sheltered by Nathan and Mary Johnson. Nathan Johnson was an officer in the Antislavery Society of New Bedford and his wife, Mary, ran a successful confectionary and catering business from the home.

Nathan Johnson was reading Sir Walter Scott's *Lady of the Lake* at the time of their visitors' stay, and Frederick Bailey, taking his new name from one of the characters of that book, became known from then on as Frederick Douglass.

DATE BUILT: Early 1800s
ADDRESS: 21 Seventh Street, New Bedford
VISITING HOURS: Private, visitors may drive or walk by
SOURCES: Telephone conversation May 21, 1994, Paul Cyr, curator, New Bedford Free Public Library. *The Underground Railroad in New England.*

Liberty Bell

Only a small piece of the old New Bedford liberty bell remains because most of it burned up in a fire. After the United States passed the 1850 Fugitive Slave Law that made it easier to capture slaves, New Bedford used this bell to warn escaped slaves of imminent danger. People would ring the liberty bell to warn the runaways when a schooner was on its way to capture fugitives.

DATE OF SIGNIFICANCE: 1850–Civil War
ADDRESS: Corner of William Street and Purchase Street, New Bedford
VISITING HOURS: Always accessible

New Bedford Whaling Museum

The New Bedford Whaling Museum has in its collection an example of a toggle harpoon invented by the Black metalsmith Lewis Temple. The contributions of other African Americans who participated in seafaring industries are also described in museum exhibits that include models of the vessels of shipbuilder John Mashow and the papers of wealthy sea captain Paul Cuffe. Mashow, who was born in South Carolina in 1805, was the son of an African American mother and a white father. His father sent him to New Bedford to learn the trade of ship building. Mashow became New Bedford's second-largest builder of whaling ships. Although he was talented enough to establish his own shipyard at the age of twenty-seven, his business was destroyed nearly thirty years later by an oversupply of whale oil on the market. The man and his accomplishments were nearly forgotten when he died in 1893.

ADDRESS: 18 Johnny Cake Hill, New Bedford
TELEPHONE: (508) 997-0046
VISITING HOURS: Mon.–Sat. 9–5, Sun. 1–5
FEES: Adults, $4.50; senior citizens, $3.50; children 6–14, $3; children under 6, free
SOURCES: Telephone call to site May 21, 1994. *African Americans*, 92.

Lewis Temple Statue

Lewis Temple, a Black metalsmith who operated a whalecraft shop in New Bedford, invented the toggle harpoon in 1848. Unlike older harpoons that often slipped out allowing the whale to escape, Temple's toggle device snapped shut and anchored firmly at a right angle. Although the harpoon greatly increased the whalers' profits, Temple did not patent his invention, and like Jan Matzeliger of Lynn, he did not benefit from his work. As a result, Temple died in poverty. Today he is honored with a statue crafted by Black sculptor James Toatley. The statue is located in front of the New Bedford Free Public Library. As one faces the library, Temple's statue is on the left; on the right is a statue of a whaleman holding the toggle harpoon invented by Temple.

ADDRESS: 613 Pleasant Street, New Bedford
TELEPHONE: (508) 991-6275
VISITING HOURS: Statue always visible
FEES: None
SOURCES: Telephone conversation May 21, 1994, Ernestine Furtado, archivist, and Paul Cyr, curator, New Bedford Free Public Library. *African Americans*, 92.

Newton

Jackson House

Many sites of the underground railroad have been identified by oral tradition but lack specific written documentation. In contrast, the Jackson House has been identified and described as such a site by an account written in 1874 by Ellen D. Jackson. Jackson told how the women of Newton used to hold sewing circles at the house to prepare clothing for fugitive slaves. Because slave owners often searched Boston for their slaves, the fugitives were often sent west of Boston to make the connection to Canada. Notice of their arrival was signaled by pebbles tossed against the window. The family rushed the visitors inside. If there was danger nearby, they hid the fugitives between two chimney supports and covered the area with boards and sacks of vegetables.

Today the house serves as the Newton City Museum, where interpreters describe the Jackson family role in the abolitionist movement. To school groups, interpreters tell about specific families who made their way to Massachusetts or Canada, and they describe the Jackson family's role on the local Vigilance Committee.

ADDRESS: 527 Washington Street, Newton
TELEPHONE: (617) 552-7238
VISITING HOURS: Mon.–Thurs. 1–5
FEES: Adults, $2; children, $1
SOURCES: Telephone conversation May 21 and May 24, 1994, Susan Abele, director. *The Underground Railroad in New England.*

Roxbury

Dillaway–Thomas House

According to oral tradition passed on by older members of the Roxbury Historical Society, the Dillaway–Thomas House, built as a parsonage by Reverend Oliver Peabody between 1750 and 1754, served as a station on Boston's underground railroad. A hidden trapdoor in the kitchen and other evidence of the underground railroad have been destroyed by a major fire in the house. The house still stands, however, and is now a part of the Roxbury Heritage Park. Located on the north side of John Eliot Square, the dwelling at one time was called Dillaway House because it was occupied by a Roxbury teacher named Charles K. Dillaway.

Before the fire occurred, the author, having heard that the Dillaway House—then boarded up and empty—was a part of the underground railroad, made a request to the Roxbury Historical Society to open the house for her inspection. Although the interior was interesting with its wide floorboards and large kitchen fireplace, the most meaningful area was the hidden trapdoor. It totally resembled the other floorboards in the kitchen, but once grasped in a certain way, it lifted to reveal in the darkness below a small rectangular area where fugitive slaves were hidden. To see such a place was an extremely moving experience. Unfortunately, knowledge of the hiding place seems to have been forgotten.

The site is operated today by the state of Massachusetts as part of the Roxbury Heritage State Park. Community groups use the house for community activities and exhibits and the garden area for concerts. The gambrel-roofed structure has retained its exterior appearance. The interior has been extensively remodeled, but sections of the original have been retained to show how it once looked. It is located in the Roxbury town square, also called John Eliot Square, an area of nineteen buildings from the eighteenth and nineteenth centuries. The John Eliot Square District is listed in the *National Register of Historic Places.*

DATE BUILT: 1750
ADDRESS: John Eliot Square, 183 Roxbury Street, Roxbury
TELEPHONE: (617) 445-3399
VISITING HOURS: Wed.–Fri. 10–4, Sat.–Sun. 12–5, or by appointment
SOURCES: Personal visit to site c1965. Telephone conversation May 28, 1994, Walter Vaughn of the Dillaway–Thomas House. *National Register of Historic Places,* 348.

William Lloyd Garrison House

William Lloyd Garrison (1805–1879), who was born in Newburyport, Massachusetts, was a well-known white abolitionist. He was born in poverty, and once was an indentured servant.

Although Garrison began his work as an abolitionist by advocating the gradual emancipation of the slaves, he became more radical in his views over time. Influenced by Black people, he founded *The Liberator,* an antislavery journal published between 1831 and 1865. The well-known journal was influential in making the antislavery cause known. Individuals in Black communities were among the newspaper's strongest supporters. In the first years of publication, almost 90 percent of its subscribers were African Americans.

Considered a radical abolitionist, Garrison founded the American Anti-Slavery Society in 1833 and was the society's president between 1843 and 1865. The first board of managers of this society included five Black abolitionists.

Garrison was well known to Black abolitionists of the day. They communicated with each other on a regular basis, discussing how best to end the institution of slavery. When the American Colonization Society proposed relocating numbers of Black Americans to Africa, Black abolitionists helped turn Garrison and other white abolitionists against that idea.

Garrison lived in this house, a two and one-half–story frame structure with clapboarding, from 1864 to 1879.

DATE BUILT: 19th century
ADDRESS: 125 Highland Street, Roxbury
VISITING HOURS: Private, visitors may walk or drive by
SOURCES: *Webster's New Biographical Dictionary,* 388. *National Register of Historic Places,* 348. *Before the Mayflower,* 144, 152, 153.

Salem

Peabody Museum of Salem

The Peabody Museum, founded in 1799 by Salem sea captains, contains in its collections some artifacts from African culture that the captains had brought back to their home port. One exhibit, *Tribal Style,* is a selection of artifacts from the museum's sub-Saharan art collection. The exhibit includes sculpture, masks, utensils, musical instruments, and weapons —priceless documents of a vanished way of life.

DATE ESTABLISHED: 1799
ADDRESS: East India Square, Salem
TELEPHONE: (508) 745-1876
VISITING HOURS: Mon.–Sat. 10–5, Thurs. 10–9, Sun. 12–5; closed Thanksgiving, Christmas, New Year's Day
FEES: Adults, $4; children 6–16, $1.50; senior citizens and students, $3
SOURCE: Ellen Soares, Peabody Museum of Salem.

Westport

Paul Cuffe Monument

Paul Cuffe was born in 1759 near New Bedford, Massachusetts, to a former slave father and an Indian mother. The family lived on a marginal farm as he grew up and had few material resources. As a young man Paul went to sea. Earning money from whaling, ship building, transporting whale oil and whalebone to Europe, and retail storekeeping, he became one of the wealthiest Black men of his day.

At the age of forty-nine, Cuffe became a member of the Society of Friends. Attending services at the Friends' Meeting House in Westport, he soon established personal and business ties with his Quaker associates. According to his own account, in 1813 he advanced over $500 in materials toward the total cost of $1,198.08 needed to build the present meeting house in Westport.

Cuffe gained an international reputation for his efforts to advance the cause of Black settlement in Sierra Leone and trade with that African nation. His work in furthering trade with Africa brought him to the attention of President James Madison. Cuffe's petition for special trading privileges to Africa received a favorable vote in the U.S. Senate.

Cuffe also sought gains in minority rights in Massachusetts. With other African Americans he submitted petitions to local and state governments seeking tax relief. The petitioners reasoned that African Americans and Indians should not have to pay taxes if they were not allowed to vote. Although the petitions were rejected, a court decision in 1783 eventually granted African Americans the right to vote.

The Friends' Meeting House in Westport, built in part through Cuffe's generosity, is open to visitors today. Cuffe, who died in 1817, was buried in the adjacent cemetery. The Society of Friends dedicated the monument at his grave, and a plaque in the town hall honors his memory.

DATE BUILT: c1813
ADDRESS: 938 Main Street, Westport
TELEPHONE: (508) 636-4963
VISITING HOURS: Call to arrange to see interior
SOURCES: Telephone conversation May 21, 1994, Jean Kennisor, member of the Westport Monthly Meeting of Friends. NRHPINF. *National Register of Historic Places,* 332–3.

Notes

1. Arthur M. Chase, *The Ashleys: A Pioneer Berkshire Family* (Ashley Falls, Mass.: The Trustees of Reservations, 1978), 20.

2. Frederick Douglass, "Men of Color, to Arms!" *Frederick Douglass's Paper* (Mar. 2, 1863), quoted in Herbert Aptheker, ed., *A Documentary History of the Negro People in the United States,* vol. 1 (New York: Citadel, 1990), 478–9.

3. Wilhelmena S. Robinson, *International Library of Negro Life and History: Historical Negro Biographies* (New York: Publishers, 1970), 28.

Works Consulted

The Academic American Encyclopedia. New York: Grolier, 1993. [electronic version]

African Americans: Voices of Triumph. Vol. 1, *Perseverance.* Alexandria, Va.: Time-Life, 1993.

African Americans: Voices of Triumph. Vol. 2, *Leadership.* Alexandria, Va.: Time-Life, 1993.

The Ashleys: A Pioneer Berkshire Family. Arthur C. Chase. Ashley Falls, Mass.: The Trustees of Reservations, 1978.

Before the Mayflower: A History of Black America. 5th ed. Lerone Bennett Jr. New York: Penguin, 1988.

Black Heritage Trail. Byron Rushing and Staff of the Museum of Afro-American History. Boston: Boston National Historical Park, National Park Service. [brochure]

A Documentary History of the Negro People in the United States. Vol. 1. Herbert A. Aptheker, ed. New York: Citadel, 1990.

Hippocrene U.S.A. Guide to Black America: A Directory of Historic and Cultural Sites Relating to Black America. Marcella Thum. New York: Hippocrene, 1992.

Historical and Cultural Atlas of African Americans. Molefi K. Asante and Mark T. Mattson. New York: Macmillan, 1991.

"Hub Museum to Restore Black Church." Diana Lewis. *Boston Globe* (6 Feb. 1989).

I Have a Dream: A Collection of Black Americans on U.S. Postage Stamps. Washington, D.C.: U.S. Postal Service, 1991.

International Library of Negro Life and History: Historical Negro Biographies. Wilhelmena S. Robinson. New York: Publishers, 1970.

"A Monument to History and High Purposes." Hal Borland. *The Berkshire Evening Eagle,* 3 Sept. 1958.

"Mum Bett's Heroism." Gerard Chapman. *The Berkshire Eagle,* 24 Feb. 1987.

National Register of Historic Places. Washington, D.C.: National Park Service, 1976.

The Negro in the Making of America. Benjamin Quarles. New York: Collier, 1987.

The Underground Railroad in New England. Richard R. Kuns and John Sabino, eds. Boston: American Revolution Bicentennial Administration, Region I, with Boston 200, the Bicentennial and Historical Commissions of the Six New England States and the Underground Railroad Task Force, 1976.

We the People: An Atlas of America's Ethnic Diversity. James Paul Allen and Eugene James Turner. New York: Macmillan, 1988.

W. E. B. Du Bois: Biography of a Race. David Levering Lewis. New York: Henry Holt, 1993.

Webster's New Biographical Dictionary. Springfield, Mass.: Merriam-Webster, 1988.

New Hampshire

Jaffrey

Amos Fortune Homestead and Burial Site

Amos Fortune (1710–1801) was an African-born slave who was brought to Massachusetts as a youth. Sold at auction at the age of sixteen, he lived as a slave until he was able to purchase his freedom at the age of sixty. Having acquired expert skills in tanning hides, Fortune moved to Jaffrey, New Hampshire, where he established his own tannery. There he lived frugally, saving his money and using it to purchase freedom for other Black slaves. One of these slaves was a woman named Violate, whom he later married. He died a man well-respected in Jaffrey for his fine work and his achievements in life. In his will he left funds to the church and school in the town.

Today, many schoolchildren learn about Fortune by reading the book *Amos Fortune, Free Man*. Although the account is interesting and often moving, some statements may lead children to develop negative stereotypes. Black children could be devastated by reading the description of all African tribes as pagan (p. 5) or by reading that after two months at sea the Africans were forgetting their language and could make only meaningless sounds (p. 26–27). Caleb Copeland, the Quaker who bought Amos, described him as part-animal, one who would run wild without the white people's influence. Caleb's wife described Amos as a poor, black lamb, a description that could be excruciatingly humiliating to a Black child. These types of statements would lead to outrage in some Black communities that are trying to instill pride of heritage in their children; the statements detract from positive aspects of the story. Sensitive and aware teachers and parents who use the book may want to explain, when reaching these statements, that the author, writing in another era, inserted some bigoted ideas that were once widely held about African Americans.

Today's visitors can see the Amos Fortune Homestead on a road named in 1995 for Fortune. Fortune purchased the land in 1789 and probably erected the house and barn soon after. Today the small, white Cape Cod cottage and the barn are private, but visitors can drive by. Tyler Brook, a waterway used by Fortune for tanning purposes, still serves as the boundary line for Fortune's homestead. With advance notice, the Jaffrey Public Library will display for visitors some original documents relating to Fortune, a compass that he owned, and the book *Amos Fortune, Free Man*.

The gravestones of Amos Fortune and his wife are in the Meeting House Cemetery at Jaffrey. His inscription reads,

> Sacred to the memory of Amos Fortune,
> who was born free in Africa a slave
> in America he purchased liberty,
> professed Christianity,
> lived reputably
> and died hopefully,
> Nov. 17, 1801, Aet. 91.

The stone for Fortune's wife reads,

Sacred to the memory of Violate
by sale the slave of Amos Fortune
by marriage his wife
by her fidelity his friend and solace
she died his widow.
Sept. 13, 1802, Aet. 73.

DATE BUILT: House, c1789

ADDRESS: Amos Fortune Homestead, 19 Amos Fortune Road (from town center take NH 137 to Amos Fortune Road, turn right); Meeting House Cemetery (Old Burial Ground), follow NH 124 west to Jaffrey Center, turn right at flashing light (behind the meeting house is a stable, and the cemetery is behind the stable); Jaffrey Public Library, 38 Main Street, Jaffrey

TELEPHONE: Jaffrey Public Library, (603) 532-7301

VISITING HOURS: House private, visitors may walk or drive by; cemetery, always open; library Mon., Wed., Fri., 11–5:30; Tues. 1–8, Sat. 9–1

FEES: None

SOURCES: Alan F. Rumrill, Historical Society of Cheshire County. Telephone call to Jaffrey City Clerk's Office Aug. 22, 1995. Telephone conversation Aug. 26, 1995, Marilyn Simons, assistant librarian, Jaffrey Public Library. Telephone call Aug. 26, 1995, Tieger Realty Company, Jaffrey. *History of Jaffrey*, 752. *Amos Fortune, Free Man.*

Littleton

Carleton House

Edmund Carleton was a white attorney who served as a stationmaster on New Hampshire's underground railroad. Although Carleton was educated as a lawyer, he left the legal profession to begin operating a lumber business. Carleton was acquainted with the Boston abolitionist leader William Lloyd Garrison and kept one of the best collections of Garrison's antislavery newspaper, *The Liberator.*

Edmund and Mary Carleton were largely responsible for founding the Littleton Anti-Slavery Society in 1837. Carleton also defended two men, Nat Allen and Erastus Brown, who were arrested for interfering with church services by making abolitionist statements. The men rejected a choice of paying fines and were sent to the county jail.

ADDRESS: 32 Carleton Street, Littleton

VISITING HOURS: Not accessible to public; visitors can walk or drive by

SOURCE: *The Underground Railroad in New England.*

Works Consulted

Amos Fortune, Free Man. Elizabeth Yates. New York: Aladdin Books, 1951.

History of Jaffrey (Middle Monadnock). Albert Annell and Alice Lehtinen. Jaffrey, N.H.: Town of Jaffrey, 1937.

The Underground Railroad in New England. Richard R. Kuns and John Sabino, eds. Boston: American Revolution Bicentennial Administration, Region I, with Boston 200, The Bicentennial Commissions of the Six New England States and the Underground Railroad Task Force, 1976.

New Jersey

Burlington City

William R. Allen School

When the Civil War ended, New Jersey was divided on the issue of school segregation. A larger number of segregated schools were built in the state's southern counties than elsewhere in the state. The William R. Allen School is an example of one of New Jersey's segregated schools.

From the earliest time of their settlement in Burlington City, African Americans wanted schools for their children. As early as 1812 an African American teacher held classes in her home. By 1844 the state had begun to share public school funds with the Black community.

In 1866 Burlington City had built a frame school for Black children. The school was so small, however—approximately 20 feet square with a ceiling about 7½ feet high—that only forty of the city's 110 to 120 Black children were able to squeeze inside. Seeing that the school clearly was inadequate, two businessmen donated land in 1868 and the city constructed the Federal Street School. From 1870 to 1900 the new schoolhouse served as the city's only school for African American students. Although a few Black students were admitted to white schools, most attended the Federal Street School. High school was not a possibility for Black students—they were refused admission.

In 1900 the city built the William R. Allen school at the Federal Street site. The new brick school, with its three rooms, was larger than the old school, and between 1914 and 1924—a period when Black families migrated to Burlington City from the South—the school was enlarged. In spite of a 1940s state constitution that explicitly forbade school segregation, Allen's student body remained almost entirely African American until the school closed in the 1960s.

After closure, the William R. Allen School reopened to house special education classes from the 1970s until the early 1980s; then the building became vacant. Today community members are discussing ways to have the schoolhouse restored so that it may be open to the public in the future. Although the interior is not accessible, it is worth driving by to see the historic 1900 schoolhouse.

DATE BUILT: 1900

ADDRESS: Mitchell Avenue, Burlington City

VISITING HOURS: Private, visitors can drive by

SOURCES: NRHPINF. Conversation Mar. 24, 1994, Mark Henderson Jr., founder of MARABASH Museum. Conversation Mar. 26, 1994, Martha Henderson, president and founder, MARABASH Museum.

Fair Haven

African Methodist Episcopal Bethel Church

Free Black residents in Fair Haven organized two separate African Methodist Episcopal congregations before the Civil War. The St. James A.M.E. Zion congregation was formed in 1833, and its members built a church on the Port Washington Road that was destroyed by fire in 1873. The second church, Bethel A.M.E. Church, was organized in 1858.

When the Civil War ended, a group of African Americans came north and joined the Black population already established in this area. In 1882 General Clinton B. Fisk, the benefactor of Fisk University in Nashville, Tennessee, donated $3,000 for the erection of a chapel. He knew some members of the Black community at Fair Haven who worked on his estate in Rumson. Others were servants or farmhands in the community. Congregation members also donated money as well as their labor for the chapel, which was dedicated in 1882 and named in honor of General Fisk. A school for African American children was soon opened nearby. The school and its successor served Black children in Fair Haven for more than sixty years.

Fisk Chapel is the oldest religious building in the Rumson-Fair Haven area. The community not only used the building for religious services but also for meetings, concerts, and social activities.

The chapel is a 1,500-square-foot, white clapboard structure. It has Gothic windows, an exposed beam at each gable, and rose windows at each end of the building. The interior has four-foot-high mahogany-finished wainscoting and a tin ceiling painted white.

In the 1970s there were plans to demolish the chapel, but people mindful of its role in the past of the area saved it. It was moved to a residentially zoned site and dedicated in 1976 as a community center. The Fisk Chapel is listed in the *National Register of Historic Places.*

DATE BUILT:	1882
ADDRESS:	Lot No. 11, Cedar Avenue, Fair Haven
TELEPHONE:	Fair Haven city clerk, (908) 747-0241
VISITING HOURS:	Privately owned by Bethel A.M.E. Church, restricted access; call the city clerk for information
SOURCES:	NRHPINF. Telephone call to site, June 13, 1994.

Gloucester Township

Solomon Wesley United Methodist Church

Members of Solomon Wesley United Methodist Church still worship in the historic church constructed in 1850, and members of the founding Davis family still attend the church. One of two Black churches in Gloucester Township, Solomon Wesley is the only one remaining from the mid-nineteenth century. The church and its cemetery remain as symbols of African Americans who were given their freedom and who established the village of Davistown.

In his 1790 will, Daniel Bates left a mile-long parcel of land, $200, and freedom to Lindley Davis, a Black woman, and her family. The stretch of land grew into a Black village known as Davistown in which most residents were Davis family members who worked on nearby farms and marl pits.

In 1850 Zachariah and Catherine Davis deeded land to Solomon and Noble Davis and three other Black men for erecting a church and establishing burial grounds. Soon after, the leaders established Solomon Wesley Church as an African Wesleyan Methodist Episcopal Church.

Construction of the one-story church with clapboard siding encouraged the development of other facilities nearby. These included the camp meeting grounds and the Davistown Colored School, built beside the church in the 1870s. The school, which no longer stands, was the only one ever for Black children in Gloucester township.

Davistown had a population of between 100 and 200 residents at its height. However, the number of people in the village and in the congregation gradually decreased, and in the 1920s many of the founding families left Davistown. Modern homes replaced the early residences, leaving the one-story frame church and the cemetery to the rear of the church as symbols of the community's history. Members of the original Davis family, as well as veterans from the Civil War, Spanish War, and World Wars I and II are buried in the Solomon Wesley Cemetery. Solomon Wesley United Methodist Church is listed in the *National Register of Historic Places.*

DATE BUILT:	1850
ADDRESS:	292-B Davistown Road (Asyla Road), Blackwood, Gloucester Township
TELEPHONE:	(609) 232-9067
VISITING HOURS:	By appointment
SOURCES:	NRHPINF. Telephone conversation Mar. 27, 1994, Reverend Johann Arnold, pastor, Solomon Wesley United Methodist Church.

Jersey City

Afro-American Historical and Cultural Society of Jersey City

The African American Historical Society Museum has exhibits from Black culture and history with emphasis on the New Jersey region. Visitors will enjoy seeing a kitchen of the 1930s, Black dolls dating back to the early 1900s, and a cluster of musical instruments including steel pan, banjo, and assorted drums. A section of statuettes is called "Black Giants in History." Panel boards illustrate the history of slavery in New Jersey, Black women's history, and the story of African American fraternal associations. A section on Africa includes dolls and other artifacts. The collection also includes African and African American art, photographs of outstanding New Jersey citizens, and posters from the 1960s Civil Rights Movement. The museum, which sponsors films, guided tours, and lectures, is housed in the former home of a sea captain who made his fortune transporting slaves from Africa.

DATE ESTABLISHED:	1977
ADDRESS:	1841 Kennedy Boulevard, Jersey City
TELEPHONE:	(201) 547-5262
VISITING HOURS:	Tues.–Sat. 10–5; closed national holidays
FEES:	None; donations encouraged
SOURCE:	Telephone conversation Mar. 26, 1994, Theodore Brunson, director.

Manalapan

Monmouth Battlefield State Park

More than 800 African Americans were among the 13,000 Americans who fought at Monmouth during the Revolutionary War. One of the Black soldiers was Oliver Cromwell from Burlington, New Jersey, who fought throughout the war and who, at the age of one hundred, still remembered the battle at Monmouth. In 1783 his discharge signed by George Washington showed that he had received the Badge of Merit for long and faithful service.

Cromwell first volunteered to fight in the American Army as a twenty-year-old farm boy enlisting as a private in the Second New Jersey Regiment. He participated when General George Washington crossed the Delaware River on Christmas night 1776, and Cromwell fought in the January 3, 1777, battle in which Americans defeated the British in Trenton, New Jersey. On June 28, 1778, when Washington attacked the British near Monmouth Courthouse, New Jersey, the battle's outcome was not decisive. Major Charles Lee, under orders from General George Washington to attack the British rear defenses, failed to carry out orders as directed, thus giving the British the chance to withdraw and complete their march to the sea.

Today, the Visitors Center at Monmouth Battlefield State Park gives information about the battle. Although there are no guided tours or markers and the land is relatively undeveloped, visitors can see the rolling terrain much as it originally appeared. The Visitors Center gift shop, a focal point of the site, includes a panel that tells about the men of color who fought at Monmouth.

DATE OF SIGNIFICANCE:	June 28, 1778
ADDRESS:	347 Freehold Road (NJ Turnpike exit 8A, then right on NJ 33 East to the park), Manalapan
TELEPHONE:	(908) 462-9616
VISITING HOURS:	Park, daily, winter 9–4:30, spring 8–6, summer 8–8; Visitors Center, daily 9–4
FEES:	None
SOURCES:	Telephone conversation Mar. 26, 1994, Richard Walling, president, Friends of Monmouth Battlefield. *Black Heroes of the American Revolution,* 3–5. The Academic American Encyclopedia. *Men of Color at the Battle of Monmouth.*

Mount Laurel

Jacob's Chapel African Methodist Episcopal Church

Built in 1859, the original Jacob's Chapel is one of New Jersey's early Black churches. Although a newer structure stands close by, the congregation has lovingly preserved the historic building and uses it today for Sunday School and for special social occasions. They have even preserved, for history's sake, one of the two original outhouses (the other one was purchased). Although siding was added to the exterior, the original church has retained its basic appearance. The small, one-story building has three windows in front, an old-fashioned double door, and three windows on each side. The interior has wood paneling up to the windows. Some of the original pews remain, but they have a new placement to make room for tables in the main area. Dr. James Still, in the 1840s one of the first Black doctors in the state, is buried in the churchyard.

DATE ESTABLISHED: Congregation, 1813; church, 1859
ADDRESS: Elbo Lane, Mount Laurel
TELEPHONE: (609) 234-1728
VISITING HOURS: Sun. service, 10–1
SOURCE: Telephone conversation Mar. 27, 1994, Edith Cobb, stewardess and missionary.

Newark

State Street Public School

The State Street School, constructed in 1845 and one of the oldest school buildings in Newark, housed the Colored School of Newark between 1869 and 1873. James Miller Baxter Jr., the first Black principal in Newark's school system, was administrator of the State Street School at this site between 1869 and 1873. The school was later moved to three other locations as facilities grew inadequate at each site. However, the State Street structure is the only home of the school still standing. Having graduated with high honors from a Quaker-operated school, the Philadelphia Institute for Colored Youth, Baxter was offered a position in Newark at the age of nineteen. Two months later, he was appointed principal of the Colored School, a position he filled with distinction. Baxter improved the quality of the curriculum, established an evening school, and improved school facilities. He also was a community leader, a founder and Past Master in the Masons, a Congressional Convention delegate, and a member of the New Jersey Central Committee. The James M. Baxter Terrace, one of the city's first housing projects, was named in his honor.

Prior to 1872 Newark's public schools were segregated, and African American children were not permitted to enroll in secondary schools. Baxter and other Black community members successfully fought for the right of Irene Pataquam Mulford to become the first Black student to enroll in the Newark High School. Although Newark passed an ordinance in 1872 allowing Black children to enroll in schools throughout the city, the Colored School continued to operate until Baxter retired in 1909. The school's closing marked an end to segregated schools in Newark.

This two-story brick building is the oldest public school building still in use in Newark. State Street School contains eight classrooms, four on each floor. A newer 1882 addition has two classrooms on each floor, bathrooms, and a small kitchen. The school, with its wooden floors, transoms, and traditional school light fixtures, retains the atmosphere of a nineteenth-century schoolhouse. Today, the historic schoolhouse is home to the school district's art department.

DATE BUILT: 1845; addition, 1882
ADDRESS: 15 State Street, Newark
TELEPHONE: Art department, (201) 268-5188; school district, (201) 733-7333
VISITING HOURS: Call or write for appointment
SOURCES: NRHPINF. Telephone call to Newark School District Mar. 28, 1994.

Princeton

Witherspoon Presbyterian Church

William Drew Robeson, the father of Paul Robeson (see Paul Robeson site in New York City), was pastor of the Witherspoon Presbyterian Church between 1879 and 1899. His son, Paul, was born in Princeton, New Jersey, in 1898. Paul rose to prominence as an American actor, singer, and spokesperson for equality and justice. Although many white Americans rejected Paul Robeson because of the strong stand he took for dignity and justice, he continued to speak out for his beliefs.

The historic Witherspoon Congregational Church was founded in 1840; its members worship today in this white clapboard, one-story structure with a balcony. The site is significant as the church of an early Black congregation and as a church associated with the family of a gifted Black American, Paul Robeson.

DATE ESTABLISHED: 1840

ADDRESS: 124 Witherspoon Street, Princeton

TELEPHONE: (609) 924-1666

VISITING HOURS: Sun. service, 11; call to arrange to see the interior

FEES: None

SOURCES: The Historical Society of Princeton, New Jersey. Telephone conversation Mar. 27, 1994, Reverend John E. White, pastor, Witherspoon Presbyterian Church.

Red Bank

T. Thomas Fortune House

Thomas Fortune, Black leader, journalist, and outspoken advocate of the rights of African American people, owned and edited three newspapers: *New York Globe, New York Freeman,* and *New York Age.* Born in slavery in 1856 in Marianna, Florida, Fortune personally experienced discrimination and unjust treatment during slavery, Reconstruction, and the early part of the twentieth century. His strong reaction against bigotry led many to criticize his uncompromising and outspoken stance.

Fortune's father, Emanuel Fortune, had learned the basics of reading and writing as well as the trades of shoemaking and tanning, and he passed some of these skills on to his son. Emanuel also was politically active—so much so that his involvement in Reconstruction politics drew the wrath of local white citizens, including having the Ku Klux Klan place the family on a list of "troublemakers" and threaten their lives. The Fortunes gave up their profitable farm and escaped to Jacksonville, Florida, where they started anew. Thomas Fortune's mother died soon after this period.

Thomas attended Freedmen's Bureau Schools where he learned the printer's trade. At the age of thirteen he became a page in the State Senate; there he became aware of the political process that exploited Black people. He entered Howard University at the age of nineteen intending to study law. He married Carrie Smiley, and they lived for a period in Washington, D.C., but lack of funds forced him to withdraw from school and foreshadowed the financial difficulties that he would face throughout his adult years. Fortune began working for the *People's Advocate.* Then, in 1881, he started his own newspaper, the *New York Globe.* Soon his acrid criticism of Republicans for abandoning African Americans led many Black members of the Republican Party to withdraw their support for his newspaper; it failed within three years.

Undaunted, Fortune began publishing *Black and White* in 1884. He criticized both the white press for its distorted images of the Black community and the Supreme Court for declaring invalid the Civil Rights Act of 1875. Then financial difficulties caused him to shut down one newspaper after another, from the *New York Globe* to the *New York Freeman,* but he then went on to edit the *New York Age.* Still politically active, in 1887 he helped to establish the National Afro-American League, one of the forerunners of the National Association for the Advancement of Colored People. He also supported Black women in their crusade for better conditions in a period when poverty, lack of respect, and racial discrimination were widespread. When white townspeople destroyed the Memphis, Tennessee, newspaper office of Ida B. Wells, a Black antilynching crusader, Fortune offered her the use of the *New York Age* facilities so that she could continue her work.

Fortune's life of onerous financial burdens contrasted with that of the well-financed, nationally known educator Booker T. Washington. Washington believed as much as Fortune did in the need to uplift the Black race, but he was far more soft-spoken and accommodating in his words to the public. The two men worked together on some projects. Washington even contributed financially to Fortune's efforts and used Fortune's services at times as a ghostwriter, but their differences in approach led to an inevitable parting of ways. Perturbed at Fortune's seemingly radical comments, Washington warned him against making politically damaging statements, but Fortune continued to speak out. He lambasted racism in the Philippines and then turned to publicly criticizing President Theodore Roosevelt for his indictment of Black soldiers after a Brownsville, Texas, race riot. Finally, Washington withdrew financial support for the *New York Age* and severed his relationship with the journalist.

Fortune, now beset with difficulties, became depressed. He suffered an emotional breakdown and withdrew from public life, staying in his home on West Bergen Place. Then in 1915 he lost his home. He later worked for several newspapers, but he never regained his former stature.

Although Fortune was depressed at his apparent failures, he actually lived a worthy life. He shared vivid and prophetic insights. In his indictment of white newspapers he spoke words that are echoed in Black communities even today. He said such newspapers "are all on the side of the oppressor, or by silence preserve a dignified but ignominious neutrality. Day after day they weave a false picture of facts—facts which must measurably influence the future historian of the times in the composition of impartial history."[1] Timothy Thomas Fortune died in 1928, but many of his insights proved accurate, and questions and issues he raised are still being debated today.

The Thomas Fortune House, where the journalist resided from 1901 to 1915, was constructed between 1860 and 1885. Originally it was a two-story L-shaped building with living room, dining room, kitchen, and rear storage room on the first floor, three bedrooms on the second floor, and an unfinished attic. The structure was enlarged in 1917 and is listed in the *National Register of Historic Places.*

DATE BUILT:	1860–1885; purchased by Fortune, 1901
ADDRESS:	94 W. Bergen Place, Red Bank
VISITING HOURS:	Private, visitors may walk or drive by
SOURCES:	NRHPINF. *The Black 100.*

Somerville

Wallace House Historic Site

John Wallace was a wealthy merchant in Philadelphia who retired to this New Jersey location just as the Revolutionary War was beginning. He was sixty years old when he built and moved into Hope Farm. Few houses were built anywhere in the colonies during the war, and this two and one-half–story Georgian residence, white with green shutters, center hall, and elegant interior woodwork, was considered a fine residence in its day.

Some of the Wallace slaves—those who tended the house—lived in three small rooms above the kitchen. The rooms were approximately 8 feet wide by 8, 10, or 12 feet long. In his will John Wallace referred to two of the slaves as "my stock of negroes." Records indicate that one slave, Phyllis, was with the family for three generations; she was highly prized by the Wallace family for her skill in cooking and completing housework duties. Little is known about the slave named Greg other than that he was advertised for sale in 1788 along with a riding chair (an open, two-wheeled riding vehicle). For unknown reasons, Greg was not sold until 1791.

The slaves first were the property of John Wallace's mother-in-law; then they became Wallace's property. After the death of John's wife, Mary, in 1784 Greg and Phyllis passed into the hands of John's son, William Wallace. William died in 1796 and there are no records left to tell what happened to Phyllis after that date. There are no records either to describe the thoughts of the "highly prized" Phyllis—to tell what she thought of the family that valued her so highly through the generations for her usefulness as a servant. We do not know how often or how deeply she yearned for freedom.

The slave quarters are open on a limited basis. Because the staircase is fairly steep and winding, visitors are allowed only to look up the stairwell. However, there is a video tour of the second floor.

DATE BUILT:	1777
ADDRESS:	38 Washington Place, Somerville
TELEPHONE:	(908) 725-1015
VISITING HOURS:	Wed.–Sat. 10–noon, Sun. 1–4; closed holidays, Mon., Tues.
FEES:	None; donation appreciated
SOURCE:	Telephone conversation May 15, 1994, James Kurzenberger, historic preservation specialist.

Tenafly

African Art Museum of the S.M.A. Fathers

The African Art Museum of the S.M.A. Fathers (The Fathers of the Society of African Missions) contains one of the finest collections of African art in New Jersey. The large exhibition area houses more than 200 objects from sub-Saharan Africa including masks, statues, textiles, beadwork, and musical instruments.

The Society of African Missions was founded at Lyons, France, in 1856. Unlike some Christian missionaries who regarded African culture as inferior, members of the Society of African Missions sought to collect and preserve artifacts from West Africa. The collection includes works in wood, brass, bronze, and ivory. The objects show the

African reverence for life in their symbols of spiritual forces and fertility. For example, young girls in Ghana tucked wooden dolls in their clothing to ensure their own fertility and their children's health and beauty.

In addition, the museum has carvings of antelope horns that were worn as a headdress in dances and pageants by the Bamana people of Mali. The collection includes Ashanti gold weights made by the "lost wax" method of casting.

Children will enjoy this site; approximately 2,000 schoolchildren visit the museum every year. There is a self-tour for children. By calling in advance, a group can schedule a ninety-minute presentation in which objects are shown close up. This is followed by a tour of the museum.

DATE ESTABLISHED:	1978
ADDRESS:	23 Bliss Avenue (County Road 501—Grand Avenue or Engle Street—to Bliss Avenue), Tenafly
TELEPHONE:	(201) 567-0450
VISITING HOURS:	Daily 9–5
FEES:	None; donations accepted
SOURCES:	Charles Bordogna, curator. Telephone conversation Mar. 25, 1994, Dr. Richard A. Barrows.

Trenton

Washington Crossing State Park

In October 1775 the Continental Congress approved a resolution that barred Black men from serving in the newly formed American Army. One month later, however, Lord Dunmore, the royal governor of Virginia, promised freedom to all male slaves who would join the British troops fighting against the colonists. As a result of Dunmore's proclamation, General George Washington reversed the resolution of the Congress and instructed his recruiting officers to enlist Black men as soldiers. In January 1776 Congress approved this decision.

Two Black men, Prince Whipple and Oliver Cromwell, accompanied Washington during the crossing of the Delaware River in 1776. Whipple had been born in Africa and was sold into slavery at the age of ten in Baltimore. He was bought as a servant by a white man named William Whipple, who lived in Portsmouth, New Hampshire. William Whipple became a general and one of George Washington's aides in the American Revolution, and Prince Whipple served during the war as a trusted bodyguard to his owner. Cromwell, another African American, was a farmer who volunteered for the colonial army when he was twenty-one years old.

Whipple and Cromwell were among the men who marched over icy roads in freezing rain in this region. In one of the important victories of the war, Washington's small army defeated the British in a surprise attack at Trenton, suffering only five casualties among the American troops. Cromwell survived the war. When he died in January 1853, one of his most-treasured possessions was his discharge paper signed by Washington in 1783 at the end of the war. Prince Whipple was given his freedom after the war, but only after he and twenty other men protested to the New Hampshire legislature that they had been born free in Africa and that under provisions of the Declaration of Independence, they should be free. His wife and several children also gained their freedom as a result of the petition. Prince, however, died in New Hampshire soon after the war ended. An engraving at the Visitors Center shows Prince Whipple in General Washington's boat.

DATE OF SIGNIFICANCE: 1776

ADDRESS: 8 miles northwest of Trenton on NJ 29, then northeast on County Road 546 to the park

TELEPHONE: (609) 737-9140

VISITING HOURS: Park, Memorial Day–Labor Day daily 8–8, rest of the year daily 8–4; Visitors Center, Memorial Day–Labor Day daily 9–5, rest of the year Wed.–Sun. 9–4:30

FEES: $2 parking fee Memorial Day weekend–Labor Day; free after Labor Day

SOURCES: *Before the Mayflower*, 446. *International Library of Negro Life and History*, 37. *Black Heroes of the American Revolution*, 16–17.

Note

1. Columbus Salley, *The Black 100: A Ranking of the Most Influential African-Americans Past and Present* (New York: Citadel, 1993), 217.

Works Consulted

The Academic American Encyclopedia. New York: Grolier, 1993. [electronic version]

Before the Mayflower: A History of Black America. 5th ed. Lerone Bennett Jr. New York: Penguin, 1988.

Black Heroes of the American Revolution. Burke Davis. New York: Odyssey Book, Harcourt Brace Jovanovich, 1976.

The Black 100: A Ranking of the Most Influential African-Americans Past and Present. Columbus Salley. New York: Citadel, 1993.

International Library of Negro Life and History. Wilhelmena S. Robinson. New York: Publishers, 1970.

Men of Color at the Battle of Monmouth June 28, 1778: The Role of African Americans and Native Americans at Monmouth. Richard S. Walling. Hightstown, N.J.: Longstreet House, 1994.

New York

Auburn

William Seward House

Senator William Seward (1801–1872) and his Quaker wife, Frances Miller Seward, lived in the house at 33 South Street, a place where fugitive slaves found shelter. Seward was governor of New York and a leader of the Whig Party's anti-slavery wing. Later, as a U.S. Senator, he made a speech in Rochester, New York, in which he described the antagonism between freedom and slavery as a conflict between enduring forces.

Although Seward was known for negotiating the purchase of Alaska from Russia in 1867, equally as important were his outspoken views opposing slavery. His speeches on the topic were said to have made an impression on then Congressman Abraham Lincoln. Seward was Lincoln's Secretary of State during the Civil War and was one of the intended victims of the plot to kill Lincoln in 1865. After Lincoln was assassinated, John Wilkes Booth's accomplice, a man named Paine, entered Seward's house and tried to kill Seward, too. Although he was severely wounded, Seward survived.

William Seward opposed slavery from his early childhood. In Florida when he was about five years old, he became friends with Zeno, a Black slave child who lived next door. One day Zeno was punished in the woodshed for some infraction and ran away from home. Seward tried unsuccessfully all of his life to find Zeno again. The incident probably influenced Seward to engage later in abolitionist activities.

As an adult, Seward provided financial support to Frederick Douglass and to underground railroad heroine Harriet Tubman. Knowing that Tubman was living in St. Catherines, Ontario, Canada, Seward wrote her. Describing her in his letter as an American hero, he urged her to live in her own country. In fact, Tubman did return to America. She came to Auburn to live and with Seward's assistance obtained a farm and a small pension from the government.

Frances Seward, who was brought up as a Quaker, gave refuge in the back of this house to fugitive slaves when her husband was a U.S. Senator. Slaves were hidden in a space above the woodshed, which they reached by stairway. While the actual room in which they hid is not open to visitors, it is still there. Visitors to the site can see the original house containing Seward's personal articles, a collection of articles that belonged to President Lincoln, and a fireplace carved by Brigham Young.

ADDRESS: 33 South Street, Auburn
TELEPHONE: (315) 252-1283
VISITING HOURS: Tues.–Sat. 1–4; closed Jan.–Mar. and federal holidays except Dr. Martin Luther King Jr. Day and Veterans' Day

FEES: Adults, $3; senior citizens, $2.50; AAA cardholders, $2.50; children under 6, free

SOURCES: Telephone conversation Apr. 30, 1994, Paul McDonald, assistant curator. Betty Mae Lewis, the historic Seward House. *The African American Presence in New York State History,* 146. *Webster's New Biographical Dictionary,* 906.

Harriet Tubman Museum*

Harriet Tubman (c1820–1913) was one of the best-known and most courageous of abolitionists. Born in slavery in Maryland, she made a remarkable escape from bondage in 1849. Having gained her own freedom, she did not rest but returned directly into the heart of danger to rescue many others. Even though Tubman was targeted for capture by slavecatchers and by the law, she made the trip back nineteen times and was credited with leading at least 300 Black men and women to freedom. Tubman never lost a person along the way. Although rewards of up to $40,000 were offered for her capture, she was never taken. She helped her own aged parents to escape to Canada.

Tubman traveled through central New York many times as she conducted people along the underground railroad. She received support from many abolitionists who lived in this area. In 1857 Tubman moved to Auburn and in the following year she brought her parents back to Auburn. With the assistance of Senator William Seward, the former governor of New York, Tubman acquired a house and land on the outskirts of Auburn. She always was willing to share with others, and her home became known as a haven for poor and elderly Black people.

Harriet Tubman continued to help others throughout her life. She aided the Union side in the Civil War and later worked to improve women's rights and African American education.

In 1896 Tubman was successful in bidding for some acres of land adjoining her home. In 1903 she deeded her entire property to the African Methodist Episcopal Zion Church to be operated as a community farm cooperative. Tubman died in 1913 in a home for the aged that she had founded. Tributes to her memory arrived from across America, and the city of Auburn erected a monument in her honor.

The Harriet Tubman House and Museum, designated as a state historic site and a national historic landmark, are located on her land. The restored house has a lean-to roof and a covered porch that extends along two sides of the house. The two-story frame structure contains Tubman's Bible and other items associated with her life. The museum, still owned by the African Methodist Episcopal Zion Church, is listed in the *National Register of Historic Places.*

Thompson Memorial A.M.E. Zion Church, which Harriet Tubman attended, and her burial site also are located in Auburn. The Harriet Tubman gravesite in Fort Hill Cemetery is marked with a small tombstone located under a large cedar tree. Thompson Memorial Church is located three blocks from Fort Hill Cemetery.

A bronze tablet at the Auburn Courthouse honors Harriet Tubman with these words:

> In memory of Harriet Tubman
> Born a Slave in Maryland About 1821
> Died in Auburn, NY, March 10, 1913
> Called the Moses of her People.
> During the Civil War, with Rare
> Courage She Led Over Three Hundred
> Negroes Up From Slavery to Freedom
> And Rendered Invaluable Service
> As a Nurse and Spy.
> With Implicit Trust in God
> She Braved Every Danger and
> Overcame Every Obstacle, Withal
> She Possessed Extraordinary
> Foresight and Judgement So That
> She Truthfully Said
> "On My Underground Railroad
> I NEBBER Run my Train off de Track
> An' I Nebber Los' A PASSENGER."

DATE BUILT: c1908
ADDRESS: 180–182 South Street, Auburn
TELEPHONE: (315) 252-2081
VISITING HOURS: By appointment
FEES: Donation
SOURCES: Jessie Thorpe, Afro-American Heritage Association, Rome, New York. NRHPINF. *National Register of Historic Places*, 496. *The African American Presence in New York State History*, 59–61, 151. *And Why Not Every Man?*, 136.

Brooklyn

Houses in the Hunterfly Road District*

Six houses on Hunterfly Road are the remaining houses from an early Black settlement called "Weeksville." This was the first major settlement of free Black people in the Bedford-Stuyvesant area.

Slavery was abolished in New York in 1827. Around that time Black people were coming to the Hunterfly Road area. They named their community for James Weeks, an African American landowner, stevedore, and community leader who chaired a committee that sought voting rights for Black citizens.

Weeksville became a refuge for Black families in July 1863 when the New York draft riots of the Civil War took place. Anger had been building among white townspeople who believed free Black workers were taking jobs away from them or driving down wages. At the same time, some poor white citizens believed they might be drafted for Civil War service while wealthier white citizens were exempted from the draft.

Civil unrest began, and white groups hurled insults and vicious comments at Black people as they walked through Brooklyn's streets. A mob of Irish workers forced their way into Lorillard and Watson, a tobacco company employing twenty-five African Americans, and tried to burn down the building with the workers, primarily women and children, inside. Although police arrived and saved the workers, tensions and fear ran high.

Eleven months later, four days of mob violence erupted in New York. The riots later were called the "draft riots," because the mobs, infuriated by seeing Black regiments pass through New York City on their way to the South, directed their greatest anger at the draft enrollment office. Roving gangs burned the Colored Orphan Asylum to the ground and lynched African Americans in the streets and in their homes. Marching through all parts of the city, gangs of men, women, and children searched houses, raided businesses employing African Americans, and lynched the Black workers. Some were drowned in the river and others were hanged from the limbs of trees. Although hundreds of African Americans fled the city, those in Weeksville and Flatbush stood their ground, arming themselves and guarding their neighborhoods and families day and night. The people of Weeksville sheltered many African Americans from other parts of the city. Many in the city were ashamed of what had happened. Later, in 1864, the people of Weeksville must have felt immense pride when the Twentieth U.S. Colored Infantry marched down Broadway behind a military band while a crowd of thousands cheered.

The houses in Weeksville were forgotten until 1968 when college students under the direction of historian Jim Hurley began a research project on Brooklyn neighborhoods. Joseph Haynes, a Black engineer and pilot, discovered the historic houses on Hunterfly Road while exploring the area from the air. The clue was a lane that ran in a different direction from the other streets and the few wood-frame farmhouses on the lane. The houses were set in a different direction because they followed the old Hunterfly Road that no longer existed.

Archaeologists, students, and volunteers dug for artifacts and found several objects, including a tintype of a woman, an old coin, and a copy of the constitution of the Abyssinian Benevolent Daughters of Esther Association of the City of New York, a Black women's group formed in 1839. The pamphlet was printed in 1853 by a firm owned by a leading Black abolitionist.

The six houses in the historical district probably were erected around 1830. The wooden-frame structures vary from one and one-half to two and one-half stories. They are unique in this area as the only surviving houses built parallel to a colonial road and as the oldest known remnants of the nineteenth-century, free-Black community of Weeksville. Three of the former dwellings have been restored by master craftsmen and trainees from the local community and now house an educational facility and African American history museum. One house was in the process of being furnished in mid-1994. A costumed guide who is a graduate of the Banks Street College of Education shows the houses to visitors. The guide has noted that visitors have commented that the old houses with their greenery convey a calm, country atmosphere, often reminding them of a grandmother's place. Visitors see some old artifacts—a stove, an old iron, a washboard, a sewing machine, a butter churn—and learn about the process of restoration. The houses on Hunterfly Road project are a New York City landmark and are listed in the *National Register of Historic Places.* In 1992 Joan B. Maynard, executive director of the Weeksville Society, received the highest award from the National Trust for Historic Preservation for this restoration.

DATE BUILT:	1838–1865
ADDRESS:	1698, 1700, 1702–04, 1706–08 Bergen Street, Brooklyn
TELEPHONE:	(718) 756-5250
VISITING HOURS:	Office hours, Mon.–Fri. 10–4; tours by 3-week prearrangement Tues.–Thurs. and some holidays; closed Sat.–Sun., holidays
FEES:	Adults, $3; children under 18, $1; senior citizens and students, $1.50
SOURCES:	Joan Maynard, executive director, Society for the Preservation of Weeksville & Bedford-Stuyvesant History. Patricia C. Gloster, The Center for African Art. Telephone conversation May 4, 1994, Anna French, administrator, Houses in the Hunterfly District. NRHPINF. *The Negro's Civil War,* 71–7, 212–13. *Weeksville Then & Now.*

Buffalo

Kush Museum of African and African-American Art and Antiquities

The Kush Museum, housed in the Langston Hughes Cultural Arts Center in Buffalo, exhibits a collection of African artifacts and several works of art by contemporary African and African American artists. The African collection concentrates on the Akan-speaking region and the Sudan region of Africa. Established in 1990, Kush Museum has programs for children of all ages. Associate Director Deborah Weeks is working with a group that plans to set up tours of underground railroad sites in the Niagara area. The Langston Hughes Institute at this site also sponsors programs for children, including summer art activities.

DATE ESTABLISHED: 1990
ADDRESS: Langston Hughes Institute, 25 High Street, Buffalo
TELEPHONE: (716) 881-3314
VISITING HOURS: Mon., Wed., Fri. 10–6
FEES: None
SOURCE: Telephone conversation June 13, 1994, Deborah Weeks, associate director, Kush Museum.

Michigan Street Baptist Church

To many fugitive slaves, Michigan Street Baptist Church was the final stop on the underground railroad for those fleeing to Canada. The church played a major role in Buffalo's Black community from its establishment during the abolitionist movement. When the church was constructed in 1845, most of Buffalo's 350 African American residents lived in the Michigan–William Street area near the downtown district. Social life for this relatively small, cohesive group centered around church activities. Reverend Dr. Edward Nash, the pastor for 61 years starting in the 1890s, was a leader in the Buffalo Urban League and the local branch of the National Association for the Advancement of Colored People.

Today the El-Bethel congregation occupies the historic building. The church has the same basic appearance that it had when constructed except for such minor modifications as the addition of an outside stairway. In the lower level visitors can look down into the underground railroad room that has a tunnel leading out to the street, mute evidence of the importance of this church as the last stop before the slaves crossed into Canada.

DATE BUILT: 1845
ADDRESS: 511 Michigan Avenue, Buffalo
TELEPHONE: (716) 854-7976
VISITING HOURS: Sun. school, 10–11:30; Sun. service, 11:30–2; Sun. evening service, 6:30–9; Wed. evening Bible study, 6:30; Thurs. children's study group, 7–9 P.M.; Sat. 10–noon
SOURCES: Telephone conversation May 14, 1994, Mr. Larry Washington, pastor's assistant. NRHPINF.

Corona

Louis Armstrong House and Archives

Corona was the home of Louis "Satchmo" Armstrong, the grandson of former slaves and a man who became a major force in bringing recognition to jazz as an art form. Armstrong was born in 1900 in New Orleans and raised by his grandmother. He loved music and sang in his church choir. As he grew up, he often visited a section of New Orleans called Brick Row, where he would listen to musicians who played in the different buildings. "King" Joe Oliver, a cornetist in one of these New Orleans groups, had a great impact on Armstrong's career.

When Armstrong was twelve years old, he committed the illegal act of firing a gun filled with blanks. He was sent to the Colored Waifs Home for Boys. Armstrong had difficulty adjusting to life in the boys home, but Peter Davis, a music teacher and janitor at the home, recognized young Armstrong's musical talent and encouraged him. Armstrong became the band leader at the home and traveled with the band whenever the group played in city parades.

Armstrong was released from the home after a year and a half. His father, who had remarried, was given custody. However, his father lacked the means to care for the boy and sent him to live with the boy's mother. By the age of sixteen, he was working at odd jobs ranging from shoveling coal in a coalyard to playing his cornet. Gradually, Armstrong began playing full-time at clubs. He learned to read music and took the opportunity to play on steamers with Fate Marable's band, visiting different cities on a six-month tour.

In 1922 Armstrong left New Orleans for Chicago, where he joined the band of his idol "King" Joe Oliver. In 1942 he married Lillian Hardin, the pianist for the band. As Armstrong became well known, he played with different bands in the United States and Europe and began to make recordings.

By 1936 Armstrong's band was earning $8,000 per week. He and his wife, Lillian, purchased the home on 107th Street in Corona, where they lived for thirty-five years. Between 1961 and 1967 the U.S. State Department sponsored Armstrong in goodwill and concert tours for America, resulting in sell-out concerts in many countries. Thousands attended an open-air concert in Africa, and President Kwame Nkrumah of Ghana gave a reception at his guest house. Armstrong experienced severe illness in 1969 and again in 1971. He died in 1971 in New York.

The Armstrong House is a two and one-half–story, red-brick, detached rowhouse. The eleven-room house was renovated during the years when the Armstrongs lived there, and much of the interior remains as it was at that time. The house contains many of Armstrong's furnishings and his musical instruments. His recordings, manuscripts, and memoirs written in longhand have been moved to an archive at Queens College, City University of New York (CUNY), where they can be reviewed and enjoyed by researchers and jazz aficionados.

DATE ESTABLISHED: Armstrong residence, 1940–1971; archives, May 24, 1994

ADDRESS: Residence, 3456 107th Street, Corona, Long Island; archives, Rosenthal Library, Queens College/CUNY, 65–30 Kissena Boulevard, Flushing

TELEPHONE: Residence, (718) 478-8274; archives, (718) 997-3670

VISITING HOURS: House, small groups by appointment, Mon.–Fri. 9–5; archives by appointment, Mon.–Fri. 9–5

SOURCES: NRHPINF. Telephone conversation May 3, 1994, Aishah Pacheco, assistant to the director.

Elmira

Woodlawn National Cemetery

Woodlawn National Cemetery is associated with John W. Jones, a stationmaster on Elmira's underground railroad. Jones was a runaway slave who had escaped from his master in Leesburg, Virginia. He settled in Elmira, situated in the Finger Lakes region of south central New York; there he became a leader of the underground railroad, personally helping hundreds of fleeing slaves.

The Woodlawn Cemetery, a Civil War prison camp, was at the rear of Jones's farm, and he was placed in charge of burying nearly 3,000 Confederate prisoners who had died during imprisonment at Camp Elmira in 1864. Jones, who once fled racism in the South, saw that the men were reverently buried. He erected wooden markers over their graves and kept a record of the name and location of each grave. As he tended the graves, he placed the name and other information about each soldier in a sealed bottle in the coffin. The information that he carefully recorded proved of value when Woodlawn became a national cemetery in 1877.

DATE OF SIGNIFICANCE: 1864

ADDRESS: 1825 Davis Street, Elmira

TELEPHONE: (607) 732-5411

VISITING HOURS: Always open; office, Mon.–Fri. 8:30–4:30, closed national holidays except Memorial Day

SOURCES: Telephone conversation Jan. 25, 1995, Brian McCade, caretaker, Woodlawn National Cemetery. *And Why Not Every Man?*, 141–2. *The African American Presence in New York State History*, 58.

Flushing

Bowne House

Oral tradition maintains that the Bowne House in a large Quaker community once was a station on the underground railroad. The town of Flushing was founded in 1645 and the dwelling, built in 1661, was home to white abolitionist John Bowne, a founder of the Manumission Society in New York. After Bowne died in 1694, antislavery sentiment was passed on through the generations in this prominent family. Mary Bowne Parsons, John Bowne's great-great granddaughter, was a Quaker abolitionist.

Today the twenty-one–room Bowne House is a national shrine to religious freedom. With its labyrinth of nooks and passages it is a favorite place for children, who can learn about colonial history and New York's antislavery movement as they walk through it. Bowne House is a city and state landmark and is listed in the *National Register of Historic Places.*

DATE BUILT: 1661

ADDRESS: 37-01 Bowne Street, Flushing

TELEPHONE: (718) 359-0528

VISITING HOURS: Mon.–Fri. 9:30–4; Sat.–Sun. 2:30–4:30; closed mid-Dec.–mid-Jan., Easter

FEES: Adults, $2; children, $1

SOURCES: Audrey Braver, director. Telephone conversation May 5, 1994, Donna Russo, executive director.

Fort Edward

Solomon Northup House

Northup House, originally built in the 1700s as Fort Edward, was built to guard the upper Hudson Valley but was abandoned after the French and Indian War. In 1777, General Burgoyne used the house as his headquarters during his march toward Saratoga. He was arrested and later joined other Loyalists in Canada.

This Fort Edward house once was the residence of Solomon Northup, a Black man who published the story of his life in a book called *Twelve Years a Slave.* In 1821, by Fort Edward board action, Solomon's father, Mintus Northup, was accepted as a free man. On Christmas Day 1829, Solomon Northup married Anne Hampton, and they began housekeeping in the Old Fort House. Northup worked with other men in repairing the Champlain Canal; he saved enough money to buy a horse and other items needed for canal-boat towing and then sought contracts for transporting rafts loaded with timber. With the earnings from this work, Solomon and Anne purchased a farm in Kingsbury in 1832.

Ten years later, however, Solomon was kidnapped and was sold into slavery in Louisiana, where he remained in bondage until he was rescued in 1853. He later told his story in a book that rivaled the popularity of Harriet Beecher Stowe's *Uncle Tom's Cabin* and that remains gripping in its descriptions of slave life.

Today the Old Fort House, the oldest frame building standing in Washington County, is a museum complex consisting of seven buildings, three of which are open for tours. Northup House was being restored at the time of this book's publication; visitors should call to find out if it is open. (For additional information on another house associated with Northup, read the listing for Bunkie, Louisiana.)

DATE BUILT:	1773; Northup residence, beginning Dec. 1829
ADDRESS:	29 Lower Broadway, Fort Edward
TELEPHONE:	(518) 747-9600
VISITING HOURS:	Mid-June–mid-Sept., daily 1–5; Dec., daily 1–4; closed all holidays and Nov., Jan.–Mar.; all groups by appointment
FEES:	Individuals, free; bus tours, $1.50 per person
SOURCES:	Telephone call to site, May 9, 1994. R. Paul McCarty, director, and Pat Turner, tour director, Old Fort House. *Old House Museum.*

Hempstead

African American Museum of Nassau County

Established in 1970, the African-American Museum is the only one of its kind on Long Island. It highlights the history and contributions of local African Americans, many of whom made significant contributions to the nation. Special exhibits include art, books, and documents. Temporary exhibits provide a continuous public showcase for artists, and traveling exhibits from other institutions place the experience of Long Island within a broader world context. One exhibit presented *The*

World of Our Grandparents, African Americans on Long Island from 1880 to 1926.

The museum is a facility of the division of Museum Services of the Nassau County Department of Recreation and Parks. Housed in a structure of approximately 11,000 square feet, it includes two galleries, an educational room, a music room, and a gift shop. The south wing is being expanded to include a theater with collapsible walls for concerts and conferences, a photography lab, and a reference room.

DATE ESTABLISHED: 1970

ADDRESS: 110 N. Franklin Street, Hempstead, Long Island (Southern State Parkway to exit 21, Nassau Road; northbound to Jackson Street)

TELEPHONE: (516) 572-0730

VISITING HOURS: Thurs.–Sun. 10–4:45; closed Mon.–Tues., holidays except Dr. Martin Luther King Jr. Day

FEES: None; charge for custom programs for groups with advance reservations

SOURCE: Mildred Clayton, museum coordinator, March 1994.

Huntington

Bethel African Methodist Episcopal Church

Bethel African Methodist Episcopal Church is the oldest surviving African American church in Huntington. When Huntington was settled in the eighteenth century, most African Americans lived in the town as slaves on large properties. By the nineteenth century Huntington also had a free Black population. The Bethel A.M.E. congregation was incorporated in 1843. Most of the African American residents worked in agriculture, domestic service, or Huntington's brickyards. The present church was designed and built in 1924 by church pastor George A. Lonzo. Prominently located on a busy village street in the city's historic district, Bethel Church, listed in the *National Register of Historic Places,* has played a central role in the spiritual life of the Black community.

DATE ESTABLISHED: 1843; African American congregation, 1860; present church, 1924

ADDRESS: 291 Park Avenue, Huntington

TELEPHONE: (516) 549-5014

VISITING HOURS: Sun. service, July–Aug. 10, rest of the year 11; Sun. school, July–Aug. 9, rest of the year 9:45

SOURCES: Telephone conversation May 1, 1994, Mrs. Jeanette Johns, wife of the pastor of Bethel A.M.E. Church. *The African American Presence in New York State History,* 118. Building Structure Inventory Form, Division for Historic Preservation New York State Parks and Recreation. *International Library of Negro Life and History,* 21. *The History of Bethel A.M.E. Church.*

Hurley

Historic Hurley

Hurley, New York, a village noted for its 250-year-old stone houses, once was the childhood home of outspoken Black activist Sojourner Truth. Although the Hardenberg house where she grew up is not open to the public, the town where slavery once existed still shows much about her early physical environment.

Before changing her name to Sojourner Truth as an adult, she was known as Isabella Baumfree. Although some believed that she was born a slave in New York's Ulster County around 1797, Sojourner claimed that she was born in Africa. She was brought to the Hardenberg house at an early age and spent the first eleven years of her life there. In the mid-1800s she spent years crusading for African American rights and women's rights, leaving a lasting impression on those who heard her speak.

Today Sojourner Truth's name is honored at several sites. In 1976 a plaque dedicated to Sojourner Truth was placed in front of the old courthouse on Wall Street in Kingston, New York. The library at State University of New York, New Paltz, is named for Sojourner Truth, and in 1986 a commemorative stamp was issued at the university in her honor.

Several houses in Hurley have links to Black history. The parsonage of the Reformed Church (1790), also called Crispell House, has a slave children's nook, an area where babies slept while their mothers did housework. A narrow stairway off the kitchen leads to the former slave quarters. Visitors may not enter the room because of the sloping stairs and the low ceiling, but they are able to look up the stairway.

The Dr. Richard Ten Eyck house (1780) allegedly was a stop on the underground railroad.

Two other houses, one on Old Route 109 and one on a side road in Hurley, are reputed to have been stations on the underground railroad. In 1790 a slave who lived at the Wyncoop house killed his master, Colonel Cornelius D. Wyncoop. Slave quarters can still be seen there.

Slave quarters for each stone house usually were located in the damp, dark basements; they consisted of cellars with several rooms. Men, women, and children slept in one room on straw or hay-covered boards placed on the cellar floor. Another room had a fireplace where cooking was done, including the food to be served to the household upstairs.

Each house usually had its own slave cemetery. Slave cemeteries were associated with the Cornelius Cool house, the William P. Cole house, the Mattys Ten Eyck house, and the Newkirk house. A cemetery on Eagles Nest, located on the top of the mountain off the Hurley Mountain Road, originated as a cemetery for white, Black, and Indian people.

In Hurley today twenty-five of its original houses from the 1700s are standing. The village has America's oldest concentration of stone houses, many with great hewn beams, floor and ceiling boards eighteen inches wide, sturdy oak doors, and thick stone walls in the basement.

A tour is sponsored by Hurley Reformed Church on Stone House Day, when about a dozen homes filled with antiques are open to the public. The tour includes the Ten Eyck house, which was part of the underground railway. A Revolutionary War encampment is set up in the streets, and there is a country fair in the church with crafts from the Revolutionary War era. Visitors may pick up a brochure giving directions for walking or driving around. They may see the village and the old Burial Ground on any day of the year.

DATE ESTABLISHED: 1700s; Hardenberg House, 1750; Hurley Reformed Church, 1850

ADDRESS: Main Street, Hurley (exit 19 [Kingston] from New York State Thruway, take US 209 S toward Ellenville; Hurley is the first exit [right] on US 209 S, about 4 minutes from the Thruway; the Hurley Reformed Church is on the right)

TELEPHONE: Hurley Reformed Church, (914) 331-4121

VISITING HOURS: Interiors open only on Stone House Day (second Sat. in July) 10–4; walking tours all year

FEES: Tour of open houses: adults $10; children 12 and under, $1; senior citizens and students, $5; parking free; bus service to outlying houses, free

SOURCES: Telephone conversation May 6, 1994, Reverend Stickley, Hurley Reformed Church. Olive M. Clearwater, co-historian for the town of Hurley. *Hurley in the Days of Slavery. Historic Hurley in the Mid-Hudson Valley. Walk, Drive Around Historic Hurley.* "Rocks 'n' Rolling, Hurley's Stones Also Its Homes."

Irvington

Madame Walker's Home

Villa Lewaro was built for Madame C. J. Walker, a nationally known cosmetics entrepreneur and possibly America's first Black, female self-made millionaire. In the early decades of the twentieth century, Madame Walker was attracted to New York City by its growing Black population and a myriad of commercial opportunities. She engaged Vertner Woodson Tandy, the first Black architect in New York State, to build an elegant three-story, red-brick townhouse at 108–110 West Thirty-sixth Street. The upper two stories served as her residence, while the lower floor housed her beauty shop and school. (The Countee Cullen Public Library later was built on this site.)

Later Madame Walker asked Tandy to build Villa Lewaro, the mansion that would become her new home. Born in Lexington, Kentucky, in the nineteenth century, he was the son of Henry A. Tandy, a prominent Lexington contractor who had erected some of that city's finest homes. The younger Tandy attended the Chandler Normal School in Lexington (see that listing in Lexington), studied architecture at Tuskegee Institute in Alabama, and continued his studies at Cornell University, where he completed the four-year program in three years. Tandy had his architectural office in New York City. Villa Lewaro is located on a beautiful five-acre site overlooking the Hudson River at Irvington-on-the-Hudson. Tandy designed the three-story residence as an Italian Renaissance palace with thirty-four luxurious rooms. The living room walls and ceiling gleamed with gold leaf, and gold-trimmed draperies hung at the windows. A marble stairway led to the second-floor bedrooms and sleeping porches. The servants' quarters were on the third floor.

After Villa Lewaro was completed in 1918, Madame Walker began entertaining some of the most influential people of the day in her splendid mansion. Unfortunately, she died just eight months afterward. Her daughter, Lelia Walker Robinson, inherited the estate, which she later willed to the National Association for the Advancement of Colored People. Upkeep for the house was prohibitive, however, and in 1930 and 1931 the NAACP sold the house and auctioned off its contents. Villa Lewaro, originally valued at $400,000, sold for only $47,000 to a private nursing home. It is one of four African American sites designated as a Westchester County Tricentennial Historical Site.

DATE BUILT: 1918

ADDRESS: N. Broadway, Greenburgh, Village of Irvington

VISITING HOURS: Private, visitors may drive by

SOURCES: NRHPINF. Telephone call June 13, 1994, Irvington Library. Westchester Historical Society. *"The Hills" in the Mid-Nineteenth Century.*

Ithaca

Alpha Phi Alpha Fraternity Founding Home

The house at 421 North Albany is associated with the founding of Alpha Phi Alpha Fraternity, a national Black fraternal organization. The fraternity had its first informal meeting at this house in 1905. The first African Americans who lived in the house were a group of seven students from Cornell University who used the house as a dormitory. Today Cornell students who are members of the fraternity still come by to see and photograph their founding house.

DATE ESTABLISHED: 1905

ADDRESS: 421 N. Albany, Ithaca

VISITING HOURS: Private, visitors may drive by

SOURCES: Telephone conversation May 22, 1994, Steven A. Centeno, community resident. Margaret Hobbie, director, DeWitt Historical Society. *Ithaca's Neighborhoods.*

Alex Haley Birthplace

The late Alex Haley (1921–1992), author of *Roots,* was born in the Cascadilla Street house and spent the first few weeks of his life here. The family included young Alex; his father, Simon, who was a graduate student; and his mother, Bertha.

Six weeks after Alex's birth, Alex and his mother went to stay with his grandparents in Henning, Tennessee, while Simon Haley stayed behind to complete his graduate studies. Simon Haley later came to Tennessee where he operated the Palmer family business. (See the Alex Haley Museum listing in Henning, Tennessee.)

DATE OF SIGNIFICANCE: 1921

ADDRESS: 212 Cascadilla Street (between Albany and Geneva Streets), Ithaca

VISITING HOURS: Private, visitors may drive by

SOURCES: Margaret Hobbie, director, DeWitt Historical Society. Telephone conversation May 22, 1994, Steven A. Centeno, community resident. *Ithaca's Neighborhoods.*

St. James African Methodist Episcopal Zion Church

St. James A.M.E. Zion Church was established by African Americans who at one time attended segregated services in a Methodist Episcopal church, that designated them as the "colored class" of the church. Upset by this discrimination, the Black members withdrew to found a church of their own. Ithaca was accessible to free Black people from different counties of New York State.

Between 1823 and 1825 the congregation had to meet in a private home but was able to build its own church on this site in the next decade. Peter Webb, the only slave in Ithaca ever allowed to purchase his freedom, bought the land for the church after he became a free person. From its earliest years, St. James Church was a station on the underground railroad. Church members along with white residents of Ithaca helped some fleeing slaves move to safety in Canada; they also provided assistance for those who chose to stay in Ithaca. One of the distinguished pastors was Jermaine Wesley Loguen, a man who had escaped from slavery in Tennessee. In the 1840s Loguen was active in the underground railroad in Syracuse, where he was a friend of Frederick Douglass. Douglass visited St. James on one occasion. Another famous guest was Harriet Tubman, who attended St. James many times.

St. James continued its history of community involvement. In 1913 several Cornell students, unhappy at the discrimination they encountered in campus fraternities, founded the Alpha Phi Alpha Fraternity in the basement of St. James Church. More recently, church members have been involved in neighborhood preservation programs.

The 1830s construction date makes this the oldest church building in Ithaca, the oldest African American church in Tompkins County, and possibly one of the oldest churches built in the United States by an A.M.E. Zion congregation. The church started out as a modest wood structure on a high stone foundation. A second story—a wood frame structure—was added in 1861, and a belfry added about 1904. Steam heat and electricity were introduced in 1913, and a large rose window was installed in 1945. Although the church has expanded many times, the original stones are still visible in its foundation. Four streets near the church still have nineteenth-century homes of African Americans. The city of Ithaca plans to designate the church and community as a historic preservation site.

DATE BUILT: 1833

ADDRESS: 116–118 Cleveland Avenue, Ithaca

TELEPHONE: (607) 272-4053

VISITING HOURS: Sun. service, 11; by appointment Mon.–Fri.

SOURCES: Margaret Hobbie, director, DeWitt Historical Society. Telephone conversation Jan. 24, 1995, Linda Thornhill, wife of pastor, St. James Church. NRHPINF. *Ithaca's Neighborhoods*, 88–90.

Lake Placid

John Brown Farm State Historic Site*

The John Brown Farm state historic site, high in the Adirondack Mountains of New York, is the home and gravesite of the white abolitionist firebrand John Brown (1800–1859). He was born in Connecticut, grew up in Ohio, and later lived in Pennsylvania. As a youth, Brown had seen a Black boy who was his friend beaten cruelly, an event that led him to believe that slavery was a sin against God. In 1855 Brown and five of his sons moved to Kansas, where Brown established a colony along the Osawatomie River. "Bleeding Kansas" had become a battleground for rival forces in favor of or against the institution of slavery. Brown was shaken by the raid a group of proslavery fanatics staged in 1856 on the capital of Kansas, Lawrence, which was noted for its abolitionist sympathies. In reprisal, Brown and some of his followers murdered five proslavery men on the banks of the Pottawatamie River a few days later. In 1859 Brown led the famous raid on Harpers Ferry, Virginia (now West Virginia). He was accompanied by twenty-two men, including five free Black men; his aim was to start an uprising that would lead to the overthrow of slavery in the South. Brown thought of himself as an Old Testament prophet and God's chosen instrument to eradicate the sin of slaveholding. Although the raid captured the town and its federal arsenal, most of the Black people in the area refused to join Brown's forces, believing that Brown's efforts would prove unsuccessful. In the end Brown and his men were besieged by a force of U.S. Marines led by Robert E. Lee. Many of Brown's party were killed in the fighting. Afterward, Brown was hanged for his rebellion against the state of Virginia. His death led to a wave of fear among white

Southerners against the abolitionists, but in the North Brown often was regarded as a martyr. The raid on Harpers Ferry fueled the passions that led to the Civil War.

Although Brown's name will be forever connected with Harpers Ferry, he regarded North Elba (now Lake Placid) as his home. A well-known abolitionist named Gerrit Smith offered parcels of his vast land holdings in this area during the 1840s to free Black men and women. This land, it was thought, would give the free people an opportunity to develop farms. In 1849 John Brown and his family moved to North Elba to help the Black settlers. Brown surveyed the land and helped the settlers build homes and plant crops. Unfortunately, the climate was harsh and there were too few markets for the settlement's products. As a result, the settlement did not survive.

The site contains John Brown's cabin, which was his last home. It also encompasses Brown's grave, the graves of two of his sons killed at Harpers Ferry, and the graves of several of his followers in the ill-fated raid.

DATE ESTABLISHED:	1850, 1895
ADDRESS:	John Brown Road (3/4 mile off NY 73, about 2 miles south of Lake Placid), Lake Placid
TELEPHONE:	(518) 523-3900
VISITING HOURS:	May 12–Oct. 31, Wed.–Sat. 10–5, Sun. 1–5; closed Mon.–Tues.
FEES:	None
SOURCES:	Telephone conversation April 30, 1994, Mrs. Alice Cotter, wife of superintendent, John Brown Farm. Ben Kroup, New York State Office of Parks, Recreation and Historic Preservation, Bureau of Historic Sites-Peebles Island, Waterford, New York. *John Brown Farm. National Register of Historic Places,* 502.

New York

Abyssinian Baptist Church

Adam Clayton Powell Sr. was born in 1865 in a one-room log cabin. Robert E. Lee surrendered at Appomattox, in Virginia, just twenty-five days later. One of sixteen children, he was the son of a former slave. The family was poor and could not afford regular schooling, but young Powell was eager to learn when he could attend school. The family moved to West Virginia when Powell was about ten years old; after attending a revival meeting there, he decided to become a Baptist minister. He graduated from Virginia Union University (then Wayland Academy) and entered Yale Divinity School. In 1908 he was selected as pastor of the Abyssinian Baptist Church in New York City.

Abyssinian Church was established in 1808 when a group of African Americans refused to continue to sit in the racially segregated First Baptist Church. They withdrew their membership and organized their own church, meeting at various locations in the early 1900s. Although the church was small and deeply in debt, within a few years the Reverend Dr. Adam Clayton Powell Sr. had built it into one of the world's largest Protestant congregations. By 1920 the congregation had purchased lots on 138th Street; three years later it dedicated a new church and community house built at a cost of more than $330,000. Powell, who adopted many of the ideas of the influential Black leader Marcus Garvey, continued to lead the congregation until his retirement in 1937. He died in 1953.

Adam Clayton Powell Jr. was born in 1908 in New Haven, Connecticut. The only son of Mattie

Fletcher Powell and Adam Powell Sr., he was noted for his intelligence, his confidence, and his oratorical skill. The young Powell attended Colgate University, graduating in 1930 and starting his career as assistant minister during the Great Depression. He led the free-meal program at Abyssinian Baptist, coordinated relief efforts throughout Harlem, and successfully garnered jobs for African Americans. The junior Powell continued to study and earned his master's degree in religious education from Columbia University in 1931.

Adam Clayton Powell Jr. succeeded his father as pastor of Abyssinian Baptist Church and served as its pastor from 1939 until 1971. Well known as a minister, Powell also was a fighter for civil rights. He organized boycotts to influence white merchants in Harlem to hire Black employees. As New York City's first Black city council member he initiated legislation to improve social and economic conditions for Black citizens. First elected to Congress in 1944, he wrote more than fifty pieces of social legislation during his time in office. Powell's flamboyant style and fearlessly outspoken speech earned him the enmity of many people, even of some Black leaders who felt that his forthright style was hurting their cause. After being stripped of his congressional seniority for defecting from the Democratic Party and for his abrasive behavior (and while he was being investigated by the U.S. Department of Justice for alleged misuse of federal funds), Powell steadfastly maintained that he was targeted because of racism and because of his power as a Black man. In 1967 the full House voted to exclude him from his congressional seat. Although the Supreme Court ruled in 1969 that the exclusion was unconstitutional, Powell did not return to serve in Washington. In 1970 he lost the primary election to another Black man, Charles Rangel. In 1971 Adam Clayton Powell Jr. retired from the Abyssinian Baptist Church. He died in 1972 at the age of sixty-three. In recognition of his many positive contributions, the stretch of Seventh Avenue that goes through Harlem was renamed Adam Clayton Powell Jr. Boulevard.

DATE ESTABLISHED: Congregation, 1808; present building, 1923

ADDRESS: 132 W. 138th Street (between Lenox Avenue and Adam Clayton Powell Boulevard), New York

TELEPHONE: (212) 862-7474

VISITING HOURS: Mon.–Fri. 9–5, call in advance to arrange a visit

SOURCES: Telephone call to this site May 1, 1994. *The African American Encyclopedia,* vol. 1, 9–10. *The African American Presence in New York State History. Webster's New Biographical Dictionary,* 814. "Adam Clayton Powell Jr.," 1273–6.

Apollo Theater

For more than four decades, the Apollo Theater, one of America's leading entertainment centers, provided a premier performance hall for Black performers and served as a center of Black cultural awareness. At one time 125th Street was famed as the "Main Street" of Black Harlem.

The Apollo originally was built as a burlesque theater catering to a primarily white clientele. In 1934 two white businessmen purchased the building, renamed it the Apollo Theater, and began presenting a variety show featuring leading Black entertainers. Louis Armstrong, Duke Ellington, Count Basie, and Ella Fitzgerald were among those who performed at the Apollo. The Apollo's shows, which included drama, dance, comedy, gospel, blues, jazz, and rhythm and blues, led to Harlem's becoming known as the premier Black cultural and intellectual center in America.

The changing economy eventually led to the closing of the theater, but there was a later rebirth. After a multimillion-dollar renovation in 1989, the Apollo reopened, once again featuring the giants of entertainment and show business.

DATE BUILT: 1914

ADDRESS: 253 W. 125th Street, at Adam Clayton Powell Jr. Boulevard, New York

TELEPHONE: (212) 749-5838

VISITING HOURS: Contact theater for schedule of performances; New Amateur Night, Wed. 7:30

SOURCES: *The African American Presence in New York State History. Four Regional History Surveys,* 114.

Ralph Bunche House

Dr. Ralph Bunche, a man born in poverty in 1904 in Detroit, Michigan, became known worldwide as a scholar, the highest ranking African American in the United Nations Secretariat, and the first Black recipient of the Nobel Peace Prize.

Bunche's father was a barber, and his mother an amateur musician. The family moved to Toledo, Ohio, then to Albuquerque, New Mexico. However, both parents had poor health, and they died when Ralph was around twelve years old. Then Ralph, his sister, his grandmother, and his aunts moved to Los Angeles, California. (See the listing for the Ralph Bunche House in Los Angeles.) An outstanding student, Bunche won medals for debate, civics, English composition, and athletics. He won an athletic scholarship to the University of California, where he was elected to Phi Beta Kappa and graduated *summa cum laude.*

Bunche then studied at Harvard University, where he earned a master's degree in 1928 and a Ph.D. in 1934. Between his master's and doctoral studies, Bunche taught at Howard University, where he organized the political science department. He later returned to Howard as a full professor and assistant to the president. He received grants to study at the London School of Economics and the Capetown University of the Union of South Africa. Bunche's work took him on a world tour from which he gained expert knowledge about different cultures.

Bunche's life was marked by many achievements. He assisted Gunnar Myrdal in research for a comprehensive study of African American life in the United States. He was the first African American to hold a desk in the State Department. He also helped to draw up the United Nations charter.

In 1948 Bunche became secretary of the Palestine Commission. One of his greatest achievements came in 1949 when his negotiations brought an end to the Arab-Israeli War. When news of the armistice agreement reached the United States, Bunche began to receive honors from all over the world, including more than thirty honorary degrees and awards. During this period, in 1950 he was awarded the Nobel Peace Prize. Continuing to act as a catalyst for peace, Bunche was appointed undersecretary general of the United Nations. He died in 1971.

The Bunche residence is a two and one-half–story home in the Kew Gardens section of Queens, New York. The English Tudor Renaissance country house has a steep gable and a main roof with slate shingles and dormers. Wood, brick, and textured stucco were used in the construction. Many interior rooms remain furnished as they were when Bunche lived in the house.

DATE OF SIGNIFICANCE: 1952–1971

ADDRESS: 115–125 Grosvenor Road, Kew Gardens, vicinity of Queens, New York

VISITING HOURS: Private, visitors may drive or walk by

SOURCES: NRHPINF. *The African American Encyclopedia,* vol. 1, 241–3. Academic American Encyclopedia.

Center for African Art

The Center for African Art's mission is to create an understanding and appreciation of African art based on a cultural, cross-cultural, and historical perspective. The museum consists of two adjoining turn-of-the-century townhouses with exhibition space in small galleries on three levels. Hallways connecting the galleries afford additional viewing space.

The museum has a variety of exhibits. The exhibit entitled *Yoruba: Nine Centuries of African Art and Thought* displays art from the Yoruba people of West Africa, including ninth- and tenth-century objects excavated from archaeological sites in Nigeria. Among the works are naturalistic terra-cotta and bronze heads, some thought to portray African kings, called *onis.*

DATE ESTABLISHED: 1983
ADDRESS: 54 E. Sixty-eighth Street, New York
TELEPHONE: (212) 861-1200
VISITING HOURS: Tues.–Fri. 10–5, Sat. 11–5, Sun. noon–5; closed Mon.
FEES: Adults, $2.50; senior citizens, students, and children, $1.50
SOURCES: Johanna Cooper for Carol Thompson, The Center for African Art. *Black Arts New York.*

Will Marion Cook House

The Will Cook residence is located in a neighborhood of Victorian townhouses built in 1891. So many outstanding, fashionable, and achieving Black African Americans lived in the community that it became known locally as "Strivers Row." Composer Will Marion Cook lived in Strivers Row in a three-story, buff-brick townhouse on West 138th Street. Cook was born in Washington, D.C., in 1869 to educated and talented parents. At the age of thirteen he began studying violin at the Oberlin Conservatory of Music. Three years later, he received funds to study violin in Germany, where he remained for nine years.

Although skilled in classical music, Cook developed interests in musical comedy and ragtime. He reached his peak as a musical composer between 1900 and 1910. Cook developed a Black jazz band and helped to organize the Clef Club's Syncopated Orchestra, comprising 125 Black musicians. When he died in 1944, he left an outstanding legacy of his compositions, innovative musical performances, and assistance for other creative artists.

Cook's residence on Strivers Row has Palladian windows on the second floor and wrought-iron balconies extending from the bottom of the first-floor windows as well as wrought-iron handrails on the steps. A cement post on one gate still bears the stern warning "Walk Your Horses," a relic from the days when exuberant ones were tempted to enter the gate at high speed. All four floors have been used since 1976 for a medical practice. The neighborhood, designated a historic district by the New York Landmarks Commission, is listed in the *National Register of Historic Places.*

DATE OF SIGNIFICANCE: Cook residence, 1918–1944
ADDRESS: 221 W. 138th Street, New York
VISITING HOURS: Private, visitors may walk or drive by
SOURCES: Telephone conversation May 14, 1994, Dr. Calvin Innis, community resident. NRHPINF.

Matthew Henson Residence
Dunbar Apartments

The Dunbar Apartments—a six-building, garden-apartment complex named for the poet Paul Lawrence Dunbar—was the first large cooperative in New York built for Black residents. The six structures contain some 511 apartments and occupy an entire block in Harlem. The Dunbar Apartments are significant architecturally and for their association with the following African American achievers who at one time lived here: Countee Cullen, poet; W. E. B. Du Bois, Fisk and Harvard University graduate, scholar, and writer; A. Philip Randolph, leader of the Brotherhood of Sleeping Car Porters and civil rights activist; actor Paul Robeson; and dancer Bill (Bojangles) Robinson. Famed explorer Matthew Henson, who is believed to be the first man to reach the North Pole, was another distinguished resident.

Matthew Henson was born in 1866 on a Maryland farm. As a young man he worked as a cabin attendant on a merchant ship. He received his first formal education from his ship's captain. When Henson was eighteen, he met U.S. Navy Lt. Robert Edwin Peary (1856–1920) and began working for him. Henson, who was highly skilled as a seaman, became one of the most highly valued members of Peary's team. Henson was able to communicate well with the Inuit people and saved Peary's life on several occasions.

In 1909 Henson was selected by Peary over five white men to accompany him on the famous expedition to the North Pole, a journey of 450 miles over ice and snow. Henson served as the trailblazer of the team that also included four Inuit explorers. Henson's task was to move ahead of the others, mark the path, build igloos at resting places, and prepare the way for the others. As a result, he was the first man to reach the North Pole. Henson recognized that when his compass no longer registered north, he had arrived at the goal, and he had the honor of placing the American flag at the Pole.

Even though Peary received many honors for this accomplishment, Henson's work was ignored for years. To support himself, Henson had to take jobs parking cars, and he worked as a messenger for the U.S. Customs Bureau in New York City, earning $900 a year at age forty-seven. Some honors and belated recognition finally came when President Truman honored Henson in 1953. President Eisenhower also cited Henson's accomplishments in 1955.

Matthew Henson lived at the Dunbar from 1925 until his death in 1955. In 1961 the state of Maryland, Henson's birthplace, placed a plaque in the State House to honor Henson as codiscoverer of the North Pole. Dunbar Apartments, the Matthew Henson residence, honored the explorer with a tablet at its Seventh Avenue entrance. The site is listed in the *National Register of Historic Places.*

DATE OF SIGNIFICANCE: Henson residence, 1925–1955

ADDRESS: 246 W. 150th Street, Apt. 3F, New York

VISITING HOURS: Private, visitors may walk or drive by

SOURCES: NRHPINF. City of New York Landmarks Preservation Commission. *The African American Encyclopedia,* vol. 3, 752–3.

Langston Hughes House

James Langston Hughes (1902–1967) was born in Joplin, Missouri. His parents separated when he was young, and he went to live with his grandmother, who told him stories about her husband, one of the Black men killed in John Brown's raid at Harpers Ferry.

Hughes worked in a variety of jobs during his lifetime—as a seaman, laundry sorter, waiter, busboy, and gardener. He lived for a while in Mexico and France, and studied at Lincoln University in Missouri. In 1926 his first book of poetry, *The Weary Blues,* called attention to his great literary ability. He gained special recognition for his poem "The Negro Speaks of Rivers." Hughes produced many other works, including the lyrics for the 1947 opera *Street Scene,* composed by Kurt Weill.

In the 1920s and 1930s a literary movement called the Harlem Renaissance highlighted the creative work of Black authors and artists. This flowering of literature and art focused on the question of Black identity, and Hughes was one of the movement's foremost figures.

The house on East 127th Street is typical of Harlem row houses built after the Civil War. Langston Hughes lived there during the last twenty years of his life. It is the best symbol of his association with Harlem and the Harlem Renaissance group.

DATE OF SIGNIFICANCE: Hughes residence, 1947–1967
ADDRESS: 20 E. 127th Street, New York
VISITING HOURS: Private, visitors may drive or walk by
SOURCES: *The African American Presence in New York State History,* 130. *Webster's New Biographical Dictionary,* 496.

James Weldon Johnson House

Civil rights leader and writer James Weldon Johnson (he changed his middle name from William to Weldon in 1913) was born in 1871 in Jacksonville, Florida. He grew up in a middle-class home. His father was a minister and a headwaiter, and his mother was a musician and music teacher. Although the Johnson boys attended the segregated Stanton School in Jacksonville, their parents taught James and their other son, John Rosamond, about literature, music, and racial pride. James never forgot the lessons about his heritage, and he set high goals for himself. Jacksonville offered no secondary education for Black students, so James attended a secondary school operated by Atlanta University and then earned his college degree in 1894 at Atlanta University.

Johnson was appointed principal of Stanton Grade School in Jacksonville and served in that capacity for four years. With a few friends he founded the *Daily American,* the first African American paper in Jacksonville. He also studied law and in 1899 was the first Black person admitted to the Florida bar. During a trip to New York in the summer of 1899 and meeting many artists in the theatrical world, he began to develop his talent for music. After returning to Jacksonville, Johnson wrote the lyrics to "Lift Every Voice and Sing," which later became known as the Negro national anthem.

Johnson and his brother returned to New York in 1900 and began a highly successful seven-year stint as the composers of more than 200 songs. The process of collaborating with others to write a campaign song for Theodore Roosevelt spurred an interest in political activity. In 1907 President Roosevelt appointed Johnson U.S. consul in Venezuela. In the next years he completed a novel, *The Autobiography of an Ex-Colored Man,* and became contributing editor of the *New York Age,* the city's oldest Black-owned newspaper.

Johnson joined the National Association for the Advancement of Colored People in 1916. He soon advanced, promoted first to field secretary, then to executive secretary, a position he held through 1930. In this capacity he increased NAACP membership dramatically by organizing branches in large cities in the South, a solid achievement considering the threats of reprisals that faced Southern African Americans for joining chapters. Johnson crusaded to halt segregation and lynchings, lobbying in support of the Dyer Anti-Lynching Bill. Even though the bill did not pass, he continued to confront Americans with the brutality of the lynchings that were taking place, and he vigorously promoted integration and political and cultural equality for African Americans. Throughout his career he stressed the view that Black Americans were active, creative, and important forces in American life.

While working with the NAACP, Johnson continued writing, publishing his own poems as well as an anthology, the *Book of American Negro Poetry.* He and his brother published two anthologies of African American spirituals. His musical work *The Creation* was produced at Town Hall, accompanied by members of the Boston Symphony Orchestra.

Johnson House is used today for a medical practice. James Weldon Johnson—author, musician, and activist—resided in this brick, five-story apartment building for more than thirteen years between 1925 and 1938, during his service as national executive secretary of the NAACP. After Johnson died in an automobile accident in 1938, he was widely mourned.

DATE OF SIGNIFICANCE: Johnson residence, 1925–1938
ADDRESS: 187 W. 135th Street, New York
VISITING HOURS: Private, visitors may walk or drive by
SOURCES: NRHPINF. Telephone conversation May 14, 1994, Dr. Fred Carter, community resident. *The Black 100,* 103–7. *The African American Encyclopedia,* vol. 3, 866–9.

Claude McKay Residence

The poet Claude McKay resided during the 1940s in the Young Men's Christian Association building. Born in Jamaica in 1890, he had moved as a young man to the United States. McKay worked at many odd jobs until he finally realized that his calling was to be a writer.

After World War I he noted with sorrow that Black soldiers who had served honorably in the U.S. armed forces returned home to face racial attacks and lynchings. Moved by this injustice, he wrote a stirring poem, "If We Must Die," later read by Winston Churchill in the British House of Commons. McKay's rousing poem was a catalyst that inspired many artists and writers of the Harlem Renaissance. Black writers finally were recognized for their creativity and ability to describe in their own words the African American experience in America.

The Great Depression was a time of financial difficulty for McKay, who also suffered emotionally. In 1937 when he published his autobiography, *A Long Way from Home,* his personal fortunes were very low. By 1942 he lacked money, he was in poor health, and he was unable to find work. He suffered a stroke, and although his last years were spent in poverty, he continued to write until his death in 1948 at the age of fifty-eight.

Claude McKay's home from 1941 to 1946 was in the Young Men's Christian Association building on 135th Street, which had residential space on its upper levels. A small plaque by the elevator confirms that McKay lived here. Many well-known African Americans also lived in the hotel at the time. The fourteen-story red brick building contains a chapel, branch offices, conference rooms, and a basement kitchen. The site is listed in the *National Register of Historic Places.*

DATE OF SIGNIFICANCE: McKay residence, 1941–1946
ADDRESS: 180 W. 135th Street, New York
TELEPHONE: Harlem Branch of the YMCA, (212) 281-4100
VISITING HOURS: Private, visitors may walk or drive by
SOURCES: NRHPINF. Telephone call May 9, 1994, to site. "If We Must Die."

Florence Mills House

Florence Mills (1895–1927) was an internationally known entertainer in the early twentieth century. Although she had appeared regularly at the Keith and Orpheum Theaters before 1921, she gained wide recognition that year as a result of her performance in the musical *Shuffle Along,* a musical extravaganza that opened at the Sixty-third Street Theater in New York. The role of Ruth Little was to have been played by Gertrude Saunders, but Saunders became ill and Mills was chosen to replace her. The show made entertainment history as a musical composed, directed, and performed by African Americans, and Mills gained fame throughout the entertainment world for her stellar performance.

ADDRESS: 220 W. 135th Street, New York
VISITING HOURS: Private, visitors may walk or drive by
SOURCE: NRHPINF.

New York Amsterdam News Building

The *New York Amsterdam News* was located at one time in the center structure of a group of four-story row houses. The narrow structure—approximately fifteen feet wide at the street side—was the newspaper's second home. James H. Anderson founded the periodical in his home in 1909 using a few sheets of paper, a pencil, and a four-by-five-foot table. The newspaper met a need in the Black community. The National Association for the Advancement of Colored People was organized during this period, and the African American community was shifting away from the accommodationist philosophy of Booker T. Washington to the social action views advocated by W. E. B. Du Bois and William Monroe Trotter.

Impelled by racially motivated lynchings that were common occurrences at the time, the *New York Amsterdam News* condemned public officials for their failure to end these atrocities. When the Dyer Anti-Lynching Bill was defeated, the newspaper spoke out, maintaining that the bill still lived on in many hearts and minds.

By 1916 the journal needed more space and moved to Seventh Avenue (now Adam Clayton Powell Jr. Boulevard). There it expanded from a local paper in Harlem to one with nationwide appeal. Editors continued to condemn the discrimination and injustice faced by African Americans and provided a powerful voice for African Americans in Harlem and throughout the United States.

In 1938 growth in circulation caused the newspaper to move again, this time to its present location on Eighth Avenue, where it has continued to be an effective voice for more than fifty-five years. The building on Adam Clayton Powell Jr. Boulevard, home of a distinguished Black newspaper for more than twenty-two years, is listed in the *National Register of Historic Places.*

DATE OF SIGNIFICANCE: 1916–1938
ADDRESS: 2293 Adam Clayton Powell Jr. Boulevard, New York
TELEPHONE: Newspaper, (212) 932-7400
VISITING HOURS: Private, visitors may drive by; newspaper operation at its current address, 2340 Frederick Douglass Boulevard, Thurs.–Fri. 11:30–12:30 or by appointment
SOURCES: NRHPINF. Telephone conversation May 12, 1994, Selvin Michael, vice president and comptroller.

New York Historical Society

The New York Historical Society contains materials associated with African American history among its collections. The extensive pamphlet collection in the society's library, which dates from the colonial and Revolutionary War periods through the Civil War, is one of the largest ever assembled on American slavery and the abolitionist movement.

DATE ESTABLISHED:	1804
ADDRESS:	170 Central Park West, New York
TELEPHONE:	(212) 873-3400
VISITING HOURS:	Tues.–Sat. and some holidays 10–5
FEES:	Nonmembers, $1
SOURCE:	Brochure forwarded by Mary Carey, reference librarian, New York Historical Society.

Paul Robeson Residence

Paul Robeson (1898–1976) was an outstanding American scholar, actor, concert artist, and humanitarian. Because he took an uncompromising stand for justice, he was widely ostracized and shunned in his own country. In spite of the hostility he endured and the damage done to his reputation, Robeson ended his career as one of the most-respected men of the century.

Paul Robeson's father, William Drew Robeson, was a runaway slave who had demonstrated his own brand of courage by fleeing to freedom. He later earned a college degree, became a Methodist minister, and married Maria Louisa Bustill, a schoolteacher. Paul was born in Princeton, New Jersey, the youngest of eight children. Because his mother died when Paul was six years old, his father raised the family by himself, requiring excellence from each of the children.

Robeson entered Rutgers University in 1915, one of the first African Americans to study at that school. In spite of racism he encountered at Rutgers, he excelled in many fields. With twelve letters in sports, he was named all-American end in football and elected to the Phi Beta Kappa society. Robeson then entered Columbia University Law School, obtaining his law degree in 1923. About that time he married a chemist, Eslanda Cardozo Goode (1896–1965). Eslanda was brilliant in her own right. She was the granddaughter of Francis Lewis Cardozo, a graduate of Glasgow University, founder of the Avery Normal Institute (see the listing in Charleston, South Carolina), and state treasurer in South Carolina during Reconstruction years. Graduating at the age of sixteen from a high school in Chicago, Eslanda placed third in statewide examinations and received a full-tuition scholarship to the University of Illinois. There she majored in chemistry. After her junior year she transferred to Columbia University with plans to enter the field of medicine. She was the first Black staff member (in histological chemistry) at the Presbyterian Hospital of Columbia University. She met Paul Robeson while working at the hospital.

Despite his brilliance, Robeson had difficulties in the practice of law mainly because of racial prejudice against Black attorneys. Recognizing her husband's artistic talents, Eslanda urged him to become an actor and singer. Robeson joined the Provincetown Players and achieved a resounding success in New York and London in the title role of Eugene O'Neill's play, *The Emperor Jones.* He also played this same role in a film. Robeson's magnificent bass voice was noted by Larry Brown, an arranger of Black spirituals; this encounter was the impetus that made Robeson a star on the concert stage. He presented Black spirituals in Greenwich Village and on other stages around the country. He was acclaimed for his rendition of "Ol' Man River" in *Show Boat.* His performance in *Othello* on Broadway in 1943 was a memorable event.

Robeson, who was proud of his African American heritage, denounced Hollywood for the way in which films portrayed Black people, and he refused demeaning roles. Due to his demonstrations against segregation and his participation in pacifist and Communist-sponsored peace meetings, a shadow fell upon Robeson's career. When a Senate Judiciary Committee called upon him to testify in 1948, he refused on the basis of violation of his privacy. As a result, concert halls around the country were closed to him and the U.S. State Department refused to renew his passport. He accepted the Stalin Peace Prize in 1952 and settled in England with his family in 1958, the same year that a Supreme Court ruling restored his passport.

Later, in 1963, Robeson returned to the United States. Despite poor health, he was honored on his seventy-fifth birthday by a near-capacity crowd at Carnegie Hall in a three-hour celebration. He died in January 1976 at the age of seventy-seven.

DATE OF SIGNIFICANCE: Robeson residence, 1939 to 1941
ADDRESS: 555 Edgecombe Avenue, New York
VISITING HOURS: Private, visitors may walk or drive by
SOURCES: NRHPINF. *The African American Encyclopedia,* vol. 5, 1376–80.

Schomburg Center for Research in Black Culture*

The Schomburg Center for Research in Black Culture is the world's most complete collection of books, photographs, rare manuscripts, films, art, and other artifacts relating to African American culture. Individuals and institutions from the United States and abroad use the collection's more than 5 million items.

The three-story stone building in the middle of Harlem originally was the 135th Street branch of the New York Public Library. When the library opened in 1905, the neighborhood was a fashionable, predominantly Jewish community. African Americans were beginning to move into the area; within fifteen years this was one of the most important Black communities in the United States. Many Black residents came to New York to fill the labor shortage created by World War I. They settled in Harlem, and many of them patronized this library, which had begun to focus on the Black experience in America.

Ernestine Rose became the branch librarian in 1920. Five years later when the Harlem Renaissance was in full flower, the Department of Negro Literature and History was established here. In 1926 its collection won national acclaim with the addition of the personal library of the distinguished Black scholar Arthur A. Schomburg.

Schomburg, who was born in Puerto Rico in 1874, came to New York City in 1901. Carnegie funds were used to acquire his collection of materials on African American culture. Included were more than 5,000 volumes, 3,000 manuscripts, and 2,000 etchings and paintings. Schomburg served as curator of the department from 1932 until his death in 1938; the collection was renamed in his honor in 1940.

The Schomburg Center is engaged today in a massive expansion project. The landmark building housing the original collections will have study and storage space for special collections, an exhibition hall, the restored American Negro Theatre, and a new auditorium. The Schomburg Center is listed in the *National Register of Historic Places.*

DATE ESTABLISHED: 1905; as center, 1926
ADDRESS: 135th Street at Malcolm X Boulevard, New York
TELEPHONE: (212) 491-2200
VISITING HOURS: Mon.–Wed. noon–8, Thurs.–Sat. 10–6, Sun. (exhibits only) 1–5

FEES: None

SOURCES: Brochure from the Schomburg Center. NRHPINF. Telephone call to site, April 30, 1994. *The African American Presence in New York State History*, 12.

Studio Museum of Harlem

The Studio Museum of Harlem is an outstanding museum devoted to the art and artifacts of Black America and the African Diaspora. Incorporated in 1967 as a working space for artists, the museum quickly became the place to view the work of emerging and prominent Black and Hispanic artists.

In 1979 the museum received the gift of a half-empty, 60,000-square-foot office building, which was converted into the acclaimed Studio Museum. Serving the Harlem community, New York, the United States, and a growing international community as well, the Studio Museum has evolved into an internationally renowned cultural institution. Museum programs include temporary exhibitions; a permanent collection; and a schedule of interpretive, educational, and developmental programs.

DATE ESTABLISHED: 1967

ADDRESS: 144 W. 125th Street, New York

TELEPHONE: (212) 864-4500

VISITING HOURS: Wed.–Fri. 10–5, Sat.–Sun. 1–6; tours by appointment; closed Mon.–Tues.

FEES: Adults, $5; students and senior citizens, $3; children under 13, $1; members, free

SOURCE: George Calderaro, public relations coordinator, Studio Museum in Harlem. Telephone call to site, Aug. 8, 1995.

The 369th Historical Society

The 369th Historical Society is named in honor of the 369th Regiment, an all-Black military unit that served with great distinction in France in World War I. The 369th Veterans Association housed at this site on Fifth Avenue preserves the historical achievements of Black Americans who served in the United States military and houses the largest collection of this type on the East Coast.

The 369th Regiment, originally called the Fifteenth Infantry Regiment, New York National Guard, was the first U.S. regiment to serve as an integral part of a foreign army. In 1918 the unit was designated the 369th Infantry and was sent to France. The U.S. government did not want to recognize a fully Black fighting unit; therefore, the 369th became the only unit in the United States to fight in World War I under a state flag—the men carried the state flag of New York throughout the war. The first Allied regiment to reach the Rhine River, the 369th fought continuously for 191 days on the front line and never had a man captured, never lost a trench, and never lost a foot of territory. The French government awarded the entire unit the Croix de Guerre for heroism and awarded the Croix de Guerre and the Legion of Honor to 171 individual men for exceptional gallantry under fire. The 369th was the first combat regiment to arrive home in America and the first to march up Fifth Avenue under the Victory Arch.

The 369th Veterans Association is located on the first floor in this building and the museum is on the second level. During Black history month many school groups come to the museum to hear talks about African American veterans and to see the displays of old equipment and the photographs of African American officers from World War I through the 1990–1991 Desert Storm campaign.

ADDRESS: 2366 Fifth Avenue (142nd Street), New York

TELEPHONE: (212) 281-3308

SOURCES: Telephone conversation Jan. 27, 1995, Gladstone A. Dell, national vice president, 369th Veterans Association. *The Historical and Cultural Atlas of African Americans,* 116–17. *The African American Presence in New York State History.*

Port Chester

Bush-Lyon Homestead

The Bush-Lyon Homestead, one of the few residences in Port Chester constructed in pre-Revolutionary War days, contains a rare example in a northern state of slave quarters, which were part of a group of outbuildings to the northeast of the main house. Although the frame, two-story slave house is not open to the public, plans are under way to make the interior accessible. Other outbuildings at the site, which is operated by the Port Chester Historical Society, include a carriage house and a corn crib.

DATE BUILT: 1750

ADDRESS: 479 King Street (Lyon Park), Port Chester

TELEPHONE: (914) 939-8918

VISITING HOURS: Thurs. 1:30–4; closed holidays

FEES: Donations accepted

SOURCES: Goldie Solomon, president, Port Chester Historical Society. Susan A. Morison, director, The Rye Historical Society. Telephone conversation May 11, 1994, James Charles, caretaker.

Rochester

Susan B. Anthony House National Historic Landmark

Born in Adams, Massachusetts, the daughter of a Quaker abolitionist, Susan B. Anthony (1820–1906) was a prominent white abolitionist, temperance worker, and leader of the movement for women's rights. The Anthony family arrived in Rochester, New York, in the 1840s. Anthony was a teacher and an agitator for women's suffrage and equal pay for women. In 1848 she met Frederick Douglass, a well-known Black antislavery speaker. Members of the Douglass and Anthony families became friends and often met to discuss political issues, including the need to put an end to slavery in the United States.

Anthony's brother, Merritt Anthony, settled near Osawatomie, Kansas, where he became a supporter of John Brown, the white abolitionist leader. In August 1856 Merritt Anthony was wounded when he joined Brown and his followers in a battle against proslavery forces. This incident caused Susan Anthony to increase her antislavery campaign. On December 2, 1859, the night of Brown's execution, she rented Corinthian Hall in Rochester and urged the people of the city to mourn his death. Some 300 citizens attended the rally, even though many prominent Rochester residents refused to honor the memory of the controversial man.

In 1861 Anthony rented the hall again and staged a three-day antislavery convention. There was great tension in Rochester because at that very moment some of the southern states were seceding from the Union. On the first night of the convention a yelling, stamping mob broke into the hall and stopped the meeting. To avoid another violent confrontation, Anthony moved the convention on the next two nights to the Zion African Methodist Church.

During the Civil War Anthony strongly supported President Abraham Lincoln's emancipation policy. The petitions she gathered helped persuade Congress to pass the Thirteenth Amendment that abolished slavery in 1865.

After the war Anthony and her close associate Elizabeth Cady Stanton organized the National Women's Suffrage Association in 1869. Anthony agitated for extension of the right to vote to women. Even though she also favored giving the vote to freedmen, she was determined that the enfranchisement of Black men would not be emphasized over the drive for women's suffrage. Some had sought the vote for Black men before seeking it for women.

Despite the friendship between Douglass and Anthony, Douglass considered Anthony's position that "no Negro shall be enfranchised while woman is not" to be less than fair. He pointed out, "Now considering that while men have been enfranchised always, and colored men have not, the conduct of these white women [Anthony and Elizabeth Cady Stanton], whose husbands, fathers, and brothers are voters, does not seem generous."[1]

Still, more things brought Anthony and Douglass together than divided them. She was one of the eulogists at his funeral in Washington. A few days later Susan's sister, Mary Anthony, spoke at a memorial service for Douglass at a church in Rochester, recalling the ties of friendship between the two families over many years.

This two and one-half–story brick house was the home of Susan Anthony, a leader in the abolitionist crusade.

DATE BUILT:	c1860; Anthony residence, 1866–1906
ADDRESS:	17 Madison Street, Rochester
TELEPHONE:	(716) 235-6124
VISITING HOURS:	Thurs.–Sat. 1–4; closed Sun.–Wed. and holidays except by appointment
FEES:	Adults, $5; senior citizens 62 and over and students, $3; children under 12, $1
SOURCES:	Telephone conversation May 5, 1994, and Aug. 10, 1995, Lorie Barnum, executive director, Susan B. Anthony House. "Griffing Papers," 469–70. *National Register of Historic Places*, 506. "Anti-Slavery Days in Rochester," 113–55. *Frederick Douglass*, 269.

Frederick Douglass Gravesite*

Rochester was the home of the famous nineteenth-century abolitionist Frederick Douglass (1817–1895). Born a slave in Maryland, he learned to read and write as a young boy. He was first taught to read by a mistress in Baltimore who later stopped the lessons because of her husband's anger at the instruction. This led to an unquenchable desire to learn to read, and Douglass traded bread for instruction from young white boys who lived nearby. When he was returned to the plantation where he had already experienced cruel treatment, Douglass became imbued with a strong desire to escape. As his master in Baltimore suspected, Douglass's new ability to read and learn had destroyed any possibility that he would remain a docile slave. In 1838 he escaped to the

North and sent for his bride-to-be, Anna, to join him. Douglass's imposing presence and his riveting accounts of slavery, led to his becoming a sought-after antislavery speaker.

Even though he was in the North, Douglass feared being picked up as a runaway and returned to his owner in Maryland; therefore, he spent some time in England. There he made some friends who collected enough funds to purchase his freedom. The same friends gave him $2,500 to use in starting an antislavery newspaper. Upon his return to the United States, Douglass settled in Rochester.

Douglass and his associate Martin Delaney (1812–1885), a man proud of his African heritage, founded the *North Star* newspaper in 1847. Its name was changed a few years later to *Frederick Douglass's Paper.* Passage of the Fugitive Slave Law caused much uneasiness among Douglass's friends who warned him that he should go to Canada for safety's sake. Douglass refused to give up his newspaper, however, and decided to stay in Rochester. He was cautious enough to move to a house on the outskirts of the city that could be reached only by a private road. His home (no longer standing) became a major station on the underground railroad. When he went each day to the paper's office at 25 East Main Street, Douglass would often find fugitive slaves sitting on the stairway. That night he would arrange for them to find refuge in other nearby cities.

Frederick and Anna had five children. They sent their daughter, Rosetta, to a fashionable girls school but was dismayed when he discovered that she was not allowed to mingle with the white students. He was also dissatisfied with the segregated colored school and hired a tutor to teach his children at home. As a result of Douglass's proddings, the board of education of Rochester finally opened all the city's schools to Black children in 1857.

Although Douglass was on friendly terms with John Brown, they differed on the means to adopt in fighting slavery. Brown believed violence would be needed to end slavery, but Douglass favored political work within the framework of the law. During the Civil War Douglass helped recruit Black men to serve in two regiments organized in Massachusetts. Two of his sons, Charles and Lewis, were the first men from New York to enlist. After the war Douglass and his sons moved to Washington, D.C., where they published a newspaper, the *New National Era.* (Two of the Douglass homes in Washington, D.C., are open to the public and are described in that section.)

When Frederick Douglass died in 1895, his body was returned from Washington to Rochester to be laid to rest in Rochester's Mt. Hope Cemetery. The city united to honor one of its most illustrious citizens. His body lay in state at City Hall, and thousands of schoolchildren filed past to pay their final respects. A military escort and band accompanied mourners to the cemetery.

Today three monuments commemorate the great abolitionist. These include a bust at the University of Rochester's Frederick Douglass Building, placed there in June 1879, a bust at the Colgate Rochester Divinity School Library, and a bronze statue of Douglass in Highland Park. Four years after Douglass died, Gertrude Thompson, his great-granddaughter, unveiled the life-sized bronze statue of Douglass. Theodore Roosevelt, then governor of New York, made the principal address at the ceremony.

DATE OF SIGNIFICANCE: 1895

ADDRESSES: Mt. Hope Cemetery, south of downtown Rochester via Mt. Hope Avenue (NY 15), Highland Park; Colgate Rochester Divinity School Library, University of Rochester Frederick Douglass Building, Rochester

TELEPHONE: Cemetery, (716) 473-2755

VISITING HOURS: Cemetery, daily, dawn–dusk

FEES: None

SOURCES: Ruth Rosenberg-Naparsteck, city historian. Elizabeth G. Holahan, president, Rochester Historical Society. Leatrice M. Kemo, Rochester Museum & Science Center. *Webster's New Biographical Dictionary,* 271, 294. "Two Episodes of Anti-Slavery Days," 213–22. "Anti-Slavery Days in Rochester," 113–55. *Frederick Douglass,* 160–1.

Memorial African Methodist Episcopal Zion Church

Memorial A.M.E. Zion Church is associated with an early pastor of the church, Reverend Thomas James. Reverend James was born in slavery in 1804 in Canajoharie, New York. When he was eight years old, his family was divided for sale. His mother was dragged from the attic where she was hiding and sold away from her children, who never saw her again. James had three masters but ran away from the third. Before coming to Rochester, he spent some time as a worker on the canals.

Reverend James later traveled to New Bedford, where he served as pastor of Zion Chapel. In his autobiography, published in 1866, he noted that Frederick Douglass, who had recently escaped from slavery, one day visited his church. He called on Douglass to speak, and the moving presentation led to Douglass's being sent on a lecture tour by the American Anti-Slavery Society. The Douglass family made Zion Chapel their religious home in New Bedford.

James returned to Rochester in 1856 and served as pastor of Zion Church. In his years there, he knew about many Black people who had tried to escape from slavery. In his autobiography he told about a runaway woman slave who had been recaptured in 1823. She was being taken to court to be returned to her master in West Virginia when fifteen or twenty African Americans overpowered the officers and took her away. They were intercepted later, and the woman was taken from them. She committed suicide rather than go back to being a slave. In 1832 another woman slave was recaptured by her owner. The rescuers, again a group of Black people, were not successful in freeing her in Rochester. However, they followed the woman and her owner east to Palmyra, New York, where they were finally able to liberate her.

Zion Church was built in the nineteenth century for a Black congregation. Today the Rochester landmark is called the Memorial A.M.E. Zion Church.

DATE ESTABLISHED:	19th century
ADDRESS:	549 Clarissa Street, Rochester
TELEPHONE:	(716) 546-5997
VISITING HOURS:	Church office, by appointment Tues.–Thurs. 9–4, Fri.–Sat. 10–2; Sun. school, 9:30; Sun. service, 11
FEES:	None
SOURCES:	Telephone conversation Aug. 8, 1995, Marjorie Anderson, secretary, Memorial A.M.E. Zion Church. Elizabeth G. Holahan, president, Rochester Historical Society. "Anti-Slavery Days in Rochester," 113–55. *A History of Negro Slavery in New York. Frederick Douglass,* 82.

Margaret Woodbury Strong Museum

The Strong Museum launched its initiative of collecting and interpreting African-American history in 1989. Museum exhibits incorporate the contributions of African Americans locally and throughout the United States. Some past exhibits (including traveling exhibits) at the Strong Museum have included *Freedom's Journals: The History of the Black Press in New York State; Field to Factory: Afro-American Migration; Black Printmakers and the WPA; The Real McCoy: Afro-American Invention and Innovation, 1619–1930; Stitching Memories: African-American Story Quilts;* and *Climbing Jacob's Ladder: The Rise of Black Churches in Eastern American Cities, 1740–1877.*

A Strong Museum conference in 1989 highlighted the Civil Rights Movement of the mid-twentieth century with a focus on the weekend of July 24–26, 1964, when Governor Nelson Rockefeller ordered 1,500 National Guard members to restore order to the streets of Rochester.

DATE ESTABLISHED: October 1982
ADDRESS: One Manhattan Square, Rochester
TELEPHONE: (716) 263-2700
VISITING HOURS: Mon.–Sat. 10–5, Sun. 1–5; closed Thanksgiving, Christmas, New Year's Day
FEES: Adults, $5; senior citizens and students, $4; children 3–16, $3; children under 3, free
SOURCES: Linda B. Tabit, lead educator for family programs, Strong Museum. Elizabeth G. Holahan, president, Rochester Historical Society. Strong Museum brochures. Telephone call to site, Aug. 8, 1995.

South Granville

Lemuel Haynes House

Lemuel Haynes, an outstanding African American minister, was born in Connecticut in 1753 of a Black father and a white mother. At the age of five months the child was taken to the household of Deacon David Rose, where he was bound out to be a servant for twenty-five years.

As a child, Lemuel received some advantages that were denied to most African Americans in the 1700s. He attended a common school in Massachusetts and had Bible studies in the Rose household. When he was young, he impressed adults with his ability to remember much of the material he had heard. He often read a sermon aloud on Saturday nights, the time of religious instruction in the Rose household. One evening when he had finished reading, the Deacon asked whose sermon he had read. He replied, "It's Lemuel's sermon." Word spread about the youth's ability, and the local parish, which lacked a minister, began calling on Lemuel frequently to conduct services.

At the age of twenty-one, Lemuel was free of his indenture. He left the Rose household and enlisted in the Minutemen, fighting with them in battles at Lexington. Following his military experience, he returned to farming and the study of theology. Encouraged by neighbors who recognized his talent, Haynes studied in Connecticut to prepare for the ministry. When he was invited to preach in Middle Granville, he may have been the first Black man in America to serve as pastor of a white church. In 1785 when Haynes was ordained as a minister of the Congregational Church, he became the first Black man to be ordained by any religious sect in North America.

Haynes encountered disrespectful attitudes from some members of a congregation in Torrington, Connecticut, and their behavior forced him to leave that church. In spite of that experience, respect grew over the years for his skill as a preacher and theologian. When Middlebury College awarded him the honorary Master of Arts degree in 1804, it was the first such degree bestowed on a Black person in America.

Haynes spent the final eleven years of his life as a pastor in South Granville, New York. He died in 1833, at the age of eighty, and his wife, Elizabeth, died three years later. Both are buried in the South Granville cemetery. Haynes was well respected in many churches in which he served and was held in high esteem in those communities for his accomplishments.

The Haynes House is the dwelling where the Reverend Haynes lived during the last eleven years of his life. The small frame house has two stories and a cellar. The interior still has a large fireplace with a Dutch oven; there are wide floorboards throughout the house.

DATE BUILT: 1793; Haynes residence, 1822–1833; restoration, 1967

ADDRESS: Parker Hill Road off NY 149, South Granville (from NY 22 in Granville turn right onto NY 149; go approximately 2½ miles to South Granville; turn left onto Parker Hill Road; the house is the second on the right on Parker Hill)

VISITING HOURS: Private, visitors may drive by

SOURCES: Telephone conversation June 15, 1994, Mitchell Van Guilder, Granville resident. NRHPINF.

Stillwater

Saratoga National Historical Park

In 1777 General John Burgoyne led a bold but unsuccessful British campaign to split the American colonies by coming south from Canada along the Lake Champlain-Hudson River Valley route. He left St. John's, Canada, on June 17 with a force of some 9,000 soldiers. Meanwhile, the Americans had brought together an army of nearly 20,000 men who surrounded the British at Saratoga about thirty miles north of Albany. Exhausted by the long march and faced with overwhelming numbers, the British were forced to surrender. Burgoyne ordered the 6,000 surviving members of his command to stack their weapons along the west bank of the Hudson. This was one of the colonists' most decisive victories. Because it so impressed the French that they agreed to recognize the rebellious Americans and aid them militarily, the Battle of Saratoga led ultimately to American independence.

The brigades that served in the Saratoga campaign were estimated to be about 4 percent Black. Black soldiers served in racially mixed units in both battles at Saratoga. Some African Americans who enlisted were free; some were slaves who remained slaves after their service; still others received their freedom after the war. For example, Peter Brewer of New Boston, New Hampshire, a Black soldier, enlisted as a private in the First New Hampshire Regiment, which fought in both battles of Saratoga. He was killed in the second battle on October 7, 1777. Another African American, Sampson Brown of the Fifteenth Massachusetts, also was killed at Saratoga. A third African American, Agrippa Hull, fought six years with the Continental army. Four years of his service were under the command of General Taddeus (Tadeusz) Kosciusko, a Polish patriot who had joined George Washington's armies. An unidentified artist painted a portrait of Hull that hangs in the historical room of the Stockbridge Library in Massachusetts.

Unfortunately, some American officers were unwilling to recognize the patriotism of the African Americans who served under them. A number of these officers were slaveowners who had grave concerns about arming Black men. In a letter General Philip Schuyler wrote to General Heath on July 28, 1777, he expressed contempt for his Black soldiers:

> . . . of the few Continental Troops we have had . . . one-third part is composed of men too far advanced in years for field service; of boys, or rather children, and mortifying barely to mention, of Negroes.[2]

Facing the threat of invasion from Canada and a thrust against Philadelphia, the Americans needed as many men as possible for long-term service in the Continental Army. Some enlisted men were farmers who had to return home at harvest time; if they had not, their families would have starved. As a result, the army decided to accept African Americans. Some were offered freedom for enlisting in place of their owners. Black soldiers served as foot soldiers, orderlies, or drummers. This was the last U.S. armed force until the Korean conflict that was racially integrated.

Today Saratoga National Historical Park includes more than 2,700 acres of battlefield sites. An automobile tour starts with maps and exhibits in the Visitors' Center; it then begins at the parking area and covers nine miles and ten tour stops. The 155-foot Saratoga Monument, which overlooks the Hudson Valley and the flats where the surrender took place, commemorates the surrender of the British forces under General John Burgoyne to American General Horatio Gates on October 17, 1777. The surrender followed two battles of Saratoga in the present town of Stillwater, and the British retreat to what is now the Schuylerville area.

DATE OF SIGNIFICANCE:	Oct. 17, 1777; park established, 1948
ADDRESS:	Park entrances, 30 miles north of Albany on US 4 and NY 32; Visitors Center, at the main section of the Historical Park along US 4 just north of Stillwater; General Philip Schuyler House and Saratoga Monument, a few more miles north in Schuylerville
TELEPHONE:	(518) 664-9821
VISITING HOURS:	Park, daily Apr.–Nov. 30 9–5; Schuyler House, Memorial Day–Labor Day, daily 9–5; monument, mid-June–Labor Day daily 9–5; Visitors Center closed Thanksgiving, Christmas, New Year's
FEES:	Adults, $3 for tour road only; children, free
SOURCES:	Paul Okey, park historian. *A Teacher's Guide to Saratoga National Historical Park.* National Park Service pamphlets and flier on the Saratoga park and on the Schuyler House.

Syracuse

Jerry Rescue Memorial

The most famous antislavery event in Syracuse was the rescue of a Black man, William Henry, who was also known as Jerry. He had escaped from slavery in Missouri and come to Syracuse via the underground railroad. He then worked for several years in Syracuse as a cabinetmaker and cooper. Jerry should have been able to live a peaceful life in freedom because the state of New York had abolished slavery in 1827; however, the federal government enacted the Fugitive Slave Law of 1850, which eliminated safe havens everywhere.

The law specified that if a white person claimed that a Black person was a fugitive, the Black person had no right to a jury trial. A white official could receive two times the usual fee if he ruled that the Black person was a fugitive rather than ruling the opposite. The law punished citizens who helped a fugitive escape. Many free Black people fled because they feared being kidnapped and sent into slavery. Reverend Samuel Ward, a Black abolitionist, spoke out against the law in an editorial in his newspaper, the *Impartial Citizen:*

> Now, this bill strips us of all manner of protection, by the writ of habeas corpus, by jury trial, or by any other process known to the laws of civilized nations, that are thrown as safeguards around personal liberty. But while it does this, it throws us back upon the natural and inalienable right of self-defense—self protection. It solemnly refers to each of us, individually, the question, whether we will submit to being enslaved by the hyenas which this

> law creates and encourages, or whether we will protect ourselves, even if, in so doing, we have to peril our lives, and more than peril the useless and devilish carcasses of Negro-catchers. It gives us the alternative of dying freemen, or living slaves.[3]

The Liberty Party of abolitionists called a meeting for October 1, 1851. On the day prior to the meeting, the county fair was in progress, and the city saw a bustle of activity: federal agents arrested Jerry on trumped-up charges of theft. Then they explained that he had been arrested as a fugitive slave.

Jerry slipped away from the officers and made a dash for freedom. Farmers had brought large loads of wood to the city and were standing waiting for purchasers. Jerry, handcuffed, began to dodge in and out among the loads of wood. A young boy, Horace McGuire, who was delivering newspapers, witnessed the flight. Years later he described the incident to the Rochester Historical Association:

> With my papers under my arm, I saw the colored man handcuffed, dodging his pursuers, among the loads of wood. Boy-like, neglectful I fear of our subscribers, I followed the crowd and witnessed the fight. Jerry fought with a determined effort to be free but was overpowered, his clothing badly torn, his face covered with blood and one of his ribs broken. A passing wagon was impressed into the service of the officers and Jerry thrown into it, one of the officers sitting on his breast and another on his legs and others leading the horses as they drove the prisoner back to the police station.[4]

The police took Jerry to the police station (today the site is known as the Jerry Rescue Site). News spread about the capture. Church bells rang, and crowds gathered. The abolitionists held a meeting that evening to plan a rescue. White abolitionist Gerrit Smith, with others, advocated using force to rescue Jerry. Authorities guarded the police station and all roads out of the city. At the same time abolitionists continued with their plans. They secured a light carriage and a pair of the fastest horses in the city.

Near midnight more than 2,000 abolitionists gathered. Proceeding to the hardware store of a sympathetic owner, they seized iron bars and axes, rushed to the prison, and overpowered the guards. Then they hurried Jerry into a carriage and scattered in all directions to confuse those on their trail. The men driving Jerry's carriage wove in and out among the streets, finally arriving at a safe house. Jerry remained there for several days, where he was given medical treatment and suitable clothing for the next part of his journey.

On October 5, 1851, Jerry's rescuers took him to Oswego, New York. The last moments before freedom had to be carefully planned. A schooner sailed out of Oswego's harbor as it normally would have, but returned after dark to meet a small boat pulled out by Jerry's friends. At last, Jerry was on his way to freedom in Canada. Jerry lived there for two years until he died in 1853 of tuberculosis.

The Liberty Party members had their convention on October 1, 1850. They never could have known when planning their meeting that the night before the meeting, 2,000 people would help with the daring rescue of William "Jerry" Henry. They rejoiced that his liberty had won the day. This incident, and the courage of the citizens in rescuing Henry, made Syracuse known nationally as being in the forefront of abolitionist activities.

In the early 1990s a monument commemorating Jerry's rescue was installed on the west side of Clinton Square, facing the site at Clinton and Water Streets where the mob had stormed the Syracuse jail in 1851 and freed Jerry. The building, which became widely known as the "Jerry Rescue Building," was demolished in 1974.

DATE OF SIGNIFICANCE: 1851

ADDRESS: Clinton Street (between Erie Boulevard W and Water Street), Syracuse

SOURCES: Judy Haven, researcher, Onondaga Historical Association. "The Rescue: Monument to our Proudest Moment." "History Preserved." *Syracuse and the Underground Railroad.*

Tarrytown

Foster Memorial African Methodist Episcopal Zion Church

Foster Memorial African Methodist Episcopal Zion Church, built in 1865 by free Black people, is the oldest Black church in continuous use in Westchester County, and may be one of the oldest in New York State. The congregation played an important role in the underground railroad.

The present-day village of Tarrytown is located on land that once belonged to an Algonquin Indian tribe. In 1681, a Dutch merchant of New Amsterdam, Frederick Philipse, purchased this area as part of his extensive manor and developed the land under the tenant farm system. Because the Philipse family was loyal to the crown during the American Revolution, the land was confiscated and sold to the tenants. The village grew from the Hudson River docks up the hill to the Albany Post Road.

In 1790 there were 357 free Black people in Westchester County, many of whom worked as farmhands or house servants. All slaves in New York were freed by law in 1827. The A.M.E. Zion denomination originated in New York City in 1796. In 1860 a congregation of the church was organized to serve the growing Black population in Tarrytown. It helped freed people in the village and also assisted runaway slaves. In the 1850s such help was an important factor in guiding fugitives up the Hudson River into Canada.

Mrs. Amanda Foster (1806–1904) was instrumental in developing the church. She was born in the household of New York Governor George Clinton but was separated from her mother when she was six weeks old. She served in different households until about the age of fifteen. Then she began working as a stewardess on a steamer. Traveling in the South with her "free papers," she was deeply moved by the sight of slavery. Amanda gave her free papers to a slave girl to help the girl escape.

Amanda married and her husband settled in Tarrytown. He operated a barber business and she opened a small confectionary store. When her first husband died, she remarried to Henry Foster, who was also a barber and who operated a livery business as well. The deeply religious couple adopted two children. The Fosters were among the few individuals who established the Tarrytown congregation. Church members met at first in a number of temporary quarters, including Foster's store. She raised funds in the early 1860s from white families who patronized her candy store and her husband's barber shop. The brick church was constructed in 1864. Amanda Foster was honored as the mother of the church. In 1886 the congregation numbered forty members and thirty-five Sunday School students. Members rented pews for three dollars per year.

In the nineteenth and early twentieth century, many social activities in the town were separated by race. Social and religious activities for the Black community centered around the church. The church assisted Black people who migrated north and settled in the Tarrytown area prior to World War I. During financially lean years church members often supported their pastor by bringing him a pound of food.

Foster Memorial Church is situated among single- and multifamily houses. Although altered since its completion in 1865, much of the early building still remains. The two-story structure is built of red brick with an artificial stone veneer. The former Foster home is directly east of the church.

In October 1984 the cornerstone was replaced at Foster Memorial A.M.E. Zion Church, marking its 120th anniversary. Members found in it a time capsule containing a roster of its members, a Sunday Service program, and a dime dated 1910. These were all later replaced. In 1982 the church was placed on the State and National Register of Historic Places. The Amanda Foster gravesite at Sleepy Hollow Cemetery was one of four African American historic sites designated as a Westchester County Tricentennial Historic Site.

DATE BUILT: Church, 1864–1865

ADDRESS: Church, 90 Wildey Street; cemetery, 540 N. Broadway, Tarrytown

TELEPHONE: Church, (914) 631-2002, or (914) 761-4786; cemetery, (914) 631-0081

VISITING HOURS: Church, Sun. 11; Sleepy Hollow Cemetery, Mon.–Fri. 8:30 A.M.–9:30 P.M.; Sat. 9–noon

SOURCES: NRHPINF. Westchester County Historical Society Library. Telephone conversation Jan. 28, 1995, May Foley, secretary, Foster Memorial Church. *"The Hills" in the Mid-Nineteenth Century.* "Foster Memorial AME Zion to Mark 120th Anniversary."

Notes

1. William S. McFeely, *Frederick Douglass* (New York: Simon & Schuster, 1991), 269.

2. Exhibit sheets, Saratoga National Historical Park, Edward A. Hoyt, researcher (Stillwater, New York: National Park Service).

3. Samuel Ward, "Editorial," *Impartial Citizen,* quoted in *The Liberator* (11 Oct. 1850), quoted in Herbert Aptheker, ed., *A Documentary History of the Negro People in the United States,* vol. 1 (New York: Citadel, 1990), 306.

4. Horace McGuire, "Two Episodes of Anti-Slavery Days," *Rochester Historical Society Bulletin* 4 (1916), 213–17.

Works Consulted

Academic American Encyclopedia. Danbury, Conn.: Grolier, 1993.

"Adam Clayton Powell Jr." Michael W. Williams, ed. In *The African American Encyclopedia,* vol. 5. New York: Marshall Cavendish, 1993.

The African American Encyclopedia. Michael W. Williams, ed. New York: Marshall Cavendish, 1993.

The African American Presence in New York State History: Four Regional History Surveys. Monroe Fordham, ed. New York: The New York African American Institute, State Univ. of New York, Albany, 1989.

And Why Not Every Man? Helene C. Phelan. Interlaken, N.Y.: Heart of the Lakes, 1987.

"Anti-Slavery Days in Rochester." Amy Hanmer-Croughton. *Rochester Historical Society Bulletin* 14 (1936): 113–55.

Black Arts New York 3, no. 6 (Feb. 1990), 1. [Newsletter of the Harlem Cultural Council]

The Black 100: A Ranking of the Most Influential African Americans, Past and Present. Columbus Salley. New York: Citadel, 1993.

"Foster Memorial AME Zion to Mark 120th Anniversary." Janis Tinsley. *(Tarrytown, New York) Gannett Westchester Newspapers,* 20 Oct. 1984.

Frederick Douglass. William S. McFeely. New York: Simon & Schuster, 1991.

"Griffing Papers." Joseph Borome. *The Journal of Negro History* 33 (1948): 469–70. Quoted in *A Documentary History of the Negro People in the United States,* vol. 2. Herbert Aptheker, ed. New York: Citadel, 1990.

"The Hills" in the Mid-Nineteenth Century: The History of a Rural Afro-American Community in Westchester County, New York. Edythe Quinn Caro. Westchester County Historical Society, 1988.

Historic Hurley in the Mid-Hudson Valley. Hurley, N.Y.: Town of Hurley. [brochure]

The Historical and Cultural Atlas of African Americans. Molefi K. Asante and Mark T. Mattson. New York: Macmillan, 1991.

The History of Bethel A.M.E. Church, Huntington, New York. Jeannette Johns. Huntington, N.Y.: The Author, 1993.

A History of Negro Slavery in New York. Edgar J. McManus. Syracuse, N.Y.: Syracuse, 1970.

"History Preserved, Woman Will Sculpt Monument to Honor 1851 Jerry Rescue." Mike Grogan. *(Syracuse, New York) Post Standard,* 1 Oct. 1988.

Hurley in the Days of Slavery. Olive M. Clearwater and John J. Hofler. Hurley, N.Y.: The Authors, 1986.

"If We Must Die." Claude McKay. In *I Am the Darker Brother.* Arnold Adoff, ed. New York: Macmillan, 1968, 63.

International Library of Negro Life and History: Historical Negro Biographies. Wilhelmena S. Robinson. New York: Publishers, 1970.

Ithaca's Neighborhoods: The Rhine, the Hill, and the Goose Pasture. Ithaca, N.Y.: DeWitt Historical Society of Tompkins County, 1988.

John Brown Farm. Lake Placid, N.Y.: New York State Office of Parks, Recreation and Historic Preservation and New York State Environmental Conservation, June 1985. [brochure]

The Negro's Civil War: How American Blacks Felt and Acted During the War for the Union. James M. McPherson. New York: Ballantine, 1991.

Old House Museum. Fort Edward, N.Y.: Fort Edward Historical Association.

"The Rescue: Monument to Our Proudest Moment." *(Syracuse, N.Y.) Herald-American,* 30 Aug. 1987.

"Rocks 'n' Rolling, Hurley's Stones Also Its Homes." Irene Gardner Keeney. *Albany (N.Y.) Times Union,* 25 June 1989.

Syracuse and the Underground Railroad. Evamaria Hardin. Syracuse, N.Y.: Erie Canal Museum, 1989. [pamphlet]

A Teacher's Guide to Saratoga National Historical Park. Rev. ed. Washington, D.C.: U.S. Department of the Interior, 1989.

"Two Episodes of Anti-Slavery Days." Horace McGuire. *Rochester Historical Society Bulletin* 4 (1916): 213–22.

Walk, Drive Around Historic Hurley. Hurley Heritage Society. Hurley, N.Y.: The Society, 1981. [pamphlet]

Webster's New Biographical Dictionary. Springfield, Mass.: Merriam-Webster, 1988.

Weeksville Then and Now. Joan Maynard and Gwen Cottman. Brooklyn, N.Y.: Society for the Preservation of Weeksville & Bedford-Stuyvesant History, 1983, 1988.

Pennsylvania

Buckingham

Mount Gilead African Methodist Episcopal Church

Mount Gilead African Methodist Episcopal Church, a small, one-room stone church, has a proud history as a part of the underground railroad. Slaves making their way north passed through this section of southeastern Pennsylvania. Mount Gilead Church was the last stop before the fugitives were smuggled into New Jersey to continue on their way to freedom. The original church was built of logs in 1832; it was rebuilt in stone in 1852.

DATE CONSTRUCTED: 1852

ADDRESS: Holicong Road, Buckingham

TELEPHONE: (215) 794-7307

VISITING HOURS: Congregation meets approximately 3 times per year; by appointment with Mr. or Mrs. William Hopkins, church caretakers

FEES: Donations appreciated

SOURCES: Telephone conversation June 16, 1994, Mrs. Mildred Hopkins, church caretaker. "Forming an Identity through the Church."

Chambersburg

John Brown House

This site is associated with John Brown, a white abolitionist who passionately advocated emancipation for Black people even if it could be obtained only through violent means. Brown led a raid at Harpers Ferry, West Virginia, in October 1859. He and his followers planned to seize the federal arsenal, free large numbers of slaves, and establish a stronghold where the freed people could live in peace. Although the rebellion was not successful, the effort aroused the country and caused many people to question the institution of slavery. The raid at Harpers Ferry and the ensuing uproar were among the factors that led to the Civil War. (See the listings for Kansas City and Osawatomie, Kansas; West Des Moines, Iowa; Akron, Ohio; Harpers Ferry, West Virginia; and Lake Placid, New York, for additional information on John Brown.)

In June 1859 John Brown rented an upstairs bedroom in this house from Abram Ritner, the owner, and lived here until mid-October. To conceal his identity, Brown called himself Dr. Isaac Smith and told people he was in the area to develop iron mines. He was quietly purchasing tools and weapons needed for the raid and storing them in a warehouse on Chambersburg's North Main Street. While living here, Brown became a part of the local community. He taught Sunday School at a church on the campus of Pennsylvania State University and preached at the Falling Spring Presbyterian Church in Chambersburg.

Abolitionist leaders, including the African American leader Frederick Douglass, visited John Brown at this site. Although they discussed plans for the capture of Harpers Ferry, Douglass did not participate in the raid. After the failure of the planned uprising, four of Brown's followers escaped and returned to this house, asking for asylum. Ritner hid them for a while in a nearby grove and gave them other assistance.

This house is Pennsylvania's only existing landmark associated with John Brown. In 1864, years after Brown's death, rebel soldiers burned the downtown section of Chambersburg to the ground. Ritner's home was located outside the center of town, however, and was not harmed.

The John Brown House is a two and one-half–story structure constructed of logs with clapboarding. The earliest section of the building probably dates from 1820 to 1840. It is listed in the *National Register of Historic Places*. The Pennsylvania Historical and Museum Commission operates the restored house, which is used today as offices of the American Heart Association.

DATE BUILT: c1820–1840

ADDRESS: 225 E. King Street, Chambersburg

TELEPHONE: (717) 263-2870

VISITING HOURS: Mon.–Fri. by appointment

SOURCES: NRHPINF. Telephone conversation June 15, 1994, Sharon Strike, division director, American Heart Association. *The John Brown House.*

Cheyney

Cheyney State University
Melrose

The Melrose residence at Cheyney University is significant in Black history for its association with Cheyney State University and with Dr. Leslie Pinckney Hill, an outstanding educator and leader from Cheyney State. The university had its start in 1828 when a Quaker philanthropist, Richard Humphrey, left a bequest of $10,000 to establish a school that would prepare teachers to instruct African American children in academics, agriculture, and the mechanical arts and trades. The training farm was established in 1837, and by 1842 the school, known as the Institute for Colored Youth, was one of the first of its kind in the nation devoted solely to the instruction of Black students.

The Institute for Colored Youth moved from Lombard Street in Philadelphia to Bainbridge Street, then to York Road. Fanny M. Jackson Coppin was one of the school's outstanding teachers. Born in slavery in Washington, D.C., in 1836, she was freed when her aunt, who earned only $6 a month, purchased Coppin for $125. Coppin attended a number of schools including Oberlin

College in Ohio, where she studied Greek, mathematics, and French. She taught former slaves who came to Ohio after the Civil War. She came to the Institute for Colored Youth in 1865 and four years later was appointed principal.

Needing more space than was reasonably available in Philadelphia for the agricultural curriculum, in 1902 the school bought the Cheyney farm, a site that had belonged to Quaker farmers John and Thomas Cheyney and that had a house, Melrose, built about 1785. The school moved to the farm in 1903 and used the former farmhouse as the president's house until 1968.

Dr. Leslie Pinckney Hill (1880–1960) led the college during a period of growth. He had graduated from Harvard University with high distinction—cum laude and Phi Beta Kappa—and served as class orator. After graduation, he headed the English Department at Tuskegee University from 1904 to 1907. While there, he married the dean of women, Jane Ethel Clark. When the position opened as principal of the Institute for Colored Youth in Philadelphia, Hill's mentor, Booker T. Washington, recommended him for the position.

As principal of the Institute, Hill transformed the school into a respected liberal arts college. Although the agricultural program continued, Hill steered the program away from the emphasis on preparing students for sharecropping and menial labor. He introduced a variety of promising agricultural practices and advanced craft skills. As the father of six daughters, Hill always advocated women's rights. Hill was active in community activities, organizing a variety of programs and encouraging Black people to remain aware of their cultural roots and heritage. He was a gifted speaker, and was often requested to address predominantly white audiences.

The Institute for Colored Youth was recognized as a teachers' college in 1902 and became a state normal school, at which time it changed its name to Cheyney State College (later University). The state began to support the college in 1922, and in 1942 it was accredited by the American Association of Teachers' Colleges. Graduates were successful not only in teaching but also in many other fields, including business, public service, and medicine.

Melrose, the house where the Hill family lived, was built in three sections, one prior to 1785, one in 1807, and one about 1850. The two and one-half–story residence originally was a single-family farmhouse with a cooking fireplace and with corner fireplaces in some rooms. The exterior remains much as it appeared when built. The 122-acre farm now forms the university campus. Melrose is listed in the *National Register of Historic Places.*

DATE BUILT: Central section, c1785

ADDRESS: Hill Drive, northwest corner of Creek and Cheyney Roads, Cheyney

TELEPHONE: (610) 399-2000

VISITING HOURS: Private; campus accessible during regular academic hours; closed summer

SOURCES: NRHPINF. *International Library of Negro Life and History,* 67.

Cornwall

Cornwall Iron Furnace

Although large numbers of slaves were brought to America to work in agriculture in the South, significant numbers were also used in both the South and the North in manufacturing operations, including the iron-making industry. In the eighteenth and nineteenth centuries iron furnaces dotted the Pennsylvania countryside, and villages with schools, churches, and shops grew around them. This industry used slave labor as early as 1766.

In 1742 Peter Grubb established the Cornwall Iron Furnace, which became the heart of a vast industrial plantation. The furnace was ideally situated for iron making because the surrounding area contained enormous quantities of iron ore, limestone, and timber. Workers continued day and night to make iron for domestic and military products.

Black workers were an important part of the operation. At the time of the American Revolution, approximately 6,000 slaves lived in Pennsylvania, ten of them in Lebanon Township in 1779. As early as April 1766, eleven Black people, slave and free, were listed in the journal at Cornwall. They worked among people of different nationalities, including a few indentured servants, most of whom came from Germany or Great Britain. In 1780 thirteen of the thirty-seven workers were Black. In that same year, however, a law passed in Pennsylvania called for the gradual emancipation of slaves; by 1792 only one Black person was listed as still working at Cornwall Furnace.

At least one slave who worked at the furnace emancipated himself. A hill in nearby Mt. Gretna is named "Governor Dick" after a slave who took on legendary fame by running away from Cornwall Furnace on April 17, 1796. On July 8 the following appeal for his capture appeared in a Pennsylvania newspaper:

> Twenty Dollars Reward.
>
> RAN away from Cornwall Furnace, Dauphin County, on Sunday the 17th of April last, a Negro man, called Dick, alias Governor Dick: he is an elderly man, bald headed, about five feet ten inches high, stout made, has a down look, is slightly marked on each of his temples with the small scores usual to some of the natives of Africa, has large feet, and a remarkable scar on the great toe of his right foot, occasioned by its being split with an axe. He is by trade a rough carpenter, and values himself greatly on his dexterity in that occupation. Had on when he went away, a new drab-coloured coatee, with metal buttons, jackets and overalls of the same, a new wool hat, and took with him some old clothes. As he lived in the early part of his life in Hartford County, State of Maryland, it is probable he has shaped his course to that quarter. Whoever secures the said Negro so that the owners may get him again, shall receive the above reward, and reasonable charges, if brought home.
>
> July 8th, 1796. Rudolph Kelker, jun.[1]

The records do not indicate whether Dick was ever recaptured.

The furnace remained in operation until 1883 when anthracite coal replaced charcoal as a fuel and made the furnace obsolete. The mines, however, continued in operation until 1974, and a surviving community nearby still reflects the period from 1857 to 1883.

Today Cornwall Furnace is one of the world's best-preserved iron-making facilities. The furnace, air blast machinery, and related buildings are still intact. The complex has a sandstone foundry with large stone furnace; Cornwall mine, the oldest continuously used iron mine in America; and a village of two-family houses constructed in the 1860s. The site also includes a Visitors Center in the Eighteenth Century charcoal house, a roasting oven, coal bins, and several other buildings. Guided tours are provided, and the Visitors Center contains exhibits.

DATE ESTABLISHED:	1742
ADDRESS:	Rexmont Road at Boyd Street, Cornwall
TELEPHONE:	(717) 272-9711
VISITING HOURS:	Tues.–Sat. 9–5; Sun. noon–5; open on Memorial Day, July 4, Labor Day; closed Mon., New Year's, Easter, Thanksgiving, Christmas
FEES:	Adults, $3.50; senior citizens over 60, $2.50; children 6–17, $1.50; children under 6, free
SOURCES:	Richard B. Stratton, Cornwall Iron Furnace. Telephone conversation Aug. 8, 1995, Karen Viozzi, guide, Cornwall Iron Furnace. *National Register of Historic Places,* 641. *Cornwall Iron Furnace.* "The Rise of an Iron Community," 15, 16, 92, 93.

Cornwells Heights

Bensalem African Methodist Episcopal Church

Bensalem A.M.E. Church, also known as Little Jerusalem, was built in 1830. It is one of the oldest African American churches in America that is still standing. The congregation dates back to 1820 when the Reverend James Miller founded it. The first members of the congregation included the Briggs, Bosley, Fraizer, and Mounts families. All of them were African Americans, who were among the original settlers in Bucks County. Most of the early church members were interred on a burial ground connected with the church.

Bensalem A.M.E. Church is a frame, one and one-half–story, one-room building. Constructed in 1830 with shiplap wooden siding, it was renovated in 1860 and 1896. In one renovation the structure was covered with shingles. In the 1960s the front was stuccoed. Reverend Ellsworth Collins, pastor of the church since 1988, notes that Bensalem Church had no indoor plumbing, including running water, until the early 1990s.

The interior features the original woodwork, including random-width floorboards, waist-level wainscoting, hand-painted board pews, and a pulpit and altar rail assembled by joinery and without nails. The church still serves the community of Bridgewater in Bucks County, Pennsylvania. Eight direct descendants of the original members are in the congregation. The building is listed in the *National Register of Historic Places.*

DATE BUILT: 1830

ADDRESS: 1200 Bridgewater Road, Cornwells Heights

TELEPHONE: (215) 245-7414

VISITING HOURS: Information on access to interior not available; visitors can walk or drive by

SOURCES: NRHPINF. Telephone conversation Aug. 20, 1995, Reverend Ellsworth S. Collins, pastor, Bensalem A.M.E. Church.

Elverson

Hopewell Furnace National Historic Site

Most people are aware of the role Black slaves played in America's agriculture, but few realize that Black people also worked as slaves, apprentices, and free laborers in America's early industries. In Pennsylvania African Americans made a significant contribution to the iron furnace industry, most often as unskilled laborers but sometimes as highly qualified workers who received pay equal to that of white workers.

Ironmasters owned Black slaves and also guided Black apprentices who worked for them for a specified number of years. In addition, they at times hired free Black people. Sometimes runaway slaves were employed for a period of time, after which they would move on to other localities.

In Elverson, Pennsylvania, Mark Bird built Hopewell Furnace on the headwaters of French Creek in 1771. Black slaves were employed there in the iron-making process, which required heavy labor. Raw materials—iron ore, limestone, and hardwood forests for charcoal—all were available in the area. Miners would dig the ore from mines or wash it from nearby streams; teamsters would then haul it to the furnace. Colliers would stack the wood and ignite it, watching the pit to ensure a slow, even burning. Finally the charcoal would be taken out, cooled, and taken by wagon to the furnace.

At the furnace the founder and workers added charcoal, limestone, and ore and periodically drained off the molten iron. Molders ladled the hot liquid into sand molds; skilled workers then cast intricate designs. Hopewell manufactured a variety of cookware and other iron products including stoves.

Laborers were scarce in the rural areas where the furnaces were situated. The furnaces had to be close to forests, the source of their fuel, and few people lived in those remote regions. To remedy this, owners used Black slaves, free Black workers who were paid, and indentured workers, both Black and white. Some poor Black parents apprenticed their children to ironmasters so that their children could learn a trade. Once the trade was learned, the ironmaster could profit by selling the unexpired time of the indenture.

Slaves were listed in furnace records by their first names as Negro Robin, Negro Samuel, Black Majer, or Black York. Some had been taken from their mothers at an early age and sold to a succession of owners before coming to the furnace. A boy named Davy, for example, was sold at the age of four for $100. He was sold again as a servant at twelve years. Within three months he went to work for an ironmaster. At the age of eighteen he became the property of a firm at the Birdsboro forge.

As the furnaces and their products became more important in the half-century after 1780, Black workers became more valuable. In the counties where iron was produced, ironmasters were the largest holders of slaves. In 1779 the Hopewell firm owned twelve slaves. Some free Black workers lived under the same conditions as white workers. They ate in the same company dining rooms and lived in homes on the iron plantation. In the early 1800s several Black men had relatively high-paying jobs as fillers, colliers, and miners. They were not admitted to the top jobs of molders and founders.

A Black community founded by escaped slaves grew up in the wooded valley of the Six Penny Creek, not far from the Hopewell Furnace, Joanna Furnace, and Birdsboro Forge. Many of the residents worked in the iron industries and founded the A.M.E. Mount Frisby Church in 1856. Two Black men who fought in the Union army during the Civil War were buried in the cemetery at the rear of the church.

Other Black people employed at the furnaces worshiped in predominantly white local churches. The records of these churches often listed their Black members. A Black man, Bill Jacobs, was buried in the cemetery of the Bethesda Baptist Church that numbered many Black and white Hopewell employees among its members. Originally Bill Jacobs had been an indentured servant who worked as a teamster before attaining the higher status of a coachman and gardener for Clement Brooks, the ironmaster of Hopewell Furnace. Because Black and white families lived near each other and sometimes worshiped in the same churches, a certain antislavery feeling developed in this area. Some white community members may have assisted escaping slaves.

By the mid-1830s Hopewell's prosperity was beginning to wane. Other companies that had developed better methods of producing high-quality iron at less expense were located closer to the urban markets. As a result, the furnace closed down in 1883, and its workers had to look for employment in towns or cities.

Hopewell Furnace, now a national historic site, has been restored as closely as possible to its appearance in the 1820–1840 period by the National Park Service. This is the finest example of an early American "iron plantation," which was the forerunner of today's iron and steel giants. Hopewell was one of Pennsylvania's most important furnace operations, producing pig iron and finished castings from 1771 until 1883. Today's visitors to Hopewell can see what a nineteenth-century iron community was like, including the restored waterwheel, blast machinery, the ironmaster's mansion, and numerous other structures. They can see a place where more than 100 Black people were employed in various capacities.

DATE ESTABLISHED:	1771
ADDRESS:	About 6 miles south of Birdsboro on PA 345; 10 miles from the Morgantown interchange on the PA Turnpike via PA 23 E. and PA 345 N.; French Creek State Park adjoins the Hopewell Furnace site; Elverson
TELEPHONE:	(610) 582-8773
VISITING HOURS:	Daily 9–5; demonstrations of molding and casting, June–Labor Day; village trades and activities, July–Aug.; closed Thanksgiving, Christmas, New Year's

FEES: Adults, $2; children under 17, free; seniors 62 and over, free; Dec.–Feb., free

SOURCES: Telephone call to site Sept. 8, 1991. Survey form completed by Richard N. Pawling, Hopewell Furnace National Historic Site. Derrick M. Cook, superintendent, Hopewell Furnace National Historic Site. Telephone conversation Aug. 8, 1995, Becky Ross, park ranger, Hopewell Furnace National Historic Site. *Hopewell Furnace.* "Negro Labor in the Charcoal Iron Industry of Southeastern Pennsylvania," 466–86. *Black Iron—Black Laborers at Hopewell Furnace (1771–1883).* "A Comparison of Negro and White Labor in a Charcoal Iron Community," 487–97.

Gettysburg

Intercultural Resource Center

The Intercultural Resource Center is located on the campus of Gettysburg College. The center's Historical Portrait Collection includes portraits of Daniel Payne, bishop of the A.M.E. Church; Major Martin Delany, the first African American field officer in the Civil War; Catherine Delany, wife of Martin Delany and an agent on the underground railroad; and Congressman Thaddeus Stevens, a white abolitionist and civil rights champion. The collection also includes a portrait of Mrs. Lydia Smith, a native of Gettysburg, who was housekeeper to Congressman Stevens. Many of the personalities featured in the Historical Portrait Collection are not widely known.

The center's records indicate that from the 1840s on, African Americans in Gettysburg met on North Washington Street for religious instruction. Daniel Alexander Payne, later bishop of the A.M.E. Church, arrived at Gettysburg in 1835 to enroll at the Lutheran Theological Seminary. On April 19, 1837, the college's board of trustees gave Payne permission to use one of the college classrooms to offer his Bible class to African Americans. Payne later became the first president of Wilberforce University. (See the entry for Ohio.)

A booklet put out by the center notes that Gettysburg is the only liberal arts college in America that provides genealogical research on African American families. The center houses census records, immigration records, Freedmen's Bureau Savings Bank records, and information about U.S. Colored Troops who served in the Civil War. Other documents include cohabitation records of former slaves in Mississippi as well as emancipation records of former slaves in Washington, D.C. The documents provide a wealth of information for African Americans in search of information about their roots. The center also houses a library of books by African and African American writers.

DATE ESTABLISHED: 1989

ADDRESS: 239 N. Washington Street, Gettysburg

TELEPHONE: (717) 337-6311

VISITING HOURS: Mon.–Fri. 9–5; closed major holidays except Labor Day

FEES: Maximum $20 per search

SOURCES: Harry Bradshaw Matthews, dean, Gettysburg College. *Gettysburg: The Intercultural Resource Center. Gettysburg Intercultural Advancement News.* "Reception Room Portrait Collection, Intercultural Resource Center." "Gettysburg College and the Intercultural Resource Center."

Kennett Square

Longwood Friends Meeting House

The community of Kennett Square, located near the Maryland border, was a crucial part of the underground railroad. The Longwood Friends Meeting House in Chester County was both a refuge for fugitive slaves and a center at which abolitionists gathered to further the cause of freedom. The meeting house, now restored, is located at the entrance to Longwood Gardens in Kennett Square.

In addition to free Black people who were active in conducting slaves on their way to freedom, white people also helped, including the Quakers who formed this meeting house in 1854. This group had been disowned by other Quakers who considered its abolitionist views too radical. Sojourner Truth, William Lloyd Garrison, Lucretia Mott, and poet John Greenleaf Whittier were abolitionists who spoke at this site.

The Longwood Friends Meeting House, an important underground railroad station, is owned today by Longwood Gardens, a public display garden that draws 800,000 visitors each year. The historic structure houses the Chester County Tourist Bureau, which has a permanent exhibit about the local underground railroad.

DATE ESTABLISHED:	1854
ADDRESS:	Chester County Tourist Bureau, Kennett Square
TELEPHONE:	(610) 388-0281
VISITING HOURS:	Apr.–Oct., daily 10–6; Nov.–Mar., daily 10–5; closed Thanksgiving, Christmas
FEES:	None
SOURCES:	Telephone conversation June 15, 1994, Pam Carter, publicity and functions coordinator, Longwood Gardens. "How the Friends and Other Friends Helped the Slaves."

La Mott

Camptown Federal District

The town of La Mott, in Cheltenham Township, is situated on part of the site of Camp William Penn, the first training camp for Black troops during the Civil War. From 1863 to 1865 Camp William Penn in Cheltenham Township was the primary recruitment and training station for the Third Regiment of the U.S. Colored Troops. Approximately 16,000 soldiers were cycled through the camp.

The town of La Mott, located about eight miles outside Philadelphia, was named for Lucretia C. Mott (1793–1880), a Quaker who worked in the antislavery, women's rights, temperance, and peace movements. Lucretia Mott and her husband, James, retired to an old farmhouse (called the "Roadside") in Cheltenham in the late 1850s. There they established a refuge for runaway slaves traveling north to safety.

Lucretia Mott, an ordained minister in the Quaker Society of Friends, traveled about with her husband to preach against slavery. She organized the Philadelphia Female Anti-Slavery Society and expressed her opposition to slavery in her writings. In 1840 she represented the United States as president of the World's Anti-Slavery Convention.

During the Civil War the Motts strongly supported the Union cause. Although Black soldiers had served in the U.S. armed forces ever since the Revolutionary War, the Military Act of 1862 was the first federal law enabling the President to call

Black men into military service. When Black troops were allowed to serve, they trained at first with white troops in Philadelphia. However, race riots broke out, ending that arrangement. Mott's son-in-law, Edward Davis, was a real estate developer, a major landholder in the area, and an advocate of the abolitionist cause. In 1863 he donated a portion of his property as a training camp for Black soldiers. The site was beyond the city limits and away from the strong anti-Black sentiments of some Philadelphians. More than 10,000 Black soldiers were housed at Camp William Penn.

The Quaker and abolitionist community in Cheltenham Township welcomed the recruits, providing friendship and a positive atmosphere. Lucretia Mott served as a spiritual leader in the community. She worked for the right of Black people to use public transportation in visits to their relatives at Camp William Penn. At the age of seventy, Mott gave inspirational sermons and speeches to the soldiers.

When the Civil War ended, Davis resumed his real estate activities. In that period integrated residential settings, even in northern cities, were rare. Davis, however, developed La Mott for both Black and white residents. He sold some of his land to wealthy white Philadelphians. In addition, he set aside thirty acres with small building lots to be sold for $150 to $250 each to Black and white purchasers. This land on the site of the former Camp William Penn was at first known as "Camptown." Davis donated land for the first school in the village; Black and white children attended it together.

The first residence in La Mott is still standing. The stone house located at Willow and Butcher Streets was built in 1854 for a tenant farmer, William Butcher, who was La Mott's first Black resident. Some of the early houses, including six houses on Keenan Street, were built with lumber salvaged from the army barracks. The house at 7310 Keenan Street, one of the original houses, has been in the same family since 1884. The house at the end of Keenan Street, a Gothic-revival cottage with an ornamental scalloped bargeboard, was constructed about 1882. La Mott's first school, which is located at Willow and Sycamore Streets, was built of local stone in 1878. The building now houses both the La Mott Free Library and the community center. The firehouse, built in 1915, also was constructed of local stone.

Davis also donated a parcel of land for the first church; it was constructed in 1888 at Cheltenham Avenue and Schoolhouse Lane. After it burned down, it was replaced by the African Methodist Episcopal Church, a brick-and-stone structure built in 1911. A state historic marker stands next to it.

Many Black people were leaders in the community. William Watson operated a brickyard from his property. Edward Davis in 1879 became La Mott's first Black real estate investor. George Elkins helped to organize the La Mott Building and Loan Association, which encouraged Black ownership by subdividing larger lots into more affordable ones. William Anderson in 1915 became Cheltenham Township's first Black police officer. Aubrey Bowser, a descendant of one of La Mott's earliest Black landowners, won a scholarship to Harvard University. He later gained prominence as a judge and was one of the founders of the National Association for the Advancement of Colored People.

Today the community has almost 4,000 residents, 80 percent of whom are Black. A national historic site, Camptown Federal District, La Mott was a major stop on the underground railroad, the first federal training camp for Black soldiers, and one of America's first planned integrated communities founded after the Civil War. In addition to the state historical marker at the A.M.E. Church, it has another one near the entrance to Latham Park. A state plaque honoring Lucretia Mott stands near the site of her home "Roadside." A granite monument honoring Camp William Penn is located outside the La Mott Community Center.

The original tradition of social and racial harmony remains a feature of La Mott today. Many descendants of the original families, including the Butchers, Bowsers, Tripletts, MacLeers, Schusters, and Millers, still reside in the community, providing a strong, positive link to the past.

DATE BUILT: First residence, 1854; first schoolhouse, 1878; current A.M.E. Church, 1911

ADDRESS: District, roughly bounded by Penrose Avenue, Graham Lane, Dennis Street, and Cheltenham Avenue; community center, in the old schoolhouse, Willow Avenue at Sycamore; library, 7420 Sycamore; church, 1505 W. Cheltenham Avenue, La Mott

TELEPHONE: Community center, (215) 635-3255; library, (215) 635-4419; church, (215) 782-1165

VISITING HOURS: Community center, Mon.–Fri. 8:30–4:30; contact other sites for visiting hours

SOURCES: NRHPINF. *Fighting for Freedom.* "Keeping up the Fight for Recognition." "Tracking the Underground Railroad." *La Mott, An Historic Community.* "A Community Seeks Its Place in History."

Oxford

Lincoln University

Lincoln University, a historically Black college, was founded in 1854 and is one of America's oldest liberal arts colleges established for students of African descent. John Miller Dickey founded the university, which was originally chartered as "Ashmun Institute" to commemorate Liberia's first president, Jehudi Ashmun (1794–1828). In 1866 the school was renamed Lincoln University in honor of Abraham Lincoln. Black professors first taught at Lincoln University in 1932.

The campus, located in a region of rolling farmlands in southern Chester County, Pennsylvania, includes twenty-seven main buildings and twenty-one faculty residences. Lincoln Hall (Ashmun Hall), built in 1866 and the oldest building on the campus, once housed all the school's facilities. Amos and Vail Halls are also two of the original buildings on the campus. The Langston Hughes Memorial Library, a newer building, houses one of the most extensive collections of African art and artifacts in the United States. It also contains personal papers of the poet Langston Hughes.

Lincoln University enrolled approximately 1,251 students in 1988–1989, 90 percent of whom were African American. From 1854 to 1954 the university's graduates accounted for approximately 20 percent of Black physicians and 10 percent of Black attorneys in the United States. Some outstanding Lincoln graduates include the late Thurgood Marshall, Supreme Court justice; Benjamin Azikiwe, president of Nigeria; Langston Hughes, poet; Kwame Nkrumah, president of Ghana; and Roscoe Lee Browne, stage and screen actor.

DATE ESTABLISHED: 1854

ADDRESS: On US 131, 45 miles southwest of Philadelphia between Oxford and West Grove

TELEPHONE: (610) 932-8300; visitor's information, ext. 289

VISITING HOURS: By arrangement with campus visitors information bureau

SOURCE: Lisa M. Collins, Lincoln University.

Philadelphia

Afro-American Historical and Cultural Museum

The Afro-American Historical and Cultural Museum, a three-story concrete, steel, and glass structure, houses an archive, a 280-seat auditorium, a gift shop, and four exhibition spaces. Stanley Arnold, museum archivist, notes that the museum was the first institution specifically built by a major city to house and interpret collections of African American culture. Its primary mission is to feature contributions of African Americans in the Philadelphia region and the state of Pennsylvania. Within the museum, visitors have viewed a variety of important exhibits, including *Climbing Jacob's Ladder: The Rise of Black Churches in Eastern American Cities, 1740–1977.*

Reaching beyond the museum walls, the staff offers visitors an African American heritage tour that reviews twenty-two sites in Philadelphia.

DATE ESTABLISHED: 1976
ADDRESS: 701 Arch Street, Philadelphia
TELEPHONE: (215) 574-0380
VISITING HOURS: Tues.–Sat. 10–5, Sun. noon–6; closed Mon., all major public holidays
FEES: Adults, $4; students, seniors 55 and over, and children 5–12, $2; group rates available
SOURCES: Telephone call to site, June 15, 1994. Stanley Arnold, archivist; Carl R. Nold, director; The State Museum of Pennsylvania. Robert Weible, chief, division of history, Pennsylvania Historical and Museum Commission, Harrisburg.

All-Wars Memorial to Black Soldiers

Pennsylvania erected the All-Wars Memorial in 1934 to honor Black Pennsylvanians who have fought in the nation's wars. The memorial's design includes an eighteen-foot column. Columbia is depicted offering laurel wreaths to twelve life-sized figures encircling the column.

DATE BUILT: 1934
ADDRESS: Lansdowne Drive, West Fairmount Park, Philadelphia
VISITING HOURS: Daily, dawn–dusk
FEES: None

Balch Institute for Ethnic Studies

Balch Institute is one of America's premier institutions that focuses on immigration and multiculturalism in the United States. Museum, library, and educational programs cover all ethnic groups. For persons involved in research, the Balch Institute Library offers a wide variety of literature on Philadelphia's African Americans, covering the period from 1865 to the present. The collection also includes photographs of some African American families and organizations in Philadelphia.

DATE ESTABLISHED: 1971
ADDRESS: 18 S. Seventh Street, Philadelphia
TELEPHONE: (215) 925-8090
VISITING HOURS: Mon.–Sat. 9–5; closed Sun., all legal holidays
SOURCE: James F. Turk, director of education, Balch Institute.

Frances Ellen Watkins Harper House

Frances Ellen Watkins Harper was well known as a reformer who worked in antislavery, women's, and temperance movements. When the Civil War ended, Harper continued her efforts to improve the civil rights of Black people. She also wrote poetry and essays on topics related to the life of African Americans.

Frances Ellen Watkins was born in Baltimore in 1825 to free Black parents. Her parents died when she was very young, and an aunt and uncle raised her. Her uncle, William Watkins, was an outstanding abolitionist and a minister in the African Methodist Episcopal Church. He operated his own school, the Watkins Academy, in Baltimore and wrote for the abolitionist paper *The Liberator.*

Even though this was a family of free Black people, opportunities were not equal for Baltimore's African Americans. Although Frances was educated, her first job at the age of fourteen was as a seamstress and nursemaid for a white family. Frances began writing during her teen years and published her first poetry book during that period. At the age of twenty-six she moved to Columbus, Ohio, where she began to teach domestic science at Union Seminary. Because she soon realized that she was more interested in working for the antislavery cause than in teaching, she directed her efforts increasingly to the abolitionist movement. One of the factors influencing her decision was that Maryland about this time passed a law prohibiting free Black people from moving to Maryland to live there; this meant that she could no longer go back to visit her family.

In the next years Frances joined her cousin, William Watkins Jr., in giving antislavery lectures in New England. She married Fenton Harper, and they had one child. After her husband's death, the administrator of the estate seized the farm she had purchased with her own savings to pay her husband's debts, leaving her almost nothing. This experience influenced her to become active in the women's movement, not only to earn a living once more but also because she began to realize the inequality of women before the law.

Harper sympathized with John Brown as he prepared for the raid on Harpers Ferry in 1859. Later, she spent two weeks with Brown's wife prior to Brown's execution. In her lectures Harper spoke about those who had participated in the raid.

After the Civil War Harper returned to lecturing, appearing at suffrage conventions and serving on committees of women's organizations. Although these groups were made up primarily of white women, many of whom accepted some types of racism, there was no other place for her to turn at that time. By the end of the nineteenth century Black feminists began organizing clubs for Black women.

Harper also continued her writing. Her book *Poems on Miscellaneous Subjects* was reprinted several times, and her poems and essays were printed in Black newspapers and journals. Her novel *Iola LeRoy or Shadows Uplifted,* published in 1892, was the first published by an African American woman.

In her travels Harper saw the poverty of the freed Black people and the abuses they suffered. She joined the struggle to attain the vote for Black people and was pleased to see the passage of the Fifteenth Amendment.

Harper moved to 1006 Bainbridge in 1870, sharing the house with her daughter. She died after a brief illness in 1911. She had spent her life working to better conditions for Black people and for women, and her writing and humanitarian efforts made her one of the nineteenth century's outstanding women.

The Harper house is a brick, three-story corner row house. Although the high, narrow house has had numerous alterations over the years, its basic structure remains intact.

DATE OF SIGNIFICANCE: Harper residence, 1870–1911
ADDRESS: 1006 Bainbridge Street, corner of Adler Street, Philadelphia
VISITING HOURS: Private, visitors may drive or walk by
SOURCES: NRHPINF. "One Great Bundle of Humanity," 21–43.

Mother Bethel African Methodist Episcopal Church*

Mother Bethel African Methodist Episcopal Church, the mother church of the A.M.E. denomination, was built on the site of the original 1793 church. The congregation began in 1793, and shortly after that Richard Allen established the A.M.E. Church.

Richard Allen was born a slave in 1760 in Delaware. A Quaker lawyer owned him, but a man named Stockley later bought him and his family. Allen was allowed to join in religious activities and became a convert to the Methodist faith. He joined the Methodist Society at age seventeen and was allowed to conduct services. His owner, Stockley, eventually came to believe that he could not reconcile his religious faith with the ownership of slaves. Although Stockley did not free his slaves, he allowed Allen and his brothers to buy their freedom for $2,000 each.

Allen received his license to preach in 1784 and became a circuit preacher, moving about to preach in three states. In 1786 Allen was asked to minister to Black people at St. George's Methodist Episcopal Church in Philadelphia. This assignment made him the first Black person to serve as pastor in a Methodist church. As increasing numbers of Black people came to the church to hear Allen preach, tensions increased, and white parishioners became irate. Black church members had a 5:00 A.M. service and were tolerated at services if they sat in "Negro pews" reserved for them, but they were not allowed to use the church for their own social meetings.

Richard Allen and Absalom Jones, another Black member of the church, responded to the discrimination by forming the Free African Society, which provided religious and social activities for African Americans. However, bigotry increased in the church, making separation inevitable. In November 1787 church members Absalom Jones and William White attempted to kneel in prayer during a church service in a section of the newly built gallery that they did not know was closed to them. The white church elders caused a commotion by directing them to move and roughly attempting to remove Jones from the church. In protest, Allen and Jones led the Black parishioners out of St. George's.

The African Americans who left St. George's Church held their worship services at the Free African Society. When the society later voted to establish an Episcopal church, Allen declined to be the pastor because he wanted to remain a Methodist, so Absalom Jones became pastor of the new Episcopal church. Allen then bought a frame blacksmith shop and had it moved to a lot he owned at Sixth and Lombard Streets (the present site of the church). In July 1794 the congregation dedicated the converted structure and named it Bethel, to make it clear that the congregation was not under the leadership of St. George's. In November 1794 Allen issued a declaration of independence, using for the first time the name African Methodist Episcopal Church.

The congregation erected a new building in 1805 and used it until 1841. Its third church building, used from 1841 to 1889, was said to have had a tunnel for escaping slaves. The present church, a three-story granite building with stained-glass windows and a tower, was built in 1889 and dedicated in 1890.

Mother Bethel Church served not only the spiritual needs but also the social and physical needs of Black people in the community. When a yellow fever epidemic struck Philadelphia in 1793, physician Benjamin Rush asked the Free African Society of Philadelphia to assist in nursing sick people and carrying the dead. Richard Allen, Absalom Jones, and William Gray took the lead in helping. Mother Bethel Church formed a paramedical staff that saved more than 200 lives during the epidemic. About 10 percent of Black people in the city died in this epidemic; 300 Black people died while helping others in the epidemic. They are believed to be buried in Washington Square or in unmarked graves at the Friends Meeting House at Fourth and Arch Streets.

In 1814 Allen together with James Forten, a Revolutionary War veteran and a wealthy Black leader in Philadelphia, organized a force of 2,500 free Black volunteers to defend Philadelphia against the British during the War of 1812. Forten, who was born of free Black parents, made a fortune in the sailmaking business and was an abolitionist leader in the city.

The church provided other services that the white city government did not extend to Black people. It also provided a forum where African Americans could discuss issues of the day. When the American Colonization Society formulated a plan to send Black people to Africa, Allen, Forten, and many others opposed the idea. In 1817 Forten chaired a meeting at Bethel Church to protest plans to send Black people to Africa by members of the American Colonization Society and those who sympathized with them. Those present at the meeting unanimously adopted a resolution that stated in part:

> Whereas our ancestors (not of choice) were the first successful cultivators of the wilds of America, we their descendants feel ourselves entitled to participate in the blessings of her luxuriant soil, which their blood and sweat manured; and that any measure or system of measures, having a tendency to banish us from her bosom, would not only be cruel, but in direct violation of those principles, which have been the boast of this republic.[2]

The congregation of Mother Bethel Church fought the racist laws known as the Black codes and opposed laws that would have prevented Black people from entering free states in the North. Church members also worked for the abolition of slavery. Today Mother Bethel Church is a memorial to Bishop Richard Allen, the outstanding American religious leader whose sense of justice and dignity led him to establish a new denomination. Allen died in 1831. Today a basement crypt houses a museum and Allen's tomb. Mother Bethel Church, one of America's earliest Black churches, is listed in the *National Register of Historic Places.*

DATE ESTABLISHED: 1794; present church, 1889
ADDRESS: 419 S. Sixth Street, Philadelphia
TELEPHONE: (215) 925-0616
VISITING HOURS: Mon.–Sat. 10–3
SOURCES: NRHPINF. *National Register of Historic Places,* 648. *The Negro Almanac,* 5th ed., 224. *Webster's New Biographical Dictionary,* 363. *Thoughts on African Colonization,* 62–63. *African Americans: Voices of Triumph,* vol. 2, *Leadership,* 124–6.

Henry O. Tanner House

Tanner House was at one time the home of one of America's best-known Black artists. Henry O. Tanner was born at Pittsburgh in 1859, the son of Bishop Benjamin Tucker Tanner and Sarah Miller Tanner. The family moved into this residence in Philadelphia about 1872.

At the age of twelve or thirteen, young Henry watched an artist paint a landscape of a hillside. This inspired in him a strong desire to become a painter, too. He was further impressed by the work of two Black artists, Edmonia Lewis and Edward Bannister, whose works were exhibited at the Philadelphia Centennial Exposition of 1876.

With his father's encouragement, Henry enrolled at the Pennsylvania Academy of Fine Arts in 1880. His teacher, the well-known painter Thomas Eakins, instructed Tanner in draftsmanship and other aspects of the artistic tradition. Tanner soon began to sell some of his paintings. Moving to Atlanta in 1888, he opened a photography studio and taught at Clark College in that city. Later he spent some time among the Black people of the Blue Ridge Mountains in North Carolina. One of his admired works titled *The Banjo Lesson* was perhaps begun at this time. (It was later completed after Turner settled in France.)

The racial discrimination in the United States was a source of depression for Tanner, who moved to Paris in 1891. Because the welcoming attitude of France appealed to him, he spent the rest of his life there. His works were accepted and exhibited in Paris salons. At the Paris Exposition of 1900 he was honored with the Medal of Honor. He died in France in 1937.

The Tanner homesite in Philadelphia is a three-story building. The interior has been altered, and the exterior wood-framed bay has been covered with aluminum siding. The Tanner residence is listed in the *National Register of Historic Places.*

DATE OF SIGNIFICANCE: Tanner residence, c1872
ADDRESS: 2908 W. Diamond Street, Philadelphia
VISITING HOURS: Private, visitors may walk or drive by
SOURCES: NRHPINF. *The Negro Almanac*, 5th ed., 225.

Temple University
Charles L. Blockson Afro-American Collection

More than one million items—rare books, photographs, slave narratives, recordings, private papers of prominent African Americans, and broadsides—make up this collection about Black Americans. The collection originated in the 1940s when its curator, Charles L. Blockson, then a ten-year-old boy in Norristown, Pennsylvania, began a search for Black heroes. The great-grandson of a man who escaped on the underground railroad, Blockson knew there had to be Black achievers other than George Washington Carver and Booker T. Washington, the men who were presented each year on "Colored History Day" in his school. When Blockson (who says that he never had a Black teacher in his life) asked one of his teachers about Black heroes other than Washington and Carver, the teacher responded that "Negroes were born to serve white people."

Stung by the statement, Blockson began his lifelong quest for information about his own heritage. He purchased books about Black people whenever he could and found many rare books whose worth had not been recognized. At Pennsylvania State, where he was a member of the football team, Blockson searched for more books whenever the team traveled. The earliest book that he found was a 1557 book on the history of Africa. The collection became extensive over the years, and in 1983 Blockson donated it to Temple University.

Today the Afro-American Collection, one of the tour sites listed by the Philadelphia Convention and Tours Bureau, is visited by scholars and lay people from many parts of the world. Blockson, the curator, is an important resource in his own right. In 1994–1995 he served as chairperson of a National Park Service committee charged with identifying underground railroad sites in the United States. His 1977 book, *Black Genealogy,* is widely used by African Americans who are searching for their roots. Blockson wrote an article on the underground railroad for the *National Geographic* in July 1984 and wrote "Sea Change in the Sea Islands" for the December 1987 *National Geographic.* In 1994 he wrote the *Hippocrene Guide to the Underground Railroad.*

DATE ESTABLISHED: Collection, 1940; donated, 1983
ADDRESS: Sullivan Hall, Temple University, Thirteenth and Berks Mall, Philadelphia
TELEPHONE: (215) 204-6632
VISITING HOURS: By appointment Mon.–Fri. 9–5; closed weekends, holidays
SOURCES: Telephone conversation Jan. 25, 1995, Charles L. Blockson, curator. *Black Genealogy. Philadelphia's Guide: African-American State Historical Markers.*

University of Pennsylvania
The University Museum of Archaeology/Anthropology

The University of Pennsylvania museum's African collection consists of more than 10,000 objects from nearly every major cultural area of the African continent, with the richest material from the West African and former Belgian Congo areas.

Most items in the collection were gathered between 1897 and 1930. Although much of the collection dates from the early twentieth century to the present, some Benin brasses and ivories date from the sixteenth to the nineteenth centuries.

Some of the objects include a mankala (an Ethiopian wooden board game with counters), a beautifully carved wooden door from the Ivory Coast, a xylophone made of wood and gourds, and a finely detailed ostrich-egg water container geometrically incised and inlaid with pigment.

DATE ESTABLISHED: 1887
ADDRESS: Thirty-third and Spruce Streets, Philadelphia
TELEPHONE: (215) 898-4000
VISITING HOURS: Tues.–Sat. 10–4:30, Sun. 1–5; closed Mon., holidays, Sun. June–Aug.
FEES: Adults, $3; children, students, and senior citizens, $1.50
SOURCE: Pam Kosty, public information officer.

Wesley African Methodist Episcopal Zion Church

Wesley A.M.E. Zion Church is a two-story stone church in the Gothic style. The church has a huge stained-glass window and a stone belltower. There are three red doors under Gothic arches on the street level. Inside, the large sanctuary with a *U*-shaped balcony seats approximately 2,000 people.

In 1784 there were over 15,000 Methodists in America, and Black people were joining this denomination in increasing numbers. To escape the uneasy racial atmosphere encountered in the white-dominated Methodist Church at Philadelphia, Richard Allen and other African Americans formed their own congregation, which was known as Mother Bethel. Allen became in time a bishop of the A.M.E. Church. Four years after the establishment of Mother Bethel, some members of the congregation became dissatisfied and decided to found their own church in 1820. This congregation is known today as the Wesley A.M.E. Zion Church and is known familiarly as "Big Wesley."

For many years the Wesley A.M.E. congregation occupied a church at 1500 Lombard Street in Philadelphia. In 1925–1926 the present-day church was built on this site, just prior to the Great Depression. Because of high construction costs, the congregation was for many years burdened with a huge debt load. Despite this handicap, its charitable members continued their outreach to the poor and hungry in the community. In one winter they fed more than 34,000 people of different races and creeds. During the Depression years they also provided clothing, paid insurance policies so as to keep some people's policies from lapsing, and operated a rent-free apartment house. In a Tuesday night service called "Joy Night," they combined prayer, music, and devotional services and collected money for the poor. By 1950 Big Wesley was out of debt. Today the church is listed in the *National Register of Historic Places.*

DATE ESTABLISHED: Congregation, 1820; present church, 1925–1926
ADDRESS: 1500 Lombard Street (corner of Fifteenth Street), Philadelphia
TELEPHONE: (215) 735-8961
VISITING HOURS: Mon.–Fri. 10–2; Sun. service 11
SOURCES: NRHPINF. Telephone conversation Jan. 29, 1995, Reverend Doctor Joseph W. Walton, pastor, Wesley A.M.E. Church.

Valley Forge

Valley Forge National Park

In 1777 Black soldiers were among those who struggled through the hard winter at Valley Forge with George Washington's Continental Army. Phillip Field, a Black man from New York, was among those who died. Another Black man, Salem Poor, survived the hardships of that winter. Salem Poor already had fought with the Massachusetts Regiment at Bunker Hill and had been cited for his bravery as a soldier. (See the entry on the Battle of Bunker Hill in the Massachusetts section.)

DATE OF SIGNIFICANCE: 1777–1778

ADDRESS: Valley Forge

TELEPHONE: Visitors center, (610) 783-1077

VISITING HOURS: Park, daily dawn–dusk; Visitors Center and Washington's Headquarters, daily 9–5; closed Christmas

FEES: Washington's Headquarters, adults, $2; youth 16 and under, free

SOURCES: Telephone call to site, June 15, 1994. *The Negro Almanac,* 5th ed., 225.

Notes

1. Gary T. Hawbaker, ed., *Runaways, Rascals, and Rogues, Missing Spouses, Servants and Slaves: Abstracts from Lancaster County, Pennsylvania Newspapers [and] Lancaster Journal, 1794–1810,* vol. 1 (Hershey, Pa.: The Author, 1987), 12.

2. From meeting of Black people in Philadelphia, Jan. 1817, in William Lloyd Garrison, *Thoughts on African Colonization, or an Impartial Exhibition of the Doctrines, Principles, & Purposes of the American Colonization Society, Together with the Resolutions, Addresses, & Remonstrances of the Free People of Color,* pt. 2 (Boston, 1832), 9–10, quoted in Herbert Aptheker, *A Documentary History of the Negro People of the United States,* vol. 1 (New York: Citadel, 1990), 71.

Works Consulted

African Americans: Voices of Triumph. Vol. 2, *Leadership.* Alexander, Va.: Time-Life, 1993.

Black Genealogy. Charles L. Blockson with Ron Fry. Englewood Cliffs, N.J.: Prentice-Hall, 1977.

Black Iron: Black Laborers at Hopewell Furnace (1771–1883). National Park Service. [flier]

"A Community Seeks Its Place in History." Will Thompson. *Philadelphia Inquirer,* n.d.

"A Comparison of Negro and White Labor in a Charcoal Iron Community." Joseph E. Walker. *Labor History* 10, no. 3 (summer 1969): 487–97.

Cornwall Iron Furnace. Cornwall, Pa.: Pennsylvania Historical and Museum Commission. [brochure]

Fighting for Freedom. Philadelphia: Civil War Library and Museum. [brochure]

"Forming an Identity through the Church: Philadelphia Places of Pride," *Philadelphia Inquirer,* 28 Feb. 1989.

Gettysburg: The Intercultural Resource Center. [booklet]

"Gettysburg College and the Intercultural Resource Center." Harry Bradshaw Matthews. *Journal of the Afro-American Historical and Genealogical Society* 8, no. 3 (fall 1987).

Gettysburg Intercultural Advancement News 4, no. 2 (Feb. 1990). [newsletter]

Hopewell Furnace. National Park Service, U.S. Dept. of the Interior. [brochure]

"How the Friends and Other Friends Helped the Slaves: Philadelphia Places of Pride." John Corr. *Philadelphia Inquirer,* 2 Feb. 1989.

International Library of Negro Life and History: Historical Negro Biographies. Wilhelmena S. Robinson. New York: Publishers, 1970.

The John Brown House. Robert N. Sieber. Harrisburg, Pa.: Bureau of Historic Sites and Properties, Pennsylvania Historical and Museum Commission, 1978.

"Keeping up the Fight for Recognition." Daniel Rubin. *Philadelphia Inquirer,* 8 Feb. 1989.

La Mott, An Historic Community. Prepared by Wallace Roberts & Todd, Planners, Urban Designers, Landscape Architects, and Architects, Philadelphia. [poster]

National Register of Historic Places. Washington, D.C.: National Park Service, 1976.

The Negro Almanac: A Reference Work on the Afro-American. 5th ed. Harry A. Ploski and James Williams, eds. Detroit, Mich.: Gale Research, 1989.

"Negro Labor in the Charcoal Iron Industry of Southeastern Pennsylvania." Joseph E. Walker. *Pennsylvania Magazine of History and Biography* 93, no. 4 (Oct. 1969): 466–86.

"One Great Bundle of Humanity: Frances Ellen Watkins Harper." Margaret Hope Bacon. *Pennsylvania Magazine of History and Biography* 113, no. 1 (Jan. 1989): 21–43.

Philadelphia's Guide: African-American State Historical Markers. Philadelphia: Charles L. Blockson Afro-American Collection/William Penn Foundation, 1992.

"Reception Room Portrait Collection, Intercultural Resource Center." Gettysburg College, 16 July 1990. [paper]

"The Rise of the Iron Community." Frederic K. Miller. *Lebanon County Historical Society* 12, no. 3a (1950): 15, 16, 92, 93.

Thoughts on African Colonization, or an Impartial Exhibition of the Doctrines, Principles, & Purposes of the American Colonization Society, Together with the Resolutions, Addresses, & Remonstrances of the Free People of Color. Part 2. William Lloyd Garrison. (Boston, 1832), 62–63. Quoted in *A Documentary History of the Negro People in the United States,* vol. 1, Herbert Aptheker (New York: Citadel, 1990), 71.

"Tracking the Underground Railroad." Sandra Long. *Philadelphia Inquirer,* 4 Feb. 1985.

Webster's New Biographical Dictionary. Springfield, Mass.: Merriam-Webster, 1988.

Rhode Island

Kingston

George and Sarah Fayerweather House

George Fayerweather, a slave owned by the Reverend Samuel Fayerweather, pastor of St. Paul's Episcopal Church in North Kingston, Rhode Island, was the founder of a leading African American family in Kingston. His son, George II, was born in slavery in 1774 and learned the blacksmith trade. When freed from slavery, George II married a Native American princess, and they built this cottage in 1820. George set up a blacksmith's shop to the right of the house; there members of this family practiced the blacksmith trade for more than one hundred years, passing the business down through the generations. The smith's shop was the heart of the town, a place where many boys watched with fascination as the smiths went about their work.

George Fayerweather II and his wife had twelve children. When he died in 1841, his son, Solomon, continued the business, serving for the next sixty years as the village blacksmith. He died in 1901 at age eighty-three. Solomon's brother, George III, also a blacksmith, married Sarah Harris, who was born in Norwich, Connecticut, in 1812, one of twelve children.

Sarah Harris's family had moved from Norwich to Canterbury, Connecticut, and as a young woman, Sarah worked there as a servant. However, she wanted to become a schoolteacher and applied for admission to the Prudence Crandall School for Girls in Canterbury. (See the listing for Connecticut.) Although Sarah was the first Black student to be admitted to the school, extreme racial hostility in the town and violent opposition to school integration finally forced Crandall to close the school.

During this period of turbulence in Canterbury, Sarah had been preparing to marry George Fayerweather III of Kingston. After their marriage George III and Sarah lived in the Helme house (no longer extant) that stood next door to the Fayerweather house in Kingston. Sarah kept in touch with Prudence Crandall; the Fayerweathers even named their first baby Prudence Crandall Fayerweather. Their residence became a center of antislavery activity in the community. Frederick Douglass and William Lloyd Garrison, famous abolitionists, were entertained in their house. Sarah lived in the Helme house until her death in 1878 at the age of 63. She was highly respected in the community, and a residence hall on the campus of the University of Rhode Island was named Fayerweather Hall in her honor.

The Fayerweather house on Moorsfield Road was restored in 1965 by the Kingston Improvement Association and today houses the Fayerweather Craft Guild.

DATE OF SIGNIFICANCE: 19th century

ADDRESS: Moorsfield Road, corner of RI 138 and RI 108, Kingston

TELEPHONE: (401) 789-9072

VISITING HOURS: Third Sat. in May–Dec. 10, Tues., Thurs., Sat. 10–4 or by appointment

SOURCES: Telephone conversation June 15, 1994, Ms. Steffanie Windus, local resident. Telephone conversation June 15, 1994, Mr. Ward Abusamra, Kingston Improvement Association. Telephone conversation Jan. 27, 1995, Claire Sweet, librarian, South Kingston Public Library. *Rhode Island's Freedom Trail. Kingston: A Forgotten History.* "A Profile in Dedication: Sarah Harris and the Fayerweather Family." *The New England Galaxy.*

Newport

Colonial Burial Ground, God's Acre

From the early days of the colony, Rhode Island slaves were often buried at the side or foot of their owners' graves. In Newport an African American section was developed in the Colonial Burial Ground and named "God's Acre." In the early part of the nineteenth century, the African Union Society developed procedures and regulations to ensure that deceased members would receive a decent funeral procession and a decent burial at this site. There is conjecture that a Black slave and mason named Zingo Stevens was the official stonecutter for the African Union Society, but this has not been substantiated. There are, however, two stones that were cut and signed in the 1760s by a Black man named Pompe Stevens. Some of the more-ornate stones in God's Acre may have been paid for by slave owners.

The Colonial Burying Ground, a national historic site, is well worth seeing. Ringed with lovely cherry trees, the grounds contain approximately 4,000 tombstones that date from as early as 1660. The God's Acre section is one of the best-preserved of such early burial grounds of Black Americans. Although the earliest stone in God's Acre dates from the 1700s, the majority of the four hundred African American burials at this site were for free Black residents of Newport.

DATE ESTABLISHED: 1600s

ADDRESS: Cemetery, Farewell Street, Newport (from the Newport Bridge take the exit to downtown Newport; turn right and go ¼ mile to the entrance)

VISITING HOURS: Dawn–dusk

SOURCES: Telephone conversation June 15, 1994, Jeanne Desrosiers, Covell Guest House. Telephone conversation June 16, 1994, John Canham, chairman, Advisory Commission on the Common Burying Ground. Telephone conversation Jan. 26, 1995, Ronald Onorato, professor of art and architectural history, University of Rhode Island. *Rhode Island's Freedom Trail.*

Quaker Meeting House

The restored building at 30 Marlborough Street is the oldest surviving Quaker meeting house in America. At this site in 1717, John Farmer, a Quaker, made an early, positive antislavery statement. Although he did not have permission to do so, Farmer tried to read his *Epistle concerning Negroes* to those attending the yearly meeting. As a result of this bold act, the Society of Friends disowned him.

Some of the Quakers owned slaves at that time, and the issue of slave ownership was a matter of contention. In 1733 the quarterly meeting of Friends approved Elihu Coleman's tract against slavery and gave Coleman permission to print his work. By 1773 the yearly meeting opposed slavery and disowned those who went against this decision. John Farmer's earlier stand had not been taken in vain.

DATE BUILT: 1699; restored, 1807
ADDRESS: 30 Marlborough Street, Newport
TELEPHONE: (401) 846-0813
VISITING HOURS: By appointment with one-week advance notice
SOURCES: Telephone conversation June 16, 1994, and Jan. 26, 1995, Ron Potvin, curator of manuscripts, Newport Historical Society. *Rhode Island's Freedom Trail.*

Isaac Rice House

Both escaping slaves and abolitionists found shelter at the home of Isaac Rice, a Black man who had been born free in 1792 at Narragansett, Rhode Island, and who had moved to Newport at an early age. Rice worked as a gardener for Governor Gibbs of Rhode Island; during this assignment Rice planted the trees in Touro Park in Newport.

In the course of his work, Rice overheard the conversations of African American servants who had accompanied their masters on their summer sojourns in Newport. As a result, Rice grew to hate the institution that bound human beings as slaves and began to work to help free the slaves.

The house on the corner of William and Thomas Streets became an underground railroad shelter. Frederick Douglass, a friend to Rice, stayed here when he came to Newport. Rice also served his church faithfully, giving generously to the Colored Union Church and Society and serving as the Society's clerk. He died in 1866.

PERIOD OF SIGNIFICANCE: 19th century
ADDRESS: 54 William Street, Newport
VISITING HOURS: Private, visitors may walk or drive by
SOURCES: *The Underground Railroad in New England. Rhode Island's Freedom Trail.*

Wanton-Lyman-Hazard House

The Wanton-Lyman-Hazard House, 17 Broadway, was once the governor's mansion and was nearly destroyed in the 1765 Stamp Act Riots. The house, a typical middle-class merchant dwelling of the 1675–1750 period, is an example of the type of dwelling in which slaves lived and worked in the North. The colonial, three-story residence was owned by patriots, merchants, and governors, most of whom owned slaves who also lived here.

One room in the house is reported to have been the slave quarters. Partial evidence for this is the back stairway leading from the kitchen to the second-story room; this stairway would not have been used by the white family members. The room is simply furnished but not in an authentic manner as a slave's living quarters.

DATE BUILT:	1675
ADDRESS:	17 Broadway, Newport
TELEPHONE:	(401) 846-0813
VISITING HOURS:	June 15–Aug. 31, Tues.–Sat. 9–5; closed Sun., Mon., holidays, Sept.–June 14
FEES:	$3
SOURCES:	Bert Lippincott, Newport Historical Society. Telephone conversation June 16, 1994, and Jan. 26, 1995, Ron Potvin, Newport Historical Society.

Portsmouth

Battle of Rhode Island Historic District

Although Black soldiers served in regular army units in most of the American colonies during the Revolutionary War, Rhode Island was an exception. Here, between 1778 and 1781, Black men were enrolled in a separate, predominantly Black unit known as the First Rhode Island Regiment. They had an extra incentive because the Rhode Island legislature had declared that every slave in the state who volunteered to serve would be declared free and would be paid a regular soldier's wages.

Between 1776 and 1779 British troops, including mercenary soldiers from Hesse in Germany, were stationed in Rhode Island. In August 1778 the Americans started an offensive against the British entrenched troops, hoping for help from the French fleet. When the French failed to give support at that time, the American forces were trapped in a difficult situation. The Black soldiers were asked to hold the line against a British assault. The British had occupied Newport and had driven the American forces from the island on which the town is located. Following up their advantage, the British troops, including their Hessian contingents, made three charges against the Americans. The Black regiment beat the aggressors back three times. This brave action enabled the American commander to organize an orderly retreat that saved the regiment from destruction. The 200 freedmen of the First Rhode Island Regiment showed great courage in repulsing veteran European soldiers.

This is the only Revolutionary War battle in which Black Americans fought as a distinct racial unit. The site today consists primarily of private houses that were not standing at the time of the battle. State route 24 is the only major road that goes into the battlefield site; the route terminates near Barker Brook and merges into West Main Road nearby. The National Association for the Advancement of Colored People has erected a marker and flagpole on a high grassy site at this interchange. The symbols commemorate the courage of the First Rhode Island Regiment in the Battle of Rhode Island.

DATE OF SIGNIFICANCE: 1778

ADDRESS: Historic District, Lehigh Hill and both sides of RI 21 between Medley and Dexter Streets; Rhode Island Black Regiment Park, left of north-bound junction of RI 114 and RI 24, Portsmouth

VISITING HOURS: Private, visitors may drive by

SOURCES: NRHPINF. *National Register of Historic Places*, 668. *Before the Mayflower*, 67. *Rhode Island's Freedom Trail*. *Black Heroes of the American Revolution*.

Prescott Farm Historic District

Tack Sisson (various sources give his name as Jack Sisson and even as Quarco Honeyman) was a Black man from Newport who served as a commando during the Revolutionary War. He became known when, in a July 1777 raid against the British, he helped to capture British General Richard Prescott. Prior to this incident the British had captured Major General Charles Lee of the Continental Army. In order to persuade the British to exchange prisoners, the Americans first had to capture a British officer. Six officers and thirty-eight men, including Sisson, set out in small boats to an area near Prescott's headquarters in a farmhouse near Portsmouth. Although guards protected the farmhouse, the darkness of midnight enabled three of the American soldiers to creep up, stealthily evading the guards. Sisson stepped forward and smashed down the doors of the general's bedroom. General Prescott surrendered, and the Americans took him away, as a newspaper later noted, "without his breeches." Prescott later was exchanged for General Lee, and Sisson later joined the First Rhode Island Regiment. The restored farmhouse where the bold capture took place stands along West Main Road at the Middleton-Portsmouth town line.

DATE OF SIGNIFICANCE: 1777

ADDRESS: Tour origin, 2009 W. Main Road, Middleton; farmhouse, Portsmouth

TELEPHONE: (401) 847-6230

VISITING HOURS: Tours (including the country store, windmill, and herb garden, but not the farmhouse, which is private) Apr.–Oct., Mon.–Fri. 10–4

FEES: Farm, free; museum and windmill, adults, $2; children, $1.50

SOURCES: Telephone conversation June 16, 1994, John Lingley, herb farmer and tour guide. *Rhode Island's Freedom Trail*. *International Library of Negro Life and History*, 32. *The African American Encyclopedia*, 1460.

Providence

Bannister House

The Bannister residence once was home to an outstanding African American painter, Edward Mitchell Bannister, and his wife, Christina. Christina Bannister was well known in her own right as a prominent person in civic and community work.

Edward Bannister was born in 1828 in New Brunswick, Canada. Orphaned at early age and poor, he moved to Boston and began working at odd jobs. He loved to draw, and by the age of ten was showing strong interest in sketching many kinds of scenes.

In 1867 Bannister read an article in the *Boston Herald* that maintained that Black people were incapable of producing art. He was determined to prove that the writer's idea was wrong. Bannister's paintings during this period were of New England landscapes. In 1870 he moved to Rhode Island and established the Providence Art Club, a group that is still active.

In spite of Bannister's talent, he encountered much racial prejudice. For example, in 1876 he was awarded a medal at Philadelphia's Centennial Exposition for his painting *Under the Oaks*. When the judges discovered that they had awarded the honor to a Black man, however, they selected another work of art for the honor. Only the demands of other competitors prevented the judges from depriving Bannister of the award. Yet he persisted in his work and, by the time of his death in 1901, Bannister had gained national recognition as a painter. Some of Bannister's work can be viewed at the Museum of Art in the Rhode Island School of Design. Several of his works are in the museum's permanent collection, but they are not always on display at any given time.

Christina Bannister, Bannister's wife, spent her years in Providence working to improve the lives of African Americans. She worked for years to raise money for a home in Providence for elderly Black people. She succeeded when, in 1890, the Rhode Island State Assembly enacted legislation incorporating a Home for Aged Colored Women. Donations from local families provided land, money to build the home, and furnishings. Mrs. Bannister saw her dream come true when the home for aged women was ready for occupancy that same year.

In 1977 the home moved to 35 Dodge Street in East Providence; it was then renamed the Bannister House in honor of Christina Bannister.

The Bannister residence on Benevolent Street, before remodeling, was a simple wood cottage.

DATE OF SIGNIFICANCE: Bannister residence, 1883–1898

ADDRESS: House, 93 Benevolent Street; Museum of Art, 224 Benefit Street, Providence

TELEPHONE: Museum, (401) 454-6507

VISITING HOURS: House, private, visitors may walk or drive by; museum, Tue.–Wed., Fri.–Sat. 10:30–5, Thurs. noon–5, Sun. and holidays 2–5, closed Mon.

FEES: Museum: Adults, $2; seniors, $1; youth 5–18 and college, $.50

SOURCES: Telephone conversation Jan. 28, 1995, Judith Davidson, reception supervisor, Museum of Art, Rhode Island School of Design. *International Library of Negro Life and History*, 47.

Brick Schoolhouse

The Brick Schoolhouse on Meeting Street was constructed in 1769 on land acquired by the town proprietors. At first the town maintained a school on the first floor, while Brown University used classroom space on the upper floor. During the Revolution, however, the building was used as a storage house for munitions and as a cartridge-manufacturing facility.

When public education was permanently established in Providence in 1800, this structure became one of the district schools. The statewide Public Schools Law in 1828 provided for public primary education for Black children under the age of ten and authorized a segregated public grammar school at this site on Meeting Street. In the 1850s, the Meeting Street School began to offer the African American students a high school education in addition to grammar school instruction. All African American children in Providence attended either the Meeting Street School or a grammar school that opened in 1837 on Pond Street.

Around 1908 the Meeting Street School became a school for tubercular children. It later served as a school for disabled children and adults. In 1987 the Brick Schoolhouse was recycled as the headquarters of the Providence Preservation Society.

DATE BUILT: 1769; Black children's school, 1828–1908
ADDRESS: 24 Meeting Street, Providence
TELEPHONE: (401) 831-7440
VISITING HOURS: By appointment
SOURCES: Amy Jordan, director of education and tourism, Providence Preservation Society. *Rhode Island's Freedom Trail.*

Civil War Monument

African American soldiers served during the Civil War in the Fourteenth Regiment Rhode Island Heavy Artillery (Colored). Their acceptance as members of the Union Army did not come easily, for public opinion at first ran heavily against the idea of arming Black men as soldiers. As the war progressed, however, Union officials realized that they needed Black recruits and encouraged them to enlist. With the exception of a few emergency situations, Black men were not used as soldiers by the Confederate army. The Confederates were fighting to maintain slavery and had good reason to believe the loyalty of African American soldiers would not be on their side.

The Civil War monument honors, among other Civil War veterans, the proud African American men from the Fourteenth Regiment Rhode Island Heavy Artillery (Colored), which was organized in 1863 and stationed for duty in 1864–1865 in New Orleans.

DATE ESTABLISHED: Design submitted, 1866; monument dedicated, 1871
ADDRESS: Kennedy Plaza, Washington and Exchange Streets, Providence
VISITING HOURS: Daily dawn–dusk
FEES: None
SOURCES: Telephone call June 16, 1994, Providence Preservation Society. *Rhode Island's Freedom Trail.*

Congdon Street Baptist Church

The frame building at 17 Congdon Street was the second meeting house built for the Black community in Providence. The First Meeting House and School stood at Meeting and Congdon Streets between 1820 and 1863 and served both as a church and as a school for Black children. Black people of all denominations met at the earlier site, and many of Providence's Black churches originated from the First Meeting House.

The church had its origins when, in 1819, African Americans and some of their white friends met to make plans for establishing a house of worship for the Black people of Providence. The group selected a lot on Meeting Street, and assisted by the Society of Friends and others, erected their house of worship and dedicated it in 1820. The original church no longer stands; the current church was built in 1874–1875.

DATE ESTABLISHED: 1820; second meeting house, 1874–1875
ADDRESS: 17 Congdon Street, Providence
TELEPHONE: (401) 421-4032
VISITING HOURS: By appointment only; contact church for information
SOURCES: Telephone call to site, June 16, 1994. Providence Preservation Society. *National Register of Historic Places*, 670. *Rhode Island's Freedom Trail.*

Fox Point

Fox Point was a neighborhood of African Americans and newcomers who arrived here from the Cape Verde Islands, a former Portuguese colony off the west coast of Africa. They settled in Providence, seeking new opportunities. In the Fox Point area they met people who were slaves or former slaves. Many were sailors or persons engaged in the maritime industry. This community of African Americans can trace its roots back to the eighteenth and nineteenth centuries.

DATE ESTABLISHED: 18th century
ADDRESS: Wickenden Street, Benefit Street, parts of N. Main Street, and Indian Point, Point Street Bridge, Providence
SOURCES: Linda A'vant, Rhode Island Black Heritage Society. Telephone information June 16, 1994, Providence Preservation Society. *Rhode Island's Freedom Trail.*

India Point

India Point was the port of entry for Cape Verdean windjammers transporting passengers and cargo between the Cape Verde Islands and New England. The African immigrants came here in search of a new life in America. A few of the older houses still are standing in this area, which is near another Black historic area, Fox Point.

DATE ESTABLISHED: 18th century
ADDRESS: Gano Street, exit 3, I-195 West, Providence
SOURCE: *Rhode Island's Freedom Trail.*

Rhode Island Black Heritage Society

The Rhode Island Black Heritage Society—the state's largest facility for preserving and documenting local and national Black historical information—is located on the main floor of the Opportunities Industrialization Center building. The society includes a library with a reading area and a large wall area for exhibits. Library and archive collections include photographs, slides, taped interviews, and artifacts from local Black homes and organizations.

The society collects, preserves, and exhibits informative materials on the lifestyle and institutions of Black citizens and makes this information available through lectures, school curricula, exhibits, and other activities. Each month it features local Black artists in the gallery space. Collections range from materials on Africans in Rhode Island in the early seventeenth century to information on recent Black migrants to the state.

DATE ESTABLISHED: 1974

ADDRESS: 46 Aborn Street, Providence

TELEPHONE: (401) 751-3490

VISITING HOURS: Mon.–Fri. 9–4:30; closed weekends, major state holidays

FEES: None

SOURCES: Alma J. Smith, library staff, Rhode Island Black Heritage Society. Linda A'Vant Coleman, executive director, Rhode Island Black Heritage Society. Telephone conversation June 16, 1994, James Clements, museum assistant. *Creative Survival.*

Works Consulted

The African American Encyclopedia. Vol. 5. Michael W. Williams, ed. New York: Marshall Cavendish, 1993.

Before the Mayflower: A History of Black America. 5th ed. Lerone Bennett Jr. New York: Penguin, 1988.

Black Heroes of the American Revolution. Burke Davis. New York: Odyssey/Harcourt Brace Jovanovich, 1976.

Creative Survival: The Providence Black Community in the 19th Century. Providence: The Rhode Island Black Heritage Society, n.d.

International Library of Negro Life and History: Historical Negro Biographies. Wilhelmena S. Robinson. New York: Publishers, 1970.

Kingston: A Forgotten History. Christian M. McBurney. Kingston, R.I.: Pettaquamscutt Historical Society, 1975.

National Register of Historic Places. Washington, D.C.: National Park Service, 1976.

"A Profile in Dedication: Sarah Harris and the Fayerweather Family." Carl R. Woodward. Reprint from *The New England Galaxy* 15, no. 1 (Summer 1973), 3–14.

Rhode Island's Freedom Trail. Carl Senna, ed. Warwick, R.I.: Rhode Island Black Heritage Society, 1986.

The Underground Railroad in New England. Richard R. Kuns and John Sabino, eds. Boston: American Revolution Bicentennial Administration, Region I, with Boston 200, the Bicentennial and Historical Commissions of the Six New England States and the Underground Railroad Task Force, 1976.

Vermont

Bennington

Old First Church

Members of the Old First Church (First Congregational Church) in Bennington were noted in the early nineteenth century for their opposition to slavery. They demonstrated these views by welcoming to their midst a Black minister, the Reverend Lemuel Haynes (1753–1833). Haynes was born in West Hartford, Connecticut. His mother was white, his father was African. Haynes served as a Minuteman April 19, 1775, in the battles of Lexington and Concord. Later he was one of three Black soldiers to participate with Ethan Allen and his Green Mountain Boys from Vermont in the Battle of Ticonderoga. The other two Black volunteers served with him on May 10, 1775, as the men stormed the British fort and captured cannons from the enemy forces. After fighting in the northern campaigns of the Revolutionary War, Haynes returned to farming. In 1778 he married a white woman, Elizabeth Babbitt. Of their nine children, one became a lawyer and another a physician.

In 1780 Haynes obtained a license to preach in the Congregational Church. He was one of the first Black ministers certified to preach by a predominantly white denomination, and he was the first African American pastor of a white church. Haynes was the first Black man to be awarded an honorary degree from an American college when Middlebury College awarded him an honorary M.A. in 1804. (The first Black college graduate probably was Alexander Twilight, who received a bachelor's degree from Middlebury College in 1823. See the next listing.)

The Bennington Museum on West Main Street in Bennington has a painting of Reverend Haynes preaching at Old First Church. (For further information on Haynes, see the section on South Granville, New York.)

DATE ESTABLISHED: 1805

ADDRESS: Monument Avenue, Old Bennington Village

TELEPHONE: (802) 447-1223

VISITING HOURS: Sun. service, 11; Memorial Day–July 1, Sat. 10–noon, Sun. 1–4; July 2–Oct. 16, daily 10–noon, 1–4; other times by appointment

FEES: Donations welcome

SOURCES: Telephone conversation Apr. 9, 1994, Nancy Andrews, secretary, Old First Church. *Before the Mayflower,* 64, 305, 444, 629, 633.

Brownington

Brownington Village Historic District

The Old Stone House in the Brownington Village Historic District is one of Vermont's most interesting sites related to Black history. The Reverend Alexander Lucius Twilight (1795–1857), who designed and erected the building, probably was one of the first Black college graduates in America and was the first Black person to serve in a state legislature. He graduated from Middlebury College in 1823 and served in the Vermont House of Representatives from 1836 to 1838.

Twilight served as headmaster of Brownington Academy (also known as the Orleans County Grammar School). Twilight may have had an office on the second floor. The school closed in 1859 and the building later was moved from its original location. The structure now houses Brownington's Grange Hall.

In the 1830s, Twilight wanted to construct a new building for the school, but the board of trustees advised against the idea and would not help. Undaunted, Twilight proceeded with help from his neighbors. For two years, between 1834 and 1836, they quarried stone from nearby fields, split and hauled the granite, and erected a four-story, thirty-room building. Many Vermonters later marveled that Twilight had accomplished this feat on his small salary as minister and headmaster.

Twilight named the dormitory/classroom building Athenian Hall. The structure, which had no indoor plumbing or central heating, may have depended on the huge kitchen fireplace and fifteen small charcoal-burning fireplaces for heat. The residents had to obtain their drinking water by draining rainwater from the roof down through pipes into the kitchen area.

Athenian Hall served the school for almost a quarter of a century. Twilight instructed local schoolchildren either in the stone building or the Orleans County Grammar School. His desk and Bible are still on view—visible symbols of a man of accomplishment.

The school closed two years after Twilight's death in 1857. A few years later his wife sold the residence, which later became a boarding house. In 1918 the Orleans County Historical Society purchased the fine old building and restored it. Today the Old Stone House contains twenty-five rooms with historical exhibits about the county. It is one of the best preserved school buildings from this era in America.

This site also contains the Alexander Twilight House, which dates from about 1820. Located next to the Old Stone House, it is perhaps the first dwelling owned by the Twilights in Brownington. The renovated homestead has farm tools and machinery on display. Across the road from the Old Stone House is the Twilight farm, which was built soon after Alexander and Mercy Twilight arrived in Brownington in 1829. The house was large enough to board several students.

The graves of Alexander and Mercy Twilight are located in the graveyard of the Brownington Congregational Church.

The Brownington Village Historic District, with the Old Stone House so closely associated with Alexander Twilight, is listed in the *National Register of Historic Places.*

DATE BUILT: Homestead, c1820; Old Stone House, 1834–1836

ADDRESS: Brownington Village, about 30 miles north of Saint Johnsbury (on I-91, take the Irasburg-Orleans exit, go east through Orleans, then take a sharp right onto VT 58; at the fork in the road turn to the left and go about 2 miles)

TELEPHONE: (802) 754-2022

VISITING HOURS: May 15–June 30, Sept. 1–Oct. 15, Fri.–Tues. 11–5; July–Aug., daily 11–5

FEES: Adults, $3; children under 12, $1; Orleans County residents, $2; special rates for student groups

SOURCES: Telephone conversation Jan. 27, 1995, Tracy Martin, site manager. *A Walking Tour of Brownington Village Historic District.*

Burlington

John Wheeler House

Vermont, the first state added to the thirteen original colonies, in 1777 also passed the first state constitution to forbid slavery. (Technically, Vermont did not become a state until 1791; it had existed for fourteen years as an independent republic.) By 1837 there were nearly one hundred antislavery societies in Vermont, and many citizens who were active in antislavery societies also were active in the underground railroad. Residents of Burlington, Vermont, and surrounding areas were very active in the abolition movement, and there were a number of underground railroad stops in this area.

Oral tradition maintains that John Wheeler, a minister and sixth president of the University of Vermont, assisted fugitive slaves who were fleeing to Canada, but there is no written documentation of the extent of involvement. He had lived in South Carolina in 1819 and had held religious services for slaves in South Carolina cities. When Wheeler returned to Vermont, he remained involved in antislavery activities.

Today the history department of the University of Vermont is housed in the Wheeler House, a brick, two-story house with basement. In the past the house served as an infirmary. The front of the house is intact, but the rear kitchen and servant wings were converted first to infirmary rooms and then to offices. The parlor and bedrooms are intact, although they are used now for university purposes.

DATE BUILT: 1840

ADDRESS: 442 Main Street, Burlington

TELEPHONE: (802) 656-3180

VISITING HOURS: By appointment Mon.–Fri. 8:30–4:30

SOURCES: Telephone conversation Apr. 8, 1994, Thomas Visser, research assistant professor of history, University of Vermont. Letter from Bridget M. Butler, administrative assistant, Department of History, The University of Vermont, 9 Jan. 1992. *The Underground Railroad in New England.*

Ferrisburgh

Rokeby Museum

In 1791 Thomas R. Robinson (1761–1851) and his wife, Jemima, moved from Rhode Island to Vermont and purchased a farm known as "Rokeby." The Robinsons were Quakers. Their homestead at the time consisted of more than 1,000 acres and encompassed a hill overlooking the Champlain Valley.

Prior to the Civil War, their son, Rowland Thomas Robinson (1791–1879), inherited the farm. Together with his wife, Rachel, he founded the Vermont Anti-Slavery Society, the first statewide antislavery organization in the nation. A leader in the local underground railroad, Robinson was also a friend of abolitionists Frederick Douglass, Lucretia Mott, and William Lloyd Garrison.

The Robinsons concealed runaway slaves in an east chamber of their house called the hidden room, which adjoined a bedroom; its entry door was not readily seen. When the fugitives left at night they were taken to their next stop at North Ferrisburgh, Charlotte, or East Montpelier. Moving north from those locations, they were helped to cross the border into Canada.

In addition to being an underground railway station, Rokeby also served as an early school, a Quaker meeting house, and the town's first library. Today the house is a museum, Vermont's only underground railway station open to the public. It displays two centuries of furnishings as well as records of the Vermont Anti-Slavery Society and items that belonged to the Robinson family. Visitors may see the room in which the fugitives hid.

DATE BUILT: House, 1780s and 1814; museum, 1962

ADDRESS: US 7 (north of Ferrisburgh off US 7), Ferrisburgh vicinity (from the south: approximately 3 miles north of Vergennes on US 7, historic site marker and front entrance sign on the right; from the north: approximately 2 miles south of the village center of North Ferrisburgh on US 7, historic site marker and museum entrance on your left)

TELEPHONE: (802) 877-3406

VISITING HOURS: May 15–Oct. 1, Thurs.–Sun. with 45-minute guided tours of the main house at 11, 12:30, and 2; tours of the outbuildings self-guided; closed Mon.–Wed., Oct. 2–May 14; office hours Wed.–Fri. 9–5

FEES: Adults, $4; senior citizens and students, $3; children under 12, $1

SOURCES: Telephone conversation Apr. 9, 1994, Jim Mullin, caretaker, Rokeby Museum. Karen E. Petersen, director, Rokeby Museum. *The Underground Railroad in New England. National Register of Historic Places*, 767.

Woodstock

Titus Hutchinson House

The Titus Hutchinson House was the home of an active stationmaster for the underground railroad. Hutchinson was a former State Supreme Court Chief Justice. He assisted slaves when they arrived from South Woodstock, then helped to move them on to Royalton or Stafford.

Hutchinson House is a large, white, frame residence on the Woodstock village square. During construction for a bridge, a tunnel was discovered that ran from the Hutchinson home to the Kedron River. (The tunnel is closed now.)

Since the early 1980s the Woodstock Historical Association (located around the corner from the Hutchinson House at 26 Elm Street) has owned Hutchinson House. Before they purchased it, the residence served for many years as an inn and a restaurant. Now the first floor houses a retail art gallery and the rest of the house contains private office space. The exterior has retained its original appearance, but some remodeling was done inside.

The house is easily accessible, as it is in the center of town. Visitors who wish to see the interior (there are no signs of the tunnel today) should refer requests to the Woodstock Historical Association.

DATE BUILT: Late 18th century

ADDRESS: One, The Green, Woodstock

TELEPHONE: Woodstock Historical Association, (802) 457-1822

VISITING HOURS: Enterprises private; make appointment to see interior by contacting the Woodstock Historical Association

SOURCES: Telephone conversation Apr. 11, 1994, Kit Nichols, assistant to the director, Woodstock Historical Association. *The Underground Railroad in New England.*

Works Consulted

Before the Mayflower: A History of Black America. 5th ed. Lerone Bennett Jr. New York: Penguin, 1988.

National Register of Historic Places. Washington, D.C.: National Park Service, 1976.

The Underground Railroad in New England. Richard R. Kuns and John Sabino, eds. Boston: American Revolution Bicentennial Administration, Region I, with Boston 200, the Bicentennial and Historical Commissions of the Six New England States and the Underground Railroad Task Force, 1976.

A Walking Tour of Brownington Village Historic District. Elaine Magalis. Brownington, Vt.: Orleans County Historical Society. [brochure]

PART 3

THE MIDWEST

Illinois

Indiana

Iowa

Kansas

Michigan

(Special Feature: Canada)

Minnesota

Missouri

Nebraska

North Dakota

Ohio

South Dakota

Wisconsin

The settling of the Midwest in the late eighteenth and the nineteenth centuries provided new opportunities and challenges for African Americans. The new territories that would become Illinois, Indiana, Iowa, Kansas, Michigan, Minnesota, Missouri, Nebraska, North Dakota, Ohio, South Dakota, and Wisconsin were attractive to white settlers because of the vast amount of land available for development. Some pioneers had heard, too, of riches to be gained from the fur trade and other commercial activities. The region was attractive to Black men and women because states in the Midwest entered the Union as free states, many of which became important underground railroad routes leading north.

Most of the Southern and Northeastern states were settled in the 1600s. The Midwest, however, was settled much later. After explorers and trappers spread word about vast wilderness regions to the west, bold and hardy men and women began moving west to seek land for themselves or to establish commercial ventures. Thriving towns grew where rivers or overland routes made possible easy transportation of goods. Of the Midwestern states, only Michigan (1668) was settled as early as the 1600s, and Nebraska (1823) and South Dakota (1859) were the last states in this region to be developed by white Americans. As the number of white settlers grew, conflicts over the land became increasingly bitter; taking of the land eventually would lead to the conquest of Native Americans and their removal from desirable land.

African Americans were an important part of the development of the Midwest, yet they often faced deliberately imposed restrictions that were designed to keep them in a subordinate position in society. Although the Revolutionary War had been fought over the issue of freedom and the right to make decisions, the liberties that white men and women sought for themselves were not extended to African Americans and Native Americans. Through the first decades of the eighteenth century, slavery still existed in the South and was a hotly debated issue in other regions of the United States. These debates led to the passage of important legislation that affected African Americans, including the Northwest Ordinance of 1787, the Fugitive Slave Laws of 1793 and 1850, an 1808 law that banned the further importing of slaves into the United States, the Missouri Compromise of 1820–1821, and the Kansas-Nebraska Act of 1854. These laws and their effect on African Americans in the Midwest are discussed in the following sections.

The Northwest Ordinance and Slavery

As the Midwest region developed, citizens throughout the United States debated the issue of slavery in the new territory. Abolitionists saw the issue as a moral one; they claimed that it was wrong to force human beings to work under inhumane conditions for the benefit of others. There were others, too, who opposed slavery, but their opposition was due more to self-interest because they believed that slaves provided competition for white workers who had to be paid wages. Another group, the emigrationists, were not opposed to emancipation, but felt that Black people, once freed, should be shipped out of the United States to colonies in Haiti, South America, or Africa. A fourth group opposed slavery in order to exclude Black Americans from the developing Midwest, which then would be settled by whites only. These ideas formed a complex web of motivations at the time Congress was writing the specifications of the Northwest Ordinance.

In July 1787 the Continental Congress adopted the Northwest Ordinance that established the Northwest Territory, land west of Pennsylvania between the Ohio and the Mississippi Rivers. The territory, called the Old Northwest, later became the states of Ohio, Indiana, Illinois, Michigan, Wisconsin, and part of Minnesota. One aspect of the ordinance—the prohibition of slavery in the Northwest Territory—made the region especially attractive to slaves who were escaping from bondage in the South. Ohio, the first state in the Northwest Territory to be admitted to the Union (1803), was situated across the river from Kentucky, a slave state. As a free state, Ohio became an attractive escape route from Kentucky and became an important link on the underground railroad. The same was true of Indiana, Illinois, Michigan, and parts of Wisconsin. The underground railroad system, a network of houses, barns, and churches where escaping slaves received food, clothing, and shelter, was extensive and effective in the Midwest.

The Prohibition Against Importing Slaves into the United States

In 1808 Congress passed a law banning the further importation of slaves into the United States. Once this legislation was passed, slave owners who wished to increase their number of slaves could do so only by purchasing them, acquiring them through inheritance, or relying on births to slaves they already owned. Slave owners found ways, however, to circumvent the law that would have decreased the number of new slaves available for purchase. Some sea captains continued to import slaves, sailing silently into numerous hidden coves and harbors. Between 1808 and 1860 they illegally imported 250,000 slaves into the United States. Many slave owners stooped to the level of slave breeding, a procedure they regarded as no more immoral than the breeding of livestock. Other white men went on raids into Northern cities where they captured fugitives or even kidnapped free Black men, women, and children and sold them into slavery in the South.

Although members of Congress had banned the importing of slaves into the United States in 1808, they were not necessarily in favor of abolishing slavery. In fact, in response to pressure from the South, they passed laws that made it easier for slave owners to capture slaves who had fled to the North and the Midwest.

The Fugitive Slave Laws

In 1793 Congress had tried to appease slave owners who were furious about losing their runaway slaves by passing the Fugitive Slave Law, making it easier for states to cooperate in the return of escaped slaves. Slave owners were disappointed, however, because the law was not very effective. Northern states already had begun to abolish slavery, and the Northwest Ordinance prohibited slavery in the region that it regulated. Antislavery sentiment was so strong in many towns in the North and the Midwest that many citizens ignored the Fugitive Slave Law and continued to support the underground railroad.

Fearing further loss of their capital—the slaves who were fleeing on foot, by horse-drawn wagon, and by boat—slave owners again angrily demanded assistance from Congress. In response, Congress passed the Fugitive Slave Law of 1850, adding provisions that strengthened the previous law. The new legislation created fear and even panic among groups of free Black people. For example, at the St. Matthews Episcopal Church in Detroit, Michigan, so many church members fled to Canada after passage of the Fugitive Slave Law that remaining members were not able to pay the debt on their new church. An African American was not allowed to testify in court if kidnapped and wrongly identified as an escaped slave. Federal commissioners who returned a person to slavery were rewarded with $10, a welcome incentive at that time. Any person who refused to cooperate with authorities in capturing a slave was punished with a fine or a jail sentence.

In spite of the new danger, many citizens, Black and white, angrily refused to cooperate with the law and even defied its provisions. For example, the African American congregation at Detroit's Second Baptist Church operated an underground railroad station in the basement of their church. At the Quinn Chapel African Methodist Episcopal Church in Chicago, members of the congregation and their friends responded to the Fugitive Slave Law by defiantly vowing to protect each other. Although more than fifty members were former slaves, they boldly vowed to defend themselves at all costs. There was no sure security, however, until Congress repealed the Fugitive Slave Acts in June 1864 and until the Union won the Civil War the following year.

The Missouri Compromise

Between the passage of the first and second Fugitive Slave Acts, the Missouri Compromise of 1820–1821 was enacted. Its purpose was to try to resolve disputes between the slave states and the free states. The area called Missouri Territory had applied to join the Union in 1818, and slave-owning citizens wanted Missouri to be a slave state. They were opposed, however, by Northerners who wanted new states joining the Union to be free states. After extensive debates in Congress and after a futile attempt to add a provision to the Missouri statehood bill that would gradually eliminate slavery in the state, Congress adjourned without passing the statehood bill.

In 1819 Alabama was admitted to the Union as a slave state, balancing representation of slave and free states in the Senate, but when Maine next applied for admission to the Union, the question of Missouri's status arose again. Henry Clay, Speaker of the House, promoted a plan in which Missouri would be admitted as a slave state and Maine as a free state, and no *additional* slave states would be created west of the Mississippi River and north of the southern boundary line of Missouri. This measure, called the Missouri Compromise, remained in existence until 1854, when it was repealed by the Kansas-Nebraska Act. Although the compromise provided a way to determine whether new states would enter the Union as slave or free states, the compromise did not solve the problem of slavery in the country.

The Kansas-Nebraska Act

In 1854, the Missouri Compromise was repealed by passage of the Kansas-Nebraska Act. This legislation divided land into two territories, Kansas and Nebraska, and specified that settlers in the border states could decide by popular vote whether each state would be a slave state or a free state. The new bill enraged opponents of slavery and deepened the split between North and South. During this period the Republican Party was founded by opponents of the bill. The test of the effectiveness of the new legislation came, however, when Kansas was opened to settlement in 1854 under the terms of the Kansas-Nebraska Act. The issue of establishing Kansas as a slave or a free state captured national interest; proslavery and antislavery groups from other parts of the country moved to Kansas to live and to fight for their side's position. For example, John Brown, a fiery white abolitionist, came to Kansas to join the fight. In 1856 he led a group of men in a battle against proslavery activists at Osawatomie. Instead of having the question of slavery in the state decided by vote, Kansas erupted instead into brutal and bloody battles and massacres over the issue. Each side formed its own government in the battle for supremacy, and the warring region became known as "Bleeding Kansas." At one point, troops had to be called out to help restore order. Although Kansas finally entered the Union as a free state, raids continued along the Missouri-Kansas border throughout the Civil War years.

Equality in the Midwest

In the twentieth century Kansas again entered the national limelight when a Black child, Linda Brown, sought to attend the all-white Sumner Elementary School in Topeka. Her case, *Brown* v. *Topeka Board of Education,* reached the U.S. Supreme Court where, in May 1954, the Supreme Court declared segregation in public schools to be unconstitutional.

In spite of barriers, there were bright instances where individuals and groups championed the cause of equality in the Midwest. Oberlin College, established in 1833 in Oberlin, Ohio, became the first college in the United States to establish a policy of nondiscrimination in admissions. Central State University and Wilberforce University, both in Wilberforce, Ohio, were among the first colleges in America operated by African Americans. In the military arena Black soldiers won respect for their performance at a number of forts in the Midwest.

Midwest Achievers

In addition to the achievements of the colleges and the African American soldiers as a group, several African Americans in the Midwest were recognized as individuals for their efforts or their achievements. One was Dred Scott, a man who sought his freedom on the basis of having lived in free territory in Illinois and at Fort Snelling, Minnesota, before being taken by his master back into slave territory in Missouri. Although he ultimately lost his legal case, his courage in carrying his plea to the courts strengthened the resolve of abolitionists to continue their work.

Other achievers from the Midwest include Paul Laurence Dunbar, poet; Congressman John Mercer Langston; Colonel Charles Young, the third Black person to graduate from West Point and the highest ranking Black military officer in World War I; Robert S. Abbott, founder of the *Chicago Daily Defender;* Jean Baptiste Point du Sable, Chicago's first settler; Dr. Daniel Hale Williams, a pioneer in heart surgery; Ida B. Wells Barnett of Chicago, a courageous fighter against racism and a researcher of the circumstances surrounding lynchings; Madame C. J. Walker, a millionaire and founder of a hair care and beauty products empire; and Alexander Clark, a civil rights leader in programs based in several states and Consul General to Liberia.

Of the individual African American achievers, one man's achievement was remarkable, even though he later was largely forgotten. The man was York, and he was the only African American member of the famed Lewis and Clark Expedition.

Work Consulted

The Academic American Encyclopedia. Danbury, Conn.: Grolier, 1993. [electronic version]

Civil War–1905

All photos by
Nancy C. Curtis, Ph.D.,
except as noted.

Emancipation Oak, Hampton Institute, Hampton, Va.

Limerick Historic District,
Louisville, Ky.

Ferry Street School,
Niles, Mich.

Dexter Avenue King Memorial Baptist Church,
Montgomery, Ala.

Estey Hall, Shaw University, Raleigh, N.C.

Joseph Price House, Livingstone College Historic District, Salisbury, N.C.

Jubilee Hall, Fisk University, Nashville, Tenn.

Interior, Jubilee Hall, Fisk University, Nashville, Tenn.

Arbor exterior, Tucker's Grove Camp Meeting Ground, Machpelah, N.C.

Arbor interior, Tucker's Grove Camp Meeting Ground, Machpelah, N.C.

Two-story "tents," Tucker's Grove Camp Meeting Ground, Machpelah, N.C.

Frank Ward's Corner Store,
Greenville, Ala.

Allen Chapel A.M.E. Church,
Yankton, S.D.

Courtesy of
Dave A. Kuehler,
Yankton, S.D.

Memorial Church,
Hampton University,
Hampton, Va.

House with wrought iron trim,
Jackson Ward Historic District,
Richmond, Va.

Pickford Hall,
Virginia Union
University,
Richmond, Va.

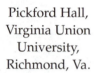

Entrances, Jackson
Ward Historic District,
Richmond, Va.

King-Tisdell Cottage,
Savannah, Ga.

Russell Historic
District,
Louisville, Ky.

Central Baptist Church,
Charleston, S.C.

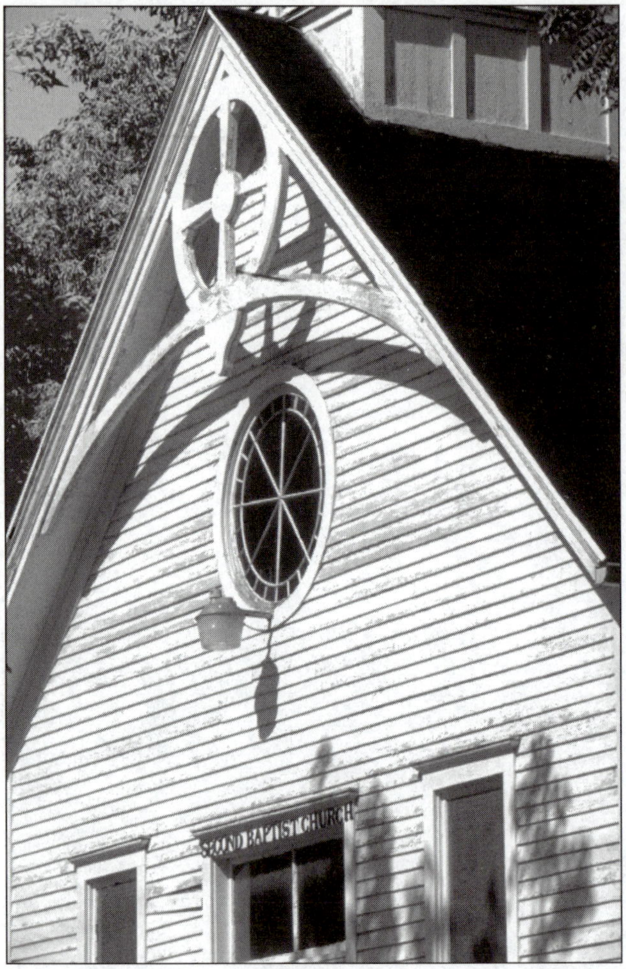

Detail, Second Baptist Church,
Adrian, Mich.

Parlor, Paul Laurence Dunbar State Memorial, Dayton, Ohio.

Illinois

Alton

Alton Museum of History and Art

In 1987 the Alton Museum established the Committee on Black Pioneers, a group charged with documenting African American cultural activities in Alton from the 1830s to the present day. Each year the museum highlights a different theme from local Black history. One exhibit, for example, featured local Black pioneers who changed conditions for the better; it also displayed the work of African American artist Regina Shaw. A room in the Alton Museum of History and Art shows how a printing press was set up for martyred white abolitionist Elijah Lovejoy. The room contains a press similar to the Lovejoy press that an angry mob threw into the Mississippi River.

Elijah Lovejoy (1802–1837) was born in Albion, Maine, the son of Reverend Daniel Lovejoy and Elizabeth Pattee Lovejoy. He graduated from Waterville College in Maine (now Colby College). In 1836 he came to Alton, at that time the most prosperous city in Illinois. Previously he had edited *The Observer,* published at St. Louis, Missouri. Because Missouri was a slave state, Elijah and his views soon became highly unpopular. He decided, therefore, to move his activities to Alton, across the Mississippi River from St. Louis. Many Alton citizens originally were from New England and other eastern states, and they believed slavery was evil. When Lovejoy began anew to edit the *Alton Observer* and to express antislavery views in the paper, many townspeople supported him. In spite of their support, however, and despite the status of Illinois as a free state, Lovejoy and his paper became targets of violence. An incident occurred when a press arrived on a Sunday morning. Lovejoy's religious convictions prevented him from caring for the business of shipping the press on the sabbath, and he left it unguarded on the wharf. That Sunday night the press was dumped into the river. The citizens of Alton condemned the act and pledged money for a new press. Two other presses were destroyed by mobs, but the Ohio Antislavery Society, hearing of the outrageous vandalism, replaced them. The rage of proslavery forces escalated, however, after the founding of a state antislavery society at Alton; soon the proslavery mobs destroyed another press. Armed abolitionists then came from nearby towns to protect a new press that was on the way from Ohio. When the press arrived on November 7, 1837, armed guards stood watch over the warehouse where it was placed. The entire city of Alton was in a state of apprehension as night fell. That night a mob came and tried to set the warehouse on fire. Lovejoy rushed out to try to stop them, and they shot and killed him, then dumped the press into the Mississippi River.

Elijah Lovejoy was buried in the Alton Cemetery, and a monument of the winged statue of Victory was erected to his memory. The statue symbolized triumph of the causes for which Lovejoy fought—freedom for Black people and freedom of the press.

Visitors should call the museum to check for current Black history themes. The African American cookbook is on sale for $8.50 at the museum and at the Alton Visitors Center, 200 Piasa Street.

DATE ESTABLISHED: Museum, 1987; memorial monument, 1897

ADDRESS: 829 E. Fourth Street, Alton

TELEPHONE: (618) 462-2763

VISITING HOURS: Tues.–Wed., Thurs., Sun. 1–4; closed Mon., Fri., Sat., Christmas, Easter

FEES: None

SOURCES: Letter from Lottie M. Pendergrass, Committee on Black Pioneers, Alton Museum of History and Art, Mar. 6, 1990. "Making History, Black History." *Dictionary of American Biography,* 434–5.

Chicago

Robert S. Abbott House

Robert Sengstacke Abbott was born in 1870 at St. Simon Island off the coast of Georgia. After attending the Beach Institute in Savannah (see the listing for Savannah, King-Tisdell Cottage), he studied at Claflin University in South Carolina and at Hampton Institute in Virginia. At Hampton, he learned the printer's trade, which proved useful in his future work. Although he had moved to Chicago to study at the Kent School of Law, Abbott was unable to earn a living as a lawyer, so he took a job working in a printing house.

Abbott wanted to print his own newspaper. He knew that the Black community had important concerns that needed to be widely shared, so he took his savings, borrowed money, and set up his first office in his landlady's dining room. In 1905 he began printing the *Chicago Daily Defender* in a small handbill size. He walked through the streets, delivering his precious first copies door to door to small Black-owned businesses. Within two decades the *Defender* was known in Black households across the country.

Abbott was brash and outspoken in his words and phrases. Where other Black newspaper writers of the day were careful not to offend white readers, the *Defender's* articles attacked racism and discrimination in searing terms. Abbott also used his newspaper for another purpose—to encourage African Americans to migrate north for better living conditions.

By 1929 Abbott was wealthy and able to publish his newspaper in a three-story building. The *Defender* became the senior partner of a chain of papers that included the *Michigan Chronicle, New Pittsburgh Courier, New National Courier,* and *Tri-State Defender.*

The most-successful Black publisher of his era, Abbott had nearly a half million dollars in cash. He purchased a fine home on South Park Way (now Martin Luther King Jr. Drive). This was in a Chicago South Side community known for the grand mansions and the opulent lifestyle of its African American residents. The Abbott house originally was built as a duplex with an elegant coach house in the rear. The interior featured carved-oak pilasters and exposed beams that framed the main rooms. Abbott lived in one section of the duplex between 1926 and 1940. When he died in 1940, Abbott's nephew, John H. Sengstacke, became the new head of the group of newspapers. The *Defender* continued to bring inspiration to thousands of Black people by offering the hope of relief from oppressive racism.

DATE OF SIGNIFICANCE: Abbott residence, 1926–1940

ADDRESS: Abbott House, 4742 Martin Luther King Jr. Drive; newspaper office, 2400 S. Michigan Avenue, Chicago

TELEPHONE: Newspaper, (312) 225-2400

VISITING HOURS: House, private, visitors may drive by; newspaper office, by appointment during business hours

FEES: None

SOURCES: Telephone call to the newspaper, June 24, 1994. NRHPINF. *International Library of Negro Life and History,* 153.

Black Metropolis

The historic area listed in the *National Register of Historic Places* under the theme of "Black Metropolis" consists of several commercial and civic buildings and a sculpture. Together they represent a once-thriving area of African American civic, commercial, and cultural activity. The structures are the Overton Hygienic Building, the Chicago Bee Building, Eighth Regiment Armory, Victory Sculpture, Unity Hall, and Wabash Avenue YMCA.

Development began in this area in the 1850s with the establishment of a grid of streets in an area three miles south of Chicago's central business district. A decade earlier African Americans had begun to leave oppressive conditions in the South. Many came to Chicago and settled throughout the city. Between 1900 and 1920 this geographic area changed from a white upper-middle class to a predominantly Black neighborhood, and several Black businesses prospered in the vicinity of State and Thirty-fifth Streets. Included in the district were the first Black-owned bank, restaurants, and theaters and nightclubs where patrons could listen to Louis Armstrong, Jelly Roll Morton, Florence Mills, and other popular entertainers.

After 1925 the Black Metropolis area began to decline. Fewer new arrivals meant a decline in the need for goods and services. White business owners began to realize the potential profits from providing services and goods to the Black population, and their businesses along Forty-seventh Street began to siphon off customers from Black enterprises. The greatest impact, however, came from financial hardships of the Great Depression years, which dealt a fatal blow to many Black businesses. Many buildings became vacant or fell into disrepair, and urban renewal projects of the 1950s and 1960s brought about the demolition of many houses and commercial buildings. By midyear 1994 a strong resurgence of interest in rehabilitating some of the buildings in the Black Metropolis area was showing results, with projects in varying stages of progress.

The Chicago Bee Building, the Eighth Regiment Armory, the Overton Hygienic Building, Unity Hall, the Victory Sculpture, and the Wabash Avenue YMCA all represent a once-thriving commercial and cultural area of the city. These structures are among the most significant Black historical landmarks in the United States and may once again be restored as places representing the pride of the community.

SOURCES: NRHPINF. Telephone conversation June 24, 1994, Alicia Mazur, preservation planner, City of Chicago, Department of Planning and Development. Telephone conversation June 24, 1994, Pat Dowell-Cerasoli, Mid-South Planning and Development Commission.

Chicago Bee Building

Anthony Overton built another landmark building in this community, the Chicago Bee Building at 3647–3655 South State Street. Overton had first published the *Chicago Bee* from his own building, the Overton Hygienic Building. Later he printed the newspaper from a storefront on State

Street. Wanting to establish one location for the complete operation, he commissioned the Chicago Bee Building in 1929 as a combination newspaper office and apartment building. The three-story art deco structure had a facade ornamented with glazed terra cotta. It was ready for occupancy in 1931.

Unfortunately, with the onset of the Great Depression, Overton's bank and insurance company began to decline, and the bank failed. Overton gave up his Overton Hygienic Building and moved the cosmetics company into the Chicago Bee Building, where the two businesses shared quarters for many years. Although the newspaper ceased publication in the early 1940s, the cosmetics firm continued to operate from the Chicago Bee Building.

Today the Chicago Bee Building, which has had few alterations, remains as a landmark, the last major structure built in the Black Metropolis area. Plans are under way to renovate the Chicago Bee Building, which the City of Chicago has owned since 1987. Renovations were to begin in 1994 and to end in the fall of 1995. Plans call for restoring the original terra-cotta finish and first-floor storefronts.

DATE BUILT:	1929–1931
ADDRESS:	3647–3655 S. State Street, Chicago
VISITING HOURS:	Visitors may drive by
SOURCE:	NRHPINF.

The Eighth Regiment Armory

The Eighth Regiment Armory at 3533 South Giles Avenue is a third landmark in the Black Metropolis area. The Illinois National Guard built it as headquarters for the country's only regiment to be commanded entirely by Black men. Originally organized as a volunteer regiment drawn from the Black community in 1898 during the Spanish-American War, the regiment served as an infantry division of the Illinois National Guard. Although their first headquarters was in a former livery stable, the men distributed petitions as early as 1910 in which they asked for better facilities. Construction started in 1914, and the building was completed the following year.

The "Fighting Eighth" served during border conflicts with Mexico in 1916 and later fought on major battlefronts in France in World War I. It was recognized as the last regiment to drive the German forces from the Aisne-Marne region before the 1918 armistice. Almost every man in the regiment who returned had some kind of decoration for bravery in action. The name of the street on which the armory is located was changed to Giles Avenue to honor Lieutenant George Giles, the highest ranking officer killed in action. The Victory Sculpture on Thirty-fifth Street and Martin Luther King Jr. Drive, erected in 1927, also honors the bravery of this regiment.

The Eighth Regiment eventually became part of several specialized military divisions housed in a new armory on Cottage Grove Avenue. The historic Eighth Regiment Armory, a three-story building with limestone trim, was used for a time for community meetings and social functions, then it became vacant. The building still appears much as it was when designed, housing a drill hall, meeting rooms, dining facilities, and reception parlors. Discussions have begun on possible ways to renovate the building.

DATE BUILT:	1914–1915
ADDRESS:	3533 S. Giles Avenue, Chicago
VISITING HOURS:	Vacant, visitors may drive by
SOURCE:	NRHPINF.

Overton Hygienic Building

Between 1908 and 1931 the Black Metropolis area gained nationwide attention as a model of Black enterprise as capital raised by the African American community put up several new buildings. One of these landmarks was the Overton Hygienic Building, which was built in 1922–1923. Pioneer Anthony Overton constructed the building, which was considered a milestone in African American business achievement in Chicago. Its construction cost a quarter of a million dollars, and it was the first structure in the Black Metropolis to offer first-class rental offices.

Anthony Overton was a business genius who emphasized integrity in business relationships. He started with a small cosmetics firm, the Overton Hygienic Company, and developed other enterprises: the Victory Life Insurance Company, the

Chicago Bee newspaper, the *Half Century Magazine*, and the Douglass National Bank—the first Black bank to receive a national charter.

Overton was born in slavery in Louisiana in March 1865. He studied at Washburn College in Topeka and earned a bachelor of law degree in 1888 at the University of Kansas. For a brief period Overton was proprietor of a general store in Oklahoma. He served as judge of the Municipal Court in Shawnee County, Kansas, and started the Overton Hygienic Company in Kansas City.

Needing larger facilities, Overton moved to Chicago. He established both his living quarters and his business in a former apartment building on South Wabash Avenue and began selling cosmetics, shoe polish, baking powder, and flavoring extracts to a wide market in the United States.

Overton broke into the publishing business in 1916 with the *Half Century Magazine* and the *Chicago Bee* newspaper. By 1922 his businesses were scattered in different buildings throughout the South Side. To consolidate them, he built the Overton Building. With more room for the different operations, Overton established an insurance company and, in 1922, the Douglass National Bank. The Black-owned bank solved many problems due to banking discrimination. A great many banks had taken funds from African American depositors but refused to employ them or give them loans.

In the Overton Building, quarters for the Douglass National Bank and Victory Life Insurance Company occupied most of the ground floor. The second floor housed quality rental offices for professionals. Overton used the third and fourth floors for his own businesses.

Overton's enterprises at first appeared to survive the Great Depression. Douglass National Bank was successful until financial panics and bank runs increased. The bank shut down in the early 1930s, and Overton's insurance company nearly became insolvent. Although the depletion of funds forced Overton to abandon the Overton Hygienic Building and to find smaller quarters in another building one block south, he retained control of the company until his death in 1946.

DATE BUILT: 1922–1923
ADDRESS: 3619–3627 S. State Street, Chicago
VISITING HOURS: Private, visitors may drive by
SOURCE: NRHPINF.

Unity Hall

Unity Hall was built in 1886 by a Jewish social organization, but became the headquarters of the People's Movement Club in 1917. This movement was started by Oscar Stanton DePriest, an African American who arrived in Chicago in 1889. DePriest became a city councilman and consistently sought jobs and better living conditions for his constituents. In 1917 DePriest, a Republican, created the People's Movement Club in order to establish a strong political base in the Black community. DePriest became the committeeman of the Third Ward in 1924. In 1928 he became the first Black person in the twentieth century and the first ever from the North elected to the U.S. House of Representatives. He served three consecutive terms before being defeated in 1934 by Arthur Mitchell, a Black Democrat.

The People's Movement Club used Unity Hall, a three-story building with red pressed-brick and terra-cotta ornamentation, as its headquarters. The interior had many small clubrooms and a large assembly hall in the rear. Later Unity Hall served for many years as headquarters for the Democratic politician William Dawson. The building later housed a church.

DATE BUILT: 1887; Unity Hall, 1917
ADDRESS: 3140 S. Indiana Avenue, Chicago
VISITING HOURS: Privately owned by a church
SOURCES: NRHPINF. *African Americans: Voices of Triumph,* vol. 2, *Leadership*, 212.

Victory Sculpture

The Victory Sculpture, located at the intersection of Thirty-fifth Street and Martin Luther King Jr. Drive, honors the courageous men of the Illinois Eighth Regiment, the first to be commanded entirely by Black men. The men served with distinction in France where they were incorporated into the 370th U.S. Infantry during World War I. By the end of World War I, General John J. Pershing had awarded the Distinguished Service

Cross for extraordinary heroism to twelve members of the "Fighting Eighth." The French government awarded the *Croix de Guerre* to sixty-eight men from the unit.

At the close of World War I, Chicago's Black community requested a memorial to honor the achievements of the Eighth Regiment. In the mid-1920s they proposed that a monument be erected in the parkway of South Grand Boulevard (now Martin Luther King Jr. Drive). The South Park Commission, which controlled the boulevard system, firmly opposed the plan, maintaining that there was no space available for a monument.

Chicago's famed Black newspaper, the *Chicago Daily Defender,* began a campaign against the commission board. Editorials urged the Black community to vote against any South Park Commission projects until the city recognized its Black war heroes. The community maintained the pressure until the commission agreed to support the memorial. Eventually the commission and the state of Illinois jointly funded the project.

French-born sculptor Leonard Crunelle designed the Victory Sculpture, a circular, gray-granite shaft with three bronze panels finished with black patination. The memorial portrays a Black soldier, a Black woman symbolizing motherhood, and the figure of Columbia holding a tablet listing the locations of the regiment's main battles.

The sculpture, the second monument erected in the United States to honor Black war heroes, was dedicated in 1936 in a public ceremony. It has since become one of the best-known landmarks of Chicago's Black community.

The Victory Sculpture is part of a plan to improve the Martin Luther King Jr. Drive from Thirty-fifth Street to the Stevenson overpass. Plans included planting trees along the way, refinishing the monument and providing special lighting for it, and raising the monument to a higher level. These changes are expected to make the underpass more visually inviting so that people would be encouraged to visit buildings in Black Metropolis.

DATE ESTABLISHED: 1936

ADDRESS: Thirty-fifth Street at Martin Luther King Jr. Drive

VISITING HOURS: Daily, 24 hours

SOURCE: NRHPINF.

Wabash Avenue Young Men's Christian Association

The Wabash Avenue YMCA opened its building to the public in 1913 after a successful three-year fund-raising drive. Julius Rosenwald, a white businessman, philanthropist, and chairman of Sears, Roebuck and Company, initiated the drive in 1911 by offering to advance $25,000 toward the erection of a YMCA building. Additional funds came from the Black community, which raised over $20,000, and from the contributions of business executives.

When the imposing five-story Wabash YMCA opened, it was one of the best-equipped of its type. Thousands of African American immigrants from the South were arriving in Chicago between 1910 and 1920, and, beginning in 1913, many were welcomed with housing and other services at the new "Y." The YMCA staff helped them find employment and provided job-training programs, including a popular auto repair class. Residents and newcomers enjoyed the assembly hall, gymnasium, and pool.

The YMCA served the community well for many years. However, by the late 1970s, the national YMCA office closed the Wabash Avenue "Y" and sold the building to a local church. The Wabash YMCA Building, which was used for a time by the church, was then purchased by a consortium of churches. With the help of a community association, the churches plan to develop the structure into a single-room occupancy building that would provide recreational and social support services, much as the old "Y" had done.

DATE BUILT: 1911–1913

ADDRESS: 3763 S. Wabash Avenue, Chicago

VISITING HOURS: Private, visitors may drive by

SOURCES: NRHPINF.

Chicago Historical Society Museum

In 1990 a major permanent exhibit opened at the Chicago Historical Museum: *A House Divided: America in the Age of Lincoln.* Museum displays focus on Black resistance to slavery, the role of Black soldiers, and the role of free Black people as abolitionists during the Civil War era.

The museum also has a small replica of Jean Baptiste Point du Sable's trading post. Du Sable, a man of mixed African ancestry, was Chicago's first non-Native American settler.

DATE ESTABLISHED: 1856
ADDRESS: 1601 N. Clark Street at North Avenue, Chicago
TELEPHONE: (312) 642-4600
VISITING HOURS: Mon.–Sat. 9–4:30, Sun. noon–5; closed Thanksgiving, Christmas, New Year's Day
FEES: Adults, $3; senior citizens and children 6–17, $1; Mon., free to all
SOURCES: Pat Manthei, public relations manager. Telephone call to site, June 25, 1994.

Du Sable Museum of African-American History*

The Du Sable Museum, one of America's oldest Black history museums, houses Chicago's most extensive collection of African American historical materials. The museum was named for Jean Baptiste Point du Sable, a Haitian pioneer of mixed African and European parentage; he was Chicago's first non-Native American settler.

The museum, which has an extensive permanent collection of African and African American art and artifacts, mounts more than six exhibitions each year. Its collection includes more than 800 artworks from the Works Progress Administration period of the Depression years and the 1960s Black arts movement. It features a monumental bas-relief carving by Robert Witt Ames that traces 400 years of African American history. The library also contains more than 10,000 volumes on African and African American life, history, and culture. Programs include tours for schools, lectures, and live performances of music and dance.

DATE ESTABLISHED: 1961
ADDRESS: 740 E. Fifty-sixth Place (Washington Park at Fifty-seventh Street and Cottage Grove Avenue), Chicago
TELEPHONE: (312) 947-0600
VISITING HOURS: Mon.–Sat. 10–5, Sun. noon–5; closed News Year's Day, Easter, Thanksgiving, Christmas
FEES: Adults, $2; senior citizens and students, $2; children under 6, free; Thurs., free to all
SOURCES: Mildred B. Jourdain, Du Sable Museum. Brochure of the Du Sable Museum sent by the Chicago Tourism Council. Brochure on Chicago museums from the Illinois Department of Commerce and Community Affairs Office of Tourism. Telephone call to site, June 24, 1994.

Provident Hospital and Training School

Dr. Daniel Hale Williams, a pioneering African American physician, was born in Pennsylvania in 1858. He grew up in a home in which his parents worked for the abolitionist cause. His father died when he was eleven. As a young man, Williams moved about the country in search of jobs. After working as a waiter, a barber, and a musician, he was fortunate to find an employer in Wisconsin who encouraged him to complete high school. After graduation, a prominent local doctor, Henry Palmer, later sponsored Williams's admission to Chicago Medical College from which he graduated in 1883.

Williams became known as an outstanding physician in the Black community. Although he treated both Black and white patients, he was acutely aware of the discrimination that barred Black patients, nurses, and interns from white-owned hospitals and training programs. To remedy this situation, he founded Provident Hospital in 1891, which was the first training school for Black interns and nurses in the United States. It was also America's first hospital serving physicians and patients without regard to race.

Williams was a staff surgeon at Provident from 1891 to 1912, except for short periods spent at Freedmen's Hospital in Washington, D.C. In 1893 he made history when a young man was brought in unconscious and bleeding internally from a stab wound to the heart. Williams opened the chest and operated, becoming one of the first physicians to perform a successful surgical closure of a wound to the heart and pericardium.

The first two hospital buildings of Provident Hospital have been demolished, and the third building—the one that opened two years after Williams's death—also is in danger of being lost. Vacant, boarded up, surrounded by a high fence, and for sale in mid-1994, the historic building is accessible only for exterior viewing. Visitors should go by only if they can view the building as a once-fine, historic brownstone that still has possibilities for restoration.

DATE BUILT: 1891

ADDRESS: 500 E. Fifty-first Street and Vincennes Avenue, Chicago

TELEPHONE: Newer Provident Hospital, (312) 572-2000 (not a historic structure)

VISITING HOURS: Vacant, visitors may drive by

SOURCES: Telephone conversation June 24, 1994, Carol Reliford, RN, Human Resource Department, Provident Hospital of Cook County. *Webster's New Biographical Dictionary,* 1061. *The African American Encyclopedia,* vol. 6, 1705–7. "The Provident Hospital Project," 457–75.

Quinn Chapel African Methodist Episcopal Church

Quinn Chapel houses Chicago's earliest Black congregation. The church was founded in 1844 when several Black Chicagoans organized a nonsectarian prayer group that met each week in the members' homes. In 1847 the group became known as part of the African Methodist Episcopal Congregation. Their church was named in honor of Bishop William P. Quinn.

More than fifty members of the congregation were ex-slaves. Some had purchased their freedom or had been manumitted, while others had escaped from bondage. Although technically free, they were bound together by a danger—even in Chicago. In 1793 the United States had passed a law, rooted in the fugitive slave clause of the Constitution, mandating that any person who was a slave in one state and escaped to another state should be apprehended and returned to his or her owner. Then in 1850 Congress passed a new and stronger Fugitive Slave Law—which placed every Black person in danger. With no more than a sworn affidavit, a white person could claim that an African American was an escaped slave and take him or her before a federal commissioner.

Any citizen could be summoned to help in capturing the fugitive; anyone who interfered with such a capture could be fined a maximum of $1,000 and imprisoned up to six months.

African Americans had no right to a trial by jury or to testify in their own behalf. Thus, there was a strong incentive to send the person back into slavery because this would reward the commissioner (the official in charge of such cases) with a fee of $10. If the suspected escapee was released, the commissioner received only $5.

Reaction at Quinn Chapel to the new fugitive slave law was immediate. The church called a special meeting, which 300 people—more than half of Chicago's Black population—attended. The group passed a resolution declaring that its members would defend themselves at all costs, even at the risk of shedding human blood. In the words of the resolution, "We who have tasted of freedom are ready to exclaim, in the language of the brave Patrick Henry, 'Give us liberty or give us death.'"[1] The group formed the Liberty Association and assigned teams of men to patrol the city and watch for possible slave hunters.

The Quinn Chapel congregation constructed their first church in 1853. True to their beliefs, they used the church as a station on the underground railroad. After the church was destroyed in the Chicago fire of 1871, church members met in several temporary locations until they could construct the present Quinn Chapel, a substantial brick and rusticated gray-stone structure, in 1892. The exterior of the church has remained virtually unchanged, and much of the interior is original. The second-floor chapel has the original wooden pews as well as the William H. Delle pipe organ purchased from the German pavilion at the 1893 Columbian Exposition. In 1940 church member Proctor Chisholm painted a mural in the sanctuary of Christ's resurrection.

Members of Quinn Chapel have been active in community affairs. They assisted in founding the Bethel A.M.E. Church, Provident Hospital, and the Wabash Avenue YMCA. Some church members have served in both houses of the Illinois legislature. Quinn Chapel A.M.E. Church is listed in the *National Register of Historic Places.*

DATE ESTABLISHED: Congregation, 1844; church, 1892
ADDRESS: 2401 S. Wabash Avenue, Chicago
VISITING HOURS: By appointment, Mon.–Fri. 10–4
SOURCES: NRHPINF. Telephone conversation June 24, 1994, Ms. Ruth Hawkins, receptionist, Quinn Chapel A.M.E. Church. *There Is a River,* 160–1.

Harold Washington Library Center

The Harold Washington Library Center, the main library of the Chicago Public Library, is the largest public library in the United States in volume. Appropriately, it is named for a man of high achievement, Harold Washington, the first African American mayor of Chicago.

Washington was born in Chicago in 1922. He graduated from Roosevelt University in 1949 and from Northwestern University Law School in 1952. Two years later he began his political career, serving as a Democratic Party precinct captain. Later he was elected to the Illinois House of Representatives and the Illinois Senate; from 1980 to 1983 he was a member of the U.S. House of Representatives.

In the February 1983 Democratic mayoral primary, Washington surprised many who had predicted that he would be defeated by incumbent mayor Jane Byrne or by Richard M. Daley, son of the late Mayor Richard J. Daley. After Washington's surprise victory in the primary election, he went on to win the mayor's seat in the April 1983 general election. Although his was a narrow victory, Washington had many loyal supporters and was reelected in 1987. The city was shocked and saddened when Washington died of a heart attack later that year.

Today the city honors its former mayor with a library that bears his name and carries an important collection of his papers. The ten-story building takes up a full city block and is designed in a classical tradition. Constructed of red granite, the library has a green roof with green metal owls perched in the corners, symbolic, perhaps, of the wisdom that resides inside. In addition to the Harold Washington Collection, the library contains a large collection of works on Black history and the Civil War.

DATE ESTABLISHED:	1991
ADDRESS:	400 S. State Street, Chicago
TELEPHONE:	(312) 747-4300
VISITING HOURS:	Mon. 9–7; Tues., Thurs. 11–7; Wed., Fri., Sat. 9–5; Sun. 1–5
FEES:	None
SOURCES:	Telephone conversation June 25, 1994, Sue Puterko, librarian. Telephone call to site, Aug. 12, 1995. The Academic American Encyclopedia.

Ida B. Wells-Barnett House

Ida B. Wells Barnett, a nineteenth- and early twentieth-century journalist and crusader, fought racism throughout her adult life. Her pioneering research and publications decried the brutal lynchings that terrorized the Black community. They were a forerunner to the work of the National Association for the Advancement of Colored People in protesting violence and senseless killings.

Ida Wells was born in Holly Springs, Mississippi, in 1862. Her father was a skilled carpenter and a man of integrity. As Ida was attending Rust College, her education was suddenly interrupted when her parents died during the yellow fever epidemic of 1878. Although only sixteen at the time, she took over the responsibility for her younger brothers and sisters and earned some money by teaching school in a town near Holly Springs.

Later Wells moved to Memphis, where she taught school and continued her teacher training at LeMoyne Normal Institute and Fisk University. About that time Jim Crow laws were passed in Tennessee, and Wells rebelled against them one day by refusing to move from the first-class section into the smoking car, which had been set aside for African Americans. Upon her refusal to follow the conductor's order, she was dragged out of the car by three white men. She filed a lawsuit against the Chesapeake & Ohio Railroad as a result. At first she appeared to have won when a court awarded her $500 in damages. However, the state had no intention of setting a precedent in favor of equal rights; the Tennessee Supreme Court reversed the decision of the lower court.

Wells next became a journalist and purchased an interest in a small Memphis newspaper, *Free Speech and Headlight*. An article by her in the newspaper denouncing the inequities observed in the Memphis school district cost her her job as a teacher, but she persisted in her efforts to expose injustice. A tragedy in Memphis in 1892 was a crucial event in Wells's life. Three Black entrepreneurs had opened a grocery store in town. Its popularity grew, drawing customers away from a store run by a white man. Resentment grew in the white community against the Black businessmen. One day a group of white thugs began to harass the Black-run store, and a group of armed Black men repelled the invaders. Three of the white attackers were shot in the confusion. The white press soon printed inflammatory articles about the Black men, portraying them as brutes who had attacked innocent white citizens. Not long afterward, a mob invaded the jail where the Black entrepreneurs were being held, seized them, and lynched them. The store run by the three Black entrepreneurs was looted and then closed down. Wells had been a close friend of one of the Black grocery store owners and his wife. Shocked at the outrage, she wrote a series of scathing articles about the lynching in her newspaper, urging Black residents to leave Memphis since there was no justice for them there.

Wells pointed out that lynchings seemed to take place when Black people began to rise up and compete economically with white people. One of her articles analyzed 728 lynchings that had taken place over a decade. She pointed out that women and children as well as men were among the victims; she hinted that many lynchings may have occurred because of interracial relationships instigated by white women. Wells was out of town when this particular article appeared. It raised a fury, and a band of white citizens burned the newspaper office to the ground and ran Wells's coworkers out of town. Wells received a warning that if she returned to Memphis, she would be hanged.

Wells stayed in the North for the next three years, lecturing in northeastern cities. She visited England for several months in 1893 and again for several months in 1894. In 1895 she ended the sojourn in the north, marrying Ferdinand Lee Barnett, a lawyer and founder of *The Conservator,* Chicago's first Black-owned newspaper. Settling in Chicago, Wells-Barnett raised a family and periodically wrote additional articles on the subject of lynching. She formed clubs for women, helped to organize the National Association for the Advancement of Colored People, went on speaking tours, and continued her outspoken attacks on lynchings and other forms of injustice. Some felt that she was too sharp in her criticism, but she never stopped crusading against lynching—the most savage act of racism.

Ida Wells-Barnett spent ten years with her husband and children at their home in Chicago on South Grand Boulevard, later called South Park Way, now renamed Dr. Martin Luther King Jr. Drive. The Barnett family moved to the three-story, fourteen-room house in 1919 where they lived until 1929. Ida Wells-Barnett died in 1931.

DATE BUILT: c1890

ADDRESS: 3624 Martin Luther King Jr. Drive, Chicago

VISITING HOURS: Private, visitors may drive by

SOURCES: NRHPINF. *When and Where I Enter. National Register of Historic Places,* 206. *The African American Encyclopedia,* 1676–80.

Junction

Old Slave House

The Old Slave House in Gallatin County, Illinois, has chilling and tangible evidence to support statements that many kidnapped slaves were kept in bondage here. Although the house is in Illinois, a free state, it was just over the border from Kentucky, a slave state. According to legend, slaves were kept in this house to provide free labor for the Equality Salt Wells in Illinois. On the third floor one can see twenty-five cells where male slaves were kept as well as family rooms for the female slaves. Iron bars over the windows allowed a modicum of ventilation and prevented attempts at escape. Even though slavery was illegal in Illinois, the owner of the Old Slave House—a man named Crenshaw—kept up his nefarious work for years. Although Crenshaw stood trial for kidnapping slaves as they escaped across the river from Kentucky, he was always acquitted. The last male slave who at one time lived in this house is said to have died in 1949 at the age of 119 years.

The slave quarters, which are open to visitors, are approached through narrow doorways leading into the small rooms. This is an important and unique historic site for those who wish to see physical evidence of what slavery was like in one nonplantation setting. Unfortunately, plans have been made to close the museum in December 1997. In 1994 the local ferry closed for good; because the house is a long drive away from urban amenities, too few visitors came after the ferry's closing to justify keeping the museum open. Perhaps with the resurgence of interest in Black history, enough visitors will drive the distance to keep the Old Slave House open.

DATE BUILT: 1834

ADDRESS: Junction vicinity, 9 miles west of Shawneetown, near intersection of IL 13 and IL 1

TELEPHONE: (618) 276-4410

VISITING HOURS: May–Oct., daily 9–5; closed winter

FEES: Adults, $4; children, $3

SOURCES: Telephone conversation June 24, 1994, George M. Fisk, the Old Slave House. Janet Armstrong, secretary, White County Historical Society. *Hammond United States Atlas*, 222.

Princeton

Owen Lovejoy Homestead

Owen Lovejoy (1811–1864) was born in Albion, Maine. He studied at Bowdoin College in Maine but did not graduate. He studied law and taught school before moving in 1836 to Alton, Illinois, where he prepared for the ministry under the guidance of his older brother, Elijah. Owen soon joined in the antislavery campaigns championed by his brother. After Elijah was killed in 1837 by mobs that repeatedly had destroyed his printing press, Owen vowed never to forsake the antislavery cause. He became minister of the Congregational Church in Princeton, Illinois. During his seventeen years as minister at the church, he repeatedly testified against slavery in spite of frequently encountered violence. In January 1843 he married a widow, Eunice Dunham; they had seven children. The Lovejoys sheltered runaway slaves in this two-story, fifteen-room frame home, and Owen wrote a book about his brother, a volume that became important in the antislavery cause. The house owned by Owen and Eunice Lovejoy became the main underground railroad station in Princeton.

Owen Lovejoy served in the U.S. Congress from 1857 until his death in 1864. While in Congress, he continued to speak out against slavery. However, he did not join in when William Lloyd Garrison, another white abolitionist, made verbal attacks on President Lincoln. Lovejoy agreed with President Lincoln's reconstruction program, which some believed was too generous to the South, and he introduced a universal emancipation bill that, after many changes, became the heart of the Thirteenth Amendment. Unfortunately, he did not live to see the amendment adopted. He died in 1864 and was buried in the Oakland Cemetery in Princeton, Illinois. In 1972 the Lovejoy house was restored to its original state.

DATE BUILT: 1838; Lovejoy residence, 1843–1857

ADDRESS: E. Peru Street (US 6), Princeton

TELEPHONE: (815) 879-9151

VISITING HOURS: May–Sept., Thurs. and Sun. 1–4; Oct., by appointment; closed Nov.–Apr.

FEES: Adults, $2; senior citizens, $1.50; students, $.50

SOURCES: Telephone conversation June 24, 1994, Ezby Collins, member of Lovejoy House board of directors. NRHPINF. *National Register of Historic Places*, 203. State historical marker. *Dictionary of American Biography*, 435–6.

Springfield

Lincoln Home National Historic Site*

This frame, two-story house was home to Abraham Lincoln, his wife, and their three sons from 1844 until 1861. The home has been restored to look as it did at that time. During this period Lincoln worked as a lawyer, a state legislator, and a congressman. After winning the 1860 presidential election, Lincoln left Springfield and never returned.

Called the "Great Emancipator," Lincoln wavered over the question of slavery during his presidency. During the 1860 presidential campaign, the Republican Party to which he belonged opposed the extension of slavery into new territories but did not oppose existing slavery in the South. Although Lincoln may have had a deep personal dislike of the institution of slavery, he adhered to the policy of the party on this matter.

In 1860 H. Ford Douglass, a Black leader from Illinois, made a speech to an abolitionist audience at Framingham, Massachusetts. He expressed regret that Lincoln had not opposed the notorious Fugitive Slave Law that made it easier to capture escaped slaves. Douglass pointed out:

> In regard to the repeal of the Fugitive Slave Law, Abraham Lincoln occupies the same position that the old Whig party occupied in 1852. . . . What did he say at Freeport? [Illinois, at the Lincoln–Douglas debates] Why, that the South was entitled to a Fugitive Slave Law; and although he thought the law could be modified a little, yet, he said, if he was in Congress, he would have it done in such a way as not to lessen its efficiency! Here, then, is Abraham Lincoln in favor of carrying out that infamous Fugitive Slave Law.[2]

Although Black abolitionist Frederick Douglass supported Lincoln's candidacy, Douglass became disillusioned as the campaign progressed. He was disturbed by Lincoln's reluctance to take a firm stand against slavery. Douglass and several other African Americans finally turned their support to the Radical Abolitionist Party, which stood firmly against slavery. Other Black community members, noting that Republicans had taken a partial stand against slavery, continued to support Lincoln and the Republican Party. Many of them rejoiced when he was elected President.

The Lincoln administration maintained that the purpose of the war was to restore the Union and had nothing to do with slavery. When General John Frémont issued a proclamation freeing slaves of all rebels in Missouri, President Lincoln worried that all Southerners might turn against the government. He softened Frémont's proclamation to the point of confiscating only slaves who had directly aided the Confederate military forces. Thousands of Missouri slaves thus lost an opportunity to be set free. These actions of the President greatly displeased the radical Republicans who wanted to put an end to slavery at any cost.

In March 1862 President Lincoln recommended to Congress that federal compensation be offered to any state adopting the gradual abolition of slavery. Although nothing came of this plan, Black people saw the policy as a positive shift and rejoiced. Their hopes were shattered again, however, on May 19 when Lincoln revoked General David Hunter's April 25 order proclaiming freedom for all slaves in South Carolina, Georgia, and Florida.

In July 1862, President Lincoln drafted an emancipation proclamation but withheld it from his cabinet until the Union Army won a great victory at Antietam on September 17 that year.

In August 1862 President Lincoln met with five Black men from the District of Columbia. Claiming that racial differences made it impossible for Black and white people to live together as equals, he advocated complete separation of the races. Black people could be colonized in Central America, he maintained, where they would work in coal mines under development there. Although Lincoln moved ahead with this plan, it never came to fruition. Later he arranged to send more than 400 African Americans from Washington, D.C., and Virginia to Haiti. Nearly 100 died from disease, starvation, or mutiny. This plan did not succeed, and it was necessary to send a ship to return the survivors to the United States.

At first, Black troops were not allowed officially to fight in the Union Army, although they could serve as laborers, carpenters, cooks, and nurses. Some African Americans built earthworks and bridges, unloaded cargoes, and served as spies and scouts. Black families had helped the Union cause by taking Union soldiers into their cabins, feeding them, and giving the weary soldiers a safe place to rest. In spite of their eagerness to serve, many white Northerners refused to fight beside Black soldiers, and many white people in the North and South believed Black soldiers would prove cowardly under battle conditions.

During the summer of 1862, as Union forces suffered a series of defeats, leaders at Washington began to realize that they needed Black participation to turn the tide. In July they agreed to enlist Black soldiers. From that point on nearly 10 percent of the Union Army was comprised of men in Black regiments.

Finally, Abraham Lincoln issued the Emancipation Proclamation on January 1, 1863. It stated that all slaves in the rebellious states would be free. Although the proclamation applied only to the Confederate states, all opposed to slavery rejoiced. In January 1865, when the war was nearly over, Congress adopted the Thirteenth Amendment abolishing slavery throughout the country.

Although President Lincoln had often compromised with the southern states on the issue of slavery, he eventually decided against it. Some Black Americans were critical because Lincoln had not done more to improve the lives of freed people, but many respected and revered him. Disbelief and grief were widespread when an assassin killed Lincoln on April 14, 1865. The *New Orleans Tribune,* an African American newspaper, expressed this grief.

> Brethren, we are mourning for a benefactor of our race. Sadness has taken hold of our hearts. No man can suppress his feeling at this hour of affliction. Lincoln and John Brown are two martyrs, whose memories will live united in our bosoms. Both have willingly jeopardized their lives for the sacred cause of freedom.[3]

DATE BUILT: 1839

ADDRESS: Visitors Center, 426 S. Seventh Street; Lincoln Home, 413 S. Eighth Street (Eighth and Jackson Streets), Springfield

TELEPHONE: (217) 492-4150

VISITING HOURS: Daily; June 1–Aug. 15, 8–8; Aug. 16–Oct. 31, 8–6; Nov. 1–Mar. 31, 8–5; Apr. 1–May 31, 8–6; closed Thanksgiving, Christmas, New Year's Day

FEES: None; visitors must obtain tickets at the Visitors Center on a first-come, first-served basis; tours last 15–20 minutes

SOURCES: Telephone conversation June 24, 1994, Andre Jordan, park ranger. Telephone conversation Aug. 31, 1995, Joyce Mavis, secretary, Lincoln Home. Telephone conversation Sept. 3, 1995, Roy Tolbert, park ranger, Lincoln Home. *National Register of Historic Places,* 211. *The Negro's Civil War,* 5, 6, 20, 41, 43, 93, 94, 98, 99, 145, 241. *New Orleans Tribune.*

Lincoln's Tomb State Historic Site

A granite obelisk on a square base, a statue of Lincoln in front of the obelisk, a bust of Lincoln in front of the tomb—these are symbols at the final resting place of President Abraham Lincoln, his wife, and three of his four children.

When a funeral train brought Lincoln's body back to Springfield for burial, a regiment of Black troops with rifles reversed led the funeral procession to the state capitol. Almost all of Springfield's Black citizens joined in expressing respect for the assassinated leader. The tomb was dedicated in 1874. Lincoln's body, earlier laid to rest above ground in a marble sarcophagus, was placed beneath the burial chamber floor in 1901 after reconstruction of the tomb.

DATE ESTABLISHED: 1874

ADDRESS: Oak Ridge Cemetery, 1441 Monument Avenue (Business Loop US 55, turn west on N. Grand Avenue to Monument Avenue, turn right, two blocks to the cemetery entrance), Springfield

TELEPHONE: (217) 782-2717

VISITING HOURS: Daily 9–5; closed New Year's Day, Veterans' Day, general election day, Thanksgiving, Christmas

FEES: None

SOURCES: Telephone conversation June 24, 1994, Nan Wynn, site manager. Telephone conversation Aug. 12, 1995, Nancy Lugo, seasonal interpreter, Lincoln's Tomb. *National Register of Historic Places,* 211. *A Guide to Historic Illinois,* 24.

Notes

1. NRHPINF for site.

2. H. Ford Douglass lecture, annual Fourth of July abolitionists' picnic (Framingham, Mass.), originally printed in *Liberator* (13 July 1860), quoted in James M. McPherson, *The Negro's Civil War* (New York: Ballentine, 1991), 6.

3. *New Orleans Tribune* (20 Apr. 1865), quoted in James M. McPherson, *The Negro's Civil War* (New York: Ballentine, 1991), 312.

Works Consulted

The Academic American Encyclopedia. Danbury, Conn.: Grolier, 1993. [electronic version]

The African American Encyclopedia. Vol. 6. Michael W. Williams, ed. New York: Marshall Cavendish, 1993.

African Americans: Voices of Triumph. Vol. 2, *Leadership.* Alexandria, Va.: Time-Life, 1993.

Dictionary of American Biography. Vol. 6. Dumas Malone, ed. New York: Scribners, 1933, 1961.

A Guide to Historic Illinois. Illinois Historic Preservation Agency, Mar. 1988. [booklet]

Hammond United States Atlas. Maplewood, N.J.: Hammond, 1989.

International Library of Negro Life and History: Historical Negro Biographies. Wilhelmena S. Robinson. New York: Publishers, 1970.

"Making History, Black History Month: Exhibit Shows Contributions Black Residents Made to Area." Mary Ann Mazenko. *The (Alton) Telegraph,* 1 Feb. 1990.

National Register Information System. Washington, D.C.: National Park Service. [computer database]

National Register of Historic Places. Washington, D.C.: National Park Service, 1976.

The Negro's Civil War. James M. McPherson. New York: Ballentine, 1991.

New Orleans Tribune, 20 Apr. 1865. Quoted in *The Negro's Civil War,* James M. McPherson (New York: Ballantine, 1991), 312.

"The Provident Hospital Project: An Experiment in Race Relations and Medical Education." Vanessa Northington Gamble. *Bulletin of the History of Medicine* 65 (1991): 457–75.

There Is a River: The Black Struggle for Freedom in America. Vincent Harding. New York: Vintage Books, 1983.

Webster's New Biographical Dictionary. Springfield, Mass.: Merriam-Webster, 1988.

When and Where I Enter: The Impact of Black Women on Race and Sex in America. Paula Giddings. New York: William Morrow, 1984; New York: Bantam, 1988.

Indiana

Evansville

Liberty Baptist Church

Liberty Baptist Church is the oldest African American congregation in Evansville. The church arose within a community living in a section of Evansville known as "Baptist Town." In 1860 there were only ninety-five African Americans in Evansville, but after the Civil War many former slaves crossed the Ohio River and settled there, seeking to leave behind the harsh living conditions of the postwar South. As a result, the Black population of the city rose to almost two thousand by 1870.

The Liberty Baptist congregation formed around 1865. Its first minister was a white man named Colonel Woods. All the deacons and members of the congregation were Black. After worshiping in inadequate quarters for a number of years, the church members erected a brick church in 1880 at a cost of about $10,000. Church members were shocked when, six years later, a tornado completely destroyed it. Undaunted, the congregation immediately began to collect funds to rebuild. In December 1886—just six months later—Liberty Baptist members were able to worship again in their new church, a structure that stands today.

Through the years this church has provided a center for religious, cultural, and political affairs in the Black community. Church members have offered day-care services, recreational activities for young people, and housing assistance.

DATE BUILT: 1886
ADDRESS: 701 Oak Street (corner of Seventh Street), Evansville
TELEPHONE: (812) 422-4628
VISITING HOURS: By appointment, Mon.–Fri. 10–2
SOURCES: NRHPINF. Telephone conversation June 17, 1994, Mr. David Fisher, custodian.

Fountain City

Levi Coffin House

Prior to the Civil War, slaves escaping from the South to freedom in Canada traveled along a great many routes. Many passing through the Midwest came through Fountain City, Indiana, which at that time was known as Newport. They received there a warm welcome and assistance from a white merchant named Levi Coffin. Originally from a Quaker community in the Carolinas, Coffin and his wife, Catherine, had come to this area in 1826 along with a group of Quakers vigorously opposed to slavery. Some years later—about 1839—the Coffins erected this house. Both Coffin and his wife joined with the free African Americans of the community in an effort to defy the Fugitive Slave Law of 1850. Some thirty families cooperated in this effort.

Coffin's home, which was built right up to the sidewalk on the main street in town, became a major stop on the underground railroad in this area. Slaves were hidden in a secret area attached to a maid's room on the second floor. This room had a ceiling sharply sloping down to a four-foot-high south wall. A low bed hid a small panel door that led to a crawl space under the roof where fugitives could hide. Many runaways remained with the Coffins for days or weeks until they had regained enough strength to continue their journey.

The Coffins also were active in establishing two schools in Randolph County—the Cabin Creek School and the Union Literary Institute—that taught freed slaves and their children. In 1847 the Coffin family moved to Cincinnati, where they continued to help approximately 1,000 additional slaves find their way to freedom. After the Civil War, the Coffins continued to assist the freedmen.

Coffin House was one of the most important underground railroad sites in the country, providing refuge for more than 2,000 slaves before and during the Civil War. The house was altered in 1910 to serve as a rural hotel but later was restored to its original condition.

DATE BUILT:	1839
ADDRESS:	113 U.S. 27 North, Fountain City
TELEPHONE:	(317) 847-2432
VISITING HOURS:	June–Aug., Tues.–Sun. 1–4; Sept.–Oct., Sat.–Sun. 1–4; groups at other times by appointment; closed July 4, Labor Day, Nov.–May
FEES:	Adults, $1; students 6–18, $.50; children under 6, free
SOURCES:	Personal visit to site, summer 1990. Telephone conversation June 17, 1994, and Aug. 27, 1995, Saundra Jackson, secretary, Levi Coffin House Association. Jeffrey Tenuth, registrar/historian, Indiana State Museum and Historic Sites, Aug. 25, 1989. Division of Historic Preservation and Archaeology. Survey and brochure from Saundra Jackson, secretary-treasurer of Levi Coffin House Association. *National Register of Historic Places,* 224.

Indianapolis

Crispus Attucks High School

During the nineteenth century, education in Indianapolis was segregated. Certain elementary schools were designated for "Coloreds only." Even though Black high schoolers were comparatively few in number, their presence was resented by the white community. In 1908 the superintendent of schools suggested that a separate high school be set up for African Americans. Nothing was done about this proposal until after World War I, when racial tensions increased and the Ku Klux Klan in Indiana grew rapidly. White citizens repeatedly petitioned for the removal of Black students from the public high schools.

In 1922 the Indianapolis school board began to make plans to build a separate Black high school despite strong opposition from the Black community. Among the groups protesting were the Black churches and the Better Indianapolis League, an African American civic organization; they forwarded protests to the school board, pointing out that separation would be divisive and unjust. Archie Greathouse, a leader of the Black community, was able to delay the school board's plans in a series of court battles. In the end, however, the courts upheld the right of the school authorities to establish a segregated school.

The school board then went ahead with construction plans and announced that some 800 Black pupils would attend what was to be known as the "Thomas Jefferson High School." The Black community was able to persuade the board to change the name to honor Crispus Attucks, a Black man who was one of the first persons to die in the Boston Massacre of 1780. (See the Boston, Massachusetts, section of this book for more information about Attucks.)

Crispus Attucks High School was completed in 1927. Until 1949 it was the only free public school for Black students in Indianapolis. Although Indiana outlawed school segregation in 1949, the school remained almost exclusively Black until the 1970s, when busing was initiated to achieve integration. Today the school is known as Attucks Middle School. Recent extensive renovations retained the original appearance of the exterior facade and the marble flooring and marble columns in the entryway. However, some interior floors were carpeted, and classrooms were enlarged to modern standards.

DATE BUILT: 1927; addition, 1938
ADDRESS: 1140 N. Martin Luther King Jr. Street, Indianapolis
TELEPHONE: (317) 226-4007
VISITING HOURS: By appointment, Mon.–Fri. 8–3
SOURCES: NRHPRF. Personal visit, summer 1990. Telephone conversation Feb. 13, 1995, Kay Gootee, school secretary.

Indiana State Museum: Freetown Village

The story of Indiana's Black history is told at the Indiana State Museum through Freetown Village, a living-history exhibit within the museum. There a house facade is set up, and a woman sits on the front porch, telling her story to those who pass by. By re-creating such scenes, the Freetown Village actors and storytellers teach Indiana's African American history. Their stories begin in the nineteenth century when many runaway slaves passed through this border state in their search for freedom. Some of the fugitives settled in Indiana, where they and other African Americans increased the state's Black population to approximately 3,000 in the 1870s.

Freetown Village actors and storytellers regularly present living history exhibits, plays, and workshops, portraying Indiana's African American community after the Civil War. Some of the actors tour midwestern states, teaching Black history by taking the roles of a barber named Isaiah Cuffee, a woman known as Mother Eudora, and other nineteenth-century villagers. Although Freetown Village actors perform regularly at the Indiana State Museum, it is a separate and independent organization.

DATE ESTABLISHED: 1982

ADDRESS: Indiana State Museum, 202 N. Alabama Street; Freetown Village office, Walker Building, 617 Indiana Avenue, Room 200, Indianapolis

TELEPHONE: Indiana State Museum, (317) 232-1641; Freetown Village, (317) 631-1870

VISITING HOURS: Mon.–Sat. 9–4:45, Sun. 12–4:45; closed Christmas

FEES: Museum, free; tours, fee

SOURCES: Ophelia Umar Wellington. Letter, Aug. 25, 1989, Jeffrey Tenuth, registrar/historian, Indiana State Museum and Historic Sites. Telephone conversation June 17, 1994, Goldie Roberts, administrative assistant, Freetown Village. Telephone conversation Feb. 16, 1995, Patti Means, executive secretary, Indiana State Museum.

Indiana Avenue Historic District

Black settlers arrived in Indianapolis before emancipation and lived near the White River as early as the 1860s. This area was open to them, to other immigrants, and to white laborers because upper-income white families found the area undesirable. In 1921 malaria had caused the death of one eighth of the city's population, and some city dwellers believed the river attracted the malaria-infested mosquitoes that had caused the pestilence. Therefore, the early newcomers found an abundance of inexpensive, unsettled land near the river, and they moved into the racially mixed area.

By the 1920s much of the city had become segregated. The 500 block of Indiana Avenue became a thriving area for Black-owned businesses; there African Americans established a restaurant, a saloon, clubs, theaters, an undertaking establishment, and the office of the *Indianapolis Recorder,* the third-oldest Black-owned newspaper in the United States. Today, the 500 block of Indiana Avenue contains eleven buildings that are historically significant as the only remaining examples of business establishments from an early, predominantly Black district. The historic avenue is of interest, too, as one of four diagonal streets laid out in the city's original 1921 plan. Where the diagonal streets intersected the regular rectangular grid, triangular building lots resulted; there some flatiron buildings were constructed to conform to the triangular lots. Two good examples of such buildings are the structures at 502–504 and 547–551 Indiana Avenue.

DATE ESTABLISHED: 1869–1935

ADDRESS: 500 block of Indiana Avenue between West, North, and Michigan Streets and Central Canal, Indianapolis

VISITING HOURS: Public and private ownership; restricted access for some places; visitors may walk or drive by

FEES: Public area, free

SOURCE: NRHPINF.

Madame C. J. Walker Urban Life Center

The Madame Walker Urban Life Center in Indianapolis is a cultural center founded by Madame C. J. Walker, an entrepreneur and the nation's first Black female millionaire. The center served as headquarters of Madame Walker's cosmetics business, housing business offices, storefronts, and a theater.

In 1867 Walker was born as Sarah Breedlove on a cotton plantation in Delta, Louisiana. The first member of her family to be born free, she lived in extreme poverty in a one-room cabin with her sharecropper parents, Owen and Minerva Breedlove, and her brother and sister, Alex and Louvenia. After the parents died from yellow fever, Alex went to Vicksburg to look for work, and Sarah went to live with her sister, Louvenia, in Vicksburg, Mississippi. Louvenia later married, but Sarah was treated harshly by Louvenia's husband; to escape this environment Sarah married Moses McWilliams at the age of fourteen. At the age of seventeen she gave birth to a daughter, Lelia. Two years later, McWilliams was killed in an accident. Mother and daughter moved to St. Louis where Walker worked hard for eighteen years as a laundress. In spite of hardships, she was able to observe well-educated, elegantly dressed African American women, and she vowed to become like them. Saving what money she could, she managed to send Lelia to public schools in St. Louis and to Knoxville College in Tennessee.

In 1906 Sarah married Charles Walker. She previously had noted the trouble Black women had in caring for their hair and had developed highly successful formulas that were well accepted. She soon was manufacturing beauty products that were sold widely and established training programs and beauty shops throughout the country. Walker, now owner of the Madame C. J. Walker Manufacturing Company, had much-larger plans than her husband had, and they divorced in 1912.

Although Walker's business was first established in Denver, she decided to consolidate her operations in Indianapolis in 1910. At first, employees manufactured the products in a building behind Walker's home, but soon she drew up plans to construct a building that would provide adequate space. Although Walker initiated these plans, the building was not completed until after her death in 1919.

The four-story Madame Walker Urban Life Center was constructed on Indiana Avenue in a commercial area of Indianapolis just northwest of the area now called the Indiana Avenue Historic District. The building had a distinctive triangular design because it had to fit into one of the area's original diagonal streets. The first floor contained storefronts and the entrance to the Walker Theater. First-floor decorations included brightly colored African motifs such as terra-cotta masks adapted from Yoruba designs.

The Walker Theater, which occupies the most space in the center, once was an Indianapolis showcase of motion pictures and traveling shows. Doorways on both sides of the stage have Egyptian or Moorish designs. The ceiling has an intricate pattern of masks, animals, and other African symbols. The building also contains a ballroom and stage on the fourth floor. Among the many businesses here were the Walker Drug Store, the Coffee Pot Restaurant, and the Walker Beauty College, an institution that trained thousands of Walker agents.

In the early fifties the neighborhood began to deteriorate, and the theater closed for a time. However, the Madame Walker Urban Life Center, Inc., purchased the building in 1979 and restored it for use as a community cultural center. The Walker Theater reopened in 1988.

Although Walker died more than seventy years ago, she left a legacy of her business acumen and her sense of dignity and worth as well as her generous philanthropy to Black charities. (For additional information on Madame Walker, see the entry for Irvington, New York.)

DATE BUILT: 1927

ADDRESS: 617 Indiana Avenue, Indianapolis

TELEPHONE: (317) 236-2099

VISITING HOURS: Mon.–Sat. 8:30–5; tours by appointment

FEES: Tours, $2

SOURCES: Letter, Aug. 25, 1989, Jeffrey Tenuth, registrar/historian Indiana State Museum and Historic Sites. Personal visit, summer 1990. NRHPINF. *The African American Encyclopedia*, 1642–4. *Madame C. J. Walker, Entrepreneur.*

Kendallville

Anderson Building

Alonzo (Lon) Anderson, a successful Black businessman, built the commercial building at 113 North Main. Anderson was born in 1845 in Terre Haute, Indiana. As a young man, he enlisted in 1864 in the Twenty-eighth U.S. Colored Regiment and marched with the regiment into Richmond, Virginia. He was mustered out of the army in 1868.

When the Civil War ended, Anderson and his brother, Jerry, took up the barbering trade in Kendallville. His brother's five children are thought to be the only Black children to have graduated from Kendallville High School until recent years.

Anderson moved his barbershop into this building in 1896. The Anderson building is in the Iddings/Gilbert/Leader/Anderson Block, a row of five connected buildings constructed in the late nineteenth century. These buildings are distinctive because of their decorative panels with raised scrollwork and rosettes.

The building at 113 North Main remained in the Anderson family until the year following Alonzo Anderson's death in 1899. It then changed hands many times, housing a buggy and implement business; a plumbing, heating, and roofing business; a store; a pool hall; and in 1983, the American State Bank and, later, the Society Bank. The bank did extensive remodeling to the Queen Anne-style building, giving the building a new brick facade.

There are no plaques to identify the Anderson Building. Be forewarned: in this Indiana town, while the author was photographing the Anderson building, a police officer drove up and took her license number. When she asked why he was doing so, he said he was investigating because she was photographing a bank. She asked him if bank robbers usually operated with a tripod and a camera. Then thinking better of it, she explained the Black history of the building to him and left. The building remains an example of Black entrepreneurship in the late-nineteenth century.

DATE BUILT:	1894
ADDRESS:	113 N. Main Street, Kendallville
VISITING HOURS:	Private, visitors may walk or drive by
SOURCES:	NRHPINF. Personal visit, summer 1990.

Rushville

Booker T. Washington School

Because Indiana legislation of 1869 called for the state to provide education for African Americans, local officials began to build segregated facilities. About 1905 the state built the Booker T. Washington School in Rushville. Students attended grades one through six here, and a large room upstairs served as a community center for social and political meetings, plays, and dances. Beginning in 1910, the National Association for the Advancement of Colored People met in the upstairs room. Local chapters of the Odd Fellows and Masons also met on the second floor. Noted educator Mary McLeod Bethune visited the school about 1919. When the Booker T. Washington School was in operation, there was only one other school for Black students in Rush county.

Dwindling enrollment and a poor economy led to the closing of the Washington School in 1932. Seventy individuals signed a petition to keep the school open, but their efforts were in vain. Yet in 1990 community residents, who remembered the school with pride, spearheaded efforts to restore the building and to reopen it. The Black community, a local preservation group, and the city of Rushville were involved in the restoration. The restoration effort, spearheaded by the dreams of local resident Billy Rae Goins, gained a national award from the Historic Landmark Foundation in 1993.

The stately two-story brick building stands in an open area on a small rise. The recessed entrance is marked by paneled wooden double doors. The interior of the school has retained much of its historic appearance. In 1990, before restoration began, there were two large classrooms in the main section of the first floor. Just inside the front entrance, a wide central stairway led upstairs; on either side of the staircase was a very narrow hall of single-file width.

Today the historic schoolhouse is used by a variety of community agencies—Head Start, the Interlocal Community Action Program, Rush County Heritage, and Big Brothers-Big Sisters. The large hall upstairs is used for community meetings. Although the building has regained its luster and a new status, community residents have insisted on keeping certain reminders of its history—the old basketball goal and the segregated wading pool outside.

DATE BUILT: 1905

ADDRESS: 525 E. Seventh at 614 Fort Wayne Road, Rushville

TELEPHONE: (317) 932-2863

VISITING HOURS: Mon.–Fri. 8–5; call in advance to arrange to see the interior

FEES: Donations welcome

SOURCES: NRHPRF. Personal visit, 1990. Conversation at Washington School July 5, 1990, Bill R. Goins, president, Booker T. Washington Community Center, Inc., and the late Reverend Peter Fletcher of Rushville, Indiana. Telephone conversation Sept. 3, 1995, Mr. Paul Davis of Rushville, who donated the schoolhouse to the community. Telephone conversation June 17, 1994, Eileen Briscoe, Community Action Representative.

Works Consulted

The African American Encyclopedia. Vol. 6. Michael W. Williams, ed. New York: Marshall Cavendish, 1993.

Madame C. J. Walker, Entrepreneur. A'Lelia Perry Bundles. Black Americans of Achievement Series. New York: Chelsea House, 1991.

National Register of Historic Places. Washington, D.C.: National Park Service, 1976.

Iowa

Cedar Rapids

Iowa Masonic Library

The Masonic Library has an extensive collection of literature and history relating to Prince Hall Masonry and Prince Hall Masonic Grand Lodges. Prince Hall, the founder of Black Masonry, was born in Bridgetown, Barbados, about 1735. His father was English and his mother was a free Black woman. Hall's training and trade primarily involved working with leather. He immigrated to Boston, Massachusetts, in 1765, where he became a minister and a leader in the African American community.

Prince Hall served in the militia during the Revolutionary War; in this same period, he organized the first Black Masonic Lodge in America. Having sought out a British regiment encamped near Boston, Hall successfully persuaded the British lodge of Masons in that group to initiate him and fourteen others into the association in March 1775. The British withdrew from Boston the following year, and Hall then organized a Masonic lodge in that city, the first in the United States for African Americans. In 1787 (the Iowa Masonic Library gives the date as September 29, 1784), Hall obtained a charter from England for the African Lodge Number 459, and five years later served as Grand Master of a recently organized interstate Grand Lodge. What is not clear is why the British favored a patriot who had served in the American Army by inducting him and others into their association. After Hall's death in 1807 the lodge changed its name to Prince Hall Grand Lodge.

DATE OF SIGNIFICANCE: The African Lodge, chartered 1784 or 1787; Iowa Masonic Library, established 1885, moved to the present building 1955

ADDRESS: 813 First Avenue SE, Cedar Rapids

TELEPHONE: (319) 365-1438

VISITING HOURS: Mon.–Fri. 8–noon, 1–5; closed most holidays

FEES: None

SOURCES: Telephone conversation May 10, 1994, Paul H. Wieck, Grand Secretary and Grand Librarian, Iowa Masonic Library. Keith Arrington, librarian. Telephone conversation Aug. 31 and Sept. 5, 1995, Ken Hurmence, deputy secretary of the Iowa Masonic Grand Lodge, and Joe Nolte, library assistant, Iowa Masonic Library. *International Library of Negro Life and History*, 21. *Historical and Cultural Atlas of African Americans. The Shaping of Black America.*

Davenport

Bethel African Methodist Episcopal Church

The Bethel A.M.E. congregation was one of several established in many states by African Americans after the Civil War. It was founded in 1875 to provide a separate worship facility for Black Methodists in Iowa. By 1909 the congregation had fifty members and had become an important central point in Davenport's Black community. As a result, the congregation was able to build the present church in 1909 on a corner lot in a turn-of-the-century Black neighborhood. The rectangular concrete building had high, round-arched, stained-glass windows and half timberwork with stucco. The pastor, William W. Williams, lived in the parsonage next door to the church. Bethel African Methodist Episcopal Church is listed in the *National Register of Historic Places.*

DATE ESTABLISHED: Congregation, 1875; church, 1909

ADDRESS: 325 W. Eleventh Street, Davenport

TELEPHONE: (319) 322-6622

VISITING HOURS: By appointment

FEES: None

SOURCES: Davenport Community Development Department, Iowa Division of Historic Preservation. Telephone conversation May 29, 1994, Pastor Moody, Bethel A.M.E. Church.

Des Moines

Burns United Methodist Church

Burns United Methodist Church was organized in 1866 in a decade when there were only thirteen Black persons in Polk County. The first African American church of this denomination in Des Moines, it was named for Francis Burns (1809–1863), who was elected in 1852 by the Northern Methodist Episcopal Church as its first Black bishop. Elected as a missionary bishop to serve in Africa, he had no authority to supervise white churches.

This congregation has had six different places of worship. The first was a building that also housed the city's segregated school for Black children. The congregation built a small chapel in 1873 and then moved to a larger building between 1885 and 1887.

In each location the church offered a variety of religious and community activities. Members sponsored Sunday School programs, literary societies, musical programs, group dinners, and charitable activities. A quartet sang in different locations around the state to raise money to purchase the present church on Crocker Street and acquired sufficient funds to do so by 1930.

Members purchased a building constructed in 1912 on gently sloping land near downtown Des Moines. The one-story brick structure with stained-glass windows and Tudor arches was located in a neighborhood of small houses and apartment buildings.

DATE ESTABLISHED: Congregation, 1866; present church, 1912; purchased by the Burns United Methodist congregation, 1930

ADDRESS: 811 Crocker Street, Des Moines

TELEPHONE: (515) 244-5883

VISITING HOURS: Office hours, Mon.–Fri. 10–4; Sun. school, 9:30; Sun. service, 11

SOURCES: Telephone conversation May 29, 1994, Reverend Leon Herndon. NRHPINF. *The Black Church in the African American Experience*, 66.

Public Library of Des Moines National Bar Association Collection

The Public Library of Des Moines is the depository for the National Bar Association's historical papers. In 1991 the association unveiled a limestone sculpture at the library as a memorial to its founders.

The National Bar Association, formerly known as the Negro Bar Association, began in Des Moines in 1925. Founders Gertrude Rush, S. Joe Brown, James B. Morris, Charles P. Howard Sr., and George H. Woodson all were active in the early legal history of Des Moines. Rush lived in Des Moines for sixty years and was the first African American woman admitted to the Iowa Bar.

DATE ESTABLISHED: National Bar Association, 1925

ADDRESS: 100 Locust Street, Des Moines

TELEPHONE: (515) 283-4259

VISITING HOURS: Mon.–Thurs. 9–9, Fri. 9–6, Sat. 9–5; closed Memorial Day–Labor Day Thurs. at 6; closed holidays

FEES: None

SOURCES: Library press release, July 5, 1991. Shirley Aluster, head of reference, Public Library of Des Moines. Telephone call to site, May 10, 1994.

Lewis

Hitchcock House

Hitchcock House, built in 1856, is one of Iowa's few remaining underground railroad stations. The two-story, sandstone house was located approximately two miles from the conjunction of the Oregon and Mormon trails. Its location is on a hill providing a 360-degree view, and its inhabitants could see anyone, whether runaway slave or slave catcher, twenty minutes before the person's arrival. The fugitives came primarily from Missouri into Nebraska City and moved from there into Tabor, Iowa, and then to Lewis, where they found safety in this house. They left by foot or by false-bottomed wagon for Anita, Iowa. The journey was risky because they had to cross a river between Des Moines and Council Bluffs; sometimes slave catchers waited at the river.

Abolitionist John Brown set up an underground railroad route through Iowa that included a stop here at the home of a sympathetic Congregational circuit-riding preacher, George B. Hitchcock. Hitchcock had moved here in 1851 and built a log cabin; then, in 1854–1856 he erected the present house with abolitionist activity in mind. Hitchcock, his wife, and their eight children provided a haven here.

Visitors can see a house with four bedrooms upstairs (there may earlier have been fewer) and a kitchen, pantry, dining area, and sickroom/birthing room downstairs. There are two basement rooms, one of which was secret. Because many buildings of that era did not have basements, visitors would have assumed that the one room, with its limestone hearth and fireplace, was all there was on that level. A large cabinet, however, covered an opening to the second half of the 60-foot-by-50-foot basement. The opening, 3.5 feet by 6 feet, concealed a hiding place that today has a few items that suggest what the furnishings might have been like at that time—wood pallets with straw tick coverings and a toilet container.

Hitchcock House was abandoned in the late 1950s or early 1960s. In 1978 a grant made possible the restoration of the house and furnishing it in the time period. Its authenticity as an underground railroad site is suggested by still-existing letters mentioning that John Brown stayed at the house or that he soon would be arriving there.

The house is operated by the Cass County Conservation Board. In addition to the house, visitors today see a barn that has displays of crafts and that shelters occasional picnics. A 1.75-mile nature trail features native plants and animals.

DATE BUILT: 1856

ADDRESS: R.R. 1, Lewis vicinity (take I-80 to Atlantic, Iowa, exit 57; go south on US 6 about 8 miles to a sign for Lewis and Hitchcock House; go south to Lewis; turn right at first street in Lewis; go approximately 1 mile; follow the sign at the top of a hill and take the road south to Hitchcock House)

TELEPHONE: (712) 769-2323

VISITING HOURS: Apr. 15–Oct. 15, Fri.–Wed. 1–5; by appointment Oct. 16–Apr. 14 and on Thurs.; guided tours by appointment

FEES: Donations appreciated

SOURCES: Telephone conversation Apr. 30, 1994, Jeff Hauser, caretaker. Telephone conversation Feb. 14, 1995, Dessie Hansen, caretaker. Flier from Hitchcock House.

Muscatine

Alexander Clark House

Alexander Clark (1826–1891) became Iowa's most prominent African American in the years following the Civil War. In addition, he was in his time one of the most outstanding Black leaders in America. Clark pressed for civil rights gains in voting and education and led the fight to enact a statewide Black suffrage amendment. When the Muscatine school board refused to admit his ten-year-old daughter, Susan, to the local grammar school because of her race, Clark sued. The celebrated case involved appeals, after which the Iowa Supreme Court ruled that a pupil could not be excluded from the public schools because of race, nationality, or religion. Because of Clark's persistence, Iowa was one of the first states to ban school segregation. Clark gained a fine education for himself, too, becoming the second African American in Iowa to graduate from the University of Iowa Law School (his own son was the first African American to do so). Black law students at the university honor him today through the Alexander Clark Society established at the university's law school.

Clark was born free prior to the Civil War to a white father and a Black mother. He matured into a well-educated individual who was successful as a business and property owner in Muscatine. His sphere of influence widened during the Reconstruction Era when he was chosen as a delegate to the 1869 National Colored Convention in Washington, D.C. There he chaired a committee that presented to Congress claims of Black soldiers and seamen. Throughout the 1860s Clark was Grand Master in the Masonic Order, overseeing Missouri, Iowa, Colorado, and Minnesota. He also owned and edited a Chicago newspaper that strongly advocated the rights of Black citizens. In 1880 President Benjamin Harrison appointed Clark minister resident and consul general to Liberia. He served in Liberia until his death the following year.

Prior to 1879 the Clark family lived in a frame dwelling facing West Third Street. In 1878 the home burned in a fire suspected to have been caused by arsonists. By December of that year, Clark had spent $4,000 on construction of a new double, brick, two-story residence with arched windows and scroll brackets. It is believed that he lived in the number 207 side of the double house, which today is one of the few double brick houses remaining in Muscatine.

When construction plans were made to build a housing project on the site, Clark House, in danger of being demolished, was moved to a sloping land area one-half block from the original site, and plans were initiated to convert the structure into a museum. Although the museum was not developed, Clark House, now listed in the *National Register of Historic Places,* remains of interest to many who drive by to see this symbol of an outstanding Black American from Iowa.

DATE BUILT: 1878; moved, 1975
ADDRESS: 205–207 W. Third Street, Muscatine
VISITING HOURS: Private, visitors may walk or drive by
SOURCES: NRHPINF. Telephone conversation May 15, 1994, D. Kent Sissel, area resident.

Salem

Henderson Lewelling Quaker House

In 1994 a fortunate and serendipitous discovery was made at this site. After a century and a half of concealment, workers remodeling floorboards in the Lewelling Quaker House found a second trap door—a secret place where fugitive slaves were concealed. The directors of the shrine could scarcely conceal their delight at the discovery. Henderson Lewelling, a Quaker who was determined to share in the abolitionists' battle, had built this house in 1840 to be a part of the underground railroad. He had built it so well that after more than a century even friends of the cause had not found out all of its secrets.

People knew, of course, about the tunnel, a dirt passageway discovered earlier when workers pulled up a floor for repair work. Today, visitors may look down into that tunnel, but the passageway leading from the kitchen to the basement is something that those who were hiding had to crawl through. Basements were unheard of in the 1840s when Lewelling built his stone house in the Quaker town of Salem as a safe place for hiding slaves. No one would have suspected the trapdoor and tunnel that led to safety in the basement. Lewelling House is interesting in its own light. When workers pulled down the plaster upstairs, they saw beams made of rough logs with the bark still on them.

There once were five other underground railroad houses in Salem, each one possibly as interesting as the Lewelling House, but they are no longer standing. The only remaining relic from one of the other houses is a large wheel once situated in an attic. A stout rope could drop from the wheel down inside the wall; a turning of the wheel could raise a portion of the first-story floor, opening up a trapdoor leading to a hiding area for fugitives.

Of the approximately one hundred underground railroad stations in Iowa, few are still standing. In addition to Lewelling House, they include the Reverend Todd House in Tabor, the Jordan House in West Des Moines, and the Hitchcock House in Lewis. These three sites are also open to the public.

DATE BUILT:	1840
ADDRESS:	From Mount Pleasant, 10 miles south on US 218, then 3 miles west on Salem Road
TELEPHONE:	Not available; to make an appointment to visit, write Lewelling Shrine, Box 28, Salem, IA 52649
VISITING HOURS:	May–Sept., Sun. 1–4; tours by appointment
FEES:	Adults, $1; students and children, $.50
SOURCES:	Vicki Baker, president, West Des Moines Historical Society. Telephone conversation May 17, 1994, Fay Heartsill, president, Board of Directors, and Judy Feeham, member of the Board of Directors.

West Des Moines

Jordan House Museum

The Jordan House Museum, a national historic site, was once a station on the underground railroad. The Victorian mansion belonged to James Cunningham Jordan, the first white settler in West Des Moines. He constructed the house in 1850 when the area was a pioneer farming settlement.

Jordan is considered to have been the chief conductor of the underground railroad in Polk County, Iowa. He made decisions about where the fugitives would stay and determined when it was safe for them to move on along the route to freedom. Community legend, family stories, and older history books document the role of this house as a station on the underground railroad. Escaping slaves on their way to freedom in Canada stayed in the kitchen or hid in a sleeping room in the basement. On one occasion twenty-four fugitives were in the house at the same time.

The famous abolitionist John Brown also stayed here on December 17, 1858. A group of slaves had been traveling through Tabor, Iowa, with their masters, and Brown helped them to escape. Brown stayed at the Jordan house again in February 1859 while planning his raid on the arsenal at Harpers Ferry. He trained followers at the Maxham farm in Springdale, Iowa, and stored ammunition at Reverend Todd's home in Tabor, Iowa. Ten months later he was hanged for treason for leading the raid. (See the listings for sites related to John Brown in Chambersburg, Pennsylvania; Harpers Ferry, West Virginia; Akron, Ohio; Lake Placid, New York; and Kansas City and Osawatomie, Kansas.)

The Italian Gothic house originally had only six rooms during the underground railroad period; more rooms were added in the 1870s. The West Des Moines Historical Society purchased Jordan House in 1978 and transformed it into a museum. A display in the basement room where the fugitives stayed tells of its story in the underground railroad. Local schools have used the house as part of their fifth grade curriculum.

DATE BUILT: 1850; addition, 1870

ADDRESS: 2001 Fuller Road, West Des Moines

TELEPHONE: (515) 225-1286

VISITING HOURS: May–Oct., Wed., Sat. 1–4; Sun. 2–5; closed federal holidays

FEES: Adults, $2; school-aged children, $.50

SOURCES: Telephone call to site, May 2, 1994. Vicki Baker, president, West Des Moines Historical Society. Flier from Jordan House Museum.

Works Consulted

The Black Church in the African American Experience. C. Eric Lincoln and Lawrence H. Mamiya. Durham, N.C.: Duke University Press, 1990.

Historical and Cultural Atlas of African Americans. Molefi K. Asante and Mark T. Mattson. New York: Penguin, 1992.

International Library of Negro Life and History: Historical Negro Biography. Wilhelmena S. Robinson. New York: Publishers, 1970.

The Shaping of Black America. Lerone Bennett Jr. New York: Penguin, 1993.

Kansas

Chanute

The Martin and Osa Johnson Safari Museum

The Martin and Osa Johnson Safari Museum features more than 350 items of West African tribal art. The artifacts include masks, dolls, jewelry, weaponry, fabrics, baskets, and a variety of drums, including ritual drums, a talking drum, log drums, and calabash drums.

DATE ESTABLISHED:	1961
ADDRESS:	111 N. Lincoln Avenue, Chanute
TELEPHONE:	(316) 431-2730
VISITING HOURS:	Mon.–Sat. 10–5, Sun. 1–5; closed Easter, July 4, Thanksgiving, Christmas, New Year's Day
FEES:	Adults, $2.50; students, $1; children 12 and under accompanied by an adult, free; tours arranged for school groups
SOURCES:	Barbara E. Henshall, curator. Telephone call to site, June 17, 1994, and Aug. 31, 1995.

Fort Riley

U.S. Cavalry Museum

Fort Riley was established as a post in 1853 to protect travelers on the Santa Fe Trail from Indian raids. Black troopers of the Ninth and Tenth Cavalry were among those stationed at Fort Riley, an arrangement that pitted one group against another for the benefit of white settlers. The Indians called the men of the Ninth and Tenth Cavalry the "Buffalo Soldiers." Because the buffalo was sacred to the Indians, the name was considered a mark of respect.

Tours of the museum are self-guided and include only a limited amount of information about the Buffalo Soldiers. However, the museum carries three books about them, and visitors can take a driving tour of the main base to see some of the buildings the soldiers would have known. The main post has buildings built in the 1854 era and later. Viewing is of the exteriors with the exception of the Custer House, which is open to the public between Memorial Day and Labor Day.

DATE ESTABLISHED: 1853
ADDRESS: Corner of Sheridan and Custer Avenues, Building 205, Fort Riley (Exit 301 off I-70)
TELEPHONE: (913) 239-2737
VISITING HOURS: Mon.–Sat. 9–4:30, Sun. noon–4:30; closed New Year's Day, Easter, Thanksgiving, Christmas
FEES: None
SOURCE: Telephone call to site, June 23, 1994.

Fort Scott

Fort Scott National Historic Site

Fort Scott was originally established to maintain peace among the Indian tribes of the region. Prior to the Civil War, however, it had a new function: to keep peace among the settlers who began to pour into eastern Kansas in search of farmland and other economic opportunities. The area became known as "Bleeding Kansas" as a result of the conflicts that frequently arose between proslavery factions and free-soil proponents who wanted to make Kansas a free state. Skirmishes and massacres took place between the two rival groups, and troops had to be sent from Fort Scott to restore order. Kansas was finally admitted to the Union as a free state in 1861.

During the Civil War Fort Scott served as an important supply and training center. The first Black combat troops were mustered into the Union Army in January 1863 and based at Fort Scott. The First Kansas Colored Infantry Regiment was among the first Black units to see action; its men were involved in seven Civil War engagements.

After the Civil War, this fort was the home base of the First and Second Kansas Colored Volunteer Infantry Regiments. Between 1869 and 1873 Fort Scott was active during the conflicts with various Indian tribes. It was abandoned as a military post in 1873.

In recent years twenty of the buildings on the old fort have been restored. The Visitors Center and fort museum display information about the First Kansas Colored Regiment and its role in the history of Kansas. Visitors with a serious interest in the nineteenth-century role of African Americans in the military may talk with base historian Arnold Schofield, who has developed an extensive database on African American soldiers in the Civil War.

Visitors also may want to see a related site, the National Cemetery in Fort Scott. It is one of the twelve original national cemeteries designated by President Abraham Lincoln. In it is a monument conceived by Fort Scott staff members and dedicated to First Kansas Colored Volunteer Infantrymen who died at the Battle of Sherwood, Missouri, on May 18, 1863. Numerous headstones in the cemetery are of African American soldiers who died during the Civil War—they are identified by the initials USCT (U.S. Colored Troops). Some Buffalo Soldiers of the Ninth and Tenth Cavalry also are buried in the Fort Scott Cemetery; although they never were stationed at Fort Scott, many lived in the town as citizens after the Civil War ended.

DATE ESTABLISHED: 1842
ADDRESS: Fort, Old Fort Boulevard; cemetery, 900 E. National Avenue, Fort Scott
TELEPHONE: (316) 223-0310

VISITING HOURS: Fort, Memorial Day–Labor Day, daily 8–6, rest of the year, daily 8–5; cemetery, Mon.–Fri. 8–noon, 12:30–4:30, grounds open daily 24 hours; closed New Year's Day, Thanksgiving, Christmas

FEES: Adults, $2; children under 16, free

SOURCES: Telephone conversation June 17, 1994, Arnold Schofield, National Park Service historian, Fort Scott National Historic Site. *National Register of Historic Places,* 243.

Hays

Historic Fort Hays

Black troopers from the Ninth and Tenth Cavalry served at Fort Hays. In 1867, shortly after arriving at the fort, African American soldiers from the Tenth Cavalry were on patrol when Cheyenne Indians suddenly ambushed the troopers. Even though they were new recruits and fighting against great odds, the men held their own as they shot their way through to rescue their own troopers.

The Fort Hays Historical Museum has completed a brochure on the Buffalo Soldiers stationed here, and two displays with photographs and text tell about three local battles in which they were involved. Visitors can see where some of the Buffalo Soldiers carved their names on the walls in the stone guardhouse. Four of the historic buildings are intact—the guardhouse, two officers quarters, and the blockhouse that served as a headquarters building. The interiors are open to visitors as part of the guided tour.

DATE ESTABLISHED: 1865

ADDRESS: 1472 US 183A, 4 miles south of I-70, Hays

TELEPHONE: (913) 625-6812

VISITING HOURS: Tues.–Sat. 9–5, Sun.–Mon. 1–5

FEES: None

SOURCE: Robert Wilhelm, superintendent.

Kansas City

John Brown Statue

In the early years of the twentieth century, African Americans at Western University collected $2,000 of their own money to erect a statue of John Brown. Although Brown, a white abolitionist, may never have visited Kansas City, his name was well known to the African Americans there. Many had escaped to freedom on the underground railroad and were well aware of the role of abolitionists.

The life-sized statue, sculptured in Italy from Carrara marble, was unveiled on the campus in 1911. The inscription on the base reads: "Erected to the Memory of John Brown by a Grateful People." (For fuller information on John Brown, see the listings for Harpers Ferry, West Virginia; Akron, Ohio; Lewis and West Des Moines, Iowa; and Chambersburg, Pennsylvania.)

DATE ESTABLISHED: 1911
ADDRESS: 2804 Sewell, Kansas City
VISITING HOURS: Outdoors; visible from dawn to dusk
FEES: None
SOURCES: "The Rise and Fall of Western University." *Historic Preservation in Kansas, Black Historic Sites.*

Larned

Fort Larned National Historic Site

Black troopers of the Tenth Cavalry Regiment were stationed at Fort Larned from 1867 to 1869 during the Indian wars. Today the buildings at Fort Larned have been restored to their 1869 appearance, and this fort offers a remarkably complete picture of a military base at that time. The Visitors Center, located in one of the historic buildings, has a ten-minute slide orientation as well as various artifacts. A guided tour on most days takes visitors through the historic structures. Holidays sometimes feature special activities—the Fourth of July, for example, features old-fashioned games in which visitors can join—hoop rolling, egg tossing, and sack races. On some weekends volunteers in period clothing are stationed at the historic sites. Of special interest is a young Black staff member who, on weekends, takes the part of a Buffalo Soldier and describes his experiences.

DATE ESTABLISHED: 1859
ADDRESS: 6 miles west of Larned, via KS 156
TELEPHONE: (316) 285-6911
VISITING HOURS: Memorial Day–Labor Day, daily 8–6; daily the remainder of the year 8:30–5; closed Christmas, New Year's Day
FEES: Adults, $2; children under 17, free; Golden Age, Golden Eagle, and Golden Access cards apply
SOURCE: Telephone conversation June 23, 1994, Felix Revello, chief ranger, Fort Larned National Historic Site.

Leavenworth

Fort Leavenworth

The Independent Kansas Colored Battery, a unit that had Black officers, was formed at Fort Leavenworth during the Civil War. In 1866, after the war, Congress decided that Black troops could serve in the regular peacetime army even though the idea met some resistance. As the Indian wars began to consume increasing attention, officials decided to use Black troops in those conflicts.

Therefore, Congress authorized the formation of the Ninth and Tenth Cavalry and the Twenty-fourth and Twenty-fifth Infantry. The Tenth Cavalry had its headquarters at Fort Leavenworth.

A highlight of the visit here is a large monument dedicated in recent years. It is the statue of a Buffalo Soldier on horseback. The museum, which is operated by the Historical Society of Fort Leavenworth, has a Buffalo Soldier display with photographs and artifacts as well as fifteen books about the Buffalo Soldiers in the gift shop.

DATE ESTABLISHED:	1827
ADDRESS:	801 Reynolds Avenue, Fort Leavenworth
TELEPHONE:	(913) 651-7440
VISITING HOURS:	Mon.–Fri. 10–4, Sat. 10–4, Sun. noon–4; closed New Year's Day, Easter, Thanksgiving, Christmas
FEES:	Donations appreciated
SOURCE:	Telephone call to site, June 23, 1994.

Nicodemus

Nicodemus Historic District

Pioneer Benjamin "Pap" Singleton led a migration to Kansas and was influential in organizing three all-Black colonies: Nicodemus, Dunlap, and Singleton. Nicodemus was established in 1877 on land designated for homesteading by families who migrated west to Kansas and were called "Exodusters."

Singleton was born a slave in Nashville, Tennessee, where he learned carpentry and cabinetmaking. Prior to the Civil War he escaped to Canada but later returned to the United States and settled in Detroit. When the war ended, he went back to Tennessee and tried to establish some Black settlements there but was stymied by racial hostility and high land prices. Seeking better conditions, he left for Kansas in 1873 and persuaded 300 Black people to go with him.

Although Singleton had little formal education, he was skilled in speaking and in promoting his ideas with enthusiastic stories about the future benefits of life in Kansas. Some educated African Americans opposed his idea of racially separate communities, but many others, tired of economic exploitation, followed him west.

W. R. Hill, a real estate agent and a primary founder of Nicodemus, led a group of migrants from Lexington, Kentucky, to the new colony. Hill and his followers arrived too late in the year to plant crops, and they had little money to buy supplies. They lived at first in burrows constructed out of the side of a hill or ravine and later moved into sod dugouts. Finally they were able to build wooden structures. Living conditions were harsh, and white settlers in Kansas did not welcome them.

Around 1887 there were 260 African Americans in Nicodemus. They had built thirty-five structures, including a general store, post office, livery stable, lumber yard, sod church, and four-room school. The community had two newspapers and a bank established by a white man. Both white and Black residents from the area were politically active and ran for political office.

E. P. McCabe accompanied Hall to Nicodemus, and they became partners in a real estate business. McCabe was elected state auditor in 1882 and 1884; he may have been the first African American elected to state office in the North.

McCabe later left for the Indian Territory, where he founded the all-Black town of Langston, Oklahoma. In 1893 he established Liberty, Oklahoma, another all-Black town.

The people of Nicodemus had high hopes because of announcements about plans to build the Missouri-Pacific Railroad. Thinking it would stop at Nicodemus, they began to expand their business ventures. Unfortunately, the railroad was not built, and the town began a long period of decline. By 1950 only sixteen people were left in Nicodemus. Its post office closed in 1953, and Nicodemus is today the only remaining town of Benjamin Singleton's Exoduster Movement. The historic district includes Sayer's General Store and Post Office (1880), the First Baptist Church (1908), and T. W. P. Hall (1939). Ruins of an original town residence lie at a distance from the district. The former residence has sod walls veneered with native limestone, a wood frame door, and partially standing walls.

In 1970 the Kansas Historical Society and the state highway commission placed a roadside marker at the site explaining the history of Nicodemus.

DATE ESTABLISHED: 1877

ADDRESS: US 24 (bounded by North Street, East Bend Road, South Street, and Seventh Street), Nicodemus

VISITING HOURS: Multiple ownership; restricted access

SOURCES: NRHPINF. Telephone call June 23, 1994, Kansas Historical Society. *Historic Preservation in Kansas, Black Historic Sites.*

Osawatomie

John Brown Memorial State Park

The Kansas-Nebraska Act of 1854 left the question of slavery in the territories to be settled by popular sovereignty. As border states were admitted to the Union, their residents would decide whether each new state would be a free or a slave state. As a result of the 1854 act, Kansas soon became a battleground of feuding factions. Free-staters moved from the North into Kansas intending to keep the territory free of slavery. At the same time Southerners from Arkansas, Missouri, and other slave states settled in Kansas, intent on gaining the territory for their side.

Slaves longing for freedom in the South had heard of the bitter contests in Kansas. Moving along the underground railroad, they came to Kansas in search of freedom. Among the Kansas towns they passed through were Lawrence, Oskaloosa, and Holton. From a station at Wabaunsee in northwestern Kansas Territory, some of the runaway slaves made their escape into the Nebraska Territory.

John Brown, the fiercely committed white abolitionist, made several trips to Kansas between 1855 and 1858. Five of his sons had settled near Osawatomie, Kansas, and invited their father to join them there. While visiting the area, Brown stayed in this cabin, which was owned by his brother-in-law, the Reverend Samuel Adair. The cabin became the headquarters of a free-state militia organized by John Brown; it was also a station on the underground railroad. In 1858 Brown sheltered eleven escaped slaves here and later escorted them to freedom in Canada. (As related elsewhere in this book, John Brown later was hanged because of the abortive raid on Harpers Ferry, West Virginia. Kansas eventually became a free state in 1861.)

The John Brown Cabin, a one-story construction with a stone chimney, was dismantled, moved, and reassembled here in 1912 in what is now the John Brown Memorial Park. In 1928 the cabin was covered with a stone pergola. The interior appears almost as it did when John Brown stopped here, and the log cabin contains a museum that honors the abolitionist who fought so passionately against slavery.

DATE BUILT: 1854
ADDRESS: John Brown Memorial State Park, Tenth and Main Streets, Osawatomie
TELEPHONE: (913) 755-4384
VISITING HOURS: Tues.–Sat. 10–5, Sun. noon–5; closed Mon., Christmas, Easter, Thanksgiving
FEES: Donations accepted
SOURCES: T. Farr, John Brown Museum. *National Register of Historic Places,* 250.

Topeka

Sumner Elementary School

When the Reverend Oliver Brown tried to enroll his daughter Linda at Sumner Elementary School, he sensed that she probably would be turned down. Although Sumner Elementary was closer to her home than the segregated "Colored" school, she was not admitted to Sumner because she was Black.

About this time the National Association for the Advancement of Colored People was leading the fight against school segregation, pressing the issue in several legal cases in different parts of the country. In 1950 Thurgood Marshall and the staff of the NAACP Legal Defense and Educational Fund that he directed selected Linda Brown's appeal as the first to be argued before the U.S. Supreme Court. This case, *Brown* v. *Topeka Board of Education,* was to make history.

At the federal appeals level, judges had ruled that the court was bound by the 1896 *Plessy* v. *Ferguson* decision that had established the legality of "separate but equal" facilities. The Supreme Court, however, announced its unanimous decision on May 17, 1954, that the doctrine of "separate but equal" had no place in public education. The court directed schools in the United States to desegregate "with all deliberate speed." The landmark decision established that separate educational facilities were inherently unequal and that they deprived students of equal protection of laws guaranteed by the Fourteenth Amendment.

Although African American children were now able to enroll in Sumner Elementary School, the doctrine of proceeding with all deliberate speed led to years of rebellion in the South against the Supreme Court ruling as "deliberate" was emphasized far above "speed."

As of February 1995, Sumner School had an enrollment of 206 students, 27 percent of whom were Black. By 1997 Sumner School will be consolidated with other elementary schools as part of Topeka's magnet school program. Use of the historic school building has not been determined as of this writing.

DATE OF SIGNIFICANCE: 1954
ADDRESS: 330 S.W. Western Avenue, Topeka
TELEPHONE: (913) 575-6865

VISITING HOURS: Call to arrange a visit

SOURCES: Telephone conversation Feb. 22, 1995, Tina Beier, secretary, Sumner School. Telephone conversation Feb. 22, 1995, June Christianson, secretary, Topeka Board of Education. *Before the Mayflower,* 375–6.

Wichita

Calvary Baptist Church
First National Black Historical Museum and Cultural Center

At the end of the Civil War, many recently freed slaves left the South and traveled west to the Wichita area seeking a better way of life. They were known as the "Exodusters," and many of these newcomers settled in the 500 and 600 blocks of North Main Street. By 1880 almost twenty-four Black families were living in this district.

The number of Black Americans in Wichita soon expanded. At the turn of the century 6 percent of Wichita's population of 25,000 people was African American. The Black community quickly set up a number of different business ventures including restaurants, two hotels, bakeries, tailor shops, a doctor's office, and the office of a dentist. In the 1950s, as this growth continued, the Black community occupied a fifteen-block area that took in North Water and North Wichita Streets. The whole area was a center of the African American community's social, business, and religious life. Urban renewal in the 1960s displaced many of these organizations.

In 1924 there were sixteen African American churches in the city. One was Calvary Baptist Church, which was erected in 1920 in midtown Wichita. The two-story building had red brick exterior walls with stone trim. Colorful stained-glass windows were inscribed with the names of church members and organizations that had donated them. The structure is one of three significant buildings remaining from Wichita's pre-urban-renewal Black community.

In 1972 the Calvary Baptist congregation moved to a new facility, and Sedgwick County later acquired the building. The First National Black Historical Museum and Cultural Center was established here in 1983, and the organization moved into the historic church structure. The museum removed pews to provide space for museum exhibits and redesigned interior space to house offices of the First National Black Historical Society of Kansas.

The museum teaches about Black participation in the history and development of Wichita and Kansas, and a Black heritage exhibit highlights achievers. There are collections of African art, old music, dolls, and other artifacts. The museum provides information on the Buffalo Soldiers. The library also contains a collection of rare and current books, prints, and papers.

DATE BUILT: 1920

ADDRESS: 601 N. Water Street (corner of Elm and Water Streets), Wichita

TELEPHONE: (316) 262-7651

VISITING HOURS: Mon., Wed., Fri. 10–2; Sun. 2–6; tours by appointment; closed all legal holidays

FEES: Donations appreciated

SOURCES: NRHPRF. Ruby Parker, director, First National Black Historical Society of Kansas.

Works Consulted

Before the Mayflower: A History of Black America. 5th ed. Lerone Bennett Jr. New York: Penguin, 1988.

Historic Preservation in Kansas, Black Historic Sites: A Beginning Point. Topeka: Kansas State Historical Society, 1977. [booklet]

National Register of Historic Places. Washington, D.C.: National Park Service, 1976.

"The Rise and Fall of Western University." Orrin McKinley Murray. Feb. 29, 1960. From the files of Wyandotte County Historical Society and Museum, Bonner Springs, Kansas. [unpublished booklet]

Michigan

Adrian

Second Baptist Church

Second Baptist Church was organized in 1866, shortly after the end of the Civil War. This was Adrian's second African American church, and many of the founding members were former slaves. Prior to the war, the church had been a stop on the underground railroad; its members provided shelter for slaves fleeing to the North.

The congregation constructed the present clapboard structure in 1900. The one-story church with a basement is located in a residential neighborhood. Minor alterations in 1985 included the installation of pews to replace the wooden folding chairs.

DATE ESTABLISHED: Congregation, 1866; present building, 1900

ADDRESS: 607 N. Broad Street, Adrian

TELEPHONE: (517) 263-2486 or (517) 263-1020

VISITING HOURS: Some Fri. and Sun. mornings; call for appointment

SOURCES: Telephone conversation Dec. 29, 1991, Reverend Russell Henagan, associate pastor Second Baptist Church. Lawrence Richardson Jr., Second Baptist Church. Personal visit, summer 1990. *Pathways to Michigan's Black Heritage.*

Dearborn

Henry Ford Museum
Greenfield Village

This open-air and indoor museum complex, the nation's largest, has displays showing the interaction of agriculture and industry in American life. Industrialist Henry Ford had historic homes and shops moved from many sites in the United States to Greenfield Village, where they were reassembled on streets and in green areas.

Several of the historic structures relate to African American history because Black families once lived in some of them. These include an 1860

Tidewater, Maryland, plantation building; two brick slave quarters from a Georgia rice/industrial plantation; an early-twentieth-century Black landowner's house that was brought to this site from near Saranson, Georgia; and a replica of the three-room cabin in which Dr. George Washington Carver was born.

The Henry Ford Museum contains inventions of Black scientist Elijah McCoy, including his hydrostatic lubricator.

DATE ESTABLISHED: Museum, 1929; buildings, 17th–19th centuries

ADDRESS: 20900 Oakwood Boulevard (bounded by Michigan Avenue, Village Road, Southfield Expressway, and Oakland Boulevard), Dearborn

TELEPHONE: (313) 271-1620

VISITING HOURS: Daily 10–5; closed Thanksgiving, Christmas, Jan. 1–mid-March

FEES: For either museum or village, persons 13 and older, $12.50; children 5–12, $6.25; senior citizens 62 and older, $11.50; for both museum and village, persons 13 and older, $22; children 5–12, $11; combination ticket is good 2 consecutive days; parking, free

SOURCES: Ed Merrell, manager of interpretation, Greenfield Village. Personal visit, summer 1990. Telephone calls to site Jan. 18, 1992, Apr. 24, 1994, Aug. 13, 1995. *National Register of Historic Places,* 367.

Detroit

Alpha Phi Alpha Fraternity House

Detroit's Gamma Lambda chapter is the third graduate chapter of Alpha Phi Alpha fraternity. The fraternity, America's oldest Greek fraternal organization for Black students, was founded in 1906 at Cornell University in New York. The Gamma Lambda chapter in Detroit was installed in 1919. Members purchased the house at 239 Eliot Street in 1939.

The fraternity's motto is "Manly deeds, scholarship, and love for all mankind." Members have carried out the ideals expressed in the motto through voter registration programs, educational programs for high school and college students, and participation in the 1950s and 1960s Civil Rights Movement.

When the Alpha Phi Alpha fraternity purchased this site in 1939, most public entertainment and dining facilities were segregated. Fraternities and sororities provided opportunities by sponsoring cultural, educational, and entertainment programs for Detroit's African American community. Currently fraternity members participate in a tutoring program in the Spain Middle School and participate in a joint project with other fraternities and the Masons to develop and revitalize the Brush Park area.

Prominent former members of the fraternity are the following: Dr. Martin Luther King Jr., Dr. W. E. B. Du Bois, and Paul Robeson. John Dancy, the former director of Detroit's Urban League, and Dr. Haley Bell, founder of radio station WCHB, are also members who were well known in the community.

The three-story Alpha Phi Alpha Fraternity House is open to the public by appointment. The site has a Michigan historical marker and is listed in the *State Register of Historic Sites.*

DATE ESTABLISHED: House, 1939

ADDRESS: 293 Eliot Street, Detroit

TELEPHONE: (313) 832-8924

VISITING HOURS: By appointment

FEES: None

SOURCES: Personal visit, summer 1990. Telephone call Dec. 1991, Mr. Kenneth Jordan, Alpha Phi Alpha House. *Pathways to Michigan's Black Heritage. Black Historic Sites in Detroit.*

Ambassador Bridge
Detroit–Windsor Tunnel

Cornelius Langston Henderson Sr. was the second African American to graduate from the University of Michigan in the field of engineering. Henderson was born in 1887 or 1888 in Detroit. His father was president of Atlanta's Morris Brown College, and Cornelius received his early education in the South. He excelled in mathematics, studying at Morris Brown College, Wayne State University, and the University of Michigan, where he received his degree in civil engineering.

Henderson designed portions of the Detroit–Windsor Tunnel as well as the Canadian approaches to the Ambassador Bridge that connects Detroit and Windsor, Canada. He also designed the Detroit Memorial Park and Toronto's General Electric Building. Henderson died in 1976.

ADDRESS: Detroit River; tunnel approached via Randolph Street, Detroit

VISITING HOURS: Always open

SOURCES: *Pathways to Michigan's Black Heritage. International Library of Negro Life and History,* 202.

Detroit Urban League

The Urban League was organized in New York City in 1910 to help meet the needs of migrants from the South. Branches later opened in other major cities in the North. In the first decades of the twentieth century, a major migration of Black people from the rural South came north seeking jobs. The Detroit Urban League office began its work in 1916 under the leadership of Forrester Washington and Henry G. Stevens. The first wave of Black migrants faced tremendous problems—housing shortages, unemployment, and a death rate twice that of their white contemporaries. The Urban League was the major organization concerned with the problems of the migrants.

The first community center under the Urban League's direction opened in 1919. It was located at 553 East Columbia near St. Antoine. The Detroit Urban League in 1919 hosted the first National Urban League meeting outside New York City.

John C. Dancy served as executive director from 1918 to 1960, a period when more and more African Americans were attracted to the city to work in the automobile factories. Although there was not a Black "ghetto" in Detroit, and although those with money could live wherever they chose (within limits), newcomers were crowded into congested tenement districts. Both races lived in the tenements, but white families had more opportunity to move to better quarters. Under John Dancy's direction, the Urban League grew to prominence as an institution that could help Black people obtain employment, housing, recreation, and other social services.

This Urban League headquarters has a Michigan historical marker and is listed in the *State Register of Historic Sites.*

DATE ESTABLISHED: 1916
ADDRESS: 208 Mack Avenue, Detroit
TELEPHONE: (313) 832-4600
VISITING HOURS: By appointment
FEES: None
SOURCES: Telephone call to site, Jan. 2, 1992, and Feb. 24, 1995. Personal visit, summer 1988. *Pathways to Michigan's Black Heritage. Black Historic Sites in Detroit.*

East Ferry Historic District

The East Ferry Historic District includes approximately twenty-four buildings, constructed around 1900. The neighborhood at one time was predominantly white, but in the 1940s it began to house many African American businesses.

Toward the end of World War I, wealthy families were beginning to move out to Detroit's suburbs. War industries were attracting thousands of African Americans to the city. By 1917, 30,000 had moved into Detroit, and some had begun to move into this fashionable neighborhood.

Landmarks still remaining include Dunbar Hospital at 580 Frederick Avenue, the former site of the Lewis Business School, Slade Gragg Academy, Fritz Funeral Home, the Omega Psi Phi fraternity house, and the Detroit Association of Women's Clubs.

The East Ferry Historic District, with its turn-of-the-century buildings that house Black businesses, is listed in the *National Register of Historic Places.*

DATE ESTABLISHED: c1900
ADDRESS: E. Ferry Avenue between Woodward Avenue and Brush Street
TELEPHONE: See individual site information
VISITING HOURS: See individual site information

Detroit Association of Women's Clubs
Detroit Association of Colored Women's Clubs

The Michigan State Association of Colored Women was founded in Detroit in 1898; its mission was to promote education and philanthropy. The association adopted its current name in 1920. In 1941 Ms. Rosa Gragg mortgaged her home, furnishings, car, and her husband's business to secure the $2,000 down payment for the elegant house on Brush Street and East Ferry Avenue.

The Detroit Association of Colored Women's Clubs consisted of eight clubs in the early years, and by 1945 it reached a peak of seventy-five clubs with a membership of 3,000 Black women. The association has had a tradition of community service, providing financial support for needy school children and senior citizens, assisting youth clubs, and awarding scholarship programs. Its motto is "Lifting as We Climb."

Gragg, whose strong commitment to the association led her to purchase this house, was inducted in 1987 into the Michigan Women's Hall of Fame. The state historic marker at the headquarters was dedicated in 1986. The headquarters building is listed in the *State Register of Historical Sites.*

DATE ESTABLISHED: Association, 1895; house purchased, 1941
ADDRESS: 5461 Brush Street (at E. Ferry Avenue), Detroit
TELEPHONE: (313) 873-1727
VISITING HOURS: By appointment

SOURCES: Personal visit, summer 1990. Telephone conversation May 26, 1994, Ms. Senora Smith, historian and active member since 1945 in the Detroit Association of Colored Women's Clubs. *Pathways to Michigan's Black Heritage. Black Historic Sites in Detroit.*

Dunbar Hospital

Dunbar Hospital, a landmark of the East Ferry Historic District, was Detroit's first nonprofit hospital for the Black community. The building later served as home to two of Michigan's first Black men elected to state and national political offices. The townhouse-style building originally was built in 1892 as a residence for a prosperous jeweler and real estate developer.

In an era of racial segregation, the Black community did not have adequate access to Detroit's hospitals. Black physicians who attended sick people in their homes eventually became overburdened by the need for health care. To address this crisis, Black physicians formed the Allied Medical Society (forerunner of the Detroit Medical Society) and raised money to establish a hospital. By 1918 the society acquired the house on Frederick Avenue and a year later opened Dunbar Hospital.

Dunbar Hospital moved to Brush and Illinois Streets in 1928 and was renamed Parkside Hospital, which operated until 1960 when the building was razed as part of an urban renewal project. While it was in existence, Parkside housed Detroit's first Black nursing school and provided advanced training for Black doctors and interns.

Charles C. Diggs Sr. and his family acquired the original buildings of Dunbar Hospital in 1928. They lived in number 580 and operated an undertaking business in 584. In 1937 he was elected as Michigan's first Black Democratic state senator. His son, Charles Jr., who lived in this house from the age of six years, succeeded his father in the Michigan Senate from 1951 to 1954. He served as Michigan's first Black member of the U.S. House of Representatives from 1954 to 1980. The Diggs family later moved from these properties. The house at 584 Frederick Avenue no longer stands.

The Dunbar Memorial Hospital Building is a red-brick townhouse-style structure on a narrow lot. The interior features an open staircase and originally had spacious bedrooms on the second and third floors. When other neighborhood buildings were cleared for urban renewal, the Dunbar Hospital Building was spared. The Detroit Medical Society purchased the site in 1978 to house its activities and to establish a museum featuring the history of medicine in Detroit's Black community. Dunbar Memorial Hospital Historical Museum exhibits include old medical equipment, photographs, and historical papers.

DATE ESTABLISHED: 1918

ADDRESS: 580 Frederick Avenue, Detroit

TELEPHONE: Detroit Medical Society/ Dunbar Memorial Hospital Historical Museum, (313) 832-7800

VISITING HOURS: Mon.–Fri. 10–5; closed most holidays

FEES: None

SOURCES: Personal visit, summer 1990. Telephone conversation Dec. 26, 1991, Ms. Dorothy Aldridge of the Dunbar Hospital Building. NRHPINF. *Pathways to Michigan's Black Heritage. Black Historic Sites in Detroit.*

Fritz Funeral Home

The Fritz Funeral Home, another landmark of the East Ferry Historic District, is one of the oldest Black-owned firms of this type in Detroit. M. Kelly Fritz came to Detroit in 1919 from Toledo, Ohio. His first business site was on Livingston and St. Antoine Streets, the central part of the Black community. The firm moved to Garfield Avenue and Brush Street, where it became the first Black firm in that area (the building was demolished in 1991).

The Fritz Funeral home moved to 246 East Ferry Avenue in 1946. The area was practically all white, and the house that Fritz chose had been built in 1914 for a prominent Jewish family. This family sold the house to a Jewish wholesale meat dealer. The next owner was Prophet Jones, a well-known religious leader in Detroit. Prophet Jones operated 246 East Ferry Avenue as a rooming house for twelve couples.

Fritz Funeral Home is a large, elegant structure, consisting of three floors and a basement. The third floor, once a dance hall and entertainment room, has a high ceiling and a hardwood floor. The original designs painted on the walls are still there, even though the third floor is now used for storage. The second floor had bedrooms for the family as well as quarters for the maid. The first floor had a large living room, a dining room, and a sun room.

In 1991 Fritz, eighty-seven years of age, personally remembered many years of Detroit history. He had seen the changes that took place when Detroit was desegregated. His son attended Northwestern High School but was not allowed to use the YMCA facilities across the street from the school because it was for white men only.

Fritz vividly remembered the trial of Dr. Ossian Sweet. When Sweet defended his home against a white mob, three white men were killed in the melée. During the trial Fritz worked as headwaiter in Detroit's Wolverine Hotel. One day Dr. Sweet, Mrs. Sweet, and famed attorney Clarence Darrow entered the Wolverine and sat down at a table for lunch. Fritz was amazed to see African Americans seated at a table in the hotel. Until then they had been allowed to stay in the hotel but were not allowed to eat in the dining room; they had to take their meals in their rooms. On that day Fritz saw the dining room integrated for the first time.

Fritz also remembered the numerous Black businesses that thrived in Detroit in the 1930s, including a wholesale coffee business, an automobile dealership, barber shops, drugstores, hotels and cabarets, dry-cleaning shops, and grocery stores. An omen of the decline of these businesses occurred about 1940 at a meeting of the local Black Business League. Detroit's mayor (possibly Mayor Frank Cousins) asked to speak to the group. In his speech the mayor stated that segregation in Detroit would soon end. A prominent Black business owner of a chain of drugstores responded by saying that integration would be a one-way street in which Black people would patronize white businesses without receiving reverse business from the white community.

According to Fritz, this prediction was correct. African American businesses began to dwindle or even disappear until there were few to patronize. Where two Black-owned barbershops once had ten chairs each, now the average barbershop for Black people had only one chair.

Fritz Funeral Home is located a block and a half east of Woodward Avenue in an area designated as the East Ferry Historic District, which is called "Preservation Wayne" because of the restoration being done in some of the buildings by Wayne State University. The home at East Ferry Avenue is significant in Black history for its association with M. Kelly Fritz, a prominent Black businessowner for more than four decades.

DATE ESTABLISHED:	1914; purchased by Fritz family, 1946
ADDRESS:	246 E. Ferry Avenue, Detroit
TELEPHONE:	(313) 871-6090
VISITING HOURS:	By appointment
FEES:	None
SOURCE:	Telephone conversation Nov. 1991, Mr. M. Kelly Fritz.

Lewis Business School Building

The former Lewis Business School Building is another landmark of the East Ferry Historic District. This structure on John R. Street near East Ferry Avenue is the second of three sites for this Detroit business. Dr. Violet T. Lewis came to Detroit from Indianapolis in 1939 in response to an invitation from the Detroit Chamber of Commerce. She soon had organized the Lewis Business College.

The college outgrew an earlier site at the corner of McGraw and Warren Avenue, and moved to 5040 John R. It adapted two old mansions for classroom and office use and used a third house as a student dormitory. Lewis and her family lived on the second floor of one of the mansions.

In the 1970s the Lewis College of Business expanded and began to offer associate degrees rather than certificates. The college moved in 1970 to 17370 Meyers in northwest Detroit.

ADDRESS:	Historic site, 5040 John R. Street; college, 17370 Meyers, Detroit
TELEPHONE:	(313) 862-6300
VISITING HOURS:	Visitors may walk or drive by
SOURCES:	Personal visit, summer 1990. *Black Historic Sites in Detroit.*

Omega Psi Phi Fraternity House

The Omega Psi Phi fraternity house, also in the East Ferry Historic District, was founded in 1911 at Howard University, the first national Greek-letter fraternity established at a Black university. In 1923 three men—Dr. DeWitt T. Burton, Francis Dent, and O. T. Davis—founded Detroit's Nu Omega graduate chapter. Nu Sigma, the undergraduate chapter, was established at Wayne State University in 1938. The Nu Omega Detroit chapter purchased this spacious house on East Ferry Avenue in 1942. The large structure served as a home for Nu Omega.

The rooms in this Victorian house were given new functions for fraternity use. The first floor has a foyer with a piano for entertainment as well as an office, a living room, and a dining room converted to a meeting room. On the second floor, two front rooms have showcases that house archives for the local chapter and the Tenth District. The second floor has a game room. Two back rooms once were used for a caretaker's quarters. The third floor has recreation rooms, including a large room with stage that is rented for parties and weddings. A basement lounge runs the full length of the house.

The Omega House is open on a regular basis on Friday afternoons and on special occasions. Fraternity members, who meet on the second and fourth Saturdays of the month, sponsor projects that match their motto: "Manhood, scholarship, perseverance and uplift." These projects include tutoring students and giving college scholarships to achieving students.

This Omega Psi Phi fraternity house has a Michigan historical marker, and is listed in the *State Register of Historic Sites* and the *National Register of Historic Places.*

DATE ESTABLISHED:	1942
ADDRESS:	235 E. Ferry Avenue, Detroit
TELEPHONE:	(313) 872-1646
VISITING HOURS:	Lounge, Fri. 6 P.M.–10 P.M.; closed Sun.–Thurs., holidays
FEES:	None
SOURCES:	Personal visit, summer 1990. Telephone conversation Nov. 29, 1991, Mr. James Wood, Omega Psi Phi Fraternity. *Pathways to Michigan's Black Heritage. Black Historic Sites in Detroit.*

Orsel McGhee House

The home of Orsel McGhee was the site of a conflict over the rights of African Americans to live where they chose. The conflict led to a United States Supreme Court decision over the issue of restrictive covenants.

In 1944 Orsel and Minnie McGhee and their two children moved into this house on Seebaldt Avenue. Their next door neighbors, Benjamin and Anna Sipes, protested, filing a legal suit against the McGhees. They claimed that a restrictive covenant prohibited Black occupancy of the house next to theirs. The McGhees received court orders to leave their home but refused to do so. Aided by the National Association for the Advancement of Colored People, with Thurgood Marshall as attorney, the McGhees appealed the case to the United States Supreme Court. The case was argued as a class action suit. In 1948 the United States Supreme Court ruled in *Sipes* v. *McGhee* that restrictive covenants could not be enforced because such covenants violated protections ensured by the Fourteenth Amendment to the Constitution. The McGhees and the NAACP triumphed, and the family remained in the home on Seebaldt Avenue. Thurgood Marshall later was named a United States Supreme Court Justice.

The Orsel McGhee House has a Michigan historical marker and is listed in the *State Register of Historic Sites.*

DATE ESTABLISHED: African American family residence, 1944
ADDRESS: 4626 Seebaldt Avenue, Detroit
VISITING HOURS: Private; visitors may drive by
SOURCES: Personal visit, summer 1990. *Pathways to Michigan's Black Heritage. Black Historic Sites in Detroit.*

Motown Museum

The famed Motown sound began in 1957 when songwriter Berry Gordy Jr. quit his job at the Ford Motor Company to devote his time to music. He borrowed $800 from his family's savings club and turned the loan into the thriving business that produced the 1960s Motown sound.

In 1969 Gordy purchased the house at 2648 West Grand Boulevard for $10,500 and established offices and recording studios there. Well-known stars and future stars—the Supremes, Michael Jackson, the Four Tops, Smokey Robinson and the Miracles, the Temptations, Lionel Richie, the Commodores, Stevie Wonder, the Spinners, and Gladys Knight and the Pips—recorded at Detroit's Motown Studio between 1959 and 1972. Their talent and Gordy's business acumen propelled Motown into a multimillion-dollar enterprise.

Although the studio moved to Hollywood, California, in 1972, visitors kept asking to see the original Motown recording studio and control room; as a result, the Motown Museum, Hitsville USA, was incorporated in 1985. Since the museum opened, thousands of tourists from all over the world have come to see studio A and its equipment used to record famous hits, the wall of photographs, and the Michael Jackson room.

The complex has four houses, two for the museum, one for offices, and one for conference rooms. Berry Gordy moved into the first house (now called Hitsville) in 1959. He lived upstairs and located the original recording studio downstairs. With the recording studio left open twenty-four hours a day, musicians came in freely to record at any hour when they felt most creative. As the business grew, Motown bought the house next door.

Today, a souvenir shop is located upstairs in the original house where Gordy and his family lived. Motown/Hitsville USA has a Michigan historical marker in the yard and is listed in the *State Register of Historic Sites.*

DATE ESTABLISHED: 1985
ADDRESS: 2648 W. Grand Boulevard (Lodge Freeway to W. Grand Boulevard exit), Detroit
TELEPHONE: (313) 875-2264 or (313) 875-2266
VISITING HOURS: Mon. noon–5, Tues.–Sat. 10–5, Sun. 2–5
FEES: Adults, $3; children 12 and under, $2
SOURCES: Personal visit, summer 1990. Telephone call Dec. 1, 1991, Ms. Barbara Leftwich Reed, Hitsville USA. Telephone call to site, Apr. 24, 1994. *Black Historic Sites in Detroit. Pathways to Michigan's Black Heritage.*

Museum of African American History

The Museum of African American History was founded in 1965 by obstetrician Dr. Charles Wright and thirty-three residents of the Detroit area. The museum originally was housed in three row houses on West Grand Boulevard close to a public library and the Carter Metropolitan Christian Methodist Episcopal Church. More space was needed, and recognizing the museum's value, the city of Detroit provided $3.5 million for construction of a new building, which was dedicated in 1987. This section of the street in the new location was renamed Frederick Douglass Street.

The museum's contemporary, trapezoidal-shaped building has red conical shapes near the entrance that symbolize African culture. The two-story, 28,000-square-foot museum includes exhibit space, a library, a laboratory, and administrative space.

In 1983 the museum initiated the African World Festival, one of Detroit's largest summer festivals, which features speakers, musicians, and special exhibits. It offers outstanding changing exhibitions such as the featured exhibit *I Dream a World,* portraits of Black women who have changed America.

DATE ESTABLISHED: 1965; new site, 1987

ADDRESS: 301 Frederick Douglass Avenue (northbound I-75 to Warren exit), Detroit

TELEPHONE: (313) 833-9800

VISITING HOURS: Wed.–Sat. 9–5, Sun. 1–5; closed Mon., Tues., and federal holidays with the exception of Dr. Martin Luther King Jr. Day

FEES: Donations welcome

SOURCES: Lenda Jackson, Museum of African American History. Personal visit, Aug. 9, 1990. Telephone call to site, Apr. 24, 1994, and Feb. 23, 1995. *Black Historic Sites in Detroit. Pathways to Michigan's Black Heritage.*

Paradise Valley/Black Bottom

Three buildings remain today from a once-thriving Detroit community known as Paradise Valley/Black Bottom. With the exception of St. Matthew's Episcopal Church (the historic building), the Lucy Thurman Young Women's Christian Association Building, and the 606 Horseshoe Lounge at Gratiot Avenue and St. Antoine Street, nothing remains but memories of a community demolished for highway construction and urban renewal.

Before the Civil War, Italian, Greek, Jewish, and Polish Detroiters began to move out of a community located between Brush and Elmwood Streets and extending from Gratiot Avenue south to Larned Street, and African Americans gradually moved in. The newcomers formed a tightly knit community that became known informally as Black Bottom. In the first three decades of the twentieth century, African Americans began leaving oppressive conditions in the South; attracted by the five-dollar-a-day wage that Henry Ford was paying to automotive workers, they migrated in waves to Detroit. By the 1930s and 1940s, local residents were referring to the commercial center of Detroit's Black community as Paradise Valley. African Americans had become the predominant ethnic group, and the streets were alive with families patronizing Black businesses, churches, and social organizations. They enjoyed restaurants, hotels, bowling alleys, grocery stores, music shops, and clubs that provided music and entertainment by nationally known artists.

St. Matthews Episcopal Church, a religious landmark in the community, was founded in 1846; it became one of Detroit's most-prominent Black churches. Although the congregation grew in the decade and a half that preceded the Civil War, church members became tense about the prospect of being captured under the 1850 Fugitive Slave Law, and many fled to Canada. They knew the federal law made it easier for slave owners to recapture their former slaves who had fled North, and they foundered in their belief that Detroit was a safe haven. So many left that remaining members could not pay their debt on the new church that they had erected on Congress and St. Antoine Streets, and the structure was never consecrated.

The church reorganized in 1881 and began to worship on the southwest corner of East Elizabeth and St. Antoine Streets. The historic brick, one-story church and parish house still stand in that location. In 1972, however, the congregation merged with St. Joseph's and began to worship at 8850 Woodward Avenue. Visitors can still drive by to view the exterior of the old church at East Elizabeth and St. Antoine Streets.

The **606 Horseshoe Lounge,** established in 1936, is the last survivor in an area that once included seventeen nightclubs. It was owned for many years by the Michael Pye family and was moved to this site from a nearby location.

As segregation decreased in Detroit, many African Americans moved to other sections of the city. The Chrysler Freeway devoured land in this community, and commercial development led to demolition of most of the old buildings.

The **Lucy Thurman Young Women's Christian Association Building** stands as a landmark of a bygone era. The Detroit Urban League helped to establish the branch in 1918 in an old building on St. Aubin and Maple Streets. The branch was named for Lucy Thurman, a nationally prominent temperance lecturer from Jackson, Michigan. In 1932 a new structure was erected on East Elizabeth and St. Antoine Streets. The thriving Lucy Thurman branch sponsored many programs but closed in 1963 after "Y" programs were integrated. The building now houses a social services agency. The Lucy Thurman YWCA received a state historical designation in 1993 as part of the Centennial Program of the Metropolitan YWCA.

DATES ESTABLISHED: St. Matthews congregation, 1846; church, c1881; YWCA branch, 1918, structure, 1932; 606 Horseshoe Lounge, 1936

ADDRESS: Church historic structure, E. Elizabeth and St. Antoine Streets; Thurman YWCA, 569 E. Elizabeth Street; 606 Horseshoe Lounge, 1907 St. Antoine Street, Detroit

TELEPHONE: St. Matthew–St. Joseph Episcopal Church, (313) 871-4750; Horseshoe Lounge, (313) 962-4124

VISITING HOURS: 606 Horseshoe Lounge, Mon.–Fri. 10 A.M.–2 A.M., Sat. noon–2 A.M.; Lounge closed Sun., most holidays

FEES: Church, none; lounge, none

SOURCES: Telephone conversation Feb. 24, 1995, Mr. Selby Jones, kitchen manager, St. Matthews–St. Joseph Episcopal Church. Telephone conversation Dec. 27, 1991, Miss Stella Jackson, St. Matthews Church. Telephone conversation Dec. 23, 1991, Ms. Ellen Bostic, Detroit YMCA. Telephone conversation Dec. 23, 1991, Mr. John W. Copeland, former executive director, St. Antoine Branch YMCA. Telephone conversation Jan. 2, 1992, Ms. Jacqueline Steingold, YWCA. Personal visit to Horseshoe Lounge, summer 1990. Telephone conversation Nov. 29, 1991, Mr. Ralph Madison, Horseshoe Lounge manager. *Black Historic Sites in Detroit. Pathways to Michigan's Black Heritage.*

Sacred Heart Roman Catholic Church, Convent, and Rectory

The Sacred Heart Roman Catholic Church complex has the only remaining buildings in an area cleared for urban renewal. It represents an important part of Detroit's African American history as the mother church of Black Catholic churches in the city and as the former site of Detroit's only Roman Catholic school for Black students. The church is significant architecturally as the sole Italianate-style church in Detroit.

Sacred Heart was established when the corner of Eliot and Rivard Streets was a rural area on the outskirts of Detroit. A German community developed in this area, and a mission school was established for them in 1874. This grew into the Sacred Heart parish; a church, convent, and school were established within a few years. By 1920 the residents of German origin began to disperse to newer residential areas in the city.

In 1911 Father Joseph Wuest had established a Black mission at St. Mary's School in an area now known as Greektown. The parish took the name of Peter Claver (1581–1654), a Spanish priest who ministered to African slaves in the Caribbean area. The new mission, which worshiped in a converted classroom for three years, moved in 1914 to a vacant church building on Eliot and Beaubien Streets. Black people were migrating to this area, and church membership among them increased. The parish dedicated a new kindergarten and primary school in 1936.

St. Peter Claver was just a block south of Sacred Heart Church. As St. Peter Claver's congregation diminished, the congregations merged. The church building at Eliot and Beaubien Streets became a community center, and in 1938 the St. Peter Claver congregation took possession of the new church.

Sacred Heart began to grow again after the merger and had at one time as many as 1,500 parishioners. The parish also maintained a grade school and Detroit's only Black Roman Catholic high school. Urban renewal eventually destroyed much of the neighborhood, and church members began to move to new areas throughout the city. They established new parishes that originated from Sacred Heart.

The Sacred Heart complex stands today in a cleared area next to the Chrysler Freeway. The church, built in 1875, is a two-story red-brick building with a wooden belfry and an eight-sided slate spire. The rectory is a red-brick building located behind the church on Eliot Street. There is a garden now where a school once stood between the rectory and the church. The school, built in 1889, was demolished in 1973. The convent, located at Eliot Street and Chrysler Service Drive, is a two-story wooden house built in the late 1870s.

Sacred Heart Church, which has stood more than 100 years in this area, is listed in the *National Register of Historic Places.*

DATE BUILT: Church, 1875; rectory, 1884; convent, late 1870s

ADDRESS: 1000 Eliot Street, Detroit

TELEPHONE: (313) 831-1356

VISITING HOURS: Church, Sun. 7–3; Sun. services, 8:30 and 10:30; Sat. evening; call for appointment

FEES: None

SOURCES: Personal visit, summer 1990. Telephone conversation, Reverend Norman Thomas, Sacred Heart Church. NRHPINF. *Pathways to Michigan's Black Heritage.*

St. James Colored Methodist Episcopal Church

St. James Colored Methodist Episcopal Church (now the New Mount Gilead Missionary Baptist Church) is housed in one of the few examples of the small frame churches of Detroit. Most of these churches were destroyed early in the twentieth century because the congregations had purchased more elaborate structures. This church is located at the corner of Vinewood and East Kirby Streets in a quiet residential neighborhood. The simple, one-room, white, frame building sheathed in clapboard has stairs leading up to the front entrance. It was constructed by members of the St. James Colored Methodist Episcopal Church, a congregation that originated in 1924 with only eight members. They met for a number of years in modest quarters.

In 1929, when the congregation had increased to forty-eight members, larger facilities were clearly needed. Reverend Alexander Turner, the newly appointed pastor, encouraged several men in the congregation to build a church. They agreed to donate their labor one day per week and soon were able to complete the present church.

In the early years a pot-bellied stove in the middle of the room heated the interior. Children sat in different areas of the room for Sunday School lessons, with the youngest placed close to the stove to ensure that they would be warm. People seated farther away were not as fortunate and often felt the cold. The church is heated now by a gas furnace in one corner of the room.

The one-room church had no basement and no facilities for social events. Therefore, when members had a tea or small dinner, they had to bring small card tables to the church and decorate them. Since there were no facilities for cooking or for refrigerating food, members brought food from home or from the parsonage next door. When the church hosted summer conferences, soft drinks were kept cold on the lawn in tin tubs that held blocks of ice.

As the Great Depression ended and the economy improved, members were able to contribute fifty cents per week rather than twenty-five cents; the minister was paid approximately $75 per month.

By 1945 the congregation needed a larger church because their small church seated only 125 persons. The white congregation of a Congregational church four blocks away from St. James planned to move away because the neighborhood was undergoing racial change. Their substantial brick church was offered for $100,000 in cash. This offer was accepted, and St. James's congregation members walked in a joyful procession to their new church, which was renamed the Carter Metropolitan Christian Methodist Episcopal Church.

The historic building on Vinewood Street was taken over by different congregations. Since the 1960s it has housed the New Mount Gilead Missionary Baptist Church.

DATE ESTABLISHED: Congregation, 1924; church, 1929

ADDRESS: Church, 5330 Vinewood Street; parish house, 3875 W. Kirby Street, Detroit

TELEPHONE: (313) 898-2802 or (313) 898-2808

VISITING HOURS: Sun. service, 11; call for appointment

SOURCES: Author's childhood church. Personal visit, summer 1990. Telephone conversation Dec. 27, 1991, Reverend Singleton, pastor, New Mount Gilead Church. Telephone conversation Dec. 27, 1991, Reverend Clyde Walker, New Mount Gilead Church. *Milestones of Carter.*

Second Baptist Church of Detroit

Second Baptist Church is the oldest Black congregation in Michigan and perhaps the second oldest in the Midwest. It was established in 1836 when thirteen former slaves withdrew from the First Baptist Church of Detroit because of discriminatory practices encountered there. Their meetings took place in a hall until they were able to purchase the First German Reformed Zion Church, which was located on the site of the present church.

Even before that date, Second Baptist was active as a station on the underground railroad. It formed antislavery societies and its members helped form the Amherstburg Baptist Association that helped escaping slaves reach Canada. Second Baptist also helped establish the Canadian Anti-Slavery Baptist Association. Second Baptist's first minister, William C. Monroe, led the congregation during its work for the underground railroad. He also established Detroit's first school for Black children, which operated in the church basement from 1839 to 1842. In 1843 and 1846 church members sponsored state conventions that petitioned for the right of Blacks to vote. The congregation was associated with a number of Americans involved in the struggle for equality. Frederick Douglass addressed Detroit's Black populace at the church in March 1859. During the Civil War Black volunteers met at Second Baptist in 1863 to form the First Michigan Colored Infantry Regiment. Fannie Richards, Detroit's first Black schoolteacher, was a church member. Much later, Dr. Ralph Bunche, winner of the Nobel Peace Prize and Undersecretary General of the United Nations, was baptized at Second Baptist in 1927. Here was held the first celebration in Detroit of the Emancipation Proclamation. A plaque in the church reads as follows:

> President Abraham Lincoln finally issued the Emancipation Proclamation on January 1,

1863. The first celebration in honor of that event in Detroit was held in the Second Baptist Church on January 6, 1863.

Second Baptist Church has occupied its present site since 1857. The original one-story church was converted to two stories in 1880, and an auditorium was added. After fire almost destroyed the church in 1914, remodeling created a new structure around the original one. The congregation constructed an activities building west of the church in 1926 and an office and educational building to the east in 1968.

Second Baptist Church has a Michigan State historical marker and is listed in the *State Register of Historic Sites* and the *National Register of Historic Places.* A tour of the church includes the underground area where slaves slept before they continued on their way on the underground railroad.

DATE ESTABLISHED:	1836
ADDRESS:	441 Monroe, corner of Beaubien, Detroit
TELEPHONE:	(313) 961-0920
VISITING HOURS:	Mon.–Fri. 10–4:30; Sun. services; tours by appointment
FEES:	None
SOURCES:	Personal visit, summer 1990. Telephone call to church Dec. 1, 1991. *Doorway to Freedom: Detroit and the Underground Railroad. Pathways to Michigan's Black Heritage. Black Historic Sites in Detroit.*

Shiloh Baptist Church

Shiloh Baptist Church, the second-oldest Baptist congregation in Detroit, was organized in 1881, growing out of the Second Baptist Church. Detroit's Black community was increasing at that period. As families moved north of Gratiot Avenue, some found it difficult to travel the distance to Second Baptist Church. Twenty-five members of Second Baptist left in 1881 to form Shiloh Baptist.

Shiloh Baptist Church held some services in homes during the early years, and early services also were held in a small hall on Gratiot Avenue, a building that no longer is standing.

Reverend Moses Hill became pastor in 1911. Under his leadership, the congregation purchased two houses on the site of the present church. They joined the houses together to accommodate the congregation and built a basement under the houses. Church member Ms. Daveen McKinney remembers hearing, as a little girl, stories about the early building. On rainy Sundays, rain came into the structure, and members had to use umbrellas inside the building.

Although there were many churches in the neighborhood, Shiloh Baptist was the first Black church to build its own edifice from the ground up, using Black contractors. Other churches had purchased existing buildings and moved into them. Shiloh Baptist broke ground for the church in 1920 and had its cornerstone observance that same year. Because of funding problems, the church was not completed until 1926.

The 1930s were the years of the Great Depression when Black people in Detroit were making pleas for decent housing. Historic Brewster/Douglas Housing Project, a federal housing project, developed around the church, which was slated for demolition when the projects were completed. However, the Reverend Solomon David Ross, pastor of Shiloh Baptist, led efforts to save the church. An independent thinker, he did not go along with the tradition in which a white minister's group served as a go-between with banks when Black churches needed loans. Reverend Ross realized that Shiloh was not being offered a fair price for the church and realized that Black churches were paying exorbitant interest rates on loans. As a graduate of Morehouse College, he was determined that Black churches should deal directly with banks rather than with white go-betweens. Under his leadership Shiloh remained in the area and was not demolished. Of approximately forty churches in the area, Shiloh was the only one to stand.

Church historian Daveen McKinney notes that in 1949 famed concert artist Paul Robeson (see listing for New York City) gave a concert at Shiloh Baptist. Robeson had been blackballed because he was outspoken against racism and because he refused to cooperate when the House Un-American Activities Committee called on him to testify. When officials would not permit him to perform in Detroit, Reverend Hill of Hartford Baptist, Reverend Ross of Shiloh Baptist, Coleman Young (later mayor of Detroit), David Moore, and others looked for a place where Robeson could perform. Ms. McKinney remembers that Robeson came to her home for a planning session for the concert, and she remembers that an overflow crowd came to hear the concert at Shiloh Baptist Church.

In 1977, under the leadership of the Reverend Dr. William Crews, the church was renovated at a cost of nearly $300,000. In the late 1980s, the Brewster projects became vacant. Shiloh Baptist still stood, an oasis in a nearly deserted community. In 1992 new housing was planned for the site where the historic Brewster projects recently had been demolished. Shiloh Baptist Church remains an important part of the history of this community. The Bentley Library at the University of Michigan in Ann Arbor has a complete copy of the church historical records and pictures. The church also has its own museum of mementos, photographs, church programs, and such memorabilia as the birth certificate of the first pastor, a document that described his color as "yellow."

DATE ESTABLISHED: Congregation, 1881; present church, 1926

ADDRESS: 557 Benton Avenue, Detroit

TELEPHONE: (313) 831-6466

VISITING HOURS: Mon., Wed.–Fri. 11–3 by appointment

SOURCES: Telephone conversation Dec. 1991, Ms. Daveen Ross McKinney, church historian, Shiloh Baptist Church. Patricia Coleman-Burns, Burns Funeral Home. Telephone conversation Dec. 1991, Mr. John Burns II. Personal visit, summer 1990. *Pathways to Michigan's Black Heritage.*

Ossian Sweet Home

The Dr. Ossian Sweet House symbolizes the determination of a Black family to live in the house of their choice. Their move first provoked violence but later served as a step in breaking down barriers of residential segregation in Detroit. The Sweets selected a one and one-half–story house in a residential district on Detroit's east side. Dr. Ossian Sweet (1895–1960) purchased the house on the corner of Garland Avenue and Charlevoix Avenue for $18,500 and moved into the house in the summer of 1925.

Sweet, a physician and gynecologist, was educated at Wilberforce University and Howard Medical School. In spite of his profession, he was not welcome in this all-white neighborhood. On hearing that their new neighbors would be Black, white residents held a mass meeting at the nearby Howe School on July 14, 1925. Intent on keeping the neighborhood white, they formed the Waterworks Park Improvement Association. Their methods were violent—the organization threatened to blow up the house on Garland Avenue if the Sweets moved in.

Sweet and his wife, Gladys—with the help of nine associates—moved into the house on September 8, 1925. They were armed and under police escort because of the threats. The next evening a crowd gathered, throwing rocks and bottles at the house, breaking windows, and finally rushing toward the house. As the crowd moved forward, gunfire came from an upstairs window. It killed a man sitting on his porch across the street and seriously injured a bystander. The next evening police arrested Dr. Sweet and ten of his companions, booking them all for first-degree murder. Eventually, only Sweet and his brother, Henry, were tried.

The National Association for the Advancement of Colored People hired famed attorney Clarence Darrow to represent Sweet. Judge Frank Murphy (later the mayor of Detroit, governor of Michigan, and member of the U.S. Supreme Court) presided over the three-week trial, which resulted in a hung jury. A second trial involving Sweet's younger brother, Henry, ended with acquittal after less than four hours of deliberation. The decision was based on the right of the Sweet family to defend their home against an attack. Sweet and his brother were released; there were no further efforts to prosecute others who were in the house at the time of the violence.

Sweet returned to his home on Garland Avenue in 1928 and lived there without further incident until 1944. He was politically active for a period but became reclusive in later life. In 1960, alone, despondent, and suffering from painful arthritis, he committed suicide.

The Ossian Sweet House is significant in the history of race relations in Detroit. His trial affirmed that citizens had a right to defend life and property and affirmed that these rights extended to African Americans. The milestone case did not usher in a period of harmony and integration in housing but moved a step in that direction because of Sweet's courageous stand.

The Dr. Ossian Sweet House is listed in the *National Register of Historic Places.*

DATE BUILT: House, 1919; Sweet residence, 1925–1944

ADDRESS: 2905 Garland Avenue, Detroit

VISITING HOURS: Private, visitors may drive or walk by

SOURCES: Personal visit, summer 1990. *Pathways to Michigan's Black Heritage. Black Historic Sites in Detroit.*

SPECIAL FEATURE

Canada

Across the Detroit River to Freedom

Runaway slaves fled to many areas in Canada in the nineteenth century. Today the province of Ontario, near Detroit, still has several historic sites related to Black Canadians that visitors are able to see by going to Windsor, Ontario, from Detroit by way of a tunnel or by way of the Ambassador Bridge. From Windsor, visitors can travel to several of the sites in a day's round-trip drive.

To fugitive slaves, few places were more symbolic of freedom than Canada. Thousands of slaves who escaped from the South stayed on in northern states of the United States. Many, however, especially after passage of the 1850 Fugitive Slave Law, did not feel safe anywhere in the United States. The law made it possible for a master to pursue "his" escaped slaves all the way into northern states and to take them back into slavery. Some free Black people felt an intense fear that they, too, might be kidnapped and sold into slavery. The northern states no longer were the promised land. Segregation and racism were rampant in politics, employment, education, public accommodations, and social affairs. For all of these reasons, many saw Canada as the true promised land. Although immigrants to Canada had to struggle for their livelihood, they were free from added burdens of legalized slavery and discrimination.

African American immigrants to Canada sometimes met Black people whose families had arrived in Canada in the 1700s. Some of those families had been among the Loyalists who founded Ontario in the 1700s. Other Black people had fought with the British during the American Revolutionary War. When the American Revolution ended in 1783, the area that would become Ontario was a vast wilderness inhabited by Native Americans and fur traders. Many white people who had been loyal to Britain during the revolution were forced into exile. Some came to Canada, taking their slaves with them. Together they cleared the land and established farms.

By 1791 opposition to slavery grew in Canada, culminating in the Anti-Slavery Act of 1793. The act prevented the further importation of slaves and limited the term of bondage of slaves already in Canada. Freed from slavery, Black Canadians began to participate in business, education, and social life. Some fought to defend the British cause during the War of 1812 and the Rebellion of 1837, in part to protect against the possibility of a return to slavery.

By the beginning of the 1800s, Canada had become a haven for slaves escaping from oppression in the United States. From the beginning of the nineteenth century until slaves were emancipated in the United States, 30,000 to 40,000 fugitive slaves made their way to Canada by means of the underground railroad. They arrived by barge, steamer, wagon, or other means.

Several well-known leaders worked directly or indirectly for the underground railroad. The most noted underground railroad leader was Harriet Tubman. Born in slavery about 1820 on a Maryland plantation, she made nineteen trips into the South, guiding hundreds of slaves to freedom in Canada. In 1851 she settled in St. Catherines, Ontario, a primary end point of her rescue efforts. Later she moved to New York. (See the listing in Auburn, New York.)

The white abolitionist John Brown chose Chatham, Ontario, as a setting for planning his raid on the federal arsenal at Harpers Ferry. In 1858, he held a series of meetings in Chatham to plan the strategy for the raid. Many Black people felt the plan would fail and stayed away. Osborne Anderson was one who did attend the meetings in Chatham. Anderson was born free in 1830 in Pennsylvania and attended Oberlin College in Ohio. In 1850 he moved to Canada, where he learned the printing trade. He met John Brown in the spring of 1850 at a convention in Chatham, Ontario. Anderson began serving as recording secretary at some of Brown's secret meetings. He later participated in the raid on the federal arsenal. John Brown and other participants in the raid either were killed or were executed; only Anderson was able to escape. As the sole survivor of the raid, he later wrote an account of the event called *A Voice From Harpers Ferry.* Although the raid was unsuccessful, it had an electrifying effect in awakening the United States to a realization that the question of slavery could not be ignored. The raid was one of the factors leading to the Civil War. (See the Harpers Ferry, West Virginia, listing.)

Black Canadians, often with support from white communities, began to develop thriving communities. The Reverend Josiah Henson, a slave who escaped from Kentucky, started a Black community where the town of Dresden is now located. His Dawn Settlement was established thirteen years before Dresden was established; thus, Henson can be considered the town's founder.

Henry Bibb, a man who escaped from slavery in Kentucky, worked with Josiah Henson to purchase land for settlement. Bibb was born into slavery in 1815 in Shelby County, Kentucky. His mother was a slave; his father was a white man whom Bibb never knew. Bibb was hired out many times to work for others; his earnings were used to pay for the education of his master's son. After enduring years of cruel treatment, he escaped, fleeing to Ohio, then to Detroit in 1842. The Fugitive Slave Law was passed in 1851, making it easier for owners to find and capture slaves who had fled to the North. Bibb fled with his wife to Canada in 1851; there, he established Canada's first Black newspaper, *The Voice of the Fugitive.* Bibb, Josiah Henson, and some white philanthropists developed a plan to purchase thousands of acres of land that would be divided for sale to individual families. Some of the revenues were to be used for educational purposes. Henry Bibb died in 1854.

In 1853 Samuel Ringgold Ward founded another newspaper for Black readers, *The Provincial Freeman,* in Windsor and later published it in Toronto and Chatham. Ward was born in slavery in 1817 in Maryland. When he was about three years old, his family escaped, moving first to New Jersey, then to New York. In 1851 he aided a fugitive slave in a well-known case, and fearing that he might be apprehended for his help, Ward fled to Canada. There he assisted fleeing slaves. He hired Mary Ann Shadd as a subscription agent for his newspaper. By 1854 Shadd was chief editor and writer for the paper, serving as editor between 1854 and 1856. The paper ceased publication by 1857 or 1858 because few of the refugees could read or afford a subscription. Shadd met John Brown when he held his meetings in Chatham; he held one meeting in the house of her brother, Isaac Shadd. Mary Shadd, who later married and settled in Washington, D.C., has been called North America's first Black newspaper woman. (See the listing for Mary Ann Shadd Cary in the Washington, D.C., section.)

Some Black families in Canada chose to live in newly established Black communities. Just outside Chatham, Reverend William King, an Irish-born Presbyterian, established the Elgin Settlement that grew into Canada's most successful self-supporting all-Black community. Some of the schools that Black families established for their own children, including the Buxton Mission School, were popular with white families because they provided an education considered superior to that in the local white schools.

When the Civil War ended and slaves had been legally emancipated in the United States, some former fugitive slaves and expatriated free Black people returned from Canada to the United States because they now felt a measure of safety. Others remained in Canada, which now had become their chosen home.

SOURCES: *An Enduring Heritage. A Salute to Historic Black Abolitionists. Kentucky's Black Heritage. The Education of the Negro Prior to 1861.*

Amherstburg, Ontario

North American Black Historical Museum and Cultural Centre

Melvin Simpson, a resident of Amherstburg, Ontario, originated the idea of founding a museum that would create pride in Black history. He was a member of the Nazrey African Methodist Church, which was built in 1848 by former slaves who had fled from slavery in the United States to freedom in Canada. The underground railroad station in Amherstburg, one of Canada's earliest Black settlements, sheltered them.

Membership at Nazrey Church numbered seventy-five at one time, but it dwindled in the 1970s until only four faithful members remained. Watching the deterioration of the church structure, Simpson realized that it could survive only as part of a museum where visitors could learn about its heritage.

The remaining church members, along with other community residents, gathered resources and started the museum in a restored log house that dated back to the 1840s. They dedicated the North American Black Historical Museum and Cultural Centre in September 1981. The museum complex consists of a restored house and the Nazrey A.M.E. Church. Inside the museum, exhibits and video programs highlight the underground railroad and the history and culture of Canada's Black citizens. The museum has maps of underground railroad routes, slave bills of sale, old newspaper stories, and the old log cabin itself in which is displayed early African American furniture.

Visitors may see other related attractions nearby in the town. In 1841 a group of African American residents met at the John Liberty Home (built about 1830) on George Street and established the Amherstburg Baptist Association. Their goal was to promote unity and spiritual growth among Black Baptists. The congregation at First Baptist Church (built in 1848) on George Street played a part in establishing the Amherstburg Baptist Association.

Across the street from the museum is the Old King Street School, constructed about 1875. The limestone building on the site of the original log schoolhouse later housed the Mount Beulah Church of God in Christ.

DATE ESTABLISHED:	Museum, 1981; other structures, 1840s
ADDRESS:	277 King Street, Amherstburg, Ontario
TELEPHONE:	(519) 736-5433 or (519) 736-7353
VISITING HOURS:	Apr. 18–Nov. 30, Wed.–Fri. 10–5; weekends 1–5
FEES:	(Canadian funds) adults, $3; senior citizens and students, $1; families, $7
SOURCES:	Personal visit, summer 1990. *Black Historic Sites in Detroit. An Enduring Heritage. The North American Black Historical Museum Celebrates the 150th Anniversary of the Abolition of Slavery Act, 1834–1984 and Ontario's Bicentennial.*

Chatham, Ontario

First Baptist Church

The First Baptist Church, a meeting house constructed in 1853 by former slaves, was the religious and social focal point in Chatham's Black community and a natural gathering place for local abolitionists. On May 10, 1858, a white abolitionist from the United States named John Brown led a meeting in this building to develop final plans for his famous but unsuccessful raid at Harpers Ferry (West Virginia). Thirty-five white and twelve Black antislavery activists were present, including Reverend William C. Monroe from Detroit, who was elected chairman at the meeting. Monroe was the first minister of Detroit's Second Baptist Church, a Black church heavily involved in underground railroad activities. Also present were two of Brown's sons, Owen and John, as well as John Kagi, a white man who was elected Brown's secretary of war; Martin Delaney, a well-known Black activist and co-editor with Frederick Douglass of the *North Star;* and the brother and the husband of Mary Ann Shadd, America's first Black female newspaper editor. (For further information on John Brown, see entries for Kansas City and Osawatomie, Kansas; Chambersburg, Pennsylvania; West Des Moines, Iowa; Akron, Ohio; Lake Placid, New York; and Harpers Ferry, West Virginia. For further information on Reverend William Monroe, see the Detroit, Michigan, section on Second Baptist Church. For further information on John Kagi's house and secret cave, see the listing for John Brown's Cave and Museum in the Nebraska City, Nebraska, section. For further information on Mary Ann Shadd Cary, see the Washington, D.C., section.)

John Brown's plans were for him and his followers to seize the arsenal at Harpers Ferry, call for an uprising of slaves in the South, and then move to a stronghold in the mountains. (Harpers Ferry was at that time in Virginia; it is now in West Virginia, which became a separate state under northern control in 1863.) The bold plan pitted a handful of abolitionists against the armed power of the U.S. government and was bound to fail. Although the October 1859 raid did not attain its goal, it aroused both proslavery and antislavery adherents across the nation and was considered one of the factors that precipitated the Civil War.

Chatham has two other early Black churches—Campbell Chapel African Methodist Episcopal Church on King Street and Victoria Chapel British Methodist Episcopal Church on Wellington Street. Victoria Chapel's congregation hosted the 1856 convention where delegates withdrew from the African Methodist Episcopal Church. The delegates formed the British Methodist Episcopal Church, thus becoming the mother church of that denomination. Fire destroyed the original 1859 Victoria Chapel in 1907, and the congregation erected the present building in 1908.

DATE ESTABLISHED:	First Baptist, 1853; Campbell Chapel, c1887
ADDRESS:	135 King Street E, Chatham, Ontario
TELEPHONE:	Kent–Chatham Tourist Bureau, (519) 354-6125
VISITING HOURS:	Historical marker, daily dawn–dusk; church, at services or by appointment
FEES:	None
SOURCE:	*An Enduring Heritage.*

Dresden, Ontario

Uncle Tom's Cabin and Museum

When the Reverend Josiah Henson and other abolitionists purchased two hundred acres of Dresden land in 1841, their intent was to establish a settlement for refugees from slavery. A previous all-Black settlement, Wilberforce, Ohio, had failed, and the new community, given the optimistic name of Dawn Settlement, was formed as a place that would offer education, work, and security.

Henson was born in Maryland in 1789, and he and his mother were sold twice before he reached adulthood. He married and in 1825 was sent with other slaves to Kentucky. Although he became an ordained minister in 1828, his owners still traded him.

Promises made to a slave meant little if a master chose not to honor those promises. Henson's master gave him permission to earn his freedom for $400. Henson patiently raised the money only to be told that the new price of freedom was $1,000. Until that point of betrayal, Josiah Henson had been a loyal and trusted slave. He even had acknowledged the institution of slavery by tacitly granting that it was reasonable to ask a man to buy his freedom. When his master went back on his word, however, and Henson learned that his master was planning to sell him again, he reassessed the situation and decided to take freedom for himself and his family by escaping.

Reaching Canada, Henson was active in founding Dawn Settlement, which established a church, a brickyard, a sawmill and a gristmill, and Canada's first vocational school. The vocational school's curriculum was designed to provide the kind of education that would help the settlement become self-supporting.

When Henson wrote a pamphlet describing his life story, the Anti-Slavery Society of Boston published it as *The Life of Josiah Henson, Formerly a Slave, Now an Inhabitant of Canada.* One of its readers was Harriet Beecher Stowe, who was moved by the account. She later used some of the incidents described by Henson in her 1852 novel *Uncle Tom's Cabin.* (Unfortunately the name Uncle Tom later became synonymous with a docile, servile personality.) (See the entries for Stowe in the Hartford, Connecticut; Brunswick, Maine; and Cincinnati, Ohio, sections.)

Today the six buildings in the museum complex include the Reverend Henson's house and the British American Institute cemetery where he and his family are buried. The complex also includes the original Dawn Settlement church, a one-story building with arched windows and wooden siding. Henson preached in this church, which was built around 1859. The site also includes a smokehouse made from the trunk of a giant sycamore tree and a cabin that housed newly arrived fugitives. The museum contains artifacts used to punish slaves as well as items and farm implements used by the early settlers.

DATE ESTABLISHED: 1841

ADDRESS: Kent County Road 40, Dresden, Ontario

TELEPHONE: (519) 683-2978

VISITING HOURS: Third weekend in May–last Sun. in Sept., Mon.–Sat. 11–5, Sun. 1–5; closed Oct.–third weekend in May

FEES: (Canadian funds) Adults, $3; senior citizens and students 12–18, $2.50; children 6–11, $2; children under 6, free; families, $10

SOURCES: Shelia E. Heflin, Owensboro, Kentucky Public Library. Larry Z. Scott, director, The Kentucky Museum. Park City Daily News, Aug. 21, 1989, Bowling Green, Kentucky. *An Enduring Heritage.*

North Buxton, Ontario

Raleigh Township Centennial Museum

Reverend William King, an Irish-born Presbyterian, was the primary force in establishing the Elgin Settlement in 1849. The settlement just outside Chatham in Raleigh Township was incorporated in 1850; in spite of initial resistance by some members of the whole community, it grew into a thriving all-Black settlement that provided a haven for escaping slaves who wanted to remain in Canada.

Isaac Riley, his wife, and four children were the first settlers in the Elgin Settlement. They arrived in 1849 and were the first to buy land here. Riley's son, Jerome, was a doctor who served in the Civil War and who helped establish the Freedmen's Hospital in Washington, D.C. Most of North Buxton's present residents are descendants of former slaves who came to Canada before the end of the Civil War.

The Raleigh Township Centennial Museum opened in 1961 as a memorial to the Elgin Settlement. It features the history and accomplishments of the settlers and displays artifacts of them and their descendants. The museum complex includes the old school, S.S. No. 13, constructed in 1863. Located next to the school are the Bethel British Methodist Episcopal Church and Burial Ground, dating from about 1870. First Baptist Church, built in 1883, is located near the B.M.E. Church. St. Andrew's Presbyterian Church, which King established in 1868, is located at the heart of this settlement in Kent County. William King is buried in Maple Leaf Cemetery in Chatham.

The George Hatter House, built about 1863, was home to a former slave from West Virginia who came to Buxton during the 1850s.

DATE ESTABLISHED: Buildings, c1863; museum, 1961

ADDRESS: (10 miles south of Chatham) County Road 6, North Buxton, Ontario

TELEPHONE: (519) 352-4799 or (519) 354-8693

VISITING HOURS: May–Sept., Wed.–Sun. 1–4:30; other times by appointment; closed Mon., Tues., Oct.–Apr.

SOURCES: *Black Historic Sites in Detroit. An Enduring Heritage.*

Works Consulted

Black Historic Sites in Detroit. Detroit: Black Historic Site Committee, Detroit Historical Department, 1989.

The Education of the Negro Prior to 1861: A History of the Education of the Colored People of the United States from the Beginning of Slavery to the Civil War. C. G. Woodson. Washington, D.C.: The Associated Publishers, 1919.

An Enduring Heritage: Black Contributions to Early Ontario. Roger Riendeau and the staff of the Ontario Ministry of Citizenship and Culture. Toronto: Durdurn, 1984.

Kentucky's Black Heritage. Frankfort, Ky.: Kentucky Commission on Human Rights, 1971.

The North American Black Historical Museum Celebrates the 150th Anniversary of the Abolition of Slavery Act, 1834–1984 and Ontario's Bicentennial. Amherstburg, Ont.: The North American Black Historical Museum, 1984.

A Salute to Historic Black Abolitionists. Richard L. Green, ed. Chicago: Empak Enterprises, 1988.

Grosse Ile

St. James Episcopal Church

Elizabeth Denison Forth represents the African Americans who not only sought their own freedom but who were generous in giving something of lasting benefit to the community. A former slave, she bequeathed her life savings for building the original chapel at this site. The funds were supplemented by the family she had worked for, and the chapel was erected.

Elizabeth (Lisette) Denison was born about 1787 in the post of Detroit, an area then part of upper Canada. The Denisons were slaves owned by William and Catherine Tucker. After William Tucker died, Elizabeth's parents were freed, but the children remained slaves. A lawsuit later filed against Mrs. Tucker requested the freedom of the Denison children. Judge Woodward ruled that the youngest child was to be free, but the older children were to remain slaves. Then Lisette and her brother heard about another ruling that stated that slaves who went to Canada for their freedom and later returned were to be considered free. Lisette and her brother went to Canada, and when they returned to Michigan, they returned free. The year was about 1815.

In 1827 Lisette married Scipio Forth, a man who operated a freight business. Their marriage was recorded in September 1827 in records of St. Paul's Church in Detroit.

Lisette showed business ability. She purchased land in Detroit and Pontiac, and with advice from some white Detroit businessmen, purchased stock in the steamboat *Michigan*. In 1831 Forth joined the Biddle household, where she worked as a servant for thirty years. She and Mrs. Eliza Falconer Biddle became good friends, and the two eventually made a vow jointly to build a chapel.

When Lisette Forth died August 1866, she had kept the vow, leaving a portion of her estate to her family and a portion to be used to build a church. This money, along with money from the Biddle family, provided funding for building St. James Episcopal Church on Grosse Ile. The frame, one-story church was built in Gothic-revival style with board-and-batten siding; corner and side buttresses; pointed, arched stained-glass windows; and a large Tiffany-glass tracery window. The original structure serves today as a chapel for a larger church built in 1958. The chapel doors are dedicated to Elizabeth Denison Forth. The congregation members revere the original chapel.

DATE BUILT: 1867

ADDRESS: 25150 E. River Road, Grosse Ile

TELEPHONE: (313) 676-1727

VISITING HOURS: Sun. services, 8, 10; by appointment

FEES: None

SOURCES: Telephone conversation Dec. 29, 1991, Reverend Scott Krejci, St. James Episcopal Church. *National Register of Historic Places*, 369. *The Ark of God. Pathways to Michigan's Black Heritage.*

Idlewild

Idlewild Historic District

The Idlewild Historic District consists of more than 1,000 acres of rolling hills, woods, and lakes. It is a resort community consisting of some 500 structures, cottages, and commercial buildings. Idlewild, which developed in Lake County, Michigan, as a self-contained community, became one of America's most popular resorts for African Americans. Middle-class professionals and business leaders came to enjoy Idlewild's attractive recreational setting away from the noise and confusion of the city.

The resort began in 1915 when two white entrepreneurs organized the Idlewild Resort Company and began marketing lots. The company erected a large clubhouse on an island in Idlewild Lake and made plans to develop a golf course and ball park. Eventually Black owners and entrepreneurs took over the business, and Black real estate agents began to sponsor tours for prospective buyers from different cities. Owners who put up small summer cottages took care to preserve the natural landscape with its many trees and shrubs.

Many influential members of the Black community built cottages at Idlewild, including Dr. Daniel Hale Williams, a well-known surgeon from Chicago and a pioneer in cardiac surgery, as well as noted scholar and historian W. E. B. Du Bois. By the 1920s Idlewild was well known to middle-class Black people in many states. As the resort continued to grow, Black businessman Herman Wilson developed Paradise Garden, a subdivision near the original settlement. One of its features was the Paradise Club, a center where Black artists could perform. The club is no longer standing.

After World War II an entrepreneur purchased Williams Island and developed it into a night entertainment place. Such well-known entertainers as Sarah Vaughn, Sammy Davis Jr., and Aretha Franklin performed here.

The boom years for the resort extended from 1920 through 1960. Affluent Black people from throughout North America came to buy land or vacation at the resort. After the 1950s, however, integration opened up other vacation and recreation areas, and a slow decline began. Some residents were disturbed by trends in commercial development in a resort that originally had a rural, recreational character. By 1970 Idlewild was nearing extinction as a community. The clubhouse was gone, and many of the cottages stood vacant.

Idlewild residents have organized recently to revitalize the community. The district still contains many of its original buildings as well as the original street plan and setting. Those who drive through may see such attractions as the Solomon House dating from 1920, the Dr. Daniel Hale Williams House (1921), and the central business district, which contains a concrete-block grocery store (around 1935) and its bar-restaurant (around 1928). Idlewild is listed in the *National Register of Historic Places.*

DATE ESTABLISHED:	1915
ADDRESS:	South of US 10 (east of Baldwin, Michigan, at the junction of MI 37 and US 10); Township office, in the fire station on Lake Drive, Idlewild
TELEPHONE:	Township office, (616) 745-3940
VISITING HOURS:	Private; the best days of the week to visit are Mon. and Fri.; call the Township Office for directions and an appointment
SOURCES:	NRHPINF. Telephone conversation Feb. 27, 1995, Mrs. Janet Gordon, deputy treasurer, Yates Township. *Pathways to Michigan's Black Heritage.*

Marshall

Crosswhite Marker

A marker at this site commemorates an incident in which neighbors helped Adam Crosswhite and his family escape to Canada. Crosswhite, who had escaped from slavery in Kentucky in 1844, brought his family to Marshall, Michigan, where they lived in relative safety. They knew, however, that there was always danger that slave catchers might try to pick them up and return them to their former owners. Therefore, they made arrangements to signal neighbors if they might need help. In 1847, three years after the Crosswhites arrived in Marshall, a group of slave catchers found them and attempted to return them to the South. When the Crosswhites gave their danger signal, their neighbors helped the family escape to safety in Canada. The slave owner then sought restitution and took to court the neighbors, who had to pay a fine of $1,925 (a very substantial amount in that era). A historical marker consisting of a boulder with a plaque marks the site where citizens defended the Crosswhite family.

DATE OF SIGNIFICANCE: 1847
ADDRESS: Near Triangle Park, Michigan Avenue and Madison Street, Marshall
VISITING HOURS: Daily, 24 hours
SOURCE: *Pathways to Michigan's Black Heritage.*

Muskegon

Jonathan Walker Memorial

The Jonathan Walker memorial, a huge obelisk with text, honors a white man who was branded on his right hand with the letters SS for "slave stealer." In 1844 Captain Jonathan Walker was captured with seven fugitive slaves off the coast of Pensacola, Florida. A federal court ordered him branded and sentenced him to one year in prison. He was the only man ever ordered branded by a federal court. John Greenleaf Whittier, the Quaker abolitionist poet from Massachusetts, commemorated this incident in his poem, "The Man with the Branded Hand."

After his release from prison, Walker moved to Muskegon, Michigan, where he died in 1862. Since 1955 the Greater Urban League in Muskegon, Michigan, has given the Jonathan Walker Award to any citizen who has worked to improve race relations.

DATE OF SIGNIFICANCE: Prior to the Civil War
ADDRESS: 391 Irwin Avenue, Muskegon
TELEPHONE: Muskegon Cemetery and Forestry Department, (616) 724-6783
VISITING HOURS: Daily, dawn–dusk
SOURCES: Telephone conversation Feb. 27, 1995, Gloria Coburn, department secretary, Muskegon Cemetery and Forestry Department. *Pathways to Michigan's Black Heritage. Webster's New Biographical Dictionary,* 1055.

Niles

Ferry Street School

Ferry Street School is a restored nineteenth-century schoolhouse for Black students. The one-room, brick building opened in 1868 as a school for "colored" children; forty-nine students enrolled. The original building opened at a cost of $2,726.28. There were only two grades, which met in the single classroom.

When the city schools were integrated in 1870, the Ferry Street School was closed. A nearby church used the building while church facilities were being remodeled. As other city schools became overcrowded, the schoolhouse was reopened in 1875. A west wing was added in 1903. Niles schools became overcrowded again, and the city began renting rooms in houses and stores, converting them to classrooms. By 1951 the city had built several new elementary schools, and the old Ferry Street School no longer was needed. The building was used for storage and briefly as a center for exceptional children. In 1975 the building was abandoned.

Concerned citizens, treasuring the historic building, began restoring the one-room section of the school to its presumed 1868 appearance. The citizens held rummage sales and raffles and sought donations for the project. The city council provided some funds for removing exterior paint. With the project completed, the building was turned over to the Niles Community School District. The Michiana Literacy Council, Rescue Read, uses half of the schoolhouse today, while the restored schoolroom is seen in the side entered through the double doors. The Ferry Street School is significant as a restored schoolhouse that originated as a one-room school for Black children.

DATE BUILT: 1868

ADDRESS: 620 Ferry Street, Niles

TELEPHONE: (616) 683-3313

VISITING HOURS: Mon.–Thurs. 10–4; closed Martin Luther King Jr. Day, Memorial Day, July 4, Labor Day, Thanksgiving, Christmas

SOURCES: Personal visit, summer 1990. Telephone conversation May 4, 1994, Phyllis Lutin, executive director, Michiana Literacy Council. *Ferry Street School.*

Remus

Wheatland Church of Christ

When Wheatland Church of Christ was organized in 1876, it was the first Black church in Mecosta County. Originally it was known as the Cross Church in honor of the Reverend Thomas Cross, who built it in 1883 and served as its pastor until his death in 1897. Although the structure has been somewhat altered, it is virtually the same church that Cross built in the nineteenth century—a simple one-story frame structure with white clapboard siding and double-entry doors. The interior has seen little alteration with the exception of carpeting and more efficient windows. The original pews are there, and two of four lights in the sanctuary that hang from long chains have the original globes.

Wheatland Church of Christ is listed in the *Michigan State Register of Historic Sites.*

DATE ESTABLISHED: Congregation, 1876; church, 1883

ADDRESS: 3025 Eleven Mile Road, Remus

TELEPHONE: (517) 967-8330 or (517) 967-8870

VISITING HOURS: By appointment

SOURCES: Telephone conversation Apr. 24, 1994, Reverend Randy Piatt, pastor, Wheatland Church of Christ. *Pathways to Michigan's Black Heritage.*

Works Consulted

The Ark of God. Isabella E. Swan. Grosse Ile, Mich.: St. James Church of Grosse Ile, 1968.

Black Historic Sites in Detroit. Detroit: Black Historic Site Committee, Detroit Historical Department, 1989.

Doorway to Freedom: Detroit and the Underground Railroad. Detroit, Mich.: Detroit Historical Department, n.d.

Ferry Street School. Niles, Mich. [flier]

International Library of Negro Life and History: Historical Negro Biographies. Wilhelmena S. Robinson. New York: Publishers, 1970.

Milestones of Carter. Detroit: Carter Metropolitan Church, 1970. [booklet]

National Register of Historic Places. Washington, D.C.: National Park Service, 1976.

Pathways to Michigan's Black Heritage. Bertha H. Miller, ed. Lansing: Bureau of History, Michigan Dept. of State, 1987.

Webster's New Biographical Dictionary. Springfield, Mass.: Merriam-Webster, 1988.

Minnesota

Rochester

Avalon Hotel

The Avalon Hotel, built in 1919, stands at the edge of downtown Rochester on North Broadway Avenue. The three-story, red-brick building, which is located next to one of the city's railroad depots, provided rental rooms in an era when African Americans faced the color barrier in accommodations.

In the early twentieth century, Rochester's Mayo Clinic grew in fame as an international medical center. Out-of-town patients coming for medical services needed short-term accommodations while they received medical treatments. White patients were housed in a variety of guest houses and hotels, but the Avalon Hotel was the only place in Rochester that accommodated Black visitors.

While some visitors came seeking medical help, others came to see the many outstanding entertainers who performed at the Avalon—well-known personalities such as Duke Ellington and his band, the Ink Spots, and boxer Henry Armstrong. Purchased in 1988 and restored, the site is now the Hamilton Music Building.

DATE BUILT: 1919
ADDRESS: 301 N. Broadway, Rochester
TELEPHONE: (507) 288-6311
VISITING HOURS: By appointment
SOURCES: NRHPINF. Telephone conversation June 20, 1994, Myrna Kay Hamilton, owner.

St. Paul Vicinity

Fort Snelling State Historical Park*

The Louisiana Purchase gave the United States jurisdiction over land extending from the Mississippi River to the Rocky Mountains. But this vast territory lay beyond American settlement and was inhabited only by fur traders and Native Americans who were still loyal to the British.

After the War of 1812, the U.S. government began to establish its presence there by erecting a chain of forts from Lake Michigan to the Missouri River.

Fort Snelling was established in 1820 near the confluence of the Minnesota and Mississippi Rivers. The outpost was used for transportation, exploration, commerce, and the protection of U.S. citizens for approximately forty years. Traders stopped at the fort while their goods were inspected; missionaries called on the fort for help as they worked with Native Americans; and government officials visited the fort for lodging and supplies.

Free Black people and slaves arrived with the U.S. Army in the early years of Fort Snelling. Some of them participated in the local fur trade. Other Black Americans, however, arrived as slaves of the military staff. Of the slaves, the one who was to become the best known in history was Dred Scott, who was born about 1795 in Southampton County, Virginia; he arrived at Fort Snelling from St. Louis in 1836 with his owner, Dr. John Emerson, the fort's new army surgeon. Earlier, Emerson had taken Scott to Illinois, a state where slavery was prohibited by the Northwest Ordinance of 1787. When Emerson took Scott to Fort Snelling, he was taking him into Louisiana Territory where slavery was forbidden by the Missouri Compromise. Emerson had ignored the ban against slavery both in Illinois and in the Louisiana Territory where he continued to treat Scott as his slave.

In 1837 Dred Scott married Harriet Robinson, another slave at Fort Snelling, who was sold by Major Lawrence Taliaferro, a federal Indian agent, to Dr. Emerson. The Scotts had a child, Eliza, during this period; Eliza was born north of the Missouri Compromise line and, therefore, was not legally a slave. However, she was treated as a slave by Emerson.

Later, when Emerson brought Scott and his family back to Missouri and sold them to a man named Sanford, Scott sued for freedom for himself, his wife, and his two daughters, one of whom was born after the family returned to Missouri. Scott claimed the right to freedom as a result of having lived in Illinois and in Minnesota Territory, regions where slavery was prohibited. Having lived in free territory, he should be considered free.

Similar claims—that a slave who had lived in a free state should be considered free even if returned by the owner to a slaveholding state—had been brought before courts in several states with varying results. A slave girl named Rachel, who at one time had lived at Fort Snelling, successfully sued for her freedom on a similar basis in a St. Louis court. Stockton, an army officer, had bought Rachel as a slave in Missouri and later took her with him to Fort Snelling, where they lived for a year. He then took her to Prairie du Chien (then in Michigan/Wisconsin Territory, where slavery was forbidden) for four years before taking her back to Missouri and selling her as a slave. Rachel was successful in gaining her freedom on the basis of having been taken to live in free territory.

Dred Scott won his case at a lower court level, but the Supreme Court of Missouri ruled that he remained a slave. The case was taken to the U.S. Supreme Court, where the court ruled against Scott. In the infamous decision Justice Roger Taney wrote the opinion of the court. He maintained that slaves were property and that any act of Congress prohibiting ownership of slaves (property) in a specific territory was not warranted by the Constitution and was, therefore, void. He also made the chilling statement that Black people did not have the rights of citizens, that for more than a century before the Constitution of the United States was adopted, they were regarded as so inferior that they had no rights that white people were bound to respect.

The 1857 U.S. Supreme Court decision was an outrage to abolitionists and increased the bitterness between the North and the South that a few years later led to the Civil War. Soon after the decision Dred Scott was emancipated, and he began working as a hotel porter in St. Louis. He died a year after gaining his freedom.

After the Civil War Fort Snelling served as a center for administering Indian affairs. During the Indian wars, the all-Black Twenty-fifth U.S. Infantry was stationed at Fort Snelling from 1882 to 1888. The fort served as a recruitment center in the twentieth century, until it was closed after World War II.

In 1963 the process of restoring buildings at Fort Snelling began. Today historic Fort Snelling consists of a large fort complex, eighteen fully furnished stone-and-wood buildings within a stone wall, erected over a 150-year period.

The History Center includes a film every thirty minutes, an exhibit area, and a museum. Although elements of Black history are covered through exhibits and through the costumed living-history program, the amount of information included about Black history may vary according to the interpreter. Restoration includes a uniformed mannequin representing a soldier from the Twenty-fifth Infantry Regiment, panels representing the service of Black soldiers, and the servant/slave quarters. Plans are made for an outdoor sculpture commemorating the role of Black people in the early years of Fort Snelling. Although Black history is a minor part of the interpretation at the fort, visitors to the site will be able to see where and how Black soldiers lived at this frontier site and will see the environment that was a part of the famed Dred Scott case. (For more information on Dred Scott, see the listing for St. Louis, Missouri.)

DATE ESTABLISHED:	1820–1824
ADDRESS:	Fort Snelling exits on MN 5 and MN 55 near the Minneapolis-St. Paul International Airport, St. Paul
TELEPHONE:	(612) 725-2428
VISITING HOURS:	Fort, daily May 1–Oct. 1, Mon.–Sat. 9:30–5 and Sun. 11:30–5, closed Nov. 1–Apr. 30 but gift shop open weekends 9–4:30 (call ahead); History Center, Mon.–Sat. 9:30–5 and Sun. 11:30–5; closed weekends and holidays in winter
FEES:	Adults 16 and up, $4; children 6–15, $2; children 5 and under, free
SOURCES:	Stephen E. Osman, site manager, Historic Fort Snelling. Telephone conversation June 19, 1994, Florence Olson, museum shop. Telephone call to site, Sept. 4, 1995. George Ryan, Minnesota Historical Society. *Webster's New Biographical Dictionary*, 897. *National Register of Historic Places*, 377. *Historic Fort Snelling. Dred Scott* v. *Sandford.*

Highland Park Tower

Clarence W. Wigington, one of St. Paul's few African American architects, designed the Highland Park water tower and belatedly was honored for his accomplishment. For many years the design was attributed to a white man, Wigington's supervisor. The tower, built in 1928, is significant both as a vital part of the city's water system and for its architectural distinction.

Clarence Wigington, who was born in Lawrence, Kansas, in 1883, attended high school in Omaha and an architectural school for a year before beginning to work for Thomas Kimball, who was at the time president of the American Institute of Architects. While employed by Kimball, Wigington studied for six years at Professor Wallace's Western School of Art. When Wigington took the city architectural examination, he received the highest grade anyone had ever scored on the test. As a young architect Wigington designed a church and two apartment buildings in Omaha as well as the administration building for North Carolina State University at Durham.

After moving to St. Paul in 1915, Wigington received commissions to design creameries at Elk River and Northfield. He also drew up the plans for the St. James African Methodist Episcopal Church at Central Avenue and Dale Street in St. Paul; the church has since been remodeled. Wigington worked on other buildings in St. Paul, including the Keller Golf Course clubhouse, the Municipal Auditorium, ice palaces, several park structures including the Harriet Island Pavilion, and schools including the Monroe School. Wigington was active in community organizations. He was a member of the Urban League, the Elks Lodge, and the Episcopal Church. He and his wife lived at 679 St. Anthony Avenue during most of their years in St. Paul.

The Highland Park Water Tower is an octagonal, brick-and-cut-stone structure consisting of a base, a shaft, and a lookout area. It has a 200,000-gallon steel tank with a circular staircase around it. One hundred fifty-one steps lead to an observation platform topped by a tile roof and small cupola. The lookout provides a panoramic view of the Twin Cities. Water is pumped from a reservoir into the tower, then flows by gravity to approximately 9,000 homes in the area.

Wigington designed the water tower in 1928, but his accomplishments were not recognized until 1976 (he died in 1967). Ironically, his supervisor's name had appeared in numerous sources as the architect of the building and still appeared on a plaque on the building. In a public ceremony in 1976 the community finally honored Wigington for his "excellence in design of the Highland Park Tower."

The tower is open to the public on special occasions. This significant landmark, designed by an African American registered architect, is listed in the *National Register of Historic Places.*

DATE BUILT: 1928
ADDRESS: 1570 Highland Parkway, St. Paul
VISITING HOURS: Daily, 24 hours
SOURCE: NRHPINF.

Holman Field Administration Building

The Holman Field Administration Building is a large rectangular structure located within the St. Paul Downtown Airport. Black architect Clarence Wesley Wigington's limestone building with its four-story octagonal control tower is considered the finest of his works. One of his Works Progress Administration projects, it was completed in cooperation with the city of St. Paul as a program during the Great Depression.

While Wigington designed many buildings for St. Paul between 1915 and 1949 (see also the entry for Highland Park Tower), all designs from his city office were stamped with the name of the city architect. Only recently were many of the structures realized to be Wigington's designs.

Of his surviving buildings, the Holman Field Administration Building is one of the best preserved. It was completed as part of a project to improve St. Paul's municipal airport, which is separate from the main St. Paul airport. The building is noted for its execution of the moderne architectural style, the fine use of salvaged Kasota stone, and the high standard of craftsmanship.

DATE BUILT: 1939
ADDRESS: 644 Bayfield Street, St. Paul
VISITING HOURS: Daily, 9–dusk
SOURCES: NRHPRF. Telephone call June 19, 1994, Capitol Air, Holman Field Administration Building.

Pilgrim Baptist Church

In 1863 a group of former slaves came to St. Paul from Missouri with their leader, Robert Hickman. That same year they founded Pilgrim Baptist Church, the second-oldest Black congregation in Minnesota and the oldest in St. Paul.

In the early years St. Paul's African American residents lived in different areas of the city. By the 1920s and 1930s, however, they began to cluster increasingly in the area that is now Concordia Avenue.

Members of Pilgrim Baptist Church worked actively to help newcomers to the area to adjust. They assisted in finding jobs, worked for better educational and recreation facilities in the community, and sought protection in the realm of civil liberties. The church history was closely related to the establishment in St. Paul of local chapters of the National Association for the Advancement of Colored People (1913), the Urban League (1923), and the Hallie Q. Brown Community Center (1929).

The first two church buildings of Pilgrim Baptist Church no longer exist. When the present church was constructed in 1928, the location matched the movement of the Black population from the old city uphill to the Rondo neighborhood. This neighborhood began to attract larger numbers of Africans in the 1920s and 1930s; it became predominantly Black in the 1950s and 1960s.

Pilgrim Baptist Church is a large structure constructed of brick with concrete trim. A series of stained-glass windows in the clerestory portray Dr. Martin Luther King Jr. and past ministers of the church.

DATE BUILT: 1928
ADDRESS: 732 W. Central Avenue, St. Paul
TELEPHONE: (612) 224-3011
VISITING HOURS: Private, visitors may drive or walk by
SOURCE: NRHPRF.

Works Consulted

Dred Scott v. *Sandford*. 60 U.S. (19 How.), 393–633.

Historic Fort Snelling. St. Paul, Minn.: Minnesota Historical Society, 1989. [brochure]

National Register of Historic Places. Washington, D.C.: National Park Service, 1976.

Webster's New Biographical Dictionary. Springfield, Mass.: Merriam-Webster, 1988.

Missouri

Canton

Lincoln School

Lincoln School, constructed in 1880, was the first and only schoolhouse built for African American children in Canton. From 1866 until Lincoln School was built, Black children attended school in a former post office building and other makeshift quarters. The first Lincoln schoolteacher, S. S. Seiler, earned only $50 per month in 1866, but lack of funds caused the school to close at the end of the school year. It reorganized in 1868, and classes began meeting in a frame house. The teacher's salary was even lower than before—$30 per month. Better facilities were needed, and classes moved to the African Methodist Church.

By 1871, a large new school was constructed for white students. The facility contrasted strongly with the inadequate facilities for Black children in the church. When parents protested against the inequity, the school board gave an inadequate response by repairing the church building and purchasing new equipment for the school. Parents of the African American children were not satisfied. They continued to petition the school board for a new school.

The school board eventually submitted a proposition to voters for funding to erect a school for Black children at a cost of $800. The proposal passed, and the city constructed the Lincoln School. The brick building, a one-room schoolhouse 42 feet by 24 feet in size, was erected on a wooded lot in the center of Canton. The teacher, M. L. Clay, received a salary of $35 per month. There was a need for adult education, and Clay organized a night school for adults at his own expense.

The original wooden floor was unsuitable because the flooding of the Mississippi River inundated the building each year. As funds became available, the wooden floor later was replaced with concrete, the wood stove was converted to gas, and indoor toilets and electricity were added.

Lincoln School operated for seventy-five years in a strictly segregated era. The school facilities remained inadequate because classrooms lacked the proper furniture, equipment, and textbooks. With the exception of Charles W. Lear, Lincoln's first Black teacher, who served as teacher for a total of thirty-two years, teacher turnover was high.

When Black students graduated from Lincoln School, they were not allowed to attend the white high school in Canton. In 1946, the school board arranged to send Black high school students on a daily round trip journey of 80 miles to Hannibal, Missouri. After the 1954 Supreme Court Decision that outlawed segregation in schools, Lincoln School closed, and Black students began to attend white schools in Canton.

Author Eleanora Tate used Lincoln School as a model for the mythical Douglass School in Nutbush, Missouri, in her stories for children and young adults. The school is listed in the *National Register of Historic Places.* It closed as a schoolhouse in 1954 and was used for years as a storage facility. As of January 1995 the schoolhouse, donated to the city of Canton by the Canton R-5 School District, had deteriorated. The Lincoln School Restoration Association, Inc., a multiethnic organization, was in the initial stages of planning the building's restoration and was having brickwork done to stabilize the exterior. Plans were made to place a plaque on the front of the school as discussions continued on the building's use as a restored schoolhouse, as a museum, or as a visitors center.

Visitors can drive by to view the exterior of the schoolhouse. It is located three blocks east of the Mississippi River at the corner of Martin Park, a municipal park in Canton.

DATE BUILT: 1880

ADDRESS: MO highway B, Canton

VISITING HOURS: Under reconstruction; visitors can drive by

SOURCES: NRHPINF. Telephone conversation Jan. 5, 1995, Carl L. Schmidt, president, Lincoln School Restoration Association, Inc., and executive vice president and cashier, Canton State Bank.

Diamond Vicinity

George Washington Carver National Monument

The George Washington Carver National Monument includes the site where Carver's birthplace cabin once stood as well as structures associated with his boyhood. Carver was born in slavery sometime between 1861 and 1864 on a farm owned by Moses and Susan Carver. Shortly after his birth Carver's father was killed while hauling wood to town on a wagon. When George was still a baby, he, his sister, and his mother were kidnapped by raiders and sold in Arkansas. Although his mother and sister were never seen again, George was returned for a price. The Carvers took George and his older brother, Jim, into their cabin and raised the boys themselves. Because George was a sickly child, he was allowed much time to explore on his own.

As a young boy, George Carver loved the woods and became a close observer of plants, rocks, and the natural surroundings. He was so skilled in nursing sick plants back to life that local people began referring to him as the "plant doctor." The Carvers were kind to the child and encouraged his explorations. When he was eleven or twelve years old, on a trip to Neosho with the Carvers, George saw a line of Black children entering a school. He waited, then went quietly to the schoolhouse and peeped through a knothole. He was astonished to see the students listening to their teacher read, just as the white children did at Locust Grove. He later begged the Carvers to allow him to attend school at Neosho. They agreed and soon watched the child start off on the eight-mile journey to Neosho; he walked off down a dusty road carrying his belongings in a bundle.

By 1876 Carver had learned all that the teacher knew at Neosho's Lincoln School. He attended three more schools, then in 1885, after a seven-year period of study, completed high school in Minneapolis, Kansas. He applied to the Highland College in Kansas, and the college accepted him. However, when he appeared in person, Highland officials turned him away because of his race. Dejected and despondent, Carver moved to the vicinity of Beeler, Kansas. One of the few Black settlers in this area, he took up homesteading with determination in 1866, filing a claim, building a small sod house, and improving his land. He persevered in spite of drought, blizzards, and poor soil. Soon local residents began to respect him for his ability to make plants thrive in difficult conditions and for his talent in construction, music, and painting.

After two years had passed, Carver had regained enough confidence to apply again to enter college. In 1888 he mortgaged his property for $300, then moved to Winterset, Iowa, where he took a job as head cook in the Arcade Hotel. In 1890 he paid his $12 tuition (which left him 10¢) and entered Simpson College in Indianola, Iowa, where he was the only Black student among 300 students. He lived in extremely meager circumstances by operating a laundry in a shack on the edge of the campus. In 1891 he transferred to Iowa State University at Ames; in 1894, near the age of thirty, he was awarded the master of science degree in agriculture. He was appointed to the faculty there, and Iowa State University later honored him by naming an administrative and classroom building Carver Hall.

In 1896 Booker T. Washington, the head of Tuskegee Institute in Alabama, offered Carver a faculty position at Tuskegee. Carver remained there for the rest of his life, teaching and pursuing the research that brought him national prominence. When he died in 1943, he was buried at Tuskegee beside Booker T. Washington. (See the listing for Tuskegee Institute National Historic Site in Tuskegee, Alabama).

The George Washington Carver National Monument is a 210-acre park. The Visitor Center/Museum has exhibits about Carver's life and films about his childhood and adult life. A twelve-minute introductory movie, *The Boyhood of George Washington Carver,* is shown on a continuous basis during the day. The nature trail includes areas associated with Carver's childhood. Be alert for poison ivy and do not drink from the springs or streams. Visitors may see the following points of interest:

Carver birthsite (The one-room cabin where Carver was born no longer exists.)

statue of George Washington Carver as a boy

Carver Spring where, as a boy, Carver collected water for household use

Williams Spring, a pond in the general area of the woods where Carver developed his interest in nature

Moses Carver House (1881) (George Washington Carver never lived in this house, which was built when he was a young man. However, he visited Moses and Susan Carver here before he went to college.)

Carver family cemetery, where Moses and Susan Carver, the owners of George and his brother Jim, are buried (Dr. Carver was buried at Tuskegee Institute in Alabama.)

DATE BUILT: House, 19th century; monument, 1943

ADDRESS: 2.5 miles southwest of Diamond (from Neosho or Carthage, take US 71A to Diamond; go west 2 miles on County V, then south about 1 mile)

TELEPHONE: (417) 325-4151

VISITING HOURS: Daily 9–5

FEES: Adults, $1; children 6 or younger, free

SOURCES: Telephone conversation Sept. 3, 1995, Dena Shaw, park ranger, George Washington Carver National Monument. Rebecca Harriett, chief ranger, National Park Service, George W. Carver National Monument. L. Bentz, board member, Madison County Historical Society, Winterset, Iowa. *National Register of Historic Places,* 410. "The Gentle Genius: George Washington Carver." *George Washington Carver.*

Fort Leonard Wood

U.S. Army Engineer Museum

During World War II Fort Leonard Wood was a segregated post established to train enlisted engineers. Because the largest proportion of Black soldiers in the combat support branches of the Army served in the engineers, thousands trained at this post.

The U.S. Army Engineer Museum consists of fourteen buildings located on a twenty-one-acre site; these buildings were built and used as temporary mobilization barracks, mess halls, day rooms, and orderly rooms and for other purposes. An Army Engineer Interpretation Section is housed in a new museum building. The site includes the original Black officers' club and the training sites of several Black engineer groups.

Since 1950, more than three quarters of a million Black men and women have passed through the integrated Fort Leonard Wood training center.

DATE BUILT:	1941
ADDRESS:	Corner of Nebraska and South Dakota Avenues, Fort Leonard Wood
TELEPHONE:	(314) 596-0169
VISITING HOURS:	Mon.–Sat. 10–4; closed Christmas, New Year's Day
FEES:	None
SOURCES:	Robert K. Combs, U.S. Army Engineer Museum. Telephone conversation Jan. 5, 1993, John Parkham, specialist.

Hannibal

Eighth and Center Streets Baptist Church

The Eighth and Center Streets Baptist Church is a major landmark of Hannibal's African American community. This historic church grew out of a congregation that had its origins in a racially mixed church long before the Civil War. Both white and Black people originally worshiped together in the small Zoar Church, which was later reorganized as the Hannibal United Baptist Church.

With the approach of the Civil War, tensions grew, and church members split along racial lines. White members formed the First Baptist Church while Black members moved to the location on Eighth and Center Streets. The trustees—described as "free persons of color"—purchased the land, which included most of the block, for $37.50. The first church they built was shared by worshipers of different denominations, and school classes met in the rear.

Between 1861 and 1865, the school's teacher was Blanche K. Bruce, a man who was born a slave in Prince Edward County, Virginia, and taken to Missouri before the Civil War. He escaped in 1861 and came to Hannibal, where he organized the school in this church. When the Civil War ended, Bruce moved to Mississippi. From 1875 to 1881, he served a full term as a United States Senator from Mississippi.

The school organized by Bruce in Hannibal was housed in the original church structure until 1870, when a free public school for African American children was built by the town. The present church structure was probably built around 1872. Pastor Oliver H. Webb and other church members worked late at night, after their regular daily work was completed, to construct it.

Eighth and Center Streets Baptist Church, a red-brick, rectangular building, is in the Romanesque revival style. The high-arched ceiling of the sanctuary still has its original tin ceiling, and twelve stained-glass windows on the main floor are inscribed with the names of the organizations that donated them. A parsonage was constructed in 1903, and lighting and heating systems were installed between 1919 and 1922.

Eighth and Center Streets Baptist Church has remained a vital part of the religious, educational, and community life of Hannibal. The church is significant also for its association with Senator Bruce.

DATE BUILT: c1872
ADDRESS: 722 Center Street, Hannibal
TELEPHONE: (314) 221-5721
VISITING HOURS: Weekdays, call in advance to see the interior; Sun. school, 9:30; Sun. service, 10:45
SOURCES: NRHPINF. Telephone conversation Sept. 9, 1995, Reverend Wesley Foster, pastor, and Hiawatha Crow, church member in charge of restoration, Eighth and Center Streets Baptist Church.

Jefferson City

Lincoln University Hilltop Campus Historic District

The Lincoln University Hilltop campus includes several buildings, largely Georgian in style, designed over a quarter-of-a-century period. These include John W. Damel Hall (1937), Richard B. Foster Hall (1923), Anderson M. Schweich Hall (1931), Benjamin F. Allen Hall (1936), Power Plant (1923), Nathan B. Young Hall (1930), and Inman E. Page Library (1948).

Lincoln Institute, named for President Abraham Lincoln, was founded after the Civil War by men of the Sixty-second United States Colored Infantry, a unit that served in Louisiana and Texas until 1866. Two white officers of the regiment noted that the soldiers would have no place to continue their education after they were discharged from the army. Although many had learned to read and write in the army, white schools would not accept them. One of the officers, Richard B. Foster, had a long-standing interest in the abolitionist movement and in providing educational opportunities for African Americans. He had been raised in New Hampshire and had graduated from Dartmouth College. For a number of years he taught in schools for African American students in Illinois and Indiana. He also participated in the John Brown raid on Fort Titus, Kansas, in 1856. After President Lincoln authorized the establishment of Black regiments, Foster volunteered to join the Sixty-second, where he rose to the rank of captain.

The men of the regiment and their white officers worked together to establish the new school. The officers' fund-raising efforts brought in $1,034.60. Soldiers of the Sixty-second Colored Infantry contributed $3,966.50 and the Sixty-fifth Colored Infantry also made a donation. Their sacrifices were great, considering that some of the soldiers contributed $100 out of a yearly wage of only $156. The Freedmen's Bureau added to the funds. At last the new school opened in an old log cabin on a place called "Hobo Hill."

The men's determination was great, even though the early structure was poor almost beyond imagination. Captain Foster described approaching the building on a rainy day when a flood had swept the bridge away. He had a half-hour detour on a route that required him to climb over several fences. The building provided little relief from the weather because it had no windows and rain leaked through from many openings in the roof. On the school's opening day, there were no tables, chairs, desks, or benches. In spite of the poor facilities, two pupils showed up, and additional pupils enrolled every day during the next few weeks.

Political leaders—both Black and white—joined forces to gain the first state appropriations for Lincoln Institute. The state legislature contributed $5,000 annually with the understanding that the school would train Black teachers. In 1871 the school acquired a new campus and completed its first building. The state of Missouri took over the operation of Lincoln Institute in 1879, adding such new buildings as a gymnasium and the president's house. The college became known as Lincoln University in 1921.

Lincoln University's leaders wanted to offer an education as extensive as that of the segregated University of Missouri, but growth at Lincoln was held back by unfavorable conditions. For example, during the early years, Jefferson City was segregated, and many young professors had to live in dormitory rooms because they could not find housing in the city.

In the 1930s the older buildings were replaced by the large brick structures still standing in the Lincoln University Hilltop Campus historic district. The university expanded to include a law school, a school of journalism, and a graduate school. During this period Lincoln University was successful in building an atmosphere of scholarship that attracted outstanding Black intellectuals to the faculty.

Today, although the majority of the student body is white, Lincoln remains unique as the only university founded after the Civil War for former African American soldiers. It is a testament to the soldiers who, recently freed from slavery, sacrificed to build a university where they and following generations would be able to obtain a quality education.

DATE ESTABLISHED:	1866
ADDRESS:	820 Chestnut Street, Jefferson City
TELEPHONE:	(314) 681-5000
VISITING HOURS:	Library, Mon.–Thurs. 8 A.M.–11 P.M., Sat. 1–5, Sun. 3–11 P.M.
FEES:	None
SOURCE:	NRHPINF.

Kansas City

Eighteenth and Vine Historic District

Of the neighborhoods historically identified with Kansas City's Black population, the Eighteenth and Vine Historic District is the only one with many buildings intact from the early years. The buildings are located along East Eighteenth Street, Vine Street, and adjacent streets in the eastern section of Kansas City. Most are commercial buildings constructed between 1885 and 1930, as well as churches, dwellings, and social halls built before 1940.

Many African Americans arrived in the earliest days of settlement, when slaves accompanied their owners to Kansas City. By 1860 there were 190 slaves in the total city population of 4,418. At first the slaves were scattered throughout the city because they lived near their owners. After the Civil War the city passed laws segregating the races. By the 1880s many Black people had moved to the riverfront area. A decade later, African Americans, who represented 10 percent of the city population, had begun to move to several other areas in the city. The intersection of Eighteenth and Vine Streets was the center of an area that became home to hundreds of Black residents between 1880 and 1890. After 1900 the Black population doubled as newcomers came from rural southern communities to Kansas City. They worked as laborers in warehouses and manufacturing facilities and as maids and janitors, laundry workers, chauffeurs, porters, shop owners, teachers, attorneys, and physicians. Most worked in low-paying occupations, and they typically rented rather than owned their homes. As the population expanded, multifamily apartments were built along East Nineteenth Street.

In the 1800s, most businesses had been owned by white citizens, while African Americans worked in the stores. Between 1900 and 1920, however, Eighteenth and Vine became a center of Black business establishments. The 1920s were years of growth when the area became dense with residences, commercial buildings, schools, and churches. During this period many residences were razed to be replaced by commercial buildings.

Kansas City rose to prominence in the 1920s as a center for music known as Kansas City jazz. The neighborhood was alive with clubs that often operated twenty-four hours a day, and musicians such as Bennie Moten; Count Basie, piano player and well-known Kansas City band leader; and Walter Page made Kansas City known as a jazz center throughout the country. Count Basie lived at 1424½ East Eighteenth Street and Bennie Moten lived at 1616 East Eighteenth Street; their residences no longer are standing.

With the arrival of racial integration in the 1960s and 1970s, many shoppers began to patronize stores in other areas and many professionals moved their offices to other sections of the city; with these changes the area began to decline. In the 1990s, recognizing the value of preserving their history, many Kansas City citizens began taking pride again in the Eighteenth and Vine Historic District and joined those who had remained there in efforts to restore and revitalize this community. The historic district is significant both for the buildings, which show the development of the early Black community in Kansas City, and for the interesting history of several of the buildings. They are arranged below in a walking tour of the area bounded by The Paseo, East Eighteenth Street, Woodland Avenue, and East Nineteenth Street. The tour, which also encompasses Vine and Highland Streets, begins on East Eighteenth Street.

DATE BUILT: 1885–1940

ADDRESS: Roughly bounded by The Paseo, E. Eighteenth Street, Woodland Avenue, and E. Nineteenth Street, including Vine and Highland Streets; see text for addresses of individual sites

VISITING HOURS: Most buildings privately owned, access varies; visitors may walk or drive by

SOURCES: Office of Housing and Community Development and Landmarks Commission of Kansas City. NRHPINF. Carolyn J. Anderson, President, Culturally Speaking. Telephone conversation Jan. 9, 1995, Rennaldo Andrews III, curator of exhibits, Black Archives of Mid-America. Telephone conversation Sept. 10, 1995, Raymond Doswell, curator, Negro League Baseball Museum. Telephone conversation Sept. 12, 1995, Renaldo R. Andrews, curator of exhibits, Black Archives of Mid-America. "18th & Vine Kansas City, Mo. Historic District, A Walking Tour."

Monarch Baseball Club

The business office of the Monarch Baseball Club was located at 1513½ East Eighteenth Street. By 1940 the office relocated in the Lincoln Building (see that listing, following). The National Negro League was organized in Kansas City in 1920, and the Monarchs were 1924 world champions of the league. Players included Leroy "Satchel" Paige as pitcher and Jackie Robinson as shortstop. The team was famous throughout the country in the 1920s and 1930s. Parades were held on East Eighteenth Street to mark the opening of the season. Leroy Paige, who became the first Black pitcher in the American League in 1948, is buried at Forest Hill Cemetery, Sixty-ninth Street and Troost Avenue. There is a memorial tombstone at his grave.

Jones Recreation Parlor

The two-story brick building housed the Jones Recreation Parlor. The owner, Junius Jones Sr., converted the building from a grocery store to a billiard parlor. Many musicians, including Count Basie and Duke Ellington, socialized at this site. The original 1911 inlaid tables are still inside. The building also houses the Jones Barber Shop.

DATE BUILT: 1881
ADDRESS: 1514 E. Eighteenth Street, Kansas City
TELEPHONE: John A. Jones Recreation Parlor and Jones Barber Shop, (816) 471-9784

1600–1610 East Eighteenth Street

The two-story, brick commercial building at 1600–1610 East Eighteenth Street was built about 1905. The storefronts have been remodeled. During the 1910s the building housed drugstores, restaurants, a clothing store, and grocery stores. Apartments and offices were on the second floor, including the local Elks' Rest Club. The El Capitan Club was an important jazz club in this building in the early 1940s. As part of the Eighteenth and Vine restoration, the city is remodeling a section of the building to house the International Jazz Museum. The exterior will retain its historic appearance.

DATE BUILT: c1905
ADDRESS: 1600–1610 E. Eighteenth Street, Kansas City

Lincoln Building

At 1601 East Eighteenth Street is a three-story landmark building that originally housed the Lincoln Furniture Company on the first floor. The Holmes Music Store occupied part of the first floor in the mid-1920s. Some sections on the first floor have their original pressed-metal ceilings. Doctors and attorneys occupied offices on the upper floors; two large dance halls on the third floor were rented out for parties and jazz performances. The Urban League of Kansas City once had its headquarters in the building.

The Black Economic Union purchased and remodeled the Lincoln Building in 1979. A variety of businesses and civic organizations are located here, including Culturally Speaking, a shop that carries books, African American art reproductions, and other multicultural wares. The Kansas City branch of the NAACP once occupied room 231 in the Lincoln Building. The building's highlight is the Negro League Baseball Museum that houses professionally designed displays of photographs and artifacts as well as interactive exhibits for fans of all ages.

DATE BUILT: 1921; remodeled, 1981
ADDRESS: 1601 E. Eighteenth Street, Kansas City
TELEPHONE: Culturally Speaking, (816) 842-8151; NAACP, (816) 421-1191; Negro League Baseball Museum, (816) 221-1920
VISITING HOURS: Culturally Speaking, Tues.–Sat. 10:30–5:30; Negro League Baseball Museum, Tues.–Sat. 10–4:30, Sun. 9–4:30
FEES: National League Baseball Museum, adults, $2; children 5–12, $1; children under 5, free

Gem Theater

The two-story brick and terra-cotta Gem Theater was constructed in 1912 as the Star Theater. The theater, which featured vaudeville and motion pictures, was converted into a nightclub in 1934. Remodeling added a cream-colored, glazed terra-cotta detail on the facade in 1924 and a large metal and glass marquee about 1940.

DATE BUILT: 1912
ADDRESS: 1615 E. Eighteenth Street, Kansas City

New Rialto Theater

The three-story New Rialto Theater originally opened in 1922 as the Highland Garden Theater. In the late 1930s and early 1940s it was known as Scott's Show Bar and the Boone Theater. The Boone Theater was named after the famed Black jazz pianist, Blind Boone.

DATE BUILT: 1924
ADDRESS: 1701 E. Eighteenth Street, Kansas City

Lucille's Paradise Band Box

Lucille's Paradise Band Box was located at 1713 East Eighteenth Street. Charlie "Bird" Parker played for a short time at this club before moving to Chicago.

ADDRESS: 1713 E. Eighteenth Street, Kansas City

Kansas City Call Building

The Kansas City Call Building has been occupied by this newspaper since 1922. The three-story section was built in 1888, and the two-story section was added around 1890. The facades were altered in the 1960s with added fronts. Chester Arthur Franklin, an influential Missouri citizen, founded the *Kansas City Call* in 1919. The late Roy Wilkins, director of the National Association for the Advancement of Colored People, once served as news editor.

DATE BUILT: 1888
ADDRESS: 1715 E. Eighteenth Street, Kansas City
TELEPHONE: (816) 842-3804

Attucks School

Attucks School is the only educational building located within the Eighteenth and Vine area. The school was named for Crispus Attucks, a Black man and the first person to be killed in the Boston Massacre. It is Kansas City's oldest continuously occupied school built for Black students. When the Kansas City school board organized in 1867, a census listed 250 Black school-aged children in the city. There had been a dramatic increase in the African American population after the Civil War, when former slaves sought jobs in Kansas City's industries. The city built Lincoln School at Tenth and McGee Streets for Black students and opened four more schools for African Americans in the 1880s and 1890s.

The city put up the first Attucks School structure in 1893 on East Eighteenth Street. The school staff consisted of a principal and two assistant teachers. By 1904 enrollment had increased, and more space was needed. The city purchased property on Woodland Avenue and in 1905 constructed the two-story school at a cost of $36,811. The new schoolhouse opened with several hundred students. Most came from the predominantly Black Paseo district near Eighteenth and Vine. By 1911, 560 students were attending, and the school was becoming overcrowded. A two-story wing containing a gymnasium, an auditorium, and classrooms was constructed in 1922. By 1950 Attucks School enrolled nearly 1,000 students, one of the highest enrollments of Black students in Kansas City's schools.

Attucks School is located on an urban lot near a manufacturing and commercial section of Kansas City. The school retains many of its original features, including hexagonal floor tiles in the lobbies, stairs with iron newel posts, wrought-iron balusters, and the original wood floors. With the onset of integration in the 1960s, Attucks became a grade school for all races. The school is listed in the *National Register of Historic Places.*

DATE BUILT: 1893; addition, 1922
ADDRESS: 1815 Woodlawn Avenue, Kansas City

Centennial United Methodist Church

The congregation of Centennial United Methodist Church organized in the late 1880s. The church purchased the Olivet Congregational Church building on this site around 1906 and razed the building. The present imposing stone structure, constructed in 1928, has a two-story portico in the Doric order.

DATE ESTABLISHED: Congregation, 1880s; building, 1928
ADDRESS: 1834 Woodland Avenue, Kansas City
TELEPHONE: (816) 421-5527

St. Paul Missionary Baptist Church

St. Paul Missionary Baptist Church (now Grace Temple Non-Denominational Church) is the oldest church structure in the historic district. It was built as a brick, one-story structure and was later remodeled.

DATE BUILT: 1918–1919; remodeled, 1942
ADDRESS: 1812 Highland Avenue, Kansas City
TELEPHONE: Grace Temple, (816) 421-3783

Mutual Musicians' Foundation Building

The Mutual Musicians' Foundation Building was constructed in 1906 as a duplex. In 1928 the Black Musicians Union Local 627 formed to protect jazz musicians and to seek consistent wages for its members. The union acquired the building and converted it into a dance hall and clubhouse where jazz musicians could meet to socialize, rehearse, and perform. It became one of America's great jazz centers. The building is listed in the *National Register of Historic Places.*

DATE BUILT: 1906
ADDRESS: 1823 Highland Avenue, Kansas City
TELEPHONE: (816) 471-5212
VISITING HOURS: Tours by appointment Mon.–Fri. 11–6

Highland Avenue Residences

In the 1950s and 1960s when integration opened up new areas of the city, many of the original neighborhood residences were razed, replaced by vacant lots and parking lots. Of an area that once extended to Twelfth Street, the Eighteenth and Vine community is all that remains. A few residences remain; they are located at 1816, 1818, 1820, 1822, and 1824 Highland Avenue.

Black Archives of Mid-America

The Black Archives of Mid-America is located just beyond the historic district but is well worth a visit. Once the site of the all-Black Hose Reel Company No. 11, the old firehouse now is home to a two-floor, 1700-square-foot museum with emphasis on the experiences of African Americans in Kansas City. Museum collections include books, periodicals, newsletters, documents, and artifacts. The archive includes the collection of the choreographer Alvin Ailey as well as letters of scientist George Washington Carver and author Langston Hughes. In addition to displays on Kansas City jazz and the Buffalo Soldiers, the museum has a special treasure—it is the meeting place of a living unit of the Greater Kansas City–Fort Leavenworth chapter of the Tenth Cavalry—the Buffalo Soldiers.

ADDRESS: 2033 Vine Street, Kansas City
TELEPHONE: (816) 483-1300
VISITING HOURS: Mon.–Fri. 9–4:30, weekends by appointment
FEES: Adults, $2 donation; children and students, $.50 donation; all welcome whether or not making a donation

Urban League of Kansas City

The Urban League of Kansas City building has a history as a community service center. In 1919 a community services organization at this site provided a place for recreation for soldiers. Later known as the Vine Street Community Center, it became affiliated with the National Urban League in 1920. The Urban League has since moved to another site.

DATE OF SIGNIFICANCE: 1919
ADDRESS: 1805 Vine Street, Kansas City

Roberts Building

The Roberts Building, with its exterior of glazed, white brick, was the site of America's first Black automobile dealership. Homer Roberts built the structure with Black real estate agent John Sears. Roberts opened his automobile dealership on the first floor and leased other spaces for stores and professional offices.

DATE BUILT: 1923
ADDRESS: 1824–1836 Vine Street, Kansas City

Ol' Kentucky Barbecue

The one-story, brick commercial building at 1516–1522 East Nineteenth Street has four storefronts oriented along both East Nineteenth Street and Vine Street. Ol' Kentucky Barbecue was known for delicious barbecued ribs and was a gathering place for young jazz musicians. Later it became known as Dixie-Lan Bar-B-Cue. The adjoining storefront to the east housed the Palace Drug Company, later known as Woods Drug Store.

DATE BUILT: 1909
ADDRESS: 1516–1522 E. Nineteenth Street, Kansas City

Sears Apartments

The Sears Apartments were built by John Sears, an African American real estate professional. The three identical two-story brick buildings were both residential and commercial. The first floors contained shops such as Lulu's Candy and Smoke Shop.

DATE BUILT: 1910–1911
ADDRESSES: 1705–1707, 1711–1713, 1715–1717 E. Nineteenth Street, Kansas City

Jamison Temple Christian Methodist Episcopal Church

Jamison Temple C.M.E. Church once occupied the building at 1813–1815 The Paseo. Now the Holy Ghost New Testament Church occupies the site. The Jamison Temple congregation was organized in 1887. The present brick building was constructed in 1926 with neoclassical details; the lotus flower capitals on the columns show an Egyptian influence.

DATE ESTABLISHED: Congregation, 1887; present building, 1926
ADDRESS: 1813–1815 The Paseo, Kansas City
TELEPHONE: Holy Ghost New Testament Church, (816) 474-6881

Marshall Vicinity

Free Will Baptist Church of Pennytown*

The Free Will Baptist Church of Pennytown is one of the most important Black historic sites in the state. Black workmen built the rectangular tile-block building among rural farmsteads. Pennytown was a Black hamlet settled by emancipated slaves who purchased their small parcels of land from white landowners. After Joe Penny made the first purchase of eight acres, other Black settlers followed his lead. Many paid between fifty and one hundred dollars for their land.

Families survived and built their community by farming, hunting, and gathering food that grew wild. Some people worked as laborers for white landowners. For all of the families, survival depended on cooperation, and they completed much of their work on a communal basis. For example, families gathered at each house on a planned date for the annual hog killing. When it was time to chop wood for the stoves, the men moved from house to house. They also hunted, trapped, and fished; in winter they hauled ice to a community icehouse. The women met on a weekly basis to make pies, cakes, quilts, and rugs, which they later raffled at the church. Funds raised from the raffles built a community fund for health insurance and other needs. Women foraged for extra food by gathering gooseberries, nuts, mushrooms, and wild greens.

Prior to 1866 worshipers had to hold services in homes or in open brush arbors. After a white landowner gave permission to build a church on his land, African Americans dismantled what had been either a former white church or school building and reconstructed it as the first Pennytown Baptist Church. This wood frame structure housed the congregation from 1886 to 1914. Church members also used the building as a school and community center. The congregation purchased the half-acre of land in 1894.

When the first church burned, a second building was constructed in 1926. To raise funds for the tile blocks, the congregation held dinners, shoebox auctions, and other fund-raisers. A local family donated pews and a piano in the 1930s that are still in use.

In the 1920s and 1930s, falling agricultural prices compelled the men of Pennytown to find work at more-distant farms. Some families began to move closer to the areas of employment. The number of families in Pennytown declined steeply in the 1930s and 1940s; by 1945 only Francis and Willa Spears remained. In 1977 Francis Spears (now deceased), the last Pennytown resident, sold his land to a petroleum company.

Farmland surrounded the church property on three sides, and the Missouri Farmers' Association sought to purchase the entire site and bulldoze the historic church. Although the inhabitants of the area had moved to other locations, they treasured the church, which reminded them of a way of life that had remained unchanged from the 1800s through World War II.

Former church members and their descendants celebrate this history in an annual homecoming at the church on the first Sunday in August. They also have initiated plans to restore the church and to open it to visitors. The Free Will Baptist Church of Pennytown, the only surviving institutional building located at a rural freedmen's hamlet, is listed in the *National Register of Historic Places.*

DATE ESTABLISHED: Town, 1871; church, 1881, 1925

ADDRESS: Off MO UU, 8 miles southeast of Marshall (from I-70 take US 65N to County Road 218; go east on County Road 218 to County Road 205; go south on County Road 205, Pennytown is located on the east side of the road)

TELEPHONE: (816) 886-7384

VISITING HOURS: Church is now closed, visitors may drive by

SOURCES: The late Josephine R. Lawrence, former head of restoration committee. Telephone conversation Jan. 5, 1995, Virginia Houston, head of church restoration committee. Cathie Forbes, Marshall Public Library.

St. Charles

African Methodist Episcopal Church of St. Charles

The A.M.E. Church of St. Charles (historically called the African Church) was built by slaves before the Civil War. The historic structure probably is the earliest Black church in St. Charles. In 1855 Jeremiah Riggs purchased land in St. Charles and sold part of it to trustees for building a church for the A.M.E. Church South. Completion of the church, with its handmade bricks and hand-hewn timbers, was a major event in the Black community. A school operated in the building, providing daytime classes for children and evening classes for adults. When the Civil War ended, church ownership was transferred to five Black trustees for $1. The congregation outgrew the small building and in 1872 constructed another church nearby.

The African Church of St. Charles is a small brick structure with a low-pitched gable roof. The building, no longer used as a church, is located on a small lot in the center of town surrounded by narrow strips of grass. Ownership of the church had changed, and by 1943 the structure was vacant. In 1947 the interior was completely remodeled for use as a private residence.

DATE BUILT: c1855; current structure, 1872

ADDRESS: 554 Madison Street, St. Charles

VISITING HOURS: Private, visitors may walk or drive by

SOURCES: NRHPINF. Telephone conversation Jan. 5, 1995, Ann King, local history librarian, Katherine Linneman Branch, St. Charles City/County Library.

Lewis and Clark Center

St. Charles was a frontier outpost on the Missouri River used by fur traders and Indians. After a long period of preparation and gathering of supplies, the Lewis and Clark Expedition embarked from St. Charles on May 20, 1804, on the long and arduous journey to the Pacific Ocean and back. York, a slave with no last name, was the only African American member of the expedition. Owned by Captain William Clark, one of the expedition leaders, York had been a constant companion to Clark from their childhood. York's physical strength, stamina, and intelligence probably were factors in his being selected to go on the grueling expedition.

The journey began in 1803 after President Thomas Jefferson gained an appropriation from Congress for an exploration of the Missouri River from its source to the Pacific Ocean. The stated purpose of the expedition was to extend commerce and to gain geographic and scientific knowledge about the wilderness region. However, a few trappers had established lucrative fur trades in some of the remote areas, and ownership of the unexplored wilderness had been contested between nations. Jefferson wanted to consolidate the U.S. claim to the region, and he urged expedition leaders to establish positive relationships with Native Americans along the way. Friendly relations would create conditions for safe passage and trading in Native American territory. Fortuitously, Louisiana was acquired by the United States in 1803, just as the journey began, making it even more important to learn about the territory.

Meriwether Lewis, 29, and William Clark, 33, men with leadership and wilderness skills, were chosen to lead the expedition. Every person in the group faced the same conditions—sweltering heat, furious storms, and raging waters. They experienced sickness, hunger, and frostbite and infestations of mosquitoes, fleas, and ticks and the sting of prickly pear thorns that slashed the feet. Some were attacked by grizzly bears, and a few barely missed being trampled by thundering herds of buffalo. They were threatened by Sioux, who were accustomed to receiving tribute from white traders who passed through their territory.

York was among the first persons who were not Native American to view these spectacular wilderness scenes, and he experienced the same trials that the other men experienced. In the Great Falls area where Clark, Charbonneau, and an Indian woman, Sacajawea, almost were swept into raging waters, York, mindless of the danger to himself, plunged into the harsh and forbidding terrain to search for them.

On one occasion York was allowed to vote with the group on an important decision, a privilege unheard of for a slave. He also helped to establish good relationships with the Native Americans. Most had never seen a Black man before, and they regarded York with awe because of his size, strength, and agility. Intensely curious, Native Americans gathered in excitement to see the Black man in the expedition; they regarded York as "big medicine," a term reserved for powerful phenomena that could not be explained.

The men met their goal of traversing the distance to the Pacific Ocean. On the return trip, they learned that many United States citizens, not having heard from them, had given them up for dead. On their arrival in St. Louis, almost everyone in town lined the waterfront to cheer for them. The expedition members, seen as heroes, received waves of acclaim as well as gifts of land. For York, however, the acclaim was brief, and he received no land. Instead, he soon was returned to his former duties as a slave.

For many years after his return, York had to devote his life to easing the life of his master. However, after having lived in near equality with the other men, he found it hard to accept his former completely subservient role. A rift grew between Clark and York—for years historians wondered why. Then, in 1988 some descendants of the Clark family discovered in an attic trunk a stack of letters that William Clark had written to his brother, Jonathan. The Filson Club of Louisville, Kentucky, a historical association that already owned a collection of Clark family papers and artifacts, acquired the newly found letters; eleven of them contained comments about York, indicating that the trouble between Clark and York began when York was taken to St. Louis. The move had separated York from his wife, and he asked to be allowed to remain in the Louisville area with her. Clark regarded the slave's request as a sign of disloyalty. Angrily Clark allowed York to visit his wife for a few weeks. When York continued to complain about not being able to live with his wife, Clark became determined not to gratify his slave's wishes, even if it meant that York would have to be sold. Clark also expressed anger that York believed he should be freed because of his service on the expedition; this was seen as impudence and insolence and was followed by a "severe trouncing" and later by a jail sentence.

Finally, Clark decided to teach York a lesson by hiring him out to a harsh master. The letters suggest that York was broken by the experience. To add to York's despair, in 1811 his wife's owner moved to Natchez, Mississippi, and York knew he would never see her again. Broken, he finally sought to make up for the rift with Clark. In 1815, still a slave, York was allowed to drive a wagon and team around Louisville for Clark's business. Eventually, York was freed. Clark helped him establish a drayage business, but the operation was not successful.

There were differing accounts about the end of York's life, but none has been verified. It is certain that he was part of a heroic nineteenth-century American experience and that he never received the acclaim and respect that he should have received for his accomplishments. Clark's letters only faintly outline York's dilemma as an African American—no matter what York's achievements were, his country still set him apart and denied him the full fruits of dignity and freedom.

Exhibits at the Lewis and Clark Center include information about York and his contributions.

ADDRESS: 701 S. Riverside Drive, St. Charles

TELEPHONE: (314) 947-3199

VISITING HOURS: Daily 10:30–4:30; closed Christmas

FEES: Adults, $1; children and students, $.50

SOURCES: *The Journals of Lewis and Clark. Lewis and Clark, Historic Places Associated with Their Transcontinental Exploration (1804–06). "I Wish You to See and Know All."* The Academic American Encyclopedia.

St. Charles County Historical Society

The St. Charles County Historical Society maintains a large file of information on Jean Baptiste Point Du Sable, a Black man who was the first permanent non-Native American settler in the area that is now Chicago, Illinois.

Du Sable was born in Haiti in 1745 to a French father and a Black mother who was a former slave. Educated in France, he lived in Louisiana as well as St. Louis, Missouri, and Peoria, Illinois. He married Katherine, a Pottawatomie Indian. In 1772 he built a trading post at the portage between the Chicago River and the Des Plaines River and began transforming the wilderness into a trading center. He continued to move about over the years, maintaining two farms and additional trading posts. In 1800 Du Sable sold his post for $1,200 and moved to St. Charles, Missouri. He died in that city August 28, 1818, and was buried in the cemetery of the St. Charles Borromeo Church. In 1968 a memorial was dedicated to him at the church cemetery.

ADDRESS: 101 S. Main Street, St. Charles

TELEPHONE: (314) 946-9828

VISITING HOURS: Mon., Wed., Fri. 10–3

SOURCE: Carol Wilkins, Archivist, St. Charles County Historical Society.

St. Louis

Scott Joplin National Historic Landmark*

The Scott Joplin residence may be the only existing structure relating to the life of the talented composer who was born in 1868 in Texarkana, Arkansas, to Giles and Florence Joplin. His father was an ex-slave and his mother was a freedwoman. As a boy, Joplin enjoyed playing the piano, and when he came to St. Louis as a young man, he began playing piano in the city saloons. He traveled with different musical groups before settling for a period in Sedalia, Missouri. In Sedalia Joplin played the piano, published ragtime music, and enrolled at the George Smith College for Negroes. At that time he published the *Maple Leaf Rag*, a composition that later sold over 1 million copies.

The Joplin residence is a two-story row house divided into flats. The second-floor east flat was Joplin's first real home from 1901 to 1903 after marrying Belle Hayden. He earned his living by composing and teaching. Many of Joplin's most popular works came off the press during the time he lived at this location. One was *The Entertainer*, a composition used in the 1970s as the theme song for the movie *The Sting*.

Joplin later moved to New York where he continued to compose. His popular compositions —later called ragtime—were recognized as an important contribution to American music. In 1911 he wrote the Black folk opera *Treemonisha*. Since publishers did not take seriously the idea of a Black opera, he had to publish the work at his own expense. He was unable to have the opera staged in New York. The Atlanta Symphony Orchestra, with the cooperation of Atlanta and Morehouse universities, gave *Treemonisha* its first full performance in 1972. Joplin did not live to see the day, unfortunately; he died in poverty in New York in 1917 and was buried in St. Michael's Cemetery in Brooklyn. After a researcher rediscovered his unmarked grave, the American Society of Composers, Authors, and Publishers honored the composer with a marker at the site. He was awarded a Pulitzer Prize posthumously in 1976.

The Scott Joplin house is located in a community of residential and industrial properties. The restoration of the residence provides for a visitors' center, modern exhibit and music galleries, and Joplin-period rooms. Long-term development plans include reviving the Rosebud Club in the building next door, a favorite location for ragtime players. The Scott Joplin residence has been designated a state historic site and is listed in the *National Register of Historic Places*.

DATE OF SIGNIFICANCE: Joplin residence, 1901–1903

ADDRESS: House, 2658 Delmar Boulevard; office, 2754 Bacon Street, St. Louis

TELEPHONE: (314) 533-1003

VISITING HOURS: Call for information

SOURCES: Annette D. Bridges, Site Administrator, Scott Joplin House State Historic Site. NRHPINF.

Old Courthouse, Site of the Dred Scott Case*

When a slave named Dred Scott sued for his freedom in the 1850s, the case highlighted the great issue of slavery, inflaming and dividing the country and its citizens. Although the decision was perhaps intended to placate slaveowners and to quiet the growing unrest over slavery, it aroused the ire of abolitionists and fanned the flames that led to the Civil War.

Scott, a slave, filed suit at the courthouse in St. Louis to gain his freedom. He was born in slavery about 1795 in Southampton County, Virginia, and came to Missouri with his original owner in 1827. His owner sold him to an army surgeon, Dr. John Emerson, who took Scott to a military post at Rock Island, Illinois, where he lived from 1834 to 1836. Illinois was a free state.

When the army transferred Dr. Emerson to Fort Snelling in 1836, he again took Scott with him. Fort Snelling was in the old Northwest Territory, an area that became the state of Minnesota in 1858. Although Congress prohibited slavery in that area in accord with the Missouri Compromise, Emerson held Scott in slavery there until 1838. While at Fort Snelling Scott married another slave named Harriet in 1836. They had two children, Eliza and Lizzie.

In 1838 Dr. Emerson returned to Missouri, taking with him Dred, Harriet, and Eliza. (Lizzie had not yet been born.) After Emerson died, his widow sold Scott to a new owner, John Sanford. In 1846 Scott filed a lawsuit against the new owner, John Sanford (erroneously spelled Sandford in the lawsuit), claiming to be a free man because he had resided in Illinois, a free state, and in the Northwest Territory. The Ordinance of 1787 (frequently called the Northwest Ordinance), adopted by the Congress of the Confederation, had forbidden slavery.

Two of three trials in connection with this famous case were held in this building. Abolitionists watched the case closely, because a ruling against Scott meant that even if a slave had lived in free territory, this did not necessarily guarantee his or her freedom.

The final decision was made in the U.S. Supreme Court at St. Louis. Chief Justice Roger B. Taney wrote the court's opinion. First was the question of whether Scott had the right to sue in a court of the United States. Taney asked:

> Can a negro, whose ancestors were imported into this country, and sold as slaves, become a member of the political community formed and brought into existence by the Constitution of the United States, and as such become entitled to all the rights, and privileges, and immunities, guaranteed by that instrument to the citizen?[1]

Taney concluded that he could not. The majority of the Court reasoned that Black people were not regarded by the writers of the Constitution as citizens; therefore, they had none of the rights and privileges guaranteed by the Constitution. Taney stated:

> On the contrary, they were at that time considered a subordinate and inferior class of beings, who had been subjugated by the dominant race, and, whether emancipated or not, yet remained subject to their authority, and had no rights or privileges but such as those who held the power and the Government might choose to grant them.[2]

Taney insisted that at the time the Constitution was adopted, slaves and their descendants were not considered citizens. Since Scott was not a citizen of the United States, Taney maintained, he could not be a citizen of Missouri; therefore, he was not entitled to sue in the courts. The Supreme Court established the precedent in this case that no Black person could be a citizen of the United States and that Black people had no rights that white people had to respect. Moreover, Taney maintained that the public history of every European nation clearly had displayed the state of public opinion in relation to the Black race, and this opinion prevailed at the time of the Declaration of Independence and adoption of the Constitution of the United States. Taney described this opinion about the Black race:

> They had for more than a century before been regarded as beings of an inferior order, and altogether unfit to associate with the white race, either in social or political relations; and so far inferior, that they had no rights which the white man was bound to respect; and that the negro might justly and lawfully be reduced to slavery for his benefit.[3]

Taney also ruled that Scott was a slave when his owner took him to Illinois; his status as free or slave, on his return to Missouri, depended on the laws of Missouri, not of Illinois.

Chief Justice Taney also declared that the provision of the Missouri Compromise, which had banned slavery in the Northwest Territory north of the latitude of 36°30′ (the southern border of

Missouri), was not valid. In addition, he wrote that the Fugitive Slave Clause of the Constitution as well as a bill forbidding the slave trade after 1808 both recognized the right to have slaves as property. He concluded that Congress could not demand that persons going into free territories should surrender their property. Thus, it was not lawful to demand that slaves, considered as property, be surrendered. This decision essentially opened the northern territories to slavery.

The Supreme Court ruling created an uproar among Black people throughout the country and among their friends, the abolitionists. Many educated people knew that when the Constitution was drafted, many Americans had been of the opinion that free Black people were citizens. Response from the Black communities was strong and quick. Black leaders C. L. Remond and Robert Purvis announced a public meeting to discuss the Dred Scott case "and other outrages to which the colored people are subject under the Constitution of the United States."[4]

Abraham Lincoln—then a candidate to be senator from Illinois—stated that he believed the decision was improperly made and should be reversed. Horace Greeley's *New York Tribune* spoke of Taney's "detestable hypocrisy" and "mean and skulking cowardice."[5] Scott's new owner freed him a few weeks after the 1857 decision. Scott began working as a hotel porter in St. Louis and died a year later.

The courthouse also had another role in Black history. Before the Civil War, slaves were sold on its steps to settle estates. Some exhibits within the courthouse describe the Dred Scott case. The actual courtroom where the trials were held no longer exists.

DATE OF SIGNIFICANCE:	1856–1857
ADDRESS:	Broadway and Market Streets, St. Louis
TELEPHONE:	(314) 425-4465
VISITING HOURS:	Daily 8–4; closed Thanksgiving, Christmas, New Year's Day
FEES:	None
SOURCES:	"Dred Scott Case," 193–9. *Dred Scott* v. *Sandford, U.S. Supreme Court. Before the Mayflower,* 178, 463. *Webster's New Biographical Dictionary,* 897.

Quinn Chapel African Methodist Episcopal Church

Between 1890 and 1920, approximately 1,000 African Americans lived in the Carondelet district of south St. Louis. Many of them, both free Black people and slaves, had lived there before the Civil War. Other freedmen came after the war, working on the river, in foundries, as domestic workers, or as draymen and teamsters. Black and white people lived together in relative harmony. Black Methodists at first worshiped under the direction of white pastors. During Reconstruction, however, they established their own congregations in south St. Louis.

The Quinn Chapel A.M.E. Church structure was built in the late 1860s as a public marketplace in the Carondelet. The Carondelet African Episcopal Church, a congregation dating from 1845, purchased the building from the city in 1880. In 1882 parishioners of Quinn Chapel A.M.E. Church dedicated the structure.

The congregation has used the same building for worship since the early 1880s, and the church has been the focal point of activities in the Black community. This was especially true during the period when Black people were barred from other social institutions. The church sponsored lectures, socials, and songfests and organized programs to help members of the community. In 1954 the church allowed twenty-five men, flooded out of their homes, to sleep at Quinn Chapel for two weeks.

Around 1900, church members added an entrance tower extension to the one-story, rectangular brick building and added to the tower an old bell dating from 1847. Except for the addition of the entrance tower and interior remodeling, the building has remained much as it was when constructed, with round arched windows of colored glass and with seven rows of pews. The building is one of a few remaining from the once-independent city of Carondelet.

The Quinn Chapel congregation reached a maximum of 150 members, then its membership began to decline as members moved to suburban areas. By the 1970s only Quinn Chapel and Corinthian Baptist remained of the early Black congregations. The historic site is listed in the *National Register of Historic Places.*

DATE BUILT: Late 1860s; purchased by Black congregation, 1880s
ADDRESS: 227 Bowen Street, St. Louis
VISITING HOURS: Visitors may walk or drive by
SOURCES: NRHPINF. *National Register of Historic Places,* 413.

The Shelley House

The Shelley House is significant because it played a role in a landmark Supreme Court decision regarding housing discrimination. The modest two-family flat on Labadie Avenue is located in a residential area that had been covered by a racially restrictive covenant that stipulated that area homes could not be sold to "people other than Caucasians and Orientals."

Prior to the Civil War, Black families, even in the South, often had lived near white families. Often they worked as servants or in restricted occupations, and the laws did not restrict them to certain residential areas. However, after the Civil War, the United States moved to become a racially segregated society. The 1896 legal decision, *Plessy* v. *Ferguson,* encouraged racial segregation.

In St. Louis, from Reconstruction, the Black population had been small, remaining at approximately 6 percent of the population. In 1916 St. Louis passed a discriminatory law that provided that no person could move to a block where 75 percent of the residents were of another race. When the law was declared unconstitutional, white people began to turn to restrictive covenants.

After World War I, the Black population began to grow and racial hostility increased. Real estate agents cooperated with these restrictive covenant agreements and segregated residential areas by sending Black people to an area called The Ville. Once a covenant was established, subsequent owners had to abide by it. Jim Crow arrangements were established, and segregation was accepted, even by the federal government. In the 1920s the National Association for the Advancement of Colored People unsuccessfully challenged such covenants.

Between World War I and World War II, the number of Black people moving into St. Louis increased dramatically, creating a critical housing shortage. The J. D. Shelleys, a family with six children, had lived in Starksville, Mississippi. One day, a young Black girl they knew was beaten, and the Shelleys decided to leave the state. They migrated to St. Louis, where they lived at first with relatives and then in overcrowded rental quarters. Seeking assistance in finding a place to buy, they learned that the owners of the property at 4600 Labadie were willing to sell in spite of the restrictive covenant. The Shelleys bought the property.

Other families in the neighborhood sued, and the Missouri Supreme Court directed that the provisions of the restrictive covenant should be enforced. The Shelleys appealed to the U.S. Supreme Court, claiming that their constitutional rights had been violated. The Supreme Court ruled that restrictive covenants violated the Fourteenth Amendment and could not be enforced by making it clear that discrimination did not have to originate with the state if state action enforced privately originated discrimination. The decision was a significant legal milestone and provided an initial impetus in breaking down the injustice of restrictive covenants. The decision did not end discrimination in housing, however, because covert discrimination continued on a widespread basis. Yet the decision had a great impact in opening up more housing and providing opportunities for African Americans to live where they chose.

The Shelleys sold the house on Labadie Avenue in 1961. In 1988, 450 people gathered at the Cote Brilliante Presbyterian Church (in the same block of Labadie as the Shelley house) to commemorate the fortieth anniversary of the *Shelley v. Kraemer* Supreme Court decision. They came to dedicate the house as a national historic site. On this occasion, J. D. Shelley, the plaintiff in the case, stood before the house that he had purchased fifty-four years before.

DATE OF SIGNIFICANCE: 1948
ADDRESS: 4600 Labadie Avenue, St. Louis
VISITING HOURS: Private, visitors may drive or walk by
SOURCES: NRHPINF. "Group Celebrates 40th Anniversary of Key Housing Case." *Race Racism and American Law.* 3A.

The Ville

Before the Civil War many free Black citizens of St. Louis worked in a variety of businesses and professions and lived in neighborhoods throughout the city. After the war, however, strict residential segregation began to develop. By the twentieth century, many African Americans had settled in The Ville. This community, originally a semirural area in the northwest suburbs of St. Louis, was later annexed to the city.

The Ville eventually became the center of a prosperous Black community, containing homes, schools, churches, businesses, and a hospital. Residents had strong and close family ties. They purchased one-story cottages and maintained them with care, sweeping the steps and gutters in front of their houses and planting beautiful flower gardens.

Between 1846 and 1863 Missouri laws prohibited the education of Black children. After the Civil War, however, the Freedmen's Relief Society organized schools and opened a school for African American children, originally named the Elleardsville Colored School number 8, in 1873 on St. Louis Avenue. The school was renamed the Simmons School in 1891. The original frame structure was replaced by a brick building in 1899.

Residents of The Ville challenged restrictive covenants that kept them out of certain blocks. Once restrictive covenants were ruled illegal by the U.S. Supreme Court in 1947, many residents of The Ville moved to other areas of the city. As more prosperous African Americans moved out of The Ville, residents from the deteriorating Mill Creek Valley area who had been displaced by an urban renewal project began to move in. Although the 1954 Supreme Court decision ended de jure school segregation, The Ville and its schools remained segregated. As Black and white middle-income families moved out of the city, segregation increased within the city. By 1970 the population of The Ville was 99 percent Black. The Ville is important in African American history. The neighborhood has a rich history, and has undergone many changes as a result of changing legislation and shifting populations.

DATE ESTABLISHED: c1900
ADDRESS: Bounded today by Dr. Martin Luther King Jr. Drive, Taylor Avenue, St. Louis Avenue, and Sarah Street, St. Louis
VISITING HOURS: Most sites private; visitors may drive or walk by
SOURCES: NRHPINF. *The Ville.*

Homer G. Phillips Hospital

The Homer G. Phillips Hospital is another significant landmark in The Ville. Its history is an interesting and instructive chapter in the history of St. Louis's Black community. Early in the twentieth century, medical facilities for African Americans were totally inadequate. Although the Black community paid taxes to construct and maintain public hospitals, such facilities were not open to them. In 1914, at the request of seventeen Black physicians, the city purchased the abandoned Barnes Medical College, renovated it, and opened it as a health care center for African Americans. The facility soon proved inadequate for the community's needs.

As a result, Black physicians enlisted the cooperation of a Black attorney, Homer Gilliam Phillips. He sought to remedy the situation by sponsoring a bond issue to fund a much-needed hospital. After years of debate, the city at last agreed to acquire a site for a new hospital as well as a school and a residence for nurses. Tragically, Attorney Phillips was assassinated on a St. Louis street before he could see the fruits of his strenuous efforts. In gratitude for his work, the hospital was named in his honor.

The Homer G. Phillips Hospital was a large complex of brick buildings; four patient wards radiated around the administration building. At the time of its construction and for years afterward, it was one of the few fully equipped hospital and training centers for Black physicians, nurses, and technicians. At its peak it employed between 800 and 900 workers. In spite of a limited budget, Phillips Hospital gained national recognition for excellence in treating the sick and injured. It has trained many graduates of America's two medical schools for African Americans as well as countless nurses, technicians, and record keepers.

Several changes came about in the 1950s. In compliance with a 1955 order from the mayor of the city, Phillips was instructed to admit all patients of every race and creed who lived in the western half of the city. In 1964 St. Louis decided to close down, for all practical purposes, Phillips Hospital, alleging the need to centralize medical services. Today it has been reduced to the status of an outpatient clinic and emergency-care center operating in an annex to the main hospital. Although the main complex is closed and boarded up, it still is worth driving by to see. Many people are amazed to see the size of the hospital complex. Homer G. Phillips Hospital, a symbol of Black pride and achievement, is listed in the *National Register of Historic Places.*

DATE BUILT:	Hospital, 1932–1936; outpatient clinic, 1960
ADDRESS:	2601 Whittier Street, St. Louis
TELEPHONE:	(314) 371-3100
VISITING HOURS:	Closed; visitors may walk or drive by
SOURCES:	NRHPINF. Telephone conversation Jan. 4, 1995, Shirley Marks, clinic manager, Homer G. Phillips Ambulatory Care, St. Louis Regional Medical Care Center.

Sumner High School

Between 1860 and 1880 the Black population of St. Louis increased more than five times, but the only schools available to African American children were inferior in quality. To add insult to injury, schools attended by white children had names while those assigned to Black children were identified by such numbers as Colored School No. 1, 2, etc. There was no high school for African Americans until 1875.

Yielding to complaints from the Black community, the school board in 1875 provided a facility no longer used by white children. It was at first simply designated as the "High School for Colored Children." Upon insistence of the children's parents, however, the name was changed to the Charles Sumner High School in honor of Senator Charles Sumner (1811–1874) of Massachusetts, a white abolitionist and vigorous champion of African American rights. Sumner High was the first high school built for Blacks west of the Mississippi River.

Initially, most subjects taught at Sumner were at the grade-school level, but in time it became a true secondary school. All the teachers were white until 1877, when the first Black instructors were hired after pressure from the African American community. To meet the need for Black teachers, a department was organized to provide two years of teacher training to graduates of the high school.

As the Black population of St. Louis grew, the original Sumner building was succeeded by a larger facility. (Both these buildings have since been demolished.) To meet the needs of an ever-expanding community, a group of Black residents petitioned the school board for a new school in a better location. After much discussion, the school board selected a site in The Ville, a stable and desirable neighborhood. The new Charles Sumner High School was designed by nationally respected architect William Ittner and completed in 1909 in the Georgian style. The substantial structure with its round arches, Palladian windows, and decorative corner quoins was the equal of any white school built at that time. Until Vashon High School opened in 1927, Sumner was the only secondary school for Black students in St. Louis.

Portable classrooms were added to Sumner High so that the normal school department could train new Black teachers. Later that department became known as the Harriet Beecher Stowe Teachers College. It performed many useful functions until 1954 when the Supreme Court decision in *Brown* v. *Board of Education of Topeka* ended legal separation in public schools. As a result, Stowe College merged with Harris Teachers College and moved to a different location.

Charles Sumner High School has been one of the finest African American schools in the country. A source of local pride for its educational standards and renowned for its cultural and social activities, Sumner has been an important milestone in Black history. The school is listed in the *National Register of Historic Places.*

DATE BUILT:	1909
ADDRESS:	4248 W. Cottage Avenue, St. Louis
TELEPHONE:	(314) 371-1048
VISITING HOURS:	Mon.–Fri. 7:30–2:10; tours by appointment
SOURCES:	NRHPINF. Telephone conversation Jan. 4, 1995, Joseph H. Du Bose, principal.

Notes

1. *Dred Scott* v. *Sandford,* 60 U.S. (19 How.), 403.
2. *Dred Scott* v. *Sandford,* 404–5.
3. *Dred Scott* v. *Sandford,* 407.
4. Stephen B. Presser, "Dred Scott Case," in *The Guide to American Law: Everyone's Legal Encyclopedia* (St. Paul, Minn.: West, 1984), 195.
5. Presser, 199.

Works Consulted

Academic American Encyclopedia. Danbury, Conn.: Grolier, 1993. [electronic version]

Before the Mayflower: A History of Black America. 5th ed. Lerone Bennett Jr. New York: Penguin, 1988.

"Dred Scott Case." Stephen B. Presser. In *The Guide to American Law: Everyone's Legal Encyclopedia.* Vol. 4. St. Paul, Minn.: West, 1984.

Dred Scott v. *Sandford.* 60 U.S. (19 How.) 393–633.

"The Gentle Genius: George Washington Carver." Peggy Robbins. In *George Washington Carver National Monument Planning and Information Packet.* Diamond, Mo.: George Washington Carver National Monument, n.d.

George Washington Carver. Diamond, Mo.: National Park Service, 1989. [flier]

"Group Celebrates 40th Anniversary of Key Housing Case." Cynthia Todd. *St. Louis Post-Dispatch,* 21 May 1988.

"I Wish You to See and Know All. The Recently Discovered Letters of William Clark to Jonathan Clark, *AE.*" James J. Holmberg, Curator of Manuscripts, The Filson Club. *We Proceeded On* 18, no. 4 (Nov. 1992).

Lewis and Clark: Historic Places Associated with Their Transcontinental Exploration (1804–06). Roy E. Appleman. Washington, D.C.: National Park Service, 1975.

The Journals of Lewis and Clark. Bernard De Voto, ed. Boston: Houghton Mifflin, 1953.

National Register of Historic Places. Washington, D.C.: National Park Service, 1976.

Race Racism and American Law. Derrick A. Bell Jr. Boston: Little, Brown, 1973.

The Ville: The Ethnic Heritage of an Urban Neighborhood. Carolyn Hewes, ed. St. Louis, Mo.: Washington University, 1975. [booklet]

Webster's New Biographical Dictionary. Springfield, Mass.: Merriam-Webster, 1988.

Nebraska

Aurora

Plainsman Museum

Although the Plainsman Museum is not a Black historical site, it has a showcase that depicts the Black history of Nebraska's Hamilton County, including that of the David Patrick family. The museum has murals, mosaics, and exhibits that trace the region's history from prehistoric times to the present, including a sod house, a schoolhouse, a log cabin, an agricultural museum, and the showcase on Black pioneers. Children especially enjoy the doll case with its collection of 800 dolls, the juke box, and the working player pianos.

Black homesteaders were among the pioneers in Hamilton County. In 1873, for example, David Patrick began to farm 120 acres of land northeast of Aurora. Another African American, Frank Harris, established a large orchard in the area in 1880. He managed this fruit farm throughout his lifetime, employing as many as thirty workers at "picking time."

Aurora also was home to General Delevan Bates, a white commander who in 1864 was appointed Colonel of the Thirtieth Infantry Regiment, United States Colored Troops. After the siege at Petersburg, Virginia (1864–1865), Bates's brigade was sent to North Carolina, where it joined General William T. Sherman's Army. A description of the service of Black regiments at Petersburg is included in the listing for Petersburg, Virginia.

DATE ESTABLISHED: 1976

ADDRESS: 210 Sixteenth Street (3 miles north of the I-80 Interchange on NE 14), Aurora

TELEPHONE: (402) 694-6531

VISITING HOURS: Apr. 1–Oct. 31, Mon.–Sat. 9–5, Sun. 1–5; Nov. 1–Mar. 31, daily 1–5; closed Thanksgiving, Christmas, New Year's Day, Easter

FEES: Adults, $4; senior citizens ages 62 and up, $3; children 5–16, $1; children under 5, free; AAA discount

SOURCES: Telephone conversation Aug. 12, 1995, Mrs. Gwen Allen, director, Plainsman Museum. Telephone conversation June 18, 1994, John H. Green, assistant director.

Bayard

Chimney Rock National Historic Site

Extensive exploration of the area that is now Nebraska began in 1804 when President Thomas Jefferson sent Meriwether Lewis and William Clark to the Missouri River to explore the Louisiana Territory for the United States. A Black servant named York was an important part of this expedition and was with the group when its members explored many sites in Nebraska, including the Chimney Rock National Historic Site. (For more information about York, see the listings for St. Charles, Missouri; Washburn, North Dakota; Spalding, Idaho; Astoria, Oregon; and Ilwaco, Washington.)

The Nebraska State Historical Society operates the Chimney Rock Visitors Center as a branch museum. The new building at the site opened in July 1994 with exhibits associated with the site. Visitors are able to see the landmark geological formation called Chimney Rock, but due to deterioration of the formation, they are not able to get close to it. Children will enjoy seeing the rugged prairie terrain that still has many dirt roads and will enjoy thinking about the wagon trains that passed through this main crossing.

ADDRESS: South of Bayard on US 26 and NE 92

TELEPHONE: (308) 586-2581 or (308) 586-2589

VISITING HOURS: Memorial Day–Labor Day, 9–6

FEES: None

SOURCES: Telephone conversation June 18, 1994, Linda Wagaman, reference assistant, Nebraska State Historical Society. *Nebraska Guide to Museums and Historic Sites.*

Crawford

Fort Robinson Museum

Fort Robinson, now Fort Robinson State Park, is a former frontier Army post whose history spans seven decades (1874–1948). It contains sixty buildings associated with the period of its active use. Black history is associated with the post because it was the regimental headquarters for the Ninth Cavalry between 1887 and 1898. Between 1902 and 1907 it served as regimental headquarters for the Tenth Cavalry. For seventeen years the post was garrisoned by Black cavalry.

Fort Robinson was established in 1874 in Nebraska's Pine Ridge country near the Red Cloud Agency. It took part in the last days of the wars between the United States and the Plains Indians. Here the Oglala warrior, Crazy Horse, met his death in 1877. Thirteen years later, Black soldiers, called the Buffalo Soldiers, patrolled the Pine Ridge Reservation in the difficult days after the Battle of Wounded Knee in 1890.

Charles Young, the third Black man to graduate from West Point in 1889, was assigned to the Ninth Cavalry that same year. He spent part of his military career at Fort Robinson. Young later became the first Black colonel in the United States Army. (See the listing under Wilberforce, Ohio.)

The Ninth Cavalry Regiment left Fort Robinson in 1898 to fight in Cuba during the Spanish-American War. The Tenth Cavalry then served at the fort until it was assigned to duties along the Mexican border in 1910.

Original and reconstructed buildings tell the story of the fort's past. Interpretive exhibits in the 1905 Post Headquarters show items from the fort's seventy-year history, including several exhibits on the Ninth and Tenth Cavalry Regiments.

DATE ESTABLISHED: 1874

ADDRESS: Fort Robinson State Park, US 20, 3 miles west of Crawford

TELEPHONE: (308) 665-2852

VISITING HOURS: Apr. 1–Nov. 1, Mon.–Sat. 8–5, Sun. 9–5; Nov. 1–Apr. 1, hours vary, phone ahead

FEES: Museum: adults, $1; children with adults, free; State Historical Society members and immediate families, free; group rates available

SOURCES: Thomas R. Buecker, curator, Fort Robinson Museum. Information page from Fort Robinson Museum.

Dorchester

Saline County Museum

Among the structures exhibited at the Saline County Museum is the Burden House, home of the only Black pioneer family in Saline County. The museum and the Burden House contain family pictures and interesting articles used by the Burden family. One picture from 1893 shows the entire family outside the home. Documents include their homestead certificate and discharge papers.

Henry Burden was born about 1844 in Petersburg, West Virginia, of slave parentage. He escaped from the Confederate Army and enlisted as a private in Company B, Seventeenth U.S. Infantry. After being honorably discharged from the Union Army on February 17, 1866, he moved to Nebraska. There he filed a homestead claim on Saline County land two and one half miles south of Pleasant Hill. Mr. and Mrs. Henry Burden and their sons, Henry and George, are buried in the Pleasant Hill Cemetery.

DATE ESTABLISHED: 1964

ADDRESS: NE 33, south of Main Street, Dorchester

TELEPHONE: Contact Ms. Norma Knoche, (402) 947-2911, or Ms. Bertha Zak, (402) 946-7441

VISITING HOURS: Sun. 2–5; other times by appointment; closed Easter, Thanksgiving, Christmas

FEES: Donations accepted

SOURCE: Norma E. Renner, board member, Saline County Museum. Telephone conversation Aug. 10, 1995, Norma Knoche, president, Saline County Museum.

Fort Calhoun

Fort Atkinson State Historical Park

York, a Black slave, traveled with the Lewis and Clark expedition when its members explored vast new territories in the western United States. The explorations may have originated with an idea that fascinated President Thomas Jefferson from his childhood. Long before the Louisiana purchase of 1803, Jefferson thought that a water route might connect the Mississippi River with the Pacific Ocean. After the land purchase, Congress appropriated funds for the discovery of this water route (that later was found not to exist). Two former army officers, also close friends, Meriwether Lewis and William Clark, were selected to lead the expedition. With them was York, a Black man who was a servant to Clark but who also was a strong contributor to the success of the expedition. York may have been the first Black American to traverse this rugged, treacherous, and marvelous terrain.

Fort Atkinson State Historic Park marks the site of Lewis and Clark's Council on the Bluff, at which they met with local Indians in 1804. From 1819 to 1827 Fort Atkinson was a United States Army Post. Today the post is partially restored and has a Visitors Center. There people can see a film about the Lewis and Clark expedition and another film depicting the process of restoring the fort. The center exhibits various artifacts and processes common to an earlier period; for example, staff members bake bread in a recently built mud oven. Walking trails lead to a blacksmith's shop, a settlers' store, the council house, and the fort itself.

ADDRESS:	US 73 to Fort Calhoun, east on Madison Street, Fort Calhoun
TELEPHONE:	(402) 468-5611
VISITING HOURS:	Visitors Center, Memorial Day–Labor Day, daily 9–5; grounds, Memorial Day–Labor Day, daily 9–7
FEES:	$2.50 per vehicle per day or $14 annually
SOURCES:	Telephone conversation June 18, 1994, Delores Holder, tour guide. "The Lewis and Clark Expedition."

Lincoln

Nebraska State Museum of Natural History
Nebraska State Historical Society

The State Museum of History has a modest amount of information about African Americans on the frontier. The museum's exhibit on the topic consists of one showcase on the second floor that features one or two pictures of the sod houses in which some Black families lived and a picture of a former slave and sharpshooter named Nate Love. Black pioneers came to the region in search of opportunity and freedom, and they settled on the Nebraska frontier as early as 1867. Staff members can talk with visitors about the settlers' experiences—the all-Black homesteading towns as well as the Ninth and Tenth Cavalry stationed at Fort Robinson.

The museum contains three floors of exhibits, including a first-floor museum store, a World War II exhibit, a third-floor general store, an exhibit about Native Americans, and a toy exhibit. The

Nebraska State Historical Society's research department, which is appropriate for adults, has the largest collection of newspapers in the state as well as photographs, history books, and census data.

DATE ESTABLISHED: 1957

ADDRESS: Nebraska State Museum of Natural History, 131 Centennial Mall North, Fifteenth and P Streets; Nebraska State Historical Society, 1500 R Street, Lincoln

TELEPHONE: Museum, (402) 471-4754; Historical Society, (402) 471-4751

VISITING HOURS: Museum, Mon.–Sat. 9–5, Sun. 1:30–5; Historical Society Library, Mon.–Fri. 10–5, Sat. 8–5, Sun. 1:30–5; closed Veterans Day, Thanksgiving, Christmas, New Year's Day

FEES: None

SOURCES: Lynne Ireland, coordinator of museum programs, Nebraska State Historical Society. Telephone conversation June 18, 1994, Domingo Colón, chief of security. *Nebraska Guide to Museums and Historic Sites.*

Nebraska City Vicinity

John Brown's Cave and Museum

The frontier town of Nebraska City once served as part of the underground railroad. Residents friendly to the abolitionist cause used to provide assistance to slaves who had escaped from the Missouri and Kansas Territories. After sheltering and feeding the fugitives, the abolitionists guided them on to Iowa, a free state. From there many of the slaves were helped to reach Canada.

This site shows how one underground railroad site operated. Located in the vicinity of Nebraska City, it was named for abolitionist John Brown, who may have assisted here. The John Kagi Cabin nearby had an underground passage that led to caves along the river, providing a safe way to move on in times of danger. John Henry Kagi served as John Brown's secretary of war during the period of the raid on Harpers Ferry. He lived in this Mayhew cabin, which was built in 1851 and which is the oldest extant building in Nebraska. The Mayhews lived in the cabin with their six sons and with Kagi, Mrs. Mayhew's brother. Captain Kagi was assigned by John Brown to the command of the rifle factory in the raid on Harpers Ferry, where he supervised the five Black men who were part of the original group that took part in the raid—Shields Green, Dangerfield Newby, Sherrard Lewis Leary, John A. Copeland, and Osborne P. Anderson. Kagi and the men whom he led were overwhelmed at the rifle factory by as many as five hundred Virginians. Only Anderson escaped. John Copeland surrendered after the others (except Anderson) were killed, but later Copeland was executed. (See the listing for Harpers Ferry, Virginia).

The cave is still there for visitors to inspect. Entered in an earlier period through a trap door in the cabin, the cave is explored now by walking down steps. Once inside, to add to the realism, there are two manikins who represent slaves; one is lying down on a bed, the other is standing up and seems to be waiting for an opportunity to leave. Visitors go through the cave and emerge at the other end to explore the rest of the site. There they will find a little village consisting of a school, a depot, a washhouse inside a barn, and an African Methodist church that was originally in Nebraska City. The museum's interior has wooden-front stores including a candy shop, a barber shop, a dentist's office, a harness shop, a shoe shop, and tool and music shops on an old-fashioned street. Visitors can explore all of this on their own.

ADDRESS: 2000 Fourth Coorso (3 miles west of Nebraska City on NE 2), Nebraska City
TELEPHONE: (402) 873-3115
VISITING HOURS: Apr. 1–Nov. 30, Mon.–Sat. 10–5, Sun. 12–5
FEES: Adults, $5; children, $2; seniors, $3; group rates available
SOURCE: Telephone conversation June 18, 1994, Marge Johnson, receptionist.

Omaha

Black Americana Museum

The Black Americana Museum is a house of African American treasures that will delight children and history fans of all ages. The museum was founded by Oran Belgrave, a cosmetologist/hairdresser who traveled from city to city teaching the art of hairstyling while keeping an eye open wherever he went for gems of Black history. Noting his interest, others have added to his collection. Here the visitor sees life-sized figures of Black heroes, each in individually appropriate settings, including leader-to-freedom Harriet Tubman; inventor Granville T. Woods; Malcolm X, orating from a podium; George Washington Carver, pouring a substance from a laboratory beaker; Louis Armstrong, making his trumpet wail in a New Orleans setting; and Muhammed Ali, preparing to float like a butterfly and sting like a bee. Also present is a figure of Matthew Henson, warmly dressed for his run to the North Pole.

For sports fans the museum contains large, life-sized cardboard sports figures and memorabilia collected from members of a Black baseball league. There are assorted hair products and implements as well as authentic "white only" and "colored only" signs collected from around the country. The doll collection here is one described by volunteer Linda Batch as "the biggest Black doll collection I've ever seen." It includes hundreds of dolls, some from England and dating from the 1800s on up to all kinds of Barbie™ dolls. Included are ceramic dolls, composition dolls, and rag dolls, but a favorite of visitors is the Topsy-Turvy Doll, which has two faces. Turn the dress up one way and the face of the doll is Black; turn the dress up the other way and the face of the doll is white.

The Black Rainbow Gallery next to the museum features the work of local multicultural artists. Complete with a reception area, the gallery provides an opportunity to show local talent.

Although the museum has an admissions charge, those who cannot pay may leave a donation of any amount they choose.

DATE ESTABLISHED: 1991
ADDRESS: 1238–40 S. Thirteenth Street, Omaha
TELEPHONE: (402) 341-6908
VISITING HOURS: Daily 11–4 including holidays
FEES: Adults, $3; children, $1.50; children under 5, free; donations accepted in lieu of standard admissions
SOURCE: Telephone conversation June 18, 1994, Linda Batch, volunteer.

Great Plains Black Museum

When the Civil War ended, a large number of Black families found their way to Nebraska. Most of these African American newcomers chose to live in Omaha. For two or three decades, they were free to live wherever they chose in the city. By the turn of the century, however, this freedom of choice diminished, and Black families increasingly were guided to the Near North Side, an area centered on Twenty-fourth and Lake Streets, or to another area in South Omaha near the stockyards. Many new African Americans arrived between 1910 and 1920 seeking industrial jobs. The growing presence of the Black immigrants was met with increasing hostility until an angry white mob lynched a Black man in a riot in 1919.

The Black history of Omaha and the surrounding region today is told in the Great Plains Black Museum, housed in the former Webster Telephone Exchange Building, a thirty-seven-room brick structure located in the heart of the Black community.

The structure is closely associated with Omaha's Black history from 1933 when American Bell donated the Webster Exchange Building to the Urban League. After a previously existing Black community center was consolidated with the Urban League, the building was remodeled for use as the Mid-City Community Center. In the 1950s, Whitney Young, later the director of the National Urban League, had his offices in this building. The Mid-City Community Center has provided a variety of services for African Americans including employment assistance, a library, a nursery, a medical and dental clinic, adult education classes, and youth groups.

The community center operated until about 1950 when the building was sold. The Exchange Building was first an apartment house, and then it became the headquarters of the Greater Omaha Community Action. Since 1975 the Great Plains Black Museum has used the historic structure.

The Great Plains Black Museum is the only museum in this area dedicated to preserving the history of the African Americans in the Midwest after the Civil War. The museum interprets life of Black people in the Great Plains from the pre–Civil War–underground railroad years to the present. Displays include information on and artifacts of Black homesteaders, including Black women of the Great Plains. Museum activities include guided tours, temporary exhibits, and films. Facilities are available for community meetings and programs, achievement projects, and arts/crafts exhibitions.

The site is listed in the *National Register of Historic Places.*

DATE ESTABLISHED: Building, 1906; museum, 1976

ADDRESS: 2213 Lake Street, Omaha

TELEPHONE: (402) 345-2212

VISITING HOURS: By appointment, Mon.–Fri. 8–4, Sat.–Sun.; open for Kwanzaa celebration Dec. 29–Jan. 6; closed Sat., Sun., Christmas Eve, Christmas Day, New Year's Eve, New Year's Day, July 4, Labor Day

FEES: $2

SOURCES: NRHPINF. R. D. Waller, assistant director, Great Plains Black Museum. *Nebraska Guide to Museums and Historic Sites.*

Jewell Building
The Dreamland Ballroom

James C. Jewell and his son lived in one of the apartments of the Jewell Building while they operated the barbershop, billiard parlor, and Dreamland Ballroom. The Jewells built the building in 1923, an era when Black people were moving into the Near North Side neighborhood surrounding Twenty-fourth and Lake Streets. During World War I expanding wartime industries had attracted

Black workers to Omaha, and the Black business district, previously at Fourteenth and Dodge Streets, shifted to this location.

From the 1920s through the 1950s, Dreamland Ballroom gained national prominence as a center for some of America's greatest jazz entertainers. Duke Ellington, Nat "King" Cole, Count Basie, Lionel Hampton, Dizzy Gillespie, Ray Charles, Dinah Washington, Sarah Vaughn, Louis Armstrong, and many others provided entertainment there.

In spite of potential loss of revenues, James Jewell refused to obtain a liquor license, thus allowing young people to attend the performances. After Jewell Sr. died in 1930, his son continued to operate the business.

During World War II the U.S. government took the Dreamland Ballroom away from the Jewell family and turned it into a U.S.O. Center for Black soldiers. A year later, when the government returned the building, Jewell sued for damages. The court awarded him $3,000 in a landmark case. The Dreamland Ballroom continued to operate until 1965, and the first-floor barbershop and pool hall were open through the mid 1970s.

In 1983 the building was sold to the community-based Omaha Economic Development Corporation. Having been vacant for years, the building was, as corporation president Alvin Goodwin said, "in disrepair and ready for the wrecking ball." Instead, the development corporation decided to rehabilitate it. The old, two-story floor plan had two storefronts on the first floor with two apartments at the rear and a dance hall with stage and a pressed-metal ceiling on the second floor. Today the two apartments have been renovated and leased. The rest of the building has been converted to office space and now houses offices of the Omaha Economic Development Corporation, the NAACP, the archdiocese, and a U.S. Post Office substation. The Jewell Building, one of Omaha's first important Black commercial buildings, a site associated with an influential Black business family, and a center of community entertainment for many years, is again an attractive and viable community structure. Designated a landmark by the City of Omaha Landmarks Heritage Preservation Commission, it is listed in the *National Register of Historic Places.*

DATE BUILT: 1923

ADDRESS: 2221–2225 N. Twenty-fourth Street, Omaha

TELEPHONE: Omaha Economic Development Corporation, (402) 346-2300

VISITING HOURS: Call for appointment

SOURCES: NRHPINF. Telephone conversation June 20, 1994, Alvin Goodwin, president, Omaha Economic Development Corporation.

Works Consulted

"The Lewis and Clark Expedition." The Academic American Encyclopedia. Danbury, Conn.: Grolier, 1993. [electronic version]

Nebraska Guide to Museums and Historic Sites. Nebraska Department of Economic Development, Division of Travel and Tourism and Nebraska Museums Roundtable. Lincoln, Nebr.: The Division, n.d.

North Dakota

Washburn

Fort Mandan

A Black man named York was part of North Dakota's early history as a member of the famous Lewis and Clark expedition. Between 1804 and 1806, explorers Lewis and Clark recorded observations about North Dakota's Indian tribes, vegetation, and game. York, who accompanied the expedition as a servant, was valued for his strength and wilderness skills as well as for his ability to make friends with the Indians encountered along the way. York participated fully in the tasks needed to make the expedition a success and had a voice in the decision-making process.

The expedition arrived in October 1804 at a Mandan Indian village. There the explorers had to cut down cottonwood trees to build cabins. Then the men lived for five months on insufficient rations.

Today Fort Mandan, which is situated in a wooded area, has a replica of the original campsite, as well as a visitors center. The Fort Mandan museum displays Indian artifacts, including arrowheads and flints. The center offers no interpretation of the role of York, the African American who traveled with the expedition; the reader, however, is aware from several passages in this book that there was an African American presence in the journey and is able to see the terrain that York traversed.

DATE BUILT:	1804
ADDRESS:	3 miles by County Road 17, in Fort Mandan Park, Washburn
TELEPHONE:	(701) 462-8129
VISITING HOURS:	Fort, open all year during daylight hours; Visitors Center, end of May–Oct. 1, Tues.–Sun. 1–5
FEES:	None
SOURCE:	Telephone call to site, June 18, 1994.

Williston

Fort Buford

Two companies of the Tenth Cavalry and Twenty-fifth Infantry, all-Black units, were among those stationed at the remote Fort Buford, a place so cold—winters often were 45° to 50° below zero—and so isolated that General Philip Henry Sheridan referred to it as "the American Siberia." The fort, built in 1866, protected railway crews from the Indians and served as a base for supplies. Soldiers stationed here, both Black and white, had more police action than the fighting action regarded as typical for soldiers. When the men arrived at Fort Buford late in the 1880s, they found a military reservation of thirty square miles with the barracks and its flagpole in the middle. Because of the large size of the village, they seldom encountered any settlers; therefore, they had few of the problems of prejudice from townspeople that other Black soldiers met. At the same time, the soldiers had few opportunities for social interaction outside their immediate setting. In addition to protecting the railway, the Black soldiers were involved in the Pullman strike.

After Fort Buford closed in 1895, the Black infantrymen were transferred to Fort Assiniboine in Montana. Today a museum at the old fort shows pictures and articles that describe the Indian wars of the 1870s. Included is a life-sized photograph of a Black soldier, who is also mentioned in the site brochure. The museum has a scale model of the fort, replicas of the soldiers' uniforms and other accoutrements, and information about barracks life. One can also examine the roller skates, balls, cards, and poker chips used by the soldiers in their leisure time. The museum provides information about such famous Indian leaders as Sitting Bull, Chief Joseph, and Chief Gall.

DATE BUILT:	1866
ADDRESS:	24 miles southwest of Williston on ND 1804
TELEPHONE:	(701) 572-9034
VISITING HOURS:	May 15–Sept. 15, daily 9–6; by appointment the rest of the year; closed major holidays
FEES:	Adults, $4; children 6–15, $2; children under 6, free
SOURCE:	Telephone conversation June 18, 1994, Charles Stalnaker, site supervisor.

Ohio

● ● ● ● ● ● ● ● ● ●

Akron

John Brown House

Famed white abolitionist John Brown (1800–1859) lived in this two-story house for two years in the 1840s. By the end of the next decade, he conceived his ill-fated plan to free the slaves after first seizing the arsenal at Harpers Ferry in West Virginia. Although the plan failed and John Brown was hanged, his ideas and the ideal of freedom continued to blaze across the country, intensifying sentiment both for and against slavery.

Brown's name was not soon forgotten. A few years after his death, Black men marched in the Civil War to the words and melody of the song "John Brown's Body," and today a memorial at Perkins Park in Akron honors him. The interpretation at this house, however, does not so much concentrate on Brown as an abolitionist but rather on Brown as a man who lived here for two years while working for Simon Perkins, the founder of Akron, Ohio. One of Brown's jobs was to care for Perkins' sheep. (For additional John Brown sites, see the Kansas City and Osawatomie, Kansas; Lake Placid, New York; Chambersburg, Pennsylvania; and Harpers Ferry, West Virginia, sections of this book.)

ADDRESS:	Brown House, 514 Diagonal Road; tours of both the Perkins Mansion and the Brown House begin at the Perkins Mansion, 550 Copley Road, Akron
TELEPHONE:	(216) 535-1120
VISITING HOURS:	Tues.–Sun. 1–5; closed some holidays, check in advance 👫
FEES:	Tours, adults, $3; senior citizens and children up to 16, $2
SOURCE:	Telephone conversation June 17, 1994, Sandy Pecimon, assistant to the director, Perkins Mansion and John Brown House.

Burlington

Macedonia Church
Promised Land Monument

Macedonia Church is one of the oldest Black church buildings still standing in America. The church was constructed on Macedonia Ridge, north of Burlington, Ohio, in the fall of 1849.

From 1799, Burlington, Ohio, had been a sanctuary for runaway and freed slaves. Additional freed people came to the area in 1849 after Virginia planter James Twyman emancipated thirty-seven slaves in his will and left them $10,000 to purchase land and homes in one of the free states. Thirty-two of the former slaves traveled 400 miles north to Ohio and settled in Burlington as free people. Farmland was deeded to them in 1849.

The freed African Americans joined with a Black congregation that had been established in the area since 1820. Before the arrival of the newcomers, church members had worshiped in individual members' cabins. When the former slaves arrived, they joined members of the existing congregation and their white neighbors in using rowboats to transport lumber across the Ohio River. They then carried the lumber up Macedonia Ridge and built the present church there.

Today the church remains much as it was when built, a one-story, twenty-by-thirty-foot, one-room frame building. The bell tower contains the original bell. The interior has the original pressed-tin ceiling. Outside and to the rear of the church is a one-story restroom structure built about 1955.

Although the congregation has dwindled to two or three African American families, they treasure the church and have a homecoming there each year, drawing families from other Ohio cities, from West Virginia, and from Kentucky. Owen Pleasant, nearly eighty-one years old in 1994, is a man with a sharp memory and a mind filled with stories of local history, as well as a descendant of one of the freed slaves who came to Ohio from Virginia. One of his ancestors bore the last name of her former owner, Twyman. Pleasant spearheaded a recent campaign to clean up the Thirty-Seventh Cemetery where the freed slaves were buried starting in 1849. Thanks to Pleasant's efforts, a monument was erected there and more than two hundred townspeople attended the ceremony. Seven and one-half feet in height, the granite monument depicts an ox cart of the type that brought the freed people from Virginia, a picture of guards with shotguns sent on the trip by the former slaveowner to protect the people as they traveled, the inscribed names of the thirty-seven former slaves, and the words "Promised Land." The cemetery, located in Burlington, is open to the public.

Macedonia Church, for many years a center of the community's activities and the mother church of many other Baptist churches, is listed in the *National Register of Historic Places.*

DATE BUILT: 1849

ADDRESS: Church, 2.3 miles north from new U.S. 52 on Burlington-Macedonia Road; Thirty-Seventh Cemetery, from downtown Burlington go to the Wal-Mart and turn right, go to Sam's Garage and turn left onto Fifth Street to the cemetery

VISITING HOURS: Interior not generally accessible; visitors may drive by

FEES: None

SOURCES: NRHPINF. Telephone conversation June 20, 1994, Owen Pleasant, descendant of one of freed slave settlers.

Cincinnati

Harriet Beecher Stowe Cultural Resource Center

The Harriet Beecher Stowe Cultural Resource Center preserves the Black history of Cincinnati and Ohio through its periodic exhibits on African American themes such as slavery and the underground railroad, African American politicians and legislators in Ohio, art from Senegal and by local Black artists.

The Harriet Beecher Stowe House on Gilbert Avenue was the home of the Reverend Lyman Beecher, head of Lane Theological Seminary, and of his daughters, Catherine and Harriet. Harriet Beecher Stowe, who lived in Cincinnati between 1833 and 1850, learned firsthand about many aspects of slavery, including the story of a slave who had escaped with her children across the icy and dangerous waters of the Ohio River. (See the entry for Ripley, Ohio.) She used some of these stories in her book *Uncle Tom's Cabin,* a work that persuaded thousands of white Americans to become involved in the antislavery cause. (For additional information on Stowe, see the listings for Hartford, Connecticut; Brunswick, Maine; and Dresden, Ontario, in the section on Canada in the Michigan chapter.)

DATE BUILT: 1830

ADDRESS: 2950 Gilbert Avenue, Cincinnati

TELEPHONE: (513) 632-5120

VISITING HOURS: Tues.–Thurs. 10–4; closed federal and state holidays; tours offered to groups

FEES: None

SOURCES: Telephone call to site, July 19, 1991. Nzingha Dahla, museum director. Dr. Sherlon P. Brown, University of Toledo. *National Register of Historic Places,* 581.

Cleveland

African American Museum

The African American Museum collects, houses, and displays information and artifacts associated with people of African descent. The displays show how African and African American contributions have been at the center of human progress from the beginning of history.

Exhibits include the inventions of Garrett A. Morgan, an inventor who lived in Cleveland. Morgan invented the first automatic traffic light, a belt fastener for sewing machines, and a smoke mask that has saved countless lives. The museum makes available a variety of self-esteem-building materials that are available for display in homes, schools, churches, and businesses. Saturday School staff members teach African history and heritage courses. One exhibit, *To Color America,* included portraits from the Smithsonian National Portrait Gallery. Another exhibit, *Malcolm X—A National Hero,* was on loan from the California Afro-American Museum.

Programs include guided tours of the museum, special and traveling exhibits, a Saturday School, Friday night forums, and a gift and book shop.

DATE ESTABLISHED: 1953

ADDRESS: Icabod Flewellen Building, 1765 Crawford Road, Cleveland

TELEPHONE: (216) 791-1700

VISITING HOURS: Mon.–Sat., 10:30–2:30; closed Christmas

FEES: Adults, $2.50; children under 12, $1.25

SOURCES: African American Museum; Dr. Sherlon P. Brown, University of Toledo. Telephone conversation Aug. 9, 1995, Donald Lynch, secretary/tour guide, African American Museum.

Karamu House*

Karamu House, founded by Russell and Rowena Jelliffe, was the first professional Black theater outside New York. It opened in 1915 as a settlement house serving the area from East Fourteenth Street to East Fifty-fifth Street between Carnegie and Woodland Avenues. In 1940 the center adopted the name *Karamu,* a Swahili word meaning "a central place of group activities."

Karamu founders Russell and Rowena Jelliffe were white social workers from Illinois who had met in school. From time to time in the settlement house they listened to Charles Waddell Chesnutt, an African American writer from Cleveland (1858–1932), as he spoke of the variety of ethnic groups in the East Thirty-eighth Street area—including Italian, Polish, Black—and expressed his belief that the races should be brought together to share their experiences. As a result of Chesnutt's suggestion, the Jelliffes began to invite people of diverse cultural and racial backgrounds into the settlement house to share art, dances, and food. Needing more space, they began raising money; fund-raising activities included the buying of individual bricks. The Child Development Center, the first new building, soon housed all activities. As more funds came in work started on two theater buildings.

Today Karamu House is a metropolitan center that provides education and diverse experiences in the performing, visual, and cultural arts; it also serves as an arena where artists can practice and demonstrate their talents. Distinguished Karamu House alumni include Langston Hughes, Robert Guillaume, and Ron O'Neal.

DATE ESTABLISHED: 1915

ADDRESS: 2355 E. Eighty-ninth Street, Cleveland

TELEPHONE: (216) 795-7070

VISITING HOURS: Gallery, pre-theater by appointment

FEES: Charge for performances and classes, discounts for members

SOURCES: Shraine L. Newman, public relations coordinator, Karamu House. Telephone conversation Jan. 7, 1995, Thelma McKinley, registrar and cultural arts and education coordinator, Karamu House. Paper from Karamu House. Karamu flier for 1989–1990 season.

Columbus

Martin Luther King Jr. Center for the Performing and Cultural Arts

From the quality of its architecture to the breadth of its programming, the Martin Luther King Jr. Center substantially enriches the surrounding community. It is housed in two renovated historic buildings—a former Knights of Pythias Temple and an elementary school whose large windows made it a wonder in its day. The Pythian Temple building (which originated as a vaudeville house before becoming the temple) was designed in 1926 by Black architect Samuel Plato, a graduate of Simmons College in Louisville, Kentucky. Plato took a correspondence course to learn the construction business; he later designed the Girls Dormitory (1909) and the Boys Dormitory (1924) at Simmons College in Louisville. He owned his own construction firm and became one of Kentucky's best-known builders. (See the Louisville, Kentucky, section for additional examples of Plato's work.)

Many famous Black entertainers performed in the 1930s and 1940s in the first-floor theater of the building, which Plato designed. Therefore, the building's use as an arts center fits its cultural heritage. In 1987 the two buildings were renovated and joined, and a main gallery was added, creating one large facility of 60,000 square feet —an arts facility that encourages creative exploration for all ages. Programs include plays, performances by dance groups, and festivals. Musicians have available a computerized MIDI laboratory, and children participate in a Summer Cultural Camp. The center sponsors a Classic Jazz Fair, a Family Fair, and Great Performances. The art gallery sponsors a variety of exhibits from quilts to contemporary art. The small gallery recently has shown the work of five African American masters as well as the work of Mexican American artists.

DATE ESTABLISHED:	1986
ADDRESS:	867 Mt. Vernon Avenue, Columbus
TELEPHONE:	(614) 252-5464
VISITING HOURS:	Mon.–Sat. 9–5, Sun. and evenings for special events
FEES:	Donations welcomed
SOURCES:	NRHPINF. Telephone conversation June 20, 1994, Barbara Nicholson, executive director.

Dayton

Paul Laurence Dunbar State Memorial*

Paul Laurence Dunbar (1872–1906) was the first Black poet after Phillis Wheatley to attain a national reputation, and he was the first to concentrate on themes about Black people and their lives.

Dunbar was born to former slaves and grew up in poverty. His mother took in washing, and Paul and his two half-brothers worked at odd jobs to supplement her income. Although Matilda Dunbar worked hard, she also took time to share songs, stories, and poems with her sons. Young Paul attended public schools in Dayton and began writing poetry at the age of seven. His teachers recognized his talent and supported his efforts. When he entered the old Central High School, he was the only Black student there. He became president of the Philomathean Literary Society and served as editor of the *High School Times* in his senior year. Teachers at the high school introduced him to literature and honored him by presenting him at the 1892 meeting of the Western Association of Writers.

Newspapers around Dayton and in Chicago began carrying Dunbar's poems and short stories. He published his first book, *Oak and Ivy* (1893), with financial assistance from William Blocher of the United Brethren Printing House. Dunbar continued to write after graduating from high school. In spite of his talent, the only job he could find was that of an elevator operator.

As Dunbar's work became better known, benefactors sent him to New York and then to England, where he gave a recital with Samuel Coleridge-Taylor, noted English composer of African and English descent, who set some of Dunbar's poems to music. On his return, Dunbar worked for a period at the Library of Congress and produced poems, articles, short stories, and his first novel, *The Uncalled.*

Returning to Dayton in 1903, Dunbar purchased this house for his mother and himself. The young writer had been plagued with health problems throughout his life. In 1899 he had a serious bout of pneumonia and later suffered from tuberculosis. Although he lived only three years in this house before dying, he had never stopped writing because writing was the central meaning of his life.

The Dunbar house, a substantial brick, two-story house with a welcoming porch, contains many of Dunbar's personal belongings. His mother continued to live in the house after his death, keeping his books, manuscripts, and even his study as they were when he was alive. Matilda Dunbar died in 1936.

The state of Ohio purchased the Dunbar home that same year, commemorating it as a historic site. Today Dunbar House is devoted to the exhibition and care of artifacts belonging to the artist and to the study of his life. A restoration and renovation returned the residence to its turn-of-the-century condition. The house is listed in the *National Register of Historic Places.*

DATE ESTABLISHED:	c1890; Dunbar residence, 1903
ADDRESS:	219 N. Paul Laurence Dunbar Street, Dayton
TELEPHONE:	(513) 224-7061
VISITING HOURS:	Labor Day–Memorial Day, Mon.–Fri. by appointment only; Memorial Day–end of Sept., Wed.–Sat. 9–5:30, Sun. noon–5
FEES:	Adults, $2.50; children under 12, $1; school groups, $.50 per person or $10 per bus; special rates for groups
SOURCES:	Personal visit, summer 1990. LaVerne Sci, manager, Dunbar House. Telephone conversation Mar. 7, 1995, Ethel Oliver, tour guide, Dunbar House. *National Register of Historic Places,* 589. National Historic Landmark Status Report. "Paul Laurence Dunbar House."

Women's Christian Association No. 2

Although the building housing the former Women's Christian Association was vacant as of mid-1994, it is worth seeing because it represents the type of housing provided for young Black women in a segregated era. In the late nineteenth century, white residents denied African Americans access to essential social services and forced them to live in restricted areas of the city. The Dayton Young Women's Christian Association restricted its facilities and programs to white females with the result that in 1889, a group of Black leaders decided to organize the Women's Christian Association. They incorporated in 1909 and purchased this building that same year. The housing, modest but graceful for its day, provided a wholesome environment for women's social activities and provided a facility where young working women could rent rooms at a reasonable cost. Services were also provided for the community from this setting. During World War I, when local Black troops were poorly housed and inadequately supplied, African American women used this site as a base for providing assistance to them.

Ironically the decline of this site began in 1918 when the white organization, the Dayton YWCA, began to provide services to the Black community. The Women's Christian Association, unaware perhaps that the group was hastening its own demise, approved of the new focus and, in cooperation, leased its building to the YWCA for a dollar per year. By 1924 the white YWCA had outgrown the leased quarters and had constructed its own building on Summit Street. At a time when the two organizations increasingly duplicated each other's efforts, the general neighborhood around this house began to decline, and the site was viewed as a less-desirable location for young women. The doors of the historic old building on Fifth Street closed in 1973.

The Women's Christian Association building, a rectangular frame building constructed in the late nineteenth century, has an entry on the right side of the facade; it is approached by a stoop with a wrought-iron railing.

The building, which is associated with the Black community's efforts to provide essential social services in an era of segregation, is listed in the *National Register of Historic Places*.

DATE BUILT: c1900; purchased by the Women's Christian Association, 1909

ADDRESS: 800 W. Fifth Street, Dayton

VISITING HOURS: Unoccupied, visitors may walk or drive by

SOURCES: Personal visit to site, summer 1990. NRHPINF. Telephone conversation June 17, 1994, Nancy Horlacher, Dayton collection librarian, Dayton/Montgomery County Library.

Harveysburg

East End School

This historic building, commonly called the East End School, was built around 1829. It served both Black children and some Indian children living in the area.

William Harvey, a white Quaker, first purchased land in this area and established the settlement of Harveysburg. He and his wife were sympathetic to antislavery ideas. Harvey's brother, Dr. Jesse Harvey, and his wife, Elizabeth, founded the East End School. Elizabeth was one of the school's first instructors. The East End School operated until the turn of the century when its enrollment began to decline. The remaining students were integrated into a nearby formerly all-white school, and the schoolhouse was closed. Later it was converted into a private dwelling.

Many years later, in 1976, the Harveysburg Community Historical Society began to write a history of the village. Recognizing the historical significance of the school, its members made plans to restore it. To raise funds, they sold cornmeal pies and sauerkraut pies at festivals and held ice cream socials. The Ohio Department of the Interior and private donors gave supplemental funds.

The school is a brick, rectangular one-story structure with six-over-six windows. Restorers provided the school with electricity and a new belfry. They repaired windows and the chimney, repaired floors and walks, and removed the partitions that had been added when the school became a residence. The schoolhouse originally had no street number, so the committee bestowed the number 1776 as an address.

Although the building was known locally as the East End School, the *National Register of Historic Places* lists it as the Elizabeth Harvey Free Black School, honoring the school's founder. Built in a Quaker town, it may have been the first free school for Black children in the Northwest Territory. It definitely was the first free school for them in Ohio. The historic building is used as a meeting place for the Harveysburg Community Historical Society, and it provides a site for the display of historical items.

DATE BUILT: 1829–1831

ADDRESS: 1776 North Street, Harveysburg

TELEPHONE: Mrs. Walter McCarren, (513) 897-6195

VISITING HOURS: By appointment

SOURCES: Wiley Smith III, acting chairperson, Department of Pan-African Studies, Kent State University. Telephone conversation May 10, 1994, Mrs. Walter McCarren, Harveysburg Community Historical Society. "First Black School in Ohio being Restored in Harveysburg."

Mount Pleasant

Village of Mount Pleasant Historic District

During the first half of the nineteenth century, Mount Pleasant was both an up-and-coming industrial center and a leading center of the abolitionist movement in Ohio. Although Mount Pleasant was primarily a Quaker community, people of other views lived here, too. Underground railroad routes from Wheeling, West Virginia, passed through southern Jefferson County and through Mount Pleasant, and tradition indicates that no slave who arrived at this community was ever taken back into captivity.

Today Mount Pleasant is a community of less than 500 individuals—it is small in size but large in pride in its antislavery heritage. Some descendants of slaves still live in this former stop on the underground railroad. Many nineteenth-century buildings remain from the period of abolitionist activity, and volunteers give tours of six of them—the Quaker Meeting House; the Benjamin Lundy Home; the 1804 log cabin of P. L. Bone, a former drummer in the Civil War; a general store; the tin shop; and the Elizabeth House Mansion Museum. The museum has a map of the local underground railroad route and the original free-labor store sign. Although most of the structures are private, visitors can walk by to view the exteriors in this two-block area.

The Quaker Meeting House is one of the most important buildings in the historic district. From the early nineteenth century it housed an association whose members worked against slavery. The brick, two and one-half–story structure has two interesting features—the separate entrances for men and women and the movable partition that could be lowered to separate the sexes.

The Benjamin Lundy House was another important antislavery site. In 1815 Lundy, a white man dedicated to the abolitionist movement, founded one of the first antislavery societies, the Union Humane Society, in St. Clairsville, Ohio. In 1821 he established his influential journal, the *Genius of Universal Emancipation*, at this site in Mount Pleasant. The Lundy House includes two attached brick dwellings that are accessible to each other through an interior door. The wing housed a free-labor store where Lundy chose to fight against slavery by selling only products not made with slave labor.

DATE BUILT: Nineteenth century; Meeting House, 1814

ADDRESS: Roughly bounded by Third, North, High, and South Streets, Mount Pleasant

TELEPHONE: (614) 769-2893 or (614) 769-2020

VISITING HOURS: Most sites private, visitors may drive or walk by; tours by appointment

FEES: Tour, $6 per person; students 5–18, $3; children under 6, free

SOURCES: Telephone conversation June 17, 1994, Sherry Sawchuk, president, Historical Society of Mount Pleasant. Reverend Lloyd G. Smith, Historical Society of Mount Pleasant. Mount Pleasant Historical Society Museum. *Webster's New Biographical Dictionary*, 627. *National Register of Historic Places*, 583.

Oberlin

John Mercer Langston House

John Langston, the son of Ralph Quarles, a white plantation owner, and Lucy Langston, a slave of African and Indian ancestry, was born in Virginia in 1829. When John was a child, both his parents died, and he was sent to Ohio in accordance with his father's wishes to live under the guardianship of the Gooch family. When he was ten years old, the Gooches decided to move to Missouri. This created a danger for John because Missouri was a slave state. It was feared that he might be forced to live as a slave. Fortunately, his half-brother intervened and sought the help of an Ohio court. As a result of this intervention, John was placed in the care of an abolitionist minister.

Langston attended a private school in Cincinnati for three years. In 1844 he entered the preparatory department of Oberlin College. After graduating from the college, he continued postgraduate studies in theology at Oberlin. His real interest, however, was in law. Rejected by law schools because of his race, Langston studied privately with attorney Philemon Bliss. Langston passed the bar in 1854 and was admitted to the practice of law.

That same year Langston married Carolina Wall, and he and his bride set up housekeeping on a farm he owned in the township of Brownhelm. He built up a professional law practice there and became a well-known figure in the town. In March 1855 the community elected him as its town clerk—perhaps the first time that an African American had won an elective office in the United States.

In 1856 Langston moved back to Oberlin, thinking that he could expand his practice in that larger community. Before long voters elected him to serve on the city council and the local board of education. When the Civil War broke out, Langston helped recruit Black soldiers for service in the Forty-fourth and Forty-fifth Massachusetts Black regiments. During the Reconstruction period Langston moved to Washington, D.C., where he worked for a time for the Freedmen's Bureau. Later he was asked by Howard University to organize a new law department. He served the university in a number of capacities—as dean of the law school, vice president, and later acting president of the university.

Next, Langston entered the U.S. diplomatic service and was stationed at posts in Haiti and Santo Domingo. Returning to the United States, he became the president of a college now known as Virginia State University at Petersburg. Turning his attention next to politics, he was elected as the first Black Congressman from Virginia in 1890. He was not reelected, however, and retired to private life in Washington, D.C. There he wrote his autobiography, *From the Virginia Plantation to the National Capital*. He died in Washington in November 1897.

The Langston House in Oberlin is the only existing house associated with this outstanding American. He lived in the home during the twelve years when he was active in politics and in his law practice in Oberlin.

DATE BUILT: House, 1855; Langston residence, 1856–1867
ADDRESS: 207 E. College Street, Oberlin
VISITING HOURS: Private, visitors may drive or walk by
SOURCE: NRHPINF.

Oberlin College

Oberlin College, like Berea College in Kentucky, was one of the first accredited colleges in America to enroll Black students in the 1800s. Established in 1833, Oberlin had an official policy of nondiscrimination in its admissions. When Lucy Sessions graduated from Oberlin in 1850, she was the first Black woman in the United States to earn a college degree.

An important center of the abolitionist movement in the Midwest, Oberlin also was involved in the underground railroad. In 1859 John Copeland Jr., a student at Oberlin College, was one of three Black men to die with John Brown in the famous raid at Harpers Ferry, West Virginia. A monument in the city park honors the three Black men who died at Harpers Ferry: John Copeland Jr., Shields Green, and Lewis Leary.

DATE ESTABLISHED: 1833
ADDRESS: Tappan Square, Oberlin
TELEPHONE: Admissions, (216) 775-8411; Campus Visit Program, (800) 622-6243
VISITING HOURS: Guided tours during school year, Mon.–Fri. 10–noon, 2:30, 4:30, Sat. 10–noon; summers, by appointment; closed last week of Mar.
SOURCES: Telephone call to site, June 17, 1994. Telephone conversation Mar. 7, 1995, Leslie Curtis, assistant, Campus Visit Program. *National Register of Historic Places,* 586.

Put-in-Bay

Perry's Victory and International Peace Memorial

Perry's Victory and International Peace Memorial is a 352-foot-high granite column that commemorates the Battle of Lake Erie during the War of 1812. This is one of the few national parks with a Black theme. Approximately one in four sailors, or 130 of the men serving on the nine vessels in the American fleet, was Black. When Oliver Hazard Perry assembled his fleet in 1813, United States armed forces were segregated. (In fact, they were not to be officially integrated until more than a century later after World War II.) Perry was dissatisfied with the men sent to him, referring to them as "a motley set—Blacks, soldiers, and boys."

His superior, Commodore Chauncey, replied, "I have yet to learn that the color of a man's skin or the cut and trimmings of the coat, can affect a man's qualifications or usefulness. I have nearly fifty Blacks on board of this ship and many of them are among my best men."[1] Thereupon, Perry tendered his resignation to the Secretary of the Navy, stating that he had not been speaking about the men's color but of their lack of training and experience. In the end Perry was persuaded to retain his command and began a rigorous training program that paid off. On September 10, 1813, the American fleet met and destroyed a British fleet of six vessels in the Battle of Lake Erie, the only instance in history when an entire British fleet was sunk or captured.

Other than their names, little is known of the men who won the historic Battle of Lake Erie in the War of 1812 and secured the old Northwest. According to the National Park Service, only three of the more than one hundred Black men who fought aboard the fleet have been positively identified. Anthony Williams fought on board the schooner *Somers*. Jesse Williams, a seaman, was wounded in the battle. Cyrus Tiffany, a Black man from Massachusetts, returned to Rhode Island with Perry and continued to serve with him until Perry's death in 1819.

Visitors to the peace monument walk up two flights (thirty-seven steps) and then take an elevator the rest of the way. There is no handicap access to the monument.

DATE ESTABLISHED:	1912–1915
ADDRESS:	South Bass Island in Lake Erie, Put-in-Bay (about 3 miles from the mainland, accessible by car ferry daily from Catawba Point and Port Clinton, Apr.–Nov.)
TELEPHONE:	(419) 285-2184
VISITING HOURS:	Third Sun. in June–Labor Day, Sun.–Thurs. 10–7, Fri.–Sat. 10–10; closing hour varies in Sept.; winter months, by appointment
FEES:	Adults, $2; children 16 and under, free; ferries $4–$8 each way for adults, depending on the speed and luxury of the boat
SOURCES:	Gerard T. Altoff, supervising park ranger. Telephone conversation June 21, 1994, Marty O'Toole, lead park ranger. "Blacks in the Battle of Lake Erie."

Ripley

John Rankin House State Memorial

Rankin House may have sheltered more than two thousand runaway slaves who were on their way to freedom. The home of the Reverend John Rankin and his wife, Jean, is situated high on a hill overlooking the village of Ripley, the Ohio River, and the Kentucky shoreline. From 1825 to 1865 the Rankins and their neighbors, including free African Americans in Brown County, took in escaping slaves and helped them on their way. At night the Rankins kept a beacon burning in the upper window of their home to show the way.

The passage of the Fugitive Slave Act of 1850, however, made the underground railroad activities of the Rankins and their friends more difficult and more dangerous. Under the terms of the law, ex-slaves located in free territory were subject to capture and return to their place of bondage if their masters could prove ownership. Anyone known to shelter runaways was subject to a heavy fine. As a result, owners, informers, and the infamous bounty hunters were quick to pursue escapees. The financial rewards for such actions were large and tempting.

Despite these difficulties, the abolitionists at Ripley persisted in their courageous work—hiding runaways, feeding and clothing them, and helping them move on to safety in Canada. Although as many as twelve persons at a time were sheltered in the Rankin home, not one was ever recaptured.

Harriet Beecher Stowe (1811–1896), the famous novelist, at one time sat here and listened to John Rankin tell the story of Eliza, a slave, who had carried her children across the Ohio River's thawing ice. Stowe modified the story a bit and used it as one of the most dramatic episodes in *Uncle Tom's Cabin.*

> The huge green fragment of ice on which she alighted pitched and creaked as her weight came on it, but she stayed there not a moment. With wild cries and desperate energy she leaped to another and still another cake;—stumbling—leaping—slipping—springing upwards again! Her shoes are gone—her stockings cut from her feet—while blood marked every step; but she saw nothing, felt nothing, till dimly, as in a dream, she saw the Ohio side, and a man helping her up the bank.[2]

The full account of this episode is, if anything, even more remarkable than the fictional version. Eliza and her husband first reached the Rankins in the middle of the night. The man had fallen into the river while leaving a boat and was covered with ice. Although the husband continued on his way to Canada, Eliza stayed behind, determined to free her six children still in Kentucky.

Returning to Kentucky, Eliza came back again to the Rankins' home; one of her children was strapped to her back in a shawl. Using a board attached to a rope, she had made her way from one treacherous ice floe to another. Eliza soon led that child to safety in Canada but resolved to make yet another trip back to Kentucky to rescue the other five youngsters. The next spring she did so. Upon reaching the home of her old master, Eliza concealed herself beneath the floor of her cabin. The next time her master and his wife left the plantation to visit friends, Eliza and the five remaining children set out, carrying bundles of clothing and other household goods. The weight of these bundles slowed them down on the eleven-mile trip to the river. Since the ferry that was to have taken them north had already left, Eliza and the children hid in a thicket along the river bank. John Rankin sent her a message that she should stay concealed until nighttime.

Disguised as a woman, Rankin then crossed into Kentucky with a group of young men as his helpers. From his home he had noted a group of thirty-one men with dogs and hunting rifles in search of the runaways. Rankin and his friends led the bounty hunters on a chase away from the river while Eliza and her children were rescued by a trusted ferryman. The story ended happily; Eliza and her children finally made their way to Canada.

Jean Lowry Rankin, the abolitionist's wife and mother of thirteen, died in 1878. She had been an integral part of efforts to help in the underground railroad. Reverend Rankin himself died in 1886 at the age of 93. Four Black men served with his sons and sons-in-law as his pallbearers. Both Reverend Rankin and his wife are buried in the Ripley cemetery.

Rankin House was purchased by the state of Ohio in 1938. The house was restored and today is used to interpret the work of the Rankin family and Ohio's contribution to the antislavery movement. Visitors may retrace the route of escaping slaves by climbing a replica of the stairway used by slaves to reach safety at the Rankin home. A book about Rankin House, *The Freedom Light,* is available at the site.

DATE BUILT:	1828
ADDRESS:	Take US 62 to the west side of Ripley, entrance road runs north off US 62
TELEPHONE:	(513) 392-1627
VISITING HOURS:	Memorial Day–Labor Day, daily noon–5; Labor Day–Oct. 31, Sat.–Sun. noon–5; closed Nov.–Memorial Day
FEES:	Adults, $2; children, $.50
SOURCES:	Telephone call to site, June 17, 1994. Telephone conversation Jan. 7, 1995, Lobena Frost, Rankin House. L 'Vera Seipelt, hostess, Ripley museum. *National Register of Historic Places,* 568. *Ripley, Ohio. Historical Collections of Brown County, Ohio. Uncle Tom's Cabin.*

Salem

Freedom Hall Museum

The Salem Historical Society's Freedom Hall Museum is a replica of a carpentry shop once used by abolitionists. The original building was constructed on Ellsworth Street in 1838. During the antislavery period, a group of antislavery activists held secret meetings in an upstairs room over the shop.

Salem was the western headquarters of Ohio's antislavery movement. Abolitionists in the town arranged to hear speakers—often at secret meetings for members of the movement. They also hid slaves in homes and barns and helped the freedom seekers escape to Canada. Many well-known opponents of slavery spoke in Salem's old Town Hall (no longer standing), including Frederick Douglass, Sojourner Truth, Parker Pillsbury, and William Lloyd Garrison. Parker Pillsbury (1809–1898) was an abolitionist born in Hamilton, Massachusetts. He traveled widely to lecture on antislavery topics.

The replica of the old carpentry shop with its meeting hall upstairs was completed in 1988, using 1845 flooring from an old Virginia courthouse. Most of the museum's memorabilia are ephemera, including baskets made by a former slave, pictures relating to slavery, some antislavery artifacts, and a bill of sale documenting the sale of Ada Carter for $400.

DATE BUILT: 1838; replica, 1988

ADDRESS: 208 S. Broadway, Salem

TELEPHONE: (216) 332-4959

VISITING HOURS: May 1–Dec. 1, Sun. 2–4; closed legal holidays and from the second week of Dec.–Apr. except by appointment

FEES: Adults, $2; children 11–16, $1; children 10 or under with parents, free; third graders from Salem, Ohio, free

SOURCES: Mrs. C. J. Lehwald, museum curator and director. Telephone conversation June 17, 1994, Ms. Josephine Rupe, director. *Webster's Biographical Dictionary*, 1185.

Sandusky

Underground Railroad Sites

Sandusky, Ohio, was noted as an abolitionist center and an important stop on the underground railroad. Its location on the southern shore of Lake Erie was highly suitable because of Sandusky's closeness to the islands in the lake and Canada. Erie County was reported to be most active in helping slaves to escape. Between forty and one hundred free Black residents lived in the town before the Civil War. As a result, the sight of escaping Black slaves did not arouse suspicion.

Most of the runaways passing through Sandusky came from Kentucky. Other Ohio communities along the underground railroad were Cincinnati, Toledo, Oberlin, and Cleveland. Some fugitives came alone, but most arrived in families or groups. One man arrived in Sandusky in a coffin with breathing holes. Although he was near death on arrival, a doctor revived him, and in a few days he was on his way to freedom in Canada.

Another group used a loophole in the law to escape. One Sunday a group of slaves with their owner boarded a ship bound for Detroit. By law, slaves were safe from arrest on Sunday. As the ship approached Canada, the captain let a small boat down and the slaves rowed to freedom. The owner could do nothing to prevent their escape.

Several Sandusky sites are associated with the city's underground railroad system. Although the interiors are not open, visitors may enjoy taking a driving tour to see the exteriors. The houses are varied and interesting architecturally as well as for the antislavery history of their former occupants.

The **Oran Follett House** (now a museum operated by the Sandusky Library) is rumored to have a room in which slaves were kept, although museum director Helen Hansen has found no solid evidence to substantiate this belief. The house is located at 404 Wayne Street at East Adams and is open to visitors. A reference room contains local history, but the exhibits do not focus on Black history.

Second Baptist Church, at 315 Decatur Street, is built around another church that sheltered fugitive slaves before the Civil War. The enclosed structure is often referred to as the "Antislavery Baptist Church." This African American congregation organized in 1849, at first coming together for the purpose of helping other Black people who were arriving from the South. They worshiped for a period in an old frame house formerly used as a church by a white congregation that had split over the issue of slavery. The Black congregation paid for the church by 1859; later they added a basement. Second Baptist was Sandusky's first Black church and was, according to member Elaine Lawson, the only church in Sandusky associated with the underground railroad. Some of its young founders were free; others were fugitive slaves. They all boldly assisted other runaways who came by way of Sandusky because from that point they could easily "island hop" to Canada. Shipping, a major industry in Sandusky, provided opportunities to smuggle slaves across to freedom.

In 1975 the congregation remodeled the church, and the old walls are no longer visible. The members, however, retain an awareness of their history. To visit the church, call in advance and make an appointment with the pastor.

The **Rush Sloane House,** 403 East Adams, was home to the best-known of Sandusky's abolitionists. Under the Fugitive Slave Act two slave owners brought suits against Sloane for helping their slaves escape to Canada. One owner lost his case on a technicality, but the other won. In 1854 a judge ordered Sloane to pay a $4,300 fine. Sloane's incensed neighbors organized a committee and raised $393. Sloane had to pay the rest himself. Sloane House is a large, beautiful structure capped with a completely enclosed widow's walk.

Other homes still existing in Sandusky were recorded by early historians as underground railroad sites. They are

Thomas C. McGee House, 536 East Washington Street.

George Barney House, 422 East Washington Street. This huge house, now painted white, still has behind it another original house from the early period.

Henry F. Merry House, 330 East Adams Street.

Joseph M. Root House, 231 East Adams Street.

Lucas S. Beecher House, West Washington Row. This limestone house, smaller than the Sloane House, has been restored inside and out.

DATE OF SIGNIFICANCE: The decades before the Civil War

ADDRESS: See individual sites

TELEPHONE: Follett House Museum, (419) 627-9608; Second Baptist Church, (419) 625-1411

VISITING HOURS: Most sites private, visitors may walk or drive by

SOURCES: Telephone conversation June 19, 1994, Jean Gardner, guide, Follett House Museum. Telephone conversation June 19, 1994, Elaine Lawson of Second Baptist Church. Helen M. Hansen, curator, Follett House Museum. "Route to Freedom." *From the Widow's Walk.*

Westerville

Benjamin Hanby House

The Hanby House in Westerville was a station on the underground railway, as was the former Hanby House in Rushville, Ohio. William Hanby was a bishop who edited the *Religious Telescope* for the United Brethren Church. He was also a founder of Otterbein College in Westerville.

Benjamin Hanby, William's son, was the most famous of the eight Hanby children. He wrote "My Darling Nellie Gray" and "Ole Shady" (also known as the "Song of the Contraband"). "My Darling Nellie Gray" told of Joe Selby, a fugitive slave who had escaped on the underground railroad and had to leave behind the woman he loved. Both songs had a strong influence on persons who believed in the antislavery movement.

Hanby House, the pre-Civil War home of the William Hanby family, has been restored and furnished as in the 1850s period. Visitors see *Gift of Song,* a seventeen-minute film that describes Hanby's life; then they can take a tour of the house. Originally Hanby House was a four-room structure with a barn behind it. Family members who were returning home knew how many slaves were hidden in the house by the number of flowers in a white vase in the window. Fugitive slaves stayed in the barn and came into the house to eat, sing, and pray. When it was safe to leave for the next stop, Mount Vernon, they departed, carefully hidden under hay and tools in a wagon. Today Hanby House still has a white vase with flowers in the window.

DATE BUILT:	1854
ADDRESS:	160 W. Main Street, Westerville
TELEPHONE:	(614) 891-6289
VISITING HOURS:	May 1–Oct. 31, Sat. 10–4, Sun. 1–5; by appointment other days
FEES:	Adults, $1.50; seniors and AAA members, $1.20; groups of 5 or more, $1.25 each; children 6–12, $.50; children under 6, free
SOURCE:	Telephone conversation June 17, 1994, Carol R. Krumm, curator.

Wilberforce

National Afro-American Museum and Cultural Center*

The National Afro-American Museum is a federal museum dedicated to the study of African American history and culture. It is located on the original eighty-eight-acre campus of Wilberforce University, the oldest Black college operated by a Black organization prior to the Civil War. The college also was a site on the underground railroad.

The National Afro-American Museum and Cultural Center is housed in a modern, one-story, 35,000-square-foot granite structure on a site overlooking a natural ravine. It was originally organized in 1972 as a joint project of the state of Ohio and the federal government. The first phase of the complex, including the newly constructed museum and the renovated Carnegie Library, opened in 1988. The museum includes exhibition space, a center for historical research, an art gallery, a children's mini museum, a theater, and an amphitheater as well as a cafeteria and picnic areas.

The museum creates a wide range of special exhibits. For example, *From Victory to Freedom: Afro-American Life in the Fifties* displayed artifacts typical of homes, businesses, clothing styles, and entertainment in the fifties. The museum also sponsored the *Holiday Festival of Black Dolls* and *Rhythm and Blues: Black American Popular Music, 1945–1955.*

DATE ESTABLISHED:	Museum, 1972; this site, 1988
ADDRESS:	1350 Brush Row Road, Wilberforce
TELEPHONE:	(513) 376-4944
VISITING HOURS:	Tues.–Sat. 9–5, Sun. 1–5; closed Mon., all holidays except Martin Luther King Jr. Day
FEES:	Adults, $3.50; students with I.D. and children, $1.50; scheduled school tours, free
SOURCES:	John E. Fleming, director National Afro-American Museum. Linda S. Buckwalter, administrative assistant National Afro-American Museum. *The National Afro-American Museum and Cultural Center. From Victory to Freedom. Holiday Festival of Black Dolls. Your Donor's Guide to Preserving Afro-American History and Culture.*

Wilberforce University
Central State University

Wilberforce University and Central State University once were housed on the same campus. Wilberforce, the older of the two universities, is the oldest college in America established and operated by African Americans before the end of the Civil War. (See the Cheyney State University listing in Cheyney, Pennsylvania, and the Lincoln University listing in Oxford, Pennsylvania, for information on other Black universities established before the Civil War.) Wilberforce University traces its history back to the time before the Civil War when the underground railroad provided safe havens and a way to freedom. Many of the free Black men and women and escaped slaves in Ohio needed an institution of higher learning. Wilberforce was established to meet this need.

The origins of Wilberforce University are intertwined with the development of an earlier school, Union Seminary. In 1844 the Ohio Conference of the African Methodist Episcopal Church selected a tract of land twelve miles west of Columbus, Ohio; there the church leaders established Union Seminary to educate young men in academic subjects, agriculture, and the mechanical arts and to provide instruction for those who wished to enter the ministry. At the same time, leaders of the Methodist Episcopal Church were starting a movement to educate African Americans from Ohio and neighboring free states; they approved the establishment of an institution called Ohio African University. The church leaders selected a site in Wilberforce (then known as Tawawa Springs), a small community with a history of underground railroad activity, and the school, the forerunner of Wilberforce University, opened in 1856.

Although enrollment at Ohio African University exceeded two hundred at the high school and college levels by 1860, the progression of the Civil War, a drop in financial support, and a $10,000 debt burden caused the school to close in 1862. School officials made plans to sell the property. Then Bishop Daniel Payne of the A.M.E. Church made an alternate suggestion—Union Seminary would move to the more-desirable location in Wilberforce. The A.M.E. Church purchased the college in 1863, and Reverend Payne was selected as president, becoming the first Black college administrator in the United States. The newly incorporated school was named in honor of the eighteenth-century British abolitionist William Wilberforce (1759–1833), who helped to end the slave trade in England.

In 1888 the Ohio legislature established Central State University, a normal and industrial school for Black students. The school had its own trustee board but educated students on the Wilberforce campus. In 1947 Central State University, the newer college, became a separate university. The historic campus where the two colleges once operated together became a part of the conference center of the National Afro-American Museum. Today, Wilberforce University, Central State University, and the National Afro-American Museum are located within a short distance of one another.

The old Wilberforce University campus has been transformed over the years. The original Shorter Hall burned to the ground on the same night that President Abraham Lincoln was assassinated, but it was soon rebuilt. The present Shorter Hall, constructed on the old campus in 1922, was the main administration center. Carnegie Library, constructed in 1909 and remodeled in 1938, was a brick structure with a full basement. The library was a gift of philanthropist Andrew Carnegie. In the spring of 1974, a massive tornado damaged many of the older buildings that were still in use on the old campus. Repairs were made to buildings on a temporary basis. Then the old campus was sold, and the Ohio General Assembly and U.S. Congress designated the campus as the location for the National Afro-American Museum and Cultural Center. The Carnegie Library structure now houses museum administrative staff as well as historical items relating to Black history and Black culture.

Wilberforce University moved to a new campus on a gently rising slope located approximately one mile from the site of the original campus. In 1974 the Old Fountain was transferred and reconstructed on the new site.

DATE ESTABLISHED: Central State University, 1947 (as an independent university); Wilberforce University, 1844; Ohio African University, 1856 (1863, as Wilberforce University)

ADDRESS: Central State, 1055 N. Bickett Road; Wilberforce University, Brush Row Road, Wilberforce

TELEPHONE: Central State University, (513) 376-6011; Wilberforce University, (513) 376-2911

VISITING HOURS: By appointment during school sessions

SOURCES: Jacqueline Y. Brown, librarian, Archives, Wilberforce University. Joan Baxter, executive secretary, Greene County Historical Society. *Wilberforce University Bulletin. International Library of Negro Life and History,* 139.

Colonel Charles Young House

Colonel Charles Young (1864–1922) was the third Black man to graduate from West Point. He was the highest ranking Black officer in World War I after serving under President Theodore Roosevelt as America's first Black military attaché. After graduating from West Point, Colonel Young was assigned to the Tenth Infantry. Later he served with both the Twenty-fifth Infantry and Ninth Cavalry.

In 1894 Young received a federal appointment as professor of science and military tactics at Wilberforce University in Ohio. He also taught French and mathematics and coached the drama and glee clubs. Young was talented in languages, including German, Italian, Spanish, Latin, and Greek. He played several musical instruments and composed music.

At the outbreak of the Spanish-American War in 1898, Colonel Young briefly was given command of the Ninth Ohio Volunteer Infantry (Colored). At their first encampment, Camp Alger in Virginia, a group of white soldiers refused to salute Young because of his color. Since they had refused to respect him, he took off his coat and made them salute the coat for its rank.

Young had several other appointments. Following service in the West, he was appointed as United States military attaché to Haiti by Theodore Roosevelt, the first African American to receive this type of appointment. When Young died in 1922, a memorial service was held in the great hall of New York College. Following the service, his body was taken to Washington, D.C., and interred in Arlington's marble amphitheater.

Colonel Young lived in this brick, nineteenth-century residence from 1894 to 1898. The house is located in Green County, approximately two-thirds of the way from Xenia to Wilberforce.

The Young House has served as the Omega Psi Phi Fraternity House, home to a national Black fraternity. Beautifully restored, the house is open to visitors by appointment.

DATE OF SIGNIFICANCE: Young residence, 1894–1898

ADDRESS: Columbus Pike between Clifton and Stevenson Roads, Wilberforce

TELEPHONE: National Afro-American Museum and Cultural Center, (513) 376-4944

VISITING HOURS: By appointment

SOURCES: Telephone call June 17, 1994, National Afro-American Museum and Cultural Center. Telephone conversation June 17, 1994, Mrs. Joan Baxter, director, Greene County Historical Society Museum. *National Register of Historic Places,* 578.

Notes

1. "Blacks in the Battle of Lake Erie," Washington, D.C.: National Park Service, 1.

2. Harriet Beecher Stowe, *Uncle Tom's Cabin* (New York: Bantam, 1981), 58.

Works Consulted

"Blacks in the Battle of Lake Erie." Washington, D.C.: National Park Service. [manuscript]

"First Black School in Ohio Being Restored in Harveysburg." Lorraine Wise. (Wilmington, Ohio) *News Journal,* 2 Feb. 1990.

From the Widow's Walk: A View of Sandusky. Helen Hansen. Sandusky, Ohio: Follett House Museum, Branch of Sandusky Library, 1991.

From Victory to Freedom: Afro-American Life in the Fifties. Wilberforce, Ohio: National Afro-American Museum and Cultural Center. [flier]

Historical Collections of Brown County, Ohio. Carl N. Thompson, comp. Piqua, Ohio: Hammer Graphics, 1969.

Holiday Festival of Black Dolls. Wilberforce, Ohio: National Afro-American Museum and Cultural Center, 27–29 Oct. 1989. [flier]

International Library of Negro Life and History: Negro Americans in the Civil War. Charles H. Wesley and Patricia W. Romero. New York: Publishers, 1970.

The National Afro-American Museum and Cultural Center. Wilberforce, Ohio: National Afro-American Museum and Cultural Center. [flier]

National Historic Landmark Status Report. Washington, D.C.: Department of the Interior, 1979.

National Register of Historic Places. Washington, D.C.: National Park Service, 1976.

"Paul Laurence Dunbar House." Columbus, Ohio: The Ohio Historical Society. [brochure]

Perry's Victory and International Peace Memorial. Washington, D.C.: National Park Service, 1989. [brochure]

Ripley, Ohio: Its History and Families. Eliese Bambach Stivers. Georgetown, Ohio: The Brown County Genealogical Society, 1965.

"Route to Freedom: Slaves Found Sanctuary in Sandusky." Mark Davidson. *Sandusky Register,* 21 Feb. 1988.

Uncle Tom's Cabin. Harriet Beecher Stowe. New York: Bantam, 1981.

Webster's Biographical Dictionary. 1st ed. Springfield, Mass.: G. & C. Merriam, 1964.

Webster's New Biographical Dictionary. Springfield, Mass.: Merriam-Webster, 1988.

Wilberforce University Bulletin. Wilberforce, Ohio: Wilberforce University, 1987.

South Dakota

Fort Meade

Old Fort Meade Cavalry Museum

Fort Meade was built in 1878 as a command post during the conflict with the Sioux Indians. From 1880 to 1888 Companies A, D, H, and K of the Twenty-fifth Infantry were stationed here. Although the soldiers were assigned to protect white settlers and Black Hills miners from the Sioux, they themselves encountered, as did the Indians, prejudice and hostility from nearby white settlers in the town of Sturgis. One such incident involved a Black soldier, Corporal Ross Hallon of Company A, who was being held in the jail on a murder charge. Townspeople from Sturgis forcibly took him from the jail and hanged him from a tree. He was buried in the nearby cemetery where the bodies of twelve other Buffalo Soldiers also lie.

Today Fort Meade is inactive as a military base, but the grounds still contain some of the original buildings. A Veterans Administration hospital operates the base, and a military academy provides training for the National Guard. The museum, which is operated by a nonprofit, nongovernment association, features a video on fort life as well as exhibits on Native American life and the experiences of the cavalry soldiers. In response to the increasing number of requests for information about the Buffalo Soldiers, the museum plans to expand that aspect of its interpretation. The current exhibit on the Buffalo Soldiers at Fort Meade includes written materials, pictures, and a coat made of buffalo skin.

DATE BUILT:	1878
ADDRESS:	1 mile east of Sturgis on SD 34 (at Sturgis, leave the interstate but continue on the same road to a four-way stop; turn right and continue one mile to the Fort)
TELEPHONE:	(605) 347-9822
VISITING HOURS:	Memorial Day–Labor Day, daily 8–7; May and Sept., daily 9–5; tours on request during winter months
FEES:	Adults, $2; children under 12, free
SOURCES:	Carrie Lavarnway, curator, South Dakota Historical Society, State Agricultural Heritage Museum. Telephone conversation June 18, 1994, Logan Lamphere, guide.

1905–Present

All photos by
Nancy C. Curtis, Ph.D.,
except as noted.

Bray Hall Administration Building,
Lane College Historic District, Jackson, Tenn.

Women's Christian Association No. 2,
Dayton, Ohio

Hotel,
Colonel
Allensworth
State
Historic Park,
Allensworth,
Calif.

Herndon Home,
Atlanta, Ga.

Afro-American
Cultural Center,
Charlotte, N.C.

Sixteenth Street
Baptist Church,
Birmingham, Ala.

Green Memorial
A. M. E. Z. Church,
Portland, Maine.
Courtesy of
Maine Historical
Society.

McCray School, Burlington, N.C.

Dunbar Hospital, East Ferry Historic District, Detroit, Mich.

Moving Star Hall, Johns Island, S. C.

Colored Masonic Temple,
Fourth Avenue Historic District,
Birmingham, Ala.

Mechanics and Farmers Bank,
Durham, N. C.

Statue, Booker T. Washington
lifting the veil of ignorance from a slave,
Booker T. Washington High School,
Atlanta, Ga.

Pastorium, Dexter Avenue King Memorial Baptist Church, Montgomery, Ala.

Martin Luther King Jr.
Birthplace,
Atlanta, Ga.

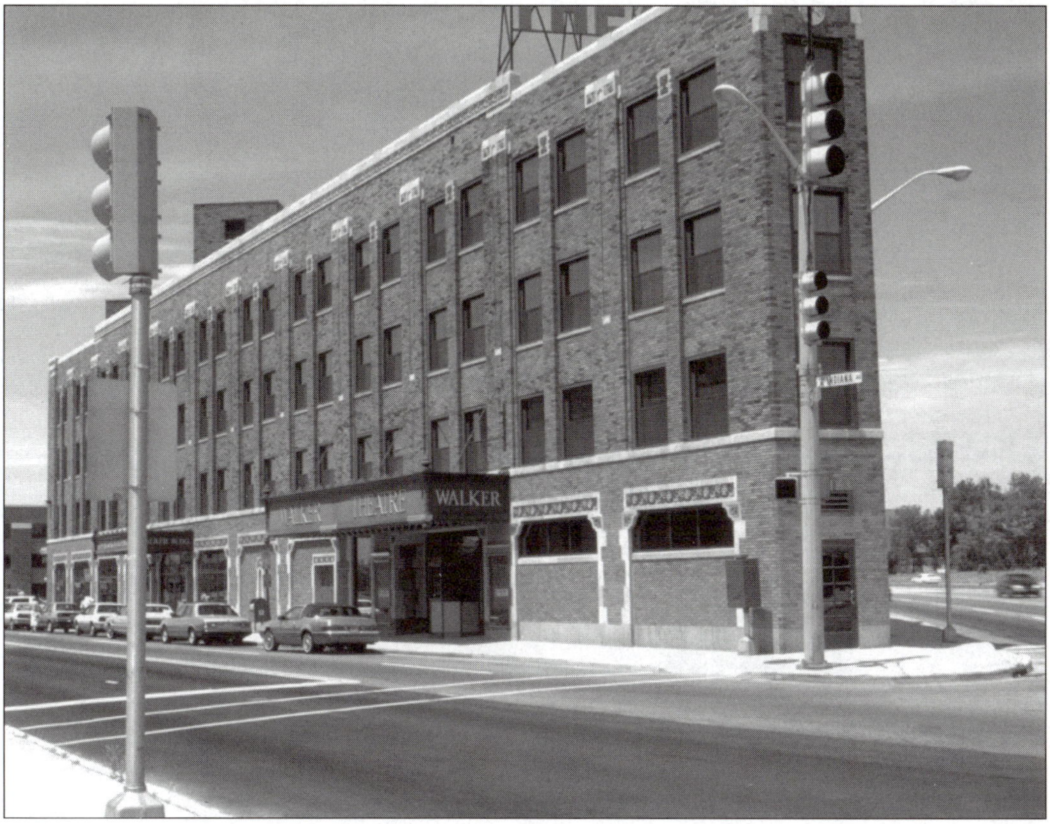

Madame C. J. Walker Urban Life Center, Indianapolis, Ind.

Jeffersontown Colored School, Jeffersontown, Ky.

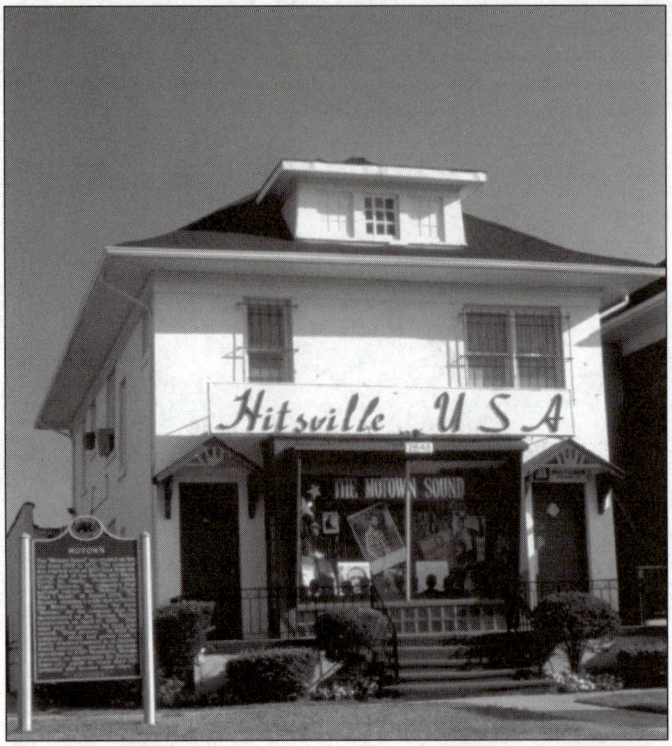

Motown Museum (Hitsville USA), Detroit, Mich.

Detroit Association of Colored Women's Clubs, Detroit, Mich.

Lake City Vicinity

Fort Sisseton Historic Park

Fort Sisseton, which was originally known as Fort Wadsworth, was established during the last half of the nineteenth century to protect settlers from the Indians. It was founded in 1864 near Lake City, South Dakota. Not far away, along the bank of the Minnesota River, lived some of the Santee Sioux. Two years before the opening of the fort the Sioux under Chief Little Crow had rebelled in an uprising that lasted for five months. Their rebellion was not without cause; the Indians could rightfully complain of unfair trading practices and broken treaties. They especially resented the white settlers who were beginning to homestead on Indian lands. The uprising was bloody. There were more than a thousand casualties, and many homes of the white settlers were destroyed. Eventually the Indian leaders were convicted. Some of them were executed, and a great many Indians fled to the west.

At this point Fort Sisseton and other forts were set up to protect the white settlers. The Indians respected the Black soldiers stationed at Fort Sisseton—men of the Twenty-fourth and Twenty-fifth Colored Infantry Regiments—whom the Indians named the "Buffalo Soldiers."

The Buffalo Soldiers of the above-named regiments as well as those of the Twenty-fifth U.S. Infantry were made up of Black men who served at Fort Sisseton from May 1884 until April 1888. The company had 92 men in 1886, 104 in 1887, and 100 in 1888.

During the 1870s the railroad began to move into the Dakota Territory, the Indians were moved from the area, and many new settlers began to arrive. In time gold was discovered in the Black Hills farther to the west. The facility at Fort Sisseton no longer seemed to be essential, and it was closed down in 1889.

Even though the fort is no longer an active military post, it is still maintained by the government. During the first weekend of June a celebration is staged to celebrate its contribution to the history of the region. A tour highlights Fort Sisseton's past; it includes visits to the barracks, guardhouse, officers quarters, post infirmary, library-schoolhouse, and trading post. Visitors can view the stone buildings and breastworks put up during the 1860s. The guardhouse has bricks carved with names of soldiers from the Twenty-fifth Infantry Regiment.

DATE ESTABLISHED:	1864–1888
ADDRESS:	Near Lake City (from Lake City go 28 miles west on ND 10, then 6 miles south)
TELEPHONE:	(605) 448-5701, or main office, (605) 448-5474
VISITING HOURS:	Memorial Day–Labor Day, daily 10–6; to request a tour after Labor Day, call the main office
FEES:	Historical Festival, adults, $2; children under 12, free; or SD park sticker (admission to any state park for the year), adult annual rate, $15; daily $2; children under 12, free; subject to change in 1996
SOURCES:	Wendy L. Lewis, visitor services specialist, Fort Sisseton State Historic Park. Telephone conversation June 18, 1994, Norma Johnson, tour services. Telephone conversation Aug. 10, 1995, Dave Daberkow, park manager, Fort Sisseton. Joanita Kant Monteith, Codington County Historical Society, Inc. Information sheet from Fort Sisseton State Historic Park. *Ft. Sisseton Historical Festival. Fort Sisseton State Park.*

Yankton

Allen African Methodist Episcopal Church

After the Civil War, several Black families, many from Alabama and other parts of the South, migrated to South Dakota. Some of them found work on the docks along the Missouri River; others worked as plasterers, barbers, domestics, or janitors. One African American, Tom Douglass, owned a restaurant. He traveled to Missouri to encourage others to migrate to Yankton. Among others, Douglass persuaded Henry and Isaac Blakey to move to Yankton, where they arrived in 1905.

In 1885 people from the African American community had built the Allen African Methodist Episcopal Church, South Dakota's oldest African American church. Other churches were soon organized. Reverend George Tillman was pastor of the Christian Methodist Episcopal Church, and the congregation of Second Baptist built its church in Yankton in 1916.

By 1920 Yankton had a population of 144 African Americans. Unfortunately, they began to face growing racial animosity. Klan cross burnings and activities were directed primarily against Catholics, but these activities also alarmed the Black community. These hostilities led to the organization of a Yankton chapter of the National Association for the Advancement of Colored People.

During the difficult years of the Great Depression, Allen Chapel and other Black churches provided leadership and places where people could share their resources and find a sense of community. Today services are led by a minister from Sioux City. The chapel is Yankton's only Black historic site.

DATE BUILT: 1885
ADDRESS: 508 Cedar Street, Yankton
TELEPHONE: (605) 665-1449
VISITING HOURS: Sun. service, 11
SOURCES: Telephone conversation June 20, 1994, Mr. Nate Blakey, community resident. "Black People in South Dakota History."

Works Consulted

"Black People in South Dakota History." Sara L. Bernson and Robert J. Eggers. *South Dakota History* 73, no. 3 (summer 1977), 241–70.

Fort Sisseton Historical Festival. South Dakota Department of Game, Fish, and Parks, Division of Parks and Recreation. [brochure]

Fort Sisseton State Park. South Dakota Department of Game, Fish, and Parks, Division of Parks and Recreation. [brochure]

Wisconsin

Beloit

Fairbanks Flats

During most of the 1800s, the Black population of Beloit was small. In 1881 some families joined together in organizing the first Black church society. The picture changed, however, during World War I when the Fairbanks-Morse Corporation—an engine-manufacturing company and the city's largest employer—recruited hundreds of Black workers from the South to work in the defense industry. Most of these workers lived in Fairbanks Flats—a development built on company land—or they lived on the west or southeast sides of Beloit.

There was some controversy about the location of Fairbanks Flats. The city of Beloit had originally intended to develop an extensive park system, a part of which would have been on the west side of the Rock River where Fairbanks Flats was built. The company disregarded the wishes of the city by buying up the land. A subsidiary of Fairbanks-Morse, Eclipse Home Makers, built twenty-four units of housing in 1917 on the land and rented the units to Black employees of Fairbanks-Morse.

Fairbanks Flats is a rare example in Wisconsin of planned segregated housing. The company deliberately set out to keep its Black workers in a segregated area on the outskirts of town. It is worth noting, too, that the company practiced discrimination not only in the location of its imported Black and white workers but also in the quality of their housing. White workers were for the most part located close to the plant in one-story cottages on curved streets in a landscaped setting. The white area was called Eclipse Park. By way of contrast, the Black workers were housed in four identical concrete-block apartment buildings. Each building consisted of six two-story units; the design was plain and undistinguished. Housed in the Fairbanks Flats were both skilled and unskilled laborers, including blacksmiths, molders, and other workers. The flats became the nucleus of the Black community. Nearby a Black YMCA was founded.

After World War II ownership of the Fairbanks Flats changed hands. People who were not employed by Fairbanks-Morse began to move into the apartments. Still those renting and living in the development were predominantly Black.

DATE BUILT: 1917

ADDRESS: 205, 215 Birch Avenue; 206, 216 Carpenter Street, Beloit

VISITING HOURS: Private, visitors may drive by

SOURCES: Cultural Resource Management in Wisconsin, study unit on Black history, State Historical Society of Wisconsin. Survey form, Historic Preservation Division, State Historical Society of Wisconsin.

Fond du Lac

Octagon House*

Octagon House, which was used as a hiding place on the underground railroad, has all the mystery and intrigue a person could want with its nine secret passageways within its octagonal shape. Research by the daughter of the present owners of the house indicates that it was not built for altruistic purposes; instead, it was designed for security reasons by a crafty and suspicious fur trader. Isaac Brown, a leading citizen in the town of Fond du Lac, built Octagon House. He traded furs and other goods with Indians but for some reason appeared to fear an attack. Therefore, he wanted a residence where he could hide both his family members and trading goods. The octagonal house was perfect; leftover spaces in the corners of the rooms made it difficult to calculate where the true ends of the walls should be, and into these nooks and crannies Brown managed to tuck nine hiding spaces. A walk-through closet hid a secret room. One fireplace was a fake. The house also had a hidden room in a wall, a fake wall in a broom closet, and a corner cupboard that a person in the know could walk behind and find a hiding place. A crawl space in the basement led two ways to the attic—by stairway and by ladder. Octagon House even had an underground tunnel leading to an adjacent woodshed.

At some point during the Civil War, Brown, who at one time was mayor of Fond du Lac, took an interest in the underground railroad and began using his highly suitable house to hide runaway slaves.

In 1975 Octagon House was slated for demolition; fortunately it was saved. Other underground railroad houses in the area have been demolished or have been kept strictly secret by owners who desire privacy. For those who want to enlarge their understanding of the underground railroad, Octagon House is an opportunity. The one and one-half–story frame and concrete house is located on a site that once was the shoreline of the Fond du Lac River. Its secrets are now open to visitors.

DATE BUILT: c1856
ADDRESS: 276 Linden Street, Fond du Lac
TELEPHONE: (414) 922-1608; special events recording, (414) 924-9393
VISITING HOURS: Call for times and tours
FEES: Adults, $6.50; children 12 and younger, $4
SOURCES: Telephone conversation June 24, 1994, Julia Hansen, The Historic Octagon House. Mr. Bob Kuhnz, Fond du Lac County Historical Society. *National Register of Historic Places,* 853.

Madison

East Dayton Street Historic District

The first Black resident reached Madison in 1847; others began arriving before the Civil War. They lived scattered around the city in rented houses, rooming houses, or apartments, and most of them worked as laborers, teamsters, or cooks or had small businesses. George and Carrie Williams came to Madison in 1850. They operated a barbershop and hairdressing salon and cleaned clothing.

Carrie William's brother, William Noland, operated a grocery, a bakery, and a saloon; he also manufactured a health tonic and worked as a veterinarian and chiropodist. Although the governor of the state appointed him a notary public in 1857, racial prejudice apparently prevented Noland from taking the position. The June 25, 1876, *Capital Times* noted that David Jones, the secretary of state, declaring that "this man is a n----r," had refused to file the required bond.

Benjamin Butts was another early Black resident. After mustering out of the Union Army at Camp Randall in Madison, he remained in the city. For twenty-eight years he operated a barbershop in the basement of the First National Bank. He later worked as a porter and messenger for the State Historical Society. In 1900 the Butts family was one of nineteen Black families in Madison.

By 1930 Madison's Black population numbered 348. The households were concentrated in south Madison around Mills, Regent, and Erin Streets and in another smaller area along East Dayton and North Blair Streets. Houses in the East Dayton Historic District are valuable because they are all that remain from the early Madison Black community. The district consists of three frame buildings that were built around the 1850s and moved from downtown early in the twentieth century. They are located in the Old Market neighborhood six blocks east of the Capitol Square in an area that originally was a cattail swamp.

The East Dayton Street area began to decline in the 1960s as new housing opportunities opened in the suburbs. Parking lots and storage yards began to claim the old area, and most of the old houses have been demolished. Those that remain are described in the listings that follow.

DATE BUILT: 1850s

ADDRESS: Old Market neighborhood, 6 blocks east of the Capitol Square, Madison

VISITING HOURS: Private, visitors may walk or drive by

SOURCES: NRHPRF. NRHPINF. State Historical Society of Wisconsin. Telephone conversation June 24, 1994, Mrs. Charlyne Hill, member of the pioneering Hill family.

Miller House

The Miller House on 647 East Dayton Street is a two-story, frame building with two units. The structure, built in 1853, was moved from downtown Madison to this site in 1908. It is associated with the William and Anna Mae Miller family, a prominent Madison family that operated a rooming house and also sought to improve conditions for Madison's Black community.

William Miller was born in Richmond, Kentucky, in 1872. He attended Berea College in Kentucky and a law school in Chicago. He was attending law school and waiting on tables at a hotel in Milwaukee as a summer job in 1901 when he accepted an invitation from Governor Robert M. LaFollette to come to Madison to work as a messenger in the governor's office.

Miller arrived in Madison during a period when many African Americans were leaving the South to escape racial tensions and discrimination. He actively participated in organizations that sought to better conditions for Black people, including the NAACP. W. E. B. Du Bois, a scholar, a leader, and an editor of the NAACP's *Crisis Magazine,* on several occasions was a guest in the Miller home.

Miller served nineteen years until his death in 1929, as messenger to Governor LaFollette. When Miller died, LaFollette, then a U.S. Senator, returned from Washington for Miller's funeral.

Anna Miller also was well educated. Born in Stanford, Kentucky, in 1877, she attended Knoxville College and Kentucky State Normal School. Anna and William Miller married in 1903. Emphasizing the importance of education for their children, they sent them to the Lincoln School in Madison, which served many families of higher income. The Millers declined to accompany Senator-elect LaFollette to Washington, D.C., because Washington's schools were segregated.

In spite of her qualifications, Mrs. Miller's career was limited to cooking for sororities and fraternities. She was an active community leader, however, and organized a literary society. She became a charter member of the local chapter of the Order of the Eastern Star.

Lucile Miller, the Miller's first child, was born in 1904. Like her parents, she was active in community affairs. She and others sought to open dormitories at the University of Wisconsin to Black students; they campaigned against segregation of the USO at Truax Air Force Base; and they helped to reorganize the NAACP in 1943. Lucile Miller lived in the family house on Dayton Street until 1978.

The building then became vacant and fell into poor condition. Fortunately, in 1986 a developer restored the house, returning the exterior to its 1908 appearance. Using old photographs and descriptions from Lucile Miller, the restorer removed asbestos shingles to reveal the original clapboards and brought back the old porches. The interior has the original wide-plank pine floors and a spindled stair rail; the garden, landscaped again, has the original lilac bush. The completed Miller House restoration received a City-County Preservation Award.

DATE BUILT:	1853; moved to this site, 1908
ADDRESS:	647 E. Dayton Street, Madison
VISITING HOURS:	Private, visitors may walk or drive by

649–653 East Dayton Street
114 North Blount Street

The three buildings at 649–653 East Dayton and 114 North Blount Streets are significant as being among the few remaining buildings from Madison's turn-of-the-century African American community. The two buildings on East Dayton were moved to this site in 1901 and 1912 and joined together with a wing. The house on North Blount Street was moved here in 1923.

John and Martha Turner and their adopted son, Alfred, came to Madison from Kentucky in 1898. John Turner, who was middle-aged when he arrived, worked in Madison as a day laborer. In 1901 the Turners moved the two-story, clapboard, commercial building to the 649 East Dayton address. They housed inside it the Douglas Beneficial Society, a self-help organization they had earlier established for Madison's Black families.

The house at 653 East Dayton Street, corner of Blount Street, was moved to the site in 1912 and a wing was added to connect the two buildings. The clapboard house has a large porch; the first-floor windows have six panes over six. The house, with one side facing Blount Street and the other facing Dayton Street, was the residence of Reverend C. H. Thomas, minister of the African Methodist Episcopal Church, and his wife, Caroline Thomas. John and Amanda Hill bought the building in 1917. Hill, a trustee of the A.M.E. Church, operated a shoe-shining parlor downtown; he and his wife also owned a grocery store in the former Douglas Beneficial Hall building. In 1923 they moved the small, clapboard-sided house to this area on Blount Street. The one and one-half–story house had a front porch with Victorian-style turned posts, a one-story wing, and a shed-roofed addition. Although the grocery store closed after John Hill's death, members of the Hill family have continued to occupy the historic properties and have kept them in good condition.

DATE BUILT:	649 E. Dayton, 1850s, moved to this site, 1901; 653 E. Dayton, moved to this site, 1912; 114 N. Blount Street, built c1850s, moved to this site, 1923
ADDRESS:	649–653 E. Dayton Street, and 114 N. Blount Street, Madison

Milton

Milton House Museum*

This site served as a hostelry on a stagecoach road; later it was an active station on the underground railroad. The hexagonal main block is of stuccoed concrete. Nearby is a one and one-half–story log cabin constructed around 1838.

Joseph Goodrich, a former New Yorker, built the main structure in 1839 as a stage stop, post office, and inn. He was a community leader who helped lay the foundation of the village. Among other contributions, he donated land for a public square and erected several buildings.

A letter written in 1955 by Mabel Davis Van De Mark, mentions the tunnel that led from the hexagonal inn to the log cabin behind the main structure. She noted, "About 1890 I visited Uncle Ezra and Aunt Libby—they managed the Milton House—and he showed me the narrow tunnel which was about five feet high and told me it was used to help slaves escape from the southern plantations north toward Canada." Van De Mark's Uncle Ezra was Joseph Goodrich's son, and he ran the Milton House Inn following Joseph Goodrich's death.

Although Wisconsin was not a heavily traveled underground railroad route, there was some antislavery activity in the state. James Clark of the State Historical Society of Wisconsin has noted that by 1840 abolitionists were active in southeastern Wisconsin; the underground railroad existed in that area. Such assistance to fugitives, if discovered, would have carried heavy penalties according to the Fugitive Slave Act of 1850. Joseph Goodrich and his friends, however, were abolitionists who did not hesitate to engage in antislavery work. An entry in a biographical dictionary about him gave the following description: "He was for many years a decided anti-slavery man, a member of the old Whig Party, and, after it, a consistent member of the Republican Party. His home was a refuge for the fugitive slave."[1]

Older people in the area passed down stories of people who were hidden at this house before being helped on their way to Canada. The tunnel, now full-height and of cement, originally was a crooked, dirt crawl space with a small room midway. Both ends of the tunnel were well concealed. Regular visitors to the inn would have had no reason to have used such an inconvenient passage from the inn to the cabin, but the tunnel did make sense as a hiding place for fleeing slaves.

Notes by Dr. Salisbury of the Milton Historical Society Archives indicate that Goodrich cared for fugitives in the basement of the inn, where they could eat and rest. If there was danger, they would crawl through the tunnel, move up through a trap door in the floor of the log cabin, and hurry on through Storrs Lake to Bowers Lake, the Otter Creek area, and Lake Koshkonong. They would not have gone through the inn itself because Goodrich did not know if all his patrons were in favor of the abolitionist program.

The site also is believed to have been associated with Sojourner Truth. Sojourner Truth, born a slave as Isabella Baumfree, later traveled across the country preaching against slavery. She may have been a guest at the Milton House, a friend of Goodrich, and possibly a speaker at the academy in Milton. The late Mrs. Nellie Daland, a local artist, painted a portrait of Sojourner Truth, using a picture in a book as a model. This portrait hangs on the wall of the Milton House Museum.

The tunnel at this site is believed to be unique as the only underground railroad segment that actually was underground and that is intact and open to the public. At the museum today, the story of the inn's role in the underground railroad is interpreted for visitors.

DATE BUILT:	1839 or 1844
ADDRESS:	18 S. Janesville Street, Milton
TELEPHONE:	(608) 868-7772
VISITING HOURS:	Memorial Day–Labor Day, daily 11–4; May, Labor Day–Oct. 15, weekends
FEES:	Adults, $3; children 5–18, $1.75; children under 5, free
SOURCES:	Doris Hoag, Milton Historical Society. "Wisconsin Defies the Fugitive Slave Law." "Underground Railroad." *National Register of Historic Places,* 858. Letter from Mabel Davis Van DeMark, 1955, from the Milton Historical Society.

Milwaukee

America's Black Holocaust Museum*

Through books, paintings, photographs, and artifacts, America's Black Holocaust Museum shows how African Americans experienced their own holocaust, similar to that experienced by the Jewish people during World War II. The story moves from slavery's beginnings in Africa to the post-Civil War Reconstruction period.

The museum, founded by James Cameron with his own privately obtained funding, opened June 19, 1988. It moved to larger quarters on North Fourth Street on November 9, 1944; there artifacts and photographs are arranged in twelve rooms and 12,000 square feet of space. Cameron, the museum's director, recommends that visitors be eight years and older because the stark quality of some of the exhibits, including realistic wax effigies of lynchings, might frighten younger children. Those who see the exhibits usually are deeply moved on seeing the atrocities that Black Americans endured.

ADDRESS: 2233 N. Fourth Street, Milwaukee
TELEPHONE: (414) 264-2500
VISITING HOURS: Mon.–Sat. 9–6; by appointment Sun., holidays
FEES: Adults, $5; children under 12, $2.50
SOURCES: Telephone conversation Jan. 7, 1995, James Cameron, founder and director. *Hippocrene U.S.A. Guide to Black America*, 373.

Milwaukee County Historical Society Museum

The Milwaukee County Historical Society Museum includes an exhibit on Blacks in Milwaukee history as well as a growing archival collection on the history of African Americans in Milwaukee. It is well adapted for use by researchers. The Milwaukee Historical Society's quarterly magazine has published several articles relating to contributions by African Americans to the growth of Milwaukee.

ADDRESS: 910 N. Old World Third Street, Milwaukee
TELEPHONE: (414) 273-8288
VISITING HOURS: Society, Mon.–Fri. 9:30–5, Sat. 10–5, Sun. 1–5; library, Mon.–Fri. 9:30–noon, 1–4:30, Sat. 10–noon, 1–4:30; closed major holidays
FEES: Exhibits, free; library, user fee $1 per day
SOURCE: Telephone conversation June 24, 1994, Kathleen O'Hara, assistant for public relations, Milwaukee County Historical Society.

Wisconsin Black Historical Society Museum

One area of the Wisconsin Black Historical Society Museum exhibits thirteen dramatic four-foot-by-eight-foot murals depicting the history of the Black people from Africa through to the present day. Artifacts are in a separate area called the Bronzeville Room. Here, the visitor sees living quarters from the 1930s and 1940s—rooms representative of typical Milwaukee Black families of that era. The living quarters, a living room and a smaller room, are small because they actually were "tight" for the immigrants who came to Milwaukee to work as laborers. The smaller room, perhaps a bedroom or combination-use room, illustrates the crowded living conditions of the era. The exhibits, along with the tour guide's explanations, promote a feeling for the sweep and scope of African American history.

DATE ESTABLISHED: 1988

ADDRESS: 2620 W. Center Street, Milwaukee

TELEPHONE: (414) 372-7677; fax, (414) 372-4882

VISITING HOURS: Mon.–Thurs. 2–6, Sat. 9–2; hours may vary, call in advance; closed Fri., Sun., major holidays

FEES: Adults, $3; children, $1.50

SOURCES: Nancy M. Moser, marketing/communications, Milwaukee Public Museum. Kathleen O'Hara, assistant for public relations, Milwaukee County Historical Society. Professor William L. Van Deburg, University of Wisconsin–Madison. Telephone conversation June 25, 1994, Clayborn Benson, director, Milwaukee Black Historical Museum.

Viroqua

Vernon County Historical Museum

Vernon County—an area located east of Wildcat Mountain—was settled as an integrated community during the nineteenth century by people of varying ethnic origins, including Norwegian, Irish, and Czech backgrounds along with a sizable number of African Americans. Black farms were interspersed with white-owned farms. Churches and schools were established and built jointly. Integration included social activities, mutual assistance on the farms, and even occasional intermarriages.

The first Black settlers in the county were Walden Stewart and Wesley Barton, both of whom came from Illinois. Stewart arrived in May 1855. He was a free Black man who had been born in North Carolina. He and his wife, Hettie, lived about twenty years in Illinois before pulling up stakes and pioneering in Vernon County. Stewart was sixty years of age when he settled at the town of Forest.

Wesley Barton founded the community of Barton Corners and became its first postmaster in 1859. Since then, Barton Corners has changed its name and is now known as Burr Corners.

Revels Valley in Vernon County is named for another early Black settler, Mycajah Revels, who came from Indiana. In 1856 six Black families migrated here from North Carolina. Some of them bought land and farmed it; others did lumberjacking; still others manufactured barrels and shingles. Some of the farmers set up a mill at which they had their sorghum, wheat, and corn ground. After children shucked and shelled the corn, the miller ground the kernels into cornmeal and corn flour. The wheat also was ground into flour. The juice from the ground sorghum was turned into syrup and molasses.

The 1870 census listed sixty-two Black settlers among eleven families. Fifty years later the 1920 census reported one hundred African Americans in the area. The numbers afterward declined as more and more young people left the farms for better employment opportunities elsewhere. Exhibits in the Vernon County Historical Museum depict the contributions of all ethnic groups to the growth of the county.

DATE BUILT: 1989
ADDRESS: 410 Center Street, Viroqua
TELEPHONE: (608) 637-7396
VISITING HOURS: May 15–Sept. 15, Tues.–Sun. 1–5; Sept. 15–Nov. 1, Thurs.–Fri. 1–4
FEES: None; donations accepted
SOURCES: Judy Gates, curator, Vernon County Historical Museum. *Our Heritage, Discover It. Black Settlers in Rural Wisconsin.*

Note

1. Files of the Milton Historical Society, Milton, Wisconsin.

Works Consulted

Black Settlers in Rural Wisconsin. Zachary Cooper. Madison, Wis.: The State Historical Society of Wisconsin, 1977.

Hippocrene U.S.A. Guide to Black America: A Directory of Historic and Cultural Sites Relating to Black America. Marcella Thum. New York: Hippocrene, 1992.

National Register of Historic Places. Washington, D.C.: National Park Service, 1976.

Our Heritage, Discover It. Viroqua, Wis.: Volunteers from the Vernon County Historical Society and the Wisconsin Humanities Committee and National Endowment for the Humanities. [brochure]

"Underground Railroad." Dr. Rachel Salisbury. Transcript of tape on the program for the Milton Historical Society, 1976.

"Wisconsin Defies the Fugitive Slave Law." James I. Clark. Madison, Wis.: State Historical Society of Wisconsin, 1955. [paper]

PART 4

THE SOUTHWEST

Arizona
New Mexico
Oklahoma
Texas

The Southwest states—Arizona, New Mexico, Oklahoma, and Texas—were scenes of rough and turbulent frontier experiences for African Americans just as they were for others who moved west in the nineteenth and early twentieth centuries. Africans were among the earliest visitors to the region, having arrived with Spanish explorers in the fifteenth and sixteenth centuries. Estevanico (also called Estevan or Esteban), a Black man born in Morocco, was part of an expedition that explored present-day New Mexico in 1539. As the slave of a Franciscan friar, Marcos de Niza, Estevan joined others in searching for the fabled Seven Golden Cities of Cibola. The men thought they would find Zuni Indian villages filled with gold and jewels. Estevan eventually was killed by the Zuni Indians, and a later expedition found neither gold nor jewels. The Spanish continued to explore the region, however, and they established settlements in the Southwest. As Spanish explorers and missionaries came to the region, Black men were among them, and they became some of the earliest settlers.

New Mexico had a varied history of ownership as Spanish territory, then Mexican territory. In 1846, after the Mexican War, New Mexico became a United States territory. The United States gained additional land in 1853 with the Gadsden Purchase, which transferred another strip of land from Mexico to southern Arizona and New Mexico.

Once the territory became a part of the United States, white settlers arrived, seeking land for their own expansion. Most of them came from states in the Southeast, and they brought with them their slaves, their strong determination to maintain the institution of slavery, and their old ideas about racial superiority. As they gained territory, the settlers passed laws designed to keep Black, Native American, and Mexican people in subservient positions.

In the years leading up to the Civil War, white settlers in the Southwest became part of a national debate over the controversial idea of "popular sovereignty." This doctrine provided that in new federal territories, the white people themselves would determine whether to permit slavery in their own territory. The debates were heated. Many Northerners argued that slavery should not be extended into newly acquired western territories, while Southerners protested any such restrictions. The divisions became so deep that they threatened to split the Union. To restore calm, U.S. Senator Henry Clay proposed a series of compromises, several of which were adopted by Congress as the Compromise of 1850. As part of this agreement, New Mexico and Utah would be allowed to enter the Union under the principle of popular sovereignty; that is, the residents would determine by vote whether to allow or prohibit slavery in their states. The Compromise of 1850 was intended to stop the arguments about slavery in the territories, but the measure proved to be only a temporary solution. The issue of slavery continued to split the Union so deeply that the question eventually was settled only by war. When the Civil War began, most white citizens in New Mexico already had views that would later place them on the side of the Confederacy.

In addition to the early Black explorers and the slaves of former Southern planters, several other groups of Black men and women arrived in the Southwest prior to the twentieth century. They became a part of the remarkable variety of cultures in the region. The different groups influenced each other positively in many ways; yet, they often clashed as different factions tried to maintain or establish territorial rights. Black families were a part of all of the groups. They were among the Mexican people who lived in the Southwest before their land became U.S. territory. They arrived as servants and slaves of the Mormons (members of the Church of Jesus Christ of Latter-day Saints) who traveled in wagon trains from Nauvoo, Illinois, and other cities to Utah, where the Mormons hoped to escape religious and social persecution. Black men and women accompanied Native Americans who were forcibly removed from southeastern states and who were dispersed to the newly designated Indian Territory in present-day Oklahoma.

Black men, women, and children also were brave fugitives who emancipated themselves by escaping west along the underground railroad. They were the free Black men and women who moved west for a better life and who were drawn in large numbers to the new all-Black towns in Oklahoma. They were among the cowboys, miners, trappers, and explorers whose colorful and daring exploits helped to create the legendary images of the West. When the U.S. government sought to establish peace among all of these groups, Black men served proudly as the Buffalo Soldiers who guarded the frontier.

This section of the book highlights a variety of sites associated with Black Americans who lived in the Southwest, with emphasis on sites built in the late nineteenth and the early twentieth centuries. The structures include sites associated with the Buffalo Soldiers, the Black communities of Oklahoma, and a variety of houses, churches, and commercial structures located throughout the region.

The Buffalo Soldiers

When the Civil War ended in 1865, Black soldiers more than adequately had shown their courage in battle. At first they had not been allowed to enlist in the war that was called a "white man's war." As the fighting raged on, however, President Abraham Lincoln and Union leaders had to admit that the war was going badly for their side. Reluctantly, the Union leaders recognized that they needed to enlist African American soldiers to tip the balance in their favor. When Congress finally allowed Black men to enlist in the U.S. Army, the bold determination and loyalty in battle of the African Americans demolished objections that they would be cowardly and unfit as soldiers. The Black soldiers were a major force in the Union's victory.

In the years following the Civil War, although there was no longer any question about their courage, prejudice against African American soldiers remained strong. In spite of the insults, the men still wanted to serve in the army. The military life, even with its inequities, was better than the life they had previously known; it provided a measure of dignity, education, and opportunity to exercise leadership.

By 1866 the U.S. government had turned its attention to preventing conflicts that arose in the western territories between Native Americans and settlers and among the settlers themselves. In the same year Congress authorized the establishment of Black regiments. Perhaps to forestall objections of white citizens to having Black soldiers stationed nearby in the developed communities, the army sent the men to remote sites. These were places that were considered undesirable because of the rugged, undeveloped land or because the climate routinely was freezing cold or miserably hot.

In this climate, the Ninth and Tenth Cavalry and the Twenty-fourth and Twenty-fifth Infantry were sent to establish order on the frontier. They were to guard telegraph and supply lines and to protect settlers in sparsely settled territories, including New Mexico. In the 1800s several companies of the all-Black Ninth Cavalry were stationed at Fort Union in Watrous, New Mexico. Approximately one thousand African American soldiers were stationed at Fort Seldon near Radium Springs, New Mexico, or passed through the site. The Black men, who themselves had suffered prejudice and discrimination, unfortunately were assigned to fight the Native Americans who were having their land taken from them. The government pitted one group against the other while refusing to give full rights to either. The Black soldiers, nevertheless, carried out their duties as assigned, protecting white settlers and trying to ensure that Native Americans remained in designated areas.

In New Mexico the Black soldiers were assigned to fight against the Apaches, and they helped to defeat Chief Victorio in the Victorio War.

In spite of the unfortunate assignment of controlling Native Americans, the Black soldiers performed well and even seemed to have gained a measure of respect from Native Americans. The Indians began to refer to them as Buffalo Soldiers, a name that may have symbolized recognition of strength and courage as well as an awareness of the common physical characteristic of short, dark hair. The name certainly was associated with the buffalo, or bison, which the Native Americans revered and respected. The soldiers began to use the name themselves and through their stellar performance, made the term a symbol of respect. Moreover, the government never was very successful in turning Native Americans and Black Americans against each other.

The all-Black units had a variety of assignments. They were sent to Arizona, where Fort Huachuca had been built to provide protection against Apache Indians. After Geronimo's surrender in 1886, and after the battles with Native Americans diminished in intensity, the fort remained to provide protection from bandits who frequented the territory and who freely crossed the borders between the United States and Mexico. In this tense situation, all-Black divisions stationed at Fort Huachuca guarded the United States–Mexico border from the late 1890s through 1931. In 1916–1917 the all-Black Tenth U.S. Cavalry, under the direction of General John J. Pershing, initiated a pursuit into Mexico to capture Pancho Villa, a revolutionary folk-hero to many in Mexico who was considered a bandit by the U.S. government. Pancho Villa had angered U.S. officials by leading several guerrilla raids into New Mexico. In retaliation, General Pershing and the men from the Tenth pursued Villa into Mexico. Although they did not capture him, Villa later received amnesty in Mexico for laying down his arms. The African American men served at Fort Huachuca through World War II; after that the fort was declared surplus.

The Buffalo Soldiers were assigned to posts in various Southwest states where they lived and worked under harsh and primitive conditions. They built many of the forts themselves after scouting under grueling conditions for suitable sites. In Texas, in a search for springs and grasslands, the men rode for miles in temperatures that often reached more than 100 degrees. Once settled in the forts in Texas, they often had to fight another enemy—racism. They had been assigned to protect white citizens, but those same citizens often taunted and jeered them, mocking their status as U.S. soldiers. Eventually, some of the soldiers had to engage in fistfights and gunfights to protect themselves.

In spite of the difficult physical and social conditions, the soldiers carried out their duties well, establishing exceptional records for their performance. Today, the Southwest region still contains some of the forts where they served, and several posts are open to visitors.

The Black Communities of Oklahoma

The Buffalo Soldiers were only one of the African American groups that were a part of the history of the Southwest. Another large and important segment was the group that began arriving in present-day Oklahoma in the 1830s. African Americans came among the Indian nations referred to paternalistically as the Five Civilized Tribes: the Cherokee, Chickasaw, Choctaw, Creek, and Seminole Nations.

The arrival of these groups in Oklahoma was the culmination of tragic and shameful events. The Indian Removal Act of 1830 had removed Native Americans from their homelands in Florida, Alabama, Georgia, and Mississippi and had included the confiscation of their homes, livestock, and personal possessions. Then they were sent to Arkansas and Oklahoma, where the land was considered undesirable. The march to Oklahoma was so harsh and brutal that thousands died along the way.

Black Americans were part of the removal that later was referred to as the Trail of Tears. They had lived among the Native Americans, in some instances as equals, in other cases as slaves. White slaveowners encouraged Native Americans to own slaves, believing that slaveowning groups would be less likely to shelter and assist runaway slaves. Fortunately, these efforts to spread racism often failed. The Seminole Indians in Florida assisted runaway slaves, and the fugitives assisted the Seminoles in return because the slaves had knowledge both of the white settlers and of effective methods of cultivating crops. The two groups lived together in remote wilderness areas, protecting each other, gathering and cultivating food, making decisions together, and sometimes intermarrying. When the Seminole Wars ended and the process of removal began, Black Americans accompanied the Native Americans to Oklahoma. Members of both groups grieved when family members died along the way, unable to withstand the savage hardships of the journey. On reaching Oklahoma, the Native Americans received land in the newly designated Indian Territory. When the Civil War ended, freed African Americans who had arrived with the Indians also received land allotments in Indian Territory.

Other African Americans separately arrived in Oklahoma Territory, drawn by glowing reports of newly established all-Black communities. The possibilities for a new type of lifestyle seemed dazzling. For the first time, many were able to dream of living their daily lives without Jim Crow's constant reminders that they were expected to stay in their places. They could walk proudly with heads held high, making their own decisions and finding work in the full range of jobs that a town had available. No longer would they be automatically directed to the most menial, dangerous, and dirty work. They could start schools for their children, and they could build homes in any part of town without wondering if they would be welcome there. They could start businesses without worrying about racial jealousy. The degree of freedom seemed much larger in scope than any they had known in the South; the possibilities were so strong and beautiful that thousands of African Americans packed their belongings and traveled to the Oklahoma towns that were all-Black or that had substantial Black communities. Hundreds arrived in Boley, Ardmore, Eufaula, Langston, Lima, Muskogee, Okmulgee, Tulsa, and Wewoka, bringing their belongings and a lot of hope. They arrived before the Civil War began, after the Civil War ended, and in the early years of the twentieth century. By the time of Oklahoma's statehood in 1907, thousands of African Americans already had made Oklahoma their home. They had established businesses, churches, schools, and a variety of social organizations.

The dream that brought African Americans to Oklahoma sometimes clashed with harsh reality. Although life was far better than many of the families had known, their communities still remained enclaves in a rigidly segregated state. Laws barred Black people from voting, and without political power, their communities could not always make choices that were in their own self-interest. Business advantages could be guided away and tax monies could be siphoned off to the advantage of white communities. Without political power and adequate funds, many of the Black communities of Oklahoma struggled for their existence. They built elementary and secondary schools, and they established Langston University in Langston, Oklahoma, which produced many leaders. Unfortunately, many of Langston's graduates had to leave Oklahoma to find jobs that matched their skills, and they took with them talent and knowledge that could have been used to build the local communities.

Today, some of the historic buildings dating from the early twentieth century remain in several Oklahoma communities. The schools, churches, a theater, community centers, military sites, museums, and the university are all important in the region's Black history.

Other Southwest Sites

Several museums feature additional interesting stories about the lives of Black cowboys, miners, explorers, soldiers, and settlers in the Southwest. The Folsom Museum in Folsom, New Mexico, has replicas of some of the artifacts discovered by Black cowboy George McJunkin. McJunkin was an alert and intelligent cowboy who worked in New Mexico. Aside from his regular work, he also taught himself some of the rudiments of science. One day he observed some unusual bison bones and he recognized that they were of a kind he had never seen. He made one of the most significant finds in American archeology, later called the Folsom fossil bed. He had discovered a site in New Mexico where more than 10,000 years ago human beings had killed a species of buffalo that later became extinct.

Early Homes in the Southwest

A few of the early homes in which Black Americans lived in the Southwest can be seen by those who drive by, but most are not open to the public. Texas has three sites with early Black housing. The Pioneer Village Museum in Corsicana contains a slave cabin that was moved from a nearby plantation and reconstructed. In Waxahachie, Texas, visitors can drive by two small shotgun-style houses that were built between 1893 and 1900. The floor plan of shotgun houses is narrow, with rooms lined up in a row, one behind another.

The third residential site, and one of the most historically significant, is the Freedmen's Town Historic District (Fourth Ward) in Houston, Texas. In Freedmen's Town narrow streets and one- and two-story frame buildings coexist with modern structures built to house white businesses. The historic dwellings are remnants of a large African American community that grew between the years following the Civil War and the years of the Great Depression. The community contained homes, businesses, churches, a baseball field, and a high school and once was Houston's economic and social center of Black residents. Today, the remnant of the historic district consists of a forty-block area with an uncertain future. The homes are private, but a drive through the district is one of the best ways to see how many African Americans lived in Houston.

The Challenge of the Southwest

Whether they came to the Southwest as explorers, as slaves, as farmers, as ranchers, as miners, or as business owners, African Americans faced the same conditions and attitudes that they faced everywhere else in the United States. Their efforts to raise themselves to positions of dignity and respect were constantly rebuffed with Jim Crow laws and other restrictions. The African Americans, however, never lost the determination to grasp the opportunities and benefits promised to them. They continued to arrive in the Southwest where they built communities, lived, worshiped, gained an education, and struggled for their existence in the face of great odds.

Works Consulted

The Academic American Encyclopedia. Danbury, Conn.: Grolier, 1993. [electronic version]

Black Indians: A Hidden Heritage. William Loren Katz. New York: Atheneum, 1986.

The Black West. William Loren Katz. Seattle, Wash.: Open Hand, 1987.

Arizona

Fort Huachuca

Fort Huachuca Historical Museum

During the war with the Apache Indians between 1871 and 1886, the U.S. Army established a military camp at the base of the Huachuca Mountains. This site served to defend American travelers and settlers in southeastern Arizona. It also was strategically located so as to cut off traditional escape routes used by the Apache Indians. In 1882 the camp was designated Fort Huachuca. After the Apache chief, Geronimo (c1829–1909), surrendered to the U.S. Army in 1886, the Army retained the fort as a protection against American and Mexican outlaws as well as against Native Americans whom they regarded as troublesome.

Beginning in the late 1890s several all-Black divisions, known as the "Buffalo Soldiers," were stationed at Fort Huachuca. First to come was the all-Black Ninth U.S. Cavalry. In 1913, when trouble broke out along the Mexican border, the all-Black Tenth U.S. Cavalry was sent to the fort. Its members were part of the expedition led by General John J. Pershing (1860–1948) in 1916–1917 into Mexico in pursuit of Francisco "Pancho" Villa. During World War I the Tenth Cavalry guarded the U.S.–Mexican border.

Between 1931 and 1941 the all Black Twenty-fifth U.S. Infantry Regiment replaced the Tenth Cavalry at Fort Huachuca. During World War II men from the Twenty-fifth were absorbed into the Ninety-third Infantry Division, and the all Black Ninety-second and Ninety-third Infantry Divisions trained at this post before being sent overseas.

After World War II Fort Huachuca was declared surplus. Beginning in the 1950s it was used again, this time as a defense site for testing electronic equipment and as the Army's Communications Command Center.

The military complex has twelve adobe residences, frame barracks, and other structures; tours of the military complex are not offered, however. The historical museum opened in 1960 in a building built in 1892. It includes the story of Black soldiers in the West.

DATE ESTABLISHED:	Fort, 1877; museum, 1960
ADDRESS:	Museum headquarters, Fort Huachuca (3.6 miles west of Sierra Vista; 70 miles southeast of Tucson following I-10 and taking the Fort Huachuca exit at AZ 90)
TELEPHONE:	(602) 533-3638
VISITING HOURS:	Mon.–Fri. 9–4, Sat.–Sun. 1–4; closed federal holidays
FEES:	None
SOURCES:	David A. Huet, Fort Huachuca Historical Museum. Telephone call to site, June 25, 1994, and Sept. 17, 1995. *Fort Huachuca. National Register of Historic Places*, 37.

Work Consulted

Fort Huachuca: Home of the Buffalo Soldier. San Diego: MARCOA, 1986. [booklet]

New Mexico

Folsom Vicinity

George McJunkin- and Folsom-Related Sites

Historian Carter G. Woodson claimed that if African Americans did not preserve their history, others would assume credit for what they had accomplished. (For more information on Carter G. Woodson, see the section on Washington, D.C.) This is what happened to an exceptionally observant cowboy named George McJunkin, whose role in discovering one of the most-important archaeological sites in North America—the Folsom fossil bison bed—was long overlooked. McJunkin's persistent requests to professional archaeologists to examine the site were ignored for two decades. Only after his death was the site more fully explored and the critically important historical significance of the findings recognized. Even then, many who heard McJunkin's story considered the Black cowboy to be only a legend of a man who had never existed. Finally George Agogino, an anthropologist at the Eastern University of New Mexico, set out to gather evidence that McJunkin was real and that he did, indeed, deserve the credit for the find at Dead Horse Arroyo (sometimes called Wild Horse Arroyo or Hereford Arroyo). Agogino learned that McJunkin's interests in collecting and exploring and his keen powers of observation had led to the discovery of the New World's first site where, more than 10,000 years ago, people killed now-extinct forms of buffalo.

McJunkin's story began somewhat obscurely around 1856 on a farm and horse ranch in southern Texas. His parents were sharecroppers; according to some accounts, they were originally slaves who had been brought to Texas from Georgia and then freed. As a child, George received a fourth- to sixth-grade education. His parents were so poor that in his teens, with their blessings, George left for new territory, finding work where he could. By 1875 McJunkin had moved to New Mexico, where he found work rough-herding steers, making cattle drives, and breaking wild horses. He was employed as a wagon boss and cow foreman and later became the manager of the Oak Grove Ranch.

McJunkin was an eager reader. On long winter days or at any time he found a few minutes on his own, he would pore happily over encyclopedias and books on anthropology and geology. His interests and knowledge were remarkable for any person of that era and location because few people near Folsom had much formal education.

Although prejudice existed where McJunkin lived and worked, he was well respected by his peers and was treated by them as an equal. Ivan Shoemaker, a man whom McJunkin taught to ride wild horses and rope and work cattle, described an incident when a number of hands from different ranches had gathered at a large Folsom ranch to help with branding.

> A number of unbranded cattle still bellowed in the corral when the men went to the main

> house for the noon meal. One hungry man realized McJunkin hadn't come in to eat. "Where's George?" [he asked].
>
> "He'll eat in the kitchen with the other darkies," the lady of the house replied.
>
> For a brief moment, silence. Then chairs creaked and boots scuffed. Every cowboy at the table pushed back, stood, and walked outside. Not a word. Without a glance at the cattle milling in the corral, they mounted and rode away.[1]

Around 1908 after a major flood in Folsom, McJunkin made his discovery of fossil bones at Dead Horse Arroyo. Realizing that no surviving species of buffalo had long, straight horns and huge bones, the cowboy consulted experts and wrote to museums, asking that recognized scientists investigate the fossils he had found. Unfortunately, no one was interested. Years later McJunkin decided to enter an "old-time contest." He built a buckboard and was traveling in it when it broke a spring. He went for help to a blacksmith in Raton and found himself talking about his discovery to an amateur archaeologist, Carl Schwachheim. It was this man who did the excavations and who, after McJunkin's death, again brought the bones to the attention of people at the Denver Museum of Natural History.

In 1921 McJunkin had begun to suffer from dropsy. He moved into a basement room in the old Folsom Hotel, where he could receive care. Although there was no doctor in Folsom, a Dr. J. H. Steele made weekly trips into Folsom to look after McJunkin. Friends and neighbors also helped as best they could. A year or two later McJunkin died at an age estimated at sixty-six years.

Four years after McJunkin's death, a new development took place. A crew brought in to further excavate the Folsom site found a broken projectile point near the rib bones of an Ice-Age bison. Finally, scientists had proof that hunters had been active there during the last Ice Age, at a far earlier date than previously believed. Paleontologists working at the site proved conclusively that the early hunters had cooperated in tracking and killing large mammals as early as 9000 to 8000 B.C.

For many years after the scientific explorations at the Folsom site, people ignored McJunkin's role in its discovery. Some archaeologists made light of stories about the Black cowboy, whom they were convinced was just a myth. Although Folsom is listed in the *National Register of Historic Places*, the nomination form still makes no mention of George McJunkin, the site's discoverer.

Beginning in the 1960s and 1970s, however, some researchers gathered information about McJunkin. Jaxon Hewett wrote an article about him for *New Mexico Magazine*. George Agogino, professor of anthropology at Eastern New Mexico University, completed extensive research on the Black cowboy/discoverer and stated that McJunkin's discovery was "the start of a new and thrilling chapter in American pre-history, the story of the Paleo-Indian who entered the New World by way of the Bering Strait well over 12,000 years ago."[2]

The Folsom site is on private land and is not open to the public. However, visitors may drive by the old Folsom Hotel where McJunkin spent his last months. Since the hotel is now a private residence, only the exterior may be viewed. A two-story house a short distance from the hotel is said to have been owned by McJunkin. The cowboy is buried in the Folsom Cemetery a few blocks away from the hotel. McJunkin's grave was originally in the back, possibly because of his race. After the road was changed, however, his grave is now in the front of the cemetery. The Folsom Museum has pictures of the dig and replicas of the Folsom artifacts. The Denver Museum of Natural History in Denver, Colorado, has one bison, mounted, from the Folsom site, along with a brief description, on the first floor in the Earth Sciences Hall.

DATE OF SIGNIFICANCE: McJunkin's discovery c1908

ADDRESS: Folsom site, 8 miles west of Folsom on the bank of Hereford Canyon; Old Folsom Hotel, ask for directions in town; cemetery, 325 Capulin Mountain Road (from the Folsom Hotel go west, continue as the street turns sharply north and the cemetery is ¼ mile on the right); Folsom Museum, junction of NM 325 and NM 456, Folsom; Denver Museum of Natural History, 2001 Colorado Boulevard, Denver

TELEPHONE: Folsom Museum, (505) 278-2122; Denver Museum of Natural History, reservations, (303) 322-7009, or paleontology, (303) 370-6448

VISITING HOURS: Folsom site, private; Folsom Museum, Memorial Day weekend–Labor Day weekend, daily 10–5, closed winters except by appointment; Denver Museum of Natural History, Sat.–Thurs. 9–7, Fri. 9–9, closed Christmas Day

FEES: Folsom Museum, adults, $1; children 6–12, $.50; children under 6, free; Denver Museum of Natural History, adults $4.50; senior citizens 65 and over and children 4–12, $2.50; children under 4, free

SOURCES: NRHPINF. Dr. Mary Ann Enders, architectural historian, State of New Mexico, Historic Preservation Division. Anya Mayans, Museum of New Mexico. Telephone conversation June 28, 1994, John Bowman, editor, *New Mexico Magazine.* Telephone conversation June 28, 1994, and Sept. 17, 1995, Kay Thompson, secretary, Folsom Museum. Telephone conversation June 29, 1994, Dr. E. James Dixon, curator of archaeology, Denver Museum of Natural History. Telephone conversation June 30, 1994, Dr. George Agogino, anthropology professor emeritus and author. Telephone conversation July 1, 1994, Mercedes Phillips, mayor, Folsom. Telephone conversation Aug. 10, 1995, Karen Arnedo, registrar, Denver Museum of Natural History. "The Bookish Black at Wild Horse Arroyo," 20. "The McJunkin Controversy," 41–47.

Radium Springs

Fort Seldon State Monument

Approximately one thousand Black soldiers, called the Buffalo Soldiers by the Native Americans, were stationed at Fort Seldon or passed through the site. After the Civil War both Black and white soldiers were stationed at ten forts in New Mexico, including Fort Seldon. The Buffalo Soldiers were involved in engagements against the Apaches, who were resisting the arrival of white settlers in the western territories of New Mexico, Arizona, and parts of Texas. The Ninth Cavalry in New Mexico and the Tenth Cavalry in Texas both participated in the war that ended with the defeat of Chief Victorio and the Warm Spring Apaches.

Fort Seldon, which was a military post for twenty-six years, now consists of adobe ruins of the soldiers and officers quarters, a few other old buildings, and a modern museum. Plaques show how the barracks once looked. Although the museum does not have a separate exhibit on the Buffalo Soldiers, it includes photographs and texts that highlight the role of the Black soldiers of the Ninth Cavalry Regiment. Visitors can see a ten-minute video before taking the self-guided tour.

DATE BUILT: 1865

ADDRESS: Radium Springs (exit 19 off I-25, then ¼ mile west)

TELEPHONE: (505) 526-8911

VISITING HOURS: May 1–Sept. 15, daily 9:30–5:30; the rest of the year, 8:30–4:30; closed New Year's Day, Thanksgiving, Christmas

FEES: Adults 16 and older, $2; children under 16, free; New Mexico residents, $1 on Sun.; New Mexico senior citizens 60 and up, free on Wed.; school groups, free

SOURCES: Jeffrey P. Brown, New Mexico State University. Telephone conversation Apr. 28, 1994, José Guzman, manager, Fort Seldon. Telephone call to site, June 26, 1994.

Watrous

Fort Union National Monument

African American soldiers were stationed at Fort Union in the 1800s. The large site included three separate military installations: a garrison of infantry soldiers and cavalry troopers and occasionally field artillery units, a quartermaster depot at which military supplies were stored, and the arsenal of the U.S. Ninth Cavalry. Several companies of the Ninth Cavalry guarded the telegraph and supply lines. During the Indian Wars of the last century, African American soldiers stationed at Fort Union fought the Apaches and guarded the biggest military supply depot in the American West.

After the Army abandoned the fort in 1981, much of the post was dismantled and stripped of articles of value, including the tin roofs. Left behind were only the walls, foundations, and cisterns.

Today Fort Union has 100 acres of adobe ruins that visitors can explore in a self-guided tour. Although only portions of the buildings remain, they are fascinating because they show the outline of what once was the largest fort west of the Mississippi. The mile-and-a-quarter-long walking tour makes a complete loop from the Visitors Center and back. The tour usually takes at least two hours, so visitors should wear comfortable clothing. There is a cutoff at the halfway point for those who do not want to take the complete tour. Inside the Visitors Center guests can ask for a handout on the Ninth Cavalry and view one of the exhibits that tells about the Ninth through photographs, a mannekin, and a short history that lists the names of men who were awarded the Congressional Medal of Honor.

DATE BUILT: 1851

ADDRESS: 8 miles northwest of Watrous on NM 161

TELEPHONE: (505) 425-8025

VISITING HOURS: Memorial Day–Labor Day, daily 8–6; the rest of the year, daily 8–5; closed Christmas, New Year's Day

FEES: $4 per car or adults 16 and older, $2; children under 16, free

SOURCE: Telephone conversation June 26, 1994, Mick Clifford, chief park ranger, Fort Union National Monument.

Notes

1. Jaxon Hewett, "The Bookish Black at Wild Horse Arroyo: How the Folsom Man Came to Light," *New Mexico Magazine* 5, no. 1–2 (Jan./Feb. 1971): 20.

2. George Agogino, "The McJunkin Controversy," *New Mexico Magazine* 49, no. 5–6 (May/June 1971), 47.

Works Consulted

"The Bookish Black at Wild Horse Arroyo: How the Folsom Man Came to Light." Jaxon Hewett. *New Mexico Magazine* 5, no. 1–2 (Jan./Feb. 1971): 20.

"The McJunkin Controversy." George Agogino. *New Mexico Magazine* 49, no. 5–6 (May/June 1971): 41–47.

Oklahoma

Ardmore

Black Historic Sites of Ardmore

During the 1830s a series of deceptive treaties and adverse court decisions created harsh circumstances for Native Americans from the southeastern United States. The Indian Removal Act of 1830 was followed by the 1831 case of *Cherokee Nation* v. *The State of Georgia,* in which the U.S. Supreme Court ruled that the Indians were not independent nations. The court ruled instead that Native Americans were subject to regulation by the federal government. After these rulings were handed down, the members of five Indian nations—the Cherokee, Chickasaw, Choctaw, Creek, and Seminole—were forced to give up their traditional homelands in the Southeast. Federal government representatives forcibly marched them from Florida, Georgia, Alabama, and Mississippi to Arkansas and to Indian Territory, an area that at first encompassed most of present-day Oklahoma. More than 4,000 of the 15,000 Cherokee died on the way to Indian Territory in a journey so devastating that it became known as the "Trail of Tears."

In Indian Territory in 1859 the Native Americans joined in a loose federation designated as the Five Civilized Tribes. The five Indian nations were described as civilized because they had adopted many of the ways and customs of white people. Among the Native Americans were significant numbers of people of Black or mixed Indian–Black heritage. Members of the Black groups had an uncertain status because slaveowners in the Southeast, recognizing the potential for alliances to form between Indian and Black people, had encouraged the Indians to become slaveowners and to regard themselves as superior to African Americans. The results of the slaveowners' efforts were mixed. Some Native Americans became slaveowners and treated their slaves harshly; others became allies of Black people. Runaway slaves found some of their strongest allies among the Seminoles, many of whom actively assisted runaway slaves. The Seminoles who did own slaves treated the slaves in a benign manner; they often intermarried with runaway slaves. Of the thousands of African Americans who accompanied the Indians on the forced march to Indian Territory, some were slaves of the Indians; others were former runaways who now were part of Indian groups as equals. Treatment of the African Americans varied in Indian Territory. For example, when the Chickasaw Indians reached Indian Territory, they began to establish farms, using Black slaves as laborers.

The end of the Civil War brought changes for members of the Five Civilized Tribes. Newly freed African Americans who had arrived with the Native Americans received land allotments in Indian Territory. The federal government claimed, however, that the Five Civilized Tribes had allied with the Confederates; in retaliation the U.S. negotiated new treaties in 1866. The treaties forced the Native Americans to give up the western half of their territory for fifteen to thirty cents per acre. The federal government then settled Plains Indians on some of the land that had been taken away, and white settlers rushed in to claim much of the unassigned land. In 1890 unassigned land officially was designated Oklahoma Territory. The Indian Territory was absorbed into Oklahoma Territory in 1907, and the union of Indian and Oklahoma Territories became the new state of Oklahoma.

Early in the 1900s—even before statehood was proclaimed—additional free African Americans were attracted to Oklahoma. They were particularly drawn to Ardmore, which had become a rail outlet for the cotton farms and cattle ranches of the surrounding area. In the 1920s Ardmore had more than 2,000 Black residents. There was a Black business district that included a grocery store, barbershop, blacksmith's shop, and rooming house and other enterprises. In an era of segregation, these businesses provided much-needed services. Three sites in Ardmore are particularly associated with the history of the African American community: the Black Theater, Douglass High School Auditorium, and the Dunbar School.

DATE ESTABLISHED: 1900s

SOURCES: NRHPINF. Telephone conversations Apr. 22, 1994, Mentha Mitchell Varner, community leader, and Nileph Jo Robinson, Head Start director. Telephone conversation Apr. 24, 1994, Elder Chester Figures, Victory Temple. New Grolier Multimedia Encyclopedia.

Black Theater

The Black Theater of Ardmore was built about 1922 in the African American business community. The two-story, red-brick building, one of the oldest Black-owned commercial buildings in Oklahoma, existed in a thriving business district. During the Great Depression, however, some families left in search of more opportunity in the big cities; as a result, a number of the business buildings became vacant or deteriorated from neglect. In 1944 the Metropolitan African Methodist Episcopal Church bought the Black Theater of Ardmore; still later it became the home of the Victory Temple congregation.

DATE BUILT: c1922

ADDRESS: 536 E. Main Street, Ardmore

TELEPHONE: (405) 226-8018

VISITING HOURS: Sun. services, 9:30 and 11; Tues. Bible Study, 7:30 P.M.; Thurs. service, 7:30 P.M.; by appointment at other times

Douglass High School Auditorium

The Douglass High School Auditorium was established in the early 1900s as Ardmore's first high school and the only high school for Black students. The Oklahoma state constitution of 1907 legalized separate schools for Black and white students, but it did not provide equal funding. Black schools received their support from countywide tax levies, while white schools received funding both from county taxes and local school district property taxes. This disparity resulted in differences in facilities. Black students, for example, did not have an auditorium until this building was constructed in 1930 near Douglass High School.

The Douglass High School Auditorium was the largest facility of its kind for African American students in southern Oklahoma. For more than fifty-three years plays, musical productions, athletic contests, and graduations were presented here. In 1969, after the school system was integrated, a new high school complex with an auditorium replaced the older one. The Ardmore Public School System continued to use the old one-story, red-brick auditorium as an administration building and area for housing school buses.

DATE BUILT: c1930

ADDRESS: 800 M Street NE, Ardmore

TELEPHONE: (405) 226-7650

VISITING HOURS: Contact Ardmore City Schools for information

Dunbar School

Dunbar is the oldest school associated with Ardmore's Black community. As the need for schools grew, the Oklahoma state constitution of 1907 stipulated that local communities should build separate schools for Black and white children. By 1910, when African Americans formed 19 percent of the city's population, Black children had to attend underfunded, segregated schools. In 1922 the school board constructed Dunbar, a one-story, red-brick schoolhouse. The structure had decorative brickwork and a masonry frieze on all exterior walks, and the landscaped site featured trees and shrubbery. In spite of discrepancies in funding, Dunbar School was a symbol of pride and cohesiveness in the community.

In the 1950s the school district remodeled Dunbar and changed its name to the H. F. V. Wilson School, honoring a principal who had been one of Ardmore's leading Black educators. School operations ceased in 1968, and the historic school was converted into the Mentha Mitchell Varner Head Start Center, named in honor of a community leader.

DATE BUILT:	1922
ADDRESS:	13 G Street SE, Ardmore
TELEPHONE:	Mentha Mitchell Varner Head Start Center, (405) 226-0759
VISITING HOURS:	Contact the Center for information

Boley

Boley Historic District

When the great majority of the Cherokee, Choctaw, Chickasaw, Creek, and Seminole nations were forcibly relocated to Oklahoma in the 1830s, they brought thousands of Black slaves with them over the Trail of Tears. (Many Indians had not enslaved the Black people but considered them to be brothers.) These Native Americans and African Americans settled in Oklahoma—then referred to as the Indian Territory—between 1830 and 1840.

After emancipation African Americans who had come to Indian Territory with the five Indian nations also received an allotment of land. Other African Americans arrived here before the Civil War ended and again in the 1880s as the Oklahoma Territory was opened up for settlement. They were fleeing prejudice and oppression in the South, and wanted to find a place where they could live independently and govern their own communities. The freed men and women established many all-Black towns, including Boley, Tatums, and Rhubarb, in the late-nineteenth century, before statehood was proclaimed in 1907.

Boley, Oklahoma, developed as an all-Black town in the central part of Okfuskee County on fertile land that had been allocated to former slaves of the Creek Indians. Building began on the 160 acres Abigail Barnett McCormick had inherited from her father, James Barnett. Thomas M. Haynes, a town founder, was selected as the site manager. Enthusiastically, he advertised the town as a place where Black people could live independently and without oppression. African Americans responded by coming to Boley from Georgia, Texas, Louisiana, Florida, Mississippi, and Alabama. On September 22, 1904, the townspeople assembled for a formal town opening. When Boley incorporated in 1905, many who had never before been able to vote could elect their town officials. Enthusiasm for the town was so high that when famous educator Booker T. Washington visited Boley in 1905, he praised it as the most enterprising and interesting of the Black towns in the United States. By 1911 Boley had a population of about 4,000.

The city's commercial district grew, encompassing three banks as well as hotels, restaurants, cotton gins, a lumber yard, a brick yard, an ice plant, a drugstore, a hardware store, and a general mercantile enterprise. Boley also boasted a three-story Negro State Masonic Temple, churches, and schools from the elementary grades through junior college. Half of the graduates of Boley's accredited Black high school went on to college. Many became successful because they were products of a good school system and had seen successful Black business leaders in their home town. The Boley Commercial Club claimed in 1912 that Boley was the largest and wealthiest Black city in the world.

Unfortunately, few state jobs were open to Black college graduates, and many skilled graduates had to leave Oklahoma to establish businesses or professional practices elsewhere. Another setback for Boley residents was that their growing political power caused resentment among the state's white citizens. Seeing that Black voters held the balance of power in many elections, the state, in retaliation, amended the constitution in 1910 with a grandfather clause. This stipulated that a person could not vote whose grandfather had not voted; it also imposed literacy tests on Black voters. In 1915 the Supreme Court in *Guinn and Beal* v. *United States* ruled the law an unconstitutional evasion of the Fifteenth Amendment. Yet, the conflicts continued until 1939 when, for a second time, the denial of the right to vote was declared unconstitutional.

A setback came when the cotton crops failed in the 1920s. Later the Great Depression brought hard times in the 1930s. More families moved on, and the population dwindled to about one-fourth of what it had been in 1911. Although fewer than 600 residents remained by 1968, Boley continued to build on its strengths. It is of national historic significance as one of the all-Black towns of Oklahoma that sought independence and self-governance for African Americans and that successfully fought all the way to the Supreme Court efforts to disenfranchise its citizens. Boley is historically significant as the largest of the Black towns established by people who wished to escape oppression and build a new life for themselves.

This historic town in the Creek Nation region of Oklahoma is listed in the *National Register of Historic Places.* Some of its historic structures are the Antioch Baptist Church (1905, reconstructed 1929), the Oliver Building (1910), Watson Building (1915), Turner's Pharmacy Building (1910), T. M. Haynes Building (1909), Boley Bank and Trust Company (1906), Frame Church Building (1904), Tieul Clothing Store Building (1921), and the Farmers and Merchants State Bank Building (c1920). Charles Coleman, president of the Boley Chamber of Commerce, maintains that the Farmers and Merchants State Bank was the first Black bank in the United States. The historic building is no longer operated as a bank but retains the bank's fine marble floors.

DATE ESTABLISHED:	1903
ADDRESS:	Historic district, roughly bounded by Seward Avenue, Walnut and Cedar Streets, and the southern city limits; Chamber of Commerce, 125 S. Pecan Street, Boley
TELEPHONE:	Chamber of Commerce, (918) 667-3943
VISITING HOURS:	Sites are both public and private; contact the Chamber of Commerce
SOURCES:	NRHPINF. Oklahoma Writers Project, from files of the Oklahoma Historical Society. Kathy L. Dickson, director of museums, Oklahoma Historical Society. Telephone conversation Apr. 25, 1994, Charles Coleman, president, Boley Chamber of Commerce. "Shaped by a Dream."

Fort Gibson

Fort Gibson Military Park*

Fort Gibson, Oklahoma's oldest military post, was built in 1824 when the region was sparsely settled. During the Indian removal period, many Black people, both slaves and freed men and women, worked at Fort Gibson or came there for business. For many of them, their legal status was unresolved. Although they claimed to be free, some members of the Five Tribes claimed them as slaves. While the African Americans awaited a decision about their status, they found sanctuary at Fort Gibson. Tradition maintains that they built at least one of Fort Gibson's still-existing buildings.

The fort also served as a center for Black refugees during the Civil War. The First Kansas Colored Infantry passed through Fort Gibson on their way from the Battle of Cabin Creek to the Battle of Honey Springs in July 1863. (The Honey Springs battlefield site, which is undeveloped today, is located about twenty-five miles from Fort Gibson.)

After the Civil War, units of several Black regiments were stationed at the fort. In 1867 Fort Gibson was the headquarters of the Tenth Regiment of Cavalry (the Buffalo Soldiers). One story about the fort suggests that after it was abandoned, the mother of the outlaw Crawford Goldsby (a.k.a. Cherokee Bill) lived in one of the Army buildings that still stands. Crawford Goldsby was of mixed Black, white, and Indian blood. His funeral was held in the building after he was hanged at Fort Smith under sentence of Judge Isaac Parker, and his grave is in the Cherokee National Cemetery at the edge of town.

Many former slaves of the so-called Five Civilized Tribes received their tribal allotments from the Dawes Commission at a temporary office in one of the old Army buildings at the abandoned fort. In the 1930s Black WPA workers participated in the restoration of the historic site.

Today, Fort Gibson consists of six original structures and five that have been reconstructed to represent the Indian removal period. Most of the original structures were completed after the Civil War. Visitors often enjoy seeing the pickets, the cannon in the stockade area, the well, the stocks, and the areas where the officers and enlisted men lived. Some buildings on the hill are being restored; these include the hospital, bake house, commissary, blacksmith shop, guardhouse, library, and schoolhouse. Although some of the buildings are privately owned, they may be viewed from the outside.

DATE BUILT:	1824
ADDRESS:	110 E. Ash Avenue (1 mile north of US 62 on OK 80), Fort Gibson
TELEPHONE:	(918) 478-2669
VISITING HOURS:	Mon.–Sat. 9–5, Sun. 1–5; closed federal holidays
FEES:	None; donations accepted
SOURCES:	Chris Morgan, Oklahoma Historical Society, Fort Gibson Military Park. Telephone conversation Apr. 23, 1994, Sally Phillips, historic site attendant, Fort Gibson.

Langston

Langston University

The city of Langston in Oklahoma Territory was advertised to Black people throughout the South as a place to be "free, equal, and independent." They were urged to come to Langston and to make a home there. Earlier, some African Americans had hoped to secure all of Oklahoma for Black people from the South. When this dream failed, they established several all-Black cities instead.

Both Langston University and the town of Langston were named for Dr. John Mercer Langston, who was a Black congressman during the Reconstruction era. However, Edwin P. McCabe, the man who founded the city, was responsible for urging the Oklahoma Territorial Legislature to pass a bill in 1897 establishing the Colored Agricultural and Normal University of the Territory of Oklahoma. The university, an institution of higher education for Black students, was founded as a land-grant college through the Morrill Act of 1890.

Settlers from the city of Langston donated the forty acres of land on which the university is situated. In a year's time they raised the money through donations, bake sales, and auctions. In 1897 the university opened, using the facilities of a Presbyterian church. The first president, Dr. Inman E. Page, started out with four faculty members and an appropriation of $5,000. The curriculum emphasized agriculture, industrial arts, and domestic classes. Students also studied trigonometry and rhetoric.

In 1942 the college was renamed for Congressman John Mercer Langston (1829–1897), a graduate of Oberlin College, school inspector general of the Freedmen's Bureau, professor of law and acting president of Howard University, and a member of the U.S. House of Representatives from 1890 to 1891.

Many outstanding Oklahomans have graduated from Langston University or taught there. Zelia N. Breaux (1884–1956) started the music department when she was eighteen years old. Dr. Isaac Walton Young (1874–1937), who served two terms as Langston president, practiced medicine in and served as mayor of Boley. Dr. W. H. Hale (1914–1974) became the first Langston graduate to serve as president of Langston University.

Langston graduate Maxine Horner, born in Tulsa in 1933, served as a state senator from District 11 in Tulsa. Elected in November 1986, she has served through the present (March 1995). Melvin Tolson (1898–1966) served as mayor of Langston four times and was professor of creative literature at Langston University. Appointed Poet Laureate of Liberia, he wrote *Libretto for the Republic of Liberia* in 1953. In 1966 the American Academy and Institute of Arts and Letters presented him with the Arts and Letters Award in Literature.

Langston professor Ada Lois Sipuel Fisher applied to attend Oklahoma University in 1946. Rejected because of her race, she made history with her court battle that led to the integration of higher education in Oklahoma. Professor Fisher, finally admitted in 1949, was the first African American to attend the University of Oklahoma Law School and later became an attorney in Oklahoma City.

Dr. Nathan Hare (1934–), scholar, writer, and major leader of the Black studies movement, was a founder of the research journal *The Black Scholar.* The son of sharecropper parents, Hare earned a doctorate in psychology and became a prolific writer. He emphasized the power of traditional African American ideas and customs in his books and journal articles. Dr. Henry Ponder, another Langston graduate, has served for many years as president of Fisk University in Nashville, Tennessee, from the 1984–1985 school year through the present (1994–1995).

Recent decades have brought an interest in African American studies. The Melvin B. Tolson Black Heritage Center, established at Langston University in 1970, houses materials about the Black experience in the United States and abroad. It also provides research materials on the Southwest, including books, microfilm, and African American newspapers and periodicals. In recent years Langston University has enrolled more than 2,000 students, of whom approximately 73 percent are African American. For many decades it was the only university in Oklahoma open to Black students, and it remains the state's only predominantly African American university.

DATE ESTABLISHED: Mar. 12, 1897

ADDRESS: OK 33 E, Langston

TELEPHONE: (405) 466-2231; visits arranged through Public Relations/Public Information Offices, (405) 466-3230 or (405) 466-3482

VISITING HOURS: Mon.–Fri. 8–5; closed New Year's Day, Martin Luther King Day, Memorial Day, July 4, Labor Day, Thanksgiving, Christmas

SOURCES: Personal visit to site, summer 1992. Telephone conversation Mar. 16, 1995, Maxine Horner, Oklahoma state senator. Kathy L. Dickson, director of museums, Oklahoma Historical Society. Public Relations Office of Langston University. "Original Entrance Declared Landmark." *Langston University, Our Heritage.* "100 Influential Black Oklahomans." "College Heights Addition, Langston City, Oklahoma Territory, April 21, A.D. 1891." *The African American Encyclopedia,* 1570.

Lawton

Fort Sill Military Reservation and National Historic Landmark*

Most of the thirteen military posts erected in the Indian Territory and the Oklahoma Territory prior to 1869 were constructed by Black soldiers of the Tenth Cavalry Regiment. Soldiers of the Ninth and Tenth Cavalry Regiments worked together to build Fort Sill in the Indian Territory. It was established in 1869 during the midst of a winter campaign against Native Americans of the South Plains. Until 1875 soldiers stationed at Fort Sill were involved in the Red River campaign against the Indians. The Black men of these cavalry units were known to the Indians as the "Buffalo Soldiers."

Lieutenant Henry Ossian Flipper, the first Black graduate of the U.S. Military Academy at West Point, was sent on his first assignment to Fort Sill, where he joined the Tenth Cavalry. One of his duties was to design a drainage ditch to eliminate standing water that had caused malaria and other sickness. When he completed this work, his commander, who came to inspect the ditch, did not believe the design could be operational because it appeared to drain in the wrong direction. The design, however, was proven to be correct, and the ditch, referred to today as "Flipper's Ditch" in honor of the accomplishment, is listed today in the *National Register of Historic Places.* (For more information on Flipper, see the entry for Fort Davis, Texas.)

Since 1911 Fort Sill has been the home of the U.S. Army Field Artillery Center and School. The fort museum consists of ten buildings, many of which date from the original foundation period. Included among them are the old post headquarters (1870), the cavalry barracks (1872), the post chapel (1875), and a warehouse that served as a school for children of the post and as an artillery classroom. Today the former warehouse is the Visitors Center, housing exhibits about the Buffalo Soldiers and their role in the history of the Indian Territory. The museum also has a children's area called Cricket's Corner, where children see an old kitchen and try out one of the old, uncomfortable saddles. Fort Sill is developing trails to the old quarry area; at an overlook there visitors can look down into the mining areas where Buffalo Soldiers blasted stones, then carried them off to use in building Fort Sill's structures.

DATE ESTABLISHED: 1869

ADDRESS: 5 miles north on US 62/277/281 to the gate entrance; museum office, Building 437, Quanah Road, Lawton vicinity

TELEPHONE: (405) 442-5123

VISITING HOURS: Daily, 9–4:30; museum's library/photo archival research collections, Mon.–Fri. 7:30–11:30, 12:30–4; closed Dec. 25–26, Jan. 1–2

FEES: None

SOURCES: Telephone conversation Apr. 25, 1994, Mr. Towana D. Spivey, director, Fort Sill Museum. *Fort Sill Museum.* "100 Influential Black Oklahomans."

Lima

Rosenwald Hall

Rosenwald Hall, a rectangular red-brick building with white clapboard sections, served the community of Lima, Oklahoma, from 1921 to 1966. During this period it was Lima's only elementary school.

Lima, one of twenty-nine all-Black towns founded in Oklahoma before statehood (twenty-five in the Indian Territory and four in the Oklahoma Territory), is one of only three such towns in existence. The towns attracted a population consisting of migrants from other regions as well as former slaves of the Indians.

The schoolhouse has a place in history as a facility constructed with funds from the Julius Rosenwald Foundation. Julius Rosenwald (1862–1932), businessman and philanthropist, was president of Sears, Roebuck, and Company from 1910 to 1925 and became chairman of the board in 1925. He established the Julius Rosenwald Fund in 1917. Influenced by the renowned African American educator Booker T. Washington, Rosenwald contributed through his fund part of the construction costs for more than 4,000 schools for Black children in 15 southern states. (Another Rosenwald school is discussed in the listing for Ahoskie, North Carolina.) Black communities needed the assistance from foundations because local funding inequities resulted in far more monies for white schools. The Rosenwald Foundation grants, supplemented with community contributions, raised the quality of educational facilities for Black children. By 1930, 10 percent of Oklahoma's African American children were studying in Rosenwald-funded schools. Of the Rosenwald Schools constructed in all-Black towns in Oklahoma, this is the only one remaining. Rosenwald Hall, a building that has retained much of its original character, closed as a school in 1966 but remained in use as a day care center from 1970 to 1985 and as a town hall since 1985.

DATE BUILT: 1921

ADDRESS: College Street, Lima

VISITING HOURS: Private, visitors may walk or drive by

SOURCES: NRHPINF. Telephone conversation Apr. 30, 1994, James Hubbard, mayor, Lima. Telephone conversation May 21, 1994, Mrs. Deborah Washington and Mrs. Tammy Hill, community residents.

Muskogee

African American Sites of Muskogee

Three churches and a mission school represent the early African American buildings of Muskogee. Muskogee, founded in 1872, became a major urban center in the Indian Territory; by 1910 it was the second-largest city in the new state of Oklahoma. Many African Americans were attracted to the city for employment opportunities in the first decades of the twentieth century, and Muskogee eventually contained Oklahoma's third largest Black community. In spite of a segregated society, African Americans here developed a thriving business district that included retail stores, a bank, a Black-owned newspaper, and offices for attorneys and physicians. There also were schools, churches, and fraternal orders.

Three churches show how early Black congregations developed in Muskogee. After missionary activity began in Indian territory in the 1830s, the Baptist and Methodist denominations became very active. The churches are included in the *National Register of Historic Places.* In addition to the churches, there is the former Manual Training High School for Negroes, a site that visitors may drive by. It may be restored in the future.

SOURCES: NRHPINF. Reverend W. R. Norful Sr., minister, Ward Chapel A.M.E. Church. Oklahoma Landmarks Inventory. Telephone conversation Apr. 24, 1994, Reverend T. G. Allen, Ward Chapel A.M.E. Church. Telephone conversation Apr. 28, 1994, Mr. Delbert Jackson, Central Missionary Baptist Church. Telephone conversation Apr. 30, 1994, Mr. Renaldo Boulware, trustee, First Baptist Church. Telephone conversation Apr. 30, 1994, Mrs. Willie Mae Robbins, Spencer United Methodist Church and Manual Training School.

First Baptist Church

First Baptist Church was constructed in 1903, four years before Oklahoma became a state. It is one of Muskogee's oldest unaltered Black churches. The one and one-half–story building is constructed of red brick, and the north side has a tower at each corner. The First Baptist congregation grew out of a Muskogee mission school established for African Americans and Native Americans in 1877. Eventually the congregation purchased land at the present site. By the 1920s the congregation of First Baptist numbered approximately 700 and was one of Oklahoma's largest Black congregations. It hosted the National Baptist Convention during the 1920s. In the 1930s the congregation actively helped the community's unemployed by sponsoring a soup kitchen at the church.

DATE BUILT: 1903

ADDRESS: Fifth and Denison Streets, Muskogee

TELEPHONE: Renaldo Boulware, (918) 687-1435

VISITING HOURS: Sun. school, 9:30; Sun. service, 11–1

Spencer Memorial United Methodist Church

Spencer Memorial, which was constructed in 1928, is located in Muskogee's Black residential community. By 1920 Methodists were the second-largest denomination in the community. An African Methodist church had been built at an earlier date, and this was the second Methodist church in the community. It is constructed of red brick with white clapboard in the gable ends. The entrance doors have surrounding colored window lights. There have been no major alterations in more than sixty years.

DATE BUILT: 1928

ADDRESS: 543 N. Seventh Street, Muskogee

TELEPHONE: (918) 682-2823

VISITING HOURS: Sun. service, 11

Ward Chapel African Methodist Episcopal Church

Ward Chapel A.M.E. Church, the city's second-oldest Black Protestant church, is one of the oldest Black churches in Muskogee that has remained essentially unaltered. The congregation organized in 1893; the present church was constructed in Muskogee's original townsite in 1904. The red-brick church has five Gothic pointed arch windows on the north side and four arched windows in the gable section.

DATE BUILT:	1904
ADDRESS:	319 N. Ninth Street, Muskogee
TELEPHONE:	(918) 682-7384
VISITING HOURS:	Sun. services, 9:30 and 11; other times by appointment

Manual Training School

The former Manual Training School building is one of the oldest African American secondary-school structures in eastern Oklahoma. It opened in 1910 at a time when Muskogee was a center for trading and processing cotton, a major railroad center, and a hub of petroleum refineries. At the time of the school's opening, 7,831 African American residents, approximately 31 percent of the city's population, lived in Muskogee, and their children needed a school. Since the 1907 state constitution provided for racially segregated schools, a bond proposal in 1909 called for building a high school for Black students in Muskogee. Thus, the Manual Training School for Negroes, a yellow-brick building with a brick parapet, was constructed. Although Booker T. Washington's philosophy of promoting vocational training influenced the curriculum, the teachers taught the full range of academic subjects as well as vocational subjects. Thanks to this training, many graduates of the Manual Training School for Negroes became leaders in the state of Oklahoma.

Students in grades 7 through 12 studied at the Manual Training School until 1953, when grades 9 through 12 were moved to a new site. Students in grades 7 and 8 continued to attend school at this site until the school closed in 1980. As of mid-1994, members of the African American community were meeting to plan a way to restore and reopen the historic school.

DATE BUILT:	1910
ADDRESS:	704 Altamont Street, Muskogee
TELEPHONE:	Mrs. Willie Mae Robbins, (918) 687-8802
VISITING HOURS:	Call for information

Okmulgee

Okmulgee Black Hospital

The historic two-story, red-brick Okmulgee Black Hospital opened to serve Black patients in 1922. Known as the Colored Hospital, it served this function until August 1956.

The town of Okmulgee, established in the Indian Territory in 1869, was the capital of the Creek Nation. Former Black slaves of the Creek Nation, freed by the Emancipation Proclamation and the Thirteenth Amendment, received up to 100 acres of land. Many chose to live in Okmulgee or close to the town. By 1910 African Americans made up about 33 percent of the population of the town. Although employment was available in mining and glassmaking, some Black entrepreneurs established businesses along East Fifth Street.

The Okmulgee Black Hospital originally had a basement, which has now been filled in. When the building was converted from hospital use, a dumbwaiter was removed, sinks and drains were taken out, and the ambulance entrance was walled in for office space. The boiler room became office space, and the coal room was converted to a food closet. The exterior has not been altered. The upstairs once was converted into a youth shelter.

Today the city of Okmulgee owns the building. Deep Fork Community Action, an antipoverty agency, occupied the first floor for several years until the early 1990s. Now vacant, the building is significant because it is the oldest building of its kind constructed for Black people in Oklahoma. Other early Black hospitals in Oklahoma no longer are standing or have been significantly altered.

DATE ESTABLISHED: 1922
ADDRESS: 220 N. Wood Drive, Okmulgee
VISITING HOURS: Vacant, visitors may walk or drive by
FEES: None
SOURCES: Elizabeth Shoun, executive director, Deep Fork Community Action Foundation, Inc. Telephone call Aug. 11, 1995, Deep Fork Community Action. Telephone call Aug. 11, 1995, Okmulgee Chamber of Commerce. NRHPINF.

Rentiesville Vicinity

Honey Springs Battlefield

Men from the First Kansas Colored Volunteer Infantry Regiment, the first Black unit to fight in the Civil War, were a strong factor in the Union victory at Honey Springs. They were part of a battle that included the most ethnically diverse group of soldiers to fight in the Civil War. African Americans, men from five Indian nations, Hispanic-American troops from Texas, and white soldiers from the North and South fought on both sides. They comprised the 3,000 Union troops and 6,000 Confederate troops that fought at Honey Springs.

In this conflict, the largest battle of the Civil War in the Indian Territory, Union troops fought under Major General James G. Blunt, while the Confederate troops fought under Brigadier General Douglas H. Cooper, a former federal Indian agent who had turned to the Confederate side. The Confederates had hoped to emerge victorious at Honey Springs and then to take Fort Gibson and establish control north of the Arkansas River. Instead, on July 17, 1863, Union forces defeated the Confederates who had challenged them for supremacy north of the Arkansas River.

The African American troops decisively proved their courage and their value in this battle. An article in the Checotah, Oklahoma, *McIntosh County Democrat* noted, "The First Kansas Volunteer Regiment (Colored) carried the day for the Union, which gained control of the upper Arkansas River with the victory."[1]

LeRoy Fischer, historian and retired professor at Oklahoma State University, notes that the battle at Honey Springs was not the first engagement for the men of the First Kansas Colored Volunteer Regiment. In June 1863, a month earlier than the Honey Springs battle, the African American troops had fought to protect a wagon train moving from Fort Scott, Kansas, to Fort Gibson in Indian Territory. By the time the battle at Honey Springs was fought, many white federal forces had been pulled out of Indian Territory to protect eastern areas of the United States, and the Union needed to have Black men fight. The Battle of Honey Springs, the first test of Black soldiers west of the Mississippi River, was considered important in determining whether Black men would fight in direct combat. Here in Indian territory, just to the north of Texas, the Black men were assigned to fight off Texans who were protecting their borders from federal forces. The African Americans were placed in the front center of Union lines, Native Americans were placed on either side of the Black men, and white soldiers, in general, were at the rear. Native Americans also were fighting on the Confederate side, where they were placed in positions on either side of the white Twentieth and Twenty-ninth Texas Home Guard.

The Indians did not do well in this type of European-style fighting in which men lined up, faced each other directly, and shot cannon and rifle volleys at each other. They were more accustomed to guerrilla-style warfare, which relied on concealment and surprise. The Black men, however, had been well-trained for this type of fighting; moreover, they had an added incentive to win because they had been told they would be made slaves if they were captured. The African Americans fought superbly. Several months later they were sworn into federal service, a procedure that provided protection for them. As a state unit they would have been subject to reprisals, but as federal soldiers they were under U.S. protection.

The state of Oklahoma has purchased 800 acres of the Honey Springs Battlefield and plans to purchase more. The state will then transfer the land to the federal government for development as a national historic site. The Oklahoma Historical Society has acquired a $627,262 federal grant to develop a museum of 3,150 square feet; two miles of hiking trails, which will extend from the museum to a bridge to be constructed over Elk Creek; and an overlook on Pumpkin Ridge. From the overlook visitors will be able to look down on Elk Creek and the bridge that was the site of the heaviest fighting of the battle. Five large granite monuments that already exist at the site will be moved to an area near the museum. One monument has an inscription honoring the First Kansas Colored Volunteer Infantry Regiment. Since the completion date for the improvements may be near the year 2000, visitors should contact the Checotah Chamber of Commerce for current visiting information. Visitors today can see a scenic location with the granite monuments and with Elk Creek flowing through the center.

DATE OF SIGNIFICANCE:	1863
ADDRESS:	¼ mile north of Rentiesville (east of US 69 and north of I-40 and Checotah)
TELEPHONE:	Checotah Chamber of Commerce, (918) 473-2070
VISITING HOURS:	Dawn–dusk
FEES:	None
SOURCES:	Telephone conversation Mar. 16, 1995, LeRoy H. Fischer, retired professor, Oklahoma State University. Artie Gipson, executive director/secretary, Checotah Chamber of Commerce. "Oklahoma Historical Society Wins $627,262 Grant for Honey Springs." *National Register of Historic Places,* 609. "Honey Springs Battlefield National Park."

Tulsa

Greenwood Cultural Center

Greenwood, a prosperous African American section of Tulsa, Oklahoma, was involved in a terrible racial conflagration in 1921. The riot was started by a rumor that a Black man had grabbed the arm of a white elevator operator. Although the operator later declined to testify, the local newspaper printed an inflammatory account, and the police took the man to jail "for his own safety." When a crowd assembled and the sheriff refused to release the man, a white mob assembled; the mood grew ugly, and carloads of armed white men soon began driving through Greenwood. They proceeded to riot, kill, burn, and loot. Although troops from nearby Fort Sill and the Oklahoma National Guard were called in, it was too late—Greenwood lay ravaged by flames. Twenty-two Black and nine white citizens were dead, and hundreds of Black people were in flight to other towns.

Greenwood eventually rose from the ashes and rebuilt. Today, visitors can see the bitter story at the Greenwood Cultural Center, through a permanent exhibit of forty-five photographs taken during the riot, *Greenwood, from Ruins to Renaissance.* In addition to the photographs, visitors can see the Mable B. Little Heritage House, a replica of a house that was destroyed during the race riot. The cultural center also has a focus on local Black history through an art gallery and the Jazz Hall of Fame.

DATE ESTABLISHED: 1989
ADDRESS: 322 N. Greenwood, Tulsa
TELEPHONE: (918) 582-1741, (918) 583-4545, or (918) 585-2548
VISITING HOURS: Mon.–Fri. 9–5; closed weekends, major holidays
FEES: Donations appreciated
SOURCES: Videotape shown on National Public Television, *Tony Brown's Journal.* Telephone conversation June 29, 1994, Betty Downing, administrative assistant, Greenwood Cultural Center.

Wewoka

Seminole Nation Museum

The Seminole Nation Museum has information about a little-known aspect of U.S. history—the association between African Americans and the Indian nations of the Southeast. Prior to 1907, when Oklahoma became a state, Wewoka was primarily a Black town. Many of its early citizens were Black slaves or freed men and women who had come west when the Seminole Indians were forced to migrate west of the Mississippi after their surrender to the U.S. armed forces in 1832. After the emancipation of the slaves, the African Americans as well as the Seminoles were allotted land in the Indian Territory.

The Seminole Nation Museum has exhibits and information associated with the Black Seminoles whose lives from the Trail of Tears to Oklahoma, Texas, and Mexico are described in two books in the museum's library. Today there are still groups of Black Seminoles within the Seminole nation, but they do not live in a specific region.

Seminole Indian guide Lewis Johnson gives tours of the 5,000-square-foot museum, pausing to illustrate the culture by playing the flute and telling stories about Seminole life. He guides visitors to exhibits displayed in chronological order; Black history is included in the tour. One room has a model of a log chickee—the Seminole home in Florida—which has a floor twelve to fourteen feet above the ground and a roof of palmetto leaves. Another exhibit shows wildlife indigenous to the Oklahoma area. There is a military room and an area that illustrates the oil boom. Another exhibit shows a wooden sidewalk and has facades of old Wewoka buildings. In accordance with museum bylaws a Black history section is in the planning stages.

DATE BUILT: 1937
ADDRESS: 524 S. Wewoka Avenue, Wewoka
TELEPHONE: (405) 257-5580
VISITING HOURS: Tues.–Sun. 1–5; closed Mon., Thanksgiving, Christmas
FEES: Donations accepted
SOURCES: Margaret Jane Norman, curator, Seminole Nation Museum. Telephone conversation Apr. 23, 1994, Jan Wyrick, director, Seminole Nation Museum.

Note

1. "Oklahoma Historical Society Wins $627,262 Grant for Honey Springs," (Checotah, Oklahoma) *McIntosh County Democrat,* 5 May 1994.

Works Consulted

The African American Encyclopedia. Vol. 2. Michael W. Williams, ed. New York: Marshall Cavendish, 1993.

Fort Sill Museum. Towana Spivey, comp. [brochure]

"Honey Springs Battlefield National Park: The Battle of Honey Springs, July 17, 1863." LeRoy H. Fischer. Oklahoma City: Oklahoma Historical Society, Jan. 1969. [monograph]

Langston University, Our Heritage: A Tradition of Quality and Pride. Langston, Okla.: Langston University. [brochure]

National Register of Historic Places. Washington, D.C.: National Park Service, 1976.

New Grolier Multimedia Encyclopedia. Danbury Conn.: Grolier Electronic Publishing. [electronic version]

"Oklahoma Historical Society Wins $627,262 Grant for Honey Springs." (Checotah, Okla.) *McIntosh County Democrat,* 5 May 1994.

"100 Influential Black Oklahomans." Henry C. Hawkins, proj. coord. Oklahoma City: Oklahoma Historical Society, 1989. [manuscript]

"Original Entrance Declared Landmark." Langston, Okla.: Langston University. [information sheet]

"Shaped by a Dream." Luther P. Jackson. *Life Magazine* (29 Nov. 1968): 72–4.

Texas

Austin

George Washington Carver Museum

The George Washington Carver Museum was the first neighborhood Black history museum in Texas. Changing exhibits include photographs, artifacts, folk crafts, and art reflecting the African-American history and culture of Austin and Travis County. The museum also features books, maps, manuscripts, and city/county reports that reflect local and national Black history.

The museum is housed in an 1,800-square-foot frame building constructed in 1927 to serve as the main Austin Public Library. After the city of Austin decided to build a larger facility, the Black community requested that this building be moved to East Austin to serve as a library for the Black community. The community named the library for noted scientist Dr. George Washington Carver.

By 1975 the community had outgrown the library, and East Austin citizens began to petition for a new library building. The new library was completed in 1980 on a site adjacent to the old facility. In 1979 the old Carver branch building was converted into a Black history museum; it opened in 1980 with one staff person, curator Louis Hicks.

Past exhibits have included quilts and quilters, the life of George Washington Carver, *Sixth Street: The Image of the Black Entrepreneur,* the folk art of Alma Gunter, and works from the Black Arts Alliance.

DATE ESTABLISHED:	Building, 1927; museum, 1979
ADDRESS:	1165 Angelina Street, Austin
TELEPHONE:	(512) 472-4809
VISITING HOURS:	Tues.–Thurs. 10–6, Fri.–Sat. noon–5; closed Sun.–Mon.
FEES:	None
SOURCE:	Telephone conversation June 25, 1994, Sylvia Owens, project coordinator, George Washington Carver Museum. Tommie J. Brown, administrative technician I, George Washington Carver Museum. State of Texas historical marker. "Black History Neighborhood Museum Is Texas First." "A Visit to the George Washington Carver Museum."

Sixth Street Historic District

Victorian commercial buildings dating from the late nineteenth century line Sixth Street, a major thoroughfare from the year of Austin's founding. Sixth Street and Congress Avenue were the major commercial districts in the city. Austin was founded in 1839 as the capital of Texas, and its streets were laid out over hills and creeks. The earliest settlers built log and rough-plank buildings. At the end of the Civil War, a burst of construction took place, including a rail line laid for a mule-drawn street railway.

When Sixth Street was at its height in the 1870s and 1880s, it had several Black businesses, including a physician's office in the 300 block and several businesses on the north side of the 400 and 500 blocks of East Sixth Street. By 1940, the area contained Black, Lebanese, Syrian, Jewish, German, Chinese, and Mexican American merchants.

The **E. H. Carrington Store** at 522 East Sixth was a highly successful Black business. Originally it was a one-story structure, but a second story was added later. Carrington, a former slave, operated a grocery at this location from 1873 to 1907. He was a community leader, known for his readiness to assist others. He often loaned money for farms and asked for little security on the loans.

Louis D. Lyons, Carrington's son-in-law, continued the grocery business through the 1920s. He was a community leader—a trustee of Samuel Huston College, which later merged with Tillotson College, and a secretary of the Friends in Need Fund, which gave funds needed for burials. Lyons Hall, on the second floor of the Carrington Building, was used for club meetings, receptions, and other social affairs in the Black community.

East Sixth Street began to decline as a commercial area in the 1940s. The number of second-hand stores and vacant buildings increased, and the electric street railways were removed. In 1968, however, an architect restored a two-story building on East Sixth Street as his townhouse. Restorations gradually increased, including the University of Texas restoration of old federal buildings for use as offices.

The E. H. Carrington Store, so important in Austin's Black business and community growth, was restored in the early 1970s by the Junior League of Austin, which uses the historic store as a thrift shop.

DATE ESTABLISHED: Late 19th-century with a few early 20th-century structures

ADDRESS: Historic district, roughly bounded by Fifth, Seventh, and Lavaca Streets and I-35; Carrington Store, 522 E. Sixth Street, Austin

TELEPHONE: Carrington Store (now Junior League Thrift Shop), (512) 477-7124

VISITING HOURS: Mostly private; Carrington Store, during business hours by appointment through the Junior League

SOURCES: NRHPINF. Telephone call June 25, 1994, Junior League Thrift Shop.

Corsicana

Pioneer Village Slave Cabin

Navarro County is rich in Black heritage and has many African-American communities, churches, and cemeteries. In 1989 an exhibit in Corsicana's City Government Center paid tribute to the county's Black history.

Pioneer Village, operated by the Corsicana Historic Association and the city's park division, is not primarily a Black historical site. However, it does have a slave cabin, a type of structure that was a significant element in African American history. The cabin is one of seven log buildings, some of which are original and were moved to the premises; others were constructed on the premises. The slave cabin is a small, one-room structure that originally stood within a plantation several miles away from Pioneer Village. Although there are a few items inside, it has not been furnished with items from its time period.

The village has some information about two of Corsicana's achieving African Americans: actor Rex Ingram and Dr. Will Coleman, one of the first Black veterinarians in the United States.

DATE ESTABLISHED: As museum, 1958
ADDRESS: 912 W. Park Avenue, Corsicana
TELEPHONE: (903) 654-4846
VISITING HOURS: Mon.–Sat. 9–5, Sun. 1–5
FEES: Adults, $1; children 6–12, $.25
SOURCE: Telephone conversation June 25, 1994, Ms. Margie Williams, assistant curator, Pioneer Village.

Dallas

Museum of African-American Life and Culture

The Museum of African-American Life and Culture, located in the Dallas Fair Park, displays traditional African sculpture and ceremonial objects, materials on African American history, and a variety of art objects. Recent exhibits have included the works of African American folk artist Clementine Hunter as well as a display of African American quilts. The museum's design incorporates African symbolism into its own architectural design that, from a top view, resembles an African cross. The museum also operates a summertime Black history camp for children.

DATE ESTABLISHED: 1974
ADDRESS: 1620 First Avenue, at the Dallas Fair Park, Dallas
TELEPHONE: (214) 565-9026
VISITING HOURS: Tues.–Thurs. noon–5, Fri. noon–9, Sat. 10–5, Sun. 1–5
FEES: None
SOURCES: Telephone conversation June 28, 1994, Barron Smith, office aide, Museum of African-American Life and Culture. *Texas State Travel Guide,* 54, 56.

Fort Davis

Fort Davis National Historic Site*

From 1867 to 1885, Black troops known as the Buffalo Soldiers were the only soldiers garrisoned at Fort Davis. The men were members of the Ninth and Tenth U.S. Cavalry and the Twenty-fourth, Twenty-fifth, and Forty-first U.S. Infantry. They left an impressive record of frontier service and became a guiding force in the development and settlement of West Texas.

After gold was discovered in California in 1848, travel routes to the West developed through Texas, including the San Antonio–El Paso Road and the Butterfield Overland Trail. Officials located the fort by Limpia Creek, which provided valuable water, and the men built the first temporary, pine-slab buildings. Fort Davis was the first military post established to guard the route west. The soldiers had the mission of protecting travelers and protecting delivery of the mail. Indian trails that led south to Mexico intersected the El Paso Road, and Apache and Comanche Indians fought to protect their territory. Fort Davis soldiers had to guard against their attacks on the wilderness stretch between San Antonio and El Paso.

When the Civil War began, this area lost Federal military protection. Texas seceded from the Union early in 1861, and Confederates occupied the fort for nearly a year. Later, Apaches destroyed the fort, which lay deserted for five years. When Federal troops returned to Fort Davis in 1867, little of value remained. The fort, however, became one of the first posts in the west to receive Black soldiers.

The end of the Civil War had brought many changes as newly freed Black people sought equality, and many Black men chose to continue to serve in the military. In June 1867 four troops of the Ninth U.S. Cavalry, a newly organized Black regiment, marched up Limpia Creek to Fort Davis. Their mission was to protect the frontier. Using stone and adobe, they began to construct a permanent post, the major installation of some fifty structures that would house up to twelve companies of cavalry and infantry.

The Buffalo Soldiers were commanded by white officers, as was the custom of the times. They served on the southwest Texas frontiers from 1867 to 1885, participating in the Indian wars of the late nineteenth century. Near the end of the 1870s, Apache warriors, led by Victorio, launched a series of attacks on the area. Black troops from Fort Davis were called on to stop the attacks. After hard-fought engagements Victorio retreated to Chihuahua, where he was killed by Mexican troops. The Buffalo Soldiers from Fort Davis then were assigned to Arizona territory, where they fought against Geronimo. The surrender of the Native American leader in 1886 brought the Apache Wars to an end.

Although white officers commanded the Black units at Fort Davis, a Black man, Lieutenant Henry Ossian Flipper, served at Fort Davis as acting commissary of subsistence. Flipper, a highly intelligent man, was the first Black graduate of West Point despite years of ostracism and discrimination. He met racism again at Fort Davis in the summer of 1881 when he was accused of embezzling government funds. Although a controversial court martial found him innocent of those charges, he was charged with unbecoming conduct and dismissed from military service. Flipper fought unsuccessfully for the rest of his life to clear his name. Even though he became successful and respected as a mining engineer and an expert on Mexico, he did not live to see his name cleared. In 1976, at the urging of his descendants and other interested citizens, the U.S. Army reviewed the court martial transcripts, found that Flipper's dismissal had been unjust, and changed the discharge to honorable. Flipper was reinterred with full military honors. (For additional information on Flipper, see the Fort Sill entry for Lawton, Oklahoma.)

The western migration resumed during the period when Black troops served at Fort Davis. The African American soldiers continued to patrol the road, escorting mail and wagon trains and mounting expeditions into the wilderness. The years of conflict came to an end as civilians settled in greater numbers on the frontier. Since the bluecoats were no longer needed, Fort Davis was deactivated in 1881.

Fort Davis, with its adobe and stone remains of the fort complex, has been restored. The fort, operated since 1961 as a unit of the National Park Service, is an excellent example of a frontier fort where Black soldiers at one time served. Half of the fifty original structures have been saved. An enlisted men's barracks has been refurnished to what it was like in the summer of 1884 when Troop H of the Tenth Cavalry occupied it. This barracks is the only one in the National Park Service dedicated to the memory of the Black enlisted men who served in the Army during the Indian wars.

The site features a Visitors Center and museum with a slide show and a self-guiding tour of the grounds and several buildings. Plan for a one- to two-hour visit.

DATE BUILT: 1854

ADDRESS: Junction of TX 17 and 118, on the northern edge of the town of Fort Davis

TELEPHONE: (915) 426-3224

VISITING HOURS: Memorial Day–Labor Day, daily 8–6; Sept.–May, daily 8–5; closed Christmas

FEES: Adults 17 or older, $2; children 16 and younger, free; Golden Eagle, Golden Age, or Golden Access Passports honored

SOURCES: John Sutton, Fort Davis National Historic Site. Mary Davis, park ranger, Fort Davis National Historic Site. Telephone conversation June 24, 1994, Mary Williams, park ranger, Fort Davis National Historic Site. *Fort Davis: Guardian of the West Texas Frontier. Fort Davis. National Register of Historic Places,* 738. *Texas State Travel Guide,* 70.

Fort Stockton

Historic Fort Stockton*

During the Civil War Confederate troops destroyed Fort Stockton. In 1867, however, Black troopers from the Ninth Cavalry arrived at the fort and rebuilt the ruined structures. Eighty-seven percent of the men stationed at this fort were African Americans. Their primary function was to defend against Apaches in the rugged West-Texas prairie—a region better known to the Indians than to the soldiers. In spite of this disadvantage, the men of the Ninth Cavalry carried out their mission well.

In one raid the Apaches raided a wagon train near the fort; then they departed, intending to cross the Rio Grande and seek refuge in Mexico. The Black soldiers pursued them and were the victors in a battle that left twenty Apache braves dead and two troopers wounded.

The town of Fort Stockton grew around the main post, which now is located two blocks from Main Street. Four of the buildings built by men of the Ninth Cavalry are still standing. The museum is in the process of furnishing a barracks that housed the Tenth Cavalry. The Interpretive Center, housed in one of the rebuilt barracks, has an audiovisual introduction to the fort and some exhibits. Another barracks building that also serves as an auditorium is partially furnished as it may have been when the Tenth Cavalry men used it in the mid-1880s.

Although some visitors may expect to see heavily barricaded structures, this was not necessary because the wide open spaces permitted the soldiers to see people who were approaching long before they arrived. In addition there was no lumber available to build barricades in this middle-of-a-desert site. Visitors who experience the sometimes 105-degree temperatures here may wonder at the fortitude of the soldiers who had to wear woolen uniforms!

DATE ESTABLISHED: Fort, 1867; museum, 1991

ADDRESS: 300 E. Third Street, Fort Stockton

TELEPHONE: (915) 336-2400

VISITING HOURS: Mon.–Sat. 10–1, 2–5; Sun. 1–5

FEES: Adults, $1; children 6–12, $.50; children under 6, free

SOURCES: Telephone conversation June 24, 1994, Carey Behrends, curator, Fort Stockton.

Houston

Freedmen's Town Historic District*

In the forty blocks of the Freedmen's Town Historic District (also called the Fourth Ward), narrow streets and one- and two-story frame buildings contrast with the gleaming modern buildings surrounding them. The older dwellings form a precious and fragile reminder of a community established by Black people just after slavery.

When Houston was founded in 1836, Black slaves and Mexican laborers cleared swampy land along Buffalo Bayou for the original town site. They were considered able to endure the malaria, snakes, insects, adulterated water, and other hardships of the work that wealthier townspeople did not want to do. The original Freedmen's Town settlement was established shortly after emancipation. It started on the southern banks of Buffalo Bayou, stretched south to Sutton Street, and led west from Milan and Travis Streets to Taft Street. African Americans worked as servants in town or as laborers on plantations. They built small shanties along Buffalo Bayou and worshiped in brush arbors or in borrowed churches.

Freedmen's Town started as a rural, sparsely settled area on the outskirts of town, but it eventually became incorporated into the city. Settlement increased in the last two decades of the nineteenth century.

Few of the earliest pre–1880 cottages have survived. Those that can be seen today are primarily small, one-story frame houses with one or two rooms. Many had porches with hand-turned posts, jig-cut brackets, and dog-toothed gingerbread trim. There were a few two-story houses and several blocks of shotgun houses. Speculators set the houses close together and close to the streets. By 1984 only twenty-four of these early houses remained in the historic district. Community leaders who worked as business owners, ministers, doctors, and teachers lived in the larger houses.

The Black population nearly doubled between 1910 and 1930, and Freedmen's Town became the economic center for Black residents of Houston. The community had a commercial district, a professional baseball field, and Booker T. Washington High School.

Although this was a growing area, fewer than 15 percent of Black residents owned their homes. In 1929 the average monthly rent for a house was $20.13. Fewer than half of the houses had indoor water; approximately 19 percent had indoor toilets. Since the streets were not paved, residents had to trudge and slosh through muddy streets in rainy weather.

Construction declined during the Depression years, and a general decline began in the 1940s. African Americans were moved out of the oldest part of Freedmen's Town to make way for San Felipe Courts, a large housing project for white residents only. Construction of downtown Houston buildings and the North Freeway cut off more of the oldest area, leaving only Antioch Missionary Baptist Church of Christ standing. The entire Black community west of Baldwin Street was razed, including the Carnegie Library and Booker T. Washington High School.

In the 1980s nearly sixty buildings within the historic district were demolished; in 1984 there were still 530 structures designated as part of the historic district. By 1991, 40 percent of the district's structures had vanished, many of the remaining buildings had deteriorated, and the rest of the area was threatened by encroachment as city developers sought more space to build and modernize. Today the forty-block area is all that remains of the oldest Black community in Houston, a community that developed from 1865 to 1934.

Sample structures in the historic district include the houses at 1109 Bailey Street, 1408 Andrews Street, 1402 Valentine Street, 1205 Andrews Street, 1001 Buckner Street, 1407 Ruthven Street, Gregory Elementary School, Good Hope Missionary Baptist Church (at the corner of Saulnier Street and Wilson Street), Alfred Smith House at 911 Andrews Street (owned and built by a Black person), and the Reverend Ned P. Pullum residence at 1319 Andrews Street (founder of the Pullum Standard Brickworks).

DATE OF SIGNIFICANCE: 1890–1935

ADDRESS: Roughly bounded by Genessee Street, W. Dallas Avenue, Arthur Street, and W. Gray Street, Houston

VISITING HOURS: Private, visitors may walk or drive by

SOURCES: NRHPINF. Telephone conversation Apr. 8, 1995, Sandra August, juvenile library-service specialist, Fifth Ward Branch Library, Houston. Telephone conversation Apr. 8, 1995, Pamela Edwards, children's librarian, Smith Library, Houston. Telephone conversation Apr. 10, 1995, Will Howard, Houston Public Library Texas Room. Telephone conversation Apr. 10, 1995, Becky Hamilton, secretary, Heritage Society, Houston. Texas Historic Sites Inventory. "A Historic Black Area in Houston Battles Developers and Decay."

Antioch Missionary Baptist Church of Christ

Antioch Missionary Baptist Church of Christ, once an integral part of the historic Freedmen's Town, was cut off from the main section of the historic community by Interstate 45 (the Gulf Freeway), and today is located in a downtown area surrounded by parking lots and modern glass-and-steel buildings. The church remains close to the historic Freedmen's Town community geographically and spiritually. The oldest African American church in Houston, Antioch Missionary Baptist Church of Christ is regarded as the mother church for other local Black congregations.

When the congregation was organized in 1866, church members were holding their services either at the First Baptist Church or the German Baptist Church. Within a few months they had built a brush arbor for their worship site. They were led by Reverend I. S. Campbell, a minister sent by the white Baptist Missionary Society.

By 1867 the congregation had grown, and its members were able to build a frame church. Their first full-time minister, Reverend John Henry (Jack) Yates, arrived in 1868. Born in slavery, Yates moved to Houston in 1865 following emancipation. He became a leader in Houston, investing in land and urging members of his congregation to buy land in Houston's Fourth Ward. Antioch Missionary Baptist Church of Christ joined Trinity Methodist Church in establishing a park that commemorated Texas Emancipation Day. Reverend Yates's son, Rutherford Yates, was a teacher and the owner of Houston's first Black-owned printing press.

When church trustees saw that the frame church was too small, they purchased land on Robin Street at Clay Street for a new church. They commissioned Richard Allen, a contractor and bridge builder, to put up the church; he completed the one-story structure in 1879. Allen, a prominent man in his own right, was active in politics. He was elected to the 1870–1871 Texas legislature, which was the first to include Black lawmakers. He also served as customs collector, city alderman, city scavenger, and first Grand Master of the Colored Masons of Texas.

Members of Antioch Missionary Baptist Church of Christ were interested in the educational welfare of young people. They contributed to the establishment of Bishop College, which opened in Marshall. The church also established the Houston Baptist Academy in 1885. This academy, later known as Houston College, educated African Americans through the 1920s.

Reverend Frederick Lights became minister in 1894. He enlarged the church to its present shape as a two-story brick building. He also was active in Houston community affairs, serving as president of an African American bank, helping to establish the Black-owned newspaper *The Western Star,* and serving as chairman of the board of trustees for the Houston Baptist Academy.

Antioch Missionary Baptist Church of Christ stands as an important historic site and a symbol of the growth of Houston's Black community. Yates House, owned by Antioch's first full-time pastor, may be the oldest residence owned and built in Freedmen's Town by an African American. On July 31, 1994, Yates House was moved from Andrews Street to Sam Houston Park to be displayed with six other historic houses brought to the park setting. Yates House is the only house in Sam Houston

Park associated with African American history. The two-story Greek-revival structure is currently being restored and will be furnished in period style and opened to the public around December 1995.

Antioch Missionary Baptist Church of Christ is listed in the *National Register of Historic Places.*

DATE ESTABLISHED: Congregation, 1866; church, 1879; Yates House, 1870s

ADDRESS: Church, 500 Clay Avenue; Yates House, Sam Houston Park, Bagby Street at McKinney Avenue, Houston

TELEPHONE: Church, (713) 652-0738; Heritage Society (for Sam Houston Park), (713) 655-1912

VISITING HOURS: Church, Sun. service 10:45, by appointment Mon.–Fri. 8–5; Sam Houston Park, guided tours Mon.–Sat. 10–3, Sun. 1–4; park tours closed New Year's Day, Good Friday, Easter, Thanksgiving and the Friday after, Christmas Eve, Christmas

FEES: Sam Houston Park tours, adults 18–64, $6; senior citizens 65 and up, $4; teens 13–17, $4; children 6–12, $2; children under 6, free

SOURCES: NRHPINF. Telephone conversation June 29, 1994, Jacqueline Bostic, office administrator, Antioch Missionary Baptist Church of Christ, and great-great-granddaughter of church founder Reverend Jack Yates. Telephone conversation Apr. 9, 1995, Linda Nwoke, church member, Antioch Missionary Baptist Church of Christ.

Menil Museum

Over the years the Menil Foundation has collected representations of Black Africans and African Americans in Western art. The museum's archive formerly included approximately 20,000 illustrations and images of Black people from the early Egyptian period to the twentieth century. Harvard University recently acquired the collection.

The museum's art at this site is closely associated with the collection of John and Dominique de Menil, which includes a major collection of African art. Displays, some of which are traveling exhibits, have featured the sacred art of Ethiopia, tribal cultures from antiquity through the twentieth century, and contemporary works by African American artists.

DATE ESTABLISHED: 1986

ADDRESS: 1515 Sul Ross, Houston

TELEPHONE: (713) 528-1345

VISITING HOURS: Wed.–Sun. 11–7; closed Mon.–Tues., national holidays

FEES: None

SOURCES: Ms. Karen C. Dalton, Menil Foundation. Telephone conversation June 25, 1994, Lauri Nelson, curatorial associate, Menil Museum. *Texas State Travel Guide,* 98.

Riverside General Hospital

Riverside General Hospital, known earlier as Houston General Hospital, was the first non-profit hospital in Houston for Black patients. It provided the first school for Black nurses; for a period it was the only hospital where Black physicians could practice. Although members of the African

American community proposed construction of the hospital, white leaders joined with them to bring the project to fruition.

Before 1919 Black patients were treated in segregated wards of charity hospitals, where services were inadequate. Union Hospital, with fifty beds, was established in 1919 and served the Black community, but it, too, was inadequate. Union Hospital's superintendent, Isaiah M. Terrell, approached Houston leaders with a proposal for a new hospital that would serve African Americans. The city donated a site, and philanthropist J. S. Cullinan pledged $75,000 for construction.

Juneteenth (June 19th), a day commemorating the emancipation of the slaves in Texas, was selected as dedication day for the new hospital. It opened in July 1926, one month after its dedication, with an African American staff and board of directors. Houston General Hospital was not a charity hospital. Families prepaid $6 per year for memberships that entitled them to a limited number of days of free hospitalization. Others paid for services as needed. This insurance plan continued until 1938.

The early years brought some financial difficulty because there were not as many patients as expected. The nursing school remained open only a few years, and by 1937 the hospital was operating at only 46 percent of capacity. In spite of the lack of adequate patients to support the hospital financially, remodeling was done through 1952 to provide more space for hospital beds and offices, to meet fire codes, and to upgrade the general appearance of the facility. After a new wing was completed in 1961, the hospital's name was changed to Riverside General Hospital.

Although the complex today provides only a fraction of its former services, Riverside Hospital has a place in Houston's history as the first nonprofit hospital for Black patients, doctors, and nurses and as a hospital that grew out of early visions and support of the Black community, supported by white philanthropists. The hospital is listed in the *National Register of Historic Places.*

DATE BUILT: 1926

ADDRESS: 2900 Elgin Street, Houston

TELEPHONE: (713) 526-2441

VISITING HOURS: By appointment through Ernest Gibson, director, or Esther Martin, public relations director

SOURCES: NRHPINF. Telephone conversation June 25, 1994, Shirley Walker, communications director, Riverside Hospital. Texas Historic Sites Inventory.

Houston Negro Hospital School of Nursing Building

The Houston Negro Hospital School of Nursing was built in 1931 with money donated by Houston philanthropist J. S. Cullinan. Closely associated with the Houston Negro Hospital, this was Houston's first residential nursing school for Black students. The master plan called for the hospital to be constructed in 1926 and the nursing school in 1931. Other structures were planned but never built. The School of Nursing Building cost more than $40,000. Students here were taught and supervised by the hospital staff.

Hospital occupancy was lower than expected in the early 1930s, and this factor threatened the existence of both the hospital and the school. The nursing school was closed in 1935, after which the building continued to be used as a dormitory for nurses working at the hospital. By the 1940s, the School of Nursing Building was vacant. It was used for a brief period in the 1950s as a facility for ambulatory cancer patients and in the 1970s as a drug-rehabilitation clinic.

The School of Nursing Building is an important landmark in Houston's predominantly Black Third Ward, representing an element in a hospital complex that was operated by Black people for the Black community.

DATE BUILT: 1931

ADDRESS: Southeast corner of Holman Avenue and Ennis Street, Houston

TELEPHONE: (713) 526-2441

VISITING HOURS: By appointment through Ernest Gibson, director, or Esther Martin, public relations director, Riverside Hospital

SOURCES: NRHPINF. Telephone conversation June 25, 1994, Shirley Walker, communications director, Riverside Hospital. Texas Historic Sites Inventory.

Jacksboro

Fort Richardson State Historic Site*

Black soldiers known as the Buffalo Soldiers lived at Fort Richardson. Although assigned to guard against attacks by Indians, the soldiers also faced the hostility of the local white population, many of whose members regarded Black men in Union uniforms with suspicion.

Fort Richardson, built in 1867, was one of the largest forts in the United States. It was part of a chain of forts designed to protect settlements against Indian raids. African American soldiers from three Tenth Cavalry companies garrisoned at the fort protected wagon trains, provided escorts for officials, and escorted the civilian mail and supply trains.

Seven original fort buildings remain. One of the buildings houses the interpretive center museum where visitors can inspect a model of the fort as well as guns, swords, eyeglasses, and other items used by the Buffalo Soldiers.

DATE BUILT: 1867

ADDRESS: 1 mile southwest of Jacksboro on US 281

TELEPHONE: (817) 567-3506

VISITING HOURS: Wed.–Sun. 8–12, 1–5; closed Mon.–Tues., Thanksgiving, Christmas, New Year's Day

FEES: $4 per vehicle; vehicle with a senior citizen over 65, free

SOURCES: Telephone conversation June 25, 1994, Cindy Massengill, office volunteer, Fort Richardson. Telephone conversation Aug. 11, 1995, Karen Sharp, office manager, Fort Richardson.

Marshall

Wiley College

Wiley College opened in 1873 in two frame buildings south of the Marshall city limits. The Methodist Episcopal Church established the institution, which was chartered by the Freedmen's Aid Society in 1882. Its founders gave the college the mission of preparing teachers and ministers for their work.

Wiley was one of the four oldest historically Black colleges founded by and currently affiliated with the United Methodist Church. It is also the oldest historically Black college chartered by the state of Texas. It was named for Isaac W. Wiley, an African American born in Pennsylvania in 1825, who became an outstanding minister, bishop, medical missionary, and educator. After studying medicine, Wiley became a medical missionary in China, where he died in 1884.

Wiley College moved in 1880 to its present site—63 acres of land in Marshall, Texas, 145 miles east of Dallas and 38 miles west of Shreveport, Louisiana. In recent years it has been in the forefront of training young people for careers in science. With funds from the National Science Foundation, it has sponsored the Wiley College Young Scholars Program, a summer science institute for high school juniors and seniors interested in science as a career.

A Texas State Historical Marker located at Wiley College reads in part:

> Founded by Freedmen's Aid Society of the Methodist Church (North) as a Co-Educational institution dedicated to the education of Black men and women freed by the Civil War, named for Bishop Isaac Wiley (1825–1884) Black religious leader. . . .
>
> In early years offered courses only in academic preparation and vocational fields, first college-level course offered, 1885; first graduate, Henry Pemberton, 1888. In 1893 Wiley College received its first Black President, the Rev. Isaiah Scott, former slave preacher.

DATE ESTABLISHED: 1873
ADDRESS: 711 Wiley Avenue, Marshall
TELEPHONE: (903) 927-3300
VISITING HOURS: During academic year or summer session; contact the college to arrange a visit
SOURCE: Ms. Dherri F. Moore, director, public relations, Wiley College. Telephone call to the site, Aug. 11, 1995.

Prairie View

Prairie View State University

Prairie View State University, established in 1876, is located on property that was named for a plantation home. At one time it was a girls school. In 1876 the property was deeded to the state, and the Texas legislature decided to establish the college for Black students on that site.

Today Prairie View is located on a 1,440-acre campus in a town east of Houston; it has become a comprehensive university that is part of the Texas A & M University system. Approximately 84 percent of the students are African American.

ADDRESS: University Boulevard, Prairie View
TELEPHONE: (409) 857-2690; for appointment, (409) 857-2626 or (409) 857-2627
VISITING HOURS: By appointment
SOURCES: Telephone conversation June 25, 1994, Anita Williams, admissions and records, Prairie View State University. *Texas State Travel Guide*, 158. *Barron's Profiles of American Colleges*, 1389.

San Angelo

Fort Concho National Historic Landmark*

Fort Concho was established in 1867 at the junction of the north and middle branches of the Concho River. African American soldiers stationed at the fort protected stagecoaches and wagon trains, took part in Indian campaigns, escorted the U.S. mail, and took part in major scouting and mapping expeditions. A community grew up around this frontier site. After military service many men of these military units remained in the area and helped form the Black community at San Angelo.

Fort Concho operated as a frontier army post until 1889. It was closed as a military post after the frontier moved farther to the west. During the 22 years that the fort was in operation, all four Black U.S. Army units served here: the Ninth Cavalry, Tenth Cavalry, Twenty-fourth Infantry, and Twenty-fifth Infantry. The Tenth Cavalry under General Benjamin Grierson served longest at this site, from 1875 to 1882. The Texas Historical Commission's historical marker at Fort Concho describes this unit in the following words:

> Following the Civil War, the United States Congress authorized the creation of six regiments of Black U. S. Army Troops. The Tenth Cavalry was organized in 1867 under the leadership of Col. Benjamin Grierson (1826–1911). The order creating Black troops also specified that they would be commanded by white officers. Facing problems of racial discrimination at the Regiment's headquarters in Fort Leavenworth, Kansas, Grierson wanted the Tenth Cavalry reassigned to the West, and they arrived at Fort Concho in the spring of 1875.

In 1882 the Tenth Cavalry was moved to Fort Davis. Transferred frequently after 1885, members of the unit eventually served throughout the world, including Cuba, North Africa, Germany, Korea, and Vietnam.

Today Fort Concho is a national historic landmark, a historic preservation project, and a museum owned and operated by the city of San Angelo. It is among the best preserved of Texas frontier military forts with twenty-three original and restored structures. Visitors can see between six and ten of the historic buildings, which are furnished with period furniture. A special exhibit in the Visitors Center reflects the history of the Buffalo Soldiers who built most of the buildings at the fort. At variable times there are presentations by a local Buffalo Soldiers living history unit. Other exhibits tell the story of the Indian campaigns and San Angelo.

DATE ESTABLISHED: 1867

ADDRESS: 213 E. Avenue D (just east of S. Oakes Street, between Avenues C and D), San Angelo

TELEPHONE: Weekdays, (915) 657-4441; weekends, (915) 657-4444

VISITING HOURS: Tues.–Sat. 10–5, Sun. 1–5; closed Mon., Thanksgiving, Christmas, New Year's Day

FEES: Adults, $2; students, senior citizens, and military, $1.50; children under 6, free

SOURCES: Telephone conversation June 28, 1994, Robert Bluthardt, director of education, Fort Concho. John Neilson, historian/archivist, Fort Concho National Historic Landmark. Roni Morales, publications director, Texas Historical Commission. *Texas State Travel Guide*, 168, 169.

Waxahachie

Waxahachie Business Structures

The buildings at 441 and 500–502 East Main Street are so old that some passersby—strangers to the town—probably would not give them a second glance. Yet buildings of this age and type have been moved on occasion to reconstructed museum villages, precisely for their value in showing what life was like in earlier, economically difficult times. Visitors to Waxahachie, seeing the old buildings in their own settings rather than in a museum, may realize what an accomplishment it was to build even such modest structures only two to three decades after slavery ended. These examples of the earliest stages of entrepreneurship may someday be restored and used again.

The building at **441 East Main** is a two-story commercial building located in a mixed residential and commercial area near the center of the town's historic Black district. For many years the lower floor of the building housed the James Funeral Parlor and later the Golden Gate Funeral Home. The Masons' Pythagoras Lodge #87, organized in 1893, used the upper floor as a lodge hall. The frame-with-brick-veneer structure has a flat roof, a porch with a shed roof, and slender round columns on brick piers. The Masonic Hall still owns the building; Golden Gate Funeral Home has a branch ofice in the building.

The building at **500–502 East Main** is the least altered of the surviving commercial buildings in Waxahachie's historic African American commercial district. Only a few of the older buildings remain. It is an open-plan, one-store masonry building with stucco veneer, wood-sash display windows, and a porch with a shed roof. The parapet on the flat roof gives a final flourish.

DATE BUILT: 441 E. Main Street, c1893; 500–502 E. Main Street, c1900

ADDRESS: 441 and 500–502 E. Main Street, Waxahachie

VISITING HOURS: Private, visitors may walk or drive by

SOURCES: Conversations June 25, 1994, local residents of Waxahachie. National Register Information System. Texas Historic Sites Inventory Form.

Wyatt Street Shotgun House Historic District

The shotgun houses on Wyatt Street represent a type of architecture that once existed in many small towns of the late nineteenth and early twentieth centuries. The houses, constructed between 1900 and 1935, are of a design that may have originated in tribal Africa. Black slaves in Haiti first introduced this architectural form to the Caribbean; then it was brought to the southern United States and used in constructing houses for Black slaves in the Mississippi Delta region. This dwelling type later could be seen throughout the South, especially in urban areas where it remained popular into the 1930s. Shotgun houses were narrow, with rooms located in a straight row without an interior hall. Supposedly a shotgun, if fired, would shoot straight through each room.

These houses in Waxahachie are important reminders of typical residences of Black laborers. The buildings have been little altered since they were constructed about 1918. Although there were at one time many other similar dwellings in Waxahachie, they have been either moved or remodeled to such an extent that they have lost their original structure and appearance.

DATE BUILT: 1900–1935

ADDRESS: East side of the 300 block of Wyatt Street, Waxahachie

VISITING HOURS: Private, visitors may walk or drive by

SOURCES: Telephone conversation June 25, 1994, resident of one of the houses. Texas Historic Sites Inventory.

Works Consulted

Barron's Profiles of American Colleges. 18th ed. New York: Barron's Educational Series, 1991.

"Black History Neighborhood Museum Is Texas First." *Austin-American Statesman/Neighbor,* 23 July 1987.

Fort Davis. Washington, D.C.: National Park Service, U.S. Department of the Interior, 1986. [flier]

Fort Davis: Guardian of the West Texas Frontier. Washington, D.C.: National Park Service, U.S. Department of the Interior, Feb. 1987. [flier]

"A Historic Black Area in Houston Battles Developers and Decay." Diana Solis. *Wall Street Journal* 124, no. 72, Apr. 12, 1991, A1, A9.

National Register of Historic Places. Washington, D.C.: National Parks Service, 1976.

Texas State Travel Guide. Austin, Tex.: State Department of Highways and Public Transportation.

"A Visit to the George Washington Carver Museum: Past, Present, and Future." Austin, Tex.: George Washington Carver Museum. [manuscript]

PART

5

THE WEST AND NONCONTIGUOUS STATES

California
Colorado
Idaho
Montana
Nevada
Oregon
Utah
Washington
Wyoming

• • •

Alaska
Hawaii

African Americans in the Western States

African Americans who arrived in the West before the twentieth century worked as explorers, traders, miners and homesteaders, servants, and laborers. Many became entrepreneurs by opening small businesses of their own. As the great railroads opened up the West, Black Americans laid miles of tracks and traveled on those tracks as porters on the trains. Families and individuals were attracted to the western territories by fertile land, by the rich fur trade, by the possibility of gaining wealth in the mines, and by the chance to start life anew in an undeveloped region that seemed to promise a greater degree of freedom. They moved to sparsely settled terrain in the western states—California, Colorado, Idaho, Montana, Nevada, Oregon, Utah, Washington, and Wyoming—because they believed there would be less discrimination there and more freedom than they had previously known. The U.S. Army, too, introduced African Americans to the West, assigning them in the late 1800s to bases in Montana, Washington, Wyoming, and Idaho. Black Americans could be found in every western state.

California's early population included many Black families; 18 percent of California's population in 1790 included people of African descent. Their history often was intertwined with the history of Mexico. Black men and women lived in Mexico when Mexico gained independence from Spain in 1821, and they were present a year later when California became a province of Mexico. Of the forty-four founding families of Los Angeles, twenty-six were of Black heritage, and most had come from the town of Rosario, in Mexico. The last Mexican governor of California, Pio Pico, was a man of mixed African heritage. A landowner and businessman, he owned Pico House, one of the major hotels in Los Angeles. Today visitors can see houses associated with Governor Pico in the old town called El Pueblo de Los Angeles in the city of Los Angeles, and in Whittier and Oceanside, California.

African American Explorers of the West

In the nineteenth century some African Americans traveled through the West as explorers. James Beckwourth, born in 1798, was a Black man who became legendary as an explorer, Army scout, trapper, and mountaineer. Said to have been a member by invitation of an Indian tribe, Beckwourth also spent time in solitary pursuits. He made a lasting contribution to California's development when he discovered an important mountain pass that began a few miles northwest of present-day Reno, Nevada, and led through the Sierra Nevadas to the goldfields of California. In 1851 Beckwourth opened a wagon road into Marysville, California, and the mining region. Serving as a guide, he led visitors through the pass, stopping at his own trading post where the travelers rested and purchased provisions. The pass that he discovered is called the Beckwourth Pass today, and the town of Beckwourth, California, is named for him.

When General John Frémont explored the far west in 1842–1844, Black men were in his expedition, including Mifflin W. Gibbs, a man who later established California's first Black-owned newspaper and became America's first Black judge. Fremont, in 1845, encouraged Californians to revolt against rule by Mexico, and African Americans were present when California was transferred to the United States in 1848 by the Treaty of Guadalupe Hidalgo. Black families had a personal interest in the outcome when Californians and other Americans debated the state's role with respect to slavery, and they were pleased when in 1850 California became the thirty-first state in the union as a free state. The process of Americanization then began in the land that once had been a sparsely settled province of Mexico.

In addition to Fremont's expedition, another important expedition in the West included a Black man. His name was York, and he was a slave. York was among the courageous men who were a part of the Lewis and Clark Expedition. Between 1804 and 1806 they explored the territory between the Missouri River and the Pacific Ocean, crossing wilderness land, most of which had been traversed only by Native Americans. York and the other men crossed the regions of Idaho now called the Nez Percé National Historical Park and the Weippe Prairie. They crossed this land weary and famished, then received desperately needed help from the Nez Percé Indians who provided them with camas roots and dried fish. After bouts of sickness and a period of restorative rest, the men constructed canoes for the final part of their trip to the Pacific Ocean. The men also stopped in Oregon where they built a camp and spent the winter. The Fort Clatsop National Memorial in Astoria, Oregon, has information about the expedition.

Western African American Settlers, Entrepreneurs, and Soldiers

In addition to the explorers, there were the African Americans who came west with wagon trains. George Washington (1817–1895), a Black man who possessed many skills useful for homesteading, traveled to Oregon Territory with a group of families in a wagon train. In 1872 he founded the town that would become Centralia, Washington. The people of Centralia honored and respected him, and a park in Centralia bears his name today.

In 1844 another African American, George Washington Bush, brought his own family and seven white companions to the Puget Sound area, where they became the first settlers in the region. Bush previously had prospered in Missouri, but a law prevented free Black people from settling there. After the group arrived in Oregon, Bush encountered racially restrictive laws again and moved on to Washington Territory. He established a farm there in the Tumwater area. His name is among those inscribed on a monument there.

William and Sarah Grose were early Black entrepreneurs in Seattle, Washington. They arrived in Seattle in 1860 and began operating a ranch and a hotel there. The house that they built for themselves in 1890 is a rare existing example of the early homes that once were associated with Seattle's Black community.

Richard Allen was another entrepreneur in the early West. He came to the small colony of San Diego around 1847 and with another African American opened a grog shop called the San Diego House (the structure is now a small retail shop in San Diego's Old Town). In Sonora, California, William and Mary Sugg were African Americans who operated a small, private hotel that they built themselves in 1850.

Moses Rodgers, a man who was born a slave, was one of the most successful of the early African American entrepreneurs in the West. After he joined the rush to the California mining country that started in 1849, he became skilled as a mining engineer, acquired a number of mines, and was first to successfully drill for gas in Stockton, California.

Mining opportunities attracted Black families to several other Western states. They found rich lodes in Idaho, Montana, Washington, and Wyoming. Some moved to the mining boom town of South Pass City, Wyoming, which, between 1840 and 1867, was the halfway point on the Oregon-California Trail.

Idaho's mines also attracted a number of African Americans in the nineteenth century. Idaho became the forty-third state in 1890, and although African Americans never made up more than one percent of Idaho's population, they lived there as miners, explorers, trappers, homesteaders, ranchers, and soldiers. Black women, because of lack of other opportunities, usually were domestic workers. By 1870, approximately twenty African Americans lived in Boise, which was Idaho's largest city and the center of mining and ranching activities. By 1900, almost half of Idaho's Black population of 293 individuals lived in Boise or Pocatello. They found work as servants, waiters, laundry workers, hotel workers, and barbers. They also established several small businesses.

Many African Americans came west for the first time as soldiers. African American units called the Buffalo Soldiers served at a number of posts that are accessible to visitors today. The Twenty-fifth Infantry, an all-Black unit from Missoula, Montana, came to Idaho in 1892 to crush labor unrest in the Coeur d'Alene mining region. The Twenty-fourth Infantry, another Black regiment, arrived seven years later with a mandate to arrest striking miners.

From Jim Crow to the Thrust for Equality in the West

As the American West developed, settlers brought their existing ideas about race and status with them. Although many white newcomers approved of slavery and segregation, California did remain in the Union during the Civil War. The segregationist side prevailed, however, when the legislature passed noxious "Black laws" that condoned open discrimination against African Americans.

All Westerners were touched by prevailing state and federal laws, especially those laws enacted when the Civil War ended and during the period of Reconstruction. In the late 1860s and early 1870s many former slaves in the South were destitute and unprotected. The Federal government passed new laws to protect them and created in this way an atmosphere of hope for all African Americans. The Fourteenth Amendment to the Constitution of the United States, ratified in 1868, ensured that former slaves were recognized as citizens and restrained state governments from abridging the rights of former slaves. The amendment insured, in law if not in practice, due process and equal protection of the laws.

The Fifteenth Amendment, passed in 1870, made it illegal for federal or state governments to deprive anyone of the right to vote because of race, color, or previous condition as a slave. Civil rights acts passed in 1871 and 1875 outlawed the use of force, intimidation, or threat to deprive any citizen of the equal protection of the law. The new law gave each citizen the right to use public accommodations, and it forbade discrimination in public conveyances, amusement places, and inns.

By the 1880s, however, the forward thrust of the Radical Reconstruction Period was weakening. Many abolitionists felt that their work was done and were annoyed that Black people were still protesting after emancipation. Many Northerners were in no mood to press for equal rights, especially as African Americans began to move north, competing with white workers for jobs. In the South and elsewhere, the new civil rights laws were widely disregarded. The poll tax, the grandfather clause, and terrorism were used to deny voting rights. Reconstruction ended in 1876 following the inauguration of President Rutherford B. Hayes. Federal troops that had provided a measure of protection for freed people were withdrawn from the South. Jim Crow practices replaced the troops' protection (Jim Crow was a pre-Civil War minstrel show character), and the new divisive laws began to replace the period of just laws. Southern state legislatures repeatedly passed legislation designed to restrict the rights of former slaves, providing a good reason for Black families to make a decision to migrate west. Unfortunately, before the nineteenth century ended, racist state and federal laws would restrict their freedom in the West, too.

In the last decades of the nineteenth century, Congress and the courts seemed to be in no mood to protect the rights of Black Americans. In 1883 the Supreme Court declared the Civil Rights Act of 1875 to be unconstitutional. The new decision specified that unless a state law or action had taken place, federal law had no power to regulate private wrongs or to regulate the conduct and transactions of individual citizens. In the 1896 *Plessy* v. *Ferguson* decision, the Supreme Court upheld the "separate but equal" principle based on a Louisiana statute that separated railroad passengers on the basis of race, thus providing a legal precedent for segregation that lasted until the 1950s. *Plessy* v. *Ferguson* encouraged the spread of segregation, affecting those who had moved their hopes and dreams to the West.

In the nineteenth and early twentieth centuries, Black Americans in the West fought hard for their rights. The thrust for equality was evident in Idaho and California. In 1870, Black Idaho pioneer John West repeatedly tested his right to vote in Boise, only to be turned away from the polls each time. The city of Boise even segregated in the afterlife—the Rose Hill Cemetery there had segregated sites for Chinese and Black burials. Many Black families came to Idaho in the early twentieth century because the state had a major Union Pacific Railroad terminal, and they found work as porters and railroad-yard workers. Beginning in the 1920s, however, Boise's Black families increasingly were confined to a neighborhood south of the railroad tracks. There was a resurgence of Ku Klux Klan activities in Boise and Pocatello, the Idaho towns with the largest Black populations. In 1923, 150 Klansmen in white hooded robes marched through the downtown area of Pocatello and lit a cross on a nearby hillside. In response to growing hostile incidents, Boise's Black community established a chapter of the National Association for the Advancement of Colored People.

In the late 1800s Black workers met prejudice in Idaho's mining camps. Barriers were set up to keep them out, or they were directed to the dirtiest and most menial jobs. Boise County passed a law in 1863 to prevent Black and Chinese people from prospecting. In 1865 the Territorial Legislature introduced a bill to bar African Americans from Idaho. In spite of the barriers, in the 1860s and 1870s Black miners continued to work in mining camps throughout Idaho.

The same discriminatory laws were found throughout the West. A Black man, Frederick Coleman, first discovered gold in San Diego County, California, in 1869. Soon other Black men arrived to stake their claims. The 1850 California census listed 962 Black residents; by 1860 there were 4,086. The possibility of gaining easy wealth also attracted white miners, and many of them protested strongly against working beside Black men in the mines. Delegates to California's 1849 state constitutional convention debated about excluding Black migrants from the state. Although the resolution was rejected, they passed laws barring African Americans from voting and from serving in the militia. Additional legislation specified that Black Americans in California could not testify in court, even if they had been cheated or assaulted by a white person. This encouraged white miners to grab land from Black miners, who were helpless to protest under the law.

Restrictive laws touched all areas of life, reaching even those who had felt secure in California. African Americans felt a stinging betrayal when, in 1852, California passed its own version of the fugitive slave law, allowing slave owners to come into the state to recapture runaway slaves.

By 1855 Black Californians had organized to fight for their rights. They held their own conventions in 1855, 1866, and 1867, and developed plans to defeat the Black laws. Mifflin Gibbs, the Black man who had been a part of John Frémont's expedition, repeatedly traveled to the capital to lobby against the Black laws.

As the new century began, Black Americans were still struggling to improve their economic and social conditions and to eliminate segregation and unjust laws. In California one group decided that the solution was to establish their own all-Black town, a haven where they would not have to endure insults and where they could be independent. In 1908, Colonel Allen Allensworth, a man who was born in slavery, left Los Angeles and, with others, established the town of Allensworth, California. The town thrived for a period but failed when developers broke their promise to provide an adequate water supply. Today, Allensworth exists as a state park visited by approximately 3,000 persons each year.

The African American Community in Los Angeles

Although Colonel Allensworth decided to leave Los Angeles, others remained there, and the Black community increased dramatically in size between 1890 and the 1920s. Biddy Mason, a remarkable Black women who was treated as a slave in a free state, became one of the community leaders. With the help of friends, she gained her freedom in a California court. Over a period of time she purchased real estate, helped to establish a church, and became a spiritual and economic leader in the community.

As the twentieth century began, the African American community in Los Angeles established associations designed to promote racial unity, education, and justice. Membership grew in the Forum, the Sojourner Truth Club, and the National Association for the Advancement of Colored People. Community newspapers emerged, providing a voice for community concerns. When white-owned hotels shunned Black visitors, a Black man, Dr. John Alexander Somerville, built the elegant Somerville Hotel (later called the Dunbar).

The city of Los Angeles shaped the adolescence of Ralph Bunche. Between 1919 and 1927 Bunche spent his teen years in a house on East Fortieth Street in Los Angeles. Dr. Bunche later became the first Black person to serve as Undersecretary to the United Nations and the first African American to receive the Nobel Peace Prize. One of his greatest accomplishments was to help establish peace in the Middle East by negotiating the 1949 armistice agreement between Egypt and Israel.

In Los Angeles as in other Black communities in the West, the years preceding the Great Depression and the years of the Depression brought contrasts in the welfare of African Americans. Those who were financially successful lived in elegant homes; they established business districts with stores, clubs, and offices for professionals. The Golden State Mutual Life Insurance Company, organized in 1924, became one of the largest African American-owned businesses of its kind in the country.

Black movie stars, such as Louise Beavers, Hattie McDaniel, and Butterfly McQueen, were among the successful in Los Angeles. Although they usually had to portray stereotyped roles, they managed to live personal lives of dignity and elegance.

The Oakland, California, African American Community

In Oakland, California, the Black community increased by hundreds of individuals after the 1906 San Francisco earthquake. Shipbuilding and wartime industries also brought more African Americans to that city. Since it was the western terminus of the Southern Pacific Railroad, many Black porters and railroad workers lived in West Oakland. Several organizations—the National Association for the Advancement of Colored People, the Afro-American League, the Brotherhood of Sleeping Car Porters, and the United Negro Improvement Association (UNIA)—were established in response to restrictions placed on the Black community. Members of the Oakland chapter of the UNIA worked hard to promote the organization's goals of Black pride, pride in Africa, and economic solidarity. Unfortunately, UNIA founder Marcus Garvey was convicted (some say wrongly) of using the mail to defraud investors. Although there was little evidence to support the allegation (a single empty postmarked envelope), Garvey was deported from the United States in 1927. The California chapter remained active for a period, continuing to operate from Liberty Hall on Eighth Street. By the mid 1930s, however, the Oakland Branch of Father Divine's Peace Mission was operating out of Liberty Hall.

The Noncontiguous States: Hawaii and Alaska

The noncontiguous states of Hawaii and Alaska are quite a distance from the western states previously described, but African Americans played a role, too, in the newest of the United States.

Pearl Harbor

Black sailors were on duty in Hawaii when the Japanese bombed Pearl Harbor on December 7, 1941. More than seventy-five naval vessels were based in Pearl Harbor, on Oahu Island, when two waves of Japanese planes struck in a surprise attack, raining destruction on the U.S. Pacific Fleet. Dive bombers, torpedo planes, and fighters hit eighteen ships, destroying more than 200 aircraft and killing more than 2,000 Americans. In those terrifying moments a Black seaman, Doris Miller, became a hero. His assignment in the segregated Navy was as a Messman Second Class on the *USS West Virginia;* like other Black seamen, he had a menial job—to serve food to white seamen and clear away their dirty dishes. In the surprise attack, Miller was called on to help carry his mortally wounded captain to safety. After doing so he returned to fire a vacated machine gun. Although he had received only minimal classroom training in use of a machine gun, he became a hero by shooting down at least two, and possibly six, Japanese Zeros. The Navy refused to recognize Miller's courage until pressured to do so by newspaper campaigns, the insistence of civil rights organizations, and direct orders from President Franklin Delano Roosevelt. Eventually he was decorated with the Navy Cross.

Alaska

African Americans were present in small numbers in Alaska as early as the 1860s. They came to Alaska in the nineteenth century as seamen and miners. Small numbers served in the U.S. Army unit assigned to maintain order after the 1867 purchase of Alaska from Russia. In 1868, at the U.S. Army base in Sitka, Alaska, six Black individuals were recorded in the population of 391 individuals.

Black men also served on whaling vessels before the turn of the century. They worked in the Klondike gold fields in the 1890s. Although some remained in Alaska after the gold rush, only 168 were recorded in the 1900 census of Alaska. Growth of the African American population remained modest in Alaska until the 1940s through the 1960s. Many came to Alaska during World War II to work on the construction of Elmendorf Air Force Base and Fort Richardson Army Base in Anchorage, Alaska. They liked the relative openness and friendliness of the Alaskan people and, impressed by the many work opportunities, many remained. The situation was ideal for those who had construction skills, who were willing to work as laborers, or who had the entrepreneurial skills to start small businesses.

Living conditions were spartan for everyone. In the early 1950s Anchorage, the largest city in Alaska, had only one main street that was paved, and there was no public transportation system in the city. In the late 1950s and early 1960s African Americans often lived in or constructed small dwellings in the Eastchester Flats and Fairview areas. Two of these modest structures are identified for this volume as typical of the era.

African Americans have been recognized only in the past few years for their heroic work in helping to construct the Alaska-Canada Highway (known as the ALCAN) under the most grueling conditions. During World War II, Black troops were assigned to help build the supply road that connected Alaska's military posts with the midcontinental United States. The 3,695 African American soldiers from the Ninety-third, Ninety-fifth, and Ninety-seventh regiments of the U.S. Army Corps of Engineers composed about one third of the military force that, with civilians, constructed the 1,500 miles of the Alaska-Canada Military Highway. When completed in 1942, the highway extended from Dawson Creek, British Columbia, to Delta Junction, Alaska.

Works Consulted

The Academic American Encyclopedia. Danbury, Conn.: Grolier, 1993. [electronic version]

"Battling the Elements on the Alcan Highway." In *African Americans Voices of Triumph, Perseverance.* Alexandria, Va.: Time-Life, 1993, 160.

"Black Angelenos: The Afro-American in Los Angeles, 1850–1950." Lonnie Bunch. Los Angeles: California Afro-American Museum, Mar. 6, 1989. [manuscript]

Black on a Background of White: A Chronicle of Afro-Americans' Involvement in America's Last Frontier, Alaska. Everett Louis Overstreet. Anchorage, Alaska: Alaska Black Caucus, 1988.

The Black West: A Documentary and Pictorial History. Rev. ed. William Loren Katz. New York: Anchor/Doubleday, 1973.

"A Guide to Black History in Los Angeles." Emily Gibson. *Los Angeles Herald Examiner,* Jan. 30, 1987.

Historical and Cultural Atlas of African Americans. Molefi K. Asante and Mark T. Mattson. New

York: Macmillan Publishing Company, 1992, 183.

The History of the East Bay Afro-American Community 1852–Present. Los Angeles: California Afro-American Museum, 1990. [brochure]

Idaho's Ethnic Heritage Historical Overviews. Laurie Mercier and Carole Simon-Smolinski, project codirectors and eds. Boise, Idaho: Idaho Ethnic Heritage Project; cosponsored by Idaho Centennial Commission; National Park Service, U.S. Department of the Interior; and Idaho Historical Society, Mar. 1990. [Files of the Idaho Historical Society, Boise, Idaho]

"Soldiers in the Shadows." In *African Americans Voices of Triumph, Perseverance.* Alexandria, Va.: Time-Life, 1993, 127, 128.

California

Allensworth (Earlimart Vicinity)*

Colonel Allensworth State Historic Park

Although Allen Allensworth was born a slave in Louisville, Kentucky, in 1842, he dreamed of freedom from an early age. In 1854, when he was twelve years old, his owner sold him to a slavemaster in New Orleans. There he learned to ride horses and gained enough skill to become a jockey. As a youth he ran away several times but was captured and was returned to slavery each time.

When the Civil War started, Allensworth, who was twenty years old, ran away again, escaping to Union Army lines where he helped tend injured soldiers. He already knew how to read and write, and he taught these skills to some of the soldiers.

After the war Allensworth worked at first as a teacher and restaurateur. Later he served as pastor of a Baptist church in Louisville, Kentucky. He then decided to join the military again and in 1866 was appointed chaplain of the all-Black Twenty-fourth Infantry—the first African American to serve as a military chaplain. In 1906 he retired from the Army as a lieutenant colonel—the highest-ranking chaplain and Black officer of his time.

Allensworth, his wife Josephine, and their two daughters, Nellie and Eva, moved to Los Angeles in 1906. He and other African Americans began planning a community where they could be independent and self-governing. They selected a promising site in Tulare County, halfway between San Francisco and Los Angeles. The fertile land was near a railway depot, and the land developer who sold them the acreage made a promise that water would always be plentiful. In 1908 the pioneers began to move into the new town of Allensworth. Soon they developed farms and built homes, a school, a church, a library, and a post office. In 1914, when Colonel Allensworth was on the way to Monrovia, California, to publicize the town, he was fatally struck by a motorcycle. He was buried with honors in a Los Angeles cemetery.

Misfortune began for the town of Allensworth about this time. The land developing company that had promised a good supply of water failed to keep its promise and siphoned off water to white-owned farms in surrounding areas. As a result, the population of Allensworth rapidly dwindled from a peak of 300 to 160. The Depression years brought additional hardships, and many families left the town during World War II. Its abandoned structures began to deteriorate.

Years later, however, the town was restored through the efforts of Cornelius Ed Pope, a Black man who worked at drafting for the state department of parks and recreation. Pope had lived in Allensworth as a child. Learning in 1969 that remaining structures in Allensworth were soon to be razed by bulldozers, he initiated successful efforts to turn the town into a state park. Restoration began in 1976, and many buildings were rebuilt to the way they looked when the town was founded.

The Visitors Center has exhibits and a film. With advance arrangements visitors can see the interiors of several buildings, including Hindsman Home, a schoolhouse, a church, a library, a hotel, a general store, Smith Home, and a drugstore.

DATE ESTABLISHED: 1908

ADDRESS: CA 43, 8 miles west of Earlimart

TELEPHONE: (805) 849-3433

VISITING HOURS: Visitors Center, daily 8–3; park, 24 hours; guided tour of interiors of several buildings, by appointment; closed Thanksgiving, Christmas, New Year's Day

FEES: Vehicles, $3 per day; overnight camping, $8

SOURCES: Personal visit, July 1992. Telephone conversation June 30, 1994, Phillip Hall, park ranger. Robert Leiterman, park ranger. NRHPINF. Manuel Bergado, chief ranger, Historic Sites. Brochure from State of California, Department of Parks and Recreation. *National Register of Historic Places, 77. California Weekly Explorer.*

Beckwourth

James Beckwourth Cabin

James P. Beckwourth—trapper, explorer, scout, and trader—became such a legend for his life of adventure as a mountaineer that a city, valley, and mountain have been named for him. He was born in Virginia in 1798, the third of thirteen children. His mother was Black, a slave in his white father's household. As a youth, Beckwourth was sent to school in St. Louis for four years. Then he was apprenticed to a blacksmith in St. Louis but ran away at eighteen to a life of adventure. He learned to hunt and to use guns, Bowie knives, and tomahawks. He became a fur trader at the age of twenty-five with the Ashley Rocky Mountain Fur Company and the American Fur Company.

Beckwourth, who communicated well with Indians, was adopted by the Crow Nation. He lived among them for six years, learning their ways and earning their respect. He was said to have been a warrior and a chieftain. Beckwourth left the Indian tribe in 1837, moving on to establish trading posts (see the listing for the El Pueblo Museum in Pueblo, Colorado) and to serve as an army scout in 1842 during the Third Seminole War. He then moved to California, to a life of travel, trapping, and prospecting for gold.

In 1850 Beckwourth discovered an important northern pass a few miles northwest of present-day Reno, Nevada, that led through the Sierra Nevadas to the gold fields of California. Before his discovery, travelers crossing in wagon trains had to take the wagons apart and hoist them up over high mountain cliffs. Beckwourth was able to open a wagon road into Marysville and the mining region. He led the first wagon train of settlers through the pass he had discovered, and thousands of travelers later traversed the Beckwourth Pass to California.

In 1852 Beckwourth built a home and trading post where westward traveling migrants could stop for food and fresh horses. He died in 1866, but the mountain pass he discovered, the mountain peak and valley, and the town nearby still bear his name. His log cabin in California stands today, much as it was when first built, near the Plumas County hamlet that bears his name.

DATE BUILT: 1852

ADDRESS: Pass, CA 70, the Feather River Highway, east of the junction with US 395, several miles north of Lake Tahoe; cabin, Rocky Point Road, south of CA 70, 1½ miles east of Chilcoot, between the towns of Beckwourth and Portola (from Beckwourth travel west on CA 70, go past Grizzly Road and turn left on Rocky Point Road; from Portola travel east on CA 70 to Rocky Point Road, turn right onto Rocky Point Road)

VISITING HOURS: Private, visitors may drive by

SOURCES: Manuel Bergado, chief ranger. *The Black West*. "A History of Black Americans in California," 72, 90–91. "State Park Units with Black Culture Influence." *A Salute to Black Pioneers.*

Los Angeles

Ralph Bunche House

The Ralph Bunche House is a frame structure in South Central Los Angeles. Dr. Bunche lived in this house from 1919 to 1927. He was born in 1904 in Detroit, Michigan, but both parents died before he was twelve, and he went to live in Los Angeles with his maternal grandmother.

An outstanding student, Bunche attended John Adams Junior High and Jefferson High School. He then enrolled at the University of California at Los Angeles, where he was elected to Phi Beta Kappa. He graduated *summa cum laude.*

Bunche earned his Ph.D. degree from Harvard University in 1934 and started on a brilliant career. He received wide recognition for his work at the United Nations, where he became the highest ranking Black person in the United Nations Secretariat. He was the first Black recipient of the Nobel Peace Prize, which was given for his peacekeeping efforts for the United Nations.

The Dunbar Economic Development Corporation is working with a private corporation to restore the home to its original appearance. The site is marked with a city cultural heritage plaque (see the New York section for additional information on Dr. Bunche).

DATE OF SIGNIFICANCE: Bunche residence, 1919–1927

ADDRESS: 1221 E. Fortieth Place, South Central Los Angeles

VISITING HOURS: Private and vacant, visitors may drive by

SOURCES: NRHPINF. Telephone conversation June 30, 1994, Louise Parsons, A. C. Billbrew Library, Los Angeles. Telephone conversation June 30, 1994, Reginald Chapple, project director, Dunbar Economic Development Corporation. "A Guide to Black History in Los Angeles."

California Afro-American Museum*

The California Afro-American Museum collects, preserves, and displays artifacts that document the African American experience in America. It is housed in a spacious, contemporary, glass-and-brick facility. Three interior galleries provide display space for changing art and history exhibits. Additional facilities include a research library with 50,000 books, archives, a meeting hall, a theater, and a gift shop.

The museum engages in research, produces publications on Afro-American artists and achievers, and presents multimedia presentations, lectures, and a cultural exchange of talented Black artists.

DATE ESTABLISHED: Building, 1984; museum, 1977

ADDRESS: 600 State Drive, Exposition Park, Los Angeles

TELEPHONE: (213) 744-7432

VISITING HOURS: Tues.–Sun. 10–5; closed New Year's Day, Thanksgiving, Christmas

FEES: None

SOURCES: Jayne Sinegal, library director, California Afro-American Museum. Telephone call to site, June 30, 1994. Aurelia Brooks, C.E.O., California Afro-American Museum Foundation. *California Afro-American Museum.* "A Guide to Black History in Los Angeles." *Museums of Southern California,* 2–3.

The Dunbar Hotel

Dr. John Alexander Somerville was born in Jamaica, the son of an Episcopalian priest. He came to California in 1902 and, as an African American, was unable to find lodging at local hotels because of racial prejudice. Undaunted, he prepared for his career by working his way through college. In 1907 he became the first Black graduate of the University of Southern California's School of Dentistry. His wife, Dr. Vada Somerville, graduated from the University of Southern California School of Dentistry in 1918.

Somerville, who once had been refused rooms in hotels, opened his own hotel in 1928. An elegant building in the Spanish hacienda style, the Somerville was built entirely by Black contractors, laborers, and craftspeople; it was financed by Black community members. The four-story, 100-room hotel in its opening year hosted the first national West Coast convention of the National Association for the Advancement of Colored People.

Lucius Lomas, another prominent Black community leader, purchased the hotel in the early 1930s and renamed it the Dunbar Hotel. It became a center for cultural, business, and social activities and hosted many prominent visitors: W. E. B. Du Bois, Thurgood Marshall, Paul Robeson, Marian Anderson, A. Philip Randolph, James Weldon Johnson, Josephine Baker, Adam Clayton Powell, Langston Hughes, Duke Ellington, Count Basie, Louis Armstrong, Joe Louis, Redd Foxx, Sammy Davis Jr., Roland Hayes, and Bill Robinson.

DATE BUILT: 1928

ADDRESS: 4225 S. Central Avenue, Los Angeles

TELEPHONE: (213) 234-7882

VISITING HOURS: Tours by appointment, Mon.–Fri.

SOURCES: NRHPINF. Telephone conversation June 30, 1994, Mr. Reginald Chapple, project director, Dunbar Economic Development Corporation. "Return of the Dunbar."

El Pueblo de Los Angeles State Historic Park

The original settlers of El Pueblo de Los Angeles came primarily from the city of Rosario in Mexico, where two-thirds of the people were of Black or mixed ancestry. Among those from Rosario who settled in the new community, 50 percent were said to be Black or mixed Black heritage. They created the foundation of the city that is now Los Angeles.

The original settlement, the birthplace of Los Angeles, is now part of a state historic park operated by the city. Although the original houses are gone, more than twenty historical buildings from the colonial period still remain. These include the facade of the Pico House, a hotel built by Pio Pico, a man of mixed Black heritage; he was the last Mexican governor of California.

Eleven buildings are open to the public and four have been restored as museums. The names of the settlers are recorded on a bronze plaque erected in 1981 to honor the city's founders. Tours start from the Visitors Center in the Sepulveda House. Pico House may be viewed from the outside, but has not yet been restored for public viewing of the interior.

ADDRESS: Park, 845 N. Alameda Street; Visitors Center, 622 N. Main; Pico House, 424–436 N. Main Street, Los Angeles

TELEPHONE: (213) 628-1274 or (213) 628-7170

VISITING HOURS: Park, daily 10–8; museums, Tues.–Sat. 10–3; guided walking tours, Tues.–Sat. 10, 11, 12, and 1 except on Thanksgiving Day and Christmas

FEES: None

SOURCES: Telephone call to site, June 30, 1994. Manuel Bergado, chief ranger. "A Guide to Black History in Los Angeles." *Museums of Southern California,* 10–13. "10 Benchmarks and Landmarks." State Park Units with Black Culture Influence. *Black Angelenos.*

Los Angeles Children's Museum

The Ethnic Los Angeles exhibit at the Los Angeles Children's Museum provides a series of innovative learning environments about cultures of ethnic groups in Los Angeles. One exhibit, *From Africa to Los Angeles,* provides a short journey through some of the sights, sounds, tastes, and textures of African American culture from the marketplaces and pyramids of the African continent to the homes and businesses of present-day Los Angeles.

DATE ESTABLISHED: 1979

ADDRESS: 310 N. Main Street, Los Angeles

TELEPHONE: (213) 687-8801 or (213) 687-8800

VISITING HOURS: During school year, Sat.–Sun. 10–5; summer, Sat.–Sun. 10–5, Tues.–Fri. 11:30–5; closed Thanksgiving, Christmas, Easter, July 4

FEES: Adults and children over 3, $5; children under 3 years, free

SOURCES: Candace Barrett, assistant director of exhibits and programs, Los Angeles Children's Museum. Telephone conversation June 26, 1994, Prima Devera, reservations and box office, Los Angeles Children's Museum.

Biddy Mason Tableau and Timeline

Biddy Mason, pioneer, midwife, and philanthropist, is honored by an exhibit at the Broadway Spring Center. The mixed-use building is built on the homestead site purchased by Biddy Mason in 1866. Elevator doors at the lobby level open to a tableau of Mason on the front porch of another Black pioneer family. Outside, a striking 8-foot-by-81-foot timeline on a wall traces her life and history.

Biddy Mason, known affectionately as Grandma Mason, was admired throughout Los Angeles for her skill as a midwife and her willingness to help others. She was born in slavery in Hancock, Georgia, and was sold about 1836 to Robert

Marion Smith, a convert to Mormonism, who took Biddy and her three daughters west with a Mississippi company of Mormons in 1848. They started out in wet, muddy weather. Biddy traveled on foot, herding the livestock behind the wagon train across Missouri and Nebraska into Utah.

When Smith left for California about 1851, taking Biddy and her children with him, he was in violation of California laws since California was a free state. Although Biddy befriended some free Black people living in San Bernardino, she continued to serve her owner as a slave.

In 1856 Smith planned to move to Texas and to take Biddy, her daughters, and other slaves south with him. Although he told Biddy that she would be free in Texas, she knew that was not true. Biddy's friends alerted authorities that the African Americans were being returned to slavery. A group that included the local sheriff rushed to Smith's camp in the Santa Monica mountains and rescued fourteen slaves, including Biddy and her daughters and some other relatives. A ruling from the United States District Court emancipated the group that Smith had held in slavery. The Black community in Los Angeles, which had financed the legal proceedings, rejoiced.

People in the Los Angeles area—both wealthy and poor families—called on Mason's help as a midwife. Soon she was able to purchase lots and to build a family homestead at 331 South Spring Street between Third and Fourth Streets. Although Mason became wealthy from real estate investments, she never forgot to return the assistance others had given her. When devastating floods of the 1880s destroyed homes, she opened an account in a grocery store to provide food for homeless people of all races. Los Angeles mourned when Mason died on January 15, 1891.

DATE ESTABLISHED: 1989
ADDRESS: Broadway Spring Center, 333 S. Spring Street, Los Angeles
TELEPHONE: (213) 626-2099
VISITING HOURS: Dawn–dusk
SOURCES: Telephone call June 26, 1994, to site. *The Story of the Negro Pioneer.* "Grandma Mason Remembered." *Biddy Mason's Place: A Midwife's Homestead, The Power of Place.* "A History of Black Americans in California," 86. *Los Angeles County Historical Directory.*

Museum of African American Art

Museum displays include sculpture from Africa as well as works by contemporary Black artists. In June 1994 the museum had just reopened, having recovered from earthquake damage to the structure. The gallery reopened with an exhibit, *Aninkra Quilt,* featuring the watercolors and monoprints of nationally known but locally based African American artist Varnette Honeywood. In addition to the changing exhibits, the museum has a gift shop gallery offering prints, books, cards, jewelry, figurines, dolls, and African imports.

DATE ESTABLISHED: Museum, 1975; at this site, 1979
ADDRESS: 4005 Crenshaw Boulevard, Third Floor, Los Angeles
TELEPHONE: (213) 294-7071
VISITING HOURS: Wed.–Sat. 11–6, Sun. noon–5
FEES: None
SOURCES: Telephone conversation June 26, 1994, Dolores Orduna, gift shop manager, Museum of African American Art. "A Guide to Black History in Los Angeles."

West Adams Historic District

The West Adams Historic District includes several homes, a historic African American business, and churches, all of which are significant to the city's African American history. The district includes the Golden State Mutual Life Insurance Company, the Louise Beavers residence, Hattie McDaniel's residence, and Butterfly McQueen's home.

Land developers laid out tracts and neighborhoods for this community in the late 1890s. They built large, luxurious homes for the rich and famous. In the late 1940s the first Black couple moved into the area, and other families soon followed. White families began to move out of the community, but they returned in the 1970s when they were attracted again by the beautiful old homes.

Golden State Mutual Life Insurance Company, at 1999 West Adams Boulevard, is one of America's largest Black-owned insurance companies. Founder William Nickerson Jr. migrated from Texas to California in 1921, seeking personal and economic opportunity. Instead, he found that the 16,000 Black residents of Los Angeles were considered such poor risks by insurance companies that they were charged high premium rates or were denied insurance coverage altogether.

Two other men, Norman O. Houston, an insurance agent from northern California, and George A. Beavers, a Los Angeles business owner and church leader, shared Nickerson's dissatisfaction. In 1924 the three men began organizing a company that would meet the insurance needs of the Black community.

Nickerson purchased a set of law books and taught himself California's insurance codes. The men then secured in advance 500 paid applications for the company they planned to develop. They were successful in raising the needed funds, and in 1925 they received a license to operate as the Golden State Guarantee Fund Insurance Company of Los Angeles.

The fledgling company started its physical existence in a 12-foot-by-14-foot second-story room at 1435 Central Avenue. The business was successful, and within seventy-nine days it was moved to new store-front offices at 3512 Central. Although many businesses collapsed during the Great Depression, Golden State continued to expand.

Nickerson died in 1945. Cofounder Houston was elected president and continued the company's growth. In 1949 Golden State dedicated the present elegant home-office building. Paul Williams, a noted Black architect, designed the five-story, art deco building located in the heart of the upwardly mobile Black community.

By 1984 Golden State Mutual ranked among the fifty largest mutual insurance companies in the nation. Today it promotes an appreciation for the African American cultural heritage by providing a showcase of California's Black pioneers and America's Black artists. The display, located at the home office, includes murals depicting the contributions of Black individuals and families to California's growth and development. The following additional historic West Adams buildings are associated with African Americans:

The **Louise Beavers Residence** at 2219 South Hobart Boulevard belonged to an African American actress who was born in Cincinnati, Ohio, in 1902. Beavers began her career as a film actress in the 1920s. As with other Black actresses through the 1950s, she was typically cast by Hollywood in the role of a maid. She played in such films as *Imitation of Life* (1934) and *Mr. Blanding Builds His Dream House* (1948). She followed another actress, Ethel Waters, in portraying the maid Beulah in the 1950s television series called *Beulah.* Louise Beavers died in 1962.

The **Hattie McDaniel Residence** at 2203 South Harvard Boulevard belonged to a Black radio and film actress. McDaniel was born in 1893 (one account gives 1898) in Wichita, Kansas, the thirteenth child of a Baptist preacher and his wife. McDaniel attended public schools in Denver, Colorado, and began her professional career at the age of sixteen or seventeen, singing in tent shows and radio programs. In the 1920s she began touring different states in vaudeville shows. In 1933 she began working on radio shows including the *Amos 'N' Andy Show* and the *Eddie Cantor Show,* and she began acting in films. McDaniel appeared in more than seventy films. Although Hollywood usually assigned the talented actress the stereotyped roles of a maid, McDaniel managed to add to her characterizations an element of assertiveness toward her white employers. The first African American to win an Academy Award, McDaniel was awarded an Oscar in 1946 for her portrayal of Scarlett O'Hara's maid in *Gone with the Wind.* McDaniel died in 1952.

The **Butterfly McQueen Home,** 2215 South Harvard Boulevard, was the residence of another well-known Black actress. Thelma (Butterfly) McQueen was born in Tampa, Florida, in 1911. Her father was a stevedore and her mother was a domestic worker. In 1935 McQueen moved to Harlem to pursue an acting career; there she joined an acting troupe, Jones's Negro Youth Group. Two years later McQueen made her Broadway debut in the George Abbott musical *Brown Sugar.* Although acclaimed for her acting talent on the stage, in films McQueen usually was limited to portraying the role of a domestic worker. She was chosen, for example, to play the role of the maid Prissy in *Gone with the Wind.* Acting assignments were scarce in the late 1940s for McQueen. She produced a one-women concert in 1951 at Carnegie Hall, but it was not a financial success. A succession of jobs followed, including waiting tables in Harlem in the 1960s. In 1975 McQueen received a B.A. degree from City College of New York; in the same year she was inducted into the Black Filmmakers Hall of Fame.

DATE OF SIGNIFICANCE: Historic district, 1940s; Golden State Mutual Life Insurance Company, 1925; company's art collection, 1949

ADDRESS: Historic district, S. Figueroa Street, west to Crenshaw Boulevard, and south from Venice Boulevard to Jefferson Boulevard; Golden State Mutual Life Insurance Company, 1999 W. Adams Boulevard, Los Angeles

TELEPHONE: Golden State Mutual Life Insurance Company, (213) 731-1131

VISITING HOURS: Movie stars' homes, private, visitors may drive by; Golden State Mutual Life Insurance Company, Mon.–Fri. 9–4:45; closed Sat., Sun., most holidays

FEES: Art exhibit, free

SOURCES: Maria Rosario Jackson, Golden State Mutual Company. "A Guide to Black History in Los Angeles." *Los Angeles County Historical Directory. The African American Encyclopedia,* 141, 1007–8, 1015–16.

Oakland

Liberty Hall

Liberty Hall in Oakland is associated with two historic African American groups: the United Negro Improvement Association and Father Divine's Peace Mission. Marcus Garvey (1887–1940) founded the Universal Negro Improvement Association in Jamaica in 1914. He came to New York and organized a branch of the association in Harlem in 1916. With the slogan, "Up You Mighty Race, You Can Accomplish What You Will," and with an emphasis on Black pride, Black nationalism, and Black economic and political power, the organization inspired African Americans in many cities.

Garvey's movement became one of the largest mass movements of Black people in the United States. In addition to emphasizing independence in America, Garvey also revived earlier attempts to send millions of Black people back to Africa. Although the latter objective was not accomplished, Garvey sowed the seeds for independence movements in the Caribbean region and Africa and for the civil rights movements in the United States.

The Oakland, California, branch, Local 188 of the United Negro Improvement Association, was chartered in 1920. Five years later the association bought the old Western Market Building on Eighth Street and renamed it Liberty Hall. A series of setbacks began soon afterward. Marcus Garvey was deported to Jamaica in 1927. Although the charges against him were questionable, the loss of the leader severely hurt the movement. The nation was entering a financial depression, and UNIA activities began a long decline after a fire severely damaged the building in 1931.

Liberty Hall began to house another organization, the main Oakland branch of Father Divine's Peace Mission. Father Divine, an African American evangelical preacher (about 1877 to 1965), was born in poverty in the South as George Baker. He began his ministry in that region. Moving to New York one year before the arrival of Marcus Garvey, George Baker acquired property in 1919 in the all-white suburb of Sayville, Long Island. There he assumed the name Father Divine and began his Peace Mission, operating a communal household during the Depression that provided free weekly banquets for all who wanted to come. He spoke out against stealing, gambling, smoking, use of liquor, evading debts, and racial prejudice of any kind. By 1926 the Peace Mission was an interracial movement.

By 1936 the Peace Mission had grown and had twenty-eight branches in California. The branch on Eighth Street was one of six in Oakland. During the Depression era the Peace Mission prepared banquets, charging only pennies per person. The facilities also included a dormitory and furniture repair shop. Although the Peace Mission movement began to decline after the start of World War II, this branch was listed in the telephone directory until 1965.

The people of Oakland have become aware of the history of Liberty Hall. Today the restored building is in use again in the old tradition of serving the community. The Jubilee West organization, which has administrative offices and a community center at 1485 Eighth Street, sponsors several programs in a youth center at this address, a thrift shop, and other services in the community. The organization's activities include a job program, a housing program, and an emergency program that distributes goods and services.

DATE BUILT: 1877; first used for the African American community, c1925
ADDRESS: 1483–1485 Eighth Street, Oakland
TELEPHONE: Jubilee West organization, (510) 839-6776
VISITING HOURS: Jubilee West organization, Mon.–Fri. 9–5 by appointment
SOURCES: NRHPRF. Telephone conversation June 30, 1994, Bill Sturm, librarian, Oakland History Room. *International Library of Negro Life and History.*

Oceanside

Santa Margarita Ranch House

The Santa Margarita Ranch House was another home of Pio Pico, California's last Mexican governor (see the listings for Pico House in Los Angeles and for Pio Pico State Historic Park in Whittier, California). The adobe structure was built in the early nineteenth century. It is a one-story residence with a veranda that encircles the house and a central patio. The original small structure was enlarged to include twenty-three rooms. The original winery was converted to a chapel and the bunkhouse to a museum. The Spanish colonial building was later sold and developed as a cattle ranch. Since 1942 it has been used as a part of a U.S. Marine base.

DATE BUILT: Main house, c1827
ADDRESS: Off Vandergrift Boulevard and Basilone Road, Camp Pendleton, Oceanside
TELEPHONE: History office, Camp Pendleton, (619) 725-5758

VISITING HOURS: Private residence, tour times vary

SOURCES: Telephone call June 29, 1994, Camp Pendleton History Office. *National Register of Historic Places,* 70.

San Diego

Richard Freeman House

Richard Freeman was born in the eastern United States. Joining the small African American colony at San Diego about 1847, he bought an adobe building. With another African American, Allen Light, Freeman operated a grog shop, known as the San Diego House, for four years.

San Diego House represents an example of early African American entrepreneurship in San Diego. The state park system plans to reconstruct the nineteenth-century adobe building as part of the Old Town in San Diego State Historic Park. The old grog shop is used now as a retail shop, Casa de Wrightington. The shop has retained its historic appearance outside but not inside, where it has been remodeled as a store. The staff members inside have no information on Richard Freeman; please do not disrupt their activities with inquiries. Visitors may enjoy seeing its exterior and surroundings in the Old Town.

DATE BUILT: 1800s

ADDRESS: San Diego House, Old Town in San Diego State Historic Park, 4002 Wallace Street; Casa de Wrightington, 2783 San Diego Avenue, San Diego

TELEPHONE: (619) 220-5422

VISITING HOURS: Casa de Wrightington, daily 8–6

SOURCES: Manuel Bergado, chief ranger, Historic Sites. Telephone conversation June 26, 1994, Tom Cline, ranger supervisor. "A History of Black Americans in California," 59.

Sonora

Sugg House

Both William and Mary Sugg were born in slavery, but each came separately to Tuolumne County. William Sugg was born in 1828 at Raleigh, North Carolina. He reached California by wagon train before 1852, working as a muleteer and bullwhacker on the journey. His traveling companions settled in the Merced area. Sugg obtained his freedom and began working in the harness business.

Mary Sugg was born in Johnson City, Missouri. She came west to California in 1851 in an eventful trip during which her group suffered a cholera outbreak and had encounters with hostile Indian groups.

William and Mary eventually came to Tuolumne County, an area where hundreds of Black people already lived. They first met at a social function and later moved to Sonora, where they married in 1855.

William Sugg began building this house on Theall Street in 1857. He and friends mixed mud and shaped it into the adobe that forms the interior walls of the home. The rooms were arranged one behind the other—a front room, a middle room, a rear living/dining room, and a 14-foot-by-16-foot frame kitchen in a wooden lean-to. The middle room served as the bedroom in which all eleven of the Sugg children were born. As the family grew, Sugg added bedrooms on the first and second floors as well as a frame kitchen. In the 1880s he built a two-story gallery across the front.

When nearby hotels were full, hotel managers referred guests to the Sugg House, where a rule stipulated that no "lewd women" could stay there. The Sugg family took in visitors until 1921, when the city began to require hot and cold running water and inside bathrooms in facilities rented to the public. Because the cost of making these conversions was more than the family could afford, the Suggs had to stop taking in boarders. In fact, the house had no indoor toilet until the 1940s.

William Sugg returned to Merced in 1877, a year after the birth of their last child. Mary Sugg remained in Sonora. Although high school classes were not offered in Tuolumne County until the late 1890s, Mary Sugg worked hard to see that all eleven children received at least an elementary school education. She died in 1915, and her grandson, Vernon Sugg McDonald, died at the Sugg House in May 1982.

Sugg House was built by a manumitted slave and his wife during the gold rush years. The house also is unique in California's gold rush country and Tuolumne County as one of the few remaining adobe buildings in the region. As of 1994 it was in use by a video productions organization.

DATE BUILT:	1857
ADDRESS:	37 Theall Street, Sonora
VISITING HOURS:	Private, visitors may walk or drive by
SOURCE:	NRHPINF.

Stockton

Moses Rodgers House

Moses Rodgers was born a slave in Missouri. While still a young man he acquired skill as a mining engineer. When the gold rush swept California in 1849, he went west to participate and moved to Hornitos, where he established a reputation as a superior mining engineer. His opinion was valued so highly throughout the state that investors often consulted him before purchasing mining claims or stock.

Rodgers acquired a number of mines in the Mariposa district. He also became a mining superintendent for the Washington mine established in 1869. In some years more than half a million dollars in gold was taken from this mine.

Rodgers married Sahra Quivers in the 1860s. They had five daughters. As the girls grew up, the family moved to Stockton because of the superior school facilities in that town. Rodgers built a fine, two-story frame home for his family on one of the best residential streets in Stockton. He continued his mining interests, becoming the first person to drill successfully for natural gas in Stockton. He didn't gain financially from his discovery, however, because he was not able to persuade investors to back the operation.

Rodgers lived in his house on South Joaquin Street until his death after the turn of the century. The house remained in the same family until 1971.

DATE BUILT: 1898
ADDRESS: 921 S. San Joaquin Street, Stockton
VISITING HOURS: Private, visitors may walk or drive by
FEES: None
SOURCES: NRHPINF. "A History of Black Americans in California," 65.

Whittier

Pio Pico State Historic Park*

Pio Pico, a man of mixed Black heritage, was the last Mexican governor of California. He served as governor in 1832 and again in 1845–1846 until his last term was cut short by the United States invasion. Governor Pico used his wealth and influence to support the development of education and banking and to develop town sites. He was an important figure in California's transition from Mexican to American rule and led in California's cultural and economic development.

After the United States acquired California, Pico spent time as a rancher, a Los Angeles city councilman, and a business-owner. He invested in the state's first oil venture and built the Pico House, a one and one-half–story adobe hotel in Los Angeles.

Pico's mansion in Whittier, an adobe structure with a veranda and a central courtyard, once was a center of social activity. Pico built the house near the San Gabriel River to ensure a ready supply of water; there was no well at the site until the 1870s. The river, however, proved troublesome—three floods in the 1880s damaged the house. The third and most severe flood inundated the mansion in 1883–1884, damaging it so seriously that the structure was rebuilt. The west wing, which had ten or twelve rooms, was not rebuilt because it led in the direction of the river. A kitchen wing was built in the opposite direction.

The state-owned mansion was restored in 1946 and opened to the public as a museum. But disaster struck again, first with the October 1987 Whittier Narrows earthquake and again in January 1994 with the Northridge earthquake. Workers removed furniture, put up a chain-link fence around Pico House, and began using an injection method to stabilize the cracked adobe walls. In inspecting the damage, workers discovered that the house had not been completely rebuilt after the 1883–1884 flood as had been thought; on the contrary, five of the rooms were from the original 1852 mansion.

Pico House is worth seeing both for its architecture and for its place in Black history. Architecturally, the mansion is interesting because its construction reflects both Spanish and American influences. The first floor, of adobe construction, is Mexican-Spanish in style. The second story shows influences from the eastern United States—construction is of wood and there are dormer windows that are not typical in California construction. In the final restoration a section with two rooms on the first floor and two on the second will be rebuilt. An old photograph shows Pico sitting on the balcony of this section and shows an American-style Victorian railing on the balcony.

Governor Pico, who was born May 5, 1801, died September 11, 1894. Although forgotten by many Californians today, Pico should be remembered again as an accomplished business person and as the last Mexican governor of California. His ethnic heritage, which included Spanish, African, Indian, and Italian ancestors, reflects the ancestry of many of today's Californians. His Black heritage, which Pico acknowledged, was the heritage of many of California's early settlers; Pico House, therefore, is a part of California's Black history.

DATE BUILT: 1852; rebuilt 1884; restored 1946 and 1995

ADDRESS: 6003 Pioneer Boulevard at Whittier Boulevard, Whittier

TELEPHONE: (310) 695-1217

VISITING HOURS: Wed.–Sun. 10–4; closed New Year's Day, Thanksgiving, Christmas

SOURCES: Telephone conversation Apr. 22, 1995, Jeanne Ekstrom, state park interpreter, Pio Pico State Historic Park. Manuel Bergado, chief ranger, Historic Sites. State Park Units with Black Culture Influence. *National Register of Historic Places.*

Works Consulted

The African American Encyclopedia. Vols. 1, 4. Michael W. Williams, ed. New York: Marshall Cavendish, 1993.

Biddy Mason's Place: A Midwife's Homestead, The Power of Place. Dolores Hayden. Los Angeles: The Power of Place, 1988. [poster]

Black Angelenos: The Afro-American in Los Angeles, 1850–1950. Los Angeles: California Afro-American Museum, June 1988. [exhibit guide]

The Black West: A Documentary and Pictorial History. Rev. ed. William Loren Katz. New York: Anchor/Doubleday, 1973.

California Afro-American Museum. Los Angeles: California Afro-American Museum. [brochure]

California Weekly Explorer. Irvine, Calif.: California Weekly Explorer, 1980. [newspaper]

"Grandma Mason Remembered." Clipping files, vol. 13, no. 1, p. 4, history department, Los Angeles Public Library. [newsletter]

"A Guide to Black History in Los Angeles." Emily Gibson. *Los Angeles Herald Examiner,* Jan. 30, 1987.

"A History of Black Americans in California." Eleanor M. Ramsey and Janice S. Lewis. In *Five Views: An Ethnic Sites Survey for California.* Sacramento, Calif.: State of California, Department of Parks and Recreation, 1988.

International Library of Negro Life and History: Historical Negro Biographies. Wilhelmena S. Robinson. New York: Publishers, 1970.

Los Angeles County Historical Directory. Janet I. Atkinson. Jefferson, N.C.: McFarland, 1988.

Museums of Southern California. Sara LeBien. Salt Lake City, Utah: Gibbs-Smith, Peregrine, 1988.

National Register of Historic Places. Washington, D.C.: National Park Service, 1976.

"Return of the Dunbar." I. Posey and F. Finley McRae. *Los Angeles Weekly,* 19–25 Feb. 1988.

A Salute to Black Pioneers. Richard L. Green, ed. Chicago: Empak, 1986.

State Park Units with Black Culture Influence. Sacramento, Calif.: California Department of Parks and Recreation. [list]

The Story of the Negro Pioneer. Kate B. Carter. Salt Lake City, Utah: Daughters of Utah Pioneers, 1965.

"Ten Benchmarks and Landmarks: Black History on View in LA." Toni Tipton. *Los Angeles Times,* Jan. 15, 1987.

Colorado

Boulder

Henry Stevens House
Oscar and Mary White House

Few of the early homes of Boulder's Black citizens have survived. Two remaining examples are the Henry Stevens House and the Oscar and Mary White House, early twentieth-century homes.

Henry Stevens, one of Boulder's best-known citizens, was born to slave parents in 1863 in Fayette County, Missouri. After emancipation the family moved to Hannibal, Missouri, where his parents apprenticed young Henry Stevens, at the age of fourteen, to a photographer. Stevens came to Boulder in 1879 and worked for three years as a photographer and creator of advertisements. He later took a job as a janitor at Boulder's First National Bank and worked there for more than fifty years.

Stevens House, which may have been constructed earlier than 1900, is typical of early housing in Boulder's Black community. Stevens lived here until his death in 1945.

Oscar and Mary White, influential citizens in Boulder's small Black community, lived in this 1,152-square-foot frame house with stucco siding. Oscar White was born a slave in Kentucky. He became a sergeant in the Union Army and served during the entire Civil War. By 1880 he and approximately seventy other Black residents were living in Boulder, Colorado. He and his wife, Mary, were charter members of Allen Chapel African Methodist Episcopal Church. Oscar White worked as a day laborer and gardener for the next fifteen years. Mary White took in laundry. The Whites' house on Goss Street had been built at least ten years before they moved into it around 1900. The Goss Street area was the center of Boulder's small Black community during the first half of the twentieth century.

DATE BUILT: Stevens House, pre–1900; White House, pre–1890

ADDRESS: Stevens House, 2220 Pine Street; White House, 2202 Goss Street, Boulder

VISITING HOURS: Private, visitors may walk or drive by

SOURCE: Colorado Historical Society, Office of Archaeology and Historic Preservation.

Denver

Colorado Historical Society Museum

Between 1994 and 1997 the Colorado Historical Society Museum has highlighted exhibits on Colorado's African Americans. Major exhibits include *Just Jazz,* the story of Black musicians, and a 1996 presentation on the Buffalo Soldiers. The impact of racism on the Black community was examined in an exhibit on the Ku Klux Klan in Colorado in the 1920s, part of a decade-by-decade series of exhibits on twentieth-century Colorado that integrates Black history into the exhibits. The Colorado Historical Society also maintains a research library on the second floor at this address. Individuals studying the African American history of the state can receive assistance with their research at the library.

ADDRESS:	1300 Broadway, Denver
TELEPHONE:	(303) 866-3682
VISITING HOURS:	Museum, Mon.–Sat. 10–4:30, Sun. noon–4:30; library, Tues.–Sat. 10–4:30
FEES:	Adults, $3; senior citizens 65 years and older and students with I.D., $2.50; children 6–16, $1.50; members and children under 6, free
SOURCE:	Jean Settles, administrative assistant, Colorado Historical Society Library.

Dr. Justina Ford House
Black American West Museum and Heritage Center*

The Dr. Justina Ford House once was the home of a prominent African American physician. The restored building now houses the Black American West Museum and Heritage Center.

Ford was born in Illinois in 1871. Her mother was a nurse, and from an early age Justina knew that she wanted to practice medicine. This was a bold dream for a Black girl in the nineteenth century, but she was determined. After graduating from Hering Medical College in Chicago, Ford practiced medicine briefly in Alabama before moving in 1902 to Denver. She received her Colorado medical license in an era when there were few Black female doctors in America. Ford was a staff member of Denver General Hospital and a member of both the Colorado Medical Society and the American Medical Society. Until her death she was the only African American female physician in Denver.

Ford specialized in obstetrics and gynecology, and she strongly believed that, if at all possible, children should be delivered at home. She is credited with delivering more than seven thousand babies during her long years of faithful practice in Denver. Her patients were of many different backgrounds, including women of Black, Mexican, Spanish, Greek, Korean, and Japanese heritage.

Although held in high esteem in the community, Ford lived modestly and never owned a car. When making home visits, she would accept payment in goods or in cash. In 1951 she received the Human Rights Award from Denver's Cosmopolitan Club. She died the following year at the age of eighty-one.

In 1911 Ford purchased a narrow, single-family residence that had been built in 1890 on Arapahoe Street. It served as both her home and her medical office until the end of her life. Years later, in 1983, the entire block on which her home stood was being cleared to make way for a parking lot. Community leaders, realizing that Ford's home was about to be demolished, raised funds to save it. The following year Historic Denver, Inc., a philanthropic organization, had the house moved to the corner of California and Thirty-first Streets. Community groups and many individuals helped restore it.

In 1986 officials of the Black American West Museum bought the Ford home and set up their museum and Black heritage center in 1990. This organization was founded by Paul Stewart, a Black man born in Clinton, Iowa, who had loved playing cowboys and Indians as a boy. His friends often made fun of him, saying that there had been no Black cowboys. Years later, Stewart met a Black cowboy who had driven cattle at the turn of the century. This meeting inspired a thirty-year search for additional information. Stewart gathered photographs, artifacts, personal possessions and memorabilia, and records of nineteenth-century Black pioneers and conducted hundreds of tape-recorded interviews with Black western pioneers. Paul Stewart founded the Black American West Museum and Heritage Center to show how Black Americans helped to settle the West by working as ranch hands, cowhands, barbers, teachers, doctors, miners, and soldiers and by establishing self-sufficient all-Black towns. Museum programs include movies, slide shows, and workshops for schools, libraries, and community groups.

DATE ESTABLISHED: House, 1890; museum, 1971

ADDRESS: 3091 California Street, Denver

TELEPHONE: (303) 292-2566

VISITING HOURS: Wed.–Fri. 10–2, Sat. noon–5, Sun. 2–5; closed Mon.–Tues.

FEES: Adults, $2; senior citizens, $1.50; children, $.75

SOURCES: NRHPINF. Mr. Ottawa W. Harris, board of directors, Black American West Museum and Heritage Center. Geraldine Stepp, project director, Black American West Museum and Heritage Center. "Museum Tells Story of Black Frontiersmen." *Colorado, Official State Vacation Guide. Dr. Justina Ford, A Legacy.* "Doctor Justina Ford, A Medical Legacy Continues," 4–5. "The Forty Years of Justina Ford." "Denver Museum Preserving Records of Black Pioneers in West."

Pueblo

El Pueblo Museum

Black trapper, explorer, and one-time Crow chief Jim Beckwourth became legendary for his exploits in America's West. He discovered a mountain pass leading to the California gold fields, a route that later was named Beckwourth Pass. (See the listing for Beckwourth, California.)

Beckwourth first came to Colorado in 1842, and with a few other trappers he built an adobe trading post that he named "El Pueblo." However, misfortune struck on Christmas Day 1854 when Ute Indians wiped out the settlement. Four years later, the trappers rebuilt the structure, using materials from the old trading post.

Today the El Pueblo Museum has a small floor-model replica of the original trading post and a diorama, approximately five feet long, that shows how it looked. The museum also has a painting of Beckwourth. Beneath it there is a brief biography of Pueblo's founder. Also in the museum are two books about him, both titled *James Beckwourth, Mountain Man.* The portion of the street just outside the museum has been named Beckwourth Plaza. Only a small part of the museum is devoted to Beckwourth, however. Most of the space is about Colorado history from the era of the Plains Indians through the early 1900s. Although Black history is not emphasized at this site, the local Black History Research Group meets in the museum each month. As a current project, association members are supporting efforts to restore the old Lincoln Orphanage, a Black historic site (see the following listing).

ADDRESS: 324 W. First Street, Pueblo

TELEPHONE: (719) 583-0453

VISITING HOURS: Mon.–Sat. 10–4:30, Sun. noon–3

FEES: Adults, $2.50; senior citizens 65 years and older, $2; members of AAA, two-for-one price; children 6–16, $2; children under 6, free

SOURCE: Telephone conversation June 22, 1994, Margie Montez, El Pueblo Museum.

Lincoln Orphanage

The Lincoln Orphanage, built in 1902, originally consisted of two buildings joined together. One of them housed young girls and older, sick women; the other took care of young boys and older, sick men. The two-story brick structure was at the time the only orphanage for Black children in a seven-state area. It continued to serve as an orphanage until 1963.

Recently the E. M. Christmas Foundation, which had purchased the old institution, handed it over to the Martin Luther King Jr. Holiday Commission and Cultural Center. After examining the building and finding that it was in excellent structural condition, the cultural center began the work of restoring it for community use in 1994. When this venerable African American institution was first erected, it stood on the outskirts of Pueblo. Today, however, it is located well within the town limits in an easily accessible area.

DATE BUILT: 1902

ADDRESS: 2713–2715 N. Grand, Pueblo

VISITING HOURS: Visitors may view the exterior dawn–dusk; for information on visiting the interior, write: Dr. Martin Luther King Jr. Holiday Commission and Cultural Center, P. O. Box 2297, Pueblo, CO 81005.

SOURCES: Telephone conversation, June 22, 1994, Ms. Ruth Steele, president, Dr. Martin Luther King Jr. Holiday Commission and Cultural Center. Telephone conversation, June 22, 1994, Margie Montez, El Pueblo Museum.

Works Consulted

Colorado, Official State Vacation Guide. Denver: Colorado Tourism Board, 1990.

"Denver Museum Preserving Records of Black Pioneers in West." William E. Schmidt. *New York Times,* July 28, 1983.

Dr. Justina Ford, A Legacy. Denver: Black American West Museum and Heritage Center, 1988.

"Dr. Justina Ford, A Medical Legacy Continues." Magdalena Gallegos. *The (Aurora, Colorado) Urban Spectrum,* Sept. 1988, 4–5.

"The Forty Years of Justina Ford." Mark Harris. *Negro Digest,* Mar. 1950, 43–45.

"Museum Tells Story of Black Frontiersmen." Tom Murray. *Colorado Black Lifestyle,* Aug. 1982.

Idaho

Boise

St. Paul Missionary Baptist Church

The Black population of Boise was quite small during the city's era of early growth, and African American worshipers may have attended church services with white congregations before St. Paul's congregation was organized. By 1909 African Americans had established their own separate church, meeting at first in a small building in Boise's commercial district. Within a year they received a donation of land south of Warm Springs Avenue.

In 1921 the Reverend William Riley Hardy, first pastor of the church, and church members built the present structure themselves. The building they created is a frame, rectangular structure with arched stained-glass windows. The interior has a raised central pulpit and pews made of oak. The church built a parsonage in the 1950s—a structure that later housed an office for the local chapter of the National Association for the Advancement of Colored People.

St. Paul Missionary Baptist Church is one of two remaining predominantly Black churches in Idaho. The building is listed in the *National Register of Historic Places.*

DATE BUILT: 1921
ADDRESS: 124 Broadway Avenue, Boise
TELEPHONE: (208) 344-0674
VISITING HOURS: By appointment, Mon.–Fri.
SOURCES: NRHPINF. Telephone conversation June 21, 1994, Mrs. Evelena Lady Ashley, wife of Pastor Bobby C. Ashley.

Spalding

Nez Percé National Historical Park

The Black man, York, who traveled with the Lewis and Clark Expedition of 1803 to 1806, may have been one of the first African Americans to explore the territory now called Idaho. York, a slave, was a man of great size and strength, and he became a valued member of the expedition. He traveled with the explorers to the areas of Idaho now within the Nez Percé National Historical Park, the Lolo Trail, and Weippe Prairie. The Nez Percé National Historical Park extends from Wallowa Lake, Oregon, to Bear Paw Battlefield near Chinook, Montana (the site of the Nez Percé surrender). The park consists of thirty-eight sites, of which Lolo Trail and Weippe Prairie are in Idaho.

In 1805 the explorers traveled over the Lolo Trail, slowly and steadily moving in the direction of the Pacific Ocean. The expedition members became the first non–Native Americans to contact the Nez Percé Indians. The journey had been very difficult, and the group was half-starved after crossing the Bitterroot Range from Montana into the Idaho territory. There they decided to rest for twelve days. Although the Nez Percés graciously provided camas roots and dried fish, the travelers were not accustomed to this type of food, and they suffered from dysentery.

When members of the expedition were well enough to continue exploration, they cut down some large trees at this site and burned out the trunks to construct five dugout canoes. In this way they were able to paddle down rivers and streams to the Pacific, their goal. This rugged and beautiful land in the Nez Percé park covers 12,000 square miles of northern Idaho. The Canoe Camp today has an exhibit of a modern dugout canoe and an interpretive marker. Although visitors are able to see the terrain through which members of the Lewis and Clark expedition traveled, the interpretive emphasis at the park is almost entirely on the Nez Percé rather than on the expedition. Visitors, however, can purchase three books at the site that describe the expedition, and a twenty-three-minute movie, *Nez Percé: Portrait of a People,* tells how the meeting with members of the Lewis and Clark expedition changed the lives of the Nez Percé.

DATE ESTABLISHED:	The Lewis and Clark Expedition crossed this area, 1805; National Historical Park, 1968
ADDRESS:	P. O. Box 93, Spalding, ID 83551 (Nez Percé County); headquarters and Visitors Center, at the park unit in Spalding, ten miles east of Lewiston, Idaho
TELEPHONE:	(208) 843-2262
VISITING HOURS:	Memorial Day–Labor Day daily 8–7; rest of the year, 8–4:30; closed New Year's Day, Christmas
FEES:	None
SOURCES:	Telephone conversation June 21, 1994, Mary Lou Tiede, business manager, Northwest Interpretive Association of the Nez Percé Branch. Telephone conversation Apr. 1, 1995, Judy Wohlert, interpreter, National Park Service, Nez Percé National Historical Park.

Work Consulted

Idaho's Ethnic Heritage Historical Overviews. Laurie Mercier and Carole Simon-Smolinski, project codirectors and eds. Boise, Idaho: Idaho Ethnic Heritage Project; cosponsored by Idaho Centennial Commission; National Park Service, U.S. Department of the Interior; and Idaho Historical Society, Mar. 1990. [Files of the Idaho Historical Society, Boise, Idaho]

Montana

● ● ● ● ● ● ● ● ● ● ●

Havre

Fort Assiniboine

When Fort Assiniboine was built in 1879, it was a Montana-Territory frontier post thirty miles south of the Canadian border. General John J. Pershing (1860–1948), an Army lieutenant at the time, led a troop of black soldiers of the Tenth Cavalry from South Carolina to Fort Assiniboine, where he directed them in raids against Native Americans. They also led raids against outlaws.

Pershing earned the nickname "Black Jack" because he was a leader of African American men. Assignments leading Black troops were not sought after at the time, and some officers refused to accept them. Pershing, however, had been raised among Black people. Some of his childhood playmates in Laclede, Missouri, were African Americans. Because of his positive stance, Pershing related to the soldiers well. He required excellence of the men in his regiment and treated them with respect and consideration.

Although the Black soldiers at Fort Assiniboine were regarded as tough and capable, there was some racism in the surrounding areas, and relationships between the soldiers and the community were strained at first. Apparently the soldiers were fully willing to protect themselves, and this resulted in a few physical conflicts.

In spite of the racism that they met at times, men of the Tenth formed a courageous, disciplined unit that became a legend in the West. Years later, in 1921, General John J. Pershing wrote these words about the Tenth Cavalry:

> It has been an honor which I am proud to claim to have been at one time a member of that intrepid organization of the Army which has always added glory to the military history of America—the 10th Cavalry.[1]

Most of Fort Assiniboine's 104 buildings were torn down in the late 1920s, leaving only fourteen standing structures. Today the buildings at old Fort Assiniboine are used for agricultural research offices, laboratories, and shops. The Fort Assiniboine Preservation Association sponsors summer tours that take approximately two hours and include all the buildings of the fort. Travel is by vehicle. Gary Wilson of the Preservation Association says that winter tours are not generally offered because Montana's usually frigid winter temperatures seem a little too cool for most visitors.

DATE ESTABLISHED: 1879

ADDRESS: Star Rt. 36, Havre

TELEPHONE: Mr. Gary Wilson, tour guide, Fort Assiniboine, (406) 265-8336; Montana Agricultural Experimental Station, (406) 265-6115; Clark Museum, (406) 265-4000

VISITING HOURS: Summertime tours Sat., Sun. at 5; winter tours by appointment

FEES: Adults, $2; students, $1; children under 6, free

SOURCES: Telephone conversation June 22, 1994, Gary Wilson, Fort Assiniboine Preservation Association. Don Anderson, superintendent, Fort Assiniboine–Northern Agricultural Research Center. "John J. Pershing at Fort Assiniboine," 19. *The Black West*, 210–12.

Helena

Montana Historical Society

Although Black culture is not a primary emphasis in the Montana Historical Society's collection, the society does have several artifacts relating to Montana's African American history, including a painting of York, the Black man who was on the Lewis and Clark Expedition. The artifacts are displayed when they fit into other temporary exhibits. Visitors may call to request information on Montana's African American history.

ADDRESS: 225 N. Roberts Street, Helena

TELEPHONE: (406) 444-2694

VISITING HOURS: Mon.–Fri. 8–6, Sat.–Sun. 9–5; closed holidays

FEES: None

SOURCE: Kirby Lambert, curator of collections, Montana Historical Society.

Missoula

The Historical Museum at Fort Missoula

Fort Missoula was established in 1877 when local settlers asked for protection in the event of conflicts with nearby Native Americans. This was the period of the Nez Percé uprising, and the fort was to be a major outpost for the entire region.

The Twenty-fifth Infantry Regiment, a unit of Black soldiers led by white officers, arrived at Fort Missoula in 1888. The men became part of an Army experiment to test the use of bicycles by the military when, in 1896, Lieutenant James Moss organized the Twenty-fifth Infantry Bicycle Corps. The plan was to find out if bicycles could successfully replace the mounted patrol-duty horses. Men from the Twenty-fifth Infantry traveled by bicycle from Fort Missoula up the Bitterroot Valley to Yellowstone Park. In another experiment, in 1897, the bicycle corps traveled 1,900 miles from Missoula to St. Louis. This trip marked the end of these experiments; the Twenty-fifth Infantry returned by train to Missoula. The Army had decided that the bicycle had only a limited potential and would not be used to replace horses.

The Twenty-fifth Infantry was one of the first Army units called to fight in the Spanish-American War of 1898. When the unit was suddenly summoned to duty, the entire population of Missoula postponed their Easter church services to turn out and bid the soldiers farewell. After serving in the Philippines, men from the Twenty-fifth were assigned to other posts.

Fort Missoula, a complex of concrete buildings with red-tile roofs, was remodeled between 1908 and 1914. During the Depression years the fort served as a regional headquarters for the Civilian Conservation Corps. After Pearl Harbor 650 Japanese Americans were interned here. The post was decommissioned in 1947, and many of the buildings were sold or dismantled.

The fort does not appear as it did when the Black soldiers were stationed here, but it remains important in Black history as a place where Black men served in the late nineteenth century. Although African American history is not a primary focus of the museum's interpretation, a portion of the permanent exhibit on the fort's history—half of a wall—tells about the Twenty-fifth U.S. Infantry and the bicycle corps. The museum staff hopes to re-create the bicycle "dash" to St. Louis in 1997, the one hundredth anniversary of Fort Missoula, and to present an exhibit about the Buffalo Soldiers.

DATE ESTABLISHED: Fort Missoula, 1877; historical museum, 1975

ADDRESS: Building 322, Fort Missoula, Missoula

TELEPHONE: (406) 728-3476

VISITING HOURS: Memorial Day–Labor Day, Mon.–Sat. 10–5; rest of year, Tues.–Sun. 12–5; closed New Year's Day, Thanksgiving, Christmas

FEES: Donations accepted

SOURCES: Telephone conversation June 22, 1994, and Mar. 29, 1995, Dr. Robert M. Brown, director, The Historical Museum at Fort Missoula. *Historical Museum at Fort Missoula. The Black West,* 219.

Note

1. William Loren Katz, *The Black West* (Seattle, Wash.: Open Hand Publishing, 1987), 212.

Works Consulted

The Black West: A Documentary and Pictorial History. 3d ed. rev. William Loren Katz. Seattle, Wash.: Open Hand, 1987.

Historical Museum at Fort Missoula. Missoula: the Museum. [brochure]

"John J. Pershing at Fort Assiniboine." Donald Smythe, S.J. *Montana Magazine of Western History* 18, no. 1 (winter 1968), 19.

Nevada

● ● ● ● ● ● ● ● ● ● ● ●

Las Vegas

Westside School

Westside School, which opened in 1922 as the first grammar school in West Las Vegas, was known as Branch No. 1, Las Vegas Grammar School. The original building had two classrooms; two back rooms were added in 1928. Children in grades one and two attended in the first years of the school, and grades three and four were added when the back rooms became available.

There were no Black students in the early days of the school. Instead, it was the first school attended by students from a nearby Paiute Indian community. In 1920, however, war-related industries began to attract Black workers from the rural South. Their arrival marked the beginning of today's West Las Vegas–North Las Vegas Black community. The first Black students began to attend Las Vegas Grammar School in 1926; for many, this was their first experience in a racially integrated school. Although different ethnic groups attended the Westside School over the years, the Black community has the strongest emotional attachment to it today. Many were pupils there while making the transition from a rural to an urban lifestyle. The school is located today in the Black community.

The Westside School complex is the oldest remaining schoolhouse in Las Vegas. The original 1922 section at Washington and D Streets was constructed in mission-revival style. It was enlarged in 1948 with the addition of eight classrooms, creating a structure built partially of wood frame and partially of concrete block. It was phased out as a school in 1967, closed that year, and then fell into disrepair. The Economic Opportunity Board purchased Westside School in 1975 and began a major restoration. Today the old schoolhouse, which is listed in the *National Register of Historic Places*, houses KCEP, a public radio station.

DATE BUILT:	1922
ADDRESS:	KCEP radio station, 330 W. Washington Avenue, Las Vegas
TELEPHONE:	(702) 648-0104
VISITING HOURS:	Contact the radio station
SOURCES:	NRHPINF. Telephone call June 22, 1994, Las Vegas Branch of the NAACP. Telephone conversation June 22, 1994, Mrs. Sylvia Staples, deputy director, Economic Opportunity Board. Inventory of Historically and Archaeologically Significant Sites within the City of Las Vegas. "Radio Station Moving into Historic School."

Works Consulted

Inventory of Historically and Archaeologically Significant Sites within the City of Las Vegas. University of Nevada–Las Vegas Library, Special Collections. [listing]

"Radio Station Moving into Historic School." *Las Vegas Review Journal,* June 26, 1983.

Oregon

Astoria Vicinity

Fort Clatsop National Memorial

Members of the adventure-filled Lewis and Clark Expedition were sent to explore the virtually unknown and vast territory of the Louisiana Purchase that the United States had bought from France in 1803. President Thomas Jefferson placed his personal secretary, Captain Meriwether Lewis, in charge of the expedition. Lewis chose William Clark as his second in command. The bold group set out from St. Louis in 1803 and returned there in 1806 after encountering many hazards and learning much about the new lands and their inhabitants during the voyage.

Among the members of the group there was a Black slave and servant named York. He became a valued member of the expedition, highly respected for his physical strength and his prowess in exploring the wilderness. His ability to communicate with the Indians proved of considerable help to Lewis and Clark. York was also a skilled hunter who knew how to live off the land. In November 1805 York, along with other members of the exhausted group, agreed with their leaders' decision to spend the winter at what is now Astoria. Together with others, York helped build Fort Clatsop on the Columbia River, where the group spent the winter of 1805–1806. When the expedition returned to St. Louis in September 1806, it was greeted with jubilation. Although York was included in the celebrations, many years passed before he received his freedom.

The Fort Clatsop National Memorial has a replica of the log fort the expedition members built in the winter of 1805. The large exhibit hall includes a modest amount of information about York's role in the expedition, but information presented about him depends on the interpreter and the questions asked by visitors. Museum features also include a seventeen-minute slide show, a thirty-minute film about the Lewis and Clark Expedition, and a canoe-landing trail. The Fort Clatsop Historic Association bookstore carries books about the famous expedition.

DATE BUILT:	1805
ADDRESS:	5 miles southwest of Astoria off US 101
TELEPHONE:	(503) 861-2471
VISITING HOURS:	Mid-June–Labor Day, daily 8–6; Labor Day–Apr. 1, daily 8–5; closed Christmas
FEES:	Adults 17 and older, $2; families, $4; U.S. citizens 65 or older Golden Lifetime Pass, $10; youths under 17, free; free Labor Day–Apr. 1
SOURCES:	Telephone conversation June 21, 1994, Alice Morton, office automation assistant, and Sandra Reinebach, business manager, Fort Clatsop Historical Association. Jeffrey Uecker, museum educator, Oregon Historical Society. *Northwest Black Heritage: The Pioneers.*

Portland

Oregon Historical Society Library Sovereign Hotel Murals

York, a Black man who traveled with the Lewis and Clark Expedition, is represented among the figures that decorate the west wall of Portland's Sovereign Hotel. Other explorers represented are Captain Robert Gray, Captain Meriwether Lewis and William Clark, and Sacajawea. The mural is huge—six or seven stories high—and is completed in a trompe-l'oeil style that incorporates the hotel windows into the design in such a way that they seem to disappear.

The Oregon Historical Society has owned the Sovereign Hotel since 1982. The library of the society has documents about Black people who homesteaded in the Pacific Northwest in the late 1800s. The collection, appropriate for adult researchers, includes a vertical file with pamphlets, clippings, books, public manuscript materials, records of African American organizations, Black-owned Oregon newspapers, oral history recordings, and personal papers of individuals.

DATE ESTABLISHED: Murals, c1988

ADDRESS: 1230 S.W. Park Avenue, Portland

TELEPHONE: (503) 222-1741

VISITING HOURS: Mural, dawn–dusk; Oregon Historical Society library, Tues.–Sat. noon–4:45

FEES: Mural, free; library, nonmembers, $4.50

SOURCES: Telephone conversation June 21, 1994, Stephen Hallberg, catalogue librarian. "Spellbinding Historic Murals on Sides of Sovereign Hotel Will Be Among Stunning Accomplishments Foreseen for 1988."

Tour of Black History through Art

Although there are few identified Black historic sites remaining in Oregon, the story of African Americans who settled the West is portrayed in a series of murals in Portland executed by Isaac Shamsud-Din. One of the leading artists of the Northwest, Shamsud-Din has created contemporary art that shows the vitality, adventure, and achievement of Black pioneers. Prudence Roberts, Senior Curator at the Portland Art Museum, described Shamsud-Din's art as "very, very colorful, densely packed with information and incidents, with vibrant color and sense of motion—murals that a family would enjoy seeing."[1]

Shamsud-Din grew up in Portland, Oregon, in the 1950s and studied art at Portland State University. During the late 1960s he served as a college lecturer in Black studies and was later selected to be Portland's visual-arts ombudsman.

As a child, Shamsud-Din wanted to learn more about his Black heritage. He eventually spent twenty years in a search that culminated in the desire to use art to preserve and share the knowledge he had gained. He was commissioned to paint a variety of murals at several Oregon sites. Some of his works in Portland are described in the following sections.

ADDRESS: See individual listings

VISITING HOURS: Contact each center to arrange visit and to be sure that the mural is currently displayed

SOURCES: Jeffrey Uecker, museum educator, Oregon Historical Society. Telephone conversation June 21, 1994, Prudence Roberts, senior curator, Portland Art Museum. Telephone conversation June 21, 1994, Sandra Tate, assistant director, Littman and White Art Galleries, Portland State University. *Northwest Black Heritage. Perspectives.*

Harriet Tubman Mural

Located at the Harriet Tubman Middle School, the 1983 work is acrylic on plaster wall. It shows the accomplishments of Harriet Tubman, an African American famed for her escape from slavery and her repeated returns to the South to lead others to freedom. The Artists in the Schools Program of the Oregon Arts Commission commissioned the work. Children enjoy seeing the mural.

ADDRESS: 2231 N. Flint, Portland
TELEPHONE: (503) 280-5630

Kwazulu

The Children's Museum in Portland commissioned this 8-foot-by-24-foot acrylic-on-panel mural by Isaac Shamsud-Din in 1984. It is on display intermittently.

ADDRESS: 3037 S.W. Second Avenue, Portland
TELEPHONE: (503) 823-2227

Pioneers—Agents of Change

The Cascade Division of the Salvation Army commissioned this 10-foot-by-8-foot acrylic mural in 1979.

ADDRESS: Moore Street Center, Portland
TELEPHONE: (503) 239-1224

Three Untitled Works in Progress

Benson High School in Portland commissioned this mural in 1985.

ADDRESS: 546 N.E. Twelfth Street, Portland
TELEPHONE: (503) 280-5100

Untitled

The Artists in the Schools Program of the Oregon Arts Commission commissioned this work in 1982. The painting, located at the Woodlawn Elementary School, is 10 feet by 11 feet in acrylic on plaster wall.

ADDRESS: 7200 N.E. Eleventh Street, Portland
TELEPHONE: (503) 280-6282

Vanport

This oil-on-canvas mural, located in the Smith Student Center at Portland State University, is one of Shamsud-Din's earlier works. The Art Department of Portland State University commissioned the 14½-foot-by-9½-foot mural.

ADDRESS: Portland State University, stairwell of the Smith Student Center, Portland
TELEPHONE: (503) 725-4522
VISITING HOURS: Mon.–Fri. 7 A.M.–10 P.M., Sat. 8 A.M.–10 P.M., Sun. 10–5; closed holidays

Note

1. Telephone conversation June 21, 1994, Prudence Roberts, senior curator, Portland Art Museum.

Works Consulted

The Oregon Historical Society Presents Northwest Black Heritage: The Pioneers. Karen Broenneke. Portland, Ore.: Oregon Historical Society. [classroom activity packet]

Perspectives. Portland Art Museum, Dec. 10–Jan. 26, 1985–1986.

"Spellbinding Historic Murals on Sides of Sovereign Hotel Will Be Among Stunning Accomplishments Foreseen for 1988." Thomas Vaughan. *Oregon Historical Society News* 32, no. 1 (Feb. 1988).

Utah

●●●●●●●●●●●

Salt Lake City

Family History Library

Alex Haley's stirring saga, *Roots,* encouraged an entire generation of African Americans to begin a search for their family histories. Unfortunately, because many found the search to be arduous and complex, they gave up before reaching their goal of constructing a family tree. For those who still want to learn more about their family heritage, the Family History Library in Salt Lake City can provide valuable assistance and encouragement.

The library does not do genealogical searches for the visitor, but staff members, some of whom are missionaries who spend a year volunteering at the site, provide a wealth of resources and suggestions. The Family History Library is owned by the Church of Jesus Christ of Latter-day Saints. Resources on the three floors in the main site and the two other buildings include computers, microfilm readers, and census information from 1790. Four hundred missionaries take turns helping at different times of the year.

Those who cannot come to Utah may call the library for the name of the regional center closest to their home. Regional centers have microfiche card catalogs and will, on request, order material from the main library. Although the Family Heritage Library is not directly a Black history site, it is a splendid Black history resource because it can encourage Black families to search for their roots.

ADDRESS: 35 NW Temple, Salt Lake City
TELEPHONE: (801) 240-2745
VISITING HOURS: Mon.–Fri. 7:30–4:45; closed weekends, July 4, Thanksgiving, Christmas, New Year's Day
SOURCE: Telephone conversation June 20, 1994, Madonna Brown, missionary volunteer, Family History Library.

Fort Douglas Military Museum

Fort Douglas was built during the Civil War, primarily to protect the overland mail route. The Buffalo Soldiers, men from the all-Black Ninth Cavalry and Twenty-fourth Infantry, were stationed at Fort Douglas between 1896 and 1900. The Twenty-fourth Infantry was assembled for the first time at Fort Douglas. Their chaplain, Colonel Allensworth, later founded the all-Black town of Allensworth, California (see the California section).

In April 1898, men from the Twenty-fourth Infantry left Salt Lake City for Cuba, where they fought in the Spanish-American War. They showed great bravery, sweeping up San Juan Hill past the wavering Seventy-first Infantry of New York.

Men of the Twenty-fourth later became the only infantry soldiers detailed to do nursing service in the yellow-fever hospital at Siboney, Cuba. Black men were assigned to the most dangerous and repulsive work in the hospital. In spite of the danger of contagion, seventy of the men went to the front and offered their services. Many were seriously weakened by illness and died of yellow fever. Survivors of the Twenty-fourth Infantry later returned to Fort Douglas amid the rousing cheers of the citizens of Salt Lake City. *The Deseret Evening News* of July 8, 1899, carried a long article commending the men for bravery and exemplary conduct: ". . . each soldier behaves as though he were upon his honor never to cast reproach upon the uniform he wears, the flag he serves or the race to which he belongs."[1]

The Fort Douglas Cemetery has a section where some Buffalo Soldiers are buried. An exhibit in the Fort Douglas museum highlights the achievements of the Buffalo Soldiers and has pictures of and information about the men and their work at Fort Douglas.

ADDRESS:	32 Potter Street, Fort Douglas Army Post (10 minutes from downtown Salt Lake City, entrance on Wasatch Drive, adjacent to the University of Utah campus)
TELEPHONE:	(801) 588-5188
VISITING HOURS:	Tues.–Sat. 10–4; closed some holidays
FEES:	None
SOURCES:	Utah Historical Society. Telephone conversation June 22, 1994, Mr. William Jaecke, staff member, Fort Douglas. "The Colored Man as a Soldier." "African-American Historical Points of Interest in Utah."

This Is the Place State Park

Within the state park the Pioneer Monument, also known as *This Is the Place Monument,* is a massive structure with several attached plaques that are larger than the wall of a house. Inscribed on them are the names of three African Americans who traveled with the 1847 pioneers: Green Flake, Hark Lay, and Oscar Crosby.

Green Flake was born in 1828 in North Carolina and lived his early life on the plantation of his owner, James Flake. In 1846–1847 Brigham Young (1801–1877) led the first wave of the migration of Mormons from Illinois to the Great Salt Lake in the Utah Territory. Green Flake was selected to travel with the advance scouts of this bold expedition. His owner entrusted him with mules, a wagon, and pioneering equipment. On his arrival in Utah, Green was to build a house for the white Flake family. The wagon was then sent back east so that the rest of the Flake family could follow other Mormons to the new settlement. In fact, when the family arrived in Utah in 1848, Green Flake had a log cabin ready for them to occupy. He continued to work for the family until his death in 1903. Both Green Flake and his wife, Martha Crosby Flake, were buried in Union Cemetery, Salt Lake City.

Hark Lay was born about 1825. His owner was a white man, William Lay. Hark Lay was about twenty-three years old when he made the journey to Utah.

A third Black pioneer, Oscar Crosby, was born about 1815 in Virginia. He was a servant in the household of William Crosby. Oscar went ahead of his owner to Utah, where he secured land, planted crops, and made other preparations for the arrival of William Crosby and his family in 1848. Later Oscar accompanied his owner to California, where a new colony of members of the

Church of Jesus Christ of Latter-day Saints was being established. Since California was a free state, he received his freedom there. Oscar Crosby died in Los Angeles in 1870.

The visitors center in This Is the Place State Park was demolished in 1995 to be replaced with a larger center in time for a June 1996 centennial celebration. Old Deseret Village in the park also was scheduled to reopen in June 1996. Old Deseret Village, a reproduction of an early Utah town from the period of 1847 to 1869, displays homes and a blacksmith shop and has demonstrations of pioneer crafts. Until the Centennial reopening, visitors to the park could see only the park with the Pioneer Monument and the Brigham Young Forest Farmhouse; after the opening they also can see the visitors center and Old Deseret Village.

This Is the Place State Park, located near the Hogle Zoo, has picnic areas and has wagon rides from May through September.

ADDRESS: 2601 Sunnyside Avenue, Salt Lake City

TELEPHONE: (801) 584-8391 or (801) 584-8392

VISITING HOURS: Park, with a visit to the Brigham Young Forest Farmhouse and to Old Deseret Village after June 1996, Tues.–Sun. 11–5; monument, Tues.–Sun. 8–10:30, Mon. 8–8; village and farmhouse displays, closed Mon.; Old Deseret Village, closed winter

FEES: Displays, adults, $1; children under 6, free; park grounds only, free

SOURCES: Telephone conversation June 19, 1994, Becky Chase, park ranger, This Is the Place State Park. Telephone conversation June 20, 1994, Edith Menna, museum director, Daughters of the Utah Pioneers Museum. Telephone conversation May 31, 1995, Dana Dmitrich, secretary, This Is the Place State Park. Eileen Dunyon, former president, Daughters of the Utah Pioneers Museum. *The Story of the Negro Pioneer.* "African-American Historical Points of Interest in Utah."

Trinity African Methodist Episcopal Church

Trinity A.M.E. Church has been a cohesive force in the life of the small Black population of Salt Lake City. When the church organized in the 1880s, it was Utah's first Black congregation. Members held services in their homes at first, and then rented quarters until they were able to construct a church. Although the territorial governor laid the cornerstone in 1891, members apparently lacked funds to complete construction, and they continued to worship for many years in homes and rented quarters.

In 1907 Mary Bright, a Black cook who had become wealthy working in the mining camp at Leadville, Colorado, donated funds needed for constructing a church. The congregation purchased land on East Sixth South Street. Hurley Howell, a member of the congregation, drew plans for the structure, and church members constructed the house of worship about 1909.

Trinity A.M.E. Church is a small, rectangular, split-level building with a square tower. Colorful leaded-glass windows provide a decorative element on the front and sides.

Trinity African Methodist Episcopal Church has been a religious, social, and educational focal point for Salt Lake City's Black community and has played a major role in the history of this community. The church is listed in the *National Register of Historic Places.*

DATE BUILT: 1909

ADDRESS: Historic site, 532 E. 700 S.; present building, 239 E. Martin Luther King Jr. Boulevard (historic street name, 239 E. Sixth S.), Salt Lake City

TELEPHONE: (801) 531-7374

VISITING HOURS: Sun. service, summer, 10, winter, 11; Bible study/prayer service, Wed. 6:30 P.M.

SOURCES: Telephone conversation June 19, 1994, Reverend Janet L. Swift, Pastor of Trinity African Methodist Episcopal Church. NRHPINF. "African-American Historical Points of Interest in Utah."

University of Utah Library Special Collections

This library contains historical information about African American settlers in Utah. The manuscript division of the library has a collection of oral interviews dated from 1889 to 1988. These cassette tapes and transcripts include at least forty interviews, primarily from people in Ogden, Utah, and from railroad workers. The collection also has a twenty-page study of African Americans in Union, Utah, in 1847; the papers of Theodore Ward, a Black playwright from Utah; and some photographs that accompany different interviews.

DATE ESTABLISHED: Library, 1969

ADDRESS: Marriott Library, fifth floor, University of Utah, Salt Lake City

TELEPHONE: (801) 581-8864

VISITING HOURS: Mon.–Fri. 8–4:30, Sat. 9–1

FEES: None

SOURCE: Telephone conversation June 20, 1994, Jennifer Breaden, senior specialist, University of Utah Library.

Brigham Young Monument

The north face of the Brigham Young Monument in Temple Square lists the names of pioneers who arrived in 1847 at the site that would become Salt Lake City. By the late 1840s, white individuals were arriving in Utah Territory and establishing settlements. Some were Mormons. Among them were three Black men—Hark Lay, Oscar Crosby, and Green Flake—who arrived with the first group of Mormon pioneers.

In 1844 after Joseph Smith, founder and first president of the Church of Jesus Christ of Latter-day Saints, was assassinated in Nauvoo, Illinois, the second leader and president, Brigham Young, and others abandoned their homes in Illinois to move west. Advance scouts migrated to the Salt Lake Valley in 1847. Among the Mormons were slaveholders who had migrated to Nauvoo from missions that the Church of Jesus Christ of Latter-day Saints had opened in the South in the late 1830s and early 1840s. Some of the Southern slaveholders migrating from Nauvoo to Utah brought slaves with them. Some Black men traveled with the advance scouts; other African Americans arrived with Mormon families in the following years.

Although all of the pioneers endured harsh conditions on the trail, the African American slaves and servants had the additional burden of ministering to the white families and caring for the animals along the way. Some of them had to walk the rugged wilderness route. Some families made the thousand-mile journey in the bitterly cold winter months. Others traveled in the spring when the roads were muddy and the rivers were swollen from rain. One group traveled when the torrents of the Platte River, which was at flood stage, almost cost them both wagons and oxen.

The slaves who worked as teamsters drove the animals and cared for them during the migration. One group of slave teamsters met abolitionists as the group camped for the night. The next morning the white family discovered that all of their teamsters had fled. Travel was not possible without teamsters and the Mormon family had to spend the winter in Iowa until they could locate more workers for this task.

The African Americans in the first advance group of 1847 were true pioneers. Their job was to find land, plant crops, and build houses for the white families who would arrive the following year. When the white families arrived, the Black people continued to work in tasks in which they had skills—farming, tending animals, cooking, caring for the children in the household, spinning, and weaving cloth. By the Compromise of 1850, Utah remained a slave state. The Mormon Church took the position that slaves could remain with their owners if they wished to do so. If the slaves wished to be free, the owners were allowed to decide according to conscience whether to sell them or free them.

The Brigham Young Monument is a large structure located at the intersection of two streets. It has a larger-than-life-size statue of Brigham Young on the top layer. Below and to each side of him are a Native American and a trapper. In the center are large plaques with names of the pioneers inscribed, including the names of three Black men who arrived in this area in 1847. For more information on the African American pioneers, see This Is the Place State Park listing in this section.

ADDRESS: Center of Main Street and Temple Square, Salt Lake City

VISITING HOURS: Dawn–dusk

FEES: None

SOURCES: Telephone conversation June 20, 1994, Edith Menna, museum director, Daughters of the Utah Pioneers Museum. Eileen R. Dunyon, former president, Daughters of the Utah Pioneers Museum. The Grolier Multimedia Encyclopedia. *The Story of the Negro Pioneer.* "African-American Historical Points of Interest in Utah."

Note

1. "The Colored Man as a Soldier," *The [Salt Lake City] Deseret Evening News,* 8 July 1899.

Works Consulted

Academic American Encyclopedia. Danbury, Conn.: Grolier, 1993. [electronic version]

"African-American Historical Points of Interest in Utah." Reverend France A. Davis. Salt Lake City: Calvary Baptist Church, 1989. [manuscript]

The Story of the Negro Pioneer. Kate B. Carter. Salt Lake City, Utah: Daughters of Utah Pioneers, 1965.

Washington

●●●●●●●●●●●

Centralia

George Washington Park

George Washington, an African American pioneer in the West, was the founder of Centralia, Washington, and Centralia's city park is named in his honor. Born in Virginia in 1817 to a slave father and a white mother, George was adopted and raised by a white family who later moved to frontier settlements in Ohio and Missouri. As the years passed, George grew to be a six-foot-tall young man known for his strength and for his expert skill in marksmanship. He also was a talented miller, tanner, cook, and weaver. In 1850 Washington and his foster parents joined other families in a train of fifteen wagons and traveled to the Oregon Territory. Washington, who married at age 50, successfully homesteaded in an undeveloped region. In 1872, on a site between the Columbia River and Puget Sound, he established the town that would become Centralia. As the town's founder, George Washington not only encouraged growth by selling lots, he also donated funds for churches and a cemetery. His generosity was especially evident in the 1893 panic when he literally saved many Centralians from starvation by bringing in wagonloads of food and by providing his fellow citizens with relief funds. When he died in an accident in 1905, the mayor of Centralia proclaimed a day of mourning.

Washington is honored with a beautiful park in Centralia that bears his name and by a plaque in the park. Visitors will enjoy strolling there and looking at the display of flowers. The only building in the park, the Centralia Timberland Library, contains a book, *The Man Who Founded a Town,* that tells George Washington's story.

ADDRESS: Main Street at Gold Street, Centralia

TELEPHONE: Centralia Timberland Library, (206) 736-0183

VISITING HOURS: Park, 24 hours; library, Mon.–Thurs. 10–9, Fri.–Sat. 9–5

SOURCES: Telephone conversation May 14, 1994, Mike Dinkins, reference librarian, Centralia Timberland Public Library. *The Black West.*

Ilwaco

Lewis and Clark Interpretive Center

The Lewis and Clark Interpretive Center incorporates into its self-guided tour a modest amount of information about York, the Black man who accompanied Lewis and Clark on their expedition from St. Louis to the Pacific Ocean between 1803 and 1806. A notebook at the front desk that tells about members of the expedition includes a paragraph on York. A large mural that includes both pictures and written information about the journey contains York's picture. He is represented, too, among some small-sized dolls downstairs.

ADDRESS: Fort Canby State Park, 3 miles southwest off US 101 at the tip of Cape Disappointment (from Portland take US 30 to Astoria, then US 101 north to Ilwaco, then follow signs 3 miles south and west to the park)

TELEPHONE: (206) 642-3029

VISITING HOURS: Daily 10–5

FEES: None

SOURCE: Telephone conversation Apr. 30, 1994, Ken Weichel, volunteer, Lewis and Clark Interpretive Center.

Seattle

Douglass–Truth Library

Funded by the city's library system and by gifts from community organizations, the Douglass–Truth Library documents the Black experience in the United States with emphasis on the Pacific Northwest. The marvelous collection, named for outstanding Black Americans Frederick Douglass and Sojourner Truth, contains 6,500 volumes, including 500 children's books, adult books, catalogues of other collections, magazines, an index of articles from local newspapers, and 1,000 files of information about local African American individuals and institutions.

The unique reference collection of children's books shows how Black characters were portrayed between 1863 and the present. They illustrate the prevailing views—from stereotypical to realistic—that existed when they were written; this provides an invaluable record for research and teaching.

The collection began in 1965 when the changing ethnic makeup of the community drew attention to the need for more books about African Americans. The Alpha Kappa Alpha sorority donated more than 300 relevant books, a gift that was supplemented by the Black friends of Yesler Branch Library and later by a 1984 library-services grant.

ADDRESS: Library, 2300 E. Yesler Way, Seattle

TELEPHONE: (206) 684-4704

VISITING HOURS: Mon.–Wed. 1–9, Thurs. 10–9, Sat. 10–6, winter Sun. 10–5 in addition to Mon.–Sat. hours; closed holidays

FEES: None

SOURCE: Telephone conversation Apr. 30, 1994, John Sheets, branch librarian, Douglass–Truth Library.

East Madison Avenue Black Heritage Sites*

Three structures related to the history of Seattle's African American community are located in the East Madison Avenue area, Seattle's oldest settlement of Black Americans. They are the First African Methodist Episcopal Church, the Mt. Zion Church, and the William and Sarah Grose House.

SOURCE: Telephone conversation Apr. 7, 1994, Esther Mumford, local Black history sites author.

First A.M.E. Church

The First African Methodist Episcopal Church has a sanctuary constructed from about 1910 to 1912 on land purchased by the congregation in 1890. An education wing was constructed next to the church about 1985. The main structure and the education wing both are two-story buildings. The sanctuary, which has a fellowship hall on the lower level, is constructed of rust-colored brick and has a tower with beige trim. First A.M.E. Church has been designated as a historic landmark by the city of Seattle.

DATE ESTABLISHED: 1912

ADDRESS: 1522 Fourteenth Avenue at E. Pine Street, Seattle

TELEPHONE: (206) 324-3664

VISITING HOURS: Office hours, Tues.–Fri. 10–4; Sun. services, 8, 11; Sun. school, 9

SOURCE: Telephone conversation June 11, 1995, Dorothy Johnson, office volunteer, First A.M.E. Church.

Mt. Zion Baptist Church

Located at the southeast corner of Nineteenth Avenue and East Madison Street, Mt. Zion Baptist Church contains a sanctuary that is a work of art in itself. The strikingly beautiful, contemporary church features motifs from the African and African American heritage. The two-level structure has a library, Sunday School office, choir room, a fellowship hall, commercial kitchen, and three large classrooms on the lower level. The upper level contains the sanctuary, administrative offices, and an educational wing. Eighteen large stained-glass windows in the sanctuary depict Black historical figures, including, among others, Prince Hall, Sojourner Truth, and Dr. Martin Luther King Jr. The windows, with their vivid shapes and colors, were created for Mt. Zion Baptist Church by a company in Cleveland, Ohio. The stained glass circles the sanctuary with portraits near the choir stand and pulpit, in the rear, and on the side of the chapel that adjoins the sanctuary. Symbolism also is contained in twelve wooden beams in the sanctuary that represent the twelve tribes of Israel and the Twelve Apostles. Created from wood from the Pacific Northwest, the beams were left unfinished to represent the unfinished status of Christians. Red and purple colors in the church represent royalty, divinity, and the blood of Christ, while skylights recreate the four gospels of the New Testament of the Bible. Symbolism is extended through the colors of ten flags that include, among others, the flag of the United States, the Christianity flag, and flags of the state of Washington, the Black Liberation Movement, the National Baptist Convention, and the National Council of Churches.

Founded by a small group of men from Tennessee, the congregation of Mt. Zion Baptist Church dates back to 1890. For most of the years from the founding date, members have worshiped at this site on Nineteenth Avenue. An earlier church structure was torn down in the early 1970s, and the present church soon was constructed on the same site.

DATE ESTABLISHED: Congregation, 1890; present building, early 1970s
ADDRESS: 1634 Nineteenth Avenue, Seattle
TELEPHONE: (206) 322-6500
VISITING HOURS: Office hours, Mon.–Fri. 9–5; Sun. services, 8, 10:45
SOURCE: Telephone conversation June 10, 1995, Reverend LaVerne C. Hall, church administrator, Mt. Zion Baptist Church.

William and Sarah Grose House

The Grose House at Twenty-fourth and Howell in East Madison stands as a symbol of the early community of Black settlers. William Grose came to Seattle in the 1860s, and in 1882 he and Sarah purchased a twelve-acre tract for use as a ranch. They operated a hotel, but it was destroyed by fire in 1889. Retiring from the hotel business, they moved into their newly built house in 1890. The large bungalow just north of the Grose House was built in the 1920s by a Grose granddaughter and her husband. The old farmhouse has been little modified since its construction, although new condominiums have consumed much of the land.

DATE ESTABLISHED: 1890
ADDRESS: 1733 Twenty-fourth Avenue at Howell Street, Seattle
VISITING HOURS: Private, visitors may walk or drive by

Dr. Martin Luther King Jr. Memorial*

A thirty-foot-tall Zimbabwean granite memorial is surrounded by a verdant four-acre park in Seattle. Designed with a wide base and gracefully narrowing to the apex, the monument symbolizes Dr. Martin Luther King Jr.'s moving statement, "I've been to the mountaintop."

Dedicated on November 16, 1991, the monument, located in an African American community in Seattle, grew out of the dream of Charlie James, a Seattle citizen who announced in 1983 that he would see that the city had a monument to the slain civil rights leader. Over a period of years other individuals joined the effort and a committee was formed. The county and state legislatures also contributed significant funds. The monument, possibly the largest such structure honoring King outside the South, is located in a lovely setting with a hill sloping down to it. It rests in a reflecting pool; a waterfall, gently with a soft musical sound, cascades from the top of the monument to the pool. Plaques embedded in the surrounding walls describe significant incidents in King's life. Children can pause here to play in the park, or they can take a moment to reflect with their families on the meaning of King's life and philosophy and his sacrifice for peace.

DATE ESTABLISHED: 1991
ADDRESS: Southeast corner of Martin Luther King Jr. Way and S. Walker Street, Seattle
VISITING HOURS: 24 hours
FEES: None
SOURCES: Telephone conversation Apr. 7, 1994, Esther Mumford, local Black heritage sites author. *A Guide to the History, Culture, and Art of African Americans in Seattle and King County, Washington.*

Tumwater

Simmons Party Memorial

George Washington Bush, an African American, led the first American settlers to the Puget Sound area in 1843, bringing his own family and seven white companions over the Old Oregon Trail. Bush was born free in Pennsylvania but moved to Missouri, where he worked as a servant for a French family. He prospered in Missouri as a cattle trader. Because he had earlier explored the wilderness as far as the Pacific Coast, he was welcomed as a guide when families wanted to go west in a wagon train. One factor in his decision to leave Missouri may have been a law that banned free Black people from settling in the state.

The group came to Oregon, and Bush settled in Oregon's Willamette Valley in 1844. He became one of the wealthiest men in the region. Oregon, however, had restrictive laws prohibiting Black people, slave or free, from entering. The group was supportive of Bush, who apparently had helped two members of the traveling party on their way to Oregon, and its members voted to go north. Bush and his son, Owen, established a farm in the Tumwater area and prospered there. By the 1850s he was one of the most successful farmers in Thurston County, Washington Territory. A generous man, he assisted his neighbors who were less prosperous. In 1854, when the validity of the land claim to his farm was threatened, his neighbors showed their respect by petitioning Congress to confirm the claim.

One of Bush's sons, William Owen Bush, was elected to Washington's first State Legislature about 1889.

George Bush's name is among those inscribed on a monument in the beautiful Tumwater Falls Historical Park. Here visitors may walk a mile-long trail that winds around the Deschutes River, with its bridges and tumbling waterfalls. A granite monument in the park, approximately twelve feet in height, contains a brass plaque with the city seal and the names of about two dozen pioneers who braved the Oregon Trail to come West and settle near Puget Sound.

ADDRESS: Foot of Grant Street, Tumwater Falls Historical Park, Tumwater

TELEPHONE: (206) 943-2550

VISITING HOURS: Winter, 8–4:30; summer, 8–dusk

SOURCES: Telephone conversation April 30, 1994, Derrick Jordan, caretaker, Tumwater Falls Historical Park. *International Library of Negro Life and History*, 58–59. *The Black West*.

Works Consulted

The Black West: A Documentary and Pictorial History. 3d ed., rev. William Loren Katz. Seattle: Open Hand Publishing, 1987.

International Library of Negro Life and History: Historical Negro Biographies. Wilhelmena S. Robinson. New York: Publishers, 1970.

Wyoming

Buffalo

Fort McKinney

In the nineteenth century Black men came to Wyoming with the United States Army. An 1866 act was the impetus for organizing two Black cavalry regiments, the Ninth and Tenth, and four Black infantry regiments, the Thirty-eighth, Thirty-ninth, Fortieth, and Forty-first. Three years later the Thirty-eighth and Forty-first merged to create the Twenty-fourth Regiment and the Thirty-ninth and Fortieth became the Twenty-fifth Regiment. Of the Black units that fought continuously on the frontier through the 1890s, some were stationed in Wyoming. They kept the peace in areas where civilians had settled. They were assigned to fight Native Americans, and they provided protection for stagecoaches and mail stations.

The Ninth Cavalry arrived at Fort McKinney in August 1885. Previously its men had had eighteen years of distinguished service in the Southwest. When they were first stationed here, there were only twelve Black people living in all of Johnson County, and the soldiers encountered some negative racial stereotypes.

Most of the tour of duty for the Ninth Cavalry was routine, even monotonous. Tasks included guard details, stable duty, and serving as kitchen police. The final days, however, for D troop of the Ninth were spectacular ones: four troops of the Ninth departed for South Dakota in a rush to rescue Colonel James Forsyth and his men who were surrounded by Indians in a valley. Ninth Cavalry troops posted at Fort McKinney also spent time on the Shoshone-Arapaho Wind River Indian Reservation at Fort Washakie near here.

Today the exteriors of the remaining buildings at Fort McKinney can be viewed. However, the buildings serve a different purpose today, and interpretation of the Black history of the site is not a priority. The Veterans Home of Wyoming now occupies the site; its staff will give a tour by appointment. Before coming to visit, families may wish to go to the Johnson County Library, which has a wealth of information on Fort McKinney—books, photographs, pamphlets, and newspaper clippings—including material about the Black troops stationed here.

DATE OF SIGNIFICANCE: Ninth Cavalry arrived, 1885

ADDRESS: 700 Veterans Lane (from Buffalo, take US 16 west [the Scenic Byway through the Big Horn Mountains] approximately 2 miles to Fort McKinney); Johnson County Library, 117 N. Adams Street, Buffalo

TELEPHONE: Veterans Home of Wyoming, (307) 684-5511; Johnson County Library, (307) 684-5546

VISITING HOURS: Veterans Home of Wyoming, by appointment Mon.–Fri. 7:30–4:30; Johnson County Library research collection, Mon.–Thurs. 10–8, Fri.–Sat. 10–5

FEES: None

SOURCES: Telephone conversation June 21, 1994, Petty Myers, history librarian, and Nancy Jennings, librarian, Johnson County Library. Telephone conversation June 21, 1994, staff at the Veterans' Home of Wyoming. Todd Guenther, curator, South Pass City State Historic Site. Frances Seely Webb Collection, Casper College. Hayward Schrock, curator Fort Caspar Museum. Helen Larsen, director, Anna Miller Museum, Newcastle, Wyoming. "The Black Regular Army Regiments in Wyoming."

Cheyenne

F. E. Warren Base Museum

In 1898 units of the Twenty-fourth Regiment arrived at Fort D. A. Russell outside Cheyenne and at Camp Pilot Butte near Rock Springs. Those who came to garrison Fort Russell arrived straight from duty in Cuba. Four companies remained in Cheyenne, while six companies continued west to Fort Douglas.

The base museum, one of the original brick structures on the present-day Warren Air Force Base, was originally named Fort D. A. Russell. The last Wednesday in July is Heritage Day and the base opens other buildings for this special event.

DATE ESTABLISHED: Fort, 1867

ADDRESS: Warren Heritage Museum, Building 210, Francis E. Warren Air Force Base, Cheyenne

TELEPHONE: (307) 775-2980

VISITING HOURS: Memorial Day–Labor Day, Wed.–Sat. 1–4; rest of year, Wed., Fri., Sat. 1–4; closed holidays

FEES: None

SOURCES: Patsy Burgess, secretary, Warren Historical Association. Telephone call to site, June 21, 1994.

South Pass City

South Pass City State Historic Site*

The discovery of gold at Sutters Mill in California in 1848 sent many people west hoping to make a fortune. By the 1860s new mother lodes had been discovered in Colorado, Nevada, Idaho, and Montana, and boom towns sprang up to accommodate the thousands of immigrants. In 1867 the Carissa mine began producing gold, and South Pass City was built to accommodate those who had joined the rush to this area.

South Pass is located five miles south of this site. At an altitude of 7,550 feet, South Pass was the lowest and easiest route across the Continental Divide. It also was the halfway point on the Oregon–California Trail, a route of approximately 2,000 miles that led from Missouri to Oregon and California. Thousands of slaves and free Black individuals traversed the trail between 1840 and 1867, and many stayed to work in the historic mining town of South Pass City. In 1868, during a presidential election, the United States marshal from Cheyenne had to escort African Americans to the polls through a mob. Black men inadvertently, because they were allowed to vote, paved the way for making Wyoming the first place in the nation to enfranchise women. William Bright, who was elected to the Territorial Legislature in 1869, introduced the first successful women's suffrage bill in the country. Wyoming then received the nickname "the Equality State."

Today South Pass City is a ghost town maintained by the state. Visitors can see the old buildings and their contents. These silent sentinals of the past belonged to African Americans, too, because Black people were a significant part of the town's heritage. Arriving primarily for mining opportunities, Black men and women worked in various businesses as well as in mining; they also experienced a race riot while here. Although only one photograph and one exhibit panel in South Pass City tell the story of the African American pioneers, their presence was large in this city, today a picturesque ghost town.

DATE ESTABLISHED: 1867

ADDRESS: 36 miles southeast of Lander (turn off at milepost 43, continue for 2 miles on a gravel road to the ghost town); or US 287 southeast from Lander to WY 28 to South Pass City Road

TELEPHONE: (307) 332-3684

VISITING HOURS: May 15–Sept. 30, daily 9–5

FEES: Adults, 18 or older, $1; children, free

SOURCES: Telephone conversation May 2, 1994, Todd Guenther, curator South Pass City State Historical Site. *Atlas of United States History.* The Academic American Encyclopedia.

Works Consulted

The Academic American Encyclopedia. Danbury, Conn.: Grolier, 1993. [electronic version]

Atlas of United States History. Maplewood, N.J.: Hammond, 1989.

"The Black Regular Army Regiments in Wyoming, 1885–1912." Frank N. Schubert. Master's thesis, University of Wyoming, Laramie, May 1970.

Alaska

Anchorage

ABC Real Estate

This small cottage was the home for many years of the ABC Real Estate in Anchorage, Alaska. The owner was a Black man named Joseph Jackson who came to Alaska in 1951. He was inspired by a friend's stories of generous paychecks in Alaska. His friend marveled about the economic opportunities available in the far north.

Carpenters were needed for many construction projects in Alaska, and Jackson, who had experience in carpentry, decided to spend about four months working in Anchorage.

When Jackson arrived, there was no housing available for him. He commented later that "Blacks as well as whites were charging $30 a day, with six in a room with double- and triple-bunk beds."[1] Jackson rented a lot made up of twelve feet of space for $25 a month. He and three other carpenters living on the lot cooked their meals in a tent out in the yard. They received the privilege of bathing once a week in the landowner's house.

Joseph Jackson later established his own business, the ABC Real Estate, operating the business out of this cottage on Fifteenth Street for the rest of his life.

ADDRESS: E. Fifteenth Street, one-half block east of Ingra, Anchorage

VISITING HOURS: Private, visitors may drive by

SOURCE: Interview with Joseph Jackson conducted by the author and reported in *Alaska Blacks Salute the Bicentennial.*

Mahala Ashley Dickerson Law Office

This remodeled home on East Fifteenth Avenue has served from 1960 to the present as the original unit of the law office of Alaska pioneer Mahala Ashley Dickerson. Dickerson graduated with honors from Fisk University in 1935 with a major in sociology. She married Henry Dickerson, and they became parents of triplet sons. By the time her sons were six years old and ready to enter first grade, she was able to realize her dream of entering the Howard University Law School. She graduated *cum laude* in 1948.

In 1948 Dickerson became the first African American female admitted to the Alabama bar. A year later she opened the first African American law office in Montgomery, Alabama. One of her accomplishments in Alabama was to rescue a Black family held in peonage by the tenant farmer system. That hiring method insured that Black families would always remain in debt and legally in bondage. Although she was able to help that particular family, she herself met discrimination in her work. When she first began practicing in Montgomery, an Alabama police officer directed her to move from the lawyer's section of the courtroom to the "colored" section. When she explained that she was an attorney, he told her that she would still have to move. Later there was an apology; forty-six years later, in July 1994, Dickerson was invited to be the keynote speaker at the annual meeting of the Alabama Bar Association.

As a young attorney, Dickerson also practiced in Indiana until 1958. Then she fulfilled a dream that brought her and her young sons to Alaska. Although there were other Black people in Anchorage, the African American population was small. At the time many Alaskans were taking advantage of the opportunity to obtain land by homesteading, and Dickerson filed her claim, too. Between 1960 and 1964 she braved rough unpaved roads, Alaskan mosquitoes, and primitive living conditions to homestead 160 prime wilderness acres on a lake in Wasilla, Alaska.

Attorney Dickerson was the first African American admitted to the Alaska bar. She purchased a building in 1960 and remodeled it to serve as her law office. Most of her early clients were white citizens who brought her a variety of general legal problems. As Anchorage's Black population grew, racism also developed, and more and more of her cases involved civil rights and gender problems. As her law practice enlarged, she built a larger office on the same lot in back of the small building. She also built a law office on her land in Wasilla.

In 1982–1983 Dickerson was elected the first Black president of the National Association of Women Lawyers. In 1982 she received the Freedom Award of the National Association for the Advancement of Colored People. In 1994 she received an honorary LLD degree from the University of Alaska.

Attorney Dickerson has quietly supported many philanthropic causes. Al-Acres, a charitable association that she founded, has given scholarships and awards to young Black students. Her autobiography, *Delayed Justice for Sale,* emphasizes that Black people in America may receive justice, but that justice is often delayed and obtained at great price. When she was a child, Dickerson says, Black children looked longingly at the municipal swimming pool in Montgomery but were not allowed to use it. When integration came to Montgomery, white citizens transformed the swimming pool into a flower bed to avoid integration so Black children could not swim there. As a result, Dickerson did not learn to swim until she was thirty-six years old. Today she has a large, beautiful swimming pool in her Wasilla home as well as a lake outside the house, and she is able to swim every day, illustrating the theme of her autobiography that African Americans often receive delayed justice, but at a price.

DATE ESTABLISHED: House, 1948; law office, 1960

ADDRESS: 1550 E. Fifteenth Street Avenue, Anchorage

TELEPHONE: (907) 276-7454

VISITING HOURS: Private, visitors may walk or drive by

SOURCES: Telephone conversation July 2, 1994, Attorney M. A. Dickerson. "Alaska Blacks Salute the Bicentennial."

Dawson Creek, B.C., to Fairbanks

Alaska Highway

During World War II, African American soldiers played a significant role in building the Alaska section of the Alaska-Canada Military Highway. In 1942 the U.S. Army, believing Alaskan territory to be under the threat of an invasion by Japan, prepared to construct a highway that would connect military posts in Alaska with those in the continental United States. The 1,523-mile highway from Dawson Creek, British Columbia, to Fairbanks, Alaska, would provide a route for trucks to bring army personnel and supplies to Alaska. Although the army recruited civilians for the grueling task, men in the all-Black Ninety-third, Ninety-fifth, and Ninety-seventh regiments of the U.S. Army Corps of Engineers were sent to Alaska to work south from Alaska to the Canadian border. There they would meet white troops who were working north from Canada. The 3,695 Black soldiers made up almost one third of the work force on the highway.

Racism prevailed in the army assignments. To prevent the Black soldiers from mixing with Native Alaskans, the army sent the African Americans to the most remote and primitive sections of the route, where they endured bitterly cold weather and had poor equipment, little fresh food, and no indoor facilities. White soldiers, in contrast, were housed in heated barracks. The Black men saw few people other than the men in their own regiments. Working conditions were grueling; the weather at times reached 70 degrees below zero. The men did construction work in the ice and snow by day and slept in tents by night. When the spring thaws came, they had to slosh through mud and dodge stinging hordes of mosquitoes.

Many of the Black men were from the South. For some, this was their first job in which they received pay equal to that of white workers. In spite of hardships and racial discrimination, their morale remained high, and they finished their assignments with distinction.

In 1946 the Canadian section of the military supply route was turned over to Canada. The entire Alaska-Canada Highway was opened to the public in the following year, and it soon became known as a spectacularly scenic highway for travelers in the far north. Although the Black soldiers' role was almost forgotten over the years, recognition came fifty years after the work was completed. The veterans celebrated the fiftieth anniversary of the highway's completion with a reunion in Tallahassee, Florida. In Alaska, an Alaskan writer named Lael Morgan gathered photographs and stories about their role; this collection became part of a 1992 fiftieth anniversary exhibit at the Anchorage Museum of History and Art.

DATE CONSTRUCTED: Completed 1942
ADDRESS: AK 2 from Fairbanks to the Alaska-Canada border
SOURCES: "Unsung Heroes." "Battling the Elements on the Alcan Highway."

Works Consulted

Alaska Blacks Salute the Bicentennial. Nancy C. Curtis, Ph.D. Anchorage: Leake Temple A.M.E. Zion Church and Great Land Visuals, 1976. [commemorative magazine]

"Battling the Elements on the Alcan Highway." In *African Americans: Voices of Triumph.* Vol. 1, *Perseverance,* 160–1. Alexandria, Va: Time-Life, 1993.

"Unsung Heroes." Lael Morgan. *We Alaskans: The Anchorage Daily News Magazine* (9 Aug. 1992).

Hawaii

Honolulu

USS Arizona Memorial*

The attack on Pearl Harbor came by surprise on December 1941. Admiral Yamamoto, chief of the Japanese Combined Fleet, had completed plans for a surprise attack that would achieve a quick and decisive victory for Japan. Before 8:00 A.M. on that morning, dive bombers began their attacks on Pearl Harbor. Ten minutes later, a bomb struck the battleship *Arizona,* causing an explosion. In less than nine minutes the ship sank, carrying more than 1,110 members of her crew to the bottom.

Doris (called Dorie) Miller was serving on the *USS Virginia* at the time. He was one of many Black men and women who served in the armed forces in World War II. Segregation prevented them from working at high levels in the service, but they were in the thick of action as others were, and they also were exposed to the brunt of the attack on Pearl Harbor.

Miller was born on a small farm near Waco, Texas, the son of poor sharecropper parents. A naval recruiting officer came to Waco when Miller was nineteen, and the young man signed up to join the Navy. He soon learned that the segregated Navy assigned Black crewmen to the hardest, dirtiest work or to support jobs as stewards and cooks; they were not eligible to train for combat roles.

On December 7, 1941, just before the attack, Miller was working as a mess attendant, or food server, on the *USS Arizona.* As bombs rained down, the ship's captain was mortally wounded, and crewmen called Miller to the bridge of the ship to help carry the captain to safety. Miller moved the captain from the bridge, then made a decision to return. He had never been trained as an antiaircraft gunner, but in spite of sirens blaring and bombs raining down, he joined his shipmates who were firing at the attacking Japanese planes. He was reported to have brought down four Japanese planes before the order came to abandon ship.

The attack on Pearl Harbor had the effect of drawing Americans together in a determination to defeat Japan and its allies. While the war was being fought for democracy, African Americans continued to face segregation in the United States, both in and out of the armed services. Nevertheless, newspapers and groups rallied for recognition of Miller, and four months later he received the Navy Cross for courageous service. He toured Black communities, encouraging the purchase of war bonds and serving as a spokesman and symbol for civil rights in the Navy and the other military services.

In spite of the national recognition he had received for heroism, when Miller returned to service, he was assigned to performing the same level of work as a mess attendant. Petty Officer Miller died two years later, in 1943, at the age of twenty-four, when the *USS Liscombe Bay* sank off Tarawa.

The Visitors Center is on the shoreline overlooking Pearl Harbor, within view of the Arizona

Memorial, and is the required first stop for visitors intending to tour the memorial. The *USS Arizona* Memorial is in the harbor along Ford Island, about a ten-minute boat ride. Tours last one hour and fifteen minutes and include a film, a Ranger talk, the boat trip out, time spent at the memorial, and the boat ride back to the Visitors Center. Because tickets are distributed on a first-come, first-served basis, it is important to arrive early, especially in summer.

DATE ESTABLISHED: Visitors Center/museum, 1980; Memorial, 1962

ADDRESS: 1 Arizona Memorial Place; Visitors Center, HI 99 (Kamehameha Highway), Honolulu

TELEPHONE: (808) 422-2771

VISITING HOURS: Daily 7:30–3; first tour at 8, last at 3; closed Thanksgiving, Christmas, New Year's Day

FEES: None

SOURCES: Mark Hertig, former museum specialist, *USS Arizona* Memorial. Telephone conversation June 22, 1994, Donald E. Magee, superintendent, *USS Arizona* Memorial. *International Library of Negro Life and History,* 227–8. "A Man Called Doris." Brochure from National Park Service Visitor Center.

Works Consulted

"A Man Called Doris:" USS Arizona *Memorial.* National Park Service. [brochure]

International Library of Negro Life and History: Historical Negro Biographies. Wilhelmena S. Robinson. New York: Publishers, 1970.

Index

C

E

F

I

M

S

Y

Z

Nancy C. Curtis is a distinguished educator and administrator whose work on behalf of students and their communities has brought her numerous honors. She earned her B.A. at Fisk University, an M.A. in Teaching at Radcliffe College, and a Ph.D. in Human Development at Harvard University. Since 1989 she has been coordinator of Black Student Achievement Programs for the Anchorage (Alaska) School District, where she also established an Early Childhood program and served as staff development specialist, principal, and teacher. Earlier administrative and teaching experience in Massachusetts included positions with Cambridge Community Schools, the Roxbury Basic Reading Program, Newton Education Development Center, and Boston University, where she was assistant professor of early childhood education. Other studies and interests, including history and photography, have led her throughout the United States and into the making of this personal record of African American heritage sites.